JOHN DONNE:
AN ANNOTATED BIBLIOGRAPHY OF
MODERN CRITICISM, 1979–1995

John Donne

An Annotated Bibliography of Modern Criticism, 1979–1995

John R. Roberts

Duquesne University Press
Pittsburgh, Pennsylvania

Published in the United States of America by
Duquesne University Press
600 Forbes Avenue
Pittsburgh, Pennsylvania 15282

Library of Congress Cataloging-in-Publication Data

Roberts, John Richard
  John Donne: an annotated bibliography of modern criticism, 1979–1995 / by
John R. Roberts.
    p. cm. — (Medieval & Renaissance literary studies)
  Includes bibliographical references and index.
  ISBN 0-8207-0353-2 (hardcover: alk. paper)
  1. Donne, John, 1572–1631—Bibliography. 2. Donne, John, 1572–1631—
Criticism and interpretation—Bibliography. I. Title. II. Medieval and
Renaissance literary studies
Z8237.R625 2004
[PR2248]
016.821'3—dc22
                                                                    2004003531

∞ Printed on acid-free paper.

To the past and present members of the Advisory Board of *The Variorum Edition of the Poetry of John Donne*

Dennis Flynn

M. Thomas Hester

William B. Hunter Jr.

Albert C. Labriola

Paul A. Parrish

Ted-Larry Pebworth

Jeanne Shami

John T. Shawcross

Gary A. Stringer

Ernest W. Sullivan II

CONTENTS

PREFACE

The primary purpose of this bibliography is to provide students, scholars and critics of John Donne with a useful aid to research. This study is the first to collect and fully annotate the vast amount of criticism and scholarship written on Donne during the period 1979–1995. The present volume is a continuation of my two previously published bibliographies: *John Donne: An Annotated Bibliography of Modern Criticism, 1912–1967* (Columbia: University of Missouri Press, 1973) and *John Donne: An Annotated Bibliography of Modern Criticism, 1968–1978* (Columbia: University of Missouri Press, 1982). This volume ends at 1995 because more recent studies were not always available, especially foreign items, and because bibliographical sources were often incomplete after that date.

The present bibliography follows, for the most part, the principles and guidelines established for the earlier volumes. The annotations are essentially descriptive, not evaluative, because I find that what is important and/or useful to one scholar is not equally significant to another. The annotations, however, are quite detailed and quote extensively from the items in order to convey a sense of the approach and level of critical sophistication. Therefore, the readers should be able to judge for themselves whether a particular book or essay will be useful for their purposes. I also have listed each item chronologically so that by reading through the bibliography readers will be able to obtain a sense of the various shifts and developments that have occurred in Donnean criticism during the 17-year period covered. Such an arrangement allows readers to observe that Donne's works have been run through many and various critical sieves (linguistic, stylistic, biographical, psychoanalytic, bibliographic, textual, feminist, new historicist, political, formalistic, etc.) and that, in a sense, work done on him represents a kind of microcosm of what has taken place in literary criticism during the past two decades. By using the three detailed indexes (author, subject and works of Donne mentioned in the annotations), users can easily locate the individual studies that interest them.

As in the previous volumes, I have tried to make this bibliography as comprehensive and complete as possible, yet even from the beginning, it was necessary to impose certain limitations. The basic guiding principle has been to include all books, monographs, essays and notes specifically on Donne written between 1979 and 1995; but, in addition, extended discussions of Donne that appear in works not centrally concerned with him have been included. Nearly all the books and many essays on metaphysical poetry or on individual seventeenth century poets contain some comment on or reference to Donne, but to have included all items that simply mention Donne in relation to Herbert, Crashaw, Vaughan, Marvell, Traherne, et al. would have extended the present bibliography far beyond manageable bounds and would have distorted the main directions of Donne criticism.

Also, brief mentions of Donne or short quotations taken from his works appearing in books and articles, as well as references in literary histories, encyclopedias, anthologies and textbooks, have been omitted. Doctoral dissertations have not been included because many of them are unavailable, especially those in languages other than English, and because a number of them have been published, wholly or partly, in later essays and books. Readers are encouraged, however, to consult *Dissertation Abstracts International* for summaries, prepared by their authors, of many (but not all) American dissertations. Some items of little critical or scholarly interest that have Donne in their title, such as original poems or pious pamphlets, are included so that users will not be obliged to track them down. Reprints of works and editions published before 1979 have been excluded; reprints of items published between 1979 and 1995 are recorded, when known, with the original entry. I have not annotated book reviews. However, I have annotated review articles (usually discussions of two or more books), and, following the annotations of books that deal *exclusively with Donne,* I have listed as many as I could find of the reviews of those books only.

Many items in languages other than English (German, French, Italian, Spanish, Dutch, Polish, Czech, Russian, Japanese, Korean, Greek, Portuguese, Swedish, Danish) have been included, but I have no assurance that I have located all items in these languages or in others. In referring to Donne's poems, I have used the abbreviations created by the editors of the Variorum Edition of John Donne's Poetry, with their kind permission.

It is a great pleasure to acknowledge and to thank all those who have generously assisted me in this project. I am especially indebted to my former research assistants, Andrew Jewell and Christian Michener, who assisted me in checking bibliographical sources, locating items, and helping me in sundry ways. I am also grateful to Yoshihisa Aizawa, Alla Barabtarlo, Susan Csaky, William R. Hooton III, Carla Waal Johns, Hirohisa Kanno, Anton Novacky, Andrea McDowell, M. Bonner Mitchell, Dennis Mueller, Edward Mullen, Seth Prezioso, Anna Slusarz, Giuseppe Soldano, Richard Todd, Mara Yanni, Seungkwon You and Russell Zguta, who assisted me with foreign language items. I wish to thank Anne Barker, Delores Fisher and Melissa McAbee, librarians, who were most helpful in locating books and essays that were unavailable at the University of Missouri Ellis Library. Many Donne scholars, critics and friends were most kind in calling my attention to lesser known material and/or by supplying me with offprints, especially Joyce Short Beck, Helen Brooks, Robert Ellrodt, Dennis Flynn, Kate Frost, Raoul Granqvist, Marshall Grossman, James Harner, Dayton Haskin, Eugene D. Hill, K. J. Höltgen, George Klawitter, Frank Kerins, Edward LeComte, Albert C. Labriola, Anthony Low, William McClung, Sean McDowell, Edmund Miller, Peter Milward, Wolfgang G.

Müller, Maria J. Pando-Canteli, Laurence Perrine, Marios Byron Raizis, Robert Ray, John T. Shawcross, R. Jason Stubblefield and Helen Wilcox. I am also very much indebted to Gerard Lowe, chief bibliographer of the Modern Humanities Research Association at Cambridge; Cheryl Adams of the Library of Congress; and David Smith at the New York Public Library for assisting me in locating hard-to-find Donne items. I also wish to thank the members of the staffs of numerous libraries, all of whom were most gracious with their time and advice, especially those at the University of Missouri Ellis Library, the British Library and the Cambridge University Library.

And to my wife, Lorraine, I owe a special note of thanks for her support, advice and assistance in proofreading the entries.

J. R. R.
Columbia, Missouri

LIST OF ABBREVIATIONS

ABR	American Benedictine Review
ACM	The Aligarh Critical Miscellany
ADEB	ADE Bulletin
AEB	Analytical and Enumerative Bibliography
AI	American Imago: Studies in Psychoanalysis and Culture
AJES	The Aligarh Journal of English Studies
Albion	Albion: A Quarterly Journal concerned with British Studies (Dept. of History, Appalachian State University, Boone, N.C.; North American Conference on British Studies)
Allegorica	Allegorica: A Journal of Medieval and Renaissance Literature
Anglia	Anglia: Zeitschrift für Englische Philologie
AngTheoRev	Anglican Theological Review
AN&Q	American Notes and Queries
ANQ	ANQ: A Quarterly Journal of Short Articles, Notes, and Reviews
AnSch	Annals of Scholarship: An International Quarterly in the Humanities and Social Sciences [Formerly *Annals of Scholarship: Metastudies of the Humanities and Social Sciences*]
ArAA	Arbeiten aus Anglistik und Amerikanistik
ARBA	American Reference Books Annual
Arcadia	Arcadia: Zeitschrift für Vergleichende Literaturwissenschaft
Archiv	Archiv für das Studium der Neueren Sprachen und Literaturen
ArielE	ARIEL: A Review of International English Literature (Calgary, Canada)
AUMLA	AUMLA: Journal of the Australasian Universities Language and Literature Association: A Journal of Literary Criticism and Linguistics
BC	The Book Collector
BHR	Bibliothèque d'Humanisme et Renaissance
BIS	Browning Institute Studies: An Annual of Victorian Literary and Cultural History
BJJ	The Ben Jonson Journal: Literary Contexts in the Age of Elizabeth, James and Charles
BkW	Book World

BMMLA	The Bulletin of the Medieval Modern Language Association
BRH	Bulletin of Research in the Humanities
BSEAA	Bulletin de la Société d'Etudes Anglo-Américaines des XVIIe et XVIIIe Siècles (Lille, France)
BSUF	Ball State University Forum
BuR	Bucknell Review: A Scholarly Journal of Letters, Arts and Sciences
CahiersE	Cahiers Elisabéthains: Late Medieval and Renaissance Studies
C&L	Christianity and Literature
CanL	Canadian Literature
Carrell	The Carrell: Journal of the Friends of the University of Miami Library
CASS	Canadian-American Slavic Studies
CE	College English
CEA	CEA Critic: An Official Journal of the College English Association (Youngstown, Ohio)
CentR	The Centennial Review (East Lansing, Mich.)
CHum	Computers and the Humanities
CIEFLB	Central Institute of English and Foreign Languages Bulletin
Cithara	Cithara: Essays in the Judaeo-Christian Tradition
CJNS	Canadian Journal of Netherlandic Studies/Revue Canadienne d'Etudes Néerlandaises
CL	Comparative Literature (Eugene, Oreg.)
CLAJ	College Language Association Journal
ClioI	CLIO: A Journal of Literature, History, and the Philosophy of History
ClQ	Colby Quarterly
CLS	Comparative Literature Studies
CML	Classical and Modern Literature: A Quarterly (Terre Haute, Ind.)
CollL	College Literature
Comitatus	Comitatus: A Journal of Medieval and Renaissance Studies
CompD	Comparative Drama
Connotations	Connotations: A Journal for Critical Debate
CP	Concerning Poetry
CQ	The Cambridge Quarterly
CR	The Critical Review
CRCL	Canadian Review of Comparative Literature/Revue Canadienne de Littérature Comparée
Criticism	Criticism: A Quarterly for Literature and the Arts (Detroit, Mich.)
Critique	Critique: Revue Générale des Publications Françaises et Etrangères (Paris, France)
CritQ	Critical Quarterly

Cross-Bias	Cross-Bias: The Newsletter of the Friends of Bemerton Honoring George Herbert 1593–1633
CrSurv	Critical Survey
CRUX	CRUX: A Journal on the Teaching of English
CSR	Christian Scholar's Review
DHLR	The D. H. Lawrence Review
DQ	Denver Quarterly
DQR	Dutch Quarterly Review of Anglo-American Letters
DR	Dalhousie Review
DSS	Dix-Septième Siècle
DUJ	Durham University Journal
EA	Etudes Anglaises: Grande-Bretagne, Etats-Unis
E&S	Essays and Studies (London, England)
ECLife	Eighteenth-Century Life
EIC	Essays in Criticism: A Quarterly Journal of Literary Criticism (Oxford, England)
EigoS	Eigo Seinen
EIRC	Explorations in Renaissance Culture
ELH	Journal of English Literary History (former title)
ELLS	English Literature and Language (Tokyo, Japan)
ELN	English Language Notes (Boulder, Colo.)
ELR	English Literary Renaissance
ELWIU	Essays in Literature (Macomb, Ill.)
EM	English Miscellany: A Symposium of History, Literature and the Arts
Emblematica	Emblematica: An Interdisciplinary Journal of Emblem Studies
EMLS	Early Modern Literary Studies: A Journal of Sixteenth- and Seventeenth-Century English Literature
EMS	English Manuscript Studies 1100–1700
Encounter	Encounter (London, England)
Encyclia	Encyclia: The Journal of the Utah Academy of Sciences, Arts, and Letters
English	English: The Journal of the English Association (Leicester, England)
ERev	The Elizabethan Review
ES	English Studies: A Journal of English Language and Literature (Lisse, Netherlands)
ESA	English Studies in Africa: A Journal of the Humanities
ESC	English Studies in Canada
ESELL	Tohoku Gakuin Daigaku Ronshu: Eigo-Eibungaku/Essays and Studies in English Language and Literature (Sendai, Japan)
Esprit	Esprit (Paris, France)

Exemplaria	Exemplaria: A Journal of Theory in Medieval and Renaissance Studies
Expl	Explicator
FJS	Fu Jen Studies: Literature and Linguistics
FMLS	Forum for Modern Language Studies
Folklore	Folklore (London, England)
FS	French Studies: A Quarterly Review
Fund og Forskning	Fund og forskning i det Konelige Biblioteks Samlinger (Copenhagen)
Genre	Genre: Forms of Discourse and Culture (Norman, Okla.)
GHJ	George Herbert Journal
Gradiva	Gradiva: International Journal of Italian Literature
GrIm	Graven Images: A Journal of Culture, Law, and the Sacred
HLQ	Huntington Library Quarterly: A Journal of English and American History and Literature
Horizontes	Horizontes: Revista de la Universidad Católica de Puerto Rico
HSELL	Hiroshima Studies in English Language and Literature
HSL	University of Hartford Studies in Literature: A Journal of Interdisciplinary Criticism
HTR	Harvard Theological Review
HudR	The Hudson Review
IAN	Izvestiia Akademii Nauk S. S. S. R. (Moscow)
Inbetween	In-between: Essays and Studies in Literary Criticism
Interpretations	Interpretations (Memphis, Tenn.)
ISJR	Iowa State Journal of Research
ISRev	Irish Studies Review
JAAC	Journal of Aesthetics and Art Criticism
JCL	The Journal of Commonwealth Literature
JD	Journal of Documentation
JDJ	John Donne Journal: Studies in the Age of Donne
JEGP	Journal of English and Germanic Philology
JELL	The Journal of English Language and Literature
JELL-CB	Journal of the English Language and Literature (Chongwon, Korea)
JEP	Journal of Evolutionary Psychology
JHI	Journal of the History of Ideas
JLS	Journal of Literary Semantics
JMRS	Journal of Medieval and Renaissance Studies
JPC	Journal of Popular Culture
JRMMRA	Journal of the Rocky Mountain Medieval and Renaissance Association (Provo, Utah)

KN	Kwartalnik Neofilologiczny (Warsaw, Poland)
KPR	Kentucky Philological Review
KR	The Kenyon Review
KRev	The Kentucky Review
L&H	Literature and History
L&LC	Literary and Linguistic Computing: Journal of the Association for Literary and Linguistic Computing
L&M	Literature and Medicine
L&T	Literature and Theology: An International Journal of Theory, Criticism, and Culture [Formerly *Literature and Theology: An Interdisciplinary Journal of Theory and Criticism*]
Lang&S	Language and Style: An International Journal
LangQ	The Language Quarterly (Tampa, Fla.)
LCUT	Library Chronicle of the University of Texas
Library	The Library: The Transactions of the Bibliographical Society
List	The Listener
Lit	Littérature (Paris, France)
LIT	Lit: Literature Interpretation Theory
LitE	The Literary Endeavour: A Quarterly Journal Devoted to English Studies
LJGG	Literaturwissenschaftliches Jahrbuch im Auftrage der Görres-Gesellschaft
LRB	London Review of Books
LRN	Literary Research Newsletter
LWU	Literatur in Wissenschaft und Unterricht (Kiel, Germany)
M&L	Music and Letters
MedPers	Medieval Perspectives
MHLS	Mid-Hudson Review
MiltonQ	Milton Quarterly
MiscMus	Miscellanea Musicologica
MLNew	The Malcolm Lowry Review
MLQ	Modern Language Quarterly: A Journal of Literary History
MLR	The Modern Language Review
MLS	Modern Language Studies
Moreana	Moreana: Bulletin Thomas More
Mosaic	Mosaic: A Journal for the Interdisciplinary Study of Literature
MP	Modern Philology: A Journal Devoted to Research in Medieval and Modern Literature
MQ	Midwest Quarterly: A Journal of Contemporary Thought (Pittsburg, Kans.)
MRDE	Medieval and Renaissance Drama in England: An Annual Gathering of Research, Criticism and Reviews

Names	Names: A Journal of Onomastics [Formerly *Names: Journal of the American Name Society*]
N&Q	Notes and Queries
NDEJ	Notre Dame English Journal: A Journal of Religion in Literature
Neohelicon	Neohelicon: Acta Comparationis Litterarum Universarum
Neophil	Neophilologus (Dordrecht, Netherlands)
NER	New England Review
NewC	The New Criterion
NLauR	New Laurel Review
NM	Neuphilologische Mitteilungen: Bulletin de la Société Néophilologique/Bulletin of the Modern Language Society
NOR	New Orleans Review
NyA	Nya Argus
NYRB	The New York Review of Books (New York, N.Y.)
Ody	Odyssey: A Journal of the Humanities
OL	Orbis Litterarum: International Review of Literary Studies
P&L	Philosophy and Literature
P&R	Philosophy and Rhetoric
PAPA	Publications of the Arkansas Philological Association
Parergon	Parergon: Bulletin of the Australian and New Zealand Association for Medieval and Renaissance Studies
PBA	Proceedings of the British Academy
PBSA	Papers of the Bibliographical Society of America
PCP	Pacific Coast Philology
PCRev	Popular Culture Review
PLL	Papers on Language and Literature: A Journal for Scholars and Critics of Language and Literature
PMLA	PMLA: Publications of the Modern Language Association of America
PMPA	Publications of the Missouri Philological Association
PNR	PN Review
Po&sie	Po&sie
PoetryR	Poetry Review (London, England)
POMPA	Publications of the Mississippi Philological Association
PQ	Philological Quarterly (Iowa City, Iowa)
PSt	Prose Studies: History, Theory, Criticism (London, England)
PURBA	Panjab University Research Bulletin (Arts)
QI	Quaderni d'Italianistica: Official Journal of the Canadian Society for Italian Studies
QJS	The Quarterly Journal of Speech
QL	Quinzaine Litteraire
QQ	Queen's Quarterly
R&L	Religion and Literature (Notre Dame, Ind.)

Raritan	Raritan: A Quarterly Review
RecH	Recusant History
Ren&R	Renaissance and Reformation (Renaissance et Réforme)
Renascence	Renascence: Essays on Value in Literature
RenB	The Renaissance Bulletin
RenD	Renaissance Drama
RenP	Renaissance Papers
RenQ	Renaissance Quarterly
RenSt	Renaissance Studies: Journal of the Society for Renaissance Studies
RES	Review of English Studies: A Quarterly Journal of English Literature and the English Language
RestQ	Restoration Quarterly
Rev	Review (Blacksburg, Va.)
RF	Romanische Forschungen (Freiburg, Germany)
Rhetorica	Rhetorica: A Journal of the History of Rhetoric
RHL	Revue d'Histoire Littéraire de la France
RLC	Revue de Littérature Comparée
RLMC	Rivista di Letterature Moderne e Comparate
RMR	Rocky Mountain Review of Language and Literature
RMS	Renaissance and Modern Studies
RoHum	Roczniki Humanistyczne: Annales de Lettres et Sciences Humaines/ Annals of Arts (Lublin, Poland)
RSLR	Rivista di Storia e Letteratura Religiosa
RSQ	Rhetoric Society Quarterly
RusL	Russian Literature
SAQ	South Atlantic Quarterly
SCB	South Central Bulletin
SCen	The Seventeenth Century
SCJ	The Sixteenth Century Journal: Journal of Early Modern Studies
SCN	Seventeenth-Century News
SCr	Strumenti Critici: Rivista Quadrimestrale di Cultura e Critica Letteraria
SCRev	South Central Review: The Journal of the South Central Modern Language Association
SCUL	Soundings: Collections of the University Library, University of California, Santa Barbara
SEA	Studies in English and American (Budapest, Hungary)
SEL	SEL: Studies in English Literature, 1500–1900
SELit	Studies in English Literature (Tokyo, Japan)
SHR	Southern Humanities Review
ShS	Shakespeare Survey: An Annual Survey of Shakespeare Studies and Production
SIcon	Studies in Iconography

SJS	San José Studies
SLitI	Studies in the Literary Imagination
SMLit	Studies in Mystical Literature (Taiwan, Republic of China)
SMy	Studia Mystica
SoAR	South Atlantic Review
SoR	The Southern Review (Baton Rouge, La.)
SoRA	Southern Review: Literary and Interdisciplinary Essays (Gippsland, Australia)
SP	Studies in Philology
SpL	Spiegel der Letteren: Tijdschrift voor Nederlandse Literatuurgeschiedenis en voor Literatuurwetenschap
SPWVSRA	Selected Papers from the West Virginia Shakespeare and Renaissance Association
SQ	Shakespeare Quarterly
SR	Sewanee Review
SSEng	Sydney Studies in English
SSt	Spenser Studies: A Renaissance Poetry Annual
Style	Style (DeKalb, Ill.)
TCBS	Transactions of the Cambridge Bibliographical Society
Text	Text: An Interdisciplinary Journal of Textual Studies
Thalia	Thalia: Studies in Literary Humor
Theoria	Theoria: A Journal of Social and Political Theory (Pietermaritzburg, S. Africa)
THES	[London] Times Higher Education Supplement
TJQ	Thoreau Journal Quarterly
TLS	[London] Times Literary Supplement
TNTL	Tijdschrift voor Nederlandse Taal- en Letterkunde (Leiden, Netherlands)
Tr&Lit	Translation and Literature
TSLL	Texas Studies in Literature and Language
UTQ	University of Toronto Quarterly: A Canadian Journal of the Humanities
W&I	Word and Image: A Journal of Verbal/Visual Enquiry
WHR	Western Humanities Review
WL&A	War, Literature, and the Arts: An International Journal of the Humanities
WVUPP	West Virginia University Philological Papers
YER	Yeats Eliot Review: A Journal of Criticism and Scholarship
YES	Yearbook of English Studies
YJC	The Yale Journal of Criticism: Interpretation in the Humanities
YJLH	Yale Journal of Law and the Humanities
YR	The Yale Review

YWES   Year's Work in English Studies
ZAA   Zeitschrift für Anglistik und Amerikanistik: A Quarterly of Language,
            Literature and Culture

Short Forms of Reference for Donne's Works

The following abbreviations of Donne's poems have been used in the annotations
for the sake of economy and convenience. I wish to express my thanks to the members of the Advisory Board and the editors of the John Donne Variorum Edition
for permission to use them.

Poems

Air   Air and Angels ["Twice or thrice had I loved"]
AltVic   A Letter Written by Sir H. G. and J. D. Alternis Vicibus ["Since
             every tree begins"]
Amic   Amicissimo et Meritissimo Ben Jonson ["Quod arte ausus es hic tua"]
Anniv   The Anniversary ["All kings and all their favorites"]
Annun   Upon the Annunciation and Passion ["Tamely frail body"]
Antiq   Antiquary ["If in his study"]
Apoth   Apotheosis Ignatij Loyolae ["Qui sacer antefuit"]
Appar   The Apparition ["When by thy scorn"]
AutHook   Ad Autorem ["Non eget Hookerus"]
AutJos   Ad Autorem ["Emendare cupis Joseph"]
Bait   The Bait ["Come live with me"]
BB   To Mr. B. B. ["Is not thy sacred hunger"]
BedfCab   Epitaph on Himself: To the Countess of Bedford ["That I might make
             your cabinet"]
BedfDead   To the Countess of Bedford: Begun in France ["Though I be dead
             and buried"]
BedfHon   To the Countess of Bedford ["Honor is so sublime"]
BedfReas   To the Countess of Bedford ["Reason is our soul's left hand"]
BedfRef   To the Countess of Bedford ["You have refined me"]
BedfShe   Elegy to the Lady Bedford ["You that are she"]
BedfTwi   To the Countess of Bedford: On New-Year's Day ["This twilight of
             two years"]
BedfWrit   To the Countess of Bedford ["To have written then"]
Beggar   A Lame Beggar ["I am unable, yonder beggar cries"]
Blos   The Blossom ["Little thinkest thou"]
BoulNar   Elegy upon the Death of Mrs. Boulstrode ["Language thou art too
             narrow"]

BoulRec   Elegy on Mrs. Boulstrode ["Death, I recant"]
Break   Break of Day ["'Tis true, 'tis day"]
Broken   The Broken Heart ["He is stark mad"]
Cales   Cales and Guiana ["If you from spoil"]
Calm   The Calm ["Our storm is past"]
Canon   The Canonization ["For God's sake hold your tongue"]
Carey   A Letter to the Lady Carey and Mrs. Essex Rich ["Here where by all"]
CB   To Mr. C. B. ["Thy friend whom thy deserts"]
Christ   A Hymn to Christ at the Author's Last Going into Germany ["In what torn ship soever"]
Citizen   A Tale of a Citizen and His Wife (noncanonical) ["I sing no harme, goodsooth"]
Commun   Community ["Good we must love"]
Compu   The Computation ["For the first twenty years"]
ConfL   Confined Love ["Some man unworthy"]
Corona   La Corona
  Cor1   "Deign at my hands"
  Cor2   Annunciation ["Salvation to all that will is nigh"]
  Cor3   Nativity ["Immensity cloistered in thy dear womb"]
  Cor4   Temple ["With his kind mother who partakes thy woe"]
  Cor5   Crucifying ["By miracles exceeding power of man"]
  Cor6   Resurrection ["Moist with one drop of thy blood"]
  Cor7   Ascension ["Salute the last and everlasting day"]
Coryat   Upon Mr. Thomas Coryat's Crudities ["Oh to what height"]
Cross   The Cross ["Since Christ embraced"]
Curse   The Curse ["Whoever guesses, thinks, or dreams"]
Damp   The Damp ["When I am dead"]
Disinher   Disinherited ["Thy father all from thee"]
Dissol   The Dissolution ["She is dead"]
Dream   The Dream ["Dear love, for nothing less"]
Eclog   Eclogue at the Marriage of the Earl of Somerset ["Unseasonable man, statue of ice"]
Ecst   The Ecstasy ["Where, like a pillow on a bed"]
ED   To E. of D. with Six Holy Sonnets ["See, Sir, how as the sun's"]
EdHerb   To Sir Edward Herbert ["Man is a lump"]
EG   To Mr. E. G. ["Even as lame things"]
EgDD   Epigraph from *Death's Duel* ["Corporis haec animae"]
Elegies:
  ElAnag   The Anagram ["Marry and love thy Flavia"]
  ElAut   The Autumnal ["No spring nor summer beauty"]
  ElBed   Going to Bed ["Come, Madam, come"]
  ElBrac   The Bracelet ["Not that in color it was like thy hair"]

ElChange	Change ["Although thy hand and faith"]
ElComp	The Comparison ["As the sweet sweat of roses in a still"]
ElExpost	The Expostulation ["To make the doubt clear"]
ElFatal	On His Mistress ["By our first strange and fatal interview"]
ElJeal	Jealousy ["Fond woman which would'st have thy husband die"]
ElNat	"Nature's lay idiot"
ElPart	His Parting From Her ["Since she must go"]
ElPerf	The Perfume ["Once and but once found in thy company"]
ElPict	His Picture ["Here take my picture"]
ElProg	Love's Progress ["Whoever loves, if he do not propose"]
ElServe	"Oh, let not me serve so"
ElVar	Variety ["The heavens rejoice in motion"]
ElWar	Love's War ["Till I have peace with thee"]
EpEliz	Epithalamion upon . . . the Lady Elizabeth ["Hail, Bishop Valentine"]
EpLin	Epithalamion Made at Lincoln's Inn ["The sunbeams in the east"]
EtAD	Epitaph for Ann Donne ["Annae/Georgii More de filiae"]
EtED	Epitaph for Elizabeth Drury ["Quo pergas, viator"]
EtRD	Epitaph for Robert and Anne Drury ["Roberti Druri/quo vix alter"]
EtSP	John Donne's Epitaph . . . in St. Paul's Cathedral ["Iohannes Donne/Sac: Theol: Profess:"]
Expir	The Expiration ["So, so, break off"]
Fare	Farewell to Love ["Whilst yet to prove"]
Father	A Hymn to God the Father ["Wilt thou forgive"]
Faust	Faustinus ["Faustinus keeps his sister"]
Fever	A Fever ["Oh do not die"]
FirAn	The First Anniversary. An Anatomy of the World ["When that rich soul"]
Flea	The Flea ["Mark but this flea"]
Fun	The Funeral ["Whoever comes to shroud me"]
FunEl	A Funeral Elegy ["'Tis lost to trust a tomb"]
Gaz	Translated out of Gazaeus ["God grant thee thine own wish"]
GHerb	To Mr. George Herbert with One of My Seals ["Qui prius assuetus serpentum"]
Goodf	Goodfriday, 1613. Riding Westward ["Let man's soul be a sphere"]
GoodM	The Good Morrow ["I wonder by my troth"]
Ham	An Hymn to the Saints and to the Marquis Hamilton ["Whether that soul which now comes"]
Har	Obsequies upon the Lord Harrington ["Fair soul, which wast not only"]
Harb	The Harbinger to the Progress (by Joseph Hall) ["Two souls move here"]

Heart	"When my heart was mine own"
Henry	Elegy on the Untimely Death of . . . Prince Henry ["Look to me, Faith"]
Hero	Hero and Leander ["Both robbed of air"]
HG	To Sr. Henry Goodyere ["Who makes the past a pattern"]
Holy Sonnets:	
HSBatter	"Batter my heart"
HSBlack	"O my black soul"
HSDeath	"Death be not proud"
HSDue	"As due by many titles"
HSLittle	"I am a little world"
HSMade	"Thou hast made me"
HSMin	"If poisonous minerals"
HSPart	"Father part of his double interest"
HSRound	"At the round earth's imagined corners"
HSScene	"This is my play's last scene"
HSShe	"Since she whom I loved"
HSShow	"Show me dear Christ"
HSSighs	"O might those sighs"
HSSouls	"If faithful souls"
HSSpit	"Spit in my face"
HSVex	"O to vex me"
HSWhat	"What if this present"
HSWhy	"Why are we by all creatures"
HSWilt	"Wilt thou love God"
HuntMan	To the Countess of Huntingdon ["Man to God's image"]
HuntUn	To the Countess of Huntingdon ["That unripe side of earth"]
HWHiber	H. W. in Hibernia Belligeranti ["Went you to conquer?"]
HWKiss	To Sir Henry Wotton ["Sir, more than kisses"]
HWNews	To Sir Henry Wotton ["Here's no more news"]
HWVenice	To Sir H. W. at His Going Ambassador to Venice ["After those reverend papers"]
ILBlest	To Mr. I. L. ["Blest are your north parts"]
ILRoll	To Mr. I. L. ["Of that short roll"]
Image	"Image of her whom I love"
InAA	Inscription in the *Album Amicorum* of Michael Corvinus ["In propria venit"]
Ind	The Indifferent ["I can love both fair and brown"]
InLI	Inscription in a Bible Presented to Lincoln's Inn ["In Bibliotheca Hospitii"]
Jet	A Jet Ring Sent ["Thou art not so black"]
Jug	The Juggler ["Thou callest me effeminate"]
Julia	Julia (noncanonical) ["Hearke newes, ô Envy"]

Klock	Klockius ["Klockius so deeply hath sworn"]
Lam	The Lamentations of Jeremy ["How sits this city"]
Lect	A Lecture upon the Shadow ["Stand still and I will read"]
Leg	The Legacy ["When I died last"]
Liar	The Liar ["Thou in the fields walkest"]
Libro	De Libro Cum Mutuaretur ["Doctissimo Amicissimoque v. D. D. Andrews"]
Licent	A Licentious Person ["Thy sins and hairs"]
Lit	A Litany ["Father of heaven and him"]
LovAlch	Love's Alchemy ["Some that have deeper digged"]
LovDeity	Love's Deity ["I long to talk with some old"]
LovDiet	Love's Diet ["To what a cumbersome unwieldiness"]
LovExch	Love's Exchange ["Love, any devil else but you"]
LovGrow	Love's Growth ["I scarce believe my love to be so pure"]
LovInf	Lovers' Infiniteness ["If yet I have not all thy love"]
LovUsury	Love's Usury ["For every hour that thou wilt spare me"]
Macaron	In Eundem Macaronicon ["Quot, dos, haec, linguists"]
Mark	Elegy on the Lady Markham ["Man is the world"]
Martial	Raderus ["Why this man gelded Martial"]
Merc	Mercurius Gallo-Belgicus ["Like Aesop's fellow slaves"]
Mess	The Message ["Send home my long strayed eyes"]
Metem	Metempsychosis ["I sing the progress of a deathless soul"]
MHMary	To the Lady Magdalen Herbert, of St. Mary Magdalen ["Her of your name"]
MHPaper	To Mrs. M. H. ["Mad paper stay"]
NegLov	Negative Love ["I never stooped so low"]
Niobe	Niobe ["By children's birth and death"]
Noct	A Nocturnal upon St. Lucy's Day ["'Tis the year's midnight"]
Para	The Paradox ["No lover saith, I love"]
Philo	An Obscure Writer ["Philo with twelve years' study"]
Phrine	Phrine ["Thy flattering picture, Phrine"]
Praise	To the Praise of the Dead and the Anatomy (by Joseph Hall) ["Well died the world"]
Prim	The Primrose ["Upon this primrose hill"]
Prohib	The Prohibition ["Take heed of loving me"]
Pyr	Pyramus and Thisbe ["Two by themselves each other"]
Ralph	Ralphius ["Compassion in the world again is bred"]
Relic	The Relic ["When my grave is broke up again"]
Res	Resurrection Imperfect ["Sleep, sleep, old sun"]
RWEnvy	To Mr. R. W. ["Kindly I envy thy song's"]
RWMind	To Mr. R. W. ["Muse not that by thy mind"]
RWSlumb	To Mr. R. W. ["If as mine is thy life a slumber be"]
RWThird	To Mr. R. W. ["Like one who in her third widowhood"]

RWZeal	To Mr. R. W. ["Zealously my muse"]
Sal	To the Countess of Salisbury ["Fair, great, and good"]
Sappho	Sappho to Philaenis ["Where is that holy fire"]
Satires	
Sat1	"Away thou fondling motley humorist"
Sat2	"Sir, though (I thank God for it) I do hate"
Sat3	"Kind pity chokes my spleen"
Sat4	"Well, I may now receive and die"
Sat5	"Thou shalt not laugh in this leaf, Muse"
SB	To Mr. S. B. ["O thou which to search"]
SecAn	The Second Anniversary. Of the Progress of the Soul ["Nothing could make me sooner"]
SelfAc	A Self Accuser ["Your mistress, that you follow whores"]
SelfL	Self Love ["He that cannot choose but love"]
SGo	Song ["Go, and catch a falling star"]
Ship	A Burnt Ship ["Out of a fired ship"]
Sickness	A Hymn to God My God, in My Sickness ["Since I am coming"]
Sidney	Upon the Translation of the Psalms by Sir Philip Sidney ["Eternal God, (for whom who ever dare . . .)"]
Sorrow	Elegia ["Sorrow, who to this house"]
SSweet	Song ["Sweetest love, I do not go"]
Stat	Stationes from *Devotions* ["Insultus morbi primus"]
Storm	The Storm ["Thou which art I"]
SunRis	The Sun Rising ["Busy old fool, unruly Sun"]
Tilman	To Mr. Tilman after He Had Taken Orders ["Thou whose diviner soul"]
Token	Sonnet. The Token ["Send me some token"]
Triple	The Triple Fool ["I am two fools, I know"]
TWHail	To Mr. T. W. ["All hail sweet poet"]
TWHarsh	To Mr. T. W. ["Haste thee harsh verse"]
TWHence	To Mr. T. W. ["At once from hence"]
TWPreg	To Mr. T. W. ["Pregnant again"]
Twick	Twickenham Garden ["Blasted with sighs and surrounded with tears"]
Under	The Undertaking ["I have done one braver thing"]
ValBook	A Valediction of the Book ["I'll tell thee now"]
ValMourn	A Valediction Forbidding Mourning ["As virtuous men pass mildly away"]
ValName	A Valediction of My Name in the Window ["My name engraved herein"]
ValWeep	A Valediction of Weeping ["Let me pour forth"]
Wall	Fall of a Wall ["Under an undermined and shot-bruised wall"]

Will	The Will ["Before I sigh my last gasp"]
Wing	Sir John Wingfield ["Beyond th'old pillars"]
Witch	Witchcraft by a Picture ["I fix mine eye on thine"]
WomCon	Woman's Constancy ["Now thou has loved me one whole day"]

Prose Works

Biathanatos	*Biathanatos* (1647)
Devotions	*Devotions upon Emergent Occasions* (1624)
Essays	*Essays in Divinity* (1651)
Ignatius	*Ignatius His Conclave* (1611)
Letters	*Letters to Severall Persons of Honour (1651)*
Pseudo-Martyr	*Pseudo-Martyr* (1610)
Paradoxes	*Paradoxes and Problems* (1633)

Other Works

OED	*Oxford English Dictionary*
Roberts 1	John R. Roberts. *John Donne: An Annotated Bibliography of Modern Criticism, 1912–1967.* Columbia: University of Missouri Press, 1973.
Roberts 2	John R. Roberts. *John Donne: An Annotated Bibliography of Modern Criticism, 1968–1978.* Columbia: University of Missouri Press, 1982.
Summa	St. Thomas Aquinas, *Summa Theologica*

1979

1. Adams, Robert M. "John Donne," in *The Norton Anthology of English Literature,* gen. ed. M. H. Abrams, 1:1059–112. 4th ed. New York: W. W. Norton. 1st ed., 1962; 2nd ed., 1968; 3rd ed., 1974; 5th ed., 1986; 6th ed., 1996.

Contains a biographical and critical introduction (1059–62), followed by selections from Donne's poetry (1062–104) and selections from *Devotions* and one sermon (1105–12), with notes. Endorses the concept of "two Donnes"—Jack and John—and calls the reading of Donne's poetry "an imaginative struggle and intellectual struggle" and "an all-absorbing experience" (1059). Sees the poetry as radically different from that of Donne's predecessors and contemporaries, stressing in particular the unique nature of Donne's conceits and his use of colloquial rhythms. Rejects the notion of a "metaphysical school" of poetry; comments briefly on the critical reception of Donne's poetry, especially in the twentieth century; and notes the importance of recognizing Donne as a coterie poet.

2. Asals, Heather. "John Donne and the Grammar of Redemption." *ESC* 5: 125–39.

Argues that the sermons offer "a provocative corpus of literary criticism" useful in the analysis of Donne's *Holy Sonnets* as well as seventeenth century religious poetry in general. Stresses in particular Donne's concept of the relationship between the Divine Word and the words of men, which is based on the logology of the Church Fathers, especially that of St. Augustine and St. Basil. Maintains that the sermons argue "the presence of the Word in words," while the poetry "demonstrates (or represents) the Word in words" (125). Discusses in detail *HSSpit, HSScene,* and *HSRound* to show that "the practice of the grammar of redemption" is "the meaning" of these poems and others (128), poems in which Donne explores and examines "the possibilities of language as reflections of God's promises in his Word" (136).

3. Barker, Arthur E. *The Seventeenth Century: Bacon Through Marvell.* Goldentree Bibliographies in Language and Literature, ed. O. B. Hardison, Jr. Arlington Heights, Ill.: AHM Publishing Co. xi, 132p.

Selected, unannotated listing of studies on seventeenth century English poetry and prose to 1975 (excluding Milton, Dryden, the dramatists, and dissertations). Includes 39 authors, aids to research, major anthologies, general studies of literary history and criticism, and studies in background information. Lists for Donne 42 modern editions, 7 bibliographies, 1 concordance, and 373 items of criticism, divided into four parts: comprehensive studies, studies of topics, studies of the poems, and studies of the prose. All of these items are fully annotated in *Roberts 1* (1973) or in *Roberts 2* (1982).

4. Bartine, David. "Rhetorical Dimensions of Primary Performatives," in *Rhetoric 78: Proceedings of Theory of Rhetoric, an Interdisciplinary Conference,* ed. Robert L. Brown, Jr., and Martin Steinmann, Jr., 1–8. Minneapolis: University of Minnesota Center for Advanced Studies in Language, Style, and Literary Theory.

Argues that the complexity of *HS-Death* results from "three simultaneous functions of personification": the personification of death "carries clues to the speaker's state of mind," "serves to constitute the audience" of the poem, and "functions as a central principle of structure for the entire utterance." Maintains, in other words, that in the poem the speaker's "ongoing constitution of the audience" and the "continuing shaping and clarification" of that audience occur "simultaneously with an increasingly complex accumulation of clues about the speaker's state of mind" (5).

5. Beardsley, Monroe. "Verbal Style and Illocutionary Style," in *The Concept of Style,* ed. Berel Lang, 149–68. Philadelphia: University of Pennsylvania Press.

Comments briefly on *ValMourn* in a theoretical discussion of the nature of verbal style or style of language, noting, for instance, the "scientific air of some key words" (158) in the poem.

6. Bloom, Edward A., and Lillian D. Bloom. "Sacramentum Militiae: Religious Satire," in *Satire's Persuasive Voice,* 160–201. Ithaca, N.Y.: Cornell University Press.

Maintains that Donne effectively uses satire in *Sat1* in order to explain allegorically how faith is needed to attain "the finality of human apprehension." Claims that Donne's injunction, "Doubt wisely," is "the soul and core" of the poem and is "a call for rational examination," noting that the satire represents "an important stage" in Donne's religious development as he

was leaving Catholicism behind him and was turning to his conscience as his "highest authority" in the mid-1590s (171). Notes also that "if wise doubt can be the satirist's appeal to conscience so equally can wise laughter, as Donne asserted in 'Paradox 10'" (172).

7. Bøgh, Knud. "Domprovsten, der lovpriste selvmord: John Donne og hans danske angribere fra 1675" [The Dean Who Praised Suicide: John Donne and His Danish Attackers.] *Fund og forskning* 24 (1979/1980): 93–118.

Reviews events in Donne's early life that led to the composition of *Biathanatos,* explains his choice of a religious vocation, and notes his elaborate preparations for his own death. Analyzes Donne's defense of suicide in *Biathanatos* as a natural impulse related to martyrdom and illustrated by the deaths of certain biblical figures, perhaps even Christ himself. Reports the response by the Danish theologian Georg Witzleben (1616–76), who wrote *Disputationum theologicarum . . .* (1675), opposing all of Donne's arguments, criticizing, in particular, Donne's tolerance of the unrepentant and his interpretation of his sources. Observes that Witzleben successfully defended his thesis in a debate at the University of Copenhagen twenty-five years before *Biathanatos* received critical attention in England.

8. Braden, Gordon. "*Viuamus, mea Lesbia* in the English Renaissance." *ELR* 9: 199–22.

Surveys adaptations of Catullus's *Carmina* 5 ("Viuamus, mea Lesbia") by English Renaissance poets, in particular Raleigh, Jonson, Thomas Campion, Thomas Randolph, Alexander Brome, William Habington, Marvell, and Donne. Points out Donne's adaptation of Catullus in *Compu* (ll. 1–5) and in *Anniv* (ll. 1–10, 25–30). Argues that, in the latter, Donne, by rejecting and transvaluing his Roman model, "attains a result far closer to Catullus's essential vision than any other Renaissance adapter does" and reproduces "the deepest concerns" of Catullus's poem— "the establishment of love as an exemplary privacy conjured from the very actions and terminology of a loveless world." Notes that while "most adapters of Catullus' poem consistently debase the distances between those two worlds," Donne "heightens it until it becomes, in fact, the great subject of his love poetry." Suggests that in *SunRis,* a poem primarily modelled on Ovid's *Amores* 1.13, Donne gives the subject "a fuller and more confident development than Catullus ever does" (218). Points out that in this poem, as well as in *Canon* and *Ecst,* the argument is not aimed at the woman but at "the enveloping world" (220).

9. **Cameron, Sharon.** *Lyric Time: Dickinson and the Limits of Genre.* Baltimore: Johns Hopkins University Press. x, 280p.

Finds similarities in the spiritual experience portrayed in several of Emily Dickinson's poems and Donne's *HSMade,* an experience in which "the self falls back on itself and finds that it is nothing" (46). Points out also that in poems such as *ValMourn, SunRis,* and *Canon* there are certain "contradictions and compressions of death and immortality that lie at the heart of the metaphysical conceit" (244). Offers a partial reading of *Goodf,* suggesting that the poem "offers barely submerged evidence" that the speaker finds it intolerable to view Christ the God suffering in Jesus the man. Thinks, therefore, that "Restore thine Image" (l. 41) may refer not only to the speaker but also to Christ and that the speaker is saying, in effect, "Allow me to see You as God rather than Jesus, as Lord rather than suffering

man." Suggests that "the power in the last few lines" of the poem "depends upon the doubling of the restoration—man's into a state of grace, Jesus' into a divinity distanced from the horrible presence of suffering" (249). Concludes that the poem gives "an extreme example of how the religious lyric can so subvert time and space, so rewrite itself into prior history, that it is left shuddering from the reality it has called into being" (250).

10. **Costa de Beauregard, Raphaëlle.** "Le compas: Instrument de connaissance occulte," in *Devins et charlatans au temps de la Renaissance,* ed. M. T. Jones-Davies, 175–85. Université de Paris-Sorbonne, Institut de Recherches sur les Civilisations de l'Occident Moderne. Centre de Recherches sur la Renaissance. Paris: Université de Paris-Sorbonne.

Discusses the symbolic uses of the compass in emblem books, astrology, art, and magic. Points out that the compass was used metaphorically to express mysterious things in a way that made them seem rational, citing *ValMourn* in which the compass creates a synthesis between two kinds of meaning, that is, between the fidelity and infidelity of the parting lovers. Calls Donne's use a "tour de force" that reveals the magic of speech (178).

11. **Cousins, A. D.** "The Coming of Mannerism: The Later Ralegh and the Early Donne." *ELR* 9: 86–107.

Calls Donne's early works "mannerist," maintaining that in them he created a "new style" in which "ideas and forms find counterparts in Italian mannerist painting" (96), thereby supplanting High Renaissance styles. Suggests that Donne's ideas about art arose out of "his fascination with skepticism" from which he fashioned "for himself a *manner,* a distinctive stylishness," and "a *method,* a way of analyzing experience" that "probes complexities yet rarely attempts more than their tentative resolution" (97). Examines Donne's aims and mannerist rhetoric in the *Paradoxes* and in *ElJeal,* but primarily in the *Satyres,* in which one finds "the most persuasive evidence that the term 'mannerist' accurately defines a moment in English literary history" because they present Donne's "considered response, and the first united response, to the ideas and forms of the High Renaissance style" (107).

12. Crennan, M. J. *In Search of Donne.* Sydney: English Association. 22p.

Challenges certain views of Donne and his poetry perpetuated by modern poets and critics who exaggerate Donne's role as a poet-reformer, as a poet with a "voracious appetite" for a "wide range of sensations and areas of knowledge as sources for his images and metaphors" that resulted in wit and paradox, and as a poet of "contemporaneity" (5) who was fully aware of the changing world about him. Comments on four portraits of Donne that show different self-images that Donne projected during his life and gives a short biographical sketch, admitting, however, that although Donne's life has "great intrinsic interest," it provides "only intermittently help in reading the poems" (9–10). Discusses several distinguishing characteristics of Donne's poetry, especially the voice and tone of the speaker, the presence of an imagined or primary audience in the poems, and the exploration of two major subjects, "love and death, or immortality and mortality" (12). Illustrates these characteristics and others by means of a detailed analysis of *HSRound, Relic,* and *Sickness.*

13. Crennan, M. J. "John Donne's Poetry: Some Remarks," in *Perspectives 79: Resource Book for H.S.C. English,* ed. Jan Fox and Brian McFarlane, 15–22. Malvern, Australia: Sorrett Publishing.

Notes that "[s]tudents often find difficulty with Donne's language and structure" and that "[a] large part of this article, therefore, is taken up with explanation rather than, strictly, criticism." Summarizes "the basic logical structure" of *SunRis, Canon, Anniv, ValMourn, Relic, HSShe,* and *Ecst* followed by "critical and evaluative remarks" on each of the poems. Comments on the elements of play, irony, tonal ambiguity, argumentation, pseudo-argumentation, and drama in the poems as well as such recurring features as the use of "the microcosm/macrocosm parallelism, the comparison of sacred and profane love, the use of astronomical and cosmological analogies," and the "conceit" (19–20). Says *ValMourn* is "remarkable, as Donne's poetry often is, for its width of reference—its *aliveness* to the world—its intelligence, and its beautifully controlled tone of assurance" (20), but claims that the "characteristic weaknesses" of many of the *Holy Sonnets* are "melodrama, and a kind of symmetry which seems, willy-nilly, to provide conclusions of a peremptory sort to any of the varying spiritual extremities of the opening lines of the sonnets," and that "[f]orm and cosmology dictate, too often, the resolutions" (21).

14. Daly, Peter M. *Literature in the Light of the Emblem: Structural Parallels between the Emblem and Literature in the Sixteenth and Seventeenth Centuries.* Toronto: University of Toronto Press. xiv, 245p.

Introduction to the study of emblematic structure in English and German literature of the sixteenth and seventeenth centuries. Chapter 1, "The Emblem" (3–53), discusses the origins and nature of emblem books, comments on forerunners of the emblem, and surveys recent critical developments in emblem theory, especially the work of Albrecht Schöne in *Emble-*

matik und Drama im Zeitalter des Barock (München: Beck, 1964; 2nd ed., 1968). Chapter 2, "The Word-Emblem" (54–102), discusses the forms and functions of emblematic imagery in English and German literature. Chapter 3, "Emblematic Poetry" (103–33); Chapter 4, "Emblematic Drama" (134–67); and Chapter 5, "Emblematic Prose Narrative" (168–84), comment on the structural affinities between the emblem and poetry, drama, and prose fiction. A brief conclusion (185–88), notes (189–223), and selected bibliography (224–33) are followed by an index of names (235–39) and an index of emblematic motifs (241–45). Comments briefly on the imagery in *ValMourn* (ll. 21–28) (65, 91) and *HSBatter* (ll. 1–4) (105).

15. D'Amico, Jack. *Petrarch in England: An Anthology of Parallel Texts from Wyatt to Milton.* Speculum Artium, 5, ed. Aldo Scaglione. Ravenna: Longo Editore. 202p.

Anthologizes English Renaissance poems that bear either directly or indirectly some recognizable thematic relationship to specific poems by Petrarch (printed in Italian with literal translations into English). Parallels Donne's *Mess* and *Leg* and Petrarch's Sonnet 21 ("Mille fiate, o dolce mia guerrera"); *SGo* and Sonnet 57 ("Mie venture al venir son tarde e pigre"); *Damp* and Sonnet 82 ("Io non fu' d'amar voi lassato unqu'anco"); *Broken* and Sonnet 124 ("Amor, fortuna e la mia mente schiva"); *HSVex* and Sonnet 134 ("Pace no trovo e no ho da far guerra"); *HSBatter* and Sonnet 140 ("Amor, che nel penser mio vive e regna"); and *Dream* and Sonnet 164 ("Or che 'l ciel e la terra e 'l vento tace").

16. Dane, Peter. "The Figure of the Pinnace in 'Air and Angels.'" *SoRA* 12: 195–208.

Argues that *Air* explores the central issue of all of Donne's love poetry:

what is love? Insists that, although the argument "largely follows a Neoplatonic line," the poem's "real concern is in no way Platonic" (200). Thinks that Donne is primarily "intent on a love actively realized" and that the speaker of the poem "rejects not sensual love but unrequited love, whether Platonic or Petrarchan," and insists that "only the lady's answering love can ensure a love relation" (201)—only she will satisfy him. Argues that the movement of the poem is "towards the visible, tangible, actual" (202) and holds that "the mutual love that is to replace the adoration of the lady's beauty is not mundane" but rather "belongs to the realm of angel and sphere, the realm of the perfect, of light, of the immutable" (204). Maintains, in other words, that "this love is not a love of the flesh but a love actualized in the flesh" and thus "does indeed come full circle" by beginning and ending with the body and with love." Concludes that, for Donne, "love is the most intimate relation between a man and a woman" and that "its closest analogue is the relation between the body and soul" (205).

17. Dolan, Kathleen H. "*Materia in Potentia:* The Paradox of the Quintessence in Donne's 'A Nocturnal upon S. Lucies Day.'" *Renascence* 32: 13–20.

Discusses the alchemical figures in *Noct,* a poem in which the speaker "is represented throughout both as the matter upon which the alchemist practices his art of reduction and transmutation" and "as the alchemist himself, performer of symbolic manipulations of matter that have a redemptive motive." Maintains that "the main business" in the poem is "the conjuring and interlocking of ideas and images" that "express annihilation," noting that the five stanzas "are arranged around a nucleus of self-negation" (13).

Believes that in the alchemical context of the poem, "separation implies transformation and eventual unity, while the experience of abyss implies a withdrawal which is privileged, a timelessness which is illuminated"; thus "all declarations of 'nothingnesse' are qualified and paradoxical, as despair is made to submit to an alchemical metaphysics" (14). An analysis of the five stanzas shows how the speaker as alchemist transmutes "his personal grief by projecting his identity into a protocosmos which, as 'first nothing,' is at once the alchemical *prima materia,* the Logos, or principle of universal coherence" and "the quintessence which emerges from nothingness to become the material sanction of the soul's ascent." Concludes that, in the poem, Donne "reveals a paradigm for the creative process itself in alchemical operations, as the opacity of experience is rendered transparent through a careful and intricate process of separation and distillation" (19).

18. Donovan, Laurence. "How John Leyden Died." *Carrell* 20: 9–24.

Compares passages from Sidney's *Arcadia,* Nashe's *Unfortunate Traveller,* and Donne's "Death's Duell" to show that Donne's language does not derive from the rhetoric of the court nor the common speech of London streets but rather is a "powerful blend of the two, of the Ciceronian and the Senecan" or "of involved scholastic argument and sensual naturalistic diction and imagery" (15). Maintains, however, that in spite of the differences, all three works "seem to solve a primary aesthetic problem which appears basic to art: they make a general specific." Analyzes the rhetoric, syntactical rhythms, diction, figurative language, dramatic effects, tone, logic, and argument of the sermon to show how Donne uses "every con-

ceivable device of direct description and sensualized rhetoric" (24) in order "to render sensual and dramatic" (17) the logical statements of the sermon, thereby not only informing his auditors but also moving them viscerally about death, both Christ's and their own.

19. Dorangeon, Simone. "L'Églogue anglaise et la théorie néo-platonicienne de l'inspiration," in *Aspects du sacré dans la littérature anglo-américaine,* 5–20. Reims: Centre de Recherche sur l'Imaginaire.

Surveys the prevalence of Neoplatonic theory of inspiration in English eclogues during the sixteenth and seventeenth centuries, especially in Spenser, Sidney, Lodge, Drayton, William Browne, and George Wither. Maintains that Donne introduced a new spirit into the tradition, for, although he borrows some elements of Italian Neoplatonism in the *Songs and Sonets,* he never suggests supernatural inspiration. Points out that, for Donne, divine fury, visits by the Muse, trances, ecstasies, and supernatural possession are treated ironically, noting in particular Donne's portrayal of Coscus, the bad poet, who is "sicke with Poetrie, and possest with muse" in *Sat2* (l. 61).

20. Dubrow, Heather. "'No man is an island': Donne's Satires and Satiric Traditions." *SEL* 19: 71–83.

Compares and contrasts Donne's *Satyres* to those of his predecessors and contemporaries in order "to define more precisely what is original in his poems" (71). Argues that although the *Satyres* are a blend of Horatian and Juvenalian elements, Donne is more indebted to Juvenal than to Horace, even in *Sat1* and *Sat4,* which are modelled on Horace's *Sermones* (I.ix). States that sometimes Donne's blend of the two Latin satirists is unsuccessful, but at other times it "produces real triumphs" (75). Compares and contrasts Donne's *Satyres* also to works by his contemporaries, such as Marston, Hall, and Guilpin, to show that the stylistic differences between Donne's poems and theirs are "as striking as the similarities" (76), the most significant difference being Donne's complex development of personae in his satires. Maintains that comparing and contrasting Donne with other satirists "highlights the idiosyncratic qualities of his poems" and "supports the conventional wisdom about his originality." Concludes that Donne's satires are "a fascinating blend of tradition and individual talent" and show that "an intelligent use of literary conventions can be a source of highly original achievements" and that "the sensibility of a single writer can readily encompass both iconoclasm and imitation" (83).

21. **Edwards, Simon.** "'Extensive and Peculiar': Some Aspects of the Literature of London," in *London in Literature,* 1–45. London: Roehampton Institute.
Examines various ways writers from the seventeenth through the nineteenth century viewed London. Suggests that *GoodM* and *SunRis* can be imagined taking place in a London bedroom. Says that "the metropolitan sophistication" of the speaker in *GoodM* is also "the achievement of an alienated genital sexuality" that "has left behind a polymorphous and rural playground of infantile sexuality" in which "Donne's claims for the totality of sexual love (at least its genital variety) insist simultaneously on its complete privacy and its universality." Maintains that in *SunRis* Donne "even more emphatically dismisses the rest of existence" while at the same time "incorporating a rich variety of imperial reference" in the poem so as "to create an erotic transcendence." Claims that Donne attempts "to hold

together, at the point of take-off into the modern world, personal experience with the developing historical process that will come to seem at an even greater distance." Points out that "personal experience will sometimes revenge itself by erecting, as already in Donne, a kind of sublime selfhood" (26).

22. **Enozawa, Kazuyoshi, and Miyo Takone.** *Bibliography of English Renaissance Studies in Japan: I, 1961–1970.* Renaissance Monographs, ed. Peter Milward, 6. Tokyo: Renaissance Institute, Sophia University. 218p.
Contains a preface (i–iv); "Japanese Scholarship and Criticism in the English Literary Renaissance: A Survey of Major Achievements during the Period 1961–71" (1–46); and an unannotated listing of English Renaissance studies in Japanese (with English translations of titles) for the years 1961 through 1970, divided into four categories for each year—bibliographies and works of reference, literary histories, general and special studies, and individual authors. Lists under Donne 74 items—books, essays, and reviews.

23. **Erlebach, Peter.** "Das Epigramm des 17. Jahrhunderts," in *Formgeschichte des englischen Epigramms von der Renaissance bis zur Romantik,* 121–84. Anglistische Forschungen, 131, ed. Johannes Hoops. Heidelberg: Carl Winter Universitätsverlag.
Believes that Donne's epigrams represent the zenith of English epigrammatic art. Maintains that most of them combine artistic perfection and technical virtuosity with traditional epigrammatic form, making them incomparably perfect examples in the history of the genre. Observes that the themes are widely varied, extending from appraisals of moral or character traits to occasional poems on contemporary events. Says that *Hero, Pyr,* and *Niobe* achieve a harmonious

blending of lyricism and epigram that was hardly ever matched. Points out that Donne obviously regarded the couplet as the primary form of the genre since thirteen of his epigrams are couplets. Concludes that although Donne's epigrams are loosely arranged, they share commonalities in content and form.

24. Erlich, Avi. "Ambivalence in John Donne's *Forbidding Mourning*." *AI* 36: 357–72.

Presents a psychoanalytic reading of *ValMourn* to show that "*all* the similes and analogies" (361) in the poem reflect the ambivalence of Donne toward mutual love, which he found both attractive and repellent. Argues that paradoxically Donne's unleashing of his "unpleasant fantasies" in the poem results in a "literary unity" (362) that shows that Donne is "not oblivious to conflict but poetically in control of it" (372). Suggests, for instance, that "the source of the speaker's repressed desire to run away" is that he is "unconsciously afraid of sexuality with his lovely lady" (366) and thus tries to convince her that spiritual love that rises above the senses is vastly superior to sexual love. Finds the stiff, twin compasses (ll. 25–32) particularly ambivalent and expressive of speaker's "infantile fantasies" that are at the root of his "sexual fears" (371). Maintains, however, that the compasses "also have a higher purpose" in that "they sublimate and manage the conflict that the speaker cannot acknowledge consciously"; in other words, the "high, metaphysical intellectuality" of Donne's simile "both elevates his love and simultaneously supplies a confession that his love is, after all, inferior" (372).

25. Ferrari, Ferruccio. "B. Jonson e 'The Tribe of Ben'—Donne e Burton," in *L'Influenza classica nell'Inghilterra del Seicento e la poesia di Robert Herrick,* 33–48. Biblioteca di cultura contemporanea, 138. Messina-Firenze: Casa Editrice G. D'Anna.

Sees Jonson and Donne as the two principal influences on the poetry of Robert Herrick, but acknowledges that, by far, Jonson's influence was the greater. Says that Herrick reminds one of Donne, especially in the way he sometimes perceives love and also in his blending together pagan and Christian elements in his poetry. Claims that, being a devoted Son of Ben, Herrick avoided the exaggeration of Donne's poetry.

26. Flynn, Dennis. "Donne and Hugh Broughton." *SCN* 37:71–72.

Comments on an ironical remark Donne made in a letter to Henry Goodyer concerning the "spurious and ridiculous rumor" that Hugh Broughton, a radical Protestant preacher living in Holland, had converted to Catholicism and for a stipend was engaged in controversy with the Jews. Thinks that Donne's wit in the letter and in related matters during his residence at Mitcham (1605–10) "suggests a qualifying element to his Anglicanism during these years." Notes also that Donne had already ridiculed Broughton in *The Courtier's Library,* in which Broughton is said to have authored an imaginary book entitled *The Sub-Savior,* "in which the illuminate, but very unilluminating, Hugh Broughton explains beyond belief that the Hebrew language is of the essence of salvation, and that his own precepts are of the essence of the language" (72).

27. Flynn, Dennis. "Donne's First Portrait: Some Biographical Clues?" *BRH* 82: 7–17.

Speculates that William Marshall's engraving of Donne (from a lost 1591 portrait by either Nicholas Hilliard or Isaac Oliver) might provide clues to the most puzzling years of Donne's life (from autumn 1587 to spring 1591) and believes that the symbolism of the portrait may shed light on how Donne handled his precarious religious situation during those years. Disputes Walton's interpretation of the portrait as a representation of "the giddy gayeties of that age" (11) and emphasizes that the sword, the plain collar, the earring in the form of a cross, and the Spanish motto translated as" Rather dead than changed" point to a militant bearing and to Donne's Catholic and Welsh ancestry. Notes that life in the military would have freed Donne from "the choices between Catholicism and security, between patriotism and conscience, which were being forced on him by public events," because in the military "[t]he code of honor included a kind of swashbuckling religious faith and an almost open toleration of Catholicism proscribed at other levels of English society" (16). Maintains that although in the portrait Donne appears as a swordsman swearing an oath of constancy, both the viewer and Donne "knew that Diana in Montemayor's poem, from which the oath is taken, was not faithful," and thus the motto becomes "a fatalistic comment on the swordsman's pose, implying that it is only a pose, albeit one Donne was to hold for several years" (17).

28. Gale, Steven H. "John Donne's 'The Calme.'" *Horizontes* 44: 59–64.

Presents a critical analysis of *Calm,* maintaining that the poem, though little studied, exemplifies "several typical Donne techniques," such as "the realism of his description, his incorporation of mythological elements, his detailed knowledge of ships, and his use of conceits," and also "supplies the reader with a better understanding of the kind of young man who would engage himself in an adventure of this type—the kind of young

man, then, that Donne himself was in 1597" (63).

29. Gardner, Helen. "Dean Donne's Monument in St. Paul's," in *Evidence in Literary Scholarship: Essays in Memory of James Marshall Osborn,* ed. René Wellek and Alvaro Ribeiro, 29–44. Oxford: Clarendon Press.

Rejects several details in Walton's account of how Donne posed for the picture from which was made his monument in St. Paul's, noting numerous errors in Walton's account of Donne's last days and pointing out that the anecdote of how the picture was painted was added to the Walton *Life* in 1658, 27 years after Donne's death. Also questions Bald's interpretation (1970) of the significance of the monument. Gives a detailed description of the monument; discusses several oddities about it; and, considering it a very "unsatisfactory" piece of work, believes that Donne did not give the directions that produced the present monument. Maintains that the facts indicate that Donne, at the urging of his physician, Dr. Simeon Fox, agreed to having a monument made in his honor and that a picture was painted showing him dressed in his shroud either before or just after his death so that the sculptor would have a likeness to use as a model. Believes that Donne wanted his monument to proclaim "that in death the Christian's trust can only be in the mercy of his Creator and the merits of his Saviour" (44).

30. Goldberg, Jonathan. "James I and the Theater of Conscience." *ELH* 46: 379–98.

Discusses the implications of the metaphor of player king that James I uses in *Basilikon Doron* and the ways that poets, such as Donne, Jonson, and Chapman, equivocate in their support of the king, using the consequent dilemma inherent in the metaphor—that, on the one hand, public and private personae should be one, but that, on the other hand, perceivers misread behavior and thus misread the inner man. Comments specifically on *Eclog*, written on the occasion of the marriage of Somerset to Frances Howard, to show how Donne used in the poem "a language that drew upon James's absolutist duplicities" (389). Maintains that "James's claim that surface events could not indicate internal motives becomes Donne's license to present a world of false surfaces" (390). Says that in the eclogue section of the poem, court-country debate establishes the artificiality of the court, which owes its creation to James, and that in the epithalamium proper the central conceit of consuming love allows Donne to make the point that a perceiver cannot make distinctions about the event. Concludes that "[t]he ambiguities of Donne's poem illustrate the equivocating possibility in James's metaphor . . . and seem appropriate to Donne's attempt to make a bid for royal largesse and yet to register his knowledge of courtly corruption" (391).

31. Golomb, Harai. "*SMAU*-Tension and Enjambment: The Contribution of the Functional Parameter of *SMAU*-Anticipation," in *Enjambment in Poetry: Language and Verse in Interaction*, 158–70. Meaning and Art: A Series of Books on Poetics and Communication in Culture, 3. Tel Aviv: Tel Aviv University, The Porter Institute for Poetics and Semiotics.

Gives a detailed analysis of three instances of enjambment in lines 208–16 of *Lit*.

32. Gransden, K. W. "*LENTE CVRRITE, NOCTIS EQVI:* Chaucer, *Troilus and Criseyde* 3.1422–70, Donne, *The Sun Rising* and Ovid, *Amores* 1.13," in *Creative Imitation and Latin Literature*, ed. David West and Tony Woodman, 157–71. Cambridge: Cambridge University Press.

Discusses the similarities and differences between Ovid's *Amores* and *SunRis*. Points out, that, like Ovid, Donne contrasts "the world of lovers and the workaday world"; asks the sun to chide schoolboys; mentions farming; refers to the sun's all-seeing eye; and wittily contrasts "domestic and cosmic imagery in the last line"; but notes that "the colloquial vigour and sardonic directness" in Donne's poem is "more dramatic than Ovid's present indicatives" that "apostrophize dawn in a series of formal exemplary topoi." Observes that in Donne's poem the lovers "proclaim their immunity from time," whereas Ovid is aware of time; in Donne's poem the classical "adynaton," in which time is delayed, "is transformed into a splendid and hyperbolic conceit" (169) that depends upon "systems and habits of thought unknown to the ancient world." Points out also that Ovid's poem is "about love's agonies not love's triumphs," whereas in Donne's poem the lovers "triumph over myth by creating their own alternative world" (171). Mentions also the common classical topos of the incompatibility of love and business in *Break* (161–62).

33. Green, Donald. "The Term 'Conceit' in Johnson's Literary Criticism," in *Evidence in Literary Scholarship: Essays in Memory of James Marshall Osborn*, eds. René Wellek and Alvaro Ribeiro, 337–51. Oxford: Clarendon Press.

Points out that nowhere in his *Life of Cowley* does Dr. Johnson define the term "conceit" and nowhere does he use the term "metaphysical conceit," noting that "the definition of 'conceit' as 'extended metaphor,' 'elaborate image,' and the like did not make its way into standard English dictionaries until around 1960." Cites a representative selection of Johnson's use of the term to show that "whatever else 'conceit' meant to Johnson, he did *not* equate it with 'metaphorical language'" (341). Concludes that for Johnson the term "is still close to its origin in French *concevoir* or Latin *conceptus*—something too obviously intellectually contrived, *voulu*, organically unrelated to the poetic occasion" and "may manifest itself in wordplay, in a combination of wordplay and imagery, or even in a true combination of images when those images are so 'heterogeneous' or so 'violently yoked together' that the reader's response is intellectual rather than emotional" or "when a trite and banal image . . . is mechanically used" (347). Concludes that the closest synonym in modern English for what Johnson meant by "conceit" is "gimmick" (347–48).

34. Hahn, Thomas. "The Antecedents of Donne's 'Holy Sonnet XI.'" *ABR* 30: 69–79.

Points out that "the ingenious and audacious" reversals, the dramatic format, the images, and the tone in *HSSpit,* in which the speaker first assumes the role of Christ on the cross and then takes on the role of persecutor, can be found in various medieval and Tudor meditations on Christ's Passion and on the Virgin Mary's compassion for Christ's sufferings. Cites in particular a fourteenth century lyric that "brings together in a remarkable way the traditional antitheses of suffering and love, guilt and sorrow, human and divine, the historical reality of the passion and the immediacy of Christ in the heart and mind of the meditator" and contains details that can be found "in a large number of late medieval and Tudor poems" (76). Points out, however, that Donne adapted "the components of the earlier literary milieu and his own Catholic background to the requirement of his temperament and to the standards of the age," creating an

"amalgam" that "intensifies and personalizes the traditional sufferings of the Savior by underscoring the sinner's own self-consciousness and his consequent participation in Christ's torment" (79).

35. Hamilton, R. W. "Donne and Castiglione." *N&Q,* n.s. 26: 405–6.

Cites two passages from Hoby's translation of Castiglione's *The Courtier* (1561) as likely sources for ll. 13–24 of *Sat1* about deserting a friend for someone better dressed. Notes also in the passage the occurrence of the word "fond" and points out that Donne uses the adjective "fondling" in the first line of his poem. Observes that Donne's usage "predates by forty-three years the earliest recording of 'fondling' as an adjective in any sense" (405).

36. Hamilton, R. W. "John Donne's Petrarchist Poems." *RMS* 23: 45–62.

Identifies three major groupings of the *Songs and Sonets*—poems of Ovidian naturalism that denigrate women, poems of Platonic mutuality in love, and Petrarchan poems of "unfulfilled, thwarted love" and comments primarily on the last category. Discusses *Mess* as a mediocre poem of unrequited love that does not "rise above the conventions upon which it draws," unlike Donne's other Petrarchan poems that creatively exploit images of the heart (*Blos, Broken, Leg*) and the God of Love (*Lov Usury, LovExch, LovDiet, LovDeity*) in order to analyze the situation of the unrequited lover. Maintains that Donne comes closest to Petrarch in *Twick,* Donne's "masterpiece" of unreciprocated love (58). Discusses *LovInf* and *LovGrow* to show Donne's progression from a Petrarchist to a Platonic position, a shift necessary when Donne speaks of mutual love rather than thwarted love because mutual love "cannot be adequately dealt with *within* the terms of Petrarchist mode" (62), as seen in *LovInf*.

37. Häublein, Ernst. "King Imagery in the Poetry of John Donne." *Anglia* 97: 94–115.

Comments on king imagery in *Sat2, Metem, Tilman, SecAn, Anniv, SunRis, ElBed, Canon, LovGrow, Dissol, ElJeal,* and several sermons. Maintains that while Donne "seems to acknowledge royal authority and dignity" and sees the king as representing "an imitation of God and His authority on earth," he also "does not refrain from criticizing the infirmities of the king" (95) and consistently describes the court as a "hotbed of vice" (97). Shows that Donne uses king imagery "to characterize, explain, define, differentiate, and concretize various *personae*" in his poems, "to elaborate his concept of Christ's followers as royal dignitaries," and to illustrate "the concept of exclusionist love." Points out that in some poems and sermons Donne's king imagery merges the secular and divine and observes that in other poems the king imagery is ambiguous because the "vehicles are morally incompatible with their tenors" (115).

38. Hester, M. Thomas. "Donne's *Apologia*." *PLL* 15: 137–58.

Disputes negative critical evaluations of *Sat2* that suggest the poem lacks unity and an effective speaker and argues that it is, in fact, "an ironic *apologia* for satire that is unified by the satirist's concern with public and private perversions of language and the presumptuous abuse of the Word" (138). Sees the Roman verse satirists as models for a tripartite argument in the poem in which the satirist ridicules the failures of contemporary poets and especially the corruption of lawyers, and follows with an admission of his own ineffectiveness. Maintains that Donne employs "this strategy in order

to articulate the same problem that occupied the classical poets: the dangers to the spiritual health of the nation inherent in the abuse of language" (141). Concludes that "the apparently incongruous collection of subjects and paradoxical stance of the satirist" are "integral to the structure and ironic strategy of the poem" (157).

39. Hester, M. Thomas. "*Genera Mixta* in Donne's 'Sir John Wingfield.'" *ELN* 16: 202–6.

Explicates *Wing* to demonstrate Donne's penchant for mixing genres, in this instance, the Greek and Roman epigram. Says that by the use of "puns, proverbs, sententiousness, and verbal tension," Donne "transforms the death of Sir John Wingfield into an event that evokes universal norms of individual heroism, national pride and enduring human achievements under the aegis of eternity" (205). Maintains that by mixing Roman wit and Greek proverbialism, Donne makes the epigram "not only a riddle and a joke but a witty *assault* fully in the spirit of Martial's comic deflations of his personal enemies in Rome" (206), in this case, the verbal assault being directed towards the Spanish Empire.

40. Hobsbaum, Philip. "Elizabethan Poetry," in *Tradition and Experiment in English Poetry,* 68–88. Totowa, N.J.: Rowman and Littlefield.

Believes that Elizabethan poetry "has remained under a cloud for generations" (68) and has been "egregiously misunderstood" because critics and anthologizers have regarded Sidney, Spenser, Daniel, and Drayton as key figures of the period, poets who wrote a kind of poetry that educated modern readers reject. Argues that if one considers Donne, Jonson, Chapman, Marston, Raleigh, and Greville—along with such translators as Stanyhurst, Golding, and Harington—as representative of the age, then "the major

Elizabethans belong to our time." Maintains that one does not have to turn to Petrarchists in order "to see the period as an incredibly rich one" and that, in fact, "the Elizabethan genius was for poetic realism," not "mock-simplicity, Petrarchan convention, and prosaic philosophising" (88).

41. Holland, Norman K. "Transacting My 'Good-Morrow' or, Bring Back the Vanished Critic." *SLitI* 12: 61–72. Reprinted in *American Critics at Work: Examinations of Contemporary Literary Theories,* ed. Victor A. Kramer (Troy, N.Y.: Whitston, 1984), 211–25.

Uses *GoodM* to argue against critics who do not acknowledge explicitly that their criticism is personal and individual. Admits his reading of the poem takes into account personal associations, including psychoanalysis, Dr. Johnson's famous phrase about metaphysical style, and even a course in the 1950s with Douglas Bush in Renaissance poetry. Says that he particularly distrusts the movement in *GoodM* from the past through the present to the future because it is a movement "from physical, earthy, fleshly love to abstract thought" (71). Judges "New Criticism" to be faulty because it closes down the meaning of a poem and finds in present-day deconstruction a similar kind of impersonality. Prefers using "I," not "we," in discussing his relationship to a poem, because, by doing so, he "opens up the closure [that] a 'scientific,' 'objective,' knowledge of literature threatens to all the myriads of different personal experiences possible for a given poem" (70–71).

42. Kawasaki, Toshihiko. "Anglican Sekkyosha no Kunou to Shinjitsu: 1622 nen Aki no Donne no Sekkyo" [Dilemma of the Anglican Pulpit—Donne's Sermons in the Autumn, 1622], in *Anglicanism to Puritanism* [Anglicanism and Puritan-

ism], 12–21. The Japan Society of Seventeenth-Century English Literature. Tokyo: Kinseido.

Comments on the sermon preached at St. Paul's Cross, 15 September 1622, and the sermon preached to the Honourable Company of the Virginian Plantation, 13 November 1622. Argues that the differences in Donne's attitude toward religion in these two sermons should be understood simply as evidence of the truth Donne attained at each stage of his religious development.

43. Kishimoto, Yoshitaka. "Josei to 'Kami no Imeiji' to Kami: Donne no 'Shunen Tsuitoshi' to *Holy Sonnets* yori" [From Women to God's Image and to God in the *Anniversaries* and *Holy Sonnets*], in *Anglicanism to Puritanism* [Anglicanism and Puritanism], 22–35. The Japan Society of Seventeenth-Century English Literature. Tokyo: Kinseido.

Comments on "image of God" presented in the *Anniversaries* and the *Holy Sonnets,* maintaining that the development of the image shows the transition of the poet's concern from women to God. Says that Donne could not take a resolute stance on religion until around 1610.

44. Larik, Asadullah. "Paradox in John Donne's Poetry." *Ariel* (Jamshoro, Pakistan) 5, no. 1: 15–23.

Discusses very briefly the use of various kinds of paradox (rhetorical, simple, logical, incarnational, and psychological) in *Canon, SGo, Flea, Fever, Prohib, Compu, Expir, SunRis, GoodM, ValWeep, ValMourn, Noct,* and *LovInf,* claiming that, although he did not invent paradox, Donne "is nonetheless the first to have used various kinds of paradoxes and explored their possibilities" (22).

45. Lawler, Justus George. *Celestial Pantomime: Poetic Structures of Transcendence.* New Haven, Conn.: Yale University Press. xi, 270p.

Discusses structural patterns in poetry as a "representation" or "mimic" of something outside the poem, which gives it meaning. Claims that "in poetry the content exists, at least partially, . . . to clarify or make manifest the nature of the structure—which structure is in turn related to some ultimate structure" (6). Contains four chapters of speculation and generalization and six chapters of practical criticism on the following structures: chiasmus and parenthesis, enjambment, coda of reversal, coda of irony, prepositionalizing, refrains, journey motifs, monopolysyllabic collisions, and oscillating imagery. Uses Donne frequently to support his positions and comments more fully on *GoodM* (the structure of which moves from "multiplicity to unity" and contains a meaningful parenthetic insertion); *HSBatter* (showing the power of enjambment and its relationship to transcendence and transformation); *Ecst, SunRis, Air,* and *Relic* (showing how Donne's "coda of irony" is used to clarify sexual meanings); and *Dream* (an example of poetic circularity).

46. Lewalski, Barbara Kiefer. *Protestant Poetics and the Seventeenth-Century Religious Lyric.* Princeton, N.J.: Princeton University Press. xiv, 536p.

Presents a revisionist theory of current views on the English religious lyric of the seventeenth century by arguing that Protestant emphasis on the centrality of the Bible and Protestant appreciation and understanding of scriptural language, biblical genres (especially the Psalms and the Canticles), biblical rhetoric, and typology fostered a theory of aesthetics that defines both the poetics of the religious lyric and its spiritual contents. Stresses that the major religious lyricists of the period—Donne, Herbert, Vaughan, Traherne, and Edward Taylor—are much more indebted to contemporary English Protestant med-

itation, emblematics, and sermon theory than to medieval Catholic and Continental sources. Supports her argument "by extrapolating from contemporary Protestant materials a substantial and complex poetics of the religious lyric" and by "examining in some detail the precepts it holds forth—regarding religious lyric genres, figurative language, symbolism, modes of meditation and self-analysis, ways of perceiving and portraying the vacillations of the spiritual life, ways of conceiving the poetic persona, and theories about rendering divine truth inhuman art" (ix). Refers to and comments on Donne throughout the study. In particular, discusses how the *Holy Sonnets* reflect "a Calvinistic sense of man's utter helplessness in his corruption" and his "total dependence upon God in every phase of his spiritual life" (25); claims that Donne in his sermons illustrates "perhaps the most creative use of typology by any seventeenth-century English Protestant" (136); points out Donne's use of various meditative traditions, especially in the *Holy Sonnets, Goodf,* and the hymns; and comments on the uses of figurative language, emblems, and Protestant sermon theory in his sermons. Chapter 8, "John Donne: Writing after the Copy of a Metaphorical God" (253–81), discusses primarily the *Divine Poems,* dividing them into six broad categories: "emblematic poems, poems based upon liturgical forms, poems of complimentary address, biblical paraphrase, poems focusing upon the Protestant drama of regeneration, and occasional meditations" (254), claiming that Donne is "the first major English poet in the devotional mode whose lyrics are influenced by a distinctive Protestant poetics" (282).

47. Linguanti, E. "Il vaso di argilla," in *Strumenti per l'analisi del testo letterario,* ed. E. Linguanti, T. Benussi, and

G. Dente, [25]–47. 2nd ed. Pisa: Libreria Goliardica, 1979–80.

Presents a detailed critical analysis of the theme, language, form, rhetorical structure, and various stylistic features of *HSDue.*

48. Low, Anthony. "Eve's Additions to the Command: Milton and Donne." *MiltonQ* 13: 20.

Points out that in the sermon "Preached to the Lords upon Easterday, at the Communion. The King being then dangerously sick at New Market" (1619) Donne uses Eve's words about death ("perchance, if we eat, we may die") to illustrate the "universal, all-too-human tendency to believe, against all the evidence that each of us personally, may somehow be exempt from death," a delusion that one can forgive in Milton's Eve but not in postlapsarian man, who has seen death and knows it is universal.

49. Mano, D. Keith. "Reflections of a Christian Pornographer." *C&L* 28: 5–11.

In discussing the nature of his fiction and the issue of obscenity, says that if there is anyone with whom he feels "a blood brotherhood" and "whose purposes and tactics" are similar to his, it is Donne. Quotes *HSBatter* and notes how in it "the sexual act can approach—in its wild animal consummation—the working of God's love in the human soul." Contrasts Donne with St. John of the Cross, noting that although "their language and imagery are similar, Donne and St. John begin from different starting blocks, different premises": St. John "has attained and needs to express," whereas Donne "needs to express so that he—and his reader—might hope to attain" (10) a mystical understanding of God.

50. Martinet, Marie-Madeleine. "Les Sibylles dans la littérature élisabéthaine: Le temps et l'esprit," in *Devins et charlatans au temps de la Renaissance,* ed.

M. T. Jones-Davies, 13–33. Université de Paris-Sorbonne, Institut de Recherches sur les Civilisations de l'Occident Moderne. Centre de Recherches sur la Renaissance. Paris: Université de Paris-Sorbonne.

Presents a historical survey of the use of the Sibyl in medieval and Renaissance literature and briefly comments on Donne's allusion to the Sibyl in *ValBook,* in which the speaker says the lady will "out-endure / Sybills glory" (ll. 5–6) if she will write in a mysterious language the story of their love, producing a work that would be a sacred book for lovers and a text for him to read when he travels far from her.

51. McCarron, William E. "Tennyson, Donne, and *All the King's Men.*" *ANQ* 17: 140–41.

Points out an allusion to *ValMourn* (ll. 25–36) in Robert Penn Warren's novel *All the King's Men,* in which Jack Burden, reminiscing about an idyllic summer spent with Anne Stanton, substitutes a stereoscope for Donne's compass in describing his youthful love. Says that, although the idea is similar to Donne's, Jack's conceit, unlike Donne's, is "simply not compelling"; rather it is "redundant, colloquial, and unpolished" (141).

52. McCarron, William E., and Jack M. Shuttleworth. "A Newly Recovered Donne First Edition." *SCN* 37: 72.

Describes a first edition of Donne's poems (STC 7045) in the Colonel Richard Gimbel Aeronautical Library at the United States Air Force Academy bearing a bookplate that reads "*Gravis Cantantibus Umbra* Edmund William Gosse" and a tipped-in leaf that reads "Edmund Gosse from Augustus Jessop Aug. 25, 1898." Notes that the edition is not listed in Keynes's *Bibliography of Dr. John Donne* (4th ed., 1973). On the title page appears a handwritten signature,

"H. Mapletoft" (unidentified), and 78 handwritten pages are appended in either late seventeenth century or early eighteenth century script with the heading "Additions to Dr Donne in the Edition 1669 8vo." Notes that throughout the edition there are occasional handwritten insertions, mostly titles of poems that appear in the 1635 and later editions, apparently in the same hand as the writer of the appended pages.

53. **Milward, Peter.** *John Donne no 'Seinaru Sonnet'* [A Commentary on John Donne's *Holy Sonnets*]. Trans. (into Japanese) by Shonosuke Ishii. Tokyo: Aratake, 179p. Revised English version published in 1988 (entry 907).

Analyzes and explains each of the *Holy Sonnets,* as well as *Corona, ED,* and *MHMary,* in a historical, philosophical, religious, literary, and biblical context to show that each sonnet is a poetic meditation based on the method and order of meditation proposed by St. Ignatius Loyola in *The Spiritual Exercises.* Also comments on the indebtedness of these poems to medieval theology and philosophy, especially the works of St. Thomas Aquinas. Suggests also that each sonnet is related to a Shakespearean play in ideas, words, and phrases. Contains a preface (iii–v) and an introduction (3–6). Divided into five major parts: (1) "To the Lady Magdalen Herbert," "La Corona," "To E. of D. with six Holy Sonnets" (7–57); (2) *Holy Sonnets* (1633) (58–124); (3) *Holy Sonnets* (added in 1635) (125–44); (4) *Holy Sonnets* (from the Westmoreland MS) (145–61); and (5) the poems in English (163–78).

54. **Morillo, Marvin.** "Donne's 'Nocturnal': A Textual Note." *ELN* 16: 278–81.

Argues for a comma at the end of l. 15 of *Noct* (found in the 1633 edition) rather than the colon found in the editions of Grierson (1912) and Gardner (1965) on three grounds: (1) the comma does not create any ambiguity in ll. 12–18; (2) the comma makes "not only good but better sense" (279) of the grouping of the lines than does a colon; and (3) with a comma "the musical phrasing seems . . . less interrupted, more solemnly sustained" (281).

55. **Morris, June.** "A Study of Humor in Donne's *Anniversaries:* 'How Witty's Ruin?'" *EM* 28–29 (1979–80): 157–70.

Examines various kinds of humor and wit in *FirAn,* especially "caricature as it develops from hyperbole" (158), and argues that Donne uses humor and wit "to temper conflicts and despair in order to keep events in perspective" (157). Maintains that Donne "manages through Elizabeth's death, the death of the world, and his own spiritual death to write a poem leading from incomprehensibleness to an understanding of his world and of himself " (169).

56. **Nagoya, Yasuhiko.** "Anniversaries Shiron" [An Essay on the *Anniversaries*]. *Aichi Kenritsu Daigaku Gaikokugo Gakubu Kiyo* [Journal of the Faculty of Foreign Studies, Aichi Perfectural University] 12: 45–85.

Suggests that Donne intended the two *Anniversaries* as parts of a series that would continue until his death rather than as companion pieces and reads the poems as the first two installments.

57. **Nassaar, Christopher S.** "The Grand and the Small: Donne's Two Hymns As Complementary Pieces." *CP* 12: 77–78.

Believes that the "full complexity" of *Sickness* and *Father* "cannot be realized unless they are read as complementary pieces in the deepest sense, showing two opposed states of mind facing death." Maintains that in the first the focus is on Donne and his size and grandeur, not on God, and that, in fact, he views himself "as something like a second Christ" (77), whereas in the second his "smallness and insignificance" are emphasized. Suggests that "these contrasting attitudes are both common to the religious mind as it faces death" (78).

58. Nelson, Byron. "'Our Brother Is Not Dead': Theme, Imagery, and the Use of Liturgy in the Funeral Sermons of John Donne and Jeremy Taylor." *WVUPP* 25: 12–20.

Compares and contrasts the funeral sermons of Donne and Jeremy Taylor. Observes that in their sermons both use imaginatively biblical texts found in the Anglican liturgy for the dead (the favorite text being the story of the raising of Lazarus) and that both "stress, with emotional vigor and unfailing assurance, the inevitability of death and the sure and certain hope of resurrection" (12). Maintains that Donne in his funeral sermons is antihumanistic; is obsessively and morbidly preoccupied with corruption of the body; is, for the most part, impersonal (although at times he presents "lively, pertinent, and affectionate details" [18] of the deceased); avoids classical references, preferring biblical ones; is very intense, often paradoxical, and anxious; and is "far-ranging in his collection and development of images" (19). Compares in particular Donne's sermons for Sir William Cokayne and for Magdalen Herbert with Taylor's sermon for Frances, the Countess of Carbery.

59. Nelson, T. G. A. "Death, Dung, the Devil, and Worldly Delights: A Metaphysical Conceit in Harington, Donne, and Herbert." *SP* 76: 272–87.

Discusses the use of scatological imagery in works ranging from the frivolous *Ajax of Metamorphosis* (first published in 1596) by Sir John Harington to the serious, devotional poems and prose of Donne and Herbert, noting that "in the same period the imagery of death, dung, devil, and worldly delights proves equally adaptable to works at opposite ends of the literary spectrum" (287). Maintains that one common trait in all of these works is "the desire to explore the relationship between matter and spirit" as well as "the insidious way in which they can become entangled, or even confused, with one another" (277). Argues that "the use of scatological imagery in inspired texts is what chiefly emboldens Renaissance writers to make use of it themselves" (281). Points out that Donne uses such imagery sparingly and tactfully. Notes that in one of his 1617 sermons, Donne compares a hypocrite's dissimulation to dung and that in *HSScene* there is a submerged metaphor of dung perhaps suggested by Harington's poem "A Dish of Dainties for the Divell."

60. Nitchie, George W. "Donne in Love: Some Reflections on 'Loves Alchymie.'" *SoR* 15: 16–21.

Rejects the view that in *LovAlch* Donne shows "disgust with the physical, with sexuality, with women, and with love" (16), and believes that the drama of the poem reveals its true intent. Suggests that "Oh, 'tis imposture all" (l. 6) refers not to love but to one who intellectualizes about love and will thus "wind up with dead flesh" (17). Also thinks that "Hope not for minde in women" (l. 23) has a positive meaning, for mind is not an issue for male or female on a wedding night when love should be an experience, not an idea. Argues that Donne, in fact, admired the minds of women and is superior among love poets. Thinks one reason for Donne's superiority in love poetry is that lovers laugh with one another in his poems, never being fully serious. Maintains that Donne and his contemporaries "still believed in a further object for human desires than that which, being human, failed to satisfy them" and that "when that is the case, you may be able . . . to laugh at your human relations, even that of love" (18).

61. Parson, E. M. *Notes on the Metaphysical Poets.* Methuen Notes: Study Aid Series. London: Methuen. 86p.

Study aid for undergraduate students for reading the poetry of Donne, Herbert, Vaughan, Marvell, and other minor metaphysical poets. In "John Donne" (1–36) gives a summary of Donne's life (1–5); a brief explanation of the terms "metaphysical," "wit," "dialectic," and "syllogism" (6–8); a general introduction to the *Satyres, Elegies,* and verse epistles, followed by *ElFatal* and *ElBed* (8–16); a general introduction to the *Songs and Sonets,* followed by six poems (16–32); a general introduction to the *Anniversaries* (32–34); and a general introduction to the *Divine Poems,* followed by *HSBatter* and *Father* (34–36). Concludes with suggested essay questions (80–81), a select bibliography (82–83), and an index of titles (84–86).

62. Pollock, John J. "A Mystical Impulse in Donne's Devotional Poetry." *SMy* 2, no. 2: 17–24.

Argues that because there has been so much attention given to his intellectual abilities and commitment to Christian humanism, Donne's "impulse toward the utter abandonment of reason in an effort to achieve a truly mystical union with the Godhead" (18) has been either overlooked or denied. Believes that *Christ,* when read in conjunction with his "Sermon of Valediction at my going to Germany," contradicts those who claim that Donne has no mystical tendencies. Regards the last statement of the poem ("To see God only, I goe out of sight: / And to scape stormy dayes, I chuse an Everlasting night") as "a daring rejection of right reason" and as "a

mystical thrust toward union with God" (20). Concludes that although Donne was a Christian humanist and adhered to the concept of right reason, "it is important for our understanding of him to recognize that in at least one of his major works he reveals an impulse toward the purely mystical apprehension of God" (21).

63. Rajnath. "From Image to Idea: A Re-examination of T. S. Eliot's Dissociation of Sensibility." *Indian Journal of English Studies* (Calcutta) 19: 149–61.

Argues that T. S. Eliot's theory of dissociation of sensibility is "not only one of his major contributions to literary criticism" but also "his most solid critical concept," and tries to show how the theory underwent "a shift of emphasis from image to idea in [the] course of the development of Eliot's career" (149). Compares Eliot's criticism on Donne and Herbert to show that "his deprecation of the former goes side by side with his exaltation of the latter" (157). Points out that the devaluation and separation of Donne from such poets as Herbert occurred when Eliot no longer emphasized "the metaphysical technique" of the so-called metaphysical poets and began to stress "his Christian point of view." Says that since Eliot was unsure of Donne's piety, he separated him from the metaphysical poets "whose religion could not be called into question" (158).

64. Redpath, Theodore. "Some Textual Problems in Donne's 'Songs and Sonnets,'" *E&S* 32: 57–79. Revised and translated into French as "Quelques problèmes textuels dans les Songs and Sonets," in *John Donne,* ed. Jean-Marie Benoist, Les Dossiers H, gen. eds. Jacqueline de Roux and François Denoèul (Herissey: L'Age d'Homme, 1983) 51–72 (entry 423).

Discusses a number of instances where he believes Helen Gardner's text of

Donne's poems in *John Donne: The Elegies and the Songs and Sonnets* (Oxford: Clarendon Press, 1965) could be improved, commenting specifically on *Mess* (l. 11), *Prohib* (l. 22), *Ind* (l. 10), *Broken* (ll. 23–24), *Will* (l. 36), *Under* (ll. 16, 25), *ValName* (ll. 9–10), *SunRis* (l. 17), *LovInf* (the title), *Lect* (ll. 9, 14, 19), *Dream* (ll. 7, 19–20), and *Twick* (ll. 2, 17).

65. Reeves, Troy D. *An Annotated Index to the Sermons of John Donne.* Vol. 1: *Index to the Scriptures.* Elizabethan and Renaissance Studies, 95, ed. James Hogg. Salzburg: Institut für Anglistik und Amerikanistik, Universität Salzburg. iii, 229p.

An annotated index to scriptural references in Donne's sermons arranged in alphabetical order by books of the Bible and the Apocrypha (*Acts* through *Zepheniah*) with citations to *The Sermons of John Donne,* edited by George R. Potter and Evelyn Simpson, in ten volumes (Berkeley: University of California Press, 1953–62). In the introduction, "The Traditional Christian Vocabulary of John Donne's Sermons" (1–32) argues that "Donne's artistry as a preacher and writer of sermons flourished within a context of strict doctrinal and semantic conservatism" (iii). Finds Donne in his sermons to be "orthodox, non-innovative, impersonal, and traditional in his use of biblical and theological terms" (1) and to be "a compendium, virtually a catechism, of Anglican theology, which in its conservatism is true to traditional Christian theology" (5). Observes also that the sermons do not reflect "the theological and doctrinal evolution that one might expect to find in a long ecclesiastical career" and that, "in keeping with his concept of preaching, [the sermons] are repetitious" (15). Presents a short glossary of selected theological terms that Donne employs in the sermons. See

also entries and Review: Jeanne M. Shami in *Ren&R,* n.s. 8 (1984): 59–62.

66. Richards, Bernard. "Donne's 'Lattices of Eyes': Possible Sources." *N&Q,* n.s. 26: 406–7.

Cites *The Song of Solomon* ii, 9 (as translated in the Bishop's Bible and the King James Bible) and St. Augustine's *Confessions,* Bk. xiii, ch. 15 as likely sources for Donne's description of the direct vision of the soul that, having shaken off "being taught by sense," no longer looks "through lattices of eyes" in *SecAn* (ll. 293–96). Also points out that the phrase "labyrinths of eares" (l. 297) is informed by "concrete physiological facts" that were available to Donne even though the *OED* does not record the specifically anatomical usage of "labyrinth" "until later in the century" (407).

67. Rivers, Isabel. *Classical and Christian Ideas in English Renaissance Poetry: A Students' Guide.* London: George Allen and Unwin. 231p.

Introduction to the intellectual contexts of Renaissance literature. Briefly comments on Donne's reaction against mythological allusions in poetry, his Protestant concept of grace, his ironic and satirical use of Neoplatonism, his view on the excessive application of Pythagorean numerology to the Bible, and his skepticism about scientific knowledge, which, however, he used "in the spirit of intellectual play" (79).

68. Rollin, Roger B. "Metaphysical Poets, Milton and the," in *A Milton Encyclopedia,* gen. ed. William B. Hunter, Jr., vol. 5, 110–14. Lewisburg, Pa.: Bucknell University Press; London: Associated University Presses.

Surveys likenesses and differences between Milton's poetry and that of the metaphysical poets and suggests that, although "there is no evidence that Milton ever read so much as a single verse by John Donne, the pre-eminent metaphysical poet of the seventeenth century, nor has investigation yielded one unmistakable echo of any of the other metaphysicals in all of Milton's poetry" (110), Milton "*was* a 'metaphysical'—at least in the very broadest sense of that elusive term" (114). Conjectures that Milton, as a boy living near St. Paul's, may have known Donne, the dean of the cathedral, and that as a student at St. Paul's School, he likely heard some of Donne's sermons.

69. Shapiro, I. A. "[John Burley's Notes on Donne's Sermons.]" *RES* 30: 194.

Reply to P. G. Stanwood (*RES* 29 [1978]: 313–20). Maintains that John Burley's notes on two of Donne's sermons (Trinity Dublin MS 419) were made "while hearing these sermons preached, or very soon afterwards" and rejects Stanwood's suggestion that possibly they were made from Donne's own working papers. Cites examples that show that Burley either misheard or missed some of Donne's words. Also questions Stanwood's suggestion that the two sermons may have been preached in Chelsea College and thinks that Chelsea parish church was a more likely site because it was the church of the family with whom Donne was staying; because it had associations with Thomas More's family, thereby making it quite attractive to Donne; and because its size would account for Burley's mishearings.

70. Sherwood, Terry G. "Conversion Psychology in John Donne's Good Friday Poem." *HTR* 72: 101–22.

Discusses *Goodf* as a poem that reveals Donne's theology and the spiritual psychology of his time. Sees the "turning" or conversion at the end of the poem as rooted in Augustinian psychology and its interpretation by later spiritual writers, such as St. Bernard of Clairvaux, John Calvin, and many of Donne's Protestant contemporaries. Points out that St. Augustine's notion of turning "pivots on a psychology of the will turned from God to the world through sin, needing a return to God through grace" (106) and that "God's correcting anger" is the agency for returning the soul to Him (108). Concludes that the poem is a dramatization of conversion: Donne's westward movement for pleasure or business opposes the eastward movement of the soul, a "tension between *aversio* and *conversio* that characterizes the fallen believer" (121); Donne's request for punishment is "the ultimate means of dissolving this tension," even though the tension must necessarily remain until one dies. Says that the poem illustrates that "penitential suffering of affliction is the way of turning, and turning is the way of being" (122).

71. Stanwood, Paul G. "Time and Liturgy in Donne, Crashaw, and T. S. Eliot." *Mosaic* 12: 91–105. Reprinted in P. G. Stanwood, *The Sempiternal Season: Studies in Seventeenth-Century Devotional Writing* 3–19 (New York: Peter Lang, 1992) (entry 1271).

Broadly defines liturgy as a religious ceremony that "memorializes or consecrates a past action in order to give to it a present and continuing significance" and argues that, in literature, liturgy functions metaphorically to convey movements of time in space and depends "upon rhetorical and verbal invention, designed to make us feel both still and active, contracted and expansive, filled with the past and alive to the present" (91). Maintains that the form, structure, and rhetoric of much of the best poetry of the metaphysicals, cavaliers, and Milton "presupposes ritual, ceremony, and liturgical action" and that although not always devotional, the poetry is "always marked by high and often exuberant ceremony which tries to defeat time." Focuses on Donne, Crashaw, and T. S. Eliot, including the latter because his poetry helps to understand the earlier poets and "his work clarifies and summarizes their themes and meaning" (92). Maintains that, although Donne and Crashaw differ greatly, "consecration, unity of experience, and publicly formalized yet personal feeling—all features of the liturgical mode—belong as much to Crashaw as to Donne" (98). Discusses *Noct,* the *Anniversaries,* and selected sermons as works in the liturgical mode.

72. Swinden, Patrick. "John Donne: 'Air and Angels.'" *CritQ* 21: 51–54.
Calls *Air* "densely argumentative" and paraphrases the conclusion this way: The speaker says, "my relation to you is that of an angel to the purified air that surrounds it; which is like my being the controlling intelligence of one of the heavenly spheres—and you being the sphere. So on the evidence of this last analogy, you give my love a geographical position, a home, and I give your love a sense of direction and purpose. Therefore our loves nicely complement each other. There is no need to argue about who is superior to whom in a situation which, I have suggested, imposes on each lover a different but equal contribution to what is clearly a very satisfactory relationship" (52). Maintains that one of the major stumbling blocks in the poem is that Donne applies the imagery of angels in the first stanza to the woman but applies it—in a confusing way—to the male in the second: "Donne has tried to shift his ground too rapidly and has overtaxed the powers of his readers' concentration." Holds that "it is at this point that critical argument must detach itself from a too slavish attention to the sixteenth-century metaphysical paraphernalia, and address itself to the basic ques-

tion about poetry: with what degree of emotional conviction, in the course of writing the poem, has Donne swapped angels?" (54).

73. Trotter, David. "The Lyrics," in *The Poetry of Abraham Cowley,* 22–55. Totowa, N.J.: Rowman and Littlefield.
Discusses Donne's influence primarily on Cowley's *The Mistress* (1647). Maintains that in Donne's love poetry, tone—"the inflection of a speaking voice"—became, for the first time, "the most important coding device" in poetry, whereby the reader does not derive pleasure "from the fulfillment of pattern, from the exact fit of semantic to metrical unit, but rather from the sense of a mind displayed at the moment when it commits itself to language, a mind which seems to invent its own patterns as it goes along" (29). Contrasts *LovDiet* and *Compu* with Cowley's "My Dyet," showing how "Donne's rakish lyrics sustain to the end their 'hyperbole above reason'" (38) and the speaker's superiority over his mistress, whereas in Cowley's poems "playful disdain" modulates "into sadism" (41).

74. Vernon, John. "Donne's Holy Sonnet XIV," in *Poetry and the Body,* 73–84. Urbana: University of Illinois Press.
Analyzes the language of *HSBatter* to show how the poem reflects the Elizabethan concept of what language is and how it functions. Comments on such matters as diction, repetition of sounds, conceits, rhyme, mirror images, sonnet structure, voice, and rhetorical devices. Stresses the centrality of the Elizabethan belief in correspondences between things, especially noting the "intimacy between words and things" (73). Maintains that the sonnet "doesn't try to tell us everything; instead, it brings us through what can be said to the verge of what can't be said"; thus the final stance of the speaker is "the hopeful, painful, anxious one of waiting"

(83–84)—all of which has been achieved by the language of the poem.

75. Watson, George. "Petrarch and the English." *YR* 68: 383–93.

Challenges the notion that Petrarch's *Canzoniere* had an important influence on English poetry. Points out that "even in early Tudor times, Petrarch was rarely imitated directly and sympathetically" (388), that Donne and his friends would not have considered Petrarch "a modern influence to be resisted," and that there was "no Petrarchan tide of fashion among the late Elizabethan poets" (389). Notes that, in the *Songs and Sonets,* "the attitude of the submissive and lamenting lover which had come to be linked with the memory of Petrarch is simply one attitude among them" and that poems such as *Twick* "belong to the medieval tradition of the love-lament" (388). Believes there are "compelling reasons . . . for thinking terms like Petrarchan and anti-Petrarchan more misleading than they are worth when applied to the great Elizabethan poets" (390).

76. Willy, Margaret. "John Donne," in *Great Writers of the English Language: Poets,* ed. James Vinson and D. L. Kirkpatrick, vol. 1, 308–12. New York: St. Martin's Press. Reprinted in *The Renaissance, Excluding Drama,* intro. by Elizabeth Story Donno, Great Writers Student Library, ed. James Vinson and D. K. Kirkpatrick (London: Macmillan, 1983), 69–72; *St. James Reference Guide to English Literature,* vol. 1, ed. James Vinson and D. L. Kirkpatrick (Chicago: St. James Press, 1985), 146–49; *Reference Guide to English Literature,* 2nd ed., vol. 1, ed. D. L. Kirkpatrick, St. James Reference Guides (Chicago and London: St. James Press, 1991), 491–93.

Presents a brief biographical sketch of Donne and bibliographical listing of editions, bibliographies, and critical works, followed by an appreciative essay on the general characteristics of Donne's poetry, commenting on its uses of "impudent colloquialism," "audacious" conceits, "paradoxical argument," "complicated syntax," "erudite allusions," "verbal ingenuity," "reason with passionate imagination," "metaphysical vision," "metaphysical subtlety," and "boldly sustained punning" (310–11). Comments also on Donne's philosophy of and/or attitude toward love as evidenced in a number of the poems.

77. Zitner, S. P. "Rhetoric and Doctrine in Donne's Holy Sonnet IV." *Ren&R,* n.s. 3: 66–76.

Sees *HSRound* as dramatizing "the situation of one who is wholly committed to a Christian view, but sees his attachment to literal reality and his placement among dogmatic alternatives [about the state of the soul after death] as a continuing source of unease to be worked into harmony." Maintains that the poem "plays observation and authentic feeling against doctrine and imagining, asserts emphatically the part of the believer yet seems to keep doctrine at a distance, even seems to denigrate it—and all this without falling into scepticism." Believes, therefore, that the poem "provides a picture of hesitation, not on the brink of belief, but within it." Conjectures that "earlier in his journey toward Anglican orders there was for Donne a kind of safety in the more conventional side of an indifferent question, whereas later [as reflected in the sonnet] he could feel free enough to accept on such an issue views more in accord with his temperamental needs." Concludes that, "[i]n any case, the tensions in this process of creeping self-conversion seem to be reflected in the rhetorical strategy" of this sonnet (75).

1980

78. Allain, Mathé. "Christ's Cross and Adam's Tree." *NLauR* 10: 18–24.

Maintains that in Donne's secular poems "time appears as a succession of discontinuous instants complete in themselves," whereas in the divine poems "time becomes continuous." Argues that Donne always viewed time "against a background of eternity towards which he had ambivalent feelings," until he began "to see his life as a point in a line stretching from the Creation to the Last Judgment and entrusted himself and his ambivalence to divine mercy" (18). Says that Donne's reaction to mutability and constancy is ambivalent: he both revels in mutability and wishes for immutability in the secular poems, but "[w]hen he fixed his affection on a steadfast woman or an unchangeable God, he gained a sense of personal continuity" that "revealed to him a different aspect of time" (21). Finds that in the *Holy Sonnets* time ceases to be "a flux of disconnected moments" and became "a continuous development" (22), and claims that *Sickness* "suggests Donne's final resolution: for the Christian whose time stretches continuously and infinitely in either direction, the passage from time to eternity is a serene one" (23).

79. Barańczak, Stanisław. "Bóg, człowiek i natura u anglielskich 'poetów metafizycznych' XVI wieku." *RoHum* 28, no. 1: 207–28.

Surveys the political, social, and religious history of the earlier seventeenth century; the early development of interest in the metaphysical poets in the twentieth century; and aspects of style and poetics of metaphysical poetry, such as the use of wit, syntactical concentration, conceits, paradox, and so forth. Points out that metaphysical poetry deals with both secular and sacred themes, often commingling the two, and suggests that the basic paradox from which all others in metaphysical poetry essentially derive is the problem of man's place in the universe. Quotes from Donne's poems to illustrate his points.

80. Beal, Peter, comp. "John Donne," in *Index of English Literary Manuscripts, Vol. I, 1450–1625, Part 1, Andrewes-Donne*, 243–564. London: Mansell; New York: R. R. Bowker.

In the introduction (243–50), Beal notes that, except for some Latin verse inscribed in two printed books, the only autograph of a poem by Donne that has survived is the verse epistle to Lady Carey (now in the Bodleian). Points out, however, that many examples of Donne's handwriting can be found in 38 surviving letters, in various documents, and in notes in a few printed books that Donne owned. Says that "probably more transcripts of Donne's poems were made than of the verse of any other British poet of the 16th and 17th centuries." Discusses Donne's poetry as part of the manuscript culture of his time, noting that only three poems were published during his lifetime. Maintains that the manuscripts of Donne's poems "offer special opportunities for studying the nature of textual transmission in the first half of the 17th century" (245). Comments in detail on the circulation of manuscript collections of the poems, especially discussing the "groups" into which modern editors have classified them, and gives a descriptive list of 69 main manuscript collections of the verse and 6 of the sermons (none in Donne's hand). Lists and briefly describes 3,998 surviving manuscript copies of the poems, 56 of the sermons, and 42 of various miscellaneous works.

81. **Boire, Gary A.** "John Donne's Cure of Love: 'The Comparison' Reconsidered." *CP* 13: 55–58.

Maintains that in *ElComp,* Donne's speaker "adapts the rhetorical techniques, imagery, and tone shared by 'love theorists' from Ovid to Avicenna to Robert Burton," men who offered scatological cures for excessive love by denigrating female beauty. Suggests that Donne's speaker "sets out deliberately to anatomize his reader's lady and, by so doing, cure him of his obsessive carnal passion for earthly (and therefore transitory) beauty" (55). Points out that "[h]aving piled filth upon filth, sore upon sore, and evil upon evil, Donne's speaker culminates his diatribe with the shocking image of diseased and violent copulation" in ll. 43–48 (57). Comments on Donne's ironic point of view in the poem, claiming that Donne's speaker becomes the "butt of an elaborate literary joke," for he unconsciously reveals that he is as much a victim of obsessive love as the reader and is "in need of his own cure" (58).

82. **Boone, Colin C.** *Praxis der Interpretation: Englische Lyrik.* Tübingen: Max Niemeyer Verlag. x, 109p.

Presents as a study guide for students preparing for literature examinations selected examples of model interpretations of English poems, including *ValMourn, Noct,* and *HSRound.*

83. **Boulger, James D.** *The Calvinist Temper in English Poetry.* De Proprietatibus Litterarum, Series Maior, 21. The Hague: Mouton. xii, 498p.

Discusses Donne briefly in various parts of this study on the influence of Calvinism on English poetry and prose. For example, contrasts the Puritan plain style with Donne's prose, maintaining that, although Donne's style is more erudite, witty, and stylistically dazzling, the plain style should not "be held synonymous with dullness and conformity to a low common denominator" (124). Suggests that perhaps a passage from one of the sermons in John Preston's *Three Sermons upon the Sacrament* that contains an extended twin compass image may have been influenced by *ValMourn,* or perhaps that both men were influenced by a common source. Compares and contrasts Donne's poetry with that of Edward Taylor and Marvell, and even more briefly, with that of Spenser, Milton, Blake, and Wordsworth. Points out that "the central tradition of religious poetry in English has been seen to run from Donne to Eliot, and to be predominately 'metaphysical' in structure and Anglo-Catholic in content." Maintains that "[t]he prominence of this tradition in literary study today is partly responsible for the critical obscurity surrounding the religious poetry of Wordsworth (and others)," and insists that "[t]he critical tools useful in dealing with Donne or Herbert are largely useless for Wordsworth or the Calvinist poets" (409). Briefly contrasts *Sickness* to Wordsworth's "Stepping Westward" to illustrate the point.

84. **Carey, John.** "Donne and Coins," in *English Renaissance Studies Presented to Dame Helen Gardner in Honour of*

Her Seventieth Birthday, ed. John Carey, 151–63. Oxford: Oxford University Press.

Surveys Donne's interest in coins as reflected in his poetry and prose, especially in *ElBrac, ValWeep, Tilman, Lit, Image, SecAn;* a letter to Sir Edward Herbert; and several sermons. Maintains that Donne had little interest in the value of coins or the coins per se, but was primarily fascinated by the relationship or correlation between the metal of the coin and the imprint on it. Maintains that Donne's poetry is "always about relationships" (154), so it is typical of him to focus his attention on the relationship of the metal and imprint, a relationship that shifts and varies as Donne examines it. Suggests that "[t]his is true of all the other relationships he concentrates upon: the interplay between faith and reason, for instance, or the relative nature of light and shadows" (154), noting that "[o]nce a relationship intrigues him, he feels impelled to probe it, modify it, reverse it, and try it out in different concentrations and in various matrices" (157). Argues that Donne's "mild obsession" with coins is "a clue which leads us to his most deeply ingrained imaginative habits, and consequently, to those problematic relationships which, as poet and theologian, most enthralled him" (163).

85. Cayward, Margaret. "Donne's 'Batter My Heart, Three-Personed God.'" *Expl* 38, no. 3: 5.

Points out an anagram in *HSBatter* (l. 6): the letters of "no end" in the line, if rearranged spell "donne," thereby "reenforcing the simile of the poet as a captured town."

86. Chanoff, David. "Donne's Anglicanism." *RecH* 15: 154–67.

Maintains that although Donne separated himself formally from Catholicism, "the Catholic commitment to order, authority, and corporate worship was part of his soul," and that "[t]he poems of 1607–09, the letters, and the cult of friendship [in his middle years] all show Donne struggling to place himself, and especially his religious experience, within a social milieu." Claims that the "sense of dejection and pain" found in *Corona, Lit,* and the *Holy Sonnets* is "largely occasioned by the inevitable failure of such a struggle," because "the milieu Donne was in search of could only be provided by the Church." Maintains that from 1593 to 1615 or 1616 Donne was in a "spiritual limbo," after which he began to work "towards a reconciliation between his inner and outer selves, the private man and the public," and "began to express the suppressed elements of his spirituality." Holds that in the sacramental and liturgical outlook expressed in the sermons and devotions of his maturity, one notices that Donne finally realized that "his true home was inside the circle of Church worship" (163). Concludes that after his ordination to the priesthood, Donne recovered "a wholeness within himself and between himself and mankind within the Anglican Church" and that "[t]he spiritual authority and reverence for sacramental forms of devotion claimed by Jacobean Anglicanism enabled him to gather the strands of spirituality that had been scattered over almost twenty years of bitterness and despair" (166).

87. Chatterjie, Visvanath. "John Donne," in *Mysticism in English Poetry,* 37–45. Calcutta: Progressive Publishers.

Says that some of Donne's religious poems are "vibrant with mystic fervour" (39), such as the opening stanza of *Christ.* Thinks that *Metem* could have been a "noble poem on the upward journey of the soul" but that Donne ended up writing "a flippant, even irreverent poem" (37) that "ends not with a bang but a whimper" (39). Finds especially appealing the "note of direct and close communion, a kind of unusual intimacy," in the *Holy Sonnets*. Suggests that even some of the love poems are "not without touches of mysticism" (44). Concludes that Donne's place as a mystic "may not be high but he is a mystic's mystic in the sense that his influence on the mystical poets who followed him was great and far reaching" (45). Compares lines from Donne to lines by Tagore. Sees Donne's intellectuality and skepticism as casting a "shadow on the most luminous of Donne's divine poems" (45).

88. Cognard, Roger A. "The Solstice Metaphor in Donne's 'Lecture upon the Shadow.'" *ELWIU* 7: 11–20.

Suggests that the "overlooked" but "obvious informing metaphor" in *Lect* is "the comparison of perfect love to the summer solstice" (11). Believes that the poem is a marriage poem commemorating Donne's wedding to Ann More and that perhaps Donne had in mind the number symbolism of Spenser's *Epithalamion* when he wrote it. Considers *Noct* as a companion poem of *Lect* in which Donne again uses the solstice metaphor, this time to commemorate the death of his wife.

89. Daniels, Edgar F. "Donne's 'The Dampe.'" *Expl* 38, no. 3: 18–19.

Reply to Roger A. Cognard's reading of *Damp* (ll. 7–8) (*Expl* 36 [1978]: 19). Believes the problems of interpretation in the lines can be solved by reading "preferre" (l. 7) as "elevate" or "advance." Paraphrases the lines: "the damp of love, by working on the doctors in the same way it worked upon the poet, will (so the lady hopes) elevate her murder of the poet to the status of a mass murder" (19).

90. Daniels, Edgar F., and Ralph Haven Wolfe. "Donne's 'The Canonization,' 32." *Expl* 39, no. 1: 46–47.

Believes that the word "sonnets" in *Canon* (l. 32) should be read as being in the possessive case and the word "build" should be understood as "to take up one's abode." Suggests that what Donne wishes to say is "We'll take up our abode in the pretty rooms of sonnets."

91. Davis, Sarah E. *John Donne: The Life and Work of a Metaphysical Poet.* Oxford: Oxford Polytechnic. 33p.

Notes in the foreword that "this book is intended for those people who have a slight knowledge, or no knowledge at all of John Donne . . . and would like to find out a little more about him." Divided into three parts: "Part One: The Life of John Donne" (3–14) presents a brief biography of Donne; "Part Two: The Types of Poetry He Wrote" (19–23) comments briefly on the love poems, *Satyres, Elegies*, verse letters, heroical epistles and epithalamia, *Metem*, epicedes and obsequies, the *Anniversaries*, and the religious poems; and "Part Three: A Selection of Donne's Poetry" (27–30) reproduces *SunRis, Fun, HSMade*, and *HSSpit*. Concludes with a brief bibliography (33). Includes six illustrations.

92. Dingley, R. J. "Donne's 'A Burnt Ship.'" *N&Q*, n.s. 27: 318.

Suggests that *Ship* perhaps "incorporates a reminiscence of the first chapter of the 1590 *Arcadia*, itself modelled on the opening of Heliodorus's *Aethiopica*."

93. Dobrez, Livio. "Mannerism and Baroque in English Literature." *MiscMus* 11: 84–96.

Argues that the term "mannerism" is fully applicable to much later sixteenth and early seventeenth century English literature and that its use by critics would have the advantage of linking certain developments in literature with the wider world of the arts—music, painting, sculpture, and architecture. Analyzes *SunRis*, passages from Shakespeare's *Othello,* and Crashaw's "Letter to the Countess of Denbigh" and "A Hymn to Sainte Teresa" to show that English literature was "progressively transformed in the course of two centuries, and that this transformation may be characterized as, in its first phase, a movement towards the dynamic, the complex and the uncertain, and, in the second, towards a grander, more affirmative vision" (96), in other words, a movement from mannerism to baroque. Argues that *SunRis* is a mannerist poem and discusses ways in which it differs "in sensibility" (89) from the poetry of Wyatt or Sidney or Spenser. Suggests that there are parallels between Donne's poem and certain works by Parmigianino, Bronzino, Pontormo, Tintoretto, Rosso Fiorentino, and Arcimboldo.

94. Donne, John. *Holy Sonnets by John Donne,* ed. with notes by Peter Milward and Shonosuke Ishii. Kenkyusha Pocket English Series, 270. Tokyo: Kenkyusha. xvi, 108p.

Contains a preface by Peter Milward in English (iii–[iv]), an introduction to the *Divine Poems* in Japanese by Shonosuke Ishii (v–xiv), table of contents (xv–xvi), the *Holy Sonnets* in English, including *MHMary, Corona,* and *ED* ([1]–28), with notes in Japanese (29–108).

95. Donne, John. *Paradoxes and Problems,* ed. Helen Peters. Oxford: Clarendon Press. c, 142p.

Contains a preface (v–vii); table of contents (ix–x); a list of references and abbreviations (xi–xiii); and a general introduction (xv–xlix). Maintains that the Paradoxes were composed in the early 1590s and the Problems between 1603 and 1609 or 1610, reviews the history of each form from classical times to the Renaissance, and identifies the influence of three authors on the Paradoxes—Martial, Erasmus,

and especially Ortensio Lando, "whose *Paradossi* Donne appears to have used as his starting point" (xxiii). Comments on general stylistic characteristics of the Paradoxes; defends the notion that they are "neither entirely serious nor merely intellectual jugglery" (xxiv); and notes Donne's concern that these youthful pieces not be widely circulated. Also in the general introduction contrasts the Problems with the Paradoxes, especially their tone, and reviews the history of the form from Aristotle to the sixteenth century, noting that the two most important books of Problems in the sixteenth century were written by Hieronimo Garimberto and Ortensio Lando and suggesting that Donne's Problems seem to be the first written in English. Comments on the subject matter, structure, moral tone, and stylistic characteristics of the Problems. Concludes the general introduction by discussing the dubia—two Paradoxes ("A Defence of Woman's Constancy" and "That Virginity is a Vertue"), two Characters ("A Scot" and "A Dunce"), "An Essay on Valour," and "Newes from the very Country." In the textual introduction (lii–xcvii) reviews the various manuscripts that contain the Paradoxes as well as printed editions; outlines their transmission in manuscript; comments on the text of the dubia; and explains reasons for basing the text of the Paradoxes on the Westmoreland MS and the problems on the O'Flaherty MS and for following the ordering of the copytexts. Presents a list of sigla (xcvix–c) followed by the text of the Paradoxes (1–22), the Problems (13–50), and the dubia (51–68). In the commentary (69–138) attempts "to defend the readings chosen in the text, to paraphrase difficult passages, and to show analogies with other texts of Donne and of his contemporaries" (vi). Has an appendix (139–42) on Lodewijk Rouzee,

who translated the Problems into Latin
in 1616 with two of the translations
reproduced. Reviews: Robin Robbins
in *TLS* (12 September 1980): 996;
D. F. Bratchell in *N&Q*, n.s. 29 (1981):
76–78; Janel M. Mueller in *RenQ* 34
(1981): 458–63; Geoffrey M. Ridden
in *L&H* 7 (1981): 250–52; John T.
Shawcross in *AEB* 5 (1981): 46–53;
Glyn Purslove in *DUJ* 74 (1982):
308–9; G. R. Evans in *RES*, n.s. 34
(1983): 73–74; Dennis Flynn in *JDJ*
3 (1984): 99–103; Jenny Mezciems in
MLR 79 (1984): 150–52; C. Mouchard
in *QL* 643 (1994): 7–8.

96. Donne, John. *The Primrose: Being at
Montgomery Castle upon the hill on
which it is situate.* Gwasg Gregynog:
Newton, Powys.

Limited edition reprint of *Prim* without notes or commentary.

97. Doudna, Martin K. "Echoes of Milton,
Donne, and Carlyle in 'Civil Disobedience.'" *TJQ* 12, no. 3: 5–7.

Notes two possible allusions to *Sat3*
in Thoreau's "Civil Disobedience"—
the imagery of the flowing stream
found in ll. 103–10 of Donne's poem
and "the portrayal of the search for
truth as an upward pilgrimage" in ll.
79–81 (6).

98. Dreher, Diane Elizabeth. "'A Growing
or Full Constant Light': A Reading of
Donne's 'A Lecture upon the Shadow.'"
JRMMRA 1: 83–86.

Argues that the shift of the shadow in
Lect from "the realm of natural phenomena to that of conjecture and
imagination" can best be understood
in terms of St. Bonaventure's method
of meditation in his *Itinerarium Mentis
ad Deum,* in which the meditator is
advised "to seek union with divine
truth by meditating on God's 'traces'
or reflections in the natural world, a
process comprised of three different
steps," namely, perceiving the truth
first on a literal level, then on an allegorical level, and finally on a moral

or tropological level. Shows that "[i]n
keeping with meditative practice, the
imagery in the poem develops cumu-
latively, drawing upon the nexus of
meanings associated with shadows in
the seventeenth century" (83). Concludes that Donne's speaker "tells his
love that they can avoid the annihilation of love represented by the threatening shadows of afternoon by fixing
their souls firmly in truth and constancy, that their love may remain 'at
this noon,' partaking of love's eternal
truth and resisting the decay implicit
in all of the cycles of nature," assuring her that "[o]nly thus can their love
transcend mutability and remain for
them a divine and 'full constant light'"
(85).

99. Dubinski, R. R. "Donne's 'La Corona'
and Christ's Mediatorial Office." *Ren&R,*
n.s. 4, no. 2: 203–8.

Maintains that the Protestant notion
of Christ's threefold mediatorial office
as prophet, priest, and king "has an
integral place" (205) in *Corona* beginning with *Cor4*. Sees *Cor4* as a meditation on Christ as prophet, *Cor5* and
Cor6 on his role as priest, and *Cor7*
on his office as king. Suggests the last
sestet of *Cor7* is a "ritualistic triple
invocation to Christ," praising him for
each of his mediatorial roles (206).

100. Duffy, John. "The Songs: 'Like Hermit
Poore' and 'So, so, leave off,'" in *The
Songs and Motets of Alfonso Ferrabosco,
the Younger (1575–1628),* 51–70. Studies
in Musicology, no. 20. Ann Arbor: University Microfilms International Research
Press.

Analyzes Ferrabosco's musical setting
of *Expir* entitled "So, so, leave off,"
noting that it was the first of Donne's
poems to appear in print when it was
published in Ferrabosco's *Ayres* (1609).
Compares it to a later anonymous setting (Bodleian MS mus.sch.f.575),
which "is more fitful, without the
melodic fullness of Ferrabosco's musi-

cal phrasing" and "is not as clearly structured and balanced" (70).

101. Ellrodt, Robert. "Angels and the Poetic Imagination from Donne to Traherne," in *English Renaissance Studies Presented to Dame Helen Gardner in Honour of Her Seventieth Birthday,* ed. John Carey, 164–79. Oxford: Oxford University Press.

Shows that Donne fundamentally follows St. Thomas Aquinas's angelology but notes how he sometimes steers a course between conflicting doctrines about angels, not committing himself firmly to any one position. Finds most interesting how Donne's choices between differing opinions about "the motions of angels or their intellectual operations" disclose "the way in which his own mind worked" (168). Suggests that Donne's attitude toward angels is characterized by a tension between "a Christian readiness to admit that speculative knowledge is unattainable and anyway superfluous for salvation" and "a persistent intellectual curiosity, an irritability of the mind" (172). Says that "Donne's interest in scholastic angelology is singular in an age when Calvinists, Platonists, and the 'new philosophers' agreed to reject it," and believes that "whim or wit" alone will not explain Donne's "original combination of genuine curiosity" and his "full awareness of the hazardous nature of this 'science'" (174). Finds that Donne's conceits and speculations about angels are most "effective" when "they convey a truth, not about angels, but about the human mind or the human predicament" (174–75). Concludes that "the claims of rationality" and "curiosity about the invisible world of spirits" have seldom been held "evenly poised— never perhaps so evenly, though in quivering equilibrium, as they were for a time in the tense and restless mind of Donne" (179). Compares and/or contrasts Donne's attitude toward angels to those held by Herbert, Milton, William Hammond, Cleveland, Cowley, Marvell, Lord Herbert of Cherbury, Crashaw, Vaughan, Traherne, and the Cambridge Platonists.

102. Elsky, Martin. "History, Liturgy, and Point of View in Protestant Meditative Poetry." *SP* 77: 67–83.

Studies the connection between liturgical presentation of time and Protestant meditative poetry and argues that the traditional Catholic view of the importance of memory in making present the major events of sacred history, both in the Mass and in private devotion, is given a different emphasis by Protestant theology, which insists that the "real presence" is an internal experience. Maintains that, although Catholic and Protestant meditative poetry often bear striking resemblances, their fundamental difference is that "the center of reformed meditative verse is not just Christ, but Christ as experienced by the meditator" (72). Argues that, "for reformed poets, applying Christ to the self often involves a union of subject and object, or the making present of Christ the object in the heart and soul of the meditating subject in a way that clearly reflects the internalized sacrifice of the Protestant Lord's Supper" (73). Claims that Catholic poets such as Southwell and Crashaw generally maintain "a distinction between subject and object" in their meditations, whereas the Protestant poet often unites the two, "so that events in the life of Christ are reenacted in his heart, as they are in the Protestant communicant" (82–83). Comments on *Goodf, HSSpit, Lit,* and several sermons in the context of Protestant meditative practices and the liturgical understanding of time and sacred history.

103. Fietz, Lothar. "John Donne: 'The Sunne Rising'—Eine Beschreibung der thematischen und rhetorischen Textstruktur und ihrer strategischen Funktion." *LWU* 13: 151–69.

By means of a functional, structural analysis of *SunRis* seeks to uncover the thematic depth structure as a function of the special viewpoint of a metaphysical poet such as Donne. Maintains that, based on the backdrop of the thematic depth structure, it becomes evident that the significant dissimilarity between the elements of the poem is nothing more than a rhetorical means of replacing the customary view of things with a new viewpoint. Sees the text of the poem as historic stage of a restructuring process in the understanding of self and the world. Believes that the structure of the poem reflects Donne's perception of the intellectual currents of his day and reveals his attempt to guide his reader through these currents.

104. Finnegan, Robert Emmett. "Donne's 'A Hymn to God the Father,' 13–18." *Expl* 39, no. 1: 38–39.

Suggests that if one reads "shore" as the past tense of "shear" in addition to its primary meaning in *Father* (l. 14), "the metaphor spinning-measuring-cutting is quite brilliantly and economically completed, albeit covertly." Suggests that the stanza indicates Donne's fear that "he will be judged at the moment of his death and be found unworthy to enter heaven, perishing eternally on the margin or *shore* which separates this life from the next." For a reply, see Ralph Haven Wolfe and Edgar F. Daniel in *Expl* 40, no. 4 (1982): 13–14 (347).

105. Gill, Roma. "Hesper/Vesper—and Phosphor." *N&Q,* n.s. 27: 318–19.

Says that Wesley Milgate in his edition of the *Anniversaries* (Oxford, 1978) is correct in saying that "Hesper and Vesper are both names for Venus when she appears as the evening star," but points out that Donne in *SecAn* (l. 198) does not intend to repeat himself by using both names but actually makes the mistake of confusing Hesper with Phosphor, which was "another name for Venus, but used only for the star appearing in the morning." Finds the same error in Donne's Problem: "Why is Venus-Starre multinominous, called both Hesperus and Vesper?" Notes that Marlowe makes a similar mistake in *Hero and Leander* (ii, 327–31). Suggests that the solution of Donne's "Problem" can be found in Pliny's *Natural History* (II.36–37).

106. Guibbory, Achsah. "John Donne and Memory as 'the Art of *Salvation.*'" *HLQ* 43: 261–74.

Suggests that Donne elevates memory above understanding and will as the most reliable faculty of the tripartite rational soul to lead man to God. Discusses Donne's views on memory "in the light of the Augustinian tradition from which it derives," explains "why Donne so closely links salvation with memory," and indicates how "his concern with memory informs his religious prose and poetry." Points out that memory for Donne is "part of the divine image which God imprinted on man at Creation" (261), was the rational faculty "least impaired by the Fall" (262), and is important "[b]ecause God, once learned, is in our memory" and thus "the way to find God is through memory" (263). Comments on "the radical concern with memory which pervades Donne's religious writings" (265). Observes, for example, that in his sermons Donne attempts to stimulate the memory of his listeners and repeatedly counsels them to "remembrances" of God and other biblical figures, maintaining that these "remembrances" will lead them to an understanding of the present and to a future salvation. Points out that memory plays a key role also in Donne's meditative poems and prose, especially in *Goodf, Devotions,* the *Holy Sonnets,* and the *Anniversaries.*

107. Handscombe, Richard. "Donne's Holy Sonnet VI: A Problem of Plainness." *Lang&S* 13: 98–108.

Analyzes *HSDeath* to show that the traditional interpretation—Christ's victory over death—is borne out by a consideration of semantics. Sees the use of the word "Death" as both personification and vocative, necessary in interpreting the "action" of the poem as an emotional debate between the speaker and Death. Considers the prosody as underscoring this debate. Analyzes the meaning of the preposition "for" (ll. 2, 3) in terms of the punctuation and resulting prosody to show how it underscores the debate and creates a pun on the four Last Things.

108. Hester, M. Thomas. "Another Allusion to Horace in Donne." *ANQ* 18: 106–8.

Points out that in *Sat5* (ll. 7–9) Donne alludes to or, better yet, responds to Horace's defense of his satirical technique in his *Satires* (I, i, 23–24). Notes that, "[j]ust as Horace [in his satire] found the jocularity of Lucilius inappropriate to the moral seriousness of satire, so Donne's satirist finds the stance of Horace inadequate under the present conditions" (107), that is, in this "Age of rusty iron" (l. 35).

109. Hester, M. Thomas. "'Carelesse Phrygius': Donne's Separatist Sectarian," in *A Fair Day in the Affections: Literary Essays in Honor of Robert B. White, Jr.,* ed. Jack D. Durant and M. Thomas Hester, 87–99. Raleigh, N.C.: Winston Press.

Suggests that Donne portrays Phrygius in *Sat3* (ll. 62–64) as a Barrowist-Separatist, an adherent of the English Protestant sect founded by John Greenwood and Henry Barrow that in the 1590s was under the leadership of Barrow, an "apocalyptic separatist and enemy of Canterbury, Rome, Geneva, Brownists, and Anabaptists alike" (92). Maintains that "'Careless' in his arrogant aloofness from the search for 'true religion' and in his shortsighted, radical intolerance, Phrygius, as the Barrowists, does not 'doubt wisely'" (96), and notes also that his rejection of all women perhaps alludes to the contempt of the Barrowists for "holy matrimony," which they regarded as simply a civil ceremony. Argues that although Donne could have had any separatist group in mind, the Barrowists are "the most likely target" of his satire and concludes that either "Separatism" or "Barrowism" is preferable to "the age's more general, and hence more slippery malediction, 'atheism'" (97).

110. Hobbs, Mary. "More Books from the Library of John Donne." *BC* 29: 590–92.

Lists 15 unsigned Latin books, in addition to those listed in Geoffrey Keynes's *Bibliography of Dr. John Donne, Dean of St. Paul's* (4th ed., 1973), in the Chichester Cathedral Library that "show Donne's characteristic neat sloping pencil lines in the margins, with occasional small brackets, as in the signed books" in the library (591).

111. Hühn, Peter. "Wirklichkeit und Bedeutung im Gedicht: Die Dichtergestalt als Medium der Realitätsvermittlung bei Carew und Gray," in *Literarische Ansichten der Wirklichkeit: Studien zur Wirklichkeitskonstitution in englischsprachiger Literatur: To Honour Johannes Kleinstück,* ed. Hans-Heinrich Freitag and Peter Hühn, 89–122. Anglo-American Forum, 12, ed. Christoph Gutknecht. Frankfurt: Peter D. Lang.

Analyzes Carew's "Elegie upon the death of the Deane of Pauls, Dr. John Donne" to show how the images and metaphors in the elegy comment in a meaningful way upon Donne's poetry and are not merely poetic adornments. Noting, for example, in the first line of his elegy Carew's use of the image of "widdowed poetry," suggests that this image is Carew's indirect reference to his understanding of Donne's special role as a poet, that is, Donne's relationship to poetry is that of a husband to his wife and the poetic works emanating from this "woman" are his children.

112. Ishii, Shonosuke. "Some New Trends in the Study of Renaissance Poetry." *RenB* 7: 10–12.

Notes the recent interest in Donne among Japanese scholars, citing in particular the edition of the *Holy Sonnets* listed above (entry 94).

113. Kuntz, Joseph M., and Nancy Martinez, eds. "Donne," in *Poetry Explication: A Checklist of Interpretations since 1925 of British and American Poems Past and Present,* 127–51. 3rd ed. Boston: G. K. Hall. First ed., 1950; 2nd ed., 1962.

Lists explications for 120 of Donne's poems published from 1925 to 1977. For annotations, see *Roberts 1* and *Roberts 2*. See also Nancy C. Martinez and Joseph G. R. Martinez, *Guide to British Poetry Explication,* vol. 2, *Renaissance* (New York: G. K. Hall, 1992).

114. Le Huray, Peter. "The Fair Musick that All Creatures Made," in *The Age of Milton: Backgrounds to Seventeenth-Century Literature,* ed. C. A. Patrides and Raymond B. Waddington, 241–72. Manchester: Manchester University Press; Totowa, N.J.: Barnes and Noble.

Contrasts two musical settings of "Sweet, stay awhile," one by John Dowland, printed in *A Pilgrimes Solace* (1612), and the other by Henry Lawes, found in British Library Add. MS 53723, to show that Lawes was more sensitive to the words of the poem than was Dowland. Points out that "[i]t is in the matter of cadence structure that the settings of Dowland and Lawes most significantly differ," observing that "[b]y the judicious use of secondary and imperfect cadences Lawes achieves a forward-moving

tonal structure that at the same time reflects the poetic argument," whereas Dowland is comparatively insensitive to cadence (266). [The poem, printed as the first stanza of *Break* in the 1669 edition, is very unlikely by Donne; it may be by Dowland.]

115. Lein, Clayton D. "Theme and Structure in Donne's *Satyre II.*" *CL* 32: 130–50.

Rejects the negative critical tradition that regards *Sat2* as disorderly and incoherent and attempts to demonstrate that the poem is "a major creative effort, a vigorous attempt on Donne's part to weld together his disparate worlds of law, love, poetry, and religion," and that it contains "a striking statement of his moral imagination" (131). Discusses how the poem is "a highly imaginative satiric experiment with fully articulated themes, coherent imagery, and supportive symbolic structures" (143). Maintains that the "profound despair and psychological uncertainties" in the poem "provide us with unique insights into the early moral world of the poet, strikingly documenting the emotional and intellectual abyss out of which the later great celebratory poems will come," and maintains that every aspect of Donne's "intellective and emotional life" is seen in the poem as "the victim of 'sluttish Time.'" Insists that *Sat2* is "the most important formal mastering of classical verse satire in English Renaissance poetry," displaying "a thorough mastery of the mode, its metaphoric style, and its principal structural manipulations." Claims that the poem "represents a significant early effort by Donne to combine his various talents in large, coherent structures." Concludes that *Sat2* shows Donne "already absorbed at this early stage in the creative process of unifying wildly distinct elements, a technique he steadily refined" and which "was ultimately to transform our lyric tradition" (150).

116. Malpezzi, Frances M. "Christian Poetics in Donne's 'Upon the Translation of the Psalmes.'" *Renascence* 33: 221–28.

Calls *Sidney* a poem of "praise of an ideal work," in which Donne "is able to expound on the source of Christian poetry, make clear the responsibility of the Christian poet, suggest the role of Christian poetry in the spiritual edification of the Church, and set a criterion of decorum for the imagery of such religious poetry" (221). Compares the poem to Donne's Lenten sermon on Ezekiel 33:32 and suggests that the similarity of language and imagery in both works makes clear that Donne regarded the role of the priest and the poet as similar. Finds in both works, for instance, the use of a complex central metaphor of tuning and an emphasis on employing scriptural expressions and style. Says that when read in conjunction with the sermon, the poem "presents a poeticized *Defence of Poesy*" and, moving "beyond theorizing," it becomes "a concrete and dramatic presentation of Christian aesthetics" (227).

117. Maurer, Margaret. "The Real Presence of Lucy Russell, Countess of Bedford, and the Terms of John Donne's 'Honour is so Sublime Perfection.'" *ELH* 47: 205–34.

Suggests that a fuller, less idealized understanding of the life of Donne's patroness, Lucy Russell, Countess of Bedford, is helpful in understanding Donne's poems addressed to her, noting that the image we have of her was primarily created by poets, Donne being in the forefront, who praised her in exchange for financial support. Observes that 350 years later she is "still collecting" on her "investment" (207). After showing how the countess's image has been idealized, discusses a basis for Donne's association with her, their "common interest in a style of courtship out of which Donne fashioned his poetic" (206). Illustrates

the lady's style of courtly negotiation by presenting "an account of her proceedings as mediator and go-between" when her brother John wished to marry the daughter of Robert Cecil, Earl of Salisbury, and argues that Donne's purpose in his poems to her is "to justify—account for as well as prescribe—[the] courtly behavior of the Lady" (222). Concludes with a reading of *BedfHon*, "a poem that not only is a courtly transaction but that also discusses the theory of such transactions" (206).

118. McGrath, Lynette. "John Donne's Apology for Poetry." *SEL* 20: 73–89.

Outlines "the kind of apology for poetry Donne himself might have made, compiling evidence from Donne's prose statements [primarily from the sermons] regarding techniques of rhetorical and poetic persuasion" and draws out "the lines of connection between Donne's statements regarding poetic persuasion and those made by Sidney in his *Apology for Poetry*" (75). Maintains that while both poets were influenced by earlier humanists, such as Juan Luis Vives and Thomas Elyot as well as by Scaliger, Minturno, and St. Augustine, Donne knew Sidney's apology very well and subscribed to most of its positions, especially the idea that poetry should persuade one to good and that content is more valuable than form. Says that for both poets the Scriptures were considered the highest poetry because they embodied truth, and both thought that secular poetry should strive for the same thing. Suggests that while Sidney draws an analogy between the creative act of God and that of the poet, Donne is more wary of the way that poetry may be abused or misinterpreted. Says that both men, however, share the idea that poetry should persuade the reader's will to action. Points out Donne's view of the relationship between poetry and the sermon, noting that, for him, "the distinction between the poet and preacher rests not so much in intention as in the source of their examples and in the degree of obliqueness required by the poet's teaching and of directness allowed the preacher." Concludes that, "though scattered, Donne's comments on poetry are consistent with themselves" and, when placed together, "show that his view of poetry was founded in a coherent and integrated aesthetic" (87).

119. Morrissey, Thomas J. "The Self and the Meditative Tradition in Donne's *Devotions*." *NDEJ* 13: 29–49.

Considers the *Devotions* as "a unique blend of traditional Christian wisdom and literary virtuosity" that utilizes both Jesuit and Anglican meditative traditions and yet departs from both in two important ways: by the manipulation of metaphors that produces "an individualized self-portrait" (29) and by the "hidden" structural device of thematic pairing of Devotions I–XI with Devotions XIII–XXIII—with Devotion XII serving as the pivot. Maintains that "[t]hese innovations are the means by which Donne achieves the metamorphosis of traditional religious concepts and beliefs into literary art while at the same time giving his art a traditional context" (30). Discusses how Donne adapts the main features of formal meditation to "the aesthetic needs of the *Devotions*" and comments on how he "individualizes the meditative tradition by applying to the tripartite method [of the formal meditation] a mastery of metaphor and literary structure" (34).

120. Moseley, C. W. R. D. "A Reading of Donne's Holy Sonnet XIV." *Archiv* 217: 103–8.

Reads *HSBatter* as an "essay on the Triune nature of God" and "the action of that nature on man," emphasizing "Donne's debt to Biblical (especially Pauline) theology and Christology" and analyzing "the movement of ideas through the poem" (103–4). Maintains that the sonnet divides into three distinct parts (ll. 1–4, 5–8, 9–14), with each part "a celebration of a property of each Person of the Trinity in turn": the first part is centered about "the idea of a creating, making God, a *Deus Artifex*" (104), "the key idea being God, as Creator, as Father, reforging his material"; the second part with its "images of besieging and war" suggests "the military triumph of Christ in the Harrowing of Hell" (105); and the third part is "an appeal for the operation of the Holy Ghost." Says that the final couplet "subsumes all the ideas in the poem into an intense appeal not to a committee but to a lover." Calls the sonnet "not a versified prayer, but prayer itself, an admirable expression of the white heat generated by intense intellectual activity" (107), and suggests that perhaps the poem is "the fruit of meditation on *Romans* VII" (108).

121. Nishiyama, Yoshio. "Erasmus to Donne" [Erasmus and Donne]. *ESELL* 71:113–46.

Calls Donne one of the prominent "Erasmian literati" and maintains that he derived many of his satiric expressions and ridiculous conceits from Erasmus. Compares the *Songs and Sonets* with Erasmus's *Colloquia*.

122. Novarr, David. *The Disinterred Muse: Donne's Texts and Contexts.* Ithaca, N.Y.: Cornell University Press. 218p.

Three chapters of this study were previously published and are annotated in *Roberts 1* or in *Roberts 2:* Chapter 1, "'The Extasie': Donne's Address on the States of Union" (17–39), first appeared in *Just So Much Honor: Essays Commemorating the Four-Hundredth Anniversary of the Birth of John Donne,* ed. Peter Amadeus Fiore (University Park and London: Pennsylvania State University Press,

1972), 219–43, in which the author gives a critical reading of *Ecst,* underscoring aspects of its wit that have been overlooked or misinterpreted in the past. Finds Donne's clever uses of the hypothetical listener and the "dialogue of one" as "the keystone of Donne's wit" (30) and argues that through these devices Donne is able to deliver an authoritative, dispassionate, and almost scientifically objective justification of bodily love as compatible with spiritual love. Sees the poem not as a celebration of mutual love but points out that its "arid air of refined doctrine provides a fertile atmosphere for crisp argument and dry wit" (38). Chapter 2, "Contextual Study and Donne's 'A Valediction: forbidding mourning'" (40–64), deals with the issue of contexts in which *ValMourn* has been read by modern critics, especially by John Freccero in "Donne's 'Valediction: forbidding mourning'" (*ELH* 30 [1963]: 335–76), and argues for two additional contexts in which to read the poem—the dramatic human situation of the poem and the erotic context—preferring these over "the contexts in astronomy, metaphysics, and alchemy" (61). Seeks "to provide affective justification for the rightness of human love in exploring the psychology of the situation which the poem implies and in showing that Donne's geometry in the poem has its counterpart in bawdy" (64). Chapter 3, "Donne's 'Epithalamion made at Lincoln's Inn': Context and Date" (65–84), first appeared in *RES* 7 (1956): 250–63. Argues that the poem is a satiric entertainment, written to celebrate a mock wedding held as part of the revels at Lincoln's Inn, possibly for the performance of the Midsummer revel in 1595. Chapter 4, "The Dating of Donne's *La Corona*" (85–93), first appeared in *PQ* 36 (1957): 259–65. Argues that *Corona* was written

"shortly before the *Holy Sonnets,* that is, late in 1608 or early in 1609" (93). Chapter 5, "Two Flamens: The Poems of Dr. Donne" (94–205), considers "Donne's career as poet after he had taken orders" and tries "to refine the chronology, the meaning, the achievement of poems he felt impelled to write after he had renounced verse" (11). Divides this chapter into sixteen parts: (1) "'To Mr. George Herbert, with my Seal, of the Anchor and Christ'": suggests that Donne wrote the poem to Herbert because he was "aware of what his ordination would mean to a young friend who shared his love of poetry and his secular ambitions" (107); (2) "'To Mr. Tilman after he had taken orders'": believes Donne had Herbert in mind as well as Tilman and that the poem was written after 20 December 1618 and before 12 May 1619; (3) "The Dating of the Sonnets in the Westmoreland Manuscript": surveys the arguments for dating three of the *Holy Sonnets* that appear only in the Westmoreland manuscript and suggests that, if they were written after Donne's ordination, they are "the most personal, the most intimately self-expressive poems Donne wrote after his ordination" (120); (4) "'O, to vex me, contraryes meete in one'": argues that "[t]he impact of Donne's recognition and acknowledgement of his inconstancy, his awareness that he has not fundamentally changed, is heightened for us if we think that he wrote this sonnet after his ordination" (121); (5) "'Since she whome I lovd, hath payd her last debt'": presents a critical reading of the sonnet, maintaining that Donne may have written the poem after his ordination and that, "if he did, it is evidence not only that he had retained his old poetic power but also that a crucial personal crisis made him reutilize that power" (127); (6) "'A Hymne to Christ, at the Authors last going into Germany'": maintains that Donne wrote the poem for his friends, not intended for public service, in order "partly to express for himself and to dramatize for others the resolution of his apprehensions about departing for Germany and partly out of a feeling that it was entirely fitting that, in his role as chaplain, he give public expression to an attitude, unexceptional and orthodox but still stamped with his own characteristic mark, which he considered proper to inculcate in those for whose religious guidance he was responsible" (130); (7) "'Translated out of Gazaeus, Vota Amico facta. fol. 160'": suggests that during his time in Germany Donne found time to translate from Latin a 12-line poem by Angelin Gazet, a Belgian Jesuit, and discusses how "fol. 160" in Donne's title may provide "a clue to the copy he saw or owned" (134); (8) "'Show me deare Christ, thy spouse, so bright and cleare'": analyzes the argument of the sonnet about Donne's yearning for a universal Church and suggests that, if it was written soon after Donne returned from Germany, "it indicates, once again, Donne's compulsion to express himself in verse at a time when he could not adequately express his deepest feelings in a more public form," and also indicates that "his poetic power had in no way diminished" (141); (9) "'The Lamentations of Jeremy, for the most part according to Tremelius'": thinks the translation "provides the best evidence for Walton's statements about Donne's interest in Church music" and that "it demonstrates that even when he was in orders he undertook to master a new form," which "he did with remarkable virtuosity" (150); (10) "'Upon the translation of the Psalmes by Sir Philip Sidney, and the Countesse of Pembroke his Sister'": stresses that the poem is "not a disinterested tribute to

work done long before" but rather was a poem seeking patronage for the deanship he very much wanted and that in this "more than in any other poem that he wrote after his ordination, Donne's motive was the motive behind his earlier poetry of patronage—self-advancement" (137); (11) "The 'Ignatii Loyolae (ἀποθέωσις) Attributed to Donne': reports the discovery of the poem in 1967 and evaluates the evidence for attributing it to Donne, concluding that "it is most unlikely that the newly appointed Dean of St. Paul's had either the time or the inclination to write such a poem at such a time" (161); (12) "The 'Stationes' in *Devotions upon Emergent Occasions*": regards these 23 Latin verses as Donne's "own imitation" of the 14 Stations of the Cross (167) and finds them "interesting" in that they show "Donne willing in his old age to attempt a mode new to him" (170); (13) "The Dating of 'Hymne to God my God, in my sicknesse' and 'A Hymne to God the Father'": dates the first as December 1623 and the second "at about the same time" (175); (14) "'Hymne to God my God, in my sicknesse'": gives a critical analysis of the poem and argues that it is "the best evidence that, as late as the end of 1623, Donne's poetic powers had suffered no diminution" (183); (15) "'A Hymne to God the Father'": presents a critical reading of the poem, contrasting it with *Sickness* and suggesting it was likely written three or four years before *Sickness;* and (16) "'An hymne to the Saints, and to Marquesse Hamylton'": explains the occasion of the poem and examines Donne's attitude towards poetry in his later years. The "Appendix: The Bridgewater Manuscript of Donne's Poems" gives a bibliographical description of the manuscript, noting it was probably written by either John Egerton, 1st Earl of Bridgewater, or his wife, Frances. Reviews: Ilona Bell in *GHJ* 4 (1980): 53–57; Robert Bozanich in *WHR* 35 (1981): 289–92; Julia Briggs in *TLS* (8 May 1981): 523; John W. Ferstel in *C&L* 31 (1981): 48–51; Raman Selden in *ELN* 20 (1981): 38–41; Jeanne M. Shami in *SCN* 40 (1981):12–13; Ted-Larry Pebworth in *QQ* 89 (1982): 899–900; Jill Baumgaertner in *RES* 34 (1983): 503–4.

123. Okuma, Sakae. "John Donne no 'Shizen-shi' soshite to Mannerism" [John Donne's "Nature Poetry" and Mannerism]. *Meiji Daigaku Kyoyo Ronshu* [Bulletin of the College of General Education, Meiji University] 138 (December): 1–22.

Analyzes *Storm, Calm,* and *ElProg,* pointing out manneristic features. Calls the elegy a perverted nature poem in which the female body is regarded as the natural world and argues that although the poem seems filled with such natural images as "Forest," "Meridian," "Hemisphere," "Canaries," "pearls," "Promontory," "Hellespont," "Sestos and Abydos," "sea," "Island," and so on, this landscape is false nature, the world of deceit. Maintains that Donne's exploration of false nature shows him to be a mannerist and suggests that his idea of the body as a representative of the physical world is akin to that of Federico Zuccaro, a theorist of mannerism, who in his *Idea de'pittori, scultori e architetti* (1607) relates the various parts of the human body to their appropriate natural phenomena, based on the microcosm/macrocosm concept.

124. Patrides, C. A. "The Experience of Otherness: Theology as a Means of Life," in *The Age of Milton: Backgrounds to Seventeenth-Century Literature,* ed. C. A. Patrides and Raymond B. Waddington, 170–96. Manchester: Manchester University Press; Totowa, N.J.: Barnes and Noble.

Surveys the pervasive influence of theology on the intellectual, emotional, political, social, scientific, and literary life in the earlier seventeenth century. Comments briefly on Donne's views on the Catholic-Protestant debate over faith and good works and on the interpretation of the Bible, especially Genesis and the Book of Revelation.

125. Perrine, Laurence. "Donne's 'Confined Love.'" *Expl* 39, no. 1: 34–36.

Argues that the speaker of *ConfL* is a libertine female, basing the argument on the fact that the poem is "a philosophical argument divorced from dramatic context" (35) and that "[t]he elements of self-interest and of psychological plausibility both support the probability of a woman speaker" (36). Notes that both Helen Gardner in her edition of the *Elegies* and the *Songs and Sonnets* (Oxford, 1965) and N. J. C. Andreasen (*John Donne: Conservative Revolutionary,* Princeton, 1967) think the source of the poem is either Ovid's *Metamorphoses* (Gardner) or his *Amores* (Andreasen) and that in both the speaker is a woman.

126. Perry, T. Anthony. "John Donne's Philosophy of Love in 'The Ecstasy,'" in *Erotic Spirituality: The Integrative Tradition from Leone Ebreo to John Donne,* 89–98. University, Ala.: University of Alabama Press.

Discusses how the Neoplatonic philosophy of love, found most fully expressed in Leone Ebreo's *Dialoghi d'amore* (1535), informs *Ecst* and how Donne also diverges from the *Dialoghi.* Agrees with, but also expands upon and modifies, what Helen Gardner says about the argument of Donne's poem ("The Argument about 'The Ecstasy,'" in *Elizabethan and Jacobean Studies Presented to Frank Percy Wilson,* ed. Herbert Davis and Helen Gardner, 279–306. Oxford: Clarendon Press, 1959). Presents a detailed reading of *Ecst* and suggests that its argument can be briefly summarized "by the pun that for Donne loving is knotty but not naughty." Argues that "[r]ather than an indecent proposal," Donne's "call to return to the body" is "an act of integration, a binding of our opposite tendencies into a unified and living being through that subtle knot that defines our humanity and that is delicately alluded to as a 'naked thinking heart' in 'The Blossom'" (5). Concludes that for Donne, "Platonism is real but secondary" (90) and that for him "both mind and body can lay claim to love's origins" (97). Briefly comments on Neoplatonic elements in *Under, NegLove, ValBook, Prim,* and *Air.*

127. Pollock, John H. "Donne's 'A Hymne to Christ, at the Authors last going into Germany.'" *Expl* 38, no. 4: 20–22.
Argues that the somber tone of *Christ* can be better understood when the poem is read against the background of Donne's "Sermon of Valediction at my going into Germany." Maintains that the somber tone of the poem "reflects Donne's awareness that he is growing old" and "his fear that God will not accept his late repentance for his sins" (21). Points out, however, that the poem ends with an affirmation of faith that he will "see God" (l. 27); in other words, "[t]hrough the very process of the poem Donne apparently has come to grips with his depression, faced it head on, and discovered finally that God is open to him even at this late stage in his life" (22).

128. Raizis, Marios Byron. "The Epithalamion Tradition and John Donne," in *Essays and Studies from Professional Journals,* 9–22. Athens: Panhellenic Association of Graduates in English.
Reprint of an essay that originally appeared in *Wichita State University Bulletin* (University Studies, No. 69) 42, no. 4 (1966): 1–15. See *Roberts*

1 (Item 1230). Comments on the Greek tradition (Sappho) and English tradition (Spenser) of the epithalamium and points out Donne's originality in the use of the genre in his three epithalamia.

129. Rao, Ananda T. "Nature in John Donne." *LitE* 2, no. 1: 61–67.
Agrees with critics who point out that Donne has little interest in the beauty of nature but notes that Donne combines an "almost Satanic curiosity of analysis" of natural things with a firm belief in a universal divine order (63). Suggests that Donne could be called "a philosopher-cum-scientist" (63) and states that, for Donne, "an object of nature is an excuse for exposition of his own personal moods and feelings, for commenting on society, and for philosophising over human experiences" (65). Cites in particular lines from *Storm* as "a representative example of Donne's use of nature in poetry" (66). Briefly contrasts Donne with the Romantic poets.

130. Reeves, Troy D. *Index to the Sermons of John Donne,* vol. 2, *Index of Proper Names.* Elizabethan and Renaissance Studies, 95, ed. James Hogg. Salzburg: Institut für Anglistik und Amerikanistik, Universität Salzburg. ii, 148p.
Presents an index of proper names found in Donne's sermons, including "major references to persons, places, organizations, and institutions, religious and national groups, and special days on the Christian calendar." Includes "biblical personages from both the Old and New Testaments; patristic, medieval and Renaissance commentators and exegetes; ecclesiastical and political figures; and Donne's contemporaries"; and also "Donne's citations from the Vulgate and other translations besides the Authorized Version." Indexes "only the sermons themselves, not the commentaries, introductions, notes and critical appa-

ratus that accompany the sermons in the standard edition" (i). Reviews: Jeanne M. Shami in *Ren&R,* n.s. 8 (1984): 59–62.

131. Richards, Bernard. "Whitney's Influence on Shakespeare's Sonnets 111 and 112, and on Donne's Third Satire." *N&Q,* n.s. 27: 160–61.

Suggests that Donne's image of the "huge hill" in *Sat3* (ll. 79–80) can be traced back to an emblem showing Hercules at a crossroads that appeared in Geoffrey Whitney's *A Choice of Emblemes* (1586). Notes that just as Hercules in the emblem "seeks honour," so Donne's speaker "seeks God's truth," and that both stress "the difficulty and the necessity for fortitude" (161).

132. Richards, Michael Reynard. "The Romantic Critics and John Donne." *BuR* 25, no. 2: 40–51.

Shows that "the Romantic critics were familiar with Donne and devoted a considerable amount of criticism to his poetry," noting that Coleridge, Hazlitt, Lamb, and De Quincey "were familiar enough with Donne so that the weight of their comments ranks him third among the Elizabethans behind Shakespeare and Spenser" (40), although Donne's popularity "was forced to await the twentieth century, Eliot, and the New Critics" (41). Discusses Coleridge's interest in Donne's language and metrics and suggests that he "appears to be the first critic who really understood Donne's poetry" (42). Points out that Hazlitt's criticism of Donne "forms a direct antithesis to Coleridge's approach of sympathy and understanding" and that his negative criticism "lies in his inability to read Donne correctly and to understand him" (45). Says that Lamb's criticism of Donne, on the other hand, is "utterly charming" (48) and that he "emerges as the sort of critic who makes a reader wish he had written more." Maintains that De

Quincey's criticism, though favorable and perceptive, is "often fragmentary and uneven" (49), the two most important aspects of his criticism being his admiration of Donne's "intricate patterns of thought and his rhetorical ability" (50). Concludes that "[o]f greatest interest is the fact that these critics admired Donne for the same reasons he is praised in the twentieth century," that is, "his dramatic immediacy, the intellectual exercise involved in any reading of his verse, and the realistic approach to his subject" (51).

133. Sadler, Lynn Veach. "'Meanes Blesse': Donne's *Ignatius His Conclave.*" *CLAJ* 23: 438–50.

Argues that, just as in many of his other works, Donne in *Ignatius* strives for "the mean between extremes" because he recognizes that "[s]eeing only in extremes reduces man's choice to either-or possibilities." Maintains that in *Ignatius* "the episodes unite to catalogue the great dichotomies of the period: either the Old Science or the New (in the Copernicus episode); either the Old Medicine or the New (in the Paracelsus episode); either a divine-right monarch or a cunning tyrant who manipulates through religion, and either accommodation between Church and State or regicide (in the Machiavelli episode); either censorship or licentiousness (in the Aretino episode); either a known world or an expanded one (in the Columbus episode); either an extremely weak Catholic hero, to whom miracles are falsely assigned (the Nerius episode), or an extremely strong and dangerous one who arrogates the trappings of heroism (Ignatius)" (443). Believes that the persona in *Ignatius* "seeks the mean between prohibitions against change and his own natural curiosity about the world and about progress," and that "[a]s he learns of the perversions of good by evil and of the dangers of extremes, he teaches an audience of Catholics,

Protestants, and simply humans, for not only is religious choice at stake but the whole pattern of making choices." Maintains that the persona "comes to see (and then mirrors for the audience) the hurtfulness of extremes," for "if one embraces extremes, his choices are delimited" and "he may be, even though he pulls back from them, tinctured by those extremes" (445). Concludes that, for Donne, the norm is always "the mean between extremes, between subservient and radical Catholicism, or between Catholicism and Puritanism, or between inaction and purposeless activity, or between no choosing and wrong choosing" (449).

134. Sanders, Charles. "Roethke's 'The Swan.'" *Expl* 38, no. 3: 26–28.

Suggests the influence of Donne's poetry on Theodore Roethke, especially *Noct* on Roethke's "The Swan."

135. Schmidt, Michael. "John Donne 1572–1631," in *A Reader's Guide to Fifty British Poets 1300–1900,* 134–45. London: Heinemann; Totowa, N.J.: Barnes and Noble.

Presents a general introduction to Donne's poetry. Compares Donne and Marlowe to highlight Donne's poetical innovations in prosody, language, use of conventions, wit, self-dramatization, and so on. Briefly comments on Donne's critical reputation from Jonson to T. S. Eliot and Allen Tate and presents a biographical sketch of Donne, claiming that "[m]any of the thematic preoccupations and radical poetic procedures in the *Songs and Sonets* and in the religious poems express a personality as complex and controversial as the verse itself" (139). Suggests that Donne's poems are "concentrated, dramatic, and realized" and are "not so much a quest for truth as a quest for effectiveness," claiming that they "generate ideas" and "do not merely decorate them" (142). Main-

tains that Donne's "actual achievement has been obscured by critics who praise his faults" and who "paint him as a contemporary, and thus deprive him of his true authority, a rich, even an alien *otherness*," and suggests that Edgell Rickword "brings us closest to Donne the poet, as he continues to be vital to us today" (143).

136. Sellin, Paul R. "The Proper Dating of Donne's 'Satyre III.'" *HLQ* 43: 275–312.

Based on the allusion in ll. 21–26 argues that *Sat3* was not likely written before the middle of 1598, after printed accounts of the expeditions of William Barents for a Northwest Passage appeared. Further argues that the poem may have been composed as late as January–June 1620, on the basis of a medallion Donne received on a visit to The Hague in December 1619 that commemorated the Synod of Dort and depicted pilgrims climbing a steep mountain that resembles the image in ll. 79–88. Believes that the meaning of the poem and the medallion have "remarkable agreement" (289) and that the likeness is probably not accidental. Maintains that this later dating of the poem would affect interpretation, placing it nearer to the sermons in theme and to the Reformed tradition in religious thought.

137. Shami, Jeanne M. "Donne on Discretion." *ELH* 47: 48–66.

Discusses the importance of discretion to Donne, which is not for him just a counterbalance to zeal, but rather "the criterion by which *all* decisions must be made and by which their integrity as right moral choices must be judged." Says that discretion was particularly important to Donne as a preacher, "whose vocation invests him with a degree of authority and power that increases the difficulty of his task as well as his responsibility to perform it well." Claims that "the dis-

cretion of choosing the means which
will minister most effectively to the
moral needs of his audience is everywhere Donne's greatest concern" (48).
Maintains that Donne sees his role not
only as one who imparts knowledge
of God, but also as one who must convince his congregation to apply that
knowledge in their own lives. Claims
that the problem of despair challenged
Donne's discretion as a preacher and
determined his homiletic method of
achieving "nearnesse" to his congregation and of assuring them that God
in Scripture and the Holy Spirit will
speak through him as preacher so that
they will understand and not lose hope.
Claims that Donne saw zeal as even
more important than discretion in moving his audience to action, but that
discretion was important in choosing
the means. Says Donne chose plainness as an aid to the understanding of
his hearers, but also eloquence and
the use of historical and biblical examples because of their persuasiveness.

138. **Shapiro, I. A.** "The Date of a Donne
Elegy, and Its Implications," in *English
Renaissance Studies Presented to Dame
Helen Gardner in Honour of Her
Seventieth Birthday,* ed. John Carey,
141–50. Oxford: Oxford University Press.
Argues that L. C. in *Sorrow* refers to
Sir Thomas Egerton, elder son of
Donne's employer, Sir Thomas Egerton, Lord Keeper of the Great Seal,
and Donne's close friend, who was
killed in Ireland in 1599. Notes that
Donne took part in the funeral of the
young man in Chester Cathedral on
27 September of that year. Discusses
how "the allusions in the poem are all
consistent with, and confirm, the conjecture" (143). Concludes that the earliest possible date of composition of
the poem is 6 September 1599, and
"its latest must be about the end of
the same month," thus making the
poem "one of the few early poems of
Donne that we can date very closely"

(145). Also describes the inclusion of
the poem among the *Elegies* in several manuscripts and in the first edition, and suggests that its appearance
in the Dowden manuscript and related
manuscripts helps identify the order
of composition of 13 of the *Elegies,*
thus providing "closer indications of
composition date than we have hitherto had for the Love Elegies" (150).

139. **Shapiro, I. A.** "Donne's Sermon
Dates." *RES* 31: 54–56.
Points out that Donne preached the
same sermon on more than one occasion, and thus cautions scholars not
to assume that "the dates attached
to Donne's sermons in printed texts
are necessarily those of their original
composition" (55). Argues that if one
wishes to study the development of
Donne's thought and theology from
the sermons, then the accurate chronological order of them is important.
Comments specifically on the possible dating of nos. 52–54 in *LXXX
Sermons* (1640) and no. 16 in *Fifty
Sermons* (1649). Maintains that even
those Donne himself dated may indicate "the date and occasion when he
preached certain sermons, to avoid the
embarrassment of repeating one when
persons who had heard it recently were
present." Thinks that "[t]his may explain why the sermons dated by Donne
nearly all relate to special occasions,
after which further repetition, except
in Donne's country parishes, would
have been impracticable" (56).

140. **Shawcross, John.** "The Book Index:
Plutarch's *Moralia* and John Donne."
JRMMRA 1: 53–62.
Calls attention "to the book index as
a possible source of information and
ideas for Renaissance authors" and
discusses in particular the significance
of Plutarch's *Moralia,* specifically an
indexed 1544 Latin version of the
work. Cites allusions or ideas in
Donne's poetry and prose that he could

have found by using the index to the *Moralia*, noting specific examples in a letter to Henry Wotton (c. 1600), several sermons, *Phrine, Sat3, SecAn, ValMourn, HSDeath, RWSlumb, Mark, Henry, FirAn, Sal,* and *Ignatius*.

141. Stanwood, P. G. "Seventeenth-Century English Literature and Contemporary Criticism." *AngTheoRev* 62: 395–410.

Argues that modern critics of English devotional literature of the earlier seventeenth century need to develop a more adequate historical sense that would allow them to participate imaginatively in the life of another time and place. Reviews nonhistorical trends in the criticism of English devotional poetry of the period and offers "from an Anglican and devotional point of view a plot of the critical course which may in the future be most profitably followed" (396). Distrusts literary genealogies or groupings of writers into "schools" and maintains that most writers of the period are better defined by their differences than by any similarities. Argues that, since most of the writers were Anglicans, critics must understand the Anglican temper, "with its distinctive ethos and its familiar threefold appeal to Scripture, to tradition, and to reason" (403). Recommends Richard Hooker's *Of the Laws of Ecclesiastical Polity* as a work that gives insights into the Anglican Church of the period. Finds objectionable the term "metaphysical," the notion of a "School of Donne," and T. S. Eliot's concept of "dissociation of sensibility." Praises those studies that try "to discover and share the culture of another time by an extension of confident sympathy and vision" (400), such as Rosemond Tuve's *A Reading of George Herbert* (1952), J. B. Leishman's *Monarch of Wit* (1951), Austin Warren's *Richard Crashaw* (1939), Helen Gardner's edition of Donne's

Divine Poems (1952; 2nd ed., 1978), and Louis Martz's *The Poetry of Meditation* (1954).

142. Sullivan, Ernest W., II. "John Donne's Probleme, 'Why was Sr Walter Raleigh thought ye fittest Man, to write ye Historie of these Times?'" *PBSA* 74: 63–67.

Notes that "Why was Sr Walter Raleigh thought ye fittest Man, to write ye Historie of these Times?" appears in eleven manuscripts, was not printed in the first or second 1633 editions of *Juvenilia* nor in the third, expanded edition, *Paradoxes, Problems, Essayes* (1652), and was published four times in the nineteenth and twentieth centuries—"always directly or indirectly from MS. Tanner 299, fol. 32, item 87 in the Bodleian Library." Points out how each of these four printed texts—by Edmund Gosse (1899), Evelyn Simpson (1924), Geoffrey Keynes (1923), and Helen Gardner and Timothy Healy (1967)—"substantially misrepresent the manuscript" (64), and gives a literal transcription of the introductory sentence and Problem from the Tanner manuscript.

143. Thomas, W. K. *The Fizz Inside: Critical Essays of a Lighter Kind.* Waterloo, Canada: University of Waterloo Press. 389p.

In "*Mors Amoris:* When Is Love Really Dead?" (109–29), presents a brief analysis of the argument of *Lect,* concluding that in the poem Donne says that "true love, that total commitment to each other, that supremacy of two-as-one, that love is dead the very moment either lover breaks that supremacy and puts self above the two together" and further that, "[w]hen that happens, it is much better to pull the plug, to remove the support equipment" (112). In "The War Sonnets of Rupert Brooke" (221–52) cites specific borrowings and/or echoes from Donne in Brooke's poems and comments on Brooke's high regard for Donne.

144. Törel, Sedat. "On Donne's Love Poems," in *Essays in English Literature,* 77–80. Ankara, Turkey: Hacettepe and Tas Books.

Presents very general, brief comments on Donne's love poems. Notes "the witty cynicism" and "cold-blooded use of conceits" in *SGo,* "the intensity of feeling" in *Ecst,* "the biting cynicism" of *Flea* (78), and "the genuine emotion" in *Twick.* Says that the "incongruous images and complex arguments" in Donne's love poems are the result of his trying to impress his readers and finds it hard to reconcile "the ecstasy, passion, love and lyricism" in some of the poems with the "deliberate cynicism, gravity of intellectual expressions, harsh reality and hard facts" of others (80).

145. Tucker, E. F. J. "Donne's Apocalyptic Style: A Contextual Analysis of *Devotions upon Emergent Occasions.*" *Interpretations* 12: 92–99.

Contends that Donne's prose needs the "same type of close contextual analysis accorded his poetry" (92) rather than the imprecise and impressionistic treatment it is customarily given. Demonstrates the methodology that he proposes by a close contextual analysis of excerpts from *Devotions,* pointing out Donne's "stylistic strategies" in relationship to the central theme of the work, which, he says, is "an apocalyptic vision based upon the *hebdomada mortium*" (93). Concludes that in the *Devotions* "[i]mages, rhetorical devices, grammatical structures, sound figures, punctuation, and rhythm all combine stylistically in one artistic whole of sense and meaning" (98).

146. Usinger, Fritz. *Opal und Pfauenfeder: Englische Gedichte deutsch.* With drawings by Rolf Schawarz. Lahnstein: Calatra Press. 18p. Limited to 300 copies.

Translates into German *SGo* (1) without notes or commentary.

147. Wiggins, Peter De Sa. "The Love Quadrangle: Tibullus 1.6 and Donne's 'lay Ideot.'" *PLL* 16: 142–50.

Agrees with those critics who point out that *ElNat* is indebted to Tibullus 1.6, a debt most evident in the retention of the Latin poet's presentation of a *praeceptor amoris* who is "vanquished by his own skill in the practice of adulterous love." Maintains, however, that Donne's poem achieves a dramatic immediacy, lacking in Tibullus's poem, by shifting the speaker's attention to the young wife rather than simply having her deliver a soliloquy or an apostrophe to the wronged husband. Says that Donne's elegy seems like "a spontaneous dialogue taking place in the heat of conflict" and provides the reader with "the pleasure of witnessing the speaker become step by step more and more ensnared in the trammels of his faulty argument and his own false position." Maintains that by adapting Tibullus, Donne is able "to probe facetiously the psychology of the faithless girl" and also to highlight the "originality of his elegy," to show how "he could treat a situation made notorious in the elegiac mode by the Roman poet" (149). Argues that the "love quadrangle, consisting of the *praeceptor amoris,* his mistress, her husband, and the shadowy fourth party with whom she uses her lessons to deceive both her husband and poet lover, is peculiarly Tibullan" and "represents a dramatic situation that Donne, among English elegiac poets, would have been the first to appreciate and the best qualified to develop to its greatest effect." Suggests that in Donne's elegy Tibullus's Delia "returns to sample life in an English boudoir" (150).

148. Wilson, Edward M. "Spanish and English Religious Poetry of the Seventeenth Century," in *Spanish and English Literature of the 16th and 17th Centuries:*

*Studies in Discretion, Illusion and Muta-
bility,* 234–49. Cambridge: Cambridge
University Press.

Discusses the importance of the influence of Ignatian meditation on both
English and Spanish poetry of the
seventeenth century and comments
approvingly on Louis Martz's *The
Poetry of Meditation* (New Haven:
Yale University Press, 1954) and
Helen Gardner's edition of the *Divine
Poems* (1952), both of whom discuss
Donne's indebtedness to post-Tridentine methods of meditation. Suggests
that Martz's case could be made even
stronger if he had taken into account
the contents of libraries of such men
as Bishop Ken and Archbishop San-
croft, both of which contained many
of the religious treatises referred to
by Martz in their original languages.
Maintains that the similarities between
English and Spanish religious poetry
of the period "is not just because
of a common climate of opinion or
because of the fact that both are eventually derived from a common mediaeval heritage" but rather because
"they are, in fact, both the results of
the same tradition of religious meditation" (245). Comments briefly on
the *Holy Sonnets,* especially their use
of urgent and everyday language, and
says that he knows no work in Spanish
that is exactly like the *Holy Sonnets.*
Concludes that "[i]n spite of the differences between England and Spain
in religion, the similarities in their
respective religious poems [are] more
important than their differences" (249).

149. **Wilson, Gayle Edward.** "Donne's
Sarcophagal Imagery in 'Epithalamion
Made at Lincolnes Inne,' vv. 37–42."
ANQ 18: 72–73.

Believes that, if one reads "tomb"
(l. 41) in *EpLin* as "sarcophagus"
(meaning "flesh eating" in Greek), ll.
37–42 "take on additional meaning
and poetic impact" (72). Points out
that, "[p]oetically expressed, the sar-

cophagus—the 'flesh-eating' tomb—
in the 'faire Temple' of the poem will
hopefully remain a 'hunger-starved
wombe' for a long time before it will
have a chance to 'fatten' on the bodies of the betrothed." Suggests that,
in effect, the lines "constitute a witty
way of satisfying the epithalamic convention of wishing the bride and
groom a long life" (73).

150. **Wilson, Scott W.** "Process and Product:
Reconstructing Donne's Personae." *SEL*
20: 91–103.

Discusses how *Triple, LovAlch, LovInf,*
and *Curse* are "informed more by the
dramatic phenomenological dialogue
between the persona and auditor than
by the interface separating author and
reader" and considers these poems as
examples in which Donne sought "to
engage his readers in a shared perspective of experience" (102). Considers the persona in these poems as
aware not only of his own reflection
but also the judgments made on it by
the reader or auditor, thus requiring
the persona to readjust his argument,
causing the reader then to readjust his.
Says "only in the physical immediacy of the metaphysical conceit can
such solipsism transcend itself" (103).
Suggests that Donne had instinctive
understanding of the reading process
whereby persona and reader or auditor are two poles that create differing
texts. Says that the task of the reader
of a Donne poem is to reconstruct "the
persona's state of mind" and that "the
task of the persona" is a "process of
becoming" that "begins when the persona views himself through the auditor's perspective and, thus confronted
by a detached mirror-image of the self
not-yet-become, attempts to compen-
sate for the shortcomings that image
reveals" (93).

151. **Zakharov, V. V.** "Opyt klassifikatsii
'Pesen i sonetov' Dzhona Donna." [The
Classification of the 'Songs and Sonnets'

of John Donne]. *Analiz stilej zarubezh-noj khudozhestvennoj i nauchnoi litera-tury* (Leningrad Univ.) 2: 20–32.

Building on Gardner's classification of the *Songs and Sonets* (1965), divides the collection into three chronological groups: 19 libertine poems (to 1598) celebrating masculine strength; 15 transitional poems (1598–1604) satirizing characteristic Petrarchan situations; and 20 philosophical poems (1604–1608) exploring the harmony between the poet and his love. Contends that stylistic differences, especially in meter and in frequency of conceits, distinguish these groups from one another. Sees in the last group the most maturity and depth because the poet reaches the end of his search for the ideal version of love. Concludes that the new classification allows Donne's mastery of form and content to be charted with greater accuracy during this period.

1981

152. Aers, David, and Gunther Kress. "'Darke Texts Needs [*sic*] Notes': Versions of Self in Donne's Verse Epistles," in *Literature, Language and Society in England, 1580–1680* by David Aers, Bob Hodge, and Gunther Kress, 23–48. Dublin: Gill and Macmillan; Totowa, N.J.: Barnes and Noble. Reprinted in *John Donne,* ed. Andrew Mousley, New Casebooks, gen. eds. John Peck and Martin Coyle (London: Macmillan; New York: St. Martin's Press, 1999), 122–34. Pages 23–34, 40–48, 200–202 reprinted in *John Donne's Poetry,* ed. Arthur L. Clements, 2nd ed. (New York: Norton, 1992), 255–70.

Attempts "to establish . . . a framework and carry out an analysis which will locate, describe, and account for versions of the self" that emerge in Donne's verse epistles (23). Examines in detail *BedfRef,* pointing out a tension in the poem between a person's inherent worth and his market or social worth, and claiming that, although it is a patronage poem, Donne emerges as the "central object of attention" (26). Points out that Donne as a Catholic was a member of an alienated group, that his marriage to a woman of higher social class increased his alienation, and that his desire to be a member of court created tension in his life and in his patronage poems. Discusses three verse epistles not written to patronesses—*HWKiss, RWThird,* and *EdHerb*—all of which assume "a simple version of the self" (41) on the surface, but when looked at more closely, reveal the same tension between inherent worth and social worth found in the poems to patronesses.

153. Aers, David, and Gunther Kress. "Vexatious Contraries: A Reading of Donne's Poetry," in *Literature, Language and Society in England, 1580–1680,* by David Aers, Bob Hodge, and Gunther Kress, 49–74. Dublin: Gill and Macmillan; Totowa, N.J.: Barnes and Noble.

Reads selected love poems in the light of Donne's letters concerning the consequences of his marriage. Explicates *GoodM* and *Canon,* seeing in them an expression of Donne's alienation from society caused by love and of his attempt to rise above that alienation by creating an alternative world, "an autonomous Utopian anti-world freed from social and historical processes with all their complex antagonisms and contingencies" (57). Discusses *HSVex* to show that Donne's longing "for a self fixed in one timeless state" "matches the dreams of lovers' transcendent and static union encountered in the *Songs and Sonnets*" (69). Considers *HSShe,* however, as "an exception to his habitual outlook" (69). Concludes with an analysis of *Christ,* written when Donne was an elite of the state church, maintaining that the hymn shows that at last Donne found that "the way to establish his self-identity was exactly the one he had always wanted—incorporation in the establishment," for after all "the life of an alienated intellectual was not one Donne could embrace" (74).

154. Aizawa, Yoshihisa. "John Donne no 'Shunen Tsuitoshi' Ko" 4. [A Study of John Donne's *Anniversaries* (4)]. *Bunkei Ronso* [Bulletin of the Faculty of Humanities, Hirosaki University] 16, no. 1: 95–107.

Part 4 of an eight-part series of articles. Discusses the *Anniversaries* and comments on Donne's secret marriage and the period of unemployment, failure, and frustration following his marriage.

155. Andrews, Michael Cameron. "Donne's 'The Ecstasy.'" *Expl* 39, no. 4: 5–6.

Disagrees with Helen Gardner's assertion in her edition of the *Elegies* and *Songs and Sonnets* (Oxford, 1965) that the "violet" in *Ecst* (l. 3) has no sexual connotations, but agrees with her that in Elizabethan literature the violet was associated with purity, modesty, and virginity. Maintains that, in fact, the violet in l. 3 has "*both* erotic and spiritual associations" and that, "[l]ike the souls of the two lovers [in the poem], the two senses interinanimate each other" (6).

156. Aramaki, Chisako. "*Holy Sonnets* ni oeru Sezoku Hyogen" [Secular Expressions in the *Holy Sonnets*], in *Yamakawa Kozo Kyoju Taikan Kinen Ronbunshu* [Essays Presented to Professor Kozo Yamakawa on the Occasion of His Retirement from Osaka University], 106–16. Toyonaka: Eihosha.

Argues that in the *Holy Sonnets* Donne treats not his personal feelings nor theological doctrines but rather fairly commonplace subjects, showing the way to the truth of God by the wordplay that mingles secularity and religiousness effectively.

157. Banerjee, Chinmoy. "Metaphysical Concreteness: John Donne's Better Hemispheres." *N&Q,* n.s. 28: 39–40.

Suggests that the "two better hemispheres" in *GoodM* (l. 17) may refer to a "hemispherical map or chart: the eyes of each lover, in reflecting the

other's face, contain the pictorial representation of half the world" and thus "the two hemispheres of the lovers' eyes constitute a hemispherical map of the world." Maintains that such a reading is consistent with ll. 12–13 in which Donne mentions sea discoverers and maps, and thinks that Donne is saying that the "lovers not only constitute a better world than the sea-discoverers find, but through the undistorted maps of their eyes they show a better representation of it than hemispherical maps." Concludes that Donne "is not merely using the hemisphere-eyes to make an abstract assertion about the perfection of love" but also "is grounding the spiritual significance in a concrete reference to the apparently distorted maps available to him" (40).

158. Bath, Michael. "Donne's 'Anatomy of the World' and the Legend of the Oldest Animals." *RES* 32: 302–8.

Discusses the history of the concept "known to folklorists as the legend of the Oldest Animals," thereby illuminating "the rich implications" (303) behind Donne's reference to the "Stag, and Raven, and long-liv'd tree" in *FirAn* (l. 115). Maintains that although Donne's reference is found only in this single line, "the conventions of the ancient formula extend into the surrounding text and the subject-matter of the poem as a whole." Notes that the lines following the reference proceed to "an inevitable and wholly predictable allusion to the Magnus Annus" and that "the precision and accuracy with which Donne uses what we must surely now call the *topos* of the Oldest Animals extends to ll. 133–4" (307). Concludes that it is interesting that "this complex of curious, but ancient and universal *topoi* should converge in a passage leading up to that moment where Donne registers the shock of the 'new Philosophy'"; in other words, "[t]he Oldest

Animals crop up in a *locus* where the received ideas of ancient learning and the corrosive effect of modern science confront each other as they do, perhaps, nowhere else in our literature" (308).

159. Bond, Ronald B. "John Donne and the Problem of 'Knowing Faith.'" *Mosaic* 14: 25–35.

Examines *HSMade* in order to show its "unusual doctrinal richness." Challenges Louis Martz's claim in *The Poetry of Meditation* (1956) that Luis de Granada's *Of Prayer and Meditation* (1612) is an analogue to Donne's sonnet, citing 2 Corinthians 4 as a more apt analogue. Dismisses both, however, as sources, claiming instead that Donne's poem "adumbrates a variety of doctrinal commonplaces" (28). Maintains that the poem is typological, using the organization of three births—generation, regeneration, and resurrection—to depict the state of the individual soul moving from a state of misery caused by sin to a state of mercy brought about by God. Concludes that the sonnet is more than "an articulation of the doctrine of grace: it dramatizes the speaker's misguided use of the doctrine in order to trace reflexively, within the poem itself, the regenerative workings of grace within the human soul" (33).

160. Brogan, T. V. F. *English Versification, 1570–1980: A Reference Guide with a Global Appendix*. Baltimore: Johns Hopkins University Press. xxix, 794p.

Presents a partially annotated bibliography of studies of English versification from 1570 to 1980. Lists 57 items for Donne, many of which are more fully annotated in *Roberts 1* and *Roberts 2*.

161. Cain, T[homas] G[rant] S[teven], ed. *Jacobean and Caroline Poetry: An Anthology*. London: Methuen. xvi, 334p.

In the introduction (1–8) rejects the conventional labels given to Jacobean

and Caroline poetry, noting that the so-called metaphysical poets do not form a unified group, school, or movement. Recognizes the great influence Donne had on other poets but finds the idea of a "School of Donne" unconvincing. Suggests that it might be more accurate to talk about a "School of Herbert." Points out, however, that many of the poets of the period were related by the political, religious, and intellectual problems of their day and, in some cases, by the strategies they used to cope with them. Includes a brief introduction to Donne's poetry and a highly selected bibliography (21–22), noting that Donne's poems "work typically towards the establishment of a surprising but convincing harmony wrought out of heterogeneous material, his wit serving not merely to surprise and impress, but to convince the reader of a truth of feeling that is inseparable in Donne from the truth of his logic" (21). Includes 25 poems or parts of poems by Donne (22–53) with explanatory notes (309–12).

162. Carey, John. *John Donne: Life, Mind and Art*. London: Faber and Faber; New York: Oxford University Press. 303p. Reprinted, 1981. Reprinted in Faber Paperbacks, 1983. New paperback edition, London: Faber and Faber, 1990. Most of Chapter 9 is translated into French by Claude Minière in *Poesie* 45 (1988): 103–17.

The introduction ([9]–14) calls Donne "unique" and states that the aim of the study is to explore "the structure of his imagination and see what makes it individual" (9) by examining "his sermons and other prose works as well as his poems" (10) and by "tracing the reappearance of words and images" throughout his works (13). Attempts to show that Donne's views on "such furiously controverted issues as original sin, election, resurrection and the state of the soul after death, were generated by recognizably the same imagination as the poems about love and women." States that the early chapters "supply the basic biographical facts [about Donne] (in so far as they are known), while examining the effects of the two vital factors in his career, his desertion of the Roman Catholic Church and his ambition, on his poetry," while later chapters "look at Donne's response to the physical and organic world, to change, to death, and to human reason." Stresses that the last chapter concentrates on Donne's "passion for fusion and interpenetration," which "if there is a single, essential quality which makes Donne Donne, this is it" (14). "Apostasy" (15–36) surveys Donne's Catholic heritage and its enduring influence on his personality and poetry, and argues that Donne's rejection of Catholicism was an agonizing experience motivated in part by his ambition for worldly success, in part by his intellectual bent that rejected blind obedience to the Church and to what he considered its superstitious practices, and in part by his reaction against his religious upbringing. "The Art of Apostasy" (37–59) discusses in more detail the ways in which Donne's apostasy is reflected in his poetry and prose, such as his anxious preoccupation with the instability of human relationships, his use of Catholic terminology and ideas in his poetry as well as elaborate blasphemies, and the pervading sense of anxiety and guilt in the religious poems. Maintains that the "Catholic notes in Donne's religious poems are remarkably clear and full" and "are the work of a man who has renounced a religion to some manifestations of which he is still, at a profound level, attached" (51). Sees a close connection between the secular and the religious poetry: "the love poems display, in their obsession with woman's incon-

stancy, a profound anxiety about his own ability to attract or merit stable affection," and "[h]is fear of damnation and of exclusion from God's love in the 'Holy Sonnets' reflects the same anxiety, transposed to the religious sphere." Notes that the disappointment and resentment that Donne directed against his inconstant mistresses "is redirected to state his own inconstancy" and also "at God, who appears negligent and inattentive" (58). "Ambition" (60–93) fills in the details of Donne's life from the 1590s to his taking of Anglican orders in 1615, and shows how his poetry reflects the events and his troubled personality during this time. Suggests that what holds the details together is Donne's "restless desire for work and worldly success," and stresses that his rejection of Catholicism gave him "a sense of separation, together with a desire to overcome it" (61), which shaped his thought and personality throughout his life. Maintains that Donne's overwhelming desire for worldly success and his poetry are "indissolubly linked" (91). "The Art of Ambition" (94–130) discusses how Donne's poetry and sermons reflect his "self-advancing, anxious, unsatisfied" personality (94) and comments on how his self-centeredness is "a major source of individuality and power" in his poems (97). Maintains that power is "the shaping principle of Donne's verse" (122) and claims that Donne uses Christianity to attack the errant ways of mankind (125). "Bodies" (131–66) considers Donne's response to the physical world and claims that "[w]hether he is writing about the human body, or animals, or plants, or inanimate objects, his effort is to engage us on other, and deeper, levels than the visual: to sensitize us, rather than to please our eyes; and to enhance our awareness both of organic life and of the solid, intransigent materials in which it inheres" (166). "Change" (167–97) shows that change "was an idea fraught with imagination and intellectual potential for Donne" and "reflected his fascination "with his own changeability" (196). "Death" (198–230) claims that Donne "was never more paradoxical than in his preoccupation with death: he felt both "drawn to suicide" and "was so re-pelled by death and its nothingness that he persistently and ingeniously animates it in his art" (229). Com-ments on his theological views on bod-ily resurrection and immortality. "The Crisis of Reason" (231–60) discusses Donne's ambivalent attitude toward reason, arguing that for Donne ideas "were plastic and, in the end, all equally questionable"; thus he "adapted them to suit his mood." Sees Donne's skep-ticism as means of freeing him "from the task of making up his mind" (250). Points out that Donne found "scientific speculation, like theological specula-tion, compelling as well as pointless" (247). "Imagined Corners" (261–79) attempts to "draw things together" and is "about drawing things together" (261). Shows how Donne delights in "imagining opposites which combined, while remaining opposites" (262), and concludes that Donne's "impulse to such conjunction, and his hypersen-sitivity to division, derive finally from his character and circumstances out-lined in the first four chapters, and in particular from his lasting sense of isolation from some greater whole" (278). Concludes with notes ([281]–96) and an index ([297]–303). Re-views: William Empson in NYRB (3 December 1981): 42–50 (entry 178); Helen Gardner in Encounter 57 (1981): 45–53 (entry 182); Timothy S. Healy in BkW 3 (3 May 1981): 9, 14; Christopher Hill in TLS (12 June 1981): 655–56; Hyam Maccoby in List

105 (1981): 747–48; Earl Miner in C&L 31, no. 2 (1981): 59–62; William H. Pritchard in HudR 34 (1981): 413–19; Richard Todd in PNR 22 (1981): 59; Margaret J. M. Ezell in EIC 32 (1982): 69–71; Daniel Karlin in English 31 (1982): 142–46; George Klawitter in BMMLA 15 (1982): 76–78; Norman R. McMillan in SHR 16 (1982): 358–59; Ruth Messenger in SCN 40 (1982): 10–12; John T. Shawcross in Rev 4 (1982): 265–73; John Stachniewski in CritQ 24, no. 4 (1982): 84–87; George Walton Williams in SAQ 81, no. 4 (1982): 471–72; Anthony Low in JDJ 2, no. 1 (1983): 111–17; Edward W. Tayler in RenQ 36 (1983): 148–51; Robert Ellrodt in EA 37 (1984): 462–63; Zensuke Taira in SELit (1984): 100–5.

163. Carey, John. "John Donne's Newsless Letters." E&S 34: 45–65.

Argues that dullness of his letters "was intended by Donne as a highly spe-cialized and functional sort of dull-ness, based on imaginative theories which tie in closely with his poems" (45). Points out that in his letters Donne generally avoids private and literary topics and that the letters can be divided into two types—those with some news, in which the news is often relegated to a postscript, and those without news. Maintains that since they do not follow classical and con-temporary models, Donne's letters reinforce "our impression of his orig-inality." Suggests that, for Donne, let-ters had "a kind of holiness" and that letter writing was for him "a spiritual exercise" (54). Notes that Donne calls letters "ecstasies" and thus "the ab-sence of news and the expression of other kinds of impersonal subject mat-ter becomes no more than what is expected" since "from the meeting of souls all temporal and external features must naturally be excluded." Suggests that "[t]he insecurity or arrogance (or both) which made Donne spurn the outer world and its doings" (55) in his letters can be found in his love poems. Concludes that "[t]he existence of Donne's newsless letters is not then, as puzzling as commentators have found it to be," since "[g]iven his imaginative predispositions, it is exactly what we should expect"; they reflect Donne's "jealous sense of identity, as well as his interest in soul transference and the integrity of love and friendship" and thereby "meet the special demands of his personality" (65).

164. Chanoff, David. "The Biographical Context of Donne's Sonnet on the Church." *ABR* 32: 378–86.

Referring to Donne's sermons, especially his first extant Paul's Cross sermon, and other writings from 1615–1618, argues that *HSShow* was "the product of a transitional phase in Donne's religious development" (379), reflecting "Donne's on-going attempt to rationalize his membership in the Anglican Communion" (386) and written during a period of his life when "he had not yet dogmatically rejected Catholicism as an honest spiritual alternative" (381). Discusses Donne's "universalism" or ecumenism, noting that for Donne the true church is any church that holds to the fundamental doctrines of the faith and that "the best of these is the one whose sacraments are most available" (384); thus the best church for Englishmen was the Church of England but for Romans the Church of Rome. Maintains that the sonnet does not reflect "any kind of religious exclusiveness" (384); neither is it an expression of Anglican orthodoxy nor a hymn to the universal church. Believes that "[t]he essence of Christ's Church," according to Donne, "is not to be identified with any of its local forms"—Catholic, Anglican, or Calvinist— but "is rather

in the relationship of the Church to its members" (386).

165. Corthell, Ronald J. "Donne's *Metempsychosis:* An 'Alarum to Truth.'" *SEL* 21: 97–110.

Argues that *Metem* is a literary paradox that is to be taken half seriously rather than as an Ovidian epic, mock epic, or satire, as some critics have suggested. Discusses how Donne's "handling of his sources and his attitude toward them are consistent with the motives and methods of paradoxy" (97). Maintains that the theme of the poem is paradoxical in that "the physical evolution or progress of the soul up the scale of being, from vegetable, to animal, to human form, is a process of moral degeneration," with "each embodiment of the soul" being "worse than its predecessor" (100). Points out that a critical feature of paradox is the concept of *serio ludere,* "a playing with serious problems of the intellectual, moral, and spiritual life" (101), which Donne uses to provoke the reader into overthrowing his argument or into making an attempt to find the truth in a relativistic world. Maintains that the poem "is founded upon the master paradox of progress and degeneration, informed by an equivocal method and purpose, and adorned with paradoxical devices," and that "[i]ts meaning and direction are repeatedly obscured by shifting tonalities and equivocation" while "[t]he reader is invited to play, *serio ludere,* a game the results of which are indeterminate" (109).

166. Corthell, Ronald J. "'Friendships Sacraments': John Donne's Familiar Letters." *SP* 78: 409–25.

Examines two groups of letters by Donne from different time periods and to different correspondents "to show that the letter was a form particularly suited to many of Donne's intellectual and literary interests" and that "it is possible to trace a development in his theory and practice that suggests connections between his art and life" (409). Claims that the first group follows the manner recommended by seventeenth century authorities on letter writing, such as John Hoskyns and Jonson, but maintains the second group shows that letter writing became for Donne "a deeply humanizing and quasi-religious experience" (410). Says the earliest surviving letters (those in the Burley MS) are brief, witty, couched in a Senecan style, and concerned principally with ideas and knowledge; some combine epistle and satire with Donne acting as a skeptical, satiric reporter, not as a participant. Maintains, however, that the letters to Henry Goodyer from Pryford and Mitcham (1602–11), written during the most disturbed years of Donne's life, are more individual in style and have as subjects Donne's personal traumas, points of religious controversy, and meditations on virtue and vice. Suggests that the most interesting feature of these letters is Donne's "preoccupation with the nature and function of letters themselves and the related tendency to define the other topics in the context of his epistolary relation to Goodyer" (416). Points out that Donne writes of letters as "sacraments," and says that they represent his "second religion, friendship" (425).

167. Costa de Beauregard, R. "Le Hiéroglyphe et le mythe des origines de la culture au XVIe siècle," in *Emblemes et devises au temps de la Renaissance,* ed. M. T. Jones-Davies, 91–101. Université de Paris-Sorbonne, Institut de Recherches sur les Civilisations de l'Occident Moderne. Centre de Recherches sur la Renaissance. Paris: Touzot.

Briefly points out that Donne considered hieroglyphics as the divine writing of the creator and as the most

ancient known writing to man, that of the Egyptians, which he regarded as the model of the highest kind of writing, poetry. Suggests that Donne believed that the poet should produce hieroglyphs that are worthy of his divine model.

168. Daniels, Edgar F. "Donne's 'Satire III.'" *Expl* 40, no. 1: 15–16.

Suggests that "hate," not "foule Devill" (l. 33), is the subject of "would allow" in *Sat3* (l. 34) and paraphrases ll. 33–35 as follows: "Your foes include first the Devil, whom clearly you strive to please, since if you hated him rather than loved him this would have allowed you to be willing to be free from his realm" (15). Argues that such a reading "meets the need for parallelism of idea, requires no syntactical gymnastics, and harmonizes with Christian tradition" (16).

169. Daniels, Edgar F. "Donne's 'The Undertaking.'" *Expl* 39, no. 3: 36–37.

Disagrees with Noam Flinker (*Expl* 36, no. 3 [1978]: 17–18), who suggests that the speaker in *Under* is an object of ridicule. Maintains that Donne often "adopts a dramatic pose and sometimes sees himself or his persona as making something of a spectacle of himself," but that *Under* "should not be categorized in this way [as Flinker does] on the grounds of logical inconsistency or tired metaphor" (37).

170. Daniels, Edgar F., and Marilyn Basel. "Donne's 'Loves Diet,' 20–21." *Expl* 39, no. 3: 35–36.

Suggests that the phrase "that that favour" in *LovDiet* (l. 3) ("And that that favour made him fat") be read as "when that that favour," noting that in Middle English and early Modern English it is not uncommon to find "when that" meaning "when," as, for example, in the first line of the general prologue to *The Canterbury Tales.*

171. Dasgupta, Debbir Bikram. "'Death Be Not Proud': An Explication." *Journal of the Department of English* (Calcutta) 17, no. 1 (1981–1982): 84–92.

Presents a close reading of *HSDeath* to show that the poem "displays a remarkable artistic and technical skill in its organization" (84). Believes that the meditative tradition alone fails to account fully for Donne's obsession with death in his poetry (both secular and sacred) and in his prose. Points out that structurally the sonnet divides into four parts (ll. 1–4, 5–8, 9–12, 13–14) and shows how point by point Donne refutes "death's claim as the destroyer" (87). Maintains that "the final impression is one of total sincerity and intensity of feeling, a real conviction generated by felt emotion, not by rhetorical blandishments" (88). Maintains that at the end of the poem Donne can stand up to death without fear because he genuinely believes that death will ultimately die while he will live eternally. Calls the sonnet "a poem of private experience" in which "Donne's personal musings re-create for us a situation" that "provides a momentary but vivid glimpse of the momentous drama awaiting enactment in Eternity" (92).

172. Davie, Donald, ed. *The New Oxford Book of Christian Verse.* Oxford: Oxford University Press. xxix, 320p.

In the introduction (xvii–xxix) explains the basis for including or excluding a poem ("Does it deserve to appear between the same covers as Herbert's 'The Collar' or his 'Church-monuments'?") and discusses the nature of Christian verse. Reproduces five sacred poems or parts of poems by Donne (68–71) with brief notes (308).

173. Donne, John. *John Donne: Canciones y sonetos,* trans. Carlos-Bolívar Gómez. Seleccion de poesía universal: Texto bilingüe. Barcelona: Plaza and Janes Editores. 237p.

Contains a general introduction to Donne and his love poetry (9–32), a note on the translation (33–34), and a bibliographical note (36–43), followed by Spanish translations of the *Songs and Sonets* (arranged in alphabetical order), with A. J. Smith's English text on facing pages (45–231). Has no notes or commentary. Includes an index (235–[38]).

174. Donne, John. *John Donne/Liebeslieder: Songs and Sonets, englische und deutsch,* trans. K. Wydmond. Stuttgart: Sunna. 211, [1]p.

Presents a brief biographical sketch of Donne (5) and a general introduction to his poetry, entitled "Das Phänomen John Donne" (6–9), followed by the *Songs and Sonets* included in Grierson's edition (1912), with English texts and German translations on opposite pages (10–181) and notes (182–210). Review: Manuel Rios Ruiz in *Nueva Estafeta* 30 (1981): 82–83.

175. Donne, John. *A Valediction Forbidding Mourning. Written by John Donne to his Wife upon his departing for France in 1611.* Staplehurst, Kent: Florin Press. [4] leaves. 175 copies.

ValMourn with a wood engraving by Graham Williams.

176. Edamatsu, Fred J. "The Message of 'The Apparition.'" *SELit* 58, no. 1: 3–21.

Argues that *Appar* is a "courting poem" that satirizes Petrarchan conventions, not an angry, brutal attack on the mistress as some critics suggest. Maintains that, endorsing the Ovidian view of love as lust, Donne uses primarily a psychological strategy to seduce the lady, rather than using Platonic arguments or logic, and that he assumes a defiant tone that "flouts the emasculated obsequiousness of the sonneteers" (12). Suggests that Donne wrote in the plain style rather than the courtly style "because it imitates reality" (15). Discusses the colloquial style of the poem, its uses of rhythm and meter, its diction and uses of sound, and the "conversational structure" of the sentences—to show that the poem is an "iconoclastic composition" (20) aimed at the insincerity and artificiality of the sonnet tradition.

177. Eddy, Y. Shikany, and Daniel P. Jaeckle. "Donne's 'Satyre I': The Influence of Persius's 'Satire III.'" *SEL* 21: 111–22.

Claims that Donne was "one of the first, perhaps the first, of the English poets to model verse satires on classical Latin models" (122). Demonstrates that in *Sat1* Donne very explicitly borrows "structural, strategic, and philosophical elements from Persius's third satire" but "transforms them in order to intensify the theme of moral inconstancy." Points out that both poems have a bipartite structure, indicated by a shift of personal pronouns. Observes that the first part of each satire dramatizes a choice between "the moral and philosophical values of a scholar and the self-indulgent immorality of society," and that the second part of each poem presents "the possible results of a wrong choice by parading figures who have already chosen the path of vice" (111). Maintains that Donne "alters his source in two directions: he maintains the integrity of the dramatic situation throughout, never losing sight of his original two characters, and he complicates the moral decision" (114). Shows that both satires can be read either as "internal debates" or as "confrontations between two characters." Claims that Donne introduces a Christian concept of sin into the poem, thus deviating from the Stoic philosophy of Persius, who subscribed to the idea that knowledge leads to virtue. Says that Donne believes that knowledge of Christian truth is no guarantee against sin; thus

"his satiric authority is undercut by an unresolved tension between Stoic and Christian ethics" (122).

178. Empson, William. "'There Is No Penance Due to Innocence.'" *NYRB,* 28 (3 December): 42–50.

Essentially an unfavorable review of John Carey's *John Donne: Life, Mind and Art* (entry 162). Suggests that Carey's mistaken notions about Donne's love poems spring primarily from his misreading of *ElBed,* a poem in which, according to Carey, Donne is "punitive" and "almost pathologically imperious" toward his mistress. Agrees with Carey, however, that the poem is "pornographic" but rejects the idea that it is sadistic, as Carey suggests (42). Believes that Carey goes wrong, at least in part, because he endorsed Helen Gardner's (1965) reading of l. 46: "Here is no pennance, much lesse innocence." Argues that the whole point of the poem is that Donne is seducing what seems to be a married lady by arguing that what he wishes her to do is not sinful. Reviews the manuscript evidence for reading l. 46 as "There is no penance due to innocence" in order to challenge Gardner's textual choice. Argues also with other of Gardner's textual choices. Challenges also Carey's thesis concerning Donne's apostasy from Catholicism and about his driving ambition for worldly success. Calls for a return to Grierson's text (1912). For replies, see Gardner (entry 31) and Justin (entry 288).

179. Evans, J. X. "Who Cast Donne's Tolling Bells?" *JRMMRA* 2: 113–16.

Basing his argument entirely on internal similarities, suggests that Donne may have been indebted for his image of the tolling bell and other images in *Devotions* to a sermon given in 1620 (and published that year and republished in 1622) at the funeral of Lady Rous by Charles Fitz-Geffrey, an Anglican clergyman and poet. Notes, however, that Donne himself earlier in *Will* (ll. 37–38) mentions such a bell and suggests that perhaps Fitz-Geffrey was influenced by Donne.

180. Flynn, Dennis. "'Sir Thomas Heywood the Parson' and Donne's Catholic Background." *RecH* 15, no. 5: 325–27.

Challenges the story perpetuated by modern biographers that Donne's grand-uncle and Catholic priest, Thomas Heywood, was executed in June 1574, when Donne was two years old. Points out that the evidence indicates that Heywood was charged only for saying Mass, a crime punishable by imprisonment and fines but not execution. Suggests, therefore, that Donne may have known him.

181. Fraser, G. S. "The Seventeenth Century," in *A Short History of English Poetry,* 112–59. Skepton Mallet, Somerset, Eng.: Open Books.

Presents a general introduction to Donne's poetry (114–20). Says that Donne is "first and foremost a poetical performer and his poems, though we hear only his side of the conversation, have often the abruptness and violence of dialogue in Jacobean drama" (115). Comments on Donne's use of conceits and paradox, his metrical roughness, and his verbal agility.

182. Gardner, Helen. "The Combination of Opposites: John Donne: A New Look." *Encounter* 57: 45–53.

Presents personal reflections on her lifelong interest in Donne and comments on the development of scholarly interest in Donne in the twentieth century, which leads into an extensive review of John Carey's *John Donne: Life, Mind and Art* (entry 162). Believes Carey's treatment of Elizabethan Catholicism is "a striking example of *suppressio veri*" (48); dislikes his treatment of Donne as ambitious; and says Carey's method of showing "the structure of Donne's imagination" "deforms his mind and his art" (49) and fragments the poetry and prose by selecting bits and pieces out of context. Praises, in particular, Carey's discussion of *Metem,* but concludes that, in spite of "all the liveliness and incidental brilliance" in the book, it lacks "historical imagination and imaginative sympathy with its subject," and its tone is "too confident in its reduction of the complexity of the poet who wrote 'doubt wisely'" (53).

183. Gottlieb, Erika. "The 'Long Nights Festival': Dialectic in Donne's 'Nocturnall.'" *AJES* 6, no. 1: 35–47.

Offers a critical reading of *Noct* to show that the poem is "profoundly religious" and illustrates "the dynamics of an unmistakably mystical aspiration." Maintains that the poem "exalts human love to the religious level" and at the same time "reveals a tendency for bringing religious love down to the human level." Maintains that "the dialectical interaction of these two contradictory tendencies" (35) shows "Donne's aspiration to reach an experience in which the contraries will coincide, where the sacred will appear the vital essence of the profane" while "the profane [will appear as] the fundamental mode for the existence of the sacred" (35–36). Points out that the poem exhibits not only tension between the sacred and profane but also between Catholic and Protestant biases, and comments on possible numerological symbolism in the poem. Concludes that the poem ends in a "mystic reversal" in which despair finally turns into "affirmation" and "through this process, to hope" (46), and suggests that the connotations and position of the metaphor of the death of the beloved as the "long nights festival" is "crucial to the understanding of the whole poem as an attempt at the integration of sacred and profane, Eternal and Temporal" (47).

184. Hall, Michael L. "Searching and Not Finding: The Experience of Donne's *Essays in Divinity.*" *Genre* 14: 423–40.

Discusses *Essays* as essays in order "to demonstrate that Donne's rhetorical strategies of exploration and displacement, of searching and not finding, reveal the subversive tastes of other essayists such as Montaigne and Bacon" (423). Considers this new genre appropriate in an age of discovery, noting that Donne's poetry frequently uses "images of journeys and voyages to describe the process of his discourse" (426). Notes Donne's use of Scripture and commentaries of the Church Fathers and other learned men in his process of discovery, but maintains that he ultimately relies on faith rather than reason in understanding God. Examines "Of Moses" for its rhetorical method and concludes that Donne "has moved from assertion to experience and in so doing has undermined the rational process by revealing its shortcomings and showing that there are things which lie beyond the powers of human reason" (429–30). Examines also "Of God," in which Donne shows through metaphor and the experience of the mind in action that human reason cannot fully understand God. Concludes that these essays draw the reader "into the experience of Donne's own private meditative journey" (439).

185. Hamilton, A. C. "The Philosophy of the Footnote," in *Editing Poetry from Spenser to Dryden: Papers Given at the Sixteenth Annual Conference on Editorial Problems, University of Toronto, 31 October–1 November 1980,* ed. A. H. De Quehen, 127–63. New York: Garland.

Points out that Donne frequently "annotates his own conceits" (140), or comments on his own lines or on his uses of conventions, citing as illustrations l. 25 of *Canon* ("So, to one neutrall thing both sexes fit"); l. 8 of *GoodM* ("And now good morrow to our waking soules"); and *Fare,* in which "the lover's cynicism comments upon the conventional 'farewell to love'" (141). Suggests that the last word of *Fare* ("Taile") "bears more than a bawdy significance: it notes the end of a tradition of love poetry" (141). Comments also on Grierson's choice of "groan" rather than "grow" in *Twick* (l. 17), noting that Grierson argues that the manuscript evidence is inconclusive and that "groan" is "much more in Donne's style" (143). Points out Gardner's preference (1965) for "grow" and Redpath's argument (1979) for "groan" and finds the latter's argument more convincing, noting that Arthur L. Clements, ed., *John Donne's Poetry* (New York: Norton, 1966), and A. J. Smith, ed. *John Donne: The Complete English Poems* (Harmondsworth: Penguin, 1971) also choose "groan."

186. Handley, Graham. *Brodie's Notes on the Metaphysical Poets: John Donne to Henry Vaughan.* Pan Study Aids. London: Pan Books. 123p. Reprinted 1991.

Presents a very brief description of several characteristics of metaphysical poetry, followed by introductions to the life and poetry of nine seventeenth century poets. Presents a short biographical sketch of Donne and comments on major features of his poetry, followed by summaries of poems with explanatory notes on each. Includes 22 poems from the *Songs and Sonets,* 3 *Elegies,* 8 *Holy Sonnets,* 4 hymns, *Calm, Sat3,* and *RWThird,* followed by 10 general study questions and/or revision exercises on Donne's poetry.

187. Hegnauer, Salomon. *Systrophe. The Background of Herbert's Sonnet "Prayer."* European University Studies, Series 14: Anglo-Saxon Language and Literature,

87. Bern: Peter Lang. 241p.

Following "Methodological Remarks" (9–22), Hegnauer divides the study into three main parts: "Induction: Phenomenology of Systrophe" (23–65) defines systrophe "from as many angles as possible" and tries "to distill the quintessence of systrophe by isolating all its pertinent features"; "Deduction: Applied Systrophe" (67–176) brings together "the pure substance of systrophe and the live poetic matter" (22) and discusses the results; "Applied Systrophe" (177–238) discusses numerous examples of systrophe in the poetry of Donne, Herbert, Crashaw, Vaughan, and others. Comments briefly on Donne's uses of rhetorical figures in *Ind, Henry, Har, HSBlack, HSSighs, HSMin, Cor5, Goodf, Sidney, Air, Ecst, Res, FirAn, Tilman,* and *Lit.* Compares and contrasts Donne's religious sensibility as reflected in his poetry with that of his contemporaries. Maintains that Donne, "though he knows and poetically represents the *ecstasis* of human love, cannot give himself up to divine transports," adding that "[f]or him vision and rapture are poetically neither real nor relevant." States that "the dogmatic axioms on which rests the Christian faith, are not questioned (nor is their justification), but at nearly every moment Donne is conscious of the fact that they are hypothetical assumptions rather than heartfelt reality, a necessary basis of faith, not verifiable" and, therefore, "[h]e takes them as the propositions of a syllogism on which to develop his theological and personal speculations" (149). Points out, in other words, that Donne's "medium of encountering the divine is neither the poetic vision nor the ecstasis, but conceit and syllogism" (150), noting that both Donne and Herbert "are painfully aware of their human deficiencies and their poetic limitations," whereas for Crashaw and Vaughan "vision was the natural path to God" (151).

188. Hester, M. Thomas. "Poetasters as 'Bellows': Donne's Inventive Imitation." *ELN* 19: 20–21.

Notes that although Donne's *Satyres* are recognized as the first to imitate classical satire in English, it is difficult to isolate specific lines he borrowed because Donne "reinvents whatever he borrows or imitates, amplifying it to fit the imaginative strategies of his own satire" (20), as evidenced in *Sat2* (ll. 13–16). Points out that Donne's image of the poetaster as "bellows" (l. 16) can be found in Horace (Satire I, iv) and in Persius (Satire V), noting that although the bellows of the Roman satirists cannot refer to an organ, as Donne's obviously does, "the picture of the poetaster as hot-air expirant is identical to the derisive point of Donne's image." Maintains that Donne's image amplifies his classical source and "exposes not only the literal dependence of the 'ideot actors' [l. 13] on the artist" but also "like its classical analogues suggests that such poetasters merit their anonymity and poverty because of the insubstantiality and hollowness of their laborious efforts." Concludes that recognition of Donne's classical source in these lines "clarifies the *two* objects of his ridicule and exemplifies once again the thoroughly original character of his imitations of classical authors" (21).

189. Hobbs, Mary. "'To a Most Dear Friend'—Donne's Bellarmine." *RES* 32: 435–38.

Announces that one volume of the annotated works of St. Robert Bellarmine, his *Disputationes de Controversiis Christianae Fidei* (Venice, 1603), that Donne bequeathed to a "dear Friend" is in the Chichester Cathedral Library and argues that the friend to whom the volume was bequeathed was Henry King, co-executor of Donne's will together with John Mountfort. Maintains that clearly the volume at Chichester is the one Donne used when writing *Pseudo-Martyr.*

190. Höltgen, Karl Josef. "Why Are There No Wolves in England?: Philip Camerarius and a German Version of Sidney's Table Talk." *Anglia* 99: 60–82.

Points out that Philip Camerarius of Nürnberg (1537–1624), in his recording of the table talk of Sir Philip Sidney during his 1577 trip as Elizabeth's ambassador to Emperor Rudolph II and other German princes, published as *Operae horarum succisivarium sive meditationes historica* (Nürnberg, 1591), recalls the "refined manners, pleasant conversation, intelligence and kindness" (69) of a certain George More, who is identified as Donne's future father-in-law, George More of Loseley Park. Suggests that this account of More "serves as a welcome corrective" to the view of More as "a hard and unreasonable domestic tyrant" (70).

191. Horrocks, Roger A. "Metrical and Grammatical Problems in 'Twicknam Garden.'" *Lang&S* 14: 172–82.

Demonstrates how "a revised [Paul] Kiparsky model" can be used to analyze *Twick,* and shows "the importance of syntactic and lexical patterns in the organization of large-scale rhythmic effects" (172). Through a detailed analysis of metrical and grammatical patterns in the poem shows that Donne's use of "a sophisticated linguistic ensemble of metrical, syntactic, semantic, and lexical patterns" creates "the total semiotic of the poem" and that "[t]he mastery of tensioning and tempo that Donne displays gives him 'finger-tip' ability to speed up or slow down at will, create effects of parallelism and positioning, smoothness or discordance." Con-cludes that "[t]he total effect has rightly been compared to that of the speaking voice—but a voice of the subtlest cadences and inflections that merits the closest critical and linguistic attention" (181).

192. Howe, Elizabeth Teresa. "Donne and the Spanish Mystics on Ecstasy." *NDEJ* 13, no. 2: 29–44.

Discusses *Ecst* in the light of the poetry and prose of St. John of the Cross and St. Teresa of Avila. Distinguishes among types of ecstasy, concluding that ecstatic union is an intermediate step on the way to union with God. Parallels the descriptions by the two saints of ecstatic union with Donne's presentation in *Ecst* and maintains that they differ fundamentally in "their perceptions of the body's ultimate role in man's existence" (38), the mystics seeing it as a prison, Donne regarding it as the proper domain for human beings. Points out other differences: for example, the two participants in Donne's poem are equals, and he introduces a hypothetical bystander who shares in the ecstasy. Concludes that "the disparities which exist between Donne's poem and the mystical writings of Santa Teresa and San Juan militate against describing the metaphysical's poem as mystical" (40).

193. Hussey, Maurice, ed. *Poetry 1600 to 1660.* Longman English Series, ed. Maurice Hussey. Harlow: Longman. x, 190p.

In "Profane" (1–11), Hussey comments on the general characteristics of Donne's secular poetry, suggesting that it "offers a series of transitions from the body's domain to the soul's that contemporary readers happily assimilated and to some extent imitated, but for which we lack the technique or lost the language" (1–2). Anthologizes ten secular poems (13–25) with a brief biographical sketch and explanatory notes (139–46). In

"Sacred" (95–103), Hussey comments on Donne's religious poetry, noting, in particular, the influence of discursive meditation on the poems. Anthologizes three sacred poems (104–6) with explanatory notes (170–71).

194. Kishimoto, Yoshitaka. "'Goodfriday, 1613. Riding Westward' ni okeru Donne no Ura no Imi" [A Hidden Meaning in Donne's "Goodfriday, 1613. Riding Westward"]. *Baika Review* no. 14: 1–11. Reprinted in *Igirisu Bungaku: Kenkyu to Kansho* [Studies in English Novels and Poetry], ed. Yoshitsugu Uchida (Osaka: Sogensha, 1982), 133–45, 218–24.

Appreciative reading of *Goodf.* Comments on a "hidden meaning" in ll. 9–10 and finds similar diction and phraseology in such poems as *ElAut, Ind,* and *Sickness.*

195. Klawitter, George. "The Narrator of Donne's 'Confined Love.'" *AN&Q* 19: 72–74.

Argues that the speaker of *ConfL* may be a man "who is merely exasperated by the stupidity of that other man who was too fearful to play the field of love-starved women, too hopeful of making one woman suffer for his trepidity" (72). Finds the strongest support for his argument in ll. 15–16, in which a ship, "a standard image for the male member riding in the female part" (73), is urged to find other harbors, citing examples from Shakespeare and Spenser as well as from *Air* (l. 18) and *ElProg* (ll. 69–71).

196. Klinck, Dennis R. "John Donne's 'knottie Trinitie.'" *Renascence* 33: 240–55.

Discusses "some major aspects of Donne's trinitarianism—its relevance to the problem of 'the many and the one,' its distinction of the attributes of the Persons, and its insistence upon the immanence of the principle of trinity in the created world, especially man" (244), and explores these concerns in Donne's poetry. Focuses on the trinity of nonentities—"absence,

darkness, death" (245), and the Augustinian trinitarian construct of being, knowledge, and love—in *Noct.* Discusses also the two central concerns of *Ecst*—the union of souls and the union of body and soul and the way they correspond to the Trinity and the Incarnation. Suggests that the most explicit treatment of the Trinity occurs in *Lit,* and discusses the difficulties of a trinitarian analysis of *HSBatter,* acknowledging, however, that the Trinity "is structurally and thematically important throughout the poem and not merely in the apostrophe of the first line" (249). Concludes that many of the *Holy Sonnets* have thematic aspects of trinitarianism, and comments on *Goodf* from the perspective of the human trinity of memory, understanding, and will.

197. Klinck, Dennis R. "*Vestigia Trinitatis* in Man and His Works in the English Renaissance." *JHI* 42: 13–27.

Demonstrates by citing examples from Donne and other Renaissance writers the belief in the doctrine of the "vestiges of the Trinity," that is, that "similitudes" of the Trinity can be found in all of creation. Explains that the biblical statement that "God made man in his own image" justified Renaissance authors' seeking the Trinity in all of creation, especially (1) in the mind and soul of man, (2) in analyses of sin based on whether or not it violated special attributes of the Trinity, and (3) in the products of the mind—the arts and sciences. Notes, for example, that Donne clearly asserts the doctrine in his sermon given at Lincoln's Inn on Trinity Sunday, 1620, and points out that it appears also in *Lit,* in which Donne lists the powers of the soul (love, power, and knowledge) as special attributes of the Father, Son, and Holy Ghost, as well as in his Second Sermon on Genesis 1:26 before the King in 1626, in which he discusses the image of the Trinity in the soul of man—understanding (Father), will (Son), and memory (Holy Ghost).

198. Little, Roger. "'Siffland mon peuple de Sibylles': A l'écoute d'une phrase de Saint-John Perse." *RLC* 217: 119–22.

Points out that Saint-John Perse's wordplay on whistling in "Poème à l'etrangère" is similar to Donne's witty use of the concept in the first sermon in *Fifty Sermons* (1649). Notes that Perse not only knew Donne's works well but also belonged to a small, elite John Donne club that proposed that one member would publish annually something on Donne. Notes that the club, after one member (Gosse) published his work, never got off the ground.

199. Llasera, Margaret. "Magnetism and English Poetry in the Earlier Seventeenth Century." *EA* 34: 16–31.

Notes that in *FirAn* (ll. 220–222, 237), Donne pictures the earth after the death of Elizabeth Drury "very much in the state of desolation" (27) envisioned by William Gilbert in his exhaustive treatise *De Magnete* (1600), and says that the "clear reference to the *magnetic* force of a world soul holding the earth together is the earliest example" that she has found "of the unmistakable influence of Gilbert on English poetry" (28).

200. Lobb, Edward. *T. S. Eliot and the Romantic Critical Tradition.* London: Routledge and Kegan Paul. xiii, 194p.

Says that T. S. Eliot had "troubling second thoughts" (17) about Donne's "unified sensibility" and that he believed conceptual thought and truth of feeling diverged in Donne's poetry. Maintains that Eliot thought Donne had no philosophy upon which to base his experience, which led him to entertain ideas rather than actually believe in them. Says that Eliot believed that for Donne, thought became an object of aesthetic delight and that its truth

or falsehood was irrelevant to the poem. Discusses Eliot's contrast of Donne and Crashaw, in which he saw Donne as a "voluptuary of thought" and Crashaw as a "voluptuary of religious emotion" (34).

201. Mann, Lindsay A. "Radical Consistency: A Reading of Donne's 'Communitie.'" *UTQ* 50: 284–99.

Discusses *Commun* and several of Donne's homilies to show that "Donne's intentions may be essentially the same in both [early, libertine] poems and homiletic prose, though expressed through different techniques: the prose comments directly and doctrinally on distorted views that the poems represent through satire and ironic technique of a perverse dramatic speaker or character" (284). Rejects the notion that *Commun* is simply high-spirited and skeptical and argues that it is, in fact, a satire on the libertine who uses women and is incapable of loving. Comments on constant and inconstant love in a number of poems and suggests that *Sat3* is the key to the intention of these poems by its equation of perverse attitudes toward religion with perverse attitudes towards women, concluding that one cannot be "indifferent" toward either. Insists that, for Donne, marriage is the center for all human relations, and demonstrates that the sermons make explicit what is implied in the poetry, addressing especially indifference, irresolution, and inconstancy in love. Holds that Donne rejects both libertine naturalism and the Neoplatonism of Augustinianism, "with its tendency to deny the possibility of true love in human relations and to make all good love mystical" (257).

202. Marotti, Arthur F. "John Donne and the Rewards of Patronage," in *Patronage in the Renaissance,* ed. Guy Fitch Lytle and Stephen Orgel, 207–34. Princeton, N.J.: Princeton University Press.

Says that Donne, who "treated literature as an avocation rather than a
vocation," "sought mainly social and
political rather than artistic patronage,
eager for the kinds of employment
that would satisfy ambitions greater
than those professional writers generally pursued" (208). Maintains that
although Donne satirized courtiers in
his satires, in his sermons he castigates himself for having "aped some
of the manners he satirized." Believes
that Donne's "metaphorics of love
reflect the dynamic of suit, service,
and recompense characteristic of a society that tied advancement to patronage" (212). Reviews Donne's early
success in the patronage system and
his ousting from it because of his pre-
cipitous marriage to Ann More. Claims
that the love poems, such as *Canon*
and *Anniv,* written during the difficult
period following his marriage, express
thwarted ambition, and points out that
from 1607 to 1615 Donne tried repeatedly, but failed, to secure a government appointment. Thinks that Donne
regretted his role as the beneficiary of
the patronage of Lucy, Countess of
Bedford, because he wanted a more
serious career than that of poet, and
points out that *Twick* and *Fun* as well
as a number of the verse epistles
express the conflicts Donne had about
his subservient patronage position.
Maintains that Donne used his religious poems of this period also "to
good advantage in his social life,"
sending the *Holy Sonnets* and *Corona*
to Magdalen Herbert and dedicating
six of the sonnets to the Earl of Dorset
(227). Maintains that the *Anniversaries*
also are closely related to Donne's
"social, economic, and political failures" (228), and points out that his
position as secretary to Robert Carr,
Viscount Rochester (later Earl of
Somerset), just before his ordination
was not edifying. Says that after his
entrance into the priesthood in 1615,
the patronage that Donne "had been
denied as a layman for the previous
dozen years he won as a churchman"
(233) by becoming a royal chaplain,
receiving an honorary degree of doctor of divinity at Cambridge, and
accepting the deanship of St. Paul's
Cathedral, and thus, at last, "obtaining some of the substantial rewards
patronage could bring" (234).

203. **McGaw, William D.** "A Note on
Donne's Phrase, 'Least truth for my subjects.'" *ANQ* 19: 140–41.

Maintains that when, in a letter to Sir
Robert Carr introducing *Ham,* Donne
wrote, "I did best when I had least
truth for my subjects," he is speaking
of poetics, not autobiography. Explains
that Donne uses "truth" here in the
medieval sense of "a representation
of the nature of things"; therefore,
"least truth for my subjects" means
"least faithfulness to the subjects (or
themes) of my poems" (140–41).
Believes that Donne is saying that "in
much of his secular work he had been
'fanciful'" and that he holds that "to
write poetry it was absolutely necessary to allow the 'fancy' to stray from
one's subject" (141).

204. **Milward, Peter.** "John Donne." *TLS*
(14 August): 934.

Objects to Christopher Hill's calling
the Jesuits conspirators and terrorists
in his review (*TLS* 12 June 1981) of
John Carey's *John Donne: Life, Mind
and Art* (1981). Comments on Donne's
attitude toward the Jesuits.

205. **Mollenkott, Virginia Ramey.** "John
Donne and the Limitations of Androgyny." *JEGP* 80: 22–38.

Discusses Donne's images of androgyny, which derive principally from
the Bible, Petrarchan love poetry, and
Neoplatonic and alchemical discourses,
and points out that such images are
frequently of the liberating balanced/
dialectical type in which each party

is equal, rather than a fusion into a One in which one party, usually the male, subsumes the female. Believes, however, that Donne's "interpretations of the social implications of his own images fall far below his imaginative heights" (23). Points out that the union of human and divine that Donne seeks is of the fusion-subsuming type but that the union of two lovers, in which the two become a third entity, is of the balanced type. Cites images in *Canon, ValMourn,* and *Ecst* and shows that they are indebted to Neoplatonic theory and Petrarchan love poetry. Discusses the imagery in the *Anniversaries* as a rare example in Donne's poetry of what Jungians call psychological androgyny. Points out androgyny in the biblical imagery in Donne's sermons and other religious works, such as *Devotions,* in which Donne evokes the concept of the mystical body of Christ, and *HSShow,* in which "a human speaker asks Christ to reveal and share the embraces of his spouse, the church, so that the speaker is both the male seeker and the female object of the search" (32). Points out that Donne often views the individual, the Church and her ministers, and even Christ and Godhead in androgynous terms. Concludes, however, that Donne did not follow "the implications of his androgynous vision to their logical conclusion: human equality" (34).

206. Mroczkowski, Przemsysław. "John Donne," in *Historia Literatury Angielskiej,* 217–19. Wrocław: Zakład Naradowy Im. Ossolińkich Wydawnictwo.

Briefly considers Donne as the father of metaphysical poetry and, therefore, as a major innovator in English poetry. Discusses how he uses startling and unusual conceits and wit in his poems to express his complex and changing view of the world. Suggests that Donne's poetry reflects the changes in his life, noting how, as a poet, he moves from being a versifier of erotic poems and simple jokes to being a writer of complex poems and hymns.

207. O'Connell, Patrick F. "The Successive Arrangements of Donne's 'Holy Sonnets.'" *PQ* 60: 323–42.

Questions Helen Gardner's ordering of the 19 *Holy Sonnets* in her edition of the *Divine Poems* (1952, rev. ed. 1978) based on manuscript evidence. Reviews the manuscript tradition of the poems and concludes that Group III manuscripts, rejected by Gardner, are, in fact, earlier versions of Groups I and II, and further, are related to the Westmoreland manuscript, written in the hand of Donne's friend, Rowland Woodward. Attempts to resolve the difficulties caused by additional sonnets in the Westmoreland manuscript, and states that his conclusion, "which is consistent with the evidence of all known manuscripts, supports Gardner's choice of the arrangement of Groups I–II (and *1633*) as Donne's definitive ordering of the 'Holy Sonnets,' and rejects her attempt to group the four sonnets added in *1635* as a related group, seeing them instead as sonnets left over from an earlier group of twelve" (334). Suggests that Donne had "strong traditional support for a decision to restrict the number of 'Holy Sonnets' to the symbolic 'twelve,'" which among other things, signified "the fullness of salvation" (338).

208. Okamura, Sachiko. "Kirisutosha Donne no Sugata: 1620 nen Zengo no Shukyoshi wo Chushin ni" [The Figure of Donne as a Christian: With Special Reference to the Religious Poems Written around 1620], in *Yamakawa Kozo Kyoju Taikan Kinen Ronbunshu* [Essays Presented to Professor Kozo Yamakawa on the Occasion of His Retirement from Osaka University], 117–29. Tokyo: Eihosha.

Comments on *HSShe, HSShow, HSVex, Tilman, Sidney, Lam,* and *Christ.* Points out that Donne ascertained the limits of the Anglican Church and became a preacher feeling distressed by many religious problems, though he served the King loyally.

209. Parain, Georges. "Metempsycosis," in *Poétiques de la métamorphose de Pétrarque à John Donne,* ed. Guy Demerson, 199–214. Institut d'Études de la Renaissance et de l'Age classique. Saint-Étienne: Publications de l'Université de Saint-Étienne.

Paraphrases the argument of *Metem,* surveys the traditional interpretation of the poem, restates the interpretation offered by Michel Butor (*Cahiers du Sud* 38 [1954]: 276–83), and, referring to these earlier interpretations, presents his own. Reads the poem as Donne's final homage to his family's Catholicism that expresses his nostalgia for his mother's womb and for his childhood religion while, at the same time, reflecting his uneasy conscience about his conversion to Anglicanism. Sees Donne as being both cynical and nostalgic; behind Donne's expression of free thought he perceives in the play of images both a nostalgia for and a sense of betrayal of his origins. Concludes, however, that because of the many ambiguities in the poem and because it is uncompleted, other interpretations remain possible. Reviews: Ulrich Schultz Buschhaus in *RF* 94 (1982): 297–301; Joan Braybrook in *FS* 38 (1984): 493–94.

210. Parry, Graham. *The Golden Age Restor'd: The Culture of the Stuart Court, 1603–42*. Manchester: Manchester University Press; New York: St. Martin's Press. xi, 276p.

Outlines "the characteristic iconography that accompanied the reigns of James I and Charles I, and in light of that iconography explores a wide range of works of art that were created within the setting of the Stuart Court, either for the express purpose of glorifying the monarch, or with the broader intention of projecting or reflecting the royal interest" (x). Comments on Donne's uses of the phoenix in *EpEliz,* calling it "the most attractive of the wedding songs" written to celebrate the marriage of James I's daughter Elizabeth to Frederick, the Elector of the Palatine. Says that Donne's motivation for writing the poem probably was the close relationship between Elizabeth and Lucy, the Countess of Bedford, "whose parents had been the Princess's guardians" (105). Briefly comments on Donne's longtime friendship with the countess, calling Donne "her most eminent literary friend" (173) and also on Donne's influence on Carew. In particular, discusses Donne's relationship with James I and Charles I and their courts (238–42). Maintains that James's primary reason for recruiting Donne for the Anglican priesthood was "to build up a learned clergy and encourage a strong preaching ministry in order to assure the Church's strength in the land" and also "to equip it intellectually for debate in an age of religious controversy" (238–39). Comments on Donne's art of preaching and says that Donne was not a sycophant: "When Donne preached, the priorities of the spirit were upheld in the Chapel Royal" (240).

211. Patrides, C. A. "The Epistolary Art of the Renaissance: The Biblical Premises." *PQ* 60: 357–67.

Maintains that letter writing in the Renaissance was influenced by the epistles in the New Testament as well as by classical models, and comments on what theologians such as St. Augustine and Calvin had to say about the relation of style to substance in St. Paul's epistles, concluding that they thought eloquence followed wisdom. Points out that Renaissance commentators, such as John Mayer, the popular Danish theologian Niels Hemmingsen, and the Italian reformer Peter

Martyr were not concerned with style as such but contributed to an understanding of the essential structure of the epistles. Calls Donne "one of the most brilliant practitioners of the epistolary art during the Renaissance," and claims that Donne merges "classical precedents and their Biblical counterpoints" in a letter that R. C. Bald (1970) called "itself virtually an essay on letter-writing." Notes also that in a sermon delivered in 1618, Donne specifically "acknowledged a particular debt to the 'form' of St. Paul's letters" (36).

212. Reeves, Troy D. *Index to the Sermons of John Donne.* Vol. 3, *Index to Topics.* Elizabethan and Renaissance Studies, 95. ed. James Hogg. Salzburg: Institut für Anglistik und Amerikanistik, Universität Salzburg. iii, 226p.

Compiles an index to topics found in Donne's sermons that complements his previously published index to the scriptures (entry 65) and index to proper names (entry 130). Includes only the sermons, not information in the critical apparatus, appendices, introductions, and footnotes in the standard edition of Donne's sermons. Cross-references both within the present volume and to items in the two other earlier volumes. Review: Jeanne M. Shami in *Ren&R,* n.s. 8 (1984): 59–62.

213. Reverand, Cedric D. "Teaching Poetry: The Negative Approach." *CollL* 8: 71–84.

Explains a four-step methodology for introducing students to close reading by discussing *Fun,* and in the process offers an explication of the theme, dramatic situation, syntax, imagery, metaphors, and diction of the poem.

214. Richards, Bernard. "Donne's 'A Nocturnall Upon S. Lucies Day.'" *Expl* 39, no. 3: 12–13.

Suggests that the "flasks" in *Noct* (l. 3) refer not to the stars, as indicated by Helen Gardner in her edition of the

Elegies and the *Songs and Sonnets* (1965) and by A. J. Smith in his edition of the poems (1971), but rather allude to "the diminished sources of energy in the Sun," and that the "light squibs" in the following line refer to "the light flashes and sunbeams emitted" during the day. Suggests that "The Sunne is spent" (l. 3) "not simply because it is night, but because his power declines in the winter" and notes also the possibility of "sexual spending" (13).

215. Richmond, Hugh M. *Puritans and Libertines: Anglo-French Literary Relations in the Reformation.* Berkeley and Los Angeles: University of California Press. xii, 401p.

Maintains that a close look at Italian poetry of the sixteenth century shows that Donne's anti-Petrarchism is much more conventional than English-speaking critics of the past have allowed, noting that even Donne's compass image in *ValMourn* was anticipated by Guarini, Tasso, and Marino and that his more general characteristics, such as "his bravura cynicism, colloquial style, and dramatic openings" were "commonplace in European lyricism since the times of the most ancient Greek poets." Concludes that "this more informed view of Donne" allows us to understand Donne, not as "an unheralded genius whose originality eludes historical explanation" but "as craftsman who gave his own distinctive and intelligible twists to accumulated literary resources, without which his memorable effects would have been impossible" (223–24). Notes, however, that a study of the cinquecento writers clearly shows that Donne is "stylistically distinct" from his models and illustrates "a temperament and social outlook at odds with the Italian tradition" (224). Finds many close affinities between Donne and Ronsard, comparing Ronsard's love poems with *Flea, HSDeath,*

HSBatter, Air, Ecst, GoodM, NegLov, Canon, Ind, SunRis, Twick, and *Noct.* Believes that, "without comprehensive and provocative precedents like Ronsard's," Donne "could not have mastered and condensed his raw materials so effectively" (251). Also points out Donnean similarities in Marguerite de Navarre's *Heptameron* and Marot's love poetry.

216. Roberts, Mark. "Problems in Editing Donne's *Songs and Sonets,*" in *Editing Poetry from Spenser to Dryden: Papers Given at the Sixteenth Annual Conference on Editorial Problems, University of Toronto, 31 October–1 November 1980,* ed. A. H. De Quehen, 14–45. New York: Garland.

Maintains that the discovery of manuscripts unknown to Grierson, such as the Colau Cothi MS in the National Library of Wales and the Dalhousie I MS in the Scottish Record Office, as well as his now dated editorial approach, necessitates that modern editors "try to go beyond" (16) Grierson's edition (1912). Insists that editors "must have a theory of the text, coherent in itself, and consistently applied" (23) and criticizes Gardner's practice in her edition of the *Elegies* and the *Songs and Sonnets* (1965) for its inconsistency. Believes that Group I manuscripts represent "the earliest substantive version of the *Songs and Sonets,*" that Group II represents revisions by Donne, and that Group III offers "a number of readings from an early version or versions of which we have no substantive record" (27). Explains his "holistic approach to editorial problems" (42) in the *Songs and Sonets,* and shows "how this theory works out in practice" (25) by discussing in detail manuscript variants in *ValMourn, Flea,* and *GoodM.*

217. Scattergood, V. J. "A Note on the Moral Framework of Donne's *The Sunne Rising.*" *NM* 82: 307–14.

Suggests that the allusion to hunting in *SunRis* (l. 7), together with the mention of "ants" (l. 8), "Sunne" (l. 1), and "Busie" (l. 1), forms an orthodox moral framework concerning the deadly sin of sloth but that later in the poem Donne defends "what might be thought indefensible" by making "a witty, and ostensibly outrageous, argument in favour of idleness" (308), from which, it was thought, "came every other vice and sin" (312). Believes, therefore, that, in addition to being "essentially a love poem" in which Donne asserts "the primacy of human love" and offers his mistress "an elaborate compliment" (313), the poem also contains "a challenge to a well established moral scheme" (314).

218. Shapiro, I. A. "Donne and Walton Forgeries." *Library,* 6th ser., 3, no. 3: 232.

Points out that the signatures of Donne and Walton on the title page of a copy of the 1629 edition of Pope Gregory the Great's *De Cura Pastorali* in the William Salt Library (Strafford) are forgeries. For a reply by Jonquil Bevan and consequent correspondence between the two, see entries 252 and 327.

219. Shaw, Robert B. *The Call of God: The Theme of Vocation in the Poetry of Donne and Herbert.* Cambridge, Mass.: Cowley. xiii, 123p.

Presents three lectures delivered in March 1981 to the members of the American Congregation of the Society of St. John the Evangelist and to friends of the community. In the preface (ix–xiii) announces his intention to focus on close readings of individual poems, noting that many of the poems considered "are not allusions to vocation so much as they are embodiments of it" (xii). In "'Many are called': The Shaping of an Idea in Theology and Poetry" (1–31), defines the Christian concept of vocation, noting two ways in which the concept is used: (1) the call of God to those he has chosen for eternal life, and (2) the occupation or place in society that God assigns to an individual. Maintains that Donne focuses on the first and fears that, although he has heard God's call, he "may lack the power to respond to it," whereas Herbert "shuns these extremes of tone and import and focuses on the second sense, on duty rather than destiny" (2). Reviews the lives of both poets, arguing that in both there was a "tension between humanist aspiration and Calvinist discipline, between self-will and the will of God" (22). Contrasts *HSDeath* with Herbert's "Death," maintaining that "the way each poet views his end is keenly suggestive of the way he views the journey toward it" (26). In "John Donne" (33–69), Shaw surveys Donne's concept of vocation, and holds that Donne was "so absorbed in the idea of vocation as the soul's final destiny that he pays relatively little attention to the nature of particular earthly calls—even to that of the priest or poet" (66), citing passages from the sermons, *Devotions,* and several divine poems to show Donne's developing theology and religious sensibility. In "George Herbert" (71–107), Shaw contrasts Herbert's focus on duty with Donne's emphasis on destiny, noting "how little troubled Herbert is by the questions upon which Donne expends such anguished speculation" (71). Insists that, "if Donne is an explorer of what we may term the vertical axis of Calvin's concept of vocation, Herbert just assiduously explores the horizontal axis" (72). Concludes with notes (111–20) and an index of names (121–23). Reviews: Lynn Veach Sadler in *C&L* 31 (1981): 85–87; Diana Benet in *MiltonQ* 16 (1982): 105–06; Dayton Haskin in *Heythrop Journal* 24 (1983): 110–11; U. Milo Kaufmann in *JEGP* 82 (1983): 446–49; Raman Selden in *TLS* (24 June 1983): 681; Joseph H. Summers in *RenQ* 36 (1983): 151–55; Anthony Raspa in *MP* 81 (1984): 424–27; Paulina Palmer in *YES* 16 (1986): 247–48.

220. **Sito, Jerzy S.** *Poeci metafizyczni.* Warsawa: Instytut Wydawniczy Pax. 206p.

Presents a brief introduction to English seventeenth century metaphysical poetry and selected poets and surveys the critical reception of the poets (5–16). Translates into Polish the inscription on Donne's tomb in St. Paul's Cathedral, *SunRis, Flea, Triple, LovAlch, Break, Canon, Lect, LovInf, ElPart, ElFatal, ElBed, Twick, ValWeep, Fever, Fun, Christ, Sickness, HSDue, HSScene, HSRound, HSDeath,* and *HSBatter* (47–81) without notes or commentary, followed by a brief biographical sketch (198–99).

221. **Sledge, Linda Ching.** "The Seventeenth Century," in *Shivering Babe, Victorious Lord: The Nativity in Poetry and Art,* 75–120. Grand Rapids, Mich.: William B. Eerdmans Publishing.

Calls the seventeenth century "the era of the finest Nativity poems in the English tongue" (75) and says that these poems "can be seen as virtual historical documents chronicling the revolutionary tenor of the time." Points out that "the scriptural theme of Christ's Nativity weaves a colorful rich thread through the ingenious, often troubled devotional poems of Donne" (76), and claims that Donne's nativity lyrics "are cast in the Laudian mold." Calls *Corona* "a throwback to medieval meditations on the life of Christ written long after the *vita Christi* has ceased to hold much meaning for the Protestant English" (78–79), and suggests it resembles a Catholic rosary meditation. Calls *Cor3* in the sequence "a spontaneous dramatic monologue in which the poet mentally seizes on details of the gospel scene to make them real to his mind and heart" (79).

222. Sleeman, Margaret. "Medieval Hair Token." *FMLS* 17: 322–36.

Examines "some very curious references in medieval and traditional literature to objects apparently made out of human hair" and discusses "the powerful associations and symbolic value which hair possessed in the medieval period" (322). Comments briefly on Donne's reference to the bracelet of hair in *Relic* (l. 6), noting that Shakespeare has a similar reference in the first scene in *A Midsummer Night's Dream*.

223. Slights, Camille Wells. "John Donne as Casuist," in *The Casuistical Tradition in Shakespeare, Donne, Herbert, and Milton*, 133–82. Princeton, N.J.: Princeton University Press.

Surveys Donne's interest in and reservations about casuistry, especially his disagreement with Catholic approaches based on the concept of probabilism, an approach most clearly identified with the Jesuits, and notes basic differences between Catholic and Anglican casuistry, primarily differences on the question of authority and individual responsibility. Maintains that throughout his life Donne "was intrigued with casuists' attempts to untangle knotty problems of conscience" (134). Cites Donne's sermon on Esther 4:16 as an example but points out that *Biathanatos* and *Pseudo-Martyr* are the prime examples of his use of casuistry. Concludes that in *Biathanatos* Donne is attempting "to establish some degree of probability for the lawfulness of suicide within the body of theological opinion rather than striving to provide the means for full assent by the individual conscience" (144). Claims that in *Pseudo-Martyr* Donne presents his "fullest exposition of his conception of casuistry and the most detailed application of these principles to a particular case" (148). Argues that Donne the prose casuist becomes Donne the poetic casuist in the *Satyres,* and discusses all five of them as the place where "Donne's interest in the laws governing human action" is more successfully combined "with the particular circumstances of individual cases" (149) than in his prose. Says that the *Satyres* focus on self-examination and practical action and that the speaker is working out his own conscience at the same time as he is exposing evil in the world. Believes that Donne's casuistical mind is evident in the *Songs and Sonets* as well, but, using *Lov-Grow* as an example, shows that the lyrics are not casuistical in the precise way that the *Satyres* are. Reviews: Daniel Karlin in *TLS* (8 May 1981): 1346; John R. Knott in *MLQ* 42 (1981): 292–94; Warren Herman Chelline in *CompD* 16 (1982): 382–83; George Hemphill in *SR* 90 (1982): x–xiii; Hugh MacCallum in *UTQ* 51 (1982): 415–17; Diane McColley in *C&L* 31, no. 4 (1982): 87–89; P. G. Stanwood in *GHJ* 6, no. 1 (1982): 42–47; James Balakier in *MiltonQ* 17 (1983): 53–54; Coburn Freer in *RenQ* 36 (1983): 476–79; Brian Gibbons in *ShS* 36 (1983): 162–63; Dayton Haskin in *Heythrop Journal* 24 (1983): 343–46; R. D. Lord in *P&L* 7, no. 2 (1983): 277–78; G. A. Starr in *MP* 81 (1983): 70–72; J. de Bruyn in *ESC* 10, no. 1 (1984); Helen Peters in *RES* 35 (1984): 225–26; Thomas N. Corns in *YES* 15 (1985): 290–92.

224. Sloane, Mary Cole. *The Visual in Metaphysical Poetry*. Atlantic Highlands, N.J.: Humanities Press. 110p.

Argues that "the impact of the simultaneous existence of emblem, meditation, and epistemological upheaval had a profound effect on the visualization one finds in metaphysical poetry" and "accounts for much that is dissimilar, as well as similar, in the visual imagery of the metaphysical poets." Maintains further that "within metaphysical poetry itself, there is a progressive tendency away from the concept that knowledge is a part of a universal system of analogies and toward an emphasis on knowledge gained directly from sensory experience" (preface). In "The Noblest Sense and the Book of Nature" (1–23), discusses the effect of the epistemological upheaval that occurred in the seventeenth century and comments on how several of the metaphysical poets regarded the visual world from which they got their metaphors. Argues that all the metaphysical poets recognized that "the visual image was no longer able to carry the full meaning it had carried for the poets of the sixteenth century" (13). Comments on a number of poems by Donne to show Donne's skepticism and epistemological concerns, his distrust of the senses and traditional approaches to knowledge, and his awareness of the inadequacy of language. In "'With Hyeroglyphicks quite dismembred'" (24–46), maintains that in metaphysical poetry the emblem and discursive meditation meet, helping to produce "those elusive characteristics that distinguish metaphysical conceits from the conceits of the Elizabethans," and says that the way in which Donne and Herbert employ emblems "denies rather than affirms the world view that the emblem originally represented" (24). In "'Cannot thy *Dove* Out-strip their *Cupid* easily in flight'" (47–72), discusses the visual imagery of Donne and Herbert and its parallels in discursive meditation and in seventeenth century emblem books, and finds in both a "psychological involvement and an immediacy that is different from the poetry of the past as it would be from the poetry of the future" (48), attributing these qualities, in part, to their specific uses of emblems and meditation. Comments on three visual

characteristics that help explain some of the peculiarities of Donne's and Herbert's conceits: (1) "the visualization of the soul as participant in the religious drama," (2) "the interiorization of the meditative image," and (3) "the equation of the persona of the poem with the object of meditation" (50). In "'Real Crowns and Thrones and Diadems'" (73–95), traces the decline of the emblematic in the visual imagery of Crashaw, Vaughan, and Traherne, and maintains that by the time of Traherne "[t]he remnants of the hieroglyphically occult that characterize the poetry of Donne and Herbert and that were consistent with their skepticism regarding the validity of sense experience have given way to something more akin to the wonder in nature itself" (94). Concludes with notes (95–105), followed by reproductions of six emblems and an index (107–110).

225. Stachniewski, John. "John Donne: The Despair of the 'Holy Sonnets.'" *ELH* 48: 677–705.

Argues for a strong Calvinist influence on the *Holy Sonnets* and finds in the poems a "dominant mood of despair." Disputes Helen Gardner's argument in her edition of the *Divine Poems* (1952) that the structure and content of the poems are influenced by Ignatian meditation and that the sonnets form a sequence, regarding them rather as "discrete *cris de coeur*" that do not progress toward peace of mind, as some critics have argued. Analyzes Donne's "technique of subverting the ostensible arguments of apparently pious or confident poems with emotions of fear, resentment, and despair" (677). Discusses in detail *HSShe* and *HSBatter* in the light of Calvinist theology. Maintains that in the *Holy Sonnets* the conflict between Donne's "personal integrity and the demands of a theology which brutalized self-esteem is the essential subject matter of the poems" (690). Thinks that the argument of many of the sonnets is "often so strained that it alerts us to its opposite, the emotion or mental state in defiance of which the argumentative process was set to work," and that the meaning of the poems "lives in the tension between the argument and the emotion" (691). Comments on several of the sonnets as illustration of this tension. Supports his belief of Donne's having been influenced by Calvinist theology by commenting on the religio-historical context in which the sonnets were written and by discussing Donne's personality and the circumstances of his life during this period, concluding that "Donne felt his dependence on God to resemble his dependence on secular patronage with its attendant frustration, humiliation, and despair" (703).

226. **Stein, Arnold.** "Handling Death: John Donne in Public Meditation." *ELH* 48: 496–515.

Discusses Donne's handling of examples of the good death and describes them as public, optimistic, penitential, instructive, consolatory, and hopeful. Suggests that the models have significant differences, however. Examines Donne's sermon commemorating Lady Danvers, George Herbert's mother, for its balance between the personal and the general, where "all the individual facts of her person and life, and especially the sound virtues she possessed and practiced, are assimilated to the general pattern which her life illustrates" (500). Then discusses the sermon preached on the death of Sir William Cokayne, which is "less remote from ordinary life" and where "the individual significance of the man is also heightened," thus "portraying a 'modern' death which serves the needs of his own time" (510).

227. **Sullivan, Ernest W., II.** "The Problem of Text in Familiar Letters." *PBSA* 75: 115–26.

Examines problems in establishing a reliable text for Donne's 233 known or suspected prose letters, problems stemming from "posthumous publication, meddling relatives, lack of accessibility to some letters or associated materials, careless printing from copy of doubtful authority, and careless editorial work by scholars with varying degrees of bibliographical sophistication." Points out, however, that, "once the critic has determined what is known about the reliability of the text of these letters," he is then able to establish "parameters for his inferences about style, audience, subject matter, chronology, sequence, etc." Concludes that, imperfect as the materials may be, study of *Letters* and Gosse's *The Life and Letters of John Donne* (1899), together with Keynes's *Bibliography of Dr. John Donne: Dean of Saint Paul's* (4th ed., 1973), articles by I. A. Shapiro (1931) and Roger E. Bennett (1941), and the 23 extant holograph letters listed in Keynes "could lead to a variety of valid analyses of Donne's familiar letters" (123). Appendix A (124–26) contains literal transcriptions of two of Donne's holograph letters in the Bodleian Library: "To the Noblest knight Sr Edward Herbert" (MS e. Musaeo 131) and "To the Most Honorable and my most Honored L: The Marquis of Buckingham" (MS Tanner 73/2*). Uses these two letters as examples of how Gosse "grossly misrepresents" (122) the originals.

228. **Tebeaux, Elizabeth.** "Donne and Hooker on the Nature of Man: The Diverging 'Middle Way.'" *RestQ* 24: 29–44.

Compares Donne's sermons to Hooker's *Laws of Ecclesiastical Polity* in order to determine the extent of Donne's adherence to Anglican theology and also to discover if he made any original theological contributions to Anglicanism. Finds that although Donne and Hooker agree on many doctrinal matters, Donne "differs significantly from Hooker on many important points" (31), such as his insistence on the pervasiveness and seriousness of human sin; his distrust of "man's ability to find God by the law of nature embedded in his heart" (37); his views on how sin "overrides the positive implications of the Incarnation"; his belief that reason, darkened by sin, "cannot be the means by which man is brought to salvation" (38); and his insistence that "preaching is necessary for salvation" (30) and that natural theology is insufficient. States that "the crux of Donne's divergence from Hooker is that Donne curtails the capacity of natural reason" and "emphasizes the essential presence of grace" (41). Concludes that Donne was not a great speculative theologian and did not expound "any definite theological system" (43). Maintains that reading Donne's sermons inductively and comparing them to Hooker's views allow us to see that Donne "is not the careful, rational, architectonic theologian that Hooker was" and that Donne's sermons "cannot be said to have contributed to the development of early seventeenth-century Anglican theology" (43).

229. Toliver, Harold E. *The Past that Poets Make.* Cambridge, Mass.: Harvard University Press. 256p.

To illustrate the idea that any text has a mixture of logos (the rational) and mythos (the intuitive), compares and contrasts Donne and Yeats, "both of whom exploit admirably the poet's advantages with historical and mythic elements" (5). Says that the fundamental distinction between Donne and Yeats is that Donne "appears dedicated to the analytic powers of logos

but subordinates them to a centralizing myth" (56), whereas Yeats creates a variety of myths but remains entangled in history. Says that Donne's poems have almost nothing to do with classical mythology, but that *GoodM* nonetheless presumes that "love has a residual element of the mythic" and concludes "with a defiance of ordinary time that carries beyond analytic limits" (51). Says that in *GoodM* "love is more than an emotion; it is a reconstruction of the self and a discovery of a world permeated by the sacred" (54). Sees in *Canon* a similar evolution, where lovers retreat from the rational world but regain it mythically when the beloved becomes the other's whole world and when both become martyrs and saints for love and poems written about them become holy relics. Says that Donne's religious poems "redefine the myth of love, or more accurately replace it" (54). Sees in *Goodf* a rivalry between the sacred and the practical world, where in meditation the speaker withdraws from the active world to that of the Incarnation, an image which fuses mythos and logos.

230. Ward, J. P. "Donne and Social Interactionism," in *Poetry and the Sociological Idea,* 76–89. Harvester Studies in Contemporary Literature and Culture, gen. ed. Patrick Parrinder. Sussex, Eng.: Harvester Press; Atlantic Highlands, N.J.: Humanities Press.

Claims that the *Songs and Sonets* provides "a comparison with the social interaction school of sociology" and suggests that this comparison will demonstrate that the poems "are not 'about' social interactions nor themselves social interactions, or parties to interaction, even when they seem to address mistresses and loved women." Points out that, for Donne, erotic love "seems more like the end of interaction" with consummation occurring "when the interactions of love are complete" (76). Argues that since love for Donne is union, it "cannot contain interaction" since "total unity ends the possibility" of interaction (77). Cites *Ecst, ValMourn,* and *Canon* as explicit examples of this union. Says that since there is no interaction in Donne's poems, there can be "no language of that interaction" (81) with which to express the nature of love; thus Donne uses poetic rather than discursive language to express it. Claims that "what we call Donne's metaphysical or extravagant imagery is, in fact, his attempt to come at this mystery by however far-fetched means" (82). Maintains that, rather than addressing the mistress, Donne's poetry "teases out amazing conceits, redoubled levels of meaning, strange inversions of grammar and logic, and shifting moods, to present a mind from which at present outside activity is excluded." Says that Donne "studied Love intellectually and the intellect lovingly" (86) and that this activity excluded social interaction.

231. Wiggins, Peter De Sa. "Giovanni Paolo Lomazzo's *Trattato dell'arte della pittura, scultura, e architettura* and John Donne's Poetics: 'The Flea' and 'Aire and Angels' as Portrait Miniatures in the Style of Nicholas Hilliard." *SIcon* 7–8 (1981–82): 269–88.

Argues that the "evocativeness and expressivity" of Donne's poetry have "antecedents and parallels" (269) in the paintings of Nicholas Hilliard and Isaac Oliver and in Italian art theory. Believes that Donne would have known, directly or indirectly, the first translation of an Italian art treatise in English, Richard Haydocke's 1598 rendering of Giovanni Paolo Lomazzo's *Trattato dell'arte della pittura, scultura, e architettura.* Quoting a passage from Lomazzo that says "a painting can seem livelier than life itself" (271), attributes Donne's liveliness to the fact that his speakers evoke in the reader "an image of a silent second character—addressee—whose words or actions influence the speaker's behavior" and thus stimulate "the reader's imagination to reconstruct . . . the very experience that gave rise to those responses." Discusses Hilliard's portrait of an unknown youth against a background of flames as a "visual equivalent of the Petrarchan love lyric" (272), as well as Donnean love lyrics. Uses *ElFatal* to exhibit that Donne's poetry shares characteristics with contemporaneous miniature painting. Concludes that "reading Donne, we go beyond empathy with his speakers to the actual creation of the unstated circumstances that make them behave as they do" (277). Discusses *Flea* and *Air,* suggesting that the major difference between them is that the latter "insists upon reconstruction of an inciting incident," while the former "compels us to wonder about its dénouement" (277). Concludes that in Donne's new kind of poetry the reader must experience "the life of each speaking character so thoroughly that he can judge of his circumstances without having to have them described" (287).

232. Wilmer, Clive. "An Art of Recovery: Some Literary Sources for Geoffrey Hill's *Tenebrae*." *SoR* 17: 121–41.

Briefly notes that Geoffrey Hill's "Lachrimae" sequence in *Tenebrae* contains "conceits and conceptions" similar to those found in Donne's poetry (125). Points out that, although these poems do not resemble any particular poem, their language "seems to owe much to Southwell and Greville and Donne" (131).

233. Winny, James. *A Preface to Donne.* Foreword by Maurice Hussey. Rev. ed. Preface Books, gen. ed. Maurice Hussey. London: Longman. [ix], 196p. First published 1970; reprinted by Charles Scribner's Sons, 1972.

Primarily intended "for those who are fresh to the poetry of Donne and realize that critical guidance is essential before this intricate verbal art can communicate to us today" ([ix]). Alters the layout of the book, includes new illustrations, and adds the following new material: (1) In "The Elegies" (146–60), says that the *Elegies* contain some of Donne's "most scandalously outspoken and unconventional love poems" (146) and that "the only thing which these poems tell us certainly about Donne is of his driving energy, his love of display, his delight in standing convention on its head." Therefore, while noting that although *ElServe* and *ElFatal* may have been written for Ann More, urges the reader to view the *Elegies* as "outrageous *jeux d'esprit,* not as autobiography" (160). (2) In "Prose Writings" (164–65), comments briefly on the sermons, noting that they contain the same passionate emotion found in Donne's poetry. (3) In "Devotions upon Emergent Occasions" (165–79), discusses the overall design and style of the *Devotions* and suggests that readers unfamiliar with seventeenth century theology may find the work easier to understand if they see it as a record of Donne's depression over his personal difficulties and as a display of his neurotic obsession with disease and death. Adds also a chronological table of Donne's life and historical events that occurred during his lifetime (3–7); eliminates separate sections on Herbert, Vaughan, and Marvell found in the earlier edition; adds a list of places to visit (190); and revises the select bibliography (191–92). Concludes with an index (193–96).

234. Yarrow, Ralph. "Admitting the Infinite: John Donne's Poem 'Batter My Heart.'" *SMLit* 1: 210–17.

Maintains that *HSBatter* asks how one can expand his consciousness to accommodate the notion of the Trinity and the Infinite, using "firstly, shock tactics to force the reader to stop in his tracks and abandon a priori conceptions; secondly, the establishment of a kind of gap or vacuum in consciousness which parallels the moment when all limits are transcended; and thirdly, the recognition of this gap as not only the result of abandoning previous categories, but also as precisely the impetus for perceptual and conceptual renewal and the ability to make sense of what previously was thought impossible." Examines each of these occurrences "in terms of the thematic and structural features of the poem" (211). Attempts to show that the structure of the sonnet as well as its particular uses of metaphor, vocabulary, and rhythm "present the action of the poem as that of an extension of consciousness beyond limits, a process achieved by the use of paradox to produce extreme flexibility" (216). Concludes that for both Donne and the reader the sonnet "becomes the place of a transformation; the record and practice of a single consciousness experiencing its complete opposite" and "thus solves the problem of the Trinity and the relationship of individual to infinite less by argument than by presentation: it becomes what it is about" (217).

235. Yuasa, Nobuyuki. "Spenser and Donne in Romantic Criticism." *HSELL* 26: 32–43.

Points out that Romantic critics generally reacted unfavorably to Donne's intellectuality and use of conceits but admired the passionate intensity in his poems. Identifies three kinds of critics: (1) radicals, such as Emerson, who liked the emotional dimension of Donne's poems, (2) judicious critics, such as Wordsworth and Coleridge, who examined Donne's poetry in depth and found numerous interesting features in it, and (3) conservative critics, such as Lamb, who, appreciated both the emotional and intellectual aspects of Donne's poems. Singles out Coleridge as the most perceptive of Romantic critics, citing in particular his observation that one must discover the time of each word in Donne's poems, not simply count syllables.

1982

236. Aizawa, Yoshihisa. "John Donne no 'Shunen Tsuitoshi' ko (5)" [A Study of John Donne's *Anniversaries* (5)]. *Bunkei Ronso* [Bulletin of the Faculty of Humanities, Hirosaki University], 17, no. 3: 119–41.

Part 5 of an eight-part series of articles. Treats the "new philosophy" and its influence on Donne's attitude toward knowledge and comments on how Donne's lines express the impact and the resultant chaos and confusion. Maintains that the mannerist world, which is broadly characterized by distorted and unquiet metaphors, especially the "serpentine line," used to intensify the emotional disturbance, is represented especially in *FirAn* (ll. 247–338).

237. Aizawa, Yoshihisa. "Nihon ni okeru Keijijoshi Kenkyu Shoshi (2)" [A Bibliography of Writings about Metaphysical Poetry in Japan (2)], in *Ouseifukko no Eibungaku* [English Literature in the Restoration Period], 1–12. The Japan Society of Seventeenth-Century English Literature. Tokyo: Kinseido.

Lists studies on seventeenth century English metaphysical poets and poetry written in Japan from April 1975 to March 1979. Includes studies of metaphysical poetry in general as well as studies of Donne, Herbert, Crashaw, Marvell, and Vaughan. Additional list of studies on metaphysical poetry in Japan from 1927 to March 1975.

238. Alexander, Gillian. "Politics of the Pronoun in the Literature of the English Revolution," in *Language and Literature: An Introductory Reader in Stylistics,* ed. Ronald Carter, 217–35. London: George Allen and Unwin.

Demonstrates "a close relationship between discourse styles and an opposition between rival or ideologically conflicting social groups." By studying the use of pronouns in specific mid-seventeenth century prose texts, including *Devotions,* the author distinguishes "a series of key historical disfunctions in the way the conservative Anglicans and the more radical Puritans saw themselves in relation to God, their fellow man and the society in which they lived" (216). Shows, for instance, that in Donne's prose meditation, the most significant pronoun is "I," whereas "you" is less important; in Bunyan's *Grace Abounding* and in Winstanley's *A Watch-Word to the City of London,* however, "you" is "relatively more significant" and "I" "less so." Maintains that the difference occurs because Donne, the "conservative Anglican," was more concerned with meditating on the "self" as "a symbol of the miserable condition of humankind," whereas the radicals "viewed the process of writing as serving the end of establishing Utopia on earth" and thus have "a message to impress upon an audience." In Donne's prose, therefore, the "I-writer assumes a central position in the discourse" and the reader becomes "an eavesdropper," whereas in the writings of Bunyan and Winstanley, "you-I" relationships become "crucial" (223). Notes that Donne's infrequent shifts from "I" to the all-inclusive "we" reflects his "belief that he is a symbol for the world," whereas in radical prose "we" is used to signal or awaken "some kind of group consciousness and collective political activity" (224). Says that for Donne, "he" and "I" are in "syntactic opposition—they never occur in the same position at the level of clause structure" (225), thereby reflecting his sense of the separation between God and fallen man; whereas in radical prose, such a dichotomy is not reflected because of the doctrine of inner light, which claimed that the divine presence is within each person.

239. Andreasen, N. J. C. "Theme and Structure in Donne's 'Satyres,'" in *Die Englische Satire,* ed. Wolfgang Weiss, 201–19. Darmstadt: Wissenschaftliche Buchgesellschaft.

Reprinted from *SEL* 3 (1963): 59–75. Annotated in *Roberts 1.*

240. Attridge, Derek. *The Rhythms of English Poetry.* English Language Series, vol. 14, gen. ed. Randolph Quirk. London: Longman. 395p.

Cites several poems by Donne as illustrations in this study of meter and rhythm in English "accentual-syllabic" verse that extends over six hundred years. Offers a detailed analysis of the meter and rhythm in *SSweet* (333–37) to show how Donne's "surface rhythms move towards and away from the metrical pattern while his metrical patterns move away from and towards the simple underlying rhythms," resulting in "verse which ranges from baroque elaboration to lucid simplicity, from the energy of vigorous speech to the calm continuities of song." Maintains that "the main site of variation [in the poem] is the metrical patterns" while "the syllables remain for the most part content with regular alternations" that are somewhat affected "by shifts in the underlying form of the verse"

(334). Concludes that, "in spite of the poem's title, both the rhythmic shaping of the whole work and the local effects of uncertainty and tension would be lost in a musical setting that imposed the same metrical framework on each stanza" (337).

241. Baumgaertner, Jill P. "The Source of Donne's Hatched Soul." *RES* 33: 296–98.

Discusses the uniqueness of the image of "a soul hatching from a shell and flying to heaven" (296) in *SecAn* (ll. 184–89). Finds the source of the image in the works of Philo Judeaus, "a first-century spokesman for Hellenistic Judaism" (296–97).

242. Bawcutt, Priscilla. "'Venus Starre' in Donne and Douglas." *N&Q,* n.s. 29: 15.

Notes that although no definite source has been found for "Problem X: 'Why Venus starre onely doth cast a Shadowe,'" it seems to belong to some tradition of astronomical lore, also familiar to Gavin Douglas, that moralizes upon the shadow-casting characteristic of the planet Venus as evidence of the paradox of erotic love.

243. Bax, M. M. H., and N. F. Streekstra. "'That's not Donne, Mr. Huygens!': Oordelen over Huygens' vertalingen van gedichten van John Donne," in *Regel voor regel: Vertalen en vertalingen: proeven en beschouwingen,* ed. K. Iwema, J. M. J. Sicking, and W. Blok, 35–51. Groningen: Nederlands Instituut van de Rijksuniversiteit Groningen.

Offers a brief history of the reception of Donne and Constantijn Huygens in The Netherlands, pointing out that admiration for both poets is not widely self-evident in the seventeenth century and only really begins to emerge two centuries later. Argues that this reception history shows very little objectivity, being based on little more than different commentators' taste for Donne's way of writing and for Huygens's rendering of it. Traces the emergence of a more objective judgment on Huygens's achievement to middle and late twentieth century formalism and proceeds to use a formalist approach to demonstrate some of the ways in which Huygens's translations of Donne differ prosodically from their sources. Devotes considerable attention to a linguistic (syntactic and morphological) model in an attempt to provide objectivity and gives linguistically based attention to the ways in which Huygens attempts to render the density of Donne's thought, asking to what extent the translations may or may not be considered more prolix than the originals. Concludes that only by applying objective approaches such as these to Huygens's achievement in translating Donne is it possible to assess that achievement fairly.

244. Bayley, Peter. "The Art of the 'Pointe' in Bossuet," in *The Equilibrium of Wit: Essays for Odette de Morgues,* ed. Peter Bayley and Dorothy Gabe Coleman, 262–79. Lexington, Ky.: French Forum Publishers.

Compares and contrasts Donne's "Death's Duell" (1630) with Bossuet's "Sermon sur le Mort" (1662) to show that, although stylistically different, both sermons are founded upon classical rhetorical techniques and reflect "strict logical and theological rigor" (264).

245. Beal, Peter, and Hilton Kelliher. "John Donne." *TLS* (12 February): 162. Presents evidence to show that the anti-Jesuitical epigram "Ignatii Loyolae" ("Qui sacer ante fuit, sanctus nunc incipit esse") discovered by P. G. Stanwood in the Cathedral Library in Durham and reported in *TLS* (19 October 1967, 984) is, in fact, the work of the neo-Latin poet Raphael Thorius (d. 1625) and "has no connection with Donne."

246. Beck, Joyce S[hort]. "Donne's Scholastic *Ars Dictaminis* in a Verse Epistle to the Countess of Bedford." *EIRC* 8–9 (1982–83): 22–32.

Examines the form and style of Donne's verse epistles, especially *BedfRef* in order to understand how Donne's scholastic *ars dictaminis* contributes to his purpose in writing verse letters. Points out that although medieval and classical *ars dictaminis* typically had a five-part pattern of *salutatio, capitatio, benevolentiae, narratio, petitio,* and *conclusio,* in Donne's hands the form is more flexible, while the style is what makes the poem a verse epistle. Says that the style of Donne's verse epistles deemphasizes the decorum and balance of the classical Horatian epistle and "may [more] accurately be called scholastic, medieval, or even Gothic" (24). Says that *BedfRef* contains the first three parts of a traditional verse letter, parts that are meant to secure the good will of the reader, but that in the *narratio* Donne amplifies the exposition of the lady's virtues "according to the scholastic principle of *manifestatio* and its literary equivalents—extended analogies, paradoxes, and syllogisms" (26). Points out that Donne makes the *petitio* into a prayer of request, rather than a song of praise, to view the countess because her outward frame implies her inner virtue, and that the *conclusio* brings him back to his original subject, Lady Bedford's virtue, which he continues to elucidate by extended analogy.

247. Bedford, R. D. "Donne's Holy Sonnet, 'Batter My Heart.'" *N&Q,* n.s. 29: 15–19. Reprinted in *John Donne's Poetry,* ed. Arthur L. Clements, 2nd ed. (1992), 333–38; revised version appears in *Dialogues with Convention: Readings in Renaissance Poetry* (Ann Arbor: University of Michigan Press, 1989), 94–104.

Reviews various interpretations of the first quatrain of *HSBatter* and argues that the opening quatrain of the poem has "as its subject an implied conceit of considerable specificity and a good deal of poetic muscle"—that of God as a potter and Donne as a pot that must not be simply mended but must be broken and remade. Argues that the conceit in the first four lines "completes the trio of metaphors" in the poem and "is not an uncontrolled outburst of whirling words, nor simply a verbal arithmetic of vaguely focused triplets, and [that] through its verbs it is as clear and as consistent as the subsequent extended metaphors" (19).

248. Bedford, R. D. "Ovid Metamorphosed: Donne's 'Elegy XVI.'" *EIC* 32: 219–36. Revised version appears in *Dialogues with Convention: Readings in Renaissance Poetry* (Ann Arbor: University of Michigan Press, 1989), 59–79.

Calls *ElFatal* one of Donne's "most sustained" and "most theatrically vital" reworkings of Ovidian conventions, noting, however, that although Donne likely had in mind Ovid's *Amores* (2.11:15–16), the poem has "a quality of passionate tenderness" that is quite un-Ovidian (222). Argues that although Donne uses Roman conventions, he adapts them to explore a serious "relationship of reciprocal and committed love" and that his use of a genre and medium "whose built-in code is often designed not to sustain" but "to deny, regret, or even wriggle out of such passionate seriousness" contributes a "special tension" to the elegy. Sees the poem as "a little piece of theatre, a miniature play in one brief scene," yet maintains that the elegy seems "to treat a real love affair, not just a literary one" (224–25). Cites specific details that make the poem seem realistic, while at the same time rejecting an autobiographical reading of it. Concludes that the reader is "teased" by "the usual ingredients and expectations of an Ovidian form—tones of self-justification or self-abasement, grandiose or ironic gesturing,

bravura expostulations, a finely discriminating sensuality, a world of jealousies, secrecies, and frustrated desires—dramatically transformed and superseded by a voice of unaffected and authentic candour" (234–35).

249. Bell, Ilona. "Circular Strategies and Structures in Jonson and Herbert," in *Classic and Cavalier: Essays on Jonson and the Sons of Ben,* ed. Claude J. Summers and Ted-Larry Pebworth, 157–70. Pittsburgh, Pa.: University of Pittsburgh Press.

Argues that Herbert's poems are perhaps more indebted to Jonson than to Donne. Focuses on one major aspect of the work of Herbert and Jonson, "a characteristic circular strategy and structure" (157) whereby the reader is included in the poetic process of discovery, noting that "this particular concept of circularity is alien to Donne" and that even when he uses a circular poetic form, as for instance in *Noct,* he does not "include the reader in the process of discovery, as Herbert and Jonson do" (167). Maintains that in Donne's poetry "circular forms and circular images do not become structural strategies to explore—or to encourage us to explore—the complexities of rewriting and rereading"; they "are either retrospective or progressive, but they are not both." Says, in other words, that "a return to the beginning of a poem, a reassessment of the speaker's 'first thoughts' in light of his conclusion, is not intrinsic or necessary to the structure and meaning of Donne's poems, as it is so often to Jonson's and Herbert's." Concludes that "[f]or both Jonson and Herbert, the poem is not ultimately a dramatic performance, as it was for Donne," but was rather "a written construct, which can be read and reread and misread and made again because it can be read from so many different points of view" (168).

250. Bennett, J. A. W. "Donne, Herbert, Herrick," in *Poetry of the Passion: Studies in Twelve Centuries of English Verse*, 145–67. Oxford: Clarendon Press.

Maintains that much of the devotional spirit in Donne's poems on Christ's Passion and cross can be found in medieval Catholic as well as sixteenth century Ignatian spirituality, citing *Goodf* as an example in which both traditions coalesce. Quotes ll. 29–32 on the Virgin Mary and says, "We shall not hear such language in English verse again—except in Crashaw, Vaughan, and, muted, in Herbert—for almost three centuries." Notes that the conceits in *Cross* might appear far-fetched "if we did not know that they had been neatly packed together, and illustrated, in the *De Cruce* of the learned [Justus] Lipsius, who duly traces them back to the Fathers" (152). Calls *HSWhat* the "direct fruit of meditation on the Crucified" and describes its medieval antecedents. Notes how in *Sickness* (l. 27) Donne "compresses into a few words the force of a long fifteenth-century meditation" (153).

251. Bevan, Jonquil. "Donne and the Walton Forgeries: A Correspondence." *Library* 4, no. 3: 329–30.

Reply to I. A. Shapiro's "Donne and Walton Forgeries" (entry 218), who maintained that the signatures of Walton and Donne in the copy of St. Gregory's *De Cura Pastorali* (1629) in the William Salt Library are forgeries. Believes the Walton signature is "*perhaps* doubtful" but that "[i]f it is a forgery it is a very good one" (329). Says she is not qualified to comment on the Donne signature but notes that both Geoffrey Keynes and R. C. Bald accepted it as Donne's signature. For a reply by Shapiro, see entry 326; for a reply by Bevan to Shapiro's reply, see entry 252.

252. Bevan, Jonquil. [Donne and the Walton Forgeries: A Correspondence.] *Library* 4, no. 3: 335–38.

Reply to I. A. Shapiro's reply to her note (entry 251). Points out that the list of Walton signatures cited by Shapiro are incomplete and some of his comments "based entirely on secondary material and unsupported by any first-hand knowledge of the primary evidence" (336). Presents additional evidence to support her original position, but says she has "no opinion about the authenticity of the inscription in Mr. Pirie's copy of Montagu's *Gagg for New Gospell*" (338) since she has not seen the volume. Points out that Walton was capable of spelling Donne's name as "don," noting its appearance in Walton's copy of Eusebius, Socrates, and Evagrius (Salisbury Cathedral Library: Lib: R.4.7). For a reply by Shapiro, see entry 326.

253. Boer, M. G. L. *De ridder met de witte pluim: John Donne, dichter-prediker.* The Hague: Uitgeverij Boekencentrum BV. 174p.

Based on a series of broadcasts for the confessional (Protestant) Dutch radio station NCRV composed in December 1981 belatedly to mark the 350th anniversary of Donne's death and transmitted in February 1982. Consists of three parts: (1) a biographical sketch of Donne in the context of the later Tudor and early Stuart periods; (2) an account of Donne as poet and preacher, treating both the secular and sacred poetry, and giving examples of the range of themes to be found in the Sermons; and (3) a discussion of Donne and The Netherlands, the historical part of which consists of accounts of Donne's 1619 visit to The Hague on the Doncaster mission and of the translations of Donne's verse into Dutch made by Constantijn Huygens in 1630 and 1633. Throughout illustrates Donne's religious development with reference to the poetry of Herbert. Quotes extensively, both in English and in a variety of Dutch translations, from Donne's work. Concludes with an account of twentieth century translations of Donne into Dutch and Frisian.

254. Booty, John E. "Contrition in Anglican Spirituality: Hooker, Donne, and Herbert," in *Anglican Spirituality,* ed. William J. Wolf, 25–48. Wilton, Conn.: Morehouse-Barlow.

Argues that Donne, Hooker, and Herbert share a common understanding of contrition for sin and that "they can help us to understand the importance of contrition in Anglican spirituality and in humanity at large." Maintains that, "above all, they affirm that true praise, joy and thanksgiving proceed out of that contrition which is the gift of divine love" (45). Finds Donne's understanding of contrition expressed primarily in *Devotions* and in the *Holy Sonnets.* Says that *Devotions,* which examines Donne's soul's health, follows a course of repentance reminiscent of Hooker—moving from a consideration of God's mercy from fear to love of God, followed by confession and detestation of sin and a weeding out of sin. Endorses Douglas Peterson's reading (*SP,* 56 [1959]: 504–18) of the *Holy Sonnets* as a poetical sequence on the subject of contrition. Concludes that "[i]t would not be incorrect to refer to the theology of John Donne as the theology of divine mercy," noting that in both the *Devotions* and the *Holy Sonnets* "the focus is not on sin but on love, God's forgiving love arousing the response of love" (35).

255. Bradshaw, Graham. "Donne's Challenge to the Prosodists." *EIC* 32: 338–60.

Maintains that Donne uses "a particular rhythmic effect" that the critic calls "sustained rise," reviews "arguments advanced by influential critics and linguists which fail to provide any convincing account of what is problematic in Donne's metrical practice," and argues that Donne "could not have written as he did without first arriving at a positive conception of the expressive function of metre, which was revolutionary in his own time and powerfully challenges assumptions that are still current today" (338). Points out that the "sustained rises" in *Sat3* "are perfectly adapted to express emotional and intellectual stress—the struggle to apprehend and control violent emotion, and the effortful process of difficult thought." Claims that "[i]t would be difficult to exaggerate the originality and importance of Donne's achievement in this poem" (352–53). Argues that in Donne's poetry "metrical rhythm is structural not accidental" and that "its function is to make expressive variations of stress possible." Maintains that, for Donne, the metrical pattern exists as "a norm that is valuable precisely on account of the expressive deviations it allows." Holds that Donne recognized "the distinction between lexical accent and metrical ictus" that allows a perfectly iambic line to include "two contiguous iambs in which there are, very perceptibly, four degrees of relative stress" (356). Suggests that perhaps it is the "sustained rise" that led Donne's contemporaries to call his verse "strong-lined" or "masculine."

256. Brodsky, Claudia. "Donne: The Imaging of the Logical Conceit." *ELH* 49: 829–48. Reprinted in *John Donne and the Seventeenth-Century Metaphysical Poets,* ed. and intro. Harold Bloom, 51–67. Modern Critical Views. New York: Chelsea House Publishers, 1986.

Questions "the status of logic as it is brought to light by the use of imagery" (830) in Donne's erotic poetry and in *Sat3.* Examines images in *GoodM* and *SunRis* in which "[s]ensual experience is imaged as itself and as the sum of all experience," thereby "admitting no external objects of comparison" (831) and defying logical examination. Likewise examines the image of the portrait or picture in *ElPict* and in *Witch,* concluding that as the referent of picture disappears in each poem, the logicality of the image of picture becomes invalid. Deconstructs images of the covering of a book to the body's soul in *ElBed* and *Ecst* to show the logic invalid as well. In discussing the equation of language with sophistry in *ElNat,* concludes that "the development of the conceit of language within the poem coherently questions its own signification" (838). Discusses *Sat3* in the context of the illogicality of images in Donne's erotic poems and judges that the figure of Truth on a high hill "is imaged without access to analogical comparisons and in the absence of even a modest display of Metaphysical wit." Noting that the figure is a commonplace one, says that "[c]ommonplace conceptions are substituted for the complex places of logical invention," and adds that "the conceit does not, or cannot, represent the truth of its own coherency, the coincidence of its logic, with its significance" (843). Suggests that when "power" is introduced in the poem, it disturbs the pattern of the imagery and "may be suggestive of the persuasive *and* critical capabilities of the poetic conceit: the power to structure imagery into apparent sense and the power to image in movement against that structure" (845).

257. **Chambers, A. B.** "Glorified Bodies and the 'Valediction: forbidding Mourning.'" *JDJ* 1: 1–20.
Maintains that the "imagistic structure" as well as the argument of *ValMourn* depends on the theology of glorified bodies after the resurrection on Judgment Day and on alchemy,

noting that both disciplines used images and symbols so much alike that it is impossible to determine at times which of the two topics is being discussed. Points out that this "duplication in imagistic usage" came about because alchemical works "regularly refer to the metaphoric 'death' of a metal and to its 'resurrection' in a glorified and golden state," and also because a number of similar symbols "appear in both systems of thought," such as "gold, thinness, airiness, circles and/or spheres, the sun, and symbolic arithmetic" (1). Examines in detail how these images inform the poem and finally culminate in a conjunction of the philosopher's stone, God, and the two lovers in the poem. Believes that Donne's intent in the poem is "to render in hyperbolic and witty terms the curious state in which we mortals exist and that, in order so to do, he is willing to employ whatever means—however ingenious, exaggerated, or, to some, even blasphemous—that he and, presumably, his audience could command" (17).

258. **Clark, Ira.** "Explicating the Heart and Dramatizing the Poet: Seventeenth-Century Innovations by English Emblematists and Donne," in *Christ Revealed: The History of the Neotypological Lyric in the English Renaissance,* 64–79. University of Florida Monographs: Humanities, no. 51. Gainesville: University Presses of Florida.
Discusses how in his sermons Donne "contrived to present himself as leading an archetypal life," presenting himself "as a saved sinner who repeated the fundamental life history of David or of Saint Augustine," in order to make a dramatic impact on his congregation by presenting himself as "a representative of Christian remorse, and by implication, salvation" (71). Maintains that in the sermons, the sacred poems, and *Devotions,* and

even in his secular poetry, Donne's "dramatic self-portrayals" are now regarded as "the axiomatic defining characteristic" of his art (72). Discusses how Donne adhered primarily to the "flexible Reformed principles of typology" (73), and points out that most frequently he turns to biblical persons as types—"Adam, Abraham, Isaac as the glad son, the seed of Abraham, Melchizedek, Jacob, Moses, Solomon, Jonah, Hezekiah, and David" (75)—noting that "[m]ost important for Donne, and for his development of the neotypological lyric, is that applying types to himself is reversible," that is, "[h]e can also apply himself to types" (75–76). Maintains that in his finest neotypological lyrics, as in his sermons, Donne "presents personally dramatic, exemplary self-portrayals through a persona so closely identified with a type that he becomes a neotype of Christ in some common seventeenth-century predicament" (77). Discusses *Sickness* as Donne's "dominant neotypological lyric" (78) and suggests that he "has released the energy in the multiple neotypological referents [in this poem] to gain more power than ever before by analyzing himself most personally and dramatically in the last, perhaps most critical scene in the archetypal life of everyman as believer," thereby bequeathing "to the neotypological lyric heritage the last characteristic essential for the fullest exploitation of its potential, an achievement realized by George Herbert" (79).

259. Corthell, Ronald J. "Style and Self in Donne's Satires." *TSLL* 24: 155–84.
Believes that the purpose of Donne's wit throughout his lifetime was "to accommodate himself to public circumstances that he recognized as corrupt because human"; in other words, his aim was "to fashion a witty self that could mediate the claims of indi-

vidual conscience and external power rather than merely defend the conscience against external power." Maintains that the *Satyres* offer "a unique opportunity for studying the relationship between Donne's self-presentation and his awareness of the political and social realities of the late Elizabethan period." Points out, for instance, that all of the *Satyres* "are informed by Donne's perception of the public consequences of a private religious commitment," a perception that is "a salient feature of Donne's style." Illustrates how all five poems "record the emergence" of Donne's "witty self that is nothing more (or less) than a style." Maintains that "the major features of this style are the principle of similitude and the paradox," noting that "Donne's similitudes define the relation of structures of power" while "his paradoxes make him unlocatable within this 'order of things.'" Points out that "from this strange position, Donne also courts those who have power; his self-presentation is rhetorical, an attempt to transcend his social estrangement" (156). Calls Donne's style in the *Satyres* "paradoxical and self-referential, but also rhetorical, socially aware, useful—a style which fashions the world in the self and the self in the world" (179).

260. Culler, Jonathan. *On Deconstruction: Theory and Criticism after Structuralism.* Ithaca, N.Y.: Cornell University Press. 307p.
Discusses the problem of self-referentiality, using *Canon* as an example, to show that the issue is "more complex and problematic" (203) than Cleanth Brooks's well-known interpretation of the poem in *The Well-Wrought Urn* (1947) would suggest. Maintains that the "self-referentiality element" in the poem "does not produce or induce closure in which the

poem harmoniously is the thing it describes [as Brooks suggests]." Argues that "[i]n celebrating itself as an urn the poem incorporates a celebration of the urn and thus becomes something other than the urn; and if the urn is taken to include the response to the urn, then the responses it anticipates, such as Brooks's, become a part of it and prevent it from closing." Insists that "[s]elf-reference does not close it in upon itself but leads to a proliferation of representations, a series of invocations and urns, including Brooks's *The Well-Wrought Urn*" (204). Says that although there is "a neatness to this situation," it is "the neatness of transference, in which the analyst finds himself caught up in and reenacting the drama he thought he was analyzing from the outside" (204–5). Concludes that, in fact, "[t]he structure of self-reference works in effect to divide the poem against itself, creating an urn to which one responds and an urn which includes a response to the urn," thus creating "a situation in which responses such as Brooks's are part of the urn in question" (205).

261. **Daniels, Edgar F.** "Donne's 'Love's Diet,' Lines 20–21." *Expl* 41, no. 1: 14–15.
    Notes the "not uncommon locution" (14) in Middle and Early Modern English of "when that" meaning "when" and suggests that in *LovDiet* (ll. 20–21) Donne uses this locution with an ellipsis: "When she writ to me, / And [when] that that favour hath made him fat. . . ." Notes also use of the locution with a similar ellipsis in *Appar* (ll. 1–2): "When by thy scorne, O murdresse, I am dead, / And [when] that thou thinkst thee. . . ."

262. **Daniels, Edgar F.** "Donne's 'The Undertaking.'" *Expl* 41, no. 1: 15–16.
    Challenges the reading of *Under* (*Expl* 36, no. 3 [1978]: 16–18) by Noam Flinker, who believes that Donne

assumes the role of a fool in the poem and intends that he be the object of ridicule. Refutes Flinker by contending (1) that there is nothing self-contradictory in the speaker's both praising the declaration of love and at the same time the concealment of it, (2) that the braver action in the poem is not a reference to concealment, (3) that there is finally no contradiction between the speaker's comment that virtue in woman is as rare as selenite and his later saying one might find this "loveliness within," (4) that there is no contradiction between the speaker saying that he wants to conceal love and then proceeding to write a poem about it, and (5) that clearly Donne is not distancing himself from the speaker's treatment of virtue in women.

263. **Donker, Marjorie, and George M. Muldrow.** *Dictionary of Literary-Rhetorical Conventions of the English Renaissance.* Westport, Conn.: Greenwood Press. xvi, 268p.
    Collection of short essays on literary and rhetorical terms that inform English poetry in the later sixteenth and earlier seventeenth centuries, arranged alphabetically, with each entry followed by a selected bibliography arranged chronologically. Cites Donne and/or his poetry and prose to illustrate the following terms: "aubade," "conceit," "couplet," "elegy," "epistle," "lyric," "song," "sonnet," "sonnets in sequence," "strong lines," and "type" and "antitype." Appendix A lists modern literary terms with references to relevant entries in the volume; appendix B lists Renaissance terms arranged by appropriate general categories; and ends with an index.

264. **Donne, John.** *Biathanatos.* A modern-spelling edition, with introduction and commentary by Michael Rudick and M. Pabst Battin. Garland English Texts, no. 1. New York: Garland. cx, 288p.

In the "Introduction" (ix–xcvi), the editors call *Biathanatos* "not only the earliest published and perhaps still the most thorough critique of the traditional Christian position [on suicide]" but also "one of the most perceptive and most wholly original accounts of suicide to be written in the entire history of the debate" (ix). Maintains that the work was written in 1608, comments on its genesis, reviews Donne's life during this period, and discusses modern critical commentary on the book. Comments also on Donne's use (and misuse) of authorities and sources, such as "the Bible and its exegetes; various civil and religious law codes, together with their commentators; Christian church fathers, moral theologians, philosophers, homilists, and religious controversialists" (xxi). Summarizes Donne's central arguments in *Biathanatos* and explains the argumentative structure of its three principal parts. Concludes by suggesting the relevance of the work to "issues which now animate moral theology and moral philosophy, particularly where they intersect in assessing the issues in suicide, partial suicide, and other forms of voluntary death" (lxxiv). "Text and Editorial Treatment" (xcvii–cx) describes the two substantive texts of *Biathanatos*, the Bodleian MS e Musaeo 131 and the 1647 quarto and comments on their relationship, arguing for the great reliability of the quarto, and explains the editorial procedures followed in this edition. Presents a modern spelling text of *Biathanatos* (1–194) based on the 1647 quarto, followed by commentary (195–278), which glosses words and passages, translates Latin passages, comments on the intellectual contexts and sources of Donne's arguments, and points out and justifies "the more important editorial decisions made in constructing the text" (195). Concludes with an index of names (279–88).

Reviews: W. Speed Hill in *JDJ* 6 (1987): 109–33.

265. Donne, John. *John Donne: Poemes,* trans. Josep M. Sobrés. Papers Erosius, 1. València: El Cingle. 36p.

Contains a brief introduction to Donne's life and poetry with a note on the text and translation (7–8), followed by translations of *Flea, Fun, Break, ElPict, GoodM, HSMade,* and *HSBatter* with English and Catalan texts on facing pages (9–28). Concludes with notes on each poem (29–36) and a table of contents [37].

266. Donne, John. *John Donne: Zwar ist auch Dichtung Sünde: Gedichte englische und deutsch.* Nachdichtungen von Maik Hamburger und Christa Schuenke. Herausgegeben von Maik Hamburger. Leipzig: Philipp Reclam, jun. 161p. Rev. ed., Leipzig: Philipp Reclam, jun., 1985.

Presents a general introduction to Donne's life, poetry, and modern critical reputation by Maik Hamburger (5–18); selections (with English and German texts on opposite pages) from *Songs and Sonets* ([19]–61), the *Elegies* (64–93), the *Satyres* (96–113), verse letters (116–37), and *Divine Poems* (140–45), with notes (146–58) and an index (159–[63]).

267. Donne, John. *The Love Poems of John Donne,* ed. and intro. by Charles Fowkes. New York: St. Martin's Press. xxi, 100p. First printed, London: Macmillan, 1982. Reprinted 1984, 1985.

Contains a biographical introduction ending with the death of Ann More (ix–xxi) and says that the collection is "for enjoyment" and, therefore, that "academic objectivity is not of the greatest importance" (ix). Presents a modernized spelling edition of the *Songs and Sonets* (1–69) (including "Song: Stay, O Sweet, and do not rise," attributed to Dowlands) and 16 selections from the *Elegies* (including "Image of her whom I love") (70–100), without notes or commentary.

268. Dreher, Diane Elizabeth. *The Fourfold Pilgrimage: The Estates of Innocence, Misery, Grace, and Glory in Seventeenth-Century Literature.* Washington, D.C.: University Press of America. x, 165p.

Quotes liberally from Donne in explaining what seventeenth century writers thought about the states of innocence, misery, grace, and glory. Suggests that Donne's tormented spirit really appreciated prelapsarian man and baptized infants. Quotes from *FirAn* to show Donne's belief in a progressive decay of the world and from *Sickness* to demonstrate his belief that "mankind was redeemed from the misery of the first [fall] by the mercy of the second Adam" (44). Quotes from a sermon and *Goodf* to show Donne's use of alchemy as a conceit for the conversion of sinners to a state of grace. Quotes from another sermon to demonstrate Donne's belief in a state of glory after death, where body and soul as well as whole families will be reunited and where their joy will be boundless.

269. Eccles, Mark. "John Donne," 44–46, in "Brief Lives: Tudor and Stuart Authors." *SP* 79: 1–135.

Notes made primarily from public records and parish registers in England for a projected, but never completed, biographical dictionary of Elizabethan authors. Records, for instance, that Donne and Christopher Brooke were sued during the Hilary term (1598–99) by the executors of William Edwardes for an unpaid debt of forty pounds. Notes information on the house in which Donne was born and on Donne's mother's administration of the estate of her second husband, Dr. John Syminges, and of a lawsuit over money brought against Syminges by Laurence Holden a year following the doctor's death.

270. Edgecombe, Rodney. "An Enquiry into the Syntax of Donne's 'The Good-Morrow' and 'The Sunne Rising.'" *ESA* 25: 29–37.

Offers "a rigorously specific examination of the syntax" of *GoodM* and *SunRis,* "breaking down their constitutive statements and noting the structural and thematic profit that Donne accrues from their assembly" (29). Shows the relevance of syntax in each poem "to the thematic line it both subserves, and, through the patterned tropes of rhetoric, often embodies," claiming that syntax is "the midwife of thought" in Donne's poems and "canalizes the poet's themes at their conceptual source and sets them coursing through the body of his stanzas." Concludes that "[a]ttentiveness to matters such as mood and voice and tense, far from drying up the spirit of a poem, ought to direct us to the very basis of its being" (37).

271. Empson, William. "'There Is No Penance Due to Innocence': An Exchange." *NYRB* 29 (4 March): 43.

Replies to Gardner (see entry 280). Maintains that those who agree with Gardner's adoption (1965) of "Here is no pennance, much less innocence" in *ElBed* (l. 46) have failed to see the point that is at issue—"that it would be heretical, not merely shocking, to call an adultery innocent." Points out that Grierson (1912) recognized this issue, which, perhaps, was the cause of his "uneasiness." Suggests that, when Grierson defended his choice of "due to innocence," he thought that, "though probably a later version and though not certainly written by the poet, it made the poem much better—ringing, decisive, and sincere."

272. Evans, Gillian R. "John Donne and the Augustinian Paradox of Sin." *RES* 33: 1–22.

Maintains that although the use of paradox in Donne's love poems is only "a merry nothing, a fashionable literary device," in his divine poems and the sermons it not only "serves a serious purpose" but is, in fact, "a philosophical device, even a theological method" (2). Argues that in his prose works and sacred poems "Donne's sense of sin runs as a connecting thread, unifying his theological reflections" and "giving a deeply felt immediacy to his use of a number of conventional paradoxes" (2–3). Maintains that although Donne's theological paradoxes are not particularly new or original, they do express a problem that troubled him persistently—"the problem of sin and the problem of evil which lies behind it." Explains the Augustinian concept of sin and evil and claims that Donne's debt to St. Augustine "is nowhere more in evidence than in his handling of these two issues" (8). Discusses how Donne's prose works and religious poems contain "a great deal of paradoxical theology," in which Donne attempted "to resolve the contradictions which troubled him personally," noting that "[n]o topic lent itself to the method so readily as that of sin and evil, regarded as Donne regarded it from an Augustinian viewpoint, because it is the very nature of evil to present paradoxes." Concludes that "Donne found himself intimately caught up in those paradoxes" (21).

273. Farr, Judith. "Elinor Wylie, Edna St. Vincent Millay, and the Elizabethan Sonnet Tradition," in *Poetic Traditions of the English Renaissance,* ed. Maynard Mack and George deForest Lord, 287–305. New Haven, Conn.: Yale University Press.

Points out that the title of Edna St. Vincent Millay's 1931 volume of sonnets, *Fatal Interview,* is derived from *ElFatal* (although the poems themselves owe little or nothing to Donne) and was dedicated to Wylie, whose final volume of poems, *Angels and Earthly Creatures* (1929), was greatly

influenced by Donne and who even strove "to become the colleague of Donne which she sometimes imagined herself" (302).

274. Fenner, Arthur. "Donne's 'Holy Sonnet XII.'" *Expl* 40, no. 4: 14–15.

Argues that *HSWhy* "achieves its power entirely by a structure of explicit argument" and has "no detailed imagery, absolutely no metaphors, scarcely anything that can be called 'figurative'" (14). Explains the argument of the poem through the use of a mathematical diagram. Finds especially impressive the last line of the sonnet in which Donne loads "every rift with ore" and "does so by sheer structure of explicit meaning" (15).

275. Fluchère, Henri. "'Beauté, mon beau souci . . . ': Fragment d'un 'Malherbe,'" in *The Equilibrium of Wit: Essays for Odette de Morgues,* ed. Peter Bayley and Dorothy Gabe Coleman, 95–108. Lexington, Ky.: French Forum Publishers.

Briefly discusses Donne's valediction poems and says that Donne's poetry is militant, aggressive poetry that explores furiously the secret corners of appearances and that its rhetoric pays no attention to rules or discretion. Compares Donne to Maurice Scève and François de Malherbe. Discusses the theological and alchemical images that describe the beauty of Elizabeth Drury in the *Anniversaries,* finding in them the extreme limits of the power of the intellect to express the ineffable. Comments also on the conceits and wit in Donne's poetry.

276. Ford, Boris, ed. *The New Pelican Guide to English Literature, 3, From Donne to Marvell.* Harmondsworth: Penguin Books. 410p.

Reprints three essays dealing with Donne that first appeared in the first edition (1956) with later minor revisions: R. G. Cox, "A Survey of Literature from Donne to Marvell" (51–93);

R. G. Cox, "The Poems of John Donne" (106–23); and Gilbert Phelps, "The Prose of Donne and Browne" (124–42). For annotations, see *Roberts 1*. Presents a new bibliographical note (384–85).

277. Fowler, Alastair. *Kinds of Literature: An Introduction to the Theory of Genres and Modes.* Cambridge, Mass.: Harvard University Press. vii, 357p.

Comments on *ValMourn* as an example of Donne's epigrammatic transformation of the love lyric, especially noting how its "strands of discourse are overlaid and compressed so closely as to make a dense texture of ambiguities, in which individual words count . . . as in the epigram" (199). Notes that the conceit of the compass comes from an epigram-madrigal by Guarini, and says that Donne "raised the amatory elegy to new heights" (223).

278. Gallenca, Christiane. "Introspection et vision du monde: La perception de la dupe chez Donne et Marston," in *La dupe elisabéthaine où l'homme trompé,* 308–30. Études Anglaises, 83. Paris: Didier Erudition.

Compares and contrasts the dupe in the satires of Donne and John Marston. Points out that both satirists, despite their differences in style and religious allegiance, primarily attack boorish young gallants and foppish courtiers who, living only for the present moment, are concerned solely with appearances and who lack a moral understanding of the world about them. Notes that both poets make clear that the dupe and the one who dupes are not necessarily opposites, for both often show a similar dishonest virtuosity. Maintains that both show that the narcissists, the vain, the egotists, and the charlatans of preciosity symbolize a compliance cut off from the world and from God. Suggests that Donne and Marston endorse two common themes: they believe that the concept of liberty is limited by itself, and they hold that true greatness of man depends primarily on his willingness to turn toward God.

279. Gardner, Helen. "A Nocturnal upon St. Lucy's Day, Being the Shortest Day," in *Poetic Traditions of the English Renaissance,* ed. Maynard Mack and George deForest Lord, 181–201. New Haven, Conn.: Yale University Press.

Speculates that *Noct* was "inspired by Donne's desolation" over the death of Ann More in 1617, thereby rejecting the earlier claim in her edition (1965) that it was inspired by the grave illness of Lucy, Countess of Bedford, in 1612. Admits, however, that the dating of the poem in no significant way increases "the value of the poem as a profound expression of the sense of utter and irremediable loss" (181). Agrees with Martz (1954) that *Noct* is "unique" among the *Songs and Sonets* because it is "fundamentally religious" (184), noting, in particular, that the title and last four lines allude to the liturgical celebrations surrounding the Feast of St. Lucy on 13 December and that the poem is, in fact, "an analysis of mortification" that "has been forced upon the speaker by the loss of what gave the world all it had of value" (186). Points out that the poem appears "in only seven closely related, very full collections and is not found in any extant manuscript miscellany" (187), a fact which supports a dating after 1615, because after his ordination Donne did not circulate his poems widely. Notes also that most of the post-ordination poems are occasional pieces, "inspired by personal circumstances, as if some strong inner compulsion made Donne break his promise in his Harington Elegy to write no more poems." Maintains that, obviously, "the most profound of his personal experiences" after his ordination was the death of his wife in 1617 (196).

280. Gardner, Helen. "'There Is No Penance Due to Innocence': An Exchange." *NYRB* 29 (4 March): 43.

Replies to Empson (*NYRB* 28 [3 December 1981]: 42–50). Rejects the idea that the mistress in *ElBed* may be a prostitute and maintains that she is more likely a rich citizen's wife than a court lady because "the ambience of similar Elegies is rather that of the city than of the court." Points out that Grierson's suggestion (1912) that the poet is writing his own epithalamium rests entirely on a note next to l. 31 in the Bridgewater manuscript, written by an unknown commentator. Maintains that if anyone can believe that this elegy, with all of its sexual innuendos, was addressed to a lady by her husband on their wedding night, then the poem deserves all that Carey (1981) says about it. Finds the notion "absurd," contending that the "brilliantly improper wit" in the elegy is a "kind of linguistic foreplay aiming to excite the mind" as the speaker's "roving hands" (l. 25) arouses her body.

281. Harman, Barbara Leah. *Costly Monuments: Representations of the Self in George Herbert's Poetry.* Cambridge, Mass.: Harvard University Press. x, 225p.

Compares and contrasts the speakers in Donne's and Herbert's poems. Observes that in Donne's secular poems speakers "are not always eager to appear" but will do so if "[p]ressed beyond endurance and impatient with their audience," and then "they speak only long enough to silence those who would threaten their safety and privacy" (41), citing in particular *Canon* and *SunRis*. Suggests, however, that "Donne's lovers, for all their reluctance to appear, experience isolation as a special version of centrality," for "as long as they cannot see anyone

else they can perpetuate the fiction that they are the only persons in the world." Points out that the speakers in Donne's sacred poems, however, "*desire* to be conspicuous" and "find privacy both isolating and threatening" and make speech "a way of insisting upon one's presence in a world that seems far more hospitable to death and disappearance" (42). Maintains that, although Donne's speaker in the *Holy Sonnets* is more desperate than the speaker in Herbert's sacred poems, speech in both "becomes a vehicle for self-manifestation in a world otherwise inhospitable to self-manifestation" (43). Also discusses the theme of the dissolution of the body in "Deaths Duell" because it "stands behind" (120) Herbert's "Church Monuments" and "Mortification," pointing out several similarities between Donne's sermon and Herbert's poems. Contrasts also the speakers in *Goodf* and in Herbert's "Affliction (I)."

282. Hester, M. Thomas. *Kinde Pitty and Brave Scorn: John Donne's Satyres.* Durham, N.C.: Duke University Press. ix, 178p.

In the "Introduction" (3–16), states that the aim of this study is "to redirect attention to the excellences" of Donne's *Satyres* "by examining the satiric strategies of these poems, individually and as a unit, within the historical and literary contexts of their composition." Maintains that, if seen from this vantage point, the poems "reveal much about Donne's early poetic and his concomitant moral-aesthetic perspective on late Elizabethan morals and manners" (3). Suggests that they also "offer a unified, sequential examination of the problems of Christian satire, a creative shaping (or re-shaping) of the generic, conventional, intellectual, and biographical materials available to Donne in the 1590s." Calls Donne "the most important and most original of the English formal verse satirists" (4) and stresses his indebtedness to the notion of the satirist as a zealous prophet in the Old Testament manner. Maintains that Donne in his *Satyres* replaces "the spokesman of Horace, Juvenal, and Persius with a speaker of Christian zeal" (15) and accommodates "the techniques of Roman satire" to the aim of Christian satire, as evidenced in "the persona, imagery, and design of the *Satyres*" (16). Chapter 1, "The Satirist as Scholar" (17–32), maintains that *Sat1* is "most instructive" about Donne's "conception of the features, limitations, and duties of Christian satire" (17). Says the poem examines primarily "the relationship between Christian satire and Christian scholarship—through a dramatic portrait of a scholar who discovers both the problematic character and the moral synonymy of his private and public commitments of Christian charity" (19). Maintains that *Sat1* "is not designed as a definition of satire" but rather it explores "the *character* of the Christian scholar" (20) whose duty as a Christian scholar "leads him to satire" (21). Shows how the "concatenation of the imagery of clothing, imprisonment, and adultery, supported by images of animals and stooping, reiterate the human condition as envisioned in Christian thought" (18) and how the poem "presents the problematic character of the Christian scholar in the world of adamant fallen nature" (32). Points out that this satire "offers an introductory study of the moral superiority and problematic conditions of Christian charity in the fallen world" (32). Chapter 2, "The Satirist as Apologist" (33–53), shows how *Sat2* "addresses the nature and potential of the satirist's medium—language" and how it "dramatically isolates the anger or 'brave scorn' of the prophetic dialectic, in order to

evaluate its applicability in a moral climate that threatens the viability of satire itself" (33). Sees the poem as "an ironic satirical apologia that is unified by the speaker's concern with public and private perversions of language and presumptive abuses of the Word" (34), which he regards as "the ultimate enemy of English morality and civilization" (35). Argues that *Sat2* "presents a tightly organized argument that accords with the Christian accommodation of ancient writings about the nature and potential of language, spoken by a poet whose own concern with the efficacy of words as vehicles of truth and instruments of persuasive 'Good workes' provides a standard against which the abuses he attacks can be judged" (38). Maintains that the satirist shows that the abuse of language by poets and by Coscus, the corrupt poet-lawyer, reflects "a world where the civilizing and sacred power of the words of God and man have been perverted into instruments of personal, material gain" (48). Concludes that Donne's speaker establishes "his criteria as a Christian satirist" by his "display of charity for sinners" in *Sat1* and by "his hatred for their sins" in *Sat2,* as well as demonstrates "his possession of the two essentials of successful oratory—good character and eloquence" (53). Chapter 3, "Satire as Religion" (54–72), argues that *Sat3* "dramatizes the satirist's initial discovery of the *devotional* nature of his satire" and "deliberates the nature of satire as much as the nature of 'true religion.'" Maintains that in this poem "the satirist finds a satisfactory balance between the charity he offered the fop" (in *Sat1*) and "the hatred that overruled it" (in *Sat2*), "through his dynamic uses of the three powers of the rational soul." Insists, therefore, that *Sat3* "examines the correct use of the satirist's own mental faculties as exemplary alternative to the failures of devotion that the poem ridicules" (54). Chapter 4, "The Satirist as Traitor" (73–97), argues that *Sat4* is a "dramatic meditation on the satirist's fearful experiences at the Elizabethan Presence Chamber," which "tests and expands the view of satire-as-religion in the previous poem," and concludes "that satire is not only a form of Christian devotion but, more important, a perilous, even dangerous, celebration of and participation in the unfolding of the Word" (73). Maintains that in this poem "the largely *private* stance of the previous poem is expanded into an examination of the problematic public role of the satirist *sub specie aeternitatis*" (74) and that it also reveals Donne's precarious position as a Catholic in Elizabethan England. Calling *Sat4* "the longest, the most complex, and most comprehensive of the five poems," explains how "its narrative [is] complicated by the conflation of horizontal and vertical levels of discourse" and "its unity [is] complicated by diverse strands of imagery" (75). Chapter 5, "The Satirist as Advisor" (98–118), argues that in *Sat5* "the satirist expands the possibilities and scope of his Christian satire by examining the role of satire *within* the legal machinery of the established state . . ., applying the satirist's established generic principles to a specific moral problem and legal situation in late Elizabethan England" (98)—"the exactions levied on suitors by the lawyers and officials of the court" (99). Maintains that this poem "illustrates not only the means but the manner in which satire can become a process of active Christian reform" (116). Appendix A, "'Careless Phrygius'" (119–27), challenges the notion that Phrygius in *Sat3* is, strictly speaking, an atheist, and argues that he does not deny God but simply denies "that any of the current churches descends from the vicarage of St.

Peter" (120). Believes that perhaps Phrygius is a Separatist, "most likely a Barrowist" (125). Appendix B, "'Becoming Traytor'" (128–33), argues that Juvenal's "Satire III" provides a classical analogue and possible source for the second half of *Sat4*. Concludes with notes (135–59), bibliography (160–72), and an index (173–78). Reviews: Lachlan Mackinnon in *TLS* (24 June 1983): 681; Robert W. Halli in *SoAR* 49 (1984): 119–23; Patrick G. Hogan, Jr., in *C&L* 33 (1984): 45–47; Norman McMillan in *SHR* 18 (1984): 258–60; David Novarr in *RenQ* 36 (1984): 667–70; Camille Wells Slights in *JEGP* 83 (1984): 235–37; Helen Peters in *RES* 36 (1985): 263–65; Edgar L. Chapman in *SCN* 45 (1987): 9–10; Raman Selden in *MLR* 82 (1987): 165–66.

283. Hughes, Kenneth James. "Donne's 'Metempsychosis' and the Objective Idea of Unreason." *CIEFLB* 18, nos. 1–2: 15–39.

Argues that the target of Donne's disguised satire in *Metem* is Elizabeth I, maintaining that when the poem was written (1601), Donne was opposed to the Tudor monarchy and the court and that, in order to protect himself, he deliberately sought "to obscure the inner meaning" (23) of the poem and consciously distorted historical facts. Sees the ape in the poem as Essex (ll. 451–60, 473–75); Tethlemite (l. 487) as Sir Robert Cecil, the leader of the anti-Essex faction; and Themech, Cain's wife, as Elizabeth, who, "married to mercantile trade in its monopoly form," finally "sums up in herself all the worst features of her ancestors" and is made out to be "the quintessence of social and political evil." Concludes that "in the interests of greater bourgeois freedom, Donne attacks neo-feudal privilege and the constraining, narrow, bureaucratic rationality that had been the creation of the Tudors as economic feudalism made a rapid transition to mercantile capitalism in extreme monopoly form within the political framework of the new centralized Tudor State." Claims that during the latter days of Elizabeth's reign "internal contradictions" between those who had plenty and those who had little "revealed themselves in all their fullness and viciousness" (37), and that *Metem* is Donne's "work of political propaganda designed beneath its surface cover to define reality by naming the Tudor monarchy as the villain for a discerning inner group of Donne's radical, bourgeois friends" (37–38).

284. Hunter, William B., Jr. "John Donne and Robert Greene." *AN&Q* 21: 6–7.
Suggests that the allusion to a starving writer in *Sat2* (ll. 13–14) is likely to Robert Greene, who died in a pitiable condition in 1592. Notes that Greene in his *Groats-worth of Witte* (1592), like Donne, calls actors puppets who are animated by poets. Points out that the reference to Greene supports the dating of *Sat2* as 1593 and emphasizes "the currency of Donne's satire" (6).

285. Hurtig, Judith W. "Seventeenth-Century Shroud Tombs: Classical and Anglican." *Art Bulletin* 64: 217–28.
Points out that "[t]he middle third of the seventeenth century in England was a period of enormously fruitful experimentation in the development of new tomb types" and that "these, for the first time since the onset of the Reformation, reflect Anglican ideas about death." Shows that these funerary "themes, and the imagery with which they are expressed, have new close parallels in the contemporary poetry, devotional literature, and sermons delivered by important Anglican preachers" (217). Discusses, in particular, how the metaphor of death as sleep that appears on tombs, mostly

tombs of women, is paralleled in Donne's *Holy Sonnets* and sermons, especially in *HSDeath*, and in his 1627 memorial sermon on Magdalen Herbert. Contrasts the tombs of women with shrouded figures reposing in peaceful sleep with Donne's tomb in St. Paul's.

286. Hyman, Lawrence W. "Humanism and 'Religious' Art." *The Humanist* 42, no. 3: 49–50.
Argues that atheistic humanists can appreciate a religious literary work without violating their "own deepest convictions" by responding not to "the correctness of the answer" given in the work but rather to "the complexity of the experience." Maintains that often "the inadequacy or failure of a poem or novel to answer the question raised is often a sign of its literary excellence," citing, as an example, *HSDeath*. Argues that "what we should be convinced of [in the sonnet] is not the argument but the experience" (49), and insists that "we should respond to the entire poem and not just to the conclusion," recognizing "the false reasoning with which the poet tries to overcome his fear," as well as "the audacious wit," "paradoxical ideas," and "contradictory feelings expressed in the regular pattern of a sonnet" (50).

287. Jones-Davies, M. T. "Paradoxes élisabéthains: 'Les guerres de la vérité,'" in *Le paradoxe au temps de la Renaissance,* ed. M. T. Jones-Davies, 105–23. Université de Paris-Sorbonne: Institut de Recherches sur les Civilisations de l'Occident Moderne; Centre de Recherches sur la Renaissance. Paris: Jean Touzot.
Discusses Donne's concept of paradox and explores his various uses of paradox in *Sat3, Sat4, ElVar, Canon,* and the *Anniversaries*. Maintains that for Donne, paradox was a means of sharpening one's judgment and of opening the way to truth.

288. Justin, Mark. "'There Is No Penance Due to Innocence': An Exchange." *NYRB* 29 (4 March): 43.

Replies to Empson (*NYRB* 28 [3 December 1981]: 42–50). Challenges Empson's reading of the first stanza of Carew's "Elegie upon the death of the Deane of Pauls, Dr. John Donne." See Empson's reply (*NYRB* 29 [4 March]: 43).

289. Kamholtz, Jonathan Z. "Imminence and Eminence in Donne." *JEGP* 81: 480–91.

Discusses how Donne was "fascinated by the smallest units of time, in the moments that cannot be sustained, when a tiny flux in time has the most profound consequences—noon, the break of day, the turn of the season, the year's midnight, the instant of death" and maintains that Donne "is drawn to those states of time when another state of time is imminent." Points out how lovers in Donne's poems "yearn to delay, to stay on the verge—of time, of love, of sex—as long as possible," but when they can no longer avoid their "descent into time," they plunge "into the material, natural world where things can be seen to bud, reach fruition, and decay"; thus "imminence gives ways to "eminence" (480). Focuses on "the transitional moments" in Donne's poetry when "lovers who have absorbed all the world into themselves are then ready to be absorbed by the world, acceding to the seduction of time's necessity" (483). Holds that Donne "juggles time, trying to redress the imbalance between the shortness of the present and the length of eternity" and says that it is this attempt "to elongate the moment" that "accounts for Donne's sense of imminence" (485). Maintains that Donne "shows his real interest in time as man halts, his progress blocked by the barrier of a single moment," when "he must make up his mind whether or not to accept the sacrifices—and gains—to be had by the rearrangements needed to pass on to the next moment" (486–87). Claims that Donne "appreciates time most exquisitely at this border" and that "[o]nce he has crossed it, objects are perceived more intensely and time is experienced less intensely" (487). Comments on Donne's treatment of time in such poems as *Lect, LovUsury, Broken, ValMourn, NegLov, Ecst,* and *GoodM.* Shows that in these poems "the purity possible when time is imminent has had to decay so that the lovers can face the inevitable complexity of their eminence." Maintains that "[b]oth the lover and the poet must sadly descend into time, where physical bodies or poetic, figurative images decay, or are gross or inadequate—but exist" (491).

290. Kaske, Carol V. "Calendrical Imagery in Sir Henry Goodere's *Epithalamion.*" *Anglia* 100: 130–34.

Discusses the "time-magnifying conceits" in *EpEliz* and in Henry Goodyer's 'The Epithalamion of the Princess' Marriage," both of which were written for the wedding of Princess Elizabeth and Frederick Count Palatine (14 February 1612–13). Notes that in the second refrain of Donne's poem "the couple's sexual prowess is able to make St. Valentine's Day last all year long." Points out that behind the conceit is the "universal lament of lovers" that the wedding night is too brief and that both Donne and Goodyer "seek to rectify the injustice" (132). Hints at Spenser's influence on Donne's poem.

291. King, Bruce. "Donne and Jonson," in *Seventeenth-Century English Literature,* 40–61. Macmillan History of Literature, gen. ed. A. Norman Jeffares. London: Macmillan.

In "Introduction to Metaphysical Poetry and Donne's Life" (40–42), briefly defines "metaphysical poetry," emphasizing wit, followed by a synopsis of Donne's life. In "Donne's Secular Poetry" (41–46), surveys the *Satyres, Elegies, Songs and Sonets,* epithalamia, and the *Anniversaries,* pointing out major characteristics of the various genres. In "Donne's Religious Poetry" (46–47), very briefly comments on the *Holy Sonnets, Corona,* and two hymns, suggesting that these poems are "stanzaically less inventive than the poems of Herbert or Donne's own secular songs" and are Donne's attempt to bring "intelligence to bear on the articulation of emotions" (47). In "Donne's Prose" (47–50), surveys *Paradoxes, Pseudo-Martyr, Devotions,* and the sermons, insisting that "[t]he use of wit, word play, ideas and conceits found in Donne's poetry is also characteristic of his prose" (47).

292. Kinoshita, Kaoru. "John Donne to Augustinianism" [John Donne and Augustinianism], in *Ouseifukko no Eibungaku* [English Literature in the Restoration Period], 89–106. The Japan Society of Seventeenth-Century English Literature. Tokyo: Kinseido.

Considers the influence of St. Augustine's *De doctrina Christiana* on Donne's interpretation of the Bible.

293. Kinoshita, Kaoru. "Sekkyosha Donne ni miru Augustinianism: Seisho no Yuben o Chushin-ni" [The Augustinianism of Donne—In Relation to the Eloquence of the Scriptures], in *Eigaku Ronshu: Ishii Shonosuke Sensei Kokikines Ronbunshi* [Essays in Honor of the Seventieth Anniversary of the Birth of Professor Shonosuke Ishii], ed. Osamu Fukushima et al., 121–32. Tokyo: Kinseido.

Discusses Donne's views on rhetoric and eloquence in light of St. Augustine's comments on rhetoric and eloquence in the Bible. Points out that Donne, like St. Augustine, appreciates eloquence and believes that the role

of the orator or preacher is to teach, persuade, and delight. Points out that there are many examples of praise of biblical eloquence in Donne's sermons and that he almost exceeds St. Augustine in his affirmation of rhetorical expression in the Bible.

294. Klaniczay, Tibor. "La poésie méditative, un genre représentatif du maniérisme: Quelques réflexions." *RLC* 56: 281–86.

Regards "meditative poetry" as the most significant genre of mannerist literature, and agrees with Martz (1954) and others that the term is more accurate and comprehensive than "metaphysical poetry," especially when one considers the antecedents of the kind of poetry that Donne wrote that can be found in languages other than English, citing in particular the work of Della Casa, Sponde, Sep Szarzynski, Herrera, Góngora, and Janos Rimay. Suggests that Christian stoicism colors the main current of mannerist poetry, which is characterized by interior questioning, intellectual tension, and spiritual anguish. Sees mannerism as the result of Renaissance man's intellectual search to make sense of a world that seems to be falling apart and to solve complex questions. Believes too much attention has been devoted to the formal aspects of mannerism while its intellectual content has been slighted. Suggests that the prose of Bacon, Montaigne, Sponde, and Paruta can be seen as prose equivalents of meditative poetry.

295. Leonard, James S., and Christine E. Wharton. "The 'Mistresse Teares' in 'Twicknam Garden.'" *CP* 15: 51–55.

Argues that "your" (l. 21) of *Twick* refers not to "lovers" (l. 19) but rather to "Love" (l. 15), and that the sense of the passage is that "the tears to be tested are those not of the 'mistresses' but of the 'lovers' themselves, whose true 'mistress' is 'Teares,'" a reading "supported by Grierson's text, which shows the word 'mistresse' in the singular objective form, not in the plural possessive required for 'lovers' to be taken as the antecedent of 'your.'" Further suggests that "the capitalized form of 'Teares' identifies it not as literal, physical tears but as an abstraction (one might even say 'deity') equivalent of 'Love' in l. 15." Paraphrases the passage thus: "Hither with crystal vials, lovers [will] come" (or "[let] lovers come") / "And take my tears, which are love's wine, / And try [i.e., test for truthfulness] your [i.e., Love's] mistress Tears at home" (54). Suggests how such a reading clarifies the argument and conclusion of the poem.

296. Logan, H. M. "The Computer and Metrical Scansion." *L&LC* 3, no. 1: 9–14.

Illustrates how computers can be employed "to provide a four-stress analysis of English poetry, incorporating some of [Joseph C.] Beaver's and [Paul] Kiparsky's modifications of the generative metrical theory" (9). Uses Donne's poetry in his analyses.

297. Low, Anthony. "The 'Turning Wheele': Carew, Jonson, Donne [and the First] Law of Motion." *JDJ* 1: 69–80.

Comments on Carew's "An Elegie upon the death of the Deane of Pauls" (ll. 79–82), Donne's *SecAn* (ll. 7–22), and Jonson's "Elegie on my Muse" (ll. 27–31) as reflecting a changing perception and understanding of the nature of motion in the seventeenth century that resulted finally in the breakdown of the Christian-Aristotelian view of the universe and the development of and final acceptance of the mechanical model. Suggests that although the theory had not been fully articulated in the earlier seventeenth century, each of the three poets "sensed that there was a menacing threat to their world in the very concept of momentum—of dead move-

ment," and also "sensed that inertia was not only a potentially destructive agent, seemingly outside human and divine control, but that it offered a shockingly accurate model of precisely what was being done to the Christian-Classical universe into which they had all been born." Notes that, although poetry kept alive the older view for many years to come, "poetry also was the first to proclaim the subtle signs of its inexorable demise" (79).

298. Lucas, John. "Edgell Rickword." *PoetryR* 72: 45–49.

Presents a tribute to Edgell Rickword (d. 1982) that acknowledges the poet's debt to and appreciation of Donne in the 1920s. Notes that although Rickword heartily endorsed Empson's view that in Donne's poetry lovers create their own world, "free from the moral and religious considerations of a post-lapsarian world," he was more influenced in his love poetry by the French decadent poets (Baudelaire, Laforgue, Corbière, Rimbaud) than by Donne.

299. Martinet, Marie-Madeleine. "Les Figures de repétition: Images de la mélancholie poétique au début du 17ème siècle." *BSEAA* 14 (June): 23–41.

Presents a detailed psychological interpretation of various metrical patterns and syntactical constructions in the valediction poems, *Twick, Noct,* and several of the *Holy Sonnets*. Comments on how metrical and syntactical patterns create a symbolic form for expressing melancholy in some of the poems. Points out also how certain repetitive metrical patterns in a poem conflict with one another, thereby creating the tone of the poem.

300. Martz, Louis L. "Meditation as Poetic Strategy." *MP* 80: 168–74.

Essentially a review of Barbara Lewalski's *Protestant Poetics and the Seventeenth-Century Religious Lyric* (1979) (entry 46) in which Martz defends his position, most fully presented in *The Poetry of Meditation* (New Haven, Conn.: Yale University Press, 1954), that Continental methods of discursive meditation had a profound effect on English religious poetry of the seventeenth century, and insists that no other devotional practices of the time "create the complex and dramatic action characteristic of the best in English meditative poetry" (168). Finds convincing, however, Lewalski's discussion of the *Holy Sonnets* in a Calvinist context, which, he maintains, "does not invalidate the presence of the Ignatian kind of meditation within the bounds of an individual sonnet" (173). Concludes that the truth probably "lies somewhere between" Lewalski's position and his, but adds, "closer to my own, I hope" (174).

301. Maurer, Margaret. "The Circular Argument of Donne's 'La Corona.'" *SEL* 22: 51–68.

Presents a reading of *Corona,* arguing that "the overall effect of its formal characteristics is to suggest that the poem is designed to present, but not resolve, a question that has human ingenuity as its significant term" (53). Maintains that what the sequence of seven sonnets "leaves unresolved" is "the issue of how the poetic act is related to the question of the speaker's salvation," even though "that issue generates the poem" (53–54). Says the poem asks, "[T]o what extent . . . does a man's apprehension of the mysteries of God's merciful disposition toward mankind indicate his own state of grace" and "assure him of his own salvation?" (54). Discusses how "the matter of the poem admits the full wealth of the circle's symbolic potential" (54), and comments on circle symbolism from the time of St. Augustine to Donne's own time. Believes that the sequence can be seen "as the self-conscious attempt of a human soul

to describe an inhumanly perfect motion." Explains that "[i]f the impulse toward a point of resolution is figured in the motion toward the center (a certain conclusion) and the impulse to progress is figured in the movement along the tangent (the employment of human faculties of reason and argument), then a reconciliation of these two motions is a circle that does not completely satisfy either impulse" (57). Discusses how the manipulation of repeated lines, artful antitheses, ingenious wordplay, paradoxical statements, subtle shifts of tone, and wit in the seven sonnets demonstrate "the limits of human ingenuity" and make clear that "[s]alvation is not a state the soul achieves in time" but rather "is a process occupying the soul until eternity." Concludes that in *Corona,* "[t]he height of Donne's power only reveals the limits of his astonishing wit" (68).

302. Maurer, Margaret. "The Poetical Familiarity of John Donne's Letters." *Genre* 15, no. 1–2: 183–202. Edited by Stephen Greenblatt as *The Forms of Power and the Power of Forms in the Renaissance.* Reprinted in *The Power of Forms in the English Renaissance,* ed. Stephen Greenblatt (Norman, Okla.: Pilgrim Books, 1982), 183–202.

Explores "the implications of seeing the relationship between Donne's letters and poems as essentially one of style or method" (183). Maintains that Donne's "particular genius as a letter-writer is his ability to conceive of a relationship that unites him to a correspondent around the message he makes the subject of the letter," after which "he selects details with an eye to the relationship he would assert, or he formulates a relationship to accommodate material with specific ends in mind" (184). Argues that the problem of reading Donne's letters "is fundamentally the issue of coming to terms with his method, of appreciating the various ways Donne uses the device of the letter to locate some image of himself within the press of chronicled events" (188). Surveys the broad range of subjects and rhetorical strategies in Donne's letters, both verse and prose, and maintains that in them "we discover a sensibility remarkably obsessed with the relationship between the self-possession out of which he writes his pretty letters and the alienation that excludes him, if only temporarily, from the events those letters might be about." Concludes that "[t]hat sensibility is the basis of what we call his familiarity . . . his ability to impress the image of himself as letter-writer on his reader" and that "[t]hat sensibility is the source of his power to dramatize and manipulate" (199).

303. McCabe, Richard A. *Joseph Hall: A Study in Satire and Meditation.* Oxford: Clarendon Press. xiv, 413p.

Notes the friendship between Donne and Hall and compares and contrasts the ideas and style of their works. Observes similarities, for instance, between Donne's *Anniversaries* and Hall's *The Arte of Divine Meditation* and between the sermons of the two preachers, noting, in particular, the influence of St. Augustine on both. Compares also their views on homiletics and notes their similar use of emblematic imagery and traditional lore.

304. Miller, Edmund. "John Donne," in *Critical Survey of Poetry: English Language Series,* ed. Frank N. Magill, 2: 821–38. Englewood Cliffs, N.J.: Salem Press.

Surveys Donne's life and works, both poetry and prose, as well as some of the major shifts in his critical reputation since the seventeenth century, concluding that "Donne's stature as a major figure is now assured" (824). Briefly comments on the *Satyres,* espe-

cially *Sat3,* the *Elegies,* especially *ElAut* and *ElBed;* the *Songs and Sonets,* especially *Canon, Flea, Ecst, ValMourn, Twick,* and *Noct;* the verse epistles; the epithalamia; the *Anniversaries; Metem;* and the *Divine Poems,* especially *HSBatter, HSMin, HSShow, Corona, Christ, Goodf;* and the Latin poems in *Devotions.* Lists major publications other than poetry and gives a highly selected bibliography.

305. Milward, Peter. "Chusei to Seibo" [Medieval Age and the Virgin Mary], in *Eikoku Renaissance Bungaku no Joseizo* [The English Renaissance Idea of Woman], ed. Peter Milward and Shonosuke Ishii, 3–23. Tokyo: Aratake.

Considers the Christian view of woman in which the Virgin Mary is regarded as the ideal woman. Demonstrates that in Elizabethan poetry the religious idea of woman is secularly expressed in the works of Donne, Spenser, and Shakespeare.

306. Nathanson, Leonard. "Sir Thomas Browne and the Ethics of Knowledge," in *Approaches to Sir Thomas Browne: The Ann Arbor Tercentenary Lectures and Essays,* ed. C. A. Patrides, 12–18. Columbia: University of Missouri Press.

Comments on Donne's ethic of knowledge and discusses his skepticism about *scientia* (the systematic understanding of the nature of things), which "arises from his conviction that *scientia* is not really relevant to man as man, that it is not a worthy human concern with value of its own." Notes that Donne condemns "promiscuous curiosity" because he thought it was "a misplacement of intellectual energy" (15). Points out that Donne in *SecAn,* as well as Thomas Browne in *Religio Medici* and Milton in *Paradise Lost,* is "painfully conscious that what man wants to know often bears little proportion to what he is capable of knowing and even less to what, in relation to life's main issues, he really needs to know" (16). Notes that in Donne's sermons the issue of knowledge takes on "an even more specifically Christian emphasis" (17), stressing the superiority of *sapientia* (the wisdom that relates man to God).

307. Newton, Richard C. "Jonson and the (Re-) Invention of the Book," in *Classic and Cavalier: Essays on Jonson and the Sons of Ben,* ed. Claude J. Summers and Ted-Larry Pebworth, 31–55. Pittsburgh, Pa.: University of Pittsburgh Press.

Suggests that the intent of the collector of Donne's poems first published in 1633 was to assure Donne a place in "the canon of English vernacular literature." Points out that Donne's poems, unlike Jonson's, do not form a unified book but are rather a collection of miscellaneous poems. Notes that "after some early interest in writing critically related poems, he seems to have adopted an essentially non-bookish attitude toward his poetry." Says that Donne showed "an indifference to the preservation of the text" and that, "[f]or subsequent poets, Donne remains a model of indifference to the responsibility of being a 'classic'" (47).

308. Okerlund, Arlene N. "The Rhetoric of Love: Voice in the *Amoretti* and the *Songs and Sonets.*" *QJS* 68: 37–46.

Contrasts the voice of the speaker in the *Songs and Sonets* with that of Spenser's speaker in the *Amoretti* to show that "the quite different voices reflect equally different perceptions of the phenomenon of love." Claims that Spenser's rhetoric, in an attempt "to rise above the commonality of normal speech and experience," serves to exacerbate "the distance between man and woman, speaker and audience," whereas Donne's "iconoclastic and conversational voice" describes "a new vision of love, one that nurtured physical, emotional, and intellectual unity." Concludes that modern readers respond more favorably to Donne than to Spenser because Donne "spoke with a rhetoric better suited to the substance and reality of love" (46).

309. Parker, Derek. "Erotic Poetry in English," in *The Sexual Dimension in Literature,* ed. Alan Bold, 183–201. London: Vision Press. Printed in Totowa, N.J.: Barnes and Noble, 1983.

Maintains that, on the whole, the success rate of erotic poems—that is, explicitly sexual poems as opposed to "love" poems—is "much lower than with poems of similar ambition on any other theme," and believes that the truly "good serious poem about sex is rare indeed." Argues that a good "sex" poet must have "a capacity for thought" that is "matched by a capacity for conveying a sturdy sexual drive," such as Donne exhibits in *ElBed.* Suggests that "[t]he constant juggling of the metaphysical with the carnal was obviously a titillating pleasure for Donne, and is no less so for the reader" (200). Finds in the poem a "combination of language and thought, wit, nicety of allusion, with the courtly compliment but also with the earthy" that is "irresistible" and suggests that "in four hundred years few other poets, if any, have equalled it" (201).

310. Patrides, C. A. *Premises and Motifs in Renaissance Thought and Literature.* Princeton, N.J.: Princeton University Press. xix, 236p.

In this collection of 12 essays on Renaissance thought (all but Chapter 10 were previously published), Donne is mentioned and quoted frequently. In Chapter 10, "'*A palpable hieroglyphick*': The Fable of Pope Joan" (152–81), comments briefly on Donne's expression of doubt in a 1626 sermon concerning the legend of Pope Joan.

311. Patterson, Annabel. "Misinterpretable Donne: The Testimony of the Letters." *JDJ* 1: 39–53.

Rejects Carey's view (1981) (entry 162) of Donne's career as "dominated first to last by a devouring ego and a prevailing sense of expediency," and argues that an examination of Donne's "personal letters, as text as well as context" (40), reveals more fully "the political pressures and inhibitions" Donne faced throughout his career and shows also that "his personal correspondence offered some release" (41). Identifies Cicero, especially in the *Letters to Atticus,* as Donne's primary model as a letter writer, but notes that Donne's letters "show rather less egocentricity than Cicero's, less introspection than one would suppose from the most frequently quoted exhibits" (42). Points out that Donne's letters contain "a curious mixture of candor and circumspection, an equivocal stance frequently expressed as ambivalence, often accompanied by the fear of being misunderstood" (42–43). Examines in particular several of Donne's personal letters to his patron Sir Robert Carr over a sermon he preached in 1627 that had upset King Charles and Archbishop Laud, to illustrate that even in his old age Donne did not sell out "in the crudely ambitious way suggested by Carey" (51). Concludes that a familiarity with the letters would have saved Carey from the contempt he expresses about Donne's political career.

312. Paulissen, May Nelson. *The Love Sonnets of Lady Mary Wroth: A Critical Introduction.* Elizabethan and Renaissance Studies 104, gen. ed. James Hogg. Salzburg: Institut für Anglistik und Amerikanistik, Universität Salzburg. ix, 222p.

Discusses similarities between Donne's poems and those of Lady Mary Wroth, noting in particular that, like Donne, her poems "show conversational, dramatic, and analytic qualities"; "display the satisfaction gained by the writer in accomplishing an intellec-

tual feat"; and often "are built upon an extended and sometimes unlikely conceit" (150). Points out that Donne and his coterie (including Lady Mary Wroth) frequently employed conventional models (Petrarchan and classical) of the time, citing in particular the use of allusions to Cupid in *LovUsury, LovExch,* and *Mess* and to fortune and stars in *ConfL.* Notes that they also often wrote on conventional topics—on absence, on dark ladies, on jealousy, on the lover's own image, and on death caused by the cruel lover. Briefly discusses imitations of Anacreon's "The Dream" by Donne, Samuel Daniel, Jonson, Shakespeare, and Lady Mary Wroth to show that, although basing their poems on a common model, each poet creates his own distinctive poem that illustrates his "own propensities for words and style" (53), pointing out that in *Dream* Donne's "talent for logic appears in his rhetorical handling of the Anacreontic model" (54).

313. Pinka, Patricia Garland. *This Dialogue of One: "The Songs and Sonnets" of John Donne.* University, Ala.: University of Alabama Press. xii, 193p.

Presents "a synthetic study" of the *Songs and Sonets* "through the personae of the poems" in order "to reveal not only each speaker's ideas about love but also his character, particularly as that character is disclosed in action—the limits of his reasoning, his parrying with his listener for advantage in an argument, his fears, his escapes into self-delusion or fiction, his penchant for impressing his listener, his involvement with his circumstances, and his ability to transcend those circumstances in order to commemorate what he truly loves" (ix). Suggests that such an approach "not only removes the autobiographical element from the poems but also defines one aspect of the dramatic mode in

Donne's poetry: the illusion of speech from one character to another, as if we were watching a play." Maintains that Donne "achieves the illusion of individuality in his personae through his deft manipulation of the relationship among the poet, the speaker, the listener, and the reader—that is, through his interweaving of the dramatic, lyric, and narrative modes within the poem" (x). Calls the *Songs and Sonets* "an unstructured colloquium on earthly love" (xi). Chapter 1, "Coming to Terms" (1–26), discusses the complex blending of the lyric and the dramatic modes in the *Songs and Sonets* by which Donne creates a "rhetorical triangle among the speaker, listener, and reader" (4), and comments on how such a blending of modes "involves time and space—the here and now" (7) that characterizes many of the poems. Discusses the seven major types of highly individualized personae Donne creates from an array of stock figures in the *Songs and Sonets* as well as several that do not fit any of the categories. Discusses also the complexity of tone in the poems, especially Donne's techniques in creating the comic tone in many of them. Concludes that "the seeming complexity" of the personae in the poems arises mostly "from Donne's modification of the lyric," noting that "by imposing a dramatic cast on it, Donne virtually asks the reader to treat the poem both as a lyric and as a dramatic speech" and "to establish with the persona the relationship of the audience to the play and of the reader to a lyric" (26). Chapter 2, "The Petrarchists" (27–49), discusses three personae found in the *Songs and Sonets*—the Parodists, who "mock the hyperbolic language" of Petrarchism; the Witty Lovers, who "find Petrarchan language appropriately rich and in an unexpected way literally accurate for expressing their complex feelings"; and the Cavalier Petrarchists, who "combine aspects of the other two characters" by mocking Petrarch's language but yet acknowledging "his sentiments and his constancy" (27). Chapter 3, "The Extremists" (50–75), discusses the Hedonists, who view love as the satisfaction of sexual appetite, "divorced from any ethical context"; the Platonic Lovers, who exclude sexual union altogether; and one Negative Lover, who totally rejects all love—all of whom "maintain a greater distance between themselves and their listeners than do the speakers in the other *Songs and Sonnets*" (50). Chapter 4, "The Dreaming Cynics" (76–104), discusses those speakers who "retaliate for women's cruelty to them by insulting, humiliating, and even terrifying their ladies," calling these "paradoxical poems of revenge" (76). Chapter 5, "Mutual Lovers" (105–57), discusses the poems that "celebrate the joys of fulfilled love" (105) between the speaker and the lady. The "Conclusion" (158–68) discusses several speakers who do not fit neatly into the seven types mentioned above and points out that the personae in the *Songs and Sonets* "are lovers of almost every stripe save the homosexual and the narcissist" and, in fact, some "only pretend to be lovers" (158). Suggests that "several essential aspects of love" become apparent in the *Songs and Sonets:* (1) "love on earth is tied to physical consummation," (2) love is often "self-deception," and (3) "no love satisfies completely" (164–65). Concludes with notes (169–83), bibliography (184–89), and an index (190–93). Reviews: Robert W. Halli in *SoAR* 49 (1984): 119–23. A. B. Chambers in *JDJ* 4 (1985): 109–20.

314. Pritchard, E. F. "Donne's 'Aire and Angels.'" *Expl* 41, no. 1:16–20.

Says that "the major critical dilemma" in *Air* is the uses of irony and argues that, in the poem, Donne "uses poetic tradition to support his ideas" and even "the very *sounds* of words to persuade the reader." Finds "a web of artifice" around such words as "haire," "aire," and "Angells" (ll. 19–24) that renders "the final irony" (ll. 26–28) "a *necessary* part of the whole." Argues that irony begins in the second stanza, in which Donne "comically" turns the "Neo-Platonists' ladder upside down" by fixing "his love in the mistress' body" only to find the "union dissolving as soon as achieved" (17). Believes that Donne needed to create a physical existence for his mistress but that her hair is a symbol that had spiritual and Petrarchan significance, so in order to transform it into something physical, Donne substituted "air" for "hair" and does so through the similarity of sounds. Suggests that Donne then needed to turn "air" into something physical, which he did through the similarity of its sound with "inhere" (or "in-hair") and "spheare." Maintains that, despite this transformation, the union ultimately dissolves as soon as "philosophical awareness" occurs in l. 25, the dissolution occurring obviously because it is unreasonable to try to use "air" as a "more suitable symbol for the mistress' physical nature than her hair" and because "spheres" do not really exist other than as lines on a map. Concludes that Donne has rhetorically attempted to make a transformation that is unreasonable and that he exposes the unreasonable nature of this transformation in order to show that neither reason nor rhetoric can "encompass the delights and difficulties of love, and the inevitability of parting after union" (19).

315. Proffitt, Edward. "Allusion in Adrienne Rich's 'A Valediction Forbidding Mourning.'" *CP* 15: 21–24.

Comments on the complex function of the allusion to *ValMourn* in Adrienne Rich's poem by the same name. Points out that "in most respects Rich's poem is opposite to Donne's": (1) Donne's poem, "through its conceits and elaborate metaphorical extension," expresses "a supreme confidence in language," whereas in Rich's poem "the very absence of sustained metaphorical extension" becomes "metaphorical, mutely reinforcing the expressed mistrust of language (metaphor) bred in the speaker by her realization of how she has been trapped by and in received definitions," and (2) Donne's emphasis is on continuance of the lovers, whereas, "in contrast (and heightened by the contrast), Rich's is on freedom" and separation (22). Comments also on allusions to the poetry of Marvell and T. S. Eliot and suggests that perhaps the allusions may indicate that Rich still needed "to separate herself from her *male* mentors (Eliot, and through Eliot, the Metaphysicals)," or perhaps "is beginning to do so here" (23). Concludes that Rich's poem is then not only about language and personal need but also about poetry: "by way of allusion, Rich conjures up a tradition that she would shed as she strikes out on her own" (24).

316. Rajan, Tilottama. "'Nothing Sooner Broke': Donne's *Songs and Sonets* As Self-Consuming Artifact." *ELH* 49: 805–28. Reprinted in *John Donne,* ed. Andrew Mousley, New Casebooks, gen. eds. John Peck and Martin Coyle. (Basingstoke: Macmillan; New York: St. Martin's Press, 1999), 45–62.

Sees in the self-consciousness of the *Songs and Sonets* a doubt on Donne's part that language can constitute truth. Points to the use of an unreliable narrator and to gaps between wit and truth, intellect and feeling as ways Donne distances his readers from accepting the propositions of his poems. Claims the *Songs and Sonets* are not only "poems about love in its variety," but also they are "poems about language itself" (806). Discusses the poems of mutual love, such as *ValMourn,* to demonstrate that even in these poems Donne undermines the truth of his assertions, especially by the use of a persona who speaks to an audience outside the dramatic experience and by the presence of other poems in the collection that overturn the assertions of the poems of mutual love. Argues that, while the fiction of *SunRis* is obvious, that of *Canon* is not, but becomes so when read in the context of "the more realistic poems" (812) in the *Songs and Sonets.* Similarly, sees the conditional ending of *GoodM* as undermining the text. Discusses Donne's use of wit and techniques of irony, paradox, and hyperbole as "self-questioning verbal devices" (815). In this light, examines *ValWeep, Air, Lect, LovGrow,* and *LovInf* and concludes that Donne's poems are "pervaded by a feeling that language is a protective fiction . . . and therefore unable to embody within itself any final reality" (819). Discusses *Fun* and *Relic,* using Paul Ricoeur's distinction between sign and symbol, and concludes that Donne's images are, for the most part, merely arbitrary signs, not symbols that embody and incarnate what they represent. Argues that the structure of the *Songs and Sonets* is not that of a typical poetic cycle but rather is "deliberately randomized . . . in order to challenge the conventional assumption of the reading process as a linear movement in which a 'truth' is progressively explored and consolidated as the reader moves forward" (823).

317. Reeves, Troy Dale. "*Sana Me Domine:* Bodily Sickness as a Means of Grace in Donne's Sermons and Devotions." *ABR* 33: 270–75.

Cites passages in *Devotions* and from selected sermons to show that Donne viewed sickness as "an existential means" of approaching and understanding grace. Maintains, therefore, that Donne's preoccupation with health, sickness, and death does not reflect a morbid or neurotic curiosity on his part but rather indicates "a preoccupation with grace" (270). Points out that Donne regarded sickness as having physical symptoms but spiritual causes; thus man "can treat only symptoms" and "grace alone can minister to causes." Says that the similarity between physical and spiritual illness led Donne to consider sickness as "a part of God's purpose, a means of manifesting His grace" (273). Notes that, for Donne, health is "not a positive possession or a good" but rather is "a neutral state, a suspension of the natural progress and inclination of fallen man toward death" (274). Concludes that at the end of *Devotions* Donne realizes that "the sound man is sound only by the power and mercy of God, who through grace . . . halts the relentless movement of man toward death" and thus that sickness shows man "his perpetual dependency upon grace" (275).

318. Richards, Bernard. "Donne's 'Twickenham Garden' and the *Fons Amatoria.*" *RES* 33: 180–83.

Demonstrates that *Twick* "has a tighter organization than previous critics have realized" and that the poem "is permeated with the recurrent image of a fountain" and, in spite of its bitter tone, "is a witty and engagingly allusive work" (180). Maintains that the speaker wishes to be transformed into a fountain in order to remain in the garden and that as an imagined fountain a "kind of retrograde transubstantiation" takes place (181), in which there is "a secular reversal" of Christ's changing water into wine at the wedding feast at Cana. Says that "[t]he fountain Donne imagines filled with his tears will not perform miracles, will not cure, but like the well of Samaria it will speak of truth" (182). Observes, however, that the reader recognizes that, "judged by the higher standard of the garden," the tears are "false," or, at least, "do not represent the highest form of truth even though they proceed from a genuine feeling." Concludes that the poem, "in its thematic movement," is "a parodic simulacrum of a higher form of authentic religion" (183).

319. Riemer, A. P. "The Poetry of Religious Paradox—T. S. Eliot and the Metaphysicals." *SSEng* 8 (1982–83): 80–88.

Maintains that T. S. Eliot's "The Journey of the Magi" can be viewed as his "homage to the metaphysicals, an attempt to replicate within the possibilities available to the modern poet some of those effects which made their poetry so richly imaginative and satisfying" (88). Notes general similarities between Eliot's poem and the poetry of Donne and Herbert. In particular, argues that Eliot may have had in mind *Goodf* and *HSDeath* when he wrote "The Journey of the Magi," and suggests several similarities between Eliot's poem and Donne's religious poetry.

320. Roberts, John R. *John Donne: An Annotated Bibliography of Modern Criticism, 1968–1978.* Columbia: University of Missouri Press. 434p.

A continuation of *John Donne: An Annotated Bibliography of Modern Criticism, 1912–1967* (Columbia: University of Missouri Press, 1973). Lists alphabetically by year and annotates descriptively 1,044 books, essays, monographs, and notes written on Donne from 1968 through 1978. Includes extended discussions of Donne that appear in books not centrally concerned with him, editions containing critical discussion, and

many items in languages other than English. Excludes mere mentions of Donne in books and articles, references in encyclopedias and literary histories, book reviews, selections from Donne's works in anthologies, and doctoral dissertations. Contains three indexes—author, subject, and Donne's works mentioned in the annotations. Reviews: Anon. in *Choice* 20 (1983): 1113; R. N. Ashley in *BHR* 45 (1983): 377–78; Albert W. Fields in *The Round Table of the South Central College English Association* 24 (1983): 5; Dietrich Rolle in *Renaissance Mitteilungen* 7 (1983): 127–28; John T. Shawcross in *AEB* 7 (1983): 156–58; Giuseppe Soldano in *Le Lingue del Mondo* (Florence) 48 (1983): 170–71; F. S. Stych in *RLMC* 36 (1983): 282–83; Ernest W. Sullivan in *LRN* 8 (1983): 83–84; Helen Wilcox in *YWES* 64 (1983): 243; Gale H. Carrithers, Jr., in *Ren&R*, n.s. 8 (1984): 149–51; Albert C. Labriola in *JDJ* 3 (1984): 113–15; Philip R. Rider in *ARBA* 15 (1984): 588; Earl Miner in *MP* 82 (1985): 323–25; Robert Ellrodt in *EA* 39 (1986): 94; Alan Rudrum in *YES* (1987): 272–73.

321. Roberts, John R. "John Donne's Poetry: An Assessment of Modern Criticism." *JDJ* 1: 55–67. Reprinted in *John Donne's Poetry,* ed. Arthur L. Clements, 2nd ed. (New York: Norton, 1992), 351–61.

Presents an overview of critical trends in twentieth century criticism of Donne's poetry. Notes that, although modern critics "tend to agree that Donne is a major poet," they do not agree "on exactly what accounts for his greatness or wherein his greatness lies" (59). Suggests that the most disturbing feature of modern Donne criticism is that it concerns itself primarily with "less than half of Donne's canon," which leads to "a synedochical understanding of and appreciation for Donne's total achievement as a poet" (62). Suggests that the "major split" in Donne criticism is between "the re-coverers," who attempt to place Donne's poetry in an historical context, and "the dis-coverers," who try "to find new things about the workings of a poet's mind and art by applying modern terms and techniques that would perhaps have been completely alien to the poet's own thinking" (62–63). Says Donne's studies have become "a self-perpetuating industry" (66), and urges critics to devote themselves to making Donne's poetry "more, not less accessible to an even wider reading audience than he enjoys at the present time" (67).

322. **Rollin, Roger B.** "The Anxiety of Identification: Jonson and the Rival Poets," in *Classic and Cavalier: Essays on Jonson and the Sons of Ben,* ed. Claude J. Summers and Ted-Larry Pebworth, 139–54. Pittsburgh, Pa.: University of Pittsburgh Press.

Discusses Jonson's dialectical relationship with Donne, noting that "[o]ne of the mind's strategies for coping with relationships can be verbal aggression—direct or indirect, conscious or unconscious; for example, fantasizing Donne hanged, and worse, forgotten; portraying Donne as a burnt-out blasphemer and heretic; ranking Donne as 'the first poet in the World'—'in some things,' an evaluation that may be read as mere hyperbole, faint damnation, or balanced criticism" (140). Analyzes *Epigrammes* 96, "To John Donne," *Epigrammes* 23, and several passages in Drummond's *Conversations* to show how Jonson's use of various strategies of the mind, such as displacement (140) and sublimation of aggressive instincts, as well as his use of puzzling syntax and semantics, reflects Jonson's ambivalent attitude toward Donne as a rival poet.

323. **Rudnytsky, Peter L.** "'The Sight of God': Donne's Poetics of Transcendence." *TSLL* 24: 185–207. Revised and translated into French by Christine Jordis as "La vue de Dieu," in *John Donne,* ed. Jean-Marie Benoist, Les Dossiers H, gen. eds. Jacqueline de Roux and François Denoël. (Herissey: L'Age d'Homme, 1983), 181–96.

Examines the effect of the new philosophy on Donne's metaphors, maintaining that "[i]n the face of the breakdown of 'correspondence' between heaven and earth, Donne had to meet the task of reinvesting his poetic art with the stamp of essential metaphor" (187). Suggests that he had two ways in which to do this: by wit that triumphs over logic, as in *Flea,* or by love that becomes transcendent, as in *Val-Mourn.* Claims that Dr. Johnson's rather than T. S. Eliot's criticism of Donne's metaphors is correct, but maintains that Donne would not have seen his practice as a failure but rather as a reflection of the loss of correspondence between heaven and earth brought about by the new science. Sees *Flea* as a poem "concerned with the status of metaphor" (188), which answers the problem by the use of wit because "there is no genuine conceptual relation between the component elements of Donne's analogy" (188–89). Discusses the metaphors in *Val-Mourn,* especially the compass, suggesting that it must be viewed as a symbol of the transcendence of spiritual love over physical love in its reference to the perfection of the circle. Claims that critics see the disproportion between emotion and fact in the *Anniversaries* as a "failure of conjunction" in the metaphors, thereby failing to see the poems as "fundamentally concerned with the status of metaphor" (196), exposing an argument between the validity of earthly versus heavenly knowledge. Concludes that in *ValMourn* and in *SecAn* Donne "relies on a hermetic strategy . . . to overcome the 'failure of conjunction' in his metaphors caused by the loss of 'correspondence' between earth and heaven" (204).

324. **Saito, Takeshi.** "Eishi ni okeru Seishi no Mondai" [Some Considerations on Life and Death in English Poetry], in *Seisho to Eibungaku no Megutte: Kanda Takeo Hakushi Sanju Kinen Ronbunshu* [Essays on the English Bible and English Literature in Honor of Dr. Takeo Kanda], ed. Toshiki Yamamoto, 1: 1–15. Tokyo: Pedilavium.

Briefly comments on *HSDeath,* saying that Donne denounces death.

325. **Sellin, Paul.** "John Donne and the Huygens Family, 1619–1621: Some Implications for Dutch Literature." *DQR* 12 (1982–83): 192–204.

Argues that Donne's presence in The Netherlands as a member of an English mission during the last half of December of 1619 and the first week of January in 1620 suggests that Constantijn Huygens "probably met Donne not in London in 1622," as usually assumed, "but in The Hague at the end of 1619, that he first heard Donne preach not in English at St. Paul's but in French at the Hofkapel in 1619, and that such acquaintance was renewed at London in early 1621, not in late." Points out that the arguments of those who deny the influence of Donne on Huygens's poetry are based on the biographical "fact" that Huygens did not meet Donne before 1622. Challenges those who hold that Huygens's contact with Donne was primarily through the "private offices of belle-lettristic Londoners" (194) by pointing out that the "tight network of specific religious and political relationships [between the two poets] harkened back to at least as early as Donne's visit to The Hague in 1619" (204).

326. **Shapiro, I. A.** [Donne and Walton Forgeries: A Correspondence]. *Library* 4, no. 3: 331–35.

Reply to Jonquil Bevan's "Donne and Walton Forgeries: A Correspondence" (entry 251). Continues his argument that the signatures of Walton and Donne in the copy of St. Gregory's *De Cura Pastorali* (1629) in the William Salt Library are forgeries. Lists twelve datable holographs in which "undoubtedly authentic" (332) Walton signatures can be found, as well as extant copies of Walton's publications "with presentation inscriptions in his handwriting" (333). Suggests reasons to think that the copy of Richard Montagu's *Gagge for the New Gospel* (1624) with an inscription that states that Donne gave the volume to Walton is also a forgery. For a reply, see Jonquil Bevan (entry 252).

327. **Shapiro, I. A.** [Donne and Walton Forgeries: A Correspondence.] *Library* 4, no. 3: 338–39.

Reply to Jonquil Bevan's reply (entry 252) to Shapiro's reply (entry 218) to her original note (entry 251). Defends his original position and answers Bevan's objections. No specific comments on Donne.

328. **Shawcross, John T.** "A Note on the Eighteenth Century's Knowledge of John Donne." *KRev* 3: 68–73.

Challenges the assumption that eighteenth century readers were unfamiliar with Donne's poetry by noting that, in addition to Tonson's 1719 edition of the poems, the very popular fourth and fifth editions of John Dryden's *Miscellany Poems* included fifteen of Donne's poems. Maintains that this anthology "helped keep at least these fifteen poems before the more popular audience" (69). Cites several eighteenth century Donnean references, discussions, and imitations not picked up in A. J. Smith's *John Donne: The*

Critical Heritage (London: Routledge and Kegan Paul, 1975) and corrects or presents additional information on several citations found in Smith's volume. Concludes that Smith's work and his additions make clear that Donne "was not so totally unfamiliar in the eighteenth century as one has been led to believe by commentary of the nineteenth and twentieth centuries" and "was better known, more reprinted, and more influential than George Herbert, Henry Vaughan, Richard Crashaw, the poetic Ben Jonson, and most of his Sons" (72).

329. **Shawcross, John T.** "Vaughan's 'Amoret' Poems: A Jonsonian Sequence," in *Classic and Cavalier: Essays on Jonson and the Sons of Ben,* ed. Claude J. Summers and Ted-Larry Pebworth, 193–214. Pittsburgh, Pa.: University of Pittsburgh Press.

Maintains that in the "Amoret" poems, which he regards as a Jonsonian sequence similar to Jonson's "A Celebration of Charis in ten Lyrick Peeces," Vaughan uses Donnean motifs, language, and metaphors "only as [a] foil" and that "the Jonsonian sequence is the key to Vaughan's form and content" (211).

330. **Shelston, Alan.** "A Note on 'The Canonization.'" *CritQ* 24, no. 2: 81–83.
Suggests alternative readings for ll. 16–17 of *Canon* ("Lawyers finde out still / Litigious men, which quarrels move") that result from syntactical ambiguities. Points out, in particular, the possible wordplay on "still" and "move." Concludes that the ambiguities in these lines contrast with the emphatic assurance of l. 18 ("Though she and I do love") and that all three lines "act out the theme to which they give verbal expression and in so doing they provide a conclusion to the stanza which is persuasive in terms of both form and meaning" (83).

331. **Smith, A. J.** "No Man Is a Contradiction." *JDJ* 1: 21–38.
Discusses Donne's concept of the liaison between the body and soul that pervades both his prose and poetry and that sets him apart from both idealists and ascetics of his time. Points out, through a discussion of *Biathanatos* and *Pseudo-Martyr,* that some of Donne's "most characteristic thinking about differences of doctrine, and the nature of a Church, grows out of a particular conception of the working of the human constitution" (22). Argues also that Donne's concept of love in *Ecst* "needed no drastic renunciation" when he became a priest because, as seen especially in his Easter sermons, he continued to affirm "the mutual dependence of soul and body as it is assured by Christ's taking flesh for pure love, and by the indivisibility of the human and divine elements in Christ's own manhood" (30). Argues that Donne "justifies human worth, and the dignity of the body itself, in the coupling of body and soul which makes us man, and the mingling of physical and spiritual elements in our make-up" (32). Points out that, for Donne, "Christ himself offers final confirmation that our nature is essentially mixed, and needs the effective union of soul and body," since Christ "shared our manhood just so long as he united body and spirit, human element and divine" (31). Further maintains that, for Donne, "Christ's mixed nature effectively seals the marriage of our flesh to divine being" and, because of Christ, "Eternal being perpetually interpenetrates the world of sense, as in a union of love, countervailing change and death" (33). Says that Donne believed that the final "dignifying of our flesh" in "a glorious resurrection of the body itself" will repair "the divorce between the body and soul made by sin" (34).

332. Somura, Mitsutoshi. "Donne Koki no Shukukonka: Sono Dentokanshu tono Kanren" [Donne's *Epithalamion* in His Later Years in Relation to the Epithalamic Tradition and Convention], in *Eigaku-ronso: Ishii Shonosuke Sensei Koki Kinen Ronbunshu* [Essays in Honor of Professor Shonosuke Ishii's Seventieth Birthday], ed. Osamu Fukushima et al., 133–45. Tokyo: Kinseido.

Shows through a comparison with Renaissance epithalamic conventions and Spenser's *Epithalamion* how Donne employs the conventions and adapts them to his individualistic expression in writing his own epithalamia.

333. Stull, William L. "Sacred Sonnets in Three Styles." *SP* 79: 78–99.

Discusses the rhetorical tradition informing religious sonnets from Henry Constable to Milton. Points out that, unlike the Petrarchan love poets of the Renaissance, who "confined themselves to the middle style aimed at pleasing a courtly mistress with flowered praise," writers of religious sonnets of the period "embraced a full rhetoric, one that encompassed all three *officia* and their corresponding styles" (78). Comments on the "passionate plainness" in the sonnets of Donne, Greville, and Jonson; the "flowered middle style" in the sonnets of William Drummond, a style that poets such as Constable and Herbert deliberately converted to the service of God; and the grand, Italianate style of Milton's sonnets. Comments on *HSMade* as an example of "the new plain style of sonneteering at its finest" (88) and calls Donne's *Holy Sonnets* examples of "the plain style of religious sonneteering at its apogee" (90). Compares and contrasts Donne's plain style with that of Greville, claiming that Greville in his later poems is "a bridge between the native plain style and the metaphysical" (91).

334. Stull, William L. " 'Why Are Not *Sonnets* Made of Thee?': A New Context for the 'Holy Sonnets' of Donne, Herbert, and Milton. *MP* 80: 129–35. Revised and expanded as "Sonnets Courtly and Christian," *HSL* 15–16 (1983–84): 1–15.

Traces the development of the English religious sonnet during the Renaissance, noting that it flourished "even as the Petrarchan vogue waxed and waned" (129). Points out that, by the beginning of the seventeenth century, sacred sonnets "were legion in England, as they had long been in Italy and France." Calls Donne, Herbert, and Milton "great Christian sonneteers" and maintains that they, "while far excelling their Tudor predecessors, write in the same literary tradition as Constable, Barnes, Lok, and Alabaster—as well as a host of minor religious sonneteers, such as Nicholas Breton, John Davies of Hereford, and William Drummond of Hawthornden" (135). Says Donne's *Holy Sonnets* are "*un*original in everything but genius" (134).

335. Sullivan, Alvin. "Donne's Sophistry and Certain Renaissance Books of Logic and Rhetoric." *SEL* 22: 107–20.

Examines various Renaissance texts of logic and rhetoric, such as Abraham Fraunce's *The Lawier's Logike,* Thomas Wilson's *The Arte of Rhetorique,* John Hoskyns's *Directions for Speech and Style,* Angel Day's *The English Secretary,* Thomas Blundeville's *The Arte of Logicke,* Richard Rainolde's *The Foundacions of Rhetorike,* and Ralph Lever's *The Arte of Reason* to show that Donne's wit "stems from the methods advocated by such texts and from the examples they contained" (107–8). Discusses the various methods of argument Donne uses, sometimes seriously, sometimes fallaciously, in his poetry, such as "argument by 'similitude' or comparison" (108); "reasoning from the adjunct to the subject" or "from subject to adjunct" (109); "reasoning by analogy" (112); argumentation by paradox and by the use of various forms of grammatical or rhetorical fallacies; and other forms of sophistical reasoning. Comments specifically on Donne's witty uses and, equally important, witty misuses of Renaissance principles of rhetoric and logic in *Jet, ElProg, Prim, Commun, ElBrac, ValMourn, LovGrow, ElBed, Fare, ElChange, Flea,* and *ConfL.* Maintains that Donne's wit clearly "belongs to a tradition of hyperbolic comparisons that permeated not merely a metaphysical school of poetry, but indeed all common methods of argumentation" (111) in his day and believes, therefore, that to estimate accurately Donne's originality one "must measure it against the practice of logic and rhetoric in the Renaissance" (119).

336. Sullivan, Ernest W., II. "Bibliographical Evidence in Presentation Copies: An Example from Donne." *AEB* 6: 17–22.

Presents a history of the bibliographical scholarship of first edition actual or intended presentation copies of *Biathanatos* to show that the various copies "having fine paper and/or manuscript corrections and/or inscriptions or letters of presentation" are related, and that John Donne the younger "intended to present all such copies." Furthermore, shows that such a history reveals "the extent to which bibliographers have overlooked the sort of evidence associated with presentation copies," and suggests "the significance of such evidence" (17) for solving "a multitude of bibliographical problems such as contemporary interpretation of the text, reliability of various states of the text, dating, printing and publication history, and the genesis and transmission of various states of the text" (21–22).

337. Sullivan, Ernest W., II. "A Donne Saying." *Library,* 6th ser., 4, no. 3: 314–16.

Points out a saying, probably by Donne and recorded by Thomas Martin, "the earliest certainly identifiable owner" of Richard Gough's copy of the first issue of the first edition of *Biathanatos* (1647), now in the Bodleian Library (Gough Norfolk 26), that reads: "A saying of Donne / I Repent me of my whole Life / save that part which I haue / spent in communion with God / & doing good" (314).

338. Tebeaux, Elizabeth. "John Donne and the Problem of Religious Authority: 'Wranglings that tend not to Edification.'" *SCB* 42: 137–43.

Surveys Donne's sermons to determine his position on religious authority and concludes that the sermons reveal that (1) Donne was "clearly aware of the conflicts among Puritans, Catholics, and reform advocates" (137); (2) that Donne's concept of reason as the source of authority did not change over the years; (3) that Donne tried to avoid contention "not only on the grounds of political wisdom but also because of his belief that many issues under scrutiny in the authority debate could never be resolved"; and (4) that, since Donne is inconsistent, "one must trace his views carefully to avoid pressing him into some theological mold that the sermons, examined in their entirety, will not support." Maintains that ultimately, for Donne, "the Church and Scripture, as interpreted by the Church, are the final, essential authority in spiritual matters because they check the weaknesses of reason." Claims that Donne's most significant diversion from Hooker on religious authority "lies in the emphasis on reason," noting that Donne "does not articulate Hooker's most basic premise, that Scripture and nature furnish all that is necessary for salvation," but rather he emphasizes that "Scripture, interpreted by the Church, supplies what is necessary for salvation." Says that Donne holds that "reason is imperfect until it is regenerated by the Holy Spirit working within the Church" (141).

339. Thomason, T. Katharine. "Plotinian Metaphysics and Donne's 'Extasie.'" *SEL* 22: 91–105.

Shows how "Neoplatonic ideas and wit interanimate" in *Ecst,* and demonstrates the closeness of the poem "in letter and spirit" to the *Enneads* of Plotinus. Also examines Donne's subtle uses of an imagined observer in the poem and comments on "the singular relationship which exists between the poem and its readers." Points out that "the initial stroke of wit" in the poem results from Donne's "turning the tables on the conventional Platonists," or rather, "it depends on Donne's inversion of their ladder of love" (93): Donne begins by presenting "the compatibility of the lovers at the level of the soul," and then, unlike the conventional Platonic lover, his speaker argues "for descent on the ladder rather than ascent." Shows thereby how much of the poem's wit "turns on the common misapprehension of the value of the natural or material world in the Plotinian scheme" (94). Argues that the "governing ideas" in *Ecst* are Plotinian concepts "of eternal order, of the essential goodness of the order itself, and of man's potential goodness" (97). Maintains that the descent of the lovers "in no way obviates the fact that the love exists simultaneously on a higher spiritual level" and that "one does not cancel the other"; in fact, "[t]he higher soul encompasses and fills the lower soul." Claims that "wit is produced by the fact that only the initiated would understand that descent after this manner is not culpable" (101). Says that "the main

opposition in the poem" is "the conventional versus the 'purer' understanding of love's mysteries" (105).

340. Thota, Anand Rao. *Emily Dickinson: The Metaphysical Tradition.* New Delhi: Arnold-Heinemann. 197, 4p.

Argues that the poetry of Emily Dickinson exhibits a profound similarity in both themes and technique to the poetry of the seventeenth century British poets. Views Dickinson as "intellectually less aggressive than Donne, as intricate in technique as Herbert, and as sensuously articulate as Marvell" (139). Maintains that Dickinson "became a major metaphysical poet of the nineteenth century, without even being very conscious of the leading metaphysical poets of the seventeenth century," but that she is "a crucial aesthetic link between the seventeenth-century metaphysicals and the twentieth-century neo-metaphysicals" (161). Mentions Donne throughout and finds numerous parallels to Donne's poetry and prose in Dickinson's poetry. Compares and/or contrasts the attitudes, themes, and techniques of the two poets and finds also many similarities between the lives of the two poets, maintaining that "both of them were extremely tortured souls" (65). Endorsing T. S. Eliot's concept, claims that both poets reveal a unified sensibility.

341. Walker, Julia M. "John Donne's 'The Extasie' as an Alchemical Process." *ELN* 20: 1–8.

Presents a reading of *Ecst* to show that each of the stanzas, either directly or indirectly, "contains some reference to the alchemical process" and "are ordered so as to constitute a complete alchemical process which yields both the physical goal of alchemy—the Philosopher's Stone—and the spiritual goal—ecstatic purification and union of souls." Maintains that "the elements, or principles of this alchemical process are the personae of the poem: the man, the woman, and the observer," with the poet himself being the alchemist (1). Concludes that seeing *Ecst* "as a process of alchemical unity and the personae as alchemical elements" adds "another dimension of meaning to the poem which, by virtue of its images of Platonic, poetic, and physical unity, has already been recognized as one of the world's greatest addresses on the union of man and woman" (8).

342. **Watanabe, Seiji.** "Eishi San-saku to Renkinjutsu Ikko" [Three English Poetical Works on Alchemy: A Study]. *Tenri Daigaku Gakuho* [Bulletin of Tenri University] 136: 52–70.

Discusses the literary uses of alchemy from Chaucer's "The Canon's Yeoman's Tale" to Jonson's *The Alchemist* and Donne's *LovAlch*. Points out that in Donne's poem, alchemy is presented with a satrical intent and is closely associated with deceit and swindling.

343. **Wentersdorf, Karl P.** "Symbol and Meaning in Donne's *Metempsychosis* or *The Progresse of the Soule.*" *SEL* 22: 69–90.

Argues that Donne's rationale for the symbolism in *Metem* can be found in the teachings of Gnostic and Hermetic philosophers, who "assumed that the forces of sexuality were universally present in all segments of the chain of being, from inanimate creation to mankind." Suggests that the experience that the soul undergoes in the course of the poem constitutes a journey "through all levels of animate creation, in a more or less hierarchical order, from the sphere of plants to that of the first humans, and then (as Donne originally planned) from primal humanity to modern man." Argues that "most and probably all of the emblematic stations in which the 'soule' temporarily resides have erotic connotations," and thus "the world in which it makes its journey is seen—for the purposes of the poem—from the standpoint of the Gnostic and Hermetic philosophies" (71). Discusses how four emblems in the poem—the mandrake, sparrow, wolf, and ape—"were used by Donne as conventional symbols of lust" (72) and explains that, in addition to the sparrow, three more emblems appear that are associated with Venus, "the goddess of sexual attraction and fulfillment" (75)—the apple, fishes, and the swan. Says that "[t]he remaining stations of the soul—sea-pie, whale, mouse, dog, and woman—are more complex in their relationship to the theme of sexual sensuality" (78). Insists, however, that, despite their diversity, all of these stations of the soul have "one element in common: their use to symbolize various aspects of human sexuality" (84). Maintains that "the theory of metempsychosis is a device for presenting the theme—a theme that would have become clearer as the poem continued—that universal sexuality is the prime motivating force in the history of mankind" (85). Suggests that, although Donne set out to show in *Metem* that the whole of history "had continually been dominated by erotic forces" (89), perhaps his growing love for Ann More taught him that "the forces of eros, while universal and inescapable, are not necessarily debasing to humanity" (90); thus he left the poem uncompleted.

344. **Wiggins, Peter De Sa.** "'Aire and Angels': Incarnations of Love." *ELR* 12: 87–101.

Restates his earlier reading of *Air* (entry 231), stressing the poem's dramatic quality and commenting on the structural symmetry of this reversed "double sonnet": "The first sestet poses the difficulty love must contend with as a passion in search of an object," and the first octave "solves the difficulty by having love discover its object in the person of the woman to whom the whole poem is addressed." Maintains that the second sestet then "poses a new problem involving love that has become aware of its object" and the second octave "resolves that problem with a request of the woman that she manifest her love for the speaker of the poem, just as angels manifest themselves by assuming bodies of air" (88). Calls *Air* one of "the most optimistic of Donne's love poems," and maintains that the speaker "engages our sympathy, because his cause is as much our own as if he were defending, not just himself, but all humanity against a charge of being tainted" (99).

345. Wilders, John. "Rochester and the Metaphysicals," in *Spirit of Wit: Reconsiderations of Rochester,* ed. Jeremy Treglown, 42–57. Oxford: Basil Blackwell.
Defends Rochester against the charges of "narrowness and simplicity," and argues that, "although Rochester's tone of voice—his grace, lucidity, and harmoniousness—is that of a court poet of the Restoration, his mind is as much aware of its complexity as were those of his predecessors" (43). Maintains that Donne expresses in his poems his awareness of his own uncertainties and doubts primarily either by using metaphors rather than similes to form paradoxes, or by creating "the impression of simultaneously believing and disbelieving his assertions by expressing an obviously simplified point of view which does not represent the whole, complex truth as he himself is capable of seeing it" (46). Maintains that such dichotomies often are expressed by means of dialogue, and notes that "many of Donne's poems read like one side of a dialogue" (47). Finds a similarity between Rochester's "Against Constancy" and Donne's *Ind*

and his "Defence of Women" in the *Paradoxes* in that both poets reveal "a divided mind unable wholly to embrace the kind of life it seems to defend" (54).

346. Williams, J. David. "Renaissance Essayists" and "Metaphysical Poets," in *Questions That Count: British Literature to 1750,* 45–47, 53, 59–63. Washington, D.C.: University Press of America. x, 87p.
Presents a list of 6 general questions about metaphysical poetry that students might ask themselves (53), followed by 32 questions on Donne's secular and religious poetry (59–63). Asks also 18 questions on Meditations XVII and XVIII in *Devotions* (45–47).

347. Wolfe, Ralph Haven, and Edgar F. Daniels. "Donne's 'A Hymn to God the Father,' Lines 13–14." *Expl* 40, no. 4: 13–14.
Responds to R. E. Finnegan (*Expl* 39, no. 1 (1980): 38–39; entry 104), who maintains that there is an "obtuse" allusion in *Father* (ll. 13–14) to the three Fates. Points out that, although the figurative use of spinning in order to express the notion of living out a life perhaps had its origin in the story of the Fates, by the seventeenth century it had long since passed into commonplace usage, that the reference to "my last thread" contains no implication of measurement, and that "shore" is not a verb suggesting shearing, as Finnegan postulates, but rather is a noun. Maintains that the expression in these lines "is clearcut and entirely consistent with the tone" of the poem, calling it "perhaps the least conceit-ridden of Donne's poems" (14).

348. Yearwood, Stephenie. "Donne's *Holy Sonnets*: The Theology of Conversion." *TSLL* 24: 208–21.
Discusses Donne's position on "the doctrinal and emotional aspects of conversion" as a critical framework

for the *Holy Sonnets* (208). Uses Gardner's ordering (1952) of the sonnets for convenience and the sermons for help in understanding Donne's views on conversion, which are "the usual Anglican Calvinist blend" (210). Suggests that three doctrines form Donne's understanding of conversion: (1) that God does all, (2) that human action—like confession—is necessary, and (3) that salvation is available to all who confess and to no one who will not. Suggests that, emotionally, the sinner starts in pride, proceeds to confession and despair, but ends in joy and confidence, which is the spiritual progress expressed in the *Holy Sonnets*. Points out that *HSDue* begins with good intentions but with a reliance on self, not God, which leads to despair; *HSBlack* corrects this pride, offering confession as necessary; and that the remaining sonnets follow the pattern mentioned above until *HSPart* when the speaker achieves both understanding and emotional acceptance, which come only by virtue of the corrective intervention of grace in *HSWilt*. Claims that *HSBatter* marks the crisis in the sequence, for fear and despair lead to the speaker's ultimate resignation to God, and *HSPart* shows his complete conversion. Claims the *Holy Sonnets* are instructions that the reader is urged to follow.

349. Yu, Chae-lk. "John Donne's Poetry and Modern Poetry." *JELL-CB* 21: 67–89. In Korean. Listed in MHRA Bibliography for 1984 (#4699). Unavailable.

350. Yuasa, Nobuyuki. "Tamashii no Shuji: John Donne no 'Shokan-shi' no Bungakuteki Imi" [The Rhetoric of the Soul: The Meaning of John Donne's Verse Letters]. *EigoS* 127: 714–17.
Examines in chronological order several of Donne's verse letters written from 1592 to 1609 to show how each letter is marked by its own mode of expression, and suggests that the changes in expression reflect different states of mind, as Donne encountered various events in his life at this time. Suggests that the literary meaning of the verse letters clarifies the process of the rhetoric of his soul and shows Donne's flexibility and development.

351. Zetterberg, Iréne. "John Donne: Motsatsernas mote" [John Donne: The Meeting of Opposites]. *Artes* 8, no. 1 (1982): 3–23.
Presents a biographical sketch of Donne, emphasizing the contrasts and changes in his life. Describes the youthful Jack and the mature John, the poetic and the religious Donne, the conservative and the unconventional thinker. Includes the major events of Donne's life and highlights of his writings. Suggests that the surviving portraits reveal various aspects of Donne's personality.

352. Zunder, William. *The Poetry of John Donne: Literature and the Culture in the Elizabethan and Jacobean Period.* Sussex, Eng.: Harvester Press; Totowa, N.J.: Barnes and Noble.
Presents a critical analysis of Donne's poetry "in itself, its inner structure and development," while at the same time suggesting "the relationship of the poetry to the age in which it was written" (ix). Chapter 1, "The Context: New and Old" (1–7), outlines the general cultural context in which Donne wrote his poems, commenting very generally on the social, political, economic, religious, and literary changes that occurred in England in the sixteenth and early seventeenth centuries. Points out, in particular, the conflict that intensified in the 1590s between "the traditional social values of a hierarchical society" and "the individualism of a generation" that refused to be limited "by traditional constraints" (3). Notes also the intellectual and

moral continuity and discontinuity with the past that continued well into the seventeenth century. Chapter 2, "The *Satires:* Society and Tradition" (9–19), analyzes the structural coherence and satirical targets of societal corruption in each of the *Satyres*. Suggests that in *Sat1* the speaker upholds the traditional, hierarchical values of the society that his inconstant companions violate; in *Sat2* he primarily "responds to the economic and social changes" of sixteenth century England; in *Sat3* Donne explores his positive skepticism toward the religious situation of his time; in *Sat4* he expresses his hope for a reformation of the corruption and affectation of the court; and in *Sat5* he directs his satire against "the maladministration of justice" (18) occasioned by corrupt legal officers and court suitors. Chapter 3, "The Love Poems: The Individual and Tradition" (21–46), attempts to show that Donne's love poems reflect the changing culture in which they were written and at the same time "register in an intimate way the inner life of Donne" (2). Finds similarities in values and techniques between Donne's poems and Shakespeare's plays, and suggests that Donne's views on love became "radical," whereas Shakespeare's "remained traditional" (31). Maintains that in the earlier love poems, change and instability dominate, while in the later love poems Donne expresses a kind of love that far surpasses the traditional view. Points out, however, that even the later poems are charged with anxiety and uncertainty because Donne is aware of the impermanence of all relationships. Suggests that Donne's uncertainty in regard to the traditional view of love led to his "poems of indirection and irony" (39). Discusses in some detail *Canon, Air, ElChange,* and *Noct*. Chapter 4, "The Verse Letters: *Friend-*

ship and Patronage (47–69), maintains that the currents of pessimism, self-deprecation, helplessness, and desire to withdraw from the world that pervade the earlier verse letters, in particular *Storm* and *Calm,* are held in check by Donne's firm belief in and assertions of friendship. Says that the earlier verse epistles are "Elizabethan," while the later ones are "Jacobean" (56), in which there is a separation between honor and love, a devaluation of faith and reason, a continuing social and political pessimism, a sense of personal insignificance, and a distrust of the traditional view of the world. Chapter 5, "The *Anniversaries:* Jacobean Donne" (71–88), says that in *FirAn* there is a pervading pessimism and "a sense of social and political disintegration" (73) but that in *SecAn* Donne turns away from worldly affairs and contemplates "an otherworld, in which the lost values of the old order are ideally imagined" (75). Compares and contrasts Donne, Shakespeare, and Webster, concluding that Donne occupies a midway position between Shakespeare, who affirms the traditional view of the world, and Webster, who has no faith in it. Chapter 6, "The *Divine Poems:* The Religious Resolution" (89–102), sees the religious poems, especially the *Holy Sonnets,* as Donne's "turning to God as a resolution of life's difficulties" (94) and as his rejection of all human relationships. Concludes that Donne's poetry "represents a series of responses to the pressures of his time," pressures that were "partly personal and partly characteristic of his class and generation," and believes that "[f]or the most part, they took place within an acceptance of the traditional view." Holds, however, that Donne accepted this view "with decreasing conviction" and with "an increasing emphasis on the resolving significance of personal experience" (102). Concludes with notes (103–15) and an index (117–21). Reviews: Lachlan Mackinnon in *TLS* (24 June 1983): 681; Heather Dubrow in *RenQ* 37 (1984): 311–13; Raymond-Jean Frontain in *C&L* 34, no. 4 (1985): 70–71; Helen Peters in *RES* 36 (1985): 263–65; Gerald Hammond in *MLR* 82 (1987): 164–65.

1983

353. Abrahamson, R. L. "The Vision of Redemption in Donne's *Devotions upon Emergent Occasions.*" *SMy* 6: 62–69.

Maintains that, for Donne, the world was "not tragic but essentially comic" because he believed that "all suffering can ultimately be redeemed by elevating the soul above temporal affairs and turning it towards God." Finds the most vivid presentation of this kind of redemption in *Devotions,* the whole theme of which is to express "the movement of the soul beyond vicissitude to a resolution with God" (62). Discusses how the Ignatian tradition of formal meditation (using the memory, understanding, and will) "provides the structure for Donne's redemptive progression" (66) in the *Devotions* and how the moral vision of the work, as conventional as its structure, comes from "the medieval tradition of *contemptus mundi.*" Maintains that what is truly original in the *Devotions* is "the passionate drama" or "imaginative vision" that Donne produces, in which the soul resolves its "dilemmas and problems in the light of the will of God" and "makes this resolution with an exuberance and sense of triumph all the more powerful for the contrast to the agony and despair which preceded it" (67).

354. Aizawa, Yoshihisa. "John Donne no 'Shunen Tsuitoshi' Ko (6)" [A Study of John Donne's *Anniversaries* (6)]. *Jinbungakka Ronshu* [Bulletin of the Faculty of Humanities, Ibaraki University] 16: 183–208.

Part 6 of an eight-part series. Examines Donne's motivation and the circumstances surrounding the composition of the *Anniversaries* and surveys the criticism on the two poems from Jonson to Herbert J. C. Grierson.

355. Aizawa, Yoshihisa. "John Donne to Rakuen no Imeiji" [John Donne and his 'Image' of 'Paradise'], in *Eibungaku Shiron* [Essays in English Literature in Honor of the 77th Anniversary of the Birth of Professor Isamu Muraoka], 110–21. Tokyo: Kinseido.

Analyzes how the image of Paradise is used in *Twick, ValName, GoodM, ElNat, ElBed,* and *FirAn.* Points out that Donne's Paradise functions as a kind of "surrogatus mundi" or a refuge of the mind and that he made Paradise into the "hortus conclusus," using a variety of traditional ideas about gardens, such as the garden as the "locus amoenus," the Epicurean garden as the "hortus deliciarum," and the biblical Garden of Eden.

356. Bann, Stephen. "Isaak Walton et John Donne," in *John Donne,* ed. Jean-Marie Benoist, 31–38. Les Dossiers H, gen. eds. Jacqueline de Roux and François Denoël. Herissey: L'Age d'Homme.

Presents a biographical sketch of Walton and discusses his published works, including his biography of Donne. Comments on Walton's acquaintance with Donne and his theory of biography. Suggests why Walton shows little concern with Donne's poetry in his account of Donne's life.

357. Barber, Charles. *Poetry in English: An Introduction.* New York: St. Martin's Press. x, 220p.

Presents a critical reading of *ValMourn* to illustrate major characteristics of Donne's secular lyrics (73–77) and also a briefer critical reading of *Sickness* to show that the religious poems of his later years "bear striking resemblances" to Donne's earlier love poems (179–81). Also comments briefly on Donne's use of "colloquial and strikingly dramatic" (39) language in the opening lines of his poems.

358. Bell, Ilona. "The Role of the Lady in Donne's *Songs and Sonets.*" *SEL* 23: 113–29.

Rejects the accusations of critics who read the *Songs and Sonets* as "an assertion of Donne's ego" more than as "a response to the lady's feelings, more as an expression of ideas he brings to the relationship than perceptions which emerge from it," and offers "a minority perspective" by arguing that in his love poems Donne achieves "an empathetic, imaginative, and varied response to the lady's point of view" (113). Presents "a revisionist reading" of several poems to show "the lady's dynamic, suasive effect upon the speaker's own intense personal moods," insisting that "what Donne *and* his speaker expressed most intensely was not egocentricity or intellectuality but empathy" (115). Argues that "the brilliance of Donne's love poems arises (at least in part) from his unprecedented capacity to elicit and articulate and respond to the woman's point of view" (116). Maintains that even in poems of "lusty frivolity" (117) and cynical wittiness, such as *Ind, SGo,* and *WomCon,* Donne "never becomes a thoroughly convincing rake precisely because he cannot ever completely ignore the woman's feelings." Through a reading of *SunRis* and *GoodM* shows how Donne, once he gives up the role of lusty bachelor, becomes a "fine lover: funny, flexible, attentive, tender, psychologically acute, and uncommonly empathetic" (119). Says that in *ValName* Donne "explains the process" of articulating and integrating the lady's point of view in a lyric poem by subordinating "his poetry to the lady's vision of herself" (124). Reads *Ecst* as a poem that records "a moment of transcendent joy, remembered as an ideal precisely because it was that unique occasion when the speaker and the lady found themselves in total harmony, thinking and wishing for precisely the same thing" (125). Reads *Dream* and *Appar* as examples of "the power and limits of empathy" (126). Concludes that, "[u]nlike his Petrarchan predecessors, when Donne writes of love he writes not of imagined love or exalted beauty but of loving and being loved, at times, of hating and being hated, not of ladies seen and admired from a distance but of a lady who is highly present, loving and criticizing, judging as well as admiring." Calls the *Songs and Sonets* "the first Renaissance poems written for adults, loving and empathetic enough to grant the woman's and the man's point of view equal credence" (129).

359. Benoist, Jean-Marie. "L'écriture de l'abyme," in *John Donne,* ed. Jean-Marie Benoist, 247–59. Les Dossiers H, gen. eds. Jacqueline de Roux and François Denoël. Herissey: L'Age d'Homme.

Presents a detailed postmodern interpretation of *Noct* that emphasizes the intertextuality between the poem and other of Donne's poems. Sees *Noct* as central to an understanding of Donne's poetry because it contains so many fields of reference found in other poems. Says that three centuries before Freud, Donne succeeded in discovering and embedding in his poem the antagonistic relationship between Eros and Thanatos, and points out that he invented a cosmology in the poem that hovers between the Ptolemaic and Copernican views of the universe and that anticipates twentieth century cosmological theories.

360. Benoist, Jean-Marie, ed. *John Donne.* Les Dossiers H, gen. eds. Jacqueline de Roux and François Denoël. Herissey: L'Age d'Homme. 319p.

Collection of previously published and original essays in French, each of which has been entered separately in this bibliography. In the "Prologue" (11–13), the editor says that the purpose of the collection is to make Donne better known among French readers and to let English readers know something of the pleasure Donne has given to French readers. Contains the following essays: (1) Robert Ellrodt, "Présence et permanence de John Donne" (17–29); Stephen Bann, "Isaak Walton et John Donne" (31–38); Jean Fuzier, "John Donne et la formalité de l'essence" (39–49); Theodore Redpath, "Quelques problèmes textuels dans les Songs and Sonets" (51–72); Philippe de Rothschild, "Traduire «Donne»" (75–86); Joseph Lederer, "Toutes ses maîtresses profanes: Réflexions sur la poésie érotique de Donne" (87–121); Jean-Loup Bourget, "John Donne: His Conclave" (125–34); Jean-Marie Maguin, "Le Phénix caché: Sens et statut de l'image occultée dans deux poèmes de Donne" (135–39); Robert Nye, "'The body is his book': La poésie de John Donne" (141–55); Charles Sisson, "John Donne et la possibilité d'une poésie religieuse" (157–62); Ray Selden, "L'incarnation, conviction de John Donne" (163–79); Peter Rudnytsky, "La vue de Dieu" (181–96); Nigel Foxell, "Un sermon de pierre" (199–211); Veronica Forrest-Thomson, "La planète séparée: John Donne et William Empson" (213–44); Jean-Marie Benoist, "L'ecriture de l'abyme" (247–59). "Poèmes choisis" ([262]–309) gives on opposite pages English texts and French translations of *ElPart, ElBed, Sappho, GoodM, SunRis, Ind, Canon, Air, Twick, ValWeep, Witch, ValMourn, Flea, Ecst, Lect, HSBatter, Goodf,* and *Sickness,* taken from the revised and corrected *Poèmes de John Donne,* translated by Jean Fuzier and Yves Denis (Paris: Gallimard, 1980). Contains also a list of important dates in Donne's life (311); a selective bibliography of bibliographies, editions of Donne's poetry and prose, and critical and biographical studies (313–17); and biographical sketches of the contributors to the volume (318–[20]). Tipped in are portraits of Elizabeth I (3), James I (1), Henry Wotton (1), Lucy Harrington (1), Robert Ker (1), Henry Percy (1), Izaac Walton (1), and Donne (2), with photos of Donne's effigy in St. Paul's.

361. Bourget, Jean-Loup. "John Donne: His Conclave," in *John Donne,* ed. Jean-Marie Benoist, 125–34. Les Dossiers H, gen. eds. Jacqueline de Roux and François Denoël. Herissey: L'Age d'Homme.

Summarizes the content and analyzes the satirical themes, baroque style, wit, and images in *Ignatius,* calling it an odd book, a potpourri, and a light work on a weighty subject. Sees the treatise as in some respects similar to a play, the hero of which is a comic who attempts to upstage the other characters, and notes the appearance of what seem like stage directions in the work. Suggests that this dramatic, comic treatment of Hell reminds one of Philippe Jacques de Loutherbourg's paintings of Hell. Discusses the prevalence and importance of images and references to blood and castration in the treatise, and believes that Donne's satire against the Jesuits is more political than religious. Says that *Ignatius* is meant to be a reflection or parody of the insignificance of the Jesuits.

362. Brady, Jennifer. "'Beware the Poet': Authority and Judgment in Jonson's *Epigrammes*." *SEL* 23: 95–112.

Comments on Jonson's expression of reverence and admiration for Donne in the *Epigrammes*. Discusses in some detail how the portrait of Donne and also that of William Camden "serve a crucial rhetorical function" in the *Epigrammes* in that Jonson presents them as "the sole exceptions to the basic assumption behind his work: the belief that even the virtuous need to be confirmed in their heroic endeavors and reminded of the conditional nature of the poet's moral validation." Points out that "[i]n the hierarchy of virtue established by the *Epigrammes*, these exceptional men stand at a remove from the struggle to attain ethical worthiness," noting that Jonson "does not try to judge them, but rather seeks their approval of his work, in much the same way as we do Jonson's approbation of us." Observes, however, that although both Donne and Camden are presented as "heroic *exempla*" (108), Jonson seems unable to define exactly their virtues and "finds it impossible to encompass the god-like minds of his mentors." Claims that, for Jonson, the achievements of both Donne and Camden "exist for us only as unattainable ideals, possibilities beyond the scope of the poet's qualifying language," and that we, like Jonson, can reverence them "but we cannot empathize with them" (109). Claims that "[b]y turning living men into monuments to their reputation," Jonson "successfully closes off one escape route his readers might take, that of self-congratulatory identification" (110).

363. Briggs, Julia. *This Stage-Play World: English Literature and Its Backgrounds, 1580–1625*. Oxford: Oxford University Press. vi, 225p.

In this survey of the intellectual, social, religious, educational, and literary backgrounds of English literature from 1580 to 1625 intended primarily for students, briefly comments on Donne's education, his marriage, his patrons, and his uses of Neoplatonism. Discusses, in more detail, Donne's religious situation and the enduring influence of Catholicism on his works. Contrasts briefly Donne and Herbert as religious poets and as sermon writers, and suggests that the differences between Donne's sermons and Herbert's resulted from the differences between Donne's "smart London congregation," who expected "something witty," and Herbert's unsophisticated congregation in a "remote parish near Salisbury" (90).

364. Brink, J. R., and L. M. Pailet. "Rhetorical Stance: The Epideictic Mode as a Principle of Decorum in the English Renaissance Lyric." *SJS* 9, no. 2: 83–92.

Argues that *Bait* belongs to the epideictic mode and that, for its full effect, it must be read together with Marlowe's "Passionate Shepherd to His Love" and Raleigh's "The Nymph's Reply to the Shepherd." Maintains also that if the three poems are not read in the order or sequence in which they were composed, "the effect on the reader or listener will not be the same." Argues that, when read sequentially, "the relationship among the three poems roughly parallels that of the confirmation and confutation in a traditional oration" (89).

365. Chernaik, Warren L. "Marvell's Satires: The Search for Form," in *The Poet's Time: Politics and Religion in the Work of Andrew Marvell*, 151–205. Cambridge: Cambridge University Press.

Compares and contrasts *Sat4* and Marvell's "Fleckno" and contrasts both poems to Horace's *Satire* I, ix, which was the model for both (169–71). Finds Donne's speaker less polite and more explicit in stating his own values than Marvell's speaker, and suggests that Donne's speaker "resembles the 'plain-dealer' figure frequently found in seventeenth-century literature" (170). Says that whereas Donne in his satire "explicitly urges the need to follow truth in one's daily affairs," Marvell in "Fleckno" "reminds us, with wry humour, how difficult it is to live up to such an ideal" (171).

366. Clausen, Christopher. "Morality, Poetry, and Criticism." *KR*, n.s. 5: 74–89.
In an essay on the moral aspects of literary works and on the role of the critic in examining the connection between literature and ethics, discusses *ValMourn*. Argues that to elucidate simply the technical finesse of the poem is "only to begin to criticize it," insisting that "[t]he famous metaphors, the twists and turns of technique, are after all in the service of expressing a moral Ideal" (80), specifically that true love goes beyond mere physical passion. Suggests that what attracts readers to the poem is "an ideal of dignity which, no matter how little intention we have to practicing it personally, we nonetheless feel to be an important and permanent virtue." Says that in the poem the lovers "come to exemplify one of the better choices that human beings can make" and thus Donne "makes possible a moral statement that readers in a later century, however they wish to formulate the matter, find moving and penetrating" (81).

367. Davies, Horton. "A Spur for the Somnolent: Wit, in the English Pulpit, 1588–1645." *Thalia* 6, no. 1: 32–47.
Discusses and cites examples of various types of wit in English sermons from 1588 to 1645: conceits, puns, paronomasia, epigrams, paradoxes, riddles, reverses of thought, extended oxymora, and ingenious titles and texts. Says that the primary function of wit in sermons was "to keep the congregation on its toes, intrigued,

delighted, amused, and, hopefully, instructed," but maintains that wit had practical purposes also—to begin a sermon, to serve as "an apology for not going deeply into all aspects of a text and its context," to apologize "for the prolixity or the brevity of the sermon," "to fasten the divisions or parts of the sermon more firmly on the mind" (41), to provide "a transition in a sermon," to make "satirical references which act as dissuasives" (42), and to mark "the conclusion of a narration or of a sermon itself" (43). Points out that "from 1640 onwards objections against the use of wit in the pulpit multiplied" (43). Cites examples of Donne's use of wit in his sermons, especially puns, epigrams, paradoxes, reverses of thought, and ingenious texts.

368. Davies, Horton. "Ten Characteristics of English Metaphysical Preaching," in *Studies of the Church in History: Essays Honoring Robert S. Paul on His Sixty-fifth Birthday,* ed. Horton Davies, 103–47. Pittsburgh Theological Monographs, gen. ed. Dikran Y. Hadidian, n.s. 5. Allison Park, Pa.: Pickwick.
Discusses ten characteristics of metaphysical preaching: "1. Wit; 2. Patristic learning; 3. Classical learning: poetic, moral, and historical; 4. Frequent citations from Greek and Latin originals, and occasional use of Hebrew etymology; 5. Biblical exegesis which not infrequently adds typological and allegorical senses to the primary literal or historical sense of Scripture; 6. Plans with complex divisions and subdivisions; 7. A Senecan, rather than Ciceronian style, often interrogative, epigrammatic, and staccato; 8. Delight in paradoxes, [r]iddles, and emblems; 9. Liking for speculative doctrines in both philosophy and particularly theology; and 10. The relating of doctrinal and devotional preaching to the liturgy, especially to the calendar of

the Christian year" (106). Cites examples from Donne's sermons, noting the frequency of Donne's quotations from the Church Fathers, especially Augustine, Jerome, Chrysostom, Gregory the Great, Ambrose, and Basil, and his use of historical exempla and "unnatural natural" history, biblical typology, Senecan style, philosophical and theological speculation and subtleties, and the Christian calendar.

369. Dixon, Peter. "Donne's 'To His Mistress Going to Bed,' Lines 7–12." *Expl* 41, no. 4: 11.

Argues that since each of the couplets in ll. 7–12 of *ElBed* treats "a single step in the progress towards full nakedness," it makes sense to see the chime as the sound made "by the operation of unlacing." Notes that laces that fastened a lady's bodice (the "busk" of l. 11) "commonly terminated in metal tags or aglets" and that when the laces were unfastened, the aglets produced "a mild tinkling sound, not unpleasing to a lover's ear." Maintains that, when read in this way, the couplet "adheres to the structural pattern of its neighbours" and is "gently witty" since "the sound of unlacing, a chime genuinely 'coming from' the mistress, does quite literally announce that her bedtime is at hand" and is also "effectively persuasive." Maintains that Donne "is not hectoring the lady, urging upon her an arbitrary hour as told by a mechanical timepiece," but rather he is "playfully arguing that her undressing (in compliance, of course, with his request) itself naturally signals her bedtime."

370. Donne, John. *John Donne: Erotische Elegien, Englisch und Deutsch,* ed. and trans. K. Wydmond. Stuttgart: Sunna. 112p.

Presents a brief introduction to the *Elegies* (9–10) followed by the 20 elegies included in Grierson's edition (1912), with English texts and German translations on opposite pages (12–106) and explanatory notes (107–12).

371. Donne, John. *John Donne: Liriche sacre e profane—Anatomia del mondo—Duello della Morte,* ed. Giorgio Melchiori. Biblioteca Mondadori. Milano: Arnoldo Mondadori Editore. lxiii, 238p. Reprinted 1992. First appeared as an Oscari Classic, 1992, and was reprinted several times thereafter.

Notes in the preface (xi–xii) the editor's two earlier works on Donne and the metaphysical poets, *John Donne: Selected Poems, Death's Duell* (1957) and *Poeti metafisici inglesi del Seicento* (1968), and his wish to present Donne to a new generation of Italian readers. The introduction (xiii–xlviii) discusses Donne as the central figure in the development of metaphysical poetry in England and comments on his critical reception. Considers the nature of metaphysical poetry, noting, in particular, its uses of wit, distinguishing euphuistic wit from metaphysical wit. Comments on the rise of so-called new philosophy and contrasts it with medieval philosophical thinking. Discusses Donne as a mannerist poet, comparing him to Michelangelo, and explains the art of meditation and its importance in shaping the religious poetry of the period. Discusses major features of Donne's poetry and explains English prosody to an Italian audience. Presents a chronology of Donne's life and publications (xlix–lii) and a bibliography of primary and secondary works (liii–lxiii), followed by translations into Italian (with English texts on the opposite page) of *EpLin, Storm, Calm, Sat3, ElPict, ElAut, ElBed,* 25 selections from the *Songs and Sonets,* 10 of the *Holy Sonnets, Cross, Goodf, Christ, Sickness, Father, FirAn, FunEl,* and "Death's Duell" (1–169). Concludes with a note on the text (171–72) and notes on individual poems (173–238).

372. Donne, John. *John Donne: Selected Poems.* Notes by Phillip Mallett. York Notes, gen. ed. A. W. Jefferson Suheil Bushrui. Harlow: Longman; Beirut: York. 104p. Reprinted 1985.

Intended for A level and GCSE students as well as first year university students. The introduction ([5]–18) gives a brief biographical sketch of Donne and a survey of the religious and intellectual background that informs his poetry. Presents summaries of the text with glosses on underlined lines of *Sat3, ElPict, ElBed,* 19 of the *Songs and Sonets,* and 12 of the *Divine Poems* ([19]–65); a general critical commentary on the *Songs and Sonets* ([66]–88); and hints for study ([89]–98); followed by suggestions for further reading ([99]–100) and a note on the author of the notes (101).

373. Donne, John. *The Songs and Sonets of John Donne,* ed. Theodore Redpath. 2nd ed. New York: St. Martin's Press. xxiv, 374p. First published, London: Methuen, 1956; reprinted with minor corrections, 1959, 1964, 1967. First paperback ed., 1967.

Enlarged, much revised edition, with a fuller textual and critical apparatus. Modern spelling and punctuation, as in the earlier edition. Follows Grierson's edition (1912) regarding the canon of the *Songs and Sonets,* but excludes *Token* and *SelfL* and adds *Image* (entitled "Picture and Dream"), which Grierson placed among the *Elegies.* Orders the poems according to "the moods of the poems"—roughly from "bitter and cynical poems," to "courting poems," to "poems expressing greater and greater satisfaction in a love relationship," to "poems of parting and of illness and death." Sandwiches in "between the poems of parting and those of illness and death, a few poems expressing a certain frustration which may or may not be resolved in the poem concerned" (xix),

and "two expressing 'Platonic' love, in the modern sense of the term" (xx). Makes no attempt to date the poems precisely and questions previous attempts, especially Helen Gardner's dating in her edition (1965). Revises and expands considerably the introduction to which has been added a detailed discussion of the relationship between Donne's lyrics and the Continental and English Petrarchan tradition, emphasizing Donne's originality in adapting the conventions for his own purposes. Also expands considerably the discussion of the individual poems and adds a new alphabetical index of titles. Contains contents (v–vii), a list of abbreviations (viii–xi), the preface to the first edition (xii–xvi), a note on the second impression (xvii), and the preface to the second edition (xviii–xxiv). Divides the introduction (1–103) into seven parts: "The Status of the 'Songs and Sonets' in English poetry" (1–2), "The Place of the 'Songs and Sonets' within Donne's Work" (3–12), "Some Approaches to the Poems" (12–21), "Some 'Psychological' Features of the Poems" (21–28), "Some 'Literary' Features of the Poems" (29–47), "The 'Songs and Sonets' and Petrarchism" (47–88), notes on the text and canon (88–103), and a note on the use of the "slur" (104). Thereafter follow the texts of the poems, each of which is followed by its own textual apparatus, critical commentary, and gloss on individual lines (106–303). Contains 13 appendices: "'The Indifferent', l. 16" (304–5); "'Farewell to Love', ll. 23–30" (306–11); "'The Prohibition', l. 22" (312–14); "'The Dream', ll. 19–20" (315–17); "'Air and Angels', ll. 24, 26–8" (318–22); "'The Ecstasy': A Note on Interpretation" (323–27); "'The Funeral', 'The Blossom', 'The Primrose', and 'The Relic': Personal Reference in these Poems" (330–33); "'Twickenham Garden', l. 17 ('groan' or 'grow'?)" (334–35); "'Twickenham Garden", 'A Nocturnal' and 'The Dissolution': Personal References in these Poems" (336–38); "The Undertaking', l. 6 ('specular stone')" (339–40); "Musical Settings of Some 'Songs and Sonets'" (341–43); and "Rhetorical Figures in the 'Songs and Sonets'" (344–58). Concludes with a select bibliography (359–70) that includes a select bibliography for the English and Continental background of Donne's love lyrics (367–70), an index of titles (371–72), and an index of first lines (373–74). Reviews: Warren Chernaik in *THES* (20 January 1984): 21; D. F. Bratchell in *N&Q*, n.s. 32 (1985): 113–14; Lucien Carrive in *RLC* 238 (1986): 235–36.

374. Donne, John. *Suicide: "Biathanatos" Transcribed and Edited for Modern Readers,* ed. William A. Clebsch. Studies in the Humanities Series, 1. Chico, Calif.: Scholars Press. xvii, 114p.

Presents a modern spelling edition of *Biathanatos* in which "terms commonly used in Donne's day have been changed to our equivalent (if debased and inflated) coinage" (ix). The introduction ([vii]–xvii) surveys the history of moral thinking about suicide from ancient times to the Renaissance, commenting in particular on the Christian position. Claims that in *Biathanatos,* Donne "stood squarely within the bounds of Christian doctrine and piety" in presenting his "audacious and fascinating argument." Points out that in *Biathanatos,* Donne insists that "the blanket condemnation of suicide sprang from a lack of charity toward the neighbor," that "[i]t presumed more than it could know in declaring that suicides could not repent," that "[i]t shackled God's grace in declaring suicide a sin for which there would be no remission," and that "[i]t blinded itself to a profound and universal human yearning for death that was

demonstrable from personal experience and historical records" (x). Notes that when "[c]ompared with other writings of moral theology by Renaissance Englishmen, this work is distinctive in that the author's personality and personal sensibilities shine through even the duller sections" (xi). Briefly summarizes Donne's life, "The Epistle Dedicatory," "The Preface," and text of *Biathanatos* ([1]–97), followed by an index of scriptural references ([99] and a glossary of names [101]–14). Review: Tom Baird in *Expository Times* 95 (1984): 156; W. Speed Hill in *JDJ* 6 (1987): 109–33.

375. Ellrodt, Robert. "De Donne à Traherne: Les formes nouvelles de la conscience de soi," in *Genèse de la conscience moderne: Études sur le développement de la conscience de soi dans les littératures du monde occidental,* ed. Robert Ellrodt, 71–81. Publications de la Sorbonne. Série «Littératures 2», 14. Paris: Presses Universitaires de France.

Calls Donne, Montaigne, and Shakespeare the heralds of the modern view of self-consciousness from which issued dramatic soliloquies, meditations, intimate diaries, and so on, and sees the change as a shift in focus from an interest in the knowledge of God to an interest in the self. Proposes to show distinctions among three aspects of self-consciousness—consciousness of the self, feeling of self, and consciousness of consciousness—as illustrated by Donne, Vaughan, and Traherne. Focuses on Donne's egotism and his fascination with himself, his love of dissection and anatomy, and his religious uncertainty, and shows how his introspection and self-reflective analysis shapes his views of love, religion, and death. Suggests that during this period new forms of self-consciousness emerged that have been felt in following centuries, and claims that the modernity of Donne's self-consciousness accounts, at least in part, for his appeal to twentieth century readers.

376. **Ellrodt, Robert.** "Prèsence et permanence de John Donne," in *John Donne,* ed. Jean-Marie Benoist, 17–29. Les Dossiers H, gen. eds. Jacqueline de Roux and François Denoël. Herissey: L'Age d'Homme.

Investigates reasons for Donne's enduring reputation from the seventeenth century to the present. Regards Donne as primarily a mannerist and compares his poetry to mannerist paintings. Endorsing, in part, Arnold Hauser's definition of mannerism, sees the mannerist movement as a style that reflects the emotional, philosophical, religious, and moral uncertainties of the late Renaissance. Comments on *Noct* as representative of Donne's mannerist characteristics. Maintains that it is not simply Donne's wit and intellectual ingenuity that has attracted readers but, more importantly, it is his skill in presenting the complexities and uncertainties of the human condition that appeals to readers of different time periods.

377. **Elsky, Martin.** "John Donne's *La Corona:* Spatiality and Mannerist Painting." *MLS* 13: 3–11.

Argues that "the visual experience of the meditative poet contemplating a composition of place resembles the spectator's relationship to the imaginative space of sixteenth-century religious painting" by comparing *Corona* to "the spatial and temporal organization" (3) of two mannerist paintings: Pontormo's *Madonna and Child and Saint* (Florence, San Michele Visdomini, 1518) and Parmigianino's *Vision of St. Jerome* (London, National Gallery, 1526–27). Argues that in *Corona* Donne, in a manner similar to that in the two paintings, "uses spatial and temporal inconsistencies" to represent past sacred events taking place in a space that the meditator can look at and enter in his own present time. Suggests that, similar to the inconsistencies of the paintings, "the inconsistencies" in Donne's *Corona* "result from the temporally illogical juxtaposition of past events themselves, as well as from including the meditator in the space and time of those past events" (6). Discusses also how the "juxtaposition of the timeless and the temporal in the liturgy has its counterpart in the narrative structure" (9) of *Corona,* and comments on how the meditator "comes to play an essential role in the circular form" of the poem, as "the work's emblematic shape serves the representation of his place in time," just as "the spatial and temporal organization" of the two Italian paintings "ultimately comes to rest on the spectator of the paintings." Concludes that in *Corona,* "the poet-spectator tries to create for himself a space that can contain historical events made present to himself in time in a way that closely resembles the representation of space and time in Pontormo and Parmigianino" (10).

378. **Erskine-Hill, Howard.** "Courtiers out of Horace: Donne's *Satyre IV* and Pope's *Fourth Satire of Dr. John Donne, Dean of St. Paul's, Versifyed,*" in *The Augustan Idea in English Literture,* 74–98. London: Edward Arnold.

First published in *John Donne: Essays in Celebration,* ed. A. J. Smith (London: Methuen, 1972): 273–307. Annotated in *Roberts 2* (Item 417).

379. **Ferry, Anne.** "Donne," in *The "Inward" Language: Sonnets of Wyatt, Sidney, Shakespeare, Donne,* 215–46. Chicago: University of Chicago Press.

Examines the language Donne uses to express his inner self in the *Holy Sonnets.* Claims that "the pointed absence of sonnets from his love poems, and his use of the form only in a few verse epistles and dedications, shows that Donne's acceptance of the sonnet as a major form for his religious verse was a deliberate and significant departure from his practice in the *Songs and Sonets*" (218). Maintains that "the choice of the [sonnet] form seems to have been dictated by his associations of it with the use of a speaker who is identified as a poet" and believes that, for Donne, writing sonnets "involved the concerns also associated with such a speaker in the sonnets of Sidney and Shakespeare" (219), especially the struggle "to find a true language for what is in the heart" (221). Contrasts *Corona* and the *Holy Sonnets* to show that, in the latter, the speakers' language is freed from "the kinds of constraints imposed by the liturgical style" of the former, noting that the speakers sound "more like Sidney's and Shakespeare's in their love sonnets" than like "liturgical petitioners." Argues that even though the speakers in the *Holy Sonnets* "do not explicitly identify themselves as poets, their language evokes in many ways the figure of the poet-lover as it was developed in the sequences of Sidney and Shakespeare, whose concerns they share" (227). Discusses several of the *Holy Sonnets* in detail to show how Donne likens the speakers "to poet-lovers who struggle uneasily with the capacity of verse to show what is in the heart" (234). Contrasts Donne's religious sonnets with his love poetry to show that in the *Holy Sonnets* Donne uses the love complaint "to raise questions about the nature of inward experience and its relation to expression which are not the concerns of the speakers in Donne's love poetry" (238). Concludes that the differences between Donne's *Holy Sonnets* and his other poems, both secular and religious, "are therefore not theological, nor are they derived from a notion of religious matter demanding a special kind of verse,"

but rather the distinctions "emerge instead from the sonnet tradition, and its associations for him with the poet's struggle to find a language that can show truly what is in the heart" (246). Reviews: Gerald Hammond in *THES* (4 May 1983): 26; Bridget Gellert Lyons in *Raritan* 4, no. 2 (1984): 109–19; Lennet J. Daigle in *SoAR* 50 (1985): 103–5; Judith Kegan Gardiner in *JEGP* 84 (1985): 259–62; Ronald L. Levao in *RenQ* 38 (1985): 177–79; Douglas L. Peterson in *MLQ* 46 (1985): 89–92; John H. Ottenhoff in *SCN* 44 (1986): 10–12.

380. Finnegan, Robert Emmett. "Numbering Donne's 'Flea.'" *AN&Q* 21: 66.

Maintains that in *Flea* "the major stresses in the poem recapitulate and support the theme that the poem represents." Notes that "the multiplication of forty-one, the number of major stresses in each stanza, by three, the number of stanzas the poem contains, results in the progression 1, 2, 3." Regards this metrical structure as a "simple numerological restatement" of the speaker's attempt to convince the lady to make him "a *tertium quid*." Notes also the amusing rhymes in the last three lines of each stanza: "woo," "two," "do"; "me," "be," "three"; and "me," "be," "thee."

381. Flynn, Dennis. "The '*Annales* School' and the Catholicism of Donne's Family." *JDJ* 2, no. 2: 1–9.

Discusses the scholarly revival of interest in English Catholicism and in the Catholic Reformation in general, influenced in part by the "*Annales* school," which sets aside "as mechanical or sterile any exclusive concern with controversial literature or other official or public expressions of conflict between great political and religious institutions" and aims rather to investigate the everyday religious lives of people, using modern "sociological, geographical, and psychological analysis" (1). Considers Donne's Catholicism "in its familial and historical contexts" (4), illustrating thereby the usefulness of the new approach. Comments, for instance, on Donne's father, John Donne, who aided his exiled father-in-law, John Heywood, in circumventing the anti-Catholic "Act against Fugitives" of 1571, and notes that both men are mentioned by Henry Machyn, a Catholic London tradesman, in whose diary "we can trace the beginnings of the oppressed, furtive, and recalcitrant Elizabethan mentality that surrounded the poet in his family and connections during the early years of his life" (5). Maintains that the key figure in Donne's early life was his maternal grandfather, John Heywood, who reflected in his life and attitudes both the continuity and discontinuity of Erasmian or Old Catholicism in England. Insists, however, that the family member who exerted "the most direct influence on Donne" (6) was his Jesuit uncle, Jasper Heywood, who, like his father, John Heywood, modeled for the young Donne the continuity and discontinuity of pre-Tridentine Catholicism. Concludes that Donne's Catholicism "was of a sort that could survive the Council of Trent only through fierce resistance on its own terms," but notes that "[d]eprived of normal conditions for spiritual and institutional development, such Catholics clung to old ways increasingly irrelevant as the sixteenth century wore on," and "[t]heir isolation became increasingly painful and confounding, and became also the source of their increasingly ineffectual ironies about religion," as seen, for instance, in Donne's "love poems, satires, and other writings" (8).

382. Flynn, Dennis. "John Donne in the Ellesmere Manuscripts." *HLQ* 46: 333–36. Notes the discovery of Donne's signature, together with that of John Phillips, "on a bond ensuring the appearance of Mary Barham before the lord keeper prior to her marriage or betrothal" (Ellesmere MS EL 5898, dated 30 August 1599). Points out that "[n]o other connection of Donne's biography to the Barhams has yet been found," and briefly suggests Donne's connection with John Phillips, if he is "the same Yorkshireman who with his brother William had been at Lincolns Inn with Donne and the lord keeper's two sons" (333). Suggests that "considering the evidence of the Ellesmere manuscripts," it is reasonable to assume that as Egerton's secretary, Donne did "very little," and maintains that "one gets the impression, especially considering the tone of the *Satyres* and other poetry of the 1590s, that even before his disastrous elopement with Ann More, Donne was going nowhere in Egerton's service" (335).

383. Fogle, French R. "'Such a Rural Queen': The Countess Dowager of Derby as Patron," in *Patronage in Late Renaissance England*, 1–29. Los Angeles: William Andrews Clark Memorial Library, University of California.
Discusses the literary connections of the Dowager of Derby, the third wife of Sir Thomas Egerton. Suggests that since Donne was private secretary in the Egerton household at the time of the marriage, it is "only reasonable to assume that there was direct contact between him and the Countess Dowager." Says that, although she "seems never to have aroused his muse, they must have been personally acquainted" (21).

384. Folena, Lucia. "John Donne: Paradiso e paradosso," in *"Fruitful beds and towery borders": Ricerche sull'idea del giardino in Donne, Marvell, Vaugham [sic]*, 76–90. Padova. Distributed by Franco Cesati Ed., Firenze.
Contrasts and compares Donne's use of garden imagery with that of

Vaughan and Marvell, pointing out that garden imagery is not as prominent in Donne's poetry as it is in the work of other poets of the period and that his use of garden images is not unique but typical of seventeenth century poets. Comments on various kinds of "gardens" in Donne's poems—the garden of the ego, which deals with the relationship of the soul with God; the garden of religion, which concerns the relationship of Christ and the Church; and the gardens of women, which involves man's erotic relationship with the opposite sex. Comments especially on garden imagery in *Twick, Ecst, FirAn, Metem, LovInf, ConfL, Sickness,* as well as several verse epistles and love elegies.

385. Forrest-Thomson, Veronica. "La planète séparée: John Donne et William Empson," in *John Donne,* ed. Jean-Marie Benoist, 213–46. Les Dossiers H, gen. eds. Jacqueline de Roux and François Denoël. Herissey: L'Age d'Homme. Translated from English by François Maguin.

Revised and expanded version of Chapter 4, "The Poet and His Tribe: Tradition and the Disconnected Image-Complex," in *Poetic Artifice: A Theory of Twentieth-Century Poetry* (New York: St. Martin's Press, 1978), 81–111. Annotated in *Roberts 2* (entry 992). Relying heavily on the work of French structuralists and related critics, describes and classifies Donne's complex uses of imagery and discusses his influence on twentieth century poets, especially William Empson and T. S. Eliot, who found in his poetry a blend of discursive and empirical imagery that they valued and attempted to adapt. Comments on Empson's reading of *Cross* and compares his "Letter V" with *ValMourn.*

386. Foxell, Nigel. "Un sermon de pierre," in *John Donne,* ed. Jean-Marie Benoist, 199–211. Les Dossiers H, gen. eds.

Jacqueline de Roux and François Denoël. Herissey: L'Age d'Homme.

First published in English as *A Sermon in Stone: John Donne and His Monument in St. Paul's Cathedral* (London: Mermaid Press, 1978); annotated in *Roberts 2* (entry 994).

387. Fuzier, Jean. "John Donne et la formalité de l'essence," in *John Donne,* ed. Jean-Marie Benoist, 39–49. Les Dossiers H, gen. eds. Jacqueline de Roux and François Denoël. Herissey: L'Age d'Homme.

Analyzes the innovative prosody and uses of rhetorical structure of *HSBatter* to show how Donne breaks down the distinction between genres, which is permitted in dramatic but not lyric poetry, and liberates meter from traditional rules and limitations. Comments on Donne's use of synalepha (the blending into one syllable of two successive vowels of adjacent syllables).

388. Gessani, Alberto. "Sacra idropisia: Saggio su *A Nocturnall upon S. Lucies Day, Being the Shortest Day* di John Donne," in *Nel labirinto: Donne, La Rochefoucauld, Nietzsche,* 27–57. Biblioteca Ianua, 7. Rome: Editrice Ianua.

Presents an Italian translation of *Noct* (27–29) and a detailed critical reading of the poem to show how it is central to an understanding of Donne's thought and how it throws light on one of the most tormented moments in European culture, the breakdown of medieval and Renaissance concepts of the world. Maintains that the poem, drawing on the ruins of Renaissance culture, expresses not only Donne's personal crisis of faith at the time but also reflects the theological tensions of the world in which he lived. Argues that the fear, desperation, and anguish Donne expresses in *Noct* can be seen as a prelude to the secular, atheistic culture that emerged in the seventeenth century and finally led to the "death of God" concept in modern times.

389. Goldberg, Jonathan. *James I and the Politics of Literature: Jonson, Shakespeare, Donne, and Their Contemporaries.* Baltimore: Johns Hopkins University Press. xvii, 292p.

Studies the "relationship between authority and its representations in the Jacobean period," denoting James I as "the primary representation of authority" but not the sole one. Considers not only the king's writings as representative of power, but also those of poets and playwrights, such as Shakespeare, Jonson, and Donne. Postulates that "language and politics—broadly construed—are mutually constitutive, that society shapes and is shaped by the possibilities in its language and discursive practices." Focuses the first half of the book on what James I called "the stile of *Gods*" (xi) and the possibilities it offered for representation, and traces "the lines of power by pursuing conventions that can be made from the king's language to that of his poets" (xii). Explores three tropes crucial to James's writing: (1) *arcana imperii* (state secrets), seeing in Donne's *Songs and Sonets* a relationship to this trope because "Donne's lovers are absolutists as much as the king" (xii); (2) the metaphor of the king as actor, discussing Donne's *Eclog* as not only using the trope of deception but also employing the king's language; and (3) the stage as history, by which the career of Donne is a model for this relationship since Donne is grounded in Jacobean absolutism. Discusses *Canon* as a poem that uses the trope of *arcana imperii,* a representation of the king's command to respect royal territory, in this case that of two lovers' domain, and shows that in *Anniv* Donne "draws upon the language of political idealization" and "absolutist ideology" (66). Discusses also the political metaphors in *Devotions* in which Donne's ill body keeps its secrets, thus representing a challenge to the physician, and suggests that Donne "reads this as an analogy for rebellion in the state, the danger of whispering plotters to the royal physician" (81). Notes also that in the *Devotions,* Donne celebrates James "as God's instrument" and also "as God's image" (215). Comments on the king's role in Donne's life and works, noting that for Donne "the court is the center and the only reality in society; not to be there is to be nowhere," and argues that "Donne's self-constitution is absolutist" (219). Discusses *SunRis* as a preeminent absolutist poem, stating that "the mystification of love, the disguise of sexuality in platonized spirituality, the parade of learning to cover ribaldry" are "characteristics of the *Songs and Sonets,* rebellious and atheistical in their manipulation of the *arcana imperii*" (107). Culls Donne's letters, sermons, and *Devotions* to show how Donne viewed his relationship with King James, and concludes that "the single metaphor—the metaphor of the hand, sustaining, lending—describes James's role in Donne's life and works, recreating him, giving him words to write" (213). Reviews: Annabel Patterson in *JDJ* 2, no. 2 (1983): 91–106; Julia Briggs in *TLS* (27 April 1984): 472; Jonathan Dollimore in *Criticism* 26 (1984): 83–86; Richard L. Greaves in *ClioI* 14 (1984): 87–89; Jean E. Howard in *SQ* 35 (1984): 234–37; L. W. Irwin in *CollL* 11 (1984): 280–84; Richard Helgerson in *RenQ* 38 (1985): 180–83; Dolores Palomo in *JAAC* 43 (1985): 411–12; Jenny Wormald in *History* 70 (1985): 128–30; Alexander Leggatt in *MRDE* 3 (1986): 324–27; Raymond A. Anselment in *MLR* 82 (1987): 445– 47; Daniel Woolf in *QQ* 94 (1987): 143–45.

390. Gottlieb, Sidney. *"Elegies upon the Author:* Defining, Defending, and Surviving Donne." *JDJ* 2, no. 2: 23–38.

Discusses the series of elegies on Donne appended to the early editions of Donne's poems to show their importance in understanding Donne's contemporary reputation and in appreciating more fully the most well-known of these poems, Carew's "An Elegie upon the death of the Deane of Pauls, Dr. John Donne." Maintains that although the elegists focus on Donne as a preacher, their comments become "relevant to our understanding of his poetry" (26). Points out that the elegies contain the expected "praise, lament, and consolation" but notes that this praise often "turns out to be surprisingly argumentative and defensive," which gives the picture of Donne as "a man deeply involved in controversy" who must be measured "against his antagonists" (28) and whose reputation must be maintained "by trampling on that of his competitors" (29). Notes also that the elegists repeatedly state the conventional theme of the death of poetry occasioned by the death of the great poet and that some even imitate Donne's style and/or ideas, thus perhaps illustrating their claim that after Donne, poets have become ineffective, or perhaps supporting the notion that "even in death Donne has generative power" (33). Discusses Carew's elegy in the light of the preceding comments, noting, in particular, "the distressing ambiguity" that runs through the entire poem: "Donne exhausts as well as adorns the art of poetry." Points out that, "[f]or all its accurate and witty praise, Carew's elegy also registers very sensitively the great pressures on those, like himself, who would attempt to write poetry in Donne's shadow," but notes that lines 71–86 show "how successfully Carew is able to resist these pressures" (35). Concludes that although the elegies (with the exception of Carew's) "contain little poetry," they "add much to our knowledge of Donne's contemporary reputation" and also "give a sometimes striking presentation of several critical and biographical problems that we, no more than they, have not been able to solve" (36).

391. Grant, Patrick. "The Cross," in *Literature of Mysticism in Western Tradition,* 103–27. London: Macmillan.

In a discussion on the centrality of the cross in Christian mysticism, presents a critical reading of *HSSpit* (115–17). Calls the poem "a typical seventeenth-century devotional poem, reconstructing the event both in the speaker's and in the reader's imagination, so that both engage, at different historical times, the continuing challenge offered by the crucifixion." Suggests that the sonnet expresses "the turbulence of a man coming to realise the paradox . . . of God's redemptive action" (115). Discusses briefly the tripartite Ignatian structure of the sonnet and the conspicuous use of the first person pronoun in it. Shows how the sonnet develops dramatically: Donne "deliberately has his speaker assume a false perspective, then to discover that the arrogance causing him to blame others, the egotistical desire, that is, to usurp divine privilege, constitutes, not an acceptance of the message of the cross, but the deepest complicity with those responsible for crucifixions" (116). Suggests that the imagery in the conclusion of the sonnet "presents the tension of faith that precedes contemplation" (117).

392. Guibbory, Achsah. "A Sense of the Future: Projected Audiences of Donne and Jonson." *JDJ* 2, no. 2: 11–21.

Discusses how Donne and Jonson "project in their work an awareness of a potential relationship between their poems and the readers of some future age, readers who may be affected, even transformed by the surviving poems, or who themselves may have a creative regenerative effect on the poetry." Argues that although Donne generally believed that "time was running out" and that "it was foolish to trust to any earthly fame," a number of his poems "betray a concern with having a future audience" (11). Cites *ValBook, Relic,* and *Canon* as poems in which Donne "envisions a large future audience that will be taught, even transformed by his poems" but believes that it is the two *Anniversaries* that "most fully reveal Donne's interest in the redemptive effect his poetry might have on the future" (13). Finds in *FirAn* "a tension between the apocalyptic feeling of an imminent end to time and Donne's desire to insure the future through poetry" (14), and maintains that the poem indicates that Donne "was attracted to the possibility that his poems might survive to affect a future age." Says that in *SecAn* Donne finds himself "isolated from his present world" and, therefore, "turns inward to his own soul and outward to the future," noting that in l. 32 of the poem he seeks "not just divine approval but an earthly fame for himself in the generations to come," and in ll. 37–38 "envisions his poems actually having a generative effect on future poets" (15). Says that, although the idea of "the poet's immortalizing power occasionally attracted Donne," it was Jonson and Herrick who "most enthusiastically embraced" the notion (16).

393. Guthke, Karl S. "Barock: Zwischen Ketzerei und Gottesdienst," in *Der Mythos der Neuzeit: Das Thema der Mehrheit der Welten in der Literatur- und Geistesgeschichte von der kopernikanischen Wende bis zur Science Fiction,* 106–79. Bern and Munich: Francke Verlag. Translated into English by Helen Atkins as "The Baroque Period," in *The Last Frontier: Imagining Other Worlds, from the Copernican Revolution to Modern Science Fiction* (Ithaca, N.Y.: Cornell University Press, 1990).

Discusses Donne's anxiety and melancholy over the philosophical and theological implications of the so-called new science, and sees him as one who, until his later life, is insecure in both the world of traditional religion and the world of the new science, which is reflected most vividly in *FirAn*. Points out Donne's familiarity with the works of Kepler, Galileo, and Copernicus, and suggests that Galileo's work, in particular, disturbed Donne because it opened up the possibility of a plurality of inhabited worlds. Believes, however, that later on, after his ordination, Donne conquered by faith any disorientation and tension he may have experienced earlier.

394. Hall, Michael L. "Circles and Circumvention in Donne's Sermons: Poetry as Ritual." *JEGP* 82: 201–14.

Maintains that in Donne's sermons "circles stand not only as images of traditional theology" but also "as deep figures of Donne's own mind or mental geometry." Discusses how Donne employs the circle "as rhetorical figure and metaphysical conceit, as theological concept and as the visible form of creation" (201), and argues that "[c]ircles also underlie the patterns of his thoughts and the shape of his expression" and represent not only "an ideal of perfection and divinity" but also "the human process for achieving that ideal through necessary indirection, by steps and degrees, through circumvention rather than by direct approaches to God and truth" (201–2). Observes also that sometimes "a certain amount of inherent conflict arises between the circles as an image (of God, creation, and eternity) or a figure of thought—both with implications of wholeness, perfection, and harmony—and the circle as a rhetorical process involving indirection and roundabout advances toward a dimly perceived though not impossible ideal of Christian knowledge and understanding." Insists, however, that "these two aspects of the circle, image and process, are closely associated in the sermons" and that "the circular form which is so characteristic of Donne's preaching style seems to emerge logically and even inevitably from his fascination with circles and roundness" (202).

395. Helgerson, Richard. *Self-Crowned Laureates: Spenser, Jonson, Milton and the Literary System.* Berkeley and Los Angeles: University of California Press. ix, 292p.

In this study of the self-presentation and literary ambitions of Spenser, Jonson, and Milton and of the "system of authorial roles in which that ambition might make sense" (2), discusses Donne as the typical amateur poet unconcerned with a public literary career, pointing out his aversion to print. Contrasts Donne with Jonson, noting that their differences are not "merely the fortuitous product of dissimilar temperaments," but rather arise from Donne's desire "to define himself in opposition to humanist ideals of sobriety, measure, and deliberation" and Jonson's intention of presenting himself "in accord with those humanist ideals and in opposition to amateur extravagance, excess, and spontaneity" (33). Argues, however, that both poets are alike "in that both are members of a single literary generation, a generation that defined itself in opposition to the generation of Sidney and Spenser" (34). Suggests that Donne's "seriousness," like Shakespeare's and unlike Jonson's, was "not the seriousness of a man writing in conformity to the dictates of truth and duty, but rather a seriousness discovered in play," as seen in "the histrionic excess

of his wit, searching out through image and attitude roles for the performing self" (39). Discusses briefly Donne as a satirist, warning against identifying too narrowly Donne's satiric personae with Donne himself, and suggesting that Donne is present in his poems "in the same way (if not always to the same degree) that any one of us is present in the gestures that declare our identity" (135). Comments briefly on Donne's influence on later seventeenth century poets, especially Cowley, Carew, Randolph, Habington, Cleveland, Waller, and Suckling.

396. Horne, R. C. "An Allusion to Nashe's *Choise of Valentines* in Donne's Second Satire." *N&Q,* n.s. 30: 414–15.

Suggests that in *Sat2* (ll. 31–38) Donne is alluding to Thomas Nashe, who was "notorious for his bohemianism and frequenting of taverns" and whose *Choise of Valentines* was often spoken of as "Tom. Nashe his Dildo." Notes also that Nashe's "base use of religious terms is a notable feature of the poem" (415). Finds no satisfactory reference, however, in Nashe's poem to Jewish usury, which forms part of Donne's description of a degenerate character in his satire.

397. Houston, John Porter. *The Rhetoric of Poetry in the Renaissance and Seventeenth Century.* Baton Rouge: Louisiana State University Press. 317p.

Believes that Donne's "extremely varied lyric production shows the range of effect that could be obtained from subtle combinations of styles" and discusses Donne's use of "low style by itself or in combination with middle-style ornaments" (70) in such poems as *Fever, GoodM, LovInf, Canon,* and *Noct.* Says that Donne's *Elegies* capture "some of the bluntness, realism, and wit in imagery that the Roman elegists had at their best" (64). Maintains that Donne's reaction to "the complex of Petrarchism, neoplatonism, and Bembism" was a search for a "new mode of expression," and that his verse "is comparable to some of the more eccentric French mannerist verse though infinitely more successful, sustained as it was by greater intellect, greater poetic talent, and greater freedom from the habit of basing newer poetic figures on the old Petrarchist analogies and techniques" (85). Maintains that although the *Anniversaries* have a formal meditational structure, they are primarily philosophical, not devotional, poems. Cites *Goodf* as a "great meditational poem in the personal vein" in which Donne "exploits the ambiguity of low style, moving from its objective, proving function to its Christian *sermo humilis* form" (193), and finally rising in diction "to suggest the austere style of the ancient rhetoricians." Says that the poem is "one of the most remarkable examples" of "evolving style in a lyric poem," a poem in which Donne crosses "the generally absolute barrier between the secular and the high devotional meditation" (194).

398. Hunter, William B. "Difficulties in Interpretation of John Donne's *Satyre 1.*" *SCB* 43: 109–11.

Argues that the 66–line introduction in *Sat1* is disordered and suggests that the poem would have more consistency if the lines were arranged in the following way: ll. 1–24, 53–64, 25–26, 37–48, 65–66, 27–36, 49–52, 67. Recognizes, however, that "there is no textual evidence . . . to support such a radical revision," and offers his rearrangement only in order to help the reader to understand the poem. Believes that Donne "deliberately introduced the disorder into the text" (110), perhaps because he was imitating the disjointed, idiosyncratic style of Persius. Also comments on the identities of the persona and the "motley humorist" in *Sat1*, suggesting various possibilities. Briefly comments on several difficult allusions in Donne's poems: (1) identifies the "one [hill]" as Luther's Wartburg, where he translated the Bible, and "no hill" as Calvin's Geneva by the lake in *HSShow* (l. 8); believes the "Hydroptique father" in *ElPerf* (l. 6) is simply thirsty for alcohol, which is supported by the reference to "hydroptique Dutch" in *ElFatal* (l. 42), an allusion to the drunken Dutch; identifies the "Schismaticks / Of Amsterdam" in *Will* (ll. 20–21) as the Dutch Remonstrants; recognizes in *Sat4* (ll. 88–89) an allusion to a proverb found in John Heywood's *Dialogue;* unscrambles the complex syntax of *Fever* (ll. 9–10); and suggests that "fidlers stop lowest" in *Sat1* refers to their leaning over their vertically held instruments (109).

399. Kennedy, Richard F. "Donne's 'The Canonization.'" *Expl* 42, no. 1: 13–14.

Maintains that "the appropriateness of the Eagle and Dove image" in the third stanza of *Canon* becomes clearer "when one realizes that the allusion may be to a popular belief that the two birds were so antithetical that, even in death, if their feathers were together, they would 'consume of themselves'" (13). Suggests that the "miracle of love" in Donne's poem is "that the masculine and feminine, normally as antipathetic as the Eagle and Dove, are united . . . not just in life, but, mysteriously, even in death, where they will 'die,' or consummate their love, as in the avian tradition" (13–14). Suggests that "the consuming of the feathers after death leads naturally to the climactic image of the stanza, the Phoenix" (14).

400. King, James Roy. "John Donne's *Devotions:* Emergent Moments," in *The Literary Moment as a Lens on Reality,* 22–36. Columbia: University of Missouri Press.

Argues that Donne "writes about a world in which the unexpected is being revealed, human beings are meeting surprising challenges, one experience is opening up as another appears to be closing down." Calls *Devotions* Donne's "most sustained and dramatic treatment of the moment" (24), and observes how Donne "etches sharply the psychological forces at work upon him at each stage of his illness, the ironies flooding in upon him, his sense of movement forward into his next set of experiences" (25). Analyzes the work to show how "the meditations appear to offer a series of clearly identifiable moments, each sharply distinct from the field out of which it grew, each shot through with ironies and emotional vectors, each in some way pointing toward potential spiritual gain" (32). Maintains that Donne characteristically "sees through physical objects and passing time to what lies beyond," and holds that his "sense of passing through and beyond situation after situation (his feelings of futurity) may indeed be the strongest experience that his treatment of certain emergent moments conveys" (34). Concludes that "the sense of the unknown future, the deepening of his experience of reality, the capacity to see through or beyond the material world, the vulnerability, and the capacity for self-transcendence" are "implied by and embodied in the concept of emergence," and "much of it we can experience too because of the way Donne offers himself and the events of his life to us" (35).

401. Klause, John. *The Unfortunate Fall: Theodicy and the Moral Imagination of Andrew Marvell.* Hamden, Conn.: Archon Books. x, 208p.

Contrasts Donne and Marvell and maintains that, unlike Donne, Marvell was not a paradoxist. Says that Donne "tended to conceive of the good in paradoxical ways, as live as he was to the powerful appeal of mixed beauty," and that he "believed that a glory, or at least a wisdom, might be distilled from corruption" (46). Suggests that Donne "seems to have found something salutary in violence," and notes that a number of the *Songs and Sonets* "dramatize contests of wit and emotions between lovers, or between lovers and unsympathetic third parties, in ways that suggest love is better off for having to overcome opposition." Observes that even in his divine poems Donne seems to find violence "almost exhilarating" (47). Points out that *HSWhat* "relies on paradoxes that Marvell could never in acknowledging make vivid for himself" (120). Suggests Marvell was reading Donne in the 1640s, and points out Donne's possible influence on "Fleckno" and "Thyrsis and Dorinda" (130).

402. Knafla, Louis A. "The 'Country' Chancellor: The Patronage of Sir Thomas Egerton, Baron Ellesmere," in *Patronage in Late Renaissance England,* 31–103. Los Angles: William Andrews Clark Memorial Library, University of California.

Sketches the life and career of Sir Thomas Egerton, emphasizing his fervently held Protestantism, his humanist interests, and his extensive patronage of a wide range of scholars, clergymen, lawyers, political economists, and literary men. Suggests that Egerton patronized Donne as part of his anti-Catholic campaign and because of Donne's effectiveness as a preacher. Notes that Donne served him as secretary and that, later on, after Donne's dismissal from his service, the two continued to see each other. Maintains that Egerton assisted Donne in obtaining ecclesiastical appointments and notes that, recognizing Egerton's help, Donne sent him in 1610 an inscribed copy of *Pseudo-Martyr,* noting "their common experiences in meeting the religious crisis caused by their recusant past" (49). Points out Donne's close connection with Egerton's son, Thomas, noting that Donne led the funeral procession when Thomas died in 1599.

403. Kolin, Philip C. "Love's Wealth in 'The Sunne Rising.'" *SCB* 43: 112–14.

Briefly surveys critical commentary on *SunRis* and argues that the poem is Donne's "wry answer to those who think that love is unprofitable and lovers indolent bankrupts." Shows how Donne "pay[s] tribute to love's wealth by contrasting it with the transient gifts of a material world linked to the sun." Maintains that "[t]hrough his metaphors, inspired by love, Donne creates his own new and richly endowed world" and that "[b]y accepting Donne's invitation to shine forever in that new world, the sun will honor a pair of lovers reaping the immortal fruits of joy and love" (114).

404. Kronenfeld, Judy Z. "Probing the Relation between Poetry and Ideology: Herbert's 'The Windows.'" *JDJ* 2, no. 1: 55–80.

In discussing Herbert's religious position on the value of externals in church worship, comments on Donne's view on the question, noting that his position shows that what may seem like opposed attitudes "may co-exist." Observes that in Donne, "emphasis on grace or God's doing as opposed to man's does not preclude a politically tinged emphasis on the value of externals in the church, considered in terms of their secular dignity and worth." Notes that Donne in his sermons maintains that one "must beware the eloquence of the preacher and not attribute to it the saving grace of God" (59), and yet, recognizing that the Bible "was written in an eloquent and high-flown style," holds that the preacher "should avoid speaking in a style unfitted for the style of the Holy

Ghost." Notes also that Donne, on occasion, "justifies the use of humanly significant (or even rich) forms in religion on the basis of the Incarnation" (60). Says that Donne recognizes "the inevitable combination of internal worth or means and external show" and, therefore, "stresses outward as well as inward glory and splendor" (61).

405. LeComte, Edward. "Donne's 'The Canonization,' Line 13." *SCN* 41: 69.

Points out that "forward spring" in *Canon* (l. 13) is an idiom meaning "early spring" and that the line can be paraphrased as "When did my chills lower the temperature of the warm weather of a spring that came early?"

406. LeComte, Edward. "John Donne the Lover." *Berkshire Eagle* (Pittsfield, Mass.) (31 March): 9.

Thinks it likely that in January of 1602 Donne, realizing that Ann More, whom he truly loved, was pregnant, hastily married her and later predated the secret marriage so that their first child would arrive nine months after the fictitious date of the ceremony.

407. Lederer, Joseph. "Toutes ses maîtresses profanes: Réflexions sur la poésie érotique de Donne," in *John Donne,* ed. Jean-Marie Benoist, 87–121. Les Dossiers H, gen. eds. Jacqueline de Roux and François Denoël. Herissey: L'Age d'Homme. Translated into French by Claudine Lederer.

Surveys complex and pervasive eroticism in Donne's poetry and prose, especially in the *Elegies,* and argues that, although he is clearly indebted to Ovid, it is not Ovid the moralist that interests him but rather Ovid the liberator of a poetry suffocated by an omnipresent moral preoccupation. Believes that Donne's early amoral sexual views came out of his sense of social inferiority, for which he compensated by an aggressive assertion of the self. Points out that Donne used the Fathers of the Church and scholastic philosophy for his own erotic purposes and how he defied not only the morality of the Church and of society but also of his own sense of guilt. Discusses the Continental and native traditions of anti-Petrarchism and of antifeminism and shows how Donne participated in both. Believes that in later life Donne developed his own brand of neo-Petrarchism, in which the playful conceits of his earlier poetry become serious and convincing. Traces the development of Donne's attitude toward love, sexuality, and femininity from that of a young elegist to that of the preacher and theologian, and maintains that Donne's erotic esotericism, his attacks on Petrarchism, his hesitant Neoplatonism, his antifeminism, and early Don Juanism all reflect his aspiration toward a kind of purification and an effort to achieve a kind of mysticism that he never quite reached.

408. Lepage, John Louis. "Eagles and Doves in Donne and Du Bartas: 'The Canonization.'" *N&Q*, n.s. 30: 427–28.

Suggests that, when referring to the union of the eagle and the dove in *Canon* (l. 22), Donne may have had in mind Du Bartas's *Les Semaines* (I, ii, 173–74) in which, speaking of *impossibilia* that "would follow on accepting the absurd hypothesis of secondary creation *ex nihilo*," he says, "breaking Natures set and sacred use, / The Dove would Eagles, Eagles Doves produce" (427–28). Suggests that Donne may be saying that "lovers create in themselves an alternative world in which contraries are brought impossibly together," a point he makes explicit in *GoodM* and *SunRis*. Points out also that the eagle and dove image points to and makes wittier the reference to the "Phoenix ridle" (l. 23), noting that "the phoenix's mysterious

power of self-regeneration is analogous to the impossible generation of doves from eagles and eagles from doves" (428). Suggests that, in the light of his reading, the comma found in the 1633 edition should be restored after line 22.

409. Low, Anthony. "John Carey and John Donne." *JDJ* 2, no. 1: 111–17.

Reviews John Carey's *John Donne: Life, Mind and Art* (1981), but also presents an "informal consideration of the present state of Donne studies" (112). Comments on several modern biographical-critical studies of Donne, especially Bald's biography (1970). Focuses particularly on various interpretations of Donne's position on religion, noting that all of the various speculations are finally "unprovable." Argues that Carey "has been handicapped by his acceptance of the reactive role thrust on him by the critical and biographical traditions, by his unwillingness to discuss the most familiar poems and passages yet once more, and therefore by his neglect of much of what is best in Donne and his work." Believes that Carey "overemphasizes the disagreeable side of his subject" but thinks that "most of what he has to say is only too probable for it to vanish at the insistence of reviewers" (116).

410. McCormick, Frank. "Donne, the Pope, and 'Holy Sonnet XIV.'" *CEA* 45, no. 2: 23–24.

Suggests that in *HSBatter* (l. 11) Donne is alluding to Henry VIII's petition to the pope to divorce Catherine of Aragon and that perhaps Donne sees a parallel between his and Henry's position: "As Henry had sought the Pope's permission to divorce a wife who had proven unable to bear him a male heir, so the poet seems in these lines belatedly to be asking permission to be released from a fruitless union of another sort [from his Catholicism] . . .

in order that he might enter a potentially more fruitful one—with the Anglican Church, in whose embraces he might enjoy the ample rewards promised by the Anglican establishment to its communicants alone" (23–24). Speculates that, on the other hand, Donne may be asking to be restored to the Catholicism he had forsaken. Believes that Donne is "painfully aware of the fundamental incompatibility of his simultaneous requests," which "is admirably illustrated in the poet's paradoxical assertion in the poem's concluding line that he can never be 'chast, except you ravish mee.'" Maintains that this paradox "dramatizes in a final figure of bold unreason, the intellectual and emotional impasse toward which the poet's quite irreconcilable religious impulses have brought him" (24).

411. McGann, Jerome J. "Romantic and Non-Romantic Works: Comparisons and Contrasts," in *The Romantic Ideology: A Critical Investigation,* 72–80. Chicago: University of Chicago Press.

Discusses briefly how Donne's "probing and skeptical intelligence" in *FirAn* "differs from anything we shall find in any Romantic poem which has developed a comparable level of *critical* (as opposed to imaginative) intensity." Notes that Donne's poem "develops its special personal force not from a Romantic self-consciousness about the grounds of human knowledge but from Donne's self-critical irony that has needed so extreme a lesson to reteach him what he knew very well all along." Points out that Donne "does not question his culture's inherited grounds of judgment for the very reason that he does not see those grounds as culturally determined": "[t]o Donne, the world's corruption (including his own) and the blessedness of heaven (the communion of saints) are not matters of ideology,"

but rather "they are matters of fact and truth" (75). Contrasts Donne's poem with stanzas from Canto IV of Byron's *Childe Harold's Pilgrimage,* in which "the expressive intensity matches Donne's lines but where the force of that expression takes its origin from an implacable nihilism" (76). Maintains that the two poets "differ not in the intensity of their verse but in the special character which the intensity assumes," noting "[t]hat character is in each case a function of sharp differences in their personal, cultural, and historical circumstances" (77).

412. Maguin, Jean-Marie. "Le phénix caché," in *John Donne,* ed. Jean-Marie Benoist, 135–39. Les Dossiers H, gen. eds. Jacqueline de Roux and François Denoël. Herissey: L'Age d'Homme.

Discusses the popularity of the phoenix image from antiquity to the Renaissance, noting how Donne employs it wittily in *Canon.* Through an examination of the phoenix myth and of Elizabethan sexual slang, finds a "hidden" allusion to the phoenix in *Fare* as well as in *Sickness.* Shows how in love poems Donne is using the profane or erotic tradition associated with the phoenix, while in the divine poem he is relying on the sacred tradition surrounding the myth.

413. Mallett, Phillip. *Notes on Selected Poems.* York Notes. Harlow: Longman. 104p. Reissued in 1988.

Contains an introduction to Donne's life and his religious and intellectual background; a note on the text of the poems ([5]–18); synopses of and notes on *Sat3* ([19]–24), *ElPict* (24–26), *ElBed* (27–28); selections from the *Songs and Sonets* (28–54) and from the *Divine Poems* (54–65); commentary on the *Songs and Sonets* (66–88); and "Hints for Study" ([89]–90), followed by examination topics and specimen answers (91–100).

414. Mashiko, Masashi. *Dan kara Waiyatto e: Eishi ni miru Ai to Warai* [From Donne to Wyatt: Love and Laughter in English Poetry]. Tokyo: Yashio shuppan. vi, 336p.

Compares the erotic and obscene poems of Wyatt, Shakespeare, and Donne. Discusses Wyatt as a lecher, Shakespeare as a sodomite, and Donne as a sensualist. Suggests that Donne was obsessed with women all his life and thinks he was, in fact, a sex maniac.

415. Maxton, Hugh. "Josef Brodsky and 'The Great Elegy for John Donne': A Note." *The Crane Bag* 7, no. 1: 62–64.

Calls Josef Brodsky's "The Great Elegy for John Donne" his "finest poem" and explains the difficulties in translating this complex poem into English. Says that Brodsky "owes much in this poem to the English metaphysical school of the seventeenth century," but points out that "the dialectics of the poem's different 'voices' remain difficult even to native speakers of English to whom the metaphysical poets are familiar" (62). Gives his English translation of the poem.

416. Nagasawa, Junji. *Eibungei-shicho no Nagare to Sugata* [The Forms and Development of English Literary Thought]. Tokyo: Hokuseido. 236p.

Surveys the characteristics of Donne's poetry and contrasts Donne the private poet with Milton the public poet from the point of view of the theory of "dissociation of sensibility."

417. Nishiyama, Yoshio. "Donne no 'Twicknam Garden' ni tsuite" [On Donne's "Twicknam Garden"], in *Eibungaku Shiron* [Essays in English Literature in Honor of the Seventy-seventh Anniversary of the Birth of Professor Isamu Muraoka], 122–34. Tokyo: Kinseido.

Presents a biographical reading of *Twick* and comments on Donne's relationship with the Countess of Bedford. Argues that Twick contains politico-religious meanings and reflects the involved political situation of the age, as well as Donne's complicated state of mind.

418. Nye, Robert. "'The body is his book': La poésie de John Donne," in *John Donne*, ed. Jean-Marie Benoist, 141–55. Les Dossiers H, gen. eds. Jacqueline de Roux and François Denoël. Herissey: L'Age d'Homme.

First published in English in *CritQ* 14 (1972): 345–60; translated into French by Annie Bénard. Annotated in *Roberts 1* (entry 479).

419. Oshio, Toshiko. "John Donne no Atarashii Sekai" [John Donne's New Worlds], in *Igirisu Bungaku ni okeru Kagaku Shiso* [Scientific Thoughts in English Literature], ed. Masao Watanabe, 80–102. Tokyo: Kenkyusha.

Discusses the worldview depicted in the *Songs and Sonets* and comments on Donne's interest in new astronomy as presented in *Ignatius*. Concludes that Donne, who was well-acquainted with new scientific discoveries and expressed them extensively in his poems, occupies a unique position in the tradition of metaphysical poetry, not merely as a man but also as a searcher for religious truth.

420. Patterson, Annabel. "Talking About Power." *JDJ* 2, no. 2: 91–106.

Review essay of four books that analyze the effects of power on Renaissance culture: Richard Helgerson's *Self-Crowned Laureates: Spenser, Jonson, Milton and the Literary System* (1983), Jonathan Goldberg's *James I and the Politics of Literature* (1983), *Patronage in the Renaissance,* ed. Guy Fitch Lytle and Stephen Orgel (1981), and *The Power of Forms in the English Renaissance,* ed. Stephen Greenblatt (1982). All four volumes contain commentary on Donne and have been annotated above.

421. Pollock, Zailig. "'The Object, and the Wit': The Smell of Donne's *First Anniversary*." *ELR* 13: 301–18.

Maintains that "the lack of decorum" and "the disconcerting quality of the relationship between the wit of the poem and its ostensible object" in *FirAn* is "not an unfortunate flaw" but is, in fact, "what the poem is about" (302). Discusses Donne's use of "a perverse substitution of wit as fancy" in *FirAn* in contrast to his use of "wit as understanding" in *SecAn,* and argues that in the first poem Donne deliberately "focuses our attention on the poet's wit and its isolation, by making a series of outrageously unconvincing claims for an object which is in reality inconsequential," that object being Elizabeth Drury (304–5). Maintains that "the poet's essentially fanciful claims for Elizabeth Drury's death, so obviously ungrounded in reality, should be seen, in dramatic terms, as an enactment of the concern which is central to the *Anatomy* as a whole, the gap between the object and the wit" (307). Explains that, "like a troubling smell, Donne's obsession with 'the object, and the wit' obtrudes itself onto our notice, pervading every aspect of the poem's structure and texture," and that "[a]s the poem's wit insistently demands that we fix our gaze on the object, the smell becomes increasingly distracting, until we finally realize that the distractions *are* the poem" (307–8). Reads the poem, therefore, as "radically indecorous," maintaining that "there is something grotesque at its heart which cannot be ignored or explained away," and insists that "[a]ny convincing account of Donne's method" in the poem "must acknowledge the madness in it" and that any attempt "to explain this madness away is to explain away the poem itself" (317–18).

422. Raspa, Anthony. *The Emotive Image: Jesuit Poetics in the English Renaissance.* Fort Worth, Tex.: Texas Christian University Press. x, 173p.

Examines the sacred verse of Donne, Crashaw, Jasper Heywood, Robert Southwell, William Alabaster, and Eldred Revett "to show how these English poets were influenced by Jesuit aesthetic verse meditation that was the counterpart to the ascetic *Spiritual Exercises*" of St. Ignatius Loyola and also to show how these poets reflect the baroque world and sensibility that Ignatian spirituality shaped and promulgated. Argues that "Jesuit poetics were constituted of three main elements—'image,' 'affections,' and 'love' and that they influenced English poets for diverse historical and literary reasons" (1). Calls Donne "the greatest of those touched by Ignatian meditation" (3), but notes that the Jesuit influence is limited primarily to the *Holy Sonnets* and *Corona,* citing Crashaw's poetry as most representative of "the flowering of the Ignatian tradition" (4). Unlike Martz (1954), focuses less on the tripartite structure of the poems and more on the broader aspects of Jesuit poetics and spirituality, insisting that Donne's views on "man, reason, and poetry" in his works "are stronger indicators of his place in the history of Ignatian aesthetics than his factual connections with Jesuit verse" (74). Proceeds, however, to comment on some specific, historical connections, such as the relation of *Corona* and the *Holy Sonnets* to *The Practice of Christian Perfection* by the Jesuit St. Francis Borgia. Discusses the psychology of sin and the role of the redemptive will in Donne's religious sonnets and his role in the development of the meditative sonnet, suggesting that Donne's poems most obviously "betray their meditative origins by depicting the understanding acting on memory and will" (75). Outlines Donne's recusant background and says that to suggest that his early spiritual environment "left him intellectually unmarked is unrealistic" (112). Observes that "Donne's approach to sacred poetry conforms to Jesuit aesthetics when these involved no fictions obscuring the clarity of Biblical prototypes," and maintains, therefore, that "[i]t is unnecessary to view Donne's practice of Jesuit or Protestant aesthetics, or both, as conflicting with either his residual Catholic sensibility or his later Anglican position" (114). Discusses also how Donne's meditative verse as well as other meditative poetry is marked stylistically by three characteristics—the use of enthymeme, metaphor of proportion, and paradox.

423. Redpath, Theodore. "Quelques problèmes textuel dans les Songs and Sonets," in *John Donne,* ed. Jean-Marie Benoist, 51–72. Les Dossiers H, gen. eds. Jacqueline de Roux and François Denoël. Herissey: L'Age d'Homme.

First published in English in *E&S* 32 (1979): 57–79.

424. Rissanen, Paavo. *John Donne's Doctrine of the Church.* Helsinki: Finnish Society for Missiology and Ecumenic. 205p.

Published dissertation (Glasgow, 1975). Presents an account of Donne's ecclesiology and sketches "the main outlines of his theological thinking" in order "to show the place which the Church held therein." Discusses Donne's "personal development and the formation of his way of thinking in order to arrive at an understanding of him on his own terms" (3). In the introduction (1–12), comments on the purpose of the study, explains his methodology, and generally outlines the following chapters. Chapter 1, "The Life and Works of John Donne" (13–62), presents a biographical sketch, focusing particularly on Donne's love life and religious life; discusses the love poems in order to emphasize the importance of communication and communion for Donne even in his search for human love; and shows how the same pattern is reflected in his religious development and outlines briefly his basic theology. Divides the discussion of Donne's ecclesiology into two main chapters: "The Church in the World" (63–116) and "The Church in Her Actions" (117–73). The first defines the place of the Church in Donne's "ontological structure, its *raison d'être* in the creation, its position in a world where the Church of Christ had recently suffered a serious split and the rise of the national state required a re-evaluation of the old ideal of the universal Church, and its relationships with the Society," and outlines "the function of the Church, given the above stated conditions and circumstances" (11). The second describes "how the Church fulfills its functions in practice" and comments on man's quest for God and the importance of scripture, preaching, and the sacraments in this search. Maintains that Donne's "preoccupation with communication and communion" provides "the *Leitmotif*" that demonstrates "how Donne's ecclesiology forms a unified structure where the different elements join each other to form a clear and logical entity" (11). Uses primarily the sermons as the main source material but also takes into account the poems and other prose writings. Concludes (174–201) by summarizing how Donne's "experience of reality affected his theological thinking in general and his ecclesiology in particular," and by presenting the results of his research, "paying most attention . . . to that which best displays Donne's originality" (177). Sees the young Donne as a person who "intensely stresses his own individuality, an ego separate and autonomous in the reality which surrounds it" (177), as evidenced, for example, in his experience with women as expressed in the *Elegies* and some of the *Songs and Sonets*. Maintains, however, that Donne's experience with Ann More "lay the beginnings of his ontological conception, which was later to become so decisive for his theology," that is, through his love for his wife he "successfully experienced the burst of an ego in its limited confinements with a shared reality of interpersonal interaction" (179). Argues that Donne's failed ambitions and isolation and later acceptance of a place in society as a priest also played an important role in his theology and his concept of the Church. Maintains that Donne drifted away from Catholicism because he could not submit "his self body and soul, to the authority of the Church" and made "a marriage of convenience" with the Church of England. Claims Donne's attitude of detachment collapsed during his crisis years at Mitcham when "the sense of isolation and separation from the world prompted him into religious meditations" (182). Says that the death of Ann More and his own serious illness in 1623 led Donne to a new relationship with God as a partner, and "in communion with God he had the *we*-experience of a shared reality in a harmonious interaction with all of God's creation" (184). Maintains that his personal development and his view of reality gave Donne's theology its characteristic shape and also shaped his view of the Church. Says that Donne saw the Church not as an institution but an event and believed that its primary function was to lead men to salvation—achieved primarily through its preaching and the sacraments. Concludes with a bibliography (202–5) but has no index.

425. Rogers, Wiliam Elford. "Gestures Toward a Literary History of Lyric," in *The Three Genres and the Interpretation of Lyric,* 176–270. Princeton, N.J.: Princeton University Press.

In a subsection entitled "Verbal Wit in Donne's 'Show me deare Christ' and Herbert's 'The British Church'" (202–20), argues that both poems deal with the same subject matter, draw on the same Christian tradition for their images and symbols, and have many verbal similarities. Maintains that the differences arise primarily "in the way the poets use the figures generated by the main symbols" (204). Distinguishes between natural wit and verbal wit and suggests that this distinction is "a means of articulating how these Metaphysical poems are like each other and thus distinctive of their literary movement" and that this distinction "can be grounded, if at all, in the genre-theory that associates lyric with reciprocal relations" (212). Says that the likenesses between Donne's poem and Herbert's are more important than the differences, "even though the differences probably are more striking" (212–13). Argues that, although both poems use verbal wit, their differences arise because Donne uses "paradoxical wit" and Herbert uses "scholastic wit." Maintains that whereas Donne questions the adequacy of any linguistic means of expressing religious truth, Herbert emphasizes the adequacy of the symbol he has chosen (218).

426. Rothschild, Philippe de. "Traduire «Donne»," in *John Donne,* ed. Jean-Marie Benoist, 75–86. Les Dossiers H, gen ed. Jacqueline de Roux and François Denoël. Herissey: L'Age d'Homme.

Discusses the difficulties of translating Donne's poetry into French by commenting on and presenting his 1975 French translations of *Sappho* and *ElBed* and by printing a second, reworked 1982 version of *Sappho* to show that the translator is never totally satisfied with his rendering and feels compelled to try again.

427. Rowse, A. L. "Father Parsons the Jesuit," in *Eminent Elizabethans*, 41–74. London: Macmillan.

Briefly discusses *Pseudo-Martyr*, calling it Donne's "most important prose work and of acute historical importance" (70). Discusses Donne's refutations of the arguments of the Jesuit Robert Parsons (or Persons), who maintained that Elizabethan Catholics must refuse to take the Oath of Allegiance. Maintains that in *Pseudo-Martyr* Donne "points the finger unerringly" at Persons for his responsibility in occasioning the suffering and death of numerous recusants.

428. Rudnytsky, Peter. "La vue de Dieu," in *John Donne*, ed. Jean-Marie Benoist, 181–96. Les Dossiers H, gen. ed. Jacqueline de Roux and François Denoël. Herissey: L'Age d'Homme.

First published in English in *TSLL* 24 (1982): 185–207; revised and translated into French by Christine Jordis.

429. Saunders, J. W. "John Donne," in *A Biographical Dictionary of Renaissance Poets and Dramatists, 1520–1650*, 39–42. Brighton, Eng.: Harvester Press; Totowa, N.J.: Barnes and Noble.

Presents a brief biographical sketch of Donne and of his works. Claims that "there is no evidence that Donne was fundamentally R[oman] C[atholic], and therefore frustrated by life" and that "[i]f anything he was a rebel against his family's Jesuitism." Says that Donne's career "was that of a normally ambitious wit" (39).

430. Schoneveld, Cornelis W. *Intertraffic of the Mind: Studies in Seventeenth-Century Anglo-Dutch Translation with a Checklist of Books Translated from English into Dutch, 1600–1700*. Publications of the Sir Thomas Browne Institute, no. 3. Leiden: E. J. Brill and Leiden University Press. viii, 270p.

Discusses Johannes Grindal's 1655 Dutch translation of the 1638 edition of *Devotions* (79–85). Examines in detail a passage from Meditation XVII, along with passages from the Expostulation and Prayer that follow it, to show that Grindal's translation "preserves a good deal of the style [of Donne's prose] but by no means all of the characteristic phrasal and rhythmic patterning." Notes that Grindal's attempt to reproduce Donne's language "sometimes results in an English rather than a Dutch word order" (85). Comments briefly also on Constantijn Huygens, first Dutch translator of Donne's poems. Says that Huygens is "untypical in the field of Anglo-Dutch translation" in that he was "one of a very small number of Dutchmen interested in English poetry." Notes that "[n]o other seventeenth-century Dutch writer came anywhere near him in the number of English poems translated by him, small though this in itself is: it amounts to no more than a dozen lyrics by John Donne and the epigrams of Archibald Armstrong" (117). In an alphabetical checklist of Dutch translations of English works published between 1600 and 1700 (163–245), lists Huygens's translation of Donne's poems and Grindal's translation of *Devotions*.

431. Selden, Ray. "L'incarnation, conviction de John Donne," in *John Donne*, ed. Jean-Marie Benoist, 163–79. Les Dossiers H, gen. eds. Jacqueline de Roux and François Denoël. Herissey: L'Age d'Homme.

First published in English in *CritQ* 17 (1975): 55–73; translated into French by Mylène Garrigues. Annotated in *Roberts 2* (entry 789).

432. Sellin, Paul R. *John Donne and "Calvinist" Views of Grace*. Amsterdam: Vrije Universiteit Boeckhandel/Uitgeverij. 61p.

The introduction (1–3) suggests that "many distinctions drawn by Anglo-American critics between Donne's religious views and those endorsed by Calvinist orthodoxy may rest not so much on misapprehension of Donne's statements as on misconceptions about the Reformed church of his time and what Calvinist orthodoxy of the sort that triumphed at [the Synod of] Dort [1619] actually thought" (3). "Predestination" (5–15) examines four sermons that Donne preached at Heidelberg and The Hague soon after the Synod of Dort in order to challenge the received view that Donne opposed the Calvinist doctrine of predestination. "Discipline" (17–25) argues that, concerning matters of discipline, Donne "identifies himself with his pastoral brethren in the Reformed church who, at that moment, were all expected to conform under oath to the tenets of the Reformed faith as defined at Dort" (24). Points out that Donne not only "speaks of himself as one with his Dutch and Walloon colleagues in the tasks of administering the sacraments and preaching the Word," but also that he "considers their calling and orders as equal to his own" (25). "Church-Government" (27–34) maintains that Donne "extends the authority of lawfully convened Reformed synods full honour" and considers their decisions as "binding on clergy in matters of doctrine" (28). Argues that Donne "would have welcomed Dort with full acquiescence, whether with respect to the parties involved or the doctrines," noting that "the issues evidently meant enough to him that he was willing later to air his views even before authorities to whom they might not prove wholly pleasing" (33). Believes that Donne was "a full-fledged Contra-Remonstrant" (34). "Perseverance" (35–47) examines two important favorable Puritan responses to Donne's preaching and piety—Constantijn Huygens's fragmentary comments on Donne's preaching (written between 1629 and 1631) and Johannes Grindal's Dutch translation of *Devotions* entitled *Aendachtige Bedenckingen* (Amsterdam, 1655). Argues that "[w]hen one

speculates about 'Puritan' responses to Donne's preaching and piety, therefore, caution should remain the watchword" (47). The "Conclusion" (49–50) succinctly summarizes the main argument of the study: "To judge by the two instances of Donne's preaching in Calvinist sanctuaries and by the reception of both his preaching and piety in the Netherlands, the idea is questionable that Donne was hostile to the basic institutions and tenets of Calvinist orthodoxy as expressed in the formulations of the Synod of Dort" (49). Concludes with notes (51–58); Appendix A (59–60), which contains a bibliographical note on Grindal's translation of the *Devotions;* and Appendix B (61), which gives an English translation of Grindal's preface to the reader. Reviews: Peter Dane in *AUMLA* 63 (1985): 75–76; Samuel M. Garrett in *Historical Magazine of the Protestant Episcopal Church* 54 (1985): 101–03; C. H. George in *Albion* 17 (1985): 84–85; Terry G. Sherwood in *Ren&R,* n.s. 9 (1985): 231–32; Roger Zuber in *DSS* 147 (1985): 206–7; Frederick H. Shriver in *Church History* 55 (1986): 536–37; Stanley Stewart in *JDJ* 7 (1988): 273–86.

433. Sellin, Paul R. *John Donne en de "Calvinistische" Predestinatieleer*. Amsterdam: Free University Press. 17p.

An oration delivered on the occasion of entering upon the office of Professor Ordinarius in English Language and Literature in the Faculty of Letters/Department of English at the Free University of Amsterdam on 1 December 1982. Investigates the sermons Donne gave in Heidelberg and The Hague shortly after the National Synod of Dordrecht in 1619, and questions current Anglo-American notions regarding Donne's enmity toward the Calvinist doctrine of predestination. An expanded version in English appears in the introduction and first chapter of *John Donne and "Calvinist" Views of Grace* (above).

434. Shami, Jeanne M. "Donne's Protestant Casuistry: Cases of Conscience in the *Sermons.*" *SP* 80: 53–66.

Despite recent critics who place Donne in "a distinctly Protestant typological tradition," one that focuses "on the literal, historical meaning of biblical personages" (53), Shami sees seventeenth century Anglican casuistry as a more useful context for examining the examples Donne uses in his sermons. Maintains that Donne was "trying to temper the extremes between zeal and discretion" (56) and believed, therefore, that "the best models" to offer his congregation were not extreme examples but rather those of a "middle nature—men like David, like Job, like Paul." Notes that, "even in applying the examples of good and rectified men," Donne continually asks his hearers "to understand how the generally virtuous examples provided by these men can sometimes tend towards errors" (60), thereby warning his congregation "against inordinate zeal" while, at the same time, warning them "against extremes of discretion" (61). Maintains that Donne's intention is "to prepare his hearers to become their own casuists," capable of making "difficult and subtle choices for themselves" (61–62). Says that Donne believed that a good example is "one which did not rely for its exemplary value entirely on its peculiar circumstance but on its applicability in forming the consciences of his hearers" (62). Shows how in two sermons, "one encouraging emulation of Esther's zeal" and "the other of Paul's discretion" (65), Donne repeats a common pattern in his sermons. Says his "use of types can best be seen as casuistical because it is not satisfied with the absolute claims of any Law, externally applied." Claims that in the ser-

mons Donne "examines historical rather than symbolically hypothetical cases of conscience, choosing his types not only for the proven rightness of their choice, but also because the procedures by which their choices were made are *exemplary*." Concludes that, for Donne, biblical types or even persons such as Elizabeth Drury, Mrs. Herbert, and James I "are exemplary not for the Image of God in them, but for the ways in which they have worked to rectify that image, not entirely depraved but yet stained, in a fallen world" (66).

435. Shawcross, John T. "A Consideration of Title-Names in the Poetry of Donne and Yeats." *Names* 31: 159–66.

Citing numerous examples, warns readers not to base critical interpretations of Donne's poems on their titles, many of which were not entitled by Donne himself but by copyists and early editors. Discusses how titles often "delimit and even diminish our reading" of a poem. Notes for instance, that if one reads Donne's epigram that begins "Both rob'd of air" without the title, the poem appears to be a "witty comment on love and lovemaking"; but if one reads the assigned title, "Hero and Leander," he is directed to see the poem as a rendering of the story of the two famous lovers, "not some generalized witty social comment." Similarly shows that the title "Klockius" given one of the epigrams "does not really lead us very far," while the title "Phryne" given another leads the reader "to an attitude before reading the poem if he knows the reference [to a Greek prostitute]" (160). Further maintains that certain titled poems, such as "Twick," may lead to erroneous biographical readings and warns in general against biographical interpretations of poems. Observes that Donne is "one often not given to specifics involving a person or event, or, in comparison with other poets, to an allusive reference or complex of background," noting that the poems in which he employs names "most frequently are public forms, the epithalamia, the epicedes, and the verse letters" (161).

436. Shawcross, John T. "The Source of an Epigram by John Donne." *ELN* 21, no. 1: 23–24.

Rejects R. C. Bald's suggestion (1970) that Donne may have personally witnessed the event that took place during the English siege of La Coruña in 1589 that is commemorated in *Wall,* and suggests instead that its source is *A Trve Coppie of a Discourse written by a Gentleman, employed in the late Voyage of* Spaine *and* Portingale (London: Printed for Thomas Woodcock, 1589), attributed to Anthony Wingfield. Points out that there is nothing unusual in Donne's having based a poem on a published account rather than upon personal experience. Cites *Ship* as another probable example.

437. Shawcross, John T. "A Text of John Donne's Poems: Unsatisfactory Compromise." *JDJ* 2, no. 1: 1–19.

Comments on problems that an editor must confront in editing Donne's poems, such as how to resolve conflicting and/or different texts in various manuscripts and early printed editions, how to order the poems within a generic category, how to order genres in a single volume edition, and how to resolve the question of classification by genre for certain poems. Argues that the ways in which editors resolve these issues will obviously affect critical interpretation of the poems. Maintains that, because of the complexity of these issues, any editor of Donne, after weighing as objectively as possible all the available evidence, will be forced nonetheless "to step in and make sense of a line," will need "to

interfere," and, "whatever textual conclusion is made, it is going to be an unsatisfactory compromise for some readers" (16). Notes, for instance, that in l. 29 of *Carey,* "the only poem we have in Donne's own hand, it is impossible to say with certainty that the next to last letter in the word "Religions" is an *n* and not a *u,* even though all other known texts of the poem have "Religions," not "Religious." Insists that an editor must decide which word to print, and inevitably some readers will be dissatisfied with his choice.

438. Sinfield, Alan. *Literature in Protestant England, 1560–1660.* London: Croom Helm; Totowa, N.J.: Barnes and Noble. viii, 160p.

This survey of English Renaissance literature in relation to Protestantism mentions Donne several times and uses examples from his poetry and prose to illustrate Protestant concepts and attitudes. For instance, quotes lines from *HSBatter* to illustrate the Protestant view that the universe was "divided by deep and perpetual strife—between God's wisdom and our benighted recalcitrance" (9), and sees the *Holy Sonnets,* in general, as reflecting Donne's acceptance of the "[P]rotestant view of his own unworthiness." In particular, discusses the influence of Protestant thinking on love and marriage in Donne's poetry (73–80). Argues that although Donne "makes explicit the irreligious basis of Ovidian love and hence challenges, outrageously, Christian thought about sexuality" in the *Elegies* and some of the *Songs and Sonets,* he probably was only joking and enjoying a bit of "witty irreverence" (53). Maintains, however, that Donne's "poems of reciprocated, fulfilling and enduring sexual love are generally his most popular," and argues that in such poems as *Canon, Anniv, GoodM,* and *LovGrow* "the pattern of feeling in them derives from the [P]rotestant conception of matrimonial harmony." Maintains, in fact, that "[t]he pressure of the [P]rotestant stress on marriage is evident even in some of Donne's Ovidian poems," which "include incidental remarks strangely respectful of marriage" (73). Maintains that Donne's "original attitude to sexual love . . . is responsible for major features of his style," and that "[h]is conceits, paradoxes and puns express the new and special complexities of reciprocal, sexual, continuing and sanctified love" (77). Says that during the Renaissance, "Donne alone achieved a significant and untrammelled assertion of human love" (80).

439. Sisson, Charles. "John Donne et la possibilité d'une poésie religieuse," in *John Donne,* ed. Jean-Marie Benoist, 157–62. Les Dossiers H, gen. eds. Jacqueline de Roux and François Denoël. Herissey: L'Age d'Homme. Translated from English by Annie Bénard.

Discusses the possibility of the revival of religious poetry in the twentieth century and comments on the appeal of Donne's sacred poetry for our age.

440. Smith, A. J. *Literary Love: The Role of Passion in English Poems and Plays of the Seventeenth Century.* London: Edward Arnold. viii, 184p.

Argues that "the true distinction of English writing about love between Shakespeare and Milton is that it takes love for a hunger of sense and spirit, which engages the intelligence no less than the feelings," and that "[i]n the tension between such divergent propensities of our nature is engendered a living metaphysic of love." Says that Donne's love poems present "a lover who zestfully accommodates himself to the precariousness of sexual desire, but also claims that he and his mistress have found a condition of mutual love which altogether preserves them from alteration" (viii). Chapter 5, "The Course of Altering Things" (87–118), contrasts Donne's view of love in the *Songs and Sonets* and *Elegies* with the highly idealized conception of love in the poems of Dante, Petrarch, and, to a lesser extent, their English and Italian imitators to show that Donne "brings love poetry agreeably down to earth from its rarefied Tuscan retreat" (95). Points out that lovers in Donne's poetry "have style as well as zest, managing the civic jungle they inhabit with a jaunty elegance" that is often "outrageously funny," and thus "challenge us to recognize ourselves and our world in the vivid little episodes they rehearse" (98). Acknowledges that "the properties of European petrarchism make up the *mise en scène* of Donne's drama of love" but insists that Donne's love poetry differs from that of other imitators "not only because of the way he uses the devices he reworks" but also "because he is always pulling even conventional materials round to point another way" and "giving them rich new life," thus making "the old familiar elements come to life in an ironic drama of sexual appetite" that is "ironically realised" in the "tense hissing deliberateness of tone and movement" and in the "incessant play of comic wit" (99). Says that often Donne "personates a lover who moves between guarded tenderness and sceptical detachment, never making an innocent commitment," noting that often "[w]hole poems act out such a mocking wariness." Maintains, however, that "[w]hat most distinguishes Donne from the idealizing love poets is his attitude to his own experience, and himself" (101). Says that Donne writes as "a venturer who has tried the extent of amorous life" and who "is well in possession of his findings," adding that "the predicaments of earlier love poets scarcely come home to us so intimately, however magnificent the poetry they engender" (105–6). Discusses *Fare,* suggesting that the poem "amounts to an intricate commentary on the lover's servitude to sense" (107) and also "deflatingly ribalds those who seek something divine in love" (115). Argues also that the way Donne's love poems relate to one another is "part of what they say," noting that the attitudes he expresses in one poem are not denied in later poems; thus "one truth isn't annulled by another" (116). Says that Donne's love poetry reminds the reader that his life is not "organized in literary categories," that man does not need "to sublimate his sensual nature," and that he also does not need "to undertake a new course of reading" in order "to develop an idea of mutual love" (117). Suggests that Donne, at times, "has more in common with Boccaccio and Machiavelli than with the idealists and transcendentalists of an opposing Tuscan tradition," for "[h]e sought his own way to master the infirmities of our condition, through the senses not in spite of them" (118). Chapter 6, "Beyond All Date" (119–30), argues that such poems as *GoodM, Canon,* and *Ecst* present lovers who "don't need to try some neoplatonic ascent to a realm of universal form beyond the world of sense and particular embodiments," maintaining that, "[o]n the contrary, what distinguishes them is . . . their achieved embodied mutualness which sets them apart from the common course of affairs in the world" (120). Notes that in some of Donne's finest poems the lovers' love is "uniquely exempt from time," and it makes them "superior to all the world's honours and riches and the sun itself; indeed their state here on earth now as human lovers must be even better blessed than they will find themselves in the life of thorough but communal bliss to come" (121). Maintains that Donne "insists that a mature love brings sense

and spirit into one" and cites *LovGrow* as a poem that "marvelously realises the perfected state of love" (129), "a love which is entirely mutual, and yet so essentially human," that it "will be proof against frailty and decay" (130). Reviews: A. B. Chambers in *JDJ* 4 (1985): 109–20.

441. Steadman, John M. "'Teeth will be Provided': Satire and Religious or Ecclesiastical Humor." *Thalia* 6, no. 1: 23–31.
    In an essay on the use of religious and ecclesiastical humor by English Renaissance writers, including Spenser, Shakespeare, Jonson, Samuel Butler, and Milton, comments briefly on Donne's "Why Puritans Make Long Sermons" in *Paradoxes,* noting that Puritans were frequently the target of satire.

442. Strong, Roy. *The English Renaissance Miniature.* London: Thames and Hudson. 208p.
    Very briefly comments on Isaac Oliver's 1616 miniature portrait of Donne, painted "in a style which, if it were not for the date on it and the dress, we would assign to the 1590s, utilizing the [Nicholas] Hilliard manner with loose brushstrokes and placing the figure against an old-fashioned blue background" (180).

443. Stull, William L. "Sonnets Courtly and Christian." *HSL* 15–16 (1983–84): 1–15.
    Revised and expanded version of "'Why Are Not *Sonnets* Made of Thee?': A New Context for the 'Holy Sonnets' of Donne, Herbert, and Milton," in *MP* 80 (1982): 129–35 (entry 334).

444. Sullivan, Ernest W., II. "*Donne Manuscripts:* Dalhousie II." *JDJ* 2, no. 2: 79–89.
    Gives a detailed bibliographical description of the Dalhousie II manuscript, now in the library at Texas Tech University, and calls it "[o]ne of the most important manuscripts of

Donne's poems to surface in this century, a manuscript that the early evidence suggests will be absolutely critical to the establishment of the texts of Donne poems it contains" (83). Notes that the manuscript contains 29 of his "most important and frequently taught poems" and "was almost certainly transcribed during Donne's lifetime" (83). Points out also that "the texts of the poems in Dalhousie II are astonishingly close to those in Donne's 1633 *Poems*" (84). Gives a complete inventory of the contents of the manuscript.

445. Sullivan, Ernest, II. "Replicar Editing of John Donne's Texts." *JDJ* 2, no. 1: 21–29.

Maintains that "[m]odern bibliographical theory and methodology have produced Donne texts more aesthetically satisfactory than anything Donne probably wrote, thereby turning Donne literary materials into the textual equivalents of 'replicars,' automobiles which reproduce the external appearance of a classic original but which incorporate modern automotive technology to make them more driveable." Points out that, "the surviving transcription of Donne's *Biathanatos* (Bodleian Library, shelfmark MS. e Musaeo 131) and the two settings of sheet 'S' in the 1647 first edition of *Biathanatos* show that the two compositors who set the different S sheets deliberately produced Donne replicarriages" (21) by restyling Donne's manuscript "to suit themselves" (22). Comments also on John Donne the younger's mislabelling and rearranging the order of his father's letters in *Letters* (1651), noting that Sir Edmund Gosse in his *Life and Letters of John Donne* (1899), while complaining of the younger Donne's edition, "commits the very same errors" (23) and produces "a highly unsatisfactory form of replicar—a modernized version of

the text with the true extent of the modernization misrepresented" (24). Points out that even Grierson in his edition of Donne's poems (1912) finally capitulated to the "desire for 'correct' punctuation that would conform to his own understanding of the poems rather than for Donne's original punctuation," thus making his edition "a replicar rather than a restored original" (25). Shows how Helen Gardner in her 1978 edition of *The Divine Poems* used the holograph of Donne's poem to Lady Carey and Mrs. Riche "to justify imposing her own ideas about metrics, punctuation, and spelling on Donne's poems" (26). Concludes that these examples show that "editing Donne's texts to make them more stylistically consistent, commercial, intelligible, or aesthetic ultimately makes them something other than what we really want, Donne's texts" (28).

446. Thompson, M. Geraldine. "The Range of Irony in Three Visions of Judgement: Erasmus' *Julius Exclusus,* Donne's *Ignatius His Conclave,* and Lucian's *Dialogues of the Dead.*" *Erasmus of Rotterdam Society Yearbook* 3: 1–22.

Compares and contrasts modes of irony in *Ignatius* with Erasmus's *Julius Exclusus* and Lucian's *Dialogues of the Dead*. Says that if the second century Greek Lucian had not understood "the value of fiction as corrective, and especially the ironic dialogue" (2), Erasmus and Donne might never have written their ironic dialogues. Suggests that although *Ignatius* "reinforces many of the themes of *Julius,*" it "diverges from it in tone and structure, and even in the modes of its irony, or ironies" (13). Points out that whereas Erasmus attacks "sins of the corrupted will," Donne in his satire "concentrates almost totally on aberrations of the intelligence—credal differences, heresies, hypothetical interpretations of ecclesiastical law." Suggests that the hell Donne creates in *Ignatius* is "closer to Lucian's Hades than to Dante's inferno" (14). Observes also that there is "little dramatic irony" in *Ignatius* but "there are countless varieties of satiric irony: mimicry, caricature, lampoon, parody, and hyperbole" (15). Suggests that in *Ignatius,* as in *Julius,* "knowledge is the ingredient that makes the agent of wrong-doing totally responsible" (19). Believes that Donne is more like Lucian than Erasmus is, especially "in his ridiculing of what some hold sacred." Cites two passages in which Donne allows his "denizens of hell" to treat, "first, the Trinity, and then the Eucharist, with ridicule or at least with misplaced facetiousness," which Christian readers find "objectionable." Says that although it is the damned who scoff, the passages have "an unpleasant ring" and are "repellent" (21).

447. Tromly, Frederic B. "Milton Responds to Donne: 'On Time' and 'Death Be Not Proud.'" *MP* 80: 390–93.

Points out that although "scholars have not been able to discover manifest borrowings from Donne in Milton's verse," there is, in fact, "at least one significant link between the poets which has been overlooked": the last line in a manuscript version of Milton's "On Time" (in Bodleian Library, MS Ashmole 36, 37, fol. 22) "clearly appropriates" the last line of *HSDeath.* Believes the link between the two poems has not been recognized, since the line under discussion does not appear in the fair copy of "On Time" in the Trinity manuscript nor in the *Poems* of 1645. Suggests that a comparison of the two lines illustrates the "'temperamental antagonism' between Milton and Donne which critics have deduced" (390). Thinks it likely that "Milton wrote the Donnean final line of the Bodleian text at an early stage

of composition and later revised it with compulsive hindsight" (391). Points out similarities in phraseology and theme in the two poems but notes that the tone and movement of Milton's poem "are so diametrically opposed to the disconcerting fragmentation of Donne's poem as to suggest that Milton was consciously creating a counterstatement" (392). Conjectures that "Milton read Donne's poem not long after its publication, found its chop-logic and ambivalence disconcerting, and responded with a poem which attempts to make good its dubious triumph over mortality" (393).

448. Wadsworth, Randolph L., Jr. "Donne's 'To Sr. Edward Herbert, at Julyers.'" *Expl* 41, no. 3: 21–23.

Argues that the last five lines of *EdHerb* "make the poem into an example," a rhetorical form, which, according to Thomas Blundeville (*The Arte of Logike* [London, 1617], 175), is a kind of argument wherein "one proceeds from one particular to prove another particular, by reason of some likenes that is betwixt them . . . In taking the first particular, you may by an unperfect induction imply an universall Proposition. And so from that universall Proposition to proceed by order of Syllogisme unto the other particular implyed in the conclusion of the Example." Shows the subtle and complex argument of the poem as a result of its concluding five lines.

449. Ware, Tracy. "Donne and Augustine: A Qualification." *N&Q,* n.s. 30: 425–27.

Suggests, with reference to his Whitehall sermon delivered on 30 April 1620, that Donne's admiration for St. Augustine "has its limitations." Argues that in the sermon Donne treats Augustine's opposition of temporal and eternal blessings ironically, recognizing that "his acknowledged master is less reliable than Scripture," his "ultimate authority." Points out that "[e]ven before his ordination, Donne emphasizes that his concern is with the alignment, rather than the opposition, of the temporal and the eternal" (427).

450. Woudhuysen, H. R. "Two More Books from the Library of John Donne." *BC* 32: 349.

Based on "an auctioneer's and a bookseller's catalogues," tentatively identifies two more books known, or believed, to be owned by Donne, both containing autographs of Donne's name: St. Isidore, Archbishop of Seville, and Martinanus Mineus Felix Capella, *Isidori originum libri viginti et Martiani Capellae de nuptijs Philologiae & Mercurij libri nouem* (Basel, 1577), and Ellis Heywood, S.J., *Il Moro d'Helisco Heivodo Inglese* (Florence, 1556). Notes that the latter is an "imaginary dialogue between [Thomas] More and six friends on the nature of true happiness" and "is set in his garden at Chelsea and dedicated to Cardinal Pole." Heywood was Donne's uncle and More's grandnephew.

1984

451. Aizawa, Yoshihisa. "John Donne no 'Shunen Tsuitoshi' Ko (7)" [A Study of John Donne's *Anniversaries* (7)]. *Jinbungakka Ronshu* [Bulletin of the Faculty of Humanities, Ibaraki University] 17: 249–67.

Part 7 of an eight-part series of articles. Analyzes the structure and meaning of the *Anniversaries,* commenting on various interpretations of "she" in the poems. Concludes that "she" means the various identities that have been suggested as well as Elizabeth Drury herself.

452. Anderson, Judith H. "Walton: Likeness and Truth," in *Biographical Truth: The Representation of Historical Persons in Tudor-Stuart Writing,* 52–71. New Haven, Conn.: Yale University Press.

Calls Walton's biography "a biographical watershed, in part because of the artificiality—the artfulness" and "in part because of its historicity" (52), and suggests similarities between Renaissance portrait painting and Walton's biographical techniques and purpose. Points out that Walton's portrait of Donne "is life-writing and should not be confused with the demands and purposes of modern biography," noting that "life-writing" is "more open, ambiguous, and potentially more artificial" than modern biography (56). Maintains that Walton's portrait of Donne is "an honorific memorial and, quite literally, a monumental work of art" (57). Discusses such matters as Walton's manner of using sources and quotations, his handling of Donne's letters, his dramatization of events, his uses of aphorisms and analogies, his interjections of his own opinion, and his subjectivity. Stresses that in Renaissance biographies "the writer constructs the life through his own memory, as well as through historical evidence and literary art," and that "[h]is involvement is thus at once historically real and doubly mind-made" (71). Concludes, therefore, that Walton's picture of Donne is "a real seventeenth-century view of a real life lived in historical time"; and "[s]een as a skillful contemporary portrayal of a late Renaissance person, Walton's *Life of Donne* is valuable, irreplaceable even by a greater, more accurate body of facts, and within the frame of its own vision, it is true" (69).

453. Auberlen, Eckhard. "Love Poetry," in *The Commonwealth of Wit: The Writer's Image and His Strategies of Self-Representation in Elizabethan Literature,* 34–39. Studies and Texts in English, ed. Joerg O. Fichte, Hans-Werner Ludwig, and Alfred Weber. Tübingen: Gunter Narr Verlag.

Compares *BedfReas* to Jonson's "On Lucy Countess of Bedford" to show that "a similar set of Petrarchist conventions could be employed for widely divergent modes of self-representation." Points out that in his poem, Jonson presents himself as "a dedicated professional who combines his praise of the Countess with a celebration of the powers of poetic imagination," while

Donne "uses the same language of Petrarchism to enrich the poet-patroness relationship with a spiritual discussion which reduces the embarrassment of the gentleman amateur forced by necessity to write an epistle mendicant" (39).

454. Baumgaertner, Jill. "'Harmony' in Donne's 'La Corona' and 'Upon the Translation of the Psalms.'" *JDJ* 3: 141–56.

Maintains that the "most profound development of seventeenth-century ideas of harmony" in Donne's poetry occurs in *Sidney,* in which he demonstrates his "facility with a musical vocabulary and his familiarity with the Renaissance musical idiom," and also in *Corona* in which Donne "goes beyond these musical mechanics to deal with a musical ideology and a consideration of harmony in its broadest definition" (142–43). Discusses both poems to show that in *Sidney* Donne depends primarily on "wordplay, pun, and traditional musical metaphors," but that in *Corona* "the harmony he is reaching toward is one which may include musical elements, but also one which does not stop with musical considerations." Points out, for example, that the seven poems in *Corona* "relate in surprising ways to the divine qualities" that Thomas Robinson in his *The Schoole of Musicke* (1603) attributes to "the seven steps of the musical scale" (147), and notes other "deep-seated connections" the sonnet sequence has not only "with Renaissance ideas of music and harmony" (151) but also with ideas found in Victor Zuckerkandl's *Sound and Symbol: Music and the External World* (1956).

455. Baumlin, James S. "A Note on the 1649/1650 Editions of Donne's *Poems*." *JDJ* 3: 97–98.

Announces a hitherto unrecorded copy of the 1649 edition of Donne's *Poems,* describes the volume, and shows how it presents "further evidence of the close relationship" between the 1649 and 1650 editions.

456. Belcher, Hilary, and Erica Swale. "Catch a Falling Star." *Folklore* 95: 210–20.

Points out the belief that, "when a star fell, its remains could be seen upon the ground, in the form of a patch or lump of jelly or slime." Examines "the nature of the various jelly-like substances which have been implicated," presents an "historical account of what has been written on the subject," and lists "some literary allusions" (210). Notes that in *Eclog* (l. 205) Donne makes reference to star-jelly: "As he that sees a starre fall, runs apace / And findes a gellie in the place."

457. Bentley, Greg. "Donne's 'Witchcraft by a Picture.'" *Expl* 42, no. 3: 15–17.

Suggests that, although *Witch* is generally seen as a conventional poem about a mistress bewitching the speaker, Donne's use of "contracted sentence structure and ambiguous imagery" makes possible an alternative reading in which the roles of the lovers are reversed and "[t]he speaker, a man who has bewitched his mistress, becomes half afraid of falling victim to his own spell, so he breaks it by breaking off the relationship" (15). Points out that "[t]he speaker not only acknowledges the woman's innocence and sincerity," but also "acknowledges, without hint of self-condemnation, his own malice and witchcraft" (17).

458. Berezkiva, V. I. "Iz istorii zhanra esse v angliskoi literature XVII veka" [From the History of the Essay Genre in Seventeenth-Century English Literature]. *Sovetskaia nauka* 6: 24–30.

Surveys the impact of "human individualism" on the seventeenth century essay and argues that a growing interest in individualism in the period manifested itself in a "new form" of prose that was characterized by an open intimacy and a confessional quality not previously seen in English letters. Sees Donne, Burton, and Browne as key figures in the development of this new form. Discusses the role of individualism and stylistic innovation in *Paradoxes, Devotions,* and select sermons. Concludes that the focus on the mind in the seventeenth century essay laid the groundwork for the prose of a "new era."

459. Booty, John. "Joseph Hall, *The Arte of Divine Meditation,* and Anglican Spirituality," in *The Roots of the Modern Christian Tradition,* ed. E. Rozanne Elder, with intro. by Jean Leclercq, 200–228. The Spirituality of Western Christendom, 2. Kalamazoo, Mich.: Cistercian Publications.

Discusses Joseph Hall's *The Arte of Divine Meditation* (1606) as illustrative of seventeenth century Anglican spirituality and suggests that the *Holy Sonnets* in the 1633 edition form a meditative sequence on the Eucharist that is not unlike Hall's meditations.

460. Chessell, Del. "A Constant Shaping Pressure: Mortality in Poetry." *CR* 26: 3–17.

Comments on *Sickness,* citing it as an outstanding poem concerning "an individual human being confronting the unimaginable fact of his imminent extinction, and imagining it—shaping for himself an idea of death that is uniquely his, because it is founded on a recognition of the distinctive qualities of his consciousness, his achievement, his very self." Says that Donne "draws his images in this poem from the commonplaces of mediaeval Christianity" but "completely remakes them, fires them with the passionate urgency of his address and transforms them into images of personal necessity, grounded in the physical reality of his sickness" (9). Shows how Donne's "courage and honesty" will not allow

him to "shy away from or stop short of the fullest imagining of what death will mean," while at the same time they "allow him to do without certainty, resting his hope in the idea of death he has realized out of the depth of his being" (12). Compares and contrasts Donne's poem with *Everyman,* Herbert's "Death," and Henry King's "The Exequy," and concludes that what these works "have in common is the effort of the imagination to come to terms with mortality—an effort that succeeds to a greater or lesser extent from poem to poem as the poet allows his idea of death to take shape from within, answering to the configurations and pressures of his peculiar self" (16).

461. Collmer, Robert G. "Donne Redone: A Literary Descent into the Vernacular." *Texas Humanist* 6, no. 6: 37–38.

Cites popular uses of and/or allusions to "Meditation XVII" of *Devotions,* "ranging from outright citations to parodies to dim echoes" (38), in twentieth century book titles (Ernest Hemingway's *For Whom the Bell Tolls* and Thomas Merton's *No Man Is an Island*), in a 1962 movie title (*No Man Is an Island*); in newspaper and popular magazine articles; in the titles of Baptist sermons; in cartoons, comic books, and advertisements; and even in bumper stickers. Suggests that "the final test of a literary work's greatness rests with its durability, not with the judgment of a few *cognoscenti,*" and maintains that "[p]uns, distortions, and echoes of a work reveal its intimacy, its permanence as [a] cultural treasure" (37). Says that Donne "has suffered (or triumphed) in being brought into the hands of everyone" and that Donne, "who redid others, has been redone" (38).

462. Cornelia, Marie. "Donne's Humour and Wilson's 'Arte of Rhetorique.'" *ArielE* 15, no. 1: 31–43.

Maintains that "far too much of Donne's poetry has been taken too seriously for too long," and thus attempts "to show by reference to standard rhetorical devices for rousing 'mirth' that Donne was not only trying to be clever" but also "was often trying to be funny" (31). Briefly traces the history of the rhetorical tradition of the art of jesting from Cicero's *De Oratore* to Thomas Wilson's *Arte of Rhetorique* and claims that "Donne was very much aware of this tradition, that he knew the devices for rousing laughter well, and that he used them freely" (32). Notes that the chief rhetorical devices for creating laughter, as presented by Wilson, were "[m]imicking, overstatement or exaggeration, punning, paradox, irony, and thwarting of the reader's expectations" (33), and illustrates Donne's use of these devices, especially in the *Elegies* and the *Songs and Sonets*. Maintains that "Donne had something of the comedian in him and as a result produced some fine comic writing" (42), and warns against reading his poetry "too solemnly" (43).

463. Crombie, Winifred. "'To Enter in These Bonds Is to Be Free': Semantic Relations and the Baroque Prose Style of John Donne." *Lang&S* 17: 123–38.

Argues that "some of those features of Donne's prose that have led to its being labeled baroque can best be described in terms of semantic relational features, that is, in terms of those semantic relations that account for the effect of linguistic context on the interpretation of clauses and sentences, and that the 'long loose' sentences [as described by Joan Webber (1963)] are, in fact, very tightly semantically structured." Supports this position by examining an extract from a sermon Donne preached at St. Paul's on 29 January 1625 "in the light of descriptive categories from text seman-

tics" and by discussing "the stylistic relevance of the description" (123).

464. DeStefano, Barbara L. "Evolution of Extravagant Praise in Donne's Verse Epistles." *SP* 81: 75–93.

Argues that Donne's verse epistles to noble ladies "are to be read literally" and that Donne "means to say that the addressees literally embody perfect virtue because they are good Christians to whom it has been revealed that they share the humanity of Christ, that they are the glory of God, and can choose to be saved." Maintains, therefore, that these poems are "in one sense, Donne's most ambitious and audacious religious expression" (76), and views them as "meditations on virtue wherein he audaciously fuses the classical epideictic tradition to Christian religiosity to create a new emphatic high style to praise man as the glory of God, a unique style which finds various fruitions in the *Anniversaries*" (76–77). Believes, therefore, that the epistles to noble ladies are "best understood in the tradition of the compelling religious ardor and passion of the medieval religious lyric rather than the sophistications of Platonism and Petrarchism" (77). Divides the verse epistles into three groups: those written between 1592 and 1595 (to male friends while Donne was at Lincoln's Inn), those composed between 1597 and 1608 (also to men while Donne sought a position at court), and those written between 1605 and 1614 (to noble ladies), and discusses the evolution of extravagant praise in each group. Insists that as long as critics view Donne's verse epistles to noble ladies (and also the *Anniversaries*) "as Platonic or Petrarchan sophistications, the suspicion of hypocrisy will continue to mar Donne's reputation," but that recognizing Donne's "radical view of virtue" "explains the need for extravagance to praise noble ladies (or to mourn the loss of an ordinary girl like Elizabeth Drury) whose good Christian lives of themselves are perfection and therein evince the present glory of God" (93).

465. Dollimore, Jonathan. *Radical Tragedy: Religion, Ideology and Power in the Drama of Shakespeare and his Contemporaries.* Chicago: University of Chicago Press. viii, 312p.

In a discussion of the Renaissance concept of cosmic decay, calls *FirAn* "probably the most famous literary exposition of decay" (97) and points out how in *Devotions* Donne "dwells imaginatively on the wholesale annihilation which decay, working at and from the centre of things, implies for a geocentric and hierarchical universe" (102). Comments also briefly on Donne's "obsessive introspection" in the *Holy Sonnets* and suggests that in almost every sonnet he "wrestles with the experienced paradoxes and contradictions of protestant subjectivity." Maintains that Donne "was preoccupied not just with the fragmentation of self and the decentring of man but also with the inherent instability of matter and the world's never absent potential to collapse back into nothingness." Believes that "[e]merging from this obsession with instability and change is a sense of the complex interrelations between power, violence, and desire, as they traverse and constitute subjectivity" (180).

466. Donne, John. *Biathanatos,* ed. Ernest W. Sullivan, II. Newark: University of Delaware Press; London: Associated University Presses. lxxi, 280p.

In the preface (vii–viii), notes that *Biathanatos* is "the first work in English (1608) to argue that suicide might not be a sin" and "remains the definitive examination of philosophical, legal, and theological attitudes toward suicide from classical antiquity to the end of the Renaissance"

(xvii). In the general introduction (ix–xxxviii), (1) discusses the biographical elements in *Biathanatos,* concluding that "even though Donne's misfortunes may have prompted his meditation of suicide and sympathy for suicides, *Biathanatos* would seem to owe more to his normal intellectual interests and mental habits than to a melancholy mood that surfaced only occasionally" (xiii); (2) examines classical, Christian, and Renaissance attitudes toward suicide to show that, considering the general tolerance toward the idea of suicide at the time as well as the extensive learned debate on the subject, Donne "could seriously defend suicide" (xvi); (3) comments on Donne's pre-ordination attitude toward suicide in the context of his other prose works, maintaining that although Donne "generally disapproves of suicide" in these early works, *Pseudo-Martyr* "proves that just after the composition of *Biathanatos* Donne found some forms of suicide acceptable to God" (xxi); (4) reviews contemporary responses to the work (xxi–xxvi); and (5) discusses the content, procedure, and rhetorical strategy of Donne's argument to show that it is "not a general defense of suicide" but rather "argues only that under certain very limited conditions suicide may not be sin," and thus becomes "a general plea for charity toward suicides and a proof that no set of rules can govern all instances" (xxx). In the textual introduction (xxxiv–lxxi), (1) presents a bibliographical description and textual history of the three extant seventeenth century texts of *Biathanatos:* the Bodleian Library manuscript (MS e.Musaeo 131), the quarto first edition, and the octavo second edition; (2) comments on post-seventeenth century reprints; and (3) presents a rationale for choosing the Bodleian manuscript and explains his editorial procedures, emphasizing that his intention is "to come as close as possible to reproducing in a print format what Donne actually wrote" (lxvii). Thereafter follows the old-spelling edition of *Biathanatos* [1]–150), followed by textual notes (151–77), a table of hyphenated words (179), explanatory notes (180–240), and a selected bibliography (241–47). Appendix A (248–50) contains preliminary materials in the Bodleian manuscript; Appendix B (251–68) lists variant readings of sheet "S" and the Bodleian manuscript. Has an index (269–80). Reviews: R. D. Bedford in *THES* (18 January 1985): 19; William B. Hunter in *SCRev* 2 (1985): 72–74; Frank L. Huntley in *RenQ* 38 (1985): 766–70; Robin Robbins in *TLS* (1 March 1985): 241; W. Speed Hill in *JDJ* 6 (1987): 109–33.

467. Donne, John. *John Donne*. Foreword and note by Mary Haltby. London: CIO. 42p.

Contains an introduction to "Masters of Prayer" by Pamela Egan (3) and a brief sketch of Donne's biography, focusing mostly on his religious life (4–6), followed by selections from his poems and prose, especially the sermons (7–42). Includes six illustrations.

468. Donne, John. *John Donne: Wiersze wybrane wybór, przekład, posłowie i opracowanie*, Stanisław Barańczek. Kraków: Wydawnictwo Literackie. 175p.

Parallel English and Polish texts. Selections from 31 poems from the *Songs and Sonets*, 6 of the *Elegies*, *Sat3*, *Storm*, *Calm*, and 23 poems from the *Divine Poems* (6–151), followed by brief notes on individual poems (154–63), a very general introduction to Donne's life and poetry and a select bibliography (165–73), and an index (174–76).

469. Donne, John. *Holy Sonnets*. Graphics by Klaus and Theo Reichenberger. Exempla lyrica and graphica. Kassel: Reichenberger. [15]p. Limited edition: 480 copies.

Reproduces six of the *Holy Sonnets,* each with a graphic. In the "Postscriptum" ([13]–[14]) briefly comments (in German) on each of the sonnets and on Donne's life and religious poetry in general.

470. Donne, John. *Shakespeare, Milton, Donne y otros: Poesía inglesa de los siglos XVI y XVII*. Historia Universal de la Literatura. Mexico: Origen and OMGSA. 150p.

Presents Spanish translations of 14 poems from the *Songs and Sonets,* 5 of the *Holy Sonnets,* 3 hymns, and a passage from *SecAn* (47–67), with no notes or commentary.

471. Donne, John. "Six Poèmes de John Donne," trans. by Groupe d'Etudes et de Recherche Britanniques (GERB), in *Cahiers sur la poésie 1*, ed. Sylvanie Marandon, 133–57. La traduction de la poésie. Bordeaux: Université de Bordeaux III.

Translates into French (with English texts on the opposite page) *GoodM, SGo, ValWeep, Flea, LovGrow,* and *HSDeath,* each followed by notes and possible variant translations of individual lines.

472. Duncan, Joseph E. "Donne's 'Hymne to God my God, in my sicknesse' and Iconographic Tradition." *JDJ* 3: 157–80.

Discusses how the iconographical tradition that shows a close relationship between the Tree of Knowledge in the Garden and Christ's cross throws light on stanza five of *Sickness*. Examines "(1) representations combining Paradise and Calvary; (2) compositions presenting the Tree of Knowledge and the Cross together, sometimes fused into one; (3) the union of the two Adams in compositions showing Adam together with Christ's redemptive blood, the Resurrection, and the Church; and (4) other iconographical parallels to the motifs" (160) in Donne's poem. Cites other seventeenth century poems that unite Paradise and Calvary, such as Herbert's "The Sacrifice," Crashaw's "The Office of the Cross," Joseph Beaumont's "The Gardin," and Vaughan's "The Dedication." Suggests that Donne's linking of the fatal tree and Christ's cross in "one place" (l. 22) gives "confident support to the other unions of opposites" in the poem—"east and west, death and resurrection, God's throwing down and raising up"—and claims that in *Sickness* "[t]hese various conjunctions of opposites, in image and in concept, are at the heart of Donne's spiritual psychology" (164–65). Concludes that Donne presents in the hymn "a more explicit geographical interpretation" of the relationship between Adam's tree and Christ's cross standing "in one place" than do previous poets and that "the visual arts provide a tradition, a context, and a mode of perception in which this is true" (165). Reproduces 14 figures (169–80).

473. Dust, Philip. "A Source for John Donne's *Seventeenth Meditation* in Rowley, Dekker, and Ford's *The Witch of Edmonton.*" *N&Q,* n.s. 31, no. 2: 231–32.

Suggests that in the seventeenth meditation in *Devotions* Donne perhaps is echoing the line "Ha! Whom tolls the bell for?" from *The Witch of Edmonton* (III.iii.75) by Rowley, Dekker, and Ford as well as "the theme of repentance and redemption that characterizes Ford's part in the play" (232).

474. Edgecombe, R. S. "Out-Heroding Herod: Hyper-Hyperbole in *King Lear* and Donne's *Nocturnal.*" *Theoria* (South Africa) 63: 67–72.

Compares and contrasts Donne's use of hyper-hyperbolic language in *Noct* with Shakespeare's use of it in *King Lear.* Maintains that both poets use the "strategy of stretching metaphor as far as it can go, and beyond" (71) in order to convey the "sense of ex-

tending sorrow beyond the conceivably sorrowful" (67). Says that in Donne's poem the result "is dogged and sullen, showing little of the dash and flourish that usually characterises his use of hyperbole." Maintains that "language, if it is dragged beyond the point of inanition into nullity itself, will drain its energy into lassitude" (72).

475. Ellrodt, Robert. "Espace et poésie de Donne à Traherne," in *Espaces et représentations dans le monde anglo-américain aux xviiᵉ et xviiiᵉ siècles,* 1–16. Société d'Études Anglo-Américaines des xviiᵉ et xviiiᵉ Siècles. Actes du Colloque tenu à Paris les 23 et 24 octobre 1981. Paris: Presses de l'Université de Paris.

In a survey of the changing meaning of the word "space" from Donne to Traherne, points out that Donne uses the word only five times in his poetry and even then only in the sense of location or place, never in a cosmic sense. Comments also on Donne's use of the word "infinite," noting that he uses the word in a metaphorical and theological sense but evidences no great fascination with the physical universe as infinite space.

476. Ellrodt, Robert. "John Donne and Mannerism," in *Litterae et Lingua: In Honorem Premislavi Mroczkowski,* ed. Jan Nowakowski, 113–21. Prace Komisji Historycznoliterackiej 44. Wroclaw: Polska Akademia Nauk.

Discusses mannerist characteristics of Donne's poetry, such as its emotional complexity; its expression of moral, scientific, and cosmic perplexity; its individualism; its aim "to communicate an impression of instantaneity" (117); its delight in "the illusions of perspective" (118); its intellectuality; and the "hallucinated intensity" (120) of its imagery. Compares Donne's poetry to mannerist paintings, especially those of Tintoretto, Rembrandt, El Greco, and Lelio Orsi. Does not suggest that Donne was definitely influenced by mannerist art but maintains rather that "the analogies must proceed from largely unconscious affinities" (121).

477. Epstein, William H. "Altering the Life-Text: Walton's *Life of Donne* and the Generic Plot of English Biography." *Genre* 17: 247–74. Expanded version appears in *Recognizing Biography* (Philadelphia: University of Pennsylvania Press, 1987), 13–33.

Points out that biographers generally recognize Walton's *Life of Donne* (1640) as "the first, major, influential English biography of a literary figure which is itself of literary merit" and observes that, although numerous critics "have identified some of the traditional narrative, generic, and symbolic structures which Walton's *Donne* incorporates," none have considered in detail "the language which inscribes those structures" or have examined "how these language-structures have been re-inscribed in and by English biography after Walton." Explores, therefore, "the etymological and connotative nuances of some of the language structures" in the biography and elaborates on "a sequential symbolic and thematic pattern through which we can begin to recognize the poetics of English biography" (247). Argues that Walton's *Donne* incorporates into English biography "a structure of conversion which implies that biographical narrative can summarily authorize the sympathetic, visionary conversion of life into text and then reconvert the miraculously preserved monument of that life-made-text into a reanimated text-made-life," a "law or principle which, perhaps more so than any other, governs the poetic of biography" (268).

478. Farmer, Norman, Jr. "Donne, Jonson, and the Priority of Picture," in *Poets and the Visual Arts in Renaissance England,* 19–30. Austin: University of Texas Press.

Points out that although Donne is not a "pictorialist writer in the sense that Sidney and Spenser are," he was, however, "aware of current conventional ways of seeing and their underlying rationale." Stresses that Donne's sermons and poetry "show how basic to his thought was the concept of seeing in pictorial terms" (19). Discusses, for instance, his interest in the imagery of mirrors and use of metaphors about obstructions to spiritual vision; his use of the picture and map as metaphors; his employment of visual tropes and analogues; and his apparent knowledge of contemporary notions of portraiture. Maintains that, in fact, "[i]n whatever Donne writes there is a persistent appeal to sight, an appeal that is frequently stated in terms of familiar iconographical combinations" (22). Claims that Donne's poetry relies on "visual models held jointly in his mind's eye and that of his reader." Comments on Donne's art collection and notes that "[h]e had his own image painted, sculpted, or engraved far more than any other poet of the age" (23). Comments on pictorial aspects in the sermons, *Anniversaries, Ignatius, Sat3, TWHence, ValName, Ecst, Canon, Damp, Break, ElNat, Phrine, Witch, ValWeep, GoodM, ElPict,* and *ElBed.* Argues that Jonson "offers a sharp contrast to Donne in his unwillingness to make concessions to the language of visible forms" and "exhibits in his poetry as much hostility to the concept of picture as Donne exhibits hospitality" (26).

479. Flynn, Dennis. "Jasper Mayne's Translation of Donne's Latin Epigrams." *JDJ* 3: 121–30.

Argues that the 60 poems included in the 1652 edition of Donne's *Paradoxes, Problemes, Essayes, and Characters* purported to be Jaspar Mayne's translations of Donne's Latin epigrams, but considered spurious by most Donne scholars, are very likely translations of Donne's poems or at least "based for the most part" on his Latin epigrams (121). Maintains that "external evidence points to the existence of a copy of Donne's Latin Epigrams in the hands of [the publisher] Humphrey Moseley and to the belief by Moseley and John Donne, Jr., that the Mayne translations published in 1652 did substantially represent Donne's Latin originals" (126). Points out that Moseley's catalogs also suggest that "by 1656 he had published both Mayne's translations and, separately, the Latin text of Donne's Epigrams" (127) (no copies known to exist) and notes that Anthony à Wood in *Athenae Oxoniensis* (1660 edition) lists among Donne's works "*Fasciculus Poematum & Epigrammatum Miscellaneorum*. Translated into English by *Jasp. Mayne*, D. D. with this title, *A sheaf of miscellany Epigrams*. Lond. 1632 oct.*" Explains that there is "the distinct possibility that Mayne for some reason may have inserted anachronisms into his translations of the poems," thereby causing scholars to suspect their authenticity. Concludes that most of the epigrams "contain nothing contradicting their claim to be based on Donne's Latin Epigrams" (128).

480. Frontain, Raymond-Jean. "Donne's Biblical Figures: The Integrity of 'To Mr. George Herbert. . . .'" *MP* 81: 285–89.
    Argues that in his Latin verse epistle *GHerb* Donne recognizes a connection between his family seal that contained a sheaf of snakes and the seal he had struck after his ordination in which a cross bifurcates to become an anchor. Maintains that Donne is aware of the significance of the serpent in Christian iconography, which symbolizes not only the "old Adam" of Genesis but also the "new Adam," who, like the bronze snake that Moses

held up to protect his people, was raised upon the cross for the salvation of mankind. Suggests that Donne, therefore, "perceives that his first seal, which he thought symbolized mortality, is intimately related to his second, which symbolizes his hope for eternal life." Believes that "[t]he ironic or paradoxical rightness of both of his chosen seals must have been proof to Donne's emblematizing imagination that he had correctly intuited and obeyed God's will by taking orders" (288). Suggests that Donne, "moved by his change in taking orders from despair of his own mortality to joy in the promise of eternal life, sought a way to emblematize his experience" and that he chose Herbert to be the recipient of the poem because he recognized in Herbert a "kindred religious sensibility" (288–89). Concludes that the poem is, therefore, more than "a mere occasional piece or an idle compliment," as some critics have suggested, and claims that it is, in fact, "a true Donnean meditation on the hidden appropriateness of seemingly contrary actions" (289).

481. Frontain, Jean-Raymond. "Donne's Erotic Spirituality: Ovidian Sexuality and the Language of Christian Revelation in Elegy XIX." *BSUF* 25, no. 4: 41–54.
    Argues that Donne regards the erotic and the spiritual as "mutually inclusive features," both of which are necessary if the experience of love is to be complete, rather than as "polarities or mutually exclusive elements between which a tension exists," and maintains that "the satisfying qualities of his eroticism results from its being perceived in relation to other, usually nominally disparate, realms of experience" (41). Insists, therefore, that Donne "creates a poetic world spanning two poles," thereby resolving "the traditional debate between the body and soul." Maintains that in

ElBed Donne transforms the undressing of the mistress into a "religious
ceremony" and overlays its sexual
aspects "with a spiritual—specifically
scriptural—gloss" (47). Argues that
Donne, in addition to conflating "the
Ovidian-erotic" and "the liturgical-
spiritual," intensifies the "erotic ritual
enactment" in the poem by "encoding Pauline and Johannine biblical references into the text" and also by
including "as a possible imaginative
element of the poem a recognizable
religious ceremony having to do with
Jesus Christ's 'Second Coming,'"
which he charges with "an undeni-
ably sexual significance" (48), thus
making the poem a sort of "apocalyptic document" that "functions ultimately as a prayer" (51). Concludes
that *ElBed* is Donne's "first major
attempt to represent the action of an
erotic spirituality" and is one of his
"most provocative" poems (53).

482. Gandelman, Claude. "The Poem as
Map: John Donne and the 'Anthropomorphic Landscape' Tradition." *Arcadia* 19:
244–51.

Suggests that in *Devotions* (when
Donne discusses man as a island) as
well as in his use of maps in *Sickness,
Mark,* and *GoodM,* "Donne's imagination may have been influenced by
the anthropomorphic maps that were
popular at the time. Notes that Donne
owned a copy of Sebastian Münster's
Cosmographia (first published in 1544
and containing a map of Europe as a
robed figure) that he later gave as a
present to his good friend, Edward
Parvish. Maintains that the influence
of the visual genre of the "landscape-
head" (often called "arcimboldianism"
after Giuseppe Arcimboldi) can be
seen in *ElProg* (ll. 41–51 and 57–66).
Suggests that the prevalence of anthropomorphic maps and landscape-bodies
in Donne's poetry is another argument
for classifying him as a mannerist.

Claims that, like mannerist pictorial
creations, Donne's female "landscape-
bodies" are "the expression of the
underlying philosophy of Mannerism
*totus in toto [est] et totus in qualibet
parte:* the world is a protean creation
and man is the world" (249).

483. Gandelman, Claude. "Le texte lit-
téraire comme carte anthropomorphe
d'Opicinus de Canistris à «Finnegans
Wake»." *Lit* 53: 3–17.

In a survey of literary uses of anthropomorphic maps from the fourteenth
to the twentieth century cites Donne
as the best example in the Renaissance
of this "phantasmagorique cartogra-
phie" (9). Points out his uses of this
visual tradition in calling man "an
island" in *Devotions,* "a flat map" in
Sickness" and lovers "two hemispheres" in *GoodM.* Notes, in particular, Donne's uses of the idea of the
anthropomorphic map in *ElBed* and
in *ElProg.*

484. Grennen, Joseph E. "Donne on the
Growth and Infiniteness of Love." *JDJ*
3: 131–40.

Offers "a more exact reading" of
LovInf "by clarifying the nature of its
roots in scholastic discussion of the
infinite" and suggests "reasons for
believing that while 'Loves Infiniteness' is a good title, it is not very
much better than 'Lovers Infiniteness,'
and indeed that the title 'Loves All'
might be more accurate than either of
the others." By comparing *LovInf* to
LovGrow hopes "to refine our appreciation of the relative merits of the
two poems" (131). Argues that, when
studied as companion poems, *LovInf*
stands out as "more successful" in
adapting academic technicalities to
the psychological or emotional currents of a man's experience in love
than does *LovGrow,* which "seems to
strain after metaphors" and "to suffer
from a contradiction in the logic which
has set the poem in motion" (138).

485. Grove, Robin. "Nature Methodiz'd."
CR 26: 52–68.

Contrasts Donne's use of couplets in
Sat3 with Pope's in "Windsor Forest,"
noting, in particular, how Donne's
couplets, "pausing, leaping forward,
stretching over line-ends, seem to
inhabit a continuous present-tense, in
which the mind is kept 'inquiring' and
scarcely able to predict what the next
move, or even the end of the present
one, will be," whereas Pope's "have
promises built into them" so that "there
will be a rhyme exactly when there
should be, that this phrase will be
answered by that, and that everything
will meet and balance and complete
itself in perfect order" (61). Notes also
that the "undeclared image" in *HSDue*
is "that of the hour-glass," which is
placed "as a *memento mori*" at the
beginning of the *Holy Sonnets* (67).

486. Halli, Robert W., Jr. "Drinking with
Donne: December 13, 1610." *JDJ* 3: 117.
An original, eight-line poem.

487. Hawkins, A. "Two Pathologies: A
Study in Illness and Literature." *Journal
of Medicine and Philosophy* 9: 231–59.

Contrasts Donne's autobiographical
account of his illness in *Devotions*
with Cornelius and Kathryn Ryan's
twentieth century description of sickness in *A Private Battle*. Identifies "the
basic structure in both narratives as
parallel to that of the case history"
and then shows how "each individual's experience is shaped by the conditions of illness appropriate to their
respective cultures." Discusses "the
way in which both authors understand
and represent sickness, as well as their
respective therapies, in terms of a particular metaphoric construct," noting
that, "for Donne, it is the analogy
between the illness of the body and
the illness of the soul," whereas, "for
Ryan, it is the analogy between illness and war." Maintains that "[t]he
stance of each towards his illness is
conditioned by the metaphoric model:
Donne's is one of acceptance, of conforming to the will of God; Ryan's is
one of resistance, of fighting heroic-
ally until the very end." Believes that
"these metaphors are functional as
well as aesthetic" and "serve as figural
modalities whereby the patient/author
hopes to transcend his illness" (231).
Comments on several differences between seventeenth and twentieth century views on sickness and maintains
that most of them are determined by
"sociocultural conditions" rather than
by "the pathological facts of the disease," especially "assumptions regarding patienthood, ideas of illness as a
private versus a social phenomenon,
and the role of the physician" (233–
34). Calls Donne's attitude toward illness "a psychology of acceptance"
and Ryan's "a psychology of resistance (248), but concludes that "[b]y
enabling the sick or dying individual
to achieve a measure of dignity and
nobility, both [stances] become vehicles of transcendence" (249).

488. Heiple, Daniel. "Lope de Vega and
the Early Conception of Metaphysical
Poetry." *CL* 36: 97–109.

Points out that, although Lope de
Vega's poetry is usually not considered "metaphysical," he was "the only
writer contemporaneous with the metaphysicals to make use of the term to
describe poetry" (98). Maintains that
the term "metaphysical poetry" resulted from "the philosophical crisis
of the seventeenth century, when conventional metaphysics was no longer
considered adequate to describe nature
and reality." Claims that "early literary
critics saw certain parallels between
the outmoded philosophical method
and certain characteristics of early
seventeenth-century poetry, such as
the contrived subtlety and learning
of the poetry, which reminded them of
the speculative philosophy of decadent

scholasticism" and that "[t]hey adopted the word 'metaphysical' because that term best characterized the type of learning they found in these poems." Concludes that these early critics "saw in the seventeenth-century poets qualities that modern readers tend to minimize" (109).

489. Hester, M. Thomas. "'All are players': Guilpin and 'Prester Iohn' Donne." *SoAR* 49: 3–17.

Points out numerous echoes of *Sat1* and *Sat4* in the fifth satire of Everard Guilpin's *Skialethia: The Shadow of Truth* (1598), and maintains that Guilpin's "imitative strategies" show not only "his considerable debt to Donne" (3) but also reflect the ways young satirists of the time viewed the genre of satire, as well as indicate Donne's importance in the literary milieu of London in the 1590s. Argues that "the specific alterations" Guilpin made in his poem "intimate that he has a different conception of the satirist and his genre" (6), but maintains that, in spite of his many modifications of his model, Guilpin wanted his readers "to recognize his debts to and adaptations of Donne's satires" (12), because he wishes to compliment and acknowledge Donne as a model, to illustrate his own familiarity with the rules of the game of satire, and to exhibit "his own ability to play that game." Contrasting the two poets, shows how Donne, unlike Guilpin, "was able to create satire which rises above and beyond the limitations of time and place" (13) and to "'remetaphorize' verse satire by dramatically evaluating and identifying this kind of genre with ethical reformation (personal and civic)" (14).

490. Hobbs, Mary. "Henry King, John Donne and the Refounding of Chichester Cathedral Library." *BC* 33: 189–205.

Outlines the history of the dissolution of the Chichester Cathedral Library during the Civil War and its refounding in the eighteenth century. Notes that the pre–Civil War library had a separate library of books belonging to Henry King, the Bishop of Chichester and the coexecutor of Donne's will, and comments on the nature and extent of the collection. Notes that, in addition to the 6 books from Donne's library (identified by Geoffrey Keynes (1973) and the 15 named by her (entry 110), there may have been many more in the collection. Points out that there is little doubt that Donne used a copy of St. Robert Bellarmine now at Chichester when he wrote *Pseudo-Martyr* (see Hobbs entry, 189). Observes that "[e]ven a preliminary examination of Donne's reading from the often very detailed marginal notes to his printed works reveals remarkable similarity between the titles and authors of the Chichester catalogue and those in the four books written before Donne's ordination" (198)— *Pseudo-Martyr, Ignatius, Biathanatos,* and *Essayes in Divinity.* Notes that Donne in these works cites more than seventy titles found in the Chichester catalogue, most by authors not commonly cited during this period, except in "the works of the Kings, Thomas Morton, and Donne himself" (198).

491. Holland, Norman N. "Transacting My 'Good-Morrow' Or, Bring Back the Vanished Critic," in *American Critics at Work: Examinations of Contemporary Literary Theory,* ed. Victor A. Kramer, 211–25. Troy, N.Y.: Whitston.

Calling for reaccepting the "I" of the critic as opposed to the "cultural 'we'" (211), reads *GoodM* as a re-creation of "the total fusion of suckling, the symbiosis we know in infancy" (213), suggesting that Donne "wants to re-create the symbiotic union of mother and infant . . . in a perfect abstract balancing of two adult and articulate lovers" (214). Acknowledging that one cannot assume Donne is himself the persona of the poem, holds that he may be, however, "making up for the loss of a child's oneness with a nurturing other" (215). Suggests that previous critical approaches to the poem are unsatisfactory because the critics have denied their subjectivity, and calls for an "identity theory" in which one "can understand someone's literary activity as a variation within a theme-and-variation picture of everything that person has done" (220). While openly acknowledging the prejudices that determined his reading of *GoodM*, suggests that his reading, nonetheless, offers a way to respond to literature "not as an abstract discipline removed from life," but rather as "a way, perhaps our best way, of articulating ourselves to ourselves, finding out who we are (our identities) and discovering why we care about the things we care about" (224–25).

492. Ishii, Shonosuke. *Eishi no Shoso: Yoshiki to Tenkai* [Various Aspects of English Poetry—Forms and Developments]. Tokyo: Taishukan-shoten. ix, 308p.

Translates into Japanese *SSweet* (99) and *Father* (192), with brief critical commentary on each poem (104–7, 208–11).

493. Karumidze, Zurab. "John Donne: Logic of Intuition," in *Three Essays on John Donne, W. B. Yeats and T. S. Eliot*, ed. Nico Kiasashvili, 9–61. Tbilisi: Tbilisi University Press. Also in Georgian as *Poeturi xatis memkvidreobit' oba: Jon Doni—Uiliam Batler leits—Tomas Sternz Elioti.*

Essay in Thai with summaries in English and Russian. Considers Donne's wit a combination of logic and intuition. Says that wit, originating out of Spanish and Italian theories of conceptism and universal analogies, "can be considered as a logical comprehension of the intuitive impressions of

experience," and that "[t]his method of expression creates [the] Conceit— an image logical in form and intuitive in content." Maintains that "[t]he poetical features of [the] Conceit are modified by the impersonal contemplation of an emotional attitude and by the realization of that attitude through the objective means of expression." Believes that "[t]he impersonal contemplation also modifies the emotive divergency of [the] Conceit" and that "[t]he result of the interpenetration and fusion of the divergent intellectual and emotional attitudes is the unique effect of poetic tension of [the] Conceit" (from English summary, 138). Discusses as examples *ValName, Fun, Dissol, ValWeep, Sickness,* and *Witch.*

494. Kawasaki, Mastoshi. *Imeiji no Shigaku: Eishi Noto* [The Poetics of Imagery: A Note on English Poetry]. Tokyo: Shinozaki Shorin. xvi, 306p.

In Chapter 4 of Part 2, "The Imagery of Rooms and Universe: John Donne's World of Illusion," discusses the room imagery in the *Songs and Sonets,* taking into account the context of Donne's personal circumstances and the seventeenth century intellectual milieu.

495. Kay, D. C. "Thomson, Donne, and Wordsworth's 'Monstrous Ant-Hill.'" *N&Q,* n.s. 31: 55–56.

Suggests that the source of Wordsworth's reference to the "monstrous ant-hill" in *The Prelude* (ll. 149–51) may be Thomson's *The Castle of Indolence* (I, xix) or perhaps Donne, who, in addition to owning a copy of Jeremias Wilde's edition of *Augustanus De Formica* (Hamburg, 1615), refers to the "triviality of the ant's endeavours" (55) in *FirAn* (l. 190); in *SecAn* (ll. 282–83); in *Har* (ll. 167–70), and in his first Paul's Cross sermon. Notes Wordsworth's interest in Donne and maintains that Donne,

Thomson, and Wordsworth "contribute to the establishment of an alternative to the ancient association of the ant" (55–56) with "thrift and useful industry" (55).

496. Kennedy, William J. "Petrarchan Audiences and Print Technology." *JMRS* 14: 1–20.

Discusses the impact of the rise of print culture on Renaissance literary history by commenting on the rise and fall of Petrarchism and on its reception and transmutation into new patterns. Maintains that Donne is a "paradigmatic example" of how "the shift from Renaissance to Baroque reflects conditions associated with print culture," noting that "[b]aroque writers seem acutely aware of print's implications for their own literary production." Believes that the "changes that Donne wrought in the rhetorical relationship between speaker and audience" suggest "a new order of culture emphasizing the distance between readers and the printed word." Observes that Donne's speakers address "a fictive audience of whose response he seems radically unsure" and thus Donne, realizing that his audience can "read into and distort" his intention, "uses all his rhetorical powers to engage its attention" (15). Suggests further that Donne's reluctance to publish his poems may reflect this wariness of how readers will respond to or distort his poems if they are in print. Thinks that Donne's skepticism about print, however, ironically "led him better to control the implications of its technology" by fully adapting "the newest and most challenging rhetorical strategies of printed texts to his own needs" (16). Illustrates the point by examining *ValBook*.

497. Kerins, Frank. "The 'Businesse' of Satire: John Donne and the Reformation of the Satirist." *TSLL* 26: 34–60.

Suggests that *EdHerb* offers "a unique commentary on the role of poetry, specifically the function of satire" (34), and that in the poem Donne "shows his younger friend his introspective satiric vision—a vision unique both in its penetration of the relationship between the individual and the world and as the finest introduction to Donne's own intricately structured *Satyres*" (37). Claims that, for Donne, the "true role of the satiric poet is finally one of inspiration—showing man as both of the world and above it" and illustrating that "[i]t is not his fallen state which condemns man but his failure to perceive his own transcendent nature" (36–37). Presents a detailed reading of the *Satyres* to show how they are "a unified artistic composition" (37). Argues that in *Sat1* Donne "exposes the limits of traditional methods of satiric authentication" and in the following four poems probes "even deeper by forcing his satirist to confront his own failings both in the social and in the spiritual realm." Stresses that Donne held that "the true satirist must first gain a precise awareness of his own diminished status in order finally to transcend it and to create a viable satire which speaks to both the spiritual and secular needs of a sophisticated society" (42–43). Shows how the plot of the *Satyres* reveals Donne's belief that "only after the attainment of self-knowledge to distinguish presumptive vanities from true merit can one reach out to the larger issue of educating humanity" (58).

498. Laurence, David. "The Protestant Roots of English Poetry: Barbara Lewalski's Protestant Poetics and Literary History." *Gradiva,* n.s. 2–3 (1984–1985): 53–75.

Essentially a detailed review of Barbara Lewalski's *Protestant Poetics and the Seventeenth-Century Religious Lyric* (1979). Approves Lewalski's attack on "the conventional wisdom that the novelties of Protestantism—its extreme doctrine of depravity and its corrosive rationalism—imply the decay of poetry, the loss of aesthetic sensibility, and the ruin of a culture and a Christianity capable of fostering true humanity" (59). Maintains, however, that, although it "will surely contribute to literary history and to criticism," Lewalski's study "is itself neither fully effective literary history nor fully effective criticism" because she "refuses to engage the larger questions her discussions nonetheless inevitably raise" (60–61).

499. Lepage, John Louis. "Sylvester's Du Bartas and the Metaphysical Androgyny of Opposites." *ELH* 51: 621–44.

Maintains that the uses of antithesis and generation of opposites in Du Bartas's *Les Semaines*, "the first major and influential work of combined science and poetry of the French Renaissance" (621), translated by Joshua Sylvester as *Divine Weeks*, "anticipate the metaphysical strain in English poetry" (624). Points out parallels between Donne's and Sylvester's uses of antitheses, noting that "[y]oked extremes, particularly of birth and death, are generally indebted in Donne to *Divine Weeks*" (628). Comments on how the metaphor of androgyny is "a Renaissance emblem for several kinds of unity in diversity, and especially an emblem of self-regeneration" (631), and notes Donne's use of it in *Canon, Metem,* and *EpLin*. Comments also on Donne's use of the phoenix in *FirAn* (l. 17) and *Canon* and Sylvester's account of the fabulous bird, and maintains that while the phoenix/hermaphrodite paradox "only has emblematic value" in Donne's love poems and the *Anniversaries,* there is a "profound difference in emphasis in the divine poetry" (638) and in *EpEliz,* in which the phoenix/hermaphrodite

becomes "his hieroglyph of perfect love" (641), both sexual and heavenly.

500. Levi, Peter, ed. *The Penguin Book of English Christian Verse.* Harmondsworth: Penguin Books; New York: Viking Penguin. 379p.

Mentions Donne briefly in the introduction, claiming that, "[a]s for fripperies, the poetry of Donne and Herbert is full of toys and ornaments" (21) and suggesting that in a few poems by both poets God seems to be "a contemporary character, dramatic and almost unpredictable" (29). Includes *Sal,* five of the *Holy Sonnets, Goodf, Christ,* and *Father,* without notes or commentary.

501. Linden, Stanton J. "Alchemy and Eschatology in Seventeenth-Century Poetry." *Ambix* 31: 102–24.

Argues that during the late sixteenth and early seventeenth centuries the literary function of alchemy underwent an important change: the satirical tradition, reaching back to Chaucer and extending through Jonson, waned and a new pattern of alchemical imagery emerged that placed "primary emphasis on positive change, purification, moral transformation and spirituality." Notes that an interesting part of this tradition is a poetic imagery that "represents the fusion of alchemy and eschatology, and of alchemy and millenarianism" (103). Points out Donne's use of the combination of alchemical and eschatological imagery in *Lit* (ll. 3–9), *Res* (ll. 2, 4–7, 12–16), and *Mark* (ll. 21–28). (These comments on Donne appear also in Linden's "Mystical Alchemy, Eschatology, and Seventeenth-Century Religious Poetry" below).

502. Linden, Stanton J. "Compasses and Cartography: Donne's 'A Valediction: forbidding Mourning.'" *JDJ* 3: 23–32.

Suggests that a possible source for the image of the compass in *ValMourn* was "the compasses or dividers (as opposed to 'directional' compasses), which for purposes both utilitarian and aesthetic are common features of Renaissance maps." Points out that, "[p]laced immediately above the numerical scale and with legs usually extended, compasses serve to indicate the scale of measurement the cartographer has adopted" and "contributed much to the richness and beauty present in early maps" (23). Notes that such dividers were especially prominent during the Elizabethan and Jacobean eras and cites a highly decorated map of "The Sea Coastes of England, from the Sorlinges by the landes end to Plymouth" in *The Mariners Mirrour* (London, 1588) by the engraver, Theodore de Bry, as a possible source or, at least, an analogue for Donne's image. Includes five illustrations.

503. Linden, Stanton J. "Mystical Alchemy, Eschatology, and Seventeenth-Century Religious Poetry." *PCP* 19: 79–88.

Maintains that in the late sixteenth and early seventeenth centuries "alchemy's literary functions and purposes undergo a marked and general change: there is a waning of the satirical tradition" and in its place there emerges "a new pattern of alchemical imagery" that emphasizes "change, purification, moral transformation, and spirituality." Argues that "an important part of this emerging tradition" is "a poetic imagery which represents a fusion of alchemy and eschatology" as well as "alchemy and millenarianism," which results in "the creation of a strikingly original and effective *concordia discors*" (79). Points out that Donne's poems, in particular, "deserve attention," and briefly discusses alchemical/eschatological images in *Lit, Res,* and *Mark.* Surveys several seventeenth century alchemical treatises that perhaps "served as models for these images" and provides "a con-

text for their understanding and appreciation" (80).

504. Linville, Susan E. "Contrary Faith: Poetic Closure and the Devotional Lyric." *PLL* 20: 141–53.

Disputes the critical contention that all devotional poetry is unpoetical or limited (1) because the genre prohibits "exposing too much of one's weaknesses or meanness or doubts" rather than "disclosing certain complexities in human nature and response that might detract from a more or less idealized poetic self" (141), or (2) because "poetry informed with theological commitment and poetry which retains complexity of response throughout are intrinsically antithetical" (142). Cites examples that, in fact, support these views but suggests there is "one very central theme that may generate disclosure in devotional poetry—both as poetic anticlosure and as personal uncovering," namely, "the unbridged gap between what the speaker knows he should feel and what he actually experiences." Discusses the poetry of the French Huguenot poet Jean Ogier de Gombauld (1570–1666) as an "especially moving illustration" (143) of this concept. Cites *HSBlack* as a sonnet which "leaves some lingering sense of unbridged gaps . . . between the desired contrite sorrow and the workings of Christ's redemptive activity" (148). Also sees *HSDue,* the first poem in the 1633 sequence of the *Holy Sonnets,* as expressing explicit unresolvedness and maintains that *HSPart,* the last poem in the 1633 ordering, is "a final dramatization of the antithetical impulses that have characterized the sonnets throughout the sequence" (152).

505. Linville, Susan E. "Enjambment and the Dialectics of Line Form in Donne's *Holy Sonnets*." *Style* 18: 64–82.

Shows that in the *Holy Sonnets* Donne employs enjambment "as an immensely powerful stylistic tool" that "is a source not only of immediacy and vigor, but also of larger organizing patterns within entire sonnets." Claims that enjambment tends to be "dramatic" not only when "it contributes to his *style parlé*," but also when it acts out "patterns of physical and mental movement." Insists that the "dialectical habits" of Donne's mind "are intermeshed with form and are inseparable from the kinetic, probative, dynamic force his lines wield" (80).

506. Love, Harold. "Dryden's Rationale of Paradox." *ELH* 51: 297–313.

Discusses Dryden's attitude toward paradox and compares it to Donne's. Claims that "paradox stands for Donne as the one essential key to the understanding of a cosmos whose organizing principles are themselves paradoxical, and of a religious faith that at every turn demands the reconciliation of irreconcilables" (304), whereas for Dryden the paradoxical image becomes simply decorative, not a valid mode of knowing.

507. Mathis, Gilles. "L'implicité dans le discours poétique," in *L'implicité dans la littérature et la pensée anglaises,* 1–23. Actes du Centre Aixois de Recherches Anglaises. Actes du Colloque de 1984. Provence: Université de Provence.

In a general discussion of the role of implicitness in English poetry, analyzes briefly various implicit meanings in *SunRis* (ll. 16–18), noting in particular the implicit intertextual evocation of the *Song of Songs.*

508. McKevlin, Dennis J. *A Lecture in Love's Philosophy: Donne's Vision of the World of Human Love in the "Songs and Sonets."* Lanham, Md.: University Press of America. vi, 115p.

Argues that the *Songs and Sonets* are a unified body of lyrics, in which Donne attempts "to establish unity within the individual, the cosmos, and

the deity," maintaining that "such a unity has a basis in Donne's bold and unique application of the traditional system of universal correspondences" (2). Believes that in the *Songs and Sonets* Donne "is conceptually creating the vision of a world of human love in which the divine and human are brought together analogously not through an appeal to faith or supernatural grace but through man's capacity to actualize the potentialities inherent in the system of universal correspondences" (3). Chapter 1, "Philosophical Background for Donne's Application of the Theory of Correspondence" (7–42), discusses the philosophical concepts of Nicholas of Cusa and Giordano Bruno as well as the poetic theories of Baltasar Gracían and Emanuele Tesauro insofar "as they have a direct bearing on Donne's use of the system of universal correspondences." Maintains that although such an investigation provides "insights into the material and the method of the *Songs and Sonets,*" it also shows that "Donne's use of the correspondences is uniquely his own," in that "he makes a daring analogy between the mutual rational love of man and woman and the unity of operation within the Holy Trinity." Argues that, for Donne, "this analogical union of mutual love is central to his vision of the world of human love," and comments on how "he applies to it the qualities which Christian theology attributes to the Trinity" (4). Chapter 2, "The Theory of Correspondences in the *Songs and Sonets*" (43–100), illustrates the use of the correspondences in such poems as *LovInf, Lect, GoodM, SunRis, Relic, Ecst, Canon, LovDeity, ValBook, ValWeep, ValMourn, NegLov, Flea, Mess,* and *Commun.* "Conclusion" (101–3), maintains that the love found in the *Songs and Sonets* "lies midway between the merely physical love of man for woman and the love of man for God" and is a love "which is primarily rational and which effects a union analogous to the processions within the Trinity," thus achieving "a conceptual union of the human and the divine." Suggests, furthermore, that Donne "imaginatively restructure[s] the universe, marred and disorganized by fallen man's mistaken sense of values, around the focal point of rational love, restoring it to its preternatural balance." Concludes that in the *Songs and Sonets* Donne "expresses, through the system of universal correspondences, the bliss of mutual human love which, in its analogy with the divine, brings together the individual, the cosmos and God," all of which "he achieves through an intellectual act which participates in the creative power of God" (102). Has a selected bibliography (105–10) and an index (113–15).

509. Mirollo, James V. *Mannerism and Renaissance Poetry: Concept, Mode, Inner Design.* New Haven, Conn.: Yale University Press. xv, 225p.

Surveys the state of scholarship on and various theories about the concept of mannerism in literature and suggests ways to improve the present confusion over the application of the term. Maintains that, since literary mannerism, unlike mannerism in the visual arts, is not "a well-established phenomenon" with "a definite enough physiognomy to claim status as an autonomous sixteenth-century style," it is best to regard it simply as "a particular artistic sensibility that expresses itself in formal and stylistic ways, on occasion, and is therefore best sought in individual literary works as a modal variety of Renaissance literary style rather than a separate autonomous phenomenon." Warns that, given the present understanding of the concept, "a statement such as Donne is a mannerist" is "so frustratingly vague as

to be almost meaningless" (68). "Postlude: Three Versions of the Pastoral Invitation of Love" (160–98), juxtaposes Marlowe's "The Passionate Shepherd to his Love," Raleigh's "The Nymph's Reply to the Shepherd," and *Bait* to show that Donne's poem can be seen as a "mannerist response" (168) to the two earlier poems. Also contrasts *Bait* to Charles Cotton the younger's "An Invitation to Phillis" to illustrate the difference between literary mannerism and literary baroque.

510. Ní Chuilleanáin, Eiléan. "Time, Place, and the Congregation in Donne's Sermons," in *Literature and Learning in Medieval and Renaissance England: Essays Presented to Fitzroy Pyle,* ed. John Scattergood, 197–216. Dublin: Irish Academic Press.

Studies the role of time in Donne's sermons, especially his emphasis on the importance of the present moment, and examines "the relation of time to other aspects of the sermon's occasion: the place and the congregation" (198). Points out that, for Donne, the sermon is "a continuation of the perennial Christian tradition of preaching, a substitute for a medieval ritual rejected by Protestantism and a commentary on the reasons for rejection or acceptance of medieval practices" (199), and that it "illuminates the *place,* usually a church, which in its fabric and its altered furnishing and decoration expresses both the continuity with and the changes from the pre-Reformation outlook on churches and their function" (199–200). Maintains that Donne's sermons "do not merely show us Donne the poet, Donne the intellectual, continuing to explore his old interests with his habitual techniques," but they also "display an acute consciousness of the special circumstances of the preacher and his congregation: their physical and historical setting and their theological justification" (214–15). Concludes that in his sermons Donne feels the necessity "to define the particular scope and attitudes of the Anglican sermon, both for himself and his congregation" (215).

511. Nicholls, David. "Divine Analogy: The Theological Politics of John Donne." *Political Studies* 32: 570–80.

Points out that "[a]nalogies have played an important part in political rhetoric" and that "among the most persistent and powerful has been the analogy between divine and human government." Argues that, although many "defenders of political absolutism" in the sixteenth and seventeenth centuries "employed the image of an absolute God as the model for civil domination," Donne, "while vindicating monarchy by analogy to the divine kingship, rejected the notion of arbitrary or tyrannical rule which was becoming increasingly popular as civil war approached." Maintains that in Donne's prose works, especially the sermons, "the trinitarian image of God" becomes for him "a model for the pluralistic state" and concludes that Donne "insisted that both divine and civil rule should be seen in the context of law" so that "ultimately the analogical relationship between the two should be governed by the univocal." Says that for Donne, "the king is in the last resort but a creature of God" (570). Points out that, although Donne's concept of God was not "merely an ideological tool for justifying by analogy the kind of polity of which he approved," the assumptions he made "about how God governs the universe" were shaped, to some extent, "by his view of how the king should govern his realm" (580).

512. Ogawa, Kazuo. *Eishi Kyoen: Shi no Ajiwai Kata* [A Feast of English Poetry: A Way of Appreciation]. Tokyo: Nan'-undo. 304p.

Offers appreciative comments on *SSweet* (183–96).

513. Olivares, Julian. "Levity and Gravity: The Interpretation of the Lucid Element in Quevedo's 'Comunicación de amor invisible por los ojos' and Donne's 'The Extasie.'" *Neophil* 68: 534–45.

Discusses the function of the ludic element in the serious love poetry of Francisco de Quevedo as it is exemplified in his poem "Comunicación de amor invisible por los ojos" and compares Quevedo's sonnet with *Ecst,* which shares with the Spanish poem "a consummate employment of the ludic element and the topic of the 'optics of love,'" that is, "the Renaissance theory of visual perception that the eyes send out invisible beams which carry the object's image back to the spectator" (535). Through an analysis of the two poems, shows that both poets "can accommodate both levity and gravity, aesthetic distance and emotional attachment, [and] wit and passion" to create poetry that is "at once entertaining and profound" (543).

514. Patterson, Annabel. "Prynne's Ears; or, The Hermeneutics of Censorship," in *Censorship and Interpretation: The Conditions of Writing and Reading in Early Modern England,* 44–119. Madison: University of Wisconsin Press.

In a subsection of the chapter entitled "'Take heed what you hear': Donne's ambiguous prose" (92–105), points out that Donne's early poetry "is scarred in places—and in significant places—by the signs of a repressive culture" and contains "a number of specific references to censorship" (92). Points out that Donne's letters, in particular, "produce, as a group of texts, an effect of strain, even of danger, in excess of generic shaping," and "show that his response to a climate of censorship and other related forms of inhibition was a constant interest in, even an obsession with, problems of interpretation and misinterpretation" (95). Cites examples also of Donne's caution, tension, and ambivalence as a court preacher and his development of strategies to avoid censure. Comments on how Donne nearly became a victim of censorship for what seemed to some to be an "oblique criticism" (100) of King Charles and Queen Henrietta Maria in a sermon delivered on 1 April 1627. Suggests that Donne was never able to solve "the problem of combining obedience [to the king] with outspokenness" (103).

515. Pebworth, Ted-Larry. "Manuscript Poems and Print Assumptions: Donne and His Modern Editors." *JDJ* 3: 1–21.
Contrasts the differing attitudes of Donne and Jonson "toward poetry as text, as artifact," noting that "Jonson's conception of text adumbrates that of the modern editor," whereas "Donne's reflects an earlier, preprint attitude that survived into the late Renaissance in the form of an antiprint bias." Argues that a major difficulty with most twentieth century editions of Donne's poetry is that the editors "have anachronistically reflected the assumptions of print culture when working with a body of poems that circulated throughout their author's lifetime only in manuscript" (1). Points out that a major feature of manuscript transmission is "its lack of stability in canon, attribution, and text," thus allowing for "none of the overall, permanent control that an author can find in print." Points out that the first published edition of Donne's poems (1633) "reflects no authorial control" and "suffers from all the consequences of that lack of control," noting that its canon is "incomplete and inaccurate," "the ordering of the poems seems haphazard," and "its texts seem not to have been set from a single

manuscript tradition." Notes that later seventeenth century editions "progressively add further canonical and spurious items" and "progressively corrupt the text" (3). Shows, as example, that, as a result of the lack of consensus among modern editors, there are "virtually as many different texts as there are editions" (5) of *Father*. Reviews the editorial practices of twentieth century editors of old-spelling editions of Donne's poems, especially those of Herbert Grierson, Helen Gardner, Frank Manley, Wesley Milgate, John Hayward, and John T. Shawcross. Concludes that, "[b]ecause most of Donne's modern editors have approached their task with the assumptions of print rather than manuscript culture, a definitive edition of Donne's poetry has yet to be published," but believes the variorum edition in progress "will carry the study of Donne's texts as far as known resources permit" and will bring "us closer to what Donne actually wrote than any previous edition" (20).

516. Pebworth, Ted-Larry, and Claude J. Summers. "'Thus Friends Absent Speake': The Exchange of Verse Letters between John Donne and Henry Wotton." *MP* 81: 361–77.
Argues that *HWNews* is the first verse letter in an exchange of three poems between the two friends, that Wotton's "'Tis not a coate of gray" is a response to Donne's poem, and that *HWKiss* is a reply to Wotton's poem. Maintains that the three poems were written "in the midst of the ominous breach between Queen Elizabeth and the Earl of Essex that lasted through July and August of 1598 and threatened to paralyze the government," that they show "the personalities of ambitious young men, each of whom is attached to a principal actor in the high drama at court," and that they reveal "a dynamic exchange between close friends who

are immersed in a political crisis that colors their relationship to each other and to events that may determine their futures but over which they have little control." Concludes that, when seen in their correct sequence and viewed in their proper biographical and historical contexts, "the individual poems in the sequence acquire an immediacy and force and subtlety heretofore unrecognized" and also that "the relationship between Donne and Wotton is clarified" (361–62). Attaches an appendix on the ordering of the two Donne poems in the manuscripts and early editions (376–77).

517. **Quitslund, Jon A.** "Sidney's Presence in Lyric Verse of the Later English Renaissance," in *Sir Philip Sidney and the Interpretation of Renaissance Culture: The Poet in His Time and in Ours: A Collection of Critical and Scholarly Essays,* ed. Gary F. Waller and Michael Moore, 110–23. London: Croom Helm; Totowa, N.J.: Barnes and Noble.

Points out that there are "a number of allusions to and transformations of Sidneian models among Donne's poems," citing the relationship between *Ecst* and *Astrophil and Stella* (Song 8) as "perhaps the most familiar example" (119). Examines *Canon* and *Astrophil and Stella* 21 to illustrate both likenesses and differences between the two poets. Observes that Donne's persona, like Astrophil, is "self-absorbed, hyperbolic, ingenious in argument, both idealistic and unprincipled," but that Donne "has made his lover more of a wit and more experienced in love and its lore than Astrophil" and "has emphasized and ironized his self-sufficiency by detaching the speaker from both society and the moral absolutes of Nature, Love, Beauty, Reason, and Virtue" (121).

518. **Raine, Craig.** "Making Love with the Light On: Poet to Poet." *List* 111 (5 April): 12–13.

Praises Donne as "a great innovator in every respect," but especially as a love poet who "went against poetic fashion." Comments specifically, but briefly, on the eroticism and sexual excitement in *ElBed,* the "hypnotic rapture" in *Ecst,* the "urgent bamboozling" in *Flea,* the "volatility of emotion" (12) in *ElComp,* and the "sexual implications" of the compass conceit in *ValMourn.* Says that, if asked to summarize why he thinks Donne is a great poet, he would say that, "whereas the rest of us kiss with our eyes closed, Donne's are wide open so he can kiss and tell," adding that Donne "probably made love with the light on" (13).

519. **Ricks, Christopher.** "William Empson: The Images and the Story," in *The Force of Poetry,* 179–243. Oxford: Clarendon Press.

Comments on Empson's criticism of Donne and the influence of Donne on Empson's own poetry. Calls Donne "the poet who means most to Empson's poetry" (181) and shows how Donne's love poems, in particular, appealed to Empson, especially their unsentimental celebration of freedom and independence.

520. **Rieke, Alison R.** "Donne's Riddles." *JEGP* 83: 1–20.

Discusses Donne's use of riddles in his poetry, especially in the *Songs and Sonets* and the epigrams, and suggests it reflects his interest in and knowledge of "the continental enigmatographers who so actively composed verse riddles during the sixteenth and seventeenth centuries," especially Nicholas Reusner, whose anthology *Aenigmatographia* (Frankfurt, 1599) Donne owned. Surveys Donne's use of various "enigmatic subgenres" in his poetry, such as "the enigmatic epigram, the numerical problem, the impossible question, the logograph, the licentious riddle, and more complex riddles which may mix characteristics of these genres" (1). Discusses in some detail the riddling elements in *Appar, Jet,* and *Noct,* as well as pointing out in less detail their appearance in a number of other poems.

521. Rohmann, Gerd. "New Aspects of Metaphysical Poetry," in *Anglistentag, 1982,* ed. Udo Fries and Jörg Hasler, 197–220. Giessen: Hoffmann.

Discusses "the metaphysical quality" of English metaphysical poetry and finds the term acceptable if we remember that it means "a new comprehension of man's physical and spiritual existence" (201). Comments on the common traits between English metaphysical poets and their European contemporaries, especially Marino, Jean de La Ceppède, Lope de Vega, Paul Fleming, and Hofmann von Hofmannswaldau, and believes English metaphysical poetry has much in common with the European baroque tradition, calling it "a philosophical form of baroque art" (205). Discusses the critical revival of interest in the metaphysical poets from the nineteenth century to the present and comments on their creative influence on practicing poets, especially Emily Dickinson, Gerard Manley Hopkins, Francis Thompson, William Butler Yeats, T. S. Eliot, William Empson, and Dylan Thomas.

522. Romein, Tunis. "Donne's 'Holy Sonnet XIV.'" *Expl* 42, no. 4: 12–14.

Comments on the two series of verbs in the first quatrain of *HSBatter,* focusing primarily on the verb "blowe" (l. 4), and suggests that perhaps God is being portrayed here as "a glass blower who uses his breath to fill the vessel and give it new form." Presents a reading that "accounts for all six of the problematic verbs" as well as "the rest of the language of the quatrain" (13).

523. Sale, Roger. "Carew as Composer," in *Literary Inheritance,* 21–62. Amherst: University of Massachusetts Press.

Discusses the influence of Donne and Jonson on Thomas Carew's poetry, maintaining that "Carew discovers who he is as he discovers them" and "creates them in the verse each taught him." Analyzes Carew's "An Elegie upon the Death of the Deane of Pauls, Dr. John Donne," calling it "a great critical achievement" that "should serve as a benchmark for critics and all others who necessarily come later, and whose subject must therefore be, in part, what it means to come later, to inherit, to compose with materials not one's own." Maintains that Carew praises Jonson "for his triumph over earlier poets" and "for creating tradition," and praises Donne "for gleaning after others had harvested, a flame, an original, who cannot be said to be an heir, and so Carew thought, would have no heirs" (52). Compares and contrasts also Jonson and Donne, claiming that "the originality of both lay in a kind of revitalizing of poetic possibility, using the language, the conceits, the ideas that had accumulated for upwards of two thousand years, but reworking their relevance— Jonson in his lifelong dedication to making all human situations an occasion for poetry, Donne in his insistent probing, so that his mind seems both taut and leaping, of the latent possibilities in his received metaphors" (53–54). Maintains, however, that "the energy and originality" of both poets "lay in no new materials" and, as a result, "no search for yet newer materials was incumbent upon their successors" (54)

524. Schleiner, Louise. *The Living Lyre in English Verse from Elizabeth through the Restoration.* Columbia: University of Missouri Press. 218p.

Briefly comments on John Dowland's song "To ask for all thy love," which is a paraphrase and simplification of one stanza from *LovInf,* noting that the difference between Donne's poem and Dowland's "filled-out, metrically regularized paraphrase is a measure of the distance between Donne's speech mode and the fluid, metrically patterned lyrics preferred by Jacobean composers" (186).

525. Schluter, Kurt. "The Influence of the Greek Prayer Hymn on the English Renaissance Sonnet: Aspects of Genre in Relation to Form of Verse." *Anglia* 102: 323–48.

Discusses how the genre of the Greek prayer hymn *(hymnos kletikós)* was adapted by the Renaissance sonneteers and comments specifically on hymnic elements in *HSDeath*. Maintains that in Donne's poem "conventional means are used, either directly or by drawing upon them somewhat obliquely, for a purpose exactly opposite to their normal use: they are turned into a means of dispraise" (337), and thus calls the sonnet "a version of the genre antihymn" (339). Points out that in the hymn one finds "a mortal in need praising and praying to an agent of supernatural power, a helper or even a saviour" but that in the antihymn, such as Donne's sonnet, one finds "a supposedly all-powerful supernatural agent [death], chidden for his assumption of fear-inspiring and threatening power, first reduced to a powerless slave and pitied as such and finally triumphed over by a mortal speaker in the surety of his own immortality" (341).

526. Shami, Jeanne. "Anatomy and Progress: The Drama of Conversion in Donne's Men of a 'Middle Nature.'" *UTQ* 53: 221–35.

Argues that Donne believes that he teaches best by examples, particularly in a context in which he can interpret God's ways, as in the sermons, as well as dramatize them, as in the *Anniversaries*. Suggests that "[a] useful way to consider the paradigm of religious experience that Donne dramatizes most often is to examine the pattern of 'anatomy and progres' that he develops, a label taken from the titles of his *Anniversaries*" but applicable also to the *Satyres*, the *Devotions*, and many of the sermons. Maintains that the overall pattern "remains fairly constant": "[a] rational and analytic 'anatomy' dissects the problem and its personal impact in an effort to understand God's justice," followed by the "progress," "an imaginative digression that intensifies and illuminates the subject, often by trying to see it from the perspective of the next world." Suggests that "both responses . . . must be corrected by the speaker's personal memory of the whole pattern of God's ways in his life," and that, "[w]hen corrected by memory of similar historical situations, both 'anatomy' and 'progress' are important dramatic techniques used by Donne to bring the lessons of the text forcefully home to his hearers and to lead them to reconciliation" (222). Illustrates this paradigm of religious experience in the *Anniversaries* and in a series of sermons on Psalm 23.

527. Shawcross, John T. "The Making of the Variorum Text of the *Anniversaries*." *JDJ* 3: 63–72.

Discusses the publication history of the editions of the *Anniversaries* and comments on some of the basic problems and questions that arose as the textual editors of the variorum edition worked on the text of the *Anniversaries*, such as choosing a copy-text, formatting, and deciding on specific readings of individual lines in the poems.

528. Shawcross, John T. "Research and the State of Studies in Seventeenth-Century British Literature (1600–1660)." *LRN* 9, no. 1: 3–19.

Reviewing the state of studies in British literature (1600–1660), comments that "[m]ost of Donne's poetry is left unread by the commentators who nonetheless allow themselves expansively inclusive statements," and that "[t]he best books on Donne are those dealing with only groups of poems, to which their authors wisely restrict their criticism." Observes that "[t]he lack of attention to the verse letters, or the epigrams, or the epithalamia is amazing in view of Donne's great popularity and the critical industry that has grown up around him." Suggests that, for the most part, critics of Donne "are going over the same old ground" (8). Concludes with a brief bibliographical survey of important works, including books on Donne (16).

529. Sherwood, Terry G. *Fulfilling the Circle: A Study of John Donne's Thought.* Toronto: University of Toronto Press. 231p. Portions of Chapter 2 first appeared in *ELH* 38 (1972): 353–74, and *SEL* 13 (1973): 53–67 (See *Roberts 2*); and Chapter 7 is a version of an essay that first appeared in *HTR* 72 (1979): 101–22 (entry 70).

Chapter I, "Fulfilling the Circle" (3–18), proposes to examine the conceptions of epistemology and psychology that inform and unite the whole of Donne's work, maintaining that the "quite orthodox formulations" of "essential metaphysical principles" found in his later religious prose are simply "the mature and complete expressions of ideas and intellectual tendencies also present in Donne's earlier thought" (4). Part 1, Chapters 2–4 (21–130), discusses "the importance of Donne's notions of reason, body, and suffering in his epistemology and psychology" as "individual notions themselves," noting, in particular, the influence of St. Augustine, St. Bernard of Clairvaux, and Luis de Granada on Donne's thought and aesthetic. Part 2, Chapters 5–8 (133–90), focuses on "the varied ways in which these notions shape important works by Donne in differ-

ent literary forms and at different times," discussing in detail *ValWeep,* the *Holy Sonnets, Goodf,* and *Devotions.* Maintains that "[t]he assumptions underlying these works prepare us, finally, for 'Death's Duell,' the conclusion to Donne's life and to this study of his thought" (18). Cites editions used (202) and includes notes (203–20) and an index (223–31). Reviews: A. B. Chambers in *JDJ* 4 (1985): 109–20; James Egan in *SCN* 43, no. 1–2 (1985): 5–6; P. J. Klemp in *C&L* 34 (1985): 86–88; Hugh MacCallum in *UTQ* 54 (1985): 409–11; Winfried Schleiner in *RenQ* 38 (1985): 370–73; Jeanne Shami in *Ren&R,* n.s. 9 (1985): 296–99; Mark Roberts in *N&Q,* n.s. 33 (1986): 227–29; David R. Shore in *ESC* 12 (1986): 459–62; Julia J. Smith in *MLR* 82 (1987): 447–48.

530. Singer, Irving. "Neoplatonism and the Renaissance," in *The Nature of Love: Courtly and Romantic,* 2: 165–208. Chicago: University of Chicago Press.

Discusses Donne's synthesis of Neoplatonic love theory with Ovidian libertinism and his creation of poems that are "neither Platonic nor libertine but somehow both at once, each perspective uniting with the other in a way that requires stereoscopic comprehension." Observes how Donne "uses the language of spiritualization to manifest the goodness of wholly sexual love between man and woman" and "transcends libertine interests in the body by denying that love can be reduced to lust alone." Maintains that, for Donne, "there is nothing in sexuality itself to prevent it from embodying the spirituality of love" (198). Further holds that by fusing Ovidian and Platonic concepts, Donne not only wished to unify the body and soul but also sought to overcome "traditional distinctions between time and eternity and between the microcosm and macrocosm" (199). Notes that, for Donne, "love consists in the mere fact of oneness between two lovers rather than a oneness with the beauty of either" (200). Observes that Donne also synthesizes the Platonic and Ovidian traditions with Christian concepts and symbolism, claiming that "profane love is *itself* sacred, that love is holy wherever it appears and most obviously in sexual consummation" (202). Points out that "though sexual love as Donne describes it is wholly compatible with marriage, he scarcely develops the concept of married love itself" (205). Comments especially on *Ecst, Canon, ElBed,* and *HSShe.*

531. **Smith, Julia J.** "Donne and Stengelius." *N&Q,* n.s. 31: 227–29.

Suggests that a comparison of Donne's writings on the name of Jesus in the sermons with those of the Benedictine monk Carolus Stengelius (1581–1663) makes clear that Donne "had both read and used" (227) Stengelius's *Sacrosancti nominis Iesu* (1613), a copy of which is known to have been in Donne's library.

532. **Smith, Julia J.** "Donne and the Crucifixion." *MLR* 79: 513–25.

Surveys traditional medieval and seventeenth century attitudes toward Christ's Crucifixion as background for understanding Donne's intense imaginative response to the event in *Metem, Corona,* the *Holy Sonnets, Goodf, Cross,* and especially the sermons, noting that it is in the latter that "the centrality of the Cross both to Christian doctrine and to Donne's own understanding of life is fully realized." Notes in Donne's portrayal of the Crucifixion a "lack of detail, either scriptural or traditional" (518); a conspicuous restraint in his descriptions of the gruesome aspects of the scene; his relatively few references to those who caused Christ's suffering; his

stress on the importance of Christ's blood "as the dominant feature" (520) in his presentation of the event; his picturing himself dying with Christ on the cross; and his insistence that in death "the hypostatic union of the Godhead with both Christ's body and soul was not dissolved" (525).

533. **Steadman, John M.** *The Hill and the Labyrinth: Discourse and Certitude in Milton and His Near-Contemporaries.* Berkeley and Los Angeles: University of California Press. xiv, 185p.

Points out that Donne adapted the new philosophy (or new science) to the *contemptus mundi* theme in *FirAn* but that, for the most part, he treated it, here as elsewhere, simply "as a source for arguments and images" (130–31). Calls Donne's ingenuity "a kind of dialectical exhibitionism" and insists that the primary function of his "extravagant analogies" and "arguments" is "to display his own *ingenium* and his versatility in inventing" (131). Warns, therefore, that even in the passage on the new philosophy in *FirAn* (ll. 205–22, 237–38) Donne "is writing as a poet and rhetorician rather than as an epistemologist" and that, in fact, "his reference to universal doubt and the conflict of rival philosophies reinforces the claims of faith." Maintains, therefore, that the poem is really "a meditation on the most traditional of themes" and that, even though "many of Donne's allusions are contemporary, the arguments they support are conventional and the attitudes they reflect, orthodox" (121–22). Comments also briefly on Donne's use of the commonplace classical and Renaissance topos of mountain climbing in *Sat3* (2–3).

534. **Stein, Arnold.** "Voices of the Satirist: John Donne." *YES* 14: 72–92. Reprinted in *English Satire and the Satiric Tradition,* ed. Claude Rawson, assisted by

Jenny Mecziems, 72–92. Oxford: Blackwell, 1984.

Discusses Donne's "imaginative uses of the 'self' as these are projected by narrator and persona," especially "the character of the satirist and his 'voices'" (72) in *Sat1, ElFatal, ElAut, HWKiss, Sat3, Devotions,* and several sermons. Discusses how Donne "creates his own satiric spokesmen" (74) who are, for the most part, "outsiders," who may amuse the reader but who "are not themselves actively amused," and who prefer rather "a certain distance most favourable to their power of inventive observation." Maintains that "[n]othing in the classical and native precedents quite corresponds to Donne's use of satiric spokesmen," noting that "[h]e invents the art of related separatenesses and near identities potential in the inherited looseness of form" (75). Stresses how the narrator in Donne's poems "creates at will the sense that he is himself there in an imagined present and is in person describing, acting, and responding," and that "[h]e is both in position and moving" and "is discontinuously and at once, with finely adjusted interstices, poet, narrator, and persona" (76). Shows how, in the sermons, Donne's satiric voice, when he speaks as an "insider," "has limited but still frequent and interesting employment" (91).

535. Stemmler, Theo. "My Fair Lady: Parody in Fifteenth-Century English Lyrics," in *Medieval Studies Conference Aachen, 1983: Language and Literature,* ed. Wolf-Dietrich Bald and Horst Weinstock, 205–13. Frankfurt: Peter Lang.

Points out that there are many details in *ElAnag* that appear in medieval parodies of the idealized description of the mistress, such as a big mouth, black teeth, rough skin, etc. Maintains, however, that like Shakespeare's "My mistress's eyes are nothing like the sun," and unlike most medieval parodies, Donne's poem is "not only destructive but presents the reader with a new type of woman in English love poetry: individual—and not conventional" (212–13).

536. Sullivan, Ernest W., II. "*Donne Manuscripts:* Dalhousie I." *JDJ* 3: 203–20.

Comments on Peter Beal's 1977 discovery of the first and second Dalhousie manuscripts in the depository of the Dalhousie family in the Scottish Record Office in Edinburgh and the purchase of the Dalhousie I (containing 44 Donne poems) by Texas Tech University in 1983. Presents a detailed bibliographical description of Dalhousie I, including a complete inventory of its contents. Maintains that the "condition, contents, date, and provenance make the Dalhousie I manuscript extremely important for the study not only of the text of Donne's poems, but also Renaissance verse miscellanies" (207).

537. Usherwood, Stephen, and Elizabeth Usherwood. "Donne at the Taking of Cadiz." *Country Life* 175 (3 May): 1226–27.

Comments on Donne's participation in the Cadiz Expedition (1596) and notes the accuracy of his observations on military life and seafaring in *Sat1* (ll. 13–18), *Storm* (ll. 29–30, 45–62), *ValBook* (ll. 59–63), *ElPict* (ll. 5–10), *Ship,* and *Wing.* Observes that Donne's accuracy is confirmed, in part, by the recent publication of a journal kept by Sir George Carew, master of ordnance to the expedition.

538. Wall, John N., Jr., and Terry Bunce Burgin. "'This sermon . . . upon the Gunpowder day': The Book of Homilies of 1547 and Donne's Sermon in Commemoration of Guy Fawkes' Day, 1622." *SoAR* 49, no. 2: 19–30.

Comments on the historical context of Donne's Gunpowder Plot sermon preached on 5 November 1622, and suggests that such a study provides "a worthy addition to our knowledge of Donne's methods of sermon construction as well as to our sense of his relationship to his church and his king" (20). Points out how Donne avoided the traditional "anti-Catholic ranting" in the sermon by shifting the emphasis "from its religious to its political dimensions," thereby treating the Gunpowder Plot "as an assault on the authority and the person of the King, rather than as a Catholic assault on reformed religion or on England itself" (24). Argues that Donne, when writing his sermon, consulted the Homily of Obedience in the Book of Homilies of 1547, which supported royal authority and which James endorsed in his *Directions for Preachers* (1622). Concludes that Donne's use of the Book of Homilies made it possible for him "to undercut the arguments of James' protestant opposition by associating them with the disobedience to royal authority manifested by the Catholic Guy Fawkes and his fellow plotters" (29).

539. **Walls, Peter.** "'Music and Sweet Poetry'? Verse for English Lute Song and Continuo Song." *M&L* 65: 237–54.

Reexamines the assumption that metaphysical poems are unsuitable for musical settings and cites a number of poems set to music by John Dowland, Thomas Morley, Alfonso Ferrabosco, William Corkine, and other songbook writers that are "reminiscent" of the *Songs and Sonets* (245) to show that "continuo-song composers active in the 1630s and 1640s were obviously interested in metaphysical poetry" and that "a considerable number of poems with metaphysical features are to be found amongst the lute-song repertoire" (252). A postscript discusses William Lawes's setting of *Appar,* noting that "those who

have written about Donne settings knew this only as the fragment in Edinburgh University Library MS. Dc.l.69 (the Cantus I part of what was originally a three-part setting)" but that "[t]he Cantus II part is now in the Bodleian Library as MS. Mus.d.238" (249).

540. **Welch, Dennis M.** "Antithetical Thinking in Science and Literature." *CentR* 28: 1–22.

Discusses "the creative thinker's use of contraries as a source of important insights into biology, physics, genetics, and literature" (1), and maintains that *Canon* "illustrates exquisitely the paradoxical nature of poetic language" (11). Points out that "[a]ccording to Donne's antithetical way of thinking [in the poem], sacred love exists in the profane, immutability in the mutable, and individual fulfillment in union with another." Maintains, therefore, that in *Canon* "we are at levels of experience different from those of natural selection, species continuity, and DNA," but that "the central complementary and creative opposition of change and continuance, diversity and unity, function throughout these various levels." Observes that "just as the chains of DNA must separate in order for them to unite with complementary nucleotides, so part of the individual person's old self must separate (or be sacrificed) in order for the person to unite with another"; thus "[p]erhaps the union of the contrasting but complementary nucleotides may even be considered analogous to the union and diversity of lovers" (12).

541. **Willard, Thomas.** "Donne's Anatomy Lesson: Vesalian or Paracelsian?" *JDJ* 3: 35–61.

Discusses *FirAn* as an "anatomy of the world," which is "a technical term in Paracelsian medicine, referring to a specific diagnostic procedure" (36), and shows how the poem is "a refutation of the world's claim to health and confirmation of its terminal illness" (52). Points out that Paracelsus provided Donne with "a set of images as well as a procedure for treating them" (48), but claims that in "the framing lines" of *FirAn* Donne is "most Vesalian" (49). Maintains, therefore, that it is the presence of both of these approaches that leads to the complications readers note in the poem: "What began as a Paracelsian anatomy of a world sufficiently dead for a Vesalian autopsy becomes, it seems, a Vesalian dissection of the Paracelsian world of correspondences" (50). Sees *SecAn* as a resolution to the crises set up by the first. Claims that *FirAn* "treats life as a long disease," whereas *SecAn* shows that "virtue can teach us how to climb higher than the stars." Concludes, therefore, that the first poem is "more of a diagnosis" that "focuses on the material world which is dying," whereas the second is "more of a prognosis" that focuses on "the spiritual world which is being born" (56). Calls the *Anniversaries* "the greatest hieratic poems in Donne's corpus, if not in all English literature" (57).

542. **Williams, Aubrey L.** "A Hell for 'Ears Polite': Pope's *Epistle to Burlington*." *ELH* 51: 479–503.

Argues that Pope's *Epistle to Burlington* is shaped "by long-standing and quite specifically Christian conceptions of the state of Hell—and its torments," and presents "a vision of the way venal and materialistic souls create for themselves a kind of hell on earth that, in various ways, is anticipatory of the Hell for which they are headed in an afterlife." Points out that, as reflected in Donne's sermons, traditionally Hell is conceived of not only as a place of physical torment but also "a state whose overwhelming affliction

is the soul's sense of its everlasting separation from God" (480). Commenting on riches, refers to Donne's sermons as expressing the typical Christian view and notes that Donne, like Pope, believes that the avaricious man begins his hell while still on earth.

543. **Wittreich, Joseph.** "'Image of that horror': the Apocalypse in *King Lear*," in *The Apocalypse in English Renaissance Thought and Literature: Patterns, Antecedents, and Repercussions,* ed. C. A. Patrides and Joseph Wittreich, 175–206. Ithaca, N.Y.: Cornell University Press.

Points out, in passing, that Donne, like other major literary artists of the Renaissance such as Spenser, Shakespeare, Herbert, Marvell, and Milton, set about resuscitating St. John's Apocalypse from the exile into which it had been cast by some churchmen and politicians. Notes that, for Donne, however, the "special attributes of its expression—the emblematic, hieroglyphic character of the book, together with its darkness and obscurity—are but devices for directing attention away from its nominal to its real subject, from its literal to its figurative sense." Maintains that Donne's interpretation of the Apocalypse in his sermons "evades the whole notion of a renovated world and envisions, instead, the spiritual resurrection of all men in this life: the resurrection from persecution by deliverance from sin by grace, and from temptation and other difficulties of human existence by death" (176). Claims, therefore, that Donne "withdraws the apocalyptic promise from history altogether, finding all reference points of the Revelation prophecy within the spiritual history of everyman" (199).

544. **Woods, Susanne.** "The Mimetic Achievement of Shakespeare, Donne, and Herbert," in *Natural Emphasis: English Versification from Chaucer to Dryden,*

237–71. San Marino, Calif.: Huntington Library.

Discusses Donne's versification, pointing out, in particular, that his poetry provides "particularly brilliant examples of the variety and sophistication of a primarily mimetic versification traceable from the late Elizabethan to the early Caroline period" (237). Stresses that Donne "brought the speaking voice convincingly into the lyric" (237–38), creating "a dramatic lyricism more various than that of his predecessors in the art, Wyatt and Sidney" (249). Notes that his verse is "characteristically rougher than the verse of his contemporaries" (249–50), and comments on how "his fabled roughness" (250) has been a major point of discussion among critics from the seventeenth century to the present. Argues that Donne "is not an effective manipulator of the rhythmic possibilities suggested by metrical forms" but is "a master of prose rhythms, particularly of the rhetorical or dramatic voice," which results in his producing "the effect of the heightened speaking voice often in spite of his meters" (253–54). Maintains that in Donne "the metrical emphases are frequently rejected in favor of phrasal rhythms," and thus he "requires his readers to make performance choices totally divorced from the meter" (254). Concludes, therefore, that "[t]he 'drama' that characterizes Donne's lyrics is more than implied character, audience, and setting, more even than the focus on conflict and tension," claiming that "it is in the very concept of the poem's rhythmic structure, which remains dependent not on the devices of the poet but on the choices of the performer" (261).

545. Wright, Ralph. "Generic Man—An Endangered Species? Some Reflections on the Abolition of Man." *ABR* 35: 167–75.

Defends the use of the generic term "man" in the Catholic liturgy and cites *HSSpit* (ll. 13–14); *HSWilt* (ll. 13–14); *HSDeath;* and the "No man is an island" passage from *Devotions* as illustrations of samples of great English literature that those with preconceived notions about the use of "man" "will no longer be free to appreciate" (171).

546. Young, R. V. "Christopher Dawson and the Baroque Culture: An Approach to Seventeenth-Century Religious Poetry," in *The Dynamic Character of Christian Culture: Essays on Dawsonian Themes,* ed. Peter J. Cataldo, 127–58. Lanham, Md.: University Press of America.

Observes that Christopher Dawson considered the baroque as "the last truly Christian culture" and discusses how seventeenth century England "provides an attractive territory to the cultural historian interested in exploring the concept" (128). Examines facets of the religious poetry of the period as a means of assessing Dawson's ideas about baroque culture in a specific setting. Maintains that, although many of the great Protestant artists of the baroque period "were truly Protestant, they were not truly part of the bourgeois culture" that flourished "in the wake of the Reformation and the disintegration of Christendom" (132). Argues that, "[a]part from Crashaw, John Donne probably furnishes the most obvious example of an English baroque poet," maintaining that "he never cast off all the marks of his Catholic upbringing" (140). Notes that much of Donne's devotional poetry shows the influence of *The Spiritual Exercises* of St. Ignatius Loyola. Rejects the notion of "Protestant poetics" as descriptive of his art. Points out many resemblances between *HSBatter* and Lope de Vega's *Rimas sacras,* especially the "passionate and daringly erotic language"

(141). Notes, however, that, unlike Lope de Vega's poems in which the tension is between "concupiscence and fidelity," the tension in Donne's sonnet is between his "longing and experience and his Reformation theology" (142).

1985

547. Ackerley, Chris. "The 'White Alps' of *Under the Volcano*." *MLNew* 17–18 (1985–86): 138–39.

Cites a possible reference to *ElFatal* (ll. 47–56) in Chapter 3 of Malcolm Lowry's *Under the Volcano* and in Chapter 4 of an earlier draft of the novel.

548. Albright, Daniel. *Lyricality in English Literature.* Lincoln: University of Nebraska Press. x, 276p.

Attempts "to provide a definition of the lyric" and to show "why such a definition is at best provisional." Believes that "lyric poetry is fundamentally an attempt to approximate the condition of music within the slightly alien and prosaic domain of words, whether through phonemic intricacies or through the frustrating of semantic reference or through the presentation of transcendental ideas or of absolute feelings." Maintains that "the lyric is not truly a genre," arguing rather that "it is a mode, discoverable in odes and dramas and novels and possibly telephone directories, through which the reader becomes aware of the illusion of music beyond the sense of the language" (ix). Cites Donne to illustrate various aspects of the argument. For instance, discussing lyrical ethics, calls *Metem* "[t]he great poem in English to demonstrate the unethicality of the lyric" (88); and, commenting on satirical poetry, cites *Sat4* to illustrate the analogical mode of satire and *Sat2* to show how Donne anticipates Swift in realizing that "[t]o

speak the language of satire tends to reduce the satirist's own speech to excrement" (137). Briefly comments on Carew's "Elegie upon the Death of the Dean of Pauls, Dr. John Donne," calling it "eloquent" in its treatment of "Donne's power to transmute and invigorate the English language" (194). Suggests that "metaphysical poetry is difficult precisely because we are not used to reading such extremely lyrical poetry," and quotes *Sat5* to show "the limit of poetic license." Says that "[m]ost poems by Donne should be read in a spirit of intellectual delirium," noting that "Donne continually uses the language of logic, of analogy, but it is only a game in which the mind delights in the reeling sensation it feels as it gropes for logical relations amid a pervasive alogicality" (250).

549. Alves, Leonard. "Well Donne, Ill Donne: The Relevance of John Donne 1571/2– 1631." *ELLS* 22: 21–41.

Presents an introduction to Donne's life and a general survey of his poetry and prose. Suggests that "the twentieth century has come round to an appreciation of Donne via the poetics of Yeats, Pound, Eliot and Wallace Stevens inter alia with the result that his reputation has been salvaged and confirmed for posterity" (23). Believes that Donne's wit is "identified with his idiosyncratic mind as revealed in his poems and thus is original and inimitable" (25). Calls Donne "a deeply religious man" who was "a victim"

(30) of the religious tensions of his day and who, "for some mysterious reason," finally "decided to turn his back on Catholicism" (34). Calls Donne "a breaker of images, a nonconformist, a rebel but above all an individualist" (41).

550. Anselment, Raymond A. "The Countess of Carlisle and Caroline Praise: Convention and Reality." *SP* 82: 212–33.

In a biographical account of Lucy Hay, Countess of Carlisle, that comments on a prose character sketch of her by Tobie Matthew and poems on her by several Caroline poets, notes that her husband, James Hay, was one of Donne's patrons and that John Donne the younger wrote an epistle to her, "To the Right Honorable Lucy, Countesse of Carleile [*sic*]," that was published in *A Collection of Letters, Made by Sr Tobie Matthew Kn* (1660).

551. Bachinger, Katrina. "Dickinson's 'I Heard a Fly Buzz.'" *Expl* 43, no. 3: 12–15.

Suggests that three of Donne's sermons on resurrection, especially his sermon at the funeral of Sir William Cokayne, preached at St. Paul's on 12 December 1626, "provided the general impulse for the creation of [Emily] Dickinson's dead but quick narrator" in "I heard a fly buzz," and that "the final nudge" likely came from *Devotions,* which appears immediately after the Cokayne sermon in Henry Alford's *The Works of John Donne, D.D.* (1839), the edition of Donne available to Dickinson. Shows how the poem is a "typically Dickinsonian reply" (13) to Donne's views.

552. Bachrach, A. G. H. "Shakespeare, the Sea, and the Weather," in *Elizabethan and Modern Studies Presented to Professor Willem Schrickx on the Occasion of His Retirement,* ed. J. P. Vander Motten, 9–20. Gent: Seminarie voor Engelse en Amerikaanse Literatur, R.U.G.

Discusses Shakespeare's poetical uses of the sea and weather and finds "amazing" (17) parallels between Shakespeare's description of and symbolic uses of sea storms and calms, especially in *The Tempest,* and Donne's description in *Storm* and *Calm,* noting, of course, that there is no direct evidence to show that Shakespeare actually knew Donne's poems in manuscript. Briefly comments also on the symbolic uses of the sea and seafaring in Donne's sermon preached at The Hague on 19 December 1619, entitled "Mundus Mare: the World is a Sea."

553. Baumlin, James S. "Donne as Imitative Poet: The Evidence of 'Satyre II.'" *EIRC* 11: 29–42.

Argues that a "spirit of emulation" and "of poetic rivalry and revisionism" informs Donne's imitation of classical models—especially noticeable in his elegies, epithalamia, and satires—and that ultimately this spirit becomes "the controlling principle of his poetry" (29). Maintains that Donne "tends not to follow or adopt a model's specific language" but rather attempts a "decorous recreation" of the "subject, structure, voice, and style" of his model; in other words, he focuses on "the decorum of a model," its "most characteristic effects," and "strives to incorporate [these] into his verse" (30). Suggests further that the classical rhetorical concept of *kairos,* "an accommodation of discourse to audience and the exigencies of time and place," "controls his strategies of emulation." Maintains that "[w]hile decorum addresses the formal properties of a work, *kairos* considers a work's efficacy as persuasion and its ability to adapt itself to change" (31). Discusses *Sat2* as an example of the "tensions between imitation and emulation, between decorum and *kairos*" (32), and shows how Donne surpasses his classical models "by asserting that language and satire itself are in need of redemption." Maintains that "[t]o write classical satire in Donne's changed circumstances *without* this recognition would be a naive exercise in imitation, an exercise in decorum without *kairos*." Shows, therefore, that Donne "closely imitates" various "stylistic features" of his classical models but that "what he rejects, ultimately, are their linguistic optimism, their methods of rebuke, and any assertion of ability to effect change in a world where both man and his language have suffered a fall." Concludes that *Sat2* thus "escapes the self-accusation of slavish imitation only by its kairotic revision and ultimate rejection of the Juvenalian model" (39). Suggests the application of these concepts to other poems.

554. **Baumlin, James S.** "Donne's Problems and the Neo-Latin Tradition." *Neo-Latin Bulletin* (El Cajon, Calif.) 3, no. 1 (Spring/Summer): 1–4.

Maintains that Donne's *Problems* are "the first to parody [the form of] the Scholastic method" as found in the *Problemata Aristotelis,* and that his parodies were "likely models" for contemporary neo-Latin writers on the Continent (1). Illustrates the point by commenting on Donne's "Why doth the Poxe so much affect to undermine the nose?" Further argues that Donne's *Paradoxes* and *Problems* are "intimately related" and that he "merges the two forms in his collection, with individual Paradoxes containing embedded Problems, and the longer Problems turning into miniature Paradoxes." Concludes that the success of both "rests, finally, on their parody of the Scholastic forms that give them shape" and on "their innovative use of such forms as vehicles for wit and satire" (3).

555. **Beck, Joyce S.** "John Donne's Scholastic Eloquence," in *Proceedings of the Tenth Congress of the International Comparative Literature Association* (1982), Vol. I, *General Problems of Literary History,* vol. ed. Douwe W. Fokkema, asst. vol. ed. Edward C. Smith, III, coordinating ed. Anna Balakian, publications ed. James J. Wilhelm, 409–415. New York: Garland.

Argues that Donne's verse letters to the Countess of Bedford "exemplify many stylistic characteristics emphasized by medieval rhetoricians and writers," such as "*amplificatio, digressio,* paradox, extended analogy, allegory, *oxymoron,* interlace, polysemous elaboration, and *discordia concors.*" Maintains that "[t]he abundance of such devices suggests that Donne's poetic in these letters can justifiably be called 'medieval,' 'scholastic,' or even 'Gothic'" (400). Discusses in particular Donne's use of rhetorical devices and figures in *BedfWrit* and *BedfTwi* and observes that, throughout his verse letters to the Countess, Donne's style is "discursive, intellectual, and elaborate" (414).

556. **Berkowitz, Steven.** "Of Signs and Seals: The New Character of John Donne." *FJS* 18: 1–27.

Offers a critical reading of *GHerb* and comments on Herbert's replies associated with Donne's gift. In an appendix, argues against Grierson's emendations (1912) of the text in both Donne's Latin poem and the English translation from that of *Poems* (1650).

557. **Birrell, T. A.** "The Influence of Seventeenth-Century Publishers on the Presentation of Literature," in *Historical and Editorial Studies in Medieval and Early Modern English for Johan Gerritsen,* ed. Mary-Jo Arn and Hanneke Wirtjes with Hans Jansen, 163–73. Groningen: Wolters-Noordhoff.

Points out that Donne's poems were not popular during the second half of the seventeenth century, with only one edition appearing in 1669, whereas

Herbert's *The Temple* was published several times. Suggests that Herbert's success is attributable to the publisher Philemon Stephens and his successors, who began publishing Harvey's *The Synagogue* and *The Temple* in one volume in 1647 and who, later on, added "An Alphabetical Table for ready finding out the chief places." Concludes that Herbert "survived through the seventeenth and into the eighteenth century, not as a metaphysical poet, but as a prayerbook" (164).

558. Bradbury, Nancy Mason. "Speaker and Structure in Donne's *Satyre IV*." *SEL* 25: 87–107.

Maintains that much negative criticism of Donne's *Satyres* arises from a failure to see them "in the context of Elizabethan psychology and literary theory" and also "from the application of inappropriate criteria" (87). Argues that, contrary to the opinion of many critics, in *Sat4* "the presentation of the speaker and the structural design are both coherent and artistic" (87–88), noting that "[b]ecause of its length and complexity," this satire "offers the greatest challenge of the five to anyone inquiring into the unity of an individual *Satyre*" (88). Shows that, although related to Horace's *Satire* I.ix, Donne's poem differs "in tone, organization, and effect" (89). Points out, for example, that because of the genuinely wicked nature of the adversary in *Sat4* and because of Elizabethan expectations regarding the genre of satire, the speaker's harsh language and melancholic temperament would seem highly appropriate to his readers, not churlish or cruel. Shows that the structure of *Sat4*, like many other verse satires, "contains a long first section satirizing vice (lines 1–154), a short middle section identifying the corresponding virtue (lines 155–74), and a long final section resuming the attack (lines 175–244),"

but, by means of a close reading of the poem, emphasizes how Donne "makes a series of innovations in order to adapt the form to his particular needs" (95). Shows, for instance, how the "accumulation of detail" in the poem "serves a rhetorical function, as does Donne's decision not to end with the climactic praise of his Mistress Truth." Insists that the tripartite structure of the poem "provides a formal unity appropriate to the genre," and that "the evocation of his Mistress Truth placed at the poem's center provides an ideal against which the corruption of the court and the debasement of language can be measured" (107).

559. Bromwich, David. "Parody, Pastiche, and Allusion," in *Lyric Poetry: Beyond New Criticism,* ed. Chaviva Hosêk and Patricia Parker, 328–44. Ithaca, N.Y.: Cornell University Press.

Argues that parody is "integral to all writing, and that, together with its neighbor, pastiche, it has a place in good standing within the larger family of allusion" (328). Claims that "[e]very parodist is a writer *madly* in love with the styles that have formed him" (330). Discusses a number of poems that "do not feel like parody or pastiche," but in fact "are closer to these than many readers suppose poetry can be." Points out how "[t]heir style is such that one cannot imagine what it would be like to read them without having read certain other poems," and yet "they do not exist for the sake of those poems" (354). Notes, for instance, an affinity in the movement and diction between Daryl Hine's "The Double-Goer" and *Canon* and suggests that one may regard Hine's poem as a "companion poem" to Donne's, "written by an idiot questioner of the metaphysical style, who takes its means for its end and by his persistence converts us to his misunderstanding" (340).

560. Bueler, Lois E. "The Failure of Sophistry in Donne's Elegy VII." *SEL* 25: 69–85.

Argues that *ElNat* is "primarily an indictment of the speaker rather than the mistress" and finds the speaker's failure "not amatory but pedagogical" (71). Regards the poem as an exploration of sophistry and holds, in contrast to traditional discussions of it, that the speaker calls himself an "idiot," not the mistress. Argues that the poem is a soliloquy in which the mistress is not only not present but is not even the audience of the address. Maintains that Donne uses sophistry pejoratively and that the poem is organized to follow the classical rhetoric of Cicero in *De inventione*. Concludes that, like all practitioners of sophistry, Donne's speaker has mastered the letter of wisdom, while missing its spirit, and has learned nothing from his failure.

561. Bump, Jerome. "Hopkins, Metalepsis, and the Metaphysicals." *JDJ* 4: 303–29.

Argues that "to focus exclusively on Hopkins' affinities with the Metaphysicals is misleading for it exaggerates their importance vis-à-vis some equally important influences which were competing and/or merged with theirs" (305), especially that of Christina Rossetti, Pre-Raphaelitism, Tractarianism, and Dante. Points out dissimilarities between Hopkins and Donne and notes both similarities and dissimilarities between Hopkins and Vaughan, Southwell, Crashaw, Quarles, and especially Herbert. Maintains, however, that "Hopkins' characteristic process of overcoming a dominating influence, whether that of the Metaphysicals or the Pre-Raphaelites, is *metalepsis or transumption,* the attempt to establish priority over the precursor, by being more true to the precursor's own sources of inspiration" (321), in particular, by being "more true to the medieval sources of their creativity" (322). Briefly contrasts Hopkins's rose imagery in "Rosa Mystica" to that of *Prim* to show how he is "more true to medieval sources" (324) than Donne.

562. Chainey, Graham. *A Literary History of Cambridge.* Cambridge, Eng.: Pevensey Press. 272p. First published by the University of Michigan Press, 1986.

Claims that Donne "possibly studied at Cambridge . . . probably in about 1588–9" (34) and notes that he was eventually awarded an honorary degree. Cites two verse letters addressed to friends at Cambridge, *SB* (Samuel Brooke, later master of Trinity Hall) and *BB* (Beaupré Bell).

563. Chambers, A. B. "Will the Real John Donne Please Rise?" *JDJ* 4: 109–20.

Review essay of Patricia Pinka, *This Dialogue of One: The Songs and Sonnets of John Donne* (1982); A. J. Smith, *Literary Love: The Role of Passion in English Poems and Plays of the Seventeenth Century* (1983); and Terry G. Sherwood, *Fulfilling the Circle: A Study of John Donne's Thought* (1984).

564. Chapman, Michael. "The Language of Poetry." *CRUX* 19: 24–34.

Suggests "several ways of developing, in pupils, an understanding and appreciation of the unique character of poetic language" and thereby "to lay a foundation for the further study of poetry, in the senior school and at university" (24). Selects *Bait* as an example and offers a worksheet of questions in order "to provide a framework for a structured yet inventive response" (34) to the poem.

565. Clark, William Bedford. "An Interview with Gary A. Stringer on the Variorum Donne." *SCRev* 2, no. 1: 80–93.

Reports an interview in which Gary A. Stringer, general editor of the variorum edition of Donne's poetry begun in 1981, describes the origin of the project, outlines the basic principles and procedures established for the edition, comments on the scholars involved and the original publisher, speculates on the publication dates for the ten individual volumes, mentions efforts to fund the undertaking, comments on several "spin-offs" from the project so far, discusses how the work will break new ground in a technical and methodological sense, and predicts the impact of the edition on future Donne studies. Indicates that the goal of the edition is to present a new text of Donne's poems and "to record the whole critical tradition on Donne, in all languages and literatures, over the last 350 years" (84).

566. Conrad, Peter. "Lyrical Nothings," in *The History of English Literature: One Indivisible, Unending Book,* 226–43. London: J. M. Dent and Sons. First American edition, Philadelphia: University of Pennsylvania Press, 1987.

Comments on Donne's critical reputation and maintains that T. S. Eliot's criticism is essentially "a manifesto of his own neo-metaphysical verse" that misrepresents Donne as "a symbolist before his time" (227). Contrasts Donne with Spenser, Herbert, and Marvell, claiming that Donne is "a fragmenter of English poetry" (229) and that "nothingness encroaches everywhere in Donne, and with it a terrifying nihilism" (230). Claims that Donne's "analytic mind delights in controlled destruction and disintegration" and that "his genius is precisely for dissociation" (235). Suggests that "[f]rom Donne emerges a tradition which explores the delighted and desolating mortality of the poem—a tradition almost of pornographic panic, extending through Marvell to the life and writing of Rochester" (239–40).

567. Donne, John. *Canzoni e Sonetti,* trans. Patrizia Valduga, with an afterword by Giuseppe Guglielmi. Piccola Enciclopedia, 9. Milano: Studio Editionale. 95p. Reprinted (with minor revisions) 1999.

Contains 30 selections from the *Songs and Sonets* with English texts and Italian translations on the same page (9–87) and no notes or commentary. In the afterword (89–95), comments on the style, metrics, and thematic concerns of Donne's poetry and prose, especially his love poetry. Calls Donne the supreme metaphysical poet and a passionate realist and briefly relates the intensity of his literary output to his life.

568. Donne, John. *The Complete English Poems of John Donne,* ed. with intro. by C. A. Patrides. Everyman's Library. London: J. M. Dent. 569p. Reprinted 1990; New York: Alfred A. Knopf, 1991. First paperback edition: 1985. Introduction (slightly revised) appears as "John Donne: The Aesthetics of Morality," in *Figures in a Renaissance Context,* ed. Claude J. Summers and Ted-Larry Pebworth (Ann Arbor: University of Michigan Press, 1989), 89–116.

In "To the Reader" (1–14), explains abbreviations, principles governing the textual apparatus, a symbol used for marking two words that should be pronounced as one, and the annotations on the text, and lists acknowledgments. Presents an out-line of Donne's life within the context of contemporary events (9–13). The introduction, "'Extreme, and scattring bright': The Poetry of John Donne" (14–45), comments on major features of Donne's poetry, such as its technical complexities and manipulation of meter; its dramatic mode and theatrical language; and its presentation of love and death. Comments briefly also on the *Satyres,* the *Elegies,* the *Anniversaries,* and the religious poems. Thereafter follows the text of the *Songs and Sonets,* the *Epigrams,* the *Elegies, Sappho,* the *Epithalamia,* the *Satyres, Letters to Severall Personages, The Anniversaries,* the *Epicedes and Obsequies, Metem,* and the *Divine Poems* (46–491), with each genre introduced briefly and with explanatory notes on individual poems. Appendix 1 (492–93) gives the arrangement of the poems in the 1633 edition; Appendix 2 (493) comments on poems attributed to Donne; Appendix 3 (494–99) presents poems on Donne by Henry King, Thomas Carew, and Ben Jonson; and Appendix 4 (500–510) gives Pope's versions of Donne's *Sat2* and *Sat4.*" Concludes with a bibliography of background studies and studies of Donne (511–56), an index of titles (558–64), and an index of first lines (565–69). Reviews: Jill P. Baumgaertner in *RES* 37 (1986): 565; Robert Ellrodt in *EA* 39 (1986): 92–93; D. F. Bratchell in *N&Q*, n.s. 34 (1987): 79–80; Raymond B. Waddington in *JDJ* 6 (1987): 135–45.

569. Donne, John. *Zwar ist auch Dichtung Sünde: Gedichte englisch und deutsch.* Nachdichtungen von Maik Hamburger und Christa Schuenke. Herausgegeben von Maik Hamburger. Reclams Universal-Bibliothek, Band 944. Leipzig: Philipp Reclam jun. 162p.

The introduction (5–19) outlines Donne's life; surveys his works, showing how they reflect the social and political events of his time; and comments on his critical reception both in the seventeenth and in the twentieth centuries. Contains English texts (Smith, 1971) and German translations on facing pages (20–165) of 26 selections from the *Songs and Sonets,* 11 elegies, 3 satires, 10 verse letters, *BedfCab,* 4 holy sonnets, and 2 hymns, followed by commentary and notes on individual poems (166–[82]). Includes 9 pen and ink drawings by Ingo Kraft. Reviews: Andrew M. McLean and J. Lawrence Gunter in *JDJ* 6 (1987): 289–93.

570. Dorrill, James. "Hardy, Donne, and the Tolling Bell." *JDJ* 4: 331–36.

Observes that critics have noted general similarities in idea, tone, and style between Donne's poetry and Thomas Hardy's poetry, but that all of the comments have been "tentative or general in nature" (331). Cites "one clear instance of Hardy's direct dependence on Donne": in his poem "Drawing Details in an Old Church" (l. 9) Hardy makes an "explicit reference" (332) to Meditation XVII from *Devotions.* Explains, however, that in Hardy's poem "Donne's belief in human solidarity" gives way "to a sense of hopeless fragmentation" and "universal and permanent isolation" (334).

571. Egan, James. "Donne's Wit of Death: Some Notes Toward a Definition." *SPWVSRA* 10: 25–34.

Cites examples from *Storm, ElNat, Twick, LovAlch, Appar, Cross, Metem,* and *FirAn* to show how Donne's "combination of irony, rhetoric, and death yields an intriguing wit." Maintains that Donne's "wit of death" is often "harsh, morbid and macabre" and that "[t]ypically, its focus is alienation, self-mockery, victimization, vulnerability, loss and humiliation" (26), but notes that his "theocentric vision acts as a form of decorum which stops his wit short of nihilism" (27). Concludes that Donne's "wit of death" is "pervasive, cutting across virtually all of the poetic genres in which he wrote," but points out that "[w]hile the early poetry frequently stresses the irreconcilability of the foolish, painful or absurd [aspects of death], the later works concede that the religious experience often resolves the contradictory states of the human condition" (32).

572. Felperin, Howard. "Canonical Texts and Non-Canonical Interpretations: The Neohistoricist Rereading of Donne." *SoRA* 18: 235–50. Reprinted as "Contextualizing the Canon: The Case of Donne," in *The Uses of the Canon: Elizabethan Literature and Contemporary Theory* (Oxford: Clarendon Press, 1990), 79–99. Surveys the development of literary criticism from nineteenth century humanism to contemporary New Historicism, defining the latter and noting how it focuses on canonical works, especially Elizabethan plays and poems, "mainly by Donne and Shakespeare," but gives them "distinctly non-canonical" readings. Claims that the aim of New Historicists is "to reread these canonical, and hitherto idealised, Elizabethan texts in a defamiliarising and demystifying way, as the encoded articulations of a historically specific system of social relations and differences" (238), noting, in particular, the breakdown of the patronage system. Discusses the similarities and differences between so-called New Critics (or formalists) and New Historicists, claiming that the latter in their readings of Donne "attempt to supply the motivations and meanings missing from the new-critical account by reinscribing the poetry within a psycho-social context" (244). Comments also on the limitations of the New Historicists' approach, pointing out that "[t]hey have produced a context, that of the politics and psychology of Elizabethan patronage, to replace the older, canonical context of the simultaneous order in which wit and love, thought and feeling, were one, and by grafting Donne's poetry into it," have attempted to make his poetry "newly meaningful" (248). Believes that, in fact, the New Historicists "have discovered in Elizabethan love poetry the portraiture of their own institutional and cultural position, a precarious, marginal and displaced position, and reframed as a context with the help of the decentring and demystifying techniques made available by a poststructuralist methodology that is itself the by-product of that

institutional and cultural breakdown" (249).

573. Granqvist, Raoul. "A 'Fashionable Poet' in New England in the 1890's: A Study of the Reception of John Donne." *JDJ* 4: 337–49.

Comments on Donne's reputation in New England around the turn of the nineteenth century, noting, in particular, the roles played in making Donne fashionable by Emerson, Thoreau, James Russell Lowell, Charles Eliot Norton, Sarah Orne Jewett, Annie Fields (wife of the famous Boston publisher), Louise Imogen Guiney, Edmund Gosse, Gamaliel Bradford, and Agnes Repplier. Notes that "Walton's stereotype of Dr. Donne, pervasive in both literary and clerical polemics during most of the nineteenth century in England, was replaced in America by the fascinating and enthralling persona of Jack Donne" (343) and that the language and imagery of his poems were "championed as exemplary" (344). Maintains that, in the 1920s, T. S. Eliot "merely transmitted" (345) a well-established critical commonplace when he commented on the fusion of emotion and thought in Donne's poetry.

574. Granqvist, Raoul. "John Donne: Kärlekens alkemist." *NyA* 8 (August): 171–75.

Uses the metaphor of alchemy to represent Donne's concern with the transcendental nature of matter and discusses his images of decay and transformation. Asserts that the poet's capacity for self-analysis and his treatment of the duality of body and soul and of relationships with women and with God are unprecedented. Finds in the *Elegies* and in the *Songs and Sonets* an analysis of human love that is presented as a confrontation of the sensual and the mystical. Believes that each of Donne's poems reveals his longing for harmony in an irrational and complex world. Reviews basic biographical facts about Donne and briefly describes his religious poems. Maintains that, throughout his life, Donne persisted in experimenting, analyzing himself, and reflecting on death.

575. Grant, Patrick. "John Donne's *Anniversaries:* New Philosophy and the Act of the Heart," in *Literature and the Discovery of Method in the English Renaissance,* 77–101. Athens, Ga.: University of Georgia Press.

Argues that the *Anniversaries* "communicate Donne's awareness that he must struggle to achieve significance for Elizabeth Drury, rather than depend upon the traditional, public content of his language to disclose allegorically the higher meaning of her life and death." Maintains, in other words, that these poems are "partly about the difficulty itself of treating the girl as a symbol," and holds that they "can be specially well understood in terms of the human heart." Says that "Donne's claim that the world lost its heart with Elizabeth Drury's death indicates both a general human disorientation (which the poetry keenly records and links specifically with the rise of science), and also the human creature's peculiar, uncertain status as embodied spirit." Claims, therefore, that in the *Anniversaries* Donne's "allusions to the heart consequently indicate a set of preoccupations which can help us to grasp what is most distinctive in his treatment of the dead girl" (79). Discusses Donne's figurative uses of the heart, especially in *Leg, Ecst,* the *Divine Poems,* and the sermons, as well as his views on and uses of the "new science." Maintains that the *Anniversaries* "are significant, less because of their obvious failure to make, as it were, a viable metaphysical symbol out of the girl's career, than for a kind of covert success, which comes from the sense they convey of why they

cannot succeed, which comes partly by a self-protective bravado and display of extravagance for its own sake" (99). Concludes that in the *Anniversaries* Donne presents "the human heart disenfranchised by science on the one hand and Calvinism on the other" and "attempts, in his treatment of Elizabeth Drury, to make of the dead girl a symbol adequate to his hope and faith and knowledge," but that "his deliberate metaphysical fabrication succeeds less in assuaging the fears and uncertainties of the human condition than in enabling poetry to find its true subject by expressing those very fears and uncertainties" (101).

576. Haefner, Gerhard. "Formen theologischer Argumentation in der religiösen englischen Lyrik des frühen 17. Jahrhunderts," in *Impulse der englischen Lyrik: Lyrik im Spannungsfeld von Politik, Gesellschaft, Interessen und Ideologien in England von der Shakespearezeit bis zur Gegenwart,* 30–47. Anglistische Forschungen, ed. Johannes Hoops, 180. Heidelberg: Carl Winter Universitätsverlag.

Discusses how Donne's religious lyrics differ from those of his contemporaries. Observes how Donne tends to cloak his theological messages in paradoxes and daring conceits that compel the reader to examine the discrepancy between logic and faith, and in analogies that require intellectual effort since they are not immediately apparent. In an analysis of *Sickness,* suggests that the fundamental theological message is that death leads to true life. Comments on Donne's struggle to picture something that basically defies depiction. Observes that the dilemma for Donne and for other religious poets of his time as well as for those of today is the fundamental, inexorable contrast between the inability of depicting theological concepts and the human need to perceive them through the senses.

577. Haffenden, John. "The Importance of Empson (I): The Poems." *EIC* 35: 1–24.

Comments on Donne's influence on William Empson, noting, for instance, that both poets express a fear of isolation and "wish to escape that fear through love," and that also both desire "to transcend the oppressive facts of the known physical world" (8–9). Believes that Empson's "kinship with Donne is deep and real" (14) and suggests that Empson "undertook a closer reading of Donne's poems than Eliot ever pretended" (15), as reflected both in his poetry and criticism.

578. Harrison, Antony H. "Reception Theory and the New Historicism: The Metaphysical Poets in the Nineteenth Century." *JDJ* 4: 163–80.

Offers an introductory essay in a special issue of *JDJ* devoted to the reception of the metaphysical poets in the nineteenth century. Rather than "recapitulate the discoveries and arguments of the essays," suggests "some additional theoretical and practical directions for studies like these, directions which have been opened up by the work of theorists in literary historiography and by reception theorists during the last two decades" (165). Surveys the work of Hans Robert Jauss (1969) and other reception theorists and discusses "ways in which reception theory may be usefully allied with the 'new historicism' in order to outline a new, theoretically informed project in literary historical studies" (167). Comments on "three descriptive rubrics" of a "truly historicist reception theory": "discursive modes of reception, subject matters of reception, and issues of reception" (171). Points out that the essays in this special issue "concern themselves with the ways in which works of literature perpetually reconstitute themselves, both as they are experienced over history by readers with changing horizons of expectations and in the works of subsequent writers, where the originary text serves as palimpsest" (178).

579. Haskin, Dayton. "Reading Donne's *Songs and Sonnets* in the Nineteenth Century." *JDJ* 4: 225–52.

Surveys the popularity and critical reception of Donne's love poetry, especially the *Songs and Sonets,* during the nineteenth century. Points out that Donne's poetry "was neither well known nor highly regarded" (225) during the first half of the century, noting that, in spite of several editions, his poetry "went pretty much unread." Observes, however, that "[b]y the 1890s Donne was being more widely and enthusiastically discussed in print than at any time since the 1630s" and that readers became "attentive to the love poetry in particular" (226), noting that "[a]bout three quarters of what was written specifically about the *Songs and Sonnets* in the nineteenth century appeared after 1890 and more than half of it was published in the five years from 1895 to 1899." Emphasizes that during this time, however, Donne's love poems "came to be interpreted as confessional poetry, revealing hidden truths that Walton and other biographers had neglected or suppressed" (227). Discusses Coleridge's appreciation of Donne's love poems, noting, however, that, for the most part, his "insight into Donne's achievement went largely unappreciated" (235). Discusses those critics who disapproved of Donne's amatory poetry in the 1860s, 1870s, and 1880s, especially George Gilfillan, Hippolyte Taine, and Edwin Whipple. Maintains that central to the Donne revival was an 1880 essay by William Minto, and discusses the critical views of the Donne revivalists of the 1890s, especially George Saintsbury, Edward Dowden, and Edmund Gosse. Concludes that, for the most part, even in the later nineteenth century there was a tendency to reduce Donne's love poetry "to a few of its moral themes, or to make of it so much pulp with which to feed vulgar curiosity about the sex life of the man who had become Dean of St. Paul's" (247).

580. Henderson, Katherine Usher, and Barbara F. McManus. "The Literary Contexts," in *Half Humankind: Contexts and Texts of the Controversy about Women in England, 1540–1640,* 99–130. Urbana: University of Illinois Press.

Surveys popular stereotypes of women in Renaissance poetry. Observes that, unlike Sidney and Spenser, in his love poetry Donne "does not employ the voice of humble suppliant to a chastely beautiful woman," but that he does employ "the popular images of women in a variety of ingenious ways." Stresses the ambivalence in Donne's portrayal of women in his poems. Points out, for instance, that in such poems as *SGo, Ind,* and *ElChange,* he "plays with the image of woman as promiscuously faithless" so hypothetically that he seems "almost certainly teasing the stereotype, perhaps to question its validity, or reveal its absurdity" (105). Maintains that "[o]f all lyric poets of the English Renaissance, Donne's work offers the greatest range of attitude towards women." Points out that "while he transcended the popular stereotypes of women in an important group of poems that celebrate the wonder and joy of mutual love that is both physical and spiritual, his work includes poems which scorn women and poems of profound sexual disillusion." Argues that the *Anniversaries* "stand as emblem of this ambivalence, for although they elevate a young woman into a symbol of all beauty and all virtue, they nevertheless participate in a theological tradition which lays upon women the heavier burden of blame for the

generally fallen condition of humankind" (110).

581. Hester, M. Thomas. "The Heritage of Donne's 'Disinherited.'" *AN&Q* 23: 135–37.

Shows how in *Disinher* Donne, being "a revisionist artist who modifies whatever he borrows" (135), "inverts" Martial's treatment of the disinherited son. Points out that in Donne's poem the "focus of the comic irony" is on "the surprising significance of a philanthropic father's final gesture" in which "the expectation that the son has been rendered poor is overturned by the moral interpretation of the worth that should be 'all' to a loving son—the goodness of his father" (136). Suggests also that Donne's epigram may be indebted to a distich from the *Catonis Disticha,* a "popular medieval and Renaissance textbook of proverbial wisdom," which reads (in English translation): "A heritage bequeathed to you will / Keep and increase: so save your good name still." Concludes that "by accommodating this popular . . . adage to the context of a *disinherited* son, Donne increases the surprise of his poem," not only reversing "the usual, expected treatment of the unfortunate-heir" but also illustrating "an unforeseen applicability for [pseudo-] Cato's advice" (137).

582. Hester, M. Thomas. "Reading Donne's Epigrams: 'Raderus'/'Ralphius.'" *PLL* 21: 324–30.

Maintains that the conclusions a reader may draw from Donne's poetry will often be "corrected, rescinded, or frustrated by the final turn of Donne's witty dialectic." Presents critical readings of *Martial* and *Ralph* as examples of works the interpretation of which may benefit from their close proximity in the manuscripts and suggests that "[t]he attitude towards the reader of epigrams intimated" in *Martial* "raises certain interpretative questions" concerning *Ralph* (325). Through an examination of several double and triple *entendres* in the two epigrams, concludes that the reader is left only with an "interpretative dilemma" and "not with the maximal closure that is supposed to characterize the epigram" (329). Believes that the aim of the wit in the two poems resides primarily in Donne's "evoking the reader's response to the evocativeness and wondrous multiplicity of language" (329–30).

583. Hobbs, Mary. "Henry King's Sermons: A Pale Imitation of Donne?" *N&Q,* n.s. 32: 78–82.

Points out close parallels between Donne's valediction sermon preached at Lincoln's Inn on 18 April 1619 and Henry King's Whitehall sermon for Lent of 1626, "the only printed examples of their both using the same text." Suggests that in his sermon King "is deliberately developing a dialogue with Donne" on his interpretation of their common text (Ecclesiastes 12:1) and that King's sermon is, therefore, a "kind of in-joke" (79) that would have delighted the King and his audience. Shows, however, that King is "no slavish imitator" and that "his argument as a whole takes a quite independent line from Donne's" (80).

584. Hodgson, John A. "Coleridge, Puns, and 'Donne's First Poem': The Limbo of Rhetoric and the Conceptions of Wit." *JDJ* 4: 181–200.

Surveys Coleridge's attitude toward punning, conceits, and wit, especially in his notebooks, lectures, and letters, noting that his puns on fleas and lice "make part of a sustained pattern of allusion, whereby these insect vermin become very icons of inferior wit and bad puns" (188). Comments on Coleridge's poem on *Flea,* entitled "On Donne's first Poem," so named because it appears as the first poem in the 1669 edition that Coleridge had borrowed from Lamb. Claims that the poem "has much to teach us about how Coleridge distinguishes wit's value from its dross," noting how in the poem "half-nothings of inferior wit give way to the greater power of the sole true wit, which bespeaks a congruence deeper than that of sound, a true analogy beneath the superficial, ridiculous likeness." Points out how Coleridge discriminates between "lower wit" and "higher wit," which "anticipates his crucial discrimination of allegory from symbol" (196).

585. Jack, Ian. "A Choice of Orders: The Arrangement of 'The Poetical Works,'" in *Textual Criticism and Literary Interpretation,* ed. Jerome J. McGann, 127–43. Chicago: University of Chicago Press.

Discusses the principal methods that editors have chosen to arrange a poet's work. Notes that Grierson (1912) published the *Songs and Sonets* in the order of the 1635 edition (with one exception), "in which these poems were first brought together and given a general title"; that Helen Gardner (1965) divided the poems into two groups, those she believed were written before 1600 and those written after 1602; and A. J. Smith (1972) arranged them alphabetically by title. Suggests that "it is not inconceivable that some day another editor may attempt to print all of Donne's poems in one chronological series," noting that one advantage of such an arrangement would be to remind us that "Donne began writing religious poetry before he stopped writing love poetry" and that "the division of his life into clearly differentiated chapters . . . lacks biographical justification" (143).

586. Kawada, Akira. "John Donne to George Herbert: Shi wo megutte" [On John Donne and George Herbert with Special Reference to Death], in *John Donne to sono Shuhen* [John Donne and Other Poets of the Seventeenth Century],

129–48. The Japan Society of Seventeenth-Century English Literature. Tokyo: Kinseido.

Discusses the similarities and differences between Donne and Herbert concerning death, commenting particularly on Donne's *HSDeath* and Herbert's "Death" and "Time."

587. Kermode, Frank. *Forms of Attention.* Chicago: University of Chicago Press. xiv, 93p.

In discussing the question, "By what means do we attribute value to works of art, and how do our valuations affect our ways of attending to them?" comments on Donne's critical reputation. Notes that even in the seventeenth century Donne's fame "began to wane very early" (70) and that by the time of Johnson his poetry "had come to seem merely quaint and out of touch with the tradition, as that tradition was formed by a later system of learning." Claims Donne's modern revival depended upon a "new view of the creative faculty, a new understanding that ratiocination might be the ally rather than the enemy of passion, [and] new understanding of history, transforming the old opinion about the late Middle Ages and the Renaissance." Observes, however, that "[i]t was also necessary that these transformations become matters of opinion; familiar ground to a reading public, not just a learned coterie" (71). Notes the importance of Grierson's edition (1912) and T. S. Eliot's criticism in making Donne, for a time, a "model of modern 'sensibility.'" Maintains that Donne "has settled into a place in our canon; but we can now see that his admission was peculiarly the work of a past epoch, an effort controlled by historical conditions we identify as quite other than our own." Concludes that Donne is "still highly esteemed, though the original tone of ecstasy has been somewhat muted," and that his

"preservation and renewal . . . has become the duty not of artists and enthusiasts, carefree adherents of opinion, but of canon-defending, theory-laden professors" (72).

588. Kim, Young-Ho. "Baroque Elements in Donne's Poetry." *Pegasus* 8: 5–19.

Argues that Donne's poetry contains many baroque elements, such as the uses of wit, rhetorical argument, shocking images, conceits and extended metaphors, hyperbole, paradox, and the grotesque as evidenced in *Sickness, Ecst,* and *ValMourn.*

589. Lawrence, Karen, Betsy Seifter, and Lois Ratner. "John Donne," in *The McGraw-Hill Guide to English Literature,* Vol. 1, *"Beowulf" to Jane Austen,* 225–37. New York: McGraw-Hill.

Contains a chronology of Donne's life (225–27), followed by essay questions and answers on *ValMourn, Flea, Canon,* and *HSBatter* (228–36) and a brief list of suggested further readings (237).

590. Love, Harold. "Manuscript versus Print in the Transmission of English Literature, 1600–1700." *Bulletin of the Bibliographical Society of Australia and New Zealand* 9: 95–107.

In a discussion of authorial attitudes toward the transmission of literature in print in the seventeenth century, contrasts Donne's attitude with that of Spenser, noting that Donne "not only rejected print, circulating the great bulk of his verse only in manuscript, but does not even look particularly distinguished in print" (99). Observes that Donne's "poetic art leads to bizarrely shaped and constantly varied stanzas" and that "[h]is stanza pattern for any given poem is determined by the requirements of the thought, without any consideration for visual effect." Suggests that because of this and his "uncompromising intellectuality," Donne "may be seen as consciously opposed to the values of the open market and the promiscuously purchasable page created by print" (100).

591. Low, Anthony. "The Complete Angler's 'Baite'; or, The Subverter Subverted." *JDJ* 4: 1–12.

Discusses how in *Bait* Donne "first draws his reader in, leading him to expect yet another smooth pastoral song," but then "[g]radually he disillusions him, as under the poet's hands, pastoralism is exaggerated, then twisted, depersonalized, mocked, and rejected" (10). Shows how Walton in *The Complete Angler* "uses precisely Donne's method in reverse and repudiates Donne's argument" by making Marlowe and Raleigh "come alive posthumously as fellow inhabitants of our human world, while Donne is relegated to the status of mere textuality" (11). Suggests that Walton's treatment of *Bait* shows "just how well Walton understands what Donne is doing in his poem" and how it expresses his "antipathy for Donnean literary privacy and revisionism" (10).

592. Low, Anthony. "John Donne," in *The Georgic Revolution,* 74–88. Princeton, N.J.: Princeton University Press.

Discusses Donne's ambivalent attitude toward the court as reflected in his poetry, especially the *Satyres.* Notes that although Donne's predecessors and contemporaries vented their criticism of the court by writing pastorals, Donne wrote only *Bait* (an untypical poem) in the pastoral mode, "which is surely extraordinary at a time when pastoral was invading comedies, romances, tragedies, epics, and satires, as well as lyrics" (74–75). Points out that, unlike Spenser, Bacon, and Jonson, Donne rejected "a public-spirited response" to the court and "retreat[ed] into privacy"—"the microcosm of the two lovers, who exclude the world, and the microcosm of the thinking and feeling self, which also

excludes the world" (75). Points out that "[e]ven when Donne is acting in the most public of offices, we find him always internalizing, always looking within, and his advice to his congregation is frequently to do likewise" (75–76). Maintains that Donne has "no fondness for any of the Virgilian forms, whether pastoral, georgic, or epic," and notes that he cites the *Georgics* "only as exemplifying the lowest kind of poetry." Observes, however, that "his poems touch on georgic subjects fairly often," such as land ownership, farming, manual labor, country life, and country people, but that "[a]lmost invariably the references are negative" (76). Cites *ILRoll* and *ILBlest* as Donne's "fullest statement of his opinion of the georgic way of life" (80), which is one of "scorn and disinterest" (83), noting that only in *RWThird* did he express a wholly favorable attitude toward georgic activity. Concludes that, for Donne, "[t]he georgic imperative—that is, the practical necessity to earn one's bread, the moral necessity usefully to multiply one's talents in the service of others, and the creative necessity to invent useful arts and discover new worlds—irritated him" and "[a]s a result more often than we might expect, he took up georgic themes and modes in order to give them the back of his hand" (86).

593. Mann, Lindsay A. "Sacred and Profane Love in Donne." *DR* 65 (1985–86): 534–50.

Argues that "Donne's portrayals of human and divine love do not support the general perception of a dualism of early profanity and later asceticism in his works." Maintains that "[r]eexamination of his poems in the light of consistent principles in his prose suggests that his deepest concern throughout his works is with the process which draws natural and spiritual, human and divine into relation, despite difficulty and failure," and that "[i]n this way he seeks to reestablish and strengthen an ideal of continuity and relation between human and divine" (548). Discusses Donne's presentation of women and love in characteristic poems from the *Satyres, Elegies, Songs and Sonets, Holy Sonnets,* and the hymns to show that "his portrayals of sacred and profane love are directed to this end" (548).

594. Martines, Lauro. *Society and History in English Renaissance Verse.* Oxford: Basil Blackwell. viii, 191p.

Discusses "the ties between non-dramatic poetry of the English Renaissance and the social world of its composition," focusing on "questions of theory, strategies of analysis, and the nature of relations between Renaissance poetry and its society" (vii). Refers to Donne as a coterie poet and a social conservative, and comments throughout on aspects of both his secular and religious poetry—its diction, figurative language, imagery, tone, and style. Envisions "the ideal reader" of Donne as one who would relate "the different aspects of his verse to the London scene, the Inns-of-Court setting, the unsettled religious milieu, the pull of elite social circles, the fickleness of patronage, a rising mood of disillusionment with the Court, the swagger of wealth and rank, a certain stage in the development of English society, financial and career pressures, the use of the new and old astronomies in social statement, and a similar use of accents drawn from late medieval philosophy and science," and then would relate these to "Donne's imagery, the learned features of his diction, alleged colloquialisms, his shifting uses of the middle and low styles, certain dramatic stances, and metrical roughness," as well as "his smart, wheedling, and *odi profanos* tones"

(124–25). Believes that "in the process of drawing his findings into a coherent whole," this ideal reader will likely discover that "the unsteadiness of Donne's social identity" shows up "in all aspects of his verse" (124).

595. Martz, Louis L. "English Religious Poetry, from Renaissance to Baroque." *EIRC* 11: 1–28. Revised version in *From Renaissance to Baroque: Essays on Literature and Art* (Columbia: University of Missouri Press, 1991), 3–38.

Sees Donne as an example of "the mannerism of anxiety," which, however, "needs to be distinguished (though not wholly divorced) from the mannerism of elegance" (1). Calls Donne "a connoisseur of art" and points out that "he had his own image painted or sculptured in five different postures," all of which were done "in a mode that can rightly be called mannerist" (6). Discusses mannerist elements in *Metem, Sat3, Corona, Father, Holy Sonnets, GoodM, ValMourn, LovInf, Cross,* and *Noct*. Points out Donne's prevailing expression of instability, ambiguity, and insecurity; his extensive use of the conditional mode; and his attempt to reconcile his divided religious allegiance into an acceptable form of "rectified devotion." Maintains that Donne "creates a spirituality that blends the Reformation with the Counter-Reformation" and suggests that, "that blending, so tormented, so strenuous, will perhaps explain why Donne has seemed unusual, even eccentric, in the course of English poetry." Suggests, however, that "he does not seem eccentric when viewed in the full European context and especially in the Spanish context, both poetical and religious" (16). Concludes that "High Renaissance, mannerism, baroque: these terms have no real existence until we give them definition, but, once defined, they may serve as tools for critical reading in the full context of European culture," adding that "it may be that the greatest value of such terms lies in this: that they serve constantly to remind us that English poetry of this era is not local in its range, but is part of the great spectrum of European art" (27). Compares and contrasts Donne to El Greco, Spenser, Herbert, Crashaw, and Vaughan.

596. Maynard, John. "Browning, Donne, and the Triangulation of the Dramatic Monologue." *JDJ* 4: 253–67.

Discusses the influence of Donne on Robert Browning's poetry, maintaining that "Browning's closest affinity as a writer of thinking in poetry, in poems that enact the process of reasoning, rationalizing, even sometimes casuistic mind at work," was Donne and his tradition. Suggests that "[p]robably many poets of the earlier modern period whom we think of in relation to Donne are as much in the tradition of Donne mediated by Browning as they are directly influenced by Donne himself" (254). Cites several affinities between the two poets, such as the attraction of "logic, argument, and the use of reason as well as feeling" in poetry (257) and the colloquial and dramatic uses of language which create a sense of "writing emerging directly from a mind at work." Sees Browning's reading of Donne as "at least a major force in helping Browning to the new poetry of argument and case-making that finds its best realization in the dramatic monologue" (258), and compares and contrasts the two poets as writers of dramatic monologues. Insists, however, that Donne's influence as well as the similarities between the two poets is "one of manner more than matter" and is "more a general approach to writing poetry than deliberate parody or verbal echoes" (259).

597. Middleman, Louis I. "Another Canon in Donne's 'Canonization.'" *ELN* 22: 37–39.

Suggests that in ll. 44–45 of *Canon* ("Beg from above / A patterne of your love!"), "'above' refers literally to the poem itself and 'pattern' to the fact that the last words of the first and last lines of every stanza are all 'love'" (37–38). Notes that the *OED* gives the following musical meaning for "canon": "A species of musical composition in which the different parts take up the same subject one after another, either at the same or at a different pitch, in strict imitation." Suggests, therefore, the poem is "indeed a canon." Notes, futhermore, that John Dowland in *Orthinoparcus (A) his micrology, or introduction: containing the art of singing song* (1609) writes: "A canon . . . is an imaginarie rule, drawing that part of the song which is not yet set downe out of that part which is set downe. Or it is a Rule, which doth wittily discover the secret of a song" (38). Says that "Dowland's first sentence is more or less a restatement of the general definition," but that "his second permits a reading of the 'love' pattern that is not amiss for such a witty and paranomasic poet as Donne." Points out that "[i]n each stanza 'love' is the end of the beginning and end of the end," or, in other words, "love is the end (purpose) of the beginning (life in this world) and the end (result) of the end (the death of the body)." Concludes that "[a]ll of this loving, though sexual, is yet also spiritual, so that it is indeed for God's sake, and not just Cupid's, that the speaker silences his interlocutor and pleads his song" (39).

598. Mueller, Janel M. "'This Dialogue of One': A Feminist Reading of Donne's 'Extasie.'" *ADEB* 81: 39–42.

From a "post-Freudian feminist perspective," examines *Ecst* "through
selective discussion of certain major
elements: the situation, the persons,
and the images that carry key meanings" (39). Characterizes the poem as
reflecting "phallogocentrism" in which
the speaker demonstrates for the hypothetical bystander in the poem "how
he takes charge of a certain 'her' intellectually and verbally . . . by using
resources of learning derived from the
all but exclusively masculine preserves
of his day" with which "he creates,
as an instrument of domination, a
monologic discourse—or, more gal-
lantly but no less revealingly a 'dialogue of one'" (42).

599. Nishiyama, Yoshio. "Hogaku-ryo Jidai
no Donne: 'Inconstancy' no Uta no
Haikei" [John Donne as a Law Student:
The Background to His "Inconstancy"
Poems], in *John Donne to sono Shuhen*
[John Donne and Other Poets of the
Seventeenth Century], 3–32. The Japan
Society of Seventeenth-Century English
Literature. Tokyo: Kinseido.

Maintains that Donne's concern for
"inconstancy" and "change" are deeply
rooted in his works. Demonstrates that
his satirical attacks on society as well
as many of his humorous expressions
are derived from the political and religious conditions of the age by commenting on several poems in the *Songs
and Sonets*.

600. O'Connell, Patrick F. "'Restore Thine
Image': Structure and Theme in Donne's
'Goodfriday.'" *JDJ* 4: 13–28.

Suggests that structurally, verbally,
and thematically *Goodf* is modelled
upon *HSLittle*. Maintains, however,
that "the most significant result of a
comparison [of the two poems] is to
highlight the ways in which Donne
has refashioned his material into a
poem in which traditional images and
ideas are used in strikingly original

ways to examine the mystery of redemption" (13). Presents a very
detailed critical reading of *Goodf* to
show how "the death of the false self
who dominated the first part of the
poem means true life, the restoration
of real identity, which is to be 'thine
image,' one who participates in the
death of Christ so as to share in his
glory." Maintains that "[b]y letting go
his self-centered individualism, the
speaker is united both to Christ and
to members of the community of faith"
and that "[h]is passage from *cupidi-
tas* to *caritas* becomes exemplary."
Concludes that Donne thus succeeds
in the poem "in giving his speaker a
representative role, in which the reader
is invited to participate, since he too
is, or is called to be, 'thine image'"
(26).

601. Okada, Hiroko. "*The Songs and
Sonnets* ni okeru Heya no Shigaku:
'The good-morrow,' 'The Sunne Rising,'
'The Canonization' wo chushin ni" [The
Poetics of Rooms with Special Reference
to "The good-morrow," "The Sunne
Rising," and "The Canonization"], in
John Donne to sono Shuhen [John Donne
and Other Poets of the Seventeenth
Century] (The Japan Society of Seven-
teenth-Century English Literature), 33–51.
Tokyo: Kinseido.

Analyzes the room imagery mainly in
GoodM, SunRis, and *Canon.* Points
out that the spatial dichotomy of
"Room/Non-Room" is one of the characteristic structures of Donne's literary world. Demonstrates that the
poetics of the *Songs and Sonets* is
based on dynamics by which lovers
make their own limited spaces and
value them, seeking their identities.

602. Otten, Charlotte F. *Environ'd with
Eternity: God, Poems, and Plants in Sixteenth and Seventeenth Century England.*
Lawrence, Kans.: Coronado Press. xix,
198p.

Comments on Donne's use of the mandrake root in *SGo, Metem,* and *Henry* (74–77); his use of a "female human navel in the middle of a watery metaphor" in *ElProg,* noting that in botany the navel is a plant that was "susceptible to sexual suggestibility" (88); and the reference to the smell of perfume ("of sweet vegetable origin") in *ElPerf* (100).

603. Pallotti, Donatella. "'That Inchanting Force': Il trattamento poetico delle forme pronominali personali nei *Songs and Sonets* di John Donne." *Analysis: Quaderni di Anglistica* 3: 23–59.

Relying on semiotic and linguistic theory, discusses how Donne's use of personal pronouns in the *Songs and Sonets* reflects his attitude toward the self, sexual love, and the world in general. Analyzes, in particular, the uses of personal pronouns in *SunRis, Blos, GoodM,* and *Canon.*

604. Parfitt, George. *English Poetry of the Seventeenth Century.* (Longman Literature in English Series.) London: Longman. xi, 236p.

Mentions Donne throughout, but primarily in "The Lyric" (18–55). Comments on major characteristics of Donne's secular and religious lyrics by contrasting them with the courtly lyrics of the Elizabethans, noting that Donne's work "is marked by extreme variations of rhythm, by its range of imagery, linguistic shock effects, and a general air of iconoclasm" (20), as well as by "wit and esotericism" and by "urgency and individualism" (21). Maintains that Donne is "revolutionary in his removal of love from court and all it implies" (26). Contrasts Donne and Jonson as lyricists and suggests their influence on other writers of the time, especially Herrick, Carew, Lovelace, Suckling, Cowley, and Marvell. Discusses also the "overlap and continuity" (42) between Donne's secular and religious lyrics, noting that

his "religious verse has exactly the same instability which marks his erotic poetry" (43). Claiming that Donne "is too individual a poet to be strictly representative, either of seventeenth-century religious experience or of its poetry" (44), compares and contrasts him with Herbert, Quarles, Wither, Vaughan, and Crashaw.

605. Parry, Graham. "John Donne: Patronage, Friendship and Love," in *Seventeenth Century Poetry: The Social Context,* 42–74. London: Hutchinson.

Maintains that, unlike Jonson's, much of Donne's poetry is "self-advertisement," written "to parade his wit, to entertain and astonish his friends, to attract patrons and generally to announce his availability for employment and advancement in the competitive circles of the Elizabethan and Jacobean Court" (42). Surveys the social dimension of Donne's poems and finds the earlier poems characterized by "excess of intellectual activity and invention cramped into couplets" (46) but considers *Sat3* an exception, noting how "[t]he search for truth in religion and for an understanding of his own spiritual condition preoccupied Donne for most of his life" (49). Finds *ElPerf* Donne's "most atmospheric" love poem, and finds wit, ingenious argument, and dramatic diction the hallmarks of the *Songs and Sonets.* Discusses Donne's circle of friends and patrons, especially the Countess of Bedford, and the verse letters he sent to them as well as comments on the *Anniversaries* and *Henry* as patronage poems. Maintains that although Donne's religious poems "served a private function of spiritual discipline, control of personal fears and encouragement of hope, they also had a social function," noting that "he circulated them to friends so that they could serve the needs of others" (68). Observes that, once Donne became a priest, most of his experience of life and his religious thinking were "channelled into his sermons" (68) and "poetry became a less important means of expression to him," citing, however, *Sickness* ("a virtuoso performance") (69) and *Father* as notable exceptions.

606. Patrides, C. A. "John Donne Methodized; or, How to Improve Donne's Impossible Text with the Assistance of His Several Editors." *MP* 82: 365–73.

Defends his textual decisions in *The English Poems of John Donne* (1985), claiming that, because of the complexity of Donne's text and the disagreement among previous editors, he has "few illusions left that Donne can ever be edited to one's satisfaction, not to mention the satisfaction of his discriminating readers" (365). Cites examples of inconsistencies and problems in the editorial work of certain major modern editors of Donne's poetry, especially H. J. C. Grierson, John Hayward, Helen Gardner, Wesley Milgate, John T. Shawcross, and A. J. Smith. Comments in some detail on the problem of punctuation in modern editions. Suggests that Grierson's tampering with the punctuation in his edition represents "a variation of the general tendency among editors to 'methodize' Donne's poetry, using punctuation much as Shawcross resorted to a forceful reduction of syllables to a presumed requisite length or as Gardner wandered in determined pursuit of 'defective' or 'clumsy' readings" (372). Rejects, therefore, the attempt of editors to regularize Donne's poetry and insists that, however eclectic or subjective a text might be, the editor of Donne's poetry should not attempt "to reduce his 'roughness' into harmony" but should allow "readings, however 'clumsy' or 'defective' in appearance, to reflect his remarkable sense of reality" (373).

607. Pritchard, R. E. "Dying in Donne's 'The Good Morrow.'" *EIC* 35: 213–22.

Argues that the last three lines of *GoodM* imply "that each lover's desire should be reciprocated, equal with the other's, should not slacken and so, unlike everything else since the Fall, not die" (216). Suggests that the view Donne expresses in these lines may have been influenced by the thinking of certain contemporary eschatalogical religious sects that practiced sexual intercourse without orgasm as "a religious sacrament, a mode of mystical knowledge, and a civilising social discipline" (217). Believes that in *GoodM* Donne "presents a new love, different from ordinary sexuality, that is associated with the discovery of reality, the establishment of the true faith, a replacement of the familiar world, an image of perfection and eternity, that recalls an original happy state, and involves an activity unlike that consequent upon the Fall." Holds that "the speaker is concerned not merely with the sexual act but with this new, ideal and transforming relationship—a relationship, however, that does not leave behind but includes, centres upon, the physical relationship that is its spirit made flesh, its embodiment and manifestation." Suggests, therefore, that the lovers by having sex without orgasm (thus no "dying" and no "slackening") "will repeat the perfect love and love-making of prelapsarian Adam and Eve" that will restore them "to a blessed, paradisal condition." Maintains that "[n]ot merely will Donne's lovers themselves not die, but their unique love will be a catalytic miracle, cancelling the effect of the Fall." Believes that such a reading is "consonant not only with Donne's frequent attempts to reconcile sexual and religious love, but also with other attempts and hopes for a Paradise Regained, entertained by many of his contemporaries, in what they thought to be 'the last days'" (220).

608. Roberts, John R. *Richard Crashaw: An Annotated Bibliography of Modern Criticism, 1632–1980.* Columbia: University of Missouri Press. 477p.

Includes 221 items from 1632 to 1980 that refer to Donne in relation to Crashaw.

609. Rosu, Anca. "Poetry as Language Presentation: John Donne Poet, Preacher, Craftsman." *Comitatus* 16: 11–28.

Argues that "[t]he literary quality of Donne's sermons contributed to the transformation of poetry from an art in which language was regarded as a material to be presented, into an art of representation, where language is regarded as a vehicle, less important than the ideas it carries" (11). Sees Donne the secular poet as the "last and most brilliant representative" of those who regarded poetry as "language presentation" and maintains that his sermons are "pervaded by an entirely different attitude toward language" (20) that can already be observed in his religious poems. Discusses Donne's theory of language as it is reflected in his poetry and sermons, noting how it was shaped by St. Augustine's theory of signification. Points out how Donne's sermons reflect his "constant effort of disciplining the figuratively rich and slippery language of the Bible towards the transparence and clarity of pure representation" (21). Maintains that "[b]y perfecting the language as representation in his sermons and introducing it in his religious lyrics, Donne not only founded the Metaphysical School but also established a poetical attitude that reaches far beyond his century." Concludes that "[t]he poetics of representation was dominant until modernism began its demolition" and that "ironically it has made us perpetually ignore the quality of the language presentation in Donne's poetry" (27).

610. Sakamoto, Yoshiyuki. "*The Anniversaries* ni okeru Choritsu no Motif: Donne no Ongaku no Image no Ichikosatsu" [Tuning Motif in *The Anniversaries:* A Study in Donne's Images from Music], in *John Donne to sono Shuhen* [John Donne and Other Poets of the Seventeenth Century], 52–82. The Japan Society of Seventeenth-Century English Literature. Tokyo: Kinseido.

Maintains that Donne's serious use of images drawn from music in the *Anniversaries* marks a turning point in his creative activity. Argues that musical references and the motif of tuning are key images by which the *Anniversaries* and Donne's later works are connected.

611. Shapiro, I. A. "Huyghens' Copy of Donne's *Letters, 1651,*" in *Elizabethan and Modern Studies Presented to Professor Willem Schrickx on the Occasion of His Retirement,* ed. J. P. Vander Motten, 229–34. Gent: Seminarie voor Engelse en Amerikaanse Literatur, R.U.G.

Discusses Constantijn Huygens's acquaintance with Donne and reports the existence of a copy of Donne's *Letters to Severall Persons of Honour* (1651) in the Birmingham University Library that he believes Huygens owned. Notes that in the center of the title page of this volume is inscribed "Constanter 1651." Presents reasons for thinking that Humphrey Robinson was the chief supplier of English books to Huygens.

612. Shawcross, John T. "Literary Revisionism and a Case for Genre." *Genre* 18: 413–34. Revised as introduction to *Intentionality and the New Traditionalism: Some Liminal Means to Literary Revisionism* (University Park: Pennsylvania State University Press, 1991), 1–19.

Challenges various kinds of "modish literary criticism" (413), especially deconstructionism and flawed reader-response theories, and argues for the authorial presence in poems. Insists that the very existence of a poem or other piece of literature implies that the author had some kind of "intent" when he wrote the piece. Identifies three "texts"—"the text, the reader's text, the author's text"—and argues that the literary critic's responsibility is "to render all three texts in all their relationships" (415). Uses Donne's *Licent* as an example of a poem "either generally inadequately read or actually misread by inattention to authorial presence" (419). Comments, in particular, on the importance of genre, which "predicates an author and authorial presence, and in turn implies meaning for the reader" (426).

613. Shawcross, John T. "Opulence and Iron Pokers: Coleridge and Donne." *JDJ* 4: 201–24.

Surveys Coleridge's critical assessment of Donne's poetry and endorses the notion that Coleridge was "among the prime movers" (203) in the resuscitation of Donne's reputation in the nineteenth century. Points out the vast number of poems by Donne that Coleridge cited, annotated, or imitated and examines his various critical comments on Donne. Analyzes a few poems to illustrate Coleridge's limited and selective understanding of Donne's poetry, especially versions of "On Donne's Poetry" and "Nature's Reply to the Suicide's Plea." Maintains that "for Coleridge Donnean metaphysical poetry depends on content, its involved treatment through conceits and syntax, a compression of thought and possible punning, and prosodic characteristics." Thinks that Coleridge's critical views "lead to [a] partial reading of Donne" and apply "to only part of the canon and then only superficially to much of that," and maintains that they also reflect "a limitation that persists today" in Donne criticism—a failure to appreciate Donne's "ironic stances" (219).

614. Shuger, Debora. "The Title of Donne's *Devotions*." *ELN* 22: 39–40.

Suggests that Donne's title *Devotions upon Emergent Occasions* "contains a Latin pun, which may be explicated roughly as: devotions upon a rising/resurrection ('emergent' from *emergo*) of one who had died ('occasions' from *occasus*, the past participle of *accidere*)" (39). Maintains, therefore, that "it is likely that Donne intended the title of his devotions to refer not only to the fact that his illness was an unforeseen and pressing opportunity," but also that "it involved the rising or rebirth of one who was near death both in body and soul." Thinks that "[t]his secondary meaning would thus connect the title with the process from doubt and questioning to renewed faith which structures each of the chapters, as well as hint at the typological significance of Donne's sickness and recovery through allusions to the rebirth of the individual in baptism and to Christ's Crucifixion and Resurrection" (40).

615. Sloane, Thomas O. *Donne, Milton, and the End of Humanist Rhetoric.* Berkeley and Los Angeles: University of California Press. xv, 332p.

Equating humanism with rhetoric, argues that Donne was "more the humanist" than Milton "because he was more the rhetorician" (xi) and believes that "our failure fully to understand the ways in which Donne and Milton are truly opposite has led to a serious misunderstanding of humanism, to say nothing of the astronomical impact of that failure on literary fortunes" (xii). Chapter 1, "In Our End Is Our Beginning, and *Vice Versa*" (1–33), contrasts Donne's funeral sermon for Sir William Cokayne with Milton's *Areopagitica* as well as *Goodf* with Milton's "On the morning of Christ's Nativity" to support his position and claims that, although "Donne in his sermon and poem does indeed *sound* more nonhumanist than Milton in his speech and poem," it is

Donne's skepticism that makes him "more humanist" than Milton (63). Chapter 2, "Rhetoric and Controversy, and *Vice Versa*" (65–144), presents an historical study of humanist rhetoric, with subsections on Erasmus, humanism, St. Augustine, Cicero, and the history of English humanist rhetorical theory. Chapter 3, "Donne's Rhetoric" (145–207), discusses *WomCon, Air, HSRound, Ecst, Pseudo-Martyr, HSSouls, HSWhat,* and several sermons as examples of Donne's use of rhetorical *controversia* or controversial thinking to show how he "fashioned a clear voice, using a discernible speaker, an identifiable audience, and, for the most part, an advocatory intention," which are "the constituents of humanist rhetoric" (164). Refutes the notion of Donne's Augustinian formalism and discusses humanist rhetoric as a habit of thought and a movement of mind found in Donne's poetry and prose. Chapter 4, "Miltonic Form" (209–78), claims that "English humanist rhetorical theory had largely disappeared by the age of Milton" and "discourse generally was losing its most distinctively humanistic feature, controversial thinking." Argues that "Milton's intentions are patently and demonstrably nonrhetorical," and suggests the best approach to his work "lies in formalism," which is "contrary to rhetorical criticism" (211). Contrasts *HSDeath* with Milton's "On Time" and *Dream* with Milton's "Sonnet 23" to show that "Donne thought controversially" but that "Milton apparently did not" (248). Holds that "Donne must have represented everything in humanism that Milton abhorred: its revelling in ambiguity and skepticism, its approach to moral issues as if they were fit subjects for cases at law, its union of words and reasons, and its disunion of God and man and Satan." Claims, in other words, that "Donne's art, which is

predicated on opposition and which proceeds by means of controversial thinking, is an art that Milton totally rejected" (249). Says Milton preferred mythological and typological thinking. In "Conclusion: Controversia *as* Inventio" (279–89), explains how he came to the views expressed in this study. Concludes with notes (291–323) and an index (325–32). Reviews: Gerald Hammond in *THES* (8 November 1985): 18; Thomas Conley in *Rhetorica* 3 (1986): 293–95; Arthur F. Kinney in *JEGP* 85 (1986): 450–54; Barbara K. Lewalski in *C&L* 35 (1986): 42–43; John F. Tinker in *QJS* 72 (1986): 213–15; Cedric C. Brown in *RES* 38 (1987): 248–49; Mary Elizabeth Green in *RMR* 40 (1987): 257–58; William J. Kennedy in *CL* 39 (1987): 281–82; Andrea Sununu in *SR* 95 (1987): lxx–lxxiv; L. A. Davies in *CahiersE* 34 (1988): 121–22; Andrew King in *P&R* 21 (1988): 73–75; Brian Vickers in *RenQ* 41 (1988): 525–28.

616. Smith, A. J. *The Metaphysics of Love: Studies in Renaissance Love Poetry from Dante to Milton.* Cambridge: Cambridge University Press. ix, 349p.

Studies "the conduct of a prolonged debate about the spiritual worth of love" among European writers from Dante to Milton, who shared "a concern with the status of love and our sexual nature which impels them to seek metaphysical reassurance in the prospect of a human bond that is not wholly subject to time, of qualities beyond flesh and blood in a fellow creature, of a providence in our chance conjunctures" (1). Mentions Donne throughout, comparing and contrasting his views on love with those of Dante, Ficino, Michelangelo, Milton, Thomas Stanley, Carew, Suckling, Rochester, Marvell, and Vaughan. Chapter 3, "Body and Soul" (187–220), focuses primarily on Donne, dividing the discussion into four sub-sections. (1) "Unchanging Union: Donne's *The Ecstasy*" (188–95), presents a critical reading of *Ecst*, calling it "one of the most extraordinary of European love poems, not least because it celebrates a mutual love by both recreating and precisely defining the bond between the lovers." Praises Donne's "utterly distinctive voice" and his "poetic intelligence which so imaginatively transforms theoretical possibility into lived experience, and realises in the movement and language itself the process of arriving at a new self-awareness." Maintains that in the poem the lovers "seek to resolve the perpetual dilemma of beings who hunger for absolutes in a world of contingency" (195). (2) "Proving the Hermaphrodite: Aristotelian Theorists of Love" (195–204), a revised version of parts of "The Metaphysic of Love" (*RES*, n.s. 9 [1958]: 362–75), discusses the views of such love philosophers as Leone Ebreo, Ficino and his followers, Tullia d'Aragone, Sperone Speroni, Benedetto Varchi, and Torquato Tasso, to show the sources of Donne's thinking on love. (3) "No Man Is a Contradiction: Donne on Self-Slaughter" (204–13) first appeared in *JDJ* 1 (1982): 21–38; (entry 331). (4) In "*The Subtile Knot:* Donne's Testament of Human Nature" (213–20), maintains that Donne's understanding of love, as expressed in *Ecst,* "needed no drastic renunciation when he took holy orders," noting that many of his sermons and divine poems "affirm the mutual dependence of soul and body as it is assured by Christ's taking flesh for pure love, and by the indivisibility of the human and divine elements in Christ's own manhood" (213). Chapter 4, "*Among the Wastes of Time:* Seventeenth-Century Love Poetry, and the Failure of Love" (221–53) (a revised version of "The Failure of Love: Love Lyrics after Donne" in *Metaphysical Poetry,* ed. Malcolm Bradbury and David Palmer [London: Edward Arnold; New York: St. Martin's Press, 1970], 41–71), surveys seventeenth century love poetry after Donne to show how it reflects changes in societal attitudes towards sex and love. Observes that, after Donne, "few poets act in the faith that the love of another human being might have absolute spiritual worth, and fewer still take sexual love to be anything other than a natural affection, which shares the decay of nature since the Fall" (252).

617. Smith, Julia J. "Moments of Being and Not-Being in Donne's Sermons." *PSt* 8: 3–20.

Maintains that the view that "man's existence is precarious" and that "time [is] fleeting and irrevocable" pervades Donne's religious writing. Maintains that Donne is often "troubled by the fear of his own nonexistence," which "gives an intensity to his persistent questioning in his sermons about death, the decay and resurrection of the body, and the immortality of the soul." Observes that Donne is "deeply interested in the mere fact of being" and that "he writes both of the greatest possible disparity between being and nothingness" as well as "of the frightening closeness of all created being to nothingness" (3). Comments on Donne's views on creation, original sin, immortality of the soul, resurrection of the body, and the afterlife as he expresses them particularly in the sermons. Concludes that Donne's belief in the General Resurrection assured him at last that "[t]he changes brought by time need no more be feared" (39).

618. Strengholt, L. "Donne als model. Donne, Hooft en Huygens in Jan de Brunes *Minne-praet.*" *Voortgang* 6: 213–47. Reprinted in *Een lezer aan het*

*woord: Studies van L. Strengholt over de
zeventiende-eeuwse Nederlandse letterkunde,* ed. H. Duits, A. M. Th. Leerintveld, T. L. ter Meer, and A. van Strien
(Münster: Nodus Publikationen; Amsterdam: Stichting Neerlandistiek VU, 1998),
239–73. Reprinted with a short coda as
"Vondel doet mee: Aanvulling op 'Donne
als model'" in *Voortgang* 10 (1989):
63–65.

Demonstrates the influence of Donne's
Eclog on the *Minne-praet* (1624) of
Jan de Brune de Jonge (ca. 1616–49)
by comparing and contrasting the two
works. Concludes that de Brune used
Donne's poem as the formal basis for
his own poem but that he drew heavily also on those he considered his
most accomplished Netherlandic fore-
bears, especially Hooft and, to a less
extent, Huygens. Shows that de Brune
was among a handful of seventeenth
century Netherlandic cultural figures
who were genuinely acquainted with
Donne's verse in manuscript and later
in print and, therefore, did not need
to rely on the translations of Huygens.
Argues that de Brune was almost certainly in possession of the 1635 and/or
1639 editions of Donne's works. Points
out how de Brune was a key figure in
Anglo-Dutch relationships in the first
half of the seventeenth century. In
"Vondel doet mee: Aanvuling op
'Donne als model,'" Strengholt suggests that a passage in de Brune's fifth
stanza can be traced to an extract from
Vondel's drama *Gijsbrecht van Aem-
stel* (1637), which strengthens the
argument for de Brune's remarkable
knowledge (for his time) of contemporary English and Dutch poetry in
their original languages.

619. Toliver, Harold. "'Householding and
the Poet's Vocation': Jonson and After."
ES 66: 113–22.

Discusses the prominent figure of the
household in the country house poem.
Points out that in *Canon* Donne

"exploits the roomy 'stanza' enclo-
sure for love's celebration" (113–14);
in *GoodM* he seeks "a domestic equivalent to empire-making, which is an
abiding paradox of the household as
noble place: it is both retreat and small
empire, harbor and community center" (114); and in *SunRis* he makes
one room an everywhere. Notes, however, that the examples from Donne
are "examples of harboring in general
rather than of the specific household
topos of the country estate poem"
(114).

620. Toliver, Harold. *Lyric Provinces in
the English Renaissance.* Columbus: Ohio
State University Press. xii, 247p.

Examines the "topography" of major
seventeenth century poets, especially
"the remoteness of so many of their
lyric sites." Claims that a "restlessness similar to that of westward exploration is detectable in the wandering
of lyric personas and in their new
terms of address." Sees this group as
"highly reactive" in the course of literary history, with Donne leading "the
first major shift" in the development
of the Renaissance lyric (ix). Chapter
5, "Donne's Silhouettes and Absences"
(95–121), examines the relationship
between Donne's *Satyres* and his love
poems, stating that "lyric for him is
often either a witty probing of rela-
tions-of-two or an enactment of communion in an enclosed place," whereas
"satire reacts to the failure of personal
relations and looks abroad to the court
and the city" (95). States further that
whereas speakers in the *Songs and
Sonets* "base true dialogue on the
openness of one party to another, the
satirist finds himself among those
whose first inclination is to impress
and use others" (96). Examines all
five *Satyres* and how they "set forth
the nature of trust and its violation"
(98). Claims that the inability in *Sat3*
to find ultimate truth "gives way to

shabby substitutions—primarily of a social sort that the other satires identify" (103). Discusses the "topography" of Donne's love lyrics—the enclosed room of the lovers—and the necessity for fidelity in love. Says, for example, that *GoodM* "recognizes that possession depends upon candor," whereas *Lect* "is preoccupied with the repercussions of deceit" (108). Suggests also that "one trademark of Donne's recurrent view of love is the way in which it controls onlookers" (110) and necessitates "the lovers to articulate love's principles and discover what they truly possess" (111). In reviewing poems where absence of love is primary, such as *Noct,* suggests that the "emptying of the enumerated world may after all be the beginning of a communion beyond specific objects and occasions" (119) and "a devotional preparation for the next world" (120).

621. Veith, Gene Edward, Jr. "Calvinism and Arminianism: The Theological Difference between Herbert and Donne," in *Reformation Spirituality: The Religion of George Herbert,* 117–32. Lewisburg, Pa.: Bucknell University Press; London: Associated University Presses.

Contrasts the theology and religious sensibility of Donne and Herbert and argues that the fundamental difference in their approach to religious experience is that Donne is an Arminian and Herbert is a Calvinist. Maintains that the "sense of insecurity and desperation in Donne's poetry derives from the Arminian position that salvation is in some way contingent upon the human will and that therefore one can fall away from grace," whereas the "sense of security and confidence in Herbert's poetry derives from the Calvinist doctrine of the perseverance of the saints, which insists that salvation is the sole work of God and therefore that it can never be lost"

(118). Suggests that "one of the strengths of Donne's religious poetry comes from his standing at a transition point between Calvinism and Arminianism, between the view that God accomplished everything for salvation and the view that the burden lies essentially on the self," and finds that "[t]his tension between the two kinds of spirituality manifests itself in the complexity of his theological positions and in the richness of his religious verse" (121). To illustrate the emotional and doctrinal differences between the two, comments on Donne's *GHerb* and Herbert's reply.

622. Verducci, Florence. "Elegiac Convention as Artistic Dilemma: *Heroides 15,*" in *Ovid's Toyshop of the Heart: Epistolae Herodium,* 123–80. Princeton, N.J.: Princeton University Press.

Reads *Sappho* as "unabashedly Lesbian" and claims that Donne's treatment of the speaker is "as macabre and as anachronistic as Ovid's." Maintains that Donne is "perfectly faithful to the central implication of Ovid's poem." Argues that Sappho's "falling in love with Phaon was a falling out of love with herself" and, "by extension, a temporary artistic suicide" but that her "return to Lesbian love, conceived by Donne as a kind of transferred autoeroticism, is central in Sappho's revivification as an artist" (143). Believes that, like Ovid, Donne understood that "Poetry comes finespun from a mind at peace" and, like Juvenal, he might have said that "A soul lacking in anxiety makes a superb poet." Concludes, therefore, that Donne "did what was necessary for Sappho" in giving her, according to Ovid, "the pleasant material for poetry" (144).

623. Vickers, Brian. "Donne's Eagle and Dove." *N&Q,* n.s. 32: 59–60.

Points out that in medieval and Renaissance iconography the eagle and the dove were emblems of the active and contemplative life, as Donne himself indicates in his sermons. Explains, therefore, that in *Canon* these emblems would suggest that "the lovers unite in themselves the virtues of the active and contemplative lives." Points out that "one of the recurrent features of the debate between the two opposed lives was to find a *via media,* which might take the form of uniting the best features of each, or following each alternately," noting that in love poetry "the latter option, with its alternation of activity and rest, would seem to be not an *impossibilia* but a practical, and desirable necessity" (60).

624. Wall, John N., Jr. "Donne's *Satyre IV* and the Feast of the Purification of Saint Mary the Virgin." *ELN* 23: 23–31.

Suggests that Donne's source for religious allusions in *Sat4* is the Anglican, not Catholic, Feast of the Purification of the Virgin, celebrated on 2 February. Maintains that there are "striking parallels" between the language of *Sat4* and the epistle in the Anglican liturgy for Sexagesima Sunday, 1597, which was used as the epistle for the Feast of the Purification that year. Notes also echoes in the poem of Psalm 15, which was "appointed for reading at Morning Prayer on that feast" (27). Believes that, regardless of his personal religious allegiance at the time, Donne used the Anglican liturgy "as an allusory frame for his description of the court" since it would carry "power precisely because of its familiarity to those who could change things at the court" and because of "its power to heighten the sense of how far that court actually was from what it claimed to be" (29).

625. Walker, Julia M. "'Here you see mee': Donne's Autographed Valediction." *JDJ* 4: 29–33.

Argues that in *ValName* Donne "has signed his name, internally, in the text itself" by using a system of English gematria, a coding system by which each letter of the alphabet is identified with a different number (29). Finds several numerological nuances in the poem and shows how Donne combines "intellectual/poetic fun-with-numbers" with his "internal signature" (31–32). Believes that the poem can be read autobiographically, maintaining, however, that "[t]his poem in which we *can* acknowledge an autobiographical Donne ironically calls into question the standard assumptions about the correlation between Donne's life and his art and thereby stresses how necessary it is that critics avoid building their arguments on blocks of biography" (33).

626. Wendorf, Richard. "'Visible Rhetorick': Izaak Walton and Iconic Biography." *MP* 82: 269–91.

Explores the emblematic and iconic properties in Walton's *Lives,* pointing out how his "frequent analogies with the visual arts, especially with the sister art of portrait painting," suggest "an affinity with . . . iconic portraiture." Argues that "it was in large part Walton's iconic cast of mind that enabled him to shape the traditional elements of contemporary biographical writing into the most sophisticated verbal portraits of the seventeenth century" (270). Discusses Walton's techniques in his life of Donne, showing, in particular, his use of iconic analogies, symmetrical structure, parallelism, abrupt transitions, temporal suspensions, and antitheses to show how biography in Walton's hands "can be more accurately charted in spatial terms" (277). Maintains that Walton "is interested less in the steady, incremental illumination of character . . . than in broader and more prolonged patterns in which one structural unit must be carefully balanced against all others" (277–78). Says that in his biography of Donne "we are asked to compare the first half of Donne's career with the second, the portrait of his youth with the likeness of a modern saint posing in his burial shroud," noting that "each of these separate revelations must be read in light of Walton's attempts to provide a summary character at the end of the work" (278). Observes that in his final version of his life of Donne, Walton's presentation of Donne became "increasingly iconic, both in its turn toward ekphrasis—the verbal description of visual works—and in its use of portraiture to accentuate its own emblematic form" (282).

627. Willmott, Richard, ed. and intro. *Four Metaphysical Poets: An Anthology of Poetry by Donne, Herbert, Marvell, and Vaughan.* Cambridge: Cambridge University Press. 184p.

In the introduction (1–16), Willmott surveys the historical, philosophical, religious, and literary background of the period; presents a biographical sketch of the four poets anthologized; and comments on aspects of the poetry—its subject matter, style, versification, imagery, uses of wit and paradox, ambiguity of tone, and dramatic qualities—concluding with a brief bibliography. "John Donne" (27–74), reproduces 15 poems from the *Songs and Sonets, ElNat,* 4 epigrams, *Sat3,* 5 selections from the *Holy Sonnets,* and 2 hymns, with explanatory notes. Concludes with an index of first lines (183–84).

628. Wymer, Rowland. "Donne's 'Biathanatos.'" *TLS* (22 March): 317.

Disagrees with Robin Robbins's review (*TLS,* 1 March 1985) of Ernest Sullivan's edition of *Biathanatos* (1984) and praises the edition by Michael Rudick and M. Pabst Battin (1982). Particularly rejects Robbins's dismissal of the personal element in *Biathanatos.*

629. Yokota, Chuzo. "John Donne to Shukyo" [John Donne and Religion], in *John Donne to sono Shuhen* [John Donne and Other Poets of the Seventeenth Century], 81–103. The Japan Society of Seventeenth-Century English Literature Tokyo: Kinseido.

Considers Donne's religious life, examining the political conditions of the age which affected his attitude toward the Catholic Church. Comments on the influence of his inner conflict about religion on his life, works, and view of death.

630. Yoshida, Sachiko. "'Junkyo' wo meguru John Donne to Robert Southwell" [Relations Between John Donne and Robert Southwell on the Idea of Martyrdom], in *John Donne to sono Shuhen* [John Donne and Other Poets of the Seventeenth Century], 105–28. The Japan Society of Seventeenth-Century English Literature. Tokyo: Kinseido.

Considers Donne's and Southwell's idea of martyrdom, noting Donne's mixed feelings about the issue, especially in *Pseudo-Martyr.*

1986

631. Adams, Robert M. "John Donne," in *The Norton Anthology of English Literature,* vol. 1, *1060–1111,* gen. ed. M. H. Abrams 5th ed. New York: W. W. Norton. 1st ed., 1962; 2nd ed., 1968; 3rd ed., 1974; 4th ed., 1979; 6th ed., 1996.

Contains only minor revision of the biographical and critical introduction of the 4th edition (1979) (1060–63), followed by selections from Donne's poetry (1063–1105) and selections from *Devotions* and one sermon (1105–11), with notes. See entry 1.

632. Alvarez-Buylla, José Benito, trans. "John Donne: Canciones y Sonetos," in *Scripta in memoriam José Benito Alvarez-Buylla Alvarez.* With an introduction by José Luis Caramés Lage and Santiago Fernandez-Corugedo. Editados por el Departamento de Lengua y Literatura inglesa y norteamericana de la Universidad de Oviedo y ofrecidos por sus amigos, discípulos y colaboradores. Oviedo: Universidad de Oviedo. 113p.

The introduction (7–35) presents a biographical sketch of Donne, commenting on the social, political, and poetical contexts in which Donne wrote the *Songs and Sonets* and noting the innovations in both style and thematic content that he introduced into English poetry; discusses his uses of the conceit, metaphor, imagery, hyperbole, irony, metrical forms, and various figures of speech; surveys the complex and dramatic situations Donne creates in the *Songs and Sonets;* and examines the view of love presented in these poems. Includes a selected

bibliography (35), followed by translations of the *Songs and Sonets* into Spanish with English texts on the opposite page (37–113).

633. Anthony, J. Philip. "Donne's 'The Relique.'" *Expl* 44, no. 2: 13–15.

Points out "metaphorical references to Christian mystery" in the last stanza of *Relic* and comments, in particular, on the metaphor of the "seales" (ll. 29–30). Notes that the speaker mentions four miracles, each of which is described as "an expression of Christian Platonic love in terms of a Christian mystery" (13), and points out that the fourth miracle (concerning the "seales") is that the lovers' love "is maintained by abstention from physical love," for "[t]o participate in physical love would break the seals, reveal the mystery, and destroy the sanctity of the Platonic relationship." Maintains, therefore, that Donne "characterizes abstention from physical love . . . as a seal which preserves the image of God created in the lovers' Platonic relationship" (14).

634. Bailin, Alan. "Metaphorical Extension." *JLS* 15 (1986): 53–65.

Examines "changes in the extension of words and phrases which are metaphorically interpreted in a text and then the changes in the extension of superordinates of those metaphorically interpreted words and phrases" (53). Briefly comments on *Sickness* (ll. 6–15) to illustrate how "no device other than the metaphorical assertion

that John Donne is a flat map is necessary to make what is asserted of flat
maps in general (i.e., of the entities
in extension of 'flat map') asserted of
both the 'real' maps in the literal
extension and the metaphorical entity
(John Donne)" (57).

635. Baldwin, Robert. "'Gates Pure and
Shining and Serene': Mutual Gazing as
an Amatory Motif in Western Literature
and Art." *Ren&R,* n.s. 10: 23–48.

Explores the motif of amorous gazing in literary and pictorial works
"with a focus on Renaissance works
and their earlier sources" (23). Calls
Ecst "the most famous lyric to speak
of mutual gazing, a poem which also
joins ocular communion with that of
the hands, evoking in the latter love's
physical dimension as well as the conjugal rite of joined hands" (38). Says
that Donne's poem is "the most majestic verbal image of mutual gazing" in
which "the sepulchral immobility of
forms seems to exclude sexual union
in favor of the more spiritual ecstasy
of souls meeting through hands and
particularly eye-beams which touch."
Notes that, "[a]fter the seventeenth
century, the motif of mutual gazing
would be more sentimental than a
mystery of *caritas* sublimating *eros*"
and that "the Renaissance fusion of
eye and spirit, in part dependent on
the incorrect optical notion of projecting eye-beams, has become a beautiful thing of the past" (43).

636. Baumlin, James S. "Donne's Christian
Diatribes: Persius and the Rhetorical
Persona of 'Satyre III' and 'Satyre V,'"
in *The Eagle and the Dove: Reassessing
John Donne,* ed. Claude J. Summers and
Ted-Larry Pebworth, 92–105. Essays
in Seventeenth-Century Literature, 1.
Columbia: University of Missouri Press.

Discusses the influence of Persius's
"protreptic zeal and diatribe style"
on *Sat3* and *Sat5,* showing, however,
how Donne transformed Persius's voice
into his own distinctly English and
personal voice and avoided "close
verbal imitation" (92) of his classical
model. Surveys Renaissance attitudes
toward Persius, noting that he was
generally viewed as a "serious moralist and proto-Christian in his teachings" and, therefore, seen as "the
satiric model most capable of conveying spiritual subjects to a Christian
audience" (93). Shows how Persius's
third satire gave Donne "the broad
thematic, stylistic, and structural model"
(94) for *Sat3* and discusses similarities
of rhetorical techniques and stylistic
elements in Persius's fifth satire and
Donne's *Sat5.* Believes that Persius
taught Donne "much about concise
expression and complexity of syntax,
rigorous argumentation, abrupt transitions in thought, hyperbolic and cate-
chetical imagery, [and] the drama and
forcefulness of second-person address"
(104). Concludes, therefore, that, "[i]n
Persius, Donne discovered the broad
outline of a deliberate and essentially
public voice whose moral exhortation,
much more than laughter or rage,
could best result in reform" (105).

637. Baumlin, James S. "Generic Context
of Elizabethan Satire: Rhetoric, Poetic
Theory, and Imitation," in *Renaissance
Genres: Essays on Theory, History, and
Interpretation,* ed. Barbara Kiefer Lewalski, 444–67. Harvard English Studies,
14. Cambridge, Mass.: Harvard University Press.

Maintains that Elizabethan satirists
"inevitably turned to *some* conven-
tionalized persona, some model of
ethos, to endow their words with ethical authority" (446) and argues that,
"for all the Elizabethan satirists, the
classical personae are the primary
models" and that any other models
are "accretions, influential but subordinate" (447). Observes, however, that
Elizabethan satire "became an ambitious experiment in *revision* as well
as imitation" and that Donne and

others "test and critically evaluate their Roman models as much as follow them" (447–48). Discusses how Renaissance criticism of the Roman satirists, such as that of Julius Caesar Scaliger, Francesco Robortello, Antonio Sebastiano Minturno, Juste Lipse, Bartolommeo Ricci, Joachim Vadian, and Pietro Crinto, "provides a firm basis for the imitative practice of the Elizabethan satirists" and then illustrates "that practice with examples of how Joseph Hall, John Marston, and especially John Donne imitate (and test) one particular Roman model, Horace" (448). Points out that for all three satirists Horace "is *not* a preferred model" and, therefore, "their adaptations of this Roman highlights for us the dialectical, evaluative, and often revisionary nature of their imitative practice" (456). Comments especially on *Sat1* to show how it "enacts Donne's search for an effective voice in classical satire" and demonstrates "his failure to find such a voice" in Horace (466). Concludes that ultimately Donne found in Persius "the best vehicle for his own serious Christian insights" but that he "could not have been secure in this choice had not he, like Hall and Marston, tested the resources of all three Roman models" (466–67).

638. **Bell, Ilona.** "'Under Ye Rage of a Hott Sonn & Yr Eyes': John Donne's Love Letters to Ann More," in *The Eagle and the Dove: Reassessing John Donne,* ed. Claude J. Summers and Ted-Larry Pebworth, 25–52. Essays in Seventeenth-Century Literature, 1. Columbia: University of Missouri Press.

Believes that three letters in the Burley manuscript were written by Donne to Ann More during their courtship and that, "[i]f so, they are the only known letters Donne wrote to Ann" and "contain the first substantive information about Donne's wooing of Ann, enabling us to examine a central moment in Donne's life (and poetry) that has remained unknown and undocumented until now" (26). Points out that, "[b]eginning with expressions of intense passion and hints of consummated love, Donne in these three letters to Ann responds to a sequence of events that created great stress for them both and made him fear, desperately, that the affair might end" (26–27). Observes that, "[i]f, as these letters suggest, Donne's love affair with Ann entailed a much wider range of feelings than we have thought, it may well have inspired a much broader, more various group of poems than we have considered" (27). Shows that in these letters Donne emerges as "remarkably attentive to Ann's feelings and desperate at the thought of losing her love," and that Ann emerges as "an independent, witty, learned lady who doubles the heat and heightens the uncertainty of Donne's love." Observes also that in the letters Donne "consistently place[s] love above personal ambition" (45). Maintains that the first Burley letter "can help us understand the unique isolation, the unconventional sexuality, and the fearful discord that often appear amid Donne's declaration of honorable love," and that the last two "can help us to see the tender, vulnerable love that underlies some of Donne's more patently angry and cynical poems" (47). Concludes that the Burley letters suggest "new ways to comprehend and assess the disturbing mixture of tones and attitudes that makes [sic.] Donne's love poems so unconventional and baffling" (48). Contains an appendix on the authenticity of the letters and a description and history of the Burley manuscript (48–52).

639. **Bloom, Harold,** ed. *John Donne and the Seventeenth-Century Metaphysical Poets,* with an introduction by Harold Bloom. Modern Critical Views. New York: Chelsea House Publishers. viii, 374p.

A collection of 13 previously published essays or parts of previously published studies on 7 major seventeenth-century poets, 4 of which are specifically on Donne: (1) John Freccero's "Donne's Compass Image" (11–26), an abridged version of "Donne's 'Valediction: Forbidding Mourning,'" *ELH* 30 (1963): 335–76; (2) John Hollander's "Donne and the Limits of Lyric" (27–36), from *Vision and Resonance: Two Senses of Poetic Form,* 2nd ed. (New Haven, Conn.: Yale University Press, 1985), 44–58 (1st ed., 1975); (3) William Kerrigan's "The Fearful Accommodations of John Donne" (37–50), from *ELR* 4 (1974): 337–63; and (4) Claudia Brodsky's "Donne: The Imaging of the Logical Conceit" (51–67), from *ELH* 49 (1982): 829–48 (entry 256). Contains an editor's note (vii–viii) describing the contents of the collection and an introduction (1–9), in which the editor says he thinks Dr. Johnson's discussion of Donne and the metaphysical poets is "still the most adequate we possess, despite the perpetual Donne revivals which go on continuously" (1), and evaluates, in particular, Johnson's skepticism about devotional poetry. Also includes a chronology of the lives of the seven poets (243–46); notes on the contributors (247–48); a selective bibliography of critical studies (249–64); and an index (265–74).

640. Bloomfield, Morton W. "The Elegy and the Elegiac Mode: Praise and Alienation," in *Renaissance Genres: Essays on Theory, History, and Interpretation,* ed. Barbara K. Lewalski, 147–57. Harvard English Studies, 14. Cambridge, Mass.: Harvard University Press.

Distinguishes between the elegy (poems of praise, lament, and consolation) and the elegiac mode ("alienated and/or sad poems which mix various moods and actions and are extremely personal") and suggests the latter are "the creation of the Romantic movement." Maintains, in other words, that the elegy is a genre, whereas the elegiac mode "is not a genre but a mode of approaching reality and was hardly named before the eighteenth century, although it is certainly to be found in earlier poetry" (148). Insists that "[t]he elegiac mode is not a new type of traditional elegy" but rather is "a new type of poem bearing only a slight resemblance to its ancestor." Notes the elegiac mode "is more romantic, more personal, and more despairing," whereas the traditional elegy "is not personal nor despairing nor lost" and, rather than expressing a personality, it is "an answer to a social and national need" (156). Surveys the history of the elegy from ancient times to the present and briefly comments on the *Anniversaries.*

641. Braden, Gordon. "Beyond Frustration: Petrarchan Laurels in the Seventeenth Century." *SEL* 26: 5–23.

Argues that seventeenth century love poetry "does not so much shut out [Petrarchism] as refract" it (8). Maintains that one reason Petrarchism was so fashionable in the Renaissance was that it "brings with it a dramatic aggrandizement of the authority of poetic imagination" and "indeed offers a kind of training ground for that aggrandizement," since often "the laurel and not Daphne might well have been the real goal all along" (10–11). Maintains, in other words, that much Petrarchism is a form of self-absorption and becomes simply "a publicizing of one's inner life as a way of gaining worldly recognition" (12). Sees in much seventeenth century love poetry, including Donne's, "not the rejection of Petrarchism but the bringing of the Petrarchan ego into the sexual arena where it must confront psychic otherness much more intensely and insistently than it previously had to do." Believes that "[t]he most convincingly hopeful picture of human love in seventeenth-century literature is of the ego's finding its way in such confrontation so that Petrarchan unattainability becomes simply a move in the negotiations of courtship" (14). Briefly comments on the note of mutuality in Donne's love poems.

642. Campos, Augusto de. "John Donne: O dom e a danação" and "Donne em dobro," in *O anticrítico,* 37–71, 73–83. São Paulo: Companhia das Letras.

Presents a brief introduction to Donne's life and poetry with translations into Portuguese (with English texts on the opposite pages) of *Ecst, ValMourn, ElBed, Relic, Twick, Triple, Witch, Mess, Flea, Expir,* and *Appar.*

643. Caramés Lage, José Luis. "Ritual, símbolo y mito en *Songs and Sonnets* de John Donne," in *Estudios literarios ingleses: Renacimiento y barroco,* ed. Susana Onega, 389–413. Madrid: Cátedra.

Discusses major innovative features of the *Songs and Sonets,* especially Donne's use of poetic devices, rhetorical techniques, wit, and stanzaic and metrical forms, to show how he creates by his use of ritual and symbol his mythic world of love. Examines the original features of Donne's concept of love, as seen in his love poetry, emphasizing his belief in the union of the physical and the spiritual in mature human love, and explores his vision of love in such poems as *Flea, SunRis, Air, Lect, Dream, Appar, ValWeep,* and *LovAlch.* Notes that Donne's complexity negatively affected his reputation for many years. Maintains that by examining closely Donne's use of ritual and symbol and by exploring the depth of his world of ideas, one recognizes Donne's uniqueness and his important contribution to the changes that occurred in English poetry in the seventeenth century.

644. Cerasano, S. P. "The Dean of St. Paul's at Court." *N&Q,* n.s. 33: 385–86.

Reports on a newly discovered document in the Public Records Office (PRO.REQ2/410/64) that indicates that Donne during his first year as Dean of St. Paul's "put his legal experience to use for the Cathedral in a property dispute" involving a John Weldon, who was Donne's household servant and lessee of church-owned property in Hackney Marsh, Middlesex. Notes that "the incident is nowhere recorded in the standard accounts of his life" (385). Suggests that the incident supports John Carey's remark (1981) on Donne's "callousness" (386).

645. Cook, Elizabeth. *Seeing through Words: The Scope of Late Renaissance Poetry.* New Haven, Conn.: Yale University Press. viii, 180p.

Examines "some of the ways in which late Renaissance poetry draws upon the multiple capacities of language to enlarge our experience of the world which language shows" and reflects upon "the kind of showing which language, peculiarly, permits." Discusses "both the range of experience to which language gives access and the compression of that range within language." Commenting on "compression for which 'metaphysical' poetry is known," asks "in what sense this poetry may be called 'compressed'" and looks at "the motivation of the period terms 'strong-lined' and 'far-fetched'" (1). Discusses how in *Metem* Donne "brings together two traditions that might appear distinct"—"the theological tradition which supposes an ubiquitous God and which attributes to the soul a freedom of movement which is the next best thing to ubiquity," and "the poetic tradition by which small, unregarded objects . . . are celebrated because of their free access to desired bodies" (95). Maintains that in Donne's poem "the directions in which and from which we are directed to look are varied" and "our customary ways of seeing are revealed as not absolute, but conditional." Claims that "[t]his mobility, which is very much part of the poem's relativistic scepticism, allows for the wonderfully precise and delicate descriptions whose tenderness points back to that providential attentiveness which is the obverse of scepticism" (126). Discusses also Donne's contribution to the genre of the flea poem by analyzing *Flea,* maintaining that "[t]he image of the flea provides a deliberately misleading focus which apparently anchors a spurious argument in a careful particularity which is not the poem's real concern," thereby constructing "a fine-meshed sieve" and passing it off for "a watertight bowl" (119). Compares and contrasts Donne to Sidney and Herbert.

646. Cowan, S. A. "Echoes of Donne, Herrick, and Southwell in Eliot's *The Waste Land.*" *YER* 8: 96–102.

Suggests that in *The Waste Land* (l. 74), T. S. Eliot is referring to Sirius, the Dog Star, as a symbol of blight and death and that he may have found a precedent in *Devotions,* noting that in the tenth meditation Donne "identifies Sirius as a source of pestilence" (97). Concludes that, whether we accept Donne's passage "as a possible source or merely a parallel, it clarifies Eliot's meaning by stressing the danger to the soul of exposure to the star of sin" (98).

647. Daalder, Joost. "The Prosodic Significance of Donne's 'Accidentals.'" *Parergon* 4: 87–101.

Argues that a careful study of the orthography and punctuation of the only known poem in Donne's hand, *Carey,* gives some insight into his "prosodic intentions" (87). Presents a transcription of the manuscript and a list of errors in Helen Gardner's pub-

lished transcription (1972). Shows how in the poem Donne "creates an impression of a speaking voice caring far less about abstract considerations of either metre or grammar than the editor of 1633" (95). Maintains that, "while syllabically regular" and "practising a degree of accentual regularity," Donne "felt quite free to produce lines which, to a smaller or lesser extent, were not capable of being read as iambic," noting that *Carey* "is not conspicuously 'rough' in this regard as some" but that the *Satyres* "provide examples" (97). Thinks that we can be fairly confident that Donne "believed in syllabic regularity" but that "our knowledge of his accentuation is likely to remain limited, since his syllabification can give us only limited information about it, while what we do know about the pronunciation of English in Donne's time is not enough to enable us to suppose that we can usefully deduce from such knowledge what degree of accentual regularity he may have intended in his verse" (99). Suggests that Donne did not always intend regularity but "wished his readers to have the iambic decasyllabic line in mind as a norm to be departed from as well as to be adhered to," and that the manipulation of stresses "is deliberate and has a vital part to play in his overall strategy" (100).

648. Davies, Horton. *Like Angels from a Cloud: The English Metaphysical Preachers, 1588–1645.* San Marino, Calif.: Huntington Library. ix, 503p.

Identifies more than 40 seventeenth century "metaphysical" preachers whose sermons have survived in print, citing 11 differentia that separate their sermons from plain Puritan sermons: "wit; patristic learning; classical lore; citations from Greek, and Latin, and occasionally Hebrew originals; illustrations from 'unnatural' natural history; allegorical exegesis; plans with complex divisions and subdivisions; a Senecan and staccato style; the use of paradoxes, riddles, and emblems; fondness for speculation; and the relation of doctrinal and devotional preaching to the Christian calendar" (2–3). Examines various kinds of metaphysical wit in sermons: "conceits, puns and paranomasia, epigrams, paradoxes, extended oxymora, and the use of ingenious texts and titles for sermons" (3). Discusses Calvinists as well as High Church preachers whose sermons are in the metaphysical mode. Considers the divisive issue of the place of learning and eloquence in sermons; analyzes the content of metaphysical sermons, their traditional as well as innovative themes; and discusses sermon techniques. Calls Donne "the greatest of all the metaphysical poet-preachers" (8) and "one of the earliest ecumenists" (342), and claims that "Death's Duell" is "probably the greatest Passion sermon in England during the seventeenth century" (374). Discusses the major aspects of Donne's sermons—their wit, their uses of learning, the sources from which he drew illustrations, and their major themes— and comments on specific merits of a number of individual sermons.

649. Davis, Walter R. "Meditation, Typology, and the Structure of John Donne's Sermons," in *The Eagle and the Dove: Reassessing John Donne,* ed. Claude J. Summers and Ted-Larry Pebworth, 166–88. Essays in Seventeenth-Century Literature, 1. Columbia: University of Missouri Press.

Demonstrates through an analysis of individual sermons that Donne "characteristically divides his sermons into three parts, often giving those three parts a typological significance, a meditative significance, or a combination of both," and claims that "[t]hese three are the sermon structures that are peculiar to Donne as to no other preacher" (168). Maintains that "[t]ypology makes

a sermon into an exploration of Scripture on the part of the preacher and his congregation" but using meditation in the sermon turns it into something "dramatic, a display of the preacher affected by the text in a manner that he hopes will speak for and to the congregation and will be imitated by them" (172). Notes that "[t]here are a few sermons, very notable ones, that are constructed as public meditative exercises" but that "more usually we find sermons either meditative in part or exhibiting a kind of generalized meditative quality" (173). Discusses and illustrates each of the three sermon structures, focusing especially on those uniquely Donnean sermons that are modelled on "meditative typology," in which "logical structure and emotive development come together" in order "to involve the congregation fully in the unfolding of the text laid before it" (188).

650. Dime, Gregory T. "The Difference Between 'Strong Lines' and 'Metaphysical Poetry.'" *SEL* 26: 47–57.

Argues that it is erroneous "to assume a close correspondence between 'strong lines' and 'metaphysical poetry'" (48), as George Williamson suggested in *ES* 18 (1936): 152–59. States that Donne's poetry is both "metaphysical" and "strong-lined" but that "the concept of 'strong lines' should not be conflated with that of 'metaphysical poetry.'" Holds that "[t]he distinction between 'strong lines' and 'metaphysical poetry' is a matter of emphasis," noting that "[f]or critics of 'strong lines,' figurative language is rarely a salient consideration," since "they are mainly interested in elliptical syntax and abstruse thought, which often result in metrical irregularity and obscurity," whereas "[c]ritics of 'metaphysical poetry,' if they do not neglect such 'strong-lined' characteristics, tend to dwell on the importance of metaphor, the 'metaphysical conceit'" (54–55).

651. **Docherty, Thomas.** *John Donne, Undone.* London: Methuen. 253p. Chapter 6 revised appears in *Post-Structuralist Readings of English Poetry,* ed. Richard Machin and Christopher Norris, 85–104 (Cambridge: Cambridge University Press, 1987).

Believes that "[m]uch of what passes for contemporary criticism of Donne contrives to ignore the historical culture which informed his writings, and the ideology which conditioned the act of writing or 'authority' itself," and laments that "[r]eaders have been content with crude and often reductionist biographical correspondences between poems and persons or events; and [that] 'criticism' has been presented as the rehearsal of older evaluations of 'the dramatic voice,' 'witty invention,' 'originality,' 'masculine persuasive force' in 'strong lines,' the 'libertine' versus the 'divine' or Jack versus the Doctor." Maintains that too little attention has been given to "the problematic of Donne as a *writer,* writing in the special historical moment of the later European Renaissance," and challenges older ways of reading Donne's poetry "with a more theoretical and critical reading," primarily by "drawing extensively on post-structural theory." Suggests "three main culturally significant and historically problematic areas which bear on Donne's writings: the scientific discourse, which troubles secular historicity itself; the sociocultural, in which woman raises certain defences in this male poet; and the aesthetic, in which mimetic writing itself becomes fraught with difficulty" and "repudiates entirely the modernist construction of Donne as poet of ethical, cultural, and political individualism in the light of the evidence produced from a consideration of his relation to these three areas" (1). Maintains that "the fact of historical change or secular mutability is replaced in the poems by a call to ritual prayer, but a prayer which turns out to be always ineffective and requiring repetition; woman further complicates any such theological impetus in the writing, making a religious escape from the vagaries of human history and from the materiality of the body appear to be madness; and mimetic adequacy as an aesthetic concept is transposed to the level of faith and fidelity, but a faith which is seen to require some kind of 'infidelity' or betrayal as its central constituent" (1–2). Believes that the modern view of Donne is "intimately linked with a self-consciously 'modernist' aesthetic and movement in poetry" and that thus, for the most part, "the Donne that we read is a post-Eliotic Donne" (3). Maintains that the aim of "undoing" Donne's texts is not to "discover the truth of Donne's meaning" but rather to produce "an understanding or knowledge which stresses the very difficulty of 'meaning' or 'intending' for a writer such as Donne" (6) and admits that this approach, "perhaps paradoxically, makes these texts more obscure: in short, it mystifies" (7). Points out that the argument of this study is tripartite: "It moves from a symptomatic reading or investigation of a psychology, outlining the limitations and problems of that psychology, through an interstitial repudiation of the image of Donne as poet of individualism, into a symptomatic reading of a cultural crux between a competing theology and ideology, and of Donne's position within that crux or crisis" (8). Believes that Donne's texts are, in a sense, "'failed' confessions" that "produce a 'catholic' spirit of guilt in their reading, together with a necessity, but impossibility, of confession to some crime" (10). Claims, therefore, that "[u]ndoing Donne simply expands the concerns of these texts, obscures and mystifies them, and makes them available for re-reading"

(11). Argues that it is "no longer a question of what Donne says, nor even strictly of what the text says [both Donne and text are silent], rather it is a question of what we the *proles* of the text, can say, and how we can construct historical meaning from working upon the raw materials of the text" (47). Illustrates this principle and poststructural theory upon which it is based in discussions principally of *SunRis, GoodM, Flea, ElAnag, ElPict, ElNat, Air, ValMourn, ElBed, Canon, Mess, Relic, Lect, Expir, Triple, Commun, ValName*, the *Anniversaries*, the *Satyres*, and several selections from *Divine Poems*, especially the *Holy Sonnets*. For example, in discussing *Flea* (53–59), focuses on the important role that telescopic vision plays in the organization of the poem and suggests that, in the poem, "what is at issue is the fact of male control of the female, through the telescopic manoeuvres of the phallus in sexual relation," and that the movement of the telescope becomes "a kind of prediction of the kind of movement which the phallus strains to attain in the text" (56). Concludes with an index (250–53). Reviews: Martin Elsky in *RenQ* 41 (1988): 520–23; N. H. Keeble in *N&Q*, n.s. 35 (1988): 529–30; Arthur F. Kinney in *Albion* 20 (1988): 302–6; Neil Rhodes in *RES* 39 (1988): 13; A. J. Smith in *TLS* 4422 (1988): 17; Julia M. Walker in *JDJ* 7 (1988): 133–39.

652. Doebler, Bettie Anne, and Retha M. Warnicke. "Magdalen Herbert Danvers and Donne's Vision of Comfort." *GHJ* 10 (1986–87): 5–22. Parts of this essay appear in Doebler's "A Case Study in Dying: Donne's Poetics of Preparation and Comfort," in *"Rooted Sorrow": Dying in Early Modern England* (Rutherford, N.J.: Farleigh Dickinson University Press; London: Associated University Presses, 1994), 183–218.

Examines the Newport heritage of Magdalen Herbert and her association with the Virginia Company in order to understand better her life and the lives of her eminent sons and to provide "a framework in which to study Donne's commemorative sermon" (5). Discusses Donne's friendship with Mrs. Herbert and notes that the first recorded evidence of their acquaintance is the first of four letters that he sent to her on 11 July 1607, in which he asks for her assistance. Surmises that Donne may have been asking Mrs. Herbert to intercede for him with his father-in-law, George More, with whom she was friendly, and perhaps to assist him also in obtaining an office with the Virginia Company since she had contacts with a number of persons associated with the company. Analyzes Donne's funeral sermon, showing how it "illustrates what persons in England knew to be Aristotle's highest ideal for friendship: the love of virtue in the friend," and also how, "[o]n a deeper level yet, it projected a great vision of heavenly comfort that included Lady Danvers and promised all Christians present a way to follow" (18).

653. Donne, John. *Holy Sonnets/John Donne,* ed. Clare Gaster; illustrated with wood engravings by Jill Barker. Winchester, Eng.: Alembic Press. 51p. Limited edition of 100 copies.

The introduction (5–9) suggests that all but the last three *Holy Sonnets* were probably written during the later years of Donne's stay at Mitcham (1606–11). Suggests that the mood of despair in some of the sonnets was caused by his rumination about his worldly ambitions and his "uneasy consciousness of his defection from the Catholic faith" (5). Calls it at worst a "Faustian despair of a man in the act of succumbing to the temptations of Satan," and at best "the despair of a frail human who was unable to concentrate on willing himself towards a closer relationship with God" (6). Points out similarities between the love poetry and the *Holy Sonnets,* calling the latter "the personal and often dramatic revelations of a man in turmoil" (9).

654. Donne, John. *John Donne: Poesía completa—edición bilingüe,* ed. and trans. Enrique Caracciolo-Trejo. 2 vols. Colección de Poesía Aire Fresco 16, dir. Alfredo Llorente Díez.) Barcelona: Ediciones 29. 261p. Revised and expanded edition, 1998.

Volume 1: The introduction (9–24), which is followed by a chronology of Donne's life (25–26), contextualizes Donne's poetry within the intellectual parameters of the seventeenth century, indicating how his poetry reflects the philosophical concerns of his day. Emphasizes Donne's use of the conceit and compares Donne's poetry to that of Baltasar Gracián. Presents a general introduction to the themes and stylistic characteristics of the *Songs and Sonets* and the *Elegies.* Contains English texts (from A. J. Smith's edition [1971]) with Spanish translations on opposite pages of the *Songs and Sonets* (29–141), the *Elegies* (144–219), the epithalamia (222–51), and the epigrams (254–61), without notes or commentary. Volume 2: The introduction (11–18) comments on the themes and stylistic characteristics of the *Satyres,* the verse epistles, and the *Epicedes and Obsequies.* Contains English texts and Spanish translations on opposite pages of the *Satyres* (19–65), *Metem* (66–109), the verse epistles (113–229), and the *Epicedes and Obsequies* (221–61), without notes or commentary.

655. Donne, John. *Mud Walls: Excerpts from the Sermons of John Donne;* with five wood engravings by Jane Lydbury. Woolley, West Yorkshire: Fleece Press [1986?]. 15p. Limited to 200 copies.

Reproduces short excerpts from the sermons with no notes or commentary.

656. Donne, John. *Selected Poetry and Prose,* ed. T. W. Craik and R. J. Craik. Methuen English Texts, gen. ed. John Drakakis. London: Methuen. xi, 299p.

The introduction (1–19) presents a biographical sketch of Donne, discusses the problem of dating the poems, comments on the general characteristics of his poetry and prose, and explains the editorial principles governing the selections and notes included in the volume. Contains 46 poems from the *Songs and Sonets,* 12 from the *Elegies,* two epithalamia, two *Satyres, Metem,* 4 verse letters, *FirAn,* 15 selections from the *Holy Sonnets, Goodf,* 4 hymns, and selections from *Devotions* and the sermons, all with modernized spelling and punctuation (23–206). The selected bibliography (207–9) lists modern texts of the poetry and prose and biographical and critical studies, background studies, and reference works, followed by explanatory notes on individual works (211–93) and a glossary of words (295–99). Reviews: Michael G. Brennan in *N&Q,* n.s. 35 (1988): 363–64; Marie L. K. Lally in *SCN* 47 (1989): 13.

657. Dubinski, Roman. "Donne's Holy Sonnets and the Seven Penitential Psalms." *Ren&R,* n.s. 10: 201–16.

Discusses the role of the seven Penitential Psalms (6, 32, 38, 51, 102, 130, 143) in Christian devotion, comments on Donne's appreciation and interpretation of them as models for prayer in his poetry and prose, and maintains, in particular, that Donne found inspiration in them when composing the *Holy Sonnets.* Argues that "[t]he spiritual situation of the Penitential Psalms forms the basis for Donne's improvisations" in the *Holy Sonnets,* observing, however, that "the improvisations are in a new key affected by the typological transference of the psalmist's situation to that of an early seventeenth-century Protestant." Maintains, however, that "it is in their nature as prayers that they most resemble the Penitential Psalms" (208). Shows how in the *Holy Sonnets* Donne "appropriates and recreates the characteristic mix of prayers found in the Penitential Psalms—lamentations, deprecations and postulations, confessions, and thanksgiving and praises," and how he, "for the most part, reworks the substance of the Psalm prayers in a new key and in his own stylistic timbre" (209). Concludes that "[t]he similarity in dramatic situation, in tone, and in a combination of parallel elements of prayer make it highly likely that the Penitential Psalms were a crucial formative influence on the 'Holy Sonnets'" (214).

658. Dubrow, Heather. "Tradition and the Individualistic Talent: Donne's 'An Epithalamium, Or mariage Song on the Lady Elizabeth . . .,'" in *The Eagle and the Dove: Reassessing John Donne,* ed. Claude J. Summers and Ted-Larry Pebworth, 106–16. Essays in Seventeenth-Century Literature, 1. Columbia: University of Missouri Press.

Shows through a study of *EpEliz* how Donne's "imaginative responses" to the generic norms of the traditional epithalamium "are central to the success of this lyric" (106). Points out that Donne "treats the interplay between sexuality and society, like so many other norms of the epithalamium, very differently from the ways Spenser and Jonson do" (108), but argues that Donne wrote epithalamia "not in spite of but rather because of the many conventions with which the genre is laden." Insists that Donne "appears to have relished the opportunity of adapting a genre some of whose norms were uncongenial to him,

[and] to have welcomed the challenge of playing the traditions of that genre against the demands of his individualistic talent" (115). Believes that in the Palatine epithalamium, as in many of his mature poems, Donne rejected "servile imitation" (to use Carew's term) "not in favor of total iconoclasm and deracination but rather for a type of creativity and originality that is rooted in the conventions of his genre" (116).

659. Elimimian, Isaac I. "The Dedicatory Letter as a Rhetorical Device: The Example of Donne." *CML* 6: 127–36. A modified portion published in Chapter 2 of *A Study of Rhetorical Patterns in John Donne's Epicedes and Obsequies* (New York: Vantage Press, 1987), 23–42.

Notes that only two of the seven poems in the *Epicedes and Obsequies* are prefaced by dedicatory letters—*Har* and *Ham*—and examines Donne's uses of rhetorical techniques in both the letters and poems, maintaining that an analysis of the letters provides a background for the poems and "highlights Donne's subject matter, his resources, and the provenance of the poems" (128). Discusses how both letters and poems are informed by the concept of virtue as described by Aristotle in his *Rhetoric*. Shows how the Harrington poem develops the concept of virtue "in the manner of the traditional seven-part structure of an oration" (130) and how the Hamilton poem also develops the concept according to Aristotelian principles. Maintains that Donne primarily uses in both letters and poems the Aristotelian ethical mode of appeal, and calls the poems "remarkable in the sense that they possess a tone of candor not immediately apparent in other Donne elegiac poems, which, although treating the themes of virtue and death, lack dedicatory letters to advance the argument Donne presents in them."

Concludes that "[t]he quality of self-denial of the letters which preface these two poems, the tone of humility exemplified in them, and Donne's frequent infusion of Christian ethical coloring, help to make his audience benevolently disposed toward him," and that "[a] study of the poems, with little or no consideration of the letters, detracts from the poems' meaning" (136).

660. Ellrodt, Robert. "Divination et esprit 'métaphysique' au dix-septième siècle anglais," in *Du verbe au geste: mélanges en l'honneur de Pierre Danchin*, 57–66. Nancy: Presses Universitaires de Nancy.

Surveys the changing attitude towards divination in the seventeenth century. Points out that Donne, in spite of the allusions to the Sibyl, the specular stone, and dreams in his poetry, was not fascinated with the issue of predicting the future, the supernatural interpretation of dreams, magic, or other forms of divination. Maintains that Donne's sense of reality and of the present kept him from ascribing supernatural or prophetic attributes to dreams. Notes, however, that in *ElFatal* Donne is innovative in attributing to the dream of his mistress the ability not only to see the future, but also to influence the lover's destiny for good or bad.

661. Everett, Barbara. "Donne: A London Poet," in *Poets in Their Time: Essays on English Poetry from Donne to Larkin*, 1–31. Boston: Faber and Faber. First published in paperback by Oxford University Press, 1991. First published as *Donne: A London Poet*, Chatterton Lecture on an English Poet (London: Oxford University Press, 1972). Also reprinted in *PBA* 58 (1974): 245–73.

Argues that Donne was "a Londoner by nature as well as by birth and breeding . . . at that crucial phase in the city's history when it took on the character by which we recognize it now" (3), and that his being a Londoner adds "something to our understanding of him as a writer" (5). Points out, for example, how *Sat1* gives detailed social observations on contemporary London life and mores, and examines a number of other poems (especially *ElFatal, ValMourn, Lect, Canon,* and *Ecst*) to show how Donne's awareness of London and the life of the city shaped his poetic vision and sensibilities. Notes that the complex tone and sense of tension in many of Donne's poems have earned him "the right to be called our first (perhaps our only) real master of the poetry of urban anxiety" (13).

662. Evett, David. "Donne's Poems and the Five Styles of Renascence Art." *JDJ* 5: 101–31.

Suggests that, in addition to the stylistic labels of Renaissance, mannerism, and baroque applied to European visual and verbal art, two additional stylistic options should be considered—realism and the grotesque. Presents "a new view of the feature known as the *linea serpentinata*—associating it not only with Mannerism, as has been the custom, but with the Grotesque—and offers "a new structural hallmark for the Mannerist style itself" and then applies "these paradigms as well as that of Realism to Donne's poetry" (101). Surveys recent scholarly discussion of mannerism, as well as recent studies of realism and the grotesque. Maintains that in the late sixteenth and early seventeenth centuries the three styles—Renaissance, mannerist, and baroque—"are based on intellectual, social, political or aesthetic systems" that are "generally stable, hierarchic, authoritarian," but that the realist and grotesque styles "are levelling rather than hierarchic, experimental rather than ideal, accidental rather than systematic" (126–27). Argues that Donne was not confined to any one of these styles but drew on them all, "whether to construct whole works of a primarily Renaissance or Grotesque character, or to color a work in one style with local admixture of another" (123). Cites *LovGrow, ValName, Fun, Prim,* and *Relic* as examples. Suggests that in the verse letters realism seems to prevail, while in the *Satyres* and the *Elegies* the grotesque is predominant, and notes that *Metem* is "a fully articulated renascence Grotesquerie, complete with poetic-realist inserts." Evett concludes that any system of categorizing "is inadequate to account for the whole complexity of an artistically rich period or a writer as complicated as Donne" but believes that his system, at least, "covers new ground" (128).

663. Flanigan, Beverly Olson. "Donne's 'Holy Sonnet VII' as Speech Act." *Lang&S* 19: 49–57.

Analyzes *HSRound* as "a mimetic speech act" to show that in the sonnet "an imagined speaker (not the poet) is performing various illocutionary acts" and that "whether they are felicitous depends on their 'fit' not with our world, historical or modern, but with the pretended world the poem presents" (51). Maintains that the sonnet "becomes a series of mimetic speech acts asserting or attesting to the faith of the speaker in a system of accepted certainties" and "is both imperative and declarative, a permissible combination in the stylistic tradition of the theological and meditative tradition it draws upon and imitates" (55). Concludes, therefore, that speech act theory "offers a formalism, a procedure for making explicable those intuitions we may have long had about a literary work" and sees Donne's sonnet as providing an excellent example of how our perceptions "may be clarified and made credible through the use of such an approach" (56).

664. Flynn, Dennis. "Donne the Survivor," in *The Eagle and the Dove: Reassessing John Donne,* ed. Claude J. Summers and Ted-Larry Pebworth, 15–24. Essays in Seventeenth-Century Literature, 1. Columbia: University of Missouri Press.

Rejecting John Carey's description (1981) of Donne as an "apostate" and William Empson's praise of him (1981) as a "blasphemer," describes Donne as a "survivor" of Elizabethan persecution of Catholics, a term which allows one "to approach the question of his Catholicism from a more historical rather than quasi-apologetic standpoint" (17). Suggests that, having ultimately survived the threat of death for years, Donne appears to have suffered from a "disintegrating, irrational guilt merely for having survived the persecution" (19). Points out that Bruno Bettelheim, who studied survivors of Nazi persecution, suggests "three possible psychological responses to the experience of trauma endured by persons like Donne: (1) one can be psychologically and even physically destroyed by the very effort to survive; (2) one can deny that the experience of having survived has had any lasting impact; and (3) one can engage in a lifelong struggle to remain aware, to recover from surviving, and to reintegrate one's personality on some new basis." Shows that "[i]n Donne's life we can see traces of each of these varied responses to surviving" (20).

665. Frye, Northrop. "The Survival of Eros in Poetry," in *Romanticism and Contemporary Criticism,* ed. Morris Eaves and Michael Fischer, 15–45. Ithaca, N.Y.: Cornell University Press.

Notes in a survey of the emergence and transformation of eros in poetry from postclassical times that the paradox of two becoming one in *Canon,* in which the two lovers become "saints in Eros' calendar," almost reads like a parody of "the Nicene Creed on the persons and substance of the Trinity" (20). Notes also that, unlike Shelley, for whom "sexual love normally includes the reintegration of nature with humanity," Donne, "with his conviction that there is nothing paradisal outside the regenerate human mind" (26), would have found such an integration impossible.

666. Garrett, John. "The Early 17th Century: Donne and Herbert," in *British Poetry Since the Sixteenth Century: A Students' Guide,* 49–55. Basingstoke: Macmillan Education. First American edition, Totowa, N.J.: Barnes and Noble, 1987.

Surveys general characteristics of Donne's poetry, stressing that it "reflects the shifting sensibilities of his age" (49), and portrays Donne's rebellion against the social and artistic disciplines that tried to restrain him. Suggests that the love poetry and the religious verse have in common a "spontaneity of diction," noting how "[t]he words strike a note which is colloquial and modern" (50). Gives a critical reading of *HSBatter,* examining the theme, diction, imagery, prosody, rhythm, syntax and structure, and sexual implications of the metaphors in the sonnet. Claims that the sexual metaphors suggest that "the speaker cannot relate to an abstract or intellectual idea of Godhead but seeks to secure the expression of God's love for him in the passionate, sensual way that he can more easily understand" (50).

667. Gaston, Paul L. "Britten's Donne and the Promise of Twentieth-Century Settings," in *The Eagle and the Dove: Reassessing John Donne,* ed. Claude J. Summers and Ted-Larry Pebworth, 201–13. Essays in Seventeenth-Century

Literature, 1. Columbia: University of Missouri Press.

Points out that although Donne apparently "enjoyed, respected, and understood music," he did not "adopt a poetic style readily amenable to musical settings," and notes that "only eight of Donne's authenticated lyrics were set to music by seventeenth century English composers." Discusses two seventeenth century settings, "The Expiration" by Alfonso Ferrabosco and "A Hymne to God the Father" by John Hilton, to show the limitations of seventeenth century song idiom "in accommodating even the simpler lyrics of Donne" (202). Maintains that a number of twentieth century composers, however, have developed "an idiom sufficiently flexible and responsive to accommodate Donne's poetry," and discusses, in some detail, Benjamin Britten's 1946 settings of nine of the *Holy Sonnets* as an example of contemporary settings that "respect the complexity" of Donne's poems "as they convey an impressive measure of their power" (206).

668. Gesalí, Esteban Pujals. "*All good structure in a winding stair:* La lírica devocional del siglo XVII," in *Estudios literarios ingleses: Renacimiento y barroco,* ed. Susana Onega, 415–36. Madrid: Cátedra.

Explores the critical revival of interest in Donne in the twentieth century and discusses the nature of English devotional poetry of the seventeenth century. Comments on the general characteristics of Donne's devotional poetry and presents a detailed analysis of the rhetorical, linguistic, and thematic complexity of *HSDeath.*

669. Gilman, Ernest B. "Donne's 'Pictures Made and Mard,'" in *Iconoclasm and Poetry in the English Reformation: Down Went Dagon,* 117–48. Chicago: University of Chicago Press.

A slightly revised version of "'To adore, or scorne an image': Donne and the Iconoclastic Controversy" that first appeared in *JDJ* 5 (1986): 63–100. See entry below.

670. Gilman, Ernest B. "'To adore, or scorne an image': Donne and the Iconoclastic Controversy." *JDJ* 5: 63–100.

Maintains that Donne's poetry is strongly influenced by the iconoclastic controversy, citing *Sat3* and *HSShow* as examples of the ambivalence Donne felt regarding images. Suggests that in his poetry "the making and breaking of images becomes Donne's figure for registering the deepest conflicts of his imagination" and maintains that he seems "to have absorbed both sides of the iconoclastic controversy into the language of his little world, where their antagonism remains fully charged" (85). Cites as examples *ElPict, Damp, Eclog, Witch, ValMourn,* and *Relic,* suggesting that in these poems there still lurks a "residual attachment to Roman ritual and imagery" (89). Claims, however, that in the divine poems Donne made "a clean break from the idolatry of the love poems" (88), but discusses how in his religious poetry Donne both shatters and sets up devotional images, illustrating the point by discussing *Cross, Goodf,* and several of the *Holy Sonnets*. Observes that, although in the sermons, as in the poetry, there are "cross-currents of attraction and repulsion" (85) toward images, Donne the preacher essentially endorses the Anglican compromise on their uses. Comments also on the paintings and maps in Donne's rooms in the deanery of St. Paul's and on the portraits and engravings made of him during his lifetime.

671. Glaser, Joe. "'Goodfriday, 1613': A Soul's Form." *CollL* 13: 168–76.

Presents a biographical reading of *Goodf,* maintaining that the poem "not only provides the clearest evidence we have as to Donne's attitudes as he moved toward ordination in the Anglican Church, but also confirms what we know from other sources about the oddly elliptical way in which his mind resolved problems and the gallery of recurrent images and concerns that haunted his imaginative life" (169). Calls the poem "a record of Donne's struggle at this point in his life" and "a remarkable glimpse of a lively and sensitive intelligence swept up in the seventeenth century's religious wars" (170). Comments on the dramatic unfolding of the argument of the poem, showing how "the speaker's Euclidian security at the beginning of the poem quickly gives way to growing uncertainty leading up to a hopeful but unreasoned gesture of faith at the end." Maintains that at the end of the poem the speaker, realizing that God has been in charge of his life all along, comes to believe that, by accepting the Anglican identity that life had thrust upon him, he will be at last reshaped "in a way that God will find useful and worthy of recognition" (174).

672. Goldberg, Jonathan. "Fatherly Authority: The Politics of Stuart Family Images," in *Rewriting the Renaissance: The Discourses of Sexual Difference in Early Modern Europe,* ed. Margaret W. Ferguson, Maureen Quilligan, and Nancy J. Vickers, 3–32. Chicago: University of Chicago Press.

In a discussion of the ideology of the family and its relationship to monarchical absolutism in the seventeenth century, Goldberg comments on Donne's marriage to Ann More and suggests that, as a frequenter of the theater, Donne "may have tried to live out a role he found there," noting, in particular, that *Romeo and Juliet* may have served as "a precedent for his behavior." Suggests also that some of Donne's poems, for instance, the *Elegies* and *Canon,* "seem to have been written with texts like *Romeo and Juliet* in mind." Points out that the ten-year "period of discontent" that Donne suffered following his marriage suggests "how closely the family and society functioned in the period, how powerful the ideology was" (8).

673. Granqvist, Raoul. "Edmund Gosse: The Reluctant Critic of John Donne." *NM* 87: 262–71.

Challenges the assumption that Edmund Gosse's *Life of John Donne* (1899) was "a decisive factor in the modern Donne revival" and "demonstrates that, for reasons of personal prestige and accidence, Gosse was pulled into the late nineteenth-century camp that was studying the poet." Claims, in fact, that Gosse basically "was antagonistic to Donne and resented his growing reputation," but that "at the time the Establishment of taste had already perpetuated the notion of Gosse's 'discovery'" (262). Surveys Gosse's criticism of Donne both before and after his writing of the biography to illustrate Gosse's hostility to Donne and his poetry, explains the circumstances behind his writing of the *Life,* and calls for a reappraisal of Gosse's role as "one of the initiators and perceptive critics of Donne" (271) in the modern Donne revival.

674. Granqvist, Raoul. "The Reception of Edmund Gosse's *Life of John Donne* (1899)." *ES* 67: 525–38.

Discusses the critical reception of the publication of Gosse's *Life of John Donne* (1899) primarily by surveying reviews of it in major literary journals and newspapers in England (and to a lesser extent in America). Argues that the reviewers "adopt to varying degrees preconceived notions about Gosse" that molded the reception of his work, and that their central concern was "the urge to establish their own position in the literary talk of the day that centred on Gosse's alleged incompetence as a scholar." Observes that even "those who were apt to defend Gosse and endorse the book also departed from the book as soon as possible to explore territories of their own," a position that "only partly benefited Gosse, although it greatly advanced Donne" (537). Believes that "[t]he direction and the emphasis of the reception are predictable because the critics more or less knew what Gosse was going to propose," which "explains why the critics were more anxious to approve or disapprove of Gosse's achievement than really examine the book" (537–38). Finds two major strands in the criticism: "criticism that evidenced factual mistakes and judged him [Gosse] extravagant and absurd in his evaluation of singular poems, and criticism that contained praises of his portrayal of Donne's fascinating and bewildering character; in short what was envisaged to be 'modern man.'" Concludes that although Gosse's book "fell into immediate disrepute," the Donne that "it mirrored gained strength and freshness" (538).

675. Guibbory, Achsah. "John Donne: The Idea of Decay," in *The Map of Time: Seventeenth-Century English Literature and Ideas of Pattern in History,* 69–104. Urbana: University of Illinois Press.

Examines the idea of history that informs Donne's work and shows that a constant feature of Donne's imagination was "his sense of decay," arguing that "Donne's pervasive, abiding concerns with time as a process of decay transcends the differences of form, genre, tone, and occasion that separate individual works" and "gives a distinctive voice to a complex, various, diverse body of writing" (70). Points out that history, for Donne, "has a clearly defined shape, with fixed, unalterable limits," and that he "finds history's pattern repeated in the life of each person, indeed in the life of every created thing" (71). Observes that Donne sees himself inhabiting a universe "where all decays" and where "the only things that grow are disease and corruption," and stresses that he "emphasizes the downward movement of history" (72), viewing it as a "process of dissolution" (74). Suggests that Donne's view of history as degenerative accounts for his belief that "the earliest state was the best" (75), which, in turn, accounts for his distrust of innovation, his view of church history, his wish to trace things to their sources (reflected in his images of the origins of fountains, springs, and rivers as well as in his images of roots), and his interest in etymology. Points out that repeatedly Donne "seeks to find some antidote for the destructive effect of time" (85), noting that in the *Songs and Sonets* "there is a fundamental tension in Donne between the desire to find in love the ability to transcend or reverse the degenerative effect of time, on the one hand, and the suspicion that man's love for woman participates in, or even accelerates, decay, on the other." Points out that in the sermons Donne's "skeptical, disparaging view of human love becomes more insistent" (87). Maintains that Donne finds a "remedy for the degenerative course of time" (88) in the Augustinian concept of memory, which, according to Donne, has the "ability to reestablish the link between human beings and God" (92), and which is "a necessary step in the process of salvation" (94). Holds that God was, for Donne, the ultimate remedy against the degenerative course of time. Points out that Donne "frequently implies that the natural, tem-

poral pattern of decline conflicts with God's force" and believes that "[i]t is this opposition between God and time that distinguishes Donne's view of history from the traditional Judaeo-Christian one, which assumes that God's providence directs the course of time" (98). Concludes that Donne believed that "[o]nly at the Resurrection, at the end of time, will we find a permanent remedy for the destructive, dissolving effects of time" (99).

676. Guillén, Claudio. "Notes toward the Study of the Renaissance Letter," in *Renaissance Genres: Essays on Theory, History, and Interpretation,* ed. Barbara Kiefer Lewalski, 70–101. Harvard English Studies, 14. Cambridge, Mass.: Harvard University Press.

Discusses various kinds of Renaissance letters—those in prose and in poetry, in Latin and in the vernacular, as well as comments on practical manuals on letter writing and letters inserted within other genres—and discusses aspects of the theory of the letter from the classical period to the Renaissance. Briefly comments on the Horatian theme of friendship in Donne's verse epistles, noting that, when writing to women, however, Donne usually swerves from "the thematic breadth of the Horatian model and tends to concentrate on love or on the nature of women"; thus these poems become "not about friendship itself, a favorite topic of the verse epistle" (79).

677. Guinness, Gerald. "Playing for Life in Donne's Elegies, Songs and Sonnets," in *Auctor Ludens: Essays on Play in Literature,* ed. Gerald Guinness and Andrew Hurley, 137–55. Philadelphia: John Benjamins.

Discusses the importance of various kinds of play in Donne's love poetry. Maintains that the argumentativeness in the love poetry is "a kind of play" and that those critics who ignore "this play element" often "go wildly astray" (137) in their judgments of individual poems. Shows, for instance, how John Carey (1981), Roma Gill (1972), and Brian Vickers (1972) "misread" *ElBed* because they fail to see its playfulness. Insists that "never has there been a poet whose sexual powers were more centred in the tongue" (138). Observes also that often the words and images in Donne's poems "play and perform as though they were on stage in a *commedia dell'arte* performance." Suggests that in *ElProg,* for instance, the reader senses that Donne is improvising and "allowing what he just said to suggest what is to follow" (142). Comments also on "the play of disorientation, wherein the poet muddles his traces, dislocates the reader's sense of place, and in extreme cases, induces a sense of dizziness or vertigo" (143), citing examples from the two elegies already mentioned as well as from *Air, Relic,* and *Leg.* Maintains that "Donne's roles in this play of love, this love-play, are more varied and conflictive than that of any other poet in the language" (147), and insists that Donne, for all his playing, is sincere because he is "*[p]laying from the heart*" (149).

678. Harland, Paul W. "Dramatic Technique and Personae in Donne's Sermons." *ELH* 53: 709–26.

Examines "the function and purpose of Donne's personae or voices in their soliloquies and implied dialogues" in his sermons in order to show that Donne "frequently uses personae to exemplify a process of growth fundamental to his understanding of human nature, to assure the auditory that a variety of religious responses may be acceptable to God, to model dialogue as a method of spiritual development, and finally, to manipulate Scripture so as to give it current value" (709). Shows how Donne's "use of homiletic

personae demonstrates his keen awareness of the individual styles and stances that made up providential history," how he delights "in the diversity of biblical and historical voices as a sign of God's bounty and his allowance of freedom by which growth takes place," and how his "ear for the diversity of biblical voices as well as his familiarity with attitudes current in his own time allows him to reproduce those voices and postures in his sermons so as to sanctify them" (724–25). Concludes that "Donne's personae and implied dialogues advance the process of the sermon towards reconciliation in a way analogous to the individual and voluntary contribution of human beings to God's providence" (725).

679. Heninger, S. K., Jr. "Sequences, Systems, Models: Sidney and the Secularization of Sonnets," in *Poems in Their Place: The Intertextuality and Order of Poetic Collections,* ed. Neil Fraistat, 66–94. Chapel Hill: University of North Carolina Press.

Compares and contrasts the *Songs and Sonets* to the sonnet sequences of Dante, Petrarch, Sidney, and Shakespeare, pointing out that Donne, like Shakespeare, "exploited the depictive possibilities inherent in Sidney's mimetic theory of poetry, the potential for the striking image and the dramatic moment" (88), and that his personae use the speaking voice so convincingly that "it obscures the historical figure who later wrote solemn sermons" (88–89). Suggests that, even more than Shakespeare, Donne modified the sonnet sequence model by using many different metrical forms, by employing complex uses of rhetoric, by minimizing narrative and emphasizing drama, and especially by modifying the traditional relationship between the speaker and his lady. Points out that Donne's poems, unlike

Sidney's, are "unabashedly sexual" and often "unabashedly promiscuous." Claims that Donne, in fact, produced a "countergenre" of the traditional sonnet sequence in which he "enlarges the range of emotional attitudes" (89) of preceding sonnet sequences and "goes beyond the confines of the theme of love" in that "[t]he usual conflict between lust and restraint becomes metonymically for him an irresolvable contention between cynicism and belief." Says that what unifies the *Songs and Sonets* is "no hypothetical lady" but rather Donne's "honest, relentless search for selfhood," and calls the collection "the most intensely human and perhaps the richest of the sonnet sequences" (90).

680. Herz, Judith Scherer. "'An Excellent Exercise of Wit that Speaks so well of Ill': Donne and the Poetics of Concealment," in *The Eagle and the Dove: Reassessing John Donne,* ed. Claude J. Summers and Ted-Larry Pebworth, 3–14. Essays in Seventeenth-Century Literature, 1. Columbia: University of Missouri Press.

Challenges the notion that Donne is "a constant presence in his poems" and argues that, in fact, Donne is "rarely there, indeed in some poems never there," and that "the urgent speaking voice we think we hear in the poem is a calculated illusion, the consequence of the collision of an unstable poem and a dislocated reader." Maintains, in other words, that "[w]hat sounds like confession is concealment, what sounds like the speaking voice is, like Don Quixote's enchanted head, masterful and duplicitous ventriloquism." Calls Donne's poems "self-animating tropes, poetry as theater," and says their subject is "the nature of illusionism itself" (3). Believes that, for Donne, "the artist remains the conjurer who disappears into his own illusions." Fears that while critics have

"radically expanded" our understanding of the context of Donne's poems, "we have come close to losing Donne as pretext or, more accurately, to losing our sense of engagement with Donne as the master of complex, unsettling, prickly poems, poems that simply will not resolve" (5). Discusses *Twick* and *Noct* as examples of poems "of hidden center, poems that use the declarative mode to elicit the interrogative, that entertain a wide range of possible readings but that leave all possibilities as merely provisional," noting that "their most striking qualities are their veiling of the center, the dissolution of the 'I,' and the consequent engagement of the reader in a continuous process of revision" (9). Shows how even *BedfTwi* is similar to the two poems mentioned above but points out that, "[f]or all the disappearing acts that Donne manages, he still remains in the verse letters a fairly stable presence in comparison with the artful dodges of his lyric poems," in which his aim "was concealment rather than revelation" (13). Concludes that "[a]ttempts to impose unity, to make the poems yield single, albeit complex, readings, usually involve constructs external to the poem," and urges an emphasis "on process rather than on conclusion, on means rather than on ends" (14).

681. Hester, M. Thomas. "Donne's Epigrams: A Little World Made Cunningly," in *The Eagle and the Dove: Reassessing John Donne,* ed. Claude J. Summers and Ted-Larry Pebworth, 80–91. Essays in Seventeenth-Century Literature, 1. Columbia: University of Missouri Press.

Argues that Donne's epigrams, although neglected by modern critics, "offer an instructive example of his poetic achievement *in parvo*" and exhibit "the daring exploration of the limitations of deriving definite conclusions from speech acts and of the traps that reside in tropes driven toward epigrammatic closure" (80). While distinguishing epigram from lyric, maintains that the two forms "find their conjunction in similar challenges to the borders of genre and metaphor as modes of signification, in the testing of the polysemous character of language and genre as metaphoric frames for Donne's poetic definition." Claims that "[t]o appreciate the wit of his more famous lyrics, we turn profitably to his formal epigrams." Examines *Wing* as "the best introduction to the complex (and complicating) generic manipulation and surprise that reached its fullest achievement in Donne's lyrics" (81), but discusses also the subtlety and complexity of Donne's "manipulation of epigrammatic strategies and conventions" in *Hero, Licent, Antiq, Wall, Phrine,* and *Cales.* Concludes that "[i]f there is a poetics of space in Donne's lyrics, that space is not bedrooms and parlors, doorways and entrances, but the spaces between word and thing," and that "one of the best introductions to Donne's play with the problematics of signification is provided by the cunning little world of his epigrams" (91).

682. Höltgen, Karl Josef. "Donne's 'A Valediction: Forbidding Mourning' and some *Imprese,*" in *Anglistentag 1985, Paderborn,* 117–25. Giessen: Hoffmann. An abriged version of Chapter 2 of *Aspects of the Emblem: Studies in the English Emblem Tradition and the European Context* (1986). See entry below.

683. Höltgen, Karl Josef. "Donne's 'A Valediction: Forbidding Mourning' and some *Imprese,*" in *Aspects of the Emblem: Studies in the English Emblem Tradition and the European Context,* 67–90. Problemata Semiotica, vol. 2. Foreword by Roy Strong. Kassel: Reichenberger. Cites various possible imprese that Donne may have had in mind when creating the compass image in *Val-Mourn,* noting that, although it is impossible to prove that Donne was familiar with any specific impresa, there is no doubt that he was familiar with "the whole convention and practice of imprese" (75). Discusses the differences between imprese and emblems and the prevalence of Continental and English books of imprese in England and the use of imprese in the early seventeenth century. Announces the discovery of a compass impresa belonging to Donne's friend, James Hay, later Viscount Doncaster and Earl of Carlisle, and discusses how it "adds a little more weight" to Walton's dating of *ValMourn* as 1611. Thinks that it is "a remarkable fact that a prominent courtier employs the compass figures for an impresa at a public celebration at about the time his friend, Donne, uses it in a poem," and notes that "[t]he motto of Hay's impresa relates more closely to the wording of the poem than any of the previously quoted examples." Does not claim that Lord Hay's impresa influenced Donne's image, noting that the influence might have worked the other way round, but suggests that Hay's impresa and Donne's compass figure indicate "a collaboration and an exchange of ideas in the social context of the growing friendship between the courtier and the poet" (90).

684. Hurley, Ann. "The Elided Self: Witty Dis-Locations in Velázquez and Donne." *JAAC* 44: 359–69. Compares *Eclog* and Velázquez's painting *Las Meninas* to show that both artists take "a certain witty delight in exposing the limitations of their respective mediums, language and paint, logic and perspective, and yet both in so doing reveal not only the limitations of these specifically human instruments but also their power" (357). Thinks that both Donne and Velázquez call into question the issue of "the possibility and even desirability of representation as a valid intentional act," and notes that in his poem Donne supplants representation "as a mode of insight with a kind of visionary stance which is for him superior to that sense perception upon which our notations of representation are based" (363). Shows that whereas Velázquez "exploits or indeed violates our assumptions about perspective to dislocate his viewer and thus release the potency of his art," Donne "demonstrates his awareness of the potency of language by wittily dislocating his readers through the exploitation of its logical property" (368). Claims that both "are thus willing to keep the relation of language to vision open and to see that incompatibility as starting point rather than obstacle" (368–69). Concludes that Donne's poem and Velàzquez's painting "enhance our understanding of how in the seventeenth century logic, perspective, epideictic art, and metaphysics intersected in disturbing, but also very intriguing, ways" (369).

685. Jones, R. T. "Meaning," in *Studying Poetry: An Introduction,* 41–57. London: Edward Arnold.

Briefly comments on the issue of sincerity in poetry by commenting on the dramatic and playful nature of *Flea.* Says the argument of the poem is "a form of love-play" (55).

686. Kay, Dennis. "Poems by Sir Walter Aston, and a Date for the Donne/Goodyer Verse Epistle '*Alternis Vicibus.*'" *RES* 37: 198–210.

Argues that Drayton's patron, Sir Walter Aston, is the author of an elegy on Prince Henry in the Bodleian Library (MS Eng. Poet. e. 37, pp. 47–48), which is "in many respects characteristic of the laments produced by Donne's circle" (204), and then argues from the date, subject matter, and circulation of that poem that *AltVic* was

probably composed in the early spring of 1613. Acknowledges that none of the information presented "can definitely establish the poem's date" but believes that "the circumstantial evidence seems compelling" (210).

687. Kelly, Kathleen. "Conversion of the Reader in Donne's 'Anatomy of the World,'" in *The Eagle and the Dove: Reassessing John Donne,* ed. Claude J. Summers and Ted-Larry Pebworth, 147–56. Essays in Seventeenth-Century Literature, 1. Columbia: University of Missouri Press.

Argues that in *FirAn* Donne "creates a speaker who is initially distanced from both poet and reader, demanding that we be an audience we initially cannot be," but that "by insisting that despite our resistance we are his audience, the speaker draws us into the anatomy," thereby causing us "to undergo a conversion to his world." Maintains that "eventually poet, speaker, audience, and reader join in celebrating both Elizabeth [Drury] and our own hope for a spiritual life" (148). Demonstrates how Donne plays the role of the biblical prophet in *FirAn* and how the audience is made to play the role of the prophet's audience, "at first skeptical of his authority, initially unable to share his vision." Observes that "[o]nly when the prophet persists in establishing his authority—through his compelling sense of urgency, through his claim to a higher source of wisdom, through his holy indignation—only then does the community finally begin to embrace his vision, to become his audience." Concludes that "[b]y creating the fiction of a speaker possessed of a sacred experience, Donne's 'Anatomy' truly unites speaker and poet, audience and reader, the fate of a mere girl and every Christian soul" (156).

688. Kim, Myong-Ok. "Eliot eui Donne bipyeong gwa Donne si eui hyeondaesung"

[Eliot's Criticism of Donne and the Modernity of Donne's Poetry]. *JELL* (Seoul, Korea) 32, no. 36: 387–406.

Maintains that a survey of T. S. Eliot's criticism shows that Eliot considered Donne modern because of his "fidelity to his feelings and emotions in his poetry" and because Donne had "his own way of bridging parts together, that is, the unique way of structural unification of parts." Notes, however, that Eliot does not adequately clarify his thinking on this point. Discusses, in particular, Donne's uses of dramatic speakers, claiming that they function as "objective correlatives" for his own private feelings, and shows how Donne presents emotion through logical reasoning and argumentation. Analyzes *GoodM*, *Fever*, and *Dream* to show how each is "unified into a fascinating and unique whole by the structural coherence of psychological reasoning" (406).

689. Kishimoto, Yoshitaka. "'Good Friday, 1613. Riding Westward': Donne no Ura no Imi" ["Goodfriday, 1613. Riding Westward": Its Hidden Meanings], in *Igirisu Bungaku: Kenkyu to Kansho 2* [English Literature: Studies and Appreciation 2], ed. Ryutaro Sugimoto and Yoshitsuga Uchida, 133–45. Osaka: Sogensha.

Offers appreciative comments on *Goodf*, focusing primarily on l. 9 ("I am carryed towards the West") as particularly important in understanding the meaning of the poem.

690. Klause, John. "The Montaigneity of Donne's *Metempsychosis*," in *Renaissance Genres: Essays on Theory, History, and Interpretation,* ed. Barbara Kiefer Lewalski, 418–43. Harvard English Studies, 14. Cambridge, Mass.: Harvard University Press.

Rejects the views of those critics who regard *Metem* as simply a *jeu d'esprit*, a "vehicle of defiant or desolate impiety" (418), or a somber meditation and maintains that perhaps "it is the kind of poem that will never lend itself to a 'satisfactory' reading (an interpretation that accounts for all major details within a design)" since "so easily does it produce confusion about its character and purpose." Points out that Donne's "approach to establishing his meaning is casual, free of a dutiful attention to consistency," and claims that "this capriciousness is no more evident than in his mingling of genres in a way that raises doubts about their compatibility" (422). Shows that in the poem all "attempts at generic form—epic, satire, theological commentary, metahistory, and allegory—are somehow checked and defeated," and that "[t]he genres are alluded to rather than embodied" (431). Maintains, however, that Donne's poem may have been greatly influenced both in matter and manner by the essays of Montaigne and points out several "points of contact" (436) between *Metem* and Montaigne's *Essais*.

691. Klawitter, George. "John Donne and the Countess of Huntingdon: The Transformation of Renaissance Woman." *Wisconsin English Journal* 28, no. 3: 10–12.

Points out that in most medieval and Renaissance poetry women "were either praised beyond belief or ridiculed in crude stereotypes," both portrayals doing "injustice to their actuality as human beings." Maintains that in his verse epistles to women Donne broke with this tradition, addressing women as equals. Comments on *HuntMan*, in which Donne "treads a fine line between insult and flattery" (11), and suggests that the poem reflects "what innovative honesty Donne brought to poetry via the verse letter." Suggests that "what earmarks Donne's appreciation of woman's equality to men more than anything else in his verse is something we have overlooked for quite some time: he actually expected women to understand his complicated lyrics" (12).

692. Klein, Jürgen. "John Donne," in *Astronomie und Anthropozentrik: Die Copernicanische Wende bei John Donne, John Milton und den Cambridge Platonists,* 194–216. Aspekte der englischen Geistes und Kulturgeschicte, ed. Jürgen Klein, Band 6. Frankfurt: Peter Lang.

Discusses Donne's penchant for wanting to deny the astronomical discoveries of his day, citing *FirAn* as an illustration of his conservatism. Observes that Donne takes the Catholic Church to task for being too progressive in *Ignatius,* a work in which he depicts the Jesuits as using recent scientific discoveries to promote their ends of reinstituting Catholicism throughout Europe and in which he describes innovators, such as Copernicus, Paracelsus, Machiavelli, and Columbus, as striving to attain higher places in hell. Maintains that Donne regarded many innovations in his day as denials of truth and tried to subordinate them to his traditional worldview. Sees Donne, therefore, as a premodern spirit and an embodiment of many contradictions. Reviews: Rainer Baasner in *Arcadia* 22 (1987): 213–15.

693. László, Gergye. "Az angol szonett-típus reneszánsz és manierista változata (Edmund Spenser és John Donne)." *Filológiai Közlöny* 32–33, nos. 3–4 (1986–87): 165–79.

Examines Renaissance and post-Renaissance manneristic variations of the English sonnet. Discusses, in particular, the structure, language, rhetorical strategies, and love philosophy of Spenser's *Amoretti,* considering his sonnets as representative of the purest form of the Renaissance concept of love. Discusses, in contrast, Donne's *Corona* and *Holy Sonnets* as examples of a new development in the history of the sonnet, showing how his sonnets deviate from the structure and thought processes of the traditional Petrarchan sonnet and commenting on how he introduces a new and different concept of love in his poems that challenges the Neoplatonic vision of love endorsed by Spenser. Concludes that Donne's mannerism makes him a transitional figure between the Renaissance and baroque periods.

694. Llasera, Margaret. "'Howrely in Inconstancee': Transcience and Transformation in the Poetry of John Donne." *BSEAA* 23: 39–56.

Discusses patterns of change in Donne's poetry brought about (1) by a "series of systems imposed by the artistic devices of pun, paradox, and metaphor that momentarily fix or create differences and similitudes," and by Donne's use of correspondences, which effect "a unification of reality and fleetingly arrest fluctuation" while, at the same time, they "bring about their own fragile transmutations"; (2) by "the theme of decay"; and (3) by "the recurring notion of transformation," in which "love, death and resurrection each involve a mutation that lifts man out of sublunary time and transience, lending the poet's vision of his ultimate metamorphosis an optimistic note" (39). Comments on the startling openings of Donne's poems; his use of dramatic personae whose attitudes shift from poem to poem as Donne explores "the many facets of himself and human nature with exceptional lucidity" (42); Donne's uses of metaphors and anamorphosis that "involve a *process* of distortion" (44); his views on death and on the decay of the body and the world, in short, his "tragic view of mutability" (46); Donne's perception of sex as "a representation of the after-life, adumbrating the spiritual union of man with God and the spiritualizing of the flesh after the resurrection" (50); and his uses of alchemical metaphors "to convey a spiritualizing process" (52). Concludes that death, "as a sexual, an alchemical, a Christian and a plain biological concept, is the fulcrum of Donne's system of understanding and being, the knot of a vast conceit that binds mortality to immortality," noting that although death is "[t]he major and most disquieting of changes in a series that leads from conception to putrefaction," it is "also the one change mysteriously welded to changelessness and is thus for the poet a fertile, if intermittent, source of hope" (54).

695. Llasera, Margaret, and Marie-Madeleine Martinet. "John Donne: *Poems*. Bibliographie selective et critique." *BSEAA* 23: 7–16.

Presents a highly selective list of modern editions, bibliographies, biographies, and critical studies on metaphysical poets in general, critical studies on Donne, and studies on specific Donne poems or collections of poems. Briefly annotates some items in French.

696. Makurenkova, S. A. "Angliiskaia 'metafizicheskaia poeziia' XVII v: K istorii poniatiia." *IAN* 45, no. 2: 174–81.

Discusses the concept of metaphysical poetry and argues that understanding the term "metaphysical poetry" allows one to understand Donne within his historical context. Reviews Dryden's discussion of Donne's wit and Johnson's critique of Donne's poetry. In passing, makes reference to other Renaissance writers, including Marlowe, Drummond, Herbert, Crashaw, Cleveland, Traherne, Carew, Cowley, and Marvell. Concludes that Donne is more widely read in Russia than the others and that readers need to gain a better understanding of English metaphysical poetry in its historical context to appreciate his verse.

697. Manning, John. "The Eagle and the Dove: Chapman and Donne's 'The Canonization.'" *N&Q*, n.s. 33: 347–48.

Suggests that the source for Donne's conceit of the eagle and the dove in

Canon (l. 22) may be a line in George Chapman's *Ovid's Banquet of Sense* (1595), but points out that Donne's conceit, "while freed from Chapman's opaque mythology, is extremely hard to pin down, because its imaginative richness resists any neat exemplary formulation." Maintains that "[i]t would be wrong to restrict any explanation of Donne's conceit to Chapman's statement," but believes that the very presence of the eagle and the dove in Donne's poem "plainly relates to their connection with the theme of wise folly and holy prophaneness" found in Chapman's poem. Concludes that "[t]he mysteriousness and suggestiveness that result from Donne's naturalizing of Chapman's mythological image must be regarded as poetic bonuses, even if we do not know how far they were consciously intended by Donne" (148).

698. Marotti, Arthur F. *John Donne, Coterie Poet*. Madison and London: University of Wisconsin Press. xviii, 369p. Portions of this study appeared earlier as "John Donne and the Rewards of Patronage," in *Patronage in the Renaissance* (1981), and "Donne and 'The Extasie,'" in *The Rhetoric of Renaissance Poetry,* ed. Thomas O. Sloan and Raymond B. Waddington (Berkeley and Los Angeles: University of California Press, 1974). Pages 246–68 and 326–46, slightly revised, are reprinted as "Donne as Social Exile and Jacobean Courtier: The Devotional Verse and Prose of the Secular Man," in *Critical Essays on John Donne,* ed. Arthur F. Marotti (New York: G. K. Hall, 1994), 77–101.

Analyzes Donne's poems as "coterie literature, as texts originally involved with both their biographical and social contexts," and discusses them "chronologically and according to audience, paying particular attention to the rhetorical enactment of the author's relationships to peers and superiors through the conflicting styles of egalitarian assertion, social iconoclasm, and deferential politeness" (xi). Relates the poetry "to the contemporary prose Donne wrote either for private circulation or for publication," and deals with "his choice of different literary forms in terms of both his changing sociopolitical circumstances and the shift from Elizabethan to Jacobean rule that brought about a realignment of genres within the culture's literary system" (xi–xii). Examines "the social coordinates of Donne's formal satires, humanist verse-letters, erotic elegies, and complimentary epistles," and defines "the markedly different contexts within which his libertine, courtly, satiric, sentimental, complimentary, and religious lyrics were originally set" (xii). Points out that this study is shaped by formalist criticism, literary and intellectual history, revisionist history, psychoanalytic theory, and post-structural criticism, and proposes a complete "reexamination of Donne's poems" in which "virtually all the poems" are discussed (xiii). Hopes that this "new historicist reinterpretation of Donne's poetry" will also serve "as a model for the kind of inquiry that might be undertaken into the work of many other writers" (xiv). In "Introduction: Donne and the Conditions of Coterie Verse" (3–24), Marotti discusses the general background of sixteenth century manuscript transmission and Donne's practice of circulating his poems among his friends and acquaintances. Believes that the basic features of Donne's poetry "are related to its coterie character," such as "[h]is creation of a sense of familiarity and intimacy, his fondness for dialectic, intellectual complexity, paradox and irony, the appeals to shared attitudes and group interests (if not to private knowledge), the explicit gestures of biographical self-referentiality, [and] the styles he adopted or invented" (19).

Maintains that Donne's poetry "with its rich interplay of text and context has been falsified since its posthumous publication in 1633 as a poetical corpus," and emphasizes that the aim of this study is "to recover some of what has been lost through the literary institutionalization of Donne" (24). Chapter 1, "Donne as an Inns-of-Court Author" (25–95), discusses Donne's poetry written roughly between 1592 and 1596, emphasizing the economic, political, and social implications in these early works. Chapter 2, "Donne as Young Man of Fashion, Gentleman-Volunteer, and Courtly Servant" (96–151), discusses those poems written roughly between 1596 and 1602, during the time Donne was involved in public life and military service, ending with his dismissal from the service of the Lord Keeper. Chapter 3, "Donne as Social Exile and Jacobean Courtier" (152–274), discusses the poems Donne wrote between 1602 and 1614, that is, during the time of his social exile for marrying Ann More and his reemergence as an active courtier again seeking preferment to the time of his entrance into the priesthood. "Epilogue: Donne's Last Poems" (275–87) comments briefly on those few poems Donne wrote after his ordination. Stresses that the chronological arrangement of this study "necessitates disintegrating some of the traditional generic groups of Donne's verse," such as the verse letters, *Satyres, Elegies,* and the *Songs and Sonets,* Maintains, for instance, that those who have read the latter as "an aesthetically unified whole have missed many of the interesting features of Donne's artful response to the poems' particular contexts of composition and reception," noting that these poems "functioned differently than they have as a collection of texts whose literary canonization was facilitated by the 1633 edition" (xii). Observes that when the poems are read separately in their original historical settings, "neat formalist distinctions between poet and person, fictive listener and real reader break down in interesting ways" (xiii). Contains notes (291–349) and an index (351–69). Reviews: Arthur F. Kinney in *CentR* 30 (1986): 538–39; Graham Parry in *THES* 717 (1986): 17; Camille Wells Slights in *MLQ* 47 (1986): 318–21; Cedric C. Brown in *RES* 38 (1987): 560–61; Heather Dubrow in *RenQ* 40 (1987): 178–81; Jeffrey Dunn in *SCN* 45 (1987): 70–71; Jonathan Goldberg in *JEGP* 86 (1987): 410–12; Andrea Sununu in *SR* 95 (1987): lxxiv–lxxviii; D. F. Bratchell in *N&Q*, n.s. 35 (1988): 87–88; Anthony Low in *JDJ* 7 (1988): 125–31; Claude J. Summers in *MP* 85 (1988): 323–27; Gerald Hammond in *MLR* 84 (1989): 124–25.

699. Mathis, Gilles. "John Donne: La Comédie du littéral et du métaphorique dans les *Songs and Sonets.*" *Bulletin de la Société de Stylistique Anglaise* 8: 69–81.

Presents a stylistic study of Donne's use of literal and metaphorical language in the *Songs and Sonets*. States that in his love poems Donne plays an ingenious game, but plays it seriously. Finds significant Donne's literal treatment of metaphorical language, which involves the double meaning of words and the mixture of poetic inexactitude with logical rigor. Identifies several consistent stylistic features in the *Songs and Sonets,* such as the primacy given to metaphorical expression, the frequency of metaphors in a series, the juxtaposition and use of words in both a literal and metaphorical sense, and the use of words with double meanings. Calls Donne an "iconophiloclaste" (81) who both loves and destroys images and who uses language not to create imaginary or fantastic worlds but rather to combat the unrealistic idealization of love and women. Suggests that through his unique use of literal and metaphorical language Donne creates an original metaphysics that reconciles the spiritual and the carnal.

700. Maynard, Winifred. *Elizabethan Lyric Poetry and Its Music.* Oxford: Clarendon Press. ix, 246p.

Discusses how Donne "in effect if not by intent led the lyric away from music," since his typical mode "is not that of song but of impassioned speech" (146), noting, however, that he did exhibit "some interest in writing verse for singing," as evidenced by the fact that "in one manuscript six of his lyrics appear under the heading 'Songs which were made to certaine Aires that were made before,'" and that "four other manuscripts give the same indication for three of the six" (147). Maintains, however, that, on the whole, his poems suggest "an absence of aptitude in Donne for writing words to music," noting that only *Father* has a "strophic setting in which words and music complement each other throughout." Maintains, however, that, "[m]ore often, his poems are astir with turbulence, and their shift of stance or emotion or thought throw up complex and non-recurring rhythms." Concludes that Donne "was well-disposed to the concept of lyrics as songs, but his own strong lines were rarely subdued to the strophic accountability needed for the practical partnership of the ayre" (149). Comments on John Dowland's reworking of *Break* and possible recasting of *LovInf,* Alfonso Ferrabosco's problematic adaptation of *Expir,* and William Corkine's setting of *Break.*

701. McGerr, Rosemarie Potz. "Donne's 'Blest Hermaphrodite' and the *Poetria Nova.*" *N&Q,* n.s. 33: 349.

Suggests that the metaphor of the "blest Hermaphrodite" to characterize the new ordained priest in *Tilman* (l. 34) may have its source in Geoffrey of Vinsauf's early thirteenth-century rhetorical treatise, *Poetria Nova,* in which Geoffrey addresses Pope Innocent III as "a 'neuter' because the pontiff is no longer mere man, but intermediary between God and mankind."

702. Merrix, Robert P. "The Vale of Lilies and the Bower of Bliss: Soft-Core Pornography in Elizabethan Poetry." *JPC* 19, no. 4: 3–16.

Maintains that in the Elizabethan era, "realistic, hard-core pornography had not yet developed an aesthetic tradition strong enough to sustain it," but that "[w]hat did develop into such a tradition was the erotic lyric and narrative poetry which employed soft-core pornographic metaphors rather than the more graphic sexual imagery used by Nashe [in *The Choice of Valentines*]," although clearly their purpose was "to stimulate the sexual imagination" (4–5). Sees the tradition of Elizabethan soft-core pornography as "an artistic amalgam of the subtle sensuousness of Ovid" and "the clever metaphors" (6) drawn from the Italian and French blazon tradition. Points out that one of the most widely used techniques in these poems is the use of metaphoric language. Notes, as example, how Donne describes his lady's breasts in *ElProg* as "Sestos and Abydos, her cleavage as the Hellespont, and her pubic hair as a forest, whereas hard-core pornography would leave little to the imagination and would lack wit and subtlety." Points out that "[d]isrobings often follow universally recognized techniques of titillation" and cites *ElBed* as an example. Points out that Donne, like many of his contemporaries, was a master at using analogies to avoid sexual explicitness, citing Donne's use of a nautical metaphor in *ElProg* (ll. 57–70) to describe the female body sexually and to describe the sex act itself.

703. Müller, Wolfgang G. "Liturgie und Lyrik: John Donne's 'The Litanie'" in *LJGG,* n.s. 27: 65–80.

Calling Donne a passionate rhetorician, maintains that a recurrent theme in his religious lyrics, often expressed in the form of a direct address to God, is the relationship between the self and God. Gives a detailed analysis of *Lit* and shows how Donne transforms the traditional litany into a lyric poem.

704. Müller, Wolfgang G. "'My Selfe, The Hardest Object of the Sight': The Problem of Personal Identity in John Donne's Poetry," in *Poetry and Epistemology: Turning Points in the History of Poetic Knowledge,* ed. and intro. Roland Hagenbüchle and Laura Skandera, 57–71. Papers from the International Poetry Symposium Eichstatt, 1983. Eichstätter Beiträge, 20; Abteilung Sprache und Literatur, 6. Regensburg: Friedrich Pustet.

Argues that Donne "used his supreme intellectual and poetic faculties in a never-ending process of self-representation and self-exploration," and that "his poems provide ample evidence for the theory that because of its subjectivity, i.e. its self-referential nature, the lyric mode of expression is better suited for treating the concerns and problems of the self than the dramatic genre." Maintains that "[t]he self-consciousness, begun in Renaissance poetry, which developed the use of the poem as an instrument of discovering and ascertaining knowledge about the self, reaches an extreme in Donne's transcending the general Renaissance desire for self-knowledge" (58). Analyzes *WomCon, LovInf, Triple, Blos, SunRis, Noct, RWSlumb, HWKiss, RWThird,* and *Har* to illustrate how "Donne's poems can be understood as attempts to arrest experience and penetrate it intellectually, the emphasis falling not on knowledge, but on the process of gaining knowledge," and to show that "the poems mirror heuristic processes and

constitute epistemological structures"
(59). Concludes that Donne's poetry
"marks a distinct rise in the level of
self-awareness and goes beyond anything to be found in earlier English
poetry," and that its epistemological
importance "chiefly resides in the rad-
icality with which the self is . . . made
the object of analysis and definition
and in the ever-present alertness to
the multiplicity of experience and personality" (69).

705. Nardo, Anna K. "John Donne at Play
in Between," in *The Eagle and the Dove:
Reassessing John Donne,* ed. Claude J.
Summers and Ted-Larry Pebworth,
157–65. Essays in Seventeenth-Century
Literature, 1. Columbia: University of
Missouri Press. Reprinted in *The Ludic
Self in Seventeenth-Century English
Literature,* (Albany, N.Y.: State University of New York Press, 1991), 49–77.
Observes that "[e]ven in such a self-
consciously witty age as the seventeenth century, Donne's poetry and
prose stand out as exceptionally playful." Argues that Donne plays "because play is always in-between—the
precise location his poetic speakers
and his preaching persona need to occupy" (157). Pointing out that Donne's
poetry, both secular and sacred, is
characterized by a contradictory fear
of both union with and separation from
the loved one, shows how play was
one way he mediated this conflict.
Claims that "[i]n order to create unity
despite apparent disunity, he plays
with witty images" (160), and that,
"[b]y placing his poems in the paradoxical play frame (by its nature in-
between), Donne can have union and
distance simultaneously" (161). Discusses also the role of play in Donne's
sermons and shows how he "came to
preach about life in between because
this was man's lot—caught between
contradictory fears of separation and
engulfment, between flesh and spirit,

between the kingdom already but not
yet come" (161–62). Maintains that
in Donne's sermons "play is as complex as his poetic play; it both brings
the congregation to the Word and distances them by his own witty words"
(164) and opens "their minds to wonder, preparing them for the grace of
faith that only God could give" (165).

706. Nuñez Roldan, Francisco, ed. and
trans. *El siglo de oro de la lírica inglesa.*
La colección Visor de poesía, 208. Edición bilingüe. Madrid: Visor. 230p.
The introduction (9–18) to this bilingual anthology surveys the development of English poetry from Wyatt
and Surrey to Milton and Marvell, citing Donne and Marvell as the most
conspicuous examples of metaphysical poetry in England. Contains a biographical note on Donne (22) and
Spanish translations (with English
texts on the opposite pages) of *GoodM,
WomCon, LovUsury, Flea, Appar,
SunRis, Triple, Anniv, Canon,
HSDeath,* and *Father,* with no notes
or commentary.

707. O'Connell, Patrick F. "'La Corona':
Donne's Ars Poetica Sacra," in *The Eagle
and the Dove: Reassessing John Donne,*
ed. Claude J. Summers and Ted-Larry
Pebworth, 119–30. Essays in Seventeenth-
Century Literature, 1. Columbia: University of Missouri Press.
Argues that when *Corona* is considered as "a single unified work" and
"not simply a detached objective presentation of Christian mysteries," it
becomes "the vehicle for a careful
investigation of the meaning of human
activity, and in particular of the vocation of the Christian artist, in the light
of these mysteries" (119). Maintains
that there is a "double consciousness"
at the heart of the meaning of the
sequence: at the beginning, seeing
himself as the "center of reality," "the
speaker's sense of his own identity is

quickly revealed to be inadequate, a projection of his own desires and delusions," but later in the sequence "the speaker progressively recognizes the illusory nature of this self, so that when the poem actually becomes the offering of 'prayer and praise' it is intended to be, the two levels of consciousness have merged." Believes that readers "are able to share both the knowledge of Donne and the experience of the speaker, to undergo the process of transformation and to reflect on the meaning of that process, an opportunity singularly appropriate in a poem whose last line, being also its first, is an invitation to read over again with deepened insight" (121). Demonstrates through a reading of the individual poems the dramatic unfolding of the notion that, "[b]y allowing Christ to assume the rightful and necessary place as the center, indeed the totality of his world, the poet is able to discover the true meaning and purpose of his own creativity." Concludes that *Corona* "provides a paradigm and interpretive key for the entire body of Donne's religious poetry, the principal subject of which is the possibility, and the difficulty, of self-transcendence (that is, prayer) in a world where the self has assumed a degree of independence unknown in previous centuries" (110).

708. **Okuma, Sakae.** *Donne, Emblem, Mannerism: Kichi no Kansatsu* [Donne, Emblem, and Mannerism: The Observation of Wit]. Tokyo: Hauosha. xv, 331p.
Considers Donne's conceits in connection with the popularity of emblems during the age of mannerism. Argues that Donne sought new styles to express his complex feelings and that his poems result from his endeavor to find new expressions. Discusses the influence of emblems on Donne's poems and the background of mannerism.

709. **Pace, Claire.** "'Delineated Lives': Themes and Variations in Seventeenth-Century Poems about Portraits." *W&I* 2: 1–17.
Studies selected seventeenth century English poems about portraits in order to "provide some illuminating insights into the writers' attitudes toward the visual arts, and their changing expectations as regards portraiture" (1). Points out that there are many references to pictures and mirrors in Donne's poetry, commenting briefly on *Damp, Witch, Phrine,* and *ElPict.* Comments briefly also on the Lothian portrait of Donne.

710. **Parker, Michael P.** "Diamond's Dust: Carew, King, and the Legacy of Donne," in *The Eagle and the Dove: Reassessing John Donne,* ed. Claude J. Summers and Ted-Larry Pebworth, 191–200. Essays in Seventeenth-Century Literature, 1. Columbia: University of Missouri Press.
Contrasts the different ways in which Donne's legacy is evaluated in Thomas Carew's "An Elegie upon the death of the Deane of Pauls, Dr. John Donne" and Henry King's "Upon the Death of my ever Desired Friend, Dr. Donne Deane of Paules." Argues that King's poem "appears to be both a response to Carew's poem and a refutation of it" (191). Points out that Carew's elegy "undoubtedly circulated in manuscript for some time previous to publication" (192) and therefore was known to King. Discusses how Carew's "fascination with Donne's achievement led him to explore the ways in which his poetry had transfigured and continues to transfigure English verse," whereas King, "charged with the duty of protecting Donne's memory, was concerned more with the man than with his works." Points out that King apparently believed that "analysis of the poetry would unearth the scandal of the amatory poems, thus undermining the edifying monument

to the saintly Donne that King and Walton labored to erect" (200).

711. Parrish, Paul. "'A Funeral Elegie': Donne's Achievement in Traditional Form." *CP* 19: 55–66.

Discusses how *FunEl* "moves toward the transforming art" of the two longer Anniversary poems "as it moves away from more conventional patterns of the [elegiac] tradition" (57). Maintains that in *FunEl* Donne "does not give his imagination free reign," as he does in the two longer poems, but rather "exercises it, distinctly and effectively, in more limited ways," and thus claims that *FunEl* "is a poem built solidly on a tradition but, more than that, it is a poem that transforms conventional motifs into experiences unique to Donne and to the *Anniversaries*" (57). Shows that, although *FunEl* contains themes and images found in *FirAn* and anticipates those found in *Sec An,* they "are asserted without elaboration and verbal ornamentation" and thus "are more immediately accessible" (60). Argues that, although *FunEl* may have been written earlier, its placement between the two longer poems has "particular value" in that it "allows a pause" between "the heady flights" of the poems on either side of it (66).

712. Pearson, David. "An Unrecorded Book from the Library of John Donne." *BC* 35: 246.

Notes that a copy of Carlo Sigonio's *De antiquo iure civium Romanorum . . . libri duo* (Paris, 1576) with Donne's signature has been found in the Durham Cathedral Library. Indicates that the book was acquired by the library sometime during the last quarter of the seventeenth century, since the library inscription on the title page is in the hand of John Milner, who was librarian at Durham between 1676 and 1705.

713. Pérez Romero, Carmen. "El soneto inglés en los periodos renacentista y bar-

roco," in *Estudios literarios ingleses: Renacimiento y barroco,* ed. Susana Onega, 199–224. Madrid: Cátedra.

Discusses the history and development of the sonnet in England from Wyatt and Surrey to Donne and comments on major characteristics of the sonnet in general. Calls Donne the great poet of the baroque and the principal metaphysical poet of England. Discusses such features of Donne's sonnets as their use of conceits, analogies, wordplay, colloquial language, and argumentative rhetoric and notes Donne's reaction against pastoralism, classical mythology, regular metrics, and Petrarchan excesses. While acknowledging Donne's original and profound contributions to love poetry, focuses on the major features of his religious poems, especially the *Holy Sonnets* and *Corona*. Notes how Donne in his religious poems often expresses his terror of death and feelings of anxiety and guilt.

714. Praga Terente, Inés. "La deuda literaria de los 'cavalier poets'," in *Estudios literarios ingleses: Renacimiento y barroco,* ed. Susana Onega, 363–88. Madrid: Cátedra.

Presents a general introduction to the cavalier poets, pointing out that they were faithful monarchists and primarily disciples and imitators of Ben Jonson. Points out, however, the importance of Donne's influence on their poetry. Maintains, in fact, that it is the confluence of Donne's and Jonson's example that shapes cavalier poetry, as seen, for instance, in Carew's "A Song: Ask No More." Notes Carew's tribute to Donne in his elegy on Donne's death and comments on the influence of Donne on Carew's *A Rapture* as well as Donne's influence on two sonnets by Suckling. Sees Herrick as the poet most indebted to the double inheritance of Donne and Jonson.

715. Pritchard, R. E. "Donne's Angels in the Corners." *N&Q,* n.s. 33: 348–49.

Points out that in Jewish and cabalistic tradition the four angels who stand at the four corners of the earth are Michael, Gabriel, Raphael, and Uriel, a tradition followed during the Renaissance by magicians, such as Heinrich Cornelius Agrippa, who in a table in his *De occulta philosophia* (1553) suggests that the whole cosmos was organized according to the tetrad. In Agrippa's table "the tetragrammaton (God's name in four Hebrew letters) heads a list of the four elements, four humours, four seasons, etc.," as well as the four corners of the earth and the four archangels that rule them. Shows how a "principle of four" (348) operates in *HSRound*—"the principle of the four humours and their planets, that are ruled over by four specific angels, who each brings a particular category to death, and also summons to the general last Judgement" (349).

716. Ray, Robert H. "Unrecorded Seventeenth-Century Allusions to Donne." *N&Q*, n.s. 33: 464–65.

Points out references to Donne in two satiric poems in *Death in a New Dress: Or Sportive Funeral Elegies* (1656) by S. F. and suggests that S. F. was probably influenced by *Coryat*. Notes also that Nicholas Hookes in his *Amanda. A Sacrifice To an Unknown Goddesse* (1653), though not mentioning Donne specifically, shows that he had closely read *Twick*.

717. Revard, Stella P. "Donne and Propertius: Love and Death in London and Rome," in *The Eagle and the Dove: Reassessing John Donne,* ed. Claude J. Summers and Ted-Larry Pebworth, 69–79. Essays in Seventeenth-Century Literature, 1. Columbia: University of Missouri Press.

Argues that Propertius, not Ovid, is the principal model for Donne's lovers in the *Elegies* and in the *Songs and Sonets*. Finds in Propertius the "very prototype of the self-examining lover: neurotic, intelligent, witty but eccentric, learned but difficult in his learning, cold and sensual at the same time, forever defining and redefining his feelings and those of his mistress" (70–71). Observes that Donne's persona, like Propertius's, (1) constantly, and with "almost deliberate contrariness," shifts his attitude toward his mistress and often uses "the backdrop of a real or imagined landscape" to compare or to contrast "his mood of despairing love" (71–72); (2) portrays his anger as despair and threatens "to expose the lady for her perfidy and to pay her back in kind," while, at the same time, expressing "an attitude of calm and amused detachment at woman's infidelity" (72–73); and (3) admits his own infidelities and suggests that "free-ranging desire is natural to both sexes," although this expression of libertinism often seems to be a defense "against his fear of the lady's inconstancy" (73–74). Sees in both Donne and Propertius "a peculiar possessiveness, an obsessive fervor, that marks even the dismissals of love and the denials of the mistress," and maintains that both regard love as "the touchstone for defining everything else, the goal toward which each strains, the transfiguring experience, the absolute in life, and the means of reaching beyond even the grave." Says that "in no classical elegist but Propertius could Donne have found so persistent a preoccupation with the mistress as the sum total of earthly experience" (74). Suggests also that "the vivid and sensual presentation of death and the grave in love poetry" (76), as well as their capacity of "examining the comic dimensions of love beyond the grave" (78), link the two poets. Concludes that Donne, "having first discovered the love poem with Ovid, went on to master its range with Propertius as his ultimate model" (79).

718. Ricks, Christopher, ed. *English Poetry and Prose, 1540–1674*. The New History of Literature, vol. 2. London: Sphere Books. 468p. First American ed., New York: Peter Bedrick Books, 1987. First published, London: Barrie and Jenkins, 1970. Paperback ed., London: Sphere Books, 1970.

Reprints, without revision, three essays on Donne from the first edition: Alicia Ostriker's "The Lyric," A. J. Smith's "The Poetry of John Donne," and John Carey's "III. Seventeenth-Century Prose" (See *Roberts 2*). Places the bibliographies that followed individual chapters in the first edition at the end of the volume and updates them (415–50) and adds a table of dates (451–57). Includes two new essays: Leslie Dunn's "Poetry and Song" (107–19) and J. C. A. Rathmell's "Ben Jonson and the Caroline Poets" (121–36), both of which only mention Donne in passing.

719. Robson, W. W. "The Seventeenth Century," in *A Prologue to English Literature*, 74–103. London: B. T. Batsford. Briefly discusses Donne, both as poet and prose writer, calling him a "strange unforeseeable genius" and an "original." Suggests that Donne was "more imaginative than any other writer of the day" (86) and characterizes him as "a self-centred poet, more interested in his own thought-processes than in the emotions they purport to clarify" (87). Calls *Ecst* a "mystical poem" and regards Donne's religious verse as "the finest devotional poetry in the language" (88). Comments briefly on Donne's life and his critical reputation in the seventeenth century and after.

720. Rollin, Roger B. "'Fantastique Ague': The Holy Sonnets and Religious Melancholy," in *The Eagle and the Dove: Reassessing John Donne*, ed. Claude J. Summers and Ted-Larry Pebworth, 131–46. Essays in Seventeenth-Century Literature, 1. Columbia: University of Missouri Press.

Discusses the *Holy Sonnets* from the viewpoint of seventeenth century and twentieth century psychology as "sick poems in the service of preventive medicine, intended to instruct as well as entertain," and as "public demonstrations of . . . spiritual malaise meant to be exemplary to disease-prone readers." Believes that the sonnets present the reader "with a kind of composite portrait of one suffering from what Renaissance psychology classified as 'religious melancholy' (and what modern psychiatry understands as a form of 'affective disorder'" (131). Suggests that, seen from this perspective, the *Holy Sonnets* "begin to look like not so much a sonnet sequence as a kind of anti-sequence, one whose main ordering principle is disorder, and specifically, mental disorder" (132). Confines the discussion "to a consideration of religious melancholy as a psychological phenomenon and as a controlling *fiction* of the Holy Sonnets" (133). Believes that the *Holy Sonnets* point readers toward the *Devotions*, where they will find "adaptational and defensive strategies" in their struggle against religious melancholy, but that the *Holy Sonnets* are "meant to vex, to be as unsettling in their own modest scale as Shakespeare's portrayal of the melancholy prince." Concludes that whether or not they "prevented or cured an affective disorder" in the intended readers, these religious sonnets "constitute powerful dramatizations of how deeply rooted melancholy is in human nature and in the human condition" (146).

721. Roussel, Roy. "Women and Fleas: The Argument of Seduction," in *The Conversation of the Sexes: Seduction and Equality in Selected Seventeenth and Eighteenth-Century Texts*, 10–36. New York and Oxford: Oxford University Press.

In a study of selected seventeenth and eighteenth century texts that discuss male authors' imaginative attempts to understand female experience, Roussel presents a detailed reading of *Flea* that attempts "to open up the space where the woman acts," thereby making the poem "a conversation between equals" (7). Sees the *Songs and Sonets* as "the record of an endless argument between the man and the woman," in which the male speaker is "continually trying to fix" the woman's position—"to mythologize her as the icon of his own meaning, to dismiss her as the simply fashionable, to trivialize her as the source of a natural but occasional pleasure." Maintains, however, that "the nervous succession of attitudes in the collection suggests the difficulty of this task" (13). Claims that in *Flea* "three elements come into play: the bite of the flea, the discourse of the man, and gesture of the woman" (14). Analyzes each of these elements and stresses that, although silent, the woman in the poem is not passive: her seductive gesture sets up "an ambivalence in the man's experience of his own masculine nature," which creates "in him a certain sense of self-difference" that "demystifies the conventional association of masculine and feminine qualities with male and female gender" (20–21). Says that *Flea* leads to the mutual understanding in poems of mature love, such as *SunRis* and *GoodM,* the latter a poem that defines "the end toward which love should develop, an understanding which finally resolves the argument of lovers" (28).

722. Sakamoto, Yoshiyuki. "*Songs and Sonnets* ni okeru Kyakuin no Hatan — careless in rhyme?" [The Failure of Rhymes in the *Songs and Sonets*] in *Bungaku to Kotoba: Ueno Naozo Sensei Tsuito Ronbunshu* [Literature and Words: Essays in Memory of Professor Naozo Ueno], ed. Toshio Kimura, Hisao Kana-seki, and Isanu Saito, 91–103. Tokyo: Nan'undo.

Examines the failure of rhymes in the stanzaic verses of the *Songs and Sonets.*

723. Serpieri, Alessandro. "Sull'uso del modello comunicazione in John Donne: 'The Funerallo' e 'The Relique',", in *Retorica e immaginario,* 269–300. Le forme del discorso, 44. Parma: Pratiche.

First appeared in *SCr* 9 (1975): 275–308 (see *Roberts 2*) and later in *Letteratura e semiologia in Italia,* ed. G. P. Caprettini and D. Corno (Torino: Rosenberg and Sellier, 1979).

724. Shawcross, John T. "The Arrangement and Order of John Donne's Poems," in *Poems in Their Place: The Intertextuality and Order of Poetic Collections,* ed. Neil Fraistat, 119–163. Chapel Hill: University of North Carolina Press.

Argues that textual criticism is closely allied with literary criticism or interpretation. Describes the various collections of Donne's poems, both in manuscript and in print, and stresses "the importance of generic arrangement and order for our reading of a poem and of a group of poems." Discusses, in some detail, "the reliability of arrangement and order of Donne's poems specifically" (121). In discussing individual groupings of Donne's poems, both reaffirms some past editorial practices and challenges others. Points out that since there is no assurance of "authorial presence" in the ordering of Donne's poems, "except for noting what seem to be relationships of some poems," one must often rely on "the nonauthorial presence of a number of scribes and at least two editors (those of 1633 and 1635)." Maintains that, in spite of some drawbacks, the major advantage of generic arrangement is that "the reader is directed to look at the poem as an example of the form, structure, and characteristics of the genre to which it is assigned, determining what is drawn from the standard and how, if at all, it is altered from the standard, all with a view toward levels of meaning" (146). Includes five appendices listing the order of specific poems according to the manuscripts and early editions.

725. Shawcross, John T. "Poetry, Personal and Impersonal," in *The Eagle and the Dove: Reassessing John Donne,* ed. Claude J. Summers and Ted-Larry Pebworth, 53–66. Essays in Seventeenth-Century Literature, 1. Columbia: University of Missouri Press.

Argues that all literature should be primarily viewed as literature, "not as biographical statement, even when biography has direct influence," and "not as philosophy, even when the work propounds strong ideologies" (53). Gives examples of misreadings of Donne's poems based on false or highly questionable biographical and/or philosophical information, especially *ElAut, Relic, WomCon,* and *Twick.* Discusses other poems that do have important biographical and/or philosophical contexts, such as *ValName, HWNews, HSWhat,* and *Dissol.* Maintains that Donne's readers "should remember the way in which he has interwoven biographical detail into the poems, the way in which they may inform us of biographical—or more usually ideational or psychological—matters, and the way in which they may represent an imaginative and artistic artifact without significantly direct biographical overtones." Insists, however, that "the major factor in evaluation of a piece of literature is the execution of the work itself and the result of that execution (the literary artifact), not what we have learned about the author" (66).

726. Stanwood, P. G., and Heather Ross Asals, eds. *John Donne and the Theology of Language.* Columbia: University of Missouri Press. viii, 376p.

The "General Introduction" (1–10) explains that the purpose of this volume is to present passages from Donne's sermons that show his basic assumptions about the nature and purpose of language and that illuminate, in particular, his "theology of language" (2). Each chapter contains an introduction followed by selected passages from the sermons. Chapter 1, "The Speech of the Trinity" (11–43), is divided into four sections: "the first on God's speech, the second on Christ's language, the third on the eloquence of the Holy Ghost, and the last on the showing forth of the threefold Word by man's song" (11). Chapter 2, "The Word Transcribed into Art" (44–68), comments on how, for Donne, art "expressed as praise and prayer is one measure of our life's sojourn" and how "[t]he life of man finds its speech in art—in the Word of God—at the meeting place where expressive sound has a harmony that is both human and divine." Notes that since Donne "cannot think of the relationship between God and man apart from the Word and the words of human art, his considerations of life and death are permeated with literary metaphors" (45). Discusses Donne's thinking on the origin and range of poetry as well as its limitations and dangers and "its special possibilities" (46). Chapter 3, "Grammar and Theology" (69–95), illustrates "Donne's concern for the study of language in all its particulars" (69), such as his insistence on the indispensability of grammar; the importance of tense, mood, and voice in verb structures; and the centrality of logic. Chapter 4, "Logic and the Son" (96–124), comments on Donne's belief in the necessity of right reason, logic, and common sense in faith, but also his recognition of the limits of reason and logic. Chapter 5, "Voice and Character—The Revelation of Self" (125–37), discusses Donne's concept of redefining human character through Christ's taking on human nature. Chapter 6, "Human Personality and the Faculties of the Soul" (136–78), comments on Donne's thinking about human personality, which is made up of the faculties of memory, understanding, and will, and discusses his views of the human being composed of body, soul, and spirit. This chapter "on human capacity, personality, and limitation, in spite of its often spoken or implied celebration of reason (or rectified nature) and with its confusion of categories, moves to proclaim the mystical joy of seeing God face to face" (140). Chapter 7, "Names and Typology" (179–217), discusses the importance for Donne of names and naming (especially of God) and of typology. Chapter 8, "Image, Idol, Example, and Imitation" (218–62), comments on Donne's attitude toward images and emblems and his warning against any form of idolatry, noting several of Donne's favorite images, such as the circle, the compass, water, wings, feet, armor, crowns, the house and court, and directions of North, South, East, and West. Chapter 9, "Hermeneutics—Interpretation and Revelation" (263–96), discusses Donne's views on the right interpretation of Scripture—literally, allegorically, tropologically, and anagogically—and the dangers of misleading or false use of Scripture. Also considers "the relationships of preaching itself to interpretation and moral behavior, and on the central role of those who listen to the preacher, who in actively hearing, learn themselves how to 'preach,' or be good models to others" (265). Chapter 10, "Genre" (297–344), discusses three major classes of genres: (1) biblical genres (prophecy, parables, epithalamia, epistles, acts, and revelations); (2) liturgical genres (confession, prayers, and psalms); and (3) pedagogical genres (catechisms and sermons). Contains a glossary of words (345–52), list of biblical texts for each chapter (353–69), a selected bibliography (370–74), and an index (375–76). Reviews: Michael Hall in *SR* 95 (1987): lxxiv–lxxvii; Allan Pritchard in *UTQ* 57 (1987): 111–12; John E. Skillen in *CSR* 18 (1988): 81–86; Baird Tipton in *Church History* 57 (1988): 371–72; Winfried Schleiner in *MP* 86 (1989): 296–97.

727. **Stein, Arnold.** *The House of Death: Messages from the English Renaissance.* Baltimore: Johns Hopkins University Press. xiii, 300p.

Explores the variety and sameness of sixteenth and seventeenth century poets who wrote about death, using Donne as a central example. Divides the study into four main parts: (1) introductory essays on background, (2) poems anticipating the poet's own death, (3) poems responding to the death of someone else, and (4) problems involving the expression of thoughts, feelings, and beliefs about death, examining particularly images of sleep, time, and love as they relate to death. "Donne's Pictures of the Good Death" (49–66) discusses Donne's presentation of the art of dying well and claims that "Donne's examples are public and optimistic, mindful of the established laws concerning penitence and alert to the practical wisdom of disciplining listeners and readers in the art of mortification, but turned finally and emphatically toward the goals of justified consolation and hope" (49). Comments on the sermon on the death of Magdalen Herbert, his funeral sermon for Sir William Cokayne, and "Death's Duell" as examples of good dying. "Imagined Dyings: John Donne" (94–110) discusses Donne's imaginative treatment of death and dying, in which "the actor-author-spectator performs" (94), pointing out the theatricality of some of Donne's *Holy Sonnets* that concern death, "the passionate and insistent language and devout reverence for God's power and goodness" (95) in *Goodf,* the violence of the metaphors in *HSBatter,* the imagery and voice in *Christ,* and the artistic excellence of *Sickness,* calling it a "master poem" (103). "The Death of a Loved One: Personal and Public Expressions" (137–59) comments on Donne's response to the death of Ann More, especially in *HSShe;* "Episodes in the Progress of Death" (160–78) discusses Donne's presentation of death in *HSDeath* and *SecAn.* Briefly comments also on Donne's reflections on the death of his daughter, Lucy, and compares and contrasts his views on death and dying with those of Raleigh and Jonson.

728. Stewart, Stanley. *George Herbert.* Twayne's English Author Series, 428, ed. Arthur Kinney. Boston: Twayne Publishers. [xvii], 182p.

Mentions Donne's relationship to the Herbert family and throughout compares and contrasts Donne and Herbert as devotional poets. Chapter 5, "The School of George Herbert" (118–56), examines the relationship between Herbert's and Donne's poetry, noting, for the most part, how the two poets differ as religious poets. Rejects, therefore, the notion that Herbert belonged to a "School of Donne," noting that "Herbert's almost polemical efforts to distinguish his aims and methods from those of contemporary love-poets express, in fact, a sentiment at the farthest pole from Donne's typical employment of religious figures— sainthood, relics, martyrology—in the service of profane love" (128). Argues for a "School of Herbert," pointing out that a number of poets, such as Crashaw, Christopher Harvey, Ralph Knevet, Thomas Washbourne, Mildmay Fane, Henry Colman, Vaughan, Samuel Speed, and Traherne, imitated or paraphrased Herbert's poetry, adopted his attitudes toward love poetry, and regarded him as a model

both as a person and as a poet. Stewart maintains that, by proposing a "School of Herbert," he does not seek "to diminish the importance of Donne, but only to acknowledge that we appreciate him and the Donneans (Lord Herbert, Cleveland, Cowley, Sherburne, Marvell, and in certain moods, Lovelace) precisely because they practiced so well the very poetic techniques from which Herbert and his followers earnestly sought to separate themselves" (155).

729. Stouck, Mary-Ann. "Structure in Ethel Wilson's *The Innocent Traveller." CanL* 109: 17–31.

Notes the use of a quotation from Meditation 18 of *Devotions* in Wilson's novel, *The Innocent Traveller* (Macmillan, 1949).

730. Strengholt, L. "Een onbekende druk van Huygens' oudste vertalingen naar Donne." *TNTL* 102: 187–206. Reprinted in *Een lezer aan het woord: Studies van L. Strengholt over zeventiende-eeuwse Nederlandse letterkunde,* ed. J. A. M. Th. Leerintveld, T. L. ter Meer, and A. van Strien (Amsterdam: Stichting Neerlandistiek; Münster: Nodus, 1998), 147–58.

Announces the discovery of the earliest known printed versions of the first four translations of Donne's poetry made by Constantijn Huygens in August 1630 and surviving in Huygens's holograph draft. Shows that the two copies of the newly discovered imprint are clearly unauthorized, bound together (differently in each case) as they are with a volume of poems by Jacobus Westerbaen entitled *Gedichten* (Leyden, 1644) and printed by Justus Livius. Demonstrates that their manifest textual corruption arises from a mixture of carelessness and incomprehension. Points out that Huygens himself did not publish these translations (of *SunRis,* parts of *ElAnag* and *ElServe,* and *ValMourn*) until 1658 and definitively in 1672.

Observes that the 1644 Westerbaen imprint furnishes the first three translations with different titles from those in Huygens's manuscript, although it does preserve the order in which Huygens dated them (8, 14, 21 [twice] August 1630 NS). Notes that the names of both Donne and Huygens are absent from the Westerbaen imprint.

731. Summers, Claude J., and Ted-Larry Pebworth, eds. *The Eagle and the Dove: Reassessing John Donne.* Essays in Seventeenth-Century Literature, 1. Columbia: University of Missouri Press. xv, 220p.

A collection of 15 original essays that "explore the critical assumptions on which Donne's reputation rests, reevaluate his most celebrated work, and draw attention to a number of relatively neglected areas of his canon, such as the epithalamia and the epigrams" (jacket). Each of the essays has been separately entered in this bibliography. The introduction (xi–xv) states that, although an "impulse toward completeness" combined with a "dichotomous way of thinking" are the hallmarks of Donne's work, there is in his poetry "an uneasy resolution" that "is related to Donne's habitual sense of conflict, which accounts for much of the poetry's power and tension" (xi). Maintains that "Donne's contradictoriness is among the ways in which he is a difficult poet and a fascinating one" and stresses that "Donne creates restless poems of remarkable suggestiveness and power, fashioning from his dichotomous vision a highly individualized style of contradictoriness" (xii). Comments briefly on the contents of the individual essays and maintains that, "despite their diversity in subject matter and approach, they intersect and reinforce each other in significant ways" and "illustrate the seventeenth-century poet's continuing vitality" (xv). Contains notes on the contribu-

tors (215–16) and an index of works cited (217–20). Reviews: Martin Elsky in *RenQ* 41 (1988): 520–23; John E. Skillen in *CSR* 18 (1988): 81–86; A. J. Smith in *TLS* 4422 (1988): 543–45; Gerald Hammond in *MLR* 84 (1989): 125.

732. Takahashi, Shohei. "Loyola no 'Muchi' to Machiavelli: J. Donne no *Ignatius His Conclave*" [Loyola's "Ignorance" and Machiavelli: Two Views of Machiavelli in John Donne's *Ignatius His Conclave*]. *Shiron* (Tohoku University) 25: 1–22.

Shows how Donne achieves his aim of exposing Jesuitical folly by two views of Machiavelli in *Ignatius*.

733. Tanner, John S. "'Here is My Space': The Private Mode in Donne's Poetry and Shakespeare's *Antony and Cleopatra*." *ISJR* 60: 417–30.

Compares Donne's love poetry and Shakespeare's *Antony and Cleopatra*, not in order to argue for influence either way, but rather "to heighten critical appreciation of both poets by situating *Antony and Cleopatra* in Donne's line of wit generally, and more specifically by measuring the similarities and differences between Shakespeare's Antony and speakers in Donne's erotic poetry" (417). Argues that the comparison shows that Shakespeare "was capable of exploiting prominent features of the metaphysical style while refashioning them into a whole at once critical of and even more paradoxical than Donne's." Claims that "[i]n comparison to Shakespeare's play, Donne's verse appears far less truly 'dramatic' than it is often thought to be" and that, "[i]n comparison to Donne's poetry, Shakespeare's play seems much more 'metaphysical' than has ever been acknowledged, for the play polarizes and surmounts the world in a manner similar to that evident in Donne's love poetry— that is, in a manner characterized by hyperbole, paradox, and the private mode." Holds, however, that "where Donne indulges his lovers' hyperbolic claims that they constitute an autonomous world, Shakespeare subjects his lovers' lyric outbursts to the constraints of an informing dramatic context" (418). Suggests that the comparison "discloses the limitation of Donne's dramatic sensibility," claiming that "his is an egoistic theatre, one in which the author's personae regularly outmaneuver any implied respondent, one in which the superiority and self-sufficiency of love's private sphere is rarely seriously challenged, as it is in *Antony and Cleopatra*" (426). Maintains that "mutual knowledge between Shakespeare and Donne of each other's work remains only a plausible supposition" (419).

734. Taylor, Donald S. "Johnson and the Metaphysicals: The Analytic Efficacy of Hostile Presuppositions." *ECLife* 10, no. 3: 186–202.

Discusses Dr. Johnson's method in defining metaphysical style and sensibility and argues that "the success of his method, especially in view of his hostile presuppositions, stems from the nature of thought itself and, consequently, of its transmissibility across time." Proposes "certain conclusions about sensibility and style studies that seem to arise naturally from these considerations" (186). Notes that Johnson's definition of metaphysical style and sensibility is supported by 16 citations from Donne, as opposed to 27 from Cowley, and comments on Johnson's view that Donne is a wit, not a poet.

735. Threadgold, Terry. "Subjectivity, Ideology and the Feminine in John Donne's Poetry," in *Semiotics-Ideology-Language*, ed. Terry Threadgold, E. A. Grosz, Gunther Kress, and M. A. K. Halliday, 297–325. Sydney Studies in Society and Culture, no. 3, Sydney: Pathfinder Press.

Based on the idea of language as "social semiotic," that is, "seeing language as actively symbolising the social system" and "its patterns of variation representing metaphorically the variation that characterises human cultures" (297), interprets "the lexico-grammatical structure of Donne's poetic discourse in terms of the higher order social semiotic of discursive formations" and argues that "Donne's discourse is ideologically transitional, encoding through presence and absence the changing epistemology of language, subjectivity and femininity which accompanied the emergence of post-Renaissance social formation" (298). Presents a "detailed systemic-functional analysis" of *ElNat* and *Leg* to show that Donne's poems can be located "at the founding moment of the bourgeois subject, but as transitional between an older discourse and the discourse of transparency which elides and positions in the elision the dominant subject of classical realism" (301).

736. Van Emden, Joan. *The Metaphysical Poets*. Macmillan Master Guides. Houndmills: Macmillan Education. viii, 96p.

Contains an introduction to metaphysical poetry (1–7); brief biographical sketches of Donne, Herbert, Vaughan, and Marvell, and comments on some major trends in seventeenth century literature (8–16); a discussion of themes in metaphysical poetry and a survey of the historical and religious background of the period (17–32); summaries and commentaries on individual poems by the four poets (33–88); and comments on the critical reception of the metaphysical poets (89–91), followed by study questions (92) and suggested further readings (93–94). Summarizes and comments on the following poems by Donne: *GoodM, SunRis, SSweet, Twick, Noct, ValMourn, Ecst, Fun, HSDue, HSDeath, HSBatter, Sickness,* and *Father* (33–56).

737. Van Hook, J. W. "'Concupiscence of Witt': The Metaphysical Conceit in Baroque Poetics." *MP* 84: 24–38.

Explores Continental baroque theory about the conceit, arguing that baroque poetics "potentially offers contemporary insights into both the metaphysical conceit and the world view it derives from and expresses" (24). Examines, in particular, the work of the Italian Renaissance theorists Emanuele Tesauro, Matteo Peregini, and Sforza Pallavicino. Points out that, after the *Songs and Sonets,* metaphors in Donne's poetry grow increasingly "less superficial," and states that "the most compelling examples of Donne's baroque metaphors come, not surprisingly, from the sermons, where their slender connections really do make a kind of imaginatively satisfying truth shine through their bold paradox" (30). Shows how the conceit differs from metaphor and is a "complex rhetorical structure" that "holds out the promise of new ways of knowing about experience," citing the witty enthymeme in *GoodM* (ll. 19–21) as an example of "the full baroque form" (35). Maintains that the aim of poets who employ the baroque conceit is "to stretch the epistemological capacities of the reader by exercising the mental faculties in unfamiliar ways" and to drive his mind "toward a new mode of awareness and vision" (38). Compares and contrasts Donne's use of metaphor and conceit with that of Herbert and Marvell.

738. Walker, Julia M. "The Visual Paradigm of 'The good-morrow': Donne's Cosmographical Glasse." *RES* 37: 61–65.

Suggests that the source for the extended image in *GoodM* (ll. 15–18) is likely the single-projection cordiform map found in William Cunningham's *The cosmographical glasse, conteinying the pleasant principles of cosmograhie, geographie, hydrographie, or navigation* (1599). Explains how the "complex elements" of Donne's "unusual and original image" become "reconciled and unified" (64) when we understand Cunningham's "double heart" map as the source.

739. Waller, Gary. *English Poetry of the Sixteenth Century.* Longman Literature in English Series, ed. David Carroll and Michael Wheeler. London: Longman. [xv], 315p.

Chapter 3, "Erected Wit and Infected Will: Cultural Contradiction in the Lyric" (72–107), identifies Donne as a Protestant poet, who, like Fulke Greville and Spenser, writes out "his contradictions and anguish into his poetry, at once fascinated by words and aware of their untrustworthiness and suspicious of their promiscuous materiality" (99). Sees Donne's obsessive concern with time, "marked by the transience of human life, the inevitability of death, the transcendent eternity of God and His constant guiding of time towards His mysterious ends" (100), and his concern with the self that is "obsessed with its own state of salvation" (101) as hallmarks of Donne's Protestantism. Chapter 7, "The Poetry of Shakespeare and the Early Donne" (215–56), discusses Donne's twentieth century reputation and sees him as "an interesting case— not only because his poetry has been used to define the transition to the next century," but also because "his career articulates so compellingly the peculiar pressures" that poetry underwent in the late sixteenth century (238). Examines Donne's Petrarchism; the variety of moods, voices, and dramatic posturings in his early poetry; and his articulation of "the characteristically anxious, over-stimulated, dislocated urban sensibility" (240) and of the dilemma of the culturally "alienated intellectual" (241). Discusses the *Satyres* as reflecting "some of the age's most crucial cultural contradictions" (242), noting "their intensity of dramatization" and their presentation of "the underlying fragility and waywardness of the self in a powerful public world" (245), and comments on the *Songs and Sonets* as "not simply love poems" but poems preoccupied with "time, mutability, and change" (247). Claims that they "make up the most powerful articulation of dislocation and self-contradiction" (249) as well as "ideological contradiction" (250) in the period, and suggests that "what we might call their glorious failure to hold together warring elements is what makes them so suggestive" (252). Concludes that, "[d]espite our century's romanticizing of him Donne was a court poet, whose self and texts alike speak of the vast power of the institutions he inhabited and which (in a real sense) inhabited him" (254).

740. **Warnke, Frank J.** "Amorous Agon, Erotic Flyting: Some Play-Motifs in the Literature of Love," in *Auctor Ludens: Essays on Play in Literature,* ed. Gerald Guinness and Andrew Hurley, 99–112. Philadelphia: John Benjamins.

In a discussion of playfully aggressive erotic flyting or the comic amorous agon in love literature from Petrarch to George Bernard Shaw, cites Donne's subtle use of the military metaphor in *Ecst* (ll. 13–16), calling the poem "his most profound exploration of the metaphysics of love" (102), and again in *ElBed* (ll. 1–8), a poem characterized by its "high-spirited bawdiness" (103).

741. **Wellek, René.** *A History of Modern Criticism, 1750–1950.* Vol. 5, *English Criticism, 1900–1950.* New Haven, Conn.: Yale University Press. xxiv, 343p.

This survey of English literary criticism from 1900 to 1950 comments briefly on the evaluation of Donne by such major English critics as Arthur

Symons, Oliver Elton, Herbert Grierson, Lytton Strachey, Virginia Woolf, Desmond MacCarthy, Ezra Pound, I. A. Richards, F. R. Leavis, William Empson, and especially T. S. Eliot, calling him "the herald of Donne's [modern] fame" (207) but showing how later on his enthusiasm waned.

742. **Wellek, René.** *A History of Modern Criticism, 1750–1950.* Vol. 6, *American Criticism, 1900–1950.* New Haven, Conn.: Yale University Press. viii, 345p.

This survey of American literary criticism from 1900 to 1950 comments briefly on the evaluation of Donne by such major American critics as Cleanth Brooks, Allen Tate, R. P. Blackmur, Kenneth Burke, and Yvor Winters.

743. **Wheatley, Carmen.** "Ambitious Shadowes: A New Portrait of John Donne?" *The Literary Review* (London) (December): 45–47.

Suggests that the eight known portraits of Donne are "all pure works of fiction, an extravagant parade of disguises, none of them definitive" (46). Notes that, on the average, Donne had his portrait painted once each decade, except for the period 1596–1616, and speculates that two portraits, dated c. 1610 and executed by William Larkin, now in the Mellon Collection at the Yale Center for British Art, are portraits of Donne and Sir Robert Drury. Further speculates that perhaps, when Donne left for the Continent in 1611 with Drury, he may have given this portrait to his distressed wife along with *ElPict* (47).

744. **Wymer, Rowland.** *Suicide and Despair in the Jacobean Drama.* New York: St. Martin's Press. xiii, 193p.

Discusses Donne's attitude towards suicide, martyrdom, and despair, and maintains that "the combined effect" of *Biathanatos* and *Pseudo-Martyr* "is to challenge the way the distinction between suicide and martyrdom was often made" (5). Argues that *Biatha-natos,* contrary to those who see it as "a sustained and witty formal paradox, a self-destroying argument about self-destruction," presents, in fact, a "co-herent and consistent case against any absolute prohibition on suicide, not by resorting to pure relativism, but, on the contrary, by utilising traditional principles of Christian casuistry" (17). Explains Donne's "intentionalist posi-tion" and points out how he "avoids making any use of classical arguments in favour of suicide" but rather pro-ceeds "entirely by means of the pre-mises and methods of Christian moral philosophy" (18). Points out that for Donne "suicide did not automatically signify religious despair" (21).

745. **Young, Bruce W.** "Thomas Hobbes versus the Poets: Form, Expression, and Metaphor in Early Seventeenth-Century Poetry." *Encyclia* 63: 151–62.

Discusses how Hobbes's literary crit-icism was "not simply a signpost pointing toward a new age of poetry" but was also "a reaction against much of the poetry of the early seventeenth century," especially the "improprieties and excesses in form, the expression, and the metaphors and imagery" used by such poets as Donne, Herbert, and Crashaw (152). Notes that Hobbes found objectionable Donne's use of unusual and complex stanzaic forms; irregular meter and rhythm; obscure, indecorous, and scientific language; compression of and double meanings of words; puns; novel, vulgar, or shocking images and metaphors; and subtlety and toughness of thought. Cites *Flea,* as well as a number of other poems, as examples of what Hobbes found most offensive in Donne's poetry. Concludes that, al-though Hobbes's literary criticism is "at times wonderfully illuminating," it is also "often shortsighted when applied to poets of the stature of Her-bert and Donne" (162).

746. **Zemplényi, Ferenc.** "Orthodoxy and Irony: Donne's Holy Sonnet No. 7 (4): At the Round Earth's Imagin'd Corners, Blow. . . ." *SEA* 6: 155–70.

Argues that although the theology in *HSRound* is "absolutely orthodox" from both the Catholic and Anglican viewpoints, "the poem's whole strat-egy is ironic." Maintains that "[i]rony plays a great part both in the begin-ning and in the ending, giving, so to speak, an ironic frame to the work," and shows how "[t]he irony is partly (but not completely) directed against poetic tradition (in the ending)" (158). Surveys a number of European devo-tional poems on the problem of sin, redemption, and salvation to illustrate that both Catholic and Protestant poets from Portugal to Hungary treated the subject with "standard formulas and well-defined topoi" (163), whereas Donne is unconventional in his son-net, in particular by expressing doubt concerning his personal salvation. Believes that the survey "puts into even sharper focus the strong origi-nality and irony of Donne's poem" and emphasizes how it "is directed against poetic tradition." Finds only Constantijn Huygens's *Goede Vrijdah* "somewhat comparable" (168). Calls Donne's sonnet "a solitary triumph of Mannerist poetry" (169).

747. **Zuber, Roger.** "Éloge du dialogue des morts: John Donne and le pamphlet gal-lican," in *La Satire au temps de la Renaissance,* ed. M. T. Jones-Davies, 127–38. Université de Paris-Sorbonne, Institut de Recherches sur les Civilisa-tions de l'Occident Moderne. Centre de Recherches sur la Renaissance. Paris: Touzot.

Comments on the enthusiastic recep-tion of Donne's *Conclave Ignati* among French Gallican lawyers in Paris soon after its publication, pointing out that they apparently found many sim-ilarities between Donne's prose work and the famous anonymous sixteenth century French Protestant work, *Satyre ménippée,* as well as Etienne Pasquier's *Le Catéchisme des jesuites* (1602). Suggests that perhaps Donne was familiar with Pasquier's anti-Jesuit work or at least consulted the same sources that inform Pasquier's satire, especially the Roman satirist Pasquino, and cites similarities in style, satirical technique, and theme. Points out, however, differences between the works of Donne and Pasquier, noting, for instance, that Pasquier, as a Catholic, was not anti-papal but only anti-Jesuit, and that Donne's satirical dialogue with the dead, heavily indebted to Lucian, is more gay and emotional.

1987

748. Aizawa, Yoshihisa. "John Donne no 'Shunen Tsuitoshi' Ko (8)" [A Study of John Donne's *Anniversaries* (8)]. *Jinbungakka Ronshu* [Bulletin of the Faculty of Humanities, Ibaraki University] 20: 229–61.

Part 8 of an eight-part series of articles. Analyzes the structure and meaning of the *Anniversaries* as occasional poetry, as poems related to the "epitaphium recens" and the "epitaphium anniversarium" traditions, as meditative poetry, and as epideictic poetry. Discusses the mutual relationships among *FirAn, FunEl,* and *SecAn.* Concludes that Elizabeth Drury's death gave Donne an occasion to vent his pent-up feelings and to confirm his way of living as well as his understanding of the meaning of life.

749. Bachrach, A. G. H. "Engeland en Huygens in zijn levensavond," in *Veelzijdigheid als levensvorm: Facetten van Constantijn Huygens' leven en werk. Een bundel studies ter gelegenheidvan zijn driehonderste sterfdag,* ed. A. Th. van Deursen, E. K. Grootes, and P. E. L. Verkuyl, 65–78. Deventer Studies, 2. Deventer: Sub Rosa.

Traces Huygens's English contacts from his last visit to London between November 1670 and October 1671 until his death in 1687. Mentions Huygens's purchase of a number of books in London on that visit (described in a letter to Sébastian Chièze on 10 December 1670) and points out that, when he died, Huygens appears to have owned over four hundred English books or books printed in England, including several editions of Donne's poems. Notes that Huygens describes his translation of *Ecst* as a "paraphrastikòmteron," and that in his dedicatory poem to Maria Tesselschade, Huygens calls his translations of Donne "shadows" that differ from their original as night does from day.

750. Bachrach, A. G. H. "*Luna Mendax:* Some Reflections on Moon-Voyages in Early Seventeenth-Century England," in *Between Dream and Nature: Essays on Utopia and Dystopia,* ed. Dominic Baker-Smith and C. C. Barfoot, 70–90. DQR Studies in Literature 2, ed. F. G. A. M. Aarts, J. Bakker, C. C. Barfoot, M. Buning, G. Janssens, W. J. Meys. Amsterdam: Rodopi.

Comments very briefly on Donne's interest in astronomy, noting, for instance, that in *Ignatius* his acquaintance with Galileo's *Sidereus Nuntius* and Kepler's *Somnium* is evident. Says that "[n]o English poet showed more direct response to the new astronomy than John Donne," noting, in particular, his interest in "the notion of a plurality of worlds." Observes that in his later years "Donne's interest in astronomy seems to have declined" (74).

751. Barnstone, Willis. "John Donne." *SR* 95: 553–54.

An original poem addressed to Donne that uses allusions to several of his poems.

752. Beal, Peter. "More Donne Manuscripts." *JDJ* 6: 213–18.

Lists manuscript sources relating to Donne's works that have come to light since the publication of Beal's *Index of English Literary Manuscripts,* vol. 1 (1980), including newly discovered main manuscripts as well as newly found manuscript copies of individual poems, new locations of previously listed manuscripts, and corrigenda. Notes that "[o]ne's conviction becomes only more confirmed that Donne was the most popular English poet of the first half of the seventeenth century" (218).

753. Beck, Joyce Short. "John Donne and William Dunbar: Poet-Satirists of the British Court." *MedPers* 2: 25–37.

While not minimizing the classical and patristic influences on Donne as a satirist, comments on the influence of the satiric medieval English and Scottish poetic and homiletic traditions on his *Satyres* and verse epistles. Compares Donne to William Dunbar, Alexander Barclay, John Skelton, and William Langland as a satirist and to Sir Thomas Wyatt as a writer of verse epistles. Relates Donne's *HWKiss* and Wyatt's "Myne owne John Poynz" to the medieval tradition of the "scholastic and satirical *sermo*" (32). Discusses how Donne follows Wyatt "in writing Scots-English verse letters which synthesize the native British satiric-prophetic tradition with the classical and medieval epistolary style" (36–37).

754. Bernard-Cheyre, Catherine. "Les Métaphores de l'amoureux dans la poésie pétrarquiste anglaise du XVIᵉ siècle, ou les jeux du miroir," in *Actes du Congrés d'Amiens, 1982,* ed. Société des Anglicistes de l'Enseignement Supérieur, 55–63. Paris: Didier.

Traces the elaborate, often playful, uses of the mirror and mirror imagery in English Renaissance love poetry from the troubadours of Provence and especially Petrarch to the poets of late sixteenth century England. Briefly comments on the uses of mirror images, metaphors, and conceits as well as other instances of optical illusions in Donne's poetry, noting, in particular, the changes he brought about in the tradition.

755. Bloom, Clive. "The Grammar of Generation and the Mark of Self-Making: A Short Analysis of John Donne, Shakespeare, and Emily Dickinson," in *The "Occult" Experience and the New Criticism: Daemonism, Sexuality and the Hidden in Literature,* 1–11. Sussex: Harvester Press; Totowa, N.J.: Barnes and Noble.

Discusses the use of the comma in *Flea* and argues that "[t]his grammatical mark, which accomplishes breakage and union, which splits yet unites, which gives significance and relationship is represented visually rather than verbally in the space occupied by the 'comma.'" Maintains that "[f]orm itself unites principles of masculinity and femininity beyond the range of its contents" (2) and that the comma "recognizes difference and reconciles difference acting without and beyond speech" (2–3).

756. Butler, Martin. "The Connection Between Donne, Clarendon, and Ford." *N&Q,* n.s. 34: 309–10.

Discusses the possible connections between George Donne, the poet's second son, and John Ford and his circle at the Middle Temple, in particular, Edward Hyde, later Earl of Clarendon, who contributed an elegy to the 1633 edition of Donne's poems. Also identifies "Sir Geo. Crymes," who, along with George Donne, contributed commendatory verses to Ford's *Perkin Warbeck,* as Sir George Grymes, a cousin of the Donne family, who made a legal complaint against George Donne in 1645 for cheating at cards.

757. Carlson, Norman E. "The Drama of Donne's 'The Indifferent.'" *SCRev* 4, no. 2: 65–69.

Argues that a close critical look at *Ind* "results not in answers, but in questions that are as lacking in persuasive answers as those raised about other works [for example, *Ecst*] that have most often exercised Donne scholar-critics." Examines the "highly unusual structure" (66) of the poem, the complex relationship between the persona of the first two stanzas and the speaker of the third, and the problem of audience, finding unsatisfactory the notion that the poem is simply a conventional argument for promiscuity. Suggests that another way of reading the poem is to assume that the lady listening to the poem "insists on being true not to the speaker, but to some other man, and that the speaker's purpose is to persuade her to direct her attention and favors towards him, at least temporarily"; and therefore, "he suggests, through the speech attributed to Venus, that in being faithful *she* is a member of a group so small . . . that they *must* be in the wrong" (68).

758. Chambers, A. B. "'Goodfriday, 1613. Riding Westward': Looking Back." *JDJ* 6: 185–201.

Maintains that "one of Donne's rhetorical strategies" in *Goodf* is "significant silence," noting that, unlike the traditional handling of Christ's Passion, in Donne's poem "there are few objects (Christ, the cross, the sun, the mother) which *might* be seen if one were only facing the right way." Points out that in his poem Donne stresses "that which is *not* seen" and emphasizes "not *seeing*" (188). Maintains that the speaker "begins by turning away the eyes of his body and then fastidiously tries to avert the eyes of his mind" and thus "never notices the existence of that richness of detail so compelling to other viewers." Calls *Goodf* "a

heavily truncated Passion Sermon" that is "preached unwillingly to the equally reluctant audience of the self" (189). Observes that, at last, Donne's speaker "perceives that his memory . . . is looking east" and "that realization immediately leads to the further awareness that Christ has been looking west toward him" (194). Notes that the poem "remains problematic" and says that it "is complete but nonetheless is not finished," for "the tense of the last line establishes future faith without claiming present certainty" (199). Suggests parallels between Donne's poem and sermons preached by Lancelot Andrewes, especially a sermon preached on Good-friday 1597, but maintains that because of their shared heritage, Andrewes's sermon "can gloss the poem without being a source for it" (192).

759. Corthell, Ronald J. "'Coscus onely breeds my just offence': A Note on Donne's 'Satire II' and the Inns of Court." *JDJ* 6: 25–31.

Maintains that *Sat2* reflects the social conflict at the Inns of Court during Donne's time there between the serious law students, like Coscus in the poem, and "the students of civility," like Donne the satirist, who "were especially anxious to cultivate courtly postures and activities that would set them apart from the lawyers and law students." Maintains that in *Sat2* Donne is defining himself and his friends in "opposition to a professional group" that he "regarded as a threat to himself and to the traditional order of society" (25). Sees the social conflict, then, as "a conflict between two systems of advancement: professionals like Coscus used the legal system, while the amateur gentlemen [like Donne] sought connections with the Court." Shows how Donne in the satire "works to gain the rhetorical upper hand over Coscus" by "tropes of courtesy" and ironic self-deprecation, thereby "privileging amateurism and recreation over professionalism and industry" (26). Sees *Sat2* as recording "an early phase" of Donne's "strained relation to the law," in which as "the prodigal law student," he "uses Coscus to focus his anxieties about participation in a changing society" (29). Concludes that *Sat2* is "a purely *symbolic* act in its evocation of Christian humanist ideals that contradict the social reality" and "in its strategy of neutralizing the contradictions by representing the satirist's self-interest as public interest" (30).

760. Dees, Jerome S. "Logic and Paradox in the Structure of Donne's Sermons." *SCRev* 4, no. 2: 78–92.

Disagrees with those critics who devalue reason and logic in Donne's sermons and looks at several examples "in which the logic of Donne's announced structure gives way in the course of the development of the sermon to a different logic, usually implicit in the Biblical text, so that the sermon is obeying simultaneously two separate logical principles, one cumulative and processive, the other disjunctive or bifurcative." Suggests that "the emotional and theological power of these sermons largely depends upon the tensions between the two logics, tensions which derive not just from Donne's interest in logic and paradox, but from something paradoxical in the very nature of his calling to be a preacher of the Word." Believes that "the fusion in Donne's sermons of recognizably discrete logical structures" results from "the peculiar intensity with which he registers a paradox inherent in the Protestant conception of the ordinances of preaching," principally that "the preacher is both absolutely necessary for man's salvation and yet utterly useless as a causally effective agent in it" (79).

Points out how Donne's view of paradox "impels him in sermon after sermon to divergent and apparently contradictory structures of thought that seem determined to expose those paradoxes inherent both in his faith and in the position he occupies vis-à-vis those whose souls' health he commands" (80).

761. Dickson, Donald R. "The Complexities of Biblical Typology in the Seventeenth Century." *Ren&R*, n.s. 11: 253–72.

Argues that an examination of seventeenth century Protestant guides to the spiritual life reveals that Protestants "continued to read the Bible—and especially to identify biblical types—using a methodology and a vocabulary not so unlike the approach they had sought to replace." Maintains, therefore, that "there is more continuity with medieval hermeneutics than has generally been acknowledged by those who advocate a distinctly 'Protestant poetics'" and believes that, as a result, "the typological wit of Protestant devotional poets may be more complex than has been recognized" (253). Examines how typology was used by Protestant reformers "as a formal method of decoding a text" (254), discussing in some detail their "fairly elaborate rules for reading Scripture typologically" (260). Points out the importance of recognizing three major kinds of typology—Christological, sacramental, and eschatological—and insists that recognizing these distinctions in kinds of types provides the student of literature "with a vocabulary for describing the complexities of typological symbolism in the seventeenth century." Cites *Sickness* as an example of how Donne's speaker "perceives his personal drama in terms of typological drama staged in Scripture" (267), and comments on the typological aspects of *HSLittle*, which "links personal and sacred history together, revealing how one essential salvation drama is being played through the archetypal patterns of the Christian *mythos*" (269).

762. Docherty, Thomas. "Donne's Praise of Folly," in *Post-structuralist Readings of English Poetry,* ed. Richard Machin and Christopher Norris, 85–104. Cambridge: Cambridge University Press.

Reprint of Chapter 6 of *John Donne, Undone* (London and New York: Methuen, 1986), 187–210 (entry 651).

763. Doerksen, Daniel W. "Magdalen Herbert's London Church." *N&Q,* n.s. 34: 302–5.

Argues that when Donne mentions the churchgoing habits of Magdalen Herbert in his funeral sermon of 1 July 1627, praising her for bringing her whole family to church, he is not specifically referring to the Chelsea Old Church where he preached his memorial sermon but is referring to the house of God generically. Noting that Sir John Danvers did not acquire his Chelsea property until after 1617, when the youngest Herbert son had already left home, suggests that, more likely, Donne is referring to the family's churchgoing practices when they resided much earlier at Charing Cross and attended services at St. Martin-in-the-Fields, where George More, his father-in-law, was a parishioner. Surveys Donne's acquaintance with Magdalen Herbert and her family.

764. Donne, John. *John Donne: Komu zvoni hrana* [John Donne: For Whom the Bell Tolls], trans. Zdenek Hron. Praha: Ceskoslovensky spisovatel. 193p.

Available only at the National Library of the Czech Republic. In the following review, Masnerova calls the volume the best collection of Donne's work available in Czech to date. Points out that it contains translations of selected poems and a few prose excerpts, without naming them. Con-

tains a biographical sketch of Donne and commentary. Review: Eva Masnerová in *Literání mesicnik* (Prague) 17, no. 2 (1988): 100–02.

765. Donne, John. *John Donne: Negativ szerelerm,* válogatta, forditotta, az utószóat és a jegyzeteket irta Ferencz Gyözö. Helikon Stúdiö. Budapest: Helikon Kiadó. 53p.

Contains Hungarian translations of 19 poems from the *Songs and Sonets, Sat2, ED, MHMary, Corona,* and *Res* (5–43), followed by an afterword (47–[50]), which gives a general introduction to Donne's life and poetry as well as a brief account of the critical reception of his poetry; notes (51–[54]); and a table of contents.

766. Donne, John. *Poesie e traduzioni,* trans. Mino Milani. Pavia: Amici di via Cardano. 74p.

Contains an Italian translation of *SGo* (58–61).

767. Donne, John. *Selected Prose: John Donne.* ed. and intro. with notes by Neil Rhodes. Penguin Classics. Harmondsworth: Penguin Books. 351p.

The introduction ([7]–30) surveys historically and critically Donne's prose works from the early paradoxes to the late sermons. States that the aim of this selected edition of Donne's prose is to show why Donne thought that he would be remembered as a great preacher rather than as a poet and "to enlarge the very partial view of Donne which is formed by an isolated reading of the *Songs and Sonnets . . .* by illustrating the considerable imaginative and intellectual continuity in his writing as a whole" ([7]). Contains a bibliography of editions and criticism ([31]–32) and a note on the texts ([33]), explaining that they are "necessarily eclectic." Contains the *Paradoxes* ([35]–50), six selections from *Problemes* ([51]–57), selections from *Biathanatos* ([59]–85), five prose letters ([87]–96), selections from *Devotions* ([97]–137), and selections from the individual sermons as well as four complete sermons ([139]–326). Concludes with notes ([327]–51). Reviews: *TLS* 4384 (1987): 397.

768. Elderhorst, Constance. "John Donne's *First Anniversary* as an Anatomical Anamorphosis," in *Explorations in the Field of Nonsense,* ed. Wim Tigges, 97–102. *DQR* Studies in Literature, 3, ed. F. G. A. M. Aarts et al. Amsterdam: Rodopi.

Argues that in *FirAn* Elizabeth Drury is an anamorphic image. Defines anamorphosis as "an ingenious perspective technique which presents a distorted image of the subject when seen from the usual point of view" but which, when seen from a particular angle, "the distortion disappears, and the image appears normal." Claims that "[t]o those on earth the image of Elizabeth Drury is distorted and seems hyperbolic" and that "[o]nly those who have remembered the faint light that is reflected from her . . . adopt the proper perspective of view" (101). Maintains that Elizabeth Drury "is necessarily out of proportion to the analysis of the anatomy" but that "the panegyric on her is not hyperbolic anymore when regarded in the light of those endowed with proper vision." Concludes that "[t]he presence of Elizabeth as an exponent of another reality, which requires a different means of perception, seems to defy the logical order to things" and "[t]he conceit not only transcends conventional figures of speech" but also "adds a non-mimetic dimension to it," thereby qualifying *FirAn* to be classified "with nonsense in literature" (102).

769. Elimimian, Isaac Irabor. *A Study of Rhetorical Patterns in John Donne's Epicedes and Obsequies.* New York: Vantage Press. xv, 120p. A modified por-

tion of Chapter 2 first appeared in *CML* 6, no. 2 (1986): 127–36.

Presents a rhetorical study of the *Epicedes and Obsequies* in four main chapters and a conclusion. Chapter 1, "Aesthetic Ego" (1–21), considers, "from the *expressive* perspective, the background of the poems, their place in Donne's aesthetic development, and their relation to his other poems, particularly the *Songs and Sonnets,*" focusing primarily on "the epideictic and the ethical." Chapter 2, "Pragmatic Vision" (23–42), comments on Donne's audience and "considers the degree to which the poet conforms to the rhetorical practices of his day, some special problems raised by the poems in the Renaissance period, and the implications of these problems for Donne's larger audience" (xi). Chapter 3, "Wit and Poesy Allied" (43–71), "examines from the *objective* perspective the thematic and stylistic orientations of the poems." Chapter 4, "Distances" (73–98), discusses "the question of inventio, imitatio, and other rhetorical sources on which an artist might depend for his argument with a view to establishing how the epicedes and obsequies fit into the categories," observing that "Donne derives materials from various sources (Christian theology or the Bible, science, the military, the court, nature, and law) and from other artists (Aristotle, Webster, and Francis Beaumont). Chapter 5, "Conclusion" (99–103), presents "a synopsis of the salient points discussed in the earlier chapters" (xii). Concludes with a bibliography (105–15) and an index (117–20).

770. Ellrodt, Robert. "L'esthétique de John Donne," in *Le continent européen et le monde anglo-américain aux XVIIᵉ et XVIIIᵉ siècles,* 50–61. Actes du colloque tenu à Paris les 24 et 25 octobre 1986, Société d'Études Anglo-Américaines des XVIIᵉ et XVIIIᵉ Siècles. Reims: Presses Universitaires de Reims.

Maintains that, since Donne did not leave a statement of his views on poetic art or on aesthetics in general, we can only imperfectly discover his attitudes by examining what he actually does in his poetry, supplemented by the various scattered comments on aesthetic issues in his poetry and prose, and by viewing him in light of the aesthetic theories of his time. Observes that since Donne is often thought of as a mannerist in his poetry, it is helpful to compare and contrast him with mannerist artists. Points out that although we do not know if Donne was aware of specific mannerist artists and/or works, we do know that he had a keen interest in painting. Discusses a number of affinities between Donne's poetry and mannerist art without suggesting any direct Continental influence.

771. **Ellrodt, Robert.** "Poésie et vérité chez John Donne." *EA* 40: 1–14.

Explores the complex issue of "truth" in Donne's poetry and shows how he uses hyperbole, paradox, irony, ambiguity, and various personae precisely in order to present the truth, not to escape from it. Observes how Donne deals with the real world about him, drawing his images from the urban milieu in which he lived and trying to make that real world intelligible to others. Maintains that Donne tries to convey a very definite meaning in his poems and does not intend his poems to be polysemic. Holds that Donne was always conscious of reality, believed in truth, and attempted to represent it in his poetry.

772. **Enozowa, Kazuyoshi.** "English Religious Poetry of the Seventeenth Century—Its Nature and Appeal for the Common Reader," in *Poetry and Faith in the English Renaissance: Essays in Honour of Professor Toyohiro Tatsumi's Seventieth Birthday,* ed. Peter Milward, 121–32. Renaissance Monographs 13.

Tokyo: Renaissance Institute, Sophia University.

Notes that the English religious poets of the seventeenth century wrote in a great variety of styles, not simply the so-called metaphysical mode. Comments on two traditions that inform the religious lyric according to modern scholars—the meditative and the baroque—and finds neither of these accounts completely satisfactory. Expresses appreciation for much of what Dr. Johnson said about the wit of "metaphysical" poetry and about religious poetry in general. Discusses the difficulties in defining "religious" poetry and in accounting for why readers find it attractive. Concludes that "religious poetry, although limited in its thematic scope, is nevertheless capable of having pleasurable effects on the common reader, if it is written by really good poets" and "[s]ince some of the seventeenth-century poets did write really good religious poetry, we may justly call them 'great' religious poets" (132). Mentions Donne only in passing.

773. **Estrin, Barbara.** "Donne's Injured 'I': Defections from Petrarchan and Spenserian Poetics." *PQ* 66: 175–93.

Argues that in *Broken* and *ValWeep* Donne illustrates "the limitations of the poetic compliment" and "concentrates on *his* wounds." Maintains that in the former he "focuses on the wound of rejection" and in the latter "on the wound of separation," which the imagined woman in the poem cannot assuage. Argues that "[e]ach poem therefore questions the poetics of substitution"—*Broken* "challenging the solace of Spenserian nature" and *ValWeep* "the consolation of Petrarchan art" (176). Presents a detailed, comparative reading of both poems to show that in *Broken* Donne "demonstrates the limits of Spenserian duplication via the empty mirror of his replicated self" and in *ValWeep* "denies Petrarchan distance through the destructive potential of the deified beloved." Suggests that *Broken* "reproduces only a broken poet," whereas *ValWeep* "turns the woman into a version of an empty self" (191). Maintains that "[f]acing the problematic time, the problematic self, and the problematic woman, Donne turns his rejection of the Petrarchan and Spenserian models, so culturally available, into a disquisition about the futility of denial" in *Broken* and about "the anguish of separation" in *ValWeep*. Believes that Donne's "refusal to accept the solace of art and his insistence on maximizing his injuries, are in their ways, homages to the real woman and the reality of his feelings about her." Concludes that "[e]ach poem is a rhetorical argument, saying 'see what an actual broken heart yields and a real physical separation means' in order presumably to find a way to avert the denial and postpone the departure Petrarch and Spenser celebrate" (192).

774. **Evans, G. Blakemore.** "Donne's 'Subtile Knot.'" *N&Q*, n.s. 34: 228–30. Suggests that the discussion of "the theory of spirits as a medium joining and interacting between soul and body" in Timothy Bright's *Treatise of Melancholie* (1586), a copy of which Donne had in his library, "affords a valuable insight into the kind of medical, philosophical, and religious backgrounds" that inform *Ecst,* especially ll. 61–68. Suggests also several "interesting coincidences between Donne's poem and Bright's *Treatise*" (230), especially certain of Bright's phrases that may have anticipated Donne's reference to that "subtile knot, which makes us man" (l. 64).

775. **Flynn, Dennis.** "Donne's *Ignatius His Conclave* and Other Libels on Robert Cecil." *JDJ* 6: 163–83. Published also as a working paper: Waltham, Mass.: Bent-

ley College, Institute for Research and Faculty Development, 1987.
Discusses Donne's functionally ambiguous and hidden, but libelous, attacks in verse and prose on Robert Cecil, Earl of Salisbury, in *Metem,* in which Donne views Cecil as "a climax of evil innovation" (165); in two satirical book titles in *The Courtier's Library;* in a farcical 1609 letter; in *Ignatius,* suggesting that in this work Donne "was shadowing Robert Cecil in the form of Loyola" (175); in a letter on Cecil's death in July 1612; and in a sermon preached in August 1622. Comments extensively on five interpretative problems or "unexplained puzzles" (169) in *Ignatius,* proposing "a solution that integrates the problems and enhances our understanding of *Ignatius* as a work with double purpose" (170), that is, not only an attack on the Jesuits but also a ridiculing of the relationship between King James I and Cecil.

776. **Fowler, Alastair.** "The Early Seventeenth Century," in *A History of English Literature,* 94–124. Oxford: Blackwell; Cambridge, Mass.: Harvard University Press.
Points out that in the earlier seventeenth century a new literary movement was underway, "a movement away from the flowing amplitude of the Elizabethans to a style compressed, concise, even charged," a movement in which "[w]it no longer showed itself in copiousness or piquant incident, but in compression," and cites Donne and Jonson as the "two contrasting figures" who led the way (94). Discusses major characteristics of Donne's poetry, such as the use of a powerful dramatic voice, colloquial diction, rhetorical and syntactical complexity, conceits, and wit. Sees many of Donne's poems as "epigrammatic compressions," pointing out, for instance, that the *Songs and Sonets* are "epigrammatic transfor-

mations of elegy—elegies compressed and sharpened" (103). Comments on major features of Donne's sermons, saying that "[n]o prose more dynamic had been achieved in English" (109).

777. Frontain, Raymond-Jean. "Redemption Typology in John Donne's 'Batter My Heart.'" *JRMMRA* 8: 163–76. Reprinted in *John Donne's Poetry,* ed. Arthur L. Clements, 2nd ed. (New York: Norton, 1992), 338–49.

Discusses how Donne's speaker in *HSBatter,* in order to communicate to God "his readiness and complete desire for salvation," employs "three images most often used in tandem by the Hebrew prophets to denounce sinful, apostate Israel: a vessel in need of repair, a usurped town under siege, and a woman trapped in a degrading sexual relationship" (163). Shows how in the sonnet "the individual's life repeats a larger pattern, just as the larger pattern is only finally understood in terms of what it reveals about the Christian's spiritual state" (163–64). Maintains, therefore, that "[r]ecognition of the poem's typological symbolism illuminates both the poem's significant prophetic dimensions and a rhetorical maneuver that it shares with other Holy Sonnets by which the speaker attempts to manipulate God in order to effect his own salvation" (164). Shows how the speaker, "[r]ather than attacking the people's complacency and denouncing a sinful nation," as the Hebrew prophets did, "storms God's ear to denounce himself" because he believes that unless God recognizes his contrition and desire to repent by giving him prevenient grace, he will be lost for all eternity. Claims that, in a sense, the speaker "prophesies to God against himself." Concludes that "[b]y describing his situation typologically, the speaker attempts to prod God into acting in the necessary way" (174).

778. Grijp, Louis Peter. "Melodieën bij teksten van Huygens," in *Veelzijdigheid als levensvorm: Facetten van Constantijn Huygens' leven en werk. Een bundel studies ter gelegenheidvan zijn driehonderste sterfdag,* ed. A. Th. van Deursen, E. K. Grootes, and P. E. L. Verkuyl, 89–107. Deventer Studies, 2. Deventer: Sub Rosa.

Notes that of the 800 works that Huygens claimed to have composed, only 39 have hitherto been known, published as *Pathodia sacra et profana* (1647), this paucity attributable to the carelessness of Huygens's literary executors. Announces the recent discovery of two more musical settings, one definitely and one probably by Huygens. Surveys the 41 now known to exist and offers a brief account of Huygens's setting of "Gaet en vatt een Sterr in 't vallen," his translation of *SGo.* Points out that the melody Huygens apparently devised was dictated by the stanza form Huygens chose for his translation, which differs in certain respects from the normative Donne original. Notes that, if an English original dating from Donne's time ever existed, it has not survived, whereas a later setting (which Huygens could not have known) is recorded in Gardner's edition of *The Elegies and the Songs and Sonnets* (1965).

779. Groner, Marlene San Miguel. "Barbara Pym's Allusions to Seventeenth-Century Poets." *Cross-Bias,* no. 11: 5–7.

Notes allusions in Barbara Pym's novels to Donne's poems: (1) *Relic* in *Excellent Women, Jane and Prudence,* and *No Fond Return of Love;* (2) *GoodM* in *Less Than Angels, The Sweet Dove Died, Quartet in Autumn,* and *Crampton Hodner;* (3) *Canon* and *Broken* in *A Glass of Blessings;* (4) *ElFatal* and *ElBed* in *Jane and Prudence;* and (5) *Curse* in *Unsuitable Attachment.*

780. Hageman, Elizabeth H. "Katherine Philips: The Matchless Orinda," in

Women Writers of the Renaissance and Reformation, ed. Katharina M. Wilson, 566–608. Athens, Ga.: University of Georgia Press.

Discusses Donne's influence on Katherine Philips, noting that her poems on female friendship abound with allusions to such poems as *Canon, SunRis, Ecst,* and *ValMourn.* Shows how Philips adapts the language and images of Donne's love poetry to express her notions of Platonic friendship.

781. Hannaford, Renée. "'Express'd by Mee': Carew on Donne and Jonson." *SP* 84: 61–79.

Maintains that two poems by Carew— "An Elegie upon the death of the Deane of Pauls, Dr. John Donne" and "To BEN. JOHNSON. Upon occasion of his Ode of defiance annext to his Play of the new Inne"—"exhibit an incisive awareness of the literary trends initiated by Donne and Jonson during the first quarter of the seventeenth century and reveal not only Carew's critical assessment of his two poetic fathers, but also something of the aesthetic aims and prejudices of Carew's contemporaries" (61). Analyzes the elegy on Donne to show how Carew "has written a stunningly Donnean poem" (70) that "functions not only as poetic mirror criticism to praise Donne's literary achievements, but also along the way comments on contemporary literary practices and popular taste, and becomes a vehicle for Carew's own critical assessment of his art" (77–78). Believes that "[t]he poem is a highly sophisticated poetic performance as much about itself as about Donne because it permits the poet through imitative stylistics and mixed genres to improvise another kind of self—a performing self" (78).

782. Harland, Paul W. "Imagination and Affections in John Donne's Preaching." *JDJ* 6: 33–50.

Points out that Donne believed that the knowledge required for salvation involved "a reordering of all the faculties and members of the human being" and argues, therefore, that discussion of Donne's persuasive method as a preacher will remain partial unless critics consider the functioning of the whole human soul, which, in addition to memory, understanding, and will, "also includes imagination and affections" (33). Shows how "Donne's understanding of human psychology and, consequently, his manner of constructing sermons to fit the working of the mind follow from his conception of the [integral] relation between the soul and body" (34). Explains that, as a result of his view that the senses and affections, if transformed, "become instruments by which we may know and praise God," Donne "preached his sermons conscious that he must engage the senses in order to restore them." Discusses also how Donne's view includes "the good uses of the imagination" (36). Maintains that Donne held that "[t]he imagination and the affections, working cooperatively, provide a significant, though limited, function in educating and rectifying the soul." Stresses that Donne's "ability to diagnose the causes of imaginative and emotional distortions frees him from a habitual distrust, common among his contemporaries, of these two faculties and allows him to find ways to put them to wise and proper uses" (48).

783. Hester, M. Thomas. "Donne's (Re)-Annunciation of the Virgin(ia Colony) in *Elegy XIX.*" *SCRev* 4, no. 2: 49–64.

Argues that generally Donne is critical of English imperialistic forays into the New World and suggests that *ElBed,* in particular, contains a "radical critique of the English adventure in Virginia." Sees the poem "as a complex literary event—as Ovidian *jeu* that approaches the boldness of

Catullus in its frank and graphic las-
civiousness, as another of the poet's
spirited send-ups of Spenser's marriage hymn, and as a sort of wry political fiction that approaches parody in
its imaginary mimicry of figures and
motifs central to the English imperial
mission in America" (50). Believes
that in the elegy Donne is attacking
Raleigh's attempts to seduce Queen
Elizabeth into supporting and endorsing his expedition to Virginia and
that "[t]he result is a sort of delightfully encoded mock Annunciation that
evokes Donne's satirical grin at the
Establishment's (or at least Ralegh's)
proposed seduction of the New World."
Shows how "[p]irating the Protestant
deification of the Virgin Queen and
Ralegh's imperial myth of the New
World possession, Donne invents a
blasphemous sub-text and an erotic
rationale for English imperialism while
outrageously mocking the mythic analogical codes of his poetic and political rivals," and demonstrates how
"[t]he various strands of metaphoric
identity in the poem operate as a sort
of equivocal typology, playing facetiously, even pornographically and
blasphemously, on the various types
with which Elizabeth was identified
in syncretic Protestant imperial mythology." Discusses, in particular, how
the woman addressed in the poem,
like Queen Elizabeth, "is consistently
identified with the iconography and
symbolism of the Virgin Mary while
being associated at the same time, or
in different comparisons, with the New
World as Eden and with Eve," while
the speaker "exploits the same mythology and typology, assuming comical,
bawdy versions of Adam, the New
World discoverer, Gabriel, and finally,
even the Word" (54).

784. Hester, M. Thomas. "Re-Signing the
Text of the Self: Donne's 'As due by
many titles,'" in *"Bright Shootes of Everlastingnesse" : The Seventeenth-Century*

Religious Lyric, ed. Claude J. Summers
and Ted-Larry Pebworth, 59–71. Columbia: University of Missouri Press.
Presents a detailed analysis of *HSDue,*
focusing primarily upon "that characteristic of Donne's verse which most
attracts us—its wit" (59). Argues that
in many ways the sonnet is "about the
problematic nature of the religious
lyric" and suggests, in fact, that it is
"an exploration of the kindness of
the religious lyric, a search for traces
of the divine Word in the typology of
the self." Shows how, "[f]ramed by
the central comparison between the
poet's witty re-creation and the divine
Maker's originary and continuous acts
of re-creation," the poem "applies that
central topos of Renaissance homiletics and poetics—man as a word
striving to communicate with The
Word—in order to explicate the limitation and powers of man to re-create
himself *in imagine dei.*" Insists, in
other words, that the sonnet is "an
anatomy of its own wit and of the central concern of the religious lyric—
the power of words to signify the self
as an image of The Word, or, in the
central terms of the poem, the capacity to 'titles' to 're-sign' the self in
humble resignation to the handwriting of God" (60). Believes that the
success of the sonnet resides primarily "in its poetic enactment of the paradox of man as a fallen image of The
Word" (70), and concludes that it is
"a poem in search of its own genre,
a poetic presentation of man's desire
for the closure of divine kindness"
(71).

785. Hieatt, A. Kent. "John Donne," in
Poetry in English: An Anthology, ed.
M. L. Rosenthal, 220–44. New York and
Oxford: Oxford University Press.
Presents a general introduction to
Donne's life and lyric poetry. Says
that in Donne's poetry the speakers
do not give in to "indulgent self-
dramatizing" but rather have about

them a convincing "honesty" (220). Comments on the uses of the conceit and wit, metrical roughness, and colloquial diction, using *Noct* as an example. Reproduces 13 poems from *Songs and Sonets, ElBed, Sat3,* 7 selections from the *Holy Sonnets, Goodf,* and *Sickness*—with explanatory notes and glosses.

786. Hill, Eugene D. "John Donne's Moralized Grammar: A Study in Renaissance Christian Hebraica," in *Papers in the History of Linguistics: Proceedings of the Third International Conference on the History of the Language Sciences,* ed. Hans Aarsfleff, Louis G. Kelly, and Hans-Josef Niederehe, 189–98. Amsterdam Studies in the Theory and History of Linguistic Science, gen. ed. E. F. Konrad Koerner. Series 3—Studies in the History of the Language Sciences, vol. 38. Amsterdam: John Benjamins.

Noting that in his sermons Donne points out that Hebrew has no conjugated present tense, discusses the possible sources of his "moralized account" of "the verbal structure of Hebrew" in which "he links morphological fact (absence of a present tense) with intended psychological effect (the arousal of expectation and faith)" (190). Suggests that, although many books on Hebrew and many moralized interpretations of Hebrew morphology were available in Donne's time, his interpretation of the lack of a present tense in Hebrew "was not a commonplace in his day" and was likely "an idea of his own devising" (192). Believes, however, that Donne's views were influenced, at least in part, by a "new way of looking at the Hebrew Bible" (194) similar to that endorsed by Martin Luther, who saw the Old Testament as "the word of promise" (195). Notes that, although Donne "anticipates much speculation" by twentieth century scholars, he differs greatly from them in that, he "assumes that he lives

in the same world as the Psalmists" and that biblical language "is structured in such a way as to point up the unity" between his and their experience (197).

787. Hill, W. Speed. "John Donne's *Biathanatos:* Authenticity, Authority, and Context in Three Editions." *JDJ* 6: 109–33.

Reviews three modern editions of *Biathanatos*—(1) by Michael Rudick and M. Pabst Battin (1982) (entry 264), (2) by William A. Clebsch (1983) (entry 374), and (3) by Ernest W. Sullivan, II (1984) (entry 466). Shows that "these three editions provide an illuminating spectrum of the options available to the editor of Renaissance nondramatic texts (109) and contrasts the editorial principles and procedures governing each of the editions. Comments on the composition and early publication of *Biathanatos,* the problems involved in choosing a copy-text and reproducing Donne's punctuation and marginalia, the issue of old-spelling "scholarly editions" versus more readable modern-spelling editions, and the professional demands made on a press that publishes old-spelling editions. See also Hill's "Letter to Editor" (*JDJ* 6 [1986]: 305) in which he withdraws the implication in his review that Associated University Presses is undercapitalized.

788. Holstun, James. "'Will you rent our ancient love asunder?' Lesbian Elegy in Donne, Marvell, and Milton." *ELH* 54: 835–67.

In an analysis of *Sappho,* argues that Sappho is a "dramatic persona" and that Donne "writes about her, not simply through her," and thus maintains that the poem's "lyric shortcomings are its dramatic successes, the product not of Donne's failure to imagine lesbian eroticism adequately, but of his success at dramatizing the decay of lesbian language from a nongay perspective" (837). Claims that the poem "presupposes a nonhierarchical language unmediated by men" and thus Donne intentionally demonstrates that Sappho "cannot create proper poetry." Maintains that even though the poem deals with lesbian eroticism "with considerable sympathy," in the end "it finally masters this eroticism by subordinating it to a patriarchal scheme of nature, history, and language" (838). Calls Donne's view "tolerant patriarchalism" and says that Donne's audience could allow such tolerance "only because it does not truly threaten the aristocratic ethic of blood tied to a morality of penetration, legitimacy, and dynasty" (846). Calls *Sappho* "an inverted epithalamion, one written from outside the wedding ceremony by a figure whose inarticulate isolation implies the fiats of patriarchal poetry" and says that lesbianism, as Donne portrays it, "can never truly threaten a cosmos ruled by patriarchal authority" because "it becomes vocal only as elegy" (847).

789. **Hutchings, G. J. M.** "Elizabethan Lyric: Poetry for Singing—Poetry for Speaking." *ESA* 30: 57–68.

Attributes the decline of English song lyric in the seventeenth century, at least in part, to the reaction of poets against Petrarchism. Says that Donne's poems typically contain an ambivalence that "makes us 'look back and revise what we thought we had caught.'" Points out that Donne's "dramatic diction, its imperatives, its colloquialisms, its passionately involved syntax, marks a dramatic change in the language of poetry" and that "that change, as a whole, is less amenable to musical setting than was the standard Elizabethan lyric." Suggests that Donne's rejection of Petrarchism "may owe something to earlier English poetry—Wyatt at his more colloquial, and perhaps Skelton" but more obviously to "Elizabethan dramatic verse" (66).

790. **Jacobs, Linda L.** "The Image of Mary Magdalene in Seventeenth-Century Poetry." *POMPA:* 62–78.

Surveys English seventeenth century poems about Mary Magdalen by Herbert, Drummond, Vaughan, Constable, Edward Sherburne, Crashaw, and Donne, poets who were anticipated by Southwell in the late sixteenth century. Comments on the ecclesiastical lore and the many traditions concerning Mary Magdalen and notes that in *MHMary* Donne indicates his awareness that church tradition had combined several biblical figures into its presentation of the Magdalen.

791. **Kerrigan, William.** "What Was Donne Doing?" *SCRev* 4, no. 2: 2–15.

Suggests that postmodernist critics (and readers) are less attracted to Donne's secular poetry because "[t]he shine is gone from the question of love in literary discourse today": it is "suddenly bereft of glamour." Examines Donne's attitudes on sexual love in his poetry and wonders why critics who speak "ponderously of phallocentric texts and invaginated texts and debate the extent to which readers should be loyal to intention" have failed to discover "these themes, and more" (4) in Donne, citing, as an example, *ElBed*. Notes that "love was the paramount subject of the English Renaissance lyric" and that in "no subsequent period in the history of English verse is love poetry a central ambition" (6). Suggests also that critics of today focus often on power, not love, thereby driving out "other human concerns, making motivation a blunt instrument and meaning a self-deceit." Says that modern criticism is split between those who see Donne as a "master rhetorician," as simply an "extravagant and resourceful self-fashioner," and those who believe that Donne evolved "something like a philosophy of love" (7). Argues that, in

fact, Donne "made an original contribution to the philosophy of love
because he rooted his reflections in
situations and *because* his poems show
us a philosophical urgency born in
the immediacies of love." Claims that
Donne is "the Heidegger of Renaissance love philosophy, the destroyer
who is also a continuer" (8). Stresses
that Donne "inherited love from two
thriving traditions, the literary [Petrar-
chism] and the philosophical [Neo-
platonism]" but found both "seriously
deficient" (9). Maintains that "[b]y
scrubbing away the layers of [Neo-
platonic] myth that lacquered the
poetic surfaces of his predecessors and
contemporaries, Donne was able to
dramatize the discovery, as if for the
first time, of the sacred significance
of sexual love" (9–10). Observes that,
for the most part, Donne also "did
away with the supplications and self-
abasements of the Petrarchan lover"
and becomes "the representative in
great poetry of bad manners and
deliberate offense" (11). Points out,
however, that he borrowed from the
Petrarchists many of their *topoi* but
that he employs them with "such emotional and intellectual *furor* that they
become, in a way they had never been
before, the plotted course of love . . . a
revelation of being-in-love through
the charted voyage of its temporal
possibilities" (12–13).

792. Kittay, Eva Feder. "Semantic Fields
and the Structure of Metaphor," in *Metaphor: Its Cognitive Force and Linguistic
Structure,* 258–98. Clarendon Library of
Logic and Philosophy, gen. ed. L. Jonathan Cohen. Oxford: Clarendon Press.
First issued in paperback in 1989.
Maintains that in *Bait* Donne "has created a metaphor which on the surface
seems plausible but which in fact is
impossible to explicate in terms of the
relations which are set up and transferred" (274). Discusses the poem as

an example "of how the topic domain
of courting is reoriented in terms of
the perspective offered by the vehicle
field belonging to the term 'bait.'"
Suggests that "[t]his perspectival reordering takes place not only by means
of drawing similarities as given in
common semantic descriptions" but
also "by setting up relations in the topic
field which mimic those in the field
of the vehicle." Says that in the poem
"we have the interesting additional
feature of parody, which involves the
reversals of relations and the absurdities into which we are led by means
of the metaphorical relations established by the poem—absurdities and
reversals which reflect back to the
matter which forms the subject of the
poem, that is, courtship, and even more
pertinently, courtly poetry, as it is this
poetry which is the instrument (the
bait) of the poet who woos his lady"
(275).

793. Klause, John L. "Donne and the
Wonderful." *ELR* 17: 41–66.
Discusses Donne's inconsistent and
qualified view of miracles, noting that
"[e]ven when he attempts to be theologically correct he betrays his need
to save something of the miraculous
from a corrosive rationalism" and that
"he feels compelled to find in his religion an essential place for the *mira,*
the wonder, that his reason has come
close to dissipating." Discusses how
Donne undertakes rationally to rescue
the notion of miracles by redefining
them "into respectability" or at least
by following "certain doctrinal emphases that Reformation thought had
brought into prominence for the sake
of minds like his own" (47). Points
out that Donne is primarily interested
in "the miraculous as a condition—
as an objective quality in things (that
which evokes wonder), and even more
as the soul's rapt experience of the
wonder-ful" (49). Maintains that, for

Donne, the miraculous becomes "that quintessence of feeling—purified from the debased intimacies of both profane and sacred 'love.'" Claims that much in Donne's literary achievement results from his "imaginative quest for the 'clean,' controlled, indeed diluted, but intense and somehow mystical experience of wonder" (55). Believes that, for Donne, "passion for the marvellous was a basic fact of his psychic life, an impulse which had to be redirected, not repressed, when he turned toward religious ends" (56). Relates Donne's love of the marvellous to his use of paradoxes, the attraction alchemy held over his imagination, and his awareness and fear of disintegration. Finds in "Death's Duell" a recapitulation of many of the themes that bear upon Donne's attitude toward the wonderful. Concludes that the mysticism for which Donne "allows himself to yearn is neither radical nor heroic" because he was "too cautious, too skeptical, too egocentric to surrender to rapture" (66).

794. **Klawitter, George.** "John Donne and Woman: Against the Middle Ages." *Allegorica* 9 (1987–88): 270–78.

Argues that to understand Donne's attitude toward women one must turn to the verse letters, especially the eight addressed to the Countess of Bedford, wherein one finds "the authentic voice of the private Donne . . . freed from the expectations of his male friends" (273). Points out that in these poems Donne expresses his belief that women are "capable of logical argumentation in poetry," thereby elevating them to the status of "equal, thinking being[s]," a point of view that required "a total readjustment of the medieval concept of inferior woman." Says that "[w]hat Shakespeare did for the status of women in drama, John Donne did for them in lyric poetry." Concludes that, "[b]y utilizing a private mode, he engi-

neered a revision in the medieval false dilemma of angel-slut womankind, once those private verse letters became semi-private through discrete dissemination by the receptors, and later public through their eventual publication" (277).

795. **Larson, Deborah Aldrich.** "John Donne and Biographical Criticism." *SCRev* 4: 93–102.

Surveys biographical studies of Donne from August Jessopp, *John Donne, Sometimes Dean of St. Paul's* (London: Methuen, 1897) to the present, showing how various critics have read Donne's poetry from a biographical point of view and how Donne's works, especially his poetry and letters, have been used to construct his biography. Comments particularly on unsettled issues surrounding Donne's courtship of and marriage to Ann More to show that "Donne's biography, more often than not, becomes what the biographer wishes to make of it" (99). Observes that "[s]o much is known about the facts that a biography of Donne seems easy to write, while so little is known about his attitudes that . . . various assumptions are equally easy to make—and to support." Hopes that studies that "depend on biographical, historical, and textual facts rather than on assumptions about Donne's personality will provide a clearer perception of Donne's life, letters, and poetry" but believes that Donne, who donned "a variety of masks in his personal letters as well as in his poetry," may, in fact, "remain elusive" (100).

796. **Lewalski, Barbara K.** "Lucy, Countess of Bedford: Images of a Jacobean Courtier and Patroness," in *Politics of Discourse: The Literature and History of Seventeenth-Century England,* ed. Kevin Sharpe and Steven N. Zwicker, 52–77. Berkeley and Los Angeles: University of

California Press. Revised and expanded in "Exercising Power: The Countess of Bedford as Courtier, Patron, and Coterie Poet," in Lewalski's *Writing Women in Jacobean England* (Cambridge, Mass.: Harvard University Press, 1993), 95–123.

Presents a biographical sketch of Lucy, Countess of Bedford, attributing her prominent role as a courtier-patroness "almost entirely to her own (Harrington) connections and to her considerable talents, brilliance, and style," not to any "financial largess." Focuses primarily on "the literary imagery through which that role was created and sustained" (52) and on the effect she "had on the literary scene—most obviously through the poems or other works addressed to her or taking her as a subject" (53). Discusses the countess's patronage of Donne, as well as of other literary figures of the period, emphasizing, however, that she "was closer to Donne than to her other literary clients" and that "for a time he was virtually her laureate." Discusses Donne's poem to her and shows how his verse epistles to the countess "develop a distinctively Donnean portrait of her agile mind, subtle wit, and exemplary character." Maintains that in his verse letters to her Donne transformed the traditional poem of praise "from conventional hyperbolic compliment or quasi-Petrarchan adulation into an audaciously witty but profoundly serious metaphysical inquiry into the bases of human worth." Discusses how specifically Donne "proposes to study, or meditate upon, or contemplate the countess (as image of God) in order to explore through her some general proposition about virtue, religion, death, or sorrow" (68). Points out that although Donne's relationship with the countess "cooled somewhat after 1613," there was "no rift" (70) between them in later years.

797. Llasera, Margaret. "Perspectives," in *Le continent et le monde anglo-améri-* *cain aux XVIIᵉ et XVIIIᵉ siècles,* 65–70. Actes du colloque tenu à Paris les 24 et 25 octobre 1986, Société d'Études Anglo-Américaines des XVIIᵉ et XVIIIᵉ Siècles. Reims: Presses Universitaires de Reims.

Discusses aspects of perspective that reflect multiplicity of view and the relativity of distance and representation in Donne's poetry. Comments on his uses of metaphors and conceits that reflect his interest in and understanding of scientific optical instruments such as the telescope, lunettes, and mirrors, and discusses his various uses of anamorphosis. Says that, like mannerist painters, Donne was a master of anamorphosis in his poetry.

798. Lockwood, Deborah H. "Donne's Idea of Woman in the *Songs and Sonets.*" *ELWIU* 14: 37–50.

Maintains that the *Songs and Sonets* "portray woman, in intellectual terms, as the essentially controllable counterpart to man," reflecting, in other words, "a world in which man's mastery of the social, and intellectual scene, is unquestioned" (33–38). Observes, however, that Donne "seems to have been aware, at least subliminally, that woman was capable of more than what she was enabled by education and duties to display." Argues, therefore, that Donne's "approach to woman in the *Songs and Sonets* is by no means merely sexist but constitutes a subtle dynamic of celebration and limitation" (38). Analyzes principally *Break, GoodM, SunRis, Curse, ConfL,* and *Commun* to illustrate the point. Observes how wit generally permits male speakers in any situation "to maintain an advantage" (43). Suggests, however, that when *ConfL* and *Break* are set against other poems in the *Songs and Sonets,* one senses "how various and complex" Donne's dramatic talent is, noting how "[h]e presents a gallery of masculine attitudes, and a briefer, still revealing sampling of feminine ones." Concludes that

Donne's poems show that he "had a clear if not a simple conception of woman, one rooted both in the Renaissance deprecation of woman and in his own 'admyring' devotion to her" (46).

799. Love, Harold. "Scribal Publication in Seventeenth-Century England." *TCBS* 9: 130–54.

Discusses how scribal publication was "an accepted and important medium for the transmission of texts during the seventeenth century, quite equal in terms of status to transmission in printed form, and by no means the preserve of the amateur writer." Shows how scribal publication was "conducted in the interests of the author, of the stationer or master scrivener, or of the intending possessor" and notes that "[l]arge numbers of works were written with scribal publication in view" and that although "many of them eventually passed into print this was by no means always welcomed by their authors" (147). Cites Donne as "[t]he best and most ambitious example of author-publication," noting that during his lifetime and for some years after his death his poetry was circulated in manuscript volumes and miscellanies. Points out that Donne "followed the practice of classical poets in issuing his poems in groups determined by genre" (138). Says that Donne used the scribal medium to control the distribution of his works at any given time but speculates that, "in the period immediately prior to the issue of the first printed edition in 1633, when there was undoubtedly a great demand for manuscripts of Donne's poems, it would have been strange if some enterprising stationer had not taken steps to satisfy it," although "there is no definite evidence for this" (139).

800. Malpezzi, Frances M. "The Weight/lessness of Sin: Donne's 'Thou hast made me' and the Psychostatic Tradition." *SCRev* 4, no. 2: 71–77.

Maintains that in *HSMade* Donne presents a "hierophanic progress, the memory's movement toward the apocalyptic revelation," which is embodied "in the speaker's imaginative rush toward death and judgment." Claims that Donne "translates his reader from the profane to the sacred, providing in his speaker a model for the internalization of the Christian Psychostasis, the weighing of the souls of the dead" (72). Presents a detailed critical reading of Donne's sonnet, noting, in particular, its relation to the visual and literary prototypes found in the psychostatic tradition. Concludes that the speaker of the sonnet "paradigmatically ponders his soul in his tropological experience of the Christian psychostasis" and that "[t]he process leaves the persona with a greater knowledge of himself and his relationship to his maker, thus preparing him for the ultimate revelation of Judgment Day" (76).

801. Mann, Lindsay A. "The Typology of Woman in Donne's *Anniversaries*." *Ren&R*, n.s. 11: 337–50.

Argues that in the *Anniversaries* Donne uses typology to emphasize "incompleteness, expectancy, and process" and that the two poems "move from a world governed by sin to redemption" but that "their movement is not represented as completed" but rather "as partial, yet successive, and cumulative." Maintains that "Donne's stress is therefore upon potentiality, upon developing and not achieved perfection," and that "[t]he poems are thus directed to evoke a specific but developing response in their readers." Believes that "[t]he symbolism of Elizabeth Drury develops from less perfect to more perfect manifestations, from mythic and historical prefigurations to biblical fulfillment," and that "[t]he biblical pattern of the poems, the recognition of providential design in imperfect human experience, is also developing, and becomes clear as the poems advance," so that "[o]nly the conclusions of each poem make their biblical pattern explicit" (337). Discusses how Elizabeth Drury is "a complex yet consistent symbolic figure whose deepest symbolic significance is biblical"; how [t]his biblical level of symbolism, typology, provides the meaning and organizing principles for the poems" (340); and how "[t]he process of the poems is a recognition of ethical values and truths of faith through acceptance of existential imperfection," which, however, "reflects in the recognition of its limitations the perfection of the spiritual" (341). Analyzes the theme, structure, and symbolism of each of the poems to show how they "echo biblical symbolic structures, not to suggest a doctrinal moral or spiritual teaching but to point beyond their hyperboles to essential truths," and to show how they "are structurally related and complete in themselves as lament and consolation." Emphasizes, however, that "the underlying pattern of the poems, of promise to fulfillment, is not complete," but rather they "set up a clear pattern" (347) that will be further clarified in Donne's sermons.

802. Martinet, Marie-Madeleine. "L'ombre de la mort dans l'angleterre du XVIIe siècle," in *Ténèbres et lumière: Essais sur la religion, la vie et la mort chrétiennes en angleterre en hommage à la mémoire d'Élisabeth Bourcier,* 31–41. Études anglaises: Cahiers et documents, 9. Paris: Didier.

Discusses the imagery of the shadow of death in seventeenth century English literature. Comments on Donne's use of shadow imagery in *Noct* and in *Devotions.*

803. Martinet, Marie-Madeleine. "Undone," in *Le continent et le monde anglo-*américain aux XVIIe et XVIIIe siècles, 62–64. Actes du colloque tenu à Paris les 24 et 25 octobre 1986, Société d'Études Anglo-Américaines des XVIIe et XVIIIe Siècles. Reims: Presses Universitaires de Reims.

Discusses how Donne uses negation in his poetry, sometimes in an obvious way by employing words that are explicitly negative, and sometimes in a more hidden way by using words that have a sense of deprivation and establish a network of meanings among the different parts of his discourse. Maintains that the greatest subtlety is found not in grammatical negations but in the play between explicit and implicit negatives. Points out examples of Donne's use of negation in *Flea, Canon, NegLov, Anniv, Noct, Fun, ElAut, ElBed, HSBatter, Christ,* and *Father.*

804. Maynard, John. "Speaker, Listener, and Overhearer: The Reader in the Dramatic Poem," in *BIS,* vol. 15: 105–12.

Focuses on the relationship of the dramatic monologue to the reader, who "[a]s overhearer rather than direct audience·of the poem . . . is drawn into a position vis-à-vis the speaker by his evaluation of, or reaction to, the speaker's rhetorical relation to the listener in the poem." Says that in the dramatic monologue there is, in effect, "a rhetoric of speaker on hearer at one remove, as a kind of vector determined by both speaker and listener" (107). Illustrates this approach by examining *SunRis* and *Flea,* choosing Donne's poems to show that "this kind of reading is appropriate for all dramatic poems with the same kind of dynamic of reader as overhearer, not merely a strategy limited to Browning's peculiarly specialized development of that type" (108).

805. Mazzaro, Jerome. "Striking through the Mask: Donne and Herbert at Sonnets," in *Like Season'd Timber: New Essays on*

George Herbert, ed. Edmund Miller and Robert DiYanni, 241–53. Seventeenth-Century Texts and Studies, gen. ed. Anthony Low, vol. 1. New York: Peter Lang.

Compares and contrasts Donne and Herbert as sonneteers, discussing the relationship of each to the rhetorical and metrical forms of traditional Elizabethan sonnet sequences. Maintains that Donne "is more faithful than Herbert to the dictates of rhetorical convention, letting enjambment and verbal interplay rather than opposition to form define his character and sincerity" (245), and illustrates this point by comparing *HSVex* and Herbert's "The Answer." Suggests, however, that in "Redemption" Herbert "approaches something like the opacity and central binding image" of Donne's sonnet. Contrasts *HSBatter* with Herbert's "Prayer (I)" to show that "[t]he extent to which diction serves to defeat ethical choice and provide opacity may be seen in the way both Herbert and Donne approach apostrophe" (249). Suggests that one "can see something like Donne's definitions of context and self in the first of the sonnets Herbert writes to his mother" (251).

806. McClung, William A., and Rodney Simard. "Donne's Somerset Epithalamium and the Erotics of Criticism." *HLQ* 50: 95–106.

Surveys the criticism on Donne's *Eclog* and argues that the disparaging comments on the poem reveal "the subversion of aesthetic by sexual values in literary criticism, at its height among the Victorians, but continuing in ferocity through the present century" (95). Shows how those associated with the events surrounding the marriage of Robert Carr and Frances Howard, as well as Donne's epithalamium, "have been subjected to a displacement of sexual outrage, whereby the language of vilification

has addressed the heterosexual affair [between the couple] directly, and the homosexual one [between Carr and King James], until recently, only evasively." Maintains that Donne's reputation, however, "has survived his association with Somerset, even if the epithalamion continues to be treated as if it were a moral transgression on the poet's part" (103).

807. McKitterick, David. "The Young Geoffrey Keynes." *BC* 36: 491–517.

Surveys the career of Geoffrey Keynes as a bibliographer and comments on the bibliographical principles and procedures that inform his work. Discusses the circumstances surrounding the publication and reception of Keynes' Donne bibliography in 1914. Points out how the bibliography was enlarged, corrected, and amended extensively in the later editions in 1932, 1958, and 1973, but notes that "essentially the book [as originally published] remained recognizable even in the fourth edition" (497). Says that Keynes first read Donne with Rupert Brooke and owned "one of the best private collections of Donne in the world" (498).

808. McNees, Eleanor. "John Donne and the Anglican Doctrine of the Eucharist." *TSLL* 29: 94–114.

Maintains that "[a]n analysis of Donne's eucharistic beliefs after his conversion from Roman Catholicism to Anglicanism allows one to place his divine poems within a securely orthodox Anglican context." Observes that Donne subscribed to "the Anglican emphasis on the sacrificial aspect of the Eucharist as opposed to the Zwinglian stress on memorial" and that he avoided Catholic, Lutheran, and Calvinist definitions of "the precise nature of the Real Presence," concentrating instead on "the individual's sacrificial preparation for 'conformity with Christ' prior to communion with him." Discusses how in his sacred poems, especially *Cross, Annun, Goodf,* and the *Holy Sonnets,* Donne dramatizes "the prospective communicant's struggle for conformity with Christ through self-sacrifice," and how he emphasizes "individual identification with Christ's crucifixion as a prerequisite for union with Christ's body in the Eucharist" (94). Shows how Donne uses puns and paradoxes "to address the task of realizing real presence within the speaker" (104).

809. McQueen, William A. "Donne's 'The Crosse.'" *Expl* 45, no. 3: 8–11.

Presents a critical reading of *Cross* to show that, although an occasional poem, written in response to the early seventeenth century Puritan attempt to abolish crosses from churches and to eliminate the use of the sign of the cross in baptism, its "emphasis is not primarily on the controversy concerning the cross but on the implicit meaning which the poet can discover in the cross." Pointing out that "[t]he word *crosse* (or variants of it) appears thirty-two times in the poem," maintains that "[t]here is a relentless focus on it and on the richness of meaning that can be garnered from its contemplation, whether of actual physical crosses or of metaphorical, spiritual crosses." Says "[t]he poem could easily be thought of as a meditation with the controversy over the cross serving as a point of initiation," and calls it "one of Donne's wittiest poems" (11).

810. Miller, Emily P. "Donne's *Biathanatos:* The Question of Audience." *MHLS* 10: 7–14.

Explores "the significant inherent conflicts" (7) in *Biathanatos,* noting that at times Donne's intended audience seems to be an elite scholastic group while at other times he addresses all Christians. Observes that his earnest analysis of the problem of

suicide is indistinguishably intermingled with paradox, satire, and humor, thereby obscuring his didactic purpose. Shows also that the implications of the metaphors Donne uses are often unclear and that *Biathanatos* reflects many of the tensions and conflicts that Donne was experiencing when he wrote the treatise. Concludes that "this paradoxically public, yet private work offers us valuable insight into the habits of the mind of both Jack Donne and Dr. Donne" (13).

811. Novarr, David. "*Amor Vincit Omnia:* Donne and the Limits of Ambiguity." *MLR* 82: 286–92.

Examines the arguments of critics who see a pun on "more" (Ann More) in several of Donne's poems, especially *Father, HSShe, Christ, ValWeep,* and *ValName,* "to determine how the pun, if it exists, may function in a particular poem and how its functions consort with other elements in the poem and with Donne's usual practice" (286). Concludes that readings of the poems based on the pun are, for the most part, "both strained and contrary to Donne's customary practice" (292).

812. Park, Tae-Ryong. "John Donne eui 'conceit' go. (On John Donne's 'conceit')." *Annual Bibliography of English Language and Literature* (Daejeon, Korea) 29: 51–68.

Listed in Modern Humanities Research Association 1987 #4975. Unavailable.

813. Parker, David. "Images of Life and Death in the Spirituality of John Donne." *Ormond Papers* (Ormond Coll. Univ. of Melbourne) 4: 75–81.

Discusses "the powerful entanglement in Donne's lyric verse of two threads of images—the thread of death and the thread of life and love," and suggests that "the devotional poems in which these two predominant strains of imagery are finally concentrated and resolved is a poetry of great emotional intensity" (75). Surveys the expression of love and death in Donne's love poetry, sermons, and religious poems. Maintains that "[t]he violent coincidence in the *Holy Sonnets* of a sense of death, arising from the poet's sinfulness, and a discerning of life, arising from Divine love, gives the poems great energy and force, and their emotion great authority" (79). Concludes that in such a poem as *HSSpit* "the identity of life and love and death in Donne is finally concentrated, in a poetry which aspires to a peace beyond understanding, and which speaks to us with authority of a life which knows pain and sorrow" (81).

814. Pawar, Malovika. "The Agony of Faith: A Comparative Study of the Holy Sonnets of Donne and the 'Terrible Sonnets' of G. M. Hopkins." *PURBA* 18, no. 2: 39–52.
Discusses "some of the similarities (and occasionally, the contrasts)" between the *Holy Sonnets* and Hopkins's "terrible sonnets" (39). Points out that "[t]he theme in both sequences is the terror of the soul at the prospect of an estrangement from God"; that, "structurally, both sequences are concerned with a progression of some kind" (40); and that both "are a fragment of the spiritual autobiography of the poet" (41). Discusses both sequences to show that the *Holy Sonnets* "depict the process of spiritual disintegration followed by reintegration through Christ" (43), whereas Hopkins's sonnets progress "from spiritual depletion to a feeling of spiritual and physical well-being" (47). Comments also on syntactical and linguistic similarities between the two sequences and discusses how each poet views God and his relationship to God. Says that both sequences are among the greatest attempts in verse to render a "cry for help" to God (51).

815. Pebworth, Ted-Larry. "Editing Literary Texts on the Microcomputer: The Example of John Donne's Poetry," in

The Donne Dalhousie Discovery: Proceedings of a Symposium on the Acquisition and Study of the John Donne and Joseph Conrad Collections at Texas Tech University, ed. Ernest W. Sullivan, II, and David J. Murrah, 41–56. Lubbock, Tex.: Friends of the University Library/ Southwest Collection.
Discusses the use of the microcomputer by the textual editors of the variorum edition of Donne's poetry in storing and organizing collations, analyzing texts, and compiling lists of textual variants. Stresses that, helpful as the computer is in "the task of organization and tabular analysis," the "final determination of a copy text of each poem and any emendations to it" (42) can only be made by a human agent, not by a machine. Describes the features of the Donne Variorum Collation Program and explains the step-by-step procedure for entering data, using *Faust* and the heading and the first two lines of *FunEl* as examples. Concludes that the goal of the textual editors is "an edition that carries the study of Donne's texts as far as known resources permit," an edition that "should bring us closer to what Donne actually wrote than does any previous edition" (49).

816. Pebworth, Ted-Larry. "The Editor, the Critic, and the Multiple Texts of Donne's 'A Hymne to God the Father.'" *SCRev* 4, no. 2: 16–34.
Discusses the textual complexity of *Father* to challenge "the implicit assumption that every literary text is inevitably singular" (16). Observes that an examination of all early manuscript and printed copies of Donne's hymn confirms that there are "three distinct texts of the poem: two similar, but substantively different versions, both addressed to Christ, in the manuscripts that circulated during Donne's lifetime and just afterwards, and a third, quite different text, addressed to God the Father, in the posthumous

printing of 1633" (19–20). Prints the three texts, commenting on how they differ, and gives in an appendix "complete textual apparatuses for the three texts, including historical collations and a stemma outlining in detail the probable textual history of the poem" (20). Notes that most modern editors have created "eclectic versions of Donne's hymn (some lines from one source, some lines from another)," thereby creating "texts that never existed before their appearance in modern editions" (24). Concludes, therefore, that "[t]he multiple texts of Donne's poetry should be presented as distinct entities in a manner that makes clear their historical evolution" (24), and that editors "should henceforth cease constructing eclectic texts of poems that exist in demonstrably multiple texts" (25).

817. **Pinnington, A[drian] J.** "Prayer and Praise in John Donne's *La Corona*," in *Poetry and Faith in the English Renaissance: Essays in Honour of Professor Toyohiko Tatsumi's Seventieth Birthday,* ed. Peter Milward, 133–42. Renaissance Monographs, 13. Tokyo: Renaissance Institute, Sophia University.

Argues that "the theological understanding of the relationship between man and God" found in *Corona* is "precisely the same as that present in the majority of the *Holy Sonnets*," and that "beneath the surface formality of the work the same spiritual anxieties can be detected" (133). Shows how, in *Corona*, as in the *Holy Sonnets*, Donne wrestles with "the question of death and the speaker's standing with God." Finds in *Corona* "a mixture of prayer and praise," a praise that is "rooted in the depiction of the speaker's own spiritual state." Concludes that "[t]he vitality of the sequence derives precisely from the interplay between these two elements—the life of Christ and that of the speaker, the mysteries of election and the ambi-

guity of the speaker's 'low devout melancholie'" (142).

818. **Radzinowicz, Mary Ann.** "'Anima Mea' Psalms and John Donne's Religious Poetry," in *"Bright Shootes of Everlastingnesse": The Seventeenth-Century Religious Lyric,* ed. Claude J. Summers and Ted-Larry Pebworth, 40–58. Columbia: University of Missouri Press.

Discusses how in *HSSighs, HSBlack, HSWhat, HSWilt, HSSouls,* and *Annun* Donne uses a device found in eight of the psalms—"the dialogue of a man with his soul" (40). Shows also how in *HSShe* and *Sickness* the device is implied. Maintains that the device "helped Donne to create the complex poetic voices of his religious poetry, by distinguishing between a speaker and the agency of his inner feeling," and that it "sanctioned for him a stance both learned and impassioned, both personal and vicarious, both univocal and congregational." Believes that these "anima mea" psalms exemplified for Donne "the combination of personal and congregational lyric voice that moves his poetry toward his priestly vocation and at every stage of that journey enriches it" (41). Points out that "[t]he history of the device in seventeenth-century English religious poetry after Donne is the history of Donnean influence and allusion as well as of biblical poetic," for "[t]he honor of the first adaptations of the trope in the seventeenth century . . . is surely Donne's, for whom it answered such complex religious, personal, poetical, and vocational needs" (58).

819. **Raspa, Anthony.** "Time, History and Typology in John Donne's *Pseudo-Martyr*." *Ren&R*, n.s. 11: 175–83.

Argues that in *Pseudo-Martyr* Donne "sought to devise for himself and his readers, both Catholic and Protestant, a viable idea of the church as a temporal thing," seeking, in other words, to understand "the manner in which the Lord transferred himself out of his individual person in the realm of eternity into his likeness of a Christian collectivity in the dimension of time" (175). Suggests that, "perversely," what *Pseudo-Martyr* tells English Catholics is "to take the Oath of Allegiance, to retain their spiritual loyalty to the spiritual authority of Rome, and to stop putting the hangman's rope around their necks," in other words, arguing rather "perversely" that "the spiritual authorities of both London and Rome are perfectly correct" (176). Shows how Donne's concept of time, history, and typology are relevant to an understanding of his unique view of the Christian Church as a temporal phenomenon. Says that Donne "tried to maintain the character of the Church as constant by claiming a typological, mystical character for it" while, at the same time, "he allowed various justifiable expressions for the structure of the Church throughout human history" based on "scholastic conceptions of matter and form." Points out that, for Donne, "[h]istory could allow many valid Christian Churches to exist, not only chronologically throughout the past, but in a variety of national states in the present as well," thereby allowing "various images of the same eternal truth to exist linearly through history and to coexist together in the present" (181). Concludes that "Donne's message in *Pseudo-Martyr,* in spite of some of his virulent anti-Catholic diatribes, was coming perilously close to telling Christians to love one another as Christ had loved them" (182).

820. Ray, Robert H. "Another Perspective on Donne in the Seventeenth Century: Nehemiah Rogers's Allusions to the *Sermons* and 'A Hymne to God the Father.'" *JDJ* 6: 51–54.

Cites references to and uses of Donne's work that appear in four works published between 1540 and 1662 by Nehemiah Rogers, royalist clergyman (1593–1660). Notes that all the allusions, except one to *Father,* come from the sermons. Says that "[t]he primary interest in Rogers's uses of Donne is what they imply about Donne's reputation and influence at this time" (51), and calls for further investigation of the early reception and influence of Donne's prose, especially his sermons.

821. Ray, Robert H. "Herbert's Words in Donne's Mouth: Walton's Account of Donne's Death." *MP* 85: 186–87.

Suggests that in the 1658 edition of *The Life of John Donne* Izaak Walton attributes to Donne just before his death a phrase from George Herbert's motto found in "The Posie" ("Lesse then the least / Of all Gods mercies"). Suggests that the quotation reflects Walton's growing interest in Herbert and his poetry at this time, noting that it is in the 1658 edition that Walton first comments on Donne's friendship with Herbert. Believes Walton inserted the motto because he "was obsessed by Herbert's poetry" and "had Herbert's motto enforced in his consciousness by [Nicholas] Ferrar and [Barnabas] Oley," both of whom had emphasized it in their works on Herbert. Concludes that "[a]dding such Herbertian humility to Donne's own preparation for death provided an easy way for Walton to further his canonization of Donne" (187).

822. Reid, David. "A Drummond Borrowing from Donne." *N&Q,* n.s. 34: 307.

Points out that ll. 1–8 of William Drummond's commendatory sonnet in Sir William Moore's *The True Crucifixe for True Catholickes* (1629) contain conceits borrowed from *Cross,* which he apparently saw in a manuscript copy of Donne's poems, since *Cross* was not published until 1633.

823. Roberts, John R., and Gary A. Stringer, eds. "A Special Issue: John Donne." *SCRev* 4, no. 2.

Contains eight original essays on Donne, each of which has been separately entered into this bibliography. All but one of the essays were presented at the first annual meeting of the John Donne Society held on the Gulf Park campus of the University of Southern Mississippi in February 1986. Points out in the preface that the essays "represent a variety of ways to understand Donne and to read his works, some traditional, some new," and that "collectively they treat of his efforts in a number of genres, including the love lyric, the erotic elegy, the divine sonnet, the hymn, and the sermons."

824. Rossi, Tiziana. "John Donne: Mística y erotismo bajo el signo de la muerte." *Hora de Poesía* 49–50: 71–77.

Discusses how the conflicts in Donne himself between erotic and sacred love, thought and feeling, and his earlier Catholicism and later Anglicanism are reflected in his poetry. Sees Donne as one who never fully reconciled these opposites and thus his poetry contains many paradoxes. Points out that one finds much human passion in Donne's religious poems and many mystical and religious elements in his love poems. Comments on Donne's pervasive obsession with death both in his life and his works and suggests that only in death, and thus in immortality, does he find the possibility of a resolution to the conflicts in his tormented soul.

825. Roston, Murray. "Varieties of Seventeenth-Century Prose," in *Renaissance Perspectives in Literature and the Visual Arts,* 279–300. Princeton, N.J.: Princeton University Press.

Calls Donne the "exemplar of mannerist prose in England" and comments on the sermons and *Devotions*. Finds in Donne's prose "the abandonment of majestic Ciceronian rhetoric in favour of a more personal idiom less

tolerant of logical progression, more immediate in its sudden tergiversations" (296), and praises especially "the sense it conveys of a process of discovery shared by author and reader." Discusses how this "emergent style was not mere fashion but symptomatic of a changing philosophical outlook" (297). Sees in Donne's sermon on the wedding of Margaret Washington in 1621 similarities with Tintoretto's *Miracle of the Brazen Serpent,* pointing out that in the sermon Donne recaptures "in words the immediacy of the preacher's own visionary experience—not universalizing the human condition into magniloquently abstract terms but, with all its significance for every Christian soul, focussing on the compelling hopes, fears, and trust of the speaker's intimate self" (300).

826. Sellin, Paul R., and Augustus J. Veenendaal, Jr. "A 'Pub Crawl' through Old The Hague: Shady Light on Life and Art among English Friends of John Donne in The Netherlands, 1627–1635." *JDJ* 6: 235–59.

Discusses and gives an English translation of an anonymous ten-stanza Dutch poem entitled "Een Gesstelijk Liedeken" ("A Spiritual Ditty") found in the so-called Conway Papers in the British Library (Additional MS 23229, fol. 169r–v), in which the soldier-speaker of the poem refers to "real places, persons, life and society in The Hague during the first quarter of the seventeenth century" (243) and, in its depiction of immorality, reminds one of Dutch genre paintings of the time, especially the "kortegaardjes" (or "figure paintings of soldiers") and the "bordeeltjes" (or "brothel scenes"). Maintains that "[t]he Conway manuscript serves to remind us that certain coarser elements in Donne's own poetry are not far removed from Netherlandish work in this vein" (246). Argues that as a solider Donne would have known firsthand the world of camp life and bordellos and maintains that by seeing certain poems, especially the *Elegies,* "as though they were poetic equivalents of Dutch 'bordello-ettes' may help to clarify their structure" and "lend better rationale to what otherwise seems but rather pointless indulgence in verbal indecency." Concludes that "for Protestants schooled in doctrines of original sin and the total depravity of man, like Donne and many of his friends in the Dutch military, acknowledging things to be what they are without illusion was perhaps a first step to salvation," and insists that, "[u]nlike Hieronymous Bosch or Jonathan Swift, notably enough, Donne eschews the scatological" (249). Includes six illustrations (256–59).

827. Sessions, William A. "Abandonment and the English Religious Lyric in the Seventeenth Century," in *"Bright Shootes of Everlastingnesse": The Seventeenth-Century Religious Lyric,* ed. Claude J. Summers and Ted-Larry Pebworth, 1–19. Columbia: University of Missouri Press.

Argues that many religious lyrics of the seventeenth century contain a mode of abandonment that seems similar to "the hopeless cries of the abandoned women of classical tradition" (5). Comments on archetypes of abandonment, loss, and vulnerability in the Psalms, Virgil, Ovid, Chaucer, Petrarch and his imitators, medieval lyricists, Shakespeare, the Renaissance humanists, and the Spanish mystics. Believes that Sappho's love complaint is, in fact, "the absolute topos for the experience of abandonment that . . . is the basis of the seventeenth century religious lyric" (8), noting how Donne in his *Sappho* clearly captures this sense of abandonment. Argues that seventeenth century English religious poets wrote "lyrics of human experience that define both sides of a

dialectical contradiction, constantly qualifying ecstasy in terms of abandonment," and that they express the "same classical sense of loss, abandonment, and vulnerability" (12) found in erotic poetry. Discusses *HSVex* as an example of "a lyric whose overt contradictory linguistic structure concentrates the drama inevitable in any dialectic of abandonment at the same time that it emphasizes, in a positive sense, its triviality," and suggests that the sonnet becomes "a model text about the nature of love, whatever kind" (16).

828. Severance, Sibyl Lutz. "Soul, Sphere, and Structure in 'Goodfriday, 1613. Riding Westward.'" *SP* 84: 24–43.

Discusses the circular structure of *Goodf,* indicating how Donne "places similar topics in sections containing equal numbers of lines as he precisely balances the parts" of the poem. Claims that "[t]hrough this symmetry Donne creates his formal trope of poem as circle, corresponding to his metaphor of soul as sphere" (24). Finds in the poem "a symmetrical nine-part pattern: 8,2,4,6,2,6,4,2,8," and argues that "the two principal metaphors of the verbal text—the sphere and the journey—are reflected and fulfilled by the shape and in the movement of the formal subtext." Claims, in other words, that in the poem "form amplifies the resonance of words" (25). Finds various numerological significances in the multiform structure of the poem and suggests that, by recognizing this complex structure and the extensive numerological symbolism that supports it, one comes to understand Donne's "profound consecration of craft and reason in 'figuring forth' a 'speaking picture' of his faith" (41).

829. Shami, Jeanne. "John Donne: Geography as Metaphor," in *Geography and Literature: A Meeting of the Disciplines,* ed. William E. Mallory and Paul Simpson-Housley, 161–67. Syracuse, N.Y.: Syracuse University Press.

Points out that often Donne's ideas "are given form and clarity through his geographical metaphors of maps," and discusses *Sickness* as the best example of his use of "the structural function of geographical metaphors" (164), a poem in which he synthesizes the medieval T-in-O map with the Renaissance flat map "into the completed vision of his poem" (167).

830. **Shami, Jeanne.** "Kings and Desperate Men: John Donne Preaches at Court." *JDJ* 6: 9–23.

Examines ways that Donne fulfilled his obligation as a court preacher and moral critic while, at the same time, he circumvented the dangers faced by those who rashly criticized the king. Shows how Donne at court "speaks ideally of the King's role (as James himself did), but in doing so challenges James personally to live up to this role and, indirectly, at least, invites his audience to discern any ironic disjunctions between ideal and real." Observes that at court Donne "also establishes his own spiritual authority as analogous, and by implication equal to, the King's," and limits the king's power in his sermons by his "claims for the sovereignty of conscience, a belief upheld in theory by James in *Basilikon Doron,* but which in practice he was reluctant to grant to any but himself." Points out, therefore, that "[i]n his court sermons Donne takes James at his word" (11). Discusses in particular Donne's sermon at Paul's Cross defending King James's *Directions to Preachers* as reflecting his "finely tuned sense of discretion." Maintains that "[b]y upholding the example of Christ as contrast to the King, by stressing the supremacy of the Law of both God and Conscience as the final moral

arbiters, and by asserting the balance of jurisdiction between church and State, Donne challenges the King's words in a King's court." Believes that "the limitations and balances which Donne's court sermons continually assert allow Donne to qualify and limit that power." Concludes that in his court sermons Donne "responds to the challenge of his vocation tactfully in sermons that serve as reminders of the delicate balance that constituted relations between Church and State in the early seventeenth century," and that these sermons "are models of the discretion required in channelling and guiding, if not absolutely controlling, the turbulent sources of political power" (21).

831. **Shawcross, John T.** "The Concept of *Sermo* in Donne and Herbert." *JDJ* 6: 203–12.

Shows how the medieval concept of *sermo*—"a conversation and a joining together of ideas, presented to lead the auditor into a heartfelt and thoughtful experience—underlies some of the poetry of both Donne and Herbert, providing a somewhat different avenue into our understanding of those poems and our appreciation of their form, structure, and imagistic components." Cites as specific examples *Dream, ValWeep, Triple, LovUsury,* and *Commun,* poems that "reflect the conversational style in setting of speaker and auditor, in tone and language" (205), and cites *Lect* as a poem that is not an example of *sermo.*

832. **Shawcross, John T.** "'What do you read?' 'Words'—Ah, But Are They Donne's?" in *The Donne Dalhousie Discovery: Proceedings of a Symposium on the Acquisition and Study of the John Donne and Joseph Conrad Collections at Texas Tech University,* ed. Ernest W. Sullivan, II, and David J. Murrah, 21–31. Lubbock, Tex.: Friends of the University Library/Southwest Collection.

Argues for the need for and the difficulties inherent in establishing a "defensible" text of Donne's poetry—"defensible if not certain; if not assuredly the author's, at least defensible" (23). Maintains that "the poet's craft is important" and that "[t]he only raw material from which we can derive valid conclusions about the craft is the text itself, so we must be sure that the text is indeed the best authorial text." Points out that most of Donne's poetry was published posthumously, that "we have only one poem and two epigrammatic book inscriptions in his own hand," and that "no study has been made of his practices of spelling and punctuation and the like (from letters and such that we do have in his own hand)." Maintains that, in establishing a defensible text, "we must study the numerous texts available in manuscript and print to try to determine what it is that he actually wrote." Insists, however, that "we can only approach such a text, at times being on surer ground than at others," but that "every means helpful to putting us in the right direction should be undertaken" (26). Evaluates the importance of the Dalhousie manuscripts in determining the text of Donne's poems.

833. **Shuger, Debora K.** "The Power Within: The Grand Style and Problems of the Self in Renaissance Literature." *BSUF* 28, no. 1: 5–19.

Examines first "the implications of the late sixteenth-century shift from ornament to passion common to both prose and poetry" and second "the differences between Renaissance love poetry and religious prose in order to suggest that the equation of the grand style with the Ciceronian or courtly styles is incorrect and that the popular association of self-expression and the plain style fits the facts of Elizabethan and Jacobean erotic poetry only

with qualifications, while the relation of self to style in religious prose demands a wholly different explanation" (5). Argues that "the development of Renaissance prose and poetry does not move from an ornate to a plain style, but from an ornate to a passionate or grand style," noting that although in poetry the plain style plays a role, it does so "only by entering into a novel combination with the grand style" (8). Argues that "poetry written after the 1590s shows more concern for being passionate and dramatic than poetry written earlier in the century," and points out that, although not usually thought of as a devotional poet in the grand style, Donne's works are, in fact, primarily characterized by their "affective power" (9) and passionate "subjectivity" (10). Observes that in the sixteenth and early seventeenth centuries "poetry tends toward a passionate plainness," whereas "prose, especially religious prose, is increasingly written in the grand style," although both "move in the direction of greater subjectivity and passion" (11). Cites Donne's sermons to illustrate their power, passion, subjectivity, and "dramatized interiority" (16), emphasizing, however, that like other Renaissance writers, he "focuses upon the self, but not necessarily the unique, individual self too complex for doctrinal formulation." Concludes that the "fusion of private and public experience expresses itself in the passionate and dramatic grand style characteristic of late Renaissance prose" (17).

834. **Smith, A. J.** "The Poetry of John Donne," in *New History of Literature, II: English Poetry and Prose, 1540–1674,* ed. Christopher Ricks, 137–69. New York: Bedrick, 1987. Reprinted from *English Poetry and Prose, 1540–1674,* ed. Christopher Ricks, History of Literature in the English Language, vol. 2

(London: Barrie and Jenkins in association with Sphere Books, 1970), 137–72. See *Roberts 2.*

835. Smith, Gary. "Gwendolyn Brooks's 'Children of the Poor,' Metaphysical Poetry and the Inconditions of Love," in *A Life Distilled: Gwendolyn Brooks, Her Poetry and Fiction,* ed. Maria K. Mooty and Gary Smith, 165–76. Urbana: University of Illinois Press.

Compares Gwendolyn Brooks and Donne as "metaphysical" poets. Analyzes the structural complexity, metaphorical language, and diction of *HSBatter* as representative of Donne's art and discusses how Brooks's sonnet sequence *The Children of the Poor* "contains many of the same stylistic difficulties one finds in Donne's *Holy Sonnets,*" noting, however, that "it also presents a distinct departure from many of his themes" (169).

836. Streekstra, N. F. "Huygens als Donnevertaler: Linguistisch-stilistisch aspecten van een vertaalstrategie," in *Huygens in Nooder Licht: Lezingen van het Gronings Huygens-symposium,* ed. N. F. Streekstra and P. E. L. Verkuyl, 25–44. Groningen: Universiteitsdrukkerij.

Discusses Huygens's translations of Donne in the light of his earlier translations from Guarini's *Il pastor fido* and from du Bartas's *La Sepmaine de la creation du monde,* in which Huygens stayed close to the prosodic and metric forms of the originals. Believes this kind of faithfulness to the original seems not to have satisfied the mature Huygens and that by the time he translated Donne in 1630 and 1633, he took greater freedoms than before. Argues that while some of these freedoms seem fairly arbitrary (for instance, the expansion of three short lines into two alexandrines in *Triple*), others seem to obey the dictate of the originals, to some extent. (For example, he translated *SunRis* in three stanzas of ten lines, conforming in this respect to the original, whereas the prosody within each translated stanza is in many respects different from Donne's.) Maintains that the complexity of Donne's stanza forms presented Huygens with difficulties that he solved by employing greater freedom than with Guarini and du Bartas. Surveys instances in which rhyme schemes are similar to Donne's and others where they are not. Observes that Huygens's translation of *Ecst* deviates more from Donne's original than any of his other translations. Contextualizes the argument by closing with a demonstration of how a modern Dutch translator of Donne, Jan Eijkelbloom, has translated some of the same poems as Huygens but adhered strictly to Donne's prosody. Concludes that Huygens's departures represent a distinct linguistic and stylistic strategy.

837. Stringer, Gary A. "When It's Done, It Will Be Donne: The Variorum Edition of the Poetry of John Donne," in *The Donne Dalhousie Discovery: Proceedings of a Symposium on the Acquisition and Study of the John Donne and Joseph Conrad Collections at Texas Tech University,* ed. Ernest W. Sullivan, II, and David J. Murrah, 57–62. Lubbock, Tex: Friends of the University Library/Southwest Collection.

Presents an overall view of the variorum edition of Donne's poetry, focusing primarily on the editorial principles and procedures governing the commentary sections of the edition. Explains the purpose of the edition and the history of its origin and describes the organization and the financial and institutional support of the project at the time.

838. Stringer, Gary A., and William R. Vilberg. "The Donne Variorum Textual Collation." *CHum* 21: 83–89.

Describes and illustrates the computer program employed by the textual editors of the variorum edition of Donne's poetry and explains how source materials are transcribed and collated.

839. Sullivan, David M. "Riders to the West: 'Goodfriday, 1613.'" *JDJ* 6: 1–8.

Points out that "riding westward" was a colloquialism in Donne's time that literally meant "going to Tyburn," that is, to the gallows located in London's West End, and believes that *Goodf* should be read "as it was understood by Donne's contemporaries, who would have recognized in it the elaborate conceit so highly dated that it has become lost since, and with it part of the poem's coherence and wit" (2). Points out that in his Easter sermon of 1619 Donne refers to death as an execution and argues that such a view of death is "the controlling metaphor" of *Goodf* and "a key to understanding it" (4). Suggests that in the dramatic unfolding of the argument of the poem, the speaker finally "sees death, physical and spiritual, as a punishment which redeems" (6). Does not believe that the poem dramatizes literally "the meditations of a man actually being carted off to Tyburn," but rather, "only symbolically, insofar as he is Everyman, and inasmuch as he is, in a minor key, by imitation, Christ himself." Concludes that the poem "records a crucial moment in a man's moral life when he becomes fully conscious of his dying, yet manages to meet it with humility and acceptance, though not without fear and trembling," acknowledging that "to ride westward is not only inevitable but finally more good than bad" and that ultimately "death means life" (7).

840. Sullivan, Ernest W., II. "'And having done that, Thou hast done': Locating, Acquiring, and Studying the Dalhousie Donne Manuscripts," in *The Donne Dalhousie Discovery: Proceedings of a Symposium on the Acquisition and Study of the John Donne and Joseph Conrad Collections at Texas Tech University,* ed. Ernest W. Sullivan, II and David J. Murrah, 1–10. Lubbock, Tex.: Friends of the University Library/Southwest Collection.

Describes the identification, acquisition, and study of the first and second Dalhousie Manuscripts, which contain 71 poems by Donne, now housed in the Texas Tech University Library. Announces the forthcoming edition of the manuscripts. Describes the contents of each manuscript and notes that Dalhousie I was probably transcribed between 1613 and 1625 and that Dalhousie II was likely transcribed between 1622 and 1628. Points out how the two manuscripts "are certainly part of the major Donne manuscript traditions" (9).

841. Sullivan, Ernest W., II. "Updating the John Donne Listings in Peter Beal's *Index of English Literary Manuscripts.*" *JDJ* 6: 219–34.

Updates the Donne section of Peter Beal's *Index of English Literary Manuscripts,* vol. 1, part 1 (1980), by identifying newly discovered manuscripts, new locations of manuscripts, and additional poems and prose, as well as additional and corrected pagination or foliation.

842. Sullivan, Ernest W., II, and David J. Murrah, eds. *The Donne Dalhousie Discovery: Proceedings of a Symposium on the Acquisition and Study of the John Donne and Joseph Conrad Collections at Texas Tech University.* Lubbock, Tex.: Friends of the University Library/Southwest Collection. vii, 71p.

Proceedings of a symposium held at Texas Tech University on 7–8 November 1984, celebrating the acquisition of the first and second Dalhousie Manuscripts, which contain 71 poems by Donne. Each of the Donne essays has been separately entered into this bibliography. Reviews: John B. Gabel in *PBSA* 83 (1989): 101–03; Paul Parrish in *SCN* 47 (1989): 9.

843. Summers, Claude J. "The Bride of the Apocalypse and the Quest for True Religion: Donne, Herbert, and Spenser," in *"Bright Shootes of Everlastingnesse": The Seventeenth-Century Religious Lyric,* ed. Claude J. Summers and Ted-Larry Pebworth, 72–95. Columbia: University of Missouri Press.

Points out that both Donne in *HSShow* and Herbert in "The British Church" "contrast the image of the Bride of the Apocalypse with distinctly unbride-like women who represent various manifestations of the visible Church" (72). Argues that "both poems are probably indebted to the conflict of Protestantism (as represented by Una) and Roman Catholicism (as represented by Duessa) in the first book of Spenser's *The Faerie Queene*," especially to "the revelation of Una as the Church Triumphant" in Book 1.12.22. Shows how "[t]he image of the Bride of the Apocalypse functions for all three poets as a mirror of their own religio-political assumptions" (73). Analyzes *HSShow* in detail, pointing out Donne's indebtedness to Spenser but also stressing how Donne expresses considerable skepticism as to the validity of Spenser's claim that English Protestantism is the true religion. Argues that, although the sonnet "expresses Donne's sincere desire for communion with Christ's spouse the Church," the extended sexual conceit in the conclusion "exposes the poet's recognition of the preposterous irony involved in any quest for true religion that identifies Christ's spouse with a temporal institution" (81). Emphasizes, in other words, that Donne resists the tendency of both Catholics and Protestants to identify the Church Triumphant with a specific temporal institution. Concludes that in the sonnet, Donne "expresses a vision [of the Church] that is at once skeptical of rival temporal institutions and also tolerant of them, juxtaposing their dubious historical records against a transcendent image of unity and love jarringly difficult to accept in human terms and impossible to equate with the unbridelike personifications of Roman Catholicism and Protestantism" (94).

844. Tarlinskaja, Marina. "Meter and Language: Binary and Ternary Meters in English and Russian." *Style* 21: 626–49. The information on Donne appears also in *Shakespeare's Verse: Iambic Pentameter and the Poet's Idiosyncrasies* (New York: Peter Lang, 1987).

Noting that a "verse meter, for example iambic or trochaic, acquires specific features as it develops on the basis of a particular language within a particular literature," singles out "common and distinctive features in variants of the same or related verse forms as they have evolved" in Russian and English. Notes that in this study "[t]he material of the typological comparison is English and Russian binary and ternary meters" and that "English and Russian iambic pentameter is compared with the Italian hendecasyllable" (626). Shows that "English metrical verse is looser than Russian" (644). Uses Donne's *Satyres* in the study.

845. Teague, Anthony. "Suffering, Trust and Hope in English Renaissance Literature." *RenB* 14: 13–44.

Suggests that Donne's life and poetry are suffused with suffering and psychological anguish and that perhaps readers are drawn to him, not because of his wit or "metaphysicality," but by "the sense of being close to a person inhabited by a nameless, limitless pain locked in the deep recesses of the soul" (30). Explores the nature of Donne's suffering and despair, claiming that "Donne always shows an inner state about which he feels that he can do nothing" (33).

846. Todd, Richard. "'So Well Attyr'd Abroad': A Background to the Sidney-Pembroke Psalter and Its Implications for the Seventeenth-Century Religious Lyric." *TSLL* 29: 74–93.

Comments on Donne's appreciation for and praise of the Sidney-Pembroke Psalter, as well as Psalm translations in other vernacular languages, and notes his attack on the translations of Sternhold and Hopkins. Suggests that in praising European translations of the Psalms Donne may have had in mind the *Souterliedekens* (1540), attributed to Jonkheer Willem van Zuylen van Nyevelt, and argues also that very likely "the example of the *Souterliedekens* . . . lies behind the Sidneys' achievement." Urges Anglo-American scholars who study the seventeenth century religious lyric to pay more attention in the future "not just to the *Souterliedekens* but to other, related, literary products of scriptural vernacularization throughout Reformation Europe" (89).

847. Turner, James Grantham. *One Flesh: Paradisal Marriage and Sexual Relations in the Age of Milton.* Oxford: Clarendon Press. xvi, 320p.

Comments throughout on Donne's interpretation of the story of the fall in Genesis and on his Augustinian attitudes towards marriage and sexuality. Observes that Donne opposed the "Puritan" notion of companionate marriage; defended celibacy and mortification; and saw in Eve's creation "nothing but a sinister depletion" of man (115). Maintains that throughout his life Donne "continued to develop and refine the cynical paradoxes latent in the fall-story" as well as "its sardonic lessons about the nature of sexuality." Points out that in *FirAn* and later in the Nethersole wedding sermon Donne "repeats with relish the outrageous proposition first made in the brash and youthful *Metempsychosis*—that 'the first wedding was our funeral,' since Eve slew her husband, and since her daughters continue to kill us 'delightfully' by sexual

depletion." Finds in *Twick,* however, "the most brilliant crossing of the sacred myth with the conventions of the world of love," and notes "a precise parallel" between it and *BedfRef* (169). Points out that Donne's "various sexualizations of the Paradise myth" in his poetry are "strangely serious" despite their "playful" contexts (170).

848. Vickers, Brian. "The Seventeenth Century, 1603–1674," in *The Oxford Illustrated History of English Literature,* ed. Pat Rogers, 160–213. Oxford: Oxford University Press. xiv, 528p. Reprinted (without illustrations) as *An Outline of English Literature,* ed. Pat Rogers (Oxford University Press, 1992), 150–99. 2nd ed., 1998.

Calls Donne and Jonson "two of the most forceful and influential writers of the [seventeenth] century" (169), and calls the *Songs and Sonets* "arguably the greatest collection of lyric poems in English" (170). Surveys Donne's poetry and discusses its major characteristics, such as experimentation with traditional forms, use of argumentative and dramatic techniques, rejection of conventional attitudes toward love, and use of startling paradox and wit. Cites *Noct* as the greatest of the love poems and *Goodf* as the greatest of the religious poems. Comments also on Donne's sermons and manner of preaching. Suggests that Donne's sermons "appeal to the ear, the mind, and the emotions" (175), and contrasts their style with the sermons of Lancelot Andrewes. Notes that Donne's individuality "expressed itself in terms of language, argument, [and] poetic form" rather than by "self-revelation" (176).

849. Waddington, Raymond B. "'When thou has done, thou hast not done.'" *JDJ* 6: 135–45.

Reviews C. A. Patrides's *The Complete English Poems of John Donne* (1985) (entry 568) and surveys the complexity of the editorial principles and procedures encountered by several major twentieth century editors of Donne's poetry, in particular, H. J. C. Grierson, Helen Gardner, A. J. Smith, and John T. Shawcross. Waddington says that if he were selecting a text for a graduate seminar, he might choose the Shawcross edition; but for a survey of English seventeenth century poetry, he would be inclined to pick Patrides's edition.

850. Wakefield, D. R., ed. *Some Trout: Poetry on Trout and Angling by Various Authors; With Etchings by D. R. Wakefield.* Wiveliscombe, Somersetshire: Chevington Press. 18 leaves. Limited edition, 75 copies.

Reproduces poems on fishing—two poems by Ted Hughes and one each by George Mackay Brown, Rupert Brooke, Andrew Young, and Seamus Heaney—and Donne's *Bait*. Includes 13 prints by Wakefield.

851. Walker, Julia M. "Donne's Words Taught in Numbers." *SP* 84: 44–60.

Reads *LovGrow* and *ElBrac* in the light of Renaissance numerology. Says that in *LovGrow* Donne "seeks out, through the processes of numerology, the 'correspondences' between love and other natural phenomenon" and that he, "through the process of the poem, enables both his speaker and the reader to understand the seeming paradox of a love which is at once perfect and yet ever increasing." Shows how Donne uses "both information and processes from numerology and astronomy as well as information from alchemy and other Renaissance and Medieval systems of knowledge to make a more powerful, yet much more subtle, statement about the nature of the two lovers and their love than critics usually acknowledge" (48). Maintains that in *LovGrow* "[t]he combination of the astrological patterns of the cosmic cycles and the numerological patterns formed by the

temporal cycles strongly suggest that the poet may be encoding information from Pythagorean doctrines (which characteristically dealt with *both* astrology and numerology) set forth in the *Timaeus*" (49). Argues that in *ElBrac* Donne presents through numerology, reversed alchemy, and rhetorical distancing a picture of an obsessive love for gold, which, unlike an obsessive love for a woman, "shatters all natural values and processes and leaves its victims with nothing" (59).

852. Walker, Julia. "The Religious Lyric as Genre." *ELN* 25: 39–45.

Maintains that during the seventeenth century the religious lyric "ceased to exist as a poetic reality at the same time it came to exist as a genre," and examines *Corona*, Herbert's "A Wreath," and Marvell's "The Coronet" to show "the increasing intrusion of a poetic presence which is neither a private man nor his private God, but a public audience" (39). Claims that the "awareness of generic tradition tipped the balance of the religious lyric increasingly from the private mode toward the public mode" and "from an external, tacit audience toward an internal or contextual audience," and that "[t]his generic awareness of audience turns the religious lyric's focus away from the experience itself and toward the presentation of the experience" (40). Argues that *Corona*, although written in a public liturgical form, has no audience other than God, the Virgin Mary, and St. Joseph, that is, "the audience does not exist *within* the poem." Says that Donne is not trying "to make a private experience into a public pattern, as he does in so many of the *Songs and Sonets*" (41). Concludes that in *Corona* "the form creates a private religious experience which neither requires nor admits the presence of a public" (42).

853. Warnke, Frank J. *John Donne.* Twayne's English Authors Series, ed.

Arthur F. Kinney, 444. Boston: Twayne Publishers. 143p.

Presents a brief, comprehensive survey of Donne's life and works. States in the preface (followed by a chronology of Donne's life) that the aim of this study is not "to advance any new knowledge about Donne or any original view of his genius" but rather "to sketch an overview that will do justice both to his position as a man and artist of his time and to those peculiar individual features that led so many intellectuals of the 1920s and 1930s to regard him as a kindred spirit." Adds that a second goal is "to see Donne and his England in the larger framework of Europe in the baroque age" and "to suggest something of the general kinship between Donne and his [Continental] coevals." Chapter 1, "Life and Career" (1–11), comments on Donne's twentieth century reputation and surveys generally his life and works, emphasizing Donne's "baroque imagination." Chapter 2, "Baroque Europe and England" (12–19), attempts to show how the literature of Donne's England participated fully "in both the intellectual concerns and the literary historical rhythms of baroque Europe" (14) and how Donne's poetry and prose reflect baroque sensibility. Chapter 3, "Juvenilia, Satyres, Early Elegies" (20–30), comments on Donne's earliest literary works and on his wit. Chapter 4, "Songs and Sonets" (31–60), discusses the general characteristics of Donne's love poetry, such as his use of a dramatic persona, irregular metrics, colloquial diction, psychological verisimilitude, and rejection of attitudes and stylistic conventions of traditional love poetry. Divides the *Songs and Sonets* into various categories—cynical poems, Neoplatonic poems, poems of idealism, and valedictory poems—and examines the problem of tone in Donne's poetry. Comments in some detail on *GoodM*,

Canon, LovInf, Noct, Air, and *Ecst*. Chapter 5, "Mid-Period Poetry and Prose" (61–90), surveys the later elegies, the epithalamia, the verse epistles, the funerary poems, *Corona, Lit,* minor devotional poems, *Pseudo-Martyr, Ignatius, Biathanatos,* and especially the *Anniversaries*. Chapter 6, "Sermons and Devotions" (91–103), comments on Donne's sermons as expressions of the baroque, commenting particularly on his Easter Day sermon of 1628, and briefly discusses *Devotions*. Chapter 7, "Divine Poems" (104–166), discusses the *Holy Sonnets* as a meditative sequence, *Goodf,* and the hymns. Suggests that in *Sickness* "[t]he themes, motifs, and techniques that had dominated his life's work— conceited imagery, radical paradox, a preoccupation with geography and cartography, dramatic tone, colloquial diction, the desperate desire for transcendence—are brought together to form a consummate masterpiece of baroque devotional poetry" (115). Chapter 8, "Reputation and Influence" (117–25), surveys Donne's fluctuating popularity and influence. Concludes that although his poetry and prose are "no longer central to contemporary literature and to thinking about literature" (124), Donne "continues to be recognized as a great lyric poet (probably the greatest love poet of the English language), as the greatest English preacher, and as a towering figure of the baroque age" (125). Concludes with notes and references (127–32), a selected bibliography (133–39), and an index (140–43). Reviews: Frederick H. Shriver in *Church History* 37 (1988): 543–45; Ann Baynes Coiro in *RenQ* 42 (1989): 585–87.

854. Wendt, George F. "'Love's Progress' According to John Donne and Theodore Roethke." *BSUF* 28: 29–36.

Comments on Theodore Roethke's relation to Donne, noting that "[r]eferences abound to Donne in Roethke's teaching notes, in his poetry note-books, and in other loose notes"; that he "copied out many of Donne's poems in his own hand and annotated criticism written about Donne," and in many ways "absorbed Donne in his own poetry." Compares *ElProg* and Roethke's "Love's Progress" in order "to show how even a limited under-standing of Donne's poem can clar-ify and enrich Roethke's" (29). Claims that in his poem Donne created a speaker "whose argument the readers are to reject and whose character is designed to evoke both revulsion and pity," and maintains that both the speaker and his argument become a "kind of *reductio ad absurdum* of the proposal that love should be physical and only physical" (30). Calls Donne's poem "an outrageous, satiric elegy, blatantly vulgar and full of obscene innuendo" (31). Concludes that, rather than seeing Donne as rejecting his own speaker and argument, it may be "more accurate to say that Donne rec-ognizes in himself the vulgar persona he has created." Suggests that Roethke "turns to Donne because he recog-nizes himself in Donne and hopes that Donne can lead him from the 'sen-sual pen' they both hate to brave the 'higher' way to love, the way that is both spiritual and physical" (36).

855. Wiggins, Peter D. "Preparing towards Lucy: 'A Nocturnal' as Palinode." *SP* 84: 483–93.

Interprets *Noct* "in the light of the St. Lucy legend," thereby corroborat-ing "that reading which sees the poem as depicting a 'transition from the dead darkness of despair to the deep darkness of resigned expectation'" (483–84). Sees the Lucy of the poem as "another—perhaps the final—man-ifestation" of "the good woman of *The Songs and Sonnets,* the one with whom the restless speaker of those poems imagines a union transcending

change." Maintains that in *Noct* Donne "grapples with the imagination of her death, testing the veracity of his claims for their love and seeking a festival vision" (484). Calls the poem "a homily preached to . . . a congrega-tion of the lustful and idolatrous—by a person who has learned from expe-rience that natural reason and its instruments, rhetoric and dialectics, are inadequate to make a real con-nection between erotic desire in this world and the fruition of desire in that 'next world' to which his beloved has departed." Claims that in the poem Donne "bears witness to this truth and, in doing so, *prepares* himself for the role of martyr as witness of the tran-scendent Word" (488). Concludes that "[i]n religious terms," the poem "rep-resents a confession and an act of bit-ter contrition" and that, "in poetic terms, it is a palinode" (490).

856. Wilcox, Helen. "Donne's Vigil," in *KM 80: A Birthday Album for Kenneth Muir, Tuesday, 5 May, 1987,* p. 145. Liverpool: Liverpool University Press.

Suggests that the word "vigil" in the penultimate line of *Noct* has a litur-gical meaning, referring not only to the anticipated joy of the feast of St. Lucy but, more importantly, to the Easter vigil, the "archetype of all vig-ils." Points out that the Easter vigil "specifically celebrates the dawning of Christ's 'light' into the darkness of sin and death" and "uses and trans-forms the very vocabulary—vigil, light, sun/son, midnight—of the final stanza of Donne's poem." Concludes, therefore, that "[i]n the light of this liturgical meaning, Donne's vigil indi-cates a faith in the cycles of time" and "marks the redemption of his grief."

857. Young, R. V. "Donne's Holy Sonnets and the Theology of Grace," in *"Bright Shootes of Everlastingnesse": The Seventeenth-Century Religious Lyric,* ed. Claude J. Summers and Ted-Larry

Pebworth, 20–39. Columbia: University of Missouri Press. Reprinted in *John Donne's Poetry,* 2nd ed., ed. Arthur L. Clements, (New York: Norton, 1992), 311–24.

Argues that the current view that the *Holy Sonnets* reflect a distinctively Protestant poetics "is based on a simplistic and inaccurate view of the theological issues of Donne's era," that it "attempts to establish the existence of an exclusively Protestant mode of poetry without determining whether the same features of theme and style are available in contemporaneous Catholic poetry," and that it "forces the Holy Sonnets into a doctrinal frame that often overlooks the equivocal resonance and play of wit in Donne's poetry" (21). Argues that the *Holy Sonnets,* despite a few scattered Calvinistic echoes, cannot be generally read "as a specifically Calvinist, nor even Protestant, exposition of grace" (23), as some critics have claimed, and notes that Donne's "view of the human will is far more Tridentine than Calvinist" (26). Finds many theological similarities between the *Holy Sonnets* and the devotional poetry of Continental Catholic poets, such as Francisco de Quevedo, Jean de la Ceppède, and Pierre de Ronsard. Illustrates how "theological categorizing" of the *Holy Sonnets* "flatten[s] out the wit and daring that are characteristic of Donne's poetry" (31). Insists that the *Holy Sonnets* contain "undeniable marks of the poet's Catholic upbringing in their themes and structures" and that "the specifically Calvinist elements are handled tentatively, even with an air of provisionality" (34).

858. Young, R. V. "'O my America, my new-found-land': Pornography and Imperial Politics in Donne's *Elegies.*" *SCRev* 4, no. 2: 35–48.

Argues that accounts of and poems about Elizabethan voyages of exploration and colonization are central to a number of Donne's *Elegies,* especially *ElBed.* Insists that the main theme of these poems is not sex but lust for gold and power. Shows how Donne "dismantles the metaphorical structures of various literary celebrations of English exploration" and "rewrites them as cynically erotic poems of unbridled desire" (37), thereby concealing his political motives. Illustrates how Donne inverts in the *Elegies* the central conceit of such imperalistic poems as Stephen Parmenius's *De Navigatione . . . Humphrie Gilberti . . . Carmen,* and George Chapman's *De Guiana, Carmen Epicum,* in which the New World and its riches are likened to a desirable female body, and points out how he mocks and ridicules sexual language used in voyage accounts, such as those of Raleigh and Keymis, highlighting thereby their "piously veiled lust" (42) for New World gold. Thinks that the voice in the *Elegies* is "equivocal" because "Donne, like a Jesuit equivocator, is concealing the identity of the speaker," thereby making it unclear whether the speaker is "a cynical adulterer or a rapacious *conquistador*" (44–45). Concludes that in the *Elegies* one cannnot be sure "when Donne is talking about a lover or a discoverer, about a woman or a country, about sex or gold, about lust or avarice" (45–46).

1988

859. Anderson, Judith H. "Life Lived and Life Written: Donne's Final Word or Last Character." *HLQ* 51: 247–59.

Considers Donne's final sermon, "Death's Duell," as "the culmination of his role as a preacher" and as "a radically verbal gesture of self-characterization" (247). Maintains that Donne "enters words and texts in this sermon as if actually to become one with them and thence with the Word" and that "[t]o an amazingly literal extent, words—as such and in themselves—become the final, defining expression and extension of his life and being," thus becoming "his ultimate, dramatic assertion of control over his own meaning" (247–48). Analyzes in detail the diction, imagery, syntax, and rhetorical structure of the introduction and conclusion of the sermon, showing how they "offer a conceptual frame for Donne's endeavor to make of life and text, of character and characterizing gesture, a single entity" (248). Suggests that "[i]t would be hard to bring life lived and life spoken and written into closer conjunction" (257) than one finds in this sermon.

860. Anderson, Judith H. "Patterns Proposed Beforehand: Donne's Second Prebend Sermon." *PSt* 11, no. 2: 37–48.

Points out that the notion "[t]hat God works according to a pattern, an idea, or a preconception and that we, made in God's image, should do likewise is a recurrent topic in Donne's sermons and one that he frequently relates to speech—to prayer and to preaching." Discusses, in particular, how in his second prebend sermon Donne "relates the presence of eternal preconceptions, eternal fore-conceits, in God to verbal practice, whether human or divine" (37) and "also effects it." Argues that Donne "finds a great deal more in language than a transparent and an incidental system of notations," and that "[h]is words are imbued with their own history, their own weight, their own significance, their own mnemonic resonance." Maintains that, for Donne, "[e]tymology and association are operative in his choice and deployment of words" and "in the way he thought not merely about but with them," thereby making them "conceptual and tangible phenomena—in a word, *res,* that is, things opaque and self-sustaining" (38). Shows that "the individual words of this sermon in themselves anticipate, reflect, or recall its shaping conceptions and variously actualize them" (39). By analyzing Donne's uses of language in the second prebend sermon, indicates "both the extent to which the sermons, especially in their final, written form, were premeditated and the extent to which Latin is a substratum of Donne's own thinking" (46).

861. Baumlin, James S. "Donne's Poetics of Absence." *JDJ* 7: 151–82.

Maintains that Donne believed in an incarnational theology of language, "one that would claim the power to transubstantiate discourse, turning poetic

285

text from an imitation to an icon" (151). Points out that "the incarnationist text claims the power to transform the interpreter, who does not read so much as *listen* to the discourse" (152). Suggests, however, that this linguistic theology begs the question whether Donne subscribes to Catholic thought or whether he is exploring the loss of sacramentalism in liturgy and rhetoric. Says that Donne shares Plato's fear of writing and of misinterpretation because of the absence of the writer from the text's space. Asks the question, "*Can* the poem-as-sacrament be transubstantive in a Catholic sense, asserting the power to re-present or incorporate the poet in the flesh of the language? Or, following the more extreme Calvinist and Zwinglian interpretations of Eucharistic theology, is the poem reduced to a commemorative event, a representation or 'Picture'?" (159). Points out that in *TWHence* Donne "describes reading itself as a sacramental event" (159) and suggests "the possibility that writing re-presents the poet to a reader-communicant in the same way that the sacrament expresses Christ's Real Presence" (160). Questions, however, if Donne is simply being ironic here, since his later theological writings explicitly repudiate transubstantiation. Maintains that "[r]eformation controversy . . . remains a subject of Donne's love poetry" and that his writing "continues to dwell in a crisis of faith, which itself remains a crisis of sacramental, performative language" (164). Comments on *Relic,* questioning the poet's attitude toward an image "simultaneously sacramental and necromantic" (163); suggests that ll. 19–22 of *Twick* are "an elaborate parody of the Roman Mass" (165); and discusses *ValName* and *ValBook,* which explore ways Donne's "incarnational rhetoric is questioned and undermined by the nature of writing itself, by the written text's loss of authorial presence" (166).

862. Baumlin, James S. "Donne's 'Satyre IV': The Failure of Language and Genre." *TSLL* 30: 363–87.

Argues that *Sat4,* based in part on Horace's *Sermo* 1.9, "reveals an ambivalence toward language" and that "the satirist condemns the words of others for their deception and abuse, at the same time noting the inability of his own words to cause reform." Maintains that "accompanying this ambivalence toward language is a skepticism about the satirist's role, whether he is ever capable of accomplishing anything other than his own self-incrimination." Reads *Sat4* in the light of the "almost universal optimism of Renaissance critics and poets," who maintained the power of satire "to curse and cure," thereby making "more startling, and more poignant" Donne's "critical testing of the genre's ability to perform and validate itself" (364). Claims that Donne is the first English writer "to discover, and enact, the limitations of classical satire," and believes that "[w]hat allows this discovery is the poet's radical reflection on the weakness of language, a reflection spurred on . . . by the culture's refusal to grant his Catholicism authority—or grant it simply the right of utterance" (366). Suggests that, in fact, the poem is not a formal satire at all but rather "an allegory on the perilous status of the loyalist Catholic at a Protestant court" (368) and shows how Donne actually repudiates the classical form of satire. Points out how in the poem Donne undermines "the possibility of writing classical satire in a fallen, Christian, Elizabethan world" and shows how *Sat4* "becomes equally self-critical, denying the premises of its own composition and asserting only skepticism toward the efficacy of its genre" (381).

863. Bennett, Stuart. "An Intermediate State of Donne's *Paradoxes* 1652." *BC* 37: 273. Identifies an intermediate state of the

1652 *Problemes, Essayes, Characters* with the dedication by John Donne the younger cancelled and suggests that the correct order of states should be (1) no. 46 listed in Sir Geoffrey Keynes's *Bibliography of Donne,* 4th ed. (1973); (2) the intermediate state, with the cancelled dedication; and (3) no. 45 in Keynes, with a reset dedication.

864. Booth, Roy. "John Donne: Ideating Nothing." *English* 37: 203–15.

Discusses how Donne "constantly represents his own compositions as volatile or transitory" and considers "the way in which his sense of himself as a 'nothing' operates in his prose and verse epistles" (203). Comments on Donne's linguistic play on the notion of nothingness and suggests that during his middle years in his verse epistles and letters Donne's "self-identification with nothing becomes obsessive, an index to his lost sense of self and role" (205). Points out how Donne envisions his poems "decomposing, reverting to their state of nothingness before creation" (210) and how he habitually represented himself and his works as "trembling on the brink of extinction" (213). Believes that Donne attempted both to make nothingness his subject and to evade it by means of his writings: "he is at times an autobiographer who paradoxically claims to have no subject." Claims that "[t]he pulpit restored to him a sense of role, which culminated in the extraordinary pose in his shroud, and allowed the literary monuments of the sermons, writings he willingly prepared for the press" (214).

865. Brennan, Michael. *Literary Patronage in the English Renaissance: The Pembroke Family.* London: Routledge. xiv, 251p.

Traces the literary and artistic patronage of the Herbert family, Earls of Pembroke, from 1550 to 1650 and examines the complexities of patronage system in general. Discusses briefly Donne's connection with the family, noting his friendship with William Herbert, third Earl of Pembroke, and pointing out that John Donne the younger was the editor of the *Poems Written by William Herbert, Earl of Pembroke* (1660) and that his motive in publishing the volume was very likely profit.

866. Brodsky, Joseph. "The Great Elegy for John Donne." *Inostrannaelia literatura* 9: 182–85.

Reprints in Russian "The Great Elegy for John Donne," an original 208-line poem written in 1963.

867. Brooks, Helen B. " 'Soules Language': Reading Donne's 'The Extasie.' " *JDJ* 7: 47–63.

Argues that in *Ecst* Donne brings about the revelation of the exemplary love of the two lovers "by making the verbal substance of their love . . . the content not only of the poem's discursive subject, but [also] of its conceptual form as well." Maintains that the poem "engages the reader in a constitutive relationship with the text by way of the silent, but implicitly responsive interlocutor," but "[b]ecause the interlocutor does not directly voice her thoughts, but whose presence nevertheless is implied by the single speaker's words, the reader is enlisted as the completing—and thus actualizing—agent of the two lovers' 'dialogue of one' " (47). Believes that "[i]n supplying the other side of the 'dialogue of one,' the reader . . . not only becomes essential to meaning" but also that, "like the two lovers, how we know and what we know as readers becomes one through the mediation of the language of love." Focuses on how Donne "meets the challenge of revealing such love" and on "significant parallels between the poem's epistemology of love and Aristotle's theory of cognition" (48). Discusses how "reading can actualize—and thus bring into existence—

both the testimony of Donne's two lovers and the subjectivity of the sympathetic reader," noting that for both the lovers and the reader "the experience is one of radical self-understanding" (57). Holds that "[h]aving cast the lovers' 'dialogue of one' in the form of the dramatic monologue, and thereby forging a creative link between the reader and text, Donne effects the promised revelation" (59).

868. Brown, Meg Lota. " 'In that the world's contracted thus': Casuistical Politics in Donne's 'The Sunne Rising,' " in *"The Muses Common-Weale" : Poetry and Politics in the Seventeenth Century,* ed. Claude J. Summers and Ted-Larry Pebworth, 23–33. Essays in Seventeenth-Century Literature, 3. Columbia: University of Missouri Press. Appears in a revised version in *Donne and the Politics of Conscience in Early Modern England* (Leiden, New York, Cologne: Brill, 1995), 110–18.

Discusses how *SunRis* resonates with Donne's "opposition to cultural constraints on love" and "his political ambition." Maintains that "[t]he poem establishes a new order that places love at the center of the generative power from which Donne was excluded" and that, by "[e]levating love above sociopolitical demands," it "playfully enacts the defiance of authority that Donne's marriage expressed" and "invests the lover's motives with a legitimacy that they were never accorded in fact." Claims that the poem "justifies love in terms of the same political order and structures of power that Donne's elopement was seen to subvert" and that the poem's persona "challenges the value of social status and power only to appropriate them and to claim the crowning position in the political hierarchy." Argues that "[o]ne of the ways in which he effects such an appropriation is by parodying the principles

and methods of casuistry or practical theology." Shows how in *SunRis* Donne's speaker "comically exploits" casuistry by arguing for "a new definition of authority, claiming that his exceptional love constitutes the standard against which political structures and social values should be measured" (24). Presents a detailed analysis of the poem to show how Donne both uses and distorts casuistical principles, noting that, like any good parody, the poem "reflects its casuistical model clearly enough to play upon the contrast" (32). Shows how in the end the speaker, by exploiting casuistical theology, "has forged a new political order in which lovers govern rather than obey society's laws" and "has empowered love with political legitimacy and, in the process, has delivered an extravagant compliment to his own lover" (33).

869. Caird, Janet. *John Donne, You Were Wrong. Poems by Janet Caird.* Edinburgh: Ramsey Head Press. 50p.

A collection of 41 original poems, the last of which is entitled "John Donne, You Were Wrong" (50), in which the poet challenges Donne's statement that "No Man is an island."

870. Carey, John. "Au sujet de John Donne," trans. Claude Minière. *Po&sie* 45: 103–17.

Translates into French most of Chapter 9, "Imagined Corners," from Carey's *John Donne: Life, Mind and Art* (1981).

871. Carr, Helen. "Donne's Masculine Persuasive Force," in *Jacobean Poetry and Prose: Rhetoric, Representation and the Popular Imagination,* ed. Clive Bloom, 96–118. New York: St. Martin's Press.

Reviews historical and contemporary views on the notion that Donne wrote with "masculine persuasive force." Says a shift occurred between the sixteenth and seventeenth centuries about the nature of men and women and claims that "[t]he anxiety over gender identity was part of a wider disruption of certainty" (100). Cites Donne as a writer who "encompasses a wide terrain of contemporary conflict and debate" about courtly love, Petrarchism, the subordination of God to ideal woman, and the passivity of the male in those traditions. Claims that Donne's use of Petrarchism brings together power and passion "so that both become attributes of the 'masculine'" (104) and sees this combination in *SunRis* and *LovInf*. Observes that in his poems to patronesses Donne reverts to Petrarchism and that any "masculine bravado is Donne's counter to his social vulnerability" (113). Disagrees with John Carey (1981) who holds that Donne's concern with woman's inconstancy was a consequence of his betrayal of Catholicism. Believes that in the "contradictory period of the early seventeenth century," it was possible for Donne "to freight sexual relations with an ontological weight that they were not again asked to carry for another 200 years" (114).

872. **Clark, Ira.** "'How witty's ruine': The Difficulties of Donne's 'Idea of a Woman' in the First of His *Anniversaries*." *SoAR* 53, no. 1: 19–26.

Points out that critics "have not generally been persuaded of any unity in the *Anniversaries*' central emblem, 'the Idea of a Woman'" and claims that "[a]ll of the multitudinous characterizations of the 'Idea of a Woman' seem more or less plausible" but that "few persuade" and "none unifies" (19). Believes that "[a]s either a transcending ideal or a mediating universal [the two major categories to which she is assigned by most critics], the woman in Donne's idea gets abstracted out of existence." Argues

that one must focus rather on the "Idea of a Woman," not on the "ideal of a human" (20). Discusses how Donne introduces into the *Anniversaries* a "self-consciously witty misogyny" and, using the "center concept of woman as human ruin" and using male-biased language, plays on the notion of "the female ruin of God's good intent" (22). Challenges, therefore, those critics who claim any transcendental significance for the woman in the two poems.

873. **Daniels, Edgar F.** "Browne's 'To the Deceased Author.'" *Expl* 46, no. 2: 19–20.

Points out how Sir Thomas Browne's elegy on Donne that appeared in the first edition of Donne's poems (1633) imitates Donne's "cryptic manner, with obscure ellipses, ambiguous pronoun references, a shocking conceit, and a puzzling summing up" (19).

874. **Docherty, Barbara.** "Sentence into Cadence: The Word-Setting of Tippett and Britten." *Tempo,* no. 166: 2–11.

Discusses Benjamin Britten's *Holy Sonnets of John Donne* (1945). Maintains that Britten's musical settings "bring before the ear the fear, starved hope, and rare consolation that were the objective constituents of Donne's universe, pursuing a rhythmic/harmonic analogue for each poem's metaphysics with only rare release, a musical equivalent of Donne's device of elaborating a philosophical or verbal conceit to the further extent to which ingenuity can extend it, presenting a musical trope disjunct from the subjective passion of the vocal line" and, in some instances "threatening to overbear it" (9). Claims that in several of the settings there is "an unsurpassed fusion of musical and poetic sensibility" (10).

875. **Donne, John.** *The Essential Donne,* ed. Amy Clampitt. The Essential Poets, vol. 8. New York: Ecco Press. 132p.

Contains an introduction (3–15) that evaluates Donne's critical reputation in the twentieth century and comments on his life and on general characteristics of his poetry. Reproduces selections (without notes or commentary) from the *Songs and Sonets,* the *Elegies,* the *Saytres,* the verse epistles, and the *Divine Poems,* as well as passages from *Sappho, Metem,* and the *Anniversaries* (17–121), arranged in "a progression, both formal and thematic, from the more accessible works to those that for one reason or another seemed to make greater demands on the reader" (15). Reproduces A. J. Smith's text (1986). Concludes with a glossary (122–31) and a biographical notice of the editor (132). Review: P. Mariani in *NER* 12 (1990): 313–20.

876. Donne, John. "Giving Thanks in Plague Times." *Christianity Today* 32, no. 17: 30–31.

Contains three excerpts from *Devotions* with brief introductory remarks by Philip Yancey.

877. Donne, John. *John Donne,* ed. with intro. by Peter Porter. Great English Poets. New York: Clarkson N. Potter, Inc. [60]p. Published in England as *John Donne: The Illustrated Poets* (London: Aurum Press).

Presents a selection of 14 poems from the *Songs and Sonets,* lines from *Coryat,* 4 of the *Elegies,* 7 of the *Holy Sonnets,* and *Sickness,* without notes or commentary. The introduction comments briefly on Donne's life and personality, emphasizing his passionate nature and his egotism. Says that Donne was perhaps "the greatest poetic innovator in the English language." Reproduces 12 paintings.

878. Donne, John. *John Donne: Liefdesgedichten, heilige sonnetten en preken.* Vertaald en van een nawoord voorzien door J[an] Eijkelboom. Amsterdam: Uitgeverij De Arbeiderspers. 74p. First issued in a shorter version in 1957.

Consists of metrically matching translations (English-Dutch) of eight poems

from the *Songs and Sonets,* two of the Elegies, an extract from *EpLin,* three of the *Holy Sonnets,* and *Father,* based on the 1633 edition. Gives translated extracts (but not the English originals) from the sermons preached at The Hague on 19 December 1619 and at St. Paul's on Christmas Day 1624, along with "Death's Duell." In the afterword, considers the nature of the harshness of Donne's verse and the difficulty it presents to the translator. Points out that Constantijn Huygens did not adhere to Donne's stanzaic forms but praises his translations as "magisterial" nonetheless. Discusses the question of Donne's apostasy, praises John Carey's *John Donne: Life, Mind and Art* (1981), and takes issue with Helen Gardner's critique of Carey (entry 182). Concludes with some thoughts on Donne's poetic identity and a note on previous translations of Donne into Dutch other than Huygens's, the last dating from 1939. Reproduces also the first page of *Carey* and the draft of Donne's wife's gravestone in holograph; most of the extant portraits of Donne (except for the Lothian portrait); and a photo of Donne's monument in St. Paul's.

879. Donne, John. *No Man Is an Island,* ed. Helen Lush. London: Souvenir. [32]p.

Contains selections from *Devotions* with illustrations by Helen Lush.

880. Dubrow, Heather. "'The Sun in Water': Donne's Somerset Epithalamium and the Poetics of Patronage," in *The Historical Renaissance: New Essays on Tudor and Stuart Literature and Culture,* ed. Heather Dubrow and Richard Strier, 197–219. Chicago: University of Chicago Press.

Offers a detailed reading of *Eclog* that disputes the common view that the marriage of Robert Carr to Frances Howard is "the outward and visible sign of subjection" that Donne experienced because of the patronage system. Argues that the poem is "far more complicated, poetically and politically, than its commentators have acknowledged" (197). Believes that "[n]either the humiliating sycophancy that most readers have found in this lyric nor the tact and integrity that others claim for it adequately describes the complexity of the Somerset epithalamium" and maintains that, in fact, "Donne's responses to the problems of patronage variously range along the entire spectrum between uncritical adulation and uncompromising criticism" (201). Reviews the scandal surrounding the marriage (and thus the problem that it posed for Donne) and records the problem that the genre itself imposed, concluding, however, that the conventions of the genre "also offered solutions" to Donne, noting how he "repeatedly invokes the motifs of the epithalamium in order to comment on the peculiarities of this particular wedding" (200) as well as "to praise the couple and to defend their behavior" (205). Points out that a numerological study of the poem reveals that the poem is composed of 11 stanzas of 11 lines, a number that St. Augustine associates with sin. Discusses the eclogue, suggesting that its "main function" is "to express and embody the problems of courting a patron" (211). Concludes by stating that the poem also demonstrates "the difficulties modern literary critics confront if they wish to study it" (213), and suggests that critics return to the approach of formalism, albeit now unfashionable, to explore the cultural tensions of the poem and warns new historical critics about the danger of broad generalizations about periods of time, ignoring changes that occur, decade by decade, year to year, in patronage as well as in the life of the poet.

881. Duer, Leslie T. "The Poet on St. Lucy's Eve: John Donne's Portrait," in *Word and Visual Imagination: Studies in the Interaction of English Literature and the Visual Arts,* ed. Karl Josef Höltgen, Peter M. Daly, and Wolfgang Lottes, 107–32. Erlangen: Universitätsbund Erlangen-Nürnberg.

Discusses Elizabethan and Jacobean portrait paintings and their settings, noting that they are "generally representational on the one hand, but icon-making and largely self-referred on the other" (107). Uses Donne's *Para* and *Noct* as poetic parallels to what happens in portrait painting. Maintains that *Para* is "both about the creation and the 'reading' of an aesthetic object, where the reading turns out to be subject to the same discontinuities as is the text" (116) and that *Noct* asks the reader to "study a painting contained within the poem and containing the poem's maker, who is the subject both of the poem and the painting" (117). Believes that the latter contains two acts, "one creative and the other critical," and that the speaker divides himself "into image and language, or into interpretable object . . . and interpreter" (118), which results in "a lively representation of a man as he is now, alive, and at the same time an effigy." Concludes that "[t]he creation of text and successor text that begins within the poem will continue beyond its own limits through the text-creating action of the critical imagination" and "[i]n so doing, it continues and expands the process which was begun within the poem by the interaction of artifact and interpretation" (119).

882. Duncan, Joseph E. "Resurrections in Donne's 'A Hymne to God the Father' and 'Hymne to God my God, in my sicknesse.'" *JDJ* 7: 183–95.

Believes that the 11 sermons on the resurrection preached by Donne between 1620 and 1630 "provide an illuminating context for the spiritual experience of the speaker" (183) in *Father* and *Sickness*. Discusses how "assurance of the spiritual resurrection and the joy in the certainty of the physical resurrection" are "at the heart of the spiritual experience" (184) in both poems and how they "are closely related and reflect successive stages in the pattern of spiritual experience discussed in the sermons." Claims that *Father* shows "a hard-won resurrection from sin through Donne's faith and repentance and God's grace and glory" while *Sickness* shows "the joy in the spiritual resurrection as an 'infallible seale' of the resurrection to glory" (185). Maintains that although *Sickness* precedes *Father* in most printed editions, "the pattern of the spiritual experience suggests reading and interpreting these poems in the reverse order. Discusses how "the two poems are bound together by their titles and relation to music, by rhyme and approximate rhyme, and by imagery" (187), and how they "are suffused with the fervor of Donne's belief in the spiritual resurrection and the resurrection to glory" (193).

883. El-Gabalawy, Saad. "The Trend of Naturalism in Libertine Poetry of the Later English Renaissance." *Ren&R,* n.s. 12: 35–44.

Points out Donne's endorsement of naturalism in several poems in which "he assumes the role of the sexual libertine, the young man of the world who glorifies inconstancy as the only constant element in love." Cites as examples *ElChange,* in which Donne "delineates the idea that the infinite variety of love mirrors the state of constant flux in nature"; *ElVar,* in which he presents "sophisticated arguments against social restraints, which have no justification in terms of the natural order" (38); *Relic,* in which he denounces "legalistic ethics that inhibit lovers"; *Damp,* in which "[m]oral qualities are portrayed as allegorical figures and reduced to figments of the imagination"; *ValBook,* in which "honour and conscience are dismissed as chimera"; *Flea,* in which Donne equates

"the lady's honour with the drop of blood sucked by the flea"; *Dream,* in which he blends "erotic realism with an opaque hint of libertine atheism" (39); and *ElBed,* in which Donne engages in "sadistic pornography" and "implicitly alludes to the Golden Age, where free love negates all religious restrictions and moral scruples" (40). Points out that Donne's libertinism is "in perfect harmony" with that of Montaigne and Tasso but notes that "these elements of naturalism are so diffused in the classical and Renaissance traditions that they cannot be traced to any specific source" (39). Suggests the possible influence of Pietro Aretino's pornographic works on Donne's libertine poems.

884. Estrin, Barbara L. "Framing and Imagining the 'You': Donne's 'A Valediction of My Name in the Window' and 'Elegy: Change.'" *TSLL* 30: 345–62.

Points out that in *ValName* and in *ElChange* Donne "comments on the aesthetics of Renaissance love poetry and its conventional image of the lover as possessor of the beloved." Maintains that "[t]he desire to know, incorporate, and control lies behind both poems, and that is why the arts play so central a role in them." Observes that though the speaker in each poem uses his knowledge of art to judge and control the woman, that knowledge comes to diametrically opposed ends (345). Maintains that in the valediction "the poet claims the woman's selfhood (the famous 'I am you' of the second stanza) but fails fully to become what he says he is," and "[h]anging on to his identity, he dwindles into the lethargy of 'near death,'" whereas in the elegy the speaker "is so absorbed by her that he loses all sense of *his* imposed perspective" and, "[l]etting go, he expands with energy and music of eternity" (345–46). Shows how in *ValName* the speaker's engraving "becomes an engravement, a burial of the lover caught in the abyss of his single self," whereas in *ElChange* "the lover is freed from the confines of his own vision as he slips into the lady's expansiveness" (353). Discusses how in the elegy the poet begins with a diatribe against the arts, calling them "flimsy, ephemeral, and feathery—as fluffy as the women they represent," but "in the ecstatic vision at the end, the arts emerge as what the poet wanted at the opening—a link to eternity, a connection that lasts" (354). Claims that, unlike the valediction, the elegy "does not use art as a vehicle for emotional control" but "presents an art that depends on movement and therefore represents the transformational mythos" (361).

885. Estrin, Barbara L. "The Lady's Gestures and John Donne's Gestes." *FMLS* 24: 218–33.

Contrasts the gesture poems of Ovid and Petrarch with *Jet, Fun,* and *Dream* and claims that Donne in his gesture poems "creates a series of love stories that contain . . . a vision of idealized likenesses" and "presents a vision of separation so unlikeable as to change the genre from its earlier prototypes." Argues that in *Break,* however, Donne "reverses the mirror of those poems, calling the man the infidel he has accused the woman of being" and, "[w]ith that story, he produces yet another likeness, turning the gesturing lady into his unbecoming—now unlikely and unlikeable—self." Observes, therefore, that "[w]orking within the genre of the gesture poem, Donne turns its traditional compliment into a threat to the lady" (231). Concludes that by "[m]aximizing the lady's potential as originator of a cycle the poet chooses to break" in *Jet* and *Fun,* "to continue" in *Dream,* and "to parody" in *Break,* Donne "underscores

the self-centeredness of Petrarch and Ovid," and by "[e]mphasizing a possessiveness that is at the core of the gift-giving cycle, Donne returns the lady's gift, rendering it the source of a story that changes the received conventions of the genre" (231–32).

886. Evans, Malcolm. " 'In Love with Curious Words': Signification and Sexuality in English Petrarchism," in *Jacobean Poetry and Prose: Rhetoric, Representation and the Popular Imagination,* ed. Clive Bloom, 119–50. New York: St. Martin's Press.

Discusses "the highly codified and restrictive" Petrarchism in English poetry of the late sixteenth century and how, in a broader sense, Petrarchism as "a discourse on love [remained] still highly influential throughout Europe of the seventeenth century." Comments on "its relationship to eroticism and the body" (120) and its correlation to other ideologies that wanted to regulate love and sexuality, especially that of the Catholic Church, and notes the relationship between Petrarchism and the views of the Marquis de Sade. Mentions the critical debate as to whether Donne was a Petrarchist or an anti-Petrarchist and suggests that he represents the baroque phase of the Petrarchan tradition. Cites *Canon* and *Ecst* as poems that defend sexual love as a necessary part of spiritual love.

887. Fallon, Robert Thomas. "Donne's 'Strange Fire' and the 'Elegies on the Authors Death.' " *JDJ* 7: 197–212.

Discusses the 13 elegies on Donne that appeared in the first edition of his poetry (1633), to which 3 more were added in the second (1635). Observes that they all dealt with the conventional theme of "the impossibility of writing elegies" but suggests that perhaps one reason for their similarity is that the poets "may have, quite simply, read one another's poems" (198). Notes also that the authors had very similar social, political, and ideological backgrounds and traces their connection to Christ Church, Oxford, and their association with John Donne the younger, who "may have provided the link between the edition of his father's poems and the elegists chosen to observe his death" (201). Finds that many of the elegists were disturbed by the appearance of poet and priest side by side and, therefore, either "diminish the importance of the early work" or "justify it in some way" (202), noting that only Thomas Browne, omitted from subsequent editions, "scorns the prudery of those disturbed by the love lyrics" (204). Believes that the mixing of sacred and profane poems in the first edition contributed to concern among Donne's admirers, a problem addressed in the second edition by ordering the poems by genre and other revisions. Suggests that Izaak Walton may have been responsible for the second edition and points out that in an epigram he suggests that the love poems were products of Donne's youthful indiscretion and therefore less meritorious than the divine poems, a view that prevailed for at least two centuries.

888. Flynn, Dennis. "'Awry and Squint': The Dating of Donne's Holy Sonnets." *JDJ* 7: 35–46.

Relying heavily on the authority of the Westmoreland manuscript, challenges Helen Gardner's dating in *John Donne: The Divine Poems* (Oxford: Clarendon, 1952) of 16 of the *Holy Sonnets* between 1609 and 1611, which is based primarily on assumptions about authorial arrangement of the poems, on the theory that the sonnets were composed as a series of sequences, on Donne's rejection of mortalism in *Pseudo-Martyr* (1609), and on identifying "E. of D." in *ED*

as Richard Sackville, third Earl of Dorset, who succeeded to his title in 1609, and assuming that this verse letter was written as an introduction to six of the *Holy Sonnets,* only three of which can be dated prior to 1609. Argues that a more likely candidate for "E. of D." is either Ferdinand Stanley, fifth Earl of Derby, or, more likely, William Stanley, sixth Earl of Derby, and that the six poems sent to him were likely love songs or verse epistles. Maintains that "nonbiographical interpretations" of the *Holy Sonnets* should be "given more consideration than is usual" and that "several possible scenarios for their composition ought to be entertained" (43). Observes that there is some evidence to suggest that the *Holy Sonnets* may have been written in the 1590s.

889. Fogelin, Robert J. "Clarifications and Elaborations," in *Figuratively Speaking,* 95–113. New Haven, Conn.: Yale University Press.

Comments briefly on the "remarkably ingenious figurative comparison" (102) of lovers to a compass in *ValMourn* as an example of a "metaphor of wit," that is, a figurative comparison that gains its "chief force by introducing, then resolving, deeply incongruous or unexpected comparisons." Points out that Donne's poem "elevates and refreshes a series of commonplaces concerning the unity of separated lovers by bringing them together under a single surprising, though remarkably apt, image" (102–3).

890. Hamilton, Lynn. "Donne's 'The Bait.'" *Expl* 46, no. 3: 11–13.

Discusses how *Bait* "parts company" with the poems that it parodies, namely Marlowe's "Passionate Shepherd to His Love" and Raleigh's "The Nymph's Reply to the Shepherd," and insists that the emphasis on Donne's indebtedness to Marlowe and Raleigh "has distracted readers from looking . . . for those peculiarities of Donne's poetry that make it distinctive," especially its "rejection of conventional sentiment and the exploration of paradox." Maintains that "[t]he central paradox in the poem resides in the words, 'For thou thyself art thine own bait' (l. 26)," which "encapsulates the drift of the poem, namely that love is the state of devouring and being devoured simultaneously" (12). Believes that in *Bait* Donne addresses the fear of "being a victim in love" and that he "rejects the assumption (one that persists into the present day) that, in love, there is always a winner and a loser." Points out that Donne indicates in the poem that "each individual in love simultaneously pursues and is pursued, triumphs and accepts defeat, devours and is devoured" (13).

891. Hart, Clive. "Flight into Union: Sexuality and Ecstasy," in *Images of Flight,* 136–92. Berkeley, Los Angeles, London: University of California Press.
Examines *Ecst* to show that "[i]n place of the more familiar patterns of union, of two desirous bodies or two loving souls, Donne substitutes a vision of the loving relationship between a single spiritual being compounded of two souls and a single 'entergrafted' body." Points out that this union "remains unrealised until the combined souls return to reanimate the immobile bodies and bring about their corresponding fusion in sexual union" (173) and that Donne "leaves us at the end of the poem focussing once more on the physical context, on the downward flight of the soul, from its aetherial ecstatic state to union with the flesh" (174). Maintains that in *Ecst* Donne "creates a witty inversion of the more familiar out-and-return journey fundamental to Neoplatonism: the emanation of created being from the godhead followed by its return and

reabsorption" (174), but points out that although his "pattern of movement—flesh-spirit-flesh rather than spirit-flesh-spirit—is a reversal of the Neoplatonic spiritual circuit, it is by no means unusual as an expression of the human quest, where the divine out-and-return journey finds its mirror image in man's search for erotic and spiritual fulfillment" (175). Notes that in *Relic* Donne boldly hopes "to sneak one last act of sexual union on earth during the turmoil of the Judgement Day—when the lovers' souls descend to repossess their bodies" (176), and that in the sermon, in which "he denounces the Islamic promise of sensual joy in Heaven, he warmly celebrates the lovable nature of the body that will ascend to Heaven with the resurrection of the flesh" (177).

892. Hatakeyama, Etsuro. "*Songs and Sonnets* ni okeru Jiko Genkyu teki Paradox" [Reflexive Paradoxes in the *Songs and Sonnets*]. *ESELL* 80: 25–49.
Discusses the self-referential paradoxes in Donne's poetry by making use of such concepts as "self-referentiality," "self-presence," "repetition," and "proliferation of representations." Examines *Canon, Relic, Triple, Under,* and *Para* to show how these poems do not contain a complete self-sufficient organic unity and are not lyrics of mutual love but rather are poems with metatextuality consciously dealing with *écriture* while seemingly treating love as their theme.

893. Hedley, Jane. " 'This bed thy center is': The Metonymic Poetry of Donne and Jonson," in *Power in Verse: Metaphor and Metonymy in the Renaissance Lyric,* 143–70. University Park, Pa.: Pennsylvania State University Press.
Uses the semiotic theory of Roman Jakobson to explain three successive stylistics in the development of the English lyric from Wyatt to Donne, and proposes that "early Tudor poetry

is metonymic, that the collective orientation of Spenser and Sidney and their Elizabethan contemporaries is metaphoric, and that Donne's and Jonson's lyrics bring metonymy once again to the fore" (2). Claims, for example, that the "symbolic importance" that Donne ascribes to Elizabeth Drury in *FirAn* has "no collective, institutional sanction," and insists that Donne's poetry is "thoroughly metonymic in its orientation" and that this subverts "the idealistic, synchronistic perspective of Elizabethan metaphoric writing" (28). Uses *SunRis* to explain metonymy and deictics, the use of which enables Donne "to give a convincing representation of spontaneous oral delivery" (32). Maintains that Donne's "insistence on the radical importance of his own personal experience" is "a refusal to give the existing political order any authority to structure his priorities" (136). Argues that the change in literary fashion in the late sixteenth century "was closely related to the demise of the cult of Elizabeth and the synchronistic, centripetal vision that had informed it" and that Donne's poems "bear witness to the emergence of a polity that was, and was experienced as being, more atomistic and incoherent." Maintains that Donne "reacted against the prevailing bias of Elizabethan poetry in both its ideological and its formal aspect" and that his poetry "supersedes the Elizabethan cultural moment from within the institution of English poesy." Claims that Donne's poetry is metonymic "in the sense of adhering to particular contexts and reacting to particular situations" (144). Claims that the *Songs and Sonets* "insist harder on their occasions than any other poems written in English" and that "the occasions they presuppose are complex and volatile" (145). Shows how several of Donne's love lyrics are "performatives" that have

"complicated settings" (146) and are "exceptionally time-sensitive" (148). Discusses *Canon* to show that "the strategy of the poem is iconoclastic not only in relation to the authority of the church and king but also in relation to the institution of 'poesy' itself" (141). Discusses *Ecst, ValWeep,* and *Flea* to show how in each, "[m]etonymy furnishes the vehicles for metaphor and then metaphor is used to master the poem's occasion in terms of the lover's feelings" (150). Regards *Canon* as the best example of a common linguistic transaction in Donne's poems: "A situation gives rise to a poem, but the poem asserts its transformative power with respect to that situation, and finally there is a move to reverse the priority of context over poem, putting the world in the poem's jurisdiction" (151).

894. Hetzron, Róbert. *Legszebb verseim: Mütfordítas-gyüjtemény* [My Favorite Poems: A Collection of Poetry Translations]. Santa Barbara, Calif.: Robert Hetzron. vii, 52p.

Translates into Hungarian *Flea, ElBed,* and *SSweet* (18–21), without notes or commentary.

895. Hollander, John. "Necessary Hieroglyphs," in *Melodious Guile: Fictive Pattern in Poetic Language,* 111–29. New Haven, Conn.: Yale University Press.

Comments on the "abstract chiasmatic scheme" in *Hero* that is "buried beneath other more prominent patterns and yet does its own work of framing and intensifying" (121).

896. James, Trevor. *The Metaphysical Poets.* York Handbooks; Longman Literature Guides, ed. A. N. Jeffares. Harlow, Eng: Longman; Beirut: York Press. 166p.

Serves as a companion to York Notes intended for students. Contains a very general introduction to the cultural, intellectual, and religious background of the earlier seventeenth century

(7–24) and a brief survey of the literary background of the period and a discussion of the major characteristics of metaphysical poetry (25–41), followed by introductions to the life and works of Donne (42–68); minor imitators of Donne, especially Lord Herbert of Cherbury, Aurelian Townshend, and Henry King (69–74); George Herbert (75–94); Richard Crashaw (95–115); Henry Vaughan (116–31); Thomas Traherne (132–42); and Andrew Marvell (143–58). Includes a chronological table (159), a brief list of suggestions for further reading (160), and an index (161–66).

897. Kim, Key Seop. "On the Measurement of Metrical Complexity." *JELL* 29: 153–67.

Discusses ways to measure the metrical complexities in the poetry of a wide variety of English poets covering four centuries. Uses examples from Donne to illustrate his theory and suggests reasons why early metricists accused Donne of writing doggerel.

898. Koppenfels, Werner von. " 'When thou hast done, thou hast not Don(n)e' ": Ent-fremdung und Verfremdung eines Meta-physical Poet," in *Anglistentag 1987 Tübingen,* ed. Hans-Werner Ludwig, 9: 154–74. Tagungsberichte des Anglistentags Verbands deutscher Anglisten. Giessen: Hoffmann.

Discusses how even Donne's contemporaries were put off by his poetic originality, considering him to be a "Copernicus in Poetry." Maintains that the obscurity in Donne's poetry and his rejection of metrical norms make his poetry difficult to translate into another language. Illustrates this point by making a detailed comparison of six different translations of *SunRis,* including one by the author himself, and concludes that it is impossible to capture all of Donne's complexity and originality in a translation.

899. Kress, Gunther, and Terry Threadgold. "Towards a Social Theory of Genre." *SoRA* 21: 215–43.

Presents "a theory of genre set in the broad framework" of what is known as "social semiotics" (215). Defines genres as "the socially ratified text-types in a community, which make meaning possible by contextualising in a megagrammatical way (a way that tells us something about the grammar) the actual linguistic or semantic patterns that constitute the lexicogrammar of texts" (216). Observes that since the Romantics, "genre" has become "a devalued term in the dominant literary/aesthetic discourse" (219), but that in classical periods "the reverse was the case." Notes, however, that in the Renaissance, genres were deliberately mixed, "producing texts which foregrounded social instability and focused on heteroglossia, the many conflicting voices of the culture" (220). Selects as an illustration *FirAn* (ll. 205–326), a multigeneric text where, "historically, we have lost, if we ever had, any sense of the 'master' genre in terms of which to read its heteroglossia" (223). Maintains that each of the "various discourses, genres, and modes from other genres" in Donne's poem "has a distinctive 'grammar' within the structure of the poem" and that "there is a 'common grammar' which bind them in some sense together as 'elegy' " (225).

900. Langley, T. R. "John Donne with Raspaberries." *CQ* 17: 166–76.

Reviews unfavorably Anthony Raspa's edition of *Devotions upon Emergent Occasions* (first published 1975; reprinted 1987), especially critical of the commentary.

901. Lerner, Laurence. "Ovid and the Elizabethans," in *Ovid Renewed: Ovidian Influences on Literature and Art from the Middle Ages to the Twentieth Century,* ed. Charles Martindale, 121–35. Cambridge: Cambridge University Press.

Calls Donne the "true English" imitator of "the sweet (or sour) witty Ovid" and points out several Ovidian themes "brilliantly recaptured" in Donne's *Elegies*—"the impassioned praise of nakedness," "the vivid torturing of the unfortunate husband," and "the love-war parallel" (125). Says that Ovid's treatment of the topos of love as war seems almost "tame" in comparison to the "vitality" of *ElWar* and praises Donne's use of wit and "verbal passion." Calls *ElFatal* Donne's "most vivid" love elegy, noting, in particular, the assertive, hence masculine, language of the poem and suggests that "what Donne takes from Ovid may be above all his masculinity: masculine cynicism, masculine power, masculine brilliance" (126).

902. Loewe, Raphael. "Abraham Ibn Ezra, Peter Abelard, and John Donne." *Tel Aviv Review* 1: 190–211.

Discusses the problems of translating post-biblical Hebrew poetry into English and uses Donne's *Corona* as a model for his translation of a 90-line poem by Abraham Ibn Erza (d. 1164) entitled "Hymn in Penitence."

903. Lorch, Sue. "Metaphor, Metaphysics, and MTV." *JPC* 22, no. 3: 143–55.

Claims that certain rock music videos are "the metaphysical poetry of the twentieth century" (143) because they, like the poetry of the seventeenth century, "explore new perceptions about the fundamental truths of existence and of the human's place in the scheme of things" (144). Contrasts Wyatt's "The lover's life compared to the Alps" to *Canon* to show that the latter does not reveal "a neat order inherent in the world," but rather "transcribes the activities of a mind searching for order and finding it in complex patterns" (148). Points out that, whereas Wyatt's poem is "simple, static, [and]

structured," Donne's is "complex, dramatic, [and] vigorous" and "does not attempt to render thought, but the mind thinking," a mind that explores "the puzzles and apparent incongruities of human experience" (149). Suggests that in music videos "the visual element serves the same purpose as paradox and conceit did for Donne, it startles; it makes an unexpected statement that urges the audience toward new awareness" (152), citing "Money for Nothing" by Dire Straits as an example. Concludes that music videos announce to us, as Donne's poetry did to his contemporaries, "that our collective mind has changed, that humanity has brought itself to a new birth in a new world" (154).

904. Low, Anthony. "Donne and the New Historicism." *JDJ* 7: 125–31.

Reviews Arthur F. Marotti's *John Donne: Coterie Poet* (1986) but discusses more broadly the issue of applying the principles of the New Historicism to the works of Donne and others. Questions whether New Historicism, "as presently constituted, can ever be made to move beyond broad and brilliant generalities to come to terms with the nitty-gritty details, the vital emotions, and the lasting significance of individual works of art" (125). Argues that New Historicists simply do not have sufficient facts about Donne's life and his relationship with patrons nor about the date of composition and specific audience of individual poems to go beyond mere "hypotheses" that are "neither provable nor disprovable in themselves." Praises the approach, however, for showing "the importance of that hidden juncture of individual or personal psychology with the broad social matrix, out of which poetry arises under various intense pressures," but sees it as "less successful in discussing individual poems or even in discriminating good poems from bad" (128). Points out how the *Songs and Sonets* both transcend and confront Donne's cultural limitations. Says that Donne, "however unwillingly or ambivalently . . . was engaged in redefining, against prevailing historical constraints and limitations, what it means to be a true poet to all ages" (131).

905. Martz, Louis L. "Donne and Herbert: Vehement Grief and Silent Tears." *JDJ* 7: 21–34. Reprinted in *From Renaissance to Baroque: Essays on Literature and Art* (Columbia: University of Missouri Press, 1991), 39–50.

Explores the theme of sighs and tears in the poetry of Donne and Herbert in order to show how the two poets are essentially different. Observes how Donne's divine poems reflect a "profound personal sense of sin and a deeply troubled theological outlook" (24), whereas Herbert's poems reveal "a sense of basic, achieved security" that "allows him to pursue his playful art" (29). Argues that Herbert's poems "dance and pirouette above the theological issues, dance over the old facts of history, liberate themselves, more than any other religious writing of the time (except for Shakespeare's plays) from the stern and warring doctrines of the time" (32), whereas in Donne's "deep anxiety to find the one true Spouse of Christ, he has devoured the entire universe of controverted divinity" and "his poetry conquers by vehement attack on the Gordian knot, by violently grasping of the terrible problems of the age and of the self" (33). Points out that Donne "seems to show a special affinity with Spain— with the vehement grief of its bleeding statues and the strenuous, anxious art of El Greco," whereas Herbert "was able to absorb the gentler lessons of devout humanism in France and Italy, the lessons of tranquillity and silent tears" (33–34). Concludes that

Donne and Herbert "are different, vastly different," and "we do them an injustice when we blur the distinctions between them" (34).

906. Mezenin, S. M. "Neizvestnye stroki Shekspira?" in *Izvestiia Akademii Nauk S.S.S.R., Seriia Literatury i Iazyka* 47, no. 6 (November-December): 559–70.

Examines metrically, semantically, and metaphorically the recently discovered poem "Shall I die?" attributed to Shakespeare and compares the poem to other works by Shakespeare as well as Donne's poetry in order to determine the poem's authorship.

907. Milward, Peter. *A Commentary on the Holy Sonnets of John Donne*. Renaissance Monographs, 14. Tokyo: Renaissance Institute, Sophia University. 110p. English revised version of *John Donne no 'Seinaru Sonnet'* (1979).

Aims to throw "new light on the devotional meaning and background" of the sonnets in *Corona,* including *MHMary* and *ED,* and the *Holy Sonnets*. Discusses each poem in both collections, "first, as meditations mainly inspired by the *Spiritual Exercises* of St. Ignatius; secondly, as deeply indebted to Scriptural and liturgical sources; thirdly, as making occasional use of mediaeval theology and philosophy, particularly that of St. Thomas Aquinas; and finally, as closely related in thought and language to the plays of Shakespeare" (3).

908. Mohanty, Christine Ann. "Penitential Sonnets 2 and 3: Anomaly in the Gardner Arrangement of Donne's *Holy Sonnets*." *N&Q,* n.s. 35: 61–62.

Agrees with Helen Gardner (1952, 1978) that the so-called 'penitential sonnets' as they appear in the 1635 edition "have far more meaning in a set of their own than they do tangled in a web of unrelated poems," but maintains that "the argument in favour of a penitential set would be further strengthened by retaining the traditional arrangement of sonnets 3 and 5, which would then reveal a sequential development undetectable in the Gardner edition," in which the two poems are reversed (2 and 3 in her edition). Argues that Gardner's reversal of the two sonnets is "unwarranted by any textual authority" and "threatens to weaken the arrangement as a whole," whereas the original order of the sonnets makes clear "the movement from one stage of penitence to the next" (62).

909. Morrison, Karl F. *"I am you" : The Hermeneutics of Empathy in Western Literature, Theology, and Art.* Princeton, N.J.: Princeton University Press. xxvi, 366p.

Morrison explores the concept of "I am you," in which he moves "from the sentence 'I am you,' as a historical artifact (Chapters 1, 2), to patterns of understanding that enabled interpreters to make sense of the sentence (Chapters 3–5), and finally to ways of understanding the enterprise of understanding that lay at the bedrock of the tradition under review, considering first verbal (Chapters 6–8) and then visual (Chapters 9–12) ways of understanding understanding" (xxv). Considers Donne's "Meditation 17" in *Devotions* in the light of the "I am you" concept, noting that Donne unites believers with God and with each other on the basis of his belief in the mystical body of Christ, which is based on sacramental, metaphysical, and epistemological reasons. Discusses also *Tilman* as an example of Donne's use of mimesis in the "I am you" concept, claiming that the closing line about the "blest Hermaphrodite" is spiritual, not sexual, and that Donne is evincing his interest in alchemy, a process by which different bodies become "concorporated," or where science proves that "I" could become "you" (48). Parts company with those who believe that Donne did not value "looking at things" (59), citing the numerous portraits he had commissioned and the many metaphors from painting that he used in his works. Surveys Donne's erotic verse in which the "I am you" concept appears, concluding that Donne found "a number of bondings that were neither participatory nor esthetic-affective, nor mimetic" but in which "[o]nly bondings in the soul involved the affects and mimetic action" (66).

910. Naulty, R. A. "Tolstoy, Donne and Metaphysics." *Colloquium: The Australian and New Zealand Theological Review* (Auckland) 20, no. 2: 29–33.

Argues that Tolstoy was not a "complete rationalist" but rather "had a settled metaphysical vision which has a mystical aspect to it." Suggests that "the kind of metaphysical reality" (29) that Tolstoy presents in his works has certain similarities to that found in Donne's poetry. Points out, however, that "the love, expressed in service to others and extolled by Tolstoy (agape) does not negate the form of love celebrated by Donne (eros) but subsumes it and moves beyond it" (32).

911. Nicholls, David. "The Political Theology of John Donne." *Theological Studies* 49: 45–66.

Discusses "the way in which the political and social structures in England, and Donne's conceptualising of these structures, influenced his theological imagery, language, and thought, particularly in his sermons" (46). Maintains that "the political analogy, which sees the king in relation to his realm as analogous to God in His relationship to the universe, and the closely connected but distinct social image of God the Holy Trinity as a model for the life of the nation, play a central and unifying role in the theology of Donne, giving it more coherence than is generally perceived"

(45–46). Argues that, contrary to the generally accepted modern view, Donne contributed significantly to theological development in the seventeenth century. Observes that, while "acknowledging a limited validity to the analogy between divine and human structures of authority," Donne "challenged the notion of God as an arbitrary and tyrannical ruler," and that while illustrating "his Trinitarian theology with reference to his political experience, he also legitimated and at times criticised political structures and policies by appealing to the image of God as perfect community and to the analogy of God's government of the universe" (65).

912. Radzinowicz, Mary Ann. "The Politics of Donne's Silences." *JDJ* 7: 1–19.

Suggests that the main barrier to "recontextualizing" Donne's poetry is not formalism but rather "Donne's own silences on topics that, if plainly addressed, would yield an ideology from historico-political evidence." Maintains that "[t]he problem with reading Donne's poetry politically is that it is so silent on politics" (1). Discusses four of Donne's silences—"about England's colonization of America, about her pacification of Ireland, about the socio-political role of exceptional women, and in English about other poets." Reads these silences as "actions, not omissions, as shaped rhetorical spaces or gestures, not accidental vacancies," maintaining that "[i]t is the *silence* itself that is politically instructive or interpretable" (2), not what the critic presumes it conceals. Argues that "no monocausal explanatory model" (13) applies to the four silences discussed but rather draws on models of historico-political interpretation by Arthur Marotti, Annabel Patterson, David Aers and Gunther Kress, and Richard Helgerson, who present "the portrait of a poet in a prerevolutionary period marked by state control of publications, whose poems were offered to a few, whose membership in an over-numerous clergy of the talented, critical, educated, underemployed was a recipe for alienation and whose very role-definition precluded open political speech in public poetry" (14). Maintains that Donne is not guilty of "ideological escapism—into ethnocentrism, sexism, or classism," and that he is "not silent as the poet of unquestioning endorsement of the socio-political status quo." Insists that in each of the four instances discussed one must rule out "the silence of pure consent," observing that in each instance he "uses the option of not saying anything more where he has asked a question" (15). Concludes that "[t]o use or to read Donne's silence, it is necessary to rehistoricize it, by recovering a clear sense of the significance of his language and his tropes, and by isolating silence within or after speech" (16).

913. Richards, Bernard. "Donne's 'Aire and Angels': A Gross Misreading." *JDJ* 7: 119–22.

Rejects Thomas Docherty's reading (1987) of "pinnance" in *Air* (l. 18) as "penis." Calls the reading "nonsensical" and an "impertinent critical excrescence" (120) and argues that it is "a hindrance rather than a help to any understanding of Donne." Says that "it is a detritus that has to be cleared away before understanding can begin" (122).

914. Ricks, Christopher. "Donne After Love," in *Literature and the Body: Essays on Populations and Persons*, ed. Elaine Scarry, 33–69. Selected Papers from the English Institute, 1986, n.s. 12. Baltimore: Johns Hopkins University Press.

Arguing that Donne's poems "record a dislike of having come," comments on the postcoital sadness and revulsion expressed in Donne's love poems and on how they are "so often driven to bend this animus upon their own previous act of creative love," which "takes shape in the recurrent phenomenon of how unhealthily the poems end" (33). Discusses in detail *Fare, LovAlch, Air, Curse, WomCon,* and *SGo,* poems that debase, demean, and degrade women and sexuality and take "perverse delight in meaning in the end something not only inadequate to, but unworthy of, the occasion he has created" (46). Does not find Donne simply witty but rather agrees with those who say that Donne's poems "practice some form of self-destruction" (53). Disagrees with critics such as Arthur Marotti, John Carey, Tilottama Rajan, and others who try to make Donne's poems amenable in some way. Says that "the occasions when Donne conquers the itch to violate his poem are those when the poem suffers no orgasm" (58).

915. Roberts, John R. *George Herbert: An Annotated Bibliography of Modern Criticism, Revised Edition, 1905–1984.* Columbia: University of Missouri Press. xix, 433p.

Lists 278 items (on George Herbert) published from 1905 to 1984 that make reference to Donne and/or his works. All items for the years 1979 to 1984 that contain extended discussions of Donne have been separately entered into this bibliography. For earlier items, see *Roberts 1* and *Roberts 2.*

916. Salomon, Willis. "Donne's 'Aire and Angels.'" *Expl* 46, no. 4: 12–14.

Argues that most readings of *Air* fail to take into account "the importance of the lightness of tone" in l. 26, which is achieved, for the most part, by the speaker's return to direct address of his beloved. Claims that "[t]he return to direct address in the last six lines asserts in the poem the dynamic, experiential quality of active courtship after

twenty-two lines of tortuous metaphysical invention." Maintains that, if approached in this way, the poem "becomes neither simply cynicism nor elevated panegyric" but rather "an 'argument' for the relation between two contexts of love: the 'metaphysical,' which defines amatory experience in terms of ultimates; and the 'rhetorical,' which defines it in terms of concrete situations" (12). Believes that what makes the poem so interesting is that "the expectation of a definition of achieved, perfected love is subverted as the poem closes" (13). Claims that in the ending Donne "pits the elaborate attempts to place love in the abstract against the most concrete implications of the poem's tone and mode of address" and that the poem "does finally arrive at the definition of love sought by its complex dialectical turns." Concludes that, although the poem acknowledges the disparity between ideal and real love, the recognition is not cynical because Donne "shows how participation in love's ritual provides the fertile basis for the invention and scrutiny of a metaphysic of love" (14).

917. Scarry, Elaine. "Donne: 'But yet the body is his booke,'" in *Literature and the Body: Essays on Populations and Persons,* ed. Elaine Scarry, 70–105. Selected Letters from the English Institute, 1986, n.s. no. 12. Baltimore: Johns Hopkins University Press.

Believes that God's willful choice to take on a body in the person of Christ, which is called "willful materialism," underscores Donne's refusal to disavow the body in poems and sermons. Relates this notion to Donne as a writer, maintaining that, "for Donne, language achieves its greatest triumph when it is inclusive of the material realm" (73). Relates Donne's concerns with language in terms of the page itself, "something that because it is cloth or paper or rag or leaf or vellum itself has sensuous properties" (75), and maintains that "[t]hus the verbal unit (word, sentence) is reconceived as a material unit, the page" (76). Refers to Donne's account of the Shroud of Turin, a material object receiving the impression of Christ's body, seeing the transfer not only as that of substance and picture, but also as that of word, for "the 'signature' of the wound is, if not a word, at least the ghostly anticipation of a word" (78). Sees all of the valediction poems as arising out of the need to establish some representative form of the body in its place and says that, "ultimately, the vehicle of representation is language, since the poem itself is offered as a place holder, occupying the person's space until he returns" (80). Says that "every material object in Donne, because it bears in its outline the evidence of inventive intelligence . . . is itself soaked in language" (92), noting especially the bell in *Devotions*, which is "progressively interiorized" (93), along with language. Concludes that, for Donne, "[m]edical science, religion, and lyric poetry animate the body, deliberately enter it, and in doing so revise it to be volitional," and that "[b]ell, lens, book, page are the repository of the peculiarly human in part because they are themselves the outcome of conscious intention" (95–96).

918. Schenck, Celeste Marguerite. " 'The Marriage Hearse': Anti-Epithalamia of Donne, Crashaw, Blake," in *Mourning and Panegyric: The Poetics of Pastoral Ceremony*, 73–90. University Park: Pennsylvania State University Press.

Briefly surveys the origin and development of the satiric epithalamium or anti-epithalamium and discusses *EpLin* as a response to Spenser's *Epithalamion*, showing how it "bawdily pits fescennine against Spenser's high-serious epithalamium, competing directly with the earlier poem in a broadly parodic manner" (75). Contrasts the two poems to show how Donne "apes the form of Spenser's poem, approximates its stanza form and mimics its refrain," (76) and deflates it "by imputing less than romantic motives to the groomsmen wanting to marry the wealthy Senators' daughters and to the fathers hastening to make rich matches for their girls" (77). Comments on two fully developed conceits in Donne's poem—"the likening of church architecture to the bride's genitals and womb" and "the superimposition of bridal rite and ritual disembowelling" (78). Believes that the poem "provided the early Donne with a conventional stage on which to exercise his poetic voice," allowing him "to dialogue with a formidable literary opponent" and permitting him "to lay aside the student years of his own poetic virginity in the course of an increasingly vigorous literary career" (79).

919. Sellin, Paul R. *"So Doth, So Is Religion": John Donne and Diplomatic Contexts in the Reformed Netherlands, 1619–1620.* Columbia: University of Missouri Press. xi, 295p.

Presents a detailed analysis of Donne's role as diplomat and divine during his visit to The Netherlands in 1619–20 "by examining in depth his participation in some of the most important social, political, and religious events of the time" (jacket). In the preface (vii–xi) indicates that the purpose of this study is "to broaden perceptions of what should be considered a significant moment in Donne's life" (vii). The introduction (1–8) outlines the major issues that the study will investigate. Comments on the difficulties inherent in understanding Donne's religious views, especially his attitude toward Calvinism, and discusses the tense political and religious situation in the Low Countries prior to the outbreak of the Thirty Years' War. Chapter 1, "John Donne as a Diplomat-Divine in the Netherlands" (9–31), argues that Donne participated fully in Viscount Doncaster's embassy to the Low Countries, "not in an informal but in an official capacity" (9–10), and suggests that, among other talents that made him valuable to the mission, Donne likely knew some Dutch and already had a reputation among the Dutch as a brilliant polemicist, preacher, and poet that "superbly fit [him] for much more than merely seeing to spiritual needs or tending foreign clergy" (30). Chapter 2, "Viscount Doncaster in the United Provinces, December 1619" (32–59), discusses Doncaster's activities in The Netherlands, arguing that his visit "was of much greater importance to Dutch policy, both domestic and foreign, and to the Continental Reformed churches than has ever been suggested" (32), and comments on Donne's experiences and personal contacts during the visit. Chapter 3, "Doncaster's Reception by the States General" (60–87), and Chapter 4, "Business in The Hague up through Doncaster's Audience" (88–108), discuss details of Doncaster's reception and political activities in The Hague, noting that Donne was "likely to have been privy to some of the behind-the-scenes activity leading to publication of the Proceedings of the Synod of Dort" and that, "right at a pivotal moment in their formulation, he was luckily at hand for consultation" (108). Chapter 5, "Donne's Preaching in The Hague" (109–34), discusses Donne's sermon, "Fishers of Men," preached most likely in the Hofkapel in The Hague, and argues that "it was designed to complement, perhaps even augment, Doncaster's postures before the Council of State and his address to the States General the day before" (109). Chapter 6, "After Doncaster's Audience" (135–

57), and Chapter 7, "Return Home" (158–84), trace the stages of the embassy's return to and reception in England, noting that Donne was awarded the commemorative medal of the Synod of Dort before he left Holland and commenting on his continuing enthusiasm "for the Bohemian cause, for Frederick's accepting the crown at Prague, and for militant support of the Calvinist Dutch against the house of Spain and Austria" (171). Argues that although not a Calvinist in outward things, Donne was not "unalterably opposed in mind, sensibilities, and spirit to doctrines, principles, or manners rooted in Geneva" (172), and suggests that his "poetic oeuvre should be reexamined from a 'Genevan' perspective" (179). Concludes with three appendices: "Appendix A. Gerard van Hamel's Speech to Doncaster at Utrecht, December 11/21, 1619" (185); "Appendix B. Doncaster's Address to the States General" (186–88); and "Appendix C. The States' Reply to Doncaster" (189–94), followed by notes (195–260), a bibliography (261–82), and an index (283–95). Reviews: Stanley Stewart in *JDJ* 7 (1988): 273–86; Roy Schreiber in *Albion* 21 (1989): 629–30; Dennis Flynn in *JEGP* 89 (1990): 224–26; David Norbrook in *N&Q*, n.s. 37 (1990): 345–46; Jeanne Shami in *Ren&R* 14 (1990): 331–33; Keith L. Sprunger in *Church History* 59 (1990): 249–50; P. G. Stanwood in *MP* 88 (1990): 75–78; C. W. Schoneveld in *ES* 73 (1992): 183–84.

920. Sellin, Paul R., and Augustus J. Veenendaal, Jr. "Een kroegentocht door oud Den Haag: Shady Light on English Friends of John Donne in the Netherlands," 13–23. *Papers from the Third Interdisciplinary Conference on Netherlandic Studies: Held at the University of Michigan.* Ann Arbor, 12–14 June 1986, ed. Tom J. Broos. Publications of the American Association for Netherlandic Studies. Lanham, Md.: University Press of America.

Shorter version of "A 'Pub Crawl' Through Old The Hague: Shady Light on Life and Art Among English Friends of John Donne in The Netherlands" in *JDJ* 6 (1987): 235–59 (entry 826). Argues that an anonymous Dutch poem entitled "Een Geestelijk Lei-deken," found in the Conway Papers in the British Library, presents a realistic view of lowlife in The Hague during the first quarter of the seventeenth century as confirmed also in Dutch genre painting of the time. Suggests that the Dutch poem shows that the coarser elements in Donne's poetry, particularly the *Elegies* and certain of the *Songs and Sonets,* "are not far removed from Netherlandish work in this view." Maintains that, in fact, "compared with Donne's, Dutch frankness pales," and suggests that Donne, as a soldier, "would have known the rough world of camp and court depicted in "Een Geestelijk Leideken" (19).

921. Shawcross, John T. "But Is It Donne's? The Problem of Titles on His Poems." *JDJ* 7: 141–49.

Encourages critics not to base critical interpretations of Donne's poems on their titles since many of them are not Donne's but the work of a copyist or early editor. Argues that a title "will direct the reader to read in a certain way, to look for certain narrative or attitudinal elements, and, unfortunately, at times, to miss certain implications which just don't fit the title" (146). Maintains that by referring to a poem simply by its first line "perhaps the reader will discover things in a poem otherwise obscured and will surely avoid readings which are otherwise extrinsic to that text" (149). Offers guidelines for giving titles to

Donne's poems: (1) "ascertain what might have been Donne's title (there may be few beyond the generic and verse letter forms)"; (2) "accept well-known titles if they do not conflict with the substance of the poem and are obvious possibilities (like 'The Flea')"; (3) "employ a well-known title that might have been Donne's but without whatever questionable additions might have accrued (like 'A Valediction' "; and (4) "omit titles and give only a short form of the first line (definitely not to make up titles like 'Recusancy')" (148), as Helen Gardner does in her *John Donne: The Elegies and the Songs and Sonnets* (Oxford: Clarendon Press, 1965).

922. Shawcross, John T. "On Some Early References to John Donne." *JDJ* 7: 115–17.

Notes six early references to Donne not included in A. J. Smith's *Critical Heritage of John Donne* (1975): two excerpts in Clement Barksdale's *Memorials of Worthy Persons: Two Decads* (1661); a response to *Biathanatos* in John Adams's *An Essay Concerning Self-Murther* (1700); an epigraph attributed to Donne in *The Prompter*, no. 166, 8 June 1736; an aphorism attributed to Donne in *The Virginia Almanack for the Year of Our Lord, 1770*; and the reprinting of six epigrams in William Oldys's *A Collection of Epigrams* . . . (1727). Challenges the notion that Donne's poetry was little known before the nineteenth century.

923. Shawcross, John T. "Scholarly Editions: Composite Editorial Principles of Single Copy-Texts, Multiple Copy-Texts, Edited Copy-Texts." *Text* 4: 297–317.

Comments on *Liar*, *HSScene*, and *Flea* as examples of poems with textual cruxes that scholarly editors must resolve. Believes that, although consistency in spelling, punctuation, capitalization, italicization, and so forth may be acceptable in nonscholarly editions of Donne's poetry, the same sort of consistency should not be imposed on scholarly editions. Argues that for a poet like Donne, where there is almost no holograph material, editorial "interference" is often required. Maintains that in scholarly editions, such as the forthcoming variorum edition of Donne's poetry, "an editor must consider individually each piece of writing and all its contexts; must decide the most accurate presentation of the text and the history of the text; and must therefore at times seem inconsistent in what is being done." Points out that "[t]reatment of some texts will offer a single text with notes and variants" (e.g., *Liar*), "some texts will offer a single text with editorial interference, discussion, notes, and variants" (e.g., *HSScene*), and "some texts will be offered in multiple versions with discussion, notes, and variants" (e.g., *Flea*) (311).

924. Sheppeard, Sallye. "Eden and Agony in 'Twicknam Garden.'" *JDJ* 7: 65–72.
Believes that a "too narrow biographical reading" of *Twick* has created misunderstandings about the poem. Argues that, contrary to much critical opinion, in the poem Donne's speaker "emerges as no ordinary loser in the game of courtly love but as a self-professed self-deceiver who suffers self-inflicted misery" and "purposefully exaggerates his plight as miserable lover frankly desiring the affections of the wrong woman" (65). Maintains that the speaker is not "a hapless victim of unrequited love" but rather is "a willing prisoner of thwarted passion," who "seeks not spiritual renewal but physical satisfaction, not grace but gratification," and that "knowing already his lady's commitment to someone else precludes his becoming her soul companion, the speaker still hopes to prompt her infidelity to ideal love." Observes, therefore, that "[r]ecognition that the speaker does not figure himself as Adam deceived by Eve in a fallen Eden is crucial in properly understanding the poem" (67). Maintains that the speaker "acknowledges himself rather than some external force as the source of his deception and misery" and that, because he fails to seduce the lady from ideal love, "the garden remains for her a prelapsarian Eden, and just because it does so, Twicknam Garden becomes for the speaker not a fallen Eden but a Gethsemane" (68). Shows how the poem is "structurally unified, its parts are logically related, and its chief ideas and figures contribute to its overall design," and discusses its "unconventional treatment of poetic commonplaces and familiar religious imagery, its patterns of ascendant and descendant values, and its ironic wit." Believes that this study "clarifies the hyperbolic nature and complimentary purpose of the speaker's complaint" and "removes familiar but unfounded suspicions" that the poem "reflects Donne's guilty response to inappropriate feelings for his patroness or his vindictive response to a rejection of him" (70–71).

925. Shuger, Debora K. *Sacred Rhetoric: The Christian Grand Style in the English Renaissance.* Princeton, N.J.: Princeton University Press. 289p.
Argues that "the Christian grand style is one of the most far-reaching and innovative developments in Renaissance rhetoric" (6) and "is not a narrowly specialized compartment of the history of Renaissance rhetoric but its most vital and reflective branch" (13), thereby challenging those who would either deny its existence altogether or who would imply that it was only an antithesis in the evolution of the plain style. Surveys the history of classical

grand style through St. Augustine and the history of sacred rhetoric from 1475 to 1675. Discusses attempts to legitimize passionate discourse in the Renaissance, the classical contribution to sacred rhetoric, and the role of imagination in emotion and thought and in the notion of the self as respondent to God. Points out that Donne's sermons "often mention rhetoric, but only to disparage it" (110–11). Frequently quotes Donne's words that "[r]hetorique will make absent and remote things present to your understanding" (195) and relates his theology with rhetoric by citing his saying that preaching and the sacraments bring Christ "nearer [to men] in visible and sensible things" (198). Notes Donne's adherence to Augustinian psychology "with its affective view of spiritual experience" (252).

926. Silberman, Lauren. "Mythographic Transformations of Ovid's Hermaphrodite." *SCJ* 19: 643–52.

Discusses "the curious fortunes of Ovid's myth of the hermaphrodite in the hands of Medieval and Renaissance mythographers and examines the literary treatment of the myth by various interpreters." Argues that "an understanding of the complex web of tradition associated with this myth" (643) is necessary for an adequate appreciation of images of the hermaphrodite in the poetry of such important poets as Rabelais, Spenser, and Donne, but does not specifically discuss Donne's use of the myth.

927. Skillen, John E. "Revisionism and Renaissance Poets." *CSR* 18: 81–86.

Reviews Diana Benet's *Secretary of Praise: The Poetic Vocation of George Herbert* (1984), P. G. Stanwood's and Heather Asals's *John Donne and the Theology of Language* (1986), Claude J. Summers's and Ted-Larry Pebworth's *The Eagle and the Dove: Reassessing John Donne* (1986), and

Richard Todd's *Opacity of Signs: Acts of Interpretation in George Herbert's The Temple* (1986)—all published by the University of Missouri Press. Comments on the influence of contemporary structuralist and poststructuralist theory on the understanding of Donne and Herbert.

928. Stanford, Michael. "The Terrible Thresholds: Sir Thomas Browne on Sex and Death." *ELR* 18: 413–23.

Argues that Thomas Browne's "responses to sex and death are the antithesis of Donne's." Calls Donne "the most *shameless* of writers" who is "[u]tterly unembarrassed by sex" and "equally unabashed by death." Notes that "the very images Browne shrinks from most violently are the most compelling for Donne" and says that Donne "embraces mortality in a nearly literal sense." Maintains that, for Donne, "sex and death are even more tightly entwined . . . than they are for Browne," and claims that "[n]o poet with the possible exception of Baudelaire has ever merged eros and thanatos so fully" (422) as Donne. Believes that Browne "is a lesser artist than Donne in part because he is a more ordinary man," but thinks that Browne's "ordinariness is part of his attraction" (423).

929. Stewart, Stanley. "Imagining Dutch Reformed Donne." *JDJ* 7: 273–86.

Reviews Paul Sellin's *John Donne and "Calvinist" Views of Grace* (1983) and *"So Doth, So Is Religion": John Donne and Diplomatic Contexts in the Reformed Netherlands, 1619–1620* (1988).

930. Sullivan, David. "The Structure of Self-Revelation in Donne's *Devotions*." *PSt* 11, no. 2: 49–59.

Argues that in *Devotions* Donne exhibits a "certain mobility in his thinking that distinguishes it from usual rhetorical discourse," but that this "apparent spontaneity" has a definite "rhetorical structure." Maintains that "the extent to which this structure is personal becomes evident when the uses Donne makes of it are compared with a similar structure in [St. Ignatius] Loyola's [*Spiritual*] *Exercises* and the very different effect he achieves with it." Shows how in both Ignatius and Donne "we see two remarkable reformulations of the place system of classical rhetoric modified to embrace narrative for didactic reasons" (57). Believes that although Donne attempts, "by allegorizing his self, to minister holy delight, we find that our eyes wander no further from that place of perennial fascination—the self—than do his own" (57–58). Says that "[a]s we read we feel it is not sickness that engrosses Donne—but his sickness" and "[n]ot sin—but his sin," and insists that "[t]hese are the real themes and obsessive preoccupations of the book and the man." Concludes, however, that we should thank Donne for his "ego-centrism" because "[i]n the structure of the *Devotions* this power transforms an old rhetorical model into a vehicle of brilliant self-presentation" (58).

931. Sullivan, Ernest W., II. *The First and Second Dalhousie Manuscripts: Poems and Prose by John Donne and Others, A Facsimile Edition.* Columbia: University of Missouri Press. x, 230p.

Presents a photographic facsimile edition of the first and second Dalhousie Manuscripts, with facing transcriptions, that contains 44 and 29 poems respectively by Donne. The introduction (1–12), preceded by a preface (vii) and table of contents (ix–x), comments on the discovery of the manuscripts in 1977 and their modern provenance, describes them bibliographically, discusses how they were compiled and transcribed, and evaluates their textual and literary significance. Maintains that "the discovery that Dalhousie I manuscript derives from papers preserved by the Essex family and that the Essex collection became the basis for British Library MS. Landsdowne 740 and, ultimately, Trinity College Dublin MS. 877 suggests that Donne's patrons and poetical coterie, rather than Donne himself, may lie behind the major manuscript collections of his poems." Points out how "the deliberate nature of the Dalhousie collection has important implications for the study of Renaissance verse and culture generally" (vii). A note on the transcriptions (14) explains the rules for expanding manuscript abbreviations and notes that the transcriptions attempt "to reproduce the manuscript text exactly, including all layers of revision by the original and later copyists," and that "[c]onjectural readings appear between vertical lines." Presents the poems with facsimile and transcription of each poem on the same page (15–189). In the explanatory notes (191–95) defines unusual words or usages; identifies persons, places, and allusions; notes problematic readings in the texts and gives traditional readings; and identifies and expands unique manuscript abbreviations. Gives a list of seventeenth century manuscript locations and sigla (197–99); lists manuscript and print locations of the poems (201–8); and lists substantive variants among the texts of Donne's poems in the two Dalhousie manuscripts as well as in the seven seventeenth century editions and/or issues of Donne's collected poems and in selected modern editions (209–22). Concludes with a selected bibliography (223), a general index (225–28), and an index of titles and first lines (229–30). Reviews: John B. Gabel in *PBSA* 83 (1989): 101–3; Michael Bath in *RES* 41 (1990): 395–97; Arthur F. Kinney in *Rev* 12 (1990): 213–27; Paul Parrish in *SCN* 48 (1990): 3; Neil

Rhodes in *MLR* 85 (1990): 913–15; John T. Shawcross in *ANQ* 4 (1991): 39–41; H. R. Woudhuysen in *N&Q*, n.s. 37 (1990): 221–22.

932. Swiss, Margo. *"Lacrimae Christi:* The Theology of Tears in Milton's 'Lycidas' and Donne's Sermon 13, 'Jesus Wept' (Whitehall, Lent [1622–23])." *MiltonQ* 22: 102. Abstract of a paper delivered at the Third International Milton Symposium (June 1988).

Maintains that Donne's sermon on Jesus weeping given at Whitehall during Lent 1622–23 can provide a commentary on Milton's "Lycidas" and suggests that "at least the authors shared familiarity with the theology of tears" and invites scholars to examine more closely "the possible influence of Donne's text upon Milton's elegy."

933. Urnov, Mikhail D. "Shakespeare's Epoch and the 'School' of John Donne: The Transition from One Epoch to the Other." *Neohelicon* 15: 51–55.

Discusses T. S. Eliot's contribution to the reappraisal of metaphysical poetry, and especially Donne's, in the 1920s and 1930s. Sees much of Eliot's evaluation of Donne as a defense of his own poetry and that of his friends. Maintains that Eliot "did not try to refute the view that this poetry was artificial" but rather "tried to change the attitude to this artificiality," and that he "never proposed to see harmony in something that had once seemed rough" but rather "insisted that it was exactly what it should be— rough." Claims that Eliot "never looked for any spontaneity in this poetry" (54) and dismissed the charge that metaphysical poetry was too difficult. Argues that, in spite of its ingenuity, metaphysical poetry "is anything but artistry, with the exception of certain lines—those flashes of poetic spirit which immediately impressed the contemporaries and

were later also appreciated according to their unquestionable artistic merit." Concludes, therefore, that if metaphysical poetry is regarded as "an epoch in the development of poetry," it was "an epoch of retreat—not in the sense of an inferior artistic level . . . but in the sense of *other merits* and *other achievements* temporarily coming to the fore and superseding the creative work proper" (55).

934. Walker, Julia M. "Left/Write/Right: Of Lock-Jaw and Literary Criticism." *JDJ* 7: 133–39.

Reviews unfavorably Thomas Docherty's *John Donne, Undone* (1986) and attacks the "stylistic opacity" and bad writing of much recent literary criticism, as exemplified by Docherty. Agrees with Docherty that Donne studies should "move from the shadow of the 1950s onto the theoretical fast-track of contemporary critical exchange" (138) but does not believe that "such a move must be predicated on the adoption of jargon-studded syntactical aberrations or on the neglect or misreading of poetry." Thinks that "[t]he idea that stylistic inaccessibility is a mark of the cognoscenti is responsible for much good criticism being badly written" (139).

935. Wall, John N. *Transformations of the Word: Spenser, Herbert, Vaughan.* Athens, Ga.: University of Georgia Press. xv, 428p.

Argues that "the fundamental identifying mark of the Church of England—the ongoing worship of Englishfolk as enabled by the use of the Book of Common Prayer—forms the indispensable frame for non-Catholic and non-Puritan religious discourse in Renaissance England and provides the definition of that 'practical piety and devotion'" (8–9) endorsed by such writers as Spenser, Herbert, and Vaughan. Briefly points out that in his sermons Donne makes clear on several occasions that "the words of the preacher are incomplete without the action of the Sacraments and the behavior of preacher and congregation in response to participation in the Prayer Book rites" (39). Maintains that, for Donne, "the corporate worship of the community is the context in which God's Word becomes effectual to the people" (45).

936. Waterhouse, Ruth. "Donne's Challenge." *Teaching of English (Sydney)* 54: 56–59.

Maintains that a major challenge for twentieth century readers of Donne's poems is "to perceive how he is using word order and the relationship of similar words or word classes as one important method of conveying (or refusing to convey) meaning" (57). Analyzes *Appar* and *HSBlack* to show how word order contributes to the whole meaning of both poems.

937. Wright, T. R. *Theology and Literature.* London: Basil Blackwell. viii, 243p.

Argues that "it is possible and even necessary to talk about God in the form of stories, poems and plays" and, therefore, in this study "attempts to continue a dialogue that has already begun between theologians and literary critics on the nature of their disciplines and the possibility of interaction between them" (vii). Points out, for example, that Donne "by describing sexual attraction in theological terms and religious experience in sexual images, canonizing his lovers and demanding to be ravished by God . . . opens up in the process the area of overlap between the two kinds of ecstatic experience" (136–37). Notes also that Donne's wit "belongs to a long tradition of Christian meditation" and that "meditation necessarily proceeds by metaphor, drawing the mind from the tangible 'realities' of the sense to the 'realities' of the spiritual world" (137). Says, by way

of illustration, that the various puns and paradoxes on the cross in *Cross* and *Goodf* are "far from trivial for they point towards the mystery at the heart of faith" (142), and insists that the great Christian symbols found in poetry should be regarded "as a richer, more emotive mode of exploring the mysteries at the heart of the Christian faith, a complementary mode of theological reflection" (152).

938. Yoo, Chung-In. "John Donne eui yeonae si e natanan 'courtly love' e daehayeo." ["'Courtly Love' in John Donne's Love Poetry."] *Journal of the English Language and Literature* (Seoul) 34: 237–54.

Suggests that Donne's love poems are influenced by the courtly love tradition as it was filtered through Petrarchan poems and Provençal love songs. Points out that Donne emphasizes spiritual love in *Canon, Noct,* and *Relic*; that in the valediction poems he portrays love as a harmonious union of the spiritual and the sensual; that in *GoodM, Under,* and *Air* he presents ideal love with "courtesy and grace"; in *LovDiet, Bait, Leg,* and other poems he becomes "licentious, tricky, playful, and deceptive"; and in *LovUsury* and *LovInf* he "stresses ironically and paradoxically the sentiments of betrayed love." Maintains that thus in the *Songs and Sonets* Donne expresses a "panoramic" view of love (254). (Taken from the English abstract.)

939. Zunder, William. "The Poetry of John Donne: Literature, History and Ideology," in *Jacobean Poetry and Prose: Rhetoric, Representation and the Popular Imagination,* ed. Clive Bloom, 78–95. New York: St. Martin's Press.

Briefly summarizes Donne's life, relating it to the changes taking place in contemporary society. Discusses *Sat3,* for example, as "a response to the religious changes of the century: to the rise of Protestantism" (79), pointing out how Donne challenges the right of the monarch to determine his subjects' religion. Calls Donne "revolutionary" (83). Discusses also Donne's degrading of the image of the sun, which is frequently a reference to the king, in such poems as *GoodM* and *SunRis,* calling the latter "a monument in the development of individualism in England" (87). Suggests, however, that Donne's commitment to the individual love relationship waned, as seen in *LovAlch* and *Noct,* and is transferred to an individual religious relationship with God, most evident in the *Holy Sonnets.* Associates Donne with the Anglican and royalist tradition of Herbert, Vaughan, and Traherne. Believes that Donne does an about-face before his ordination, observing that "the radicalism" of *Sat3* and *SunRis* "gives way to the absolutism of James I" (92). Suggests that Donne ended his career "in a state of self-alienation" (93).

1989

940. Aizawa, Yoshihisa. "Nihon ni okeru Keijijoshi Kenkyu Shoshi (3)" [A Bibliography of Writings about Metaphysical Poetry in Japan (3)], in *17 Seiki Eibungaku to Europe* [The Heritage of European Culture in English Literature of the Seventeenth Century], 45–62. The Japan Society of Seventeenth-Century English Literature. Tokyo: Kinseido.

Presents a bibliography of studies on metaphysical poets (including Donne, Herbert, Crashaw, Marvell, Vaughan, and Traherne) and metaphysical poetry in general, published in Japan from April 1979 to March 1984. Contains also an additional list of studies on metaphysical poetry in Japan from 1927 to March 1975. Items on Donne (1979–84) have been included and annotated in this bibliography; for pre-1979 items, see *Roberts 1* and *Roberts 2*.

941. Anderson, Judith H. " 'But We Shall Teach the Lad Another Language': History and Rhetoric in Bacon, Ford, and Donne." *RenD,* n.s. 20: 169–96.

Discusses how in the first third of the seventeenth century, Francis Bacon, John Ford, and Donne, when taken together, "offer a spectrum of views on the relation of poetry to history and of words to material reality." Observes that Bacon regards words as "images of matter" and poetry as "idealized, hence untrue," whereas Donne and Ford disagree with Bacon's view, "though both are sensitive to it and pointedly include it in their own work." Says that Donne is "a tentative constructor of counterfeit worlds,

which are always qualified, often threatened, and sometimes undermined by an awareness of what is excluded." Observes, however, that Donne does not share Bacon's "distrust of language" but shows "an ironic awareness at once of its limits and illusions and also of its significant powers," thereby remaining "more committed to the possibilities of verbal constructs than to the material world, more to one kind of truth than to another" (192). Finds resemblances between Ford's *Perkin Warbeck* and *Canon*.

942. Bedford, R. D. *Dialogues with Convention: Readings in Renaissance Poetry.* Ann Arbor: University of Michigan Press. x, 204p.

Chapter 2, "Conventions of Imitation: Donne and the Metamorphosis of Ovid" (59–79), is a revised, expanded version of "Ovid Metamorphosed: Donne's *Elegy XVI*" in *EIC* 32 (1982): 219–36. Argues that, although there are many resemblances between Donne's erotic poetry and Ovid's, there are also "profound and inevitable differences." Points out, for example, that the Ovidian games Donne plays in his poems "are complicated by the Christian assumptions and values of the world into which Donne projects his squibs," and that his use of theological language "reinforces a special kind of *nequitia* [naughtiness] unavailable to Ovid" (63). Believes, however, that the most important discovery Donne made was the dramatic element in Ovid's poems, which was perhaps reinforced by the influence of the Elizabethan theater. Discusses *ElFatal* as Donne's "most sustained" and "most theatrically vital" (67) reworkings of Ovidian conventions. Chapter 4, "Conventions of Devotion II" (94–104), is a revised, expanded version of "Donne's Holy Sonnet, 'Batter My Heart'" in *N&Q*, n.s. 29 (1982): 15–19. Reviews various earlier interpretations of the first quatrain of *HSBatter* and argues that the implied conceit has "considerable specificity and a good deal of poetic muscle"—that of God as a potter and Donne as a pot that must not simply be mended but completely broken and remade. Insists, therefore, that it is not simply "a gesture of disorganized and uncontrolled sensationalism" nor "an outburst of whirling words, nor simply a verbal arithmetic of only vaguely focused triplets," but rather is "internally consistent" (102). Chapter 3, "Conventions of Devotion I: Vented Wit and Crossed Brains" (81–93), discusses the relationship between wit and devotion in seventeenth century devotional poetry and comments on Donne's attitude toward wit and uses of wit in *Cross, Corona,* and *Lit.*

943. Bevan, Jonquil. "Henry Valentine, John Donne and Izaak Walton." *RES,* n.s. 40: 179–201.

Comments on the career of the Rev. Henry Valentine (1600?–1644), Donne's assistant and parish lecturer at St. Dunstan's-in-the-West and later vicar at St. Nicholas, Deptford, who was also Izaak Walton's nephew-in-law, and shows how a knowledge of Valentine's life "connects John Donne and Izaak Walton in a manner not previously known," how it "helps illustrate Donne's influence upon his immediate successors in the Church," and how it also "sheds a little new light on Walton's use of sources in his *[Compleat] Angler*" (180). Discusses the undistinguished elegy that

Valentine contributed to the first edition of Donne's poems (1633) that shows his familiarity with Donne's poetry and prose, and comments on the influence of Donne on Valentine's sermons.

944. Campbell, Gordon. "John Donne," in *The Renaissance (1550–1660),* 220–41. Macmillan Anthologies of English Literature, vol. 2, gen. eds. A. Norman Jeffares and Michael Alexander. Houndmills: Macmillan Education.

Presents a brief introduction to Donne's life and works (220), followed by 11 poems from the *Songs and Sonets,* 3 poems from the *Holy Sonnets, Image, Sat1,* "Defence of Woman's Inconstancy," a selection from *Devotions,* and part of a sermon, with explanatory notes.

945. Chaudhry, Rita. *The Dramatic Experience in Donne's* Songs and Sonets. Amritsar (India): Guru Nanak Dev University Press. 206p.

The introduction (1–20) maintains that Donne's development of various personae "to give imaginative expression to different moods of and attitudes to love" (10) makes the *Songs and Sonets* dramatic rather than lyric poems and suggests that the influence of the contemporary theatre may have played a role in Donne's mode of expression. Rejects the notion that the use of personae renders a poem less sincere and argues that, in fact, it "brings feeling closer to experience, narrows the distance between two vital areas—poetry and life—and makes the flight between them easy and natural" (14). Discusses briefly the four major components in a dramatic poem—the speaker, the listener, the situation, and the interaction—each of which is more fully explored in following chapters. Chapter 1, "Speaker I" (21–55), discusses generally the wide range of nontraditional speakers that Donne adopts in the *Songs and Sonets,* focusing on those who are scorned or scornful lovers, especially in *Appar, Damp, Leg,* and *Will,* or on those who are disillusioned and cynical, particularly in *LovUsury, Commun, Ind, WomCon,* and *SGo.* Chapter 2, "Speaker II" (56–90), discusses fulfilled lovers in the *Songs and Sonets* who "celebrate the joys of a mutually shared love and extol it as an almost perfect relationship," notably in *GoodM, SunRis, Canon, ValMourn,* and *Ecst,* and Platonic lovers, especially in *Relic* and *Under.* Chapter 3, "The Listener" (91–117), examines the crucial role of the addressee in the *Songs and Sonets* in contributing to the drama of the poem and points out how the listener "provokes the speaker by his attention or lack of it, his approval or resistance, his sympathy or hostility" (93). Suggests four broad categories of listeners—"active and combative listeners," "active and participating listeners," "passive recipients of the speech," and auditors who can be called "third parties" (102–3)—and illustrates each category by discussing specific poems. Chapter 4, "Situation" (118–50), comments on "the framework within which the characters speak, argue, perform, and interact" and how the situation "fixes the time at which the speech occurs as well as the context in which it is uttered" (118). Points out that in the *Songs and Sonets* Donne creates a wide variety of situations "in order to exploit the possibilities of drama in them" (120) and uses complex techniques "to unfold and develop the situation of the poem" (123). Examines in particular four common situations found in the *Songs and Sonets*—seduction, the dawn, parting, and death. Chapter 5, "Interaction" (151–79), discusses how the speaker and listener "act and react towards each other in a particular situation," noting that in a dramatic poem, "more than physical gesture

and movement, action has to do with the words of the speaker" (151). Illustrates these observations by discussing the interaction between the speaker and listener in *Flea, Dream, SSweet, Expir, Blos,* and *Canon.* The conclusion (180–89) emphasizes that Donne was an innovator in departing from the conventions of courtly love poetry and developed a new style of love poetry that influenced not only contemporary but also later poets, particularly Browning. Concludes with notes (190–94), select bibliography (195–200), and an index (201–6).

946. Claes, P. "Donne naar de Wijze van Huygens." *De Revisor* 16: 78–79.
Reproduces an edited text of *Triple* and Constantijn Huygens's translation of the poem, prefaced by a pastiche translation in Huygens's idiom.

947. Corthell, Ronald J. "Donne's 'Disparitie': Inversion, Gender, and the Subject of Love in Some Songs and Sonnets." *Exemplaria* 1: 17–42.
Believes that the *Songs and Sonets* have remained "relatively untouched by recent ideological interpretations of Renaissance culture" (17). Discusses *Ind* and *ConfL* to show that, although Donne's wit does not directly challenge ideology, it is not orthodox either in reflecting ideology. Maintains that in *Ind* "various cultural materials are patched together in a parody of ideological production which opens ideology to scrutiny" (22). Calls *ConfL* "an inverted 'Indifferent' for women," in which the speaker "inverts a more radical myth of origins to critique orthodox views on sexual relations" (23). Concludes that the poem "thematizes the interplay of orthodoxy and heterodoxy by representing it as a play of language"; thus "the 'defense' of orthodoxy proceeds by linguistic entrapment, that is, by reversing the equivocal movement of heterodoxy" (24). Noting that paradox is a "marker

of Donne's writerly texts," points out "the ideological significance of this sort of rhetoric" (25). Uses Fredric Jameson's ideological criticism to resolve the contradictions in Donne's "notoriously difficult poem" (26) *Air*, which is "about both love and talking about love" (31). Maintains that his "ideological work" is an attempt "to see the poem as an interrogation of its own intention through its foregrounding of . . . traditional materials" (34), and thus claims that the "meaning" of the poem resides in its open-endedness. Insists that *Air* can only be properly understood if it is seen in the historical context of the position of women.

948. Creevy, Patrick J. "John Donne's Meditations upon the Magnitude of Disease." *SCUL* 72: 61–73.

Discusses Donne's philosophical and theological view on sickness and disease as reflected in the "Meditations" only of *Devotions*. Points out that in the "Meditations" "disease aggravates especially the ineluctable sense man has of his own unrelatedness, of his separation from the forces of nature and from the divine" (61).

949. Cunnar, Eugene R. "Donne's Witty Theory of Atonement in 'The Baite.'" *SEL* 29: 77–98.

Calls *Bait* Donne's "intense and witty defense of mutual love as 'erotic spirituality'" (78), a love in which the sacred and sexual are united, and argues that the poem, perhaps addressed to Ann More, is also "an ironic defense of human love that argues that woman as representative of the power of human sexuality may be a means of spiritual revelation and atonement," and that "man's capture of the woman or the woman's capture of man may share something with God's tricking the devil and capture of the human soul for salvation" (79). Through a detailed reading of the

poem shows how Donne, therefore, "emphatically repudiates the artificial idealism of Marlowe, the cynical realism of Ralegh, and the Petrarchan inspired fantasies" of his contemporary readers primarily by "his witty and paradoxical manipulation of the fishing/bait metaphor" in the poem. Discusses how both the secular and sacred traditions behind this central trope inform the poem. Believes that the "abrupt shifts and witty reversals" in the poem "not only undermine the male fantasy of domination, but also may be Donne's way of renouncing his own ambitions for the possibility of mutual love" (92). Claims that *Bait* becomes, in fact, Donne's "witty way of telling Ann More that their mutual love has atoned for his courtly and male ambitions" (92–93).

950. Danielson, Cam. "Christian Instruction: Donne's Personal Style." *ABR* 40: 1–12.

Contrasts the sermon styles of Donne and Lancelot Andrewes and suggests that "Andrewes' preaching style creates an objective distance between himself and the scriptural text in order to convey the force of an interpretation independent of personal bias" but that "Donne does not separate himself as a meditative reader from his role as a preacher" (8). Discusses the importance of literature, especially the works of the Fathers of the Church, and the role of meditation in Donne's preaching style, both of which suggest Donne's affinity to basic principles of monastic theology.

951. Demoor, Marysa. "The Whisper of John Donne in Dante Gabriel Rossetti's 'The Stream's Secret.'" *N&Q*, n.s. 36: 190–91.

Comments on Rossetti's admiration for Donne's poetry and claims that several lines in Rossetti's "The Stream's Secret" reflect ideas and images in *GoodM*.

952. Donnelly, M. L. " 'To furder or re-presse': Donne's Calling." *JDJ* 8: 115–24.

Explores "one curious phenomenon of Donne's relentless pursuit of worldly favor: his application of tropes of divinity in the poetry of patronage," focusing not on "their transparent serviceability as a grammar of praise" but rather on "their function as a story or scheme justifying to himself (and to anyone sharing his ideology) his applications for favor" (115). Argues that "some of the tropes of divinity constitute the central and characteristic matter of analogy and representation through which Donne re-creates and imposes meaning on his experience" and that "they in fact articulate Donne's rationalization of his situation as suitor to the great and powerful"; in other words, "their analogy serves to quiet his anxiety of pride and conscience" (118). Shows how "the language of divinity and the distinctions of the schools afford Donne more than an extended range of hyperbolic vocabulary, on the one hand, and ingeniously intricate arguments, on the other," and how "the hair-splitting distinctions and multiplied categories of scholastic divinity offer plausible and elegant refinements for his construction and rationalization of models of his relationship to his various patrons" (119).

953. Dougill, John. "John Donne," in *The Writers of English Literature*, 22–26. Annotations by Yoshihisa Aizawa. Tokyo: Macmillan Language House.

Presents a brief introduction to Donne's life and works. Calls Donne "one of the most original of all writers" and the *Songs and Sonets* "arguably the greatest collection of lyric poems in English" (22).

954. Dubinskaya, M. P. "A Book from John Donne's Library." *Kolletstii-knigi-avtografy* 1: 95–102.

In Russian. Reports a book from Donne's library, R. Recyvall's *Bibliotheca Hispanica* (STC 19619), which is in the State Public Library, having arrived there via Henry King, Anne King, Charles Cotton, Gottingen University Library, and the Hermitage.

955. Dupas, Jean-Claude. "Figures de la répétition," in *Tropismes 4: La répétition,* ed. Jean-Jacques Lecercle, 211–27. Centre de Recherches Anglo-Américaines. Paris: Université de Paris X, Nanterre.

After a theoretical description of kinds and levels of repetition, discusses in some detail the binarity exhibited in Donne's poems. Observes that Donne characteristically presents a series of hypotheses, rather than providing answers to the complex issues he treats. Through a discussion of individual poems, both secular and sacred, comments on how Donne typically plays with various kinds of contrarieties and contradictions, such as the tension between and ultimate reconciliation of eros and agape.

956. Duyck, Rudy. "V. S. Naipaul and John Donne: The Morning After." *JCL* 24: 155–62.

Points out that, although he showed little interest in metaphysical poetry while studying at Oxford, V. S. Naipaul parodied *Relic, Fun,* and especially *GoodM* in his African novel, *A Bend in the River* (1980). Calls his parody "a caustic extrapolation of Donne's poems into the modern world" (161).

957. Easthope, Antony. "Eliot, Pound and the Subject of Postmodernism." *CIEFLB* 1, no. 2 (December): 1–10.

Offers a poststructuralist analysis of *ElBed* as an example of "confessional discourse" in which Donne's speaker sees himself as "the interrogator of whom the woman should reveal the inwardly concealed truth about her sexuality, a truth of course veiled in her but to which he presumes immediate and transparent access" (2). Claims that the speaker's "(would be) transcendental position" is that of "a bearer of knowledge, a coherent point for the intersection of a range of discourses (geographical, medical, theological, mythical)," and thus he is "a mastering subject for whom his mistress is a corresponding and complementary object" (2–3). Maintains that "the rhetorical strategy" in the poem is "to contain the process of representation, to disavow it by promoting in its place a coherent represented." Further points out that, on the one hand, "the speaker's diegetic reality is substantiated" since "his knowledge moves forward from clothed 'appearance' to the 'naked truth' behind which is claimed as a final reality, an object reciprocally constituting the speaker as a fully present subject," while, on the other hand, "the linguistic process of the text, phonetic and semantic, is effaced by the vivid dramatisation of speaker in a particularised situation, a scenario so persuasively and fluently scripted that we are led to forget it is scripted at all." Concludes, therefore, that the reader "is interpellated into identification with a represented speaker who is a full subject and the bearer of knowledge," and that thus the text "secures a position for the classical humanist subject" (3).

958. Easthope, Antony. "Foucault, Ovid, Donne: Versions of Sexuality, Ancient and Modern," in *Poetry and Phantasy*, 47–62. Cambridge: Cambridge University Press.

Employing the theories of Foucault, contrasts Donne's view of sexuality in *ElBed* to Ovid's in *Amores* 1.5.26–48, showing thereby the differences between Ovid's attention to the body and pleasures "primarily in relation to themselves" and Donne's mobilization of "a proliferation and heterogeneous range of discourses for and around sexuality." Discusses how Donne's poem "pursues its object of desire through a series of substitutions for it, displacements of sexual drive into the pleasure of looking, into verbal innuendo and witty circumlocutions, into metaphors that persistently replace Ovid's concrete description of the physical with some abstraction." Shows that Donne's idea of sexual intercourse differs markedly from Ovid's "in the degree to which sexual drive has been transformed or sublimated into narcissism" (57) and claims, therefore, that *ElBed* is really "an expression of self-love" (57–58). Maintains that, unlike Ovid's speaker, who wants transient and bodily sexual pleasure, Donne's speaker desires neither the woman nor sexual satisfaction but rather wants "a transcendent object, one whose perfect atemporal image may return to him an equally perfect reflection of himself" (58). Says that in Donne's elegy, a poem in which scopophilia becomes narcissistic, the speaker simply "uses the idea of the woman's body and intercourse with her as a vehicle for his own idealised image of himself, his Eden, his paradise." Concludes that Donne's poem therefore "makes possible a narcissistic phantasy for which there is no precedent in Ovid but which conforms entirely to the ideological promotion of individual inwardness in the courtly love tradition" (59).

959. Ellrodt, Robert. "Aspects de la conscience du corps dans la poésie de la Renaissance anglaise de Spenser à Milton," in *Le Corps à la Renaissance: Actes du XXXe Colloque de Tours 1987*, ed. Jean Céard, Marie Madeleine Fontaine, and Jean-Claude Margolin, 199–211. Paris: Aux Amateurs de Livres. Revised and expanded in *Les Figures du corps dans la littérature et la peinture anglaises et américaines de la Renais-*

sance à nos jours, ed. Bernard Brugière (Paris: Publications de la Sorbonne, 1991), 37–49.

Discusses aspects of and the evolution of body consciousness in English poetry from Spenser to Milton. Compares and contrasts Donne's views on the body with those of Spenser, Sidney, Shakespeare, Milton, and Traherne. Points out that Donne does not focus on the physical description of lovers in his poems, but notes his abiding interest in anatomy and vivisection in such poems as *Fun* and *ElComp* as well as in his prose works. Suggests that Donne's sensuality is primarily tactile and that sight, hearing, and smell play a much lesser role because these senses do not put the individual in contact with real substance. Observes that Donne is more interested in clasped hands and tongues that roll about each other and that thus he is not a voyeuristic poet but rather one who prizes caressing and penetration. Claims, however, that the appetite Donne attempts to satisfy is complex and more than simply a desire for physical contact. Believes rather that it is a desire to make the beloved a part of his own body.

960. Evans, Robert C. "John Donne, Governor of Charterhouse." *JDJ* 8: 133–50.

Through an examination of the Assembly Books, unavailable to R. C. Bald when he wrote his biography, shows that Donne from 1626 to 1631 was "one of the most active and conscientious" of the governors of Charterhouse, a charitable foundation that provided lodging and education for impoverished boys and men. Discusses how the Assembly Books reveal Donne's intimate involvement with "the routine management and supervision of the institution" and show "the kinds of issues—including socially controversial ones—that he and the other Governors confronted,

and how they dealt with them." Maintains that these records present "a fuller sense of how Donne spent a good deal of his time, energy, and attention in the last five years of his life" (133).

961. Flynn, Dennis. "Donne and a Female Coterie." *LIT* 1: 127–36.

Points out that Donne wrote his poetry for a female coterie as well as a male one and discusses the special appeal of his poetry for a female audience. Comments on Donne's connection with well-educated and sophisticated women and his humanist family background. Points out the emphasis on mutuality in love in *WomCon* and offers a reading of the poem, the speaker of which may be either an educated man or educated woman, that "assumes a courtly audience of female readers (including Ann More)," thereby suggesting the need "to revise hitherto stable or unstable conclusions drawn from reading the poem without much regard to biography" (133). Discusses also several of Donne's epigrams, especially an early Latin one translated by Jasper Mayne, "Upon one who for his wives fault took it ill to be called Cuckold," that perhaps was addressed to Donne's mother.

962. Flynn, Dennis. "Donne and the Ancient Catholic Nobility." *ELR* 19: 305–23.

Discusses how "the desolation of the Catholic peerage became part of Donne's formative experience and deeply influenced him throughout his life," and comments on "the politics of Donne's Catholic humanist heritage as a descendant of Sir Thomas More in the midst of the Elizabethan persecution of Catholics." Maintains that "Donne and his family lived through important and historic developments in which they were active participants more often than passive sufferers" and that "their sacrifice and repression took place in significant social and political contexts" (306). Examines, therefore, "the long history of association between Donne's family, the ancient nobility, and the Tudor Court" (307). Argues also that the Latin epigrams translated by Jasper Mayne are Donne's and suggests they provide important biographical information about Donne's life since a number of them are based on observations of the Spanish conquest of Antwerp in the spring of 1585. Points out that as early as the 1590s Donne had "experienced a certain familiarity with the Court," and that his "witty disdain" of it in his early poems cannot be explained away as "mere posturing" but, more likely, "had a subversive appeal specifically intended for readers delighted to share Donne's 'inside' commentary on the society of the Elizabethan Court, seen from the critical perspective of the family of Sir Thomas More" (323).

963. Frantz, David O. "The Context of Erotica: Marston, Donne, Shakespeare, and Spenser," in *"Festum Voluptatis": A Study of Renaissance Erotica,* 208–52. Columbus: Ohio State University Press. Focusing on the *Elegies,* maintains that much "lip service" has been given to the sexual elements in Donne's poetry but laments that discussion always "stops just short of analyzing precisely those elements in the elegies that make them so outrageous, so witty, so shocking, so memorable— the bawdy and obscene," and argues that, if these matters are ignored, "the full impact of the poems will be missed" (219). Calls *ElComp* "a virtuoso performance" and insists that "what gives us the sense of impudence and insolence carried off with wit" is "the startling sensuality" of Donne's imagery, observing that, if Donne had not used repulsive comparisons, sexually aggressive images, and strong sexual language, "the wit, the tone,

and the pose of the speaker would simply not work" (220). Maintains similarly that in *ElNat* one feels "the full power of the wit involved, the impudence of the stance taken by the lover, and the assumptions about the true nature and end of love" (221) only when one recognizes the sexual nature of the poem's imagery. Discusses *ElProg* too as a "bravura performance" and as "exemplary of Donne's elegies," and shows how the poem reflects Renaissance erotica. Concludes that Donne in the *Elegies* shows himself fully capable of being pornographic, erotic, bawdy, and even obscene, but insists that his manipulations of poetic convention, his outrageous logic and argument, and his deftness with puns and metaphors, and even his witty use of bawdy "surely earn our admiration" (229).

964. Granqvist, Raoul. "Lusten och döden: Teman i John Donnes poesi." *Kulturtidskriften Horisont* 2, Argang 36: 6–19.
Discusses Donne's awareness of contemporary scientific discoveries and other ideas typical of the Renaissance world view and finds in the poems spontaneity, questioning, and emotional truth rather than logic and balance. Explores in particular the themes of dualism, love, and death, and reviews critical reaction to Donne's diction and imagery. Presents also key biographical facts about Donne and supports the idea of a Swedish edition of his poems. Concludes with translations into Swedish of *ElBed, Sappho,* and *Flea,* with brief commentaries on each of the poems.

965. Gray, Dave, and Jeanne Shami. "Political Advice in Donne's *Devotions:* No Man Is an Island." *MLQ* 50: 337–56.
Argues that Donne in *Devotions* "offers political advice to the young Prince Charles, to whom the *Devotions*

was dedicated, but that the circumstances at the end of 1623 forced him to make his advice circumspect" (338). Maintains that the phrase "No Man is an *Iland*" has political resonations, "reminding the prince, his advisers, and the larger audience of readers that even private actions have public consequences" and that "the heir apparent and his advisers have a responsibility not to act merely as private persons" (340). Discusses how in his dedication Donne "publicly affirms his authority as a political counselor" and "signals to his readers the kind of advice the *Devotions* will develop." Shows that Donne's advice "concentrates on two related themes: the vulnerability and public responsibilities of the king," both of which "are illustrated by the metaphor of the king as heart of the kingdom" (346), and shows how "[t]wo public responsibilities of kings, the importance of counsel and the need to govern openly, are dramatized through the metaphor of the physician" (349). Argues that in the *Devotions* "the political and personal elements are interdependent" and that Donne's "anatomizing" shows that "self-analysis leads to self-awareness, which is the foundation for public action" (255–56). Points out that at the time "Charles's actions had shown him insensitive to the public responsibilities of his growing political role, embarked on the course of personal rule that made him indifferent to public opinion, careless of his reputation, and confident that he could rule without recourse to the established and authorized means of governing." Concludes, therefore, that the *Devotions* "challenges the prince to consider the public significance of his private actions, to accept the responsibility to govern openly and honestly, and to accept the counsel of those 'physicians' who, like Donne, were

authorized to help him with his task" and, at the same time, "challenges those physician-counselors to persist in their counsels and not to vaporize into destructive rumors" (356).

966. Greene, Thomas M. "The Poetics of Discovery: A Reading of Donne's Elegy 19." *YJC*: 129–43.

Presents a detailed reading of *ElBed*. Observes that although typically the Latin love elegy is "a voyeur's delight," in Donne's poem the mistress "stays oddly invisible" and argues that the poem is, in fact, "a tissue of coverings, analogical garments which apparel the 'full nakedness' the text seems to celebrate but actually withholds." Maintains that although the elegy could be read as simply "a cheap exercise in clever but self-evident sophistry," the "rapturous elements" (136) and the theological and ecclesiastical imagery cannot be easily dismissed or regarded simply as blasphemous. Considers, therefore, the possibility that the metaphors, "however glib, however ostensibly blasphemous, provide the most accurate index of the desires that can only be admitted by this ribald seducer *as* blasphemy," and that "perhaps the recovering of the mistress's body with analogies corresponds to a swerve away from common carnality." Argues that Donne's speaker, who regards himself as a member of "an elite priesthood," seems to "sacramentalize" the flesh, "making his mistress the instrument of a priestly institution" and sexual pleasure " 'dignified,' paradisal, mystically 'unbodied' " (138). Believes that his wish to possess her "becomes a synecdoche for ulterior fantasies of possession, vague, limitless, otherwise unutterable," and that her body becomes "the medium for an experience of sacred possession, sacred knowledge, and sacred revelation." Says that the poem "osten-

sibly directed to a woman ends by
concealing her," and "a poem that
looks literally phallocentric drifts away
from the phallic" to a conclusion that
"serves to call into question the most
obvious functions of the speaker's
power." Suggests that perhaps the
seduction scene is only hypothetical
and that what is important to the
speaker is "his *self*-discovery, his naming or metaphorizing of his truest and
deepest desires" (142).

967. Ferencz, Gyōzō, ed. "John Donne,"
in *Donne, Milton és az angol barokk*
Költöi. välogatta, 9–93, 351–54 (Lyria
mundi). Budapest: Európa Könyvikadó.
Translates into Hungarian 41 poems
from the *Songs and Sonets,* 4 selec-
tions from the *Elegies* (including
Image), and 29 poems from the *Divine
Poems* (9–93) by Vas István, Eörsi
István, Jékely Zoltán, Ferencz,
Kálonky Lászlö, Orbán Ottö, Molnár
Imre, Károlyi Amy, Kios Zsuzsa,
Szabó Lōrinc, and Mezie Balázs.
Includes a brief biographical sketch
of Donne and a general introduction
to his poetry by Gyōzō Ferencz
(351–54).

968. Guite, A. M. "The Art of Memory
and the Art of Salvation: The Centrality
of Memory in the Sermons of John Donne
and Lancelot Andrewes." *SCen* 4: 1–17.
Examines the treatment of memory
in the sermons of Donne and Lancelot Andrewes in the light of the
Augustinian tradition they inherited
and highlights "the ways in which
their contribution enriched and modified that tradition" (1). Discusses
how both preachers blended "philosophical and patristic material with
profoundly imaginative interpretations
and reworkings of biblical texts in
such a way as to provide for their
auditors a pattern or method whereby
they can so use their own memories
as to achieve the *conversio,* or continual turning and re-turning towards

God, as the necessary prelude to divine
enlightenment, which is at the heart
of Augustine's teaching" (4). Examines two of Donne's sermons to
exemplify his views on the "central
role for memory in the process of salvation" (8)—a sermon on Psalm 38
delivered at Lincoln's Inn in the spring
or summer of 1618 and his "Sermon
of Valediction at my going into
Germany," preached also at Lincoln's
Inn on 18 April 1619.

969. Halley, Janet E. "Textual Intercourse:
Anne Donne, John Donne, and the Sexual
Poetics of Textual Exchange," in *Seeking
the Woman in Late Medieval and
Renaissance Writings: Essays in Feminist
Contextual Criticism,* 187–206, ed. Sheila
Fisher and Janet E. Halley. Knoxville:
University of Tennessee Press.
Argues that a search for Donne's
wife's "historical presence in the writings of her husband not only displaces
the historical woman with masculine
desire but also occludes the actual
traces of her history inscribed in his
text." Believes that Ann "offers, then,
a case study in the feminist project of
recovering lost and silent women—a
case study that warns us to examine
carefully the forms, and the limits, of
our knowledge" (188). Maintains that,
"rather than demand that an over-
whelmingly masculine historical
record make Ann Donne *present* to
us, we might ask whether, in the man's
writing, we can read the woman's
absence" (190–91). Discusses how
several of Donne's letters, especially
those to Henry Goodyer, "provide fundamental information about her relation to the gendered exercise of literacy
in her era and class" (192). Claims
that Ann emerges as "functionally illiterate" (193) but shows how Ann's
illiteracy "is complemented" by
Donne's literacy, "her text by his reading, so that she is whole only when
she is joined by him" (195). Argues

that although Ann is absent from many of Donne's texts, "their strategies depend on her passionate presence outside of them." Insists that by refusing to find "reliable references" to Ann's "actuality" in Donne's works, "we are freed to observe the uses of her exclusion and of his literacy in a cultural practice of literary exchange that belongs as insistently to her history as it does to his" and in which her "history is inscribed as a sequence of displacements" (196).

970. Harvey, Elizabeth D. "Ventriloquizing Sappho: Ovid, Donne, and the Erotics of the Feminine Voice." *Criticism* 31: 115–38.

Presents a detailed reading of *Sappho* and argues that in Donne's poem "the otherness of a classical text (Ovid's) and the otherness of woman (Sappho) are domesticated and re-shaped into an image of the self, a process that is mediated both by ventriloquism and by voyeurism" (126). Contends that Donne "borrows the feminine voice as a way of acting out his rivalry with Ovid," but that "he controls its dangerous plenitude by domesticating its alterity and ultimately turning it into a version of himself" (129). Observes that Ovid makes Sappho heterosexual so that "she will be vulnerable to his erotic and poetic mastery," whereas Donne "marginalizes her within a utopian world that—despite its allusion to the fertility of the Golden Age—is narcissistically sterile." Maintains that Donne's borrowing of the feminine voice seems "to provide an intensified version of intertextuality, for where a system of diachronic textual echoes and citations continually subverts the ontological security of a text, its discrete historical boundaries, and its status as self-contained property, the phenomenon of transvestite ventriloquism provides in addition a powerful critique of phonocentrism"

or, in other words, "while all textual 'voices' are constructions, tenuously connected with their referents and ambiguously tethered to the authorial presence that supposedly stands behind them, critical discourse has traditionally relied on the implicit presence of a stable author who manipulates these personae or voices." Concludes, therefore, that "ventriloquistic crossdressing, particularly when the borrowed voice belongs to an actual poet, transgresses the laws of gender, propriety, and property by undermining in a fundamental way the conventional relationships between author and voice, making visible in the process the radical contingency of poetic and authorial identity" (131).

971. Haskin, Dayton. "New Historical Contexts for Appraising the Donne Revival from A. B. Grosart to Charles Eliot Norton." *ELH* 56: 869–95.

Surveys the critical and moralistic assumptions of those late nineteenth and early twentieth century critics who engaged in biographical readings of Donne's works, as well as those who rejected such readings, and places the controverted issue of Donne's sensuality within the cultural contexts of the time. Shows in particular how the anti-biographical position, strongly advocated by Charles Eliot Norton, "represented a powerful response to and rejection of the assumptions and methods operative in the work of the most publicized Donne revivers in England, Grosart and Gosse." Explains, in particular, why Norton's reluctance to comment on Donne's sex life was "quite deliberate and calculated" (871), and discusses how Norton's disagreement with Grosart, in particular, can best be understood "within the context of a Victorian culture that was not so much refusing to recognize sex as it was finding ways of talking about it as a powerful and decisive secret, a secret that was to be shared by a group of initiates." Maintains that Norton found in Donne's life and works "complex moral and aesthetic issues that were quite beyond the interests of Gosse and Grosart" (876), and observes that, in late nineteenth century America, interest in Donne was "less obviously moralizing" than it was in England (882). Believes that the attacks that Norton made on "the incompetence of Grosart and Gosse were on the whole justifiable," and that "time has vindicated his criticisms." Explains Norton's personal and aesthetic reasons for insisting "so strenuously that Grosart and Gosse were incompetent Donne scholars" (883). Shows also how Norton fitted Donne's poetry "into a theory of the history of Western art that he had developed many years before" (887), and suggests that his criticism serves as an interesting context for T. S. Eliot's criticism of Donne.

972. Howison, Patricia M. "Donne's Sermons and the Rhetoric of Prophecy." *ESC* 15: 134–48.

Maintains that by examining Donne's confrontation in his sermons of obscure texts, "we see his explicit recognition of the relative inadequacy of human language." Explains that "this recognition causes him neither to attempt to project himself into a visionary state nor to admit defeat" but rather becomes "a statement of interpretive principle by which he counters paradox with paradox, and so attempts to mediate to his hearers an obscure text without compromising the obscurity which is part of its truth" (136). Illustrates how this "interpretive principle" works by examining Donne's treatment in two of his sermons of two prophetic texts, one from the Old Testament prophet Micah (2:10) and the other from the Book of Revelation (7:9). Concludes that in both sermons Donne "acknowledges the importance of the form of prophetic texts and affirms their essential obscurity by the form of his own interpretation of them" (146), and that he "shows figurative language glossed by figurative language, paradox by paradox—and, in terms of Scripture, the paradox of words, with all their ambiguities and inadequacies, glossed finally by the paradox of the Word, the Incarnation" (146–47).

973. Johnstone, Peggy Ruth Fitzhugh. "Donne's 'Love's Growth.'" *Expl* 47, no. 3: 8–10.

Argues that references in *LovGrow* suggest that Donne's poem was written after 1613 in response to Galileo's description of his observations of the planet Venus. Maintains that "[i]f this hypothesis is correct, then the title refers not only to love, but also the planet Venus, named by ancient astronomers after the goddess of love and beauty, who also symbolized the creative force that sustains all life." Shows how the poem's "form, imagery, and argument support this interpretation" (9). Suggests that, "like the image of the planet Venus growing smaller as it becomes a full sphere, love [in the poem] expends itself as it becomes more complete" (10).

974. Jones, David L. "To Write True Things: The Metaphysical Realism of Keith Douglas." *Ody* 11, nos. 1–2: 29–35.

Discusses Donnean qualities in three poems by Keith Douglas (1920–44), noting that in them one finds "a paradoxical and analytical approach which mixes a lyric speech with a harsher, more realistic speech—the sort of rough lyricism often found in Donne's poetry" (29).

975. Jordan, Richard Douglas. "'Harmony Was She': Donne's *Anniversaries* and the Neoplatonic Elizabeth Drury," in *The Quiet Hero: Figures of Temperance in*

Spenser, Donne, Milton, and Joyce, 62–121. Washington, D.C.: Catholic University of America Press.

Maintains that, although a real person, Elizabeth Drury becomes in the *Anniversaries* a "symbolic figure of heroic proportions," adding that, in fact, she is "perhaps the most elaborately realized symbolic hero in English literature—a heroic figure who did little more than die" (62). Calls the *Anniversaries* "renaissance analogical thinking at its best" (63), noting how Elizabeth's soul, which becomes representative of all souls as it is separated from its body by death, is the subject of the poem. Discusses how Donne treats Elizabeth's soul as analogous to the Soul of the World, the *anima mundi,* an idea central to Christian Neoplatonism, and maintains that he "limits, orders, and develops his poems by concentrating on the most significant of analogical parallels" (68) that he found in Christian Neoplatonic sources. Points out that Donne orders the poems in a "broadly sketched chronological structure"—*FirAn* on the first five books of the Old Testament and *SecAn* "on time and the soul's movement toward the apocalypse" (69). Discusses how "[t]he great cycle of creation, decay, and regeneration" is presented in *FirAn* "in all its parts" (82) and suggests how we, in the corrupt world, are directed to an earlier perfection and to a future return. Discusses also the typological aspects of the poem, in which biblical allusions "point toward the presence of Christ . . . and toward the soul as *alter christus*" (85). Sees the poem as "Donne's own pentateuch, and his own creation (and decreation) myth, and a typological prophecy of the return of man to God" (90). Discusses how *FunEl* serves as a "fulcrum" (93) between the two major poems. Shows how *SecAn* does not have its full meaning on its own

(96) but must be read as a continuation of the first poem, noting that "the reader must carry over into this poem" the various meanings given to the figure of Elizabeth in the first poem and in *FunEl* since the figure is not further developed in the second poem, "though different aspects of its meaning are explored" (96). Says that in the poem Elizabeth's soul becomes "both actually and symbolically a redeemed soul" and that "her body represents—as far as anything mortal can—the Idea, the Divine thought, realized in matter" (99). Compares the two poems to the two parts of Herbert's "Easter Wings" and argues that the poems are meant to be a consolation, if rightly understood. Speculates about what a "Third Anniversary" might have been.

976. Kermode, Frank. "William Empson: The Critic as Genius," in *An Appetite for Poetry,* 116–35. Cambridge, Mass.: Harvard University Press.

Evaluates William Empson's intense interest in and criticism of Donne. Argues that Empson was fundamentally wrong to regard Donne as *the poet* of the new philosophy, a view that shaped many of his writings on Donne. Maintains that although he "made jokes about Kepler and Tycho Brahe and Galileo," Donne "habitually thought about the world in pre-Copernican terms, and treated the New Philosophy as further evidence that all human knowledge was extremely fallible" (128). Believes, therefore, that Empson "was imitating a Donne of his own imagining" and notes that he "reacted like a wicked animal if anybody seemed to disparage his scientist-poet" (129).

977. Kerrigan, William, and Gordon Braden. "Petrarch Refracted: The Evolution of the English Love Lyric," in *The Idea of the Renaissance,* 157–89. Baltimore: Johns Hopkins University Press.

Comments on Donne's radical modification of Petrarchism in his love poetry, claiming that "[t]he peculiarity of Donne's love poetry stems in part from the absence of three related themes, each of them familiar in English Petrarchism: he does not encrust the physical image of the woman with elaborate tropes, he does not register distress over the impending decay of the woman's beauty, and he is not especially interested in the usual Petrarchan way of preserving her beauty, poetic immortality" (176–77). Discusses how Donne "abandons the unconsummated Petrarchan verse of the sixteenth century, which yearns for a first time but made do with lesser favors, and gestures toward the Ovidian experiments of the seventeenth century, which characteristically presuppose consummation." Suggests, in fact, that Donne "fuses Petrarch and Ovid by presenting an exclusive devotion enjoying full sexual consummation" (177) but observes that Donne, like many other seventeenth century love poets, "encountered defects in [sexual] union" and expresses in his poems a kind of "postcoital depression." Says that one reason why the evocation of Christ's resurrection in *Canon* "should not be written off as schoolboy irreverence is Donne's likely assumption that the [sexual] act *needs* redemption" (183).

978. Kerschbaumer, Marie-Thérèse. *Neun Canti auf die irdische Liebe.* Kalgenfurt: Wieser Verlag. 39p.

Contains three original cantos in German based on *GoodM* (4–5, 33, 37). Drawings by Helmut Kurz Goldenstein.

979. Kim, Young-Nam. "John Donne and the Problem of 'Unified Sensibility.'" *JELL* (Daejeon, Korea) (30 May): 1–20.

In Korean. Finds unconvincing T. S. Eliot's argument that Donne's poetry reflects a unified sensibility and ar-

gues that, when examined in the light of rhetorical principles of his time, Donne's poems "do not have such fusion [of thought and feeling] as Eliot describes" but rather "are connected or related by the concept of resemblance and relatableness in which natural reason plays an important role." Analyzes *ValMourn* "to show how Donne's poetry was affected by the intellectual climate of his age" (20).

980. Larson, Deborah Aldrich. *John Donne and Twentieth-Century Criticism.* Ruther-ford, N.J.: Fairleigh Dickinson University Press; London: Associated University Presses. 208p.

The introduction (13–17) outlines some of the major issues in Donne criticism of the twentieth century and suggests that the purpose of the present study is "to determine why Donne's poetry provokes such a range of critical and emotional responses, why it is apparently so difficult to read Donne's poetry objectively without reference to his life and personality, why his works, more than those of other poets, proved congenial to the New Critics, why his poetry is difficult to classify, and why his attitudes toward women, religion, and science have been so controversial" (17). Chapter 1, "The Image of Donne from 1633 to 1897" (18–43), surveys critical responses to Donne from 1633 to 1897, "showing that commentary on Donne's poetry from these centuries has been partially responsible for some of our own century's debates." Examines "three complex issues for pre-twentieth-century critics: Donne's and Ben Jonson's comments on Donne's poetry; Donne's meter and supposed rebelliousness; and his life, wit, and morality." Chapter 2, "'I did my best when I had least truth': Biographical Criticism" (44–89), discusses how Donne's life "has provoked extensive biographical speculation and many conflicting interpretations of the facts of his life and the meaning of his works." Chapter 3, "Donne Refashioned: Eliot and the New Critics" (90–112), evaluates the role of T. S. Eliot and the New Critics in "encouraging close analyses of poems" and argues that "the New Critics' adoption of Donne contributed to subsequent misinterpretations of and attacks on Donne by critics and scholars eager to refute New Critical methods." Chapter 4, "Donne and Literary Tradition" (113–35), arguing that "Donne's place in the history of English literature has not yet been convincingly established," discusses "nine categorizations—including Petrarchan, baroque, and mannerist—to show that into whichever classification Donne is placed, he does not exactly fit," and maintains that "[s]cholars insisting on a certain label for Donne become Procrustean, misreading the works to make them fit or faulting Donne for not 'succeeding' in poems that do not neatly fit the categories." Chapter 5, "Donne's Views on Women, Religion, and Science" (136–60), examines studies that focus on Donne's views on these three subjects and "traces reactions to Donne's supposed morbidity, egocentricity, skepticism, and libertinism in order to show that his works both encourage and defy attempts to understand the personality behind them" (jacket). The conclusion (161–63) speculates on the future of Donne criticism and is followed by notes (164–71), a list of works cited (172–91), a list of works consulted (192–99), and an index (201–8). Review: Eugene D. Hill in "John Donne: In and Out of Fashion" *AnSch* 9 (1992): 455–63.

981. Liu, Yameng. "The Making of Elizabeth Drury: The Voice of God in 'An Anatomy of the World.'" *JDJ* 8: 89–102.

Argues that in *FirAn* the name "Elizabeth Drury" "signifies simply a well-articulated *discourse* or *enunciation,*" or "a 'song' to use Donne's term" (88), and that Donne in the poem assumes a "God-like speaking voice," comparing himself not only to "the maker of the Mosaic song" but also to "the maker of man and the world" (91). Discusses how "recognition in the poem of a self-conscious apotheosis on the part of the speaker-poet, and of the poem-song as the creation of this deified figure, makes available a fresh perspective from which many of the thorny and controversial problems arising in the reading of the poem can be attacked" (92), and especially "helps to de-problematize the numerous logical inconsistencies concerning the characterization of Elizabeth Drury and her function in the structure of the poem" (93). Suggests further that the poem reflects "the shady, carefully guarded core of Donne's view on poetic creation," observing that he "appears to be suggesting that just as it was the nothingness that gave rise to God's desire to create the world, so the impulse of poetic creation springs from *absence* or *void*" or, in other words, that "poetic creation is, in the final analysis, a creation *ex nihilo*" (95). Argues that "[t]he privileging of poetry over history, and especially the analogy between God and the poet, between the Mosaic 'song' and Donne's 'verse,' unmistakably echo Sir Philip Sidney in his *Defence of Poetry*" (90), but that, unlike Sidney's, "Donne's creative act turns out to be more a process of interacting with and overcoming a co-existent destructive tendency, and his poem more a treatise on the *difficulty* or *problem,* than one on the ease of success, of creation" (98). Claims that Donne believes that just as God "redeemed the inevitable loss of his law and prophets with the 'song,' so likewise he "undertakes to redeem the inevitable loss of all 'shee' represents and the unavoidable death of the ideal world with his 'verse'" (99).

982. Lloyd-Evans, Barbara, ed. "John Donne," in *Five Hundred Years of English Poetry: Chaucer to Arnold*, 281–300. New York: Peter Bedrick Books.

Presents a brief biographical sketch of Donne, followed by 11 poems from the *Songs and Sonets*, 3 sonnets from the *Holy Sonnets*, and *Sat3*, with explanatory notes.

983. Low, Anthony. "Love and Science: Cultural Change in Donne's *Songs and Sonnets*." *SLitI* 22: 5–16.

Discusses how Donne's love poetry reflects the revolutionary changes that were occurring in the scientific thinking of his day. Maintains that Donne was "among the first to develop and give expression to the innovative ways of thinking that were beginning to form the cultural opening and the conceptual basis of the 'New Science'" and that "there is no question that in his poetry the new imagery of science has vanquished and fragmented the old imagery of courtly love" and "has proven to be clearly the stronger of the two" (8). Observes that Donne "often presents the difficulties of love more as dead scientific conundrums to be solved dispassionately or dissected than as living social dynamics to be lived through and humanly resolved" (14). Concludes that "[n]ot only the details of new scientific discoveries—new stars, comets beyond the moon, spots on the sun—energize his poetry," but also "[a]t a deeper level Donne learned from science possibilities for new ways of seeing and new ways of thinking which had the potential not only to turn the physical world upside down but love, society, and individual consciousness as well" (16).

984. MacLure, Millar. *Register of Sermons Preached at Paul's Cross, 1534–1642.* Revised and augmented by Jackson Campbell Boswell and Peter Pauls. Centre for Reformation and Renaissance Studies, Victoria University, University of Toronto: Occasional Publication, vol. 6. Ottawa: Dovehouse Editions. 151p.

Originally published as part of *The Paul's Cross Sermons, 1534–1642* (Toronto: University of Toronto Press, 1958). Lists the sermons Donne preached at Paul's Cross from 24 March 1617 to 22 November 1629.

985. Makurenkova, S. A. "Byl li Dzhon Donn Dzhonom Donnom?" [Was John Donne John Donne?] *Filologicheskie nauki* 2: 74–77.

Discusses variant seventeenth century spellings and pronunciations of Donne's name within the context of Donne's biography. Outlines the history of Donne's name in Renaissance England and the normalization of its spelling over time, as well as Donne's habit of punning on his name. Claims that although Pushkin brought Donne to the attention of Russian readers in the nineteenth century, Donne's work received no critical notice in Russian scholarship until the publication of Hemingway's *For Whom the Bell Tolls* and the subsequent translation of Donne's work into Russian. Also discusses the correct spelling and pronunciation of Donne's name in Russian.

986. Malpezzi, Frances M. "Adam, Christ, and Mr. Tilman: God's Blest Hermaphrodites." *ABR* 40: 250–60.

Shows how Donne, drawing on biblical, patristic, medieval, and Neoplatonic sources for his image of the "blest Hermaphrodite" in the last line of *Tilman*, "deftly defines the priestly vocation and explores the minister's amatory relationship to God and to his congregation" (250). Points out also that a "survey of the analogues to Donne's image not only reveals the long standing and pervasive tradition of an androgynous deity but [also] involves current theological issues as it reminds us of the way our assumptions about gender affect our metaphors for the divine." Discusses how in the final image of the poem Donne calls upon three traditions: "the androgynous Adam; the hermaphrodite as a symbol of love; and the biblical, patristic, and medieval image of Jesus as mother," and how "[i]n the culmination of these traditions, the figure of the hermaphrodite vitally underscores Donne's perception of the nature and responsibilities of God's minister" (251).

987. Manlove, Colin. "Comparisons," in *Critical Thinking: A Guide to Interpreting Literary Texts,* 86–106. New York: St. Martin's Press.

Compares and contrasts the theme, argument, tone, imagery, structure, and form of *HSDeath* and Dylan Thomas's "And Death Shall Have No Dominion" to illustrate how such an approach provides "a way into the poems" and also provides "two quite different approaches to the same subject," thereby extending "our understanding of the range of possible poetic answers to death" (98).

988. Marotti, Arthur F. "John Donne, Author." *JMRS* 19, no. 1 (Spring 1989): 69–82. Material from this essay appears in a revised version in *Manuscript, Print, and the English Renaissance Lyric* (Ithaca, N.Y.: Cornell University Press, 1995).

Considers "some of the ways that, over the course of time and in spite of his own efforts to the contrary, Donne was absorbed into the evolving literary institution to emerge as an author in the modern sense of the term," and "examines some of the processes by which Donne was canonized as a major English author" (70). Traces the publication history of Donne's poetry and the consequent evolution of his reputation as a poet—from the publication of the first edition in 1633, which transformed him "from a literary amateur into a canonical English author, from someone writing for manuscript circulation for coterie readers, sometimes within the framework of social and political patronage, into an 'author' in the modern institution of literature" (74), to the publication of major editions of the twentieth century. Argues that "[i]n order for Donne to be installed in literary history as an author in the modern sense of the term, his identity had to be secularized: he had to be extricated from the immediate sociocultural contexts in which he had functioned and in which his verse was received during his lifetime and in the extended period after his death, and relocated in the newly emerging institution of literature in which texts and authors were defined differently" (79). Maintains that "the comments of Dryden, Bishop Hurd, and other eighteenth-century poets and critics underscore the secularization of Donne's identity and his emergence as one of a line of English poets" (80), and that, likewise, Bell's 1779 edition of Donne's works, "along with Johnson's act of literary-historical contextualization of Donne in the life of Cowley, placed him in the company of authors whose cultural identity was defined by the modern era's assumptions about literature and the author-function" (81). Believes it is important to "reimmerse Donne's texts in the social world that elicited them and follow their vicissitudes in the media of manuscript and print, alert to the interesting social history of writing in which they participated" (82).

989. Martz, Louis L. "The Generous Ambiguity of Herbert's *Temple*," in *A Fine Tuning: Studies of the Religious Poetry of Herbert and Milton,* ed. Mary A. Maleski, 31–56. Medieval and Renaissance Texts & Studies, vol. 64. Binghamton, N.Y.: Medieval and Renaissance Texts and Studies. Reprinted in *From Renaissance to Baroque: Essays on Literature and Art* (Columbia: University of Missouri Press, 1991), 64–83.

Briefly comments on Donne's Arminian and anti-Calvinistic theology as reflected in the sermons. Cites a passage from a sermon that "shows Donne's mind firmly set against the exclusive tenor of the theology represented by the Lambeth Articles and by the chief representative of English Calvinist theology, William Perkins" (35). Says that in the *Holy Sonnets* Donne "seems to be pondering, with fearful anxiety, how he might come to terms with Calvinist orthodoxy, while using essentially Jesuit methods of meditation as part of his quest for a solution," but that "in his late sermons preached before King Charles in 1629, he had clearly adopted an Arminian, anti-Calvinist position" (48–49). Compares Donne's views with those of Herbert in *The Temple*.

990. Masselink, Noralyn. "Donne's Epistemology and the Appeal to Memory." *JDJ* 8: 57–88.

Reviews the arguments among critics concerning "the roles and relative importance of memory, understanding, and will" in Donne's sermons and argues that Donne "appeals to memory neither *instead of* nor *in addition to* reason, but rather because memory is a *necessary condition* for the function of reason," and that, for Donne, "working in the Aristotelian-Thomistic tradition, memory is a prerequisite for understanding" and, without it, "reasoning is impossible." Maintains, then, that Donne approaches "the intellect or reason by *means* of the memory." Argues that, although Donne was indebted to St. Augustine, readings of his sermons that "explore only this influence while ignoring the Thomistic parallels are incomplete" (57). Discusses, therefore, affinities between the sense-oriented, Aristotelian epistemologies of Donne and St. Thomas. Maintains that throughout the sermons Donne "consistently advocates the same process of approaching God—a process rooted in sensory perception of God's effects rather than direct illumination" (64), and that he holds that "only after our resurrection will our knowledge of God truly be a direct and complete illumination" (67). Points out that Donne believed that the preacher, by directing the attention of his auditors to "examples of God's handiwork and by providing images of His creation for their consideration," provided them with "the materials necessary for the initial seeing and understanding of God which precede faith." Maintains, therefore, that Donne "works to make sure the images he provides are vivid and concrete and likely to be retained in his listeners' memories where they can be worked on by the intellectual light" (71). Concludes that throughout the sermons Donne asserts that "in this world our initial knowledge of God, as limited and potentially distorted as that may be, does, indeed, derive from our sense perceptions of his creation" (83).

991. Morse, David. "The Private World of Donne, Burton and Browne," in *England's Time of Crisis: From Shakespeare to Milton: A Cultural History,* 256–318. New York: St. Martin's Press.

Argues that, though by no means a recluse, Donne "always sought to shelter and guard his identity from the world" and that "even in the midst of advancement and conformity he always saw himself as being at odds" (264). Attributes Donne's feeling of being apart to his Catholic upbringing as a member of a persecuted minority and discusses how "Donne, in the depths of his interior being, was permanently scarred by the experiences of his youth." Explores his fascination with suicide, noting that he was attracted to the notion "not so much because it was something that he directly contemplated as because it was a possibility that was constantly in his mind" (265). Believes that, in addition to his Catholic experience and the various misfortunes of his early life, Donne's fundamentally pessimistic attitude toward life was also "deeply conditioned by his sense that the world was in a state of progressive deterioration and decay" (267). Illustrates Donne's conflicts and tensions by commenting on *Biathanatos,* the *Anniversaries,* the *Satyres,* the *Songs and Sonets,* the verse epistles, the religious poems, and the sermons. Concludes that "[a]ll his life Donne was torn between a desire to attract attention and a fervent wish to blend into the wallpaper," and that he ends his life desiring only that God "will reassemble all his multiple identities and weld them into a new and pristine being that is no longer subject to division" (289). In the struggle to reconcile his public and private self, compares and contrasts Donne with Burton and Browne.

992. Mueller, Janel. "Women Among the Metaphysicals: A Case, Mostly, of Being Donne For." *MP* 87: 142–58. Reprinted in *Critical Essays on John Donne,* ed. Arthur Marotti (New York: G. K. Hall, 1994), 37–48.

Discusses women as subjects, readers, and imitators of Donne's poetry and points out the central role women played in its production and reception. Claims that Donne is "the last English poet to sustain the force of the great, centuries-old Continental tradition of love lyrics that had celebrated femininity for offering the male poet a privileged access to ideality and divinity as well as a means of grounding his selfhood through intimacy with a person figured to and by this self as other" (143), and calls him, therefore, "the last English poet of the metaphysics of heterosexual love" (144). Shows how Donne "acutely delineates a whole range of male attitudinizing about love" and insists that "it is the speaker's play of mind—not social contexts, norms, and practices—that determines the roles of women in Donne's verse" (145). Reviews Donne's various reactions to women and various masculine poses he adopts in his love poetry and discusses how he "had to discourse differently of love, or had to discourse of a different love," when he wrote the verse epistles, the *Anniversaries,* and his sacred poetry, poems in which, for the most part, he "proves capable of displacing the flesh while retaining the spirit at the center of a male-female relationship" (149). Compares and contrasts the representation of women in Donne's poetry to that in the poetry of Crashaw, Marvell, Herbert, Vaughan, and Emily Dickinson.

993. Nash, Walter. *Rhetoric: The Wit of Persuasion.* Oxford: Basil Blackwell. x, 241p.

Analyzes *HSDeath* as an example of "affective rhetoric" (34–37). Discusses how the argument of the sonnet is "quite close to that of classical forensic oratory, except that the process of *confutatio* is absent" (34). Observes, however, that although a Petrarchan sonnet, the "prosodic basis of Donne's argument in this poem is the distich," that is, "he proceeds two lines at a time." Shows how deftly Donne unites two different themes in the sonnet—

"the theological assertion of faith in the resurrection and the therapeutic management of the fear of dying" (36). Shows also how Donne's artful use of pronouns finally involves the reader personally in the poem. Discusses also the "figurative rhetoric" of *HSRound* (143–45), showing how between the octave and sestet of the sonnet there is "a change of tone symptomatic of a change of authorial role, of stance." Points out how the octave "is crowded with figures" while the sestet is "much less so," and that "[t]he resultant impression of the octave is one of hectic, high-voiced excitement, an exhilaration at once virile and morbid, a pathological state of tension," whereas the sestet "supplants this with a healthier sense of reality" (144). Concludes that in this sonnet "Donne's figuration is imaginatively conceived, as the embodiment and symptom of a changing psychological state" (145).

994. Parfitt, George. *John Donne: A Literary Life*. Literary Lives, gen. ed. Richard Dutton. New York: St. Martin's Press. viii, 140p.

Focuses on "selected aspects" of Donne's life and work "in the context of the times" in which he lived and seeks to highlight "those features which are most alive in our times." Emphasizes "the period between Donne's marriage in 1601 and his ordination in 1615," stating that "[t]he last period of his life and its main literary product, the sermons, are treated more briefly because they have limited interest now" and that "the treatment of the early years is limited by the gaps in the surviving evidence" (viii). Chapter 1, "1572–1601" (1–39), outlines Donne's early life; comments on his familial and religious background; surveys his early poems, especially the *Satyres,* the paradoxes, epigrams, and the *Elegies;* and discusses Donne's youthful view of women. Chapter 2, "1601–1615"

(40–100), surveys Donne's life from the time of his marriage to his ordination, focusing primarily on the negative consequences of his marriage and his attempts to overcome them; comments on his coterie poems, especially the epithalamia, the verse letters, *Pseudo-Martyr, Ignatius,* the *Songs and Sonets,* the *Holy Sonnets,* and *Corona.* Suggests that during this period Donne should not be seen "as one figure so much as a multiple made up of the interaction of personality with the shaping qualities of the modes in which he is working and the specific circumstances which bear upon his adoption of these modes and not others" (71). Chapter 3, "1615–1632" (101–25), discusses Donne's life from the time of his ordination until his death and comments on Donne as a preacher, on his doctrinal position on certain theological issues, and on the sermons as literary products. "An Appendix on Criticism of Donne's Writings" (126–28) briefly surveys Donne's critical reputation before the twentieth century and during both the early and late twentieth century, with suggested readings followed by notes (129–36), a selected bibliography (137–38), and an index (139–40). Review: Patrick Demers, *JRMMLA* 12 (1991): 167–68.

995. Patrides, C. A. "John Donne: The Aesthetics of Morality," in *Figures in a Renaissance Context,* ed. Claude J. Summers and Ted-Larry Pebworth, 89–116. Ann Arbor: University of Michigan Press.

Reprints (slightly revised) the introduction to *The Complete English Poems of John Donne,* ed. C. A. Patrides (London and Melbourne: J. M. Dent, 1985), 14–45.

996. Pebworth, Ted-Larry. "John Donne, Coterie Poetry, and the Text as Performance." *SEL* 29: 61–75.

Discusses the textual implications of Donne's having been a coterie poet.

Points out that "[f]or the seven poems printed for general circulation during his lifetime, Donne was forced at the point of their imminent publication to treat their texts as objects destined to endure, in other words, to treat them as stable artifacts," but "[f]or the other 187 poems in his canon, Donne allowed himself the coterie poet's freedom of treating texts as scripts for performances, with all the flexibility and impermanence that such a concept implies" (61–62). Maintains that Donne's coterie poems were composed for specific occasions, "whether or not those specific occasions can now be determined with exactitude," and that "the word 'performance' applied to coterie poetry does not necessarily entail an oral presentation" but rather simply designates "an unenduring presentation of a text to a necessarily restricted audience" (64–65). Insists that "[w]hat we recognize as a peculiarly Donnean sensibility arises not from a consistent vision, but from an ethos of performance, one that tailors perspective to particular occasion" (65), and maintains that Donne viewed the text of most of his poems "not as artifact but as performance" (73). Comments, therefore, on problems that modern textual scholars must face as a result of the coterie nature of Donne's poetry, such as multiple texts of individual poems, noncanonical poems in manuscript collections, and scribal errors or "corrections" or "improvements" in the transmission of texts.

997. Pebworth, Ted-Larry, and Ernest W. Sullivan, II. "Rational Presentation of Multiple Textual Traditions." *PBSA* 83: 43–60.

Proposes that textual editors "provide, rather than a single 'authoritative' text, the entire texts of all authoritative versions of works when the entire texts are essentially variant . . . and at least the portions containing variants in all probably or possibly authorial versions when the differences are less universal" (44). Proposes also that "in the textual apparatus editors provide, rather than a single comprehensive historical collation of all versions of the text, independent historical collations for each authoritative and probably authoritative version of the whole or partial work" (45). Illustrates the proposal for universally variant versions by discussing the textual complexities of *Beggar,* showing how a critical edition of Donne's poetry should present the poem in a format that "recognizes the multiple, authoritative versions of the poem, clarifies the transmission of their texts, and allows users of the edition to reconstruct easily any exemplar from any textual tradition" (47). Illustrates the proposal "[w]hen multiple versions do not differ universally, or when their variants are not of equal authority" by discussing the text of Walton's "A shorte Hymne by Sr Hen: Wotton," which is "extant in three distinct versions of varying authority" (49). Appendix A (57–58) presents the sigla for *Beggar* and Appendix B (59–60) the sigla for Wotton's poem.

998. Richards, Bernard. "The 'Bed's Feet' in Donne's 'A Nocturnal Upon St. Lucy's Day.'" *N&Q,* n.s. 36: 28–29.

Maintains that the term "bed's feet" (l. 7) in *Noct* refers to the foot of the bed, "the part at the bottom of the mattress where the feet rest" (28). Points out that if Donne is saying that life flows out from the feet, his view is "physiologically somewhat unusual for the time" (29).

999. Roebuck, Graham. "Donne's Visual Imagination and Compasses." *JDJ* 8: 37–56.

Considers "some representations of compasses in the age of Donne" and thereby "seeks to probe the relationship of visual representation to poetic conceit in order to enhance our understanding of Donne's imagination: its range, depth and, especially, its centrality to the thought of the age." Points out that although Donne's use of the compass in *ValMourn* is "a commonplace of the period, what the poet does with it by extending its range of reference is rare and subtle indeed" (37). Contrasts Donne's use with that of Henry Peacham in his *Minerva Britannia* (1612) and suggests that "there is something restless and urgent" about Donne's "treatment of visual elements in some of his late lyrics and the later Epicedes and Obsequies which places them beyond the class of, say, the ingenious, the apt and the pleasing" (40). Maintains that Donne's visual imagination was formed primarily by "the woodcuts and, especially, the copper engravings of printed books, maps, and cartes" (41). Surveys critical attempts "to identify the particular visual trigger of Donne's conceit" (45) of the compass and comments on "the navigational and cartological arcana" operative in *ValMourn*. Insists, however, that in the poem, as later in *Har*, "the visual image disappears into the circle" and, "for the expert reader, even more radically, so has the printed line of symbols itself been subsumed into the abstraction of the circle, expressive of all to the self" (54).

1000. Sawday, Jonathan. "Reading Renaissance Poetry," in *Bloomsbury Guide to English Literature,* ed. Marion Wynne-Davies, 201–22. London: Bloomsbury Publishing. Reprinted in *Bloomsbury Guides to English Literature: The Renaissance,* ed. Marion Wynne-Davies (London: Bloomsbury Publishing, 1992), 15–36.

In a general essay on Renaissance poetry, claims that "[n]o poet could be said to be more alive to the possible presence of the female in his writing than John Donne, but then no poet

so determinedly ensures that she remains so absent when compared to the true centre of his poetry—the fascinating object of contemplation that the poet's own self presents." Suggests that "[t]he urge to render things 'transparent', a desire to peer beyond surface representation, together with the triumphant discovery of the dramatic speaking voice, and the continual awareness of the poetic self as both the subject and object of his writing, combine to make Donne and Donne's poetry almost inseparable" (214). Discusses how Donne's poems reflect a "shifting poetic awareness of a created sense of selfhood" (215).

1001. Schleiner, Winfried. "Donne's Coterie Sermon." *JDJ* 8: 125–32.

Calls Donne's sermon preached at Whitehall, 12 April 1618, a "coterie" sermon, "a descriptive and non-evaluative term describing a sermon hovering in the elusive space between political allegory, moral application, and edification" (123), and suggests that the imprisoned Robert Carr (Earl of Somerset) in a letter to King James pleading for a pardon is perhaps referring specifically to this sermon. Acknowledges that the claim is tenuous since he is unable to date the letter and unable to prove definitely that Somerset is referring to this specific sermon. Surveys Donne's friendship with Somerset and suggests that possibly in the sermon Donne, in a veiled and oblique way, is asking the king to show mercy to Somerset and that, in his letter, Somerset is reminding the king of this occasion.

1002. Seelig, Sharon Cadman. "In Sickness and in Health: Donne's *Devotions upon Emergent Occasions.*" *JDJ* 8: 103–13.

Notes that the mood of the conclusion of *Devotions* is "remarkably anxious, doubtful, and uncertain, leading one to question both the permanence and the significance of [Donne's] recovery" (103), but rejects the notion that this is simply "a moment of existential doubt" (104). Shows how the *Devotions* is "both progressive and cyclical" (106), thereby preparing the reader for the conclusion. Argues that the rhetorical point of the conclusion is that "sickness and health are not only opposites but [also] notions whose values are radically dependent on their context." Maintains that in the *Devotions* physical illness is "at first an image of the sickness of sin" but that "by the end of the work, health of the body, formerly a cause for rejoicing, may be seen as that which separates the soul from its heavenly goal." Concludes, therefore, that "[t]he God whom Donne sees as both a circle and a straight line provides the vision by which he understands that to be lowered here is to be raised in heaven, to see that what in human terms is a victory, a return to health, is in theological terms a postponement of the goal, and that fear of relapsing, contrary to our first impression of the matter, may be taken as a sign of hope and of health" (112).

1003. **Slights, William W. E.** "The Edifying Margins of Renaissance English Books." *RenQ* 42: 682–716.

Surveys the extent, style, and functions of printed marginalia in Renaissance English books and points out that, "[w]ith a clear view of both Roman Catholic and Puritan excesses in the area of contentious biblical commentary in the latter half of the sixteenth century, Donne chooses to minimalize the marginal apparatus of his sermons and sets a kind of standard for the genre." Notes also that Donne could assume that his readers would consult the King James version of the Bible, "an authorized translation, one unencumbered by the impenetrable masses of doctrinally slanted

marginalia in editions such as the Geneva Bible of 1560" (692).

1004. **Smith, A. J.** "The Death of Virtue: From Hyperbole to Havoc," in *Italy and the English Renaissance,* ed. Sergio Rossi and Dianella Savoia, 107–21. Milano: Unicopli.

Traces the transformations of the conceit of the sickness and death of the mistress, given "definitive form and authority" by Petrarch, from Dante to Donne, stressing in particular "the drastic difference between Donne's handling of it and Petrarch's, or for that matter anyone else's." Calls Donne "the most radical of all European poets" and shows how he exploits in different ways the conventional conceit "for ends entirely his own" (107). Discusses in detail *Fever* to show how in this poem the conceit "is put in the service of an end which is far removed from Petrarch's, and wholly distinctive" (110). Analyzes also *Noct* to show how it "presents an extreme development in a love poem of the conceit of the mistress's death" (115). Finally examines lines from *FirAn* in which Donne "systematically develops the petrarchan conceit to show the dependence of all the world's vital virtues upon the personal qualities of a dead girl, a girl whom we know he had never even met" (119), as a way of illustrating his view of "an accelerating decline of the cosmos and of the human constitution towards havoc, ruin, and general dissolution" (119–20).

1005. **Strengholt, L.** "Constantijn Huygens' Translation of John Donne's 'A Valediction, forbidding mourning,'" in *In Other Words: Transcultural Studies in Philology, Translation, and Lexicology Presented to Hans Heinrich Meier on the Occasion of His Sixty-Fifth Birthday,* ed. J. Lachlan Mackenzie and Richard Todd, 173–83. Dordrecht: Foris Publications.

Translated into English by Richard Todd. Examines the autograph of Huygens's translation of *ValMourn,* entitled "Vertreck," and presents an inventory of "the various cancellations and improvements" (173) Huygens made in the process of arriving at his final version of the poem. Shows how on several occasions Huygens actively strove towards "an increasingly precise rendering of Donne's words" (178) and also points out how examination of Huygens's corrections gives us "a deeper understanding of the translated text itself" (179). Points out, for example, that Huygens's failure to see any erotic wordplay in ll. 26 and 32 "may help us see that it is simply our own century's preoccupation with the erotic that renders the possibility of word-play in this area unavoidable" (181). The appendix presents a literal translation into English of "Vertreck."

1006. Strier, Richard. "John Donne Awry and Squint: The 'Holy Sonnets,' 1608–1610." *MP* 86: 357–84.

Argues that in many of the *Holy Sonnets* of 1608–1610 "[t]he Protestant imprint is clear enough, but the underlying matter does not fully 'take' the print" (358), and that therefore they "are awry and squint as poems, reflecting rather than reflecting on the confusions and uncertainties of Donne's spiritual life." Maintains that many of the sonnets "are simply not very successful as poems" (359). Believes that "the pain and confusion" that Donne expresses in these poems "is not that of the convinced Calvinist but rather that of a person who would like to be a convinced Calvinist but who is unable to be so and unable to admit that he is unable to be so" (361). Discusses several of the *Holy Sonnets* to show how they reflect "Donne's difficulties with and occasional successes at imprinting Calvinism" on

his soul. Maintains that those that are unsuccessful are marred by Donne's attempt to evade or his failure to acknowledge his theological confusion, while others that avoid such "incoherence and sophistry" are "psychologically coherent, theologically coherent, and poetically successful" (377). Holds that when Donne attempts "to present fully positive, non-terrifying visions of divine love," he fails to produce "distinguished poetry" (378), and suggests that *HSWhat* best reflects Donne's "inability in this period to conceive of divine love in terms of a loving relationship" (380), calling the poem "an exercise that does not come off, another failure at poetically rendering divine love apart from images of force" (381). Regards *HSMin* as a successful poem that perhaps "leaves us puzzled at the content of what Donne is saying" but "not at why Donne is saying something that he does not seem to mean" (382). Maintains that viewing the *Holy Sonnets* "in their proper biographical context and without historical preconceptions about the horrors of Protestantism or aesthetic preconceptions about the necessary greatness of these poems" makes it possible for us "to see their actual, peculiar shapes more clearly" and "to make better use of all the poems as human documents—in general and in Donne's biography—and better to honor and appreciate those that are truly artistic successes" (384).

1007. Strier, Richard. "Sanctifying the Aristocracy: 'Devotional Humanism' in François de Sales, John Donne, and George Herbert." *Journal of Religion* 69: 36–58.

Describes "devout humanism" as "a movement that set out to show Christianity to be fully possible within the bounds of ordinary and recognizable aristocratic life" (37) and cites, as the major text of the movement, St. François de Sales's *Introduction to the Devout Life* (1656). Points out echoes of the aims and ideals of Salesian spirituality in *Lit* and in some of Donne's sermons in which he stresses the compatibility of service to God and of Christian values with wealth, privilege, and aristocratic attitudes and behavior. Suggests that "Donne's version of 'the devout life' is even more courtly than that depicted by François de Sales" (44).

1008. Sullivan, Ernest W., II. "'John Donne, Anne Donne, Vn-done' Redone." *ANQ* 2: 101–103.

Discusses the possible genesis and transmission of the famous anecdote/pun and suggests that the source may be Archibald "Archie" Armstrong (d. 1672), the official court jester of King Charles I, whose account was embellished by King Charles and finally revised and included in the 1675 edition of Walton's *Life of Donne*. Armstrong in his *A Choice Banquet* (1660) reports that Donne, frolicking on his wedding day, chalked the pun on his kitchen door. Maintains that "if the anecdote/pun is authentic and authorial (all versions share the identification of Donne as the author of the pun) and if Archie's version of the anecdote is correct, then Donne wrote his own epithalamion and the sexual ambiguity of 'Un-done' resonates far more strongly than in Walton's account." Concludes, therefore, that it is quite possible that Donne "coined the pun" and that "it had a very different context" than the one given it later on by Walton and others (103).

1009. Sullivan, Ernest W., II. "Who Was Reading/Writing Donne Verse in the Seventeenth-Century?" *JDJ* 8: 1–16.

Identifies 275 volumes published in the seventeenth century by 55 different authors that contain more than 750 complete or partial printings of Donne's verses that provide evidence for a "relatively limited, yet relatively certain, means for establishing Donne's seventeenth-century audience" (2). Argues that this information, although not affecting "our present perception of Donne's seventeenth-century audience as verbally skilled intellectuals," shows that "a great many more authors were reading/writing Donne verse a great deal more frequently and over a much greater span of time than has been thought" and therefore requires us to revise "the current perceptions that Donne had an almost exclusively manuscript (and therefore very restricted) audience during his lifetime" and that his "audience disappeared in the Restoration" (5). Points out also that Walton's biography, musicians, and translators "extended Donne's influence beyond English literature" (7) and that his poems appeared in letters, poetical miscellanies, and self-improvement and writing guides. Holds that this survey indicates the likelihood that Donne's poetry had more "commercial and social value for lower levels of Renaissance society than presently believed" (15).

1010. Sun, Suli. "Contrastive Study of Lyric Patterns of Chinese and English Love Poems." *Wai Guo Yu* 3, no. 61 (June): 44–47.

In Chinese. Quotes the first stanza of *Flea* in this brief comparative study of lyrical patterns in English and Chinese love poems.

1011. Thompson, Thelma B. "Religious Doctrines in the Seventeenth-Century English Hymn," in *The Seventeenth-Century English Hymn: A Mode for Sacred and Secular Concerns,* 55–96. American University Studies, Series 20, Fine Arts, vol. 5. New York: Peter Lang.

Discusses how seventeenth century hymns reflect the political, religious, social, and scientific concerns of the age. Discusses how *Father* reflects Donne's Calvinistic belief in original sin as well as in personal sin and notes that it was set to music and sung during Donne's deanship at St. Paul's. Briefly comments on the various versions of Donne's hymn. Maintains that "[t]he form of the hymn enhances the meaning and together they fuse into a vibrant, poetic unity" (58). Calls the poem "metaphysical and witty" (59), noting, in particular, Donne's pun on his family name.

1012. Vicari, E. Patricia. *The View from Minerva's Tower: Learning and Imagination in "The Anatomy of Melancholy."* Toronto: University of Toronto Press. x, 250p.

Compares Donne and Robert Burton in their use of natural philosophy in their writings, noting many similarities "but also an important difference" (26). Emphasizes that for Donne "scientific knowledge was something to be played with" and that "he uses snippets of it as a craftsman uses bits of coloured tile in a mosaic." Maintains that "[h]e detaches himself, as it were, from such ideas by manipulating them for a rhetorical purpose rather than examining them to see what truths, if any, they contain, and what might be the metaphysical implications of such truths" (27). Points out that since Donne's interest in science lay primarily in "its curiosity and novelty as a source of analogies," his "interest waned," and that "[a]fter 1614 allusions to any kind of astronomy are rare in his sermons and poetry, whereas Burton continued to pursue information on this subject and ponder upon it until his death" (28). Notes Donne's interest in Paracelsus but points out that he "could not arrive at a final evaluation of the man or his work" (64).

1013. Wada, Tetsuzo. *Keijijoshi-ron-Soko* [Tentative Essays on the Metaphysical Poetry]. Tokyo: Chuseki-sha. 227p.

Consists of five essays: (1) on T. S. Eliot's comments on metaphysical poetry, (2) on Herbert Read's views on metaphysical poetry, (3) on Dante, (4) on Blake, and (5) on T. S. Eliot. Comments on the major metaphysical characteristics of Donne's poetry, primarily as those are discussed by Herbert Grierson, T. S. Eliot, and Herbert Read and as seen in *Relic, ValWeep,* the *Anniversaries,* and *Calm.*

1014. Walby, Celestin J. "The Westmoreland Text of Donne's First Epithalamium." *JDJ* 8: 17–35.

Argues that the copy of *EpLin* in the Westmoreland manuscript is "the least corrupted, earliest extant recension of the poem." Discusses how it "provides a stronger reading at important points of difference with the 1633 edition," how emendations of the 1633 text with Westmoreland made by Grierson and Milgate in their editions "adversely affect the interpretation of the poem," and how the Westmoreland text supports those who interpret the poem as a parody of Spenser's *Epithalamion* (18). Concludes that the Westmoreland text is "bibliographically superior to all other early copies of the work, including the 1633 first printing"; that it "preserves the poem in a state closest to the authorial holography"; that its adoption as copy-text is "justified by its textual authority" and "avoids the anachronism of eclecticism inherent in the creation of a 'critical text'"; and that it "clarifies several cruxes in the work, and supports the reading of the poem as parodic or satiric" (26). Includes two appendixes: (1) the text of the poem based on the Westmoreland manuscript, with expanded abbreviations (29–32); and (2) a scheme based on omission of words (32) and a second based on verbal alterations (33) followed by sigla of manuscript sources (34) and a note on Appendix 2 (34–35).

1015. Westerweel, Bart. "The Well-Tempered Lady and the Unruly Horse: Convention and Submerged Metaphor in Renaissance Literature and Art," in *Convention and Innovation in Literature,* ed. Theo d'Haen, Rainer Grübel, and Helmut Lethen, 105–22. Utrecht Publications in General and Comparative Literature, 24. Ams-terdam: John Benjamins.

Comments on conventional horse imagery in Renaissance iconography and literature and discusses a "submerged metaphor" of horses and horseback riding in *Goodf.* Argues that in Donne's poem "the (unmentioned) horse as an emblem of the pursuit of pleasure and the riding of the horse as a conflict between body and soul" (116) would have been readily recognized by his contemporary readers. Observes that in *Goodf* "the horse carries its rider one way, while God, the divine rider of man, tries to curb, check him by penitential corrections until he is fit to take the other direction." Maintains that "[w]hat in other contexts is expressed in concrete detail (reins, bit, whip and spur) is only suggested" in Donne's poem, but shows how "the horse as an emblem of passion has an important part in the action though it does not even occur in the text" (117).

1016. Wright, Nancy E. "The *Figura* of the Martyr in John Donne's Sermons." *ELH* 56: 293–309. Reprinted in *John Donne,* ed. Andrew Mousley, New Casebooks, gen. eds. John Peck and Martin Coyle (Basingstoke and London: Macmillan; New York: St. Martin's Press, 1999), 182–97.

Observes that the Jacobean clergy "used biblical *figurae* both to veil and reveal their intended criticisms of the king's appropriation of theological discourse" and that "[i]n the language of their sermons, the peculiar function of *figurae* of hidden allusion in classical rhetoric informs the meaning of biblical *figurae* or types." Points out, furthermore, that "[t]hese *figurae* locate the authority of language in the Divine *Logos,* Christ, to whom the preacher as well as biblical types such as John the Baptist are witnesses." Examines, therefore, Donne's sermons "spoken in response to the censorship imposed by King James I in 1622 as a paradigm of the functions of language as both the medium and the object of conflict in Jacobean England" (294). Analyzes, in particular, Donne's sermon preached in James's presence on 15 September 1622, in which he ambivalently responds to the king's *Directions for Preachers,* showing how he "circumvents secular restrictions appropriating the authority and use of language by using biblical *figurae* and texts not only as rhetorical proof but also as exempla of a particular form of religious discourse, *martyria* or testimony" (306).

1017. Yancey, Philip. "A Wrestling Match with the Almighty." *Christianity Today* 33, no. 12: 22–26.

Reflects on how suffering in Donne's life and his dealing with it, especially in the *Devotions,* changed the author's understanding of pain and suffering. Discusses how Donne confronts in his meditations, poetry, and sermons the fear of dying, the meaning of life and suffering, and the crisis of death. Says that, for Donne, the turning point came "as he began to view death not as the disease that permanently spoils life, but rather as the only cure to the disease of life," and when he fully recognized that "only through death—Christ's death and our own—can we realize a cured, sinless state" (26).

1990

1018. Arndt, Murray D. "Distance on the Look of Death." *L&M* 9: 38–49.

Calls *Devotions* "an instructive paradigm" of Donne's "lifelong failure to resolve some wrenching pain" (38). Maintains that, in spite of its technical finesse and "perceptive insights into the human condition," *Devotions* is flawed: "the *general* effect of the reflections is not nearly so strong as it needs to be" and "in the end there is no thunder, but, instead, one long, trailing argument" (40). Argues that in *Devotions,* Donne "managed to distance himself from his own experience through elaborate structural devices, the interplay of carefully tensed styles, and a constantly active and paradoxical wit," and that this "effort to distance himself from the experience finally cost him the passionate involvement, indeed the mystical surrender," that he yearns for in the *Holy Sonnets.* Maintains that, "instead of willing surrender, Donne's response was intellectual control" (41–42). Concludes that in *Devotions,* Donne presents "a rational method of controlling suffering, not a passionate surrender to its terrible divinity" (47), and thus the work expresses "an inefficient and perhaps impossible way to achieve the sort of surrender Donne desired" (48).

1019. Baker-Smith, Dominic. " 'Th'old broad way in applying': John Donne and his 'Litanie,' " in *A Day Festivall: Essays on the Music, Poetry and History of Scotland and England and Poems Previously Unpublished in Honour of Helena Mennie Shire,* ed. Alisoun Gardner-Medwin and Janet Hadley Williams, 48–58. Aberdeen: Aberdeen University Press.

Discusses how in *Lit* Donne combines an ancient liturgical form and the personal, "the formal with its private application" (49). Says that the poem "becomes a dramatisation of the process by which, through grace, the private does become public; and as such it has an oblique reference to Donne's own intermediary position, adopting a devotional tradition but rectifying it by a reformed attentiveness to the absolute initiative of grace." Analyzes the poem to show "the ingenuity of Donne's performance as he wrestles to particularise the broad outlines of the liturgical form" (52) and "to put his personal petitions in a canonical form" (56). Believes that in *Lit* Donne attempts to save and to rectify "a literary artifact which projected the Church he so desperately needed" in those "difficult years that preceded *Pseudo-Martyr*" (57).

1020. Baumlin, James S. "From Recusancy to Apostasy: Donne's 'Satyre III' and 'Satyre V.' " *EIRC* 16: 67–85.

Argues that *Sat3* is, in part, "an invective against the political enforcement of conscience, an argument, admittedly oblique, for religious tolerance, and thus an argument against contemporary court policies," a poem which thus "flaunts the poet's recusancy." Sees *Sat5* as Donne's attempt "to retract the treasonous political attack of this earlier poem" and as "an apostate poet's hasty—and expedient—revision of his earlier recusant satire" (69). Maintains that *Sat5* "may publicly announce the poet's own apostasy and identification with Royal power" but believes that "still his heart mourns for the Catholic and his perilous political circumstances." Holds that "the poet seeks still to protect the rights of conscience, placing charity above the blind and prejudicial application of law" (82).

1021. Bonnefoy, Yves. "Traduction inédite de deux poèmes de John Donne," in *Traduire la poésie*, 2–5. *Palimpsestes* 2. Paris: La Sorbonne Nouvelle.

Translates into French *Christ* and *Sickness*, without notes or commentary.

1022. Chambers, A. B. "Crooked Crosses in Donne and Crashaw," in *New Perspectives on the Life and Art of Richard Crashaw*, ed. John R. Roberts, 157–73. Columbia: University of Missouri Press.

In an intricate stylistic comparison of three versions of Crashaw's "On the bleeding wounds of our crucified Lord," comments on Donne's "mind-teasing" (158) uses of the image of the cross in *Cross*. Suggests that in the poem Donne argues that "all images, including the poem itself and the multiple crosses to which it refers, are individually inadequate to the reality which nonetheless collectively attempt to signify" and that "single imperfections, in effect, are crossed out by self-canceling replication so that cross-eyed vision is doubly crossed and an uncrossed Christ is revealed" (161).

1023. Choi, Ye-Jung. "John Donne eui Anniversaries: Jashin eui segae reul chiyu haryeoneun noryeok" [John Donne's Anniversaries: An attempt to heal the world and himself]. *English Studies* (Seoul National University, Korea) 14: 23–36.

Surveys earlier criticism on the *Anniversaries* and presents a detailed analysis of both poems to show how, in them, Donne envisions a healing of the corruption of the world as well as a healing of the spiritual sickness that he recognizes in himself. Maintains that in *FirAn* Donne reveals the disease and corruption of the world by dissecting it, whereas in *SecAn* he presents Elizabeth Drury as the symbol of the human capacity to overcome the world's sin and pollution and as the symbol of the reconciliation of inner conflict. Stresses, therefore, that Elizabeth is not individualized but generalized in the poem. Points out how Donne, through Elizabeth, invites the reader to participate in the process that she symbolizes. Discusses also how the two poems reflect Donne's faith and religious sensibility and how they show his moving towards his commitment to the Church of England as a preacher.

1024. Chung, Hae Sung. "John Donne eui si e natanan sarang eui yangsik" [The Mode of Love in John Donne's Poetry]. *JELL* (Daejeon, Korea) 31: 61–83.

Discusses how Donne rejected Petrarchism and gave witty and unconventional expression to a wide range of amorous moods, but observes that many ideas in his love poetry are similar to those found in the medieval courtly love tradition. Discusses *Twick* and *ValWeep* as examples of the medieval mode of appealing to a proud mistress by means of sighs and tears, comments on *GoodM* and *Anniv* as examples of lovers making their own microcosm through the consummation of their love, discusses *Ecst* and *Flea* as examples of how souls are united through the body, and comments on *Commun* and *SGo* as examples of cynical love.

1025. Clark, James Andrew. "The Plot of Donne's *Anniversaries*." *SEL* 30: 63–77.

Maintains that the *Anniversaries* are informed by "a teleological principle" that "can properly be called a plot," and discusses how Elizabeth Drury's life, "as rendered in these poems, reveals a principle of order, though incompletely realized, and an energy of procession, though imperfectly discharged." Claims that "[h]er mourners become readers of narrative" and that "Donne's readers become mourners, driven to find a proper end for her story" (63). Shows how a teleological reading "looks for that narrative wholeness which gives the *Anniversaries* a relation like that between desire and satisfaction, a movement through tension to pleasure," and argues that it makes clear that the two poems "are not timeless at all but bound to time" and that "their course may hold much ambivalence and disunity" (64). Sees a triangle in the plot in which Donne as narrator and surrogate hero wavers between Elizabeth Drury "as both the goal and the model for his quest" and the world, which is both "scene" and "antagonist." Shows how a fictive audience, plural in the first poem and singular in the second, "is closely tied to the working out of Donne's narrative drives" (65). Calls the story "abstract or allegorical rather than mimetic," and shows how syntax and imagery work against each other, concluding that "one process wavers between two competing metaphors" which the speaker tries to yoke together "by violent syntax" (67). Analogizes the duality or contradictions of the *Anniversaries* to the Psalms, to St. Paul's "Epistle to the Romans," and to Book 4 of Plato's *Republic* and observes that Donne's poems are most like the story of Leontius in *The Republic* because they bring Donne's desire and aversion about death into conflict. Concludes that "[t]he narrative premise of the *Anniversaries* is thus Donne's

attempt to maneuver among his contrary impulses toward the world in its systems and scales." Shows that "[w]hat gets him over his conflict—and thus what gives the poems as narrative an ending—is finally a change in his defensive strategies" (72), and points out how "a kind of freedom eventuates from the logic of morality in the *Anniversaries*, the central figure of this plot no longer squandering but sublimating his desires" (74).

1026. Clements, Arthur L. *Poetry of Contemplation: John Donne, George Herbert, Henry Vaughan, and the Modern Period.* Albany: State University of New York Press. xvii, 306p. Pages 45–57, 257–58 reprinted in *John Donne's Poetry,* ed. Arthur L. Clements, 2nd ed. (New York: Norton, 1992), 231–42.

The preface (xi–xvii) indicates that the purpose of this study is to show "precisely to what extent and in what particular qualified ways" the poetry of Donne, Herbert, and Vaughan can be viewed in terms of the "ancient-medieval-Renaissance contemplative tradition" (xiv) and to show not only how "that tradition may elucidate these poets' works" (xvi) but also how the tradition connects these poets with modern poets and with modern science. Chapter 1, "Contemplative Tradition" (1–18), presents an overview of the "ancient-medieval-Renaissance contemplative tradition, or more precisely, different aspects of it as it existed in the Renaissance and was known to seventeenth-century and later writers," which includes "stages, types, and characteristics of mystical experience, the kinds of 'vision,' and some key contemplative ideas, such as regeneration and the distinctions between the two selves and between meditation and contemplation" (2). Chapter 2, "John Donne: 'We two being one, are it'" (19–79), considers "the contemplative dimension" of several of Donne's best-known secular and sacred poems "in terms of the general guidelines to mystical life as set forth in the previous chapter, and in an effort to determine . . . the spiritual state of being and progression imaginatively revealed in Donne's poetry" (19). Presents a detailed reading of *Ecst,* since it affords "a point of reference for the reading of other Donne poems which have contemplative elements in them" (24), and comments also on *Canon* and *SunRis.* Considers the contemplative tradition "in some of its various historical, philosophical and theological as well as literary aspects and sources" (58) to suggest how it may have contributed to Donne's view and presentation of faithful or true love. Emphasizes that although "the philosophical, theological, and literary aspects of contemplative tradition may provide sources, contexts, and direction" for Donne, the poems of true love in his canon "are more meaningful because they grew out of his own mystical experiences" (65). Discusses also Donne's *Holy Sonnets* as "representative of his divine poems with regard to the question of meditation and contemplation" (65), and suggests that Donne "appears more readily to have found union and godlikeness in the secular poems which celebrate extrovertive mystical experience than in the divine poems that seek introvertive mystical experience" (68). Analyzes in some detail *HSBatter* as a fairly "representative Holy Sonnet" and as "representative of the divine poems in general" (69). Concludes that the *Holy Sonnets* "do not advance beyond the stage of Purgation" and are, therefore, "meditative rather than contemplative" (76) and that the other divine poems "do not attain their end [which is the Vision of God], not even temporarily or partially, and are not, strictly speaking, mystical poems" (77). Claims, in

fact, that "Donne appears, on the evidence of the poetry, to have been more religious when he was less religious" (78). Chapter 3, "George Herbert: 'Was ever grief like mine?' " (81–127), compares and contrasts Herbert with Donne and stresses that "[w]hereas Donne's divine poetry is characterized by fear and trembling and uncertainty, Herbert's poetry frequently comes after conflict to assurance about salvation" (90). Chapter 4, "Henry Vaughan: " 'I saw Eternity the other night' " (129–72), compares and contrasts Vaughan with Donne and points out that, unlike Vaughan, Donne "writes of a love that accepts and affirms bodiliness as a valid part of holiness and that re-integrates polymorphously erotic sexuality and spirituality," adding that "[t]he best expression of the Vision of Eros in the English language, Donne's poems of true love are genuinely mystical and so appropriately expressed in genuinely mystical language" (170). Chapter 5, "Contemplative Poetry and the Modern Period" (173–239), points out similarities and differences between Donne and modern writers, especially D. H. Lawrence. "Appendix A: Grouping of the Songs and Sonnets and a General Dating of Poems" (241–45), divides Donne's poems into four groups: (1) "poems of inconstant, false, or incomplete love," (2) "poems of faithful or true love, usually both physical and spiritual," (3) "poems of Platonic love," and (4) "poems which, because of uncertainty or inapplicability, do not readily fall into one of the first three groups." Discusses also the issue of dating the poems. "Appendix B: A Selected Bibliography of 'The Extasie' " (246–250) lists major twentieth century studies of *Ecst.* Concludes with notes (251–80), works cited (281–96), and an index (297–306). Reviews: Bridget Gellert Lyons in *GHJ* 13 (1989–1990): 98–106; Stanley

Archer in *SMy* 13 (1990): 120–22; Anthony Low in *JDJ* 9 (1990): 183–87; D. F. Bratchell in *N&Q*, n.s. 38 (1991): 382–84; Ross C. Murfin in *DHLR* 23 (1991): 274–75; Maria Lichtmann in *Journal of Religion* 72 (1992): 311–12; John R. Mulder in *RenQ* 45 (1992): 203–05; Alan Rudrum in *RES* 43 (1992): 425–27.

1027. Coiro, Ann Baynes. " 'New-foundland': Teaching Metaphysical Poetry from the Other Side," in *Approaches to Teaching the Metaphysical Poets,* ed. Sidney Gottlieb, 81–88. Modern Language Association of America, Approaches to Teaching World Literature, gen. ed. Joseph Gibaldi. New York: Modern Language Association of America.

Argues that metaphysical poetry should be read "in a context as richly political—that is, historical and cultural—as possible" and rejects the idea of reading it "in a timeless realm of close reading" or "in a timely realm of any one feminist theory" (81). Discusses how Donne's poetry can be taught from a feminist viewpoint and points out the significant role that women play in Donne's poetry. Comments on how Donne's poems "are ideally suited to teaching a number of key literary principles, especially the concept of persona" (83), and discusses specific techniques for teaching *GoodM* and *Break* that encourage students to "examine their own assumptions and the assumptions and gender constructions of Donne and all the other metaphysical poets" (85–86). Comments also on feminist readings of *ElBed*.

1028. Cookson, Linda, and Bryan Loughrey, eds. *The Metaphysical Poets.* Longman Critical Essays. Harlow, Eng.: Longman Group. 137p.

A collection of ten essays by divers hands intended for students. The following essays discuss Donne and have been entered separately into this bibliography: Cedric Watts, "The Conceit of the Conceit" (9–18); Ronald Draper, "The Intellectual Ingenuity of John Donne" (33–45); Pat Pinsent, "Form and Meaning in Donne and Herbert" (79–87); David Lewis, "Drama in Donne and Herbert" (98–108); and Nigel Smith, "The Metaphysical Penguin" (110–16). Each essay is followed by "Afterthoughts" or questions posed for student reflection. Concludes with "A Practical Guide to Essay Writing" (119–30), "Style Sheet" (131–35), and "Suggestions for Further Reading" (137–[38]).

1029. Cunnar, Eugene R. "Illusion and Spiritual Perception in Donne's Poetry," in *Aesthetic Illusion: Theoretical and Historical Approaches,* ed. Frederick Burwick and Walter Pape, 324–36. Berlin: Walter de Gruyter.

Observes that throughout his poetry and prose Donne "reveals an acute interest in and knowledge of visual metaphor and structure that, in turn, reflects his concern about the problematics of visual perspective." Points out how "[t]he discovery and employment of linear perspective in the Renaissance raised serious theological, philosophical, and epistemological questions concerning the knowledge of God, the relationship between subject/knower/viewer and object/known/viewed" as well as "the relationship between word and referent in language and metaphor." Argues that, for Donne, these questions "were central to his understanding of God and to his representation of that understanding in poems and prose" (324). Shows that he "makes clear distinctions between perception and vision that lead to his rejection of conventional linear perspective as an organizer of reality or as a means to God because it is an illusion," and thus he seeks "alternative perceptive modes that underlie his poetic and narrative structures articulating his desire for the vision of and union with God" (325). Illustrates Donne's "struggles with the problematics of visual illusion and quest for a visual mode compatible with his theology" by discussing *Christ* and passages from *Essays in Divinity, Devotions,* and several sermons. Surveys several of "the historical problematics of perspective" that Donne encountered, in particular "the visual epistemology of Nicholas of Cusa, one of Donne's primary sources for the problematics of perspective" (326).

1030. Daley, Koos. "Donne and Huygens Travel Westward." *Dutch Crossing* 40: 23–30.

Compares Constantijn Huygens's rough draft and manuscript corrections of his seventeenth century translation of *Goodf* with Donne's original text to show how changes that Huygens made in his translation reflect subtle differences between his religious attitudes and Donne's. Notes, for instance, how "[t]he calvinist Huygens tries both to emphasize his participation in Christ's sacrifice and to temper the honour Donne gives to Mary as mother of Christ" (24). Concludes that the persona in Donne's poem "finds himself in the early and middle stages of the regenerative process" and "his emotional state is that of a Christian experiencing emotional doubts, anguish, even despair," whereas the persona in Huygens's translation "considers himself as an established member of the elect" (26).

1031. Daley, Koos. *The Triple Fool: A Critical Evaluation of Constantijn Huygens' Translations of John Donne.* Bibliotheca Humanistica and Reformatorica, vol. 46. Nieuwkoop: De Graaf Publishers. vii, 231p.

Chapter 1, "Introduction" (1–18), discusses the problems associated with translating poetry from one language to another, especially as they are related to Huygens's translation of 19 of Donne's poems into Dutch, and comments on Huygens's views on translation and his skill as a translator. In Chapter 2, "Donne's Heritage" (19–40), discusses Donne's sociocultural and literary heritage in order to understand his "participation in the history and literature of his age" (19). Comments on Donne's life, the centrality of rhetorical tradition in his poetry, and his reaction to Petrarchism. Chapter 3, "John Donne: Riddling, Perplexed, Labyrinthical Soul" (41–63), comments on major characteristics of Donne's poetic style and his attitudes toward sex and love to show that "[w]hat makes Donne's poetry so difficult to interpret and therefore so difficult to translate is its multivalency, its protean quality" (50). Comments on the terms "metaphysical," "wit," and "conceit," and maintains that when reading Donne's poems "we get the same illusionary experience we perceive in viewing Rembrandt's paintings or [Maurits] Escher's graphic art" because "[t]here is no resolution in his poems" (60). Chapter 4, "Constantijn Huygens: Uomo universale" (65–93), examines Huygens's life, his talent as a poet and translator, his contributions to Dutch letters and culture, and his relationship with England and particularly his relationship with Donne. Chapter 5, " 'When thou hast done, thou hast not Donne': Huygens as Translator of Donne" (95–135), compares *SunRis, Goodf,* and *Ecst* with Huygens's translations and argues that the translations "change Donne's complex thought process and multiplicity of perspectives" and "consistently lack the force and exuberance of the originals" (96). Maintains, however, that Donne's "light-hearted songs such as *SGo* and *Triple* suffer least in translation," noting that the translation of *Triple,* the last poem Huygens translated, "captures the tone and sentiment of the original faithfully" (130) and "was well received by the 'Muiderkring' poets, the elite circle of which Huygens was a member" (131). Chapter 6, "Traduttore, Traditore" (137–64), evaluates Huygens's "viable and vital contributions to the multidimensional functions of translation" (137). Discusses translation as intertextuality and shows how Huygens's "personal, spiritual, and political circumstances form the context" in which he translated Donne's poems; shows also how translation functions as critical interpretation. Discusses reasons why Huygens's translations, "with some significant exceptions, are adequate at best and do not function in a dynamic equivalence," pointing out how he often "selects, excludes, and reforms" (144) what he finds in Donne's poems and how he transforms Donne in order "to defend himself against total immersion in the abyss of poetic influence" (145). Also compares and contrasts Dutch and English as languages with a common background and, using lines from *Dream,* illustrates "the typical broadening and redundancy apparent in most of Huygens' translations of Donne" (154). Also analyzes corrections Huygens made when he translated *Goodf* to enhance our "appreciation for and understanding of the translation process" and to show how the translation reflects "the subtly different religious attitudes of Huygens and Donne" (156). An appendix (165–223) prints the poems by Donne in the order in which Huygens translated them along with Huygens's translations (taken from *Gedichten,* vol. 2, ed. J. A. Worp [Groningen: Wolters, 1893]), followed by a list of works cited (225–31). Reviews: Paul Claes in *SpL* 32 (1990): 205–7; N. F. Streekstra in *TNTL* 107

(1991): 127–35; A. van Strien in *De Niewe Taalgids* 85 (1992): 247–52.

1032. Diehl, Huston. "Discovering the Old World: The Renaissance Emblem Book as a Cultural Artifact," in *Approaches to Teaching the Metaphysical Poets,* ed. Sidney Gottlieb, 68–74. Modern Language Association of America, Approaches to Teaching World Literature, gen. ed. Joseph Gibaldi. New York: Modern Language Association of America.

Explains how emblem books can be used in classrooms to "provide insights into what is unique and distinctive about seventeenth-century culture, and what may, if unrecognized, separate us from the culture's art and artifacts" (68), thereby serving as a way into discussions of metaphysical poetry. Suggests, for instance, that when students "see how the emblem writers apply images from the past to their own time and place," they "become sensitive to the way Donne adapts conventional images to personal experience, uses erotic images in sacred poetry, and plays with images drawn from his contemporary world" (74).

1033. Donne, John. *John Donne,* ed. John Carey. The Oxford Authors, gen. ed. Frank Kermode. Oxford: Oxford University Press. xl, 488p.

Contains an introduction (xix–xxxii) to Donne's life and personality and to major characteristics of his poetry and prose; a chronology (xxxiv–xxxvii); and a note on the text (xxviii–xl), followed by Donne's English poems and a large selection of his prose (1–417) with notes (419–79), a list of further readings (480), and an index of poem titles and first lines (481–88). Attempts to arrange the works "in the chronological order of their composition, as far as possible," but acknowledges that not all of Donne's works can be dated exactly. Points out that, in the case of the *Songs and Sonets,* which have "no clues to dating at all," the poems are simply printed together as a group and inserted "into the chronological run at the earliest date at which there is any evidence of their existence" and that similarly the epigrams "are printed as a group in this way" (xxxviii). Presents page references for those who wish to study the *Satyres, Elegies,* or *Holy Sonnets* as distinct groups. Both spelling and punctuation of the texts are eclectic. Reviews: Marie-Madeleine Martinet in *DSS* 173 (1991): 454–55; T. R. Langley in *CQ* 22 (1993): 188–210; Robert Ellrodt in *EA* 47 (1994): 82–83.

1034. Donne, John. *John Donne: Selected Poems,* ed. Richard Gill. Oxford Student Texts, ed. Victor Lee. Oxford: Oxford University Press. ix, 169p.

Following acknowledgments and biographical notes on the editors (vii) and a foreword (ix) that describes the series, presents 25 poems from the *Songs and Sonets,* 4 from the *Elegies,* 7 selections from the *Holy Sonnets, Goodf,* and 3 hymns (1–51); notes on each poem (53–116); and a section entitled "Approaches" (119–62), which presents short discussions, critical questions, and literary exercises on such topics as Donne and love, Donne and religion, Donne and his age, Donne's language, and metaphysical poetry in general. Concludes with a chronology of Donne's life (163–65); suggested further readings (166–67); a section entitled "Tasks" (168–69) that contains basically a set of essay examination questions for students of Donne's poetry, followed by several illustrations and an index of titles and first lines.

1035. Donne, John. *John Donne: Selections from Divine Poems, Sermons, Devotions, and Prayers,* ed. John Booty. Preface by P. G. Stanwood. Classics of Western Spirituality. Mahwah, N.Y.: Paulist Press. viii, 309p.

Contains a foreword (1–2); a preface by P. G. Stanwood (3–8), who discusses the Anglican spirit of Donne's religious poetry and prose and especially the centrality of the mystery of the incarnation in Donne's works; and an introduction in which the editor discusses Donne's life (11–20), outlines Donne's spiritual journey as reflected primarily in his works (21–31), and comments on Donne's divine poems as a meditative sequence and on the sermons, *Devotions,* and prayers (32–64), calling these works "classics of West-ern spirituality, and therefore helps to those embarked upon spiritual journeys now" (31). A discussion of the texts used in the collection (65–67) is followed by notes to the introduction (68–72). The texts are divided into four sections, each of which is followed by notes: (1) 29 selections from the *Divine Poems* (73–115), (2) selections from 8 sermons (117–250), (3) passages from *Devotions* (251–86), and (4) selections about prayer or actual prayers (287–300). Concludes with a selected bibliography (301–6) and an index (307–9). Review: Arthur L. Clements in *SMy* 14 (1991): 77–79.

1036. Draper, Ronald. "The Intellectual Ingenuity of John Donne," in *The Metaphysical Poets,* ed. Linda Cookson and Brian Loughrey, 33–45. Longman Critical Essays. Harlow, Eng: Longman Group.

Points out that the intellectual quality of Donne's poetry is quite different from that of modern poetry. Maintains that "[h]is commitment to reason is fundamental" and that his poetry "is intellectual in the sense that it employs a linguistic mode suited to the needs of the conscious intelligence and is dedicated to the arts of argumentative persuasion." Points out that in the *Songs and Sonets* especially, "traditional assumptions about love are often stood on their head with a typically youthful delight in being provocative," but notes that "the tactics matter more than the strategy," and "[i]nvariably the means by which an end is achieved count for more than the end itself, which may be suspect, or even manifestly absurd" (34). By discussing such poems as *WomCon, SGo, Flea, SunRis,* and *ValMourn* "shows how Donne's love poems display the varied content of a flexibly vigorous mind, bold in its engagement with amorous experiences of all kinds and brilliantly adept in taking a debater's role for or against almost any notion that might be proposed— a mind which delights in its own intellectual ingenuity and is capable of intense feeling, but which cannot easily be pinned down" (45).

1037. Dubrow, Heather. "John Donne," in *A Happier Eden: The Politics of Marriage in the Stuart Epithalamium,* 151–200. Ithaca, N.Y.: Cornell University Press.

Based, in part, on three earlier essays: "Donne's 'Epithalamion made at Lincolnes Inne': An Alternative Interpretation" in *SEL* 16 (1976): 131–43; "Tradition and the Individualistic Talent: Donne's 'An Epithalamium, Or mariage Song on the Lady Elizabeth . . .'" (entry 658); and "'The Sun in Water': Donne's Somer-set Epithalamium and the Poetics of Patronage" (entry 880). Discusses Donne's three epithalamia to show how they "illuminate both their genre and their author" (151) and "offer textbook examples of the tensions associated with their literary type and with marriage in Renaissance England" (152). Maintains that though Donne's "preoccupation with love and sexuality made the genre attractive to him, wedding poems did not come naturally to him" (153), in part because the genre is "intensely communal in its values," whereas typically Donne sees "the community as a source of entrapment rather than support" (153), and in part because of his "ambiva-

lent attitudes to women, sexuality, and wedlock" (154). In a reading of *EpLin,* rejects the view that the poem is simply a parody of Spenser's "Epithalamion" and claims that its oddities, infelicities, and incongruities result from a shifting "back and forth between parody and imitation" (161) and from the "disturbing interplay of sanctioned male aggression, willing female submission, holy violence, and unholy bawdiness" (164). In a reading of *EpEliz,* sees Donne working through "many of the problems stemming from his attitudes to wedlock and, in particular, those revealed by his earlier image of the bride as a sacrificial lamb" (165) in *EpLin.* Discusses how "[t]hroughout this poem, we find traces of the problems and anxieties typically inscribed in Stuart epithalamia" but, at the same time, we see how Donne "delimited those tensions through a series of restorations, renewals, and reconciliations," "evokes a vision of rebirth through prosodic and semantic allusions to cycles," "lauds equality and mutuality," and "reconciles his vision of the wedding and his own role within it with the literary authority of his generic tradition, the religious authority of the bishop who married the couple, and the political authority of the king and court" (177). In a reading of *Eclog,* discusses how "[t]he moral problems posed by this wedding generated literary ones" (178) for Donne and how he adapted and manipulated epithalamic conventions, not always successfully, to effect a solution, noting how he "trenchantly sandwiches criticism of the couple between his compliments to them" (181). Notes the tension Donne felt because of the pressures of the patronage system that required him to defend and celebrate the marriage of Somerset and Frances Howard and the moral pressures he felt to criticize it, and shows how "[s]ome of the apparent contradictions in the poem stem from Donne's attempts to serve a variety of masters—and to turn at least some of them into his servants instead" (182). Comments on how Donne uses numerology to criticize the wedding and shows how he "develops techniques to distance himself and his audience from the occasion he is forced by the constraints of patronage to celebrate" (192). Discusses *Eclog* to show that its main function is "to express and embody the problems of courting a patron" (195). Concludes that the ambiguities and tensions in the Somerset epithalamium "reflect the fact that Donne was pulled between the moral necessity to condemn the wedding and the financial necessity to praise it— and also perhaps, between his desire to absent himself from the court and his urge to participate in courtly rituals, even morally dubious ones" (199–200).

1038. Fish, Stanley. "Masculine Persuasive Force: Donne and Verbal Power," in *Soliciting Interpretation: Literary Theory and Seventeenth-Century English Poetry,* ed. Elizabeth D. Harvey and Katharine Eisaman Maus, 223–52. Chicago and London: University of Chicago Press, 1990. Reprinted (revised) in *John Donne,* ed. Andrew Mousley, New Casebooks, gen. eds. John Peck and Martin Coyle (Basingstoke: Macmillan; New York: St. Martin's Press, 1999), 157–81.

Claims that "Donne is sick and his poetry is sick," but that "he and it are sick in ways that are interestingly related to the contemporary critical scene." Says that "Donne is bulimic, someone who gorges himself to a point of satiety, and then sticks his finger down his throat and throws up," but that "[t]he object of his desire and of his abhorrence is not food, but words, and more specifically, the power words can exert" (223). Sees in Donne "the need first to create a world and then endlessly to manipulate those who are made to inhabit it" (224). Cites *ElAnag* as an instance of Donne's ability "to say anything or many things as he combines and recombines words and letters into whatever figurative, and momentarily real, pattern he desires" (225). Discusses *ElComp* as an instance of the instability of meaning that characterizes Donne's use of language. Observes how "the speaker of elegies *always* imagines himself [like God] as a center of stability and control in a world where everyone else is plastic and malleable." Argues, however, that "this self-dramatization of an independent authority can be sustained only if the speaker is himself untouched by the forces he exerts on others," for if that force were "to turn back and claim him for its own by revealing itself to be the very source of *his* identity (which would then be no longer his) he would be indistinguishable from those he manipulates and scorns; he would be like a woman and become the object rather than the origin of his own performance, worked on, ploughed, appropriated, violated." Adds that the "suspicion that this may indeed be his situation is continually surfacing" (228), as seen in *ElComp, ElChange,* and *ElFatal,* and concludes that by "playing *all* the parts, the practitioner of masculine persuasive force denies himself a part of *his own*" (235). Sees the same instability and irony in the *Satyres,* poems in which Donne "presents a speaker who refuses to recognize himself in the indictment he makes of others" (239). Discusses the *Holy Sonnets,* in which the persona is no longer the shaper, but God is, noting, however, that Donne's God is made in the image of Donne himself—a "self-aggrandizing bully" (241). Says that in these poems Donne "assumes the posture of a woman," spreading "his legs (or cheeks)," noting that this stance does not indicate "a significant (and praiseworthy) change in his attitude toward women and power" (242). Rejects past criticism of Donne that is "a series of critical romances of which Donne is the hero" (250), and instead sees Donne as "always folded back into the dilemmas he articulates" (251).

1039. Francus, Marilyn. "An Augustan's Metaphysical Poem: Pope's *Eloisa to Abelard.*" *SP* 87: 476–77.

Maintains that Pope's *Eloisa to Abelard* "takes on the characteristics of the Metaphysical devotional poem." Discusses how "the divine and the erotic unite as Eloisa fuses Abelard's 'idea' with God" and suggests that "[t]his Metaphysical recognition is taken to its extreme" (476). Points out, however, that "instead of eroticizing the divine into a lover, as Donne, Herbert, and Crashaw did, Eloisa elevates her lover to the divine" and "becomes a pagan St. Teresa, whose religious ecstasy belongs to the cult of Abelard, not to God" (483). Observes that the metaphysical poets themselves, several of whom were divines, did not easily resolve "the conflict between the erotic love of man and the ecstatic love of God" (483–84). Cites *HSShe* and *Christ* as examples of how the rival claims permeate Donne's poetry.

1040. Franssen, Paul. "Pope's Janus-Faced Imagery," in *Centennial Hauntings: Pope, Byron and Eliot in the Year 88,* ed. C. C. Barfoot and Theo d'Haen, 65–85. DQR Studies in Literature, 8. Amsterdam: Rodopi.

Discusses the relationship between Pope's imagery and metaphysical imagery, concentrating primarily on his use of conceits, density of meaning, and tone, noting his use of double entendre and puns. Compares and contrasts Pope to Donne, pointing out, for instance, that Pope's verse "is rarely as dense as the strong lines of Donne" (82) but that his opening lines "can be as shocking and dramatic as Donne's" (84), although "[u]sually his tone is more urbane than Donne's." Concludes that "[m]any of Pope's images are merely witty, perhaps most, and the importance of the Metaphysical element in his writings should not be exaggerated; but it should not be altogether neglected either" (85).

1041. Frontain, Raymond-Jean. "Donne's Imperfect Resurrection." *PLL* 26: 539–45.

Points out that since "resurrection became a central trope of his imagination" in both his religious and secular works, it is surprising that Donne left unfinished *Res,* the one poem in which he meditated at length on this mystery (539). Maintains that perhaps the word "imperfect" in the title (if it is Donne's) and the fact that the poem remains unfinished have critical significance. Argues that, having described "in derogatory terms" the imperfect "resurrection" of the physical sun, the speaker of the poem "has described as much as can be put into words" (544) and that, therefore, he ends the poem because he realizes that "[a]ny description of the Resurrection [of Christ] is in its very attempt imperfect" and that "the imperfect resurrection of the 'old Sun' is all that the human eye has seen and speech can tell" (545).

1042. Frost, Kate Gartner. *Holy Delight: Typology, Numerology, and Autobiography in Donne's "Devotions Upon Emergent Occasions."* Princeton, N.J.: Princeton University Press. xvi, 178p.

The preface ([xi]–xvi) briefly comments on the occasion of the *Devotions* and its critical reception, indicates that the study is based on an examination of "premodern poetics" and of "the conventions of devotional literature" (xii), presents an outline of the following chapters, and explains the object of this study. Chapter 1, "The

Devotions and the Tradition of Devotional Literature" (3–14), places Donne's book "within the tradition of English devotional literature, especially within the traditions of the meditation (both Augustinian and Ignatian) and the *ars moriendi,* both of which have been held up by critics as models for Donne's work." Chapter 2, "The *Devotions* and Spiritual Autobiography" (15–38), makes the case that the *Devotions* is "a form of spiritual autobiography, part of an ongoing tradition that manifested itself in the English Renaissance in forms as varied as the sonnet sequence and the revelatory essay." Chapter 3, "Personal and Political Typology in the *Devotions*" (39–77), discusses "the complex use of biblical typology in the *Devotions,*" which "points back to the tradition of spiritual autobiography within which Donne worked and forward to the historical circumstances of the book's composition." Shows how "[t]he reliance on underlying number structures, manifest in so many early autobiographies, is derived from a poetic rooted in pre-Copernican cosmology." Chapter 4, "Donne and the Tradition of Number Symbolism" (78–105), explores Donne's "adherence to that poetic." Chapter 5, "Structural Significance in the *Devotions*" (106–57), comments on "the autobiographical and numerologically structured calendars, based on the hexaemeral week and the solstitial day, which underlie the discursive fabric of the *Devotions*" (xiii). Chapter 6, "An Afterword" (161–66), discusses how Donne presents in the *Devotions* "a 'liturgical self': a sense of being that is at once private and public, in service of personal salvation and at the same time committed to the spiritual fate of king and nation; a sense of being in harmony with the movement of the seasons and the temporal progress of the Incarnation and

Redemption" (164). Points out that "[w]e no longer possess that world and that perspective" but "we cannot deny its validity for those who lived and wrote within its hierarchical confines" (165). An appendix, "Ocular Proof: The Spiritual Autobiography of Opicinus de Canistris" (167–70), discusses, "as an example of the kind of underlying schema that must have preceded a work like Donne's," the "spatially organized autobiographical chart" (xiii) of Opicinus de Canistris (1296–ca. 1350). Contains illustrations and an index (171–78). Reviews: Robert C. Evans in *SCJ* 23 (1992): 185–86; S. K. Heninger in *RenQ* 45 (1992): 410–12; Eugene D. Hill in *AnSch* 9 (1992): 455–63; Edwina Burness in *ES* 74 (1993): 206–7; Albert C. Labriola in *R&L* 25 (1993): 75–80; Terry Sherwood in *JEGP* 93 (1994): 576–78; P. G. Stanwood in *JDJ* 13 (1994): 181–85.

1043. Gardiner, Anne Barbeau. "Donne and the Real Presence of the Absent Lover." *JDJ* 9: 113–24.

Discusses how in *ValMourn* Donne uses the mystery of the Real Presence of Christ in the Eucharist "to reveal the potentially infinite depths of human love" (144) and, in the process, explores Donne's eucharistic theology in the context of contemporary debates over how exactly Christ is present in the Eucharist. Maintains that the poem presents a "view of bodily Real Presence which most readers (except the followers of Zwingli) in seventeenth-century Britain and Europe shared." Observes how in the valediction Donne "takes as a paradigm for the most exalted human love Christ's love for the Church, a love which will not allow him to be Absent," which permits him "to give an almost infinite depth to the promise of the lover, who on the brink of a journey pledges not merely to return to his beloved but also, in an incomprehensible, numinous, but still substantial manner, to remain all the while Really Present" (123).

1044. Gelfert, Hans-Dieter. *Wie interpretiert man ein Gedicht?* Arbeitstexte für den Unterricht. Stuttgart: Philipp Reclam jun. 192p.

Compares an unidentified German translation of *HSDeath* with Andreas Gryphius's "Es ist alles eitel." Says that Gryphius's poem conveys a tone of personal affliction and a feeling of great authenticity that is expressed in straightforward simplicity, whereas Donne's poem is a highly complex portrayal of fear, hope, salvation, faith, and doubt, giving it a profundity that is evident to the reader even in translation.

1045. Gorbunov, A. N. "Time Category and the Concept of Love in English Poetry at the Turn of the XVII Century (Spenser, Shakespeare, Donne)." *Shekspirovskie chtenia* [Shakespeare Readings] 7: 299.

In Russian. Discusses how Donne in the *Songs and Sonets* "brings together conflicting views of love . . . without giving marked preference to any of them" and how "[u]nstable harmony" is achieved only in his later religious hymns (from English summary).

1046. Gottlieb, Sidney, ed. *Approaches to Teaching the Metaphysical Poets.* Modern Language Association of America, Approaches to Teaching World Literature, gen. ed. Joseph Gibaldi. New York: Modern Language Association of America. xii, 177p.

Preceded by a preface to the series (xix) and a preface to the volume (xi–xii), Part 1, "Materials" (3–32), reviews and evaluates sources relevant to teaching the metaphysical poets—editions, anthologies, reference works and bibliographies, background and general critical studies, studies of individual poets (Donne, Herbert, Vaug-

han, Crashaw, Marvell), and teaching aids (3–32). Part 2, "Approaches" (35–149), contains 18 essays covering different aspects of the period, of the metaphysical poets as a group and individually, and specific poems. These include the following: an introductory essay by Annabel Patterson, "Teaching against the Tradition" (35–40); seven essays on general topics and background material, including E. R. Gregory, "Vivifying the Historical Approach: Exercises in Teaching Seventeenth-Century Love Poetry" (41–47); William A. Sessions, *"Tottel's Miscellany* and the Metaphysical Poets" (48–53); Gene Edward Veith, Jr., "Teaching about the Religion of the Metaphysical Poets" (54–60); Albert C. Labriola, "Iconographic Perspectives on Seventeenth-Century Religious Poetry" (61–67); Huston Diehl, "Discovering the Old World: The Renaissance Emblem Book as Cultural Artifact" (68–74); P. G. Stanwood, "On Altering the Present to Fit the Past" (75–80); and Ann Baynes Coiro, " 'New-found-land': Teaching Metaphysical Poetry from the Other Side" (81–88); five essays that focus mainly on course content: Robert H. Ray, "Ben Jonson and the Metaphysical Poets: Continuity in a Survey Course" (89– 95); Faye Pauli Whitaker, "Metaphysical, Mannerist, Baroque: A Seminar for Undergraduates" (96–102); Steven Marx, "Teaching in the School of Donne: Metaphysical Poetry and English Composition" (103–8); Mark Reynolds, "Teaching the Metaphysical Poets in a Two-Year College" (109– 13); and Bridget Gellert Lyons, "Poetic Affinities: Metaphysical and Modern Poets" (114–19); and five essays on approaches to individual poets: Nicholas Jones, "Teaching Donne through Performance" (120–26); Richard Strier, "Songs and Sonnets Go to Church: Teaching George

Herbert" (127–31); John R. Roberts, "Richard Crashaw: The Neglected Poet" (137–43); and Heather Dubrow, "Teaching Marvell" (144–49). Concludes with a list of contributors and survey participants (150); a list of works cited (151–69); an index of works by Donne, Herbert, Vaughan, Crashaw, and Marvell mentioned in the volume (170–71); and an index of names (172–77). Only essays that contain significant comment on Donne have been annotated separately in this bibliography.

1047. Graziani, René. "Donne's 'Anniversaries' and the Beatification of Elizabeth Drury by Poetic Licence," in *The Craft and Tradition: Essays in Honour of William Blissett*, ed. H. B. de Groot and Alexander Leggatt, 59–80. Calgary: University of Calgary Press.

Maintains that "Donne's model of an anniversary is a saint's feast with its official paradox of death as birth" and argues that "[o]ne result of recognizing that Elizabeth Drury's role of saint is more than a local conceit is that it explains such features of the *Anniversaries* as the heavy accent on earthly birth as immersion in corruption and gives extra point to other celebrated images such as the phoenix, decapitation and the trumpet" (60). Examines "the birth paradox and the image of Elizabeth Drury as a saint separately" (61). Believes that Donne may have had in mind the series of anniversary poems (or *natalicia*) composed by Paulinus, Bishop of Nola (353–431), for the feast of St. Felix, poems in which "the birth-in-death of a saint's feast day [is] very prominent" (63). Shows how in *FirAn* Donne "adopted a strategy of making physical birth appear in the worst possible light, making the release of the soul at death appear extremely desirable" (64), and how in *SecAn* he envisions Elizabeth Drury as "the soul liberated and pur-

suing its proper aspirations to unobstructed powers and blisses, and reconstituted as a poetic, spiritual example to a world in process of decomposing without her" (65). Claims that Elizabeth Drury "generates *two* feasts, the anniversary of her death/birth and the christening of the world" (68). Discusses how Donne's portrayal of Elizabeth as a saint "is qualified by his Anglican beliefs which entail rejection of certain features" (70), such as attributing miracles to her.

1048. Gregory, E. R. "Vivifying the Historical Approach: Exercises in Teaching Seventeenth-Century Love Poetry," in *Approaches to Teaching the Metaphysical Poets,* ed. Sidney Gottlieb, 41–47. Modern Language Association of America, Approaches to Teaching World Literature, gen. ed. Joseph Gibaldi. New York: Modern Language Association of America.

Presents a series of classroom exercises intended to introduce students to the historical and literary background relevant to reading the seventeenth century love poets. Suggests, for instance, that by having students compose their own anti-Petrarchan sonnets, they "are able to enter imaginatively" into the anti-Petrarchan sentiments in Donne's poems "far more easily than if they had merely been told about educational practices or that Petrarchism had a vogue in the 1590s and then fell off sharply in popularity" (46).

1049. Grey, Mary. "The Core of Our Desire: Re-imaging the Trinity." *Theology* 93: 363–72.

Maintains that it is important "for feminist theology to re-image the concepts of transcendence and immanence in such a way as to break free from the sexist interpretations of patriarchal theology" (363). Says that "[n]owhere in the context of trinitarian doctrine is the blatantly violent interpretation of transcendence more exposed than in John Donne's sonnet on the Trinity" (i.e., *HSBatter*). Disparages the sonnet for using "the language of rape and seduction" (365) as a vehicle for describing Christian love and suggests that it was Donne's poem that "inspired Oppenheimer to code-name that atomic bomb 'Trinity,' "—an example of "apocalyptic destruction, heavily disguised as love." Believes, therefore, that "there is urgent need to re-image transcendence and immanence" (366).

1050. Guibbory, Achsah. "Donne, the Idea of Woman, and the Experience of Love." *JDJ* 9: 105–112.

Discusses issues of gender that are implicit in the psychology of *Air*. Believes that the shift in the speaker's attitude of "reverence" in the first half of the poem to "condescension" in the second is psychologically "quite understandable—both in terms of Renaissance thinking about women and sex, and as a distinctly male response to the experience of sexual love that is not only the product of Donne's historical moment but recognizable today." Maintains, therefore, that the last lines of the poem are "almost inevitable as a culmination of the experience of love that the poem has been describing." Sees the poem as "a lyric with a 'before and after' meditative structure" in which the speaker contrasts his experience of love before he had sexual intercourse with the lady with a newly acquired "understanding of love" (105) after intercourse. Observes that once his sexual desire has been consummated, the speaker's "entire sense of the woman" and "his relation to her" change (106). Points out that the notion that "consummated love was destructive to men" was "legitimized by medical thinking" (108) of the day and maintains that in the second half of the poem the speaker expresses "his fear

of being absorbed in and depleted by the physical and emotional experience of sexual love." Holds that "[t]he poem's movement thus shows how this man's desire for love undergoes change, a re-evaluation, as the desire for intimacy, at odds with a need to preserve individuality, gives way to a desire for separation." Claims that the poem, therefore, "expresses a gendered, male experience of love" (108). Believes that in the end "Petrarchan idealization of women and Platonic dualism of body and spirit have been replaced with a relational model that is hierarchical in its definition of the difference between women and men, body and spirit" (109), and thus the poem finally "attributes a superior purity to the male" (111).

1051. Guibbory, Achsah, ed. "Interpreting 'Aire and Angels.' " *JDJ* 9, no. 1 (special issue).

This special issue of the journal contains the following 12 essays on "Aire and Angels" (all of which have been separately annotated in this bibliography: R. V. Young, "Angels in 'Aire and Angels' " (entry 1127); Stella P. Revard, "The Angelic Messenger in 'Aire and Angels' " (entry 1095); Phoebe S. Spinrad, " 'Aire and Angels, and Questionable Shapes" (entry 1109); Michael C. Schoenfeldt, "Patriarchal Assumptions and Egalitarian Designs" (entry 1100); Judith Scherer Herz, "Resisting Mutuality" (entry 1055); John T. Shawcross, "Donne's 'Aire and Angels': Text and Context" (entry 1104); John R. Roberts, " 'Just such disparitie': The Critical Debate About 'Aire and Angels' " (entry 1098); Arnold Stein, "Interpretation: 'Aire and Angels' " (entry 1112); Albert C. Labriola, " 'This Dialogue of One': Rational Argument and Affective Discourse in Donne's 'Aire and Angels' " (entry 1068); Janel Mueller, "The Play of Difference in Donne's 'Aire and Angels' " (entry 1079);

Camille Wells Slights, "Air, Angels, and the Progress of Love" (entry 1107); and Achsah Guibbory, "Donne, the Idea of Woman, and the Experience of Love" (entry 1050).

1052. Guibbory, Achsah. " 'Oh, Let Mee Not Serve So': The Politics of Love in Donne's Elegies." *ELH* 57: 811–833. Reprinted in *Critical Essays on John Donne,* ed. Arthur F. Marotti (New York: G. K. Hall, 1994), 17–36; reprinted also in *John Donne,* ed. Andrew Mousley (Basing-stoke: Macmillan; New York: St. Martin's Press, 1999), 25–44.

Argues that in the *Elegies* love is not simply a metaphor for politics but is itself political, involving "power trans-actions between men and women" (811). Discusses Donne's "depictions of amatory relationships—his representation of the female body, sexual relations, and sexual difference—to show how he represents power relationships in love and how love repeatedly intersects public politics" (811–12), claiming that in these poems "the public world of politics and the intimacies of the private world are often inseparable." Emphasizes that there is a "persistent misogyny" in many of the *Elegies,* and rejects the notion that these cynical, often degrading poems are simply "rhetorical posturing" or "exercises in witty manipulation of literary convention" (812). Shows that in the *Elegies* "[t]ensions over submission to a female ruler are strikingly evident in Donne's representation of private love relationships" (813), and points out their "politically resonant language." Sees Donne as rejecting and mocking the conventions of courtly love through "a ritualized verbal debasement of women" (814), often by representing the female body as grotesque and often "defining the essence of woman as her genitals" (818). Argues that Donne's rejection of courtly love con-ventions, which were closely identified with Queen Elizabeth, has political implications as does his decision to write erotic elegies rather than sonnets. Maintains that even in poems of seduction Donne uses seduction to complement his strategy of debasing women because his aim is to restore male sovereignty over female sovereignty, all of which had clear political overtones in the 1590s. Believes that in the *Elegies* Donne remains "conservative, even reactionary" (826) in his views of women, and thinks that in later life Donne may have regretted having written the *Elegies* because he realized their subversive elements. Suggests that perhaps *ElBed* and *ElProg* were refused a license in 1633 not only because of their eroticism but also because of their political subtexts. Sees in the *Elegies* a "central tension" in their emphasis on male superiority and dominance, and, at the same time, female "unruliness" and "subversion of permanent male rule," and thus maintains that in them "power (whe-ther in private, interpersonal relations, or in public, social ones) is seen as radically unstable" (829).

1053. Hammond, Gerald. *Fleeting Things: English Poets and Poems, 1616–1660.* Cambridge, Mass.: Harvard University Press. 394p.

Contains no extended discussion of Donne but cites throughout examples from his poetry and prose to illustrate various critical observations. For example, notes less interest in how Donne's use of the compasses in *ValMourn* shapes our "attitudes toward love in absence" than how it gives us a "new perception of compasses," making us "less likely to look again at a pair of compasses as if they were inanimate measuring instruments" and persuading us "to see them as potentially alive, slender pieces of steel packed with emotion" (1). In another instance, deploring that "often critical discussion ignores the things and explores only the idea," points out that seventeenth century readers would have recognized in *GoodM* (l. 4) that the term "sevensleepers" was "a dialect word for a dormouse" and argues that the opening lines of the poem have more life if the reader sees "the image of lovers as a couple of mice, awake after hibernation, for whom one little room really would be an everywhere" (2). Compares and/or contrasts Donne with Jonson, Milton, Carew, Cleveland, Cartwright, and Lovelace.

1054. Hawkins, Anne Hunsacker. "A Change of Heart: The Paradigm of Regeneration in Medical and Religious Narrative." *Perspectives in Biology and Medicine* 33: 547–59.

Discusses the "regenerative paradigm," which is a "belief that it is possible to undergo a process of transformation so profound as to be experienced as a kind of death of the 'old self' and rebirth to a new and very different self" (547), a process that "transcends cultural boundaries" and is expressed "in varied literary forms in different eras and cultures." Points out how spiritual autobiographies of the seventeenth century are "strikingly similar" to pathographies of the twentieth century. Comments briefly on *Devotions* as a narrative that deals with "physical illness as a means for spiritual growth" but which "also insistently interprets the physical dimension as a metaphor for the spiritual" (549).

1055. Herz, Judith Scherer. "Resisting Mutuality." *JDJ* 9: 27–32.

Responds to R. V. Young's "Angels in 'Aire and Angels'" (entry 1127) as well as to responses to Young's essay by Stella P. Revard (entry 1095), Phoebe S. Spinrad (entry 1109), and Michael C. Schoenfeldt (entry 1100).

Maintains that there is "hardly a word" in *Air* "that cannot be read upside down or inside out," noting that "there is nothing constant in this text." Sees the poem as "the parodic playing off of conflicting apprehensions of divine and phantasmic love" but believes that the textual spaces "remain distinct, unresolvable, whatever glossary or archive we employ for the text's (necessary) elucidation" (27). Disagrees, therefore, with Young that historical and philological investigation will resolve the difficulties in the poem, insisting that "how we read, indeed what it is that we read, remains unsettled and unsettling" (28). Concludes that *Air* "may be inscribed ideologically in the putative disparity between man's active and woman's responsive love" but rejects the notion that "it valorizes this as a celebration of mutuality" (30).

1056. Hester, M. Thomas. "The Titles/ Headings of Donne's English Epigrams." *ANQ* 3: 3–11.

Acknowledges that the manuscript titles of Donne's 23 epigrams may not be his, but maintains that it is useful "to test the propriety of a title by using the poem's strategies or wit as a guide." Argues that such an approach cannot "determine whether any of the manuscript titles are Donne's" but "it can suggest the most likely, the most perceptive, or the most instructive titles in the manuscripts for the epigrams, it can indicate how some Renaissance readers interpreted the poems, and it can provide data about the provenance and state of the many Donne manuscripts." Points out that four of the epigrams simply "move the name of the satirical epigrammatist's victim to the head of the poem" and that "none of these titles is essential to the display or enactment of the poet's wit"; six have titles that "identify the subject of the poem which does not appear verbatim in the poem itself" and are, therefore, "essential," since "omitting them modifies the reader's experience" and forces the reader "to surmise the subject being described" (3); seven "create more troublesome choices" because "the titles of all seven are frequently omitted in the manuscripts overall" (4) and "because of their interpretative or designatory character" (5); and a final group "creates the most interesting problems, because of both their manuscript history and the possibility that they offer titles that Donne may have composed." Maintains that "[t]hese are the only titles that offer interpretative guidelines for the poems, or the only ones that accentuate wittily the central play of the poem they head" (6). Believes that since the titles "remain problematical" (9), it is best not to invent new titles but to assign "headings" that are found in the manuscripts since many of them "bespeak an understanding of the wit and dexterity of the poems so succinctly that one is tempted to claim they are Donne's" (10).

1057. Hester, M. Thomas. " 'This cannot be said': A Preface to the Reader of Donne's Lyrics." *C&L* 39: 365–85.

Discusses how Donne uses the recusant art of equivocation as a witty strategy in his poems to comment on current theological or political issues and to express covertly his Catholic sympathies. Discusses, in particular, the "strategy of denial—or stratagem of deniability—in the love lyrics . . . in order to offer a 'preface' to a reading of how and why those works tell us how and why they *will not tell*" (368). Maintains that Donne's "dramatic dialogues about human sexuality frame a speaker who uses the terms and arguments of the current Recusant position concerning the hermeneutics of the Sacraments and a protesting, scornful auditor who is given those of the current Protestant position"

(373), and shows how "the doctrinal vocabulary used to present his outrageous metonymies transfers the terms identified with the warring parties in the controversy about the Sacrament and the government's statutory responses in that war to the speaker's defense of and the auditor's response to his (libertine) amatory creed of sexual incarnation" (374). Comments in some detail on *Canon, Ecst,* and especially *Flea,* the latter described as "[t]he most outrageous, the wittiest, and the most thorough application of the terms of the 'currant' debate in which Catholics asserted that the 'mysteries' of divine love were to be read not only in the 'booke' of Scripture but also in the 'body' of the Eucharist" (377). Suggests that the Elizabethan policy of persecuting those who supported Catholicism might explain why Donne, wishing not to become a casualty, chose to remain a manuscript poet who limited the circulation of his poems to a select coterie, and also might explain why, "even after we uncover the striking theological lexicon embedded in the hyperbolic conceits of his poems, it remains difficult to 'decipher' the precise spiritual and political beliefs of their inventor" (382).

1058. Hodge, Robert. "Literature and History," in *Literature as Discourse: Textual Strategies in English and History,* 201–36. Baltimore: Johns Hopkins University Press.

In a study based on social semiotics, regrets the separation of English and history in schools and universities and presents "reasons for the separation as well as strategies for overcoming it" (201). Comments on Terry Sherwood's *Fulfilling the Circle: A Study of John Donne's Thought* (1984) and William Zunder's *The Poetry of John Donne: Literature and Culture in the Jacobean Period* (1982) to show why historians do not value literary criticism and scholarship. Urges literary critics to make better use of literary texts in their work, noting, as an example, that "Donne's poetry, along with his other writings, could provide evidence for attitudes to love, marriage, and religion, themes that social historians are very much interested in" (223), but warns that when using literary texts one must be aware of their "complex modality" (225). Suggests ways in which English and history "could be reconstituted to become parts of a single historical enterprise," using Donne as an example to show "how he can be read not as a canonical poet but as the focus for a set of documents in a history of attitudes towards love, marriage and the family in seventeenth century England" (225). Examines "the ways in which his semiotic position was established by contemporaries" (226), discusses the Lothian portrait, and presents a transformational analysis of *Canon* to show that it "announces a revolution in gender-relations which goes beyond customary practice in the period" (231).

1059. Holdsworth, R. V. "The Death of Death in Donne's Holy Sonnets 10." *N&Q*, n.s. 37: 183.

Suggests that, in addition to 1 Corinthians 15:26, 54, most often cited by editors as Donne's source for his assertion in the conclusion of *HSDeath* that death will die, he may have had in mind Hosea 13:14. Notes that, "[i]f Donne had this verse in mind he must be remembering either the Geneva Bible of 1560 . . . or the Bishop's Bible of 1568, for instead of 'death, I will be thy death' the Authorised Version (1611) has 'death, I will be thy plagues.'" Points out that "[a]ll three bibles provide a cross-reference directing readers of the better-known passage in 1 Corinthians to the verse in Hosea" (183).

1060. Hopkins, David, ed. *English Poetry: A Poetic Record, from Chaucer to Yeats.* London: Routledge. xii, 269p.

A collection of "poetic responses by English poets to one another's work" (ix). Reproduces eight poems to or about Donne—with notes on each (117–24), written by Jonson, Richard Corbet, Lord Herbert of Cherbury, Carew, Sidney Godolphin, Dryden, Coleridge, Hartley Coleridge, and John Clare.

1061. Idziak, Malgorzata. "John Donne and the Seventeenth Century Maps." *Studia Anglica Posnaniensia* (Posnan) 24: 37–45.

Discusses parallels between Donne's poems and "the design" of sixteenth and seventeenth century maps and "considers the implications of these similarities for our reading of Donne's poetry" (37). Comments on how *Sickness* "reminds one of the maps which had their margins richly decorated with miniature paintings representing the story of redemption," and points out how the poem "develops the motif of a mystical journey" and gives an "account of a mystical expansion of the self" (39). Observes how in *ElProg* Donne "assumes the role of a cosmographer exploring the body of his beloved lady and describing in detail the perils which await those who uncunningly set out on the journey from the wrong harbour," and notes the prevalence of "cartographic metaphors" in the poem (40). Discusses Donne's use of the cordiform map in *GoodM* and his notion that one who draws a map tames an unknown region in *FirAn, ElBed,* and *SunRis.* Suggests also the use of conventions of seventeenth century cartography in *ValMourn.*

1062. Jones, Nicholas. "Teaching Donne through Performance," in *Approaches to Teaching the Metaphysical Poets,* ed. Sidney Gottlieb, 120–26. Modern Language Association of America, Approaches to Teaching World Literature, gen. ed. Joseph Gibaldi. New York: Modern Language Association of America.

Recommends, as a teaching technique, classroom performance of Donne's poems, maintaining that from this exercise "students can learn to overcome the initial difficulties of syntax, meter, and semantics [in the poems]; can explore their rich poetic structure, discovering possibilities for otherwise-ignored turns of phrase and changes of tone; and can present to the class a finished reading that vividly plants the words of the poem in the ears and in the minds of all in the class" (120). Illustrates the technique by commenting on several of Donne's love poems, but primarily on *LovGrow*. Explains how a performance of *Relic* enhanced an understanding of the poem.

1063. Kay, Dennis. *Melodious Tears: The Funeral Elegy from Spenser to Milton.* Oxford: Clarendon Press. 296p.

Discusses the development of the funeral elegy from Spenser to Milton and claims that "just as the sonnet was an aggregative form in which practitioners defined their individuality against their predecessors, so with the elegist" (4). Chapter 4, "Donne's Funeral Poems and *Anniversaries*" (91–123), observes that "[t]he importance of Donne's *Anniversaries* in the history of the English elegy is immense" and that "an entire elegiac tradition . . . derived from them" (91). Maintains, in fact, that "[f]rom 1611 Donne was the poet of the *Anniversaries*" and "[t]hereafter when he came to compose funeral verses he did so . . . as the acknowledged master—indeed the inventor—of the form" (116). Considers Donne's career as an elegist chronologically to show that "his funeral verses—most particularly those composed during the years

1609–14 when funeral elegies apparently constituted his major poetic occupation—represent a development from faltering imitation to generic innovation of the highest order of sophistication and accomplishment" (91). Comments on *Sorrow, Ham, BoulRec, BoulNar, Mark, Har,* and especially the two *Anniversaries* to show how Donne gradually constructed "an idiom which might accommodate praise of the dead both with general philosophical and religious meditations and with dramatically enacted consolation." Points out how Donne's funeral verses "constitute a highly significant development" of the elegy and how he "enlarged the repertoire of elegy, by moving towards increasingly inclusive and reflective forms and away from the immediate circumstances of death and burial." Emphasizes that "the followers of Donne had before them vernacular models that were simultaneously innovative and based on reputable classical precedent" and "[t]hey had a new model of the poet's role." Says that, "[l]ike Spenser, Donne gave a voice to a generation" but that, "[u]nlike him, he achieved this initially—and primarily—through his funeral verse" (123). Chapter 5, "Elegies on the Death of Prince Henry" (124–203), discusses the ingenuity and intellectual complexity of *Henry* and maintains that it shows "the way the flexible, musical, compendious form of Donne's commemorative writings increasingly resembles the form of the sermons he was soon to write" (193). Maintains that in the poem Donne "seems to have used the elegy as an opportunity to particularize the general considerations of the earlier pieces" and "dramatized a process of consolation that was both an education in individual meditation and understanding, and a panegyric inseparable from a particular event," similar to the "intensity of particular application" found later in *Har* (196). Holds that "[f]rom 1613 the elegy was a canonically laureate form: but it was also established as poetry of social gesture, as a medium for self-examination, and as a form in which writers could learn to imitate, recognize, and investigate the elements of their art" (203). Discusses the influence of Spenser and Sidney on Donne as an elegist and comments on his influence on a great number of poets, especially Thomas Campion, Edward Herbert, Henry Goodyer, Chapman, Jonson, John Webster, Henry Burton, John Cleveland, Richard Niccols, Cyril Tourneur, Thomas Heywood, John Davies, William Drummond, George Garrard, and Milton.

1064. Kesler, R. L. "The Idealization of Women: Morphology and Change in Three Renaissance Texts." *Mosaic* 23, no. 2: 107–26.

Argues that the emergence of the sonnet form, "while locally assigning 'spiritual,' 'natural,' or 'holistic' values to women, worked consistently to undermine both the efficiency and relevance of those ideals, offering in their place its own mode of conceptualization, based in literacy and the compartmentalization and repeatability of its own form" (107). Maintains furthermore that the sonnet sequence functioned "to segment, regularize, and re-assemble its perceptual field by the imposition of its own structure, breaking 'reality' into the individual units of the individual sonnets and allowing the re-integration of the sequence only out of these pieces," and that "[w]ithin the sonnet, the 'scattering' or fragmentation of women became the emblem for this process" (108). Maintains that, in time, "woman's role in the sonnet became increasingly irrelevant" and "she suffered the final indignity of no longer being

worth dividing," which finally resulted in works like *Robinson Crusoe,* in which the main character is "primarily absorbed in a process of self-definition" and is defined not in term of nature but "in terms of his mastery and control over it" (117). Says that "Donne's earlier lyric poems mark an intermediate point in this process," noting that "[w]hile a Donne poem 'talked' to the woman (or rather lectured to her), its primary object of description was not the woman at all, but the poem's argument, its vehicle . . ., and the celebrated structure of the metaphysical conceit" (117–18). Maintains that in a Donnean love poem the speaker becomes "defined by a process of egotistical self-dramatization, within which 'the woman' serves only as an admiring and respectful audience" (118). Claims that *FirAn* is "about fragmentation itself as a recognized and pervasive condition that exiled such former ideals to the ultimate peripheries of experience." Sees the poem as "simultaneously experimental and retrospective, an attempt to balance its own compulsive 'modern' tendencies toward analysis against a nostalgia for unity and the more holistic representational structure of the past" (118). Claims that "[w]hat lay behind Donne was the 'ideality' of the sonnets and an at least nominal role for women" and "what lay before him was another order of poetry and description all together, an order in which the male subject was free to define himself more totally within his isolation, beyond the sight of women and beyond the necessity of their symbolic involvement" (123). Concludes that "the placement and displacement of the image of the idealized woman in Renaissance poetry was nothing more than the cycling of one particular symbolic function from centrality toward marginalization, as the structural context supporting it underwent a process of change" (125).

1065. Kinney, Arthur F. "Confronting Nightmares: The Dalhousie Manuscripts." *Rev* 12: 213–27.

Reviews *The First and Second Dalhousie Manuscripts: Poems and Prose by John Donne and Others: A Facsimile Edition*, ed. Ernest W. Sullivan, II (1988) (entry 931). Comments on the publication history of Donne's poems and on problems associated with editing them. Describes the Dalhousie manuscripts, comments on their history and discovery, and notes their importance for the study of Donne, concluding that they also clearly "provide ample evidence of the importance of transcribing and studying miscellanies generally" (225).

1066. Kishimoto, Yoshitaka. *Donne to sono Ippa: Shi no Ronri to Tenkai.* [Donne and His Followers: The Logic and Development of Poetry]. Osaka: Sogensha. 221p.

The preface, "Donne's Originality" (7–11), describes Donne's distinctive uses of logic and metaphor. Chapter 1, "Spenser, Marlowe, and Donne" (14–45), contrasts *EpLin* with Spenser's *The Epithalamion*, pointing out how Donne uses bold and obscene metaphors whereas Spenser uses moderate and restrained ones. Also compares *Bait* with Marlowe's "The Passionate Shepherd to his love" and with Raleigh's "The Nymph's Reply to the Shepherd," noting the realistic attitude and twisted logic in Donne's poem. Chapter 2, "Donne's Love Poetry" (48–134), comments on the logical development and intellectual handling of metaphors in *ElBed, Ind, Flea, Prim, Dream, LovAlch, SunRis, GoodM, ValMourn, Canon,* and *Noct.* Chapter 3, "Religious Poetry" (136–57), comments on five of the *Holy Sonnets* and *Father,* suggesting that these poems are successful when

Donne presents his own sincere feelings and does not simply attempt to express Christian doctrine.

1067. Kusunose, Toshihiko. *John Donne no Sekkyo: Henreki to Fukkatsu* [John Donne's Sermons: Pilgrimage and Resurrection]. Kyoto: Apollonsha, iii, 206p.

Chapter 1 considers the 16 years from Donne's ordination in 1615 to his death in 1631, dividing them into three periods: 23 January to 20 October 1621; 22 November 1621 to 27 March 1625; and 3 April 1625 to 31 March 1631. Chapter 2 discusses the consecutive sermons preached at Lincoln's Inn in 1618. Chapter 3 traces Donne's inner conflict till his ordination, examining *Paradoxes and Problems, The Courtier's Library, Biathanatos, Pseudo-Martyr, Ignatius,* and *Essays in Divinity.*

1068. Labriola, Albert C. " 'The Dialogue of One': Rational Argument and Affective Discourse in Donne's 'Aire and Angels.' " *JDJ* 9: 77–84.

Examines how Donne in *Air* playfully adapts the explanations of angels given by medieval scholastic philosophers, especially their use of "analogy by predication" (77), and comments on Donne's witty commingling of the sacred and profane in the poem. Shows how "the lady who is the angelic subject becomes by the analogy of predication more accessible and knowable" and how the speaker "creates a sensible presence from an angelic nothingness." Maintains that "[t]he speaker is challenged to fashion his beloved so that she is at once more corporeal than angelic nothingness and yet more rarefied than a sensible presence" and that "[h]e meets the challenge by predicating an analogy that likens her to the manifestation of an angel in condensed air, whereby the form and some details of the figure become evident but full material presence does not" (78). Observes that "[t]he argument that spiritual love may manifest itself corporeally is developed by implication, against a frame of reference involving the love of the godhead for humankind" that results in "wordplay and the double entendre in the poem, which result in predicated analogies of coarse and obscene wit that parody the sexual enactment of the mystery of divine love." Maintains, therefore, that *Air* is "outrageously blasphemous" (79), and proceeds to discuss the promiscuous punning and playful analogies in the poem. Concludes that "[t]he witty tour de force that ends the poem occurs as the speaker by analogy imparts to himself both the angelic and sensible natures that he attributed to his beloved," and that finally the speaker "likens himself to the angel of the Annunciation, whose discourse and interaction with Mary are the sensible signs of otherwise mysterious activity" (82).

1069. Labriola, Albert C. "Iconographic Perspectives on Seventeenth-Century Religious Poetry," in *Approaches to Teaching the Metaphysical Poets,* ed. Sidney Gottlieb, 61–67. Modern Language Association of America, Approaches to Teaching World Literature, gen. ed. Joseph Gibaldi. New York: Modern Language Association of America.

Maintains that it is important for students to examine Christian iconography in order "to regain the sensibility of the Middle Ages, the Renaissance, and the seventeenth century" and comments on how "[v]isual analogues provide the context and establish the outlook for interpreting the poetry of John Donne, George Herbert, and Richard Crashaw" (61). Discusses, for instance, how the traditional iconography of the Annunciation and the Resurrection elucidates Donne's divine poems, especially the *Holy Sonnets.* Maintains that the iconographical

approach shows students that the imagery of metaphysical poetry is not obscure but traditional—"indeed, conventional"—and that thus they "conclude that the ingenuity of such poetry is attributable to the synthesis and the interrelation of conventional images, resulting in an enlarged range of associations and a multiplicity of meanings" (67).

1070. Lewis, David. "Drama in Donne and Herbert," in *The Metaphysical Poets,* ed. Linda Cookson and Bryan Loughrey, 98–108. Longman Critical Essays. Harlow, Eng.: Longman Group.

Maintains that Donne "was able to synthesise the essence of [Elizabethan] drama" into his poetry and discusses dramatic elements in his poetry, especially the use of a range of personae (the cynical lover, the constant lover, the unrequited lover, the mutual lover, the embittered lover), the creation of settings or dramatic situations, and the employment of extravagant and explosive language and passionate intensity similar to that of contemporary plays. Suggests that the "dramatic concept, impact, and the actual use of language" at the end of *ElFatal* are "remarkably similar" (104) to lines from Shakespeare's *Romeo and Juliet.* Compares and contrasts Donne and Herbert as dramatic poets and suggests that, as readers of Donne and Herbert, "we are cast in the role of the audience, and as in a theatre we participate in the drama by responding to the voice, and [by] becoming caught up in the action or situation" (108).

1071. Low, Anthony. "Donne and the Reinvention of Love." *ELR* 20: 465–86.

Argues that in his later love poetry Donne was "a chief actor and influence in what may be called the 're-invention of love,' from something essentially social and feudal to something essentially private and modern" and maintains that "he accomplished this reinvention partly through a brilliant and unexpected redirection of the communal" (466). Surveys Donne's changing attitudes toward love, beginning with the *Satyres,* and points out that in them "sexual love is reduced to a subordinate but fully congruent place in a universally grim, treacherous, self-seeking society, a society that lacks true community in its legal and political relationships as in its writings, since the chief concern of its members is personal gain." Observes that in the *Elegies* Donne "views love and sexuality as matters for Ovidian game-playing" (470) and that, "[a]t best, it gives the lover brief pleasure and a sense of superior cleverness for having overcome obstacles, out-machiaveled other schemers, and bested rivals" and, "at worst and more predictably, his schemes collapse and his pleasures turn to self-loathing and disgust" (470–71). Maintains, however, that it was Donne's courtship of and marriage to Ann More—and the resultant dashing of his hopes for preferment—that "drove him to a new kind of love poetry that came to dominate English and Western culture" (472). Believes that Donne "was among the earliest and most powerful proponents of love as shelter and defense against the world" (473). Comments on "the influence of community and festivity on Donne's invention of a private and sacred love" (480) and sees him as "anticipating the whole Romantic complex of individualism, self-assertion, and 'natural supernaturalism'" (483). Maintains that "[w]hat Donne proposes in his most idealized love-lyrics is a union between lovers that is essentially communal, sacred, and religious in a certain sense, but neither Christian nor social" (485). Concludes that Donne's later love poems show that "somehow the individual can cut himself loose from the conventions of the social order and instead construct, on the basis of his private experience, a psychological space within which he can safely live, love, and discover new truths of feeling" (486).

1072. Lyons, Bridget Gellert. "Poetic Affinities: Metaphysical and Modern Poets," in *Approaches to Teaching the Metaphysical Poets,* ed. Sidney Gottlieb, 114–19. Modern Language Association of America, Approaches to Teaching World Literature, gen. ed. Joseph Gibaldi. New York: Modern Language Association of America.

Explains a course designed "for senior honors majors in English that paired major poets of the seventeenth century with twentieth-century poets" and "was organized around four pairs of poets: Donne and Eliot, Jonson and Yeats, Herbert and Frost, and Marvell and Stevens" (114). Discusses specifically how Donne and Eliot were compared and contrasted in the class and how each was seen as "a poetic innovator in his time" (115), and mentions specific issues of style and content discussed in individual Donne poems. Suggests that "the comparative format had the virtue of heightening the students' awareness of literary history and locating some issues of style and self-presentation common to the two periods" (119).

1073. Mackenzie, Donald, ed. *The Metaphysical Poets*. The Critics Debate, gen. ed. Michael Scott. Houndmills: Macmillan Education. 128p.

Explains in the general editor's preface (7–8) that the purpose of the series is to assist students by delineating "various critical approaches to specific literary texts," by helping them "come to terms with the variety of criticism," and by introducing them "to further reading on the subject and to a fuller evaluation of a particular text by illustrating the way it has been approached in a number of contexts" (7). "Part

One: Survey" (15–44) surveys criticism on the metaphysical poets, discussing the work of three major critics before 1921 (Johnson, Coleridge, and T. S. Eliot), followed by an account of the criticism written after 1921, which contains a section on Donne (31–34). "Part Two: Appraisal" (45–117) rejects the notion that Donne founded a "school" but maintains he did establish a style, and discusses characteristics of Donne's style and how that style was adapted by later poets. A section on Donne (63–79) focuses on his poetic innovations, his mastery of rhetorical syntax, and his "recurrent impulse towards the ideal of a centred stability and seclusion" (65). Comments specifically on the *Elegies,* especially their Ovidian indebtedness; discusses the *Songs and Sonets,* calling them "the most *exhilarating* body of love poetry in English" and commenting on their "range of moods and stances in love" (70), their intensity and wit, and their experimentation with lyrical forms and stanzaic patterns; and comments on Donne's religious poetry, highlighting its uneven quality. Thereafter follow discussions of Herbert, Vaughan, Crashaw, and Marvell (79–114) and a conclusion (115–17) in which metaphysical poetry is characterized as often extravagant and strange but "a poetry where extravagance can be disciplined into acrobatic play, a poetry offering at its best, the most civilised and resourceful body of lyric in English" (117). Concludes with a bibliography and suggestions for further reading (118–25) and an index (126–28).

1074. Makurenkova, S. "Tvorchestvo Shekspira i Danna: v sisteme khdozhestvennyx" [The Works of Shakespeare and Donne within the Aesthetic Framework of Coleridge]. *Shekspirovskie chtenia:* 166–76.

In an effort to introduce literary criticism on Donne to a Russian audience, examines Coleridge's perception of Donne in reference to his views on Shakespeare. Focuses initially on Coleridge's use of two terms, "homoiusian" (similar to) and "homousian" (of the same substance), which derive from fourth century debates about the relationship of Christ to God the Father, explains the meanings of these terms, and points out that Coleridge thought that Donne was similar to but not of the same "substance" as Shakespeare. Surveys Coleridge's criticism of both Donne and Shakespeare and maintains that although the two are similar in their use of wit, imagery, conceit, and paradox, the distinguishing feature of Shakespeare's work is its dramatic nature. Concludes that Coleridge's views on Donne and Shakespeare within the framework of the homoiusian/homousian debate allows for new ways to examine both poets.

1075. Martin, Bernard. *The Poetry of John Donne.* Horizon Studies in Literature, gen. ed. Penny Gay. Sydney: Sydney University Press in association with Oxford University Press Australia. viii, 72p.

The general preface (iii–iv) explains that the series is intended to aid high school and undergraduate students and their teachers "by offering detailed, close analysis [of several of Donne's poems] allied to an overview informed by recent trends in criticism and scholarship" (iii). The author's foreword (vii–viii) notes that this study "deals with a small selection from Donne's poems and aims mainly at explication." Chapter 1, "A Most Laborious Student" (1–6), and Chapter 2, "A Great Writer of Conceited Verses" (7–18), discuss briefly Donne's life, his intellectual background, and general characteristics of his poetry, particularly his uses of wit and conceits.

Chapter 3, "A Great Visiter of Ladies" (19–23), comments on Donne as a love poet in general. Chapter 4, "Sexuality and Love" (24–34), analyzes *Flea* and *SunRis*. Chapter 5, "A Valediction: Forbidding Mourning" (35–47), and Chapter 6, "The Canonization" (48–57), present critical readings of the two poems. Chapter 7, "Contraryes Meet in One" (58–67), comments on the *Holy Sonnets,* especially *HSBatter,* and discusses *Sickness.* Concludes with a list of further readings (68–72).

1076. Marx, Steven. "Teaching in the School of Donne: Metaphysical Poetry and English Composition," in *Approaches to Teaching the Metaphysical Poets,* ed. Sidney Gottlieb, 103–8. Modern Language Association of America, Approaches to Teaching World Literature, gen. ed. Joseph Gibaldi. New York: Modern Language Association of America.

Suggests ways that the study of the metaphysical poets can help students write better English. Maintains that the study of diction and style "is uniquely enriched by the study of metaphysical poetry," and that "an approach to literary interpretation through the rhetorical topics of diction and the use of the dictionary can lead students to original critical insights, specifically into the metaphysical poets and into other literature as well" (103). Comments specifically on how *Canon* is used to teach the importance of choosing the right word, the nature and uses of ambiguity, the use of figurative language, and how to use the *OED.* Notes how a student outlined "the arrangement of contraries created by connotative diction" in *Flea* and suggests that the student's "investigation of Donne's microscopic subtlety" inspired her "to compose with analogous precision" (107).

1077. McKenzie, D. F. "Speech-Manuscript-Print." *LCUT* 20, nos. 1–2: 87–108.

Discusses how speech, manuscript, and print were complementary modes of expression in the seventeenth century and comments on how Donne belongs primarily to a manuscript culture. Observes that Peter Beal in his *Index of English Literary Manuscripts* (entry 80) points out "the existence of some 4,000 seventeenth-century manuscript copies of individual poems by Donne" and that these probably represent "only a fraction of the number once in existence" (96). Notes that Donne did not intend to publish *Biathanatos,* so "its posthumous printing in 1646 is no evidence of some new liberal dispensation" (97). Suggests that "the reluctance of many to speak or write in type may well have been, not fear of the censor (as is too readily claimed), but a psychological response to technological change" (109).

1078. Mohr, Mary Hull. "Lucy Harington and John Donne: Reinterpreting a Relationship," in *A Humanist's Legacy: Essays in Honor of John Christian Bale,* ed. Dennis M. Jones, 49–62. Decorah, Iowa: Luther College.

Discusses the verse epistles addressed to the Countess of Bedford between 1608 and 1610 to show how the relationship between Donne and the countess matured from patronage to friendship. Observes how the letters that "started out as a bid for favor developed into friendship" and how "elaborate compliment changed to advice." Points out that "[a]lthough there is no evidence that Donne and the Countess were close from 1611–1614, Donne was surprised that she could not in 1614 wholeheartedly support his decision to take Holy Orders." Suggests that the reason "[w]hy she could not is explained by her understanding of the role of the clergy, an understanding revealed in the epistle dedicatory of Nicholas Byfield, to whom the Countess did give patronage at approximately the same time as Donne made his decision to enter the church." Maintains, however, that Donne's decision "did not cause a permanent rift" between them, that they "continued to see each other," and that the countess finally "seems to have accepted his decision," although "their relationship must have been tempered by his role as clergyman" (59).

1079. Mueller, Janel. "The Play of Difference in Donne's 'Aire and Angels.'" *JDJ* 9: 85–94.

Offers a feminist reading of *Air*. Identifies the speaker's anxiety: "the Self, sexually magnetized toward union with an Other, feels its boundaries loosening and thus comes to fear losing either its own sense of identity or the bliss of union." Believes that "[b]y playing with and playing out verbal formulations of difference—and whatever difference these can be made to make in his relation with his beloved—this speaker strives to regain self-control," which hinges on his "achieving a controlled articulation of what this love means, mainly to him but by extension to his beloved" (85). Highlights "the significance of the gap that widens between asserted control and manifest indeterminacy as the speaker pursues his discursive play with difference" (86). Argues how "[p]laying upon and beyond Petrarchan tropes for representing the differential roles of male and female," the speaker in the second stanza "performs an inversion on his earlier situation: she dispossessed him of himself, his love now possesses him of her." Maintains, therefore, that "[w]ithin these poetic confines, the imperious rhetoric registers a triumph of self-repossession" and the speaker

"asserts his control and his prerogatives for action" (88). Suggests that the poem is, in fact, "a Renaissance sonnet sequence, albeit a minimal instance of a sequence, in containing just two sonnets" (89), the second a response to and finally reversal of the first by asserting male superiority. Concludes that the speaker's claim that the "particular differential construction of sex and gender" he enunciates will always be so "is reduced when readers candidly confront the gaps and obfuscations which authoritative utterance, for all its bravado, repeatedly suffers in this poem" and when they "compute the costs of such rhetoric to all of the parties involved" (92).

1080. Nishiyama, Yoshio. *Yuutsu no jidai: Bungou John Donne no kiseki* [A Melancholic Age: The Course of Life of a Great Writer, John Donne]. Tokyo: Shouhakusha. 329p.

Chapter 1 presents a background study of London in Donne's time. Chapter 2 discusses portraits of Donne and his view of death. Chapter 3 traces the life of Donne as a law student. Chapter 4 gives a detailed explication of the valediction poems and *Twick*. Chapter 5 comments on the tradition of sermons Donne inherited from contemporary preachers and discusses a sermon Donne preached to the members of the Company of the Virginian Plantation. An appendix presents a consideration of Donne's wit.

1081. Norbrook, David. "The Monarchy of Wit and the Republic of Letters: Donne's Politics," in *Soliciting Interpretation: Literary Theory and Seventeenth-Century English Poetry,* ed. Elizabeth D. Harvey and Katharine Eisaman Maus, 3–36. Chicago: University of Chicago Press.

Examines Donne's views on monarchy and regards as incomplete the view of earlier scholars who claimed that Donne was politically and religiously conservative. Argues that Donne's relation to the Caroline establishment was not "as singlemindedly careerist and sycophantic as is often assumed" (26). Points out, however, that Donne had little room to maneuver independently in a world of courtly power. Claims that the view of Donne as a monarchist and High Anglican poet stems from Walton's biography and was continued on through the New Criticism. Says that New Historicists emphasize the difficulty of Donne's sustaining opposition to the dominant power structure. Observes that Donne "constantly seeks to become part of a society from which he feels alienated" while, at the same time, "he desires also to maintain a critical distance" (6). Traces Donne's religious and political views to show how they do or do not make him a conservative.

1082. Ober, William B. "John Donne as a Patient: *Devotions Upon Emergent Occasions*." *L&M* 9: 21–37.

Discusses *Devotions* from a medical perspective. Speculates that Donne's illness was likely caused by "epidemic louse-born typhus fever" (25). Glosses the text to show how Donne reacted to his illness, stressing that, although not completely unconcerned with physical matters, "Donne's mind focused on his soul and his illness as a spiritual experience" (26). Maintains that Donne "viewed his illness as a proper visitation from God" and "accepted it with good cheer because it was a sign of salvation" (27). Examines the role of the physician in the *Devotions,* the emotional tensions Donne experienced as a patient, and the treatment prescribed for his recovery. Speculates that "writing the *Devotions* during his convalescence was therapeutic for Donne and also gave him much pleasure" (35).

1083. Osmond, Rosalie. *Mutual Accusation: Seventeenth-Century Body and Soul Dialogues in Their Literary and Theological Context.* Toronto: University of Toronto Press. xiii, 284p.

Chapter 6, "Aspects of Body and Soul in Seventeenth-Century Poetry" (115–38), discusses Donne's view of love in his poems, which "derives from the Aristotelian concept of the body as the instrument of the soul, enabling the soul to exercise its faculties." Maintains that "no other writer has examined the body/soul relationship in love with such a combination of cerebral reflection and bodily passion" (116). Points out that, although he asserts "the primacy of spiritual love," even "a spiritual love that is able to exist independently of the physical," he also insists on "the importance of the body." Briefly comments on *Air* and *Ecst* to show how Donne combines Aristotelianism and Christian theology to support his view that, "[i]f the essence of love is spiritual, its actuality, on earth, can only be expressed through the body" (117). Chapter 7, "Body and Soul Analogies" (139–60), comments on Donne's literal and figurative uses of the terms "body" and "flesh" and his use of the body/soul relationship in the creation of ingenious analogies. Points out, for instance, how Donne sees "the body as a house of clay, describes the bones as timbers, the walls as flesh, the windows as eyes"; how he sees the grave as "the house of the body" (141); and how he sees "the external elements of worship" as analogous to the body.

1084. Patterson, Annabel. "All Donne," in *Soliciting Interpretation: Literary Theory and Seventeenth-Century English Poetry,* ed. Elizabeth D. Harvey and Katharine Eisaman Maus, 37–67. Chicago: University of Chicago Press.

Examines a nonliterary meeting Donne attended probably in 1610 that is recorded in a Latin poem to show how "a writer subsequently canonized may be resituated in his original environment" and also "how 'literary' assumptions may be profitably modified by cultural history" (37). Believes that unfortunately much of Donne's "sociohistorical environment has been disregarded in critical practice as having no explanatory value" for understanding Donne "the literary entity" (39). Reviews the limitations of Donne's recent biographers from R. C. Bald (1970) to John Carey (1981) as well as critics, especially New Critics, and wishes that "we might be able to look at the whole Donne and see him not as a monster of ambition but as a mass of contradictions" (42). Disputes the contention of those editors who reject Donne's authorship of *Citizen* arguing that the poem was written "when Donne could not himself decide between Jack and Dr. Donne" (47). Sees *Pseudo-Martyr, Ignatius,* and *Eclog* as reflecting Donne's "self-division and equivocation" (51). Examines the doubts and divided opinions of the 1614 Parliament at which Donne was present as an important context for understanding Donne. Says that "when Donne eventually succumbed to James's insistence that he take orders, it may have been less out of naked ambition than out of despair for any secular change" (60).

1085. Patterson, Annabel. "Teaching against the Tradition," in *Approaches to Teaching the Metaphysical Poets,* ed. Sidney Gottlieb, 35–40. Modern Language Association of America, Approaches to Teaching World Literature, gen. ed. Joseph Gibaldi. New York: Modern Language Association of America.

Patterson rejects the notion that there is a tradition of metaphysical poetry and explains how she engenders skepticism in her students about such labels. Says she introduces Donne by discussing *Flea* because students are amused by its wit and also "see instantly that there is nothing particularly learned or difficult or esoteric about it, that the central metaphor is, on the contrary, bodily and mundane" (40–41). Maintains that the tensions the poem raises "can be put to good use in a corporate attempt to decide why the poem engages and divides its audience and in what its outrageousness consists" (40).

1086. Perrine, Laurence. "Explicating Donne: 'The Apparition' and 'The Flea.'" *CollL* 17: 1–20.

Maintains that *Appar* and *Flea,* but especially *Appar,* "have been badly misread by an astonishing number of scholars and critics" and suggests, when examined together, "each may throw light upon the other" (1). Through a close reading of each poem shows that both "present an often-rejected lover taking a new and 'far-out' approach to winning a woman's favors"; that "in tone the two poems are radically different," *Appar* being "dark and menacing" and *Flea* being "light and playful"; and that the speaker of *Appar* "attempts to attain his goals by threats" while the speaker of *Flea* hopes to obtain his objective "by obviously specious reasoning" (7). Maintains that in *Appar* the speaker "attempts to win his lady's favors by maximizing her fears of what will happen to her if she refuses," while the speaker in *Flea* "attempts to win them by minimizing his lady's fears of what will happen if she consents" (7–8). Concludes that the speaker's methods in *Appar* are "ingenious and sinister" while those of the speaker in *Flea* are "ingenious and witty" (8). An appendix (8–15) presents an annotated list of commentaries on *Appar,* arranged chronologically, that shows that the "prevailing interpretation" is that "the central emotion expressed is *hate* or anger and that the speaker's motivation is *revenge*" (8), a position rejected in the preceding analysis of the poem.

1087. Peterson, Douglas. *The English Lyric from Wyatt to Donne: A History of the Plain and Eloquent Styles.* 2nd ed. East Lansing, Mich.: Colleagues Press. xxxii, 391p.

Reprints the first edition of 1967 (Princeton University Press) with a new preface (ix–xxxii) that refines and expands the discussion of the plain style as it appeared originally. Agrees with J. V. Cunningham in "Lyric Style in the 1590's" (*The Collected Essays of J. V. Cunningham* [Chicago: Swallow Press], 1976), who differentiates between two kinds of plain style, the native and classical. Points out that "in the native plain style there is normally a regular coincidence between syntactical and verse units," whereas "in the English version of the classical plain style metrical units are normally subordinate to syntactical units." Claims that Donne is the "inventor" of the classical plain style in English and Jonson its "perfecter" (xiv). Suggests that the distinction between the two plain styles clarifies "the nature of Donne's relationship to earlier native verse traditions" (xv). Contrasts *HSRound* with Greville's *Caelica*, no. 87, to illustrate the differences between the classical and native plain style.

1088. Pezzini, Domenico. "La poesia della passione nella tradizione letteraria inglese: Dal 'Sogno della Croce' à R. S. Thomas." *RSLR* 26: 460–507.

Discusses the poetry of Christ's Passion and cross in "The Dream of the Rood," in medieval religious lyrics of the thirteenth to fifteenth centuries, in the poetry of Donne, and in poems of R. S. Thomas to show how the Christian faith has been embodied and expressed in English culture over the centuries. Comments on the relation-ship between poetry and theology. In a section on Donne (488–97), sees him as a bridge between medieval and modern religious sensibility and discusses how the theme of Christ's Passion and his cross occupies a central place in Donne's Christology. Comments on the importance of and complex uses of the theme in several of the *Holy Sonnets, Lit, Cross,* and *Goodf.*

1089. Pfister, Manfred. "Noticias de nuevos mundos: El diálogo entre los poetas isabelinos y los viajeros." *Casa de las Américas* 30, no. 180: 96–113.

Discusses representations of the New World created by poets during the sixteenth and seventeenth centuries, noting that often they departed radically from the views held previously. Maintains that stories of discovery and exploration provided poets with new images that replaced well-worn Petrarchan images and other stereotypical rhetorical devices used by earlier poets. Regards Donne as a major example of a poet who drew upon the literature of exploration for his images and conceits and cites examples from *Storm, Calm, ElPict, GoodM, SunRis,* and *ElBed.* Observes that Donne holds to the generally accepted view of the New World as an opportunity for obtaining riches and colonial expansion.

1090. Pinsent, Pat. "Form and Meaning in Donne and Herbert," in *The Metaphysical Poets,* ed. Linda Cookson and Bryan Loughrey, 79–87. Longman Critical Essays. Harlow, Eng.: Longman Group.

Discusses how in Donne's poems line length and rhyme reenforce meaning, citing as examples *Flea, SunRis, Ecst,* and *ValMourn.* Contends that "the kind of stanza which Donne creates, in these and many other poems, is organically linked to the movement of the action between the persona and the implied other participant(s)" and that "[t]he choice of line length and rhyme pattern appears to be part of this overall concept, subsumed to the main idea of the poem" (81–82). Contrasts Donne and Herbert, examining, in particular, *ValWeep* and Herbert's "The Pulley" to show how the strengths of each poet "are revealed in their manipulation of the form," and to illustrate "the kinds of differences between them" (84).

1091. Radzinowicz, Mary Ann. "Reading Paired Poems Nowadays." *LIT* 1: 275–90. Discusses how *Storm* and *Calm* as paired poems comment on each other, observing how "[e]choes and cross-references create a tension between sameness and difference in the pair—repetition signaling similarity and increment, complementarity." Suggests that the poems "make poetry out of the discord between man's need for and resistance to grace" (278). Regards the "storm-calm pair" as part of a series, including *ElPict* and *Christ,* and suggests that the whole series should be read "for its complex voice doubling, neither wholly impersonal nor dramatic; for its extending and developing a complex group of inter-related responses to reality, not for any monologic self-referentiality; and for rejecting transcendence in order to expose irrational mental states as well as rational, so as to end with a self-discovery that includes the dis-sentaneous" (279). Comments also on Katherine Philips's sequence of response and answer poems that echo Donne's love poems as well as *Storm, Calm,* and several of the verse letters. Concludes that paired poems, dialogue poems, and response poems "take their value nowadays not from arguments of their organicity, self-referentiality, impersonality or uniqueness, but from their unstable combination of the rational with the irrational, from their refusal to transcend their historical moments, from their irresolute admix-

ture of self-representation with detachment, and finally from their class or gender representativeness as much as their individuality" (287).

1092. Raizis, Marios Byron. *The Metaphysical Poets of England.* Athens: Gutenberg. 136p. Greek version, with original works included in English, 1998. Contains a general introduction to the metaphysical poets (7–14), explaining the history of the term "metaphysical poets" and commenting on major characteristics of their poetry, especially its syntactical concentration, use of conceits and wit, dramatic immediacy, argumentative structure, conversational language, and intellectual dynamism. Regards the metaphysical poets as not entirely different from their contemporaries but rather as men who "concentrated on stylistic features and philosophical lore that the others had not emphasised in their verse, or had used sparingly" (13). Thereafter follows introductions to the lives and works of Donne, Herbert, Marvell, Crashaw, Vaughan, Traherne, and Cowley, with selections from their poetry and discussions of selected key poems (15–123). "John Donne (1572–1631)" (15–53) gives a brief historical account of Donne's life and comments on general characteristics of his poetry, followed by explications of *ElBed, SGo, Flea, Relic, Ecst, Val-Mourn, HSMade, HSDeath,* and *Sat3.* "In Retrospect: The Metaphysical Panorama" (125–32) recapitulates the main points of the study, showing likenesses and differences among the poets surveyed and stressing that the metaphysical poets "did not revolutionise English poetry, secular or devotional" but rather "they merely brought a fresh and salutary breath of manneristic novelty to it" (132). Concludes with a selected bibliography (133–34) and a biographical sketch of the author with a list of his major publications (135–36).

1093. Ray, Robert H. "Ben Jonson and the Metaphysical Poets: Continuity in a Survey Course," in *Approaches to Teaching the Metaphysical Poets,* ed. Sidney Gottlieb, 89–96. Modern Language Association of America, Approaches to Teaching World Literature. gen. ed. Joseph Gibaldi. New York: Modern Language Association of America.

Argues that a too rigid separation of the metaphysical poets from Jonson or Jonson's exclusion altogether in college survey courses of seventeenth century literature distorts for students the continuity in English poetry. Discusses how Jonson can be integrated into the study of the metaphysical poets. Discusses similarities between Donne and Jonson, noting in particular, how Jonson's "To John Donne" "reveals some interesting connections in wittiness and friendship between Donne and Jonson" (93). Insists that "students who read metaphysical poetry without knowing Jonson do not really understand all the components of that poetry" (95).

1094. Ray, Robert H. *A John Donne Companion.* New York: Garland. ix, 414p.

The preface (vii–x) explains the purpose of this reference volume and its organization and format. Comments on bibliographies, resources, and tools helpful to researchers (3–5) are followed by a Donne chronology (7–11), a survey of Donne's life (13–22), and a list of his works (23). Thereafter follows the Donne dictionary (25–368), in which items are arranged alphabetically and include persons in Donne's life and works; places associated with him; characters, allusions, central ideas, and major concepts in his works; difficult or ambiguous words and phrases found in the poetry and prose; summaries of the best known of Donne's poems and prose works; other important writers who influenced Donne; and key literary terms. Concludes with a selected bibliography divided into six sections: Donne's works (369–70); bibliographies, concordances, and indexes (371); biography (371–73); reputation and influence (373–74); and critical studies (375–413), which is further subdivided into background studies (375–76), general studies of the poetry and prose (377–80), studies on individual poems or groups of poems (380–408), studies on individual prose works (408–13), and general background studies (414). Reviews: D. F. Bratchell in *N&Q* n.s. 38 (1991): 382–83; Eugene D. Hill in *AnSch* 9 (1992): 455–63.

1095. Revard, Stella P. "The Angelic Messenger in 'Aire and Angels.'" *JDJ* 9: 15–18.

Responds to R. V. Young's "Angels in 'Aire and Angels'" (entry 1127). Discusses the importance of the concept of angels as messengers in *Air*. Argues that the poem is not just about women and men in love, but is also "about the relationship between spiritual and corporeal states—and the inevitable and necessary movement from the one to the other." Maintains that in the poem the speaker "wants to know how to attain love" and that "the angelic messenger puts him in mind to learn," and that for him "to know and understand what love is, it must as a heavenly concept or idea travel downward" (15). Says that "[t]he means for its descent, as the medium for dissemination of all information originating in heaven, but descending to earth, must be the angel" (15–16). Suggests that in stanza one the problem is "how the spiritual idea may take proper earthly form" and that the problem in the second stanza is "just the opposite: how the spiritual may retain its integrity in a physical context." Maintains that, in order to learn "how spiritual love may manifest itself on earth," the poet "needs the agency of the angel or muse" and believes that "[t]he very words of the poem that the poet, inspired by the angel, delivers to us are the aural message" (16). Maintains that in the conclusion of the poem Donne "is not speaking of the difference between men and women, but of the difference between intellectual love, conceived first by man, and embodied love, realized through the man's love of woman," and that he is simply acknowledging that "[a]ny spiritual message realized . . . will never in its earthly embodiment be the same as the wordless word the angel knew before he brought his message to earth." Claims "it is just this disparity that Donne also implicitly deals with" (17).

1096. Reynolds, Mark. "Teaching the Meta-physical Poets in a Two-Year College," in *Approaches to Teaching the Metaphysical Poets,* ed. Sidney Gottlieb, 109–13. Modern Language Association of America, Approaches to Teaching World Literature, gen. ed. Joseph Gibaldi. New York: Modern Language Association of America.

Suggests ways of teaching metaphysical poetry to students in two-year colleges who often have little experience or interest in reading poetry. Mentions specific exercises in critical analysis, using such poems as *SGo, Ind, Canon, Flea, ValMourn,* and the *Holy Sonnets.* Believes the various activities suggested "make even the difficult poetry of the metaphysical poets accessible and appealing to students who are neither literature majors nor sophisticated readers" (113).

1097. Rickey, Mary Ellen. "Donne's 'The Sunne Rising,' Lines 19–20." *Expl* 48, no. 4: 241–43.

Points out that in *SunRis* (ll. 19–20) Donne suggests that his mistress and he are "a compaction of royalty,"

which becomes "a true crux for his entire argument" (241). Maintains that "these second-stanza kings are types of the kings or magi who sought and found the Christchild at Bethlehem" (242). Points out that medieval sculptors and painters often showed these saintly kings as lying together "in one bed, under a common coverlet, wearing their crowns" with an angel appearing above them pointing to the star. Suggests several cathedrals where Donne may have seen this depiction. Claims that "[t]he biblical kings, not unlike Donne's metaphorical ones, have seen the Word made flesh," that "[t]hey operate according to a set of divine instructions nicely corresponding to the transcendent vision of the persona addressing the sun" in the poem, and that "[t]hey surpass the earthly politics of King Herod, just as the lovers do the mundane activity of the hunting king" in the first stanza. Concludes that Donne's "seriocomic trope of kings in one bed pleases us in something of the same way that the biblical kings have instructed and delighted centuries of viewers" (243).

1098. Roberts, John R. "'Just such disparitie': The Critical Debate About 'Aire and Angels.'" *JDJ* 9: 43–64.

Presents a historical survey of representative critical comment on *Air* from 1912 (Grierson's edition) to 1989. Maintains that "[n]o other poem in Donne's canon has been given so many completely contradictory readings," and observes that, because of its difficulty, many Donne critics shy away from the poem altogether or mention it only briefly in their studies. Points out that "[t]he major critical crux in the poem . . . has always been the apparent disparity of tone between the last six or perhaps three lines and the rest of the poem" (43). Claims that "[m]uch of the recent criticism of the poem tells us more about the critics that write it and about their critical theories and methodologies than it does about Donne's poem" (61), and chides "those who explain Donne's poem in such complicated, jargon-ridden language that even educated and sophisticated readers feel put off and intimidated." Concludes that there has been "an array of bewildering and contradictory interpretations" of *Air* and that "there are no signs that indicate the debate will end in the near future" (62).

1099. Roebuck, Graham. "Elegies for Donne: Great Tew and the Poets." *JDJ* 9: 125–36.

Notes that when "Death's Duell" was published (1632), it contained only two commendatory poems, one by Henry King and the other by Edward Hyde, and asks why there were not other elegies written at the time of Donne's death. Speculates why Hyde wrote his elegy and suggests that he is "the likely impresario behind the line-up of elegies" that appears in the first edition of the poems in 1633. Points out that Hyde was a member of the Great Tew, "the renowned circle of humanist, liberal theological, scientific and ecclesiastical thought" (127) that found especially attractive Donne's "Erastian arguments for the subordination of religious to civil authority" (128), and suggests how Hyde and other of the elegists, men associated with Great Tew, "arrayed their forces against the anticipated eloquence of the poets, to be led by Jonson himself, in order to appropriate the memory of Donne" (131). Points out that "thus the contestants for legacy of Donne aligned themselves in the funeral and commemorative elegies" with "the poets on the one hand and the guardians of the Church, both lay and cleric, on the other" (133).

1100. Schoenfeldt, Michael C. "Patriarchal Assumptions and Egalitarian Designs." *JDJ* 9: 23–26.

Responds to R. V. Young's "Angels in 'Aire and Angels'" (entry 1127). Disagrees with Young's view of the hierarchy of the sexes in the poem and argues that *Air* cannot be read simply as expressing the superiority of men's love. Agrees with Young that it is wrong to refashion Donne's views of Renaissance patriarchy to suit modern tastes but believes that the conclusion of the poem "continues to assert simultaneously the superiority of male and of female love, and in so doing installs a space for the imagination of sexual equality within a discourse of masculine hierarchy" (26).

1101. Schoenfeldt, Michael C. "'That Ancient Heat': Sexuality and Spirituality in *The Temple*," in *Soliciting Interpretation: Literary Theory and Seventeenth-Century English Poetry,* ed. Elizabeth D. Harvey and Katharine Eisaman Maus, 273–96. Chicago: University of Chicago Press.

In an essay devoted primarily to examining eroticism in Herbert's poetry, comments on how Donne, like Herbert, identifies "the erect penis with sin, rebellion, and aggression." Points out that Donne explains that God chose circumcision to seal his covenant with Abraham because the penis is the most rebellious part of the body and thus, "[a]s the penis becomes a synecdoche for mortal depravity, circumcision comes to represent the severing of our capacity for sin" (280). Observes also that in both *Sat3* and *HSShow* Donne "converts religious choice into a question of sexual preference" (285) and that in *HSShow* and *HSBatter* he sexualizes very explicitly his relationship with God (290). Contrasts Donne and Herbert, noting that "[w]here Donne's God adopts erotic terminology to test the interpretive and moral capacities of his followers, Herbert's God assumes sexuality to attest his total absorption of sinful humanity" (292).

1102. Serrano, Celia Florén. "Some Aspects of Rhyme and Suffixation in *Lucrece*," in *Proceedings of the I National Conference of the Spanish Society for English Renaissance Studies,* ed. Javier Sánchez, 83–93. Zaragoza: Librería General.

Compares the results of a statistical study of rhyme and suffixation in Shakespeare's *Lucrece* with results of a similar study of the *Anniversaries* and Books 1 and 2 of Milton's *Paradise Lost*. Concludes that the three poets show more similarities in their use of grammatical suffixes than in the use of lexical suffixes, that all three "abound in grammatical suffixes at the end of verse position," that the suffix *ing* "hardly ever take[s] final position in Donne or Milton, while it is significant in Shakespeare," that Milton "does not use the syncopated form of the suffix for the past/past participle," and that "*eth* is almost totally absent in Donne and totally absent in Milton." Maintains, however, that "coincidence stands out far more than disparity" (92). Notes also that Shakespeare shows a "preference for nominal suffixes for the final position" but that Donne does not (92–93). Concludes that "suffixation helps rhyme considerably in *Lucrece* but that "[t]he results can be attributed only partially to Shakespeare's style as the variation the other two poets show proves" (93).

1103. Sessions, William A. "*Tottel's Miscellany* and the Metaphysical Poets," in *Approaches to Teaching the Metaphysical Poets,* ed. Sidney Gottlieb, 48–53. Modern Language Association of America, Approaches to Teaching World Literature, gen. ed. Joseph Gibaldi. New York: Modern Language Association of America.

Argues that comparing the poems in *Tottel's Miscellany* with those written by the metaphysical poets allows the contemporary student to enter directly into "what was a central experience for any poet or reader of the Renais-sance: a sense of the past." Maintains also that "[i]ntertexuality helps students understand the relation of the metaphysical poets to the poets in Tottel's 1557 collection, the first anthology of modern English lyric verse." Suggests, for instance, that by comparing Donne's "defiantly anti-Petrarchan" *Ind* with Wyatt's "Divers Doth Use," "students discover that, for sarcasm and cynicism about human love, Donne cannot match the ferocity of Wyatt, when expectation may have led them to think otherwise" (48). Holds that students can find in Tottel's collection "what remained quintessentially metaphysical: the language of meditation, a dramatic voice in a style both colloquial and musical" (51).

1104. Shawcross, John T. "Donne's 'Aire and Angels': Text and Context." *JDJ* 9: 33–42.

Discusses how both the text and context of *Air* influence the interpretation of the poem. Maintains that "the position of a poem alongside other poems may be meaningful, to the reader at least, even if not so intentionally arranged by an author," since "as the reader moves from one poem—its subject, treatment, attitude, effect, language—to another, various comparisons or contrasts or developments of these poetic elements may be experienced, and thus its 'context' rather than its being read in isolation may offer meaning." Insists that "what text is read, and the instabilities of that text, will predicate its interpretive possibilities" (34). Maintains that the ambiguities in *Air* are "underscored by not only its imagery but also by its positioning among the Songs and Sonets" (37).

1105. Shawcross, John T. "Notes on an Important Volume of Donne's Poetry and Prose." *JDJ* 9: 137–40.

Describes the contents and explains the importance of a "privately owned volume, which binds together exempla of John Donne's 1633 *Poems,* a poetic manuscript, and the 1633 *Juvenilia* (first edition), with a prose manuscript" that was "incompletely and erroneously described" (137) by Peter Beal in *JDJ* 6 (1987), 215.

1106. Shuger, Debora Kuller. "Absolutist Theology: The Sermons of John Donne," in *Habits of Thought in the English Renaissance: Religion, Politics, and the Dominant Culture,* 159–217. Berkeley and Los Angeles: University of California Press.

Argues that Donne "consistently and insistently deploys language associated with absolute monarchy in his treatment of the divine" and that "he stresses precisely that aspect of absolutism most alien to the modern mentality: the configuration of ideal relations in terms of domination and submission." Regards Donne as "representative of the mainstream of English Reformation theology" (164) and suggests that his religious writings "differ from those of his contemporaries primarily in the *degree* to which he stresses the analogy between God and kings" (165). Maintains that "[w]hether speaking about literal or metaphoric kings he almost invariably echoes the main themes of Jacobean royalism" and "depicts divine/human interaction as analogous to seventeenth-century absolute monarchy" (166). Discusses how Donne's "politicization of the divine image leads to a spirituality based on awe and subjection" (168). Insists that Donne's theology is absolutist "not by implication or inference but quite literally and explicitly," observing that "[t]he sermons insist on the analogy between God and king and furthermore locate the point of contact in *power*." Demonstrates that the analogy "involves more than a simple comparison between temporal and spiritual centers of authority,"

maintaining that "[i]t is a psychagogic rather than cosmological analogy" (169). Points out that, for Donne, "[t]he theological corollary of royal absolutism is radical monotheism" (169) and suggests that his monotheism "includes two related elements: the unlimited power of God and the representation of such power as terrifying and destructive" (170–71). Says that Donne's God "strongly resembles a Renaissance nobleman," who is, "above all, concerned to maintain His superiority" (175). Discusses how Donne's "valorization of guilt, his depiction of a demonic selfhood, and vilification of man belong to the discourse of absolutist theology" and are "based on the principles of power and submission" (184), noting that he even treats marriage "in terms of power" (185). Comments on Donne's conception of God and Christ and his views on the role of sin, guilt, fear, pain, and personal holiness, all reflective of his theology of power and submission. Points out also that in the sermons Donne's "repeated references to textual difficulties, disagreements among the fathers, differences between ancient and modern expositors seem designed to erode the belief in a single, accessible meaning of the holy text," and notes that Donne's "own hermeneutic furthers this destabilization by replacing the spiritual sense of medieval exegesis with the principle of accommodation" (205). Suggests that this "denaturalization of text and dogma reinforces authority by breeding doubts and fears that then yearn for closure and intelligibility" (207), which places "church and priest rather than some objective and relatively impersonal text at the center of the redemptive process as it unfolds in history" (207–8). Concludes that "[b]oth as strategy and substance, then, theology duplicates politics," and "Donne's God, his preaching, and his king are all analogously related, all participants in absolutist structures of domination and submission" (209).

1107. Slights, Camille Wells. "Air, Angels, and the Progress of Love." *JDJ* 9: 95–104.

Discusses how various interpretations of the concluding three lines of *Air* have led critics to "implausible readings" of the poem, in which they postulate "a female auditor too stupid to understand, too much in love to notice, or too sophisticated to mind that she is being insulted." Argues that "the fictive audience implied by the poem is not a gullible aristocrat, a coyly reluctant mistress, or a Jamesian heroine, but a woman, perhaps a wife, who has shared love with the speaker and who now accuses him of diminished romantic ardor." Maintains that "[i]t is she who has initiated the making of comparisons, contrasting her undiminished devotion with his neglect" and that "[h]is final assertion of a universal and unalterable disparity between women's love and men's is a response to her charge of a particular and personal disparity." Suggests that the speaker "explains his changing response as the adoption and rejection of inadequate theories of love and concludes by proposing a relationship based on his masculine superiority." Claims, therefore, that "[b]y tracing the speaker's amatory progress," *Air* "displays a sequence of cultural paradigms of love, from Neo-Platonic and Petrarchan forms of romanticism to the emergent ideal of companionate marriage" (98). Concludes that the poem, "through the progress of a love story, examines the decline and development of ways of loving among sophisticated men and women during the decades ending the sixteenth and beginning the seventeenth centuries" (103) and "wittily mocks traditional idealizing modes of love that were becoming old-fashioned and increasingly appearing unrealistic," and "exposes the coercion embedded in the emerging ideal of companionate marriage, warning that, within a gender hierarchy presupposing female inferiority, the price women pay for love is condescension and subjection to control" (104).

1108. Smith, Nigel. "The Metaphysical Penguin," in *The Metaphysical Poets,* ed. Linda Cookson and Bryan Loughrey, 110–16. Longman Critical Essays. Harlow, Eng.: Longman Group.

Observes the influence, especially on students, of Helen Gardner's introduction to *The Metaphysical Poets* (1957, revised 1966 and 1972) in defining "metaphysical" poetry and challenges her notion of a "tradition" of metaphysical poetry as well as her inclusion of certain poems and poets in her anthology. Asks if metaphysical poetry, as Gardner envisions it, has become "an educational drug which blinds us to the necessity of a vibrant tradition of public verse meant to flourish in the good life of a nation." Maintains that most metaphysical verse was "occasional, frivolous, largely written to circulate in the restricted milieu of one's friends" and was considered only a "distraction, at best produced to manifest certain skills of eloquence and wit at the point of one's initiation into manhood, before one progressed to weightier matters, like affairs of state" (112). Warns that when one reads *The Metaphysical Poets,* "it is well worth pondering how it has been organised, what ideas have dictated the choice of poems" (116). Mentions Donne throughout, claiming, for instance, that his poetry was not widely read in his lifetime and that much of his poetry is simply role playing and the fulfilling of literary conventions.

1109. Spinrad, Phoebe S. "'Aire and Angels' and Questionable Shapes." *JDJ* 9: 19–22.

Responds to R. V. Young's "Angels in 'Aire and Angels'" (entry 1127). Suggests that a number of images of the lady in *Air* are "highly sinister in the context of Renaissance spirit-lore" and that, like similar images in such poems as *Ecst* and *Canon,* "they call into question Petrarchan notions of love" (19). Comments on the angelology of such Protestant contemporaries as Ludwig Lavater, Reginald Scot, and James VI of Scotland to show how their ideas may have shaped Donne's view of angels. Argues that ultimately the poem stresses mutuality: "[t]he 'spheare' of the lady's love is both the less-pure element of air (but still pure, remember) that enables man's love to be made palpable, and the cosmological sphere that emphasizes man's place at the center." Notes that "[w]ithout the heavenly sphere, the center is itself a referentless pile of debris, and without air to make spirit visible, the spirit cannot act effectively in the human world." Suggests that in the conclusion of the poem the speaker acknowledges that "[n]either the female sphere unoccupied nor the male love with nothing to occupy produces culminative love, any more than the unclothed spirit or untenanted air/matter produces an apparition," and that, "should the so-called dominant male attempt to produce love without the enabling envelopment of the female, the result is onanism—impure and simple" (22).

1110. **Stanwood, P. G.** "On Altering the Present to Fit the Past," in *Approaches to Teaching the Metaphysical Poets,* ed. Sidney Gottlieb, 75–80. Modern Language Association of America, Approaches to Teaching World Literature, gen. ed. Joseph Gibaldi. New York: The Modern Language Association of America.

Maintains that "the knowledge, hard and strenuously learned, that the present is made up of the past and the past of the present is surely the basis to literary study and to the educated imagination" (75), and comments on ways of making students aware of this concept. Discusses ways of introducing Donne to students, explains how Donne can fit into a survey course on seventeenth century literature, discusses writing assignments given students, and comments on an end-of-term seventeenth century "feast" planned and executed by students by which they learn "to live in the seventeenth century, to know and enjoy it as a social, historical, and literary epoch" (80).

1111. **Steadman, John M.** *Redefining a Period Style: "Renaissance," "Mannerist" and "Baroque" in Literature.* Pittsburgh, Pa.: Duquesne University Press. vii, 206p.

Challenges "current assumptions concerning the interrelationship between our concepts of historical periods and the criteria we commonly employ to define and differentiate varieties of literary style," especially "the application (or frequently, misapplication) of terms and values derived from the visual arts to the arts of discourse." Discusses "some contemporary stereotypes of Secentismo: the differentiation of mannerism and baroque, their relationship to Renaissance styles, and their links with *concettismo* and metaphysical poetry" (1). Chapter 7, "The Metaphysicals" (124–42), discusses the various interpretations of the term "metaphysical poetry" and suggests that at best it "can be used only as trope" and "is rarely valid in the literal sense." Maintains that the distinguishing feature of English and Continental poetry of the seventeenth century is a "conscious preoccupation with *ingenio*" or the "ideal of wit" (128). Discusses how Donne outstripped earlier poets "in converting the *topos* of love as philosophy into fresh inventions and ingenious sources of wit" (131). Chapter 8, "Metaphysical and Baroque" (143–58), argues that "[g]eneralizations about baroque art and metaphysical poetry are necessary and inevitable, but also dangerous" and notes that one "must necessarily recognize differences and variations not only in national styles, but even in the style of the same writer or artist at different stages and in different genres and subjects" (146). Argues that critics "have exaggerated the unity of the metaphysical tradition, both in England and on the Continent, seeking a common denominator for writers as diverse as Marino and Quevedo, Góngora and Herbert, Crashaw and Donne, instead of stressing the differences between them" (148). Concludes that "the distinctions between a 'classical' Renaissance phase, a 'mannerist' phase, the 'high baroque,' and the 'neoclassical' or 'late baroque' are usually inadequate as historical and stylistic categories" and that "they will not of themselves enable the reader to pinpoint the work historically or to assign it a fixed and determined place in literary tradition" (158).

1112. Stein, Arnold. "Interpretation: 'Aire and Angels.'" *JDJ* 9: 65–76.

Discusses the general issues and problems involved in the interpretation of poetry. Maintains that, although Donne was a coterie poet who preferred not to publish his poems, we should not assume that "he did not value his writing, or took no pains in creating its impromptu air of freshness, or in creating the exact character of what he wished to say" (67) and yet acknowledges that "in interpretation many differences are affected by what one is looking for or prepared to see" (68). Cautions that "[t]here are many ways to misinterpret, no less easily by booming confidence in the accuracy of one's knowledge and its application than by

the assurance of the reliability of one's own intuition and its functioning" (70). Disagrees with Helen Gardner's interpretation of *Air* in *The Business of Criticism* (Oxford: Clarendon Press, 1959), claiming that she errs in taking a detached comment from one of Donne's sermons as relevant to an interpretation of the poem. Contrasts her interpretation with that of A. J. Smith in "New Bearings in Donne: 'Aire and Angels,'" *English* 13 (1960): 49–53, agreeing with Smith that the poem is witty and ingenious but differing with him "in matters of emphasis and because of silences in his discourse." Offers a brief interpretation of the poem, stressing how "[t]he whole performance arranges for silence in the woman's role" (74).

1113. Stephens, John, and Ruth Waterhouse. *Literature, Language and Change: From Chaucer to the Present.* The Interface Series, gen. ed. Ronald Carter. London: Routledge. xvii, 293p.

Analyzes an extract from Donne's "Sermon Preached at Pauls upon Christmas Day, 1624" "to show the syntagmatic/paradigmatic structuring and to bring out other features which are perhaps less obvious in a normal prose format" (48). Shows that "[b]y inviting the audience to perceive the variety of ways in which the normal conventions of language are played with (and against), the rhetoric [in this sermon] functions to involve the audience in the gradual layering of meanings into a richly associative discourse" (51). Using the first stanza of *GoodM* as an example, discusses how Donne reacted "against the enriching of semantic density" (57) in lyric poetry that had been going on since Wyatt, pointing out that "[a]ny intensity in this stanza does not depend on semantic density, but on the spare and tightly controlled relationships which activate the penumbra of associations evoked by the signifiers." Maintains that Donne's language "depends very much on a syntagm/paradigm relation which is close to that of ordinary speech, even though it is more tightly patterned than speech," and observes that "there are rhetorical devices in it which activate a range of associations, but lexis on the whole is not very Latinate and elevated, and can become quite colloquial" (58). Analyzes *HSBlack* to show "the extent to which the syntagmatic/paradigmatic interrelationship controls and yet allows play and flexibility of interpretative activity when it interacts with a highly conventional verse form" (59). Briefly discusses Adrienne Rich's use of Donne's poem in her "A Valediction Forbidding Mourning" (200–201).

1114. Stewart, Garrett. "Graphonic Tension in English Poetry," in *Reading Voices: Literature and the Phonotext,* 145–91. Berkeley and Los Angeles: University of California Press.

Maintains that "it is Donne among the immediate successors of Shakespeare who offers the most arresting reactivations of the lexical code from within its own erosion" (145). Points out that "Donne's texts everywhere demonstrate the hold that semantic sense has on the textual sensorium: the reader's relentless tendency to control the phonemic in the form of the morphemic, to bracket free play by syllabification" (145–46). Maintains that "[d]espite appearances to the contrary—despite lettering and spacing—even Donne's penchant for mono-syllabism subserves the interdependence rather than the discreteness of lexical sequencing," noting that "[h]is words are often overrun by each other, under mutual siege" (146). Illustrates the idea by commenting briefly on *Pyr* and *LovExch.*

1115. Strier, Richard. "Songs and Sonnets Go to Church: Teaching George Herbert,"

in *Approaches to Teaching the Metaphysical Poets,* ed. Sidney Gottlieb, 127–31. Modern Language Association of America, Approaches to Teaching World Literature, gen. ed. Joseph Gibaldi. New York: Modern Language Association of America.

Shows how studying Herbert's poetry "in the context of Donne's provides a number of pedagogical opportunities, although it also presents a number of dangers" (127). Argues that the *Songs and Sonets,* not Donne's religious verse, are "the perfect context in which to study Herbert's lyrics." Maintains that, "[l]ike Donne, Herbert is a master of nonundercutting irony" and that "[d]emonstrating that phenomenon is one of the great challenges of teaching Herbert." Maintains that, "[l]ike the *Songs and Sonets, The Temple* must be shown to be remarkable not only for the variety of tones that different poems in it embody but also for the variety of tones that individual poems embody," and that students need to recognize that "Herbert, like Donne, simultaneously represented and criticized his deepest emotions" (131).

1116. Sullivan, Ernest W., II. "Updating the John Donne Listings in Peter Beal's *Index of English Literary Manuscripts, II." JDJ* 9: 141–48.

"[P]romotes another manuscript to Peter Beal's list of main manuscripts (those having more than ten complete or partial Donne poems (*Index of English Literary Manuscripts* [London: Mansell, 1980, I, ii, pp. 250–59); locates additional, previously unrecorded poems within manuscripts already listed in Beal's *Index;* and completes two entries in Beal's *Index* and two in his 'More Donne Manuscripts,' *John Donne Journal* 6 (1987), 213–218" (141).

1117. Tomlinson, T. B. "Donne's Poetry and Belief in 17th-Century England." *CR* 30: 5–39.

Challenges the assumption that Donne lamented the passing away of old certainties, such as a divinely ordered universe, and argues that "to take any of Donne's poems as evidence of some anguished despair is to misread both the poems and their significance in the late-sixteenth and early-seventeenth centuries" (25). Suggests that even in *SecAn* the "language and rhythms" have a "buoyancy" that "virtually belies what the poem has in other terms announced" (27) and rejects the view of those who see the poem "as part of a kind of self-imposed apprenticeship to what later became a fully-fledged religious life and poetry." Cautions against "any developmental thinking about Donne," stating that "[e]ven the young man's Songs about love, whatever the later Dean of St. Paul's may have wished, must be allowed still their own say" (34). Maintains that even though we know of Donne's many personal problems and disappointments there is little anguish in Donne's poems and prose, and insists that "[w]e cannot even assume that the past, or daily experience, had any relevance at all to his later poetry," citing *Christ* as an example, a poem that shows that "important religious poetry is possible even in cases where the poem in question is obviously completely indifferent to the author's most immediate situation and to the larger circumstances surrounding this" (35). Believes that in the longer religious poems Donne "writes much more impressively, and far beyond the range of either conventional belief and practices" (37), than he does in the *Holy Sonnets*. Maintains that Donne's "later religious poems are exceptional, both in his own poetic career and in the seventeenth century generally" and questions "whether the age was as fully and completely 'a religious age' as it is often supposed when contrasts are made either with our own century or with whichever period the 'new science' is said to have first controlled." Holds that "[i]n general, both Elizabethan and seventeenth-century England were strongly secular in temperament, outlook and action" but that Donne's later religious poems show "a truly and deeply religious sensibility in action" (39).

1118. Toulmin, Stephen. "The 17th-Century Counter-Renaissance," in *Cosmopolis: The Hidden Agenda of Modernity,* 45–87. New York: Free Press.

Regards Donne as representative of the counter-Renaissance and suggests that in reaction to the assassination of Henry IV of Navarre, Donne "produced in 1611 two complex and problematical poems" [*sic*]—*Ignatius* and *FirAn* (63). Suggests that *Ignatius* "is so odd that many scholars ignore it" and that "some of the standard editions of Donne's *Collected Poems* even omit it." Believes that the "exaggerated idolization" of Elizabeth Drury is not Donne's point in *FirAn,* but rather, "[h]er death gave him the chance to enumerate all the things he deplores in his own time" (64), especially the New Science. Calls the poem "an Elegy for cosmic and social decline" (66). Sees Donne as a conservative who dislikes innovation in theology and science.

1119. Traister, Daniel. "Reluctant Virgins: The Stigma of Print Revisited." *ClQ* 26: 75–86.

Discusses briefly how Donne shared the reluctance of most Tudor and Stuart Court poets to have their poetry published. Notes, however, that, while only the *Anniversaries* and a few scattered poems were published in Donne's lifetime, "[h]is religious writings, including his sermons, had frequently appeared in print before his death." Observes that "[s]ermons were Donne's job," and that "getting them

published was part of it, in a way
hat his poetry—even his religious
poetry—evidently was not" (80).
Maintains that not until the end of the
seventeenth century and the beginning
of the eighteenth century did print culture come "to dominate the thinking
of authors in ways we now automatically, anachronistically, and unthink-
ingly assume" (86).

1120. Van Hooff, Anton J. L. "A Longer
Life for 'Suicide': When Was the Latin
Word for Self-Murderer Invented?" *RF*
102: 255–59.

Discusses the origin and development
of the word "suicide." Finds its first
use in English in the 1643 version of
Thomas Browne's *Religio Medici* and
notes its absence in the first edition
of 1642. Points out that Donne
"employed as the title for his writing
the Greekish *Biathanatos*, i.e. the one
who is killed violently" (257).

1121. Veith, Gene Edward, Jr. "Teaching
about the Religion of the Metaphysical
Poets," in *Approaches to Teaching the
Metaphysical Poets,* ed. Sidney Gottlieb,
54–60. Modern Language Association of
America, Approaches to Teaching World
Literature, gen. ed. Joseph Gibaldi. New
York: Modern Language Association of
America.

Maintains that when the religious
dimension of metaphysical poetry is
dealt with historically and phenome-
nologically, it is not "an obstacle for
twentieth-century students" but may
rather "be a bridge for them into the
poetry" (54). Believes not only that
theology helps eludicate poetry but
also that poetry helps explain theology. Discusses, for instance, Donne
as representative of "Arminian syn-
ergism" in contrast to the "divine mon-
ergism" of Herbert to show that the
metaphysical poets, like the students
themselves, are "pluralistic." Observes
that when students read more deeply
such poets as Donne and Herbert,

"they often find themselves realizing
that their own religious tradition is
richer, more complex, and more intellectually open than they had dreamed"
(57). Insists that this approach is
intended "to affirm the student's own
religious understanding and to help
the student understand the spirituality of others" (59).

1122. Waddington, Raymond B. " 'All in
All': Shakespeare, Milton, Donne and
the Soul-in-Body Topos." *ELR* 20: 40–68.

Traces the notion that "the soul exists
as an indivisible whole both in the
entire body and in every individual
part of the body" (40) from Plato to
the Renaissance and shows how this
philosophical topos ("all-in-all") was
imaginatively adapted and transformed
(often comically) in Renaissance
poetry and prose. Observes that "the
notion that one's entire soul dwells in
each and every part of the body, when
particularized, becomes inescapably
risible" (48) and cites as a most striking example two personal medals of
Pietro Aretino that feature on the
reverse side a satyr whose features are
composed of penes and testes. Comments on the use of the "all-in-all"
topos by Shakespeare and Milton and
discusses in detail Donne's complex
use of it in *Air*. Regards Donne's poem
as a serious, though not solemn, presentation of mutual love between two
lovers, a poem that "describes an
achieved sexual relationship that, perhaps wholly unexpectedly, has come
to mean more than the speaker anticipated" (61). Shows that Donne was
working with "a nexus of philosophical and religious commonplaces" and
that "[f]or all the dramatic twists of
thought and rhetoric, the movement
from soul to body to soul to body is
a hyper-determined pattern." Suggests
how Donne links the conceit of the
"all-in-all" topos with that of Ficino's
"miracle of reciprocal love," in which

lovers exchange souls, and how the reciprocal love defined in the poem is reenforced by the stanzaic pattern (a double Petrarchan sonnet, each of which has an inverse structure). Concludes that "Just such disparity" (l. 26) at the end of the poem "really means 'no disparity'" (68).

1123. Watts, Cedric. "The Conceit of the Conceit," in *The Metaphysical Poets,* ed. Linda Cookson and Bryan Loughrey, 9–18. Longman Critical Essays. Harlow, Eng.: Longman Group.

Points out that conceits are not always successful and that "[t]he emphasis on mental gymnastics, on ostentatious cleverness, in typical metaphysical poetry can give the impression that the poet is an intellectually conceited person" (11). Suggests that "the grand paradox of Donne at his best is that, just as he exploits an extreme tension between the theoretical metre and the irregular rhythms of colloquial utterance, so he exploits a marked tension between intense feeling and almost neurotic mock-logic." Notes that it is "the illusion of fervent immediacy and spontaneity which seems to sustain the whole." Maintains that "[w]hat gives identity and personality to his work is largely its effective mimicry of an argumentative voice: its particular tones, pacings, stumblings, emergences into eloquence after struggles with entanglements" (15). Illustrates this point by analyzing ll. 79–82 of *Sat3*.

1124. Whitaker, Faye Pauli. "Metaphysical, Mannerist, Baroque: A Seminar for Undergraduates," in *Approaches to Teaching the Metaphysical Poets,* ed. Sidney Gottlieb, 97–102. Modern Language Association of America, Approaches to Teaching World Literature, gen. ed. Joseph Gibaldi. New York: Modern Language Association of America.

Discusses the content and critical approach used in an undergraduate seminar entitled "Metaphysical,

Mannerist, and Baroque." Begins the seminar by requiring the reading of the *Songs and Sonets* in full and by analyzing in detail *Flea* and *ValMourn* because these two poems "provide a balance of serious and ribald wit, incorporate traditional elements handled in an original way, and express two attitudes towards love," as well as speak out of "a dramatic situation in which both the persona and the person addressed are clearly imagined" (97). Ends the section on Donne by reading the *Holy Sonnets* and *Goodf* to show "the extent to which the techniques used in the *Songs and Sonets* are confined to the treatment of secular love and the extent to which subject matter is the controlling force in the structure of Donne's poems" (98).

1125. Williams, John, ed. *English Renaissance Poetry: A Collection of Shorter Poems from Skelton to Jonson.* 2nd ed. Fayetteville: University of Arkansas Press. xxxv, 416p.

First published in 1963. The preface (xi–xxxv) discusses how the short poem in the English Renaissance went through three phases—an early one informed by the native tradition, an intermediate one shaped by the Petrarchan tradition, and "one which assimilates and completes the practices of the earlier phases" (xii)—and regards Donne as representative of this latter phase. Shows how Donne's poetry reflects the native and Petrarchan traditions and how he attempted "to reconcile the opposing tendencies" of both. Claims, however, that he "worked mainly within the Petrarchan tradition, which is hyperbolic, violent, decorative, and metaphorical" and that "[m]any of his poems are deliberate parodies of Petrarchan subjects and conventions," while "many others, such as the Holy Sonnets, clearly are not." Maintains, however, that "between these lies a very large body of poetry . . . in which the two traditions are in violent conflict" (xxvii). Warns that "because of Donne's uncertainty in the matter, his reader must often remain unsure whether Petrarchism is being parodied or whether it is being seriously employed for serious ends." Claims that "[i]t is here, in the not fully resolved conflict between Native and Petrarchan practice, that Donne achieves the 'originality' that has been so overevaluated by so many readers and critics." Maintains that, in fact, Donne "offers very little that is new to the technique of English poetry" but that he is "truly original precisely where he should be, in his excellence as a poet, which is an excellence that, in a number of poems, surmounts the limitations of schools or movements, not by ignoring their implications but by understanding them" (xxviii). "John Donne: 1572–1631" (337–71) presents a brief biographical and critical commentary, followed by 17 selections from the *Songs and Sonets,* 2 from the *Elegies,* 6 from the *Holy Sonnets, Goodf,* and 3 hymns—without notes or commentary.

1126. Yancey, Philip. "John Donne: As He Lay Dying," in *Reality and the Vision,* ed. Philip Yancey, 173–86. Dallas, Tex.: Word Publishing. Reprinted in *The Classics We've Read, The Difference They've Made* (New York: McCracken Press, 1993), 228–46.

Maintains that Donne's view of pain and suffering in *Devotions* is quite modern. Says that the treatise is "trenchant without being blasphemous, profound without being abstract or impersonal," and that it "combines the raw humanity of modern treatises with the reverent sagacity of the ancients" (174). Suggests that "what sets Donne's work apart is his intended audience: God himself" and discusses how "[t]he presence of God looms like a shadow behind every thought, every sentence" (177). Points out that *Devotions* "does not answer the intellectual questions about suffering" but that it records "Donne's emotional resolution, showing us a step-by-step process of transformation" (179). Claims that for Donne the turning point came when "he began to view death not as the disease that permanently spoils life, but rather as the only cure to the disease of life" and when he accepted that "only through death—Christ's death and our own—can we realize a cured, sinless state" (183).

1127. Young, R. V. "Angels in 'Aire and Angels.'" *JDJ* 9: 1–14.

Argues that *Air* "emerges as a more resonant and intelligible poem—though certainly not a less intricate poem—when it is read in the light of the precise features of Scholastic angelology" (1). Maintains that the poem is a "subtle and elaborate dismantling of a Petrarchan trope, the lady as angelic presence," and "manages the figure in a way that discloses Donne's fundamental objection to the Petrarchan/Neo-Platonic treatment of love" (2). Shows how *Air* "begins by invoking the conventional Petrarchan conceit of the desirable woman as a remote and unapproachable angel" but "closes with an analogy based on the Thomist conception of angels." Argues that superficially the poem is "a witty thrust in the war between the sexes" but that "at a deeper level it embodies a philosophical proposition regarding the proper relationship between men and women and thus seeks to establish a basis for peace" (3). Maintains that Donne, like St. Thomas, does not regard human beings as "angelic pure intelligences tragically trapped in bodies, but rather [as] bodily creatures animated and informed by specifically human souls" and that "[s]ince we are not altogether spiritual in our nature, our natural human love is not fulfilled on a purely spiritual realm" (5). Shows how the first half of *Air* "moves from a generalized desire for beauty to the desire for a specific woman whose beauty is animated by her soul and exists in its complete form only in the composite, not in a purer form in the soul alone," and that the second part of the poem arrives at a "radically Thomist conclusion" that "rewrites the Petrarchan implications of the initial angel trope" (8). Says that in the conclusion the lady is "no longer an angel—emissary or image of divine transcendence"— but rather "it is the love of the man that is 'angelic' insofar as it calls forth and shapes the responsive love of the woman, even as an angel shapes the air into a manifestation of his presence" (9), all of which "confirms that the poem closes with an assertion of the priority of the masculine role" (11). See the responses to the essay by Stella P. Revard (entry 1095), Phoebe S. Spinrad (entry 1109), Michael C. Schoenfeldt (entry 1100), and Judith Scherer Herz (entry 1055).

1991

1128. Abraham, Lyndy. "'The Lovers and the Tomb': Alchemical Emblems in Shakespeare, Donne, and Marvell." *Emblematica* 5: 301–20.

Discusses the appearance and significance of emblems depicting lovers in the tomb in alchemical books of the sixteenth and seventeenth centuries, such as the *Rosarium philosophorum* (1550), Johan Mylius's *Philosophia reformata* (1622), and Daniel Stolcius's *Viridarium chimicum* (1624). Points out how in *Mark* Donne equates the grave with the alembic, noting that "[t]he alchemical vessel as grave was clearly a place of death and putrefaction, but because the [Philosopher's] Stone was conceived there, it was also a place of conception, or renewal" (303–4). Observes that typically "[t]he lovers' deathly embrace [as seen in the emblems] inevitably led to renewal and regeneration" and "[t]heir sacrificial dissolution facilitated a union at a higher level" (304). Points out that the idea of love in a tomb appears in such poems as *Anniv, Relic, Para, Canon, Noct,* and *Ecst*. Comments in some detail on the alchemical elements in *Ecst* and suggests how Donne may have been influenced by several emblems in the *Rosarium*.

1129. Allinson, Mark. "Re-Visioning the Death Wish: Donne and Suicide." *Mosaic* 24, no. 1: 31–46.

Investigates "the way that Donne's attitude toward suicide sheds light on our understanding of his character." Using post-Jungian archetypal psychology, aims "to provide an inter-disciplinary theoretical framework for the numerous literary debates concerning the causes and implications of Donne's preoccupation with death and corruption" (31). Argues that Donne's suicidal desire is "fraught with ambivalence: death is both abhorred and desired," and examines this ambivalence "to show its effects in the literature." Discusses how "a continuing fascination with death and suicide is a product of the controlling archetype in Donne's psychic constellation: what Jungian and post-Jungian psychology would call the archetype of the Herculean hero, the strongman of the psyche" (33). Suggests that Donne's "continuing melancholic preoccupations with suicide and death mean that, although unable or unwilling to realize an experience of ego death, he nevertheless understood, even though he literalized his psychic need, that this was the path to transformation." Speaks of Donne as an "insecure Herculean captain of his soul, guiding it with strict control to its literalized point of transformation" (40). Maintains that the analysis of Donne's psychology presented here "establishes a consistent theoretical frame in which the poems may be read . . . as spiritual autobiography" (41).

1130. Arnold, Duane W. H., ed. and comp. *Praying with John Donne and George Herbert.* Introduction by Richard Harries. The Praying With Series. London: Triangle. xvi, 127p.

In the introduction (ix–xiii), Richard Harries compares and contrasts the

spiritual sensibilities of Donne and
Herbert. Suggests that Donne's religious writings, in addition to being
appreciated for their own sake, encourage us "to bring our whole self before
God, all our passions and disquiet, our
fear, our loathing and longing alike"
(xii). Gives short biographical sketches
of both poets (xiii–xvi), followed by
selections from Donne and Herbert
(poetry and prose) intermingled by
themes—Confession and Contrition,
Supplication and Preservation, Adoration and Thanksgiving ([1]–121).
Concludes with an epilogue (125) and
notes (126–27).

1131. Arshagouni, Mary. "The Latin 'Stationes' in John Donne's *Devotions upon
Emergent Occasions*." *MP* 89: 196–210.
Examines the Latin "stationes" or
headnotes in *Devotions* to show how
"their integral relationship with the
English devotions creates an unusual
narrative and dramatic work." Maintains that the *Devotions* "is anything
but a loose collection of twenty-three
individual meditations directed inward
upon the meditator with little consciousness of its effect on the reader."
Believes that "this work represents
Donne's most mature, perhaps most
complex work: a remarkable, sustained
prose-poem that not only expresses
conflicting and powerful internal emotions but also consciously provides its
readers with a touching model of the
experiences of God's elect in confronting the inexorable course of human
sinfulness that characterizes life on
earth." Concludes that "in this work,
perhaps more than any other in
Donne's canon, poet and preacher
stand united" (210). Comments on
"the linguistic play between the Latin
headnotes and English devotions"
(201) and shows that their relationship is closer than that between the
English headnotes and the devotions.
Shows also that the Latin phrases

rather than the English serve as "a
guide to the themes and emphases of
the *Devotions*" (202) and as "a key
to a far more unusual narrative structure" than often thought (206).

1132. Arshagouni, Mary. "Politics of John
Donne's *Devotions Upon Emergent Occasions:* or, New Questions on the New
Historicism." *Ren&R*, n.s. 15: 233–48.
Examines "the historical and political
context" of the *Devotions*, considers
"the way in which Donne's life and
writings have been politicized," and
questions "the appropriateness of
applying a new historicist methodology for interpreting a work like the
Devotions" (233). Challenges, in particular, the New Historicist reading of
the *Devotions* by Robert M. Cooper
in *New Essays on Donne,* ed. Gary A.
Stringer (Salzburg: Institut für Englische Sprache und Literatur, Universität Salzburg, 1977), 192–210. Argues
that "[f]ar from expressing criticism
of public policy, whether foreign or
domestic, the *Devotions* is rather an
anatomy of Perseverance, an experience appropriate only to the elect who
despite their assurance of salvation,
can never be free from sinfulness while
on earth." Calls the treatise "a dramatization of the emotions which afflict
the godly as they attempt to humble
themselves before God, repent their
sins, and bear their crosses patiently
as they await their final moment of
peace, a peace that comes with a final
escape from—and not an engagement
in—the world of politics, diplomacy,
and worldly men." Concludes that
"[a]wareness of the true political and
historical situation leading up to the
publication of the *Devotions* reveals
that in this work, a Donne psychologically distressed by the failure of
his mission with Doncaster to persuade King James to act decisively
on behalf of the Palatinate offers a
striking and profound turning away

from the world of politics as he realizes the suffering that this world inevitably brings and laments his failure to escape from its miseries into the eternal comfort of Heaven." Believes that a New Historicist reading "ironically points up how 'antihistorical' a work the *Devotions* in fact is" and makes clear "why ultimately in the *Devotions*—and perhaps this is Donne's point—piety and poetry transcend politics" (244).

1133. Baumlin, James S. *John Donne and the Rhetorics of Renaissance Discourse.* Columbia: University of Missouri Press. xiv, 333p.

"Prelude" (1–35) discusses four major rhetorical perspectives: (1) "an incarnational rhetoric" in which "truth is presumed to be singular, accessible to reason, and fully expressible in language"; (2) "a transcendental rhetoric" in which "this same truth, though singular and stable, retreats from language at the same time that it defeats or transgresses formal logic and the palpable realities of the senses"; (3) "a skeptical rhetoric" in which "language fails altogether to express a truth that is presumed to be unstable and ultimately unknowable"; and (4) "a sophistic rhetoric" that, "while assuming this same instability . . . compensates by claiming to invent truth, to create a world out of words." Maintains that "each reading in the interpretive history of Donne's poetry has situated itself within at least one of these perspectives" and proposes to examine "their dynamic interplay" (8). States that this study examines "the ways literary form is simultaneously enabled, sustained, and de-stablized by the multiplicity of rhetorics potentially resident within each text, and the ways these different rhetorics offer alternative perspectives or orientations for reading" (11). Chapter 1, "Reading the Theologies of Language" (39–66), "describes the problems these multiple rhetorics have brought to the interpretive history of Donne" and, "as a reading of others' interpretation," "this chapter simultaneously complements and complicates their more orthodox, unified readings by asserting the very terms they seek to refute—the equal claims of skepticism and fideism in Donne's epistemology, the continuing influence of Roman Catholicism upon an Anglican's writings, a consummate rhetor's mistrust of rhetorical argument, a gifted writer's radical questioning of literary-discursive form." In Chapters 1, 2, 3, and 4 Baumlin "reads Donne's early prose and the *Satyres* as documents in the competing rhetorics of Reformation theology," poems in which "self-conscious assertions of skepticism continually question, test, and strain their literary-discursive form. Chapter 2, "Satire and 'Self-Guiltiness' " (67–93), combines and alters two previously published essays; "Generic Context of Elizabethan Satire: Rhetoric, Poetic, Theory, and Imitation," in *Renaissance Genres: Essays on Theory, History, and Interpretation,* ed. Barbara Kiefer Lewalski (1986), 444–67 (entry 637), and "Donne as Imitative Poet: The Evidence of 'Satyre II' " in *EIRC* 11 (1985): 29–42 (entry 553). Chapter 3, "The Politics of Private Conscience" (94–118), revises and expands "Satyre IV: The Failure of Language and Genre" in *TSLL* 30 (1988): 363–87 (entry 862). Chapter 4, "The Reformation, and Retraction, of Satire" (119–56), reshapes material in "Donne's Christian Diatribes: Persius and the Rhetorical Persona of *Satyre III* and *Satyre V*," in *The Eagle and the Dove: Reassessing John Donne,* ed. Claude J. Summers and Ted-Larry Pebworth (1986): 92–105 (entry 636), and "From Recusancy to Apostasy: Donne's 'Satyre III' and 'Satyre V' " in *EIRC* 11 (1990): 67–85 (entry 1020). Chapter 5,

"Sacramental Theology and the Poet-ics of Absence" (159–90) expands in "Donne's Poetics of Absence" *JDJ* 7 (1988): 151–82 (entry 861), and "explores the linguistic theology of the valedictory poetry especially, observing the ways skepticism time and again undermines the poet's incar-nationist arguments." Chapter 6, "Incarnationism and Tran-scendence" (191–229), "examines the theological basis of Donne's transcendent rhetoric (the second alternative to the poet's failed incarnationism)." Chapter 7, "Skepticism and Sophism" (230–62), "describes the movement from skep-ticism to sophism." Draws several paragraphs in Chapter 8, "The Four Shapes of Rhetoric" (263–91), from "Decorum, *Kairos,* and the 'New' Rhetoric" (*Pre/Text* 5 [1985]: 171–83); from "Persuasion, Rogerian Rhetoric, and Imaginative Play" (*RSQ* 17 [1987]: 33–43); and from "*Psyche/Logos:* Mapping the Terrains of Mind and Rhetoric" (co-authored with Tita French Baumlin) (*CE* 51 [1989]: 245–61), and "attempts to orchestrate all four rhetorics in a perspectivist reading of selected lyrics," showing how "these four perspectives are dialectically related" (12) and "assume a theological character, modeling themselves upon the speech-acts of the priest-celebrant, the mystic, the agnostic, and the creator-god" (13). "Coda" (292–306) argues that in the Renaissance "genre-concepts arise out of the dynamic matching of form and function—a rhetorical model that directs reading and writing alike" (294), and that rhetoric "provides an interpretive procedure as well as a means of literary production." Main-tains that "interpretation situates it-self in the dynamic interplay between rhetoric and genre" (295). Holds that "rhetoric must either validate the genre by enacting its aims, or else the rhetoric will implicitly test, strain, and

subvert the form" (304) and that, "[l]ike rhetoric, genre never remains static in interpretation" since "the form itself undergoes a process of restate-ment as meanings and expectations are sustained, qualified, undermined, and revised" (305). Maintains, there-fore, that "genre-concepts change not just between but within literary works themselves" and "that which gives an initial shape to the text is inevitably reshaped by the reading experience," thus "[t]he relationship of a text to its genre-concept is therefore neither sta-ble nor assured," since "genre enables a reader's interpretation of a text that, in some problematic way, constitutes an author's intentions at the same time that it distorts and exceeds those intentions through the unpredict-able supplementarity of a reader's meaning" (306). Concludes with a bib-lio-graphy (307–25) and index (327–33). Reviews: Jill P. Baumgaertner in *RenQ* 45 (1992): 606–9; Eugene D. Hill in *AnSch* 9 (1992): 455–63; Mary Arshagouni Papazian in *ANQ* 5 (1992): 150–52; George L. Pullman in *RSQ* 22 (1992): 73–76; Michael L. Hall in *SR* 101 (1993): 596–98; Nora-lyn Masselink in *JEGP* 92 (1993): 242–44; Paul A. Parrish in *SCN* 51 (1993): 44–45.

1134. Benet, Diana Treviño. " 'Woman, do you know this nail?': A 'New' Donne Anecdote." *ANQ* 4: 181–84.

Reports an anecdote about Donne to the effect that he once solved a mur-der case while Dean of St. Paul's. According to the story, Donne, com-ing upon a skull of a man in the parish cemetery of St. Dunstan and noticing that it had a nail in it, confronted the dead man's widow, who instantly con-fessed to the murder. The account appeared in *The European Magazine* in 1820, although it was anticipated by a letter to the editors of *The New Monthly Magazine* in 1815 in which an unknown A. Z. sought information about the anecdote. Suggests that the probable source of both the query and the anecdote was Laetitia Pilkington's *Memoirs* (1754), in which she claimed she heard the story from Dean Swift.

1135. Bredbeck, Gregory W. *Sodomy and Interpretation: Marlowe to Milton.* Ithaca, N.Y.: Cornell University Press. xv, 261p.

Points out the reference to homoeroticism in *Sat1* (l. 40) but maintains that Donne "invokes sodomy not as a specific condemnation of male-male eroticism but as part of a larger attack on undifferentiated debauchery, in which 'prostitute boy' and 'plumpe muddy whore' are equivalent—though prurient—terms" (16). Points out also that in *Fare* (ll. 24–25) Donne refers to the Elizabethan medical theory that each orgasm shortens the life of the male (104).

1136. Brown, Meg Lota. "Interpretive Authority in Donne's *Biathanatos,*" in *Praise Disjoined: Changing Patterns of Salva-tion in Seventeenth-Century English Liter-ature,* ed. William P. Shaw, 151–63. New York: Peter Lang. Appears as part of Chapter 3 in *Donne and the Politics of Conscience in Early Modern England* (Leiden: E. J. Brill, 1995), 76–83.

Points out that *Biathanatos* differs from official church teaching on suicide, which condemns it under all circumstances. Maintains that Donne "advances the casuistical principle that no law, whether natural, positive, or divine, should condemn an action in disregard of circumstances" and thus he believes that "categorical arguments against suicide are both unreasonable and unjust" (151). Maintains, therefore, that in *Biathanatos* Donne defends "the casuistical doctrine that we must support our judgments with fully debated reasons" (152), a thesis he owes to Protestant casuistry. Gives a brief overview of critical commentary on the work. Notes that *Biatha-*

natos does not end with a definitive statement on suicide because Donne's aim "is not to become another authority on the subject," but rather he wants "to demonstrate the contingency of moral judgments and the need to weigh all sides of an issue before deciding on its moral status" (154). Notes that throughout *Biathanatos* Donne insists that his readers "should discriminate among the many opinions cited" and "should assume responsibility for their judgments, rather than rely on the authority of another" (154–55). Rejects the opinion of those who believe that because it is "replete with legalistic distinctions and citations" (157) from classical philosophers, Christian fathers, casuists, and jurists, *Biathanatos* is really a parody and should not be taken seriously. Shows that actually Donne is rather conservative in his views on suicide but that he gives the opinions of those who favor it so that his readers will "identify and resist their fallacies" and "formulate their own counter-arguments" (162). Suggests, therefore, that the paradoxical nature of the work "includes absurd examples and contradictory propositions in order to exercise the reader's logical and moral judgment" (162).

1137. Burns, D. A. "A Potpourri of Parasites in Poetry and Proverb." *British Medical Journal* 303, no. 6817: 1611–14.

Points out that "many verses have been composed with fleas, lice, and scabies as the main subject matter" (1611) and cites (with brief discussions) several examples, including *Flea.* Says that "the flea has attracted more attention from poets than any other insect" (1613).

1138. Chandra, Naresh. *John Donne and Metaphysical Poetry.* Delhi: Doaba House. 325p.

Discusses the nature of metaphysical poetry and examines Donne's poetry in the light of his definition. Chapter 1, "Introduction" (1–52), surveys previous attempts to define metaphysical poetry, focusing primarily on the work of Dr. Johnson, Augustus Jessop, Edmund Gosse, T. S. Eliot, George Williamson, Helen Gardner, Clay Hunt, and J. B. Leishman, followed by the author's own view. Maintains that "metaphysical poetry is not all of one kind" and argues that "[t]here are at least two kinds, the European and the English, the first beginning in intellect and ending in emotion; the second, beginning in emotion and ending in intellect" (52). Chapter 2, "Elizabethan Poetic Convention" (53–66), surveys the beliefs and attitudes about love found in the Elizabethan poets, a view which he calls "Spenserian erotic idealism" (53), and comments on the influence of Plato, Ovid, and Petrarch in shaping these ideas and poetic conventions. Chapter 3, "Revolt Against the Convention" (67–78), shows that Donne was alone in rejecting Elizabethan attitudes and conventions. Chapter 4, "Satyres and Verse Letters" (79–91), discusses these poems "to show that the crude rudiments of the qualities which distinguish metaphysical poetry are not altogether absent from them" (91). Chapter 5, "Poetry of Love" (92–137), comments on the main characteristics of *Songs and Sonets,* dividing them into three major categories: (1) "those that scoff at love poetry of a false idealism derived from Petrarch and other sources and later developed into a religion of love," (2) "those which make the scintillating experience of true and intense love the ground for the display of a rare wit, and speculations on the relationship between physical and spiritual, between body and soul even in sexual love," and (3) "those which take the theme of love as a pretext for the display of turns and twists of thought which cuts across both the

above categories" and in which "wit has a great role to play" (92). Chapter 6, "Elegies" (138–47), calls these poems the "least metaphysical of Donne's poems" (139) but notes their remarkable uses of wit. Chapter 7, "Epithalamions" (147–60), suggests that these poems show that Donne "is not outside the tradition of English poetry" but "is quite aware of the tradition, and even consciously tries to be in it, without merging his identity into it" (160). Chapter 8, "Epicedes and Obsequies" (161–75), looks at Donne's funereal poems, noting how they exhibit "certain characteristics of metaphysical poetry" as well as "certain tenets of his religious philosophy" (161). Chapter 9, "'An Anatomie of the World'" (176–95), and Chapter 10, "Of The Progresse of The Soule" (1976–215), analyze the two anniversary poems and suggest that in them Donne "has come closest to the European concept of metaphysical poetry, that is, poetry in which the poet gives expression to his own convictions and beliefs about life and the world, or the belief of an age, in a sustained argument in which abstract ideas and concepts are conveyed through the vehicle of sensuous images" (176). Chapter 11, "The Progresse of the Soule—Poema Satyricon" (216–28), discusses the theme and structure of the poem and regards it "worth looking into for specimens of descriptive poetry" and for "its reflections on sundry subjects" (228). Chapter 12, "The Sacred Poetry of Donne" (229–76), surveys the Divine Poems, considering them as inferior to Donne's secular poems and to those of certain other contemporaneous religious poets, such as Herbert, Crashaw, and Traherne. Complains that the pervading sin-consciousness in Donne's religious poetry "drags him down from the exalted state to one of doubt and fear" (276). Chapter 13, "The Significance of Donne's Poetry" (277–319), examines Donne's "contemporaneous and abiding significance" by placing "his poetry against the poetry of his contemporaries, and by assessing them all in relation to the poetry of the immediate past and of succeeding ages." Discusses, therefore, Donne's poetry in relation to that of Spenser, Sidney, Chapman, Daniel, Drayton, Marlowe, Shakespeare, and Jonson and comments on Donne's profound influence on the course of English poetry. Suggests that "the greatest significance of Donne's poetry is that if we want to understand modern poetry, we must begin with the study of the poetry of John Donne" (319). Contains a select bibliography (321–25).

1139. **Chapman, Wayne K.** "Yeats, Donne, and the Metaphysicals: Polemics and Lyrics, 1896–1929," in *Yeats and English Renaissance Literature,* 142–84. New York: St. Martin's Press.

Discusses the influence of Donne on Yeats. Points out that "[a]lthough it appears that most formal aspects of Donne's work failed to attract Yeats's attention until comparatively late, the Irish poet was long an admirer of Donne's natural-sounding poetic voice and his racy contrapuntal image-making ability," noting that especially "Donne's lyric mixing of the erotic and the philosophic struck a nerve in Yeats as early as the 1890s." Notes, however, that "[t]hose admired characteristics of Donne's poetry remained, largely, outside Yeats's register until he initiated a series of imitative exercises after his marriage in 1917," but that "until he made them his property, he was indebted to Donne for an ambience, a guise, which he could exploit in verse without having quite to bare his soul to the general public" (145). Points out specific borrowings of Yeats from Donne's poems as well as themes and philosophical ideas.

Discusses also the influence on Yeats of the critical thinking of H. J. C. Grierson, who presented Yeats with a gift copy of his edition of Donne's poems in 1912 and became a friend and mentor.

1140. **Clucas, Stephen.** "Poetic Atomism in Seventeenth-Century England: Henry More, Thomas Traherne and 'Scientific Imagination.'" *RenSt* 5: 327–40.

Discusses how in the seventeenth century "the atom haunted the imagination of its detractors and its supporters—writing in both poetry and prose" and examines "the metaphorical configurations used to exorcise or reinforce its burden of heterodoxy" (328). Cites Donne's *FirAn* as "an excellent example of the hostility and fear which the idea of atomism provoked in the popular imagination," in which atomism functions "as part of a moral typology of the discontinuous and the continuous in nature: the separate, the divided, the multiple, are perceived as evil, and the homogeneous, united, and complete are perceived as good" (329). Points out Donne's uses of anti-atomism in *Julia* and in *Har,* in which Donne's view is "symptomatic of the great distaste and revulsion felt for the atomic hypothesis in the early seventeenth century—when atheism and social discontent were felt to threaten the stable structures of Christian society and its monarch" (329–30).

1141. **Cousins, A. D.** *The Catholic Religious Poets from Southwell to Crashaw: A Critical History.* London: Sheed and Ward. xiii, 204p.

Explains in the preface that there is no extended discussion of Donne in this study since "[r]ecent work on Donne's sacred poetry, most notably that of Barbara K. Lewalski (which is reinforced by John N. King's account of English Reformation Literature) persuasively suggests that both its theology and its literary strategies are Protestant, as of course Donne himself was when he wrote it" (xii). Compares briefly, however, the poetry of Robert Southwell, Henry Constable, William Alabaster, Patrick Cary, and especially William Habington to Donne's poetry.

1142. Daley, Koos. " 'And Like a Widow Thus': Donne, Huygens, and the Fall of Heidelberg." *JDJ* 10: 57–69.

Contrasts *Lam* and Constantijn Huygens's translation of the same text as "private expressions of grief over the fall of Heidelberg" (58), which occurred on 6 September 1622, and comments on the political and poetical connections between the two men during this time. Discusses Donne's sermon of 1622, preached on the anniversary of the Gunpowder Plot, as a public warning to James I as well as to Prince Charles (the future king) of the dangerous political and religious situation caused by James's pro-Spanish and, therefore, pro-Catholic diplomacy at the time. Notes how the sermon "bristles with warnings against Catholicism" (65) and closes "with a strong plea for unity within the church and the kingdom, a unity that was almost destroyed by the Gunpowder Plot of 1605, and that was once again in danger by the King's political course" (68).

1143. Daley, Koos. "Traduttore, Traditore: Huygens as Translator of Donne," *CJNS* 12, no. 2: 11–16.

Examines Constantijn Huygens's "view of translation as expressed in his letters, his preface, and his introductory poem to his Donne translations" undertaken in 1630 and 1633. Discusses the meter, rhyme scheme, and syntax of his translation of *SunRis* "to evaluate his claims about the status of translation and the role of the translator," and compares Donne's original and Huygens's translation "to illustrate the relation between form and meaning and the problems Huygens faced when rendering a poet as complex and idiosyncratic as Donne" (11). Shows how in the translation Huygens "seems reluctant to translate Donne's hyperbolic allegations about the superiority of love and rejects as unacceptable its mystical, almost religious, qualities." Concludes that Huygens "might have been an equal to Donne on an intellectual level, but he could never quite distill Donne's soul into his version" (14).

1144. DiPasquale, Theresa. "Ambivalent Mourning: Sacramentality, Idolatry, and Gender in 'Since she whome I lovd hath payd her last debt.' " *JDJ* 10: 45–56.

Reads *HSShe* as Donne's attempt to cope with the sadness caused by Ann More's death and "to define who and what he has lost and, in so doing, to redefine himself." Believes that his wife's death deprived Donne not only of the woman he loved, but also "of a human sacrament, a tangible sign that both reveals and conceals divinity." Points out that the mood of the poem is, therefore, "a mixture of passionate devotion and ingenious anxiety." Argues that the sonnet's "imagery and theme evoke in particular the unresolved conflicts in Donne's sense of the sacramental," and that "[h]is response to the absent presence of Anne parallels his response to the Eucharist," and that "his fears about marriage reflect his fears about the efficacy of both Baptism and the Eucharist" (45). Shows how throughout the sonnet Donne's "on-going desire for Anne is ridden with guilt" since there is a direct connection "between his conjugal activities and their lethally fruitful consequences," and how, "[u]nable to separate devout apocalyptic yearnings from potentially idolatrous desire, he remains suspended between a sacramental mystery—Anne the earthly bride—and an anagogical mystery— God, the celestial bridegroom" (48). Maintains that throughout the poem Donne's diction "shows how much he still clings to a husband's role, which he must abandon in order to become a Bride in the heavenly wedding feast." Concludes that Donne's dilemma is that he cannot look at the example of Ann's femininity "without responding to it as a man" and maintains that "[h]e looks to the absent bride of Christ that he may become, like her, a responsive and utterly wifely creature; but in doing so, he makes present to himself the earthly bride he still desires"; thus "[i]n showing her husband how to welcome the Bridegroom, Anne can't help but remind him of how good it felt to be one" (54).

1145. Donnelly, M. L. "Saving the King's Friend and Redeeming Appearances: Dr. Donne Constructs a Scriptural Model for Patronage." *YES* 21: 107–20.

Reprinted in *Patronage, Politics, and Literary Traditions in England, 1558–1658,* ed. Cedric C. Brown (Detroit, Mich.: Wayne State University Press, 1993), 79–92.

Discusses Donne's sermon, preached on 24 March 1617, the anniversary of James I's accession, from an outdoor pulpit at Paul's Cross, in which his "thoughts on patronage took public form." Traces "connexions and associations from the 1617 sermon back through his [Donne's] earlier, secular writings and forward through later sermons and poems" in order "to shed light on his conception and rationalization of the patronage relationship" (107). Points out that "Donne habitually tried to lay hold of patterns of worldly success in his culture by casting his reflections on politics and society into theological language" (108) and shows how in the sermon Donne

"glorifies the king's favour as an aspect of God's grace, while at the same time implying the weighty responsibility which rests upon the dispenser of favour as he imitates and enacts the beneficence of the Godhead." Observes how in the sermon, by establishing "moral virtue as the precedent condition for the patronage relationship," Donne defends "a congruence between virtue and worldly reward that would justify power in its distribution of favour" (116). Concludes that "Donne could react to the model of the patronage system that he constructed out of the conceptions of divinity, not by rebelling against the medium, favour, defining it as alienating, but by committing himself ever more desperately to laying hold of it, opening himself to its power, even sanctifying it through the analogies he used to understand and describe its operations, all in the fervent hope that, in God's good time and with God's help, grace and favour would eventually be his, and help him realize his ambitions, and actualize his gifts and virtues in an effectual calling" (120).

1146. Dubinski, Roman R. "Donne's 'A Litanie' and the Saints." *C&L* 41: 5–26.

Discusses Donne's view on saints as found in his sermons and examines "the spectrum of views about prayer and the saints that were advanced by apologists and catechists for the Catholic and the various Reformed Churches" (6). Discusses how in his treatment of the invocation of the saints in *Lit,* Donne has fashioned a form of prayer for his friends that would defuse objections by those of either Catholic or Reformed inclinations. Points out that "[b]ecause Donne does not dismiss or ignore commemoration of the saints, he addresses Catholic sensitivities on this subject" and "accepts the doctrine that the saints, both on earth and in heaven, are filled with love for each other and voluntarily pray for each other." Maintains that, furthermore, Donne believes that "as heroes of faith the saints in heaven deserve special note and gratitude for their continuing prayers on behalf of their fellow servants on earth"; thus he "does not repudiate commemorations of the saints just because Catholics have abused them." Argues, however, that "at the same time the invocations are distinctly Protestant and offer rectified devotion to the saints." Discusses how "the first four invocations honor the primacy of God and the other persons of the Trinity in the merciful work of salvation" (23), and how Donne "carefully directs his prayers to God and not to the Triumphers," cautioning "believers about putting their trust in the prayers of the Triumphers" and "emphasizing that their trust should be in God alone." Thus sees *Lit* as a poem that best reflects "the spirit of the Anglican *via media*" (24).

1147. Dunlap, Rhodes. "Air and Angels," in *Reference Guide to English Literature,* vol. 3, 1450–51. ed. D. L. Kirkpatrick, 2nd ed., St. James Reference Guides. Chicago: St. James Press.

Presents a critical reading of *Air* and argues that the main point of the poem "is not the disparity but the smallness of the disparity" between men's and women's love. Believes the poem was written after Donne's marriage and during a time when he was reading Neoplatonic love theory, and suggests that "Donne's treatment of reciprocity in love might be compared with Leone Ebreo's definition of perfect love (in *Dialoghi di Amore,* 1535) as a transformation of the lover into the beloved." Points out that Donne's "theory of angelic bodies" comes from St. Thomas Aquinas (*Summa,* I, li. 2) (1451).

1148. Dust, Philip C. "Donne's 'The Dampe' as a Gloss on Spenser's *Faerie Qveene,* Book I." *SSt* 12: 219–21.

Published in 1998. Argues that the lady addressed in *Damp* "is very much a Duessa-figure in her immorality and her destructive abilities." Notes that "[e]pic love and war in *The Faerie Qveene,* Book I are parodied in Donne's treatment of the lady's sexual conquest of him in a joust" (219), and suggests how various lines in Donne's poem can serve as a gloss on Spenser's poem.

1149. Ellrodt, Robert. "Aspects de la conscience du corps dans la poésie de la Renaissance anglaise de Spenser à Milton," in *Les Figures du corps dans la littérature et la peinture anglaises et américaines de la Renaissance à nos jours,* ed. Bernard Brugière, 37–49. Paris: Publications de la Sorbonne.

A revised and expanded version of an essay with the same title published in *Le corps à la Renaissance: Actes du XXXe colloque du Tours,* ed. Jean Céard, Marie Madeleine Fontaine, and Jean-Claude Marolin (Paris: Aux Amateur de Livres, 1989), 199–211.

1150. Fortier, Mark. "The Muse in Donne and Jonson: A Post-Lacanian Study." *MLS* 21, no. 4: 90–104.

Presents a post-Lacanian psychological interpretation of the Muse as "the Other" and "the internalization of the mother" (91), and studies the Muse of Donne and Jonson, focusing on "a generalized pattern, a troubled relation to the Muse as Other, and a (wished for) resolution and loss of poet and Muse in God." Says that "[t]o trace the pattern of references to the Muse in the poetry of John Donne is to see the Muse as imaginary lover or wife of the poet, half of a (discursively, erotically, religiously) unsatisfying relationship between parts of the self, in (apparent) contrast with relationships between 'real' lovers, or, so he asserts, between other poets and their Muses." Claims that, "[i]n Donne, the world of the Father, God, the patron, social advancement, is set apart from the poetic ego and his intimates, the lover, the Muse and poetry, with which he shares a domestic seclusion" (93). Discusses how "[h]is dissatisfaction with his Other leads Donne, finally, to desire the annihilation of his Muse, and of his ego, in a surrender of the self, a perfection of the self, a death of the self, in God" (94), and that "[t]he sacrifice of the poet's own Muse—and hence his own ego—will perfect him by annihilating him as individual, as human," thus leaving "no poetic ego, no individual Muse, but only Christ as divine poet, a poet with a perfect Muse, a Muse such as this life never affords" (98).

1151. Fowler, Alastair, ed. *The New Oxford Book of Seventeenth Century Verse.* Oxford: Oxford University Press. xlv, 831p.
The introduction (xxxvii–xlv) challenges the notion that Donne and the metaphysical poets "overthrew Tudor conventionality, and introduced a style of concrete sensuous particularity." Maintains rather that Donne "was in many ways a conventional, traditional, and even a retrospective poet" (xxxvii), but at the same time admits that Donne's "brilliance illuminated or challenged most of his contemporaries" (xxxviii). Suggests that "[n]o recovered genre was more significant historically than epigram" and calls Donne's love poems "epigrammatic love elegies" (xxxix). Notes, in particular, Donne's wit and its influence on later poets. Includes 36 of Donne's poems (modernized text) with notes (104–39). Concludes with additional notes (800).

1152. Gibbs, Lee W. "John Donne: 1571–1631," in *The Middle Way: Voices of*
Anglicanism, 29–38. Foreword by John Booty. Cincinnati, Ohio: Forward Movement Publications.
Calls Donne "the most famous preacher of his time," "*the* metaphysical poet of Anglicanism" (29), a "champion" of the Church of England, and claims that he was the first "to coin the famous phrase *via media* to describe its essence and spirit" (33–34). Presents a biographical sketch of Donne, emphasizing his religious background and development. Notes that Donne "was not an original theologian" and maintains that the primary intention of his religious essays and sermons was to explain and defend "the doctrine and ritual of the Anglican church" (34). Sees Donne as an orthodox Anglican in all respects who "came to believe during the course of his life that in the Church of England there is a near approach to the early church" (35). Maintains that "[t]he keynote of all of Donne's devotional writing is passionate repentance" (36) but that his "final focus is not on sin but on love" (37).

1153. González Fernández de Sevilla, José Manuel. "La poesía metafísica de John Donne y Francisco de Quevedo." *Neophil* 75: 548–61.
Compares and contrasts Donne and Francisco de Quevedo as metaphysical poets, maintaining that they are fundamentally alike and that in their poetry they differ only in certain nuances. Discusses how both poets reflect the sociohistorical temper of their times, how their personal histories are the most decisive factor in shaping their poetry, and how both assume an existential posture that allows them to face boldly the radical themes of human existence. Maintains that both poets were obsessed with the thought of death and compares and contrasts their views on death as expressed in their poetry.

1154. Harada, Jun. *Donne Context.* Tokyo: Kenkyusha. iv, 339p.

Examines Donne as an egoist and maintains that his texts should be clearly understood in the context of their composition. Maintains that Donne's poems are witty and rhetorical self-expressions composed of very intricate imagery to reflect his paradoxical way of life.

1155. Heffernan, Thomas. *Art and Emblem: Early Seventeenth-Century English Poetry of Devotion.* Renaissance Monographs, 17. Tokyo: Renaissance Institute, Sophia University. Chapter 1, "The Book of Scripture and of Nature and Early Seventeenth-Century English Emblem Poetry of Devotion," is reprinted in *Yearbook of Interdisciplinary Studies in the Fine Arts* 3 (1992): 531–81.

"The Book of Scripture and of Nature and Early Seventeenth-Century English Emblem Poetry" (1–28) presents a reading of *Noct* as a "nudum emblema" or "naked emblem," that is, a picture-poem that lacks an actual hieroglyphical picture, and comments on Donne's possible sources in contemporary emblem books and in Christian tradition. "Donne: Imitating the Antitheses of the Divine Artist" (57–60) discusses *HSBlack* as "an emblem poem—a verbal picture of an invisible reality spoken of as visible," and as "a hieroglyph, a shadowy sign that points to a higher and better meaning hidden within the Soul's sinful condition." Maintains that "[i]n this hieroglyph the visualized Soul conceals and gradually reveals the truth and beauty hidden in the Soul's capacity to be reformed," and attributes the "underlying notion" of the poem, "shown by the antithesis of black and white," to St. Augustine, "who linked psychology of the individual soul and sacred history" (60).

1156. Hellegers, Desiree E. "The Politics of Redemption: Science, Conscience, and the Crisis of Authority in John Donne's 'Anniversaries.'" *NOR* 18: 9–18.

Maintains that the *Anniversaries* "reflect Donne's concern with preserving the voluntarism of God and the interpretive freedom of the individual, concerns which are embodied in his acceptance of justification by Grace." Says that "[t]he metaphor of the two books, the Book of Scriptures and the Book of Nature, is a constitutive element" of the two poems, "in which Donne attempts to mediate between two equally appropriate representations of the transcendence of God: unitary order and postlapsarian chaos," and that "[i]n this respect, the poems illustrate the complex relationship between Protestant theology and science and the extent to which disputes over nature of the physical world are both implicated in and extend seventeenth-century debates over the nature of language" (9). Points out that "Donne's skepticism about science is rooted in his profound suspicion of claims of disinterested interpretation" (10) and that he sees the "New Philosophy" as "simply the latest of many towers men have built throughout history to threaten God" (12). Believes that Donne sees the imperfection of nature and language as proof of man's dependence on Grace, and contrasts Bacon's experimentation and its emphasis on "endless progress" with Donne's belief that human knowledge is not progressive. Suggests that Donne attributes "a redemptive function to the fallenness of language" (15) and that metaphor serves "a socially redemptive function" because of "its capacity to embody multiple and conflicting interpretations." Concludes that "[p]oetry and interpretation are, for Donne, the paradigmatic Protestant acts of worship" and "embody both the quest for unity and the impossibility of ever attaining it" (18).

1157. Hester, M. Thomas. "Genre, Grammar, and Gender in Donne's *Satyre III*." *JDJ* 10: 97–102.

Argues that *Sat3* is Donne's response to the Church of England's claim to rid the country of idolatry. Maintains that, as in *Sat2* and *Sat4*, "the poem appropriates the terms and lexicon of current religious controversy" to show that the major threat to English souls is the idolatry of "an England ruled by Cecil and Protestant nominalisms, which have created a world in which only parodies of 'our Mistresse faire religion' ([l.] 5) prosper—thoroughly in line (from Donne's Catholic perspective) with the Lutheran-Calvinist heresy's *deus absconditus,* its metonymical Eucharist, and its displacement of the spiritual by the political in all aspects of English 'devotion'" (97). Calls the concluding couplet of the satire "a crisp epigrammatic reminder" that the preceding lines serve "primarily as a dramatic *satirical* warning about a 'currant' eternal problem: the loss of free will and the absence of 'true religion' in late Elizabethan Protestant England" (98). Supports this reading of *Sat3* by pointing out "that it is a *late* Elizabethan poem contemporaneous with the Lambeth Articles and an increase in the enforcement of the penal laws against recusants; that it is a *manuscript* poem circulated among a circle of like-minded readers; and that it is above all a *satire*" (98). Believes that *Sat3,* "as an Elizabethan manuscript satire," reveals more about "the difficulty and danger (spiritual and physical)" that Donne confronted "in his search for the 'Presence' of God in Elizabethan England" than it does about which Christian sect he later chose and that, "as such, it offers a glimpse into the psychological dynamics that animate in equally equivocal textures his elegies, lyrics, and even his holy sonnets" (101). (From a colloquium on *Sat3* held during the John Donne Society conference in 1992; see also essays by Paul Sellin (entry 1183), Gary Stringer (entry 1192), and Camille Slights (entry 1186).

1158. Hester, M. Thomas. "'Impute this idle talke': The 'Leaven' Body of Donne's 'Holy Sonnet III,'" in *Praise Disjoined: Changing Patterns of Salvation in Seventeenth-Century English Literature,* ed. William P. Shaw, 175–90. New York: Peter Lang.

Argues that the *Holy Sonnets* present "a moral interrogation of the central issues of the English (Counter) Reformation debate about justification doctrine" and that "[a]s dramatic meditations which affirm man's limited powers of recreation (which is common to both Catholic and Protestant thought), the poems display the tensions inherent to, and the psychic questions raised by, the application of Protestant doctrine of imputation to the human condition." Further maintains that the *Holy Sonnets* do not show us "a former Catholic moving toward a 'conversion' to Protestantism" but rather "a Catholic confronting the limitations of Reformed doctrine" (177). Analyzes *HSScene* as a poem that directly considers the issue of imputation and shows how the poem dramatically suggests that "[a]ny doctrine of justification which imputes merit without admitting that the believer undergoes any real ontological change . . . is merely a *covering up* of the necessity for interior renovation (that is essential to Catholic dogma)." Claims, therefore, that Donne "plays out the inherent (verbal) limitations of the Protestant imputation and the shaky dualism it infers, or seems to imply for him" (186). Concludes that the sonnet "dramatizes the fond rational foundations of any mechanical doctrine of justification that evades the problematics of human virtue and the mystery of imputation at the same time that it explores the desperate foundation of such doctrine in the human desire for signification" (190).

1159. Hester, M. Thomas. "The *troubled wit* of John Donne's 'blacke Soule.'" *Cithara* 31, no. 1: 16–27.

Presents a detailed reading of *HSBlack* and claims that the sonnet can be better understood "through comparison of its central paradox with the dramatic exposition of that doctrine in *Everyman*." Maintains that "[s]uch a perspective suggests that the achievement of Donne's sonnet derives in large measure from the manner in which it engages the doctrine of prevenient Grace as it is expostulated dramatically in the play, not in order to endorse explicitly the Catholic view of the doctrine but in order to explore the psychological and moral questions attendant to the application of the Protestant or Reformed view of imputation to that doctrine current at the time of the poem's composition" (16). Maintains that the sonnet is "another of Donne's rhetorical enactments of the equivocal dynamics of human desire," noting that "the figurative repetitions and changes the poem undergoes convey dramatically the desire for and the insufficiency of man's attempts to transfigure his 'selfe.'" Maintains that the sonnet "tempts us to read a personal attempt [on Donne's part] to locate himself within— or in between—the Catholic and the Protestant readings of 'Christs blood'" but adds that "it survives not just as a record of that dilemma, but as a dramatic evocation of the motions of moral consciousness—fully cognizant of the inherent limitations of its humanity, puzzled by and in wonder of the eternal motions of Grace." Concludes that "[t]his ability to dramatize the dynamics of human paradox

remains the major achievement of Donne's poetry of wit" (24).

1160. Hill, Geoffrey. *The Enemy's Country: Words, Contexture, and Other Circumstances of Language.* Stanford, Calif.: Stanford University Press, xiv, 153p.

Briefly comments on the uses of rhetoric, syntax, conceit, and metaphor in Donne's verse letters to Sir Henry Wotton written between 1597/98 and 1604.

1161. Hiller, Geoffrey. "'Where thou doost Live, There let all Graces Be': Images of the Renaissance Woman Patron in Her House and Rural Domain." *CahiersE* 40: 37–51.

Examines how aristocratic women patrons during the late Elizabethan and Jacobean periods, especially Mary, Countess of Pembroke; Lucy, Countess of Bedford; and Margaret, Countess of Cumberland, "are portrayed in the considerable corpus of literature addressed to them by those who wished to gain or maintain their patronage." Draws "some conclusions not only about the writers' ideal of a female patron but also about patronage itself—what aspects of it, apart from simple monetary reward, were the most coveted by the aspirant and appreciated by her protégé." Notes that what becomes most evident is "the value placed on the psychological as well as the material security" that belonging to an aristocratic household gave the writer. Notes that often the patroness "is idealised as the beneficent mistress of a cultural community or as a semi-deified figure presiding over her garden or estate which resembles a poetic Arcadia," and "[h]er surroundings are a literary haven characterised by the companionship and intellectual stimulus provided by herself and other writers in her circle" (37). Observes that Donne addresses Lucy, Countess of Bedford, "as a goddess" and "metamorphoses Twickenham into a church filled with worshipping poets who sound her praise like organs and interpret her words like priests" (38), lauds her "for her keen discernment in selecting those worthy to be her intimate circle" (40), and praises her "in terms of the effect her radiant personality has on her domain" (44). Concludes that the aspects of patronage that writers "valued most highly" and "hoped in part at least to enjoy" were "companionship, intellectual stimulation, liberal hospitality, [and] security in a community which under a patroness's benevolent rule epitomized moral and social order" (46).

1162. Hirsch, David A. Hedrich. "Donne's Atomies and Anatomies: Deconstructed Bodies and the Resurrection of Atomic Theory." *SEL* 31: 69–94.

Discusses Donne's "metaphorical appropriation of anatomic and atomic theories" in both his poetry and prose and suggests "some of the difficulties Donne confronts in representing the self as a unified object," noting that "representation," in this case, means "both a symbolic process of denying spatial and temporal absence through the manipulation of words and images, as well as the re-presentation of one's soul and scattered bodily parts, aspects of self separated with death's decay." Maintains that "[b]y anatomizing the representative body to the limits of material dissection, Donne attempts to discover a radical immutability of selfhood which could refute his fear of dissolving into nothingness," but ceases his anatomy "once he cuts to the material permanence of atoms," since "the atom as the limit to the self's deconstruction might also serve as the origin of that self's reconstruction" (71). Holds that Donne's interest in the atomic debate "stems from his concern with permanence in the face of what seems to him an unavoidable recognition of decay and loss" (73), nowhere better illustrated than in *FirAn*. Surveys several poems and his prose works to show that Donne's "conception of self is deeply rooted in the integrity of his personal body, and that without some assurance of physical permanence, purely spiritual immortality is somehow incomplete" (80). Maintains that "Donne's belief in the immutability of atoms is prerequisite to his acceptance of the possibility of physical resurrection" (86) but that he finally realizes that "human reason cannot account for the mysteries of resurrection," and thus the significance of the atom must at last defer to "the Absolute Signified, God" (87).

1163. Keller, James R. "A Note on the Phrase 'His Purple Wrapped' from Donne's 'Hymn to God, My God, in My Sickness.'" *SCN* 49: 44.

Suggests that, in addition to several other interpretations, the phrase "his purple wrapped" in *Sickness* (l. 26) also refers to the purple liturgical vestments worn by Catholic priests during Lent. Discusses how "the clerical vestments represent the central theme of Donne's poem: the good Christian must endure pain, sickness, and death in order to attain the joys of heaven and freedom from corruption." Suggests also how "the entire first stanza initiates the liturgical motif that culminates with the image of a priest dressed in penitential robes at the end of the poem."

1164. King, John N. (with the assistance of Robin Smith). "Recent Studies in Protestant Poetics." *ELR* 21: 283–307.

Presents a bibliographical account of recent scholarship "concerning the conventions, techniques, genres, and theory of Protestant literature written during the English Renaissance and Reformation (c. 1525–1675)," which "emphasizes studies of poetry" but also "includes analyses of dramatic literature, imaginative prose, literary criticism, and selected literary and stylistic studies." Focuses on "the inter-relationship of literature and religion" and "excludes purely historical and theological studies" (283). Includes Donne (296–97, 306). All items mentioned that were published between 1979–1995 are annotated in this bibliography. For all items before 1979, see *Roberts 1* or *Roberts 2*.

1165. Kirkpatrick, D. L., ed. *Reference Guide to English Literature.* 2nd ed. Vol. 3. St. James Reference Guides. Chicago: St. James Press. xviii, 1445–2143p.

Contains four brief critical essays on individual Donne poems by Rhodes Dunlap, Peggy Nightingale, Chris Roark, and William Zunder, each of which has been separately entered in this bibliography.

1166. Klawitter, George. "John Donne and Salvation Through Grace," in *Praise Disjoined: Changing Patterns of Salvation in Seventeenth-Century English Literature,* ed. William P. Shaw, 137–49. New York: Peter Lang.

Maintains that, while Donne was "acutely concerned with salvation and damnation throughout his life" (137), he was "no more obsessed with death and its after effects than were other Renaissance writers" (138). Provides a background for Donne's theology of grace, noting how Reformation and Counter Reformation theologians developed their thinking from the same medieval traditions. Points out that, although Donne's attitude toward grace seems orthodox, we must remember that he was an "English Catholic," not a Presbyterian or Puritan. Cites eight references to grace in Donne's poems that show "the power of grace to change human nature" (142) and discusses in particular *Goodf* and *Tilman.* Examines *HSBlack* as an example of the problem of "the grace to begin

grace" (144), which is solved by repentance and by receiving the Eucharist and in which "the initiator of 'automatic' grace is the sinner him-self" (148). Concludes that "[f]or Donne, a man of action, there is no question of sitting around waiting to be worked upon from above" (149).

1167. Kruzhkov, Grigorii. "Dama v zele-nom." *Novyi mir: Literaturnii khudozh-estvennyii obshchestvennii politicherskii zhurnal* 3, no. 4: 147–53.

Translates into Russian *ElFatal* and *ElComp* with no notes or commentary.

1168. Laird, Edgar S. "Love 'Elemented' in John Donne's 'Valediction: Forbidding Mourning.'" *ANQ* 4: 120–22.

Comments on Donne's use of the learned term "elemented" in *ValMourn* (l. 16) to describe "sublunary" lovers. Traces the term back to "the medieval Latin term and concept from which it was derived: *elementata*" (120) and notes that it could still be found in several Renaissance dictionaries. Maintains that a correct understanding of "elemented" "helps to locate the sublunar lovers more precisely at a very low point on the scale of being and thus separates their love more widely from the love which the poem celebrates" (121).

1169. Levi, Peter. "Visionary Poets," in *The Art of Poetry,* 81–105. The Oxford Lectures 1984–1989. New Haven, Conn.: Yale University Press.

Maintains that there are visionary passages in Donne's poetry and sermons but that he "never maintains vision-ary intensity throughout an entire sec-ular poem." Says that although *Noct* is "thrilling and faultless," contain-ing "a series of breathtaking insights and devices," the reader knows that "the metaphors are only metaphors" because Donne "several times changes them." Holds that, in spite of "mo-ments of great intensity," neither *Noct* nor *Ecst* "as a whole can be called visionary." Cites *HSRound* as an example that shows that Donne was "capable of unearthly visions" (93), but claims the sonnet "droops away into religious melancholy about sin, as so many of Donne's religious poems do." Believes that Donne was "too passionate for innocent visions" and "too thoughtful for simple ones," thus "his greatness lies elsewhere" (94).

1170. Llasera, Margaret. "Optique baroque: Un aspect de l'imaginaire de la modernité dans la poésie anglaise de 1600 à 1700," in *Y a-t-il un imaginaire de la modernité?: Actes du colloque tenu à l'Université de Paris-X Nanterre sous la direction de Maurice Robin et d'Armand Himy les 11 mars, 20 mai et 10 juin 1988,* 195–209. Confluences 3. Nanterre: Université de Paris-X.

Based on an extensive examination of Renaissance treatises on optics, shows how optical theories filtered down to baroque poets, who were intrigued with the mechanics of vision and various kinds of distorting illusions. Discusses, in particular, the complex and prevalent uses of images, metaphors, and conceits derived from an interest in mirrors, the telescope, the microcosm, and other anamorphoses. Cites several examples from Donne's poetry—his use of reflective tears in *ValWeep,* of the telescope in *Har,* and of theories of sight in *Ecst, GoodM,* and *Canon.* Discusses also the relationship of perspective to wit and metaphor and the growing antagonism between poets, who viewed the world metaphorically, and emerging scientists, noting, for instance, Bacon's distrust of metaphor.

1171. Lewalski, Barbara Kiefer. "Writing Women and Reading the Renaissance." *RenQ* 44: 792–821.

In a survey of women writers of the Renaissance, discusses briefly the Countess of Bedford's patronage of Donne; her influence on his poems, especially the verse epistles and poems that they exchanged with each other; and Donne's admiration for her as a poet. Suggests that the countess's "poetic exchange with him at the death of Cecilia Bulstrode affords some insight into the poetic transactions of her circle" (799–800).

1172. Mahler, Andreas. "Profanierung des Sakralen—Sakralisierung des Profranen. Beobachtungen zur Entsubstantialisierung des religiösen Diskurses in der frühen Neuzeit," in *Deutsche Shakespeare-Gesellschaft West Jahrbuch,* ed. Werner Habicht, 24–45. Bochum: Ferdinand Kamp.

Discusses *Sat3* as a return to the private, personal expression of religion in which faith is understood as a question of subjective self-discovery and self-determination. Sees the satire as a remarkable statement on tolerance. Points out how the satire as a genre was adapted for the purposes of religious discourse and suggests that Donne's transforming a previously profane genre into something sacred anticipates his use of sacred parody in his later religious poems.

1173. Martz, Louis L. *From Renaissance to Baroque: Essays on Literature and Art.* Columbia: University of Missouri Press. xiii, 277p.

Includes 12 essays, 11 of which were previously published. The final essay, "Vaughan and Rembrandt: The Protestant Baroque" (218–45), is new, but does not discuss Donne. Only 4 of the essays discuss Donne: "English Religious Poetry: From Renaissance to Baroque" (3–38) first appeared in *EIRC* 11 (1985): 1–28 (entry 595), and here the account of Donne's portraits has been substantially revised; "Donne and Herbert: Vehement Grief and Silent Tears" was originally published in *JDJ* 7 (1988): 21–34 (entry 905); "Donne's *Anniversaries* Revisited"

(51–63) appeared in *That Subtile Wreath: Lectures Presented at the Quatercentenary Celebration of the Birth of John Donne,* ed. Margaret W. Pepperdene (Decatur, Ga.: Agnes Scott College, 1973): 29–50, and is here extensively revised; and "The Generous Ambiguity of Herbert's *Temple*" (64–83) was originally published in *A Fine Tuning: Studies of the Religious Poetry of Herbert and Milton,* ed. Mary A. Maleski (Binghamton, NY: Medieval and Renaissance Texts and Studies, 1989): 31–56 (entry 989).

1174. Matar, N. I. "John Donne, Peter Sterry and the *Ars Moriendi.*" *EIRC* 17: 55–70.
Discusses the influence of Donne's meditations on the art of dying on Peter Sterry, the Puritan advisor to Cromwell, whose unfinished treatise, "The State of a Saints Soul and Body in Death" (1683), is called "one of the most eloquent statements on the *ars moriendi* in seventeenth-century theological imagination" (55). Maintains that "while Donne wrote from the literary and social tradition of the art of dying, Sterry was formulating for his followers the theology of that art" (58) and proceeds to examine that theology, especially Sterry's emphasis on death-as-love. Discusses how inspired by Walton's portrait of Donne's death and by the deaths of his interregnum associates, especially Major General Harrison and Sir Henry Vane, Sterry "articulated from his own deathbed a unique explication of the art of dying in Restoration England," affirming, like those before him, "the love/joy/mystical union analogy with death" but also presenting "an extensive theological and historical perspective on death" (64). Concludes that Sterry's purpose was "to leave to the persevering [Puritan] saints the testimony of the Puritan martyrs and the art which would enable them, even at Tyburn,

to love death in preparation for the eschaton" (67).

1175. Morgan, Paul. "Hypertext and the Literary Document." *JD* 47: 373–88.
Surveys "some recent developments in textual studies," identifies "areas where a hypertext form would be of assistance to textual and literary scholars in examining multiple texts of single works," and proposes "a model of how such a literary hyperdocument might be constructed and used," using "the Guide hypertext software" (373). Maintains that since numerous manuscript versions of Donne's poems circulated in his lifetime, "varying not only in content, but [also] in the contextual poems in the documents which contained them," all of these versions "have their own validity." Maintains that "the generic and other relationships of these texts, with their differing contexts and intended audiences, is an important and fruitful field of enquiry," but that in printed editions "all this can only be hinted at by the use of appended tables and diagrams" (378), thereby privileging the printed copy-text. Reports the creation of a hyperdocument, using six poems from the *Songs and Sonets* that exist in 28 manuscript collections, suggesting that it was "this multiplex of variant transcriptions which constituted the *Songs and Sonets* as far as Donne and his contemporary audience were concerned, not solely the printed version which only appeared two years after the poet's death." Says that the aim of the hyperdocument is "to make easily and coherently available" the "complexity and richness of texts of a work, as [they were] originally circulated" (380).

1176. Mościcki, Krzysztof. "Was John Donne a Mystical Poet?" *KN* 38, no. 2: 91–107.
Argues that, when mysticism is properly understood, Donne "was not a mystical poet in any of the phases of

his literary work." Notes that, "[p]ara-doxically, it is his later, religious phase . . . that is completely devoid of mystical qualities," and suggests that, "in that period, his earlier richness and rapidity of poetical wit seem to be missing" and he "appears to have lost this sense of unity and totality of being, which he had so fully expressed in his [earlier] conceits" (94). Points out, however, that Donne's love poetry "does have certain features that could be called quasi-mystical, being evoked by certain elements of poetic diction such as hyperbole and conceit" (94). Cites several examples from the *Songs and Sonets* but concludes that none of the poems "could be classified as mystical, since the crucial element of the mystical experience, which is man's submission to and union with the Absolute, is missing" (100). Discusses how *Ecst*, for all its references to mysticism, is not a mystical poem in the ordinary sense of the term. Believes that the "close link between poetry and mysticism" is the cause for some critics applying "the terminology of mysticism to the analysis of Donne's poetry." Concludes that, although Donne uses the tradition of mysticism in his conceits, "neither he can be called a mystic, nor his poetry mystical" (106).

1177. Nardo, Anna K. "John Donne at Play in Between," in *The Ludic Self in Seventeenth-Century English Literature,* 49–77. SUNY Series, The Margins of Literature, ed. Mihai I. Spariosu. Albany: State University of New York Press.

Reprinted from *The Eagle and Dove: Reassessing John Donne,* ed. Claude J. Summers and Ted-Larry Pebworth (Columbia: University of Missouri Press, 1986), 157–65 (entry 705).

1178. Nightingale, Peggy. "A Valediction: Forbidding Mourning," in *Reference Guide to English Literature,* ed. D. L. Kirkpatrick, 2nd ed., vol. 3, 1918. St.

James Reference Guides. Chicago: St. James Press.

Comments on *ValMourn* as representative of Donne's art: "it is an expression of intense feeling carried by a series of clever and witty comparisons; the speaking voice of the poem addresses an imaginary listener directly; and generally that voice employs a fairly natural syntax, frequently settling for half-rhymes." Points out the sexual double entendres, noting that "under the surface where the departing lover speaks movingly of the depth and spiritual strength of their love, there is a constant undercurrent of physical passion." Concludes that Donne's "art conceals its artifice, and intellect combines with poetic instinct to produce a poem which is both emotionally and critically satisfying."

1179. Patterson, Annabel. "John Donne, Kingsman?" in *The Mental World of the Jacobean Court,* ed. Linda Levy Peck, 251–72. Cambridge: Cambridge University Press.

Maintains that "more than any other Renaissance poet, Donne challenges us to conceive of subjectivity in environmental terms, to see how socio-economic and political circumstances interact with a particular temperament to produce the historical person, who is both partly conscious of the rules by which he must play and partly the director of all his roles." Says that "if any single writer might be said to exemplify 'the mental world of the Jacobean court' as well or better than James himself, Donne is he" (251). Points out, however, that Donne has a "deep ambivalence about the world in which he both desperately wanted and deeply disdained to participate" (252). Examines Donne's works written during the reign of James I, especially *Biathanatos, Pseudo-Martyr, Ignatius, Eclog,* and *SecAn,* to show that they were "conditioned by the style of James's court, character, politics, publications, and James's dealings with parliament" (254). Argues, however, that Donne "was never so simply the king's man as the newer historical criticism has asserted," and suggests that "some of the current paradigms in history proper could be profitably modified by looking at 'literary' evidence" (255). Points out also that the love poems are "riddled with political terminology" and that "by no means all of it situates the speaker on the side of royal absolutism" (268). Believes that "Donne's membership in the 1614 parliament" was perhaps his "last bid for personal freedom" but that "events conspired against him" and in the following year he "bowed to the king's pressure and agreed to take orders, so that a clerical appointment might follow" (272).

1180. Roark, Chris. "The Anniversaries" in *Reference Guide to English Literature,* ed. D. L. Kirkpatrick, 2nd ed., vol. 3, 1464–65. St. James Reference Guides. Chicago: St. James Press.

Discusses the argument of the *Anniversaries.* Points out that primarily Donne offers "a meditation on human existence spurred by feelings of lost human potential which accompany the death of someone young" and celebrates "the power of the poet to depict the ideal." Examines several critical cruxes in both poems and the ways in which critics have attempted to solve them. Maintains that Donne "challenges generations of readers to make sense of the colliding relationship between the extreme praise of Elizabeth Drury and the debased world this figure stands against, or otherwise [to] respond to the energy this conflict generates, insuring his subject an audience through time" (1464). Calls both poems "complex explorations of the contrasting and simultaneous processes of the soul's putrefaction and purification" (1465).

1181. Roebuck, Graham. "Donne's *Lamentations of Jeremy* Reconsidered." *JDJ* 10: 37–44.

Rejects claims that there are echoes of the Authorized Version (1611) in *Lam,* describes "the kind of paraphrase or translation Donne is attempting," and suggests "its relationship to his life" (39). Maintains that Donne's work is a translation when he translates his primary source, Tremellius, and is a verse paraphrase when he paraphrases the Geneva Bible, noting that "in both cases there are passages in which Donne expands somewhat his sources with a modicum of poetic license, appropriate to his conception of the highest matter and noblest form" (41–42). Believes that "it would make sense" to date the poem as early as the 1590s, perhaps sometime after May 1592 when Donne entered Lincoln's Inn and the ravages of the plague had "virtually closed down London" (42).

1182. Scodel, Joshua. "Reconceiving the Dead: Donne and Carew on Donne," in *The English Poetic Epitaph: Commemoration and Conflict from Jonson to Wordsworth,* 113–39. Ithaca, N.Y.: Cornell University Press.

Maintains that, although Donne wrote few epitaphs and that the few he did write "reveal little of his genius," *BedfCab* is "a major though neglected poem with important ramifications for Donne's treatment of death throughout his writings" (113). Shows how in the poem Donne "depicts an intense reciprocity between the living and the dead well outside the mainstream of both English poetic tradition and Protestant theology" and suggests that the epitaph "attracted no imitators because it was too daring an expression of a highly personal poetic and theological vision" (114). Presents a detailed reading of the poem, pointing out many "resemblances of theme and tone" between the epitaph and

Donne's other writings, "both secular and sacred" (114). Points out how the poem "is reminiscent of medieval Catholic epitaphs, not in specific doctrinal content but in its sense that the living and the dead are bound to mutual spiritual improvement" (122). Discusses also "An Elegie upon the death of the Deane of Pauls, Dr. John Donne," in which Carew "seeks not only to define Donne's achievement but also to relate it to his own" (129). Shows how in the concluding epitaph of the elegy Carew "legitimize[s] his own secular values by hallowing the whole of Donne's accomplishment, profane as well as sacred" (133), and "overturns the proclamations of expressive failure in the elegy," thereby testifying "not only to Donne's but also to Carew's poetic power" (134). Shows also the political ramifications of the epitaph in which Carew presents Donne as a servant of the Caroline state and himself indirectly as "a poetic supporter of royal power" (138), concluding that thus his epitaph "exemplifies the polemicization of the dead" that becomes "a central feature of the mid- and late seventeenth-century epitaph" (139).

1183. Sellin, Paul R. "*Satyre III* No Satire: Postulates for Group Discussion." *JDJ* 10: 85–89.

Argues that *Sat3* "is not a satire, and certainly not one in the same sense as the other satires"; that there is "no certain proof" that it "was designed to function as a pivotal third poem in a suite of five Romanesque satires"; and, therefore, that critics should treat the poem as "an independent entity, not as a part of a larger whole" (89). Discusses how *Sat3* differs from Donne's other satires and from Roman satire, points out that its place and numbering in the manuscripts vary, and argues that it was written later than the other satires, certainly after 1598 and more likely after 1600. From

a colloquium on *Sat3* held during the John Donne Society conference in 1992; see also essays by M. Thomas Hester (entry 1157), Gary Stringer (entry 1192), and Camille Slights (entry 1186).

1184. Shawcross, John T. *Intentionality and the New Traditionalism: Some Liminal Means to Literary Revisionism.* University Park, Pa.: Pennsylvania State University Press. 236p.

Chapter 1, "Introduction: Literary Revisionism: Definitions and Devices (1–19), first appeared as "Literary Revisionism and a Case for Genre" in *Genre* 18 (1985): 413–34 (entry 612), in which the author insists that the very existence of a poem or other piece of literature implies that the author had some kind of "intent" when he wrote the poem. Comments on *Licent* as an example of a poem "generally inadequately read or actually misread by inattention to . . . authorial presence" (7), and discusses the importance of recognizing the intertextuality between Carew's "Secrecy Protested" and *Damp*. Mentions Donne's poetry throughout primarily by way of illustration: Chapter 2, "Poetic Genre and Its Implications" (23–35), contrasts *Sat1* and *Sat5* as examples of the genre of verse satire. Chapter 5, "Genre and Seventeenth-Century Poetry" (63–76), suggests that *Christ* is "misclassified, mistitled" because, in terms of genre, it is "more correctly a prayer" than a hymn (71). Chapter 8, "Henry Vaughan's 'Amoret' Poems: A Jonsonian Sequence," repeats the argument in "Vaughan's 'Amoret' Poems: A Jonsonian Sequence," in *Classic and Cavalier: Essays on Jonson and the Sons of Ben,* ed. Claude J. Summers and Ted-Larry Pebworth, (entry 329) that explores Vaughan's debt to Donne in his Jonsonian sequence, concluding that he only used Donne's poetry as "a foil" (116). Chapter 13, "The Self as Poetry in Marvell's Work" (169–84), finds Donnean echoes in

Marvell's "The Coronet" and "The Definition of Love". Chapter 14, "Rochester's Poetry and Its Seventeenth-Century Antecedents" (185–95), mentions Donne's influence on Rochester's poetry.

1185. Shawcross, John T. "Some Further Early Allusions to Donne." *JDJ* 10: 79–83.
Notes the following eighteenth century allusions to Donne not included in A. J. Smith's *John Donne: The Critical Heritage* (1975): (1) an appropriation of *SGo* in a letter by William Warburton to Thomas Birch, dated 27 May 1738 (MS Additional 4320 in the British Library); (2) a listing of the *Poems* (1635) and the quotation of *ConfL* in Thomas Hayward's *The British Muse, or a Collection of thoughts Moral, Natural, and Sublime, of Our English Poems* (1738) and in its second edition entitled *The Quintessence of English Poetry* (1740); (3) three references—one to *Metem* and two to *Eclog*—in Walter Harte's *The Amaranth: Or, Religious Poems* (1767); (4) a letter in *The Barbados Gazette* (18 July 1733) containing a poem entitled "On Reading Dr. Donne's Poems," which was reprinted in volume 1 of *Caribbeana . . .* (1714); (5) an anonymous poem, *A Sorrowful Ditty; Or, the Lady's Lamentation For the Death of Her Favourite Cat. A Parody* (1748) that plays with the last stanza of *Canon* and perhaps the stanzaic form of *SGo;* (6) "Observations on the Life of Dr. Donne, Dean of Paul's" in volume 2 of *State-Worthies: or, The Statesmen and Favourites of England From the Reformation to the Revolution* (1766); (7) an allusion to *Metem* in Richard Farmer's second edition of *An Essay on the Learning of Shakespeare* (1767) and repeated in a letter of Henry Headly in *Gentleman's Magazine* (October 1786); (8) comments on Donne's life in the second edition of *Anecdotes of Some Distinguished Persons . . .* (1796); (9) a reference to Donne's prosody in *The Progress of Satire: An Essay in Verse* (1798); (10) a reference to Donne's sermon on Mrs. Herbert in volume 1 of *The Lives of the English Regicides . . .* (1798); and (11) two revised lines from *Sat2* in the undated *Liberty Deposed, or the Western Election. A Satirical Poem. In Three Books.*

1186. Slights, Camille Wells. "Participating Wisely in *Satyre III*." *JDJ* 10: 91–95.
Argues that *Sat3* presents very little about Donne's religious beliefs and "nothing at all about his allegiance to an institutionalized church" but rather "offers as a model of correct behavior conscious engagement with contemporary social practices and institutions" (91). Maintains that Donne "saw religious faith as unavoidably involved in the social, political, and economic as well as the narrowly spiritual—and that he wanted to show the problem of religious allegiance at least in part as a question of how to relate to the existing social order" (92). Holds that in the poem Donne "recommends the dialectical process of participating in human debate, a process the poem enacts by considering the question of religious truth in terms specific to the legitimation crisis of early modern Europe through a speaker who questions, argues, chastises, and exhorts his fictive auditor and the reader." Insists that *Sat3* is "most interesting and significant when seen in the context of Donne's other verse satires, which as a group explore the problem of how to participate in human society without compromising personal integrity," and maintains that, "in its insistence that we must know the bounds of human power in order to 'rightly obey power,'" the poem "complicates and disrupts any attempt to see in Donne a dramatic conversion from alienation and moral isola-

tion to absorption within an absolutist power structure" (94). From a colloquium on *Sat3* held at the John Donne Society conference in 1991; see also essays by M. Thomas Hester (entry 1157), Paul Sellin (entry 1183), and Gary Stringer (entry 1192) and Camille Slights (entry 1186).

1187. Smith, A. J. *Metaphysical Wit.* Cambridge: Cambridge University Press. xii, 270p.

Discusses "the reason for the central importance of wit in the thinking of the metaphysical poets, and argues that metaphysical wit is essentially different from other modes of wit current in Renaissance Europe." Surveys "[f]ormal theories and rhetorics of wit . . . for both their theoretical import and their appraisals of wit in practice," considering "fashions of witty invention . . . in Italian, French and Spanish writings" in order "to bring out the nature and effect of various forms of wit: conceited, hieroglyphic, transformational, and others from which the metaphysical mode is distinguished." Finds "the basis of Renaissance wit in the received conception of the created order and a theory of literary innovation inherent in Humanist belief, which led to novel couplings of time and eternity, body and soul, man and God." Maintains, however, that "metaphysical wit distinctively works to discover a spiritual presence in sensible events" and "traces its demise in the 1660s to changes in the understanding of the natural world associated with the rise of empirical science" (foreword). Surveys the limitations of previous critical and/or scholarly evaluations of Donne's wit and explores the uniqueness and range of Donne's wit and its philosophical underpinnings in both his secular and sacred poetry and prose, citing numerous examples. Distinguishes Donne's mode of wit "from other forms of wit which were current in seventeenth-century Europe in that it does not aim at figurative enlivenment" but rather "sets itself to apprehend metaphysical issues, as it were sensibly and immediately in the contingent occurrences of the world" (151). Points out that Donne's "true legacy" to those poets following him "shows up in metaphysical endeavour rather than in the trappings of a metaphysical style, or in Cavalier attitudes" (235). Compares and contrasts Donne's wit not only to that of his predecessors, both English and Continental, but also to the wit of Herbert, Crashaw, Cartwright, Suckling, Marvell, Cowley, and Lancelot Andrewes. Reviews: Mary Arshagouni Papazian in *JEGP* 92 (1993): 431–34; John Lennard in *EIC* 44 (1994): 140–47; Gerald MacLean in *MP* 92 (1994): 99–104.

1188. Smith, Bruce R. *Homosexual Desire in Shakespeare's England: A Cultural Poetics.* Chicago: University of Chicago Press. xii, 329p.

Considers Donne "a spokesman for the moral arguments against sodomy," noting that the Renaissance view of homosexuality is "wittily sketched" in *Metem* (ll. 468–772), in which Donne equates homoeroticism with bestiality. Observes that it is "this cosmic context, this Christian context" (174) that Donne endorses when he addresses the issue of homosexuality in the *Saytres,* specifically in *Sat1* (ll. 84–85) and *Sat4* (ll. 127–28). Notes that Donne says that men who act out their homosexual desires are not only immoderate, effeminate, decadent, and "abuse nature," but most damning of all, "they extinguish the soul that makes man Man" (181), thereby relinquishing their "social" and even "psychological identity" (185). Observes that for Donne sodomy meant primarily "a man lusting after a boy" but that, "[o]n the sexual potentiality in male bonding, so difficult to see be-cause so pervasive and so undefined," he remains "silent" (186). Also in passing contrasts Donne and Shakespeare as love poets, noting that Donne's poems in manuscript apparently circulated more widely than did Shake-speare's sonnets perhaps because of the homosexuality expressed in the latter, which required greater privacy and secrecy.

1189. Spurr, Barry. "Salvation and Damnation in the *Divine Meditations* of John Donne," in *Praise Disjoined: Changing Patterns of Salvation in Seventeenth-Century English Literature,* ed. William P. Shaw, 165–74. New York: Peter Lang.

Maintains that Donne's "preoccupation with grace and the conviction of sinfulness are at the heart of his religion" and that "[t]he most characteristic feature of Donne's spiritual emotion—its striking extremity—arises out of the daunting contrariety between these two heterogenous destinies of the Christian life." Insists, therefore, that "[t]here is no 'grey area' in Donne's Christianity," noting that "for all his professed Anglicanism he was decidedly not a poet of compromise." Contrasts Donne with Herbert's "quiet assurance" (165) and says it is "the defining paradox of Donne's vocation as a religious poet that the nearness of God is most keenly known in the ignorance of grace" (167). Likens Donne's attitude to that of the dark night of the soul in St. John of the Cross and suggests that he anticipates the desolation found in the poems of Gerard Manley Hopkins. Maintains that the *Holy Sonnets* "are dominated by Donne's delineation of the probability of his damnation" (168), citing as examples *HSMade, HSDue,* and *HSBatter.* Suggests that the source of Donne's attitude is "his recusant childhood," and concludes that the *Holy Sonnets* "portray a

scrupulosity in faith unto death of Jesuit inspiration," reflecting "the meticulous and remorseless self-questioning in which, in a family of martyrs, [Donne] had been thoroughly schooled" (173).

1190. Stachniewski, John. "John Donne: The Despair of the 'Holy Sonnets,' " in *The Persecutory Imagination: English Puritanism and the Literature of Religious Despair,* 254–91. Oxford: Clarendon Press.

Revised and expanded version of an essay with the same title in *ELH* 48 (1981): 677–705.

1191. Stringer, Gary A. "Donne's Epigram on the Earl of Nottingham." *JDJ* 10: 71–74.

Reports a hitherto unnoticed epigram to the Earl of Nottingham in the Crewe/Monckton Milnes manuscript (now at Meisei University in Tokyo), which "on both thematic and bibliographical grounds may be tentatively ascribed to Donne" (71).

1192. Stringer, Gary A. "*Satyre III* Colloquium: Stringer, Sellin, Slights, Hester." *JDJ* 10: 79–83.

Discusses the colloquium on *Sat3* held during the John Donne Society conference in 1992, commenting briefly on the contributions of each of the panelists and suggesting ways that "further attention to Donne's status as a manuscript poet could modify or refine the arguments they make" (80). Points out that *Sat3* appears in 29 surviving seventeenth century manuscripts and all seventeenth century editions. In a chart gives the ordinal position of the poem in these artifacts. Illustrates by selected examples how unsettled the matter of Donne's prosody is and gives evidence that Donne revised the poem. Concludes that *Sat3,* as well as many of Donne's other poems, should be seen "as a progressing 'work' constituted over the course of time by several participating 'versions'" and that critical interpretation must "take into account the structural and thematic implications of the poem's evolutionary nature" (81). See also essays by M. Thomas Hester (entry 1157), Paul Sellin (entry 1183), and Camille Slights (entry 1186).

1193. Summers, Claude, and Ted-Larry Pebworth. "Donne's Correspondence with Wotton." *JDJ* 10: 1–36.

Discusses how the verse and prose letters that Donne exchanged with Henry Wotton illustrate "Donne's mastery of two distinct yet related forms of discourse" that "are equally referential and occasional" and how they "vividly document the course of a relationship lived out under the shadow of the political tensions of the declining years of Elizabeth's long reign." Shows how the correspondence "partakes of the cult of friendship that was important to both men" and describes their friendship, insisting, however, that the letters are "firmly rooted in and decisively shaped by concrete and immediate realities" (1). Maintains that "[m]ost of the surviving correspondence in prose and verse may be grouped in relation to four distinct episodes centering on the political fortunes of the young courtiers: the crisis of the summer of 1598 occasioned by Essex's quarrel with the queen and his self-exile from Court; Essex's Irish campaign of the spring and summer of 1599, in which Wotton participated; the disgrace of Essex in the autumn and winter of 1599–1600; and the revival of Wotton's fortunes at the accession of King James" (2–3). Shows how these events "provide the context and dictate the rhetorical strategies of the correspondence" and "help explain several salient features of the exchanges between Donne and Wotton, especially their obliquity, discretion, self-consciousness, and ten-

sion." Proceeds, therefore, with "a contextual/conjectural reconstruction of the surviving correspondence" which (1) "provides a glimpse into a dangerous world of intrigue and instability as seen through the eyes of young men at once attracted to that milieu and repulsed by it"; (2) "offers a fascinating record of a friendship affected variously by the stresses of politics and finally altered altogether by the success of one colleague and the frustration of the other"; and (3) reveals important biographical information ("especially Donne's alleged partisanship toward Essex") and gives "psychological insights into the personality of each participant." Maintains that the correspondence shows how Donne "grows from a brash young man affecting a fashionable cynicism into a more astute observer of the political scene." Insists also that the letters (both prose and verse) "are crafted works in their own right" (3) and "revealingly embody creative responses to important public crises even as they also record the tensions and rewards of a significant personal friendship" (32).

1194. Tayler, Edward W. *Donne's Idea of a Woman: Structure and Meaning in "The Anniversaries."* New York: Columbia University Press. xiii, 190p.

Discusses the structure and meaning of the *Anniversaries,* examining not only *FirAn* and *SecAn* but also Joseph's Hall's "To the Praise of the Dead" that preceded *FirAn* and Donne's *FunEl* that followed it as well as Hall's "The Harbinger of Progres" that preceded *SecAn.* Maintains that by 1612 "[t]he five poems had become a book" and the *Anniversaries* "had become in the technical, generic sense 'companion poems,' radically altering the purpose and meaning of the first edition of 1611" (ix–x). The introduction (1–19) argues that the

Anniversaries must be read in the light of the seventeenth century philosophical theories and convictions that inform them. Surveys the various interpretations of the "she" of the poems and maintains that "she" is, in fact, Elizabeth Drury. Argues that "[i]nstead of asking what she symbolizes, we need to know what Donne, in an age before Descartes and Locke and Coleridge, could have meant by the word *idea*" (19). Chapter 1, "The Idea of a Woman" (20–33), explores the history of the word "idea" to clarify what Donne meant when, reputedly responding to Jonson (according to Drummond's account), he said that in the *Anniversaries* he had described "the Idea of a Woman and not as she was." Discusses "the meanings acquired by *idea* in its relation to *species* during the second half of the sixteenth century" (27), noting that "*species* could refer to the intelligible form of an object, that which can be 'seen,' to adopt the old metaphor, by the 'eye of the mind'" (28). Maintains, therefore, that "Donne told Jonson that he described the intelligible species of a virtuous woman" (31). Chapter 3, "The Watch-Tower (1)" (34–51), points out that Donne makes clear in the *Anniversaries* that "[t]o see Elizabeth Drury and to read the poems we need 'better eyes,' which in accord with the ancient equation between seeing and knowing implies the need for a better mind," and that "a better mind for Donne, though not for us, depends on virtue" (42). Maintains that Donne is saying, in other words, "you can't see her if you are not good, for you have 'vulgar sight' and stand in need of 'better eyes'" and that "[t]hose of lesser wit and purblind vision find themselves deterred by 'incomprehensiblenesse' and perceive only imperfectly or not at all the subject of The Anniversaries" (43). Chapter 3, "The Watch-Tower (2)" (52–67), examines the Renaissance epistemology that informs the *Anniversaries*. Discusses, in particular, how William of Moerbeke's translation of Aristotle's *De Anima* "established the vocabulary, the terms of discourse, that were used habitually to describe mental operations in Renaissance England: phantasia, phantasma, sensibile, sensitivum, intelligibile, intellectus patiens, intellectus agen, and the like," which, during the period became "the language of imagining and thinking" and the "vocabulary of cognition" (53). Examines also Lodowick Bryskett's *A Discourse of Civill Life* (1606), which illustrates "the ways in which the mind deals with the 'incomprehensibleness' of sense perception" (61). Chapter 4, "Beauties Best (1)" (68–90), maintains that the *Anniversaries* "have suffered mainly from imperfect appreciation of the ways in which they are constructed—the relation of the parts to the whole and the whole to the parts" (75) that has resulted in the inability of critics "to reach even tentative agreement about the *subject* of the poems—the identity and the significance of 'she'" (80). Surveys various interpretations of the structure of the *Anniversaries*, observing that a proper understanding of the structure "vitally affects our understanding of other aspects of the poem—imagery, tone, theme, and the like" (81), and that "the *meanings* we ascribe to a poem depend upon the structure that we find in the poem or that we manage to impose on the poem" (80–81). "Beauties Best (2)" (91–113) presents a "schematic representation of the skeletal structures" of the *Anniversaries* "to reveal exactly how Donne effected the transition from the first to the second poem," to "provide graphic illustration of the organization that the poet consciously imposed on his varied materials," to show that "this structure may be apprehended without recourse to theories epideictic, Jesuitical, or funereal" (89), and to make clear that "the organization of The Second Anniversary proceeds to a series of carefully calculated variations from the norm established by the first poem, and ends with an astonishing yet significant departure from the norm" (90). Explains how "Donne uses the three-part divisions of the five main sections created in The First Anniversary as the basis for the meaningful variations in The Second Anniversary" and then "leaves behind this carefully articulated system of comparisons and contrasts to simulate the nature of the soul in ecstasy, using structure first to imitate the three-part movement of reason, memory, and will in this-worldly 'meditation' and then using the calculated conflation of the elements of that structure to mimic the activity of the soul in otherworldly 'extasee'" (113). The "Conclusion" (114–35) summarizes the argument of the study, stressing that "in [the] mix of Aristotelean cognition and Christian Neoplatonism—lies the rationale for Donne's praise of Elizabeth Drury" (132). Concludes that in the *Anniversaries* "the poet corresponds to poem corresponds to reader—if all are good, and if the reader knows it," and that "[t]he distinction between subject and object collapses into a series of equivalences—between poem and poet, between poem and subject, between poem and reader," because "[e]levated to their essential status as 'Idea' they are one and the same" (135). Includes notes (137–84) and an index (185–90). Reviews: Eugene D. Hill in *AnSch* 9 (1992): 455–63; Dennis Flynn in *JDJ* 13 (1994): 187–92; Richard Harp in *BJJ* 1 (1994): 238–41; John

Klause in *JEGP* 94 (1995): 548–51; John Mulryan in *Cithara* 36 (1996): 34–36; L. E. Semler in *Parergon* 15 (1997): 265–67.

1195. Tebeaux, Elizabeth. "Memory, Reason, and the Quest for Certainty in the *Sermons* of John Donne." *Renascence* 43: 195–213.

Argues that recent studies of Donne's sermons have focused too exclusively on his indebtedness to St. Augustine's views on memory and have failed to show how "Donne's comments on memory also illuminate his perspective on reason and its role in salvation," claiming that "the value Donne places on reason in the believer's quest for certainty surfaces during the definition of his stance on memory." Outlines, therefore, Donne's position on memory and then traces "the points at which his position on reason becomes tentative and difficult to capture" (195). Shows that an examination of "Donne's passages on memory and then reason and the relationship of memory and reason in the believer's quest for certainty suggests that any attempt to circumscribe and describe Donne's theology is never final." Concludes that "Donne's position on reason defies rigid definition" because "Donne is sometimes a sceptic" and "[a]t other times he endorses the importance of reason" (210). Calls Donne "an analytical nightmare" (211) and stresses that his "position on reason is neither consistent nor easy to capture" (212).

1196. Todd, Richard. "Carew's 'Crown of Bayes': Epideixis and the Performative Rendering of Donne's Poetic Voice." *JDJ* 10: 111–27.

Discusses the elegies appended to the first edition of Donne's poems (1633) in order "to examine the complexity of some of the developments the funeral elegy was undergoing during the early Stuart period in England, at a time when the classical practice it was imaginatively conscripting was being subjected to quite revolutionary changes in epistemological perception." Maintains that the discussion "will serve to contextualize Thomas Carew's act in allowing his own elegy to perform its way self-consciously through conceits familiar to the reader of Donne's religious poetry, ultimately troubling itself to a point where it settles on one conceit in particular, becoming consumed by the fire it contrives to kindle." Shows how "Carew's performance thus culminates in nothing less than a rendering or burning down of elegy to epitaph, in a process that is itself a tribute to the energizing dynamism Carew seems [to] have sensed in and been attracted to in Donne's religio-poetic discourse." Examines "the complex and shifting generic and performative relationship between 'elegy' and 'epitaph'" (111), and discusses Carew's poem "in the context of a fictive enactment of (at least part of) the drama of an ancient rite" (113), arguing that Carew "uniquely employs his epideictic formula to conclude that neither this nor indeed any other epicede is fit for its subject," and thus proceeds "by destroying the epicede" and "replacing it with a four-line epitaph" (116).

1197. Wolny, Ryszard. "Image of Death in John Donne's Love and Religious Poetry." *Filologia Angielska* 5: 179–89.
Argues that the pervasiveness of death both in Donne's love poetry and sacred poetry is untypical of seventeenth century poetry in general. Notes that 32 poems in the *Songs and Sonets* have allusions or references to death and that the presence of death is even more evident in his religious poems. Attempts to find "the source of Donne's enormous interest in death, together with a social and psychological moti-

vation for it" and examines "the image of death that constantly appears and re-appears in some of his love and religious poems, providing for it, at the same time, a wider seventeenth-century literary context." Attributes Donne's preoccupation with death primarily to guilt and isolation caused by "his unhappy conversion from Catholicism to Anglicanism" (180). Comments on Donne's paradoxical attitudes towards and uses of death in his poetry and concludes that fundamentally "for Donne death of the body is simultaneous with its resurrection and, what is more, with the resurrection of his soul from the deadly sin of betrayal" (189).

1198. Young, Robyn, ed. "John Donne," in *Poetry Criticism: Excerpts from Criticism of the Works of the Most Significant and Widely Studied Poets of World Literature,* vol. 1: 120–62. Detroit, Mich.: Gale Research.
Contains a biographical sketch of Donne (with a portrait) and a critical introduction to his works (120–21), lists Donne's principal works (121–22), and presents critical excerpts from books and essays, arranged chronologically (from Donne's time to 1987) (122–60), followed by a list of suggested further readings (160–62). All items from 1979 to 1987 are included in this bibliography.

1199. Zunder, William. "Batter My Heart (Holy Sonnet 14)," in *Reference Guide to English Literature,* ed. D. L. Kirkpatrick, 2nd ed., vol. 3, *1483–84.* St. James Reference Guides. Chicago: St. James Press.
Critical line-by-line analysis of *HSBatter,* briefly commenting on Donne's use of metaphors, imagery, paradoxes, alliteration, enjambment, shifting tone, and the sonnet form. Says that "the theology of the poem is typically Protestant" (1483).

1992

1200. Akiba, Ryuzo. "Donne no 'A Nocturnal upon St. Lucy's Day,' matawa 'Chaos no Shi' " ["A Nocturnal upon St. Lucy's Day: A Poem of Chaos"], in *Renaissance to 17 Seiki Eibungaku* [Renaissance and Seventeenth-Century English Literature], 23–43. The Japan Society of Seventeenth-Century English Literature. Tokyo: Kinseido.

Argues that *Noct* is the most philosophical and religious of Donne's love poems, especially commenting on the influence of St. Augustine on Donne's thought.

1201. Albrecht, Roberta J. "Montage, *Mise en Scène*, and Miserable Acting: Feminist Discourse in Donne's *Holy Sonnet X.*" *ELN* 29, no. 4: 23–32.

Maintains that the *Holy Sonnets* "is based upon structuring principles similar to those of the cinema" (24) and that Donne uses both "*mise en scène* and montage, and that the latter, in particular, gives the sequence as a whole a meaning greater than that of the sum of its parts." Believes that the first 12 sonnets "consist of two series of six each, forming something like a diptych, with each sonnet in the one half corresponding very closely to its counterpart in the other." Notes, however, that the second series (12–7) "has been inverted so that Donne, instead of doing what might have been expected, giving us a parallel structure, has created one gigantic chiasmus" (24). Examines in particular the relationship between *HSScene* and *HSBatter* to show how the reader "is forced constantly to revise, to re-read

the one poem in the light of its counterpart" (25). Maintains that the male speaker of the latter poem adopts the role of a female transvestite ventriloquist, creating thereby "an ambiguity of the same sort as counterpoint does in music or as montage does in film" (30). Concludes that the speaker "is motivated by pride and imprisoned by masculine discourse so that when he seeks to accomplish salvation, he fails" and "is trapped in an endless now, ever going around in circles" (31).

1202. Austin, Frances. "John Donne (1572–1631)" in *The Language of the Metaphysical Poets,* 18–46. The Language of Literature, gen. ed. N. F. Blake. London: Macmillan; New York: St. Martin's Press.

Discusses Donne's language, especially his use of striking images; colloquial diction; technical, Latinate, and monosyllabic words; mostly abstract and unremarkable adjectives; and syntactical words, verbs, and pronouns. Comments on the close relationship between the syntax, including ellipsis, and meter in Donne's poems, which accounts for their forcefulness, harshness, speechlike quality, and compression of meaning. Notes that "[k]nowledge of the emblem tradition helps the reader to understand the strange pictorial quality that Donne often draws" (41). Maintains that "[p]erhaps the principal rhetorical device that Donne uses, apart from conceits and emblems, is repetition in all its many forms" (42), which allows for various kinds of wordplay. Shows how Donne's language is "ratiocinative" and how he "argues through his vocabulary, syntax and images, forcing the reader to use powers of reasoning to reach the meaning" (46).

1203. Badenhausen, Richard. "Wilfred Owen on John Donne: 'You've got a hell of a breath.'" *MQ* 33: 181–92.

Comments on Donne's influence on Wilfred Owen, especially the influence of *HSDeath* on Owen's sonnet "The Next War." Points out how Owen, like Donne, "enjoyed turning traditional forms, attitudes, and styles against themselves," pointing out that whereas Donne adapted the sonnet to religious meditation, Owens brought to it "a graphic description of wartime conditions" (191).

1204. Bates, Catherine. "The Semantics of Courtship," in *The Rhetoric of Courtship in Elizabethan Language and Literature,* 25–44. Cambridge: Cambridge University Press.

Points out that the meaning of the verb "to court" in Elizabethan English meant most often court rhetoric, as seen in Donne's use of it in *Will* (l. 22), in which he wills "courtship" to a university, "where he assumes the art of civil conversation is wanting" (30). Notes also that in *Sat1* (ll. 21–24) and in *HSVex* (ll. 9–10) Donne suggests that, "in its flattering mode, courting epitomizes fraudulence and dissimulation" (31).

1205. Beck, Joyce Lorraine. "Negative Subjectivity in Luce Irigaray's 'La Mystérique,' Donne's 'A Nocturnall Upon S. Lucies Day,' and Crashaw's 'Glorious Epiphanie.'" *SMy* 15: 3–17.

Shows how the account of mystic discourse and subjectivity in Luce Irigaray's *Speculum de l'autre femme* (Paris: Éditions de Minuit, 1974) elucidates *Noct*. Disagrees with those critics who find in the poem "nothing but unrelieved pessimism" and sides with those who have perceived in it "a

movement from grief to some kind of resolution, from utter darkness to the beginnings of a mysterious illumination" (7). Analyzes the poem to show that "[t]his new beginning is made possible through the poet's pursuit of the negative path of mystical unknowing, a *via negativa* in which the speculative subjectivity of what Irigaray calls 'self-identity-as-sameness' is overcome" (10). Observes that "[t]he paradox of *lux ex tenebris*, light out of darkness, is the central figure" (14), not only in *Noct* but also in *BedfRef*. Compares *Noct* with "the mystical discourse of illumination" (16) in Crashaw's "Glorious Epiphanie."

1206. Brown, Meg Lota. "'Though it be not according to the law': Donne's Politics and the Sermon on Esther." *JDJ* 11: 71–84. Appears as part of Chapter 3 in *Donne and the Politics of Conscience in Early Modern England* (Leiden: E. J. Brill, 1995), 91–96.

Maintains that Donne "was not a champion of democracy or even of the limited liberty that Milton espoused" but "was a political moderate under a coercionary regime." Holds that "[m]ore conservative than insurgent, he was a supporter of monarchy and—when he believed circumstances warranted—an apologist for autocratic governance." Insists, however, that "Donne's political analyses, like his support of monarchy, were never unequivocal" and that "[h]is politics were often inconsistent—at times apparently absolutist and at times apparently subversive—because they were typically casuistical." Notes that around 1615 Donne preached a sermon "in defense of unlawful religious assembly" in which "he denied the authority of the monarch to enforce unjust conformity" (71), but that a decade later he "urged unrelenting and severe pressure on religious non-conformists," insisting on the divine right of the king. Maintains that "it is the circumstances of the specific cases under consideration that shape the politics of each sermon," claiming that "[s]uch casuistical contingency informs Donne's politics throughout his works." Examines, therefore, "Donne's politics through his use of casuistry, focusing on the 1615 sermon on Esther as representative of the interpretive principles that inform Donne's politics throughout his career" (72). Shows how Donne in the sermon "encourages the congregation to cultivate casuistical habits of mind so that they will be prepared to adjudicate their own cases of conscience" (79) and discusses how "casuistry was particularly well-suited to Donne's interpretive practices and politics" (80).

1207. Burnley, David. "John Donne," in *The History of the English Language: A Source Book,* 249–54. London: Longman.
Begins with a brief biographical sketch of Donne followed by comments on the spelling, punctuation, and distinctive use of verb and pronoun forms in "Meditation 17" of the *Devotions,* noting also in the passage that "[t]he rhetorical conception of the style, preferring parallel, balanced short clauses, ensures that the syntax echoes the patterns of simple speech" (249–50). Reproduces *SGo* and *GoodM* "to illustrate the use of the apostrophe in order to aid the reader in scanning the lines, where it indicates the elision of *e* in the inflexional endings -*ed* and -*est*." In the notes (253–54), Burnley briefly comments on how Donne's pronunciation "can be deduced from the rhymes" (250).

1208. Butler, Guy. "John Donne—A New Contemporary Reference." *N&Q,* n.s. 39: 357–60.
Points out in Robert Tofte's very free translation of the Italian *Dello ammogliarisi piacevole* (1594), entitled *Of Marriage and Wifing* (1599), a personal attack on Donne and suggests reasons for Tofte's antagonism. Suggests that the attack provides evidence of "Donne's being sufficiently well-known by mid-1599 to form a target, in literary circles at least." Notes that Tofte's volume, along with ten others, were ordered by the Archbishop of Canterbury on 4 June 1599 to be burned and suggests that the reason was that Tofte had linked Donne's name in his attack with that of the powerful Rich family. For a reply, see I. A. Shapiro in *N&Q,* n.s. 41 (1994): 61–62 (entry 1455).

1209. Cain, T. G. S., and Ken Robinson. "Introduction," in *Into Another Mould: Change and Continuity in English Culture 1625–1700,* ed. T. G. S. Cain and Ken Robinson, 1–17. London: Routledge.
In a discussion of the pressures of change and continuity simultaneously shaping literature and audiences in the seventeenth century, briefly comments on how Donne "responds to the serious *magi* of Paracelsus" (11) while, at the same time, he regards the "new philosophy" as confirming that the universe "was in sharp decline" (14). Says that Donne's "relative lack of interest in classical imitation did not indicate a lack of respect for classical writers, but rather his pessimistic sense of the decline of the modern world" (15–16), whereas "[c]lassical imitation implied for most practitioners a faith in the potential for improvement of the poet's society that Donne simply did not have" (16).

1210. Carey, John. " 'The Flea' by John Donne." *ERev* (Oxford) 3: 32–33.
Presents an analysis of *Flea* to show how various interpretive possibilities "complicate and deepen a poem which, on the surface, registers only crude masculine triumphalism." Concludes that "the poem seems confident,

clever and fairly shallow" but that "its changes of tone, and its concealments, and its doubt about whether to be dramatic (public) or undramatic (private), give it the subtlety and indecisiveness that distinguish Donne's lyrics from those of lesser metaphysical poets" (33).

1211. Carrithers, Gale H., Jr., and James D. Hardy, Jr. "Love, Power, Dust Royall, Gavelkinde: Donne's Politics." *JDJ* 11: 39–58.

Maintains that Donne as a preacher was "*ipso facto* a political figure" but argues that "his politics may best be constructed largely, in terms of his theology and the Prayer Book liturgy, the tropes of religious life, and the fact of dialogue" (39). Insists that "Donne's politics were God-oriented, heaven-oriented, eternity-oriented, and dialogic" and "were centered on his God and his God's loving call, and his own and his auditors' charitable response to it, as against the rising current of civil, ecclesiastical, or technological shows and idolatries." Points out how this orientation is "implicit in the innumerable metaphors and metonymies of Christian journey" and is "synecdochially suggested by the *moment* of loving revelation or graced *retorqueo,* as opposed to the moment of apocalyptic loss or the endlessly disjunctive moments of tychastic time" (42). Maintains that Donne believed that "the City of God, present here and even now, very now, in the mysterious workings of grace, was the true end of humankind" and that "it was understood to surpass incalculably, to outrank ontologically, the *civitas terrena*" (42–43). Illustrates these elements through an analysis of several of Donne's sermons, pointing out that, while criticizing James I and his court, Donne "hedged enough to keep his post, his freedom, and his ears" (46). Concludes that, for all its political

ramifications, Donne's "preaching itself manifested a sort of parable or allegory of the Biblical, Augustinian, liturgical journey of right ordered loves" (54).

1212. Chambers, A. B. *Transfigured Rites in Seventeenth-Century English Poetry.* Columbia: University of Missouri Press. xii, 275p.

Discusses the connection between liturgy and poetry in the seventeenth century, in which poets "regularly wrote verse that might accurately be called a 'reappropriation' and or 're-creation' of liturgical materials" (5), as found, for example, in *Lit,* Donne's personal adaptation of a public prayer, and *Canon,* a love poem using "the vocabulary of prayer" (21). Shows how patterns of liturgical rites and liturgical language were translated or transfigured into poetry, both sacred and profane, and discusses in some detail the liturgical dimensions of *Father, Annun,* and *Corona.* Shows how *Noct* is a "serious parody" (118) in which Donne "turns divinity inside out or upside down to stake out a profoundly serious position" (120). Includes a revised version of " 'Goodfriday, 1613. Riding Westward': Looking Back" that first appeared in *JDJ* 6 (1987): 185–202 (entry 758), and "Crooked Crosses in Donne and Crashaw" that first appeared in *New Perspectives on the Life and Art of Richard Crashaw,* ed. John R. Roberts (1990).

1213. Daley, Koos. " 'Good Friday': Donne, Huygens and the Protestant Paradigm of Salvation," in *The Great Emporium: The Low Countries as a Cultural Crossroads in the Renaissance and the Eighteenth Century,* ed. C. C. Barfoot and Richard Todd, 43–58. DQR Studies in Literature, 10. Amsterdam: Rodopi.

Contrasts Donne's religious anxiety, fears, and uncertainty with Constantijn

Hugyens's "steadfast faith in God's grace" and the sense of religious "security" (44) that this conviction gave him and shows how Huygens's translation of *Goodf,* the only sacred poem of Donne's that Huygens translated, "evinces the cross-currents between two Christian poets and marks the crossroads where the two men met" (45). Maintains that Donne's poem is "a fusion of drama and meditation based on the Protestant poetics of sin and salvation" (47) but that it "illustrates a Christian in the early and middle stages of the journey from sin to salvation—a Christian who is still anxious and distrustful and who experiences emotional vacillations," while Huygens in his translation imposes on the poem his own distinctively Protestant convictions of salvation "[t]hrough his crucial departures from Donne's text, the knitting together of phonetic and syntactical units, and the crucial changes he made in his rough draft." Maintains that it was "[n]ot until shortly before his death, when Donne preached his last sermon on Friday, 25 February 1631, did he mirror Huygens's steadfast reliance on God's grace and the peace such piety could bring" (54).

1214. Dime, Gregory T. " 'The New News at the New Court': Recent Historicist Interpretations of Metaphysical Poetry." *ELWIU* 19: 3–19.

Discusses a selection of recent critical works on Donne and Marvell to show how metaphysical poetry "presents a singular challenge to the new historicists and thus provides a unique litmus test with respect to the validity of their approach." Suggests that such a survey "will enable us to delineate the broader cultural movement of which the new historicism itself is an aspect" (3). Discusses how "[c]ountercultural critics readily take the oxymoronic, antithetical quality of

Donne's poetry, its paradoxical wit, as testimony to the poet's inner conflicts," and how "the intellectuality of Donne's verse is diagnosed as signalling resistance to the upwelling of subconscious urges, even sexual pathology" (9), and how they "eagerly interpret the darkness of Metaphysical poetry as an emblem of psychological repression or oppressive political machinations" (13). Believes that although "[c]ountercultural criticism anathematizes ahistoricism," it "too frequently lacks the periodization that would prevent it from becoming anachronistic itself." Claims that these "new" critics often "mistake Donne's experimentation with, or attack upon, poetic conventions as a sign of revolt against society in general or prevailing political authority" and thus "with Romantic lens" seek to project a Jacobean image that simply mirrors "their own sociopolitical aspirations and concerns" (14).

1215. Donne, John. *John Donne's Poetry,* ed. Arthur L. Clements. 2nd ed., A Norton Critical Edition. New York: Norton. xvii, 377p. First edition, 1966.

Explains in the preface (xi–xiii) that, with the assistance of Philip Brady, 19 poems (with glosses and textual notes) have been added (5 elegies, 4 satires, 6 verse epistles, and 4 divine poems); that 7 new essays have been included; that the selected bibliography has been updated and expanded; and that indexes of first lines and title have been added. Notes that the primary text of the poems remains the 1633 edition, with a few exceptions that are indicated in the textual notes, and that the texts, glosses, and textual notes have been reedited and updated. Thereafter follows the preface to the first edition (xv–xvii), the texts of the poems (1–129), and the textual notes (130–35). The section on criticism excludes two essays found in the first edition: C. S. Lewis, "Donne and Love Poetry in the Seventeenth Century" from *Seventeenth-Centuries Studies Presented to Sir Herbert Grierson* (1938): 64–84, and A. L. Clements, ["The Paradox of Three-in-One"] from "Donne's 'Holy Sonnet XIV,'" in *MLN,* 76 (1961): 484–89. The following are added: A. L. Clements, ["Eros in the *Songs and Sonnets*"] from *Poetry of Contemplation: John Donne, George Herbert, Henry Vaughan, and the Modern Period* (1990): 45–57, 257–58; John R. Lauritsen, "Donne's *Satyres*: The Drama of Self-Discovery" from *SEL* 16 (1976): 117–30; David Aers and Gunther Kress, "'Dark Texts Needs Notes': Versions of Self in Donne's Verse Epistles" from *Literature, Language and Society in England, 1580–1680* (1981): 23–34, 40–48, 200–02 (entry 152); R. V. Young, "Donne's Holy Sonnets and the Theology of Grace" from *"Bright Shootes of Everlastingnesse": The Seventeenth-Century Religious Lyric*, ed. Claude J. Summers and Ted-Larry Pebworth (1987): 20–39 (entry 857); R. D. Bedford, ["The Potter-Clay Image"] from "Donne's Holy Sonnet, 'Batter My Heart'" in *N&Q,* n.s. 29 (1982): 15–19 (entry 247); Raymond-Jean Frontain, ["Redemption Typology"] from "Redemption Typology in John Donne's 'Batter My Heart'" in *JRMMRA* 8 (1987): 163–76 (entry 777); and John R. Roberts, "John Donne's Poetry: An Assessment of Modern Criticism" from *JDJ* 1 (1982): 55–67 (entry 321). Contains a selected bibliography (362–70), an index of titles (371–73), and an index of first lines (375–77).

1216. Ferrell, Lori Anne. "Donne and His Master's Voice, 1615–1625." *JDJ* 11: 59–70.

Compares and contrasts Donne and Lancelot Andrewes as preachers, noting how they "represent different styles of churchmanship, evidence of a generational gap present in the Jacobean church." Points out that Donne's sermons "reflect an enthusiasm for the ministry of preaching that hearkens back to the rhetoric of earlier English reformers" (59). Argues that they "provide a perspective on the religio-political destabilization of the later Jacobean reign" and claims that "[a]n examination of his position on conformity and Calvinism will reveal the fragmentation of a rhetoric designed to define and defuse extremes." Places the sermons "in the context of the court *milieu*," since "his religious concerns reflect the needs of the monarch he served as apologist" (60), and explores "his public views on theology" (61) to show that "[t]he dictates of court policy rather than the dictates of private conscience determined the broad themes of Donne's sermons" as well as "many of the implications he drew from those themes." Maintains, however, that "his quasi-sacramental theory of the reciprocal operations of preaching lend a unique quality to his conformist politic" (67) and says that, in contrast to the predominate ecclesiastical style of the Jacobean court, "Donne's divinity is oriented towards the power of the minister's voice, and of the word preached," and that his sermons, therefore, were "perfectly suited to deliver the frustrating mixed messages of the 1620's—a decade poised between Calvinist consensus and Laudian provocation" (67–68). Concludes that Donne's "preaching-centered ecclesiology was (to borrow a phrase) politically correct from 1615–1625" but "his theology less so, at least until 1622." Maintains that "[a]fter James's death, however, the situation was neatly reversed" and Donne "may be seen as the true representative of a Jacobean *via media,* as long as we remember that after 1625 the 'middle way' was a road less travelled" (68).

1217. Fishelov, David. "Yehuda Amichai: A Modern Metaphysical Poet." *OL* 47: 178–91.

Compares the modern Israeli poet Yehuda Amichai to Donne to show that although both poets use "striking similes," "elaborate on the similarities between the two dissimilar concepts introduced by the similes," use "pseudo-logical and pseudo-causal formulations," create "dramatic situations" in their poems, and treat "the tension between religious concepts and secular experiences," "these close affinities . . . should not, however, cloud the significant differences between them." Observes that "these shared poetic characteristics ultimately highlight the modernist nature of Amichai's poetry—with its tendency for fragmentation, exploring man's internal world, and expressing an existential point of view" (178).

1218. Fleissner, Robert F. "Donne's Compasses Re-Figured: The Ambivalent Finale." *ANQ* 5: 16–18.

Shows how Donne, like Dante, plays with "the paradox inherent in the circle image" (16) in ll. 35–36 of *ValMourn*. Notes that "two basic actions are being described: first, the speaker's geometric completion of the circle figure, symbolizing both his constant love for his addressee and hers for him" and, second, his ending up "where he began." Points out that, in addition to the circle being a symbol of divine perfection and constant love, "[a]n ambivalent bawdy hint also emerges in Donne's wordplay, in that the circle, partly a symbol of earthly love, could be an indirect allusion to the female sexual organ (a yonic symbol)" (17) and notes that "erect" in the last stanza of the poem may refer to the clitoral stimulation experienced by the waiting mistress. Concludes that "for something to be a circle in the divine sense and yet not be one . . . is, if startling, simply part of the challenging, paradoxical nature of the metaphysical conceit itself" (18).

1219. Freeman, Arthur. "Donne's Puns." *TLS,* 10 July, 14.

Comments on Donne's love of puns. Notes that in a newly discovered book that was in Donne's library, Filippo Gesualdo's *Plutosophia* . . . (Padua, 1593), Donne has inserted in his own hand the name Xantippa, the shrewish wife of Socrates, in an alphabetical list of historical or mythological men and women. Suggests that Donne's misogyny might explain the insertion but claims that "the point of the poet's embellishment lies in a bilingual pun." Notes that "Gesualdo had described and headed his double alphabet of men and women—not once but twice, just above it—as 'uno di Huomini, e l'altro de Donne . . . de gli Huomini, e delle Donne.' "

1220. Frontain, Raymond-Jean. " 'With Holy Importunitie, with a Pious Impudencie': John Donne's Attempts to Provoke Election." *JRMMRA* 13: 85–102.

Maintains that the use of the imperative in the *Divine Poems* is "part of the speaker's frantic attempt . . . to provoke his own election." Analyzes "the problem faced by believers like Donne who find their desire to be subsumed into the sacred intensified to a fever pitch by their recurring failure to be so" and then considers "the rhetorical campaign undertaken by the speaker of the [*Holy*] *Sonnets* to be 'imputed righteous.' " Argues that Donne "models his use of the imperative upon a similar operation in certain psalms which simultaneously implore and assure the Lord's action on the speaker's behalf," maintaining that Donne's posture is "the defensive stance of a speaker acutely conscious of impending fragmentation and dissolution" (86). Believes, in other words, that "[a]cutely and painfully conscious of the theological implications of his unworthiness, and of the consequent dire necessity of God's providing him with the prevenient grace that will justify him, the speaker of the *Holy Sonnets* must rhetorically provoke divine intrusion into his personal history, that its end might be revealed" (91), and that he "found hope that he could break this impasse in the process of his election by a peculiar situation and set of poetic operations in the Psalms" (96). In order "[t]o demonstrate how essential an impulse the imperative is for Donne when seeking completion or union with an empowering, salvific figure—whether God or woman," examines his use of the imperative also in *ElBed*. Argues that, in spite of obvious differences, "the dynamics of the situation [in both the *Holy Sonnets* and in *ElBed*] are radically similar" (101).

1221. Gill, Roma. "Labyrinths." *N&Q*, n.s. 39: 71.

Notes that in his sermon preached on St. Paul's Day 1628, Donne characterizes the atheist as a "Riddling, perplexed, *labyrinthical* Soul" and asks if anyone knows a common source for this idea—"other than the Minoan."

1222. Grossman, Marshall. "Housing the Remains of Culture: Absolute Monuments to Absolute Knowledge." *Surfaces* 2 (Section 10): 18.

Studies "the dialectic of desire and commemoration as they constitute the discourse of cultural nostalgia" in Donne's poetry (abstract). Concentrates on the year 1611 when Donne wrote *FirAn* and asks the question: "Is there some useful analogy between Donne's experience and conditions and the experiences and conditions that lead us to ask 'What remains of culture and tradition'?" Says that the "shee" of the poem is neither Elizabeth Drury nor the Virgin Mary, but rather is, "generically, the chaste and unattainable female cynosure of the neoplatonic tradition" (8). Says that "[a]s

the literary conventions of neoplatonic epideixis become increasingly visible as such, the experience they had mediated fades from view" (9) and that "significance was irreparably disjoined from substance" (10). Believes that what remains "of the world remaining still" is "a mediating voice . . . comprising a remembered spirit and an always already archaic form" (13).

1223. Hamilton, Ian. "John Donne the Younger," in *Keepers of the Flame: Literary Estates and the Rise of Biography*, 7–15. London: Hutchinson.

Discusses the role of Donne's son in preserving and perpetuating his father's literary reputation, noting that probably he is the first literary custodian "to have been given an entry in the *Dictionary of National Biography* and to have had his character and motives scrutinized in the scholarly periodicals" (1). Points out that "[a]lthough not officially his father's literary executor, John Jr. decided to appoint himself custodian of the literary side of the estate" since "no one else seemed to be in charge, least of all Henry King" (7), the official executor. Admitting that it is impossible "to reconstruct a precise and plausible chronology of John Jr's involvement in his father's literary estate" (9), speculates on his efforts to gain control of it. Suggests that he was principally responsible for the survival of Donne's prose. Comments also on John Jr.'s own *Donnes Satyr; containing a short map of Mundane Vanity, a cabinet of Merry Conceits, certain pleasant propositions and questions with their merry solutions and answers* (1662).

1224. Harland, Paul W. "Donne's Political Intervention in the Parliament of 1629." *JDJ* 11: 21–37.

Discusses how Donne in his sermon preached at Whitehall on 20 February 1628/29 "spoke in terms that supported the traditional role of Parliament and cautioned the king against arbitrary rule, even though he was a royal chaplain indebted to the king's favour" (21). Points out, however, that "given the conditions of censorship and the restrictions placed on authorized speech, Donne could only make such pronouncements obliquely, using analogies between kingship and divine governance, making implicit comparisons between recent historical events and scriptural examples, and by employing theological language that had political overtones" (21–22). Suggests that an examination of the sermon "adds to the increasing body of evidence that the view of Donne as a sycophantic supporter of divine right is dubious." Points out how in the sermon Donne promotes "values obviously contrary to royal inclination such as the rule of law, counsel based on free and unflattering speech, as well as openness and accessibility in government" (22). Maintains that, "despite Donne's deference towards the office of king, his auditory, familiar with recent political events, could appreciate his tactics" and would recognize how "[h]e was using his reputation to affirm the supremacy of law, to encourage broadly-based counsel, to warn against the vice of flattery, to celebrate accessibility, to support the value of free speech in a subject, and to remind courtiers of their duty in providing their sovereign with honest advice." Concludes that Donne "had demonstrated to these courtiers, in the sermon itself, how 'to handle the matter wittily and handsomely' so that their efforts might prevent political disintegration" (32).

1225. Harmon, William. "Paronomastics: The Name of the Poet from Shakespeare and Donne to Glück and Morgan." *Connotations* 2: 115–25.

Comments on how various writers have played on their names in their works, citing Donne's paradoxical play on his name in *Father*.

1226. Harvey, Elizabeth D. *Ventriloquized Voices: Feminist Theory and English Renaissance Texts.* London and New York: Routledge. Chapter 3 re-printed in *John Donne*, ed. Andrew Mousley (Basingstoke and London: Macmillan; New York: St. Martin's Press, 1999), 135–56. Chapter 4, "Ventriloquizing Sappho, Or the Lesbian Muse" (116–38), first appeared in *Criticism* 31 (1989): 115–38 (entry 970).

Chapter 3, "Matrix as Metaphor: Midwifery and the Conception of Voice" (76–115), focuses on "the trope of male birth," contextualizing it "within the historical debate on midwifery," and examines poetic texts that "use the metaphor of pregnancy and birth to image their own textual origins at the same historical moment that birth and the interior of the female body were becoming subject to male medical scrutiny and economic control" (8). Concentrates on "the way voice as a construct coheres in a particular constellation of metaphors that is frequently found in Renaissance poetry: the image of the pregnant male poet giving birth to voice, being impregnated or impregnating his muse, or serving as a midwife to poetic birth" and examines books on midwifery of the period "in order to contextualize the trope in historical and medical terms." Discusses Donne's "imaging of birth and the figure of the midwife in a number of poems," particularly in *ElBed, ValWeep,* and *BB* and "most specifically in the *Anniversaries*" (78). Maintains, in fact, that "no other of Donne's poems so explicitly express [a] ligature of speech, sexuality, and pregnancy than his two elegies written to commemorate the death of Elizabeth Drury" (106) and claims that in the poems "Donne's references to pregnancy and birth are contiguous with the discourses of theology and physiology, which themselves furnish a linkage between pregnancy and voice" (107). Juxtaposes the *Anniversaries* and Julia Kristeva's writings on motherhood, especially her "Stabat Mater" (1987), to show how both poets "rely on the image of the Virgin Mary, a figure that represents the bifurcation of maternity and sexuality," but that "Donne uses a virginal maternity as a source of his (ventriloquized) voice," whereas Kristeva "provides a historical and psychoanalytic explication of the Virgin's contribution to a more general theory of maternality" (8–9). Maintains, however, that the juxtapositions of these texts "interrogate motherhood as a discourse or an act that can be owned or appropriated, either by the male midwives and physicians who colonize and eventually medicalize childbirth, or by feminists who seek to repossess the experience of maternity in language" (9).

1227. Haskin, Dayton. "John Donne and the Cultural Contradictions of Christmas." *JDJ* 11: 133–57.

Points out that Donne's Christmas sermons reflect a negative attitude toward celebrating Christmas, that *Eclog* is "deeply implicated in traditional Christmas celebrations," and that as early as 1594 Donne had declined the offer to serve as "Steward of Christmas" at Lincoln's Inn (137). Maintains that "[i]n acknowledging objections to the celebration of Christ's birth Donne was evincing a certain sympathy with those who were, with increasing vehemence, leveling the charge that the feast of Christmas has no basis in the Bible, that it was a belated innovation, and that it involved popish appropriation of pagan rites and superstitions" (141). Observes that Donne "never talked about any ways of celebrating Christmas besides those that involved prayer and meditation" (142) and sug-

gests that if we take the sermons and *Corona* "as a fair index of Donne's personal attitudes, then we could say that what he loved best about Christmas was not festivity, nor camaraderie, nor traditional spirit, but its allophanic potential: above all, the revelation that God, who is wholly Other and on so many grounds rightly perceived to be our utmost Enemy, is as weak as any human lover." Stresses that in Donne's sermons Christmas Day is seen as "the first of Christ's two great comings, relevant to his hearers chiefly for what it tells us about the second" (149). Comments on the publication history of the Christmas sermons and laments how the Potter and Simpson edition repositions the seven sermons "in order to facilitate constructing a fictional narrative of 'development'" (151).

1228. Hatakeyama, Etsuro. "Donne no Jikogenkyu-teki Text to 'Ai no Hitoku' no Dento" [Donne's Self-Referential Texts and the Convention of "Secrecy in Love"], in *Renaissance to 17 Seiki Eibungaku* [Renaissance and Seventeenth-Century English Literature] (The Japan Society of Seventeenth-Century English Literature), 44–65. Tokyo: Kinseido.

Points out that Donne's self-referential texts function as conscious rhetoric and can be understood as a parody of courtly love, especially the convention of "Secrecy in Love." Comments primarily on *Under* and *Damp* by way of illustration.

1229. Healy, Thomas. "Gendered Readings," in *New Latitudes: Theory and English Renaissance Literature,* 145–78. London: Edward Arnold.

Points out that the sexual fantasies Donne conjures up in *ElBed* cause "problems for the modern reader, raising questions about exploitation of the female arising from constructions of women by male authors" (145). Shows how in the poem Donne "portrays masculine desires of conquest without responsibilities" and observes that it is "a public performance, addressed to a readership almost certainly envisaged to be male, showing Donne at play—sexually, but especially verbally—as the empowered male poet" (146). Points out that "[i]nscribing the female from a male position such as Donne's can incite much critical hostility among current readers" (146–47), especially feminist critics, and examines the presentation of women in Renaissance texts, observing that usually they are portrayed as "either leading men to destruction or salvation," as "either hastening bodily corruption, decay and death, or promoting immortality, permanence and salvation," and that often "beneath the apparent ideal lurks a corrupter" (168). Discusses how Donne's love poetry "abounds in a skilfull manipulation of these two reductive types of female roles so that he can gain control of women." Cites as an example *GoodM*, in which the speaker recognizes that "[h]e has been deluded and his lover is not the source of perfection he believed," and "[r]ather than being a second Eve who would restore him to deathless Eden, she is the first Eve who causes him once more to lose Eden, draining his sexual vigour and diminishing him" (170). Points out that "[r]eading through gender, we become aware of masculine partiality in depicting the world," noting that "[c]elebrations of secular love are almost always reflections of male wit trying to cope with emotional obsession, and supposed victimisation by imagined female deceptions" (171).

1230. Heffernan, Thomas. "The Book of Scripture and of Nature and Early Seventeenth-Century English Emblem Poetry." *Yearbook of Interdisciplinary Studies in the Fine Arts* 3: 531–1.

Reprints Chapter 1 of *Art and Emblem: Early Seventeenth-Century English Poetry of Devotion* (Renais-

sance Monographs, 17), Tokyo: Renaissance Institute, Sophia University, 1991.

1231. Hill, Eugene D. "John Donne: In and Out of Fashion." *AnSch* 9: 455–63.

Reviews recent critical works on Donne: James S. Baumlin, *John Donne and the Rhetorics of Renaissance Discourse* (1991) (entry 1133); Heather Dubrow, *A Happier Eden: The Politics of Marriage in the Stuart Epithalamium* (1990) (entry 1037); Kate Gartner Frost, *Holy Delight: Typology, Numerology, and Autobiography in Donne's* Devotions Upon Emergent Occasions (1990) (entry 1042); two essays in Elizabeth D. Harvey and Katharine Eisaman Maus, eds., *Soliciting Interpretation: Literary Theory and Seventeenth-Century English Poetry* (1990); Deborah Aldrich Larson, *John Donne and Twentieth-Century Criticism* (1989) (entry 980); Robert H. Ray, *A John Donne Companion* (1990) (entry 1094); John M. Steadman, *Redefining a Period Style: "Renaissance," "Manner-ism," and "Baroque"* (1990) (entry 1111); and Edward W. Tayler, *Donne's Idea of a Woman: Structure and Meaning in* The Anniversaries (1991) (entry 1194).

1232. Hina, Horst. "Octavio Paz como traductor de poesía inglesa." *Brispania* 1: 81–105.

Discusses Octavia Paz's views on poetic translation, emphasizing that, for Paz, the translator's task is to recreate the original, not merely paraphrase it. Points out that in his book of essays, *Traducción: Literatura y literalidad* (1971), Paz introduced the poetry of T. S. Eliot, Erza Pound, William Carlos Williams, Wallace Stevens, e. e. cummings, and Donne to the Spanish-speaking world. Comments on Paz's translation of *ElBed*, in which Paz underscores the erotic elements in the poem as well as the connection between eroticism and religion. Notes that Paz recognized Donne as the most representative baroque poet in English and compared his poetry to that of Gracián and Góngora. Points out that Paz chose not to include the English text of Donne's poem with his translation because he did not want his translation compared to the original, which would violate his notion of re-creational translation.

1233. Holmes, M. Morgan. "Out of Egypt: John Donne and the Quest for Apocalyptic Re-Creation." *C&L* 42: 25–40.

Examines Donne's "treatment of apocalyptic transformation in order to demonstrate its centrality to his understanding of the re-creation of the body and soul in this life and the next," focusing primarily on his apocalypticism as it is revealed in *Essays in Divinity*, "a work that most clearly expresses Donne's fusion of physical and spiritual quests for empowerment" (25). Points out that for Donne the events in the Book of Revelation provided him with "a master metaphor for a release from the world of time" and observes that he "appropriated Christian eschatology in order to speak about the present" (26). Discusses how "[t]he unity that the Apocalypse brings to human experience by abolishing all conventional spatiotemporal relations provided Donne with a metaphor of total incorporation capable of sustaining his own search for immediate knowledge and experience of divine glory" (28). Maintains that Donne's views "conform to a tradition of idealist exegesis that repudiates an understanding of Revelation based on particular historical events and instead locates the drama of apocalyptic transformation in the individual soul" (29). Shows how the *Essays in Divinity* is "crucial in articulating the relation between knowledge, being, and the Apocalypse which was fundamental to Donne's later theological discourses and self-representation," noting that, for Donne, "knowledge of ultimate reality was a matter of perceiving the divine in the world and in the self" (36) and that, for him, "[t]he valorization of the primacy of individual cognition in apocalyptic re-creation unites heaven and earth through the medium of the self" (37).

1234. Johnson, Carol Siri. "'That hidden mysterie': Sources of Misogyny in Donne's *Songs and Sonets*." *JEP* 13: 195–203.

Discusses Donne's misogyny in the *Songs and Sonets* from a psychoanalytical viewpoint, noting that his portrayal of women "is split into two distinct images: the all-loving, and the hateful and hating" (195), reflecting the basic tenets of pre-oedipal psychology. Maintains that the "positive" poems are those "in which Donne feels a strong connection to the 'gratifying breast,'" citing *SunRis* and *GoodM* as expressing "an early childhood unity at its best." Considers other poems in this grouping, such as *Commun* and *Leg*, as reflecting "equivocal moments in which anger intrudes." Says that the most "negative" poems, such as *WomCon*, *Curse*, and *LovAlch*, "express the 'frustrating breast' and are unequivocally misogynistic" (196). Claims that Donne's poems "cover the full gamut from initial love with the 'gratifying breast' expressed in close, pre-natal union with the lover, to an envious rage and desire to spoil with 'bizarre objects' in the paranoid-schizoid stage, to the mourning and reparation of the depressive stage." Maintains that although Donne "never fully reaches an understanding of love," he does portray "a vivid inner world in which women, however maligned, loving, or dangerous, are granted a real power," and concludes that "[f]ear, denial and envy" (202) of the power of women are the source of Donne's misogyny.

1235. Kanno, Hirohisa. *"The Songs and Sonnets* no 'Dokusha'" [The Reader in *The Songs and Sonnets*], in *Renaissance to 17 Seiki Eibungaku* [Renaissance and Seventeenth-Century English Literature] (The Japan Society of Seventeenth-Century English Literature), 66–89. Tokyo: Kinseido.

Argues that Donne's consciousness of readers is evident in how he can establish the relationship with them in each poem as well as what literary effects he can give them, demonstrating that in a literary space constructed by the speakers and the listeners who play various parts, the readers are also demanded to play variously changeable roles in the poems.

1236. Keller, James R. "The Science of Salvation: Spiritual Alchemy in Donne's Final Sermon." *SCJ* 23: 486–93.

Argues that in "Death's Duell" Donne "reveals the occulted similarities between the mystic experiments of the alchemists and the magical transformation of humanity in the process of Christian salvation," demonstrating thereby that "Christ shared many qualities with the alchemist's philosopher stone." Maintains that Donne "emphasizes this correspondence by employing the language of alchemy in his description of death and salvation" and "employs this pseudo-scientific description in his sermon in order to elucidate the often vague and esoteric principles of Christian salvation" (486). Believes that in this, his last sermon, Donne "attempts to justify the grotesque horror of death by transforming it into a deliberate and exacting process whose objective is eternal life." Maintains that "the language of the hermetic experiment helps to revive Christian platitudes that have

all but lost their meaning" and thus "[t]he exhausted Christian archetypes are regenerated by the mystic figure of Christ as the alchemist's *magnum opus*, transforming base humanity into spiritual gold to be 'laid up in god's treasury'" (493). Points out also that "[t]he use of the terminology of alchemy to describe spiritual rebirth is not foreign to Donne's other works" (491).

1237. Kerrigan, William. "Seventeenth-Century Studies," in *Redrawing the Boundaries: The Transformation of English and American Literary Studies,* ed. Stephen Greenblatt and Giles Gunn, 64–78. New York: Modern Language Association of America.

Discusses the impact of post-1960 critical theories on seventeenth century studies, observing how "the new work sees itself in a destructive opposition to the pedagogical aims of Renaissance humanists" (66) and "suffers from a shallow engagement with the dynamics of generational transmission" (67). Suggests that of all the new approaches "[f]eminism alone . . . has earned its rhetoric of self-canonization" by rescuing women writers of the Renaissance that were "largely ignored by previous generations of scholars." Maintains that "theory-based contributions of the last decade [to Donne studies] seem rather minor in relation to the vast body of detailed explication produced by the New Criticism" (68). Says that "[e]xplicating the psychopolitical subtext" of *ElBed* "has become a minor contemporary genre" and surveys "this nascent tradition" in order to explain that "no theoretical book has enough evidence, accurately represented, to warrant delimiting a new era in seventeenth-century studies" (69). Notes that "[w]ork on the vexed problem of the symbolic meaning of 'shee' in the *Anniversaries,* once a thriving enterprise, seems to have fallen off without achieving an altogether satisfactory conclusion" but predicts that "it will come back, since the most exciting mysteries, the venerable ones that struck even our grandparents, are impossible to replace" (70). Expresses reservations about Arthur Marrotti's *John Donne, Coterie Poet* (1986) (entry 698), John Carey's *John Donne: Life, Mind, and Art* (1981) (entry 162), and Thomas Docherty's *John Donne Undone* (1986) (entry 651) and praises M. Thomas Hester's *Kinde Pitty and Brave Scorn: John Donne's Satyres* (1982) (entry 282) and Achsah Guibbory's essay on Donne in *Map of Time: Seventeenth-Century English Literature and Ideas of Pattern in History* (1986) (entry 675).

1238. Klawitter, George. "Verse Letters to T. W. from John Donne: 'By You My Love Is Sent,' " in *Homosexuality in Renaissance and Enlightenment England: Literary Representations in Historical Context,* ed. Claude J. Summers, 85–102. Binghamton, N.Y.: Harrington Park Press.
Maintains that the sexual metaphors in the verse letters that Donne wrote to Thomas Woodward, younger brother of his close friend, Rowland Woodward, "reflect a homoerotic undercurrent and demonstrate affection that most readers of Donne associate only with his heterosexual love poems" (85). Points out that, although one need not conclude that Donne acted upon the homoerotic fantasies contained in his letters, the tender feelings he expresses in them show that Donne's affections were not exclusively focused on women. Suggests that the poems to T. W. form a kind of brief sonnet sequence that contains a narrative account of Donne's deep affection for the young man that moves from "excitement and anticipation" to a final resignation "to the reality of a cooled friendship" (99). Regrets that

most critics when discussing the verse letters "are careful to avoid letting any taint of affection for male friends tarnish Donne's courtier-turned-priest image" (100).

1239. Larson, Deborah Aldrich. "John Donne and the Astons." *HLQ* 55: 635–41.
Points out that a commonplace book in the Huntington Library (HM 904, c. 1630–50), chiefly in the hand of Constance Aston, contains a reference to Donne and echoes of his poems in poems by Constance and Herbert Aston, her brother, that have not been previously noted. Suggests that "[t]his literary connection between Donne and the Astons adds to the likelihood of a personal connection between Donne and Walter Aston" (638), who, like Donne, suffered various repercussions because of a secret and illegal marriage. Suggests that perhaps one reason for Walter Aston's admiration of Donne's poetry was his empathy with Donne's personal history. Points out that "[h]e apparently passed on an interest in Donne to his children, Herbert and Constance, who echoed Donne in their own poetry." Concludes that "the coincidence of Walter Aston's and Donne's marital circumstances may indicate the kind of relationship Donne's contemporaries assumed between the poet's life and his poetry" (639).

1240. Long, John C. "Foucault's Clinic." *The Journal of Medical Humanities* 13: 119–38.
Examines Michel Foucault's "ideas about the clinic from the point of view of a clinician" and endeavors "to show how doctors and patients talked about disease before and after the birth of the clinic." Shows how "this language operates in Renaissance woodcuts, nineteenth-century paintings and modern lithographs about disease; in poetry about sickness by John Donne, Walt

Whitman, and L. E. Sissman; and in a contemporary medical journal" (120). Briefly comments on Donne's account of disease and sickness in *Devotions* and *Sickness,* in which "symptoms are more important than signs of disease." Observes that in the eighteenth century "[d]isease is no longer a particular set of symptoms, but a specific anatomical lesion" and, "[a]s a result, John Donne's chronological series of symptoms is subordinated to explorations of lesions in tissues" (126–27).

1241. Lucarelli, John. "John Donne's 'La Corona' as Sonnet Sequence," in *The Western Pennsylvania Symposium on World Literatures, Selected Proceedings: 1974–1991, A Retrospective,* ed. Carla E. Lucente, 61–65. Greensburg, Pa.: Eadmer.

Maintains that *Corona* is a sonnet sequence that "illustrates in sound and form, as well as sense, the Christian paradox: 'The first shall be last and the last, first.'" Discusses how "[t]his structurally implied paradox serves to heighten all the statements of paradox within the work, to emphasize the verbal complexity of its puns, to call attention to the syntactic complexities of its ambiguities, and, perhaps, to strengthen its compressed allusions" (61). Points out that although *Corona* deals with divine love, its "surface conventions" resemble those of the traditional secular sonnet sequences that focused on human love. Observes, however, that in *Corona* "the speaker takes on the passive role associated with the female," while God "is given the active, traditionally male, role" (64). Thinks that *Corona* lacks the "concentrated energy" of Donne's later religious poems and "makes use of some paradoxes which had become theological commonplaces by the seventeenth century" (65).

1242. Manlove, Colin. "The Metaphysical Poets," in *Christian Fantasy: From 1200 to the Present,* 93–101. Notre Dame, Ind.: University of Notre Dame Press; Houndmills: Macmillan.

Argues that a "potential gap between imagination and devotion is most strikingly seen in the metaphysical poets— particularly Donne, who puts a form of his own personality squarely at the centre of interest" (94). Analyzes *HSRound,* in which "all the imaginative force of the poem in the octet has to be set aside for the speaker's development in the sestet" (96) and in which "there is a gap between free visualisation and its application." Claims that in the poem "[t]he imagination operates with some licence" and that "the image [of Judgment Day] amasses to itself an interest not wholly absorbed by the rest of the poem." Analyzes also *HSBatter,* in which "the sense seems more closely integrated with the (still violent) imagery" (97) but which displays "an imagination which has so delighted in various images for the speaker's plight that the gravity of that plight has been lost" (98).

1243. Malpezzi, Frances M. "'As I Ride': The Beast and His Burden in Donne's 'Goodfriday.'" *R&L* 24, no. 1: 23–31.

Maintains that Donne in *Goodf* "by casting his speaker as a rider imbues his poem with added spiritual ramifications as he places this speaker within a very definite religious, literary, and visual tradition" (24). Discusses how Donne uses the image to illustrate the analogy of the subjection of the body to the soul, suggesting thereby, on a metaphorical level, "the paradigmatic earthly pilgrimage through life to death and eternal life in the celestial city of the new Jerusalem, a journey impeded by the animalistic appetites of the flesh which must be forcibly subdued if the soul is to reach its intended destination"

(26). Shows how "Donne's rider must be transformed during the course of the poem from a poor horseman to the ideal Christian militant." Maintains that the juxtaposition of the image of the horse and rider and Christ crucified at the center of the poem "emblematizes for us the consequences of all such errant wanderings" and "reminds us not only of the unruly flesh but of the terminus of such diversion" (26). Maintains, therefore, that "[t]hrough the image of his errant rider Donne exemplifies the unbridled corporate pride and lust of humanity which led to Christ's sacrificial assumption of mortal flesh . . . to ransom sinners who had descended to the level of the beast" (27). Points out that in the conclusion of the poem the rider/speaker "is no longer a weak horseman, transported by his appetites," but rather "recognizes that the bit and bridle of God's afflictions can transform him into a true Christian militant," and "[w]hile he continues westward in his journey through life to death, he has been spiritually oriented" and "travels the *via purgativa,* ready to accept the afflictions God gives him to help rein in the unruly beast he rides to salvation." Concludes that the speaker, therefore, "reflects the human condition," that the image of the horse and rider juxtaposed with the image of Christ crucified "reminds us of the way uncontrolled flesh can cause the pilgrim to deviate from his goal," and how "the suffering Christ teaches him the value of the bit and bridle" (29).

1244. Mann, Lindsay A. "Misogyny and Libertinism: Donne's Marriage Sermons." *JDJ* 11: 111–32.
    Examines Donne's "three published marriage sermons, as well as his pervasive treatment of marriage and related topics throughout the sermons and devotional prose," in order "to suggest a developing consistency of principles in Donne." Maintains that Donne's "mature prose develops the arguments of the earlier love poems, at times directly echoing their language and imagery," and thereby challenging "the common view of discontinuity or reversal in Donne's career" (111). Points out that in the sermons Donne "engages and resists both libertine naturalism and ascetic mysticism as contrary extremes which meet in denying the human responsibility to fulfill a vocation in the world," just as in the love poetry he "charted a similar course for love between the extreme of libertine naturalism (mere body) and the extreme of Petrarchan Neoplatonism (mere soul) by celebrating a love which is personal, mutual, and equal and joins the lovers in body and soul—like the companionate ideal of Christian marriage" (113). Observes how the cynical love poems are "ironic inversions of asceticism" that "dramatize naturalism" and, like the sermons, "attack romantic pretensions and idealizations in the name of natural feeling and passions," but at the same time, "ironically expose the reductive insufficiency of a mere naturalism through the limitations of their speakers." Observes that in his poems of true love Donne "reproduces in their imagery and arguments the pattern of his doctrine of marriage," in which he repudiates "dualistic extremes" and dramatizes "the responsive act of mutual relation, mutual love, and mutual support" found in the sermons (123). Points out that in these poems, and especially in the valediction poems, Donne celebrates a love that is "consistent with the affirmation in Donne's sermons of the permanence of love, the profound obligation to love and mutual support through the vicissitudes of time, in imitation of a divine pattern and a divine injunction" (124).

1245. Masselink, Noralyn. "A Matter of Interpretation: Example and Donne's Role as Preacher and as Poet." *JDJ* 11: 85–98.

Maintains that in both his poetry and sermons Donne relies more heavily than do his contemporaries "on examples (concrete images or models) to illustrate rules (abstract universals)." Points out, however, that "[w]hereas Donne the poet creates examples to promote singularity, innovation, and change, Donne the preacher relies on examples to denounce the very qualities he lauds in the poems" (85). Notes, however, that in both genres Donne "assumes the role of arbiter of truth" and "*he* determines which examples point to moral laws peculiar to a specific occasion and which we may embrace as precedents having universal application and significance" (85–86). Maintains that, in general, in his sermons Donne suggests that "God's universal laws are not to be determined from singular examples" (93) and that he warns of "the dangers of heeding the call of singular 'prophets' claiming new revelations and generating conflict with the church universal" (95). Suggests that "in the sermons Donne may actually cloak his own religio-political views in language which is purposely resistant to definitive interpretation." Compares Donne's view on religion and the church in the sermons with that expressed in *Sat3* and *HSShow* to show that, "despite stylistic differences," there are "more similarities than differences" (95). Insists that "when it comes to defending the Church, the public and private voices converge" and that "[i]n both the sermons and the religious poems, Donne decries extremes," always seeking to defend the Church "without explicitly identifying her with any particular earthly church" (96). Concludes that Donne "clearly is willing in both the sermons and at least two poems to say what the church is not" and that, "[b]y embracing his role as interpreter of examples and by refusing to identify 'the Church' in more specific religio-political terms, Donne the preacher maintains his independence, the character trait we find so attractive in Donne the poet" (97).

1246. Masselink, Noralyn. "Wormseed Revisited: Glossing Line Forty of Donne's 'Farewell to Love.'" *ELN* 30, no. 2: 11–15.

Surveys various interpretations of l. 40 of *Fare* and suggests an alternative reading in which the speaker is saying that "if all his other attempts [to reject love] fail, another remedy is at hand": he can apply wormseed to his tail (i.e., his behind) "in order to purge himself of the 'worms' (the winds and humors of passion) within." Suggests that perhaps there is "an ironic undercutting implied by the application at the tail (the milder method of purging): the speaker *is* willing to purge himself, but is unwilling to take the drastic steps (ingestion of the herb) necessary for a complete purgation." Suggests, in other words, that perhaps "the speaker has not yet completed his farewell to love" (14).

1247. Matar, N. I. "The Date of John Donne's Sermon 'Preached at the Churching of the Countesse of Bridgewater.'" *N&Q*, n.s. 39: 447–48.

Argues that "Donne's polemical focus on the Jews" in his sermon "Preached at the Churching of the Countesse of Bridgewater" situates it "in the summer of 1621 when the issues of Jerusalem and of the 'restoration' of the Jews were being discussed in London on a theological and political level" as a result of the publication in March of that year of Sir Henry Finch's *The Calling of the Iewes* (447). Points out that in the sermon Donne reiterates "current ecclesiastical policy" and discredits "Jewish millenarianism that other Anglicans had denounced in that year and that had been deemed by James I to be dangerous to his authority" (448).

1248. McNees, Eleanor J. "The Eschatology of Real Presence: Donne's Struggle Toward Conformity with Christ," in *Eucharistic Poetry: The Search for Presence in the Writings of John Donne, Gerard Manley Hopkins, Dylan Thomas, and Geoffrey Hill*, 33–68. Lewisburg, Pa.: Bucknell University Press.

Argues that "[t]he Anglican stance toward the Eucharist with its denial of transubstantiation but its assertion of Real Presence lends John Donne a model for the poetic paradoxes in both his secular and sacred lyrics." Discusses how three specifically Anglican views on the Eucharist that Donne adhered to after his ordination inform his "poetics of the real presence": "(1) the eucharistic elements were not (as in transubstantiation or consubstantiation) changed in *substance* but rather in *use;* (2) the sacrament operated on the faithful as a *seal* of grace, not merely as a representational *sign;* and (3) the celebration of Holy Communion was fundamentally a *sacrifice* recalling Christ's Passion and exacting contrition in the communicant" (33). Shows how the divine poems "attempt to emulate the language and ritual of the sacraments, especially of the Passion and its extension in the Eucharist" (38), and work toward an "internal transformation." Suggests that the secular lyrics, on the other hand, "emphasize visible transubstantiation without proper penitence," bypassing "the sacrificial struggle toward purgation" and thus only depicting "a false resurrection." Discusses *Ecst* as a poem that "stands midway between Donne's secular and divine poems" and moves, like the eucharistic ceremony, "from an emphasis on the physical presence of

the elements—the two bodies—to the spiritual union of souls" (40), thereby showing Donne "playing with both Roman Catholic and Protestant doctrine but ultimately refusing to make either transubstantiation or consubstantiation support the real presence of the lovers' union" (41). Discusses *Canon, Twick,* and *Relic* as poems that "exaggerate specific eucharistic elements and reinforce Donne's complaint that Roman Catholics emphasize miracles over faith" (45). Maintains that the Eucharist becomes "the only point of intersection of the divine and temporal" in Donne's sacred verse, signifying "the *idea* of the Resurrection in its promise of redemption from sins through communion." Suggests that Donne is thus "poised between the Catholic reliance on Incarnation and the Protestant focus on Eschatology" and that "[t]he Anglican Eucharist allows both to meet and absolves Donne from membership in either Catholic or Calvinist camps." Discusses how in his longer divine poems Donne "is almost exclusively absorbed with the mystery of the Incarnation and Resurrection," noting that the *Holy Sonnets* "compact the persona's struggle toward death and resurrection into pleas to God to punish him so that he will be worthy of salvation, whereas the longer hymns and monologues protract that struggle" (51). Maintains that "[a]lthough the language of the secular and divine lyrics is similar, the real difference arises in the separate goals the words serve." Points out that "[t]he divine lyrics continually transform secular denotation to sacred connotation as the eucharistic ceremony transforms secular food into the spiritual food of Christ's body and blood," noting that "[w]ithin this sacramental framework, the divine lyrics are chary of such overtly Roman Catholic practices as miracles and transubstantiation," whereas in the love poems Donne "is able both to parody Roman Catholic practices and make them appear to reenforce earthly love." Maintains, therefore, that Donne is "less indulgent" in his divine poems and "[i]nstead of seeking visible transformation, he focuses on the sinner's struggle for union with an invisible God," a struggle that "tends to make the human lovers' unions appear too easy." Concludes that the Anglican view of the real presence "provides a model for Donne's compression of diverse images into an illusory paradox" and that, "[b]y incorporating eucharistic symbols in his poetry, he can juxtapose secular and sacred in the love lyrics and commingle them in his divine poems" (67), thus making paradox his "chief poetic tool" (68). Review: Robert Archambeau in *R&L* (1993): 103–4.

1249. Mueller, Janel. "Lesbian Erotics: The Utopian Trope of Donne's 'Sappho to Philaenis,'" in *Homosexuality in Renaissance and Enlightenment England: Literary Representations in Historical Context,* ed. Claude J. Summers, 103–34. Binghamton, N.Y.: Harrington Park Press.

Calls *Sappho* "a verse elegy which stands alone" not only among Donne's works but also "in the entire literary production of the Renaissance for its celebration and defense of a passionate lesbian relation binding the two women of its title" (103). Shows how Donne "successfully overturns Ovid's influential portrayal of Sappho as an aging voluptuary reclaimed for heterosexuality, the virulent homophobia of Renaissance humanists, and the coy idealizations and transient evocation given to lesbian affectivity by the very few Renaissance writers (including Shakespeare) who touched on the subject at all" (103–4). Argues that when *Sappho* "is set in the context of Donne's other love elegies in

verse as productions by a young intellectual moving in sophisticated London circles and writing for a coterie audience, lesbianism looks like a master trope for positively resolving a dilemma that confounded Montaigne and many other authors of the age," namely, "[c]ould the perfections of love and friendship be united in a relation of equality between two persons?" Points out that "[g]ender hierarchy and separate socialization precluded a heterosexual construction of any such equality in the Renaissance" and that "the greater opprobrium cast on male homosexuality in this era must have influenced Donne's decision to figure his equal lovers and friends as a lesbian couple." Believes, however, that "[t]he disclosive power" of Donne's poem "goes far beyond the entailments of a specific choice of poetic representation" and that he "really undertakes to imagine the pleasures, sustenance, and ideological implications by which lesbianism, as a mode of loving and being, resists patriarchal disposition and diminution of women." Holds that Donne "anticipates the advances of twentieth-century feminists . . . as he poetically articulates possibilities and knowledge that were otherwise denied expression by Renaissance culture and its exponents" (104).

1250. Müller, Wolfgang G. "Das Paradoxon in der englischen Barocklyrik: John Donne, George Herbert, Richard Crashaw," in *Das Paradox: Eine Herausforderung des abendländischen Denkens,* ed. Paul Geyer and Roland Hagenbüchle, 355–84. Stauffenburg Colloquium, 21. Tübingen: Stauffenburg Verlag.

Analyzes various kinds of paradox and maintains that paradox is the most decisive means of expression linking Donne to Marvell and Traherne. Maintains that in Donne's lyric poetry paradoxes have the function of expressing intensely felt problems, such as the "I-You" relationship and complex issues of time, love, and death. Points out, for instance, that repeatedly Donne defines the "I" as "You" or views the "I" and "You" as one, often deriving new and startling effects. Maintaining that a discussion of paradox in baroque poetry must also consider imagery, points out how in Donne's lyrics the conceit is a metaphoric picture that displays surprising and often paradoxical analogies between widely diverse images. Observes also that Donne's art of employing paradox can be seen in his elaborate uses of wordplay, citing as an example the play on "death-die" in *HSDeath*.

1251. Norbrook, David, and H. R. Woudhuysen, eds. *The Penguin Book of Renaissance Verse 1509–1659*. Penguin Classics. London: Penguin. xliv, 910p. Published with minor revisions and an additional index in Penguin Books, 1993.

Poems selected and introduction by David Norbrook; volume edited by H. R. Woudhuysen. Contains *Calm*, lines from *Sat4, ElBed, ElPict, SunRis, Canon, LovGrow, ValWeep, Val-Mourn, Noct, HWKiss, Sat3, Goodf, Sickness*, three selections from the *Holy Sonnets*, and lines from *SecAn* and *Triple*, arranged by topic and accompanied by explanatory notes.

1252. Oliveros, Alejandro. *La mirada del desengaño: John Donne y la poesía del barroco*. (Ediciones del Rectorado.) Valencia, Venezuela: Universidad de Carabobo. 199p.

A collection of 14 brief essays, only 6 of which discuss Donne. (1) "La poesía de la crisis religiosa en Inglaterra" (63–69) surveys the religious poetry of England during the sixteenth and seventeenth centuries. Contrasts Donne with Spenser and Herbert and translates into Spanish *Leg* and *HSSpit*. (2) "El rostro en el espejo de la muerte

acerca de la vida de John Donne" (77–106) presents a survey of Donne's life and poetry. (3) "Anatomía del mundo" (107–23), considers *FirAn* as Donne's most metaphysical poem; surveys the critical reception of the poem, noting that in the twentieth century it has been regarded more highly than in the past; and discusses its structure, metrics, syntax, diction, and imagery as well as its philosophical concepts and baroque themes. (4) "Rasgos comunes: Donne, Quevedo, Sponde, Colonna, Miguel Angel" (125–36), compares Donne primarily to Francisco de Quevedo, analyzing the metaphysical style and baroque themes in their poetry, especially the theme of death. (5) "John Donne y Don Luis de Góngora" (137–42) suggests that Donne knew the baroque poetry of Spain and likely was impressed by the 1605 collection of Luis de Góngora in which he would have found a vision of life similar to his own. Compares the themes and style of the two poets, noting that both were dependent on aristocratic patronage. (6) "El Mundo como representación en cuatro poemas del barroco inglés" (143–65) translates into Spanish and discusses *HSScene*, analyzing the meditative and Ignatian elements in the sonnet and commenting on it as a prime example of English baroque poetry. Appendix 1, "Sobre Devociones de John Donne," reprints an essay that originally appeared in *Imagen* (Caracas) no. 73 (1970): 15–31. Notes (187–98) are followed by a table of contents (199).

1253. Pando Canteli and María Jesús. "The Treatment of the Feminine in Donne's Love Poetry: Some Traces of the Roman Elegy," in *Actas del III congreso internacional de la Sociedad Española de Estudios Renacentistas Ingleses (SEDERI)* [*Proceedings of the III International Conference of the Spanish Society for*

English Renaissance Studies], ed. María Luisa Doñobeitia, 243–53. Granada: SEDERI.

Discusses how Donne, borrowing from the Roman love elegy, "recreates an image of woman" that serves "to subvert the codes of the extended idealized notion of the lady in an unrequited relationship" and to entertain "an audience likely to enjoy these kinds of compositions and that could, somehow, be mirrored in the experiences depicted in poems" (243). Explores, in particular, Donne's treatment of women in *ElJeal* and selected poems in the *Songs and Sonets* to show "how the male speaker's attitude toward her reflects a relationship of power and tension between the speaker, his world, and the woman addressed" (244). Points out how the woman in *ElJeal* "is deprived of authority and dominated by the male speaker's voice" (246) and how in such poems as *Jet, Leg, Mess,* and *Ind* the woman is presented as treacherous and fickle and as "an object of pleasure, created by and for men's sake and always in a subordinate position to men" (251). Concludes that "[t]he contempt for the feminine so frequently displayed by Donne's speakers suggests not only that the sphere of power enjoyed by women was considerably diminished, but [also] that the 'masculine persuasive force' was exercised most potently" (251–52).

1254. Papazian, Mary Arshagouni. "Donne, Election, and the *Devotions upon Emergent Occasions.*" *HLQ* 55: 603–19.

Questions the generally accepted scholarly assumption that *Devotions* "represents an upward movement toward God by Donne as an Everyman" (603) and argues rather that he creates a speaker "who, as prayer 1 puts it, is elect 'from the beginning,' and who undergoes an experience peculiar to his kind." Discusses how "[r]ecognizing that Donne presents the speaker as elect from the opening prayer raises some new possibilities for interpreting the work—for understanding the character of the speaker, the overall focus and movement of the work, the unusual open-ended conclusion, and the nature of Donne's self-presentation" (604). Surveys the Anglican position on predestination and examines Donne's references to election in his sermons to show that Donne's own statements "echo orthodox Reformed conceptions of election and reprobation" (607). Argues also that "[a]lthough Donne may well make use of Protestant meditative techniques in the *Devotions,* this tradition fails not only to explain fully its overall structure but also to account for the emotional twists and turns experienced by the speaker during the course of his illness, arguably the essence of the work's affective power" (608). Maintains that although "there is a "movement from anxiety to peace in each individual devotion," thereby marking "the necessary role of affliction for the elect, no similar linear movement marks the overall progress of the work." Shows how "[t]he internal cycle, in short, betrays the speaker's election" and "is not paralleled by the kind of upward progress that most readers expect to see in the work" (611). Believes that "[i]nstead of being simply a meditative exercise on sickness, the *Devotions* rather presents a dramatic account of the speaker's fall into affliction" (615), but since he is assured of salvation, he is not seeking grace. Maintains that "[i]n the *Devotions,* we witness a speaker who longs not for physical recovery . . . but for death" (615–16). Concludes that "[i]n the light of Donne's own words in his sermons, the *Devotions,* and final will and epitaph, then, it seems hard to deny the conclusion that Donne fashioned his persona and himself as elect" and thus "was able to face suffering, pain, and, finally, death itself with the peace and equanimity of spirit" (616).

1255. Pebworth, Ted-Larry. " 'Let me here use that freesome': Subversive Representation in John Donne's Obsequies to the Lord Harington." *JEGP* 91: 17–42.

Argues that *Har* is "an accomplished occasional poem, deeply rooted in contemporaneous political controversies and tensions, and unavoidably circumscribed by considerations external to itself," in other words, "a poem that can be fully understood and appreciated only in light of the complexities of its occasion and the contexts of its composition." Examines, therefore, the historical and biographical contexts of the poem not only to explain its "peculiarities" but also to shed light on its "political subtext" and to show how it illustrates "Donne's solution to a personal and professional dilemma" (18). Thinks the poem "can, in fact, be best appreciated not as an expression of Donne's philosophical perspective but as his subversion of the concerted representation of his subject by the young man's political and religious supporters" (19). Shows how in the poem Donne "praises by means of negative formulas and indirection" and how "this practice (coupled with the poem's accusatory tone and pointed references) subtly reveals his deep-seated ambivalence about Harington's accomplishments" (31). Argues that "the force of the poem is directed not to attack Harington but to reshape him," that it "attempts to deny the other public representations of him as a champion of Puritanism and militancy by seeing him as a privately virtuous youth who would have modified his extreme views had he been given longer to live" (41). Maintains that "even as (and especially because) it depicts Harington as a pri-

vate rather than public individual and implicitly denies his political significance, Donne's obsequy is a political poem" (41–42) that is "most remarkable for its deft use of conspicuous silences and noticeable absences as tools of subversive representation." Believes the poem is a "testimony not merely to Donne's ingenuity but also to his integrity, his refusal to abandon his religiopolitical views in order to please a patron" and that it marks publicly "his determination never again to put himself in such a position" (42).

1256. Poley, Roger. *English Prose of the Seventeenth Century, 1590–1700.* Longman Literature in English Series, gen. eds. David Carroll and Michael Wheeler. London: Longman. xii, 325p.

Surveys various genres of English prose from 1590 to 1700—fiction, history, biography, autobiography, the Bible, the sermon, devotions and meditations, politicized religious treatises, the essay, and so on. Comments on Donne's sermons (110–15), calling Donne the preacher "a Christian psychologist, an investigator and mover of emotions, an Augustinian who regarded love and fear as essential motives to the discovery and obedience of Christian truth" (111). Points out in the sermons "the restlessness, the inventiveness and the gap-bridging that we might call baroque" and also notes "the organisation, the delight in antithesis and rounding off that is associated with the Ciceronian style" (112–13). Finds in the sermons anxiety, tension, sometimes uncertainty, imaginative flights that go beyond decorum, and self-dramatizing. Believes that Donne's "greatness as a preacher lies in his ability to capture the perceptions and feelings of a specific congregation for specific theological ends" (114). Also comments on how the *Devotions* (123–25) reflects a typical Donnean characteristic—the "analogical imagination." Discusses how the style of the *Devotions* "is part of the meaning" (124) and concludes that the *Devotions* "show how inherently literary the practice of meditation in this period can be, encouraging expressiveness with discipline" (125).

1257. Raizis, Marios Byron. "Hoi metaphysikoi poihtes tes Anglias" [The Metaphysical Poets of England]. *Philologike Protochronia* (Athens) 49: 54–58.

Presents a general introduction to English metaphysical poetry of the seventeenth century for the Greek reader. Comments on Donne's critical reception and on major features of his poetry, such as its intellectuality, novelty, and use of elaborate conceits. Discusses *Ecst* as an example of Donne's technique and art.

1258. Ray, Robert H. "Donne's 'To His Mistress Going to Bed,' Lines 33–35." *Exp* 50: 203–4.

Points out a bawdy pun in ll. 33–35 of *ElBed*: "Donne is punning on 'whole' as the female 'hole' revealed by nakedness." Suggests that "[t]his implication is reinforced by the further bawdy meaning of 'taste' as to enjoy a woman sexually" (203). Notes a similar allusion to "hole" in *ElProg* (ll. 31–32, 36).

1259. Robinson, Ken. "Putting Words to Wonders." *EIC* 42: 299–319.

Cites *GoodM* as an example of a poem that plays on the gap between experience and language "as a way of puzzling about the tension between the pre-verbal and the verbal, dependence and independence as experienced within the moment." Suggests how the poem "expresses the emotional complex of 'maternity and genitality,' of being merged and pre-verbal and being separate and verbal" (305) and "confronts the complex in terms of

the paradox of the eternal moment, the experience of being outside considerations of time and space that lovers can feel in [a] high-charged state of emotional union" (305–6). Sees the poem as a "tonal puzzle" because "[i]t is impossible to tell whether it should be read as a one-sided expression of male dominance and sexual power or whether it betokens a relationship that is so jealousy-proof, so certain, that it is possible for the couple to share a joke about the speaker's past sexual life." Says that "[a]t the root of the poem's problematic status lies the fact that the lover speaks at all instead of simply staring into his mistress's eyes," for "[t]he moment of total union requires silence" and "[t]o speak is to constitute a self distinct from the other." Notes that "[t]o speak with Donne's hyperbolic and pyrotechnic wit is to deepen the self-consciousness" (306).

1260. Ronberg, Gert. *A Way with Words: The Language of English Renaissance Literature.* London: Edward Arnold. ix, 207p.

Discusses the language of English Renaissance poetry and prose in order to acquaint students with "the linguistic habits and niceties of the period" (3). Comments on phonology and spelling, vocabulary and meaning, syntax and rhetoric, uses of pronouns and verbs, and the sentence. Draws illustrative examples from Donne's poetry throughout and gives a brief rhetorical analysis of an extract from his second prebend sermon preached at St. Paul's on 29 January 1625.

1261. Sabine, Maureen. *Feminine Engendered Faith: The Poetry of John Donne and Richard Crashaw.* Houndmills: Macmillan. xvi, 301p.

Maintains that, although "[i]t is a critical commonplace that no two seventeenth-century English poets could be as antithetical as Donne and Crashaw," their common love for the Virgin Mary "provides an important point of apposition." Discusses how "[t]he ebb and flow of interest in the sacred motherhood from the poetry of Donne to that of Crashaw highlights the shifting sexual politics of seventeenth-century religion and of the devotional language invigorating it" (ix). Chapter 1, "Unspeakable *Domina*" (1–42), shows how the Virgin Mary "exerts a retentive hold over Donne's imagination which affected the religious orientation of his poetry and his fitful movement towards Anglican communion." Points out that, because of the objections of the Reformers, Donne had to conceal his devotion and that, as time went by, "[v]arious women could only partially satisfy an inbred Catholic longing for the continual protection of Guardian Mother." Chapter 2, "Crowned with Her Flesh" (43–77), discusses *Corona* and *Lit* to suggest that "Donne quieted this longing by refashioning time-honoured devotions to Mary and keeping these in secret circulation among a nucleus of friends sympathetic to his Catholic turn of mind." Points out that, although *Corona* "strives for medieval solemnity, Donne drew upon the drama and escapades of his Catholic youth for inspiration as well as for relief from his subservience to patronesses," and that "[p]oetic employment of rosary techniques tranquillised and uplifted his spirits while substantiating his belief that continuing identification with Mary as *Deipara* or the God-bearer was vital to inner well-being." Maintains that in *Lit* Donne "struggled to follow a 'rectified devotion,' yet still occasionally relapsed into acclamation of Mary" (xi). Chapter 3, "Refuse the Name of Mother" (78–110), argues that in the *Anniversaries* Donne "found

an outlet for his involuntary Catholic instinct to honour the Virgin Mary while declaring his formal determination to refrain from invoking her once and for all" but that, in fact, "in making her deficiency the *modus operandi* of the *Anniversaries*, Donne lent a hand in the decomposition of the Marian ideal" (xii). Maintains that "[i]n projecting a feminine figure remote from maternal involvement in the cares of men, the *Anniversaries* were works of evasive iconoclasm" (xii–xiii). Notes that in *HSShow,* "wary of resurrecting Mary's union as Mother with the body of Christ, Donne overworked the metaphors of a spousal relationship" (xiii). Chapters 4, 5, 6, and 7 discuss Crashaw's praise of Mary in his religious poems and comment on how "he pursued a feminine vision of faith when seventeenth-century religion was largely the patrimony of men" (xiii–xiv), concluding that Crashaw "triumphantly restores Our Lady to the majesty that predecessors such as Donne and his father had helped to eclipse" (xv). Includes notes (236–81), a selected bibliography (282–94), and an index (295–301). Reviews: Peter Hyland in *SCN* 51 (1993): 45; Anthony Low in *C&L* 42 (1993): 608–9; Nancy E. Wright in *SoRA* 27 (1994): 232–35; Paul A. Parrish in *JEGP* 94 (1995): 244–46.

1262. Salenius, Maria. " 'They Came Early': On the Presentation of Women in One of John Donne's Sermons," in *"As They Say": Many Happy Returns: Essays in Honour of Saara Nevanlinna,* 108–15. Helsinki: University of Helsinki. Discusses Donne's sermon, given at St. Paul's on Easter 1630, in which, commenting on the women who came to Christ's tomb on Easter morning, he, somewhat uncharacteristically, speaks of women "in a most gentle and approving spirit" (108). Analyzes the sermon to show how Donne not only gives "the women at the grave the main focus in the events of Easter morning" but "also recognizes them as the first bearers of the gospel of salvation" and suggests that "not only these women in the text of the Gospel but all women have a theological purpose" (113).

1263. Shami, Jeanne. "Introduction: Reading Donne's Sermons." *JDJ* 11:1–20.

Provides an introduction to volume 11 of *JDJ*, which is devoted to Donne's sermons. Examines why modern scholars, for the most part, have neglected not only Donne's sermons but sermons in general and stresses their importance in understanding the culture of the time. Comments on Donne's reputation and popularity as a preacher in his own day and laments that at the present time "sermon scholarship constitutes only a fraction of the total output, and is inversely proportional to the total amount of Donne material being discussed." Suggests that, as literary scholars, "we need to reconsider how we generalize from the sermons, how we gain access to those texts, how we can quote effectively from the sermons; how we understand them as historical as well as literary documents, and, finally, how we can promote a less fragmented approach to their use" (5). Argues that Donne's sermons "need to be re-assessed from the full range of critical positions available to modern scholars," noting that, "[a]s it is, there is little overlap in Donne studies between literary, historical, and theological approaches of the sermons: literary assessments of his rhetorical and homiletic devices, of style, are carefully insulated from historical assessments of Donne's place among contemporary preachers; theological labels are applied to the entire body of his work; political assessments are achieved by quoting fragments of sermons out of context without due consideration of the time, place, and cultural circumstances informing the sermons; and it is unclear whether historians and literary critics are engaging in a productive dialogue about Donne as well as some of the other important preachers of the period" (11–12). Points out some new directions in scholarship on Donne's sermons that are developing, as reflected, in part, in the essays included in this volume, and suggests what more needs doing.

1264. Shell, Cheryl. "The Foe in Sight: Discovering the Enemy in Donne's *Elegie XIX*." *WL&A* 4, no. 2: 1–18.

Explains the metaphor of military conflict in *ElBed*, noting how "love and war have been figurative partners for centuries" (6). Discusses how the speaker, hoping to achieve more than "just sexual conquest," desires "full conquest of his enemy: to place all her territories, her present and future treasures, and her body under his control." Maintains, in other words, that "he wants to make her his wife" but recognizes that sexual conquest is "the first step in that process," and "the important one, because it makes all subsequent steps legal" (12). Argues that having been envisioned by Donne as an "archetypal enemy" and as "the target of progaganda for the war between the sexes," the lady in the poem "will continue to be treated like the monstrous other, as the rich spoils of war who can be captured, exploited and even enslaved but who will never be worthy of trust, never really be transformed or tamed." Maintains that "she will remain dangerous, antagonistic, immoral, and along with yielding her treasure she will continue to produce her conqueror's justifiable response: surveillance, restraint, confinement." Suggests, in other words, that Donne, by creating woman as "an archetypal foe to man," concludes that she "must forever remain 'in sight' " (15).

1265. Sinfield, Alan. "Protestantism: Questions of Subjectivity and Control," in *Faultlines: Cultural Materialism and the Politics of Dissident Reading,* 143–80. Berkeley and Los Angeles: University of California Press.

Maintains that Donne's Protestantism "is strongly infused with the anxious contradictions of Calvinism" and that "[a]bout half of the Holy Sonnets end with the condition of Donne's soul in *question*—unaffected by his devotional efforts, awaiting God's mysterious judgment." Claims that Donne's theology "is close to the center of English Calvinism, in the sense that any move toward God depends on God moving first," leaving "the human person without influence over his or her salvation" (147). Points out how Calvinistic theology led to "the creation of self-consciousness, of interiority," a savoring of "the nuances of one's spiritual condition" (159), and sees in the *Holy Sonnets* "a self-conscious deployment and cultivation of self-awareness" (159–60).

1266. Singh, Brijraj, ed. *Five Seventeenth-Century Poets: Donne, Herbert, Crashaw, Vaughan, Marvell.* Delhi: Oxford University Press. xii, 297p.

An anthology designed to meet the needs of Indian students. The introduction (1–33) comments on attempts to define the poetry of the seventeenth century as either "metaphysical" or "meditational," concluding that neither label is satisfactory. Briefly comments on how Donne's poetry is rooted "in the burdens and uncertainties" of his times, noting that "to be free from them by means of a woman's or God's love is a desire that underlies a good deal of his poetry" (8). "John Donne" (34–110) presents (1) a brief biographical sketch of the poet and com-

ments on the early publishing history of the poems; (2) an introduction to the *Satyres,* followed by *Sat3*; (3) an introduction to the *Elegies,* followed by 5 elegies; (4) an introduction to the *Songs and Sonets,* followed by 18 poems; and (5) an introduction to the religious poems, followed by 4 selections from the *Holy Sonnets, Goodf,* and *Father.* Each poem is preceded by a brief commentary and followed by explanatory notes. Includes a bibliography (31–33) and an index of first lines (295–97). Review: W. B. Hutchins in *SCN* 53 (1995): 14.

1267. Skulsky, Harold. *Language Recreated: Seventeenth-Century Metaphorists and the Act of Metaphor.* Athens, Ga.: University of Georgia Press. 294p.

Discusses "how figurative language behaves in a major tradition of English poetry: seventeenth-century lyric" (1), in order "to show how the notion of figurativeness can illuminate a body of great poetry" and "to show how the poetry can return the compliment by illuminating the notion of figurativeness—and the tragicomedy of human interaction in which figurativeness arises" (2). Presents the classical account of figuration, based primarily on Aristotle, and the Christian view, as seen primarily in the theories of St. Augustine. Cites Donne's poems throughout as illustrations. For example, discusses the uses of pseudo-metaphor and profane wit in *LovGrow, Fever, ElAut,* and *Expir,* maintaining that "as a mock metaphorist he blithely exploits his hearers' figurational charity to rule out literal readings," he "signals figurative senses that don't exist," and he "talks nonsense" but "when he talks nonsense, he doesn't refuse commitment," rather he "celebrates it" (76). Comments on the dramatic uses of diversionary *litterae* in *Ecst, ValMourn, Appar, WomCon, Noct,* and the *Holy Sonnets,* in which "a speaker either tries and fails to get his scheme taken literally, or manages to miss the point himself" (25). Discusses the uses of dramatic irony in *Twick* and the elaborate and powerful exploratory metaphor in *Sickness*. Considers these poems fundamentally as "miniconversation[s] inside the wider conversation of the culture" in which they grow, as speech-acts and "(self-announced) *performances*" (224).

1268. Smith, A. J. "John Donne." *Dictionary of Literary Biography: Seventeenth-Century British Non-Dramatic Poets*, ed. M. Thomas Hester. First Series: vol. 121, 77–96. A Bruccoli Clark Layman Book. Detroit, Mich.: Gale Research.

Contains a list of Donne's works and editions of his works (77–79), followed by a discussion of his critical reputation (79–80) and of the major characteristics of his poetry and prose and accompanied by a biographical sketch (80–94). Concludes with a selected bibliography of editions of Donne's letters, bibliographies, biographies, and modern critical studies (94–96). Maintains that Donne's "standing as a great English poet, and one of the greatest writers of English prose, is now assured" (79). Sees the dramatic immediacy of the poems, their impassioned reasoning, striking images, subtle uses of argument, wit, and the subversion of conventions as the basis of their appeal, noting how Donne "confronts us with the complexity of our own natures" (92). Discusses also Donne's prose, especially *Devotions* and the sermons, stressing how "[o]ver a literary career of some forty years Donne moved from skeptical naturalism to a conviction of the shaping presence of the divine spirit in the natural creation." Concludes, however, that "his mature understanding did not contradict his earlier vision" and that "the amorous adventurer nurtured the dean of St. Paul's" (94).

1269. Spiller, Michael R. G. *The Development of the Sonnet: An Introduction*. London: Routledge. x, 241p. 2nd ed., 1993.

Mentions Donne as a sonneteer throughout, pointing out, in particular, his experimentation with the sonnet form. Notes his uses of dramatic rhythms, enjambment, medial pauses, compression, and "violent ellipsis" (179–80). Compares Donne to Guittone d'Arezzo, calling the latter "the John Donne of early Italian poetry" (20), and suggests the possible influence of Donne on Herbert's sonnets.

1270. Spurr, Barry. *The Poetry of John Donne*. Glebe (NSW, Australia): Wild Woolley. 26p.

Presents a general introduction for students to Donne's life, followed by analyses of *SunRis, GoodM, Canon, Relic, ValMourn, HSBlack, HSBatter, HSShe,* and *Sickness*.

1271. Stanwood, P. G. *The Semipiternal Season: Studies in Seventeenth-Century Devotional Writing*. Seventeenth-Century Texts and Studies, gen. ed. Anthony Low, vol. 3. New York: Peter Lang. xiii, 185p.

A collection of mostly previously published essays, five of which deal specifically with Donne: (1) "Time and Liturgy in Donne, Crashaw, and T. S. Eliot" (3–19), which appeared in *Mosaic* 12 (1979): 91–105 (entry 71); (2) "'Essential Joye' in Donne's *Anniversaries*" (31–42), which appeared in *TSLL* 13 (1971): 227–38; (3) "Word and Sacrament in Donne's Sermons" (43–54), which is new and annotated below (entry 1273); (4) "John Donne's Sermon Notes" (75–83), which appeared in *RES* 29 (1978): 313–17; and (5) "'Thou Art Indeed Just, Lord': Hopkins, Donne and Herbert and the Sonnet of Affliction" (181–85), which is new and annotated below (entry 1272).

1272. Stanwood, P. G. " 'Thou Art Indeed Just, Lord': Hopkins, Donne, and Herbert and the Sonnet of Affliction," in *The Sempiternal Season: Studies in Seventeenth-Century Devotional Writing,* 181–85. Seventeenth-Century Texts and Studies, gen. ed. Anthony Low, vol. 3. New York: Peter Lang.

Compares similarities in theological outlook and use of poetic imagery and techniques in *HSSighs,* Herbert's "The Sinner," and Gerard Manley Hopkins's "Thou art indeed just, Lord." Shows that "[t]his trinity of sonnets locates an attitude of suffering, disappointment, wretchedness," "asks the question of why one's best hopes end in disorder," and "asks for joyful resolution" (183). Points out that in their affliction all three poets "discover that the Redeemer Himself is both calling and responding" and that "in affliction there is joy and paradise at last" (185).

1273. Stanwood, P. G. "Word and Sacrament in Donne's Sermons," in *The Sempiternal Season: Studies in Seventeenth-Century Devotional Writing,* 43–54. Seventeenth-Century Texts and Studies, gen. ed. Anthony Low, vol. 3. New York: Peter Lang.

Focuses "primarily on eucharistic celebration, or the sacramental sense in Donne, especially in the sermons," and suggests that "Donne's interest in the issues of life—and death—is representative of the most compelling feature of Anglican spirituality—its incarnational theology" (43), as that tradition is represented by Richard Hooker's *Of the Lawes of Ecclesiastical Polity* and Jeremy Taylor's *Holy Living.* Maintains that "most of Donne's sermons, ending so often at a moment of supreme exaltation and desire, lead to a celebration of the eucharistic feast" (44). Observes also that in his Christmas sermons Donne "gives prominence" to the Incarnation, the "doctrine that underlies so much of

his work," and "is able to manifest well that sacramental sense inherent in it" (46). Holds that in Donne's sermons there is a general impulse "toward temporal collapse, the finite in the infinite; or, in sacramental terms, the Word made flesh, and Christ's death, Resurrection, Ascension, and coming again in glory" (47), thus emphasizing that "[m]ortality leads upwards where word and sacrament, time and eternity, are one" (53).

1274. Strien, A. van. "17 Augustus 1630: Huygens sturrt Hooft twee vertalingen uit de gedichten van John Donne—Constantijn Huygens, de virtuoos," in *Nederlandese literatur, een geschiedenis,* ed. M. A. Schenkevel-Van der Dussen, 218–24. Groningen: Nijhoff.

Elucidates the context for Constantijn Huygens's letter to Peter Corneliszoon Hooft (1581–1647) dated 17 August 1630, in which Huygens enclosed fair copies of his translations of *SunRis* and most of *ElAnag,* praising Hooft (who had no English) by remarking that these Donnean poems are commensurate with Hooft's *inventio* and *elocutio.* Argues that this gesture exemplifies the way in which until the very end of his long life Huygens was able to gain and keep the admiration of a small circle of the kind of admirers he sought.

1275. Summers, Claude J. "Donne's 1609 Sequence of Grief and Comfort." *SP* 89: 211–31.

Observes that the *Epicedes and Obsequies* "are seldom taken seriously or read sympathetically on their own terms as poems of grief and sorrow" because they are "at once occasional and idealized" (211). Maintains, however, that "[e]ven as they are implicated in the details of their occasions, they strive toward a condition of impersonality" and "even as they participate in the poetics of patronage, they aspire to the timelessness of art" (211–12). Discusses, in particular, a "closely knit group of poems written within a very short time" (*BedfShe, Mark, BoulNar,* Lady Bedford's "Death be not proud, thy hand gave not this blow," and "Elegie: Death") that "illustrates Donne's characteristic balance of the personal and the impersonal in a project of epideictic idealization that never entirely transcends its immediate context." Argues that the five poems "form a dynamic sequence of grief and comfort," a sequence "most remarkable not for its philosophy or even its striking imagery and ingenious arguments, but for its revelation of Donne's rhetorical agility, his tentativeness and tactfulness, his willingness to revise positions, and, especially, his persistent awareness of audience and occasion." Shows how the poems "gain in clarity and poignance when seen as a dynamic exchange, rooted in the specific circumstances of their occasions" and how they "are yoked together by their self-referentiality, their linked images, and their common problem of discovering meaning in the face of death" (212). Discusses how the poems are "highly complex social transactions between Donne and Lady Bedford" in which the poet seeks "to discover in the senselessness of particular losses some meaning to death" and attempts "to find in the meditations prompted by those specific deaths [namely the deaths of Lady Bridget Markham and Cecilia Bulstrode, both friends of the Countess of Bedford] some abstract truth that can offer concrete comfort" (213). Acknowledges that the sequence is not "uniformly successful" but shows how "its failures no less than its triumphs are informative" and that "both can be accounted for by reference to contexts external to the poems" (230–31). Discusses, in particular, how "the Countess directly shapes Donne's

discourse by her own poetic responses" and how "her influence sometimes cramps as well as liberates Donne's poetic imagination" (231).

1276. Swiss, Margo. "Donne's Medieval Magdalene: Apostolic Authority in 'To the Lady Magdalen Herbert, of St. Mary Magdalen.'" *ESC* 18: 143–56.

Maintains that in *MHMary* Donne departs from the post-Reformation representation of the Magdalene and turns to an earlier tradition in which her apostolic authority and function were "firmly and widely established in both patristic and medieval contexts" (143). Discusses also how the poem reflects "the affective theology of twelfth-century Cistercian practice" (144). Presents a detailed reading of the sonnet in which Donne as preacher-poet regards the Magdalene as "the first Christian preacher of the Gospel" and "exhorts his designated reader, Magdalen Herbert, to active ministry" (147). Observes that Donne claims in the poem that "[a]s an exemplar of feminine beauty, moral virtue, and ministerial service, the Magdalene (in her biblical precedent and in the person of Magdalen Herbert) presides as authoritatively over his spiritual as over his literary salvation" (147). Discusses how Donne, by dedicating his sacred poems to Mrs. Herbert, "engages with the medieval tradition of St. Mary Magdalene's role as witness and evangelist of Christ" and how in his sonnet he is concerned "not merely with patronage, even in its most exalted form, but with apostolic authority in its most Catholic sense" (151).

1277. Venkatasubramanian, Meenakshi. "Donne's *Devotion 14.*" *Expl* 50: 133–36.

Points out that in Devotion 14 of *Devotions* Donne "yokes together the human drama of [his] illness and the larger Christian drama in which he sees himself participating simultaneously," "a process that hinges on the use of the words *crisis* and *critical*" (133–34).

1278. Vessey, Mark. "Consulting the Fathers: Invention and Meditation in Donne's Sermon on Psalm 51:7 ('Purge Me with hyssope')." *JDJ* 11: 99–110.

Discusses Donne's treatment of patristic texts in general in his sermons by examining his sermon on Psalm 51. Points out that, with the exception of St. Augustine, the patristic writers mentioned in the sermon add little to its exegetical argument, serve mostly as "stylistic ornaments or elements of rhetorical *elocutio*," and were most likely drawn from "the preacher's memory or his notebooks" rather than from the works themselves (104). Notes that even in his use of St. Augustine in the sermon he probably "relied on his earlier notes or some other secondary source" (105). Suggests a plan of study that (1) would extend "this kind of analysis to Donne's patristic references to a larger sample of his sermons"; (2) would examine Donne's mode of recourse to the Fathers "in the context of Renaissance theories and practices of excerption, compilation and quotation" and would explain "how he went about acquiring his own stock of commonplace material and what other stories he raided"; (3) would "reconstruct the full apparatus of patristic scholarship within which he worked"; (4) would study his citations of the Fathers "as an integral part of the verb artistry of his sermons" (106); and would explain "how Donne used patristic reference to establish a character for himself as a Christian interpreter." Concludes that although "[m]odern readers of Donne's sermons are naturally impressed, as his seventeenth-century listeners must have been too, by the tokens of his patristic learning," there lurks the suspicion that "much of what we have taken for erudition is more

rightly considered a form of display" (107).

1279. Vickers, Brian. "The Seventeenth Century, 1603–1674," in *An Outline of English Literature*, ed. Pat Rogers, 150–99. Oxford: Oxford University Press. Reprint of Chapter 4 from *The Oxford Illustrated History of English Literature*, ed. Pat Rogers (Oxford and New York: Oxford University Press, 1987) (entry 848).

1280. Wallerstein, Nicholas. "*Adversative Conjunction:* The Poetics of Linguistic Opposition." *LangQ* 30, nos. 1–2: 47–61.

Outlines "the general use of adversative conjunction in (primarily) English and American poetry" and contends that "the adversative is not merely a grammatical convenience, but sometimes a highly functional tool of rhetorical strategy" (47). Points out that Thomas O. Sloane in "A Rhetorical Analysis of John Donne's 'The Prohibition'" (*QJS* 48 [1962]: 38–45) observed that "the contrastive function of the adversative conjunction is what the Ramists called 'the discretive axiom,'" citing as an example *Prohib* (51).

1281. Wheeler, Angela J. *English Verse Satire from Donne to Dryden: Imitation of Classical Models.* Anglistische Forschungen, 214. Heidelberg: Carl Winter. 368p.

Surveys formal verse satire from Donne to Dryden, observes that, apart from *Sat4,* "his most conscious imitation of classical satire" (115), "Donne's debt to Roman satirists for individual lines is . . . negligible" but that "it is evident that Donne looked to the Roman satirists for method, manner and ideas." Claims that "Donne's sophisticated and subtle borrowing resulted in a type of satire which was quite unique in English literature at the beginning of the 1590's" (120), noting, in particular, that Donne differs from his models—Horace, Juvenal, Persius—by introducing religion into his satires. Says that "[t]he fixing of the label 'Horatian,' 'Persian' or 'Juvenalian' to Donne's satires is impossible, for Donne was all, and at the same time none" (121). Points out, for example, that even in *Sat4* Donne simply "uses the framework of Horace's satire as a peg on which he hangs a tirade on court-life in general" (117), and that *Sat1* captures "the gay spirit of Horace's satire" (118) but contains no direct borrowings. Throughout, comments on various aspects of Donne's satires, in particular, the use of classical names, obscene language, medical imagery, obscurity, and especially irregular versification, which may have been Donne's "attempt to reproduce the irregular rhythms of everyday speech" (70–71). Compares and contrasts Donne as a satirist to Guilpin. Reviews: Kirk Combe in *N&Q*, n.s. 41 (1994): 100–101; Stephan Lieske in *ZAA* 43 (1995): 273–74.

1282. Wilcox, Helen. *"Catching the Sense": The Wit of Seventeenth-Century English Poetry.* Groningen: Phoenix Press. 24p.

Surveys the nature and importance of wit in seventeenth-century English literature, citing Donne as "an author of prodigiously witty works" who exploits "the creative anarchy of language" while at the same time facing up to the fact that "there are things in heaven and earth that may be beyond words—and then [writing] about these" (9). Notes that Donne's awareness of "the gap between earthly wit and heavenly values is so powerful that it praises by the contrast it evokes, and by default" (10).

1283. Wilcox, Helen. "John Donne." *De Gids* 155, no. 5: 413–15.

Argues that it is not incongruous to consider the death of an author alongside "literary" (i.e., fictional) deaths, since Donne's death was, as far as it could be a controlled and scripted drama, the climax of his lifelong preoccupation with mortality, as seen in his poems, letters, *Devotions,* and sermons. Discusses aspects of Donne's last days—a mixture of narcissism and self-abnegation in the commission and contemplation of his deathbed portrait, the public spectacle of "Death's Duell," and his commemoration in St. Paul's Cathedral by an upright effigy awaiting resurrection. Highlights a number of paradoxes appropriate to Donne, including the idea of his deathbed as a "temple" (*Flea*), and the fact that, in Donne's view, his "last scene" was actually the prologue to an eternal drama. Translated into Dutch by Christel van Boheemen. (From an English summary provided by the author.)

1284. Wiltenburg, Robert. "Donne's Dialogue of One: The Self and Soul," in *Reconsidering the Renaissance: Papers from the Twenty-First Annual Conference,* ed. Mario Di Cesare, 413–27. Medieval and Renaissance Texts and Studies, 93. Binghamton, N.Y.: Medieval and Renaissance Texts and Studies.

Argues that Donne "presents a fundamentally internal and non-progressive dialogue between two concepts of the inner life, the self and the soul—a dialogue that is exploratory, inconclusive, and thereby faithful to its subject, Donne in love" (414). Suggests that "for Donne and other equal heirs of the Renaissance and the Reformation, to whom both ways of describing and organizing the inner life are available and urgent, there is a primary need to adjudicate, to satisfy, and, if possible, to reconcile, the competing claims—both compelling, both legitimate—of the self and the soul" (418). Shows how Donne makes the questions posed by the "competing imperatives" of the views about self and soul central to his poetry by asserting that "the experience of love is neither of successful or frustrated ascent, but of vigorous claim and counterclaim, which no single form or sequence of forms can adequately represent" (419–20). Maintains that in the *Songs and Sonets* "the promiscuous juxtaposition" of the individual poems "makes Donne's most important and characteristic point about the self and the soul in love" and shows how the poems are primarily "the domain of the self," in which Donne assumes conflicting "moods, postures, and points of view" and presents "the thematic emphasis on variety and inconstancy as not only inevitable but positively good" (420). Maintains, however, that the soul also "appears regularly . . . though less frequently" (422) in the love poems and suggests that in *ValMourn* "both self and soul seem fully reconciled" (423). Discusses also how the religious poems "show a similar pattern of claim and counterclaim, of dialectical imperatives in conflict, with the difference that the very fact of conflict is usually a source not of challenge or delight but of anxiety and melancholy" (424). Claims that "Jack Donne and Doctor Donne, Pico and Augustine, self and soul, are present from the beginning and continue in pleasurable, anguished, fruitful, unresolvable conversation to the end," and concludes that "it is Donne's peculiar quality and courage to insist throughout that we have both something like a self and something like a soul (as we have also soul and body) and that the claims of both must be, if not quite satisfied, recognized" (426).

1285. Yanni, Mara. *Sense of a Self: Subjectivity and Language in John Donne's Songs and Sonnets.* Athens: Gnosis. 162p.

Reevaluates the *Songs and Sonets* as an example of the way early poetical texts construct or undo the sense of a self. Examines ways the various discourses of the text challenge traditional Renaissance notions of lyric subjectivity and probes the problem of Donne's literary self as both agent and object of his writing. Claims that Donne's practice in the *Songs and Sonets* suggests a departure from the normative patterns of articulating subjective experience in poetry through a new conception of the self and a new mode of lyric expression. Believes that the striking feature of this text is that it draws attention to the problem of the self by deconstructing in an explicit manner the humanist conviction that views the existence of a unified self as an actual possibility, and finds this approach new and different from the way the "terror" of the self's dissolution is dealt with in the sonnet sequences of Sidney, Spenser, or Shakespeare. Maintains that in the discourse of the self, stability of language has always implied a way to fix identity in the world. Argues that her grouping of Donne's poems involves, therefore, a number of distinctions, all of which point to the ways the language as well as the thematics of the text generate the sense of self—in particular that of a literary self. Holds that the representation of the self is problematic in the *Songs and Sonets* and maintains that Donne's choice of an oblique mode for inscribing subjective experience (the inconspicuousness of the poet, unreliable speakers, and rhetorical indeterminacies) suggests a deep distrust in the semantic and representational functions of language as well as an entropic subjectivity. Maintains that Donne's practice also involves a vigorous resistance to the insufficiency of language and the dissolution of meaning, a continuous struggle for asserting a unitary presence in the text through a creative deployment of the power of words. Discusses how these distinct and opposing attitudes towards language materialize into two different modes of discourse—"ironic" and "figural." Points out that the predominance of either mode in individual poems has serious implications for the quality of subjective experience or the kind of literary presence registered in the text: by stressing difference and disjunction, the duplicitous language of irony produces a split subject, whereas figural language disguises difference as likeness through an imaginative assent to the inference of totality and identity. Concludes, therefore, that subjectivity in the *Songs and Sonets* is constructed in the dialectic exchange between these two modes of discourse. (Annotation from a synopsis provided by the author.)

1286. Young, Margaret. "Elegy for John Donne," in *Elegies and Love Songs,* 61–74. Moscow, Idaho: University of Idaho Press.

An original short story in which a hippie father is nicknamed John Donne and to whom his wife reads the *Holy Sonnets* as he is dying of lung cancer.

1993

1287. Addison, Catherine. "From Literal to Figurative: An Introduction to the Study of Simile." *CE* 55: 402–19.

Argues that "some similes are 'literal comparisons'—or, at least, comparisons that approach the literal more closely than the figurative," but that others "are, to varying degrees, figurative, if 'figurativeness' be the distinctive feature of metaphor" (404). Points out that "conceits can be either metaphors or similes, the form taken not contributing markedly to the principal effect of the figure, which is its shock value" (410). Cites Donne's figure of the compasses in *ValMourn* as an example of a conceit that is an "extremely figurative" simile, noting that in the poem the speaker tries to persuade the lady "to accept the appropriateness of his unfamiliar image to their exact situation, against the odds and tradition" (411).

1288. Arnold, Erin L. "Relevance of John Donne to Medical Career Preparation." *The Pharos* 56, no. 3: 33–35.

Discusses *Devotions* as "an example of how literature can play a critical role in a premedical curriculum" by providing the student "with a unique interpretation of disease and its effects on the patient and physician" (34). Maintains that "[a]side from providing an abundant collection of rich imagery and metaphors, Donne's *Devotions* also provides an in-depth investigation of the significance of the emotions that accompany disease," "makes the experience of contracting a disease identifiable for the student by creating imagery that relies on the five senses," and presents "a model of communication—rooting explanations of abstract ideas in concrete senses" (35).

1289. Berman, Antoine. "Critique des traductions John Donne." *Po&sie* 59: 3–20.

Prepublication by Michel Deguy of the introduction of *Pour une critique des traductions: John Donne* (Paris: Gallimard, 1995), 11–31. See entry 1481.

Contains a tribute to Berman, who died in 1991, along with a bibliography of his publications.

1290. Berman, Antoine. " 'Le defi du prosaique': Une critique des traductions françaises de John Donne," in *Traductions, passages: Le domaine anglais,* ed. Stephen Romer, 25–35. Publication des Groupes de Recherches Anglo-Américaines de l'Université François Rabelais de Tours, 10. Tours: Université de Tours.

Prepublication excerpts from *Pour une critique des traductions: John Donne* (Paris: Gallimard, 1995). See entry 1481.

1291. Berry, Philippa. "Authorship Overshadowed: Death, Darkness and the Feminisation of Authority in Late Renaissance Writing," in *What Is an Author?* eds. Maurice Biriotti and Nicola Miller, 155–72. Manchester: Manchester: University Press. Distributed in the USA and Canada by St. Martin's Press.

Argues that in Walton's description of Donne's last sermon "the advent of death coincidentally affirms the

449

closest possible identity between the author and his text" and, "in its implicit relationship of pulpit and tomb, the passage accords a strange supernatural authority to Donne's last appearance as preacher." Notes, however, that "[i]ronically, it communicates this conviction through a striking reversal of that priority of word over image which is held to have been central to Protestant theology, for it stresses the extraordinary visual impact made by the dying man" (157). Maintains that it was Donne's "ghostly demeanour" that "gave his last sermon the authority of a revealed truth" and that, "paradoxically, his performance authorised Donne's words by displacing him as author" (158). Concludes, therefore, that Walton's account "suggests that the relationship between the visual and the verbal in late Renaissance English culture was rather more complicated than is often assumed" (159). Observes that "certain Renaissance texts also associate a crisis in authorial identity with a . . . positive conception of shadowing, pointing to creativity's dependence on the apparent nothingness of darkness" and that "these figurative shadows . . . sometimes acquire feminine substance." Notes that "[i]t is to just such a feminine darkness that Donne's metaphorically annihilated poetic persona cedes his authority" in *Noct*, adding that in "Death's Duell" Donne "relates his theme of the 'issues from death' to man's lifelong connection with an originary (and implicitly dark) maternal space," thereby associating "a female creative act not only with the presence of death in life, but also with a second birth which coincides with death" (162). Concludes that such "motifs of a paradoxical, dark vision . . . provide us with new insights into the themes of authorial death which figure so prominently in late Renaissance literature" (170).

1292. Bethea, David. "Joseph Brodsky as a Russian Metaphysical: A Reading of 'Bol'shaia elegiia Dzhonu Donnu.'" *CASS* 27: 69–89.

Presents a close reading and contextualization of Joseph Brodsky's elegy to Donne ("Bol'shaia elegiia Dzhonu Donnu"), "one of the first major poems of Brodsky's early maturity" (70), written in 1963. Suggests that *Devotions* "provides the most illuminating gloss" (76) on Brodsky's poem and sees it as "a modern Russian attempt to answer Donne's riddle" (77) concerning the fate of the soul after death. Notes that Brodsky's emphasis "is exclusively on the pain of parting, on exile rather than on reunion," and that his poem "has no cosmic or microcosmic circles" but rather "only images of tragic separation" (83–84). Maintains, therefore, that although Brodsky's poem deals with "the metaphysics of Donne (the *efflatus* of the soul from the body), the actual terms of his argument, their combinatory possibilities, are apparently his own, or at least do not owe their derivation to medieval scholasticism" (84); his poem is "a modern version of *ecstasis*, but not the *ecstasis* of John Donne" (85).

1293. Biester, James. "Gender and Style in Seventeenth-Century Commendatory Verse." *SEL* 33: 507–22.

Points out that "[p]oems commending poets in the seventeenth century were expected to treat the poet as miraculous, or capable of producing wonder; praise the poet's wit, either for its boldness or, later in the century, for its restraint; and praise the style of a male poet as 'manly'" (507). Suggests that a study of these poems "provides insight both into the obstacles facing female poets in the seventeenth century, and into the shifts in poetic style during the course of the century," and "help[s] us to determine what contemporary poets thought of each other in particular, and of the art of poetry in general." Maintains that "[n]o poem was as instrumental in establishing wit, wonder, and manliness as the obligatory topoi or commonplaces of eulogies for poets" than Carew's elegy on Donne, noting that "[i]n the years following its publication in 1633, failure to employ these categories almost meant failure to commend the poet addressed." Points out that, "[i]n the early seventeenth century 'masculinity' was associated with the compressed, strong lines of Donne and others" even before Carew wrote his poem and discusses how the term "manly" was applied to style that was "notable either for its rhythmic roughness or for its figurative boldness" (508). Comments on Carew's elegy in which Donne's "pithy vehemence and wit are juxtaposed to the shallow, bodily voluptuousness of his effeminate predecessors" in order to show that "Donne's poetry is the only begetter of strong, manly verse." Notes, in particular, that Carew's "sexually charged mining image" [in ll. 37–44] functions "as a reminder of the intellectual depth of Donne's verse" as well as "of its value as a result of its scarcity, novelty, and inherent worth" (510).

1294. Bruster, Douglas. "Female-Female Eroticism and the Early Modern Stage." *RenD* 24: 1–32.

Explores the presentation of female-female eroticism in early modern English drama, concluding that, "[i]n contrast with other venues, the early modern stage rarely imagined mutually pleasurable erotic relations among the female bodies it represented" but rather imagined "erotic and eroticized relations consonant with current narratives of heterosexuality, with potentially unequal levels of power and pleasure" (3). Observes that, in general, "[i]n early modern England, sug-

gestions of sexual practice among females gravitate strikingly toward coterie discourses" and that "only there do we find its most radical, positive expression" (4), citing *Sappho* as an example of "a rare positive fantasy of female homoerotic practice" (5). Notes, however, that it is unclear what the poem may have meant to Donne's coterie audience.

1295. Carpenter, Peter. "Taking Liberties: Eliot's Donne." *CrSurv* 5: 278–88.

Discusses T. S. Eliot's appropriation of and critical commentary on Donne's poetry and prose and his eventual moving away from Donne's influence. Points out that Eliot's "pronouncements as an advocate for Donne are still influential" and that "they exploited the element from which later he tried his hardest to detach himself: the close relationship in the seventeenth century between the orator and the poet" (278). Notes that one purpose of Eliot's reworking of Donne "was to register the pattern of the past in the consciousness of the present age," and shows how in *The Waste Land* Eliot's transformation of Donne "is only part of the series of cultural recognitions and tests that the poem embodies" and "is a loaded advocacy and memory of one powerful influence among many" (285). Believes that "[w]hat survived of Donne for poetic propaganda and Eliot's special praise, was a quality of voice" (287).

1296. Chambers, Diane. "'Salvation to All That Will Is Nigh': Public Meditation in John Donne's 'La Corona.'" *EIRC* 19: 161–72.

Emphasizes the public nature and interconnectedness of *Corona*. Maintains that the sequence presents "a meditation on the life of Christ that is focused on a central theme revealed in the last line of the first sonnet: *'Salvation to all that will is nigh,'*" that is, that "salvation is near at hand," and discusses how the remaining six sonnets "show how this salvation is accomplished through the incarnation, death, and resurrection of Christ" (161). Discusses the significance of both the circularity of the sequence and its linear progression, which "takes the reader from one aspect of Christ's life to another, each adding to the understanding of Christ's nature and his purpose on earth" (164). Shows how, gradually, the reader "becomes more involved in Christ's life, sees the offer of salvation, and offers in return prayer and praise" (165). Explains also how *Corona* is "a public meditation in that the meditator/reader is drawn into a community of believers who have all chosen salvation" (170).

1297. Coldiron, A. E. B. " 'Poets be silent': Self-Silencing Conventions and Rhetorical Context in the 1633 Critical Elegies on Donne." *JDJ* 12: 101–13.

Maintains that although the 12 elegies appended to the 1633 edition of Donne's poems "seem to perform many of the functions expected of funeral elegy: praise, lament, consolation; asking the essential questions about death; attempting to gain control over unimaginable absence," they, in fact, "contain not only qualified praise, defensive lament, and ironic, unconvincing consolation, but [also] elegiac material handled such that concerns other than Donne and his death become paramount" (101). Discusses how these poems "reveal a sub-genre [the critical elegy] stretched to its limits: mainly, as an inherently agonic kind of poetry with deeply self-obviating conventions; and from the start, as a sub-genre whose rhetorical contexts—occasion, audience, subject, conventions, even purpose—are blurred and multiplied." Concludes that these elegies "reveal how very

much critical elegy's conventions are complicated by its special literary focus" (110).

1298. Collmer, Robert G. "Elizabeth Drury in the United States." *JDJ* 12: 131–38.

Discusses the history of the poorly restored portrait of Elizabeth Drury, presumably painted by Paul van Somer (1576?–1621), which now hangs in The Elms in Newport, Rhode Island, a gift of Klaus von Bulow to the Preservation Society of Newport County. Notes the difference between the present portrait and photographs of the original portrait that appear in both R. C. Bald's *Donne and The Drurys* (1959) and volume one of Edmund Gosse's *The Life and Letters of John Donne* (1899).

1299. Corns, Thomas N. *The Cambridge Companion to English Poetry: Donne to Marvell.* Cambridge Companions to Literature. Cambridge: Cambridge University Press. xx, 306p.

A collection of 14 original essays by divers hands, 6 of which discuss Donne and have been separately entered into this bibliography: David Loewenstein, "Politics and Religion" (entry 1355); Elaine Hobby, "The Politics of Gender" (entry 1345); Arthur F. Marotti, "Manuscript, Print, and Social History of the Lyric" (entry 1359); Alastair Fowler, "Genre and Tradition" (entry 1331); Brian Vickers, "Rhetoric" (entry 1388); and Achsah Guibbory, "John Donne" (entry 1337). Reviews: John R. Roberts in *SCN* 52 (1994): 43–44; Andrew Hadfield in *N&Q*, n.s. 42 (1995): 91–92; Neil Rhodes in *MLR* 91 (1996): 193–95; Alan Rudrum in *RES* 47 (1996): 256–58; Michael Schoenfeldt in *RenQ* 49 (1996): 654–55.

1300. Crockett, Bryan. " 'Holy Cozenage' and the Renaissance Cult of the Ear." *SCJ* 24: 47–65.

Discusses the "metaphysical" sermons of Donne, Thomas Playfere, Ralph

Brownrig, Thomas Adams, and Lancelot Andrewes as works in "a performative mode both informed by and informing Renaissance drama." Maintains that "the peculiar cultural conditions developing out of the Protestant Reformation engendered in England a 'cult of the ear,' a sensibility marked by a heightened aural receptivity to performances evoking a sense of wonder by their manipulations of paradoxical terms" (47). Maintains that the paradoxes of the metaphysical preachers "resonate with the root paradigm of Christ's martyrdom," that "[i]n each case the illogic of paradox serves to subvert or transcend the categories of structured thought, evoking an experimental resolution of contraries," and that "[s]uch an extra-rational resolution tends toward communitas rather than structure" (63). Notes that in his sermons Donne tends "to subordinate the eye to the ear" and believes that "the aural reception of the preacher's words is a sine qua non of salvation" (50). Comments on the use of paradox in his sermons, noting that, for Donne, "the preacher's task is to evoke in the audience a peculiar state of psychological tension involving both fear and comfort" (62).

1301. Cunnar, Eugene R. "Fantasizing a Sexual Golden Age in Seventeenth-Century Poetry," in *Renaissance Discourses of Desire,* ed. Claude J. Summers and Ted-Larry Pebworth, 179–205. Columbia: University of Missouri Press.
Points out that Donne, like many other seventeenth century poets, often endorses the myth of a sexual Golden Age "in which uninhibited and ever-potent male desire and sexuality supposedly prevailed, free from shame, guilt, responsibility, and social custom" (180), thereby allowing for the creation of "sexual fantasies in which there is a perfect love dominated and controlled by the male for male plea-sure and desire" (180–81). Argues that "the appeal to a male myth of a sexual Golden Age does not represent an appeal to mutual freedom but instead embodies a male power play—a discourse of desire—supporting patriarchal assumptions about and control over the nature of women" (181). Examines briefly "representative examples within the historical evolution of the myth from the classical through the Renaissance period" (182)—commenting on both writers and artists—and then discusses uses of the myth in seventeenth century poetry, where it shows up "generally in the context of libertine, Ovidian, or anti-Petrarchan verse" (194). Comments on Donne's use of it in *ElVar, ElBed, Fare,* and especially *Ecst,* in which "the speaker's argument ultimately turns on the control and fulfillment of his desire, which, in turn, marginalizes the woman" (198). Concludes that, "[f]or most poets, the myth became a way to displace or sublimate their own sexual fears and anxieties while controlling the woman for male desire" (204).

1302. Daley, Koos. " 'A Crowne of Prayer and Praise': Donne and Huygens at Prayer." *CJNS* 14: 96–102.
Examines how Donne and Constantijn Huygens "sought to realize a delicate paradoxical balance between self and creator, in poetry that is simultaneously lyrical and sincerely religious" (96) by comparing and contrasting *Corona* and Huygens's *Heilighe Daghen.* Analyzes each of the poems in *Corona* to show how Donne's sequence illustrates the conflicts that he, as a religious poet, attempted to resolve, concluding that he comes "dangerously close to distancing both reader and poet by the linguistic tour de force of weaving together words, lines, and sonnets through repetition, antithesis, ploce, puns, and paradoxes" (98).

Maintains that, although there are many affinities between the two poets, there is "a strong personal conviction in Huygens' series, with none of the doubt" found in Donne's sequence. Points out that "[t]he troubling uncertainties and fear of rejection" that Donne expresses by his "use of a conditional clause at a key moment in the circular movement of the sonnets" in *Corona* are absent from *Heilighe Daghen*. Concludes that whereas Donne's speaker weaves "an uncertain maze where grace may be deliberately withheld, Huygens' speaker walks with the confidence of grace received" (101).

1303. Dean, Leonard F. "Richard Kirk and the Teaching of English." *SR* 101: 567–70.

In a tribute to Richard Kirk as a poet and teacher, whom Dean calls "a natural New Critic with a style of his own" (570), speculates on how Kirk, in contrast to Thomas M. Greene (1989) (entry 967), would have read *ElBed*.

1304. Dime, Gregory T. "The Eliot Tradition in the Criticism of 'Metaphysical' Poetry." *YER* 12: 1–8.

Examines influential studies of Donne that often appropriate (often without citation), misunderstand, modify, and/or transform T. S. Eliot's criticism on the metaphysical poets "for their own purposes" and "thus maintain an active relationship to his criticism." Comments specifically on the work of George Williamson, *The Donne Tradition: A Study in English Poetry from Donne to the Death of Cowley* (Cambridge, Mass.: Harvard University Press, 1930); Basil Willey, *The Seventeenth-Century Background: Studies in the Thought of the Age in Relation to Poetry and Religion* (London: Chatto and Windus, 1934), Cleanth Brooks, *Modern Poetry and the Tradition* (Chapel Hill, N.C.:

University of North Carolina Press, 1939); John Crowe Ransom *The World's Body* (New York: Charles Scribner's Sons, 1938); Leonard Unger *The Man in the Name:Essays on the Experience of Poetry* (Minneapolis, Minn.: University of Minnesota Press, 1956); Rosemond Tuve, *Elizabethan and Metaphysical Imagery: Renaissance Poetic and Twentieth-Century Critics* (Chicago, Ill.: University of Chicago Press, 1947); Louis Martz, *The Poetry of Meditation: A Study in English Religious Literature of the Seventeenth Century* (New Haven, Conn.: Yale University Press, 1954); Odette de Mourgues, *Metaphysical, Baroque, and Précieux Poetry* (Oxford: Clarendon Press, 1953); Wylie Sypher, *Four Stages of Renaissance Style: Transformations in Art and Literature 1400–1700* (Garden City, N.Y.: Doubleday, 1955); and John Carey *John Donne: Life, Mind and Art,* (1981) (entry 162). Points out that, "[i]n general, these critics interpret the notion of 'unified sensibility' as involving a pronounced emotional element, and so foreground the 'romantic' character of Eliot's concept," and "also exceed Eliot's own stress on the importance of the 'conceit' in 'metaphysical' poetry" (1).

1305. Di Nola, Gerardo. "John Donne e Tommaso Campanella," in *Tommaso Campanella: Il nuovo prometeo: Da poeta-vate-profeta a restauratore della politica e del diritto,* 105–49. Collana Lumen, 9. Bologna: Edizioni Studio Domenicano.

Compares and contrasts Donne's *Holy Sonnets* with the poetry of the Italian Dominican theologian, philosopher, and astrologer Tommaso Campanella (1538–1639), showing how their philosophical and religious ideas inform both their lives and poetry and observing how both men are intrigued by self-analysis and by the metaphysical questions of their day. Discusses how both poets share similar eschatological and anthropological viewpoints and how the themes of sin, grace, death, and eternal life pervade their poetry. Discusses also how both focus heavily in their works on the theme of repentance and contrition and are ever conscious of the fragility of human life and of the available strength that comes only from God. Comments on similar theological views that Donne and Campanella share, such as the centrality of Christ in effecting man's salvation, the importance of God's love in bringing about man's salvation and the necessity of man to respond to that love, and the power of prayer. Shows how each poet incarnates the values of Christian theology in their poetry in their own unique ways. Presents a selected bibliography of modern English editions and Italian translations of Donne's works and a brief list of modern critical studies (255–56) and a chronology of Donne's life and works (263–64).

1306. DiPasquale, Theresa M. "Donne's Catholic Petrarchans: The Babylonian Captivity of Desire," in *Renaissance Discourses of Desire,* ed. Claude J. Summers and Ted-Larry Pebworth, 77–92. Columbia: University of Missouri Press.
　　Maintains that in Donne's love poems "the attitudes and utterances of unrequited lovers are often reminiscent of specifically Roman [Catholic] piety." Discusses how Donne's "Petrarchan speakers—faced with the rejection of their faith in favor of sexual pragmatism, jolly promiscuity, or mutual devotion—speak in defensive counter-Reformation accents" and how "[t]heir discourses of desire uphold a creed of nonfulfillment, assert the efficacy of erotic relics and sacraments, and proclaim invalid any love doctrine that challenges the orthodoxy of frustra-

tion." Argues, in other words, that, for Donne, "Petrarchism is love's papistry, the Babylonian captivity of desire" (78). Illustrates this point by discussing how the Petrarchan speakers in *LovDeity, Fun,* and *Twick* "redefine both love and desire in order to uphold the ways of their tradition-bound faith" (78) and find ways to "play out the drama of invidious sexuality" (92).

1307. Donne, John. *John Donne: A Fragment.* Los Angeles: Robin Price. [8]p.
　　Consists of one folded and continuous page with lines from *ValMourn* and art work.

1308. Donne, John. *John Donne: Poésie.* Introduction, translation, and notes by Robert Ellrodt. Collection La Salamandre. Paris: Imprimerie Nationale. 463p.
　　Contains an introduction (7–[38]); notes on the introduction (39–[41]); a biographical sketch of Donne (42–44); a selected bibliography of Donne's works and of biographical and critical studies (45–[47]); a note on the English text (48–[49]); a note on the translation (50–[51]), followed by selections from the *Songs and Sonets, Elegies, Satyres, Metem, Verse Letters, Anniversaries,* and *Divine Poems,* with English texts and French translations on opposite pages ([52]-419); notes on the poems (421–[60]); index of poems (461–[64]); table of contents ([465]); note on other works by Ellrodt ([467]); and a list of other works in the same collection ([469]–[70]). In the introduction, intended for French readers, sees Donne as an original and innovative modern poet who broke with poetic tradition and opened up the domain of satire to love poetry. Discusses Donne's use of dramatic personae, his intelligence and wit, his search for certitude of being, and his philosophy of love and death and its resultant psychological expression. Examines the "metaphysical" dimension of his poetry in which Donne tries

to make existence intelligible. Maintains that Donne develops from a "spiritual mannerist" as a secular poet to a baroque writer of hymns and sermons. Surveys Donne's knowledge of Spanish, Italian, and French poets and compares and contrasts his art with theirs and finds the greatest affinity of Donne to Michelangelo and Maurice Scève. Stresses, however, Donne's singularity and notes that the English metaphysical poets are all different. Reviews: M. Baccelli in *Europe* 72 (1994): 211–12; Claude Mouchard in *QL* 643 (1994): 7–8; Armand Himy in *EA* 48 (1995): 184–88.

1309. Donne, John. *John Donne: Selected Poems.* Selected by Ian Hamilton. Bloomsbury Poetry Classics. London: Bloomsbury Publishing. 127p.

Presents 32 selections from the *Songs and Sonets, Sat3,* 4 selections from *Verse Letters to Severall Personages,* and 19 selections from the *Divine Poems,* with no notes or commentary.

1310. Donne, John. *John Donne: Selected Poems,* ed. Shane Weller. Dover Thrift Editions, gen. ed. Stanley Applebaum. London: Constable; Ontario: General Publishing Company. ix, 77p.

Presents a new selection of poems reprinted from *John Donne: Complete Poetry and Selected Prose* (Nonesuch, 1929) with modernized spellings. Calls Donne "the foremost poet of the Jacobean age" and says that his work, both secular and sacred, is "one of the finest treatments in English literature of the themes of fidelity and betrayal, conviction and skepticism" (v). Reproduces 31 selections from the *Songs and Sonets,* 4 epigrams, 6 elegies, *EpEliz, Sat1, Sat2,* 5 selections from the verse letters, *Mark,* 29 selections from the *Divine Poems* (1–70), followed by an alphabetical list of titles (71–73) and an alphabetical list of first lines (75–77). No notes or commentary.

1311. Donne, John. *Perché l'oro non sporca le dita?: Paradossi E Problemi.* Intro. and trans. Fabio De Propris. Rome: Castelvecchi. 152p.

Presents the first Italian translation of the *Paradoxes and Problems.* In the introduction (1–4), comments on Donne's life and general characteristics of the *Paradoxes and Problems,* especially their wit, intellectual ingenuity, and humor. Sees paradox as the basic principle governing not only Donne's work but also his life and the times in which he lived. Bases the translations ([16]–106) on Helen Peters's edition (Oxford, 1980) (entry 95), followed by explanatory notes ([107]– 50). In a note on the text (151–52), outlines the publication history of the *Paradoxes and Problems,* discusses dubia, indicates his indebtedness to Helen Peters's edition, and presents a list of modern editions of Donne's works.

1312. Donne, John. *Pseudo-Martyr.* Edited, with introduction and commentary by Anthony Raspa. Montreal: McGill-Queen's University Press. lxxxix, 427p.

In the introduction, divided into six parts, discusses the historical, political, and theological contexts in which *Pseudo-Martyr* was written and published. Stresses that *Pseudo-Martyr* "led Donne to raise all the moral, literary and philosophical issues that were to concern him for the remaining brief twenty years of his life" and suggests that it is "vast not because it is his first major published work, but because it represents the literary synthesis of the ideas of a major writer embarking comparatively late in life on a literary career which a political situation enables him to set into motion" (xii). Part 1, "The Occasion of Donne's Writing" (xiii–xxxvii), calls *Pseudo-Martyr* "a journalistic work in the sense that it addresses itself to a current political situation in a topical fashion." Points out that its purpose was "to convince English Catholics that they could take the Oath of Allegiance without betraying their Roman faith" (xiii), although "[t]he issue of the relations between secular and spiritual powers . . . often in *Pseudo-Martyr* appears to have interested Donne more than the oath itself" (xxii). Part 2, "The Meaning of Donne's *Pseudo-Martyr*" (xxxviii–liv), points out that in attempting to explain his apostasy from Catholicism there is "an implicit suggestion that Donne is still trying to convince himself that his religious convictions are settled," but he "has still not succeeded in reassuring himself that what he is saying, even though it is central to his life, is true beyond question" (xl). Discusses Donne's arguments in which he urges English Catholics to swear allegiance to their Protestant king. Part 3, "Copies of the First Edition" (lv–lviii), lists the names of the holders of the known 82 copies of the first edition of *Pseudo-Martyr*. Part 4, "The Edition of 1610" (lix–lxx), comments on the text and publication history of the only printed edition of *Pseudo-Martyr*, noting that there are no holograph or other seventeenth century manuscripts of the work. Part 5, "Biblical and Manuscript Sources" (lxxi–lxxvii), points out that Donne used two (and perhaps three) Bibles for his biblical references in *Pseudo-Martyr*, comments on his preparation of the manuscript, and examines his complex system of annotation. Part 6, "The Text" (lxxviii–lxxxix), explains that the two copies of *Pseudo-Martyr* "serve conjointly as copy texts for the present edition" (lxxviii) and points out that variants in existing copies of the 1610 edition suggest that Donne "kept popping in and out of the printer's shop to cast an anxious eye on the sheets of his first book as they left the printer's frame" (lxxix).

Explains emendations made in the text—by correcting typographical errors, changing some punctuation and capitalization, and modernizing in some instances orthography and typography. Presents the text of *Pseudo-Martyr* (1–268), followed by commentary ([269]–418) and a finding list ([419]-27), in which is listed "titles of publications and documents (such as papal decrees) and the names of the principal authors and historical figures that are often pivotal to understanding the meaning of Donne's lines" ([419]. Reviews: Robert C. Evans in *SCJ* 25 (1994): 1013; Andrew Hadfield in *N&Q,* n.s. 41 (1994): 562–63; Graham Roebuck in *UTQ* 64 (1994): 150–53; Terry G. Sherwood in *ESC* 20 (1994): 474–76; Judith Scherer Herz in *Ren&R,* n.s. 19 (1995): 79–81; Mishtooni Bose in *RES* 47 (1996): 84–85; Elizabeth Hodgson in *EMLS* 2 (1996): 101–103; E. M. Knottenbelt in *Heythrop Journal* 37 (1996): 232–34; R. V. Young in *RenQ* 49 (1996): 657–58.

1313. Eliot, T. S. ["The Conceit in Donne"], in *The Varieties of Metaphysical Poetry,* ed. Ronald Schuchard, 119–38. The Clark Lectures at Trinity College, Cambridge, 1926, and The Turnbull Lectures at The Johns Hopkins University, 1933. London: Faber and Faber. First American edition, New York: Harcourt Brace, 1994.

In the fourth Clark Lecture, Eliot discusses how "the acceptance of one orderly system of thought and feeling results, in Dante and his friends, in a simple, direct and even austere manner of speech, while the maintenance in suspension of a number of philosophies, attitudes and partial theories which are enjoyed rather than believed, results, in Donne and in some of our contemporaries, in an affected, tortuous, and often over-elaborate and ingenious manner of speech." Maintains that the interest in images for Dante and his Italian contemporary love poets "lies in the idea or feeling to be conveyed" and that "the image always makes this idea more intelligible," whereas in Donne "the interest is dispersed" and "may be in the ingenuity of conveying the idea by that particular image" or "the image itself may be more difficult than the idea," or "it may be in the *compulsion,* rather than in the *discovery,* of resemblances" (120). Illustrates Donne's use of the conceit by commenting on *Fun, Relic, Blos, ValMourn,* and the *Anniversaries.* Maintains that Donne cannot be ranked with Shakespeare, Dante, Guido, or Catullus but believes that "of certain secondary modes he is an indisputable master; his is a mind of the *trecento* in disorder; capable of experiencing and setting down many super-sensuous feelings, only these feelings are of a mind in chaos, not a mind in order" (133). Believes, however, that none of his followers "can compete with Donne in power of thought, in power of sensualizing thought," and "are apt to be excellent, in so far as they are not metaphysical" (134). Attempts "to show the sensuous interest of Donne in his own thoughts as objects" and "to show that his interest naturally led him to expression by conceits" (138).

1314. Eliot, T. S. ["The Conceit in Donne and Crashaw"], in *The Varieties of Metaphysical Poetry,* ed. Ronald Schuchard, 265–80. The Clark Lectures at Trinity College, Cambridge, 1926, and The Turnbull Lectures at The Johns Hopkins University, 1933. London: Faber and Faber. First American edition, New York: Harcourt Brace, 1994.

In the second of the Turnbull Lectures, drawn in part from the third, fourth, sixth, and seventh of the Clark Lectures, Eliot announces his intention to show how "the acceptance of an orderly system of thought results,

with Dante and his friends, in a simple, direct and even austere manner of speech, while the maintenance in suspension of a number of philosophies, attitudes and partial theories which are enjoyed rather than believed, results in Donne and some of his contemporaries, in an affected tortuous and often over-elaborate diction." Maintains that "[t]he interest of Dante lies in the idea or the feeling to be conveyed" and "the image is there to make the idea more intelligible, the feeling more apprehensible, the vision more visible," whereas, "[i]n Donne, the interest is dispersed, it may be, in the ingenuity of conveying the idea by that image" and "the image may be more difficult than the idea" or "the interest may lie in the compulsion, rather than in the discovery of resemblances" (265). Claims that "[i]n Dante we find complete coherence and integrity, in Donne disintegration, in Jules Laforgue the conscious irony of conflict between feeling, and the intellectual interpretation and dignity which feeling wishes to give itself, and reason" (268). Contrasts the imagery, conceits, and wit of Donne and Crashaw, seeing Donne as a "voluptuary of thought" and Crashaw as a "voluptuary of religious emotion" (276).

1315. Eliot, T. S. ["Cowley and the Transition"], in *The Varieties of Metaphysical Poetry,* ed. Ronald Schuchard, 185–206. The Clark Lectures at Trinity College, Cambridge, 1926, and The Turnbull Lectures at The Johns Hopkins University, 1933. London: Faber and Faber. First American edition, New York: Harcourt Brace, 1994.

In the seventh Clark Lecture, Eliot discusses Abraham Cowley as "a symbol of the change from seventeenth- to eighteenth-century England," claiming there is "no figure at once as mediocre and so important as Cowley" and noting that, "[w]ith

Cowley, all problems are reduced in size and artificially simplified" (185). Discusses Donne's influence on Cowley and calls him "the link between Donne and Dryden" (188). Primarily contrasts Donne and Cowley, maintaining that Cowley "was a poor metaphysical" but that "no one could mimic Donne so well and so badly without a power of appreciation" (190). Claims that Donne and Crashaw are "metaphysical by their types of mind, and therefore metaphysical in virtually everything they wrote," whereas the lesser metaphysical poets of the seventeenth century, such as Cowley, are "metaphysical either at moments, or through acquiring certain mental habits of association of ideas, or are sometimes not metaphysical at all" (199). Concludes that "[t]he essential differences between Dante and Donne, and Dante and Crashaw, are, to sum up, these: that in Dante there is a system of thought to which is exactly equivalent a system of feeling, whilst with Donne there is only a kind of flow of thought to which is equivalent a flow of feeling; and that Dante alters or transforms his human feeling into divine feeling when applying it to divine objects, whilst Crashaw applies human feeling, though of intensity equal to any ever applied to human objects, almost unaltered to divine objects" (200).

1316. Eliot, T. S. ["Crashaw"], in *The Varieties of Metaphysical Poetry,* ed. Ronald Schuchard, 161–83. The Clark Lectures at Trinity College, Cambridge, 1926, and The Turnbull Lectures at The Johns Hopkins University, 1933. London: Faber and Faber. First American edition, New York: Harcourt Brace, 1994.

In the sixth Clark Lecture, Eliot argues that "Donne's mind is typical of his age, but his poetry is not altogether typical of the poetry of his age" and, therefore, he examines Crashaw's

poetry "to indicate his most important differences from Donne." Claims that Donne "represents the transition from the sixteenth to seventeenth century," whereas Crashaw "represents the more serious aspect of the *Caroline* mind" and is "more representative of the mind of Europe" (161). Says that "Donne might be called a voluptuary of thought" and that "Crashaw could be called a voluptuary of religious emotion" (168). Distinguishes between Donne's conceits and those of Crashaw and "between the metaphysicality of Donne and the metaphysicality of Crashaw" (180). Believes that "[i]n Donne you get a sequence of thoughts which are felt," whereas "in Crashaw . . . you have a sequence of feelings which are thought" (183).

1317. Eliot, T. S. ["Donne and the Middle Ages"] in *The Varieties of Metaphysical Poetry,* ed. Ronald Schuchard, 67–92. The Clark Lectures at Trinity College, Cambridge, 1926, and The Turnbull Lectures at The Johns Hopkins University, 1933. London: Faber and Faber. First American edition, New York: Harcourt Brace, 1994.

In the second Clark Lecture, Eliot challenges the notion that Donne possessed a medieval mind as proposed by Mary Paton Ramsay in 1917. Argues that whereas Ramsay judges Donne "by what he read and the terms (scholastic) which he uses, and concludes that his mind was mediaeval," he judges him "(apart from the large proportion of his reading which is not mediaeval at all) by the way in which he read" and finds him "to be exactly of his own moment in time." Maintains that, for Donne, "[t]radition has little weight," that "he wishes to read everything, and is willing to take something from everywhere, and is not too nice about coherence" (83). Points out that Ramsay suggests that Donne's "mind is of the Middle Ages, though his feelings are of the Renaissance," but Eliot believes that "where the feelings are, there will the mind be also." Maintains, therefore, that he seeks Donne's mind "in the examination of his own sensations and ideas and emotions" (84) and believes that "[i]t is not so much in the thought, as in the development of the thought, that Donne's metaphysical peculiarity resides" (87). Insists that Donne was "wholly a man of his own time" and points out, in particular, that "the air which Donne breathed was infused with Jesuitism," a typically Renaissance phenomenon that deflected the center of philosophical interest "from what it was for the Middle Ages" and marked "an important alteration in human attitudes" (89), including Donne's.

1318. Eliot, T. S. ["Donne and the *Trecento*"], in *The Varieties of Metaphysical Poetry,* ed. Ronald Schuchard, 93–117. The Clark Lectures at Trinity College, Cambridge, 1926, and The Turnbull Lectures at The Johns Hopkins University, 1933. London: Faber and Faber. First American edition, New York: Harcourt Brace, 1994. An abbreviated version of this lecture was translated into French by Jean de Menasce and published as "Deux attitudes mystique: Dante et Donne" in *Le Roseau d' or* 14 (1927): 149–73; it is also included as an appendix in *The Varieties of Metaphysical Poetry* (309–18).

In the third Clark Lecture, Eliot contrasts the religious mysticism of the twelfth and thirteenth centuries as represented by Richard of St. Victor and the mysticism of the sixteenth century as represented by St. John of the Cross, St. Teresa of Avila, and St. Ignatius Loyola to show that from the time of Dante to the time of Donne, there was a major difference in the notion of the body and soul. Points out that the Italian love poets (in particular Dante, Guinizelli, Calvacanti, and Cino) stress

the notion of the contemplation of beauty and the dignity of the love object, whereas Donne argues for the union and possession of the beloved in his poems. Presents an analysis of *Ecst* to show Donne's view of the fundamental dualism between body and soul, a modern notion that would be essentially foreign to the Italian writers of the fourteenth century. Also compares *Ecst* to Lord Herbert of Cherbury's "Ode."

1319. Eliot, T. S. ["Donne's Longer Poems"], in *The Varieties of Metaphysical Poetry,* ed. Ronald Schuchard, 139–59. The Clark Lectures at Trinity College, Cambridge, 1926, and The Turnbull Lectures at The Johns Hopkins University, 1933. London: Faber and Faber. First American edition, New York: Harcourt Brace, 1994.

In the fifth Clark Lecture, Eliot discusses the *Satyres,* the *Elegies,* the *Verse Epistles, Metem,* and the *Anniversaries* "to determine how far the metaphysical, and how far the conceited, enter into these poems" (139). Suggests that all of the longer poems, except for the *Anniversaries,* are "less metaphysical," but points out that there are elements in them that "became completely developed" in Donne's metaphysical poetry (140), and regards them as steps "in the development of a metaphysic wit" (145). Registers a strong dislike, however, for *Metem.* Discusses the *Anniversaries* as "the most metaphysical of all Donne's metaphysical poems" (151) and maintains that "nowhere did he rise to greater heights of verbal and metrical beauty" than in these two poems, claiming that "everything we find in his lyrics, everything that we find in his sermons, is here" (157).

1320. Eliot, T. S. ["Introduction: On the Definition of Metaphysical Poetry"], in *The Varieties of Metaphysical Poetry,* ed. Ronald Schuchard, 43–65. The Clark Lectures at Trinity College, Cambridge,

1926, and The Turnbull Lectures at The Johns Hopkins University, 1933. London: Faber and Faber. First American edition, New York: Harcourt Brace, 1994.

In the first of the Clark Lectures, Eliot states that the purpose of the series is "to arrive at a systematic description of the common characteristics" of seventeenth century English metaphysical poetry and "to seek for a definition of the nature of metaphysical poetry in general." Points out the renewed interest in the metaphysical poets at the time (1926) and suggests that there is "a consciousness or a belief that this poetry and this age have some peculiar affinity with our own poetry and our own age, a belief that our own mentality and feelings are better expressed by the seventeenth century than by the nineteenth or even the eighteenth" (43). Says that he speaks not as a scholar but as "a craftsman who has attempted for eighteen years to make English verses, studying the work of dead artisans who have made better verses" (44), and states that his interest in defining metaphysical poetry is "to know what value the term 'metaphysical' as applied to verse can have for the present day" (45). Maintains that "in certain periods the revolution of the sphere of thought will so to speak throw off ideas which will fall within the attraction of poetry, and which the operation of poetry will transmute into the immediacy of feeling" and states that "[i]t is these moments of history when human sensibility is momentarily enlarged in certain directions" that can be called "the metaphysical periods" (52–53). Says that metaphysical poetry "occurs when an idea, or what is only ordinarily apprehensible as an intellectual statement, is translated in sensible form; so that the world of sense is actually enlarged" (53–54), citing as an illustration Donne's "fusion and identification of *souls* in sexual love" (54).

Says that metaphysical poetry "elevates sense for a moment to regions ordinarily attainable only by abstract thought, or on the other hand clothes the abstract, for a moment, with all the painful delight of flesh" (55). Comments on three exemplars of metaphysical poetry—Dante in the thirteenth century, Donne in the seventeenth century, and Baudelaire in the nineteenth century, along with their followers—and outlines the rationale for the following seven lectures.

1321. Eliot, T. S. ["Laforgue and Corbière in Our Time"], in *The Varieties of Metaphysical Poetry,* ed. Ronald Schuchard, 281–95. The Clark Lectures at Trinity College, Cambridge, 1926, and The Turnbull Lectures at The Johns Hopkins University, 1933. London: Faber and Faber. First American edition, New York: Harcourt Brace, 1994.

In the third Turnbull Lecture, based in part on the first, third, and primarily the eighth of the Clark Lectures, Eliot discusses the poetry of Jules Laforgue and Tristan Corbière to show greater disintegration between the unification of thought and feeling than one finds in Donne and the seventeenth century poets. Compares Laforgue to Donne and Corbière to Crashaw. Discusses his reasons for suggesting that in histories of literature "Dante deserves ten pages, Donne one, and Laforgue a footnote" (290). Summarizes his views on the nature of metaphysical poetry, emphasizing that metaphysical poetry demands that the poet "have a philosophy exerting its influence, not directly through belief, but indirectly through feeling and behaviour, upon the minute particulars of a poet's daily life, his quotidian mind, primarily perhaps his way of love-making, but also any activity" (294). Concludes that he "cannot see much prospect of metaphysical poetry issuing from the liberal or rad-

ical political cosmologies of the immediate future" (295).

1322. Eliot, T. S. ["The Nineteenth Century:
Summary and Comparison"], in *The
Varieties of Metaphysical Poetry,* ed.
Ronald Schuchard, 207–28. The Clark
Lectures at Trinity College, Cambridge,
1926, and The Turnbull Lectures at The
Johns Hopkins University, 1933. London:
Faber and Faber. First American edition,
New York: Harcourt Brace, 1994.

In the eighth Clark Lecture, Eliot discusses primarily Jules Laforgue and
Tristan Corbière as examples of nineteenth century metaphysical poets and
compares Laforgue with Donne and
Corbière with Crashaw. Eliot maintains that his purpose in the Clark
Lectures "has been to define metaphysical poetry in general; its place,
past, present and future; by implication to define what may rightly be
called metaphysical but is merely conceited; and to establish the place of
some of our seventeenth-century
poetry in this conception." Points out
also that he has tried "to distinguish,
in the seventeenth century, the metaphysical from the conceited, and at
the same time to indicate the way in
which the metaphysical naturally tends
to the conceited, and the conceited to
the metaphysical." Considers seventeenth century Italian poetry to be
"conceited without being metaphysical" and insists that during the seventeenth century the metaphysical
"flourished only in England." Points
out that he has focused on Donne and
Crashaw because "all the other poets
usually included can be included under
one or the other or under some cross-
breed of both: for these are the two
great innovators" (225). Notes that he
dealt with Cowley "merely in order
to show how easy the metaphysical
poetry transforms itself into the
Augustan," as he has "tried to show
in connection with Donne, how read-

ily the Elizabethan poetical impulse,
working on such a mind and with such
a training and interest as Donne's,
becomes the metaphysical" (226).
Concludes that he believes the thirteenth century produced the "best
poetry" and that, "if we are to acquire
any conscious control over the quality of our poetry, we shall do well to
study the conditions under which were
produced the poetry of Dante, and of
that greatest of English poets, who
came soon after him [Chaucer]" (228).

1323. Eliot, T. S. ["Toward a Definition of
Metaphysical Poetry"], in *The Varieties
of Metaphysical Poetry,* ed. Ronald
Schuchard, 249–63. The Clark Lectures
at Trinity College, Cambridge, 1926 and
The Turnbull Lectures at The Johns
Hopkins University, 1933. London: Faber
and Faber. First American edition, New
York: Harcourt Brace, 1994.

In the first Turnbull Lecture, drawn
in part from the first three earlier Clark
Lectures, Eliot announces his intention to define metaphysical poetry and
to discuss what is meant by "metaphysicality," a quality not shared by
all the poets designated as "metaphysical poets." Comments on a common "metaphysicality" in Dante,
Donne, and Laforgue, observing that
"[a]mong them all, ideas are felt, and
feelings are transformed by ideas"
(256–57). Rejects the idea of Donne's
medievalism and cites the prevalence
of Jesuitism in his thinking. Points out
that in his poetry Donne focuses "on
the idea in his mind, rather than upon
the object to which the idea refers."
Maintains that "[t]o contemplate an
idea, because it is my idea, to observe
its emotional infusion, to play with it,
instead of using it as a simple meaning, may bring curious and beautiful
things to light, though it lend itself,
this petting and teasing of one's mental offspring, to extremities of torturing of language," noting, however,

that it is not "so much vocabulary that is tortured, as it is the idea" (262).

1324. Eliot, T. S. *The Varieties of Metaphysical Poetry*. The Clark Lectures at Trinity College, Cambridge, 1926, and The Turnbull Lectures at The Johns Hopkins University, 1933. Edited and introduced by Ronald Schuchard. London: Faber and Faber. xiii, 343p. First American edition, New York: Harcourt Brace, 1994.

Presents an annotated edition of the previously unpublished Clark Lectures given at Trinity College, Cambridge, in 1926 and the Turnbull Lectures given at The Johns Hopkins University in 1933. The Clark Lectures, entitled "On the Metaphysical Poetry of the Seventeenth Century with Special Reference to Donne, Crashaw, and Cowley," consists of eight lectures: "Introduction: On the Definition of Metaphysical Poetry" (43–65) (entry 1320); "Donne and the Middle Ages" (67–92) (entry 1317); "Donne and the *Trecento*" (93–117) (entry 1318); "The Conceit in Donne" (119–38) (entry 1313); "Donne's Longer Poems" (139–59) (entry 1316); "Crashaw" (161–83) (entry 1316); "Cowley and the Transition" (185–206) (entry 1315); and "The Nineteenth Century: Summary and Comparison" (207–28) (entry 1322). The Turnbull Lectures, entitled "The Varieties of Metaphysical Poetry," consists of three lectures: "Toward a Definition of Metaphysical Poetry" (249–63) (entry 1323); "The Conceit in Donne and Crashaw" (265–80) (entry 1314); and (3) "Laforgue and Corbière in Our Time" (281–95) (entry 1321). Each of the essays has been entered separately into this bibliography. In the introduction (1–31), the editor traces the development of Eliot's interest in the metaphysical poets beginning in 1917 and discusses the circumstances that led up to his being invited to give the Clark Lectures as well as the events surrounding the

actual presentation of the lectures. Comments also on Eliot's plans (later abandoned) to publish the lectures in book form, his abbreviating and revising them for the Turnbull Lectures in 1933, and the historical odysseys of the two surviving copies of the lectures—one now at King's College Library, Cambridge, and the other in the Houghton Library at Harvard. Noting that Eliot's original typescript and reading copy is lost, explains in "Notes on the Text and Editorial Principles" (33–36) that the copy-text for the present edition "is the top copy of the fair copy (King's) that was prepared with a single carbon (Houghton) shortly after the lectures were delivered," which was typed (with numerous errors) by a "professional speed-typist" (33). Contains also Eliot's preface to the Clark Lectures (44) in which he announces his intention of revising and rewriting the lectures for a book to be entitled *The School of Donne,* which was to be part of a trilogy entitled *The Disintegration of the Intellect* and would have also included a volume on Elizabethan drama and a volume on the Sons of Ben Jonson. In an introduction to the Turnbull Lectures (231–44), the editor discusses the preparation of the lectures, drawn essentially from the earlier Clark Lectures, and their reception at John Hopkins. Comments also on the many other lectures Eliot gave during his one-year stay in America in 1933. Concludes with textual notes on the Clark Lectures and the Turnbull Lectures (299–307); an appendix containing a French translation of Clark Lecture 3 (308–18) by Jean André Moise de Menasce and published as "Deux attitudes mystique: Dante et Donne" in *Le Roseau d'or* 14 (1927): 149–73, with the editor's comments; an appendix that lists the Clark lecturers from 1884 to 1992–93 (319–22); an appendix that lists the Turnbull lecturers from 1891 to 1984

(323–25); an index to the lectures (327–34); and an index to editorial material (335–43). Reviews: Jewel Spears Brooker in *SoR* 59, no. 4 (1994): 107–13; Robert Craft in *Book World* (22 May 1994): 4; Paul Dean in *NewC* 13 (1994): 75–78; Eric Griffiths in *TLS* (8 July 1994): 3–4; Frank Kermode in *LRB* 16 (1994): 13–15; William Logan in *EIC* 44 (1994); 162–70; Dominic Manganiello in *C&L* 43 (1994): 420–22; C. H. Sisson in *PNR* 49 (1994): 49; James S. Torrens in *America* (17 September 1994): 26–27; William H. Pritchard in *AnSch* 64 (1995): 452–56; Michael Coyle in *ArielE* 27 (1996): 179–81; Steven Helmling in *SR* 104 (1996): xxiv–xxvi; James F. Loucks in *ANQ* 9 (1996): 33–37; Jan Gorak in *DQ* 33 (1998): 33–39.

1325. Empson, William. "Donne's Foresight," in *Essays on Renaissance Literature: Volume One: Donne and the New Philosophy,* ed. John Haffenden, 200–206. Cambridge: Cambridge University Press.
   In this previously unpublished draft of an essay, Empson repeats his argument that Donne "foresaw the coming theological row about life on other planets, from 1600 at the latest, and used the idea in the love-poetry" (200). Comments on the growing debate over the plurality of worlds among seventeenth century thinkers and suggests that "Donne of the love poetry used both the thoughts of Nicholas Hill and those of the Family of Love" (203).

1326. Empson, William. *Essays on Renaissance Literature: Volume One: Donne and the New Philosophy,* ed. John Haffenden. Cambridge: Cambridge University Press. Published also in paperback.
   A collection of four previously published and four previously unpublished drafts of essays on Donne (63–258), preceded by a preface (ix–xii), a note of sources and acknowledgments

(xiii–xvi), and an introduction (1–61), and followed by notes (259–90) and an index (291–96). The four previously published essays are "Donne and the Rhetorical Tradition" (63–77) first published in *KR* 11 (1949); "Donne the Space Man" (78–128) first published in *KR* 19 (1957); "Donne in the New Edition" (129–58), first published in *CritQ* 8 (1966); and "Rescuing Donne," first published in *"Just So Much Honor": Essays Commemorating the Four-Hundredth Anniversary of the Birth of John Donne,* ed. Peter Amadeus Fiore (University Park: Pennsylvania State University Press, 1972) (159–99); with emendations provided by Empson in an offprint of the essay given to Frank Kermode. The previously unpublished essays are "Donne's Foresight" (200–206) (entry 1325), "Copernicanism and the Censor" (207–19), (3) "Thomas Digges His Infinite Universe" (216–19), and "Godwin's Voyage to the Moon" (220–54) (entry 1327), followed by "Appendix on Galileo" (255–58). Only previously unpublished essays that discuss Donne specifically have been separately entered into this bibliography. In the introduction, reviews and evaluates Empson's writings on Donne and considers "why—during the last 30 years—they have been patronized as *divertissements,* more or less irrelevant to the proper business of Donne scholarship" (2). Points out that early on, Empson regarded as his chief opponents "the reactionary forces of the Christian religion, with T. S. Eliot as its literary high priest" (4), and "believed that Donne's celebrations of love amounted to a defiant doctrine, challenging canon law and received morality" (6), and that Empson "sought to credit Donne with being purposefully provocative, slicing through convention, with his imagery not incidental but integrative." Discusses how

Empson saw *ElBed* as "a crucial measure of Donne's outrageousness" (7) and how he believed that "Donne's unorthodoxy may be appreciated only if you allow for the full seriousness of his interest in the new science" (15). Discusses Donne's knowledge of the new science and its proponents and agrees with Empson that, "given Donne's up-to-the-minute fascination with the emerging new astronomy, and his known predisposition to affront authority, it is far from impossible to believe that he took advantage in his poetry of the potent philosophical implications of the Copernican revolution—not only to snub church and state, but to aver the autogeny and supreme value of human love" (46). Discusses in detail Empson's disagreements with Helen Gardner, especially her editorial methods. Notes that in 1967 Empson stated that no one had ever refuted his interpretation of Donne and that he still believed that Donne "meant what he said, and had experienced what he described," concluding that "the onus of proof lies with the denier—who says that Donne never experienced mutual love, but cooked up fantasies about it, from his reading of pious and theoretical authors, while neglecting his wife" (61). Reviews: Eric Griffiths in *TLS* (30 July 1993): 6–7; Frank Kermode in *LRB* 15 (1993): 15–17; Charles Rosen in *NYRB* 40 (1993): 72–77; Eugene R. Cunnar in *ELN* 32 (1994): 74–78; Pamela Gossin in *Isis* 85 (1994): 692–93; Stephen Greenblatt in *LRB* 16 (1994): 31–32; J. McCue in *Agenda* 31 (1994): 309–11; David Pasco in *N&Q*, n.s. 41 (1994): 419, 21; David Fuller in *DUJ* 56 (1995): 159–68; John Lucas in *MLR* 90 (1995): 142–44; David Norbrook in *TLS* (10 May 1996): 27; Brian Patton in *RenQ* 49 (1996): 879–80; D. E. Richardson in *SR* 104 (1996): 305–11; Michael Keefer in *Ren&R*, n.s. 21 (1997): 65–67.

1327. Empson, William. "Godwin's Voyage to the Moon," in *Essays on Renaissance Literature: Volume One: Donne and the New Philosophy,* ed. John Haffenden, 220–54. Cambridge: Cambridge University Press.

In this previously unpublished draft of an essay, Empson argues that Donne's presentation in his love poetry of the lovers colonizing a separate planet was influenced by Francis Godwin's *The Man in the Moon* when it was first drafted in 1597. Suggests that Donne's first use of the theme appears in *GoodM* and that "[t]he most impressive poems by Donne using lovers on planets were probably written to his wife after their runaway marriage" (224) but dates *GoodM* before their meeting. Argues that there is definite proof that Donne had read *The Man in the Moon* by the time he wrote *FirAn* and comments briefly also on Donne's knowledge of Kepler.

1328. Farmer, Stephen. "Donne's *The Ecstasy*." *Expl* 51: 205–7.

Argues that the analogy of "equal armies" in stanzas 4 and 5 of *Ecst* "introduces the relationship between the body and soul that dominates the rest of the poem" (205) and that, "[b]y creating multiple connections among its parts, by defining 'we' first as the body, then as the soul, the analogy suggests that any division between the speaker's physical and spiritual selves is insignificant or illusory" (206–7). Concludes that "[t]his vision of human beings as mysteriously and wonderfully indivisible must have been profoundly important to Donne, who cherished the Christian doctrine of the body's resurrection and felt deeply troubled by the prospect of a soul's being eternally severed from its physical frame" (207).

1329. Faust, Joan. "John Donne's Verse Letters to the Countess of Bedford: Mediators in a Poet-Patroness Relationship." *JDJ* 12: 79–99.

Observing that critics have not discussed "why Donne chose to offer his praise [of patronesses] in letter form rather than in the more traditional lyric poem," considers "what the implications of this choice are with regard to content and correspondent." Maintains that an examination of the verse letters Donne addressed to Lucy, Countess of Bedford, "reveals that the more interactive, purposeful form of the verse letter allows the poet not only to praise a much-needed patroness, but also to create a relationship with her where none existed before" and "can be seen as individualized, meaningful correspondences with a powerful, like-minded woman." Suggests that, "[v]iewed in the light of Donne's relationship with Bedford, these verse letters become much more, not less, than 'legitimate poems' that did indeed engage Donne's whole mind during a period of poverty and frustrated ambition at Mitcham" (79). Shows how Donne "chose the verse letter form to initiate and sustain ties with this important patroness and friend because the flexibility of this rhetorical style allowed him to demonstrate his understanding of and ability to function within Bedford's courtly world" (80). Points out that, "[s]ince the subject of these verse letters is not only the growing relationship between Donne and Bedford, but also the general interdependence of patroness and client in the Jacobean patronage system, the letters serve as metacommunicative links between Donne and the Countess" (80–81). Maintains, in other words, that "[t]he verse letter is both poem and letter, and its intermediary form mirrors its subject, the necessity of intermediaries for court success" (81). Discusses how "[b]y forming his

verse letters into rhetorical extensions of a rhetorical self, Donne was able to frame both his epistles and himself to the interests and concerns of Lady Bedford, and to the intricacies of the Jacobean patronage system he hoped to enter through her help" (95).

1330. Ferry, Anne. "Titles in George Herbert's 'little Book.' " *ELR* 23: 314–44.

Discusses "the casual and inconsistent habits of titling shorter poems" (315) during the Renaissance as reflected in the first edition of Donne's poems. Observes that "[t]he arrangement and titles of the poems in the 1633 volume . . . are attributable to some combination of Donne's own habits, the practices of copyists, the accidents of transmission, the decisions of the editor, [and] the vagaries of printing." Maintains that the edition "is fairly representative" of seventeenth century practice and discusses how it "reflects some of the commonly held assumptions about poems and their titles shared by writers, copyists, printer, and readers in the earlier seventeenth century" (317).

1331. Fowler, Alastair. "Genre and Tradition," in *The Cambridge Companion to English Poetry: Donne to Marvell,* ed. Thomas N. Corns, 80–100. Cambridge Companions to Literature. Cambridge: Cambridge University Press.

Discusses the relationship between genre and tradition during the seventeenth century. Comments on Donne's brilliance in mixing of epigram and elegy, for instance in *FunEl* and *ElBed,* and his mixing of epigram and emblem in *ValName* and *ValMourn.* Notes that Donne's classical epigrams themselves are "comparatively undistinguished." Maintains that Donne gave the classical love elegy "a new acuteness of thought and economy of diction" (86). Points out also that the roughness of Donne's satires resulted not from "incompetence or negligence" but from an incorrect understanding of the etymology of the word "satire" (spelled "satyre") and from "false doctrine out of Renaissance Italian genre theory" (95).

1332. Frontain, Raymond-Jean. "Moses, Dante, and the *Visio Dei* of Donne's 'Going to Bed.'" *ANQ* 6: 13–17.

Points out that there are several references to theophanic experiences in *ElBed* that "combine to support the speaker's plea to his mistress that she reveal herself completely to him as she undresses for bed and so allow him to experience an ecstasy that is simultaneously sexual and spiritual." Maintains that the poem "turns upon the parenthetical qualifications made within lines 38–43" and thus the poem is "a self-consciously powerless but audacious speaker's petition to be permitted the full extent of the woman's revelation," in which "'[k]nowledge' of her will entail both sexual orgasm and the impartation of a mystical knowledge whose exact nature cannot be specified to the general reader" (13). Cites additional theophanic references in the poem in ll. 17–18 and ll. 13–14 and maintains that by such allusions Donne "attempts to integrate the sexual and the spiritual" (16).

1333. Frost, Kate. "John Donne, the Number 23 and the Tradition of Spiritual Autobiography," in *Medieval Numerology: A Book of Essays,* ed. Robert L. Surles, 135–42. Garland Medieval Casebooks, vol. 7; Garland Reference Library of the Humanities, vol. 1640. New York: Garland.

Explores in *Devotions* "the complex ramifications of the number 23, particularly in its association with the rich tradition of medieval spiritual autobiography." Discusses "the early associations of the number with the hexaemeral tradition, with Divine Justice, and, concomitantly, with the Second Coming and the Advent liturgy" and demonstrates "its association with the vertical structure of the universe, the tradition of the Harrowing of Hell, and with the solar ecliptic—emphasizing its connection with the winter solstice and the theme of moral conversion" (135). Comments also on "the implications of the number when it is associated with autobiography, its use by Dante, Henry Suso, and Donne (with some side excursions into Ficino and Milton)" (135–36). Concludes by referring to "the recent discovery of a twenty-three part, fourteenth century illustrated manuscript autobiography that lasted at least from the thirteenth through the seventeenth centuries" (136). Shows how "[i]n its twenty-three part structure, the *Devotions* presents a complex, numerologically structured artifact which mirrors the structure of the hexaemeral week, the solstitial day, and a year-by-year progression through the ecliptic of his [Donne's] own life" (139–40), suggesting that "the latter seems directly derived from Dante's architectural arch of the ages of man in the *Convivio*" (140).

1334. Gabrieli, Vittorio. "Thomas More and John Donne." *Moreana* 30, no. 115–16: 168.

Notes that R. C. Bald, *John Donne: A Life* (New York: Oxford University Press, 1970) says that John Donne the younger bequeathed "Thomas More's Head" to Sir Christopher Guise, but that it is unclear whether the "head" is a portrait or bust. Notes also that Donne himself "bequeathed to a friend of his the portraits of two eminent Italian theologians, Paolo Sarpi and Fulgenzio Micanzio, whom he may have met in Venice early in 1600." Points out also Donne's reference to Thomas More in *Biathanatos* as "a man of the most tender and delicate conscience that the world saw since Augustine."

1335. Garrett, Cynthia. "The Rhetoric of Supplication: Prayer Theory in Seventeenth-Century England." *RenQ* 46: 328–57.

Presents "a critical interdisciplinary study of the more prominent English prayer guides, particularly those written during the period from 1600–1660 when interest in private prayer was at its height" (328), and argues that they "reveal a complex theory of prayer which acknowledges, at times even embraces, the contingent and imperfect nature of communication with the divine" and show "an intense ambivalence over God's nature, human emotional experience, and the possibility of true communication between human and divine beings, an ambivalence which has wide implications for the study of post-Reformation English views of God, language, and the self" (329). Points out how Donne's views on prayer reflect the thinking of contemporary prayer manuals, such as viewing the prayer as "a persistent and importunate child" (339); offering "advice on how to manipulate God most effectively, suggesting that praise works best"; agreeing that "emotional appeals for God's favor are more likely to succeed in bending God to the prayer's will" (344); and distrusting spontaneous or unpremeditated prayer because it may "express a false, earthly self instead of the true, spiritual self" (351). Maintains that Donne thus preferred set prayers.

1336. Gorbunov, A. N. *Dzhon Donn i angliiskata poezia XVI–XVII vekov.* Moskva: Izd-vo Moskovskogo Universiteta. 186p.

In the introduction (3–5), calls the sixteenth and seventeenth centuries the golden age of English literature and indicates that the primary purpose of this study is to show a Russian audience unfamiliar with English literature of this period the unique place that Donne occupies in the develop-ment of English poetry. Chapter 1, "English Poetry of the 16th Century: The Forerunners of Donne" (5–85), surveys the flowering of English poetry during the sixteenth century and comments on the work of such poets as Wyatt, Sidney, Spenser, Shakespeare, Marlowe, Chapman, Daniel, Raleigh, and Southwell as a context for understanding the uniqueness of Donne's contribution to the development of English poetry. Chapter 2, "The Poetry of John Donne" (86–137), discusses major characteristics of Donne's poetry, stressing how it bridges the Renaissance with the seventeenth century but also separates and sets the two periods apart. Points out both the original quality of Donne's poetry as well as its traditional roots. Chapter 3, "English Poetry of the 17th Century and Donne" (138–86), discusses the poetry of Donne's contemporaries and successors, especially the poetry of Jonson, Lord Herbert of Cherbury, Henry King, Francis Quarles, Herbert, Carew, Lovelace, Suckling, Herrick, Vaughan, Crashaw, Marvell, Traherne, and Cowley.

1337. Guibbory, Achsah. "John Donne," in *The Cambridge Companion to English Poetry: Donne to Marvell,* ed. Thomas N. Corns, 123–47. Cambridge Companions to Literature. Cambridge: Cambridge University Press.

Surveys major characteristics of Donne's poems, such as their dramatic immediacy; use of colloquial language and conversational tone and rhythms; the combination of passionate intensity and intellectual analysis and argument; the prevalance of verbal wit; and the extensive use of puns and conceits. Maintains that "[b]ecause his poetry speaks to needs and desires that seem to persist despite cultural and historical differences, Donne is accessible, compelling, and engaging," although his poetry is often "difficult and complicated." Stresses that in his poetry Donne "expresses radically contradictory views" and finds the prevalence of contrarieties a "distinguishing feature" of his poetry (123). Maintains that "[l]ove and salvation are not only the two great subjects of his poetry" but also "preoccupations that gave dramatic shape to his life" (125), but warns against biographical readings of individual poems. Suggests that "[w]it, logic, equivocation, and dramatic immediacy all contribute to the central concern of Donne's poetry—the exploration of the individual's experience of love, mortality, and the divine," observing, however, that "the process of examining emotional experience inevitably produces poetry of contradictions" (128). Points out how Donne's poetry also reflects the intellectual, social, political, and religious concerns of his age. Surveys major features of the *Satyres*, the *Elegies*, the *Songs and Sonets*, the *Anniversaries*, and the *Divine Poems* to show that Donne's poetry "expresses the instability and infinity of human desire" and "articulates a persistent desire to have everything, to experience an ever increasing 'joy' and 'fulfilment'" (144).

1338. Guillory, John. "Ideology and Canonical Form: The New Critical Canon," in *Cultural Capital: The Problem of Literary Canon Formation,* 134–75. Chicago: University of Chicago Press.

In an account of the New Critical revision of the English canon, challenges Cleanth Brooks's reading of *Canon* in *The Well Wrought Urn: Studies in the Structure of Poetry* (1947) (first published in *The Language of Poetry* [1942]), in which Brooks exemplifies his notion of paradox and claims that *Canon* is "an intensely serious parody of a sort that [modern] man, habituated as he is to an easy yes or no,

can hardly understand" (161). Discusses the ideology of Brooks's criticism and claims that one of its implications is that "much of English literature after Dryden is defective in terms of wit, ambiguity, paradox" and thus "[t]he history of English literature is the history of the decline of literary culture itself" (167).

1339. Halpern, Richard. "The Lyric in the Field of Information: Autopoiesis and History in Donne's *Songs and Sonnets.*" *YJC* 6: 185–215. Reprinted in *Critical Essays on John Donne,* ed. Arthur F. Marotti (New York: G. K. Hall, 1994), 46–76; and in *John Donne,* ed. Andrew Mousley (Basingstoke: Macmillan; New York: St. Martin's Press, 1999), 104–21.

Discusses the question of lyric autonomy by invoking "the theory of autopoiesis or self-referring systems" that offers "a model of language and culture radically different from that of poststructuralism" (187). Explains the distinctive features of autopoiesis and explores "the ways in which a theory of autopoietic systems can shed new light on the question of lyric autonomy." Primarily focuses on "issues raised by the historical reading of the Renaissance love lyric" (187–88); situates the *Songs and Sonets* "within a history of sexuality which at once respects the formal boundaries of the lyric and questions some of the assumptions behind a Foucauldian understanding of sexuality"; and locates "those areas in which autopoietic and Marxist theory can achieve, if not harmony, then at least a productive conflict" (188).

1340. Hamilton, Ian. "John Donne the Younger," in *Keepers of the Flame: The Making and Unmaking of Literary Reputations from John Donne to Sylvia Plath,* 1–15. New York: Paragon House; London: Hutchinson.

Discusses the life of Donne's son, John Jr., and his role in the publication of his father's literary works and comments on Donne the younger's own minor publication, *Donnes Satyre; containing a short map of Mundane Vaneity, a cabinet of Merry Conceits, certain pleasant propositions and questions, with their merry solutions and answers.*

1341. Haskin, Dayton. "The History of Donne's 'Canonization' from Izaak Walton to Cleanth Brooks." *JEGP* 92: 17–36.

Surveys the history of reading *Canon* from Walton's biography of Donne (1640) to Cleanth Brooks's essay on the poem in "The Language of Paradox" in *The Language of Poetry* (ed. Allen Tate, 1942), which was later revised and included in his *Well Wrought Urn: Studies in the Structure of Poetry* (1947). Reviews also both "new historicist and deconstructionists attacks on the New Critical approach" in order "the better to appreciate the sharp discontinuity that Brooks wrought in Donne studies when he brought 'The Canonization' to the center of Donne's canon" (19). Notes that, until the nineteenth century, the poem received little critical attention and discusses how, "without ever explicitly mentioning the poem, Walton's *Life and Death of Dr. Donne* long served as a severe restraint" on its interpretation, "until, at the end of the nineteenth century, that same *Life* was suddenly seen to provide grounds for interpreting the poem in ways almost diametrically opposed to those in which it had previously been read" (18). Regards the views expressed in Walton's *Life* as the primary reason why "the poem was only belatedly fitted into what might have seemed an obvious biographical context, a context from which Brooks's interpretation asked readers again to prescind" (19). Points out that in the nineteenth and early twentieth centuries *Canon* "was rarely singled out

for attention"; that "a few readers nonetheless thought highly of it and made comments that, if we were to combine them with one another, might be said to constitute the embryo from which a New Critical approach developed"; and that, "while readers began to refer other lyrics by Donne to episodes in his life," biographical readings of *Canon* "emerged relatively late" (26–27). Points out that Walton in his *Life* "suppressed reference to any poetry that other readers may have associated with the passionate period of [Donne's] courtship" and notes that Edmund Gosse (1899) is the first to challenge Walton by seeing *Canon* as Donne's defense of his marriage. Maintains that "nearly all interpretations of the poem before Brooks were constrained by biographical assumptions" derived from Walton's *Life*. Observes that, "in view of the fact that even the New Criticism (which sought temporarily to bracket out biographical considerations) and deconstruction (which renders all biographical accounts problematic) have not succeeded in eradicating all interest in Donne's relationship with Ann More, Walton's *Life* remains potentially relevant to any interpretation" of *Canon*, even though "Walton had aims that necessarily precluded explicit mention of the very work that for three centuries he de facto interpreted more powerfully and influentially than any other interpreter, with the happy and ultimately liberating exception of Coleridge" (36).

1342. Hatakeyama, Etsuro. "'The Extasie' ni okeru Fushi Kozo" [The Ironical Mechanism in 'The Extasie']. *SELit* 69: 217–32.

Discusses *Ecst* as a parody to examine its mechanisms of irony, focusing on the narrator's metastructural discourse and its function as a strategy of parody on Neoplatonic love theories and poems.

1343. Hester, M. Thomas. " 'Let them sleepe': Donne's Personal Allusion in *Holy Sonnet IV.*" *PLL* 29: 346–50.

Points out that the "surprising sestet" in *HSRound* "recalls the precise details of St. John's vision [of the Apocalypse in Revelations 6:9–11]—details that would have struck a sensitive personal note for the author by recalling general as well as personal conditions of his situation." Maintains that this biblical allusion "helps to explain the chord of frustration with which this poetic meditation concludes" (346). Believes that in the sestet Donne expresses his fear, shame, and confusion about his abandonment of his family's Catholic faith. Concludes that "this poem is representative of the Holy Sonnets as the site for Donne's meditative attempts to appraise the moral virtues of the rivals in the Counter-Reformation debate," a site where he tries out "different versions of grace" and struggles to become an Anglican "without betraying his family tradition" (550).

1344. Himuro, Misako. " 'The Good Morrow' and the *Legenda Aurea.*" *N&Q,* n.s. 40: 177–79.

Gives reasons for thinking that the immediate source for Donne's knowledge of the Seven Sleepers of Ephesus mentioned in *GoodM* (l. 4) was probably either Jacobus Voragine's *Legenda Aurea* or William Caxton's version in *The Golden Legend* (1483).

1345. Hobby, Elaine. "The Politics of Gender," in *The Cambridge Companion to English Poetry: Donne to Marvell,* ed. Thomas N. Corns, 31–51. Cambridge Companions to Literature. Cambridge: Cambridge University Press.

Argues that male-dominant poetry of the seventeenth century gives one a "distorted impression of the probable social realities" (31) of the actual relationships between men and women of the period. Notes that "one of the most striking differences between social reality and poetic representation" was the assertion in poetry of "female omnipotence in male/female relationships," whereas, in fact, "women's subordination to men was axiomatic in the legal and economic organization of society, and firmly reinforced in ideological formulations that insisted the subordination was natural" (32). Cites *ValMourn* and *Anniv* as examples in which the union of lovers is not equal but "divided by a power differential" (34). Notes also that in many love poems of the period "women are admonished for refusing sex with a would-be lover, but in the social world women were supposed to be chaste" and that "[i]n men's poetry of the period, these self-contradictory ways of thinking about female sexuality produce curious effects." Cites, in particular, "male fearfulness about women's sexual capacity," which is "most famously dramatized" in *Appar* (37), and male concern about women cross-dressing found in *ElFatal,* in which "what is really being protected here is not the woman, but gender differentiation" (43).

1346. Hurley, Ann. "Donne's 'Good Friday, Riding Westward, 1613' and the *Illustrated* Meditative Tradition." *JDJ* 12: 67–77.

Argues that, in addition to the texts of devotional manuals and treatises, the illustrations they contain and the messages they convey about "the danger inherent both in pictures and in that picture-making faculty of the mind, the imagination," provide another link between Donne's religious poems and Counter-Reformation meditational practices. Traces "the development whereby the act of meditation, initially described as simply stimulated by graphic description, becomes full and explicitly modeled on the activity of the painter, by looking at representative examples of meditative manuals from the late 13th century to the early 17th" (68). Points out that throughout his life Donne was very interested in "the role of the image, and particularly the picture-making faculty of the human imagination." Focuses on *Goodf* to show how the dynamic of picture-making is central to its full meaning, maintaining that the poem is "the product not only of a meditative tradition but also of habits of seeing as modified and intensified by meditative practices." Discusses how Donne dramatizes the meditative tradition "by bringing vividly to life some of the theories underlying the use of real images for religious practice" (76). Shows how Donne's poem concerns itself with "the highly dynamic nature of a stage in the meditative process and with the central role of the image-making faculty in his speaker's life" (77).

1347. Kelchner, Heidi. "Dryden's *Absalom and Achitophel*." *Expl* 51: 216–18.

Points out that the notion that "bastards are somehow superior to their legitimate brothers because they were conceived in illicit passion was a common idea in the Renaissance" (216). Points out that Donne, however, in "Why have Bastards best Fortune" created an "inverted encomium" in which "[p]arodying earlier serious examinations of the phenomenon," he "rejects all previous explanations and, through sinuous twists of logic, ends up defending illegitimacy by attacking a hypocritical society that he considers more sinful than the bastard himself." Notes that Donne states that "mistresses are so commonplace that their love nests have become as stale as the marriage bed" (217).

1348. Kelliher, Hilton. "Donne, Jonson, Richard Andrews and the Newcastle Manuscript." *EMS* 4: 134–73.

Refutes H. W. Garrod's proposal (*RES* 21 [1945]: 38–43) that Donne's Latin poem *Libro*, addressed to Richard Andrews, a London doctor, was written in March 1612 and suggests sometime between 1624 and 1631 as a more likely date. Presents a detailed bibliographical description of the Newcastle manuscript (MS. Harley 4955), written between 1630 and 1634 by John Rolleston, secretary to William Cavendish, Duke of Newcastle, which contains 98 poems by Donne as well as verses by King James I, Jonson, Richard Andrews, and others. Discusses the importance of the manuscript to the text and canon of Donne and Jonson and comments on Andrews's poems, which have been generally overlooked by scholars. Suggests that the connection between Donne and Andrews, and their connection with Jonson, adds "something to our knowledge of the Duke of Newcastle's circle" (163). Concludes with a biographical sketch of Richard Andrews and a first-line index to Andrews's verses in Harley 4955.

1349. Kelly, Tom. *John Donne in Jarrow.* Jarrow: Here Now. 25p.

A collection of original poems, one of which is entitled "John Donne in Jarrow" (3).

1350. Klause, John. "The Two Occasions of Donne's *Lamentations of Jeremy*." *MP* 90: 337–59.

Conjectures that *Lam* probably was composed "not once but twice," the first version probably having been written in the late 1580s or early 1590s, "when Donne, still a Catholic, traveled abroad at a distance from the sufferings of his English coreligionists after the defeat of the Spanish Armada," or perhaps in 1596–97, when, as *Sat3* indicates, he was searching "the grounds for belief in the several institutionalized forms of Christianity"; and the second version, "the one we now possess, being produced one or two decades later, probably in the haste which may explain some of its pedestrian lines, and certainly for purposes different from those of his initial effort" (338). Bases his theory, in part, on a letter Donne wrote to Sir Henry Goodyer in 1608 in which he indicates he is sending along a translation of a work for the Countess of Bedford that he had made at sea some years earlier and that now appears in a new version. Discusses how the translation could be read as comment on the sufferings and/or delinquencies of English Catholics. Thinks that "when Donne undertook to translate Lamentations for a second time, he felt compelled to emphasize his Protestant credentials by openly announcing his reliance on the version of Tremellius (like him a convert, though from Judaism to Calvinism), whose Latin translation of the Old Testament was widely used by Protestants." Observes that "[a] text like Lamentations with potentially Catholic applications, turned into English verse by a man with a Catholic past and militantly Catholic antecedents and connections, would not be intended for wide circulation" but "would have to carry some overt sign of Protestant legitimacy—both for the eyes of the countess and for the sake of his own converted conscience" (358). Suggests *Lam* may be seen as "barter in [Donne's] quest for patronage" (359).

1351. Langley, T. R. "Having Donne." *CQ* 22: 188–210.

Presents a very detailed, negative review/analysis of the re-issued edition of John Carey's *John Donne: Life, Mind and Art* (1990, first published in 1981) (entry 162) and his *John Donne* (1990) (entry 1033). Calls the first "a sensational book, red-blooded, full of vigorous observations, bold in its endeavours to flesh out art with biography" but finds its perspectives "frequently, deliberately, and damagingly partial" and believes that Carey's treatment of Donne's prose "is often

more pornographically eclectic than it is seriously expository; more intent on fabricating an image, evoking a frisson, than following an argument" (207). Finds unwarranted and confusing the attempted arrangement of the poetry and prose in the edition and says the notes are weak and sparse.

1352. Larson, Deborah Aldrich. "Donne's Contemporary Reputation: Evidence from Some Commonplace Books and Manuscript Miscellanies." *JDJ* 12: 115–30.

Comments on Donne's popularity in the seventeenth century as evidenced by the large number of his poems (or poems falsely attributed to him) that appear in commonplace books and miscellanies. Argues that "the evidence from commonplace books, manuscript miscellanies, and marginalia seems to show that much of Donne's fame and notoriety was not due to his poetry per se but rather to his marriage and his ministry. Maintains that "[w]hile some who were Donne's friends (reading Donne's versions of his poems) admired his wit, the varying metrical and rhyme patterns, and the conceits, many more were intrigued by the proximity of the illegally married poet, to whom graphically sexual poetry was attributed, and the saintly Dean of St. Paul's who preached about sins of the flesh." Points out that "[t]o the minds of many of those writing commonplace books or miscellanies, the division [between John and Jack Donne] that Walton had been promulgating since 1635 about Donne's life had no basis in fact" (126).

1353. Lewalski, Barbara Kiefer. "Exercising Power: The Countess of Bedford as Courtier, Patron, and Coterie Poet," in *Writing Women in Jacobean England*, 95–123. Cambridge, Mass.: Harvard University Press.

Expanded and revised version of "Lucy, Countess of Bedford: Images of a Jacobean Courtier and Patroness," in *Politics of Discourse: The Literature and History of Seventeenth-Century England,* ed. Kevin Sharpe and Steven H. Zwicker (Berkeley and Los Angeles: University of California Press, 1987), 52–77.

1354. Little, Geraldine Clinton. "John Donne," in *Out of Darkness,* 1–10. Lanham, Md.: University Press of America.

Presents a brief, nonscholarly introduction to Donne's life with some general comments on Donne as a coterie poet in a manuscript culture. Notes that the poetry is intellectual, witty, and "vigorously passionate" (9) and says that today Donne "is regarded as one of the world's greatest poets" (10).

1355. Loewenstein, David. "Politics and Religion," in *The Cambridge Companion to English Poetry: Donne to Marvell,* ed. Thomas N. Corns, 3–30. Cambridge Companions to Literature. Cambridge: Cambridge University Press.

Discusses how the world of politics, religion, and literary culture intersected during the seventeenth century. Points out that Donne "reveals in his poetry a fascination with the world of Stuart politics and kingship, as well as a sense of unease about that world of seemingly unlimited power which he himself was never able fully to participate in," and observes that he "appropriates the extravagant language of kingship, power, and absolutism . . . and brings it right into the private world of his love poetry" (6). Notes, however, that in poems like *Anniv,* in which Donne "appropriates the analogy of kingly power to characterize the intensity of a mutual relationship, he can also register unease with the analogy's more treacherous implications" (7). Suggests that Donne's "agonistic and intensely introspective *Holy Sonnets* offer powerful examples of his Calvinistic terror of damnation and sense of sinfulness," noting that in these poems his "awesome heavenly

monarch possesses a power not unlike that which James I attributed to kings" (11).

1356. Love, Harold. *Scribal Publication in Seventeenth-Century England.* Oxford: Clarendon Press. xi, 379p. Draws heavily upon "Manuscript versus Print in the Transmission of English Literature, 1600–1700," *Bulletin of the Bibliographical Society of Australia and New Zealand* 9 (1985): 95–107 (entry 590); and "Scribal Publication in Seventeenth-Century England," *TCBS* 9 (1987): 130–54 (entry 799). Reprinted as *The Culture and Commerce of Texts: Scribal Publication in Seventeenth-Century England,* foreword by David D. Hall (Amherst: University of Massachusetts Press, 1998).

Points out that it was not until the appearance of such editions as the Oxford Donne in the 1950s and 1960s and Ernest W. Sullivan's edition of the Dalhousie miscellanies in 1988 (entry 931) that "the transmissional challenges posed by scribal publication fully revealed themselves to literary scholars" (7). Discusses how Donne was committed to a manuscript culture. Comments on the transmissional history of *Biathanatos* as an illustration of a work not intended originally for publication that circulated privately before it finally left the private for the public realm. Discusses also the circulation of Donne's poems among his coterie as "scribal publication," noting that he "not only rejected print but does not even look particularly distinguished in print" since his art "leads to bizarrely shaped and constantly varied stanzas" (146).

1357. Low, Anthony. *The Reinvention of Love: Poetry, Politics, and Culture from Sidney to Milton.* Cambridge: Cambridge University Press. xiii, 258p.

Argues that "cultural, economic and political change transformed the way poets from Sidney to Milton thought and wrote about love" and shows how "from the late sixteenth century poets struggled to replace the older Petrarchan tradition with a form of love in harmony with a changing world, and to reconcile human love and sacred devotion" (jacket). Views Donne as a "pivotal figure in the reinvention of love"—a "new kind of private love: idealized, Romantic, mutual, and transcendent in feeling." Maintains that later in life, Donne "wrote some of the strongest devotional poems in the language," and explores "some of the difficulties he had in transforming his early loves . . . into the sacred love of God," noting that "[s]ome of the same personal characteristics and attitudes that made Donne so innovative as a lover of women—among them his active, insistent masculinity—proved impediments to his loving God but also were sources for much of the conflicted, paradoxical baroque power of his best divine poems" (3). Devotes two chapters exclusively to Donne: Chapter 2, "John Donne: 'Defects of Loneliness'" (31–64), is a slightly revised combination of two previously published essays: (1) "Donne and the Reinvention of Love," *ELH* 20 (1990): 465–86 (entry 1071); and "Love and Science: Cultural Change in Donne's *Songs and Sonnets*" in *SLitI* 22 (1989): 5–16 (entry 983), Chapter 3, "John Donne: 'The Holy Ghost is amorous in his Metaphors'" (65–86) appears under the same title in *New Perspectives on the Seventeenth-Century English Religious Lyric*, ed. John R. Roberts (Columbia: University of Missouri Press, 1994), 201–21 (entry 1436). Other chapters compare and contrast Donne with Herbert, Crashaw, Carew, and especially Milton. Says that although Donne and Milton "did not invent companionate marriage," they gave it "a fresh set of perceptual underpinnings," "established the little world of privacy and of magical transcendence," and "separated mar-

ried love from its classical connections with the Church, the local community, and society, and even (sometimes) from those with God" (205).

1358. MacGregor, Tiree, and C. Q. Drummond. "The Authorship of 'Fair Friend, 'tis true, your beauties move.'" *JDJ* 12: 153–68.

Surveys arguments for the authorship of "Fair Friend, 'tis true, your beauties move," attributed both to Ben Jonson and Sidney Godolphin, concluding that "a careful stylistic analysis . . . argues very strongly that the poem was written by Sidney Godolphin" (153), perhaps with the help of his mentor, Jonson. Shows how the poem was written by "a Caroline poet with an admirable appreciation of Donne and, especially, Jonson" (156). Sees the influence of Donne in the poem's "personal quality and structure of the argument" (156) as well as in the poet's "sensitivity to the kind of concession and reasonableness for which Donne is noted" (157). Suggests that the poem contains rhetorical effects similar to those in *ValMourn*.

1359. Marotti, Arthur F. "Manuscript, Print, and the Social History of the Lyric," in *The Cambridge Companion to English Poetry: Donne to Marvell*, ed. Thomas N. Corns, 52–79. Cambridge Companions to Literature. Cambridge: Cambridge University Press. Material from this essay appears in a revised version in *Manuscript, Print, and the English Renaissance Lyric* (Ithaca, N.Y.: Cornell University Press, 1995).

Discusses how both manuscript and printed systems of transmission of poetic texts "thrived and interacted" throughout the seventeenth century but notes that "[i]n the manuscript system, the social history of the lyric is more visible," even though "both media were part of a process of cultural change that shaped the modern institution of literature" (52). Discusses

Donne as a coterie poet who circulated his verse primarily among friends and patrons. Maintains that, although there is little specific evidence about the particular social occasions for which Donne wrote most of his poems, it is clear that "many of his poems [including his religious lyrics] were associated with particular social milieux or occasions" (54). Comments on how the printing of the first edition of Donne's poems (1633) "had a marked impact on the relationship of lyric poetry to print culture" (67–68), noting that by midcentury "lyric poems themselves were perceived less as occasional and ephemeral and more as valuable artifacts worth preserving" (68).

1360. Miller, Philip. "Simic's 'Cabbage.'" *Expl* 51: 257–58.

Suggests that Charles Simic's poem "Cabbage" that appears in *God and Devils* (1990) is a subtle parody of *Flea* and Marvell's "To His Coy Mistress."

1361. Mincoff, Marco. "Baroque Literature in England," in *Shakespeare and His Contemporaries: Eastern and Central European Studies,* ed. Jerzy Limon and Jay L. Halio, 11–69. International Studies in Shakespeare and His Contemporaries. Newark: University of Delaware Press; London: Associated University Presses.

Discusses the characteristic differences between Renaissance and baroque in both dramatic and nondramatic literature in England. Regards Donne and the other metaphysical poets as baroque poets, commenting on such features as their uses of "ingenious wit," "compression of utterance that leads to obscurity," and especially "the metaphysical conceit," which "does not seek beauty or convention but surprise" and becomes "an expression of a personal attitude or apprehension or reality, the realization of the unity underlying the outer forms of experience." Cites *Flea* as a poem that "far

more than the elaboration of a conceit is the expression of a complex and original thought" (33). Maintains that Donne, "with his introspection and organic imagery, his long and complex trains of thought, is evidently baroque," adding that "he would seem to have been slightly ahead of his time" (63).

1362. Mueller, Janel. "Troping Utopia: Donne's Brief for Lesbianism," in *Sexuality and Gender in Early Modern Europe: Institutions, Texts, Images,* ed. James Grantham Turner, 182–207. Cambridge: Cambridge University Press.

Argues that *Sappho* is a "conspicuous exception" (183) to the treatment of Sappho by Renaissance English adapters of Ovid's "Sappho to Phaon" in the *Heroides*. Maintains that "[i]n Sappho's name Donne writes his way beyond the confines of a Renaissance social context by imagining a synthesis of love and friendship that she and her Philaenis alone seem to make possible" (184). Presents a reading of Donne's poem to show how he revised Ovid's treatment of Sappho and how his "affirmative representation of lesbian sexuality, in particular, contrasts starkly with the insistent homophobia of the commentaries and poetic histories in which the text of the *Heroides* and the myth of Sappho were transmitted to Renaissance readers" (187). Shows how Donne undermines Ovid's portrayal of Sappho "by picking out elements from the humanist commentary that can be set to work against the grain of Ovid's poem" (190). Discusses how he presents active sexual lesbianism as "emotionally and morally positive" (192) as he imagines how the Renaissance ideals of friendship and ideals of marriage might be conjoined and shows how this "utopian figuration on the erotic plane . . . carries utopian connotations onto an economic plane as well"

(200–201). Concludes that lesbianism as presented in *Sappho* "opens a utopian dimension in the history of sexuality" (203).

1363. Norbrook, David. " 'This blushing tribute of a borrowed muse': Robert Overton and His Overturning of the Poetic Canon." *EMS* 4: 220–66.

Discusses versions of Donne's poems (as well as others) that appear in a manuscript collection of verse and prose writings written as a tribute to his wife by the Puritan Robert Overton entitled "Gospell Observations and Religious Meditations, etc." (1671 or 1672), now in the Princeton University Library, to show "the way in which a committed republican confronted a literary culture whose traditions were monarchist" (220). Maintains that "Overton's admiration for Donne was not diminished by the gulf between his republican Fifth Monarchism and Donne's monarchist Anglicanism," and thus he "draws heavily on the *Anniversaries* and other elegies." Notes that "[a]mongst the character-istic changes in Overton's versions are a tendency to tone down Donne's more grisly descriptions in order to retain a more idealized portrayal of his [Overton's] wife's physical body, and a shift from Donne's nostalgic glance back to 'the golden times' to an apocalyptic vision of 'bes[t] future time.' " Observes that in addition to "the poems of Donne the cleric who had repudiated youthful vanities," Overton shows "an active interest" in Donne's love poems and imitates certain of the *Songs and Sonets,* which he found attractive because of their "sense of exploring mutuality in love that goes beyond Petrarchan conventionality" (234). Discusses Overton's "corrections" of specific Donne poems. Notes that he "seems to have been particularly interested in Donne's use of alchemical imagery to figure the

relations between lovers" (236) and also shows that "[o]ccasionally the political implications of Overton's appropriation of Donne become explicit" (237). An appendix (246–63) lists the contents of the manuscript, indicating the Donne adaptations by page number.

1364. O'Connor, Garry. *Campion's Ghost: The Sacred and Profane Memories of John Donne, Poet.* London: Hodder and Stoughton. 246p.

An historical novel "based upon a diversity of factual sources" and the author's "own speculation about the nature of John Donne from his poems and his prose writings," noting that his interpretation of Donne's charac-ter "differs largely from [R. C.] Bald's" (243). Review: Arnold Hunt in *TLS* (20 August 1993): 20.

1365. Pallotti, Donatella. "*Periculosa et pestilens quaestio:* Interrogative Discourse in Donne's *Holy Sonnets,*" in *English Studies in Transition: Papers from the ESSE Inaugural Conference,* ed. Robert Clark and Piero Boitani, 167–84. London: Routledge.

Discusses Donne's use of interroga-tive discourse in the *Holy Sonnets,* a discourse that "becomes a site of con-troversy, where different points of view and/or voices are brought into unresolved collision or contradiction" (168). Maintains that the *Holy Sonnets* "neither impose a one-sided evalua-tion of the religious and personal prob-lems they raise, nor urge the reader to believe that some fiction 'is so' " but rather invite the reader to produce his own answers. Stresses that "[t]he truths these sonnets appear to com-municate are, in fact, often called into question, and in most cases, chal-lenged" and "the 'authority' of the poetic subject is inevitably under-mined, its privileged position as source of meaning and action radically threat-ened, its traditionally *constituted* unity eroded." Notes that there are 27 questions in the *Holy Sonnets*, "one question every 9.8 lines" (169), and that they "occupy strategic positions" (171). To illustrate the functions performed by questions in the *Holy Sonnets*, discusses in some detail *HSDue* and *HSMin*, poems in which conflicts are not resolved, questions are left unanswered, and "different, conflicting voices can be heard" (178). Maintains that the *Holy Sonnets* "reflect a sense of personal urgency, a painful oscillation between contradictory attitudes, [and] a fluctuation between two definitions of the self" (179).

1366. Pando Canteli, Maria J. " 'One like none, and lik'd of none': John Donne, Francisco de Quevedo, and the Grotesque Representation of the Female Body." *JDJ* 12: 1–15.

Maintains that although for Donne female bodies are "a place for pleasure and power, a space to conquer and dominate, a microcosm where all the joys of the world come together," they are also "the meeting ground where the loathsome and the comic, the ludicrous and the dreadful merge" and that "it is at this point that a grotesque representation of the body, of the *female* body emerges." Argues that Donne's tone in a number of poems "clearly moves beyond realism/naturalism toward the hyperbolic and distorted world of deformity, degradation, and dehumanization: in short, toward the grotesque." Locates Donne's "treatment of the grotesque in a broader context of European literature" (2) by pointing out similarities between his and Francisco de Quevedo's treatment of the female body. Discusses the techniques Donne uses in mocking and ridiculing the female body in *ElAnag* (contrast and displacement), *ElComp* (contrast; repulsive, scatological imagery; dehu-

manization), and *ElAut* (exaggerated physical decay, repulsive deformity, and dehumanization). Comments also on how "[t]he subversive power of the grotesque moves beyond the mere aesthetic codes of a mysogynistic diatribe into the arena of ideological implications" (11).

1367. Patterson, Annabel. "*Quod oportet versus quod convenit:* John Donne, Kingsman?" in *Reading Between the Lines,* 160–209. Madison: University of Wisconsin Press. A portion reprinted in *Critical Essays on John Donne,* ed. Arthur Marotti (New York: G. K. Hall, 1994): 141–79. An earlier version appeared as "John Donne, Kingsman?" in *The Mental World of the Jacobean Court,* ed. Linda Levy Peck (Cambridge: Cambridge University Press, 1991), 251–72. Contains also reworkings of "All Donne," in Soliciting Interpretation: *Literary Theory and Seventeenth-Century English Poetry,* ed. Elizabeth D. Harvey and Katharine Eisaman Maus (Chicago: University of Chicago Press, 1990), 37–67.

Maintaining that "[t]he story of Donne's politics is one of self-division and self-contradiction" (163), argues that "we will learn more about both Donne and his culture by noticing the contradictions than by trying to smooth them away" (164). Emphasizes that Donne "was never so simply the king's man, never so simply careerist or absorptive of absolutist monarchism as twentieth-century literary critics (with the exception of [Arthur] Marotti) have been led or chosen to believe." Supports this position by examining primarily (but not exclusively) Donne's works between 1606 and 1615, a period "when he was clearly engaged in an intellectual agon with his environment" (165). Maintains that "[p]erhaps more than any other Renaissance poet Donne challenges us to conceive of subjectivity in environmental terms, to see how socio-economic and political circumstances interact with a particular temperament to produce the historical person, who is both partly conscious of the rules by which he must play and partly the director of all his roles" (166). Claims that the *Satyres* "can do more to explain the political Donne" than the *Songs and Sonets* or even his sermons (168) and believes that his "transitional years, especially, were marked by contradiction and its writerly symptoms: on the one hand a continuation into the new reign of satirical, even subversive and unpublishable writings" and, "on the other, the use of his extraordinary intellect and eloquence for official purposes" (178). Illustrates Donne's dilemma by examining *Citizen,* calling it "a significant exhibit in the cultural afterlife of the Essex rebellion, a tribute to the role played in that event (or in those that led up to it) by difficult intellectuals like Donne and his friends" (183). Examines *Biathanatos, Pseudo-Martyr, Ignatius,* and *Eclog* to illustrate Donne's use of subtle rhetorical techniques and equivocation in criticizing the world of the Jacobean court. Examines the doubts and divided opinions of the 1614 Parliament, at which Donne was present, as an important context for understanding Donne's political allegiances and conduct. Observes also that Donne's love poems are "riddled with a specifically political terminology, by no means all of which situates the speaker on the side of royal absolutism" (202), and briefly comments on the subtle political overtones of his first Paul's Cross sermon (24 March 1617). Concludes that Donne inhabited "a highly developed if unstable world of articulated choices, in which *quod oportet* negotiated with *quod convenit,* Jack with the Doctor, in which there were both a disposition and an equally strong

indispositon to bear a slavish yoke" (209).

1368. Pinka, Patricia G. "Donne, Idios, and the Somerset Epithalamion." *SP* 90: 58–73.

Points out that many critics cite Donne's *Eclog* as "one of the most sycophantic tributes" written on the occasion of the wedding of Frances Howard and Robert Carr but argues that, in fact, "more than the others it exhibits the poet's struggle with and self-castigation for celebrating the wedding and his general outrage at the politics of the court" (59). Discusses how Donne "drives a wedge between himself and the commemoration by adopting the persona of a shepherd" and then "through a series of echoes, historical references, and self-references, he equivocates his celebration, castigates the court, and disparages himself not only for his rampant ambition but also for his idiotic hope to secure court appointment" (63). Shows how in the poem there is "an anti-epithalamion within an epithalamion within a pastoral eclogue, an anti-persona within the persona for John Donne, and an additional character, Allophanes, who, in sounding like another, echoes—or has the potential to echo—everyone in and just outside the poem" and indicates how "[t]his structural strategy provides the satiric leverage Donne needed to commemorate the marriage of his patron, to debase that commemoration, and to disparage himself and his motives for writing the epithalamion in the first place" (70).

1369. Politi, Jina. "'The Written and the Unspoken,'" in *English Studies in Transition: Papers from the ESSE Inaugural Conference,* ed. Robert Clark and Piero Boitani, 51–71. London: Routledge.

Maintains that *BoulNar* lends itself to a double reading: in the first "the mourning subject finds himself thrust in the *topos of inexpressibility,* that vast desert of absence and silence" (51); in the second this topos gives way to "the topos of unequal quantities" (54). Shows that both topoi assert that "between the passionate subject and language there is an unbridgeable abyss." Claims that "[t]he elemental passions of the soul always exceed the limits of language, break the dam of arbitrary signs and return the subject to the source of its being, the before-language" (56).

1370. Radcliffe, David Hill. "Donne in Meditation: Method and the Varieties of Discourse," in *Forms of Reflection: Genre and Culture in Meditational Writing,* 1–40. Baltimore: Johns Hopkins University Press.

Compares the genres Donne used "to anatomize his society with the kinds of criticism some recent writers have used to anatomize that same society." Maintains that "Donne's meditational works illustrate how generic structures are used to combine and oppose literary formations and social institutions." Points out that Donne "wrote meditations in prose and verse, in Catholic and Protestant forms, in sacred and secular genres, for public and private occasions" and that they are "almost always tied to historical and social circumstances." "In describing how Donne alters discursive procedures in response to historical circumstances," addresses the issue of "how a study of genre might address . . . the need to reformulate relations between text and context, literature and history, and individual authors and social collectivities" (5). Analyzes the *Anniversaries* to show that they "attempt to make history by altering relations between kinds of discourse and to authorize these changes by appealing to historical origins and philosophical first principles." Examines "how their meditational structure combines the various kinds of discourse Donne seeks to reform" and considers "how Donne's poetic and typological figures combine literary and historical discourses in ways that attempt to validate his proposed reformations" (14). Discusses how Donne "methodically interprets historical texts in ways that lend authority to his own critical procedures" and "uses his logical-typological structure to demonstrate how apparent ruptures in literature, society, and history are necessary parts of a grand design, subversive moments that finally confirm the unity made manifest by the critic's interdisciplinary method" (26). Examines also *Essays in Divinity,* which "retain the topical disposition of the *Anniversaries* and the conceit of creating and populating a new world through meditational discourse" but "drop the epideictic elements, curb the satire, return to manuscript circulation, and returning to prose, yield up the claims of vatic inspiration." Compares Donne's "critical procedures to the discursive strategies he contests in both works," showing how both, in different ways, make "a bid for preferment by opposing the art of meditation to competing discourses handling similar material" (30). Situates the *Anniversaries* and *Essays in Divinity* "in a dynamic field of intersecting and opposing literary kinds" and argues that "[t]he variety and complexity with which these literary kinds combine results from the variety and complexity of seventeenth-century social institutions" (39).

1371. Raspa, Anthony. "Donne's Model: Henry IV." *Ren&R,* n.s. 17, no. 4: 41–50. Maintains that in *Pseudo-Martyr* Donne, in discussing the relationship between the state and religion, "establishes Henry IV of Navarre, king of France, as one of his models of a competent and tolerant king" because of "his moderation, his steadfastness and fearlessness amid religious conflicts between Catholics and Protestants in his own country, and in the face of the power of the papacy." Observes that in *Pseudo-Martyr* Donne "calls upon the English Catholics to swear allegiance to James I as a political leader, in the same manner in which French Catholics and Protestants swore allegiance to Henry" (41).

1372. Reeves, Eileen. "John Donne and the Oblique Course." *RenSt* 7: 168–83.

Discusses "the alliance of poetry and technology" in Donne's poetry and prose "by first demonstrating the relevance of a technical issue—the loxodromic problem of early modern cartography"—to selected passages in Donne's sermons and poems and then "by suggesting specific parallels between cartographic and poetic representation" in *ValMourn* (169). Points out that both in the sermons and in the poem "man is invariably assigned a spiral course" (173). Argues that *ValMourn* is based, in fact, on "the metaphor of the oblique course, an essential navigational concept," and shows how it is "appropriate both to the specific occasion of Donne's poem and to its larger and more philosophical claims," grounding, as it does, "the spiral path of human love in a particularly apt metaphor." Notes, moreover, that Donne's speaker saying that he must "obliquely run" (l. 34) is "another way of describing the *cursus obliquus* or 'oblique course' and a literal translation of 'loxodrome'" (181). Shows how the poem "reflects a long tradition in geometry" (182).

1373. Revard, Stella P. "The Sapphic Voice in Donne's 'Sapho to Philaenis,'" in *Renaissance Discourses of Desire,* ed. Claude J. Summers and Ted-Larry Pebworth, 63–76. Columbia: University of Missouri Press.

Argues that, although there are elements of Ovid's "Sappho to Phaon" in *Sappho,* Donne's aim "is to adopt the voice of the original Sappho, rather than that of Ovid's poetical Sappho" and discusses how Donne's poem "goes beyond the Ovidian model and explores some of the attitudes towards love notable in Sappho's poetry" (64). Points out that Donne seems to allude in his elegy to extant poems and fragments that "depict, however briefly and obliquely, Sappho's attitude toward young girls and toward love" (69) and notes that in Donne's poem "female speaks to female, not male to female as in Catullus's imitation, or female to male as in Ovid's" (73). Analyzes *Sappho* to show that Donne "initiates a dialogue with the ancient poet, going further than others had in attempting to fathom the love of woman for woman that inspired her lyrics" but noting that "[f]inally, however, this dialogue breaks down into a Donnean monologue, so marked by the characteristic intellectual curiosity of his other poetry that it persuades us that this elegy clearly belongs to his canon with as unique a voice as that of the ancient lyric poet that it purports to imitate" (76).

1374. Rhodes, J. T. "Continuities: The Ongoing English Catholic Tradition from the 1570s to the 1630s." *JDJ* 12: 139–51.

Discusses how the English Catholic tradition survived during the period from the 1570s to the 1630s through the writing of books on the lives of English martyrs and saints; the preservation of relics, pre-Reformation ecclesiastical art, vestments, and spiritual books; and documentation of traditional Catholic customs and the perpetuation of pre-Reformation English spirituality. Points out the importance of English Catholic exiles on the Continent in the survival of Catholicism in the seventeenth century but maintains that "their influence should not be allowed to obscure the ongoing English tradition of Catholicism that reached back to the time before the reformation." Cites examples to show that "English Catholics, in England and in exile, cared about their past" (147). Briefly comments on Donne's Catholic ancestry.

1375. Ruf, Frederick J. "Lyric Autobiography: John Donne's *Holy Sonnets*." *HTR* 86: 293–307.

Presents "an outline of the possibilities and limitations of *lyric* autobiography" (295) by examining the *Holy Sonnets*, which "record a spiritual crisis in powerful and effective terms" and give us a view of Donne's life "that is intimate to a degree that few other works can rival," bringing us "close to Donne in astonishing fashion" (298) as "he exemplifies the stages of salvation." Discusses how the poems "present a different sort of person than a narrative of the events might present" (299). Points out that "[n]arrative presents the illusion of comprehensiveness with (perhaps) hundreds of pages and dozens of people and events," whereas the *Holy Sonnets* present 19 "emotional moments and the illusion that these are the moments that most matter," noting that "[w]hat allows these nineteen moments to outweigh the narrative scope in the poet's eyes is their depth" (302). Observes also that "[t]he narrator's voice simply speaks, whereas the lyric voice beseeches, condemns, and also listens" (303), and thus "[t]he narrative voice principally presents and observes, whereas lyric voice interacts" (304) and "models a self caught up in one moment that expressly has no sequel" (305). Maintains that the lyric voice "forces us to encounter some depth that unsettles, shakes us, and changes us" and thus "Donne's lyric voice—*any* lyric

voice—is the voice of a self in a particularly deep sense." Observes, however, that this intimacy also has its limitations, for "[i]t may be partial, biased, skewed, cryptic," filling "the entire stage" and giving us "no context and no competing voices" (307).

1376. Scodel, Joshua. "The Medium Is the Message: Donne's 'Satire 3,' 'To Sir Henry Wotton' (Sir, more than kisses), and the Ideologies of the Mean." *MP* 90: 479–511.

Maintains that Donne's early poetry "uses the notion of the [Aristotelian] mean so central to his contemporaries in order to articulate a new ideological vision" (479) and argues that, "[r]ejecting his contemporaries' use of the mean to justify prevailing religious and sociopolitical formations, he adapts the mean instead to enlarge the sphere of individual freedom." Discusses how in *Sat3* Donne "spurns the English church's self-description as the via media in order to advocate a mean of skeptical inquiry between acceptance and rejection of any of the rival Christian denominations" and how in *HWKisses* Donne "eschews his contemporaries' use of the mean to glorify a fixed position in the social hierarchy—the middle state—and advances instead a means that justifies a socially mobile self's freedom to maneuver" (480). Through a detailed analysis of *Sat3* shows that Donne "uses skepticism re-constructively to imagine a self finally saved from self-destructive extremes," noting that although Donne "questions the validity of any given ecclesiastical and political formation, he does not doubt God's ultimate benevolence and man's eventual ability to find his proper place in the world." Then, through an analysis of HWKisses, shows how Donne "undertakes to de-fine a sphere of individual freedom without involving a transcendental guarantor" and "adapts the mean to imagine a personal space between—and thus beyond—oppressive social realities." Points out that in the verse epistle Donne "enunciates a highly original ethics, however, by advocating a mean that challenges conventional sociopolitical norms as much as 'Satire 3' challenges religiopolitical ones" (501).

1377. Semler, L. E. "John Donne and Early Maniera." *JDJ* 12: 41–66.

Discusses Donne and mannerism, reasserting "the intimate relationship between the *linea serpentinata* and Mannerism" and demonstrating "the way in which a Donnean *persona* is analogous to a visual *sprecher* figure." Discusses in detail *Storm* and *Calm,* two early verse epistles that "evince an artistic sensibility and poetic style that embody [an] early-manneristic poetic, which at times points towards the developing refinements of the Maniera." Maintains that "[t]he more radical early-mannerist preoccupations with anxiety, disorder and disturbing emotive expression occur in these verse epistles in conjunction with an occasional and calculated 'fluency' and grace, providing a rich example of a poetic that seems legitimately to invite the application of not only the more general style term, *early Mannerism,* but also, at times the more distinguished and complex term, *early Maniera*" (42). Maintains that Donne's "particularly probing and emotive searching out of the contraries of life's experiences is best expressed by a combination of a particularly serpentine mode of discourse and a drawing together of utterly unlike words and things in the expression of the chaotic and contradictory nature of the universe he depicts" (62). Shows how "[t]his expression is characterized by controlled manipulation of perspective and gracefulness, complex deployment of *figures* as poetic

difficultà, calculating use of *sprecher* and reader involvement strategies, and a thoroughly personal expression of deep scepticism which only succeeds because it is expressed through a congenial aesthetic, one that is searched out and built up from the passion within" (62–62). Calls this "Donne's personal and powerful *maniera,* his individual expression of what could be seen as the beginning of the English poetic best designated *early Maniera*" (63).

1378. Sena, Jorge de, trans. "John Donne," in *Poesia de 26 séculos: antologia, tradução, prefácio e notas de Jorge de Sena (De Arguíloco a Nietzsche),* 2nd. ed. 163–64, 355–56. Coimbra: Fora do Texto.

Translates into Portuguese *SGo* and *HSDeath* (163–64), without notes or commentary. Presents a brief introduction to Donne's life and poetry (355–56), calling Donne one of the major poets of the English language.

1379. Shullenberger, William. "Love as a Spectator Sport in John Donne's Poetry," in *Renaissance Discourses of Desire,* ed. Claude J. Summers and Ted-Larry Pebworth, 46–62. Columbia: University of Missouri Press.

Observes that frequently Donne introduces an observing third party in his love poems, thereby suggesting that there is "something in the dynamic of desire that requires triangulation, the insertion of a potentially disruptive outsider in a love scenario hopefully scripted for two" (46). Discusses, therefore, "the specific and characteristic ways in which Donne creates a visual field in his amatory poetry and stations an observer in relation to it." Examines a number of poems to show "the way in which the activity of seeing, represented so frequently by the incursion of a third party, operates in the poetry as a social, psychological, and aesthetic phenomenon: socially, as an index of the conditions under which love could be made in the late Elizabethan and early Jacobean household; psychologically, as an expression of Donne's anxiety about being watched and longing to be watched; and aesthetically, as a way of implicating the reader and the act of reading in the poem" (48). Shows how Donne "introjects the public discourse of the poem into the apparently private and privileged discourse of the poem's love making" and argues that it is "the reader who is the actual object of the poet's rhetorical self-display, both the admirer and judge of the play of wit, both the 'thou' being addressed and the silent observer whom Donne variously resists, browbeats, condescends to, cultivates, and purifies" (60). Maintains that Donne "inserts an erotic spectator in so many of his love poems, then, for several reasons, not the least of which is to inscribe within the fictive speech a reminder to the reader that the pleasure of the text is a voyeuristic pleasure" (61). Maintains that in Donne's love poems "[t]he verbal pleasure in making poetry and in its being read becomes so intermixed with the pleasure in the love scenarios it conjures as to absorb or supersede the specifically sexual pleasure that is the ostensible goal and subject of the poetry." Concludes that "[t]extuality, textual performance, becomes the source of its own pleasure, but Donne knows that pleasure is completed by a witness, one whose imaginative participation in the text makes it as real as it will ever be" (62).

1380. Smuts, Malcolm. "Cultural Diversity and Cultural Change at the Court of James I," in *The Mental World of the Jacobean Court,* ed. Linda Levy Peck, 99–112. Cambridge: Cambridge University Press.

Argues that the cultural history of the court of James I cannot be understood simply by judging it by the work of only a few great artists such as Jonson and Inigo Jones. Points out, for example, that "Donne, who after his marriage and dismissal from Egerton's service was never a part of the court circle, nevertheless influenced court literature" (103) and "had more impact on cultural life than much more prominent figures" (106). Points out also that Donne's *Satyres* "incisively dissect the corrosive effects of luxury, ambition and power upon a ruling elite" (108).

1381. Stanwood, Paul G., Diana Treviño Benet, Judith Scherer Herz, and Debora Shugar. "Excerpts from a Panel Discussion," in *Renaissance Discourses of Desire,* ed. Claude J. Summers and Ted-Larry Pebworth, 259–76. Columbia: University of Missouri Press.

Excerpts from a panel discussion in response to the papers presented on the general theme of "Discourses of Desire: Sexuality in Renaissance Nondramatic Literature" at the ninth biennial Renaissance conference held at the University of Michigan-Dearborn, 19–20 October 1990.

1382. Stiebel, Arlene. "Subversive Sexuality: Masking the Erotic in Poems by Katherine Philips and Aphra Behn," in *Renaissance Discourses of Desire,* ed. Claude J. Summers and Ted-Larry Pebworth, 223–36. Columbia: University of Missouri Press.

In a discussion of various techniques used to mask and, at the same time, reveal lesbian love in the poems of Katherine Philips and Aphra Behn, cites examples of borrowings from Donne's poetry in their poems .

1383. Streekstra. N. F. "Spheares en hemelbollen bij Donne en Huygens," in *In de zevende Hemel: Opstellen voor P. E. L. Verkuyl over literatuur en kosmos,* ed. H. van Dijk, M . H. Schenkeveld-van der Dussen, and J. M. J. Sicking, 169–76. Groningen: Passage.

Uses Thomas de Keyser's 1627 portrait of Huygens in the National Gallery in London with its background emblems of map, compass, lute, book, and two globes to explore Huygens's fascination with these subjects in his own work, a fascination that he shared with Donne. Comments on cosmological elements in *SunRis* and *SGo* and devotes several pages to an analysis of *Goodf,* commenting on Koos Daley's "back-translation" into English of Huygens's Dutch version of the poem (entry 1031).

1384. Strier, Richard. "Radical Donne: 'Satire III.'" *ELH* 60: 283–322. Revised and expanded version appears as "Impossible Radicalism: Donne and the Freedom of Conscience," in *Resistant Structures: Particularity, Radicalism, and Renaissance Texts* (Berkeley and Los Angeles: University of California Press, 1995), 118–64.

Attempts "to restore a nineteenth-century and early twentieth-century sense of the young John Donne, a sense of boldness, radicalism, and free-thinking" that could be called "an Empsonian sense of young Donne" (283). Presents a detailed critical reading of *Sat3* to show that "its radicalism is its deepest and poetically most distinguished strain" and that "such a view is not anachronistic" (284). Argues that, written in the 1590s, the poem expresses Donne's "suspension of commitment" to any one religious position and that "its ultimate import is to stand as a defense of such suspension" (285). Claims that "[t]he integral soul, standing still, refusing to be bound, waiting for a personal revelation that may or may not come, is the final positive image" in the poem and suggests that Donne seems to say "[t]hey also serve who resist and doubt." Insists that there is no "criticism of or fetters on the autonomous self here" and that "[i]n terms of intellectual history, Donne can be seen to have shown, in the strongest parts of the third Satire, the perhaps surprising compatibility of three of the most radical notions of the European sixteenth-century: Erasmus's 'philosophy of Christ,' Castellio's vindication of doubt, and Luther's conception of conscience" (312–13).

1385. Stringer, Gary A. "Breaking the Bibliographical Code in Seventeenth-Century Manuscripts and Printed Editions of (Mainly) Donne's English Epigram." *AEB* 7: 192–204.

Shows how "study of material forms in which the texts of John Donne are inscribed or printed in seventeenth-century artifacts can often yield meaning equal in importance to that of the words of which the texts are composed" (192). Believes that the editing of Donne poems "has not been done right so far—partly because the body of data constituting the linguistic code for Donne is dauntingly vast, partly because previous scholars have not devised an acceptable theory for editing Donne, and partly . . . because the bibliographical code embedded in the Donne artifacts remains almost entirely uninterpreted." Selects examples from *Mark,* from a prose letter entitled "To the Countesse of Bedford, Sister to the Lord Harrington," and primarily from Donne's English epigrams to illustrate "something of the variety of information that may be derived from careful study of the Donne manuscripts and early printed editions" and suggests "the impact of that information on critical interpretation" (193). Claims that "the primary effect" of the perspective developed in this essay "is to demystify these texts, to domesticate them and reveal them as dynamic rough-and-tumble forces in the culture, both shaping and shaped by the realities amongst which we live" (199). Presents seven figures (200–204).

1386. Sullivan, Ernest W., II. *The Influence of John Donne: His Uncollected Seventeenth-Century Printed Verse.* Columbia: University of Missouri Press. xvii, 215p. Presents a bibliographical study of Donne's uncollected seventeenth-century printed verse. In the introduction (1–51), which is preceded by a list of short titles and first lines of Donne's poems and dubia (xi–xvii) and a list of abbreviations for libraries, maintains that editors, by focusing on the seven collected editions/issues of Donne's poems and virtually excluding the uncollected printings, have "produced a significantly incomplete understanding of the canon, chronology, texts, audience, uses, and thus the influence of Donne's printed verse in the seventeenth century." Points out that previous scholars "have identified 46 titles having 65 reported seventeenth-century editions and issues that contain 77 entire and 62 partial uncollected printings of Donne verse" and "have identified 6 titles (including 2 that print no English verse) in 7 editions/issues printing 48 complete and 1 partial translation of Donne's verse" (1). Indicates that "the present census expands the number of titles to 83; the number of editions/issues to 239; and the number of uncollected printings of entire and partial poems to 207 and 653, as well as 7 titles (including 2 that print no English verse) in 12 editions/issues printing 59 entire and 24 partial translations." Notes that "the present work also lists 110 editions/issues of works printing 238 obvious adaptations and 3 titles in 4 editions printing 129 dubia presently considered possibly Donne's." Explains how this study "has far-reaching implications involving historical, literary, and cultural aspects of Donne's influence." Discusses how it shows (1) that "[s]ubstantially more Donne verse (including 6 Latin and 7 English verses not included in the Donne canon by his editors) was available in significantly greater quantity to a print audience earlier, later, and more consistently throughout the seventeenth century than has been previously thought"; (2) that "[u]ncollected printings will have to play a far more important role in establishing the texts of Donne's verse and the facts of Donne's life (including his influence on seventeenth-century continental verse) than they have to date"; (3) that it must be recognized that Donne was "an extraordinarily popular poet not only among the intelligentsia, but also among the functionally illiterate" (2); (4) that "Donne's verse became part of the discourse of an entire society," and that it "had influence because his verse had commercial, social, and personal value (based primarily on 'wit' in all its manifestations) for a large and diverse audience over a long period" (3) "Donne's Uncollected Seventeenth-Century Printed Verse" (52–[192]) explains the format of the bibliography (52–54) and lists of "Works Containing Donne Verse" (55–159), "Works Containing Translations Only" (160–161), "Works Containing Adaptations Only" (162–81), and "Works Containing Dubia Only" (182–[191]). Concludes with a chronology of printings (193–95); a selected bibliography (197–99); an index of verse, translations, adaptations, and dubia (201–5); an index of authors, compilers, contributors, and translators (206–7); an index of short titles of works (208–9); and an index of first lines (210–15). Reviews: Eugene R. Cunnar in *ELN* 32 (1994): 74–78; Donald L. Guss in *SoAR* 59 (1994): 146–48; W. Speed Hill in *PBSA* 88 (1994): 513–15; Alan Rudrum in *AEB* 8 (1994): 70–75; A. S. G. Edwards in *MP* 93 (1995): 256–59; Judith Scherer Herz in *Ren&R,* n.s. 19 (1995): 79–81; Patricia Pinka in *SCN* 53 (1995): 12; Robin

Robbins in *N&Q,* n.s. 42 (1995): 492–96; Paul Parrish in *SCR* 13 (1996): 61–62; Neil Rhodes in *MLR* 31 (1996): 194–95; Alan Rudrum in *RES* 47 (1996): 256–58; Harold Love in *Text* 10 (1997): 402–5.

1387. Summers, Claude J., and Ted-Larry Pebworth, eds. *Renaissance Discourses of Desire.* Columbia: University of Missouri Press. vii, 284p.

A collection of 14 original essays, with excerpts from a panel discussion (entry 1381) and an introduction by the editors, followed by notes on the contributors and an index. The introduction points out that the essays in this collection "explore the discursive representations of sexuality in non-dramatic literature of the late Renaissance, clarifying Renais-sance ideas and ideals about love and sexuality and examining the manifestations of those ideas and ideals in literature" (4–5). Notes that the essays "are historically grounded and critically based" but "vary widely in their historical perspectives and critical techniques and in their scope and focus" (6). Comments briefly on each of the essays to show how they "contribute to a fuller understanding of the complexities and range of seventeenth-century discourses of desire, while also helping chart the outlines of the period's sexual ideologies and anxieties" (12). The following essays, each of which discusses Donne, have been entered separately into this bibliography: William Shullenberger, "Love as a Spectator Sport in John Donne's Poetry" (46–62) (entry 1379); Stella P. Revard, "The Sapphic Voice in Donne's "Sapho to Philaenis" (63–76) (entry 1373); Theresa M. DiPasquale, "Donne's Catholic Petrarchan: The Babylonian Captivity of Desire" (77–92) (entry 1306); Eugene R. Cunnar, "Fantasizing a Sexual Golden Age in Seventeenth-Century Poetry" (179–205) (entry

1301); and Arlene Stiebel, "Subversive Sexuality: Masking the Erotic in Poems by Katherine Philips and Aphra Behn" (223–36) (entry 1382).

1388. Vickers, Brian. "Rhetoric," in *The Cambridge Companion to English Poetry: Donne to Marvell,* ed. Thomas N. Corns, 101–20. Cambridge Companions to Literature. Cambridge: Cambridge University Press.

Discusses the importance of rhetoric in seventeenth-century English poetry, noting that "[e]ach of the major English poets uses rhetoric individually, according to genre, mood, [and] purpose, adapting it to his own idiom and poetic style" (107). Shows that "in Donne's love poetry rhetoric serves to express and dramatize a whole range of feelings and attitudes towards its subject-matter" (113), citing examples of his use of anaphora, parison, antimetabole, hyperbole, antithesis, asyndeton, polysyndeton, epanalepsis, exclamatio, anadiplosis, epizeuxis, and ploche.

1389. Wollman, Richard B. "The 'Press and the Fire': Print and Manuscript Culture in Donne's Circle." *SEL* 33: 85–97.

Believes that recent critics who focus too exclusively on Donne's being a coterie poet who shunned print are "ironically replicating a tradition that begins as early as Walton in his hagiographic *Life of Dr. John Donne*" in that both suggest that Donne in his poetry is "merely exercising his wit" (85), cares little if his art endures, and regards his poetry primarily as an ephemeral performative act. Argues that "[t]he print-based standard, however, is not the only existing standard in the seventeenth century" and that "it is erroneous to privilege print over manuscript in analyses of Donne's work." Maintains, therefore, that "[a] more thorough understanding of Donne's relationship to manuscript culture is essential to interpreting correctly his attitude towards print" (86). Shows that Donne was "far from casual about his unpublished works" and that "his letters and poems demonstrate an obsessive desire to preserve his identity through his writing." Claims that "manuscript transmission [of his writings] among a close circle of learned friends provides Donne with some measure of authorial control" and a middle way to place his writings "between the rigid fixity of print and the complete destruction of his works." Maintains that Donne "was aware of his immense popularity" and "was not afraid of the physical survival of his poems but of the proliferation of misinterpretations by readers" (88). Maintains also that "[m]anuscript, as Donne demonstrates, preserves to a greater extent the oral expression of the writing by inviting a closeness with the reader that becomes more and more difficult, if not impossible, to achieve in print" (89), noting that Donne's expression of regret about printing the *Anniversaries* does not show a disdain for "professionalism" but "confirms for him that in print he can no longer control the rampant misinterpretation of his poem" (94). Concludes that manuscript circulation "does not make Donne less of an author, but simply defines a different way of being an author in an age that provides widely variant responses to the competing pressures presented by two equally acceptable systems of literary transmission—manuscript and print" (93).

1390. Zickler, Elaine Perez. " 'Not in nothing, nor in things': The Case of Love and Desire in Donne's *Songs and Sonets*." *JDJ* 12: 17–39.

Maintains that "a casuistical subjectivity" informs all of Donne's writings "much as a psychoanalytic subjectivity informs modern writing" and sees the influence of casuistical discourse "not only in his overt staging of cases *per se*, but [also] in the pre-novelistic, divided subject of literary representaton which is discernible in his writing." Argues that "the importance of casuistical discourse to Donne's writing inheres in his radical restructuring of dialogue, and in an epistemology embodied in the psychoanalytic notion of transference" (17), noting that this transferential model is "structural, dramatic, and imaginative" (18). Maintains that in the *Songs and Sonets* "transference love defeats both courtly love and Petrarchism on the one hand, and libertinism on the other," and that the poems "point toward an ideal of love that is always in the future of the subject, neither denied nor granted, but always in process," so that "love is both an enabling relationship and a condition for knowledge of the other." Shows that in Donne's poems "the problem of love and desire involves charting a path through the twin tyrannies of mastery and submission" (18) and that "the language of love and desire is imbricated with sexuality and sensuality as well as epistemology, cognition, and spirituality" (22). Discusses how the reader of Donne's poems "must be engaged casuistically" and how "it is the reader who psychoanalyzes or is psychoanalyzed by these poems" (31). Illustrates the argument by discussing in some detail *EpEliz, ElBed, NegLov, LovAlch, Fare, Ecst, ElComp,* and *Air*.

1994

1391. Baumgaertner, Jill Peláez. "Political Play and Theological Uncertainty in the *Anniversaries*." *JDJ* 13: 29–49.

Argues that, in addition to seeking the favor of the Drurys, Donne wrote the *Anniversaries* to attract the attention of King James and his heir, Prince Henry, godson of Elizabeth I, whose queenly and virginal "presence lurks just under the surface of the poems" (38). Notes that "within seven months of Henry's investiture, and soon after the death of Elizabeth Drury, Donne was writing a poem in which he seemed very purposely to be invoking images and myths which had recently been re-introduced in the Prince's honor" (39), but that after the prince's death in 1612 Donne no longer makes references to Elizabeth as a second Virgin Mary since the notion "would no longer serve to ally [him] with the court mythologies" (40). Discusses how *FirAn* is "infused with much more of a Roman Catholic spirit" than is *SecAn* (41), a poem which "anchors Donne more firmly within a Reformation context" (42). Suggests that Donne's theological predicament "seems similar to that of the English church at the time, which was its own creation—neither Catholic nor avowedly Lutheran nor completely Calvinist—but rather a combination of elements uniquely English" (43). Suggests that, in writing the *Anniversaries,* Donne, "attempting to prove himself ready once again for a public appointment, was actually proving to James that he was exactly the kind of Catholic the King wanted in his church" (44). Points out that James was eager to establish "a middle ground in religion" and argues that, "[m]otivated by the desire for personal aggrandizement, Donne seemed after a similar middle ground in his political posturings, which very naturally included his religious position." Concludes that "[i]n attempting to attract the attention of the Drurys through the publication of these poems, Donne also revealed his astute awareness of the acceptable political metaphors of the time, metaphors which would do two things at once: lavishly memorialize the dead child, and compliment the Prince of Wales," noting that "for this brief moment in history—1610–1612—these metaphors were viable" (46).

1392. Baumgaertner, Jill Peláez. "Rereading John Donne: The Art of *Trompe-l'oeil*." *Cresset* 57, no. 7: 4–9.

Analyzes the effects of trompe l'oeil in Battista Angolo del Moro's painting *A Vision of the Holy Family near Verona* and suggests that its "ludic quality has some connections with the exaggerations, the riddles, and the jarring effect of the seventeenth-century metaphysical poem," especially Donne's religious poems. Maintains that "[t]o look for consistency in Donne is to miss the point," because "[t]he dislocation of the reader is the point." Argues that "we must read with our eyes open to the cultural, theological, and political inconsistencies in his verse in addition to indications that

489

in his poetry at least he never completely resolves his problem of doctrinal allegiance." Insists that "[t]he greatest obstacle in the way of clear and fresh readings of Donne's poems is the interpretive tradition that has already been established, a tradition which has ignored some of the major flaws in his poetry and has even held up some of its weaknesses as strengths" (8). Examines the theological inconsistencies and confusion in *HSBatter* and *HSShow*.

1393. Baumlin, James S. "Dialogue and *Controversia* in English Renaissance Literature: Historicizing the Reader's Response." *PMPA* 19: 1–20.

Argues that "Renaissance literature is characteristically open to dialogue; that its orientation 'toward the listener and his answer' results from authors' pervasive training in humanist rhetoric; that both dialogue specifically and rhetoric generally assume multiple, competing perspectives and the possibility that one's arguments can be refuted; and, finally, that the age's dialogism reveals habits of controversial thinking which are themselves premised in an attitude of skepticism." Claims that "[a]ll of these elements— dialogism, rhetoric, controversial thinking, and skepticism—are the intellectual offspring of humanist education." Focuses primarily on English love poetry in order "to suggest ways to synthesize these many facets of humanist intellectual culture within a student- and reader-centered pedagogy" (5). Cites *Flea* as an example of dialogism, noting that the poem "presents two arguments simultaneously: the poet's and, indirectly, the lady's." Points out that "the former asserts, and the later refutes, argument by analogy" (10) but that in the end it is "the reader's turn to respond, to take the place of the lady and refute, or else succumb to the poet's verbal

seductions." Maintains that as readers of Donne, "we are to 'resist' his arguments, finding 'better reasons against them.' " Believes that even such serious love poems as *Ecst* and *GoodM* "must be read dialogically and against a background of doubt." Notes that *Canon* "begins precisely as a counter-argument or answer to an imagined interlocutor's skepticism" (11). Maintains that "[e]arly humanists' claims regarding rhetoric's power to persuade, though boldly asserted by Sidney and Shakespeare, are by Donne's time rendered either ironic or naive" and that "the intensity of skepticism toward humanist rhetoric increases throughout the seventeenth century" (12).

1394. Beier, Nahla M. "Irresolvable Dialectics: Donne's Sense of Disunity." *EIRC* 20: 127–41.

Maintaining that "Donne's seemingly playful manipulations of visual conventions and logical tenets usher the reader into a radically avisual and alogical realm of comprehension," focuses "on a relatively unexamined group of poems that constitute Donne's metaphysical failures, or moments that lose sight of the transcendent end." Observes that "[t]he logical disparities displayed here seem neither playful nor deliberate, but are nonetheless crucial to understanding the divided nature of Donne's mind, and the means by which he overcomes his inner divisiveness" (128). Discusses the dialectical structure of such poems as *LovDiet, Storm, Dissol, Prohib,* and *LovInf,* poems that "tellingly duplicate at large the most basic syntactical structure of Donne's poetic style." Maintains that "[i]t is the simple and hitherto unexplored level of syntax that may provide us with important clues to Donne's successes as well as his failures in intimating transcendence" (129). Discusses how Donne often "creates a kind of unresolved dialectic, an opposition of parts incapable of synthesis except in superficial ways" and maintains that "[t]his particular dialectical movement does not remain in Donne only at the syntactical level of the sentence, but can be seen at work throughout the structure of a number of poems in *The Songs and Sonnets*" (134).

1395. Belsey, Catherine. "John Donne's Worlds of Desire," in *Desire: Love Stories in Western Culture*, 130–49. Oxford: Blackwell. Reprinted in *John Donne,* ed. Andrew Mousley (Basingstoke: Macmillan; New York: St. Martin's Press, 1999), 63–80.

Discusses sexual desire in Donne's poems, maintaining that desire "has its own political history" and that "Donne's poems in particular belong on the threshold of its modernity" (134). Reads *ElBed* as "a text of desire" since "the action is all explicitly at the level of fantasy" (136). Maintains that the poem is "about love and not about woman who is its object" (139) and shows that, whereas Donne's Ovidian model "is a seemingly transparent narrative of sexual pleasure, Donne presents an intricate, knotty, difficult, dazzling formulation of desire." Finds the sexual relationship in *SunRis* "marginally more reciprocal" (140) and calls the poem "an affirmation of radical subjectivism," observing that it "teases and tantalizes the reader to the degree that it is at once utopian about love and explicitly witty at the expense of the utopia it depicts," a poem in which "love evades a final definition" and "so remains indeterminate" (142). Maintains that although *GoodM* "moves very much closer to portraying the kind of sexual relation that the twentieth century perceives as ideal" (143), when examined closely, one finds that "true ideal, equal lovers are immobilized, frozen like figures on a Grecian urn, in a state of perfect reciprocal excitement which remains ungratified for ever" (146). Concludes, therefore, that "[d]esire in Donne's love poetry is a world that remains paradoxically unknown, and that elicits in consequence a corresponding anxiety, which is registered in the texts as undecidability." (147). Points out, however, that paradoxically this is the "historical moment at which desire becomes the basis of a lifetime of concord" and that poems like Donne's are part of the foundation of the historical development of "conjugal partnership, where love and consent ensure the harmony of the family and the proper inculcation in the next generation of consensual assumptions, beliefs, meanings" (147).

1396. Benet, Diana Treviño. "Introduction to Cluster on 'A Valediction forbidding Mourning.'" *JDJ* 13: 125–26.

Comments on papers given by Janice Whittington (entry 1469), Judith Herz (entry 1428), and Graham Roebuck (entry 1450) as part of a colloquium on *ValMourn* at the ninth annual John Donne Society Conference. Points out that these critics suggest that "the story surrounding the poem's creation is probably fiction," that "the poet such a context seems to imply is likewise questionable," that "the meaning typically ascribed to the poem's most striking image has been in error," and that "the text itself is a product, to a certain extent, not of the author but of editorial choices." Concludes that the essays "remind us of the extent to which the author and text we read are the author and text we (and others like us) dispose or even create" (126).

1397. Benet, Diana Treviño. "Sexual Transgression in Donne's Elegies." *MP* 92: 14–35.

Maintains that an understanding of the public debate over the role of women in Donne's time allows one to see the *Elegies* "in a cultural context that explains their characteristic features, so alien to the traditionally idealizing bent of most vernacular love poetry" (14). Rejects the idea that in these poems Donne "wrote in flagrant disregard of erotic convention or that he expressed a general hatred of women" and holds that the *Elegies* "are not bizarre, misogynistic love poems," noting that they are "less interested in the inner world of emotion than in the outer world of social interactions." Maintains, therefore, that the poems "take their typical concerns and themes from the controversy [over the role of women], focusing on people whom it pinpoints as sexual transgressors: aggressive or uncontrollable women, a would-be cross-dresser, an effeminate man, men overcome by women, powerless husbands, and an anarchic lover." Argues that "the woman question interested Donne in the potential fluidity of gender identities," and that in the *Elegies* "this interest produced a major thematic emphasis on the sexual transgressions of the masculine woman and the feminine man." Maintains that, "unlike most of the contributors to the public controversy, Donne was more inclined to explore sexual transgression than to pass any particular judgment on it" (15). Reads the *Elegies,* therefore, not as love poems but as "topical and often satirical social commentary" (33), and believes that they "depict a world as various and complicated as men and women can make it by transgressing against the sexual roles assigned by their culture" (35).

1398. Bevan, Jonquil. *"Hebdomada Mortium: The Structure of Donne's Last Sermon." RES* 45: 185–203.

Maintains that the original layout of a text may "affect its sense, may indeed be part of it," and that thus "the physical arrangement of the text on its page must be respected as much as any other original feature." Argues that "this is the case with Donne's last sermon" (185), "Death's Duell." Points out several characteristics of the first edition of the sermon that are lacking in modern editions, such as eliminating or moving marginal and division notes and reorganizing paragraph divisions. Discusses in detail the elaborate, numerologically complex, seven-paragraph structure of the sermon and also its tripartite overall structure, showing why it is important to a fuller understanding of the sermon that it be read "with careful attention to its layout on the page" (203). Discusses reasons for thinking that Donne himself prepares the sermon for publication.

1399. Borkowska, Ewa. "Donne and God's Playground," in *From Donne to Celan: Logo(theo)logical Patterns in Poetry,* 13–53. History of Foreign Literatures, ed. Aleksander Abłamowicz. Katowice: Wydawnictwo Uniwersytetu Ślaskiego.

Attempts to show "a gradual dissipation of homogeneous aesthetics and art as manifest by literary examples from J[ohn] Donne through G. M. Hopkins down (up) to Rilke and [Paul] Celan" and argues that "[i]n this perspective baroque poetry, with its multiocularism and multiplication of motifs, becomes essential as it anticipates contemporary groundlessness, unpossession and fragmentation characteristic for a scopic regime of modernism" (7). Discusses Donne's "deified vision of nature and the ludic self that indulges in rhetorical perorations, tampering with language and nonplussing the reader by verbal rodomontade." Comments on Donne's "Spinozist language: passive (defensive), active (aggressive) and hermeneutic-constructive in which the poet articulates his *concetti,*" a language that "turns out to be fallacious, duplicitous, never unequivocal 'cloven language' which nonetheless, renders most tellingly baroque allegorical imagery, the Nietzschean *stilo representativo* whose verbal excesses are appeased by *musicum carmen* of conceits as well as epigrammatic verses." Maintains that "[t]he rhetorical acrobatics and logo(theo)logical patterns Donne's poetry demonstrates evince the poet's rebellion against the literary canon which postulated a restrictive function of language and verbal ascesis" and "shatters the limitation of *imaginatio* intelligible for the multitude and promotes language of *ratio* (active-aggressive) which requires that the reader disentangle the conceptual imbroglios with the help of hermeneutic-constructive abilities." Claims that Donne's poetry "manifests perfect synchronization of the erotic and the divine language in all heretic idolatry of secular theology." Depicts Donne's verbal power, therefore, "as anticipative of modernist aesthetics of fragmentation, 'finite infinity,' self-biathanatos and intellectual love of God of which Spinoza becomes a chief advocate." Believes that "Donne's poetic excesses of 'no reasons but proofs,' semi-theological and scientific, cannot aim at other than a secular salvation and, as such, serve the poet to liberate the Scripture from an authoritarian regime by employing the language which counteracts the long observed canon in favour of new logo(theo)logical patterns in which wordplay, game, phonic effects and verbal luxuriance cease to be blasphemous because of their apostatic connotation" (8). Holds that "God is not eradicated from Donne's writing but approached in the way accessible to the universal audience, neither religious nor entirely secular, the reader who celebrates the 'intellectual love of God' rather than devoted veneration" (8–9).

1400. Brooker, Jewel Spears. "Eliot, Descartes, and the Language of Poetry: A Review Essay." *SoAR* 59, no. 4: 107–13.

Reviews the publication of T. S. Eliot's Clark and Turnbull Lectures, entitled *The Varieties of Metaphysical Poetry: The Clark Lectures at Trinity College, Cambridge, 1926, and the Turnbull Lectures at The Johns Hopkins University, 1933,* ed. Ronald Schuchard (London: Faber and Faber, 1933; New York: Harcourt Brace, 1993) (entry 1324). Discusses how this publication "will make a permanent difference in our understanding of Eliot and of twentieth-century literature and criticism" (107–8), especially by clarifying Eliot's concept of intellectual history, in which Descartes emerges as the villain in the decline of belief and the disintegration of the intellect, and by showing that "Eliot's theory of decay is rooted in philosophic and linguistic analysis rather than in nostalgia or personal taste" (110). Points out that "[t]his account of intellectual history is replicated in Eliot's account of literary history" and notes how Eliot "seems to rank Donne at or near the top of his hierarchy," but "[w]hat becomes clear when the discussion of Donne is contextualized is that Eliot did not consider Donne a first-rate poet at all." Suggests that if Eliot's views expressed in the lectures had been widely known in the twenties, "it would have made an enormous difference in twentieth-century literary criticism and in the revision of the canon that is usually linked to Eliot's infatuation with Donne and his contemporaries." Claims that in Eliot's view "Donne is Adam after the fall, the first representative of the romantic or modern mind in English poetry" and that, "in literature, Donne is the counterpart of Descartes" (111).

1401. Chaudhry, Rita. "The Moment in John Donne's Major Love Poems." *ACM* 7, no. 2: 192–208.

Points out that the "moment of speech" in the *Songs and Sonets* is "a crucial point of time when the characters of the poems speak, perform, and interact," and that it "implies not only a specific context of time and place but also the circumstances which inspire the interplay of feelings, thoughts, beliefs, and compulsions." Notes that, for the lovers, the moment of speech is "a moment of commitment or of rejection, a time to affirm or to scorn, a time of sharing or of parting, an instant to rejoice or to mourn." Discusses how Donne's major love poems are built on this depicted "emotional and intense moment" (192). Discusses the various techniques Donne employs "to unfold and develop the moment of speech" (194) in a number of his love poems and observes how he develops essentially "four crucial occasions for speech—the moment of awakening, parting, rejection, and death" (196). Concludes that "each of the four moments of speech captures the speaker in control of his situation," noting that "even though the moment is stressful, it does not reduce the lover to a state of helpless despair nor does it provoke him to speak without reserve or with absolute candour," for "[e]ven a highly tense moment fails to illumine the hidden springs of his being." Notes that "[i]n certain poems of parting and of mutual love, however, the lover struggles to persuade, convince, or influence his mistress at a peak moment in their relationship" and "is less guarded, highly argumentative, and more inclined to reveal his innermost feelings." Believes that "Donne's convincing portrayal of even the orthodox love situations indicates his special ability to develop them as moments of significant and eloquent speech" (208).

1402. Colman, Warren. "Love, Desire, and Infatuation: Encountering the Erotic Spirit." *Journal of Analytical Psychology* 39: 497–514.

Arguing that "romantic love is simply a modern variant of an experience well known to antiquity," presents a "brief historical review of erotic love in Western culture, with particular reference to Plato's *Symposium*," and explores "the sexual and spiritual phenomenology of erotic love" (497–98). Maintains that it was "Donne who was supremely able to celebrate spirituality and sexuality together and in so doing probably came closest to Plato's original intent, which was not to denigrate sexuality but to recognize it as a route to something which lies beyond itself" (505). Cites *Ecst* as an example.

1403. Corthell, Ronald. "The Obscure Object of Desire: Donne's *Anniversaries* and the Cultural Production of Elizabeth Drury," in *Critical Essays on John Donne,* ed. Arthur F. Marotti, 123–40. New York: G. K. Hall.

Presents a psychoanalytic reading of the *Anniversaries* in an attempt to balance "recent new historicist critique of representation [in the poems] against a psychoanalytic notion of identification in order to argue for the importance of desire in the process of producing and interpreting the *Anniversaries*." Examines the logic of desire in the poem's "construction of the subject of Donne," which includes "the speaking subject who produces (and is produced by) Elizabeth Drury as the Idea of a Woman for Sir Robert Drury in the two *Anniversaries;* the academic subject 'John Donne' produced by readings of the *Anniversaries;* and the reading subject who produces (and is produced by) that 'John Donne' and who thereby also instantiates a relationship between the Renaissance and the present." Emphasizes "the psychological investment in the work of producing Elizabeth Drury as the centering 'shee' of the poem" in "all three processes of subjectification" and explores "the role of desire, particularly in the form of identification, in this production of the enigmatic 'shee'" (124). Stresses "the relationship between representation, identification, and the idea of a woman in the production of the subject of the *Anniversaries*" (124–25) and shows that "the signifying economy of loss and recuperation that produces the empowered reading subject of the *Anniversaries* is also a male economy of desire" (125). Discusses the psychological dimensions of the poet-client and patron-reader relationships of the poems and suggests that "1) the extravagance of the *Anniversaries* might in fact resonate to the felt loss of Robert Drury; 2) that the loss of a daughter can be seen as a defining instance of the narcissistic loss described by Freud; and 3) that the *display* of such loss participates in a tradition of melancholy writing devoted to recuperating male loss" (130).

1404. Coyle, Martin. "The Subject and the Sonnet." *English* 43: 139–50.

Speculates about "the idea of the subject in Renaissance poetry," particularly in the *Holy Sonnets* and Shakespeare's sonnet sequence. Points out that "the subject" simply means "the figure in the text who speaks and who finds (in this case) himself defined by difference from other figures—especially God and Christ—or defined by knowledge of time" (139) and notes that the primary focus of this study "is on the process of turning inwards" (140). Discusses *HSSpit* and *HSBatter* as "texts which articulate the struggle that characterises the subject" (140–41). Comments on how the first poem is "about the efforts of the speaker to supplant Christ through identification with Him and through recognition of their differences" (143). Points out that in the second poem, "[e]ven as the speaker seeks for union with God so the text utters the desire for subjectivity that separates the speaker from God." Concludes, therefore, that "Donne's religious poems

document one area of the crisis of subjectivity in the Renaissance" and contrasts them with Shakespeare's sonnets to show that "perhaps the religious sonnet marks a cul-de-sac as far as the subject is concerned" since "the subject-speaker is always-already limited by the premise of the poem" (49). Concludes that Shakespeare's sonnets analyze while the *Holy Sonnets* record "the crisis of the subject in its recognition of its difference from other figures" (150).

1405. Crispin, Ruth K. "Originality, Hidden Meanings and the Canon: Reading Donne, Góngora and the Critics in Their Days and Ours." *Neohelicon* 21, no. 2: 87–108.

"In this study of the canonical status of poets like Donne and Góngora," Crispin examines "the ontology implicated in the creation, refashioning and indeed interpretation(s) of the canon" (87). Contends that "Metaphysical/Baroque poetry and all endeavors like it . . . are always in a sense outside the canon, because they are outside any canonical mode of thought." Surveys major critical statements about Donne and Góngora that marginalized both poets for a time after their deaths "to see how the Auerbachian taxonomy of 'Hebraic' and 'Greek' can account for the bases of these poets' acceptance or rejection," and then turns to "criticism which ushered in and followed their re-admission to the canon, early in this century, to illustrate how, within the modernist revival of Baroque itself, these distinctions resurface and influence the reading and the canonical judgment of this poetry" (90). Maintains that "the Spanish, like the English Baroque—and in contrast to, for example, Renaissance poetry—seeks knowledge of a different order, a knowledge whose truths are revealed by poetry and language rather than by the visible world," and that "its urgency is not simply to create art (as one might argue for a work like Sidney's *Astrophil and Stella*) but to manipulate with art." Concludes, therefore, that baroque art is "dynamic, vital, skeptical and other, not ideal, not classical, not decorous—and very often, like the barbarian other, not welcome" (106).

1406. Davies, Stevie. *John Donne*. Writers and Their Work. Plymouth, U.K.: Northcote House in association with the British Council. ix, 84p.

Surveys Donne's poetry and analyzes parts of his sermons. In "The Person" (1–29), discusses major characteristics of Donne's poetry (speech-rhythm, dramatic situations, colloquial spontaneity, violent intensity, complex intellectual syntax, conceits, wit, seeming modernity, elaborate uses of rhetoric) and argues that, although "the large general patterns and sweep of Donne's individual life" is useful "as a way of guessing out hints and clues to configurations of meaning in his poetry," more important are "the cultural, historical, and religious forces (often stormily contradictory)" that "cross-biased to shape Donne and to which he was constrained to form a vivid complex of attitudes and responses" (9) and that bred in him a kind of "skepticism that made him doubt even his own self" (11) and appears in the very structure of his poems and in his "eccentric and skewed vision, errant logic, tense shifts, extremism verging on self-parody, insecure but categorical self-assertion" (12). Maintains, however, that in his total belief in God, Donne "parts company with modern alienation" even if he is "seldom sure of God's relation to his own unstable self" (12). Reads the poems in the light of Donne's intellectual and religious conflicts and sees a relationship between his poetry and Continental baroque and mannerist art. In "The

Male" (30–54), Davies challenges the tradition of male criticism that praises Donne for the "virility" of his poetry and prose and suggests that such congratulations are "the trophies of a kind of linguistic colonialism which finds virtue in aggression and self-authentication in irreverent rhetorical self-display" (32). Discusses Donne's obscenity, especially in the early poems, and his misogyny "formed on fear, anger, and insecurity as well as desire for approbation in a patriarchal world" (32–33). Comments on how often Donne dehumanizes woman, seeing her as "an edible commodity" or "usable goods," "game to be flushed out and killed," or "a mindless piece of flesh without individuality" (34). Argues that in the *Divine Poems* Donne moves on to "a more transcendent realm of sexual paradox in which, abdicating his male gender though not his 'virile' style, he could represent himself as the female partner, according to that ancient scriptural tradition derived from the biblical Song of Songs in which the human soul and the Church are figured as the Bride or beloved of Christ." Maintains, however, that this "transsexual identification did not call for a revision of misogynistic attitudes" since "humanity stood as female to God's male" and because "human nature incorporated all those defects Genesis and Christian tradition visited upon woman" (51). In "The Soul" (55–75), Davies discusses Donne's religious sensibility as it is reflected in his poetry and prose and comments on his religious development, especially his "journey towards ordination," maintaining that Donne really wanted in life "power, prestige, rank, and riches," not Holy Orders (55). Finds in the sermons and most of the *Holy Sonnets* an awareness of "inner foulness" (56), "apocalyptic horror" (57), and a pervading sense of death and decay. Sees in the *Holy Sonnets* an expression of fear, despair, rebelliousness, and self-division that "assumed a Faustian emergency status" (63). Praises the hymns as "spiritual testaments which count among the most precious of our heritage" (67). Concludes with notes (77–78), a select bibliography (79–82); and an index (83–84). Reviews: Maria Salenius in *NM* 96 (1995): 110–11; Graham Parry in *Inbetween* 5 (1996): 195–98.

1407. DiPasquale, Theresa M. "Cunning Elements: Water, Fire, and Sacramental Poetics in 'I am a little world.'" *PQ* 73: 403–15.

Argues that "to appreciate the emotional force—and, ultimately, the metapoetic implications" in *HSLittle* one must recognize "the typological relation between the Flood and baptism," noting that "the water of the Deluge is a 'figure' of baptism (1 Peter 3:20–21)" (203–4). Notes that the speaker realizes that there can be no second baptism just as there will be no second Deluge and thus fears that his actual sins will not be forgiven. Discusses how in the sonnet the speaker finally "leaves behind the fears inspired by his meditation on one sacrament—baptism—to find hope in the thought of another—the Lord's Supper" (406) and "seeks a eucharistic renewal in the very flames with which, according to his typological analogy, he 'must be burnt'" (406–7). Holds that "the speaker hopes that, 'in eating' the sacrament of Holy Communion, he will be restored to the house of God, the Church which he first entered through the saving flood of baptism" (407–8). Shows how, "[r]elying upon the doctrines articulated in the rite of the 'Communion of the sick'" of the Anglican Church, the sonnet "remedies private desperation with liturgically informed belief" (408). Discusses also how

Donne's "eucharistic consecration of the fire imagery" in the poem "redefines and transforms the sonnet itself" (409), as he puts fire "to a new and spiritually profitable use." Concludes that in the sonnet "the healing flames of a eucharistic fire save Donne from a burning fear that he has lost the grace of Baptism: the response to fire is fire, the answer to fears about sacramentality is sacrament, and poetic utterance remedies the despair that was spoken into being through poetry" (410).

1408. Doebler, Bettie Anne. *"Rooted Sorrow": Dying in Early Modern England.* Rutherford, N.J.: Fairleigh Dickinson University Press; London: Associated University Presses. 296p.

Studies the "theme of death, despair, and comfort in seventeenth-century literature," emphasizing "the importance of social and historical context to theological, literary, and philosophic convention" (11). Calls Donne "the best human example in the period of one who explicitly and artistically made death the center of his work, both in poetry and in the great body of his sermons" and claims that in his work he "becomes a case study of the interaction among poetic image, life, and word in bringing together a poetics of comfort for seventeenth-century English people." Maintains that "[t]he articulation of a life—the articulation of a process by which people came to a faith in the relationship between life and death—is embedded in the rich expressive forms of Donne's work" (12). Mentions Donne throughout this study, but devotes Chapter 9, "A Case Study in Dying: Donne's Poetics of Preparation and Comfort" (183–218), exclusively to his "poetics of comfort." Maintains that "[t]he late poems, the devotions, and the last sermons of Donne reflect both the end of the breaking away from the structure of his early beliefs and the gradual moving through a more vital relation to a *communitas,* a process and a state that in turn eventually moves him into the larger society that reconciles structure as principle of order and convention and the warmly spontaneous and ambiguous phase of community" (189). Discusses *Ecst* and *Canon* as representative of Donne's early perspective by which he "moves through the yeasty liminality of *communitas* toward *societas,*" poems that reflect "cultural and communal codes that prepare the reader for Donne's fullest image of belonging, the one that moves him more deeply into the resolution of *societas,* the Communion of Saints" (191). Maintains that in the *Devotions* Donne "tolls the advent of the paradoxical resolution of a soul that had ever been on the threshold between individualism and community" (196). Finds that "[t]he most appealing voices in the Divine Poems, the devotions, and the sermons . . . owe their character, however, not to theology but to the personal intensity by which Donne expresses his longing for perfect integration into the ideal *societas:* the ultimate loving communion with the divine." Believes that "[t]he comfort of that communion, which he embodies in the few funeral sermons that he preaches during the last fifteen years of his life, is strong evidence of his own personal perspective" (199), noted especially in his funeral sermon for Magdalen Herbert in 1627. Discusses how in his poems and prose works Donne "plays upon many of the ideas, themes, conventions, and even metaphors that were part of the commonplace store of Renaissance association with death" (204), "including the two symbolic traditions of the dance of death and the *ars moriendi,* and the rituals of mourning and consolation that developed in a culture where sudden death was so frequent and frightening a

guest" (204–5). Sees *Sickness* as Donne's "most mature experience of the Communion of Saints and the community of love" and "his most fully realized example of . . . *societas*" (217).

1409. Doerksen, Daniel W. "Preaching Pastor versus Custodian of Order: Donne, Andrewes, and the Jacobean Church." *PQ* 73: 417–29.

Argues that an examination of Donne's sermons shows how his position is "the unashamedly Protestant one of the Jacobean church" (418). Sees Donne as a moderate Calvinist and contrasts his sermons with those of Andrewes, who is clearly a Laudian. Notes that Donne's emphasis on evangelical preaching contrasts with the views of the Laudians who "felt that preaching was getting too much emphasis in the Jacobean church" (421). Maintains also that, in general, Donne was "notably less sacerdotal than the Laudians" and was "not personally a stickler for following all the rules" 423), whereas the Laudian "seemed to care most about the keeping of church rules" (424). Concludes that Donne was "not part of the disgruntled Laudian minority but participated wholeheartedly in the Calvinist Jacobean mainstream, where in fact he had much in common with the conforming puritans" and that, "[w]hereas Andrewes and the Laudians tended to think of themselves primarily as custodians of order, Donne found his fulfillment as a preaching pastor" (425).

1410. Donne, John. *Dzhon Donn: Izbrannoe iz ego elegii, pesen i sonetov, satir, epitalam, i poslanii: s dobavieniem graviur, portretov, not i drugikh illustatsii, a takzhe s predisoviem i kommentariiami perevodchika,* ed. and trans. G. Kruzhkova. Moskva: Moskovskii Rabochii. 172p.

Contains a preface ([6]-[7]) and a general introduction to Donne's life and times and to his poetry and reputation

([9]-22), followed by translations into Russian of 9 elegies, 27 selections from the *Songs and Sonets,* 4 of the *Satyres,* 2 epithalamia, "*Storm,*" and "*Calm*" ([25]-116). Presents brief introductions to each of the genres included in the volume, a brief bibliography, and notes and commentary on each of the translated poems ([117]-72), followed by a table of contents. Includes 45 illustrations.

1411. Donne, John. *John Donne: Paradoxes et Problèmes,* trans. Pierre Alferi. Paris: Editions Allia. 85p.

Presents a French translation of *Paradoxes and Problems* with brief notes (11–[77]), based on the English text established by Helen Peters (1980), followed by a postscript by Pierre Alferi (79–[83]) in which the translator comments briefly on the history of the publication and date of composition of the two works, outlines Donne's life and works, and comments on the literary traditions in which Donne's works participate, stating that, although literary paradoxes existed in English before Donne's time, he seems to be the first author of Problems in English. Concludes with an index (85–[86]).

1412. Donne, John. *John Donne: Poems.* Selected and introduced by A. H. Ninham. Kidderminster, Worcestershire: Joe's Press. 43p.

Contains 13 poems from the *Songs and Sonets;* lines from *ElBed, Eclog, CB, FirAn,* and *ElComp;* 2 epigrams; 2 poems in *Corona;* 2 of the *Holy Sonnets;* and *Annun,* without notes or commentary (1–35). In the introduction (36–43), calls Donne's love poems "typical love poems, running through the gamut of emotions from desire through sex to loathing and love and, as ever in Western poetry, death" (36–37). Praises Donne's wit, his "incisive explorative imagination" (38), and his humor. Says that Donne is

"slippery, psychologically, ontologically, metaphysically" (40). Discusses *Annun* as one of Donne's "best poems," calling it an excellent example of his "brilliant dialectical poesie" (40). Sees Donne as a "deeply yearning but also deeply critical religious poet" (42). Contains a selected bibliography (44–45).

1413. Donne, John. *John Donne: Selected Poems.* With an introduction by Christopher Moore. New York: Gramercy Books; Avenel, N.J.: Distributed by Outlet Book Company. 223p.

Presents a very brief introduction to Donne's life and poetry (11–12), followed by the *Songs and Sonets,* the *Elegies, Sappho, EpLin, Sat3,* 5 verse epistles, *FirAn, FunEl, Corona,* 19 *Holy Sonnets, Cross, Res, Annun, Goodf, Tilman, Christ, Sickness,* and *Father* (15–216), followed by an index of titles and first lines (217–223). No notes or commentary. Modern spelling text.

1414. John Donne. *John Donne: Trois des derniers poèmes,* trans. Yves Bonnefoy. Coedited by Yves Prié and Thierry Bouchard. Losne: T. Bouchard. 25p. Limited edition: 800 copies.

Translates into French *Christ, Father,* and *Sickness,* with English poems on facing pages. No notes or commentary.

1415. Donne, John. *The Works of John Donne.* The Wordsworth Poetry Library. Ware, Hertfordshire: Wordsworth Editions. xiv, 300p.

Contains a brief introduction to Donne's life and poetry with a select bibliography (v–viii). Says that "the vitality, the individuality, the paradoxical modernity of this complex seventeenth-century man speaks with piercing directness to readers of the late twentieth century" (viii). Contains 54 poems from *Songs and Sonets,* 19 epigrams, 20 elegies, and *Sappho.* No notes or commentary.

1416. Dundas, Judith. "'All Things Are Bigge with Jest': Wit as a Means of Grace," in *New Perspectives on the Seventeenth-Century English Religious Lyric*, ed. John R. Roberts, 124–142. Columbia: University of Missouri Press.

Maintains that although wit was often identified with levity and as "not only a breach of decorum in religious poetry but as a sign of lack of faith" (124) by some seventeenth century poets and critics, poets such as Donne, Herbert, and Marvell demonstrate that "wit has a particular role to play in the conversion of sinners and may be decorous according to the principles of both art and religion" (125). Discusses how these poets "articulate a new decorum for religious poetry" by which wit "becomes a net in which to catch sinners, making the poets fishers of men" (126). Comments on the varieties of wit in Donne's religious poems: his use of personification or *prosopopoeia,* figures of repetition or *anadiplosis, antimetabole, adynaton, meiosis,* conceits, metaphors or *catachresis,* and musical and visual images. Discusses, in particular, wit in *Corona, Sidney, Mark,* and several of the *Holy Sonnets* and notes comments on wit in Donne's sermons.

1417. Edgecombe, Rodney Stenning. "Donne's *Nocturnal Upon S. Lucy's Day, Being the Shortest Day." Expl* 52: 142–45.

Suggests that when Donne, mourning the death of his wife, wrote *Noct,* he turned to Spenser's *Epithalamion,* "a radiant affirmation of conjugal love in all its festive summer brilliance, taking it as an archetype of human happiness to be set in contrast to the archetypal misery of his bereavement." Sees the poem as "an anti-epithalamion, a poem about solitary survival rather than procreative communion" 143), in which Donne commemorates the longest night of the year in contrast to Spenser's comment on being married on the shortest night of the year. Discusses how Donne in his poem "alludes to Spenser's autobiographical happiness and at the same time inverts it in his autobiographical unhappiness" (144) and points out parallels between the two poems.

1418. Estrin, Barbara L. "Donne," in *Laura: Uncovering Gender and Genre in Wyatt, Donne, and Marvell,* 149–223. Post-Contemporary Interventions, ed. Stanley Fish and Fredric Jameson. Durham, N.C.: Duke University Press. Pages 149–79 reprinted in *John Donne,* ed. Andrew Mousley (Basingstoke: Macmillan; New York: St. Martin's Press, 1999), 81–103.

This poststructuralist, psychoanalytic study challenges the notion of certain feminist critics who hold that the woman in a Petrarchan poem is always silenced or objectified by the male speaker and proposes a way of "reading the female consciousness back into" (14) poems by Wyatt, Donne, and Marvell. Views Petrarchism "as a series of anamorphic representations imbricated by three principal spaces: the main plot, with Laura as Daphne— or woman who denies sexuality; and the two subplots—with Laura as Eve, or woman who returns sexuality; and Laura as Mercury, or woman who invents her own life by escaping configuration altogether" (9). Comments on how "the three Lauras complicate the Petrarchism of Wyatt, Donne, and Marvell" (11). Divides the section on Donne into three chapters ([147]-223). Rejects the claims that Donne is a misogynistic poet and discusses how in *Broken* and *ValWeep* Donne "bemoans the effects of Petrarchism gone awry by demonstrating how Laura-Daphne inspires a failed poem"; how he argues in *Dream* that, by returning his desire, Laura-Eve inspires her own poems; and how Donne, speaking as a woman, in *ElChange* "voices Laura-Mercury's abstractions, following her into an eternity not yet defined." "Small Change: Defections from Petrarch and Spenserian Poetics" (149–79), a revised and expanded version of "Donne's Injured 'I': Defections from Petrarchan and Spenserian Poetics" (*PQ* 66 [1987]: 175–93; entry 773), discusses Donne's relationship to the lady in *Broken* and *ValWeep,* in which "the imagined listening woman, who is herself aware of the way women are conventionally idealized, shapes the poem she is in and the future poems the poet might write" (152). Maintains that in *Broken* Donne "demonstrates the limits of Spenserian duplication via the empty mirror of his replicated self" and that in *ValWeep* he "denies Petrarchan distance through the destructive potential of the deified beloved." Maintains that *Broken* "reproduces only a broken poet," whereas *ValWeep* "turns the woman into another version of an empty self" (174). Argues that in these poems Donne "turns his rejection of the Petrarchan and Spenserian models, so culturally available, into a disquisition about the futility of denial . . . and the anguish of separation" and maintains that "[h]is refusal to accept the solace of art and the insistence on maximizing his injuries are, in their ways, homage to the woman's power." Points out that each poem presents "a rhetorical argument" that attempts "to find a way to avert the denial and postpone the departure Petrarch and Spenser celebrate" (175). "Sylvia Transformed: Returning Donne's Gifts" (180–200) discusses *Jet, Fun,* and *Dream,* poems in which the lady's "gestures determine the discourse" (152) and in which Donne "expands the vehicle of the gesture poem" and "complicates its terms by challenging the gesturing woman and her gift" (182). " 'A Pregnant Bank': Contracting and Abstracting the 'You' in

Donne's 'A Valediction of My Name in the Window' and 'Elegy: Change' " (201–223), a revision and expansion of "Framing and Imagining 'You': Donne's 'A Valediction of My Name in the Window' and 'Elegy: Change' " (*TSLL* 30 [1988]: 345–62; entry 884), discusses how the lady "breaks down all barriers so that the poet speaks her ideas and so relinquishes all ties to the ideal of a biologically gendered self" (152). Shows how in *ValName* the speaker's engraving "emerges an engravement, a burial of the lover caught in his single self," whereas in *ElChange* "the lover is freed from the confines of his own vision as he slips into the lady's expansiveness and recognizes the connection between a fluid self and the larger movements and music of the world" (212). Points out that Donne, speaking as a woman in the elegy, begins with a diatribe against the arts, calling them "flimsy, ephemeral, and feathery—as fluffy as the women they represent," but "in the ecstatic vision at the end, the arts emerge [as] what the poet wanted at the opening—a link to eternity and a connection that lasts" (213). Reviews: Nathan P. Tinker in *EMLS* 2, no. 2 (1996): 1–5; Gordon Braden in *MP* 95 (1997): 91–97; Richard Harrier in *Rev* 19 (1997): 185–93; William J. Kennedy in *CLS* 34 (1997): 189–90; Andrew Hadfield in *English* 46 (1998): 139–45; Diane Purkiss in *MLR* 93 (1998): 176–78; Elizabeth Harris Sagaser in *RenQ* 51 (1998): 310–11; R. V. Young in *BJJ* 5 (1998): 288–99.

1419. Feinstein, Sandy. "Donne's 'Elegy 19': The Busk between a Pair of Bodies." *SEL* 34: 61–77.

Comments on the various possible implications of Donne's reference to the busk in *ElBed* (l. 11). Notes that in ladies' fashions of the time the busk was "one of the primary means to create the stiff, erect, masculine visual effect that was achieved by flattening the chest and stomach and elongating the waist" (64), a stay inserted into the bodice. Discusses Donne's bawdy wordplay on the busk but argues that he "is doing more than toying with a bawdy image." Explains how the busk "may also be a metaphor for power as well as for its contraries, power-lessness and impotence" (69). Maintains that although in the conclusion of the elegy "the narrator may be the only one we know for sure is naked, it is a nakedness that dresses itself in questions about the body and the part it plays in defining sexual roles of men and women—questions that are left unanswered and provoking as the one that finally closes the poem" (72–73).

1420. Fischler, Alan. " 'Lines Which Circles Do Contain': Circles, the Cross, and Donne's Dialectic Scheme of Salvation." *PLL* 30: 169–86.

Focusing primarily on Donne's *Divine Poems,* attempts "to bring together and relate his most significant references to circles and, on the basis of these and his ideas about the figure of the cross, to propose a geometric model which embodies his scheme of salvation" (170). Shows how Donne's "linear imposition [of the cross upon an image of human and divine circles] resolves both the geometrical metaphor for, and spiritual reality of, humanity's alienation from God" and shows how "the cross not only provides the connections between the divine and human circles but is itself a meeting place for these two contraries—in other words, the cross, too, becomes an emblem of the final synthesis" (178).

1421. Fleck, Jade C. "A Grammar of Eschatology in Seventeenth-Century Theological Prose and Poetry," in *Reform and Counterreform: Dialectics of the Word in Western Christianity since Luther,* ed. John

C. Hawley, 59–76. Religion and Society, 34, gen. eds. Luther Martin and Jacques Waardenburg. Berlin: Mouton de Gruyter.

Discusses how *HSRound* "focuses on spiritual fulfillment of eschatological prophecy without abandoning final, literal fulfillments," noting how "[t]ense substitutions and shifts depict repentance in an eschatological light" (66). Points out that the shift from the present tense in the sestet to future in the octave "corresponds with a shift in emphasis from the eschaton to realized eschatalogy" and that "[t]he speaker's imaginative projection into the future and meditation upon the last judgment result in a retreat to the present for sober examination of his spiritual condition." Observes that "[s]trikingly, the present tense also refers to the eschaton" and that "[t]hese 'futuristic' presents convey the certainty and suddenness of the eschaton as literal, future event," and, at the same time, "suggest that the speaker is already 'there,' at the last judgment, since present repentance has eschatological consequences" (67). Contrasts and compares Donne's eschatalogical views with those of Milton.

1422. Friedman, Donald M. "Donne, Herbert, and Vocation." *GHJ* 18 (1994–95): 135–58.

Examines the lives and religious sensibilities of Donne and Herbert to determine what might have accounted for "the apparent reluctance, and the final yielding, to assume the responsibilities of priesthood," and considers "what influence the two men might have had on each other's course toward that fulfillment" (137). Points out that both men "seem to have delayed in the hope of worldly position" and that "each was troubled by a sense of unworthiness (matched, perhaps, by a measure of distaste for the common view of the priesthood as itself unworthy of men of ability and standing)," but maintains that "none of the events that surrounded the decision to end delay and to act can explain satisfactorily the change" (151). Discusses how Donne and Herbert regarded the call to the priesthood differently and came to accept it in different ways. Comments on the personal relationship between Donne and Herbert and suggests that they did not accede fully to a priestly vocation until after the deaths of the one person closest to them, Ann More, in Donne's case, and Magdalen Herbert, in Herbert's case, noting that "although Donne accepts ordination as priest in 1615, it is not until after his wife's death that he becomes Dean of St. Paul's, a post that defines the remainder of his life," and that Herbert "marries and is ordained priest some three years after his mother's death." Maintains that "[i]n both men the call they answered eventually appears to have been dim, intermittent, and for a long time drowned out by the importunities of other sounds and other voices," but eventually Donne "found his voice by inviting, or allowing, God to speak through him" as a preacher, whereas Herbert "called God into his letters so urgently, eloquently, and persuasively, that he heard a voice that told him how better to speak his praise" (154).

1423. Frontain, Raymond-Jean. "Donne's Emblematic Imagination: Vision and Reformation of the Self in 'The Crosse.'" *PAPA* 20, no. 1: 27–51.

Claims that *Cross* is Donne's "most explicit poetic meditation upon the nature of divine language, as well as one of his most telling examples of how man must respond to such language" (28). Argues, therefore, that the poem is not "the idle and overly ingenious game of wit that it is so often dismissed as being" but rather is "a poignant meditation both upon

a physical universe in which every action somehow reveals the animating mystery at its center, and upon the individual's need to reform himself in that most sacred image of Christ." Sees in the poem Donne's response to "the Baconian desacramentalization of the medieval analogical universe," as "an expression of Donne's wonder at how physical nature continually bears witness to the Word-made-Flesh," and as "his pained incredulity at Puritan objections to the use of material crucifixes in worship" (29). Claims that the "particularly Donnean feature" of the poem is "the self-consciousness of its effort to assert the significance of spiritual correspondences in the physical world" (39). Points out how Donne displays "an essentially emblematic sense of self" (40) and how the linguistic excesses in *Cross* suggest his attempt "to reappropriate the power of a eucharistic language" (41), his "last-ditch effort to reassert the sacral meaning of the universe." Discusses how the poem "offers insight into the imaginative power that language had for Donne" (42) as he attempted "to assert the analogical world's inhering holiness and meaningfulness to a generation that he saw as divisive" (43).

1424. Frost, Kate Gartner. "The Lothian Portrait: A New Description." *JDJ* 13: 1–11.

Presents a very detailed description of the Lothian portrait which the author examined, while it was undergoing minor restoration, in September 1993, with the assistance of John Dick, Keeper of Conservation at the Scottish National Galleries. Suggests the need to examine in more detail "the problem of the unknown artist and date of composition, iconography, and political and biographical ramifications" (1) of the portrait. Reproduces four figures.

1425. Guillén, Claudio. "On the Edge of Literariness: The Writing of Letters." *CLS* 31: 1–24.

Briefly comments on Donne's "somewhat playful theory" of letter writing, citing his prose letter to Sir Thomas Lucey and *HWKiss,* in which Donne suggests that letter writing "amounts to the sharing of a soul by two persons, not excluding the bodies," thereby placing "himself firmly at the very core of the tradition of the familiar letter" (8). Notes that "the overarching concern and chief preoccupation [in the tradition] is the conveyance of affection, friendship, or love" and that "[t]he principal message then is the act of communication itself or the will-to-communicate" (9).

1426. Harding, Anthony John. "'Against the stream upwards': Coleridge's recovery of John Donne," in *Milton, the Metaphysicals, and Romanticism,* ed. Lisa Low and Anthony John Harding, 204–21. Cambridge: Cambridge University Press.

Argues that although it is a commonplace for scholars to give Coleridge "much of the credit for initiating the nineteenth-century revival of interest in Donne's work," they have not recognized "just how anomalous is the emergence of Samuel Taylor Coleridge as one of Donne's earliest champions, how it runs counter to most of our assumptions about romanticism, and, in particular, how far it challenges one influential recent interpretation of the relations between the Romantics and the seventeenth century" (203), namely that "British romanticism was—predominantly and in its definitive or most significant works—radical, utopian, prophetic, visionary, tending to republicanism in politics and dissenting protestantism in religion" (204–5). Maintains that "in almost every respect, the qualities that Coleridge admired in Donne are contrary to those that go to make up this picture of British romanticism and what it derived from the seventeenth century." Points out that Coleridge "praised Donne's lyrics for their toughness of mind, the compression and paradoxical nature of their thought, and the close weave of their versification, their ruggedness . . . not for visionary intensity or prophetic power" and that "he commended Donne for his emphasis on the place that the Church, its teachings and liturgy, must hold in the life of the believer" as well as "his ability to see how the measures taken to consolidate the separation from Rome had damaged the Church of England—clearly not the view of a thorough-going Protestant" (205). Maintains that in his praise of Donne, Coleridge "seems to have felt himself to be rediscovering a true voice of English poetry," noting that "[t]his eagerness for a national tradition undoubtedly had an element of chauvinism in it" (211). Points out also that "[t]he attention Coleridge paid to Donne's versification and the meticulousness of his observations on Donne's meter testify to a much more lively interest in prosody than one might expect from a Romantic." Believes that Coleridge primarily admired Donne for his "subtle exploration of genuine intellectual problems" and his "freedom from reforming zeal." Concludes that "Coleridge's response to Donne is a dramatic example of the way in which a writer of one age constructs from the records of a complex past the image of the predecessor that writer needs" (218).

1427. Hassel, R. Chris, Jr. "'How infinite in faculties': Hamlet's Confusion of God and Man." *L&T* 8: 127–39.

Points out that Donne "likes playing with the conceit of creation as a discourse of the Trinity" (130) and that he "follows Augustinian tradition when he links this discourse of the

Trinity in the act of creation with the idea of the three moral faculties of persons made in the image and likeness of the threefold God" (131), that is, the memory, understanding, and will. Discusses how one of Donne's sermons helps to contextualize "the irony of Hamlet's characteristic frustration with the inadequacies of his reason, memory, and will" (132) and helps us "understand Hamlet's self-conscious thwarting of his reason and his memory and his ungracious complaining when they still work well enough to frustrate his perverse will" (134).

1428. Herz, Judith Scherer. "Reading [out] Biography in 'A Valediction forbidding Mourning.'" *JDJ* 13: 137–42.

One of three essays delivered at a colloquium on *ValMourn* at the ninth annual John Donne Society conference. Maintains that Walton's account of the composition of the poem is fictitious and contains several inaccuracies and inconsistencies but shows how "the details of Walton's claim, the uses he put it to in the final, 1675 version of Donne's Life (the only one in which it appears), the ways in which that claim has subsequently functioned even when it is disputed and rejected, together provide a useful exemplum of the perils of biographical criticism and, more particularly, of the perils of such an approach when applied to Donne's imagined relations with his wife" (137). Argues "that biography, understood as when was the poem written, what does it reveal of John [Donne] and Anne [More], where was Donne going, what was he doing, is not an approach that is likely in this instance to yield much gold, and beaten too thin will surely shatter." Believes "the biographer may look to the poem for potential evidence of Donne's interest in a range of subjects, from theology to astronomy and

alchemy," but insists that "this is quite different from making biography read the poem" (141).

1429. Hester, M. Thomas. "'Ask Thy Father': Rereading Donne's *Satyre III*." *BJJ* 1: 201–18.

Argues that it is important when reading *Sat3* "to take into account Donne's intended audience"—not only the persecuted English Catholic readers of his time but also their persecutors, which accounts, in part, for "the equivocal manner of Donne's witty application of those Recusant tropes he embeds in the urbane, even Horatian, texture of his meditative address" (202). Suggests that the "most striking feature" of the poem "is not its urbane religious tolerance" but rather "the *absence* of 'true religion' which it discovers in Elizabethan England" (208). Shows that, when read "in the lexical arena of the late Elizabethan sectarian wars, *Sat3* is "remarkable for its 'daring' invocation of religious toleration in an age of rigid censorship and religious suppression" as well as for "its inscription of major themes, texts, allusions, and attitudes of the Recusant position" (211). Concludes, therefore, that "[a]s a satire which evokes the tropes and polemical strokes of English Catholic critiques of the state of religion in Elizabethan England," *Sat3* "seems closest to the pre-Tridentine church of Donne's family tradition" (212).

1430. Hester, M. Thomas. "Donne and the Court of Wards." *ANQ* 7: 130–33.

Points out that in the portrait of Graius in *Sat3* (ll. 55–62) Donne equates the corrupt practices of the English Court of Wards and the penal laws against Catholics and ridicules both as forms of oppression. Notes that "[o]ne form of this ridicule, as conveyed by the *triple-entendres* on 'still' as a deadly form of foolish consistency, is the suggestion that the bride of Christ has been replaced in English Reformed worship by a sort of self-serving cult of Elizabeth" (130–31), a form of idolatry and a kind of "sectarian, political prostitution" (131). Observes that when Donne chooses the Court of Wards as the "vehicle for his metaphoric portrait of the idolatry possible in English Protestantism, he focuses attention on a frequently corrupted instrument of the 'Establishment' ideology which English Catholics especially saw as a violation of their ancient rights." Discusses how "Donne himself would have found the machinations of the Court of Wards personally relevant" (132), noting that a newly discovered letter of Anne Brooke to Robert Cecil, dated 30 May 1599, shows that for Donne, "the association of English sectarian 'idolatrie' and the machinations of the Court of Wards was not just an 'idle' conceit for him" (133).

1431. Hurley, Ann. "Colliding Discourses: John Donne's 'Obsequies to the Lord Harington' and the New Historicism." *Ren&R,* n.s. 18, no. 3: 57–76.

Argues that *Har* "is more profitably approached by readings which deemphasize the valorization of personality and presence which have so dominated Donne studies in the past. Maintains, for example, that "by focusing on a variety of discourses, rather than a single personalized 'voice,' one discovers in this poem a richly complex fabric of cultural, economic and social ideologies" and that it is thus "restored to readability and its cultural contexts recaptured for future discussion" (57).

1432. Johnson, Jeffrey. "Gold in the Washes: Donne's Last Going into Germany." *Renascence* 46: 199–207.

Argues that, by reading *Christ* "in the context of Donne's own Valediction sermon that complements it, one more clearly perceives the ingenuity of Donne as he celebrates the paradox

of repentance" (199). Points out that "[w]ithin the adversities confronting him in the spring of 1619, Donne discovers once again that suffering is the means for the power of God to enter the world" and that "it is only by sharing in the suffering of Christ that those within the Church are able to be conformed to Christ" (199–200). Insists, therefore, that Donne's sermon and hymn "are not morose, self-indulgent expressions in which he longs for death" and that they do not "reveal the mind of man who is seeking to escape from the difficulties of life" (201). Presents a reading of the valediction sermon and the poem to show how both have a similar "circular structure, in which Donne presents himself in a posture of humble repentance as he reads his trip to Germany typologically" (203). Points out that in the sermon, as in the poem, Donne "finds gold in the washes," that is, "in the tribulations he associates with his impending journey, he finds the way to Christ through penitent obedience." Observes that "[t]he interface here between sermon and hymn plays upon the parallel that Renaissance alchemists frequently drew between the philosopher's stone and Christ, by whom the base matter of our adversity is transformed into the precious metal of our redemption" (204).

1433. Klause, John. "Hope's Gambit: The Jesuitical, Protestant, Skeptical Origins of Donne's Heroic Ideal." *SP* 91: 181–215.

Points out that, although Donne often "spoke as though it were a mark of rational honesty to resist the allure of heroes or models," they "were for him a deep necessity" and "also an expediency" (184). Observes that Donne "was never able to obliterate the influences of his Catholic youth," noting that his mother "had raised him to be a recusant hero" and that he decorated the Deanery at St. Paul's "with pictures of the Virgin Mary, St. Joseph, and Mary Magdalen," thereby "creating a scene symbolic of the persistence in Donne's life of voices that might be severely muted but never entirely silenced" (185–86). Maintains that "[w]hat heroes Donne needed he professed to find not in the present or the immediate past, where familiarity might stain or trivialize an ideal, but in the scriptures, where figures like Job, David, and Christ himself were lodged safe from medieval superstition and from the disillusionment born of too much knowledge," although St. Augustine he regarded as "sufficiently ancient, brilliant, bold, and in Donne's own case, spiritually atavic, to earn his deep reverence." Maintains that "[t]hese were, however, heroes to whom Donne resorted, not who pressed themselves upon him and caused him grief." Explores how "he contended with and resisted certain haunting examples [from his youth] as he tried to 'fashion' himself according to an image that he wished privately to define" (197). Discusses, in particular, his rejection of the soldierly model of the Jesuits and their ideas about martyrdom, noting especially his hostility toward St. Ignatius Loyola, and yet comments on the many spiritual principles of the Jesuits that attracted Donne and influenced his thinking. Observes that whereas the Jesuits maintained that they were willing "to risk their lives for certainties," Donne lacked that kind of faith and assurance and thus he "developed for himself a different kind of hero, one who endured the rigors not of faith but of hope" (207). Claims that, for Donne, "although hope had sometimes to suffer deception in order to exist, sometimes to deceive in order to preserve itself, its prevarications were somehow legitimate" (211). Notes that one of his special heroes

of hope was St. Mary Magdalen and points out his great admiration for Paolo Sarpi. Believes, therefore, that Donne's self-fashioned hero finally "was a Protestant, who might live with 'too little' truth as long as there were hope of more, hope which he could not harbor were he compelled to die for 'too much.'" Concludes that "[b]ecause Donne could not escape the Jesuits cleanly, his hero was a martyr—but a *surviving* 'witness' to the authentic value of personal necessities that were smaller yet no less important than truth" and thus ultimately "his hero was a temporizer" (215).

1434. Klawitter, George. *The Enigmatic Narrator: The Voicing of Same-Sex Love in the Poetry of John Donne.* Renaissance and Baroque Studies and Texts, gen. ed. Eckhard Bernstein, 14. New York: Peter Lang. xiii, 271p.

In the introduction ([ix]–xiii), maintains that reading certain of Donne's poems as expressing a man's love for another man "may heighten our understanding of obscure passages" but insists that whether Donne "did or did not toy with male lovers in his poetry cannot in any way be construed to prove that he did or did not experience male coupling himself" (x). Points out that the intent of this study is "to let the enigmatic narrator speak in his own voices and to suggest meanings for those voices that critics of Donne have in the past ignored or suppressed" (xii). Chapter 1, "Early Verse Letters to Young Men: 'By you my love is sent'" (1–26), which is an expanded version of "Verse Letters to T. W. from John Donne: 'By You My Love Is Sent,'" in *Homosexuality in Renaissance and Enlightenment England: Literary Representations in Historical Context,* ed. Claude J. Summers (Binghamton, N.Y.: Harrington Park Press, 1992), 85–102 (entry 1238), explores the sexual

metaphors in Donne's early verse letters to T. W. (Thomas Woodward)
and E. G. (Everard Guilpin) and suggests that they reflect "a highly
charged homoeroticism" (16). Chapter
2, "Donne's Verse Epistles to Women:
'Raised by love, but not throwne
down'" (27–45), parts of which were
previously published as "John Donne
and the Countess of Huntingdon: The
Transformation of Renaissance Woman"
in *Wisconsin English Journal* 28, no.
3 (1986): 10–12 (entry 691); and "John
Donne and Woman: Against the
Middle Ages" in *Allegorica* 9 (1987–
88): 270–78 (entry 794), discusses
how Donne in verse letters to women
"engineered a revision in the medieval
false dilemma of angel-slut womankind" by elevating women "to the
status of an equal" capable of understanding "his complicated lyrics" (45).
Chapter 3, "Sappho's Narrator: 'My
selfe I'embrace'" (47–61), comments
on the complex voice of the narrator
in *Sappho,* shows how the poem is
directed to stimulating sexually a male
audience, and argues that the narrator is likely a male. Chapter 4, "The
Barnfield Connection: 'Come live with
mee, and bee my love'" (63–74), discusses *Bait* to illustrate how "historical context can tell us things about
the narrator we have not considered
before" (63) and suggests specific links
between Donne's poem and Richard
Barnfield's homoerotic *The Affectionate Shepheard,* arguing that possibly Donne presents in *Bait* a male
narrator and his male lover. Chapter
5, "What the Times Tell Us: 'Suck'd
[we] on countrey pleasures'" (75–94),
examines the varieties of sexual
practices during Donne's time and
the playful use of sexual metaphor
by Renaissance poets in order to
appreciate better "Donne's own sexual wit" (75). Chapter 6, "What the
Manuscripts Tell Us: 'That I might
play on the[e]'" (95–112), examines

the manuscript tradition of the *Songs
and Sonets*, arguing against any biographical reading of the poems, rejecting any specific chronology or
ordering of the poems, and especially
challenging the notion of seeing "a
female presence in a poem where no
evidence proves that she is actually
there" (100). Maintains that the poems
"have to speak for themselves and
reveal, if at all, the rationale for the
ordering of the poems" (112). Chapter
7, "The Streetwise Fop: 'A thing more
strange'" (113–24), examines the
sexual intent in *Sat1* and *Sat4,* showing how they were "public verses,"
whereas the *Songs and Sonets* were
"private, or purported to be so, many
of them ostensibly meant for an audience of one, to be read in private"
(124). Chapter 8, "Love, Language,
and the Narrator: 'More fat, by being
with men'" (125–43), identifies 36 of
the poems in the *Songs and Sonets* as
genderless and argues that when no
specific audience is indicated there
is "no reason to presume a female
lover" (132). Discusses in particular
ValMourn, Break, and *ConfL,* maintaining each can be read as male to
male and arguing that the narrator in
the *Songs and Sonets* "experiments
with various love relationships, some
with women, some with men" (143).
(The discussion of *ConfL* first appeared as "The Narrator of Donne's
'Confined Love,'" in *ANQ* 19 [1981]:
72–74; entry 195.) Chapter 9, "Tone
and the Audience of One: 'Kill mee
as Woman'" (145–68), discusses the
various tones in the *Songs and Sonets,*
"ranging from euphoric to sad" (145).
Discusses in particular *Anniv, GoodM,
Air, ValBook, LovExch, Expir,* and
Damp, poems addressed to a single
person, to show that the poems "run
the gamut from earthy to Platonic and,
it seems reasonable to conclude, capable of being interpreted in a context
larger than heterosexuality" (165).

Chapter 10, "Tone and the Audience of Many: 'Forget the Hee and Shee'" (169–93), discusses the various tones in poems not addressed to single persons but to a general audience, in particular *Relic, NegLov, Under, Ecst, Twick, Curse, Fare, LovAlch,* and *SelfL.* Insists that "[t]hroughout the *Songs and Sonets* Donne's enigmatic narrator is found, fumbling through words to express messages that can be variously understood, variously explicated, dependent only upon the strength of a reader's imagination" (193). Presents in the Appendix (195–208) six tables: (1) a numbering of the *Songs and Sonets* as they appear in the 1633 edition, (2) the order of the poems in selected manuscripts, (3) the number of poems in the *Songs and Sonets* found in each of the manuscripts mentioned above, (4) groups of poems addressed to ungendered persons, (5) the incidence for appearance of an individual poem within the context of poems written to an ungendered person, and (6) the number of manuscripts in which a poem appears. Concludes with notes (209–46), works cited (247–64), and an "Index to Donne's Works" (265–71). Reviews: Mario DiGangi in *RenQ* 50 (1997): 339–40; Michael Morgan Holmes in *Journal of Homosexuality* 36 (1998): 128–35.

1435. Kullmann, Thomas. "Höfischkeit und Spiritualität: Dramatische Elemente in der <<Metaphysical Poetry>>." *LJGG,* n.s. 35: 121–37.

Discusses the dramatic elements in Donne's secular and religious poetry and considers the cultural and historical significance of the use of drama in Renaissance nondramatic poetry. Comments on the dialogue in *SunRis,* a poem in which the male speaker chides the sun, and suggests that the dramatic pattern in the poem is similar to what is described as courtly

forms of conduct by Castiglione, Giovanni della Casa, and Stefano Guazzo in their conduct books. Emphasizes that Donne's use of the dramatic is not limited to his love poems but also is prevalent in his religious poems in which the speaker engages in a dialogue with God. Concludes that by using dramatic elements, the metaphysical poets were able to combine clarity of expression and detailed psychic description.

1436. Low, Anthony. "John Donne: 'The Holy Ghost is Amorous in His Metaphors,'" in *New Perspectives on the Seventeenth-Century English Religious Lyric,* ed. John R. Roberts, 201–221. Columbia: University of Missouri Press.

First published in Anthony Low's *The Reinvention of Love: Poetry, Politics and Culture from Sidney to Milton* (Cambridge: Cambridge University Press, 1993), 65–86 (entry 1357).

1437. Low, Lisa, and Anthony John Harding, "Milton, the Metaphysicals, and Romanticism: Reading the Past, Reflecting the Present," in *Milton, the Metaphysicals, and Romanticism,* ed. Lisa Low and Anthony John Harding, 1–19. Cambridge: Cambridge University Press.

This essay, introductory to a collection of 12 original essays that reevaluate "the interrelationship between romanticism and the seventeenth century" in the light of "new strategies of reading" (3), surveys past criticism that saw links and affinities between the two periods and challenges certain of those assumptions. Shows that "the presence of the metaphysical poets in, to, or behind the Romantics remains a question that somehow refuses to be settled." Notes that during the nineteenth century Donne was "relatively obscure" (8) and suggests that perhaps the most relevant aspect of Donne's poetry as far as romanticism is concerned is "something like the modern sense of self" that appears in the *Holy Sonnets*. Observes that "by the time of Donne, the hold that medieval theology exercised on people's minds was weakened, religious beliefs were more diverse, and the private decisions of the individual conscience were beginning to acquire a new importance," conflicts and challenges that emerged again during the Romantic period. Insists, however, that "[t]his is *not* to say that the seventeenth-century poets were Romantics or proto-Romantics," and proceeds to point out "important differences" (8). Suggests, though, that *Goodf* is "closer to Wordsworth than mere chronology might have suggested," noting that some lines nearly parallel those of Wordsworth, that "Donne's poem resembles Wordworth's in tone" in "Tintern Abbey," and that "[i]n both poems there is intense self-consciousness" (13). Maintains that "the high and petitioning tone of personal meditation, the immediacy and candor of the diction, the violence of feeling, and the sense of the frail self on the verge of disaster appear from our perspective very similar" (13–14).

1438. Lull, Janis. "Distributed Donne: A Response to the Problem of His Titles." *Ren&R*, n.s. 18, no. 4: 53–64.

Maintains that since "[m]ost of the titles traditionally associated with Donne's poems did not originate with the biographical Donne," the use of these titles by modern editors expands "Donne's authorial 'self' to include the literary judgments of the poet's first readers as well as their own literary judgments." Believes that "[a]ssimilating such non-authorial choices to the self of the author has two things to recommend it: it is consistent with the practices of the interactive literary subculture to which Donne chose to belong, and it offers an alternative for those who can no longer believe in intentionalism as the only principle of editorial choice" (53).

1439. Lull, Janis. *The Metaphysical Poets: A Chronology*. New York: G. K. Hall; Toronto: Maxwell Macmillan Canada; New York: Maxwell Macmillan International. vii, 227p.

The introduction (1–5) presents a brief cultural and political sketch of seventeenth century England and comments on the relationship between literature and the historical and religious events of the century. "Biographical Sketches of Recurrent Figures" (7–26) presents brief biographies of persons (from George Abbot to Christopher Wren) "whose names recur throughout the chronology that follows," except for the "biographies of the six metaphysical poets themselves nor usually of their relatives, since the chronology itself is intended to provide such information." Omitted also are "rulers of England, with the exception of Oliver Cromwell" (7). "The Metaphysical Poets: A Chronology" presents a chronological account of political, religious, social, cultural, and other notable events that occurred from 1572 (the date of Donne's birth) to 1695 (the death of Vaughan). Concludes with "Secondary Works Consulted" (217–19) and an index (221–27).

1440 Makurenkova, S. A. *Dzhon Dann: Poetika i ritorika*. Moskva: Akademiia. 206p.

Presents a general introduction that places Donne's poetry into its seventeenth century contexts. Chapter 1 reprints "Byl li Dzhon Dzonom Donnom?" from *Filologischeskie nauki* 2 (1989): 74–77 (entry 985). Chapter 2 offers an expanded version of "Angliskaia 'metafizicheskaia poeziia' VIII v: K istorii poniatiia" (*IAN* 45, no. 2 [1986]: 174–81; (entry 696), and presents as part of an overview of Donne's twentieth century reputation a brief commentary on Donne scholarship in Russia by Z. A. Karumidze and A. Gorbunov. Chapter 3 surveys the history of rhetoric and poetics from Aristotle through the Renaissance and sees Donne as the proponent of a new concreteness, which was informed by Ramist dialectic. Chapter 4 compares Donne's poetry with that of his Elizabethan contemporaries, principally Shakespeare and Marlowe. The final chapter assesses Donne's views of death as presented in "Death's Duell" within the context of post-Reformation spirituality.

1441. Marotti, Arthur F., ed. *Critical Essays on John Donne.* Critical Essays on British Literature, gen. ed. Zack Bowen. New York: G. K. Hall; Toronto: Maxwell Macmillan Canada; New York: Maxwell Macmillan International. ix, 185p.

A collection of seven critical essays on Donne, only one of which has not been previously published—Ronald Corthell's "The Obscure Object of Desire: Donne's *Anniversaries* and the Cultural Production of Elizabeth Drury," 123–140 (entry 1403). Included are Achsah Guibbory, "'Oh, let mee not serve so': The Politics of Love in Donne's *Elegies*" (17–36), from *ELH* 57 (1990): 811–33 (entry 1052); Janel Mueller, "Women among the Metaphysicals: A Case, Mostly, of Being Donne for" (37–48), from *MP* 87 (1989): 142–51 (entry 992); Richard Halpern, "The Lyric in the Field of Information: Autopoiesis and History in Donne's *Songs and Sonnets*" (49–76), from *YJC* 6 (1993): 185–215 (entry 1339); Arthur F. Marotti, "Donne as Social Exile and Jacobean Courtier: The Devotional Verse and Prose of the Secular Man" (77–101), from *John Donne, Coterie Poet* (Madison and London: University of Wisconsin Press, 1986), 246–68, 326–46 (entry 698); David Aers and Gunther Kress, "'Darke texts need notes': Versions of Self in Donne's Verse Epistles" (102–22), from *L&H* 8 (1978): 138–58; and Annabel Patterson, "*Quod oportet* versus *quod convenit:* John Donne, Kingsman?"

(141–79), from *Reading Between the Lines* (Madison: University of Wisconsin Press, 1993) 160–209 (entry 1367). Each of the essays has been separately entered into this bibliography. In the introduction (1–16), the editor surveys the history of Donne criticism in the twentieth century, noting how, "[m]ost recently, new historicist, cultural materialist, feminist, and deconstructive critics have redefined the texts of this early-modern author in terms of new notions of textuality, culture, literary production and reception, and gendered writing and reading" (1). Discusses, therefore, how "scholars have paid increasing attention to the historical circumstances of English Renaissance literature and to the ideological assumptions of both the texts themselves and of the critics interpreting them" and suggests that the essays in this collection demonstrate that Donne "has benefitted from this new wave of historical criticism, including work with specifically feminist emphases." Comments briefly on the essays to show how each approaches "the historical embeddedness of literary texts and their interpretation in markedly different ways" (5). Concludes with an index (181–85). Review: Dana E. Aspinall in *RenQ* 49 (1996): 880–81.

1442. Martz, Louis L. "The Poetry of Meditation: Searching the Memory," in *New Perspectives on the Seventeenth-Century English Religious Lyric,* ed. John R. Roberts, 188–200. Columbia: University of Missouri Press.

Traces the steps in the creation of *The Poetry of Meditation: A Study of English Religious Literature of the Seventeenth Century* (1954) and of *The Paradise Within: Studies in Vaughan, Traherne, and Milton* (1964), noting that his first introduction to discursive meditation occurred following a classroom discussion of the structure of

Donne's *Anniversaries*. Shows how his historical studies of meditational modes were grounded in the New Criticism and yet have some affinities with the New Historicism, therefore calling his work "New Critical Historicism" (193). Maintains that the term "poetry of meditation" should be applied only to religious poetry and should not replace the term "metaphysical poetry." Acknowledges that religious poetry in the seventeenth century was influenced by many factors, not just meditation, and maintains that his study does not fail to recognize these other influences, in particular, the literary forms of the Bible. Points out also how his studies relate to more recent studies of "Protestant poetics" and Reformation theology and suggests ways in which his studies of both Catholic and Protestant meditation could be improved. Concludes, however, that he believes the basic argument of *The Poetry of Meditation* is valid, but that "it needs, and has been subjected to, constant modifications and supplementation" (200) by others as well as by himself.

1443. Murphy, Andrew. "Gold Lace and a Frozen Snake: Donne, Wotton, and the Nine Years War." *ISRev* 8 (1994): 3–8.

Points out that "a surprising number" of important English writers in the early modern period showed an interest in Ireland, including Donne. Discusses *HWHiber,* in which Donne chastises Henry Wotton for failing to write to him while he has been in Ireland. Shows how the verse letter "sheds interesting light on English attitudes to Ireland at a crucial point in Anglo-Irish history" (3). Comments on how Donne's letter "exhibits a profound anxiety over the effect of the Irish experience on English national and cultural identities" (7).

1444. Pebworth, Ted-Larry. "Manuscript Transmission and the Selection of Copy-Text in Renaissance Coterie Poetry." *Text* 7: 243–61.

Using Donne's poetical canon as an example, argues that W. W. Greg's theory and practice in the selection and treatment of copy-text "does not work well (and indeed, in some cases is not even technically possible) in the case of works whose textual histories betray all three of the following features: an extensive and complicated manuscript transmission during the author's lifetime, a first publication after their author's death—sometimes long after—from copies of doubtful authority, and an absence of holographic copies" (244). Describes "the state of Donne's poetic texts," noting that "what is said about the transmission of his texts fits equally well—though on a smaller scale—the poetical texts of most of the other coterie poets at the turn of the seventeenth century" (245). Discusses, for instance, differences in accidentals in the 1633 first printing of *Carey* and Donne's holograph to show that "the poet follows older, freer conventions of capitalization, spelling, and punctuation, while the printer tends towards 'modernizing' all three" (249), thereby illustrating the problem of selecting the 1633 as copy-text, which most modern editors have done. Observes also that "of the twenty-one non-authorial seventeenth-century manuscript copies of Donne's verse letter known to survive, not a single one matches Donne's holograph in accidentals, and most do not even come close" (251). Suggests, therefore, that "in works where authorial accidentals are essentially unrecoverable, after detailed and careful study of all surviving artifacts, an editor should base his or her choice of copy-text on verbal authority insofar as it can be determined and forthrightly admit the lack of authority in the resulting edition's accidentals" (261).

1445. Pritchard, R. E. "Donne's Image and Dream." *JDJ* 13: 13–27.

Argues that *Image* is "a notably subtle and searching poem, exploiting and exceeding the conventional expectations, both formal and thematic, of late Elizabethan Petrarchist verse, reflecting a critical stage in Donne's career" (13). Explores the play of language, the elaborate structure and form, the "shifts and twists of meaning, [and] the sense of juggling illusions and balancing instabilities" that are "appropriate to Donne's theme of simultaneously existing alternative apprehensions of reality" (18). Points out also an "undercurrent of indecent innuendo" (20) and suggests that, "at some level, the poem deals with the relationship in Donne's psyche between his mother and his proposed wife" (23). Shows how Donne "exploited" Petrarchist sonneteering, "breaking down and remaking the sonnet form with all its cramping associations, undermining Petrarchist half-truths and posturing, and developing the ambiguities of language to explore and release fundamental anxieties." Discusses how the medal or image in the poem is "a complex figure of female authority and desire, comprehending the young woman, the mother, and the Queen, the supreme giver and denier." Maintains that ultimately Donne says that "[a]s the image is multiple, so is his self" and thus "dream-world and waking-world, formally interspliced, seem interchangeable in their unsatisfactoriness and unreality." Notes that "[a]t the heart of the poem is a sense of deep dissatisfaction, that seeks to appease deficiency by elaborating discourses of desire, whether idealistic, or obscene, or both, that nevertheless serve only to suggest the insufficiency of reality to satisfy need" (25).

1446. Rambuss, Richard. "Pleasure and Devotion: The Body of Jesus and Seventeenth-Century Religious Lyric," in *Queering the Renaissance,* ed. Jonathan Goldberg, 253–79. Durham, N.C.: Duke University Press.

Discusses the "homoerotic incendiariness" (271) of *HSBatter,* maintaining that "[e]xpressing sheer impatience with divine measures to date, Donne metaphorically aligns the extremity of his longing for redemption and spiritual satisfaction with the desire to be taken and ravished by God in what amounts to a kind of trinitarian gangbang" (272). Says in the poem that "we find Donne imagining and embracing a limited experience with his God in terms of a homosexual bondage and rape fantasy," noting that, "[f]ar from thinking himself a woman in this scenario, Donne remains aggressively priapic throughout" and "bawdily calls up the suggestion of anal penetration." Argues that "religious poetry of the seventeenth century—devoutly fixated on the incarnation of its deity as fully human and indicatively male—is fundamentally queer in ways recent criticism has refused to acknowledge or has obscured" (273).

1447. Revard, Stella P. "Christ and Apollo in the Seventeenth-Century Religious Lyric," in *New Perspectives on the Seventeenth-Century English Religious Lyric,* ed. John R. Roberts, 143–167. Columbia: University of Missouri Press.

Discusses how English religious poets of the seventeenth century allowed their classical education and knowledge of Continental neo-Latin poets to inform their sacred poems, focusing primarily on how they treat the figure of Apollo that was handed down to them by Neoplatonic and Christian humanist poets of the fifteenth and sixteenth centuries. Points out that poets from Donne through Milton and Crashaw had to confront the problem of how to treat the symbol of Apollo and that "[t]he different religious and, to a degree, political orientation of the poets involved—Anglican, Puritan, or Roman Catholic—dictated different solutions to the problem, principally because the figure of Apollo had become by the seventeenth century a potent symbol in the iconography of the Roman Catholic Church and was becoming also a potent political symbol for the Stuart monarchy." Discusses, therefore, how "[r]eactions to the Christianized and royalized Apollo intimately involved a poet's political and religious persuasion" (144). Observes that Donne associates Apollo with Christ and suppresses the presence of Apollo as a pagan sun god in his poetry. Points out that he seems "particularly inclined to the sun-son pun in poems that concern the Resurrection or Ascension" (151), such as *Corona*, *Res*, *Goodf*, and *Father*.

1448. Roberts, John R., ed. *New Perspectives on the Seventeenth-Century English Religious Lyric*. Columbia: University of Missouri Press. viii, 335p.

A collection of 11 original essays and one previously published essay on the seventeenth century English religious lyric. The following eight essays deal significantly with Donne and have been separately entered into this bibliography: Helen Wilcox, " 'Curious Frame': The Seventeenth-Century Religious Lyric as Genre" (9–27) (entry 1470); Michael Schoenfeldt, "The Poetry of Supplication: Toward a Cultural Poetics of the Religious Lyric" (75–104) (entry 1454); P. G. Stanwood, "Liturgy, Worship, and the Sons of Light" (105–23) (entry 1460); Judith Dundas, " 'All Things are Bigge with Jest': Wit as a Means of Grace" (124–42) (entry 1416); Stella P. Revard, "Christ and

Apollo in the Seventeenth-Century Religious Lyric" (143–67) (entry 1447); R. V. Young, Jr., "Donne, Herbert, and the Postmodern Muse" (168–87) (entry 1474); Louis L. Martz, "The Poetry of Meditation: Searching the Memory" (188–200) (entry 1442); and Anthony Low, " 'The Holy Ghost is Amorous in His Metaphors' " (201–21) (entry 1357). In the introduction (1–8), the editor comments on each of the essays to show how, taken together, they form a cohesive whole, noting that they address three major issues: Is the religious lyric a genre, or is it only a lyric poem on a religious subject? Is the term "religious" in "religious lyric" too narrowly applied? To what extent do these religious poems also participate in and reflect the social, political, and cultural contexts of the period in which they were composed? Concludes with a selective, though extensive, bibliography of modern studies of the seventeenth century religious lyric from 1952 to 1990 (269–321); notes on the contributors (323–27); and an index of works cited (329–35).

1449. Roe, John. "Italian Neoplatonism and the Poetry of Sidney, Shakespeare, Chapman, and Donne," in *Platonism and the English Imagination,* ed. Anna Baldwin and Sarah Hutton, 100–116. Cambridge: Cambridge University Press.

Examines the Neoplatonic features in the *Songs and Sonets,* especially in *ValMourn, Noct,* and *Under,* but maintains that Donne "makes his greatest and undoubtedly most challenging statement about the impact of the Neoplatonic on love poetry" (114) in *Ecst.* Analyzes the argument of the poem to show that its "erotic statement neither parodies Neoplatonism . . . nor does it end by submitting to its orthodoxy" but rather "celebrates the erotic as a valued element of the process." Concludes that "[b]ecause of his success in finding an authoritative role and position for the erotic in what is normally, in Neoplatonic philosophy, the exclusive preserve of the soul," Donne in *Ecst* is "the most original and adventurous of Elizabethan poetic thinkers to engage in the Platonic mode" (116). Contrasts Donne with Chapman and Shakespeare.

1450. Roebuck, Graham. "'A Valediction forbidding Mourning': Traditions and Problems of the Imagery." *JDJ* 13: 143–49.

One of three papers delivered at a colloquium on *ValMourn* at the ninth annual John Donne Society conference. Discusses the imagery of the poem. Believes that the movement of the poem may have been suggested by Giordano Bruno's *De Imaginvm, Signorvm, & Idearum compositione* (1591) in which, like Donne, Bruno "presents, as in his title, an ascending Platonic hierarchy of image to sign to idea" (147). Observes that in *ValMourn* "stanzas 1, 2, 3 present images ascending from body to heaven; stanzas 4 and 5 signs—of dull sublunary folk, and of those refined by love, while the rest of the poem moves into the realm of idea" (147). Concludes by discussing the mathematical complexity of the spiraling compass image or figure in the conclusion of the poem.

1451. Rollin, Roger B. "John Donne's *Holy Sonnets*—The Sequel: *Devotions Upon Emergent Occasions*." *JDJ* 13: 51–59.

Sees Donne's *Devotions* as "a kind of sequel to his miscellany of sacred sonnets" and, in a sense, "Dean Donne's valedictory to Sonneteer Donne" (51). Maintains that the central theme in the *Devotions* is "essentially the same as that of Donne's sonnets—the effects upon a susceptible Christian of what might be called 'spiritual malaise,'" a "psychological condition [that] has been clinically described in the annals

of modern as well as seventeenth-century medicine." Believes that "[g]oing largely untreated in Donne's *Holy Sonnets,* it is considerably ameliorated if not cured in his *Devotions*" (51). Holds that both works are "ultimately directed towards the psychical and spiritual health of readers" (51) and should be regarded as "autobiographical *fictions*" (52). Sees the *Holy Sonnets* as a case study of religious melancholy and "thus a negative lesson in holy living," whereas the *Devotions* presents "a positive lesson in holy dying, a typically Donnean innovation upon the tradition of *ars moriendi*" (53). Insists that both the *Holy Sonnets* and the *Devotions* "exemplify that the general thrust of seventeenth-century devotional literature is more public than private, that writers of devotional texts tend to perceive their works not so much as confessional as exemplary and hortatory, as vehicles for the diagnosis of spiritual malaise and as sources of remedies, as, in the end, acts of *caritas* more than of self-expression" (53). Shows how the *Devotions* is "the penultimate act of the divine comedy of John Donne, wherein are largely resolved most of the complications that lent such dramatic tension to its earlier acts, including the act we now think of as his *Holy Sonnets*" (57–58).

1452. Roth-Schwartz, Emma L. "John Donne's 'Nocturnall Upon S. Lucies Day': Punctuation and the Editor." *JDJ* 13: 81–99.

Observes that "[n]either analysis of the first editions nor collation of manuscripts will get us any closer to the punctuation that John Donne actually used" (82) and briefly surveys various, eclectic punctuation practices of modern editors in the light of this problem. Discusses the punctuation of significant twentieth century recensions of *Noct,* maintaining that such an examination "can show us something about the nature of the questions to be asked," will illustrate "the kinds of problems we face," will allow us to "outline the yet-to-be-undertaken empirical studies" that need to be done, and will let us survey "the work that has already been done to bridge the gulf between Donne's punctuation and our own" (83). Envisions "an eventual edition of Donne's poetry that bases its punctuation on a careful study of his habits insofar as we can know them" and on "those of editors during his lifetime," an edition "that eliminates egregious modernism" and that "subdues the urge to clarify meaning once and for all." Concludes that "try we must, against our natural inclinations, to refrain from meddling in what he [Donne] left unsaid and to attempt to transmit, even in an imperfect state, the *most* meanings, not just the clearest, that can be justified on empirical grounds" (93).

1453. Sanders, Andrew. "Andrewes and Donne," in *The Short Oxford History of English Literature,* 192–200. Oxford: Clarendon Press. Revised ed., 1996.

Contrasts both the content and style of the sermons of Donne and Lancelot Andrewes and comments on specific characteristics of Donne's sermons, such as "his delight in verbal and stylistic flourish," his use of "illustrative metaphors," and his focus on "sin, death, and judgment" (195). Comments on Donne's religious background and his rise in the Church of England but maintains that "[n]othing in Donne's intellectual and religious development can, however, be easily categorized" (196). Points out that "[m]ental conflict for Donne was dynamic," as evidenced in both his secular and religious poetry, and comments on the more salient characteristics of his poetry, especially his use of wit, his fascination with both "ancient learning" and

"new advances in science and geography" (197), the skepticism of his early erotic verse, and the "conversational casualness" (198) and dramatic immediacy of the poems. Believes that "[t]hroughout Donne's work, however, the real triumphs are those of Death and Resurrection" (199). Concludes that the "intertwining of humility with glory, of theatre with devotion, of the mortal body with its representation in art, of playfulness and seriousness, of rules and the bending of rules, are characteristic of the kind of international baroque art of which Donne's life and work form part" (200).

1454. Schoenfeldt, Michael C. "The Poetry of Supplication: Toward a Cultural Poetics of the Religious Lyric," in *New Perspectives on the Seventeenth-Century English Religious Lyric,* ed. John R. Roberts, 75–104. Columbia: University of Missouri Press.

Argues that seventeenth century English religious lyrics cannot be interpreted "in deliberate isolation from the social and cultural forces" that form their contexts. Illustrates "the genesis of the very assumptions that still hinder our full comprehension of the seventeenth-century religious lyric by attending to the social resonances of religious poems by Donne and Herbert, and by indicating that something significantly different is going on in the religious poems of Vaughan, Herrick, and Traherne" (75). Points out the social resonances in the religious poems of Donne and discusses how "the social circumstances of Renaissance England conspired with Donne's own dependent status and his verbal prowess to create an enormously rich language of devotion— a language that Herbert would use with even greater precision, but that would be progressively dulled in the course of the turbulent century" (80). Shows, in particular, how the religious lyric "absorbed and then rejected social conversation as a model for discourse with the divine" (102). Points out how Donne in the *Holy Sonnets* "approaches his God through strategies that are strikingly similar to those he employed toward his mortal patrons" (83) and stresses that in his religious poems Donne repeatedly turns "to social relationships as a vehicle for representing his relationship with the divine" (85). Maintains that Donne "developed a rhetoric of supplication that could record at once the sincere desire for submission and the lingering ambitions of the self," noting that "he learned how the acknowledgment of creatureliness and indebtedness could place claims on one's benefactor," and "he discovered the ingratiating force of fervent submission," lessons he learned from "Jack Donne, the antecedent self whose secular practices he purportedly abjured" (86).

1455. Shapiro, I. A. "It's No Allusion to Donne." *N&Q*, n.s. 41: 61–62.

Reply to Guy Butler, "John Donne—A New Contemporary Reference," *N&Q*, n.s. 39 (1992): 357–60 (entry 1208). Maintains that Butler is mistaken in attributing a reference to Donne in a passage he quotes from Robert Tofte's translation of *Dello Ammogliarisi Piacevole* (1594), entitled *Of Marriage and Wifing* (1599), and claims that Tofte "is merely quoting proverbs familiar long before Donne was born and long after he died." Further argues that "[t]he speculations built on this misinterpretation are unsustainable" and that "[m]isunderstanding of sources underlie all the hypotheses advanced" (61) by Butler.

1456. Shawcross, John T. "More Early Allusions to Donne and Herbert." *JDJ* 13: 113–23.

Notes 30 heretofore unrecorded seventeenth and eighteenth century allusions, brief notices, and/or references to Donne and Herbert. Points out that "[t]he significance of unearthing these growing numbers of citations is the refutation of that old chestnut that Donne was not read or appreciated after 1650 or so, until Samuel Taylor Coleridge and then a half century later Robert Browning discovered him" (113).

1457. Shelburne, Steven. "The Epistolary Ethos of Formal Satire." *TSLL* 36: 135–65.

Points out that, "[a]ccording to Horace, satire originated not in moral outrage, or in melancholy, or in the railings of a satyr figure, or in nihilism, but rather in fraternal amity" (135), and that he "locates its origins not in the mythic but rather in the recent Roman past, and explicitly in the circle of Laelius and Scipio," whose friendship "had been celebrated by Cicero in *Laelius De Amicitia*. Maintains that "later satirists are able to evoke this ethos [of friendship] through a prototypically Horatian and Ciceronian genre, the one that is conventionally associated with the idea of friendship—the familiar verse epistle. Argues that "[i]n the English Renaissance, the epistolary ethos is the natural complement of formal satire, with which it combines to fulfill the ancient prescription of epideictic as *laus et vituperatio*" (136). Discusses three, often overlapping ways that the "epistolary ethos [of friendship] may be introduced into formal satire": (1) in "the epistolary satire, where the satire itself takes the form of a letter to a friend," as seen in *HWKisses;* (2) in "a discussion within a satire of the tenets of friendship provoked by a dramatic confrontation with a former or putative friend," as seen in *Sat1* and *Sat4;* and (3) in a "defense of the satirist, for whom friendship of good men is . . . a guarantee of virtue" (145). Points out that "[a] more subtle but perhaps more pervasive use of Ciceronian ideals of amity involves their being implied in their violation" and notes that although often "the verse epistle, satire's countergenre, is not formally incorporated in the satire, it still has a sort of shadow presence that occasionally makes itself felt" (147), again as seen in *Sat1* and *Sat4*. Discusses how, for Donne, as for his contemporaries, Marston and Guilpin, "engagement in satire itself provokes an examination of Ciceronian ideals, just as the genre of formal satire calls up the countergenre of the verse epistle" (158). Concludes, therefore, that "[i]n their investigations of the efficacy of satire and in their attempts to defend the genre, Renaissance satirists return the epistolary ethos of Ciceronian amity to the central place it occupied, according to Horace, in the satire of the ancients" (158–59).

1458. Sorlien, Robert Parker. "Apostasy Reversed: Donne and Tobie Matthew." *JDJ* 13: 101–12.

Discusses the friendship between Donne and Tobie Matthew, showing how Matthew's conversion to Catholicism "complicated both his life and his relations with Donne, whose own shifting religious convictions contributed to the uneven course of their friendship" (101). Comments on the extant letters exchanged between the two that documents their early close friendship as well as their later strained relationship and presents a biographical sketch of Tobie Matthew, comparing and contrasting him to Donne.

1459. Sprigley, Michael. "Alchemical Regeneration: Paracelsus, Dorn and Donne." *Studies in Spirituality* (Netherlands) 4: 146–64.

Discusses "the relationship between the view of Paracelsus and his followers in the sixteenth century concerning the nature of Christ and alchemical regeneration," and points out that "from about the middle of the century Paracelsus was accused by opponents of being an Arian in rejecting the divinity of Christ." Maintains that "[t]his links Paracelsus with the Radical Reform movements of his time with which he shared the belief in the divinization of the human being," a belief "expressed by Paracelsus and his followers in terms of a universal alchemy operating both in mind and matter" and clearly expressed in the works of Gerhard Dorn, his distinguished sixteenth century disciple, especially in his *De Speculativa Philosophia* (1612). Points out that, "[l]ike Paracelsus, Dorn claims that the regeneration of the human being and of matter follow parallel stages" (164). Calls *Ecst,* a "deeply Paracelsian poem" (152), discusses how alchemical language and ideas "pervade" Donne's poem, and suggests that they are derived primarily from Dorn's work (158). Maintains that in *Ecst* Donne suggests "a parallel between the incarnation of lovers in their body in order to reveal the true nature of love, and the Christian incarnation by which the revelation of the nature of true love was made" and that this parallel "is in line with the deification motif in the thought of Paracelsus and Dorn" and "is consistent with Donne's own investigation into the heterodox ideas of the period before he finally became an Anglican minister." Maintains further that this view is "also in line with the unitarian view held by Paracelsus and others that Christ was the Son of God, fully human, and therefore imitable," and that, therefore, *Ecst* "proclaims that human love between a man and woman could also bring about their divinization, and lead to a species of salvation" (162).

1460. Stanwood, P. G. "Liturgy, Worship, and the Sons of Light," in *New Perspectives on the Seventeenth-Century English*

Religious Lyric, ed. John R. Roberts, 105–123. Columbia: University of Missouri Press.

Argues that, no matter what other influences shaped it, "liturgy defines religious lyric poetry, whether the poet's designs are obvious or implicit in the resulting work" (105), and shows how liturgy, taken in its broadest sense, suggests "shape, form, repetition, order, [and] the regulation of private feelings into normalized, public expression." Surveys briefly devotional poetry that explicitly manages form in a liturgical setting (for instance, the canonical hours) as well as that which contains an implicit form, in which the poet "does not deliberately set out to write in a liturgical form, yet in avoiding the form comes inevitably to have it" (106). Points out the liturgical aspects of the *Holy Sonnets* and that *Corona* performs "an interpretive ritual in a liturgical cycle" (112). Observes also that *Noct,* though in the *Songs and Sonets,* was "probably imagined to be a solemn hymn to suit the canonical office of nocturn" (113), and notes how *Goodf* "assumes a devotional attitude appropriate to the present memory of the Passion" (114).

1461. Streekstra, Nanne Frederik. *Afbeeldingsrelaties: Een taal-en letterkundig essay over Huygens' Donne-vertalingen.* Groningen: University of Groningen. xiv, 388p.

Published doctoral dissertation. Presents a linguistic-philological and literary study of Huygens's Dutch translations (1630 and 1633) of 19 of Donne's poems. Chapter 1 discusses the textual problems in deciding on a copy-text of Huygens's translations, choosing the *editio definitiva* of the *Koren-bloomen* (1672) and choosing as Donne texts Helen Gardner's edition (1965) for Huygens's first batch of translations, and the 1633 edition for the second batch. Chapter 2 pro-

vides "an all embracing critical evaluation of the secondary sources regarding the literary Donne-Huygens connection in general, together with a detailed survey of the various descriptive contributions over the years, particularly in relation to the stylistic and linguistic aspects of the translations" (384) and "offers an analytical overview of the evaluations of Huygens' Donne translations" (386). Chapter 3 presents a detailed comparative grammatical and stylistic analysis of Donne's and Huygens's translations of Tremelius's *Lamentations of Jeremy,* discusses Huygens's Donne translation in the light of his earlier work as a translator, and explores the linguistic difficulties in translating poetry from one language to another. Review: Ad Leerintveld in *TNTL* 112 (1996): 172–76.

1462. Strier, Richard. "Lyric Poetry from Donne to Philips," in *The Columbia History of British Poetry,* ed. Carl Woodring and James Shapiro, 229–53. New York: Columbia University Press.

Maintains that the "modern concept of the lyric, of the (relatively) short, primarily non-narrative poem, was invented in seventeenth-century England" (229), noting that Donne, Jonson, and Herbert are the most important lyricists of the earlier seventeenth century. Calls Donne "not a professional poet" but "a professional intellectual" and says his poetry was his way "to show his wit, his skill, his learning, his rhetorical command" (230). Insists, however, that although his poems were "self-display and self-advertisement," they were "also much more than that" and that "any account that does not attempt to suggest this 'more' is as misleading as an account that overly idealizes the poems and treats Donne as an 'author.'" Points out that "[t]he pressure of intellection—of a complex, skeptical, probing intelligence—is one of the most distinctive features of Donne's verse" and that it "penetrates the surface and is felt in the structure of even his lightest and slightest pieces." Discusses how Donne transformed the classical models of elegy and satire in his early poems, noting that "[f]rom the beginning of his poetic career, Donne was writing a kind of antipoetry" (231). Maintains that Donne's primary importance as a poet rests on the *Songs and Sonets* and explores the wide range of attitudes towards love in the collection. Discusses the *Holy Sonnets,* suggesting that "perhaps the choice of a form which he was not fully comfortable with unconsciously reflected a deeper discomfort" (235). Points out that, later on, Donne "turned from the holy sonnets to stanzaic religious lyrics, as he was able to recapture some of the spontaneity and range of his great love poems" but notes that "even these poems have difficulty maintaining their affirmative stance." Suggests that Donne's "lifelong self-scrutiny and self-fascination culminates in a brilliant, self-mocking refrain [in *Father*] about the difficulty of self-abandonment" (236). Compares and contrasts Donne with Jonson, Herbert, and Marvell and comments on the influence of Donne and Jonson on the cavalier poets. Concludes with a brief list of suggested further readings.

1463. Sullivan, Ernest W., II. "1633 Vndone." *Text* 7: 297–306.

Discusses the eclectic nature of the text of Grierson's edition of Donne's poetry, first published in 1912, and shows that the provenance of the first edition of 1633, which Grierson and others have used principally as a copy-text, is "ambiguous at best" and is "un-Donne in its contents, texts, and textual tradition." Points out the omissions in the 1633 edition, noting that "its 148 Donne poems are only 69 percent of the 216 to appear in the

Variorum Edition of the Poetry of John Donne" (301), and shows how "(t)he sexual, political, and theological censorship of *1633* suggests that Grierson may have misplaced his faith in the editor's freedom or willingness to show 'the side of Donne which his poetry reveals.'" Discusses how recent collations "of every artifact" of the *Anniversaries* and *Epicedes and Obsequies,* undertaken for the first volume of the variorum edition, show that, "even disregarding their scant provenance and the evidence of censorship, the texts of *1633* would make poor copy-texts" (303).

1464. Summers, Claude J. "Marlowe and Constructions of Renaissance Homosexuality." *CRCL* 21: 27–44.

Challenges the conclusions about homosexuality in early modern England in Alan Bray's *Homosexuality in the Renaissance* (London: Gay Men's Press, 1982) and questions the impact that Bray's conclusions "have had on the study of Renaissance literature" (27). Disagrees with Bray's notion that "there were no homosexuals (by whatever name) in Renaissance England, only individuals who committed sodomitical acts without ever recognizing themselves as sodomites" (28). Argues that "sodomitical discourse is not co-extensive with the discourse of homoeroticism in the period and that Bray's construction of Renaissance homosexuality as exclusively sodomitical is misleading, for it fails to accommodate the co-existing constructions of homosexuality in the period's poetic discourse" (30–31). Cites *Sappho* to illustrate "the insufficiency of Bray's construction" and shows that in the poem Donne "fails to represent lesbianism as sodomitical" and actually "rejects the sodomitical construction to figure lesbianism as a utopian trope." Points out that, "[a]s his satires and epigrams demonstrate, Donne was certainly capable of representing homosexuality as sodomitical" but observes that both *Sappho* and his early letters to T. W. indicate that "he did not invariably do so." Claims that "Donne's transcendence of his culture's official, morally and legally sanctioned, concept of homosexuality is paradigmatic of the way thoughtful individuals in the Renaissance could question the narrow range of meaning propagated by a society that was never as hegemonic as it aspired to be" (31).

1465. Vander Ploeg, Scott D. "Reflexive Self-Reference in Donne's 'The Triple Foole.'" *KPR* 9: 39–45.

Maintains that in *Triple,* as elsewhere in his poetry, Donne "shows a penchant for reflexive self-reference," and argues that the fictional poet that Donne creates in the poem "embodies a type of poetic stance that Donne deploys for ironic effect." Sees *Triple,* therefore, as an example of Donne's "awareness of the fact of his poetic activity," a poem that reflects "a more thoroughly metapoetic, self-referential awareness than is typically granted him" (40). Emphasizes that although his "own experience of the world contributes to the world he presents," Donne "creates personae as independent entities rather than representatives of some facts of his own personality." Maintains, in other words, that in his works "Donne should be granted the ability to intend differences from, as well as similarity to, his own personality." Shows how in *Triple* "the poet who created the poem is not in the condition of the speaking persona" (43). Insists that Donne is "first and foremost a creative artist" and that "his works deserve to be treated as 'creations'" and not used for "a biographical romp to prove his nasty recusancy or his rakish youth" (44). Concludes that Donne is "a wise poet"

and "not the fool" and that the persona in *Triple* is clearly not intended to reflect some aspect of Donne's "foolish personality," for "Donne was nobody's fool" (45).

1466. Von Koppenfels, Werner. "Discovering the Female Body: Erotic Exploration in Elizabethan Poetry," in *ShS,* ed. Stanley Wells, 127–37. Cambridge: Cambridge University Press.

Discusses how Marlowe's globe conceit in *Hero and Leander* "appears to have inspired a whole Elizabethan geography of desire by turning the discovery or uncovering of the desired female body into an adventurous journey of exploration, conquest, and Eldorado-like gratification." Comments on *ElBed* as a prime example of this kind of sexual wit. Points out that the voyeurism in Donne's poem is "of a refined kind" but that "in the final hymenic celebration of 'full nakedness', the wordplay on 'discovering' is ubiquitous" and "is repeated, and carried further, by means of a blasphemous pun on 'revelation' in the literal and physical sense of 'unveiling.'" Maintains that "worldly cynicism" is "the predominant mode" in *ElProg,* calling it "the most notorious of Donne's elegies" and an "eroticosatyricon," which "turns both the traditional downward progress and all its laudatory *blasons* upside down" (134–35). Notes that in it "there is no voyeuristic revelation" but that "the shock of cynical argument remains paramount" and that its conclusion is "positively anaphrodisiac in effect." Maintains that in Donne's poetry, "desire for, and loathing of, the female body can exist side by side," and that in some poems "the creed of mere carnality reaches almost the point of sexual disenchantment and disgust" (135).

1467. Watson, Robert N. *The Rest Is Silence: Death as Annihilation in the English*

Renaissance. Berkeley and Los Angeles: University of California Press. xiv, 416p.

Argues that "the fear of death as annihilation produced a crisis in English Renaissance culture, a crisis discernible in both Shakespearean drama, which criticizes and parodies traditional promises of immortality, and Metaphysical poetry, which experiments with new versions of those promises" (1). Maintains that "[t]hese plays and poems show deformations from the first impact of the disastrous collision between modern Western narcissism and modern Western skepticism" (11). Mentions Donne throughout, but devotes Chapter 5, "Duelling Death in the Lyrics of Love: John Donne's Poetics of Immortality" (156–252), entirely to him. Argues therein that "[m]any of Donne's trademark gestures—his conceited valedictory departures, his pursuit of an abstract mutuality with his beloved, his misogyny when that mutuality falters—can be productively read as displacements of his anxieties about his mortal body." Maintains that "[h]is egoism would have made him especially susceptible to the annihilationist fears of his culture" and claims that "his secular lyrics reveal a desperate and elaborate mythmaking in which erotic love compulsively undertakes the salvational work ordinarily performed by Christianity" (46). Discusses this "broadly consistent mythology Donne assembled in order to reassure himself that the embrace of his body and mind was unbreakable," explains from a psychological and existential viewpoint "what may have necessitated and shaped this mythology" (159), and sees "annihilationist anxiety at the psychological core of Donne's writings" (164). Maintains that, in later life, Donne replaced "his erotic fixation with a religious one" and "ceases to seek immortality from the mutual affirmations of seduction" as he "turns

instead to a merger with women's creative power." Believes that "Donne's vengefulness, directed in the misogynistic lyrics against the women whose failures of reciprocity mirrored his fallible mortality, turns against heretics and his own sinfulness in the sermons and the Holy Sonnets" (250). Chapter 6, "Word Without End: The Comforts of George Herbert's *Temple*" (253–304), contrasts the perspectives of Donne and Herbert concerning death and annihilation, noting that Herbert, in contrast to Donne, "seems ostentatiously unanxious about death, yet that very ostentation suggests an effort to answer an unspeakable terror—if not for himself, then for his troubled companions" (46). Points out that "[t]he cure for mortal isolation that Donne seeks through the physical penetration of his mistress and the intellectual penetration of his reader, Herbert achieves more chastely through an inward catechistic exchange with God, reproduced as dialogue with the responding reader," and that he "recasts the conventions of love-complaint into poems of spiritual frustration addressed to an elusive God" (256). Contrasts Herbert's "gynocentric eroticism" to Donne's "erotic *agon*" (261).

1468. West, William N. "Thinking with the Body: Sappho's 'Sappho to Philaenis,' Donne's 'Sappho to Philaenis.'" *RenP*: 67–84.

Maintains that a rhetorical analysis of *Sappho* "reveals not only a departure from Donne's usual diction in his suppression of metaphor and his use of only a single conceit" but also "a strong connection between this altered diction and the representation of gender." Holds that, in the poem, Donne "accepts the initial premises of his culture about gender and language" but that he "inverts the valorization so that the qualities associated with female speech come to seem more positive than the so-called 'masculine' ones." Discusses how Donne "tries to devise alternative strategies of speaking that will give Sappho a voice that is, in terms of Jacobean England, recognizably feminine without reducing her to silence or ineffectuality" (68). Argues that the poem "requires a double reading—once as Donne's poem and once as Sappho's" (74), and shows that, "[w]hile accepting and reinscribing the limitations placed on female language in his period, Donne manages to recover from the devalorized qualities of surface, body, and indistinction a utopian space for female community and equality." Maintains that "Donne's complex layering of levels of legibility valorizes female discourse and opens up a space in which such rigorously nonmetaphorical language can appear, but finally cannot do so without setting it into a metaphorically established frame that gives it a meaning and connects it to familiar masculine forms of knowledge." Concludes, however, that "Donne's position as a male should in no way force us to ignore or, more dangerously, to subordinate in a gesture of masculine hierarchizing, Sappho's voice to Donne's," noting that "[t]he silencing of homoerotic desire in this poem, if it occurs, occurs at the level of reading what's done as Donne instead of seeing the possibility of the reverse" (83).

1469. Whittington, Janice. "The Text of Donne's 'A Valediction forbidding Mourning.'" *JDJ* 13: 127–36.

One of three papers delivered at a colloquium on *ValMourn* at the ninth annual John Donne Society conference. Comments on the text of the poem based on 12 selected manuscripts and on 7 seventeenth century editions. Shows how "[e]ach artifact . . . offers its own variants, whether in spelling, grammar, word choice, structure, metrics, or a combination," and that "those variants alter the reading of the poem" (129). Maintains, therefore, "any sophisticated interpretation of the poem ought to demonstrate an awareness of the textual evidence" (130). Appendix 1 "shows how difficult choosing a copy-text can be when there are three families of textual transmissions"; Appendix 2 shows "the original artifacts of 020 [Dowden manuscript], TT1 [Dalhousie I manuscript], and H06 [O'Flahertie manuscript]; and Appendix 3 "identifies the families and the readings on the lines which help delineate the families" (127).

1470. Wilcox, Helen. " 'Curious Frame': The Seventeenth-Century Religious Lyric as Genre," in *New Perspectives on the Seventeenth-Century English Religious Lyric,* ed. John R. Roberts, 9–27. Columbia: University of Missouri Press.

Explores the issue of whether or not we mean anything more by the phrase "seventeenth-century religious lyric" than simply the devotional poems of a "loose compendium of poets, inclusion among whom is simply an accident of history" (10). Maintains that, although these poets did not all share the same theology or religious doctrines, they all did agree that the English language had the potential "to express, as much as any human system of expression could, the experience of the divine" (11). Explains how these religious poets had in common "a strong linguistic theology, an active interest in expressive poetic structures, and a commitment to the emblematic function of devotional verse," all of which may be seen as ways of dealing with, and gaining, *transcendence*" (18–19). Points out that "[l]anguage, form, and image in the poems are devices of human wit to discover spiritual perspectives, often through startling reworking of the familiar" (19), and that these poems have a sort of "creative disrupting and transcending of the normal patterns of time and space," as well as of "certain kinds of limitations inherent in the short poem" (20). Observes also that typically in the poems "the individual voice and text are themselves transcended in their effort to achieve a spiritual transcendence" (21). Discusses also how these poets were consciously attempting to reshape and convert secular poetry to sacred ends. Concludes that the religious lyric is, in fact, a genre "not so much by birth (for it was undoubtedly not newly created by these poets) but by *baptism*," that is, "the lyric was converted and born again, as it were, through the offices of this group of poets" (24). Comments on *Father* to show how, through a "precise linguistic sensitivity, the majestic simplicity of the redemption is conveyed" (13), and discusses the "serious game-playing" (18) with images in *Cross*.

1471. Wilcox, Helen. "Squaring the Circle: Metaphors of the Divine in the Work of Donne and His Contemporaries." *JDJ* 13: 61–79.

Discusses "the metaphorical language employed by Donne and his contemporaries in their attempts to describe, converse with, or attend upon God" (61). Points out that "no language can exist which is able fully to match or express God" and therefore "description or evocation of the divine must proceed by the use of likeness or connection," which is "the essence of metaphor," and "would suggest that metaphor is a sheer necessity for religious understanding" (63–64). Surveys Donne's idea of metaphor and the sources of his metaphors—primarily the Bible, especially the Psalms and the Songs of Songs, and mathematics—and discusses how Donne uses

metaphors "as ways of defining the divine, knowing and being known, and understanding the mysteries of faith" as well as "to open up a discussion or argument" (71). Comments also on the limits of metaphoric language, noting that "metaphors for the divine have only a limited function— they are for other human readers, and not for God (their focus) at all" (77). Concludes that "the relationship of the gendered individual to metaphor, and the relationship of individuality to linguistic creation" (78) need to be further explored.

1472. Williams, Gordon. *A Dictionary of Sexual Language and Imagery in Shakespearean and Stuart Literature.* 3 vols. London and Atlantic Highlands, N.J.: Athlone Press. xvii, 569; 571–1122; 1123–1616p.

Cites examples from Donne's poetry to illustrate the use of sexual language and imagery in the sixteenth and seventeenth centuries. See, for instance, *agricultural imagery, Aretino, brothel, country, dildo, effeminate, life shortened by coitus, rot, succuba,* and *usury.*

1473. Yamawaki, Yuriko. *Keijijo-shijin John Donne—Renaissance ni Ikita Gendaijin* [John Donne: A Metaphysical Poet—A Modern Man Living in the Renaissance]. Tokyo: Kindaibungei-sha. 197p.

Consists of two parts: a survey of Donne's earlier life and works entitled "The Progress of the Soul," and a survey of his later life and works entitled "Meditation on Life and Death." Attempts to re-create the interior life of Donne through a critical examination and analysis of his poetry and prose, with an emphasis on his inner conflicts. Sees the development of Donne's inner life as relevant to the experience of modern man. Relies heavily on biographical sketches by Izaak Walton, E. M. Simpson, Hugh

Faussett, Herbert Grierson, J. B. Leishman, and Pierre Legouis.

1474. Young, R. V., Jr. "Donne, Herbert, and the Postmodern Muse," in *New Perspectives on the Seventeenth-Century English Religious Lyric,* ed. John R. Roberts, 168–187. Columbia: University of Missouri Press.

Argues that the devotional poetry of Donne (as well as the other metaphysical poets) continues to fascinate modern critics precisely because "it addresses essentially the same issue that holds a central place among the deliberations of contemporary literary theory: the capacity of the speaking self to define its identity in meaningful utterance and the relationship between the words of its discourse and an absolute source of significance." Believes that the devotional poet and the deconstructionist are alike "in deploring the secular humanist's illusion of self-sufficiency" and thus sees "the confrontation between seventeenth-century poetry and contemporary literary theory" as "an academic version of the conflict of faith and unbelief." Thus believes that "its outcome has more than academic interest" (187). Comments on how Donne "becomes, as a result of his peculiar circumstances, a paradigm case of the alienation endemic to the period of the Protestant and Catholic Reformations," a man who "expresses an especially acute experience of the age's general sense of lost spirituality" (171), observable especially in the *Holy Sonnets, Corona,* and *Christ.* Maintains that Donne is "as aware as any deconstructionist that his own personal presence is insufficient to guarantee the significance of his signifiers" (173). Discusses how Donne "stands on the brink of the abyss between the analogical realm of Catholic Christianity and the deconstructed world of contemporary literary theory" (177).

1995

1475. Amelinckx, Frans. "L'apport de John Donne à l'oeuvre de Suzanne Lilar," in *La Belgique telle qu'elle s'ecrit: Perspectives sur les lettres belges de langue française,* ed. Renée Linkhorn, 259–69. Belgian Francophone Library, vol. 4, gen. ed. Donald Flanell Friedman. New York: Peter Lang.

Discusses Suzanne Lilar's personal affinity to Donne and her references to his poetry in her writings. Points out especially her appreciation of Donne's attitude on love, both profane and sacred; on his mystical quest for unity; and on his complex attitude toward the human body.

1476. Anon. "John Donne," in *The Metaphysical Poets: With an Introduction and Bibliography,* 9–43. Wordsworth Poetry Library. Ware: Wordsworth.

Reproduces 3 *Elegies, Calm,* 20 poems from the *Songs and Sonnets,* 9 of the *Holy Sonnets,* and 4 hymns, without notes or commentary. Includes a one-paragraph biographical sketch of Donne (119–20), noting that "he is widely regarded as the greatest of the metaphysical poets" (120).

1477. Barnaby, Andrew. "Affecting the Metaphysics: Marvell's 'Definition of Love' and the Seventeenth-Century Trial of Experience." *Genre* 28: 483–512.

Maintains that the "Baroque fascination with the possibilities and limits of knowing haunts Donne's great love lyrics," citing in particular *Ecst* as an example. Says that the poem is "both an attempt to assign a specific meaning to love and a retrospective description of the experimental procedure designed to achieve that meaning." Holds that the poem recounts "the procedure whereby a privately held notion is tested against the physical reality from which it claims to derive" and that "the poem's narrative stands finally as the experimental report which others must verify in terms of their own experience" (499). Maintains that Donne's love poems, as well as metaphysical poetry in general, "may be considered as just one among a number of generic forms marking a transitional moment in a vast project of cultural transformation," noting that, "[i]n the constant attention they give to their own epistemological conditions, these forms are determined to address their topics not only by dissecting their component parts but also by rendering an intelligible account of the representational practices being employed in that dissection." Compares *Ecst* to Marvell's "The Definition of Love" to show that both poems examine love "as an intellectual question, a problem of knowledge, rather than as one of affectionate, playful entertainment (Dryden) or of moral sentiment (Johnson)" (500).

1478. Bauer, Matthias. "Paronomasia celata in Donne's 'A Valediction: forbidding mourning.'" *ELR* 25: 97–111.

Discusses how the language of *ValMourn,* "by means of paronomasia, reflects and realizes its theme of unity-in-separation" (97). Points out that in the poem there are "certain common sounds or letters which reveal the connection between two seemingly dis-parate words" and that "[a] similar correspondence exists between theme and imagery." Shows how parono-masia "serves to connect the very dif-ferent and seemingly unrelated images of the poem by bringing together dif-ferent but similar-sounding words" and claims that this rhetorical device "illuminates its own function as well as the subject of the poem" or, in other words, it "substantiates on the level of *verba* what is put forward by the conceit on the level of poetic *res*" (98). Points out the use of concealed paro-nomasia and homonymic wordplay in Donne's title and discusses how these devices also connect the images of the poem. Maintains, therefore, that the theme of the poem, "the spiritualiza-tion of love," is "verbally linked to the religious sphere . . . by a carefully designed pattern of Latin references" (104), homonyms, and concealed paro-nomasia. Suggests a possible secret allusion to Ann More in the compass image of the poem.

1479. Bawcutt, N. W., and Hilton Kelliher. "Donne through Contemporary Eyes: New Light on His Participation in the Convocation of 1626." *N&Q,* n.s. 42: 441–44.

Discusses new evidence that sheds ambiguous new light on Donne's par-ticipation in the Convocation at Westminster Abbey on 8 February 1626, where he gave an oration in Latin to mark his assumption of the office of Prolocutor: (1) the Latin text of Dr. Leonard Mawe's laudatory introduction to Donne and (2) a let-ter that records the reaction to Donne, Mawe, and a third speaker, Dr. Samuel Harsnett, by a contemporary eyewit-ness, probably John Scudamore. Believes that the praise of Donne by Mawe and Harsnett, though extrava-gant, "demonstrates the status and rep-utation he had achieved at this state

in his career" and suggests that the letter shows that, although the writer evidently admired Donne, he found the compliments paid him by the speakers excessive and "was repelled by the fulsome and obsequious flattery of the bishops" (444).

1480. Belsey, Catherine. "Worlds of Desire in Donne's Lyric Poetry," in *John Donne and Modernity,* ed. Armand Himy and Margaret Llasera, 83–102. Confluences XI, Centre de Recherches sur les Origines de la Modernité et les Pays Anglophones. Nanterre: Université Paris X.

Discusses in Donne's love poems "the imperatives of empire characteristic of the energetic and optimistic begin-nings of English expansionism" (84), observing that frequently in them "the process of erotic discovery" involves "both a sexual and social mastery." Explores the kind of love that "per-sistently finds a meaning for itself in images of discovery and mapping, cosmography and conquest," and examines "the nature of the worlds of desire which appear so frequently in these love poems of the early modern period." Discusses the politics of desire inscribed in these texts, "which in-cludes but also exceeds the difference of gender," and, arguing that desire "has a political history," discusses how "Donne's poems in particular belong on the threshold of its modernity" (86). Discusses in *ElBed, SunRis,* and *GoodM* "the uncertainty of the lover, registered above all in the indetermi-nacies of the texts," and how "[t]he object of desire is unsure" and "ambig-uous" and "its realisation in the subject is indefinite, to the degree that the transcendent union lovers seek is in-compatible with sexual satisfaction." Maintains, therefore, that it is "[n]o wonder the worlds which were grad-ually opening up to the gaze of Renais-sance explorers and cartographers seemed the appropriate emblem of desire," since these territories seemed "vast," "perhaps limitless," "enticing, rich and beautiful," and also "dangerous, to the degree that they were uncharted both geographically and anthropologically." Concludes that "[d]esire in Donne's love poetry is a world that remains to some degree unknown and that elicits a corresponding anxiety in the subject of the enunciation" (100). Maintains, however, that, "paradoxically, this is the historical moment at which desire becomes the basis of a lifetime of concord," when "the modern nuclear family is increasingly defined . . . as the centre of society, the place where social values are learned and reproduced." Observes that "the privileged, intimate world" of *SunRis* and *GoodM* is "in the process of becoming the foundation of conjugal partnership, where love and consent ensure the harmony of the family and the proper inculcations of consensual assumptions, beliefs, meanings" (101).

1481. Berman, Antoine. *Pour un critique des traductions: John Donne.* Paris: Gallimard. 274p. Introduction was first published as "Critique des traductions John Donne" by Michel Deguy in *Poésie* 59 (1993): 3–20 (entry 1289); and excerpts appeared in " 'Le Defi du prosaique': Une critique des traductions françaises de John Donne," in *Traductions, passages: Le Domaine anglais,* ed. Stephen Romer. Tours: Université de Tours (1993), 25–35 (entry 1290).

In the "Note de l'éditeur" the author's widow, Isabelle Berman, indicates that her editorial changes in her husband's manuscript have been minor, mostly checking quotations for accuracy, filling in blanks, reordering some sections, and correcting the table of contents. The "Introduction" (11–31) presents a summary of the book, outlining its contents, methodology, and purpose. Part 1, "Le projet d'une critique «productive»" (33–98), explains Berman's method of analyzing translations, which he calls "productive" criticism, and evaluates various theories of translation. Part 2, "John Donne, traductions et retraduction" (99–228), applies his theory outlined above to translations of Donne's poetry, evaluating in detail the work of four translators, focusing primarily on their translations of *ElBed*: Auguste Morel (1924), Yves Denis (1962), Philippe de Rothschild (1983), and Octavio Paz (1971). Berman dislikes Denis's and Rothschild's translations, calling the first a disaster and berating it for attempting to translate Donne into archaic French and viewing the second as a flawed, unsuccessful, even childish production, which, nonetheless, has a quality of enthusiasm about it. Approves of Morel's almost unknown translation, calling it unaffected and somewhat successful in its attempts at archaism, and thinks that Paz's free translation (or what Paz calls his "adaptation") is also reasonably successful and has the force of Donne's original. Considers *ElBed* a unique and beautiful poem and a prime example of Donne's metaphysical poetry. Notes that Donne's poetry as a whole is generally unavailable in France and argues that the translations by Yves Bonnefoy (1990) (entry 1021) and Robert Ellrodt (1993) (entry 1308) are among the best in French. Discusses more briefly in this section also the Fuzier and Denis translation of *Sappho* (143–48) to illustrate the weakness of their approach to translating Donne. Part 3, "De la réception de la traduction Denis et Fuzier en 1962" (229–54), analyzes the critical reception of the Fuzier and Denis translation, especially the reviews of Jean Grosjean and Pierre Legouis, discussing the "mirages" that blinded them in their evaluations and discusses the critical atmosphere of the 1960s both in poetry and criticism that shaped the reviewers. Concludes with a bibliography (259–68) and an index (269–74). Reviews: Martine Broda in *Critique* 51 (1995): 758–66; Claude Mouchard in *QL* 666 (1995): 6–7; Lieven D'hulst in *RHL* 96 (1996): 348–49; Peter France in *Tr&Lit* 5 (1996): 114–16.; Sabine Prokhoris in *Esprit,* n.s. 223 (1996): 207–11; Jacky Martin in *CahiersE* 51 (1997): 93–99.

1482. Blair, David. "Inferring Gender in Donne's *Songs and Sonets.*" *EIC* 45: 230–49.

Shows how the gender of the speakers in *Break* and *ConfL* is established through a "process of disguise followed by disclosure," maintaining that until a "point of self-clarification" is reached at the end of the second stanza in each, they "might, as it were, 'go either way'." Believes, in fact, that in the case of *ConfL* it is not clear "which way the poem does in the end 'go'" (239). Maintains that these poems are "not unique among the *Songs and Sonets* in deferring thus the disclosure of gender-specificity" and cites *Commun, Under, SunRis, Ecst, Blos, LovAlch,* and *Leg* as examples of poems in which "a presumption of maleness inhibits us from recognising the degree to which any or all of those poems might be heard to participate in the kind of ambivalence and self-disclosure" more readily recognized in *Break* and *ConfL.* Notes also that several poems "give no formal indication of the gender of the speaker and thus do not explicitly self-clarify at all" (240). Warns, therefore, that "we should be cautious in presuming Donne to be constructing male personae except where the text explicitly specifies otherwise" (240–41). Observes that in such a poem as *ValWeep* "there is a complete collapse of differentiated behaviours into a mutuality which generates androgyny" (241). Maintains that "[t]o the extent that the poem specifically withdraws from or blurs any systematic differentiation of sexual roles it correspondingly accommodates the question of whether it is the male voice or the female which conducts the poem" (242). Discusses the androgyny or possible bisexuality in *ValMourn* and comments on how *WomCon* "collapses apparent sexual difference and orthodox sexual politics" (247) and possibly embraces "ironies dependent on sexual ambivalence rather than those more brutal ones nurtured in the relentlessly masculinist culture on which Donne tends, though not invariably, to rely" (248).

1483. Blank, Paula. "Comparing Sappho to Philaenis: John Donne's 'Homopoetics.'" *PMLA* 110: 358–68.

Challenges "the idea that homosexual desire has its source in sexual 'sameness,' in an identity with another," and discusses how *Sappho* "participates in a common Renaissance discourse of likeness in love," observing that Donne's Sappho "appeals to physical identity—the 'sameness' of the bodies of the two women—as the basis of an idealized passion." Maintains, however, that in Donne's poem "difference emerges as the only inviolable, invariable feature of erotic experience with another" and that "sameness is exposed as rhetorical rather than material, a contingency produced by Donne's comparative method." Argues that "[b]y comparing Sappho to Philaenis, Donne's poem suggests that sameness has to do not with the 'nature' of homosexuality but with a cultural 'homopoetics' that makes such likenesses and produces sexual identities" (abstract, 520).

1484. Brooks, Helen B. "Donne's 'Goodfriday, 1613. Riding Westward' and Augustine's Psychology of Time," in

John Donne's Religious Imagination: Essays in Honor of John T. Shawcross, ed. Raymond-Jean Frontain and Frances M. Malpezzi, 284–305. Conway, Ark.: UCA Press.

Examines "the internal cohesion" of *Goodf,* arguing that "Augustine's conception of time and its relation to the faculties of the human soul provide an illuminating framework for the way the poem—and the speaker—achieves its true meditative aim: the coalescence of the soul's faculties with its true object of desire: the timeless image of God." Points out "striking parallels . . . between the poem's unifying element—its attempt to evoke an enduring image upon which the mind can focus itself—and the psychology of time Augustine develops in the concluding chapters of the *Confessions* and employs in the structuring of the book itself." Observes that "[b]oth Augustine and Donne held to a Christocentric theology in which redemption depends on renewal of the defaced, salvific image of God within" and that both view human existence as "a life-long struggle to free oneself from the ravages of time, that is, from the transitory, worldly distractions that repeatedly fail to satisfy the soul's unmitigated longing for union with God." Shows how *Goodf* "articulates that ongoing struggle" (286). Maintains that, for Augustine, "the primary task before humans is to arrest the passing into non-existence of that which occupies the soul's attention, namely, the *imago Dei* in Whose likeness the soul is created, but which has been obscured through the soul's transitory preoccupations," and that Donne's poem "verbalizes such an experience." Discusses how "the unity of the speaker's meditative experience derives from an act of *distentio* in which the soul's attention, though looking to both the 'past' (the historical Crucifixion) and the 'future' (the

salvation of the soul), is all the while fixed on the timeless significance of the historical Crucifixion as it recurs in time, and here specifically on Good Friday, 1613" (290). Concludes that Donne's poem "succeeds not only in capturing the redemptive experience of the soul's meditation on the Passion of Christ, but also in evoking in the reader a corresponding modality of mind as the requisite human matrix in which this timeless image repeatedly comes to life" (300).

1485. Brown, Meg Lota. *John Donne and the Politics of Conscience in Early Modern England.* Studies in the History of Christian Thought, ed. Heiko A. Oberman et al., 61. Leiden: E. J. Brill. 159p.

Part of Chapter 4 appeared as " 'In that world's contracted thus': Casuistical Politics in Donne's 'The Sunne Rising,' " in *"The Muses Commonweale: Poetry and Politics in the Seventeenth Cenbtury,* ed. Claude J. Summers and Ted-Larry Pebworth (Columbia: University of Missouri Press, 1988), 23–33 (entry 868); part of Chapter 2 appeared in *Ren&R,* n.s. 15 (1991): 101–14 (entry 1136); parts of Chapter 3 appeared as " 'Though it be not according to the law': Donne's Politics and the Sermon on Esther," *JDJ* 11 (1992): 71–84 (entry 1206), and as "Interpretive Authority in Donne's *Biathanatos,*" in *Praise Disjointed: Changing Patterns of Salvation in Seventeenth-Century English Literature,* ed. William P. Shaw (New York: Peter Lang, 1991), 151–63 (entry 1136).

Examines "the responses of Donne and his culture to post-Reformation debate about authority and interpretation" and argues that "the legal and epistemological principles, as well as the narrative practices, of casuistry provided an important resource for those caught in the welter of conflicting laws and religions." Focuses on Donne's poetry and prose but also looks at "the culture encoded in those works—at the historical, theological, and political discourses in which Donne's view of authority and interpretation took shape." Draws upon "the hermeneutics of casuistry in both Protestant and Catholic polemics" and "locates Donne in contemporaneous debate about the limits of knowledge and the cultural construction of authority" (1). Argues that "casuistry acknowledges the pressure of epistemological anxiety and the indeterminacy of language—that it recognizes, as does Donne throughout his works, that language and law are ambiguous, moot, unstable" and yet, at the same time, "enables one, however precariously, to impose form on uncertainty, to justify action on the basis of probability and circumstantiality, to reason towards practical responses to the conflicting claims of absolutist authorities" (2). Shows "the ways in which Donne invokes the principles and methods of practical theology" in order "to augment our understanding of the intellectual and emotional conflicts that inform his works, as well as our appreciation of the playfulness, tension, and vitality of his writing" (3). In Chapter 1, "Introduction: 'Nothing without perplexities'" (1–34), and Chapter 2, "The Politics of Conscience: Contexts and Controversies" (35–65), examines "the epistemological and historical contexts of Donne's casuistry, particularly the Renaissance controversy about valid criteria for judgment"; explains "the importance of casuistry for Donne and his contemporaries as a method of treating uncertainty and justifying action"; and looks at "specific controversies, political and religious, that precipitated the pressing need for, and the enormous popularity of, practical theology." Chapter 3, "Case Divinity and the Argument of Donne's Prose" (66–98), focuses on "problems of moral decision and action, problems of knowledge and definition in the secular context of the *Paradoxes and Problems* and the theological context of the *Essays in Divinity,* and discusses in some detail "these problems in three casuistical texts: *Biathanatos, Pseudo-Martyr,* and the sermon on *Esther 4.16.*" In Chapter 4, "'In that the world's contracted thus': Casuistry and Beyond in the *Songs and Sonets*" (99–138), explores how Donne's love poems "assimilate and wittily subvert practical theology's response to epistemological and linguistic uncertainty"; examines "the casuistical dilemmas that confront Donne's personae"; and discusses how Donne "playfully burlesques the methods of casuistry when addressing those dilemmas" (7). Illustrates these observations by commenting on *Twick, ValBook,* and *Anniv* and, in even more detail, on *ValMourn, Canon,* and *SunRis.* Chapter 5, "Conclusion" (139–43), summarizes the main thesis of the book and suggests other subjects that merit further scholarly investigation. Concludes with a selected bibliography (144–53), an index of names and places (154–57), and an index of subjects (158–59). Reviews: Ceri Sullivan in *N&Q,* n.s. 42 (1995): 495–96; Daniel W. Doerksen in *SCJ* 27 (1996): 804–5; E. M. Knottenbelt in *Heythrop Journal* 37 (1996): 232–34; Jeanne Shami in *JDJ* 15 (1996): 213–17; William B. Robinson in *Journal of Church and State* 39 (1997): 806–7; Annabel Patterson in *RenQ* 51 (1998): 1388–89.

1486. Burke, Victoria. "John Donne and the True Church." *English Review* 5: 32–35. Explicates *HSShow* to show how it reflects Donne's "confusion about the possibility of achieving Christ's true Church on earth" (34).

1487. Cain, Tom. "Donne and the Prince D'Amour." *JDJ* 14: 83–112.

Appears in a special issue of the *JDJ* on new uses of biographical and historical evidence in Donne studies, edited by Dennis Flynn. Supports those who challenge the notion that Donne was a high-church monarchist and "tries to add something to our understanding of his political values by examining his relationship with one of the leading figures in the Donne coterie, the lawyer, MP, and wit Richard Martyn" (84), an avowed opponent of absolutist policies and the abuse of the royal prerogative. Maintains that "while Donne's private views cannot simply be equated with those of his friends, it is most unlikely that he was markedly out of step, before or after his ordination, with men who were and remained close to him, and who were so much involved in the genesis of his work" (84–85). Shows that a number of men in Donne's coterie, but especially Martyn, were "strong opponents of absolutism not just in the 1590's, when biographers have conventionally allowed Donne to be critical of the establishment, but up to and beyond his ordination in 1615" (95).

1488. Coakley, Sarah. " 'Batter my heart . . .'? On Sexuality, Spirituality, and the Christian Doctrine of the Trinity." *GrIm* 2: 74–83.

Argues that *HSBatter* "acknowledges more explicitly than any textbook on Christian doctrine . . . the intrinsic, if initially puzzling, connections between sexuality, spirituality, and the Christian doctrine of the Trinity" and discusses "its implications for contemporary and especially feminist theology" (74). Maintains that Donne's genius "lay in his perception that within the Christian provenance, trinitarianism both reflects and permeates our most basic preoccupations—with sex, power, pain, death, and political arrangements," and observes that,

influenced by Augustinianism, "he perceived his own ensnarement to sin, his own tragic sense of disjunction between human and divine loves, as capable of resolution only by divine, invasive intervention" (75). Maintains that in both his love poetry and the *Holy Sonnets* Donne seeks an "integrated understanding of sexual and divine loves," noting that "[h]is early erotic poetry and his *Holy Sonnets* invite collocation," since "divine and human loves feature in both" (82).

1489. Correll, Barbara. "Symbolic Economies and Zero-Sum Erotics: Donne's 'Sappho to Philaenis.' " *ELH* 62: 487–507.

Presents a reading of *Sappho* "to suggest a link between the crisis of signification Donne presents in his 'lesbian' poem and the masculinist crisis that structures his heteroerotic poems," and to address "the limits of some feminist criticism of Donne that reads his masculinism more conspiratorially and less than problematically" (489). Argues that "the poem is both utterly characteristic and thus continuous with the other *Elegies*; a different way of addressing the kind of failure that marks the success of the heteroerotic poems." Maintains that "[t]he failure that Donne sees paralyzing women's same-sex love and undermining signification" in *Sappho* is also "the failure of difference that haunts other poetic works in the Donne canon, for it is one in which the poetic speaker's most dedicated, even frantic gestures of overcoming loss—turning a profit on loss—point toward the failure to overcome" (490). Places the elegy "in the context of Donne's poetic *oeuvre* and in a symbolization process that encompasses a historically and economically embedded cultural masculine crisis" (490–91). Discusses how Donne "reduces the fertility of a cultural female voice to stagnant futility" (494) and how the poem "offers the male poet transvestite voyeuristic pleasures of dislocation without threatening masculine poetic authority." Shows how the elegy is "a failed poem, or a *tour de force* poem that brilliantly and innovatively performs failure," or, in other words, "zero-sum erotics" (497).

1490. Creswell, Catherine J. "Giving a Face to an Author: Reading Donne's Portraits and the 1635 Edition." *TSLL* 37: 1–15.

Discusses how the Marshall engraving that appears in the 1635 edition of Donne's poems functions as an emblem, which Walton in his epigraph interpreted as illustrating how Donne was converted from being a rake to being the dean of St. Paul's. Argues, however, that Walton's interpretation "rests on a mistranslation [of the motto]" that surrounds the portrait and on "a misapprehension of Donne's meditation upon emblems, portraiture, and reading" (3). Maintains that, "[r]ather than suggesting a unifying narrative or even a lively image of the author, the portrait perhaps most clearly evokes Donne's fascination with the interdependent yet conflicted relation between visual images and texts" (4). Argues that, rather than revealing Donne, "the emblem-portrait foregrounds not the portrayed subject but the very procedures of portraiture, its own and its subject's constructed, fictive nature" (11). Maintains that the subject of the engraving, as well as the subject of the Lothian portrait, "is reading—not as perception but as an act of figuration." Holds that "[r]eaders of these portraits, thus, will not uncover the true Donne but only perform the painting's trope of prosopopoeia." Concludes that "[t]o read Donne's self-portraiture—whether his emblem paintings or dramatic self-meditations—is to uncover not a face but a rhetorical figure" (12).

1491. Creswell, Catherine J. "Turning to See the Sound: Reading the Face of God in

Donne's *Holy Sonnets*," in *John Donne's Religious Imagination: Essays in Honor of John T. Shawcross,* ed. Raymond-Jean Frontain and Frances M. Malpezzi, 181–201. Conway, Ark.: UCA Press.

Maintains that the *Holy Sonnets* reflect "an iconoclastic skepticism about the truth of images" and "a movement away from vision." Points out that "Donne's rejection of truth as vision, like his rejection of individual revelation, is an insistence upon interpretation over immanent seeing, often thematized as a move toward 'hearing' the Word or turning to the 'voyce.'" Claims that "[t]his emphasis upon 'hearing' suggests Donne's rejection of the possibility of any direct phenomenal access to truth and marks his turn to the more problematic task of reading." Insists that "[i]n their contemplation of the Word Incarnate, the *Holy Sonnets* reflect . . . mistrust of the iconic image," and that "the figure of Christ within these sonnets remains resolutely verbal and opaque." Maintains that "the truth or efficacy of the figure within the *Holy Sonnets* lies not in its appearance . . . but in its interpretation" and that "the iconoclastic or material figure resists interpretation as mere perception, as mere 'seeing' or 'unveiling.'" Discusses how "[t]his skepticism about the truth of figures stems from Donne's reconceptualization of the Word and the status of praise," concluding that "[t]he ultimate confrontation with God, as Donne characterizes it, is movement away from vision" (184). Presents a detailed reading of *HSBatter* to show how the speaker "moves from the figures of praise to the figures of address and in doing so redefines the project of the sonnet and the very status of the subject" (187–88) and to show how his "demand to be literally battered is the demand for the destruction of false icons" (193–94). Concludes that the "revision of the poetics of praise" in the *Holy Sonnets* "functions as an ethical critique" (195) and "is the call for a revelation that would turn from seeing as knowing, for a praise that would gesture to a space beyond its own tropic light" (196).

1492. DiPasquale, Theresa M. "Receiving a Sexual Sacrament: 'The Flea' as Profane Eucharist," in *John Donne's Religious Imagination: Essays in Honor of John T. Shawcross,* ed. Raymond-Jean Frontain and Frances M. Malpezzi, 81–95. Con-way, AR: UCA Press.

Argues that *Flea* "functions simultaneously on each of several mutually contradictory levels" and maintains that "by inscribing the speaker's argument in eucharistically charged language, Donne has insured that his signs and verbal gestures will be as polyvalent and as open to debate as the signs and gestures of the sacrament." Believes that the poem "may be read as a Petrarchan tribute, a libertine entrapment, or a true lover's persuasion" (82), although "the outcome of the seduction is—as any undergraduate will tell you—'left up to the reader.'" Explores "two different ways of reading the seduction as successful," each of which "depends upon a different reading of the images and arguments presented to the lady who is the 'reader' within the text"—the first being "an anti-Petrarchan, libertine reading, based upon the principles of radical iconoclasm," and the second being "a response rooted in an Anglican semiotic, which finds in the speaker's signs and gestures an invitation to genuine erotic communion." Argues further that "this second way of reading the poem helps to explain some intriguing parallels between the woman in the lyric and Ann More Donne as her witty husband constructs her in a letter" (83) to his father-in-law, George More.

1493. Docherty, Thomas. "Donne: The Body Without Organs, the Mechanics of Love and Truth," in *John Donne and Modernity,* ed. Armand Himy and Margaret Llasera, 51–61. Confluences XI, Centre de Recherches sur les Origines de la Modernité et les Pays Anglophones. Nanterre: Université Paris X.

Argues that Donne is "a fine example not only of an incipient modernity, but also of a postmodern within that modernity" (51–52), and attempts to show that "Donne's engagement with the fundamental reassessments of space and time that are constitutive of the modern break is conditioned by an attitude which uncannily prefigures the notion of the 'body without organs.'" Reassesses "the concept of 'love' in Donne" and examines "'love' as an early modern cultural problematic, related to philosophy and criticism in general." Addresses the issue in three parts: (1) explores "the implications of Donne's engagement with the body as space," (2) examines "the theme and theory of representation at work in Donne," and (3) opens Donne "to a kind of schizanalysis" (52). Argues that in Donne "the body without organs appears in the form of the body without organisation, even without erotic organisation," a "body in time rather than in the stability of space." Maintains that "[i]t thus figures in the texts as a body which is dysfunctional with respect to representation" and that "[b]ecause it prioritises the temporal over the spatial deictic, because it prioritises the temporal present over the spatial, the body enters in Donne into the function of a *mecanique des fluides*," is "a body which cannot be represented because it can never have been present in the first place" (59), and "is, as it were, a schizophrenic body, understanding schizophrenia here not in strictly clinical terms, but as a defining characteristic of a disjunctive relation between the Subject and its language" (59–60). Believes, therefore, that "Donne's poetry could be considered in fact less as modern and more as the site of an incipient post-modernism: not only contaminated by a proto-Nietzschean 'active forgetting' (which allows it its energy), but also contaminated by that schizophrenia which Jameson has characterised as a recurring element in the postmodern condition." Concludes by discussing how love in the late Renaissance was "profoundly problematic" (60).

1494. Doerksen, Daniel W. " 'Saint Paul's Puritan': John Donne's 'Puritan' Imagination in the Sermons," in *John Donne's Religious Imagination: Essays in Honor of John T. Shawcross,* ed. Raymond-Jean Frontain and Frances M. Malpezzi, 350–65. Conway, Ark.: UCA Press.

Maintains that although Donne was "not a Puritan, some of his most distinctive passages in the *Sermons* are marked by what may properly be called a 'puritan' imagination," and argues that "Donne in his attitude toward Puritanism is not a mere time-server, but someone who identifies fully with the official position of the Jacobean church, including its acceptance of conforming Puritans" (350). Comments on how Donne "shared with the Puritans their evangelical vision, their concern for a whole-hearted and practical Christianity, and their view of preaching as a chief means of propagating the gospel," and shows that Donne, like Richard Sibbes, a conforming Puritan, "regarded appeals to the imagination as a vital means of stirring the hearers of a sermon" (361). Cites passages from the sermons that reflect Donne's moderate "Puritan" imagination.

1495. Donne, John. *Donne: Poems and Prose.* Selected by Peter Washington. Everyman Library Pocket Poets. London: David Campbell. 256p.

A collection of 32 poems from the *Songs and Sonets,* 3 elegies, 5 satires,

6 verse letters, *FirAn,* 13 selections from the *Holy Sonnets* and 2 poems from *Corona,* 6 poems from the *Divine Poems,* and selections from *Paradoxes and Problems, Ignatius,* sermons, *Essays in Divinity,* and *Devotions,* with no notes or commentary. Has an index of first lines.

1496. Donne, John. "Sonnet X," trans. Jean Fuzier. *Rimbaud Revue* Année 3, no. 4 (April): 8.

Translates into French *HSDeath*—with accompanying English text and without notes or commentary.

1497. Donne, John. *John Donne: Poems and Selections,* ed. Robert van de Weyer. Fount Paperbacks. London: Harper Collins. x, 165p.

Presents a brief introduction to Donne's life and writings (vii–x) in which Donne is called "a rascal, a witty pamphleteer, and, in his later years, a preacher of great learning and spiritual insight" (vii), followed by 30 selections from the *Songs and Sonets,* 32 selections from the *Divine Poems* (41–63), 5 sermons, and 5 selections from the *Devotions,* without notes or commentary. Modern spelling texts.

1498. Donne, John. *John Donne: Poemas eróticos,* trans. Helena Barbas. Lisbon: Assírio and Alvim. 191.

The introduction (7–35) presents a biographical sketch of Donne, a survey of philosophical and intellectual concepts of his time, a discussion of the nature of English metaphysical poetry, and an introduction to the *Songs and Sonets* followed by a brief bibliography (36) and a chronological table of Donne's life and works (37–38). Thereafter follows a translation of the *Songs and Sonets* into Portuguese with English texts on the opposite pages. Concludes with notes on the poems (186) and an index of titles in English and Portuguese (188–91).

1499. Donne, John. *The Variorum Edition of the Poetry of John Donne. Vol. VI: The Anniversaries and the Epicedes and Obsequies,* gen. ed. Gary A. Stringer. Text eds. Ted-Larry Pebworth, John T. Shawcross, Gary A. Stringer, and Ernest W. Sullivan, II; chief editor of the commentary, John R. Roberts; commentary ed. Paul A. Parrish; contributing eds. Donald R. Dickson and Dennis Flynn. Bloomington and Indianapolis: Indiana University Press. lvii, 689p.

Presents a newly edited text based on an exhaustive study of all known manuscript and printed copies of the *Anniversaries* (including *FunEl*) and the *Epicedes and Obsequies,* followed by a chronological summary of critical comment on these poems from Donne's time to 1989. Contains a table of contents (ix–xi), acknowledgments (xii–xv), a list of short forms of reference for Donne's works (xvi–xxii), a list of abbreviations used in the commentary (xxiii–xxvi), sigla for textual sources (xxvii–xxxvii), and a list of symbols and abbreviations used in the textual apparatus (xxxviii). Thereafter follows a general introduction, explaining the origin and plan of the edition, the purpose and scope of the commentary, the materials available and textual theory governing the edition, procedures for choosing and emending the copy-text, the general organization of the edition, the reportage of textual variants, and bibliographical conventions in the apparatus (xxxix–li). Presents an introduction to volume 6 that explains the order and arrangement of the poems in the volume and an overview of the critical reception of the poems included and outlines the organization of the material within the volume (lii–lvii). Thereafter the volume is divided into two main sections: (1) the presentation of the texts, a textual introduction, and textual apparatuses for the *Anniversaries* (5–100) and the texts, textual introductions, and textual apparatuses for each of the *Epicedes and Obsequies* (101–233), with an appendix on a funeral elegy, probably written by the Countess of Bedford, that has been linked to Donne's elegies on Cecilia Boulstrode (234–36); and (2) a chronologically arranged summary of critical commentary on the *Anniversaries,* divided into general commentary; dating and early printings; Donne, the Drurys, and Patronage; the identification of "she" in the poems; the poet and his audience, the structure of the poems, language and style; and the *Anniversaries* and other works (239–365), followed by notes and glosses on individual lines and words in *FirAn, FunEl,* and *SecAn* (366–536), followed by a general commentary on the *Epicedes and Obsequies,* with commentaries on each of the individual poems with notes and glosses on individual lines and words (537–655). Concludes with a list of works cited (656–77), an index of authors cited in the commentary (678–685), an index of titles (686), an index of first lines (687), and biographical sketches of the editors (688–89). Reviews: Albert C. Labriola in *SCN* 53, nos. 3–4 (1995): 45–47; Claude J. Summers in *EMLS* 1.3 (1995): 6.1–10.

1500. Donne, John. *The Variorum Edition of the Poetry of John Donne. Vol. VIII: The Epigrams, Epithalamions, Epitaphs, Inscriptions, and Miscellaneous Poems.* gen. ed. Gary A. Stringer. Text eds. Ted-Larry Pebworth, Gary A. Stringer, and Ernest W. Sullivan, II; chief editor of the commentary, John R. Roberts; commentary ed. William A. McClung; contributing ed. Jeffrey Johnson. Bloomington: Indiana University Press. lxiii, 509p.

Presents a newly edited text based on an exhaustive study of all known manuscript and printed copies of the epigrams, epithalamia, epitaphs, inscriptions, and other miscellaneous poems, followed by a chronological summary of critical comment on these poems from Donne's own time to 1990. Contains a table of contents (ix–xv), acknowledgments (xvi–xix), short forms of reference for Donne's works (xx–xxvi), abbreviations used in the commentary (xxvii–xxxi), sigla for textual sources (xxxii–xlii), and symbols and abbreviations used in the textual apparatus (xliii–xliii). Thereafter follows a general introduction to the edition, explaining the origin and plan of the edition, the purpose and scope of the commentary, the editoral stance of the editors, organization of the material within the volumes, style of presentation, bibliographical conventions in the commentary, textual materials and textual theory governing the edition, procedure for choosing and emending copy-texts, introductions and textual apparatuses, reportage of variants, and bibliographical conventions in the apparatus (xliv–lvi). Contains an introduction to volume 8 that offers a critical overview of the poems included and the order and arrangement of them in the volume (lvii–lxiii). Presents the texts and apparatuses of the epigrams with a general textual introduction to the epigrams, followed by textual introductions and apparatuses for individual epigrams (5–172) and the texts, textual introduction and textual apparatus for the epitaphs and inscriptions (175–213) and the miscellaneous poems (217–251), including the dubious "The Apotheosis Ignati Loyolae" (252–53). Appendix 1, prints a controversial group of epigrams (originally in Latin) attributed to Donne and translated into English by Jasper Mayne that first appeared in the 1652 issue of *Paradoxes, Problems, Essayes, Characters* (254–269); Appendix 2 prints poems associated with the epi-

grams: appropriations, translations, answers, and attributions (270–76). Thereafter follows the general commentary on the epigrams (281–89); commentary on individual epigrams, including notes and glosses on individual lines and words; general commentary on the epithalamia (333–41); commentary on each of the epithalamia, including notes and glosses on individual lines and words (342–424); general commentary on the epitaphs and inscriptions (427–28); commentary on the individual epitaphs and inscriptions, including notes and glosses on individual lines and words (429–51); and commentary on individual miscellaneous poems (455–66), including notes and glosses on individual lines and words and also including "The Apotheosis Ignati Loyolae" (467–71) and the dubious epigrams attributed to Donne and translated by Jasper Mayne (427–80). Concludes with a list of works cited (481–93), an index of authors cited in the commentary (494–98), an index of titles (499–503), an index of first lines (504–7), and biographical sketches of the editors (508–9). Reviews: Albert C. Labriola in *SCN* 54 (1996): 1–2; Anthony Low in *SEL* 37 (1997): 193–94; Brian Vickers in *AEB* 10 (1999): 107–11.

1501. Dubrow, Heather. "Resident Alien: John Donne," in *Echoes of Desire: English Petrarchism and Its Counterdiscourses*, 203–48. Ithaca, N.Y.: Cornell University Press.

Argues that Donne "neither embraces Petrarchism enthusiastically, as some revisionist readers assert, nor rejects it under the guise of participating in it, as others claim," but rather "complicating—but not canceling—his debt to that tradition, Donne uses modes of distancing . . . to establish himself as both inside and outside

Petrarchism" (204–5). Maintains, in other words, that, "as his own vocabulary suggests, he is a visitor to, perhaps even a temporary resident in, a foreign country, following its customs and talking its language yet never forgetting or allowing us to forget that he is no native" (205). Shows how a study of "the interplay of cultural and intellectual history" that shaped Donne's life, making him both an "insider and outsider" in the society about him, "bears on his Petrarchism" (210) and how his "approach to Petrarchism is shaped . . . by his reactions to the imbricated cultural circles of the court, the patronage system, and the Inns and by his ambivalent responses to his literary milieu and to the process of imitation" (211). Maintains that "the patterns of Petrarchism influence Donne's self-fashioning and the fashioning of his speakers in that the Petrarchan lover provides both a model to emulate and one to reject." Shows how "both the lyrics in which Donne adapts Petrarchism and those in which he mocks it help to define the nature of Petrarchism for him and his readers" (214). Discusses a number of Donne's major and minor poems to show his complex uses of the Petrarchan tradition, insisting that he "does not reject the [Petrarchan] tradition completely, subscribe to it wholeheartedly, or condemn it under the guise of participation—but rather establishes his status as both insider and outsider at once" (247). Claims that Donne's "counterdiscourses produce in the reader a reaction that accords to the amalgam of distance and contiguity which is at the heart of Donne's stance towards Petrarchism" (248).

1502. Ellis, Jim. "The Wit of Circumcision, the Circumcision of Wit," in *The Wit of Seventeenth-Century Poetry,* ed. Claude J. Summers and Ted-Larry Pebworth, 62–77. Columbia: University of Missouri Press. Discusses the prevalent topos of Christ's circumcision in seventeenth-century religious poetry and prose in which "[t]reatments of the event inevitably circle around to a demand that the reader circumcise the foreskin of his or her heart, an operation [that the author calls] a circumcision of wit." Observes that "[w]hat the poetry often simultaneously calls for and enacts is a particular way of reading the body of Christ, and subsequently our own bodies" (62). Argues that "[j]ust as Christ's circumcision marks the divide between the order of law and the order of grace (which become, in effect, two orders of law)," it also divides "two hermeneutic regimes" and that "[t]he reading strategy that follows after Christ's circumcision, that which employs a circumcised wit, functions as the literal circumcision did to mark out a community and to demonstrate submission to the law" (62–63). Comments on "this circumcised wit in relation to the poetry of circumcision" and further suggests that "this form of wit is historically linked both to the emergence of the individual during this period and to the escalating challenge to both religious and political communities that culminated in the English civil war" (63). Illustrates these ideas by discussing Donne's witty use of circumcision in his sermons in which he tells his audience not to read circumcision literally but urges them "to read the body and the world with a metaphysical wit" (71). Shows how in the sermon Donne, "[b]y associating the Puritans with the Jews of the Old Testament" and "by connecting that with a naive or literal reading style" marks out "a community of believers: those who seal a contract with God by circumcising their wit" (76–77).

1503. Ellrodt, Robert. "The Search for Identity: From Montaigne to Donne," in *John Donne and Modernity,* ed. Armand Himy and Margaret Llasera, 7–23. Confluences XI, Centre de Recherches sur les Origines de la Modernité et les Pays Anglophones. Nanterre: Université Paris X.

Discusses the similarities between Montaigne and Donne "in their search for identity" and accesses "its novelty and significance in the history of European thought" (7). Shows that for both Donne and Montaigne "the first fruits of self-analysis were perplexity and a sense of failure" (10). Examines "the multiple causes that may be assigned to their search for identity," concluding that none of them would have proven decisive "without an intense self-consciousness," that is, the ability "to act, feel and think, while distancing oneself from the action, the feeling and the thought" (13) and "to be acutely aware of doing so on the spur of the moment." Suggests that "[t]his spontaneous reflexivity accounts for the blend of passion and irony (especially irony directed at oneself) in so many of Donne's poems" (14). Maintains that "there was in poetry, from the *dolce stil nuovo* to the Renaissance, no full display of the kind of self-consciousness" defined in the essay. Claims, therefore, that Donne and Montaigne "were in many respects unprecedented in their questioning of personal identity" (19). Observes that for both men, who so often perceived the self as "fragmentary and changing," death imparted to the self "an ultimate and intimate stability and substantiality" (22). Maintains that Donne finally perceived that "[t]he self in its wholeness can only survive through the resurrection of the flesh" and that "man will only discover on the Day of Judgment what he could not discover in his life" (22). Suggests that this "yearning for an epiphany of the self" was "Donne's innermost and deepest desire" (23).

1504. Fine, Aaron M. "Handfuls of Dust." *TLS* (12 May): 15.

In a reply to John Newton's suggestion in "Another Handful of Dust" (*TLS* [28 April 1995]: 18) that T. S. Eliot perhaps borrowed the phrase "a handful of dust" in *The Waste Land* from Charlotte Mew's *The Farmer's Bride,* points out that a probable common source for both poets was *Devotions,* Meditation 4.

1505. Flynn, Dennis. "A Biographical Pro-lusion to Study of Donne's Religious Imagination," in *John Donne's Religious Imagination: Essays in Honor of John T. Shawcross,* ed. Raymond-Jean Frontain and Frances M. Malpezzi, 28–44. Conway, Ark.: UCA Press.

Discusses how Donne's Catholic lineage and his social circle influenced his religious imagination, noting that as a result of the religious persecution of his family and friends "[i]mprisonment and exile were and were to be frequently occurring themes in Donne's imagination" (29). Insists that "we should no more separate study of Donne's life and writings from his and his family's religious persecution than we would separate study of the writings of Solzhenitsyn or Wiesel from theirs." Points out that "as a member of a group directly afflicted by enormous and penetrating social developments, Donne wrote out of an experience that his contemporaries *could* not ignore, that therefore never ceased to dominate *his* outlook, and that may appear as an element in anything he wrote" (34). Outlines in some detail Donne's and his family's association with members of the ancient Catholic nobility. Comments on Donne's concept of honor and on the honor extended to him by his contemporaries to show that "Donne's contemporaries regarded him not as a desperately ambitious, place-seeking, social-climbing son of a hardware salesman, but as a person of remarkable honor" (35). Discusses how "[t]hroughout his life Donne's association with Northumberland and other members of the ancient Catholic nobility was an honor association with a social class whose power can be seen to have been in decline, doomed to eclipse by the political skill and power of Tudor politicians" (40).

1506. Flynn, Dennis. "Donne, Henry Wotton, and the Earl of Essex." *JDJ* 14: 185–218.

Appears in a special issue of the *JDJ* on new uses of biographical and historical evidence in Donne studies, edited by Dennis Flynn. Examines assumptions concerning Donne's early relationship with Henry Wotton. Challenges Walton's notion that they were close friends at Oxford in the 1580s and argues that, more likely, the two men were "drawn together in the 1590s when Donne somehow came to have knowledge of Wotton's book" (188) *The State of Christendom: or, A Most Exact and Curious Discovery of Many Secret Passages, and Hidden Mysteries of the Times*, written in the spring or summer of 1594. Suggests also that Donne and Wotton may have met during the Cadiz voyage of 1596 and, if so, this fact could "help solve another problem: the controverted question whether Donne, like Wotton, was a supporter of the Earl of Essex" (197). Argues that Donne more likely served under Raleigh on the expedition, not Essex, and that, although "no admirer of Raleigh," Donne was not, therefore, "a partisan of Essex" (203). Maintains that Donne "did not think of his service on the Cadiz expedition as a matter of 'waiting upon' Essex" and notes that "[a]ll the Cadiz and Azores writings pointedly exclude the Earl as a focus of admiration" (210). Shows that "Donne's references to

Essex in the period from 1596 to 1601 are consistently framed in sarcastic tones" and that, in comparisons with Raleigh, for whom Donne had a low opinion, Essex "does not come off well" (211). Concludes, therefore, that "Donne's attitude toward Essex was not, like Wotton's, that of an outsider seeking entrance to a privileged circle" but rather that "his service under Essex was an outgrowth of his and his family's having been at Court long before Wotton was, and in particular of their long-standing associations with the ancient Catholic nobility, including the house of Percy" (212).

1507. Flynn, Dennis. *John Donne and the Ancient Catholic Nobility*. Bloomington: Indiana University Press. viii, 245p.

Places Donne in the ancient Catholic tradition of his formative years and discusses the significance of this background on his life and works. States that the purpose of the study is "to present new facts, previously unknown or unnoticed, facts that suggest reasonable conjecture and imply the need for reconsideration of a whole range of assumptions underlying the work of critics" (16), especially those who regard Donne as simply a social climber whose driving ambition for social acceptance and financial security motivated almost all aspects of his life and works. Emphasizes that Donne's family was on very easy terms with the nobility long before his birth. "Introduction: Portrait of a Swordsman" (1–16) presents an interpretation of William Marshall's engraving and argues that Donne had a long-standing relationship with the court and that his eminent Catholic family greatly influenced his formative years. Concludes that Donne's link to the ancient Catholic nobility was "a matter of honor that remained a presence throughout his life" (5). Part 1, "Donne's Catholic Heritage"

(17–79), traces the persistent Catholicism of two generations of Donne's family and discusses those relatives of Donne who were "active participants more often than passive sufferers" (19) of religious persecution, especially Thomas More, William Rastell, John Heywood, Ellis and Jasper Heywood, Donne's mother and father, and his stepfather, Dr. John Syminges. Describes the social, political, and religious environment of the London into which Donne was born and spent his early years and portrays the heroism of beleaguered Catholics who maintained their religious belief in the midst of state-enforced Protestantism. Maintains that once readers have an understanding of the fuller context of Donne's family and its precarious position in the political struggles of the time, they can better appreciate the difficult decisions Donne made in his later life. Part 2, "Donne and the Ancient Nobility" (83–172), discusses how, through the underground missionary work of Donne's Jesuit uncle, Jasper Heywood, his family formed an alliance with the powerful Percy and Stanley families and that from this alliance sprang Donne's lifelong friendship with Henry Percy, ninth Earl of Northumberland, "whose continental travels early in the 1580s seem to have been related to the early travels of Donne and to the schemes of Catholic exiles for an invasion of England six years before the eventual Armada" (16). In recording the activities of the Percys, postulates that Donne would have experienced the reality of their persecution and would have himself felt threatened. Points out how some Catholics, like Donne's stepfather, accommodated themselves in varying degrees to the established church, while others, like Donne's mother, did not, thereby presenting the young Donne with "an incongruity that would have inevitably produced

conflict" (114). Speculates that Donne likely accompanied Stanley, the Earl of Derby, to the court of Henry III in 1585 and that he remained for a short time in Paris and thereafter proceeded to Eu, where preparations were underway for the invasion of England, and then to Antwerp to observe the Duke of Parma's invasion of the city. Suggests Donne's presence in Antwerp is reflected in a series of Latin epigrams (no longer extant) that were translated into English by Jasper Mayne. Speculates further that Donne and William Stanley traveled together to Spain and Italy between the spring of 1585 and the spring of 1586 and that, upon returning to England, Donne served at the earl's court. The conclusion (173–81) reiterates that Donne's Catholic heritage and social circle "were factors shaping Donne's character in ways that have been less apparent to us than to his contemporaries" and that "both were associated in poignant ways with notions of imprisonment and religious exile" (175). Concludes, therefore, that "[w]e should no more separate study of Donne's life and writings from his and his family's religious persecution and exile than we would separate the writings of Solzhenitsyn and Wiesel from theirs" (176). In an appendix (183–94), Flynn repeats his earlier argument, first advanced in 1984 (entry 479), that the epigrams translated by Mayne are indeed translations of Donne's poems and argues that the epigrams present important evidence about Donne's early life and travels. Reviews: Rodney Delasanta in *C&L* 45 (1996): 427–30; Elizabeth Hodgson in *EMLS* 2 (1996): 104–7; Maureen Sabine in *JDJ* 15 (1996): 203–11; T. M. McCoog in *Catholic Historical Review* 83 (1997): 343–44; Barry Spurr in *SCJ* 28 (1997): 259–61; Celestin Walby in *R&L* 29 (1997): 71–75; Chanita Goodblatt in *RenQ* 51

(1998): 675–76; Steven W. May in *ANQ* 11 (1998): 51–53; John R. Roberts in *SCN* 57 (1999): 151–55.

1508. Frontain, Raymond-Jean. "Discovering the Way to New Elysium: Carew's 'A Rapture,' the Renaissance Erotic Pastoral, and the Biblical Song of Solomon." *PAPA* 21, no. 1: 39–67.

Compares Carew's "A Rapture" with *ElBed* "[i]n order to specify the way in which the biblical Song of Solomon licensed Renaissance erotic writing in general, and sanctioned Carew's expression of an erotic spirituality in particular." Maintains that "Donne's elegy is a particularly useful foil because, despite the important work done on the erotic pastoral and on Carew's contribution to such a tradition, the Song of Solomon has rarely been cited as a justification for pastoral libertinism," and shows that "Carew's departures from Donne's model are clearly in this direction" (40). Discusses how Donne's elegy served as a model for Carew's poem and how both poems attempt "to enact an erotic spirituality" (53) but points out a significant difference: "Donne's speaker invites his partner into a closed room and, within that room, to 'loves hallow'd temple, this soft bed' " (54), while, "[l]ike the lovers of the biblical Song who find the city an inhibiting place, Carew's speaker and his woman friend escape the world of the city and court to practise freely love as nature (which includes human nature) intends it." Maintains that "[i]t is Carew's reliance upon the biblical Song of Solomon . . . which allows him to present human sexuality in pastoral terms that are simultaneously religious and erotic," and holds that "A Rapture" "depicts the perfect harmony of humankind with nature by conflating the desired woman's body with the pastoral landscape, a garden to be explored and savoured" (55).

1509. Frontain, Raymond-Jean. " 'Make all this All': The Religious Operations of John Donne's Imagination," in *John Donne's Religious Imagination: Essays in Honor of John T. Shawcross,* ed. Raymond-Jean Frontain and Frances M. Malpezzi, 1–27. Conway, Ark.: UCA Press.

In this essay, which serves as an introduction to the whole collection, argues that Donne's imagination was essentially religious and emphasizes that he "increasingly came to see poetry . . . as a religious activity." Argues that even in the *Elegies* and in the *Songs and Sonets* love is seen as a religious experience that allows lovers to transcend "worldly, everyday concerns," launching them out of this world "into a realm of transcendent meaning" (2). Maintains that, for Donne, "love is not polarized between body and soul, or between the erotic and the spiritual," but rather "is capable of uniting the two, the physical being the typological adumbration of the spiritual, in an understanding of sexuality that depends heavily on incarnational theology." Insists, in fact, that "the very genius of Donne's greatest love poems lies in their determination to make of love as deeply spiritual an experience as it is erotic" (5). Suggests also that "the threat of dissolution animates nearly every part of Donne's canon" (8) and comments on this theme primarily in the *Satyres, Metem,* the *Anniversaries,* and *Lam,* noting that "the speaker of a Donne poem seems always setting out in hopes of arriving at a more sacred place" (11) and that his greatest challenge is "how to negotiate the transition from the realm of the profane to the sacred" (13). Maintains further that Donne's poetic development "can be mapped in terms of his shift from secular to sacred models" (13) and argues that he "found in the creating power of religious language his passport across

the mysterious border from dissolution to transcendence" (16–17).
Concludes by pointing out how the
essays in the collection attempt "to
erase boundaries, too much of which
prove artificial or are the constructs
of earlier criticism's imagination" (19),
and by explaining how they show
"how much of a piece Donne's work
was" (22).

**1510. Frontain, Raymond-Jean, and
Frances M. Malpezzi, eds.** *John Donne's
Religious Imagination: Essays in Honor
of John T. Shawcross.* Conway, Ark.:
UCA Press. xii, 446p.

A collection of 23 original essays,
each of which has been separately
entered in this bibliography. Contains a preface (ix–x), which stresses
that "Donne's religious life—and the
imaginative works that his religion
inspired—are among the most troublesome set of paradoxes and problems to emerge from the English
Renaissance" (ix). Notes that "[i]nso-
far as it was possible, the essays that
follow are organized according to
the arrangement of Donne's poems
in John Shawcross's edition of the
Complete Poetry (1967)" and that
those on Donne's prose "are loosely
organized according to the prose
works' dates of publication" (x).
Contains also a dedication of the collection to John T. Shawcross, entitled
" 'To his dear name addrest': In Honor
of John T. Shawcross" (414); notes
on texts and citations (xi); brief biographical sketches of the contributors
(439–42); and an index of Donne's
works (443–46). Reviews: Jill Peláez
Baumgaertner in *C&L* 45 (1996):
430–32; Robert C. Evans in *SCJ* 27
(1996): 609; Joshua Eckhardt in
Cresset 60 (1997): 26; Robert W.
Halli, Jr., in *ANQ* 10 (1997): 55–58;
Stanley Archer in *SCN* 56 (1998): 6–7;
Catherine Gimelli Martin in *SCRev*
15 (1998): 54–55.

1511. Frost, Kate Gartner. "Magnus Pan
Mortuus Est: A Subtextual and Context-
ual Reading of Donne's 'Resurrection,
Imperfect,' " in *John Donne's Religious
Imagination: Essays in Honor of John
T. Shawcross,* ed. Raymond-Jean Frontain
and Frances M. Malpezzi, 231–61.
Conway, Ark.: UCA Press.

Argues that *Res* "is not incomplete"
but rather "is a finished poem concerned with unfinished time" and is
"connected to the liturgy of Holy
Saturday and to the subject of the
Harrowing of Hell and Christ's consequent 'hasting to heaven' through
the levels of the cosmos." Maintains
that "[i]n shaping his work the poet
drew widely and wittily on the Holy
Saturday topos as it was manifested
in the premodern disciplines of
alchemy, cosmology, mythography,
and arithmology" (231). Believes that
understanding *Res* "entails habits and
skills unfamiliar to the modern reader,"
since "one must subordinate the custom of deriving total meaning from
sequential order to an overview of the
work that may entail a perception of
its schematic structure and the relation of its contexts and subtexts to that
structure." Examines, therefore, "the
discursive surface text [of the poem]
in a process of verbal recognition
according to the multiple seventeenth-
century meanings and connotations of
its language" and shows how "[t]his
exploration of primary definitions and
their alternatives reveals not specific
references to but rather a fabric of
association with the poem's exegetical, cosmological, mythographic, and
alchemical contexts" (233), each of
which is examined in some detail.
Presents a subtextual and contextual
reading of *Res* that examines the language, mathematical structure, and
liturgical aspects of the poem to show
how they "ratify the testimony of the
contexts, revealing a poem concerned
with Christ's triumph over the fallen

universe and the sinful human heart" (243), and how they support the claim that "the appearance of incompleteness is deliberate and that the Latin tag is a final twist of Donne's wit" (244).

1512. Gabrieli, Vittorio. "John Donne, Thomas More e Roma." *RLMC* 48: 235–62.

Discusses Donne's familiarity with Italian Renaissance writers and thinkers and his knowledge of the Italian language, speculates on his visits to Italy and his Italian acquaintances, and comments on his evolving negative attitude toward post-Tridentine Catholicism. Notes especially the influence of Machiavelli on *Ignatius*. Comments on Donne's familiarity with the works of his eminent ancestor, Thomas More, contrasting their religious views and sensibility and their very different understanding and appreciation of sexual love and the body.

1513. Gandelman, Claude. "John Donne et la tradition de la carte anthropomorphe," in *Le corps dans tous ses états,* ed. Marie-Claire Rouyer, 137–42. Bordeaux: Presses Universitaires de Bordeaux.

Places Donne at the heart of the tradition of the anthropomorphic map and suggests the likelihood of his familiarity with the body-maps of Arcimboldo. Discusses Donne's implicit and explicit use of maps in his poetry and prose, especially his fondness for cartographic metaphors. Comments, in particular, on Donne's metaphorical descriptions of the human body as a map, as exemplified, for instance, in *ElProg*. Sees Donne as a precursor of Baudelaire, James Joyce, Jorge Luis Borges, and Henri Michaux in this respect.

1514. Gregory, Michael. "Generic Expectancies and Discoursal Surprises: John Donne's *The Good Morrow*," in *Discourse in Society: Systemic Functional Perspectives. Meaning and Choice in Language: Studies for Michael Halliday,* ed. Peter H. Fries and Michael Gregory, 67–84. Advances in Discourse Processes, vol. 50, ed. Roy O. Freedle. Norwood, N.J.: Ablex.

Presents a detailed linguistic analysis of *GoodM,* observing that as a discourse the poem has "at least two potential communicating community contexts and generic situations; the one centers on John Donne and his audience(s); the other is created by the language of the poem." Comments in much detail on the "discourse 'plot' (i.e. phrasal description)" of the poem "based on a trifunctional semiological analysis of the proposition and predications and their morphosyntactic and grapho/phonological realization" (71). Maintains that his *explication du texte* indicates that "discourse, unlike sentence, is rule-*referenced* rather than rule-governed" (84).

1515. Grierson, Herbert J. C., ed. *Metaphysical Lyrics and Poems of the Seventeenth Century.* 2nd ed., revised by Alastair Fowler. Oxford: Oxford University Press. xix, 320p.

First edition published in 1921. Contains a preface to the 1995 edition (v–ix) by Alastair Fowler, who discusses the historical importance of Grierson's anthology and his purpose—to challenge Palgrave's disparagement of the metaphysical poets in his highly influential *Golden Treasury of Songs and Lyrics* (1861), which at the time was the "representative view" (v). Comments on the evolving critical understanding of "metaphysical" poetry over the centuries, noting, in particular, the important role T. S. Eliot played in the modern Donne revival. Notes that the present edition retains all the poems in Grierson's original anthology, "although some poems he included are no longer thought of as Metaphysical" (viii). Points out that the texts have been revised; that orthography and punctuation have been modernized, although some obsolete spellings have been retained; and that the notes are much more extensive and modernized. Contains a table of contents (xi–xvii), a list of journal abbreviations (xviii–ix), Grierson's original introduction (1–36) and his selection of poems (37–229), notes on the poems (231–304), a list of books cited (305–14), suggestions for further reading (315–16), and an index of first lines (317–20).

1516. Halli, Robert W., Jr. "Cecilia Bulstrode, 'The Court Pucell,'" in *Subjects on the World's Change: Essays on British Literature of the Middle Ages and the Renaissance*, eds. David C. Allen and Robert A. White, 295–312. Newark: University of Delaware Press; London: Associated University Presses.

Discusses the life of Cecilia Bulstrode and reassesses her representation by such notable seventeenth century figures as John Roe, Ben Jonson, Edward Herbert, the Countess of Bedford, and Donne. Concludes that critics have often misinterpreted the literary works in which she appears and that, in fact, she was "a woman notable for integrity of character, intellectual attainments, and personal magnetism" (305). Comments briefly on *BoulNar* and *BoulRec* and a passage in a letter about her addressed to Henry Goodyer.

1517. Hanshaw, Larry. "The Literary Influence of Alchemy." *PCRev* 6: 61–73.

Discusses the alchemical symbolism in *Dissol*, stressing primarily how Donne uses "the ambivalence of the term dissolution to convey the same complexity of emotions he felt because of his loved one's death" (67). Shows how he employs the alchemical term to indicate the disintegration of his beloved's body and of his emotional disintegration and also to define the

"the inseparable nature of the relationship" (68) that exists between the lovers and "the regenerative power of his loved one" (68). Points out that Donne's speaker finally "feels renewed and transformed into a man who unexpectedly rejoices in the wealth represented by the lasting nature of the bond he feels with his previous love" (69).

1518. Harland, Paul W. "'A true transubstantiation': Donne, Self-Love, and the Passion," in *John Donne's Religious Imagination: Essays in Honor of John T. Shawcross*, ed. Raymond-Jean Frontain and Frances M. Malpezzi, 152–80. Conway, Ark.: UCA Press.

Discusses how three of Donne's poems on Christ's passion—*Cross, HSWhat,* and *Goodf*—and various passages in the sermons "enact the drama of the ego breaking out of the prison of destructive self-preoccupation into a liberated state of true self-love which best expresses itself as willing and disinterested giving." Points out that "Donne's explorations within the self may thus be seen to animate the familiar Renaissance trope that a human being was a little world: to know and to love the self was a method ultimately of knowing and loving the greater world beyond it." Claims that "a study of Donne's writing on Christ's passion records the transformation of degenerate self-love into the regenerate variety, a distinction that Donne makes throughout his *Sermons*" (162). Discusses how in the works mentioned above Donne illustrates that "genuine love of the suffering Christ allows the self to transform itself into its best nature, to reflect Christ, and thereby to love itself fully" (163), and how in them he makes clear that "the world with all its problematic complexity is not to be shunned" since "it is by exposure to the world and by the difficult attempt to discriminate good from evil that the image of God is restored within an individual" (177).

1519. Hartwig, Joan. "Donne's Horse and Rider as Body and Soul," in *John Donne's Religious Imagination: Essays in Honor of John T. Shawcross,* ed. Raymond-Jean Frontain and Frances M. Malpezzi, 262–83. Conway, Ark.: UCA Press.

Discusses the figure of the horse and rider in *Sat1, ElNat,* and *Goodf,* observing that the figure "has roots in classical tradition as well as a pervasive history in works of religious imagination, both verbal and visual" (262). Discusses how in each of these poems Donne "builds upon awareness of traditional associations between horse and rider as body and soul, although each presents a different version of the rider and of the horse." Maintains that in *Sat1* "the soul and body demonstrate a divisiveness that undermines all efforts to make the horse and rider appear harmoniously unified: they fail the training program"; that in the elegy "the lustful rider discovers that, although he has skillfully trained his horse, he has failed to alter the nature of the animal"; but that in *Goodf* Donne "demonstrates the potential for horse and rider, through submission and control, to be shaped by divine force into an harmonious image, unifying body and soul" (278).

1520. Hester, M. Thomas. " 'Miserrimum dictu': Donne's Epitaph for His Wife." *JEGP* 94: 513–29.

Points out that Donne's epitaph for Ann More is the only work that "we know for certain Donne wrote for his wife" (514) and maintains that "[f]or this reason alone it merits more attention than we have given it, especially in the light of the ways in which it (inevitably) confronts the grim realities of death—especially the death of this *femina lectissima* as possibly the result of his love for her—and for the ways in which its response to that event would seem to underscore the contrarious psychological tensions endemic to all those claims about the 'power' and 'wonder' of love that were central to the bold assertions of Donne's lyrics" (514–15). Suggests ways in which this Latin epitaph "evinces many of the tensions, paradoxes, and fears that animate the poet's better known lyrical-sermonic-meditative *valedictions*" (515) and explores its "meditative, confessional, and inventive wit" (516). Translates the epitaph into English showing how Donne exploits "the copious variety of the Latin idiom in order to figure forth his 'wonder' at the life and death" of his wife (517). Describes also how the poem contains "a sort of trans-lingual transaction in which the rich variety and conciseness of the Latin begins to drift into English puns, its timeless stability seemingly infected with the current and timely multivocal puns of the living tongue in imitation of the poem's confronting the mortal consequences of Anne's devotion" (523). Suggests that in the epitaph Donne portrays himself as "mirror and *doppelgänger* of the divine *Infans*" (524) and that "Donne-as-infant transforms the inexpressibility topos (*infans* = speechless) into a public pledge which professes their marriage to be a figure for that eventual reunion in which he, like Hannah and Mary, will be joined to the *Infans*" (525). Discusses each line to show how the epitaph is one of Donne's "most eloquent testaments to the 'vex[t] contraryes' . . . of that immense, powerful and penetratingly painful desire for 'more love'—that feverish egocentric desire for the irresistible folly of human love—even while it confesses his devotion to and his desire to express his devotion to the eternal Passion that rewrites all desires *hoc loco*" (529).

1521. Hester, M. Thomas. "The Shape of 'the mindes indeavours': Donne's First Anniversarie," in *John Donne's Religious Imagination: Essays in Honor of John T. Shawcross,* ed. Raymond-Jean Frontain and Frances M. Malpezzi, 113–21. Conway, Ark.: UCA Press.

Discusses the metaphoric shape of *FirAn,* which "derives from the central metaphor of neo-Pythagorean aesthetics and Renaissance cosmology— the planes of correspondence in the macro-microcosm." Maintains that "[s]uch a perspective provides several insights into the central meaning of the poem—specifically, by showing that the speaker of the poem has a much more positive or optimistic attitude towards man's condition and the value of his own art than studies of the poem's rhetoric have intimated or claimed" (113). Discusses specifically how "the metaphoric shape of thought" in *FirAn* is "that of a spiral" and how "the poem's structure figures forth a mind in a widening gyre that ascends beyond this world to the circumference of *Sapientia*" (114). Shows that Donne's poem "exemplifies that not only all 'structure' but, indeed, the truth which the human reason can attain is realized in the 'winding' ascent of the mind towards God" and that "[b]oth the necessary beauty and the truth about the capabilities of the rational soul, the stairway to Truth and the exemplary motions of the rational soul, are figured in his poems as a spiraling ascent towards its own eternal Image in time." Concludes that "[t]he poem intimates, then, not just the 'gyre' of imperfection in which man's fallen consciousness endlessly spins, but, more accurately, the fuller response and fuller self-expression which natural man can achieve" (120).

1522. Himy, Armand. "Donne and the Question of Dualism," in *John Donne and Modernity,* ed. Armand Himy and Margaret Llasera, 37–50. Confluences, XI, Centre de Recherches sur les Origines de la Modernité et les Pays Anglophone. Nanterre: Université Paris X.

Discusses "Donne's extraordinary discovery of the text of the body" and comments on "what implications this leads to in the field of theology" (38). Shows how Donne deciphers "the metaphysical enigma of the hieroglyphs of the body" and is fascinated by its paradoxes. Points out how "[a]ll the perplexing aporias of duality are reviewed by Donne with the characteristic delight of a brilliant intellect" (42). Comments on Donne's views on the relationship of the body and the soul and suggests that it "is best described by incarnational conceptions" (47). Discusses also Donne's understanding of what happens to the body in death and shows how the concept of the resurrection of the body is "quite central in Donne's theological thought" (45), noting that, for him, "what was important in the resurrection of the body was the resurrection of selfhood, of the same ego" (49).

1523. Himy, Armand, and Margaret Llasera, eds. *John Donne and Modernity.* Con-fluences XI, Centre de Recherches sur les Origines de la Modernité et les Pays Anglophones. Nanterre: Université Paris-X. 102p.

A collection of six essays on Donne adapted from papers read at a colloquium at the University of Paris X in Nanterre on 19 March 1993, each of which has been entered separately into this bibliography.

1524. Hurley, Ann. "More Foolery from More?: John Donne's Lothian Portrait as a Clue to His Politics," in *So Rich a Tapestry: The Sister Arts and Cultural Studies,* ed. Ann Hurley and Kate Greenspan, 72–87. Lewisburg, Pa.: Bucknell University Press.

Argues that the Lothian portrait of Donne participates "in a specifically visual tradition" and that "Donne's selection of the details of his portrait were deliberate choices made with that tradition in mind." Discusses how the portrait "uses a literary tradition which has been depoliticized to deflect visual allusions which are highly political" (75). Believes that "[b]y taking advantage of the coincidence that one gesture, the crossed-arms posture, exists independently in two traditions, painting and poetry," the Lothian portrait "uses the verbal tradition of the melancholic lover to deflect the dangerous implications of its visual associations with Roman Catholic devotion" (81). Maintains that Donne's selection of a "Catholic pose of devotion" for the portrait, "as seen from the perspective of a visual rather than a verbal tradition, implies that he was considerably more visually erudite than has heretofore been acknowledged by Donne scholars" (84). Points out further that the way in which "the verbal tradition of the melancholy lover, invoked by the witty text encircling the head of the poet, is used to deflect the more politically dangerous visual allusions of the pose . . . calls into question current critical assumptions about linguistic dominance in Renaissance conjunctions of words and images." Concludes that "establishing Donne's connections with the visual culture of his time" provides "a clue to his political and cultural circumstances with a specificity that confirms some of the conjectures of his recent biographers" concerning his Catholicism. Points out also that a fifteenth century portrait of a cross-armed court fool by Jean Fouguet, entitled *Le Gonella,* suggests that "the pose itself has a history of association with politically risky but witty foolery in the context of sacred things, a history well in keeping with both the ancestry and the literary career of John Donne" (85).

1525. Innocenti, Loretta. "'A Lecture upon the shadow': Truth and Representation," in *Counting and Recounting: Measuring Inner and Outer Space in the Renaissance,* ed. Paola Bottalla and Michela Calderaro, 129–48. Proceedings of the conference held at the Faculty of Magistero on 14 October 1991. Trieste: La Mongolfiera.

Discusses how "[t]he Renaissance inherited from the past an idea of poetry as a false and deceiving practice, but transformed it, first by defending the need for illusions, as a counterpart to naked truth, and secondly, by defining the boundaries of an autonomous territory proper to poetry and art" (137). Points out how the early Renaissance "breaks the bipolarity of false and true, by re-evaluating the similar, the probable and the possible of verisimilitude," and how the late Renaissance goes even further, "setting poetry, and art in general, in the paradoxical space of the barrier between the opposing terms of false and true," enabling "the two terms of the opposition to be simultaneously present" (140). Maintains that paradox and oxymoron are privileged figures in metaphysical wit "since they reconcile contrary qualities or attributes" and "make the two poles of a semantic opposition melt and merge into one image, into *discordia concors.*" Points out that Donne's poetry "particularly reveals this paradoxical attitude, at different levels and in several ways." Notes that it appears most simply in "the direct utterance of paradoxes" as found, for instance, in his religious poetry, "where paradox appears as the form proper to a mystical experience," but observes also that Donne believes that human love, "as a sort of mystical experience, is best known or represented through the paradoxical statement of *coincidentia oppositorum*" (143). Maintains, however, that in

Donne's poetry there is a more complex way of showing paradoxical coincidence, which is "carried out on a discursive level: the mingling of logic and rhetoric, the use of argumentative techniques like syllogisms, which are proper to the demonstration of truth and the revealing of errors, together with metaphorical premises, which are not subject to demonstration, since they can be verified and accepted only as poetic likeness" (144). Discusses *ValBook* and *Lect* to show how a viewer can change "his relationship with what surrounds him" and thus alter "his perception of reality" (145). Concludes that Donne's poetry "represents the extreme paradox of a man wandering like a lost atom in a protean universe, a man who goes on representing himself as a fixed, unvarying point from which the world can be measured and, more than that, from which the world can be transformed into poetry" (148).

1526. Jensen, Phebe. "'The Obedience Due to Princes': Absolutism in *Pseudo-Martyr*." *Ren&R*, n.s. 19, no. 3: 47–62.

Points out that "[a]bsolutism existed on a spectrum, from radical formulations that demanded completed obedience even to evil monarchs, to moderate beliefs in the balance between monarch's prerogative and subject's liberties," and that "any account of Donne's absolutism must situate him along this graduated line." Examines the "contemporary political resonances" in *Pseudo-Martyr* to show that, although it "aligns itself with absolutism, it does so in a very complex and ambivalent manner, rejecting political patriarchalism and adopting a moderate sense of the obedience due to the monarch" (47). Argues that "not only does *Pseudo-Martyr* align itself with moderate absolutism" but also that it "stresses the continuities between Catholic/Protes-

tant political positions as much as it insists on their differences" and maintains that "[i]t is in this way only a partially obedient text, and one which suggests reservations toward the secular authority it supposedly defends" (48). Acknowledges that *Pseudo-Martyr* "has little in it that could have been offensive to main-stream absolutist thought," but stresses that "its tensions and ambivalences should make us leery of ascribing too great a reverence for authority even in the now-emerging Dr. Donne." Suggests that "*Pseudo-Martyr's* awareness that terms from one side of an opposition so easily slide into their counter principle is oddly reminiscent of the metaphorical mechanics of much of Donne's poetry." Observes also that *Pseudo-Martyr* "suggests that Donne's life-long involvement with Catholic doctrine and controversy shaped not only his spiritual and psychological constitution, but also his political attitudes as well" (64).

1527. Johnson, Jeffrey. "Wrestling with God: John Donne at Prayer," in *John Donne's Religious Imagination: Essays in Honor of John T. Shawcross,* ed. Raymond-Jean Frontain and Frances M. Malpezzi, 306–23. Conway, Ark.: UCA Press.

Discusses how Donne's discussion of prayer is based on "the teachings of the Church, the model of Christ, and the particular needs of the self" (308). Discusses how "[i]n defining the central place of prayer in the Christian life, Donne availed himself of a wide spectrum of theological sources," noting that "he was well aware that prayer had not in fact given rise to significant partisan debate either in the Reformation or in the Christian tradition as a whole." Further shows that Donne found "in New Testament accounts of Christ at prayer a model not only for persistence in making his requests known to God, but also for conform-

ing himself to God by humbly submitting to His will." Argues that it is
"within these orthodox contexts that
Donne argues for a 'religious impu-
dency' in prayer, the body of Christ
wrestling with God to secure its divine
blessing." Shows also that "[t]he man-
nered use of paradox and typological
analogy as figures for the act of prayer,
mannerisms which themselves define
Donne's style, sit comfortably alongside traditional teachings about the
centrality of prayer and its constitutive
function for the Christian community."
Claims that "Donne could therefore
remain, as usual, at his most public
when he was at his most private, as
illustrated in the hymns and the
Devotions, in which the prayers stemming from Donne's personal suffering also articulate the petitions of and
for the common body of Christ" (321).

1528. Kelly, David. "The Canonization of
John Donne." *SSEng* 21 (1995–96): 3–41.
Presents a critical reading of *Canon,*
noting that in the poem Donne "imagines a kind of immortality being con-
ferred upon him for his loving and his
poetry-making" and that although "he
is being ironic, blasphemous and
obscene all at the same time," that is
exactly "how it turned out." Discusses,
therefore, how Donne himself has been
"canonized in the secular, literary
sense" (7) and how his poetry has
become a "cultural monument" (8).
Comments on ways of reading *Lov-
Alch* to show that "our own inclinations, our own biases, are somehow
bound up with and implicated in our
approach to canonical texts and our
ways of arriving at the meaning, and
therefore the value, they appear to
hold for us" (13). Surveys Donne's
fluctuating critical reception to show
that "the vicissitudes of Donne's career
in and out of (or at least to the side
of) the canon may be taken as exemplary of that canon's propensity for

transformation and evolution" (17).
Points out, for instance, how *LovGrow*
is "an excellent example of the sort
of poem Eliot would have valued and
the sort of poem Johnson would have
derided and, perhaps, considered val-
ueless" (23). Maintains, therefore, that
"social and political and cultural actu-
alities contribute to the changing
systems of value through which we
appraise poetry" and that "poetry itself
responds differently to those actuali-
ties as they change over time." Argues
that "[n]o doubt it is because we still
respond to it as Eliot did that we still
value the poetry of John Donne" (25).
Maintains that Donne remains important because he invented "a genuinely
searching poetics" and because he
"utterly transformed the poetic legacy"
(26) that he inherited from the Elizabethan poets. Argues that Donne's
poetry "arguably marks the moment
in English literature when modern
love comes into being" and discusses
how it fell out of favor when a very
different ideology of romance was
invented during the neoclassical
period. Discusses how Donne's poetry
reflects the fact that "love and the narrative of romance were in the process
of disengaging themselves from one
codification—that of courtly love—
but had not yet been encoded in the
next major form—the bourgeois sentimental myth" (29). Comments on several of the *Holy Sonnets* to show how
Donne explores "the spirituality of
love on the one hand, or the romance
of faith on the other, in wholly new,
imaginative ways" (35). Concludes
that Donne's poetry re-mains valuable because it is "a lyrical dramatization of the exploring self and the
exploring soul in its moments of
extreme emotional and spiritual intensity, and from the midst of this intensity brings into view—and so brings
into being—the elemental forms of
our modern sensibility" (41).

1529. Klawitter, George. "John Donne's Attitude toward the Virgin Mary: The Public versus the Private Voice," in *John Donne's Religious Imagination: Essays in Honor of John T. Shawcross,* ed. Raymond-Jean Frontain and Frances M. Malpezzi, 122–48. Conway, Ark.: UCA Press.

Maintains that in his public sermons Donne expresses a "consistent Protestant orthodoxy" regarding the Virgin Mary, but not so in "his private devotional poetry." Points out that of the "Marian dogmas that surface in Donne's poetry, divine motherhood and perpetual virginity were easy for Donne to accept, as they were for Elizabethan and Jacobean Protestants generally," whereas if "he ever held to a third doctrine, an immaculate conception for Mary, we cannot tell for certain from his writings, but as for invocation of the Virgin, we have proof positive that Donne underwent a change in faith" (122), for "in 1608 he praises Mary's intercessory powers, but in 1616 he denounces them as spurious" (123). Examines Donne's references and allusions to Mary in his poems and sermons, commenting also on "some recusant Marian poetry contemporary to Donne" by way of comparison, and surveys Marian theology in both the Catholic and Reformed traditions "in order to settle Donne within a theological context" (123). Believes that "Donne's private beliefs may be more accurately reflected in his poems than in his sermons" (137). Concludes that "when he speaks in the private voice of a worshipper, Donne's poetry suggests that ideas learned early are not easily discarded," but that "when he speaks in the public voice of the preacher, Donne's sermons reflect orthodox [Protestant] doctrine" (138).

1530. Kuno, Sachiko. "John Donne no 'Goyo Sekko'—St. Paul's Cross, 1622" [John Donne and the "Time-Serving" Sermon— St. Paul's Cross, 1622], in *17 Seiki to Eikoku Bungaku* [Seventeenth-Century English Literature in Its Cultural Context], 56–77. The Japan Society of Seventeenth-Century English Literature. Tokyo: Kinseido.

Considers the different evaluations of Donne's sermon preached at St. Paul's Cross, 1622, examining in detail the contents of the sermon, the contemporary response to it, and Donne's own thoughts on the result of the sermon. Argues that Donne continues to question his religion after ordination.

1531. Labriola, Albert C. *"Christus Patiens* and *Christus Victor:* John Donne's Ultimate Reality and Meaning." *Ultimate Reality and Meaning* 18: 92–101.

Summarizes Donne's life, his literary reputation, and major hallmarks of metaphysical poetry, especially the witty conceit, as illustrated in *ValMourn.* Maintains that Donne's religious poems manifest "the same hallmarks" as his secular poems and that, through his influence, "English religious poetry in the metaphysical style became a richly literary and profoundly confessional mode whereby Herbert, Crashaw, and others foster an interactive relationship with the Lord, and, in the language of Christian Platonism, contemplate the ultimate reality and meaning associated with his transcendence" (95). Explains that, for Donne, "the ultimate reality and meaning include a twofold conception of the Lord: first, as a suffering servant (*Christus Patiens*); then, as a conqueror over the powers of darkness, death, and Satan (*Christus Victor*)" (96). Discusses in particular *Corona,* the *Holy Sonnets,* and *Goodf* to show how Donne's "ingenious use of conceits enables him to fuse mental and affective processes in ways previously unrealized" (101) and how his speaker "becomes the spokesperson of the spiritual community to which he belongs" (101).

1532. Labriola, Albert C. "Donne's 'Hymne to God My God, in My Sicknesse': Hieroglyphic Mystery and Magic in Poetry." *BJJ* 2: 1–7.

Argues that *Sickness* is "an invocation of the holy name, an attempt by the speaker on his deathbed to be inscribed with the hieroglyphic identity of Jesus, who preceded him in death and underwent thereafter a resurrection and ascension heavenward." Claims that, "[i]n fact, the climax of the speaker's virtual identification with Jesus occurs when he invokes the Lord as follows: 'So, in his purple wrapp'd receive mee Lord,'" noting that the purple wrap "signifies the blood of Jesus, which surrounded his body at the Passion and Crucifixion" (3). Discusses in detail the hieroglyphic inscription and Christogram in the fourth stanza of the poem. Explains how the speaker "seeks assurance of safe transit to the hereafter as if he were traveling in a vessel surmounted by mast and yard in the form of a cross, through a route of travel demarcated cartographically by crisscrossed lines, along a wavy way under the protection of the *waw* [Jesus], and with the name of Jesus as a hieroglyph in his heart, its inscription following the chiastic arrangement across lines 18–20 of the poem" (6).

1533. Labriola, Albert C. "Sacerdotalism and Sainthood in the Poetry and Life of John Donne: 'The Canonization' and Canonization." *JDJ* 14: 113–26.

Appears in a special issue of the *JDJ* on new uses of biographical and historical evidence in Donne studies, edited by Dennis Flynn. Examines the trope of sacerdotalism and the conceit of sainthood in *Canon*. Presents "an innovative interpretation of the poem's title," arguing that the speaker of the poem is a canon and that his beloved is a canoness; comments on "the claustration of the lovers" in the poem; and discusses the lovers "in the context of sacerdotalism." Contends that the conceit of sainthood also "informs two other works by Donne—the epitaphs that he composed for Ann More, his wife who died in 1616, and for himself," and maintains that "sacerdotalism" in *Canon* and "sainthood in the two epitaphs, will provide a unique interpretation of one of the best known of the Songs and Sonets and an innovative understanding of the spousal relationship of John and Ann More Donne" (113). Discusses several allusions and references to sacerdotalism in *Canon*, concluding, however, that "the tone of the poem is satiric or parodic" and that the speaker and his lover "embody the sacerdotal abuses of the Church of Rome or, more probably, their vestigial presence in the Church of England" (120). Maintains, however, the conceit of sainthood in the two epitaphs conveys "earnest aspirations toward sainthood" and recounts "a spousal union that contrasts strikingly with the relationship of the lover and his beloved" in *Canon* (121).

1534. Larocco, Steve. "Contentious Intimations: John Donne, Richard III, and the Transgressive Structures of Seduction." *Exemplaria* 7: 237–67.

Rejects the claims of critics who hold that the dominant relation between men and women in Donne's love poetry "takes a manifest patriarchal urge to subdue the woman as Other and that this urge requires that the man coerce the woman into fulfilling his language and desires, that he usurp her freedom" (240). Examines "the nuances of transgressivensss inherent in the dynamics of seduction" (245) in Donne's love poetry, contrasting them with those in Shakespeare's *Richard III* to show that "[s]eduction, for Donne, is not driven by the same desire for appropriation or closure that moved Richard" (258). Points out that even in such an aggressive poem as

ElBed Donne's "prurient solicitations do not assume or require capitulation by the woman." Maintains that the elegy "is an open-ended, if offensive, game of seduction, and as such manifests but indefinitely defers the poet's dream of sexual possession." Discusses how in *Flea,* "Donne's most renowned poem of seduction," the speaker "also defers sexual possession" and "flirts with the transgressive dynamics that informed Richard's seduction of Anne, but without trying to institute the fantasy of omnipotence which ultimately consumed Richard" (258). Argues that in *Flea* Donne's speaker "engages the seductive realm for its own pleasure" and maintains that "[h]is desire is not to subdue or colonize the woman in any simple sense . . . but rather to provoke, to identify with, to imitate, and perhaps to envy and love the woman's challenge to him." Holds that "[i]n the woman, and in seduction, he imagines a subversion of many of the patriarchal codes and laws which oppress them both" and that "in seduction, he imagines a woman whose appearance, mobility and silent initiative can engender a circulation of power, signs and contentious intimacy which can depose, momentarily, the father's law." Concludes, however, that "[t]his does not mean that desires for mastery never surface in Donne's poetry" but "does suggest that such desires are entangled with other desires" (267).

1535. Lein, Clayton D. "John Donne." *Dictionary of Literary Biography, vol. 151, British Prose Writers of the Early Seventeenth Century,* ed. Clayton D. Lein, 114–39. A Bruccoli Clark Layman Book. Detroit, Mich.: Gale Research.

Contains a list of Donne's works and editions of his works (114–16) followed by a discussion of major stylistic characteristics and thematic con-

cerns of individual prose works (*Paradoxes and Problems, The Courtier's Library, Biathanatos, Pseudo-Martyr, Ignatius, Essayes in Divinity,* the sermons, and *Devotions*). Presents a biographical sketch of Donne (116–36) and relates the prose works to Donne's life, showing how they manifest features of Donne's poems, such as wit, clever argumentation, rhetorical and philosophical paradox, intellectual subtlety, the analysis of minds and motives, interest in science and familiarity with Continental writers, structural and linguistic virtuosity, and so forth. Maintains that "Donne's early prose, like his early poetry, reacted against the copious rhetorical styles favored by Elizabethan writers" and "flirted with the pointed, asymmetrical curt style," but that later on "he comes to a compromise with Ciceronian style," building "elaborate sentences but in the meditative, or 'loose' Senecan style." Notes, however, that Donne's long and rhythmical sentences "recapture something of the harmoniousness and authoritativeness of Ciceronian utterance" (134). Concludes with a selected bibliography of editions of the letters, bibliographies, biographies, and critical studies (136–39).

1536. Linsley, Joy L. "A Holy Puzzle: Donne's 'Holy Sonnet XVII,'" in *John Donne's Religious Imagination: Essays in Honor of John T. Shawcross,* ed. Raymond-Jean Frontain and Frances M. Malpezzi, 202–13. Conway, Ark.: UCA Press.

Suggests that *HSShe* is centrally important in Donne's "transition from the poetry of earthly love to that of heavenly love" and presents a detailed reading of the sonnet that "reveals Donne's subtle analysis of his spiritual problems, points out the theological, emotional and gender conflicts present in the poem—as well as their uneasy resolution—and suggests a possible artistic motive for Donne's producing such an intriguing and puzzling text" (202). Shows how Donne "employs spiritual and artistic strategies in coping with the loss of the earthly beloved and with dangers posed thereby to his love affair with God." Argues that the poem is "meaningfully obscure" and is "a holy puzzle that partly conceals the poet's deep grief and his methods of coping with it" (203). Maintains that Donne's sonnet is "very self-protective in that it is written for the few who understand the nature of his loss and who accept his grief for what it is, a grief too deep to express except to those who break through the puzzles of this work" (209–210). Sees the sonnet as "one of Donne's parting poems, a final valediction to the earthly Ann" (210).

1537. Llasera, Margaret. "New Alchemy," in *John Donne and Modernity,* ed. Armand Himy and Margaret Llasera, 63–82. Confluences XI, Centre de Recherches sur les Origines de la Modernité et les Pays Anglophones. Nanterre: Université Paris X.

Maintains that "Donne's interest in alchemy is not a throwback to an outdated system of beliefs" but rather is "part and parcel of seventeenth-century developments" (64) that "were to exert a growing appeal as the century progressed." Examines in particular his "interest in spiritual alchemy that foreshadows this growing literary and eschatological trend"; discusses "the erotico-mystical imagery of the 'chemical wedding' that was to prove popular in love poetry"; and comments on "the scientific side of his thought concerning the structure of matter" (65). Discusses alchemical thought and allusions in several of Donne's love poems and sacred poems, pointing out that references in his love poetry to rooms, gold mines, pregnancy, regeneration, and tears have

alchemical connotations and that not only his vocabulary but also "his attitude towards matter" (80) reflects those of the alchemists and minerologists. Stresses that "in a universe where the mineral, vegetable, animal, and spiritual orders are intimately linked, alchemical thought, and superimposed upon it, spiritual alchemical thought provides a vivid and concrete conceptual framework, stretching from stones in the earth to planets in the sky, that reinforces the Christian framework and that helps thinkers to grasp and to make sense of the whole cosmological system" (73–74).

1538. Machacek, Gregory. "Donne's 'The Indifferent.'" *Expl* 53: 192–94.

Offers a reading of *Ind* that "emerges from a reconsideration of the poem's implied audience" (192). Argues that the poem is addressed to "two women who have discovered that they are both lovers of the speaker and have confronted him concerning his infidelity." Maintains that "the advantage of this reading is that one needn't explain away the plural 'mothers'" (l. 11) and suggests further that the reference may be "a veiled boast that the listeners' mothers too have been among those the speaker has been able to love!" (193). Believes the shift to the past tense in the final stanza "takes the speaker's bravado one step further" by suggesting that "he has found himself in this very position—confronted by two women, each of whom thought she was his one-and-only—before!" (193–94). Suggests, therefore that perhaps "[t]he speaker has been compelled to utter the preceding two stanzas on a previous occasion, with results (Venus seeking out and rebuking the few existing 'heretics in love') that he relates in the third stanza for the benefit of his latest lovers" (194).

1539. Malpezzi, Frances. "Donne's Transcendent Imagination: The Divine Poems as Hierophantic Experiences," in *John Donne's Religious Imagination: Essays in Honor of John T. Shawcross,* ed. Raymond-Jean Frontain and Frances M. Malpezzi, 141–61. Conway, Ark.: UCA Press.

Maintains that "Donne's religious imagination transcends the particularities and limits of his time and place," that he is "more than a seventeenth-century Protestant writer (with whatever qualifiers we want to attach to Protestant)" (141), and that he "is even more than a Christian writer whose values are firmly entrenched in western culture" (141–42). Argues that "placing Donne within the context of the history of religions illumines the cross-cultural dimensions of his religious imagination." Discusses how Donne "not only perceived the world as imbued by the sacred, but also clearly believed the principal events of sacred experience, those preserved in Scripture, are repeatable and accessible to humanity" (142). Maintains that "[t]hroughout his devotional writing Donne views the world from this perspective of *homo religiosus,*" who sees "the visible and tangible world as saturated with sacred meaning" (143) and who is "able to recognize the spiritual significance of the created universe because he is never far from the sacred events of mythical time" (146). Maintains that "religious poetry for Donne is a vehicle for keeping souls in tune with God" and that, "[b]ecause of this aesthetic, Donne's divine poems are often hierophantic experiences, manifestations of the sacred," by means of which he "not only asserts the sacrality of life, but returns the speaker, and consequently, the reader to the sacred time and/or space of Christian mythology, either making participants in the poem contemporary with divine events and placing them in the presence of the deity or demonstrating the way these events structure, imbue with meaning,

and sacralize profane experience." Concludes that "[t]o see Donne operating from the context of *homo religiosus* means to recognize his relationship not only to those seventeenth-century British writers who shared his ideology nor only to Christians such as Augustine who came before him and helped shape his doctrine," but also it means "recognizing what he has in common with all those who through the centuries and across continents have been moved by the religious impulse," thereby ultimately revealing "the transcendent power of his poetry and hence its enduring value" (156).

1540. Manley, Lawrence. "Essential Difference: The Projects of Satire," in *Literature and Culture in Early Modern London,* 372–430. Cambridge: Cambridge University Press.

Argues that during the late sixteenth century in England, the development of verse satire based on classical models represented "an alternative form of ethical innovation in response to the disorienting effects of urbanization on traditional values" (372). In this context discusses Donne's *Satyres,* pointing out how their primary emphasis "falls not on social injustice but on fraudulence, hypocrisy, dissimulation, and pretence" (382). Discusses, in particular, the importance of the Inns of Court in providing Donne and other satirists with "a community which was in many ways autonomous but at the same time contiguous with London's competing centers of wealth and power" (390), the targets of their satires. Sees Donne's *Satyres* as pitting "an anti-social integrity against the fear of social isolation, an attempted moral accommodation to society against a sweeping indictment of it" (396). Comments on how in these poems Donne "attempts to reconcile his perceptions to his imagined status in the social structure, to his dramatized roles as scholar-wit, jurist, theologian, courtier, and office-holder," stressing, however, that "in the course of the five satires his penetration more and more deeply toward the inner circles of his society pushes him, as satirist, further and further toward that soulful isolation which alone can authenticate his being and vision" (397). Believes that "all of Donne's satires tend to end on a note of surprised disillusionment, as if, in the process of unfolding, they exhaust all hope in the project of selection and refinement they set out to perform" (402).

1541. Marotti, Arthur F. *Manuscript, Print, and the English Renaissance Lyric.* Ithaca, N.Y. and London: Cornell University Press. xx, 348p. Contains revised versions of "Manuscript, Print, and the Social History of the Seventeenth-Century Lyric," in *The Cambridge Companion to English Literature,* ed. Thomas N. Corns (Cambridge: Cambridge University Press, 1993), 52–79 (entry 1359); "The Trans-mission of Lyric Poetry and the Institution-alizing of Literature in the English Renaissance," in *Contending Kingdoms: Historical, Psychological, and Feminist Approaches to the Literature of Sixteenth-Century England and France,* ed. Marie-Rose Logan and Peter Rudnytsky (Detroit, Mich.: Wayne State University Press, 1991), 21–41; "John Donne, Author," *JMRS* 19 (1989): 69–89 (entry 988); "Malleable and Fixed Texts Manuscript and Printed Miscellanies and the Transmission of Lyric Poetry in the English Renaissance" and "Manuscript, Print, and the English Renaissance Lyric," in *New Ways of Looking at Old Texts: Papers of the Renaissance English Text Society, 1985–1991,* ed. W. Speed Hill (Binghamton, N.Y.: Medieval and Renaissance Texts and Studies in conjunction with the Renaissance English Text Society, 1993), 159–73, 209–73; and "Poetry, Patronage, and Print," *YES* (1991): 1–26. Discusses Donne's poetry as part of the manuscript culture of the six-

teenth and seventeenth centuries. Points out that his verse "is found in more surviving manuscript documents than the work of any other English Renaissance poet" (24) and also that "[m]ore poems are misattributed to Donne than to any other English Renaissance poet" (158). Maintains that Donne's poetry is also "the most striking case of textual malleability" (147) and that "[w]hat happened to Donne's poems historically, especially in the manuscript system, deserves study—for the Donne poems people actually read, transcribed, and modified are part of a fascinating social history of literature that idealistic scholarship has largely ignored" (148). Surveys manuscripts containing Donne's poems and shows how "the texts were 'corrupted' in their transcript transmission—not only by small-scale verbal changes that appeared in due course but also in the more deliberate efforts to rewrite his texts." Discusses three kinds of changes in particular: "(1) the titling, retitling, and discursive ascription of particular poems, (2) the excerpting of parts of whole poems to create new pieces, and (3) the wholesale revision of particular texts or the plagiaristic imitation of them" (150). Maintains that "[t]he paradoxical effect of the extended transmission of Donne's poetry in manuscript through the seventeenth century is that it both reinforced his importance as an eminent 'author' and immersed his work, often without ascription, in a large body of poetic writing whose textual instability and vulnerability to appropriation as literary property worked against the isolation of individual authorship and the fixing of authorized texts" (159). Believes that the publication of the first edition of Donne's poems (and also Herbert's) in 1633 was "a watershed event that changed the relationship of lyric poetry to the print medium, helping to normalize within print culture the publication of poetry collections by individual authors." Maintains that thereafter "lyric poems themselves were perceived less as occasional and ephemeral and more as valuable artifacts worth preserving in those monumentalizing editions that were among the most prestigious products of print culture" (247). Discusses how the first printed edition of his poetry "began the process that led to Donne's conversion from coterie poet to English author" and how later seventeenth century editions of his poetry "not only effectively canonized Donne within the literary institution emerging within print culture, but also helped to reinforce the prestige of single-author collections through the rest of the century" (250).

1542. Martin, Catherine Gimelli. "Pygmalion's Progress in the Garden of Love, or The Wit's Work Is Never Donne," in *The Wit of Seventeenth-Century Poetry,* ed. Claude J. Summers and Ted-Larry Pebworth, 78–100. Columbia: University of Missouri Press.

Presents "a subtle and revisionist reexamination" of the wit in the *Songs and Sonets.* Reacts "against recent criticism of Donne," especially the work of Jonathan Goldberg and Thomas Docherty; applies to Donne's love poetry the Freudian theory of play; and argues that Donne's "poetics are not 'imperial,' but rather 'bourgeois.'" Maintains that Donne's "conversion of private lovemaking into a public display intended for courtly or coterie audiences clothes a celebration of the body in the language of power." Concludes that Donne,"[b]y self-consciously enlarging the scope of gendered human interchange in the private sphere," enlarges "the private sphere itself" and that he, therefore, participates "in an implicitly subversive critique of the hierar-

chical limits imposed by the divine right ideology of the Stuart court" (5). (Taken from editor's summary.)

1543. McCullough, Peter. "Preaching to a Court Papist?: Donne's Sermon before Queen Anne, December 1617." *JDJ* 14: 59–82.

Appears in a special issue of the *JDJ* on new uses of biographical and historical evidences in Donne studies, edited by Dennis Flynn. Examines Donne's sermon preached before Queen Anne at Denmark House on 14 December 1617 in order "to cast some new light on the perennial question of Anne's rumoured Roman Catholicism," to "demonstrate again the crucial importance of reading Donne's sermons with their specific occasions in mind," and to suggest "the possible significance for Donne's career of realignments in court politics after 1616" (60). Analyzes Donne's sermon to show that it is "an extended condemnation of church papistry addressed directly to Anne herself" (70) and intended to inspire the Queen "to move from outward conformity to full communion" with the Church of England, maintaining that "the covert practice of Catholicism estranges a prince from the faith of her birth and baptism" (75).

1544. Osterwalder, Hans. "'Nor ever chaste, except You ravish me': The Love Imagery in John Donne's Secular and Religious Poems." *ArAA* 20: 199–210.

Analyzes "some of the most salient instances of the metaphoric expression of love in some of Donne's seminal secular and religious poems." Argues that by putting the secular and religious poems side by side, it becomes apparent how Donne uses "the paradoxical reversal of the images of love." Points out how "the vehicles for human love are drawn from Christian Neoplatonism, whereas in some of the Holy Sonnets rape and prostitution are the chief metaphors" (200). Discusses the love imagery in *Ecst, ElBed, Canon, HSBatter,* and *HSShow* to show how "physical union of the lovers in the secular love poems is spiritualized by the Neoplatonic and Christian imagery" and how in the religious poems "the intensity of God's love for man is rendered by images derived from physical love in order to give it a palpability which religious, spiritual images cannot convey" (209). Believes that in Donne's best poems the spiritual and the erotic, the ideal and the real, the Neoplatonic and Ovidian are held together in a delicate balance.

1545. Papazian, Mary Arshagouni. "Literary 'Things Indifferent': The Shared Augustinianism of Donne's *Devotions* and Bunyan's *Grace Abounding*," in *John Donne's Religious Imagination: Essays in Honor of John T. Shawcross,* ed. Raymond-Jean Frontain and Frances M. Malpezzi, 324–49. Conway, Ark.: UCA Press.

Maintains that the "standard distinctions" between Donne's *Devotions* and John Bunyan's *Grace Abounding to the Chief of Sinners* (1666), "particularly those of genre (meditation vs. autobiography) and style (figurative vs. plain), are neither necessarily related to Donne's and Bunyan's theology, nor do they need to be explained as reflections of two different faiths." Argues rather that "the genre and style, to the extent that they are actually different, should be seen as the literary equivalents of religious *adiaphora* (or 'things indifferent'), that is, church practices not necessarily related to the issue of salvation." Maintains that both Donne and Bunyan "though they indeed disagreed on questions of church discipline and ceremonies, can be shown to share an essential Reformed Augustinian theology that emerges from Augustine's

Confessions and the late anti-Pelagian works, which permeated and united various parts of the Protestant movement and indeed their two works." Argues, therefore, that the *Devotions* and *Grace Abounding* "do not represent two separate, opposing, and ultimately incompatible faiths, but rather two manifestations of the same spirit divided only by time, genre, and style." Discusses both works in the context of Augustinian theology, thereby placing Donne "squarely in the context of the broad Reformation traditions, including that of the conformists." Maintains that such an approach will show that the *Devotions* is also "a spiritual autobiography in an acknowledged tradition" and "will allow us to recognize Donne's spiritual affinity with Bunyan and the inconsequentiality of their two different, and nondefining styles" (325).

1546. Patterson, Annabel. "Afterword." *JDJ* 14: 219–30.

In this postscript to the special issue of the *JDJ* on new uses of biographical and historical evidence in Donne studies, edited by Dennis Flynn, comments on the critical evolution in recent Donne studies, in particular the emergence of different versions of New Historicist and biographical approaches to his poetry and prose. Comments on the historical or contextual contributions to Donne studies made by six of the seven essays in the issue and, by way of her own contribution, analyzes several sermons Donne delivered at Lincoln's Inn following the death of Donne's friend Richard Martyn, in which the "idealistic skepticism" of *Sat3*, "with its demands that each man determine and keep his own Truth, is here expanded to the corporate and national body of believers" (228). Concludes that "[t]he renewed scholarly interest in history, in religion, in prose and in John Donne leaves plenty of room for further debate, further defining of what we mean by 'context,' and, best of all, further discoveries" (229).

1547. Pebworth, Ted-Larry. "John T. Shawcross: Editor of John Donne," in *John Donne's Religious Imagination: Essays in Honor of John T. Shawcross,* ed. Raymond-Jean Frontain and Frances M. Malpezzi, 415–25. Conway, Ark.: UCA Press.

Evaluates John T. Shawcross's contribution to Donne textual studies, calling his edition of *The Complete Poems of John Donne* (1967) "the most significant and helpful one-volume edition of Donne's poetry yet to appear." Maintains that "[i]ts significance and helpfulness lie primarily in its sensitivity to the early transmission of Donne poetry, which occurred primarily through manuscript circulation" (415). Surveys the textual history of Donne's poems to show how Shawcross's edition "reflects a depth and breadth of objective textual investigation never before attempted by an editor of Donne's poetry" (422) and that, when compared to one-volume editions published since 1967, Shawcross's edition is "luminous in its textual scholarship and exemplary in its good sense." Notes Shawcross's involvement with the forthcoming variorum edition of Donne's poetry, remarking that although the variorum editors "will produce an edition of Donne's poetry that is quite different from John Shawcross's," they "will owe an inestimable debt to his pioneering work with the manuscripts" (424).

1548. Pilshchikov, Igor A. "Coitus as a Cross-Genre Motif in Brodsky's Poetry." *RusL* 37: 339–50.

Points out that the modern Russian poet Joseph Brodsky, in his 1960 poem "Elegy to John Donne," very specifically noted Donne's intertranslatable use of sacred and erotic language and suggests certain similarities between Donne's use of sexual language in his love poems and in his sacred poems and Brodsky's employment of similar language in his poetry. Discusses how, on the whole, Brodsky's "attitude to eros is foreign to the Russian tradition" (342) and illustrates how in his poems the sexual and metaphysical "do not form a shocking contrast, but describe each other" (349).

1549. Price, Michael W. " 'Jeasts which cozen your Expectatyonn': Reassessing John Donne's Paradoxes and Problems." *JDJ* 14: 149–84.

Appears in a special issue of the *JDJ* on new uses of biographical and historical evidence in Donne studies, edited by Dennis Flynn. Believes that critics have taken too literally Donne's several comments in his letters to Wotton and Goodyer on the triviality of his *Paradoxes and Problems* and notes that, "[w]hether explicitly acknowledged or not, this literal interpretation, in turn, has become the basis (or justification) for critics' own dismissals of, apologies for, and embarrassment about the Paradoxes and Problems." Offers, therefore, "an alternative interpretation" of Donne's comments, "including overlooked commentary which appears in the works themselves," and argues "for interpreting Donne's characterizations ironically, not literally." Maintains that Donne "merely appears to trivialize" the *Paradoxes and Problems* and that this "appearance of triviality facilitates the safe transmission of provocative ideas buried in a subtext, thereby circumventing the dangers posed by the unsafe conditions in which Donne wrote." Holds that, "[n]ot merely dismissals, Donne's characterizations cleverly call attention to . . . a rhetorical strategy by which Donne dissimulates a subtext—

alerting initiated coterie readers to interpret the works ironically" (150). Concludes that the *Paradoxes and Problems* are "indeed trifles, jests, and *jeux d'esprits*—but not as critics have believed" and insists that "their surface triviality disguises their underlying meaning" (151). Discusses four selections to show how "[m]etacommentary" within the *Paradoxes and Problems* "corroborates an ironical interpretation of Donne's dismissive characterizations in the letters" (166).

1550. Rambuss, Richard. "Christ's Ganymede." *YJLH* 7: 77–96.

Discusses the "devotional outpourings of some seventeenth-century male lyric poets" over the naked body of Christ and maintains that it is in this "closet of devotion" that such poets as Donne, Herbert, Crashaw, and Traherne and others "can more or less self-consciously reassign in same-sex configurations (male devotee, male God) the conventional terms and postures of Petrarchan love lyric" (79) as they "court" Christ. Suggests that their use of "stock amorous conceits" leads to "a form of devotion that turns on an affectively, even erotically, expressive desire for the body of Jesus." Cites as an example the speaker's "rapturous gaze" (80) on Christ in *Goodf* (ll. 21–25) and presents an analysis of *HSBatter* in which "the poet's intense longing for spiritual satisfaction is metaphorized in terms of a rather explicit fantasy of divine abduction and ravishment, one that is framed . . . in terms that cut back and forth across genders, across 'eroticisms,' across desires both sacred and illicit" (82). Argues that the "erotics of salvation" in the sonnet are clearly "homoerotic ones" (86) as the speaker fantasizes being sodomized. Notes also that in *HSShow* "salvation comes by a divinely sanctioned debauchery" (89).

1551. Rambuss, Richard. "Homodevotion," in *Cruising the Performative: Interventions into the Representation of Ethnicity, Nationality, and Sexuality,* ed. Sue-Ellen Case, Philip Brett, and Susan Leigh Foster, 71–89. Bloomington: Indiana University Press.

Repeats essentially his argument in "Pleasure and Devotion: The Body of Jesus and Seventeenth-Century Religious Lyric," in *Queering the Renaissance,* ed. Jonathan Goldberg (Durham: Duke University Press, 1994), 253–79, that in *HSBatter* Donne, "pursuing his own fantasia of erotic excess" (80–81), asks God to give him "a trinitarian gang-bang" (81). Challenges those critics who suggest that the persona of the poem places himself before God as female. Insists that in the poem Donne wants "to take it like and as a man" and instructs "his master every step along the way in what he wants to bring him off to spiritual satisfaction" (82).

1552. Ramsey, Allen. "Donne's 'Epithalamion Made at Lincolnes Inne': The Religious and Literary Context," in *John Donne's Religious Imagination: Essays in Honor of John T. Shawcross,* ed. Raymond-Jean Frontain and Frances M. Malpezzi, 96–112. Conway, Ark.: UCA Press.

Rejecting the opinion that *EpLin* is indecorous and coarse, argues that "the dissonant tone in the poem is justifiable when set in its historical and religious milieu" (97). Shows how Puttenham in *The Arte of English Poesie* and Donne in his poem, rejecting "the celebratory acclaim accorded the bridal party in typical Renaissance wedding treatises," focus on "the anguish of the bride," who, for Puttenham, is "a virtual victim, a pawn who perpetuates family genealogies and estates" but who, in Donne's poem, "stands at the threshold of marriage, frightened and alone, but her plight is alleviated by the promise of a Christian marriage" (98). Shows how Donne is "innovative in his approach, especially in bringing to the poem the timely language of the religious significance of the occasion" (101). Through an analysis of the poem and two marriage sermons shows that Donne believed that, "in consummating the marriage, the sacrifice of virginity embraces a divine mystery, the tripartite promise of eternal life—through the resurrection, through procreation, and through the marriage with Christ" (108). Maintains, therefore, that the poem's energy "is generated largely by Donne's religious inspiration" (110).

1553. Reeves, Eileen. "Reading Maps," in *So Rich a Tapestry: The Sister Arts and Cultural Studies,* ed. Ann Hurley and Kate Greenspan, 285–314. Lewisburg, Pa.: Bucknell University Press; London: Associated University Presses.

Points out that "[t]he seventeenth century abounds in the association of maps and texts" and that "the theme was a frequent feature of more canonical works of literature." Says that "[i]t is perhaps within the poetry and the sermons of John Donne that references to the literary dimension of map-making are the most common and most learned." Cites *ValMourn* (l. 34) as an example of "a translation of a contemporary issue in both map-making and navigation, the *cursus obliquus* or *loxodrome*," a concept that also shows up in the sermons, and discusses how the whole poem is based on "the metaphor of the oblique course" (288). Maintains that in the valediction poem "the *cursus obliquus* of the ship that bears the poet away is the visible counterpart of the unseen spiral suggested by the poem's metaphysical tendencies" and suggests that "Donne's first readers would have seen the serpentine lines traced in this voyage as the analogue to the difficult

lines of which the poem itself was composed." Claims that the poem offers us "one of the closest associations of literature with cartography" (289).

1554. Roberts, John R. "John T. Shawcross: Critic of John Donne," in *John Donne's Religious Imagination: Essays in Honor of John T. Shawcross,* ed. Raymond-Jean Frontain and Frances M. Malpezzi, 426–38. Conway, Ark.: UCA Press.

Surveys and evaluates John T. Shawcross's contribution as a critic to Donne scholarship. Notes that from 1964 to 1991 Shawcross published 21 essays on Donne, a major edition of Donne's poetry, and several important book reviews concerned primarily with Donne. Maintains that Shawcross's scholarly publications on Donne "are not simply a reshuffling of what is already known but are original and thought-provoking contributions to our understanding of the poet," and stresses that his "masterful command of the textual history of the poems and his vast knowledge of the historical, political, and social contexts in which they were written, combined with his very keen critical insights and clear prose style, make his work a joy to read" (436). Contains a chronological list of Shawcross's publications on Donne from 1964 to 1991 (436–38).

1555. Rosen, David. "Anatomical Comparisons, Metaphysical Conceits: Poets, Physicians, and the Motions of the Heart." *Caduceus* 11: 185–206.

Argues that "by examining the work of [William] Harvey and the changing paradigms of English poetry we can find a relationship between the scientific and poetic communities of early modern England" (185–86). Discusses how "the two communities shared a discourse that embeds similar underlying assumptions that fostered a new, common direction." Holds that "[d]iscourse, a precondition of discovery, was being radically re-shaped by poets," and that "[u]nderstanding that discourse is helpful in understanding how Harvey discovered the circulation of the blood" (186). Shows that Harvey "frequently relies on symbols that had become crucial to the cultural discourse, a discourse shaped in large part by the great shapers of Elizabethan language, the poets," and that "it is the power of the image of the circle to illustrate the heart's form, placement, and function that shapes Harvey's discovery" (198). Maintains that "[t]he center from which and to which circulation occurs is a dominant trope of the day" and that Donne's work "offers the most familiar and striking examples." Points out that Donne's poetry "testifies to his acquaintance with anatomical detail," that "he is one of the first writers to use the word 'skeleton,'" and that "he seems to understand the sutures of the skull" (199). Cites *FirAn* as an example of a work that "underscores the need to shift views, to shift paradigms, to see differently," and shows similarities in diction and use of illustration, especially the use of the image of the circle, in *ValMourn* and Harvey's *De Motu Cordis* (200).

1556. Sabine, Maureen. " 'Thou art the best of mee': A. S. Byatt's *Possession* and the Literary Possession of Donne." *JDJ* 14: 127–48.

Appears in a special issue of the *JDJ* on new uses of biographical and historical evidence in Donne studies, edited by Dennis Flynn. Discusses A. S. Byatt's extensive and subtle uses of Donne's poetry in her novel *Possession* (1991) and then suggests how the novel combines biographical and critical themes that perhaps offer new insights into the life and poetry of Donne. Comments also on Byatt's interest in and use of the poetry of

Robert Browning and T. S. Eliot and their keen interest in Donne. Claims that a "longing for a relationship of unbroken trust is the originating impulse of Byatt's romance *Possession* as it is the deep buried feeling in Donne's finest love poems" (143).

1557. Schuchard, Ronald. "Eliot and Ignatius: Discovery and Abandonment in Donne." *Modern Schoolman* 73, no. 1: 1–16.

Notes that "[t]hough Eliot began studying Donne in 1906, and writing on him in 1917, he seems not to have explored Donne's Jesuit background or picked up a copy of Ignatius's *Spiritual Exercises* (1548) until he began preparing his Clark Lectures" (1) in 1925. Points out how Eliot in those lectures identifies Ignatius and the Jesuits "with the psychological transformations that took place in the religion and mysticism of the sixteenth and seventeenth centuries and develops his lectures "on the premise that under Jesuit influence Donne takes a psychological rather than an ontological attitude towards objects, ideas and emotions in his poetry" (3). Comments on the evolution of Eliot's views on Donne and finally his disenchantment with him as he discovered Dante. Discusses also Eliot's evolving understanding of and attitude toward Ignatius, Jesuit spirituality, and the *Exercises* to show that although "his expressed attitude towards Ignatius changed," his negative attitude "toward Jesuitism did not" (8), and that finally "he found it impossible to come to temperamental or intellectual terms with the Ignatian method of the *Spiritual Exercises*" (15). Claims, therefore, that "[t]he gradual diminishment of Donne's importance to Eliot was hastened by his study of Ignatius" and notes that "by the mid-1930's both had essentially disappeared from the center of Eliot's critical consciousness" (13).

1558. Scodel, Joshua. "John Donne and the Religious Politics of the Mean," in *John Donne's Religious Imagination: Essays in Honor of John T. Shawcross,* ed. Raymond-Jean Frontain and Frances M. Malpezzi, 45–80. Conway, Ark.: UCA Press.

Discusses how Donne "transforms the notion of the ethical mean, which was central to his contemporaries' defense of the religiopolitical status quo, in order to articulate a new ideological vision" and how his "spirited and independent engagement with classical and patristic thought gave him a vital critical distance, however, from his culture's dominant habits of mind" (45). Shows how in *Sat3* Donne "transformed and endowed with intense religious significance both Aristotelian ethics and skeptical epistemology in order to articulate his personal vision of the true religious mean" and observes how in "the religious prose Donne composed after joining the English church," he "draws eclectically and idiosyncratically upon classical, patristic, and Scholastic formulations in order to outline a less radical but still independent vision of the proper religious mean." Concludes that "[t]his later vision allows Donne to embrace the church of England without relinquishing his sense of himself and all sincere believers as questing individuals" (70).

1559. Shami, Jeanne. "Donne's 1622 Sermon on the Gunpowder Plot: His Original Presentation Manuscript Discovered." *EMS* 5: 63–86.

Announces the discovery in December 1992 in the British Library of a manuscript presentation copy of Donne's 1622 sermon on the Gunpowder Plot corrected in his own hand (Royal MS 17 B.XX) and describes the manuscript in detail. Notes that "[m]anuscript sources exist for only nineteen sermons, out of a total of one hun-

dred and sixty, and, to date, no 'authorial' manuscript has been identified" (63). Maintains that "[t]he implications of such a discovery are profound" and discusses how "[t]he manuscript and its corrections yield important new information about the process in which Donne's sermons were produced and transmitted," require a reconsideration of "the textual status of the only early printed version of the sermon," and "reveal much about the political considerations impinging on Donne in the pulpit in 1622" (65). Points out that "[t]he manuscript indicates that Donne's copy of the sermon made immediately after delivery is more dramatic in syntax and diction" than the later printed text, that a comparison of the manuscript and the 1649 text "reveals that Donne substantially revised this sermon for publication" (80), and that "[t]he two states of the sermon suggest that Donne changed his sermons not only for stylistic or rhetorical reasons but also for political ones." Points out that "[m]any of the revisions indicate that Donne's intentions changed" and that "in 1622 he was wary of criticizing the King openly, as he did in the revised version" (81). Comments on Donne's handwriting and presents in an appendix a list of Donne's autograph corrections of the manuscript.

1560. Shami, Jeanne. "Donne's Sermons and the Absolutist Politics of Quotation" in *John Donne's Religious Imagination: Essays in Honor of John T. Shawcross,* ed. Raymond-Jean Frontain and Frances M. Malpezzi, 300–412. Conway, Ark.: UCA Press.

Addresses "two related problems: the increasingly popular view of Donne's religious politics as absolutist, and the politics driving the modern critical use of Donne's sermons as evidence to prove this view." Challenges "the opinion that Donne as preacher merely echoed and publicized Divine Right propaganda" and rejects the notion that "the political content of the sermons is little more than a display of outward conformity to an absolutist system which Donne may (or may not) have supported personally, but which he promoted enthusiastically and without reservation from the pulpit." Maintains that "[s]uch a view grossly oversimplifies Donne's complex relationship with the court and is based on an interpretive method and style of argument that have never been adequately analyzed," and insists that "Donne as a royalist propagandist, in fact, distorts our understanding of Donne's political position." Maintains that Donne should be placed "among others who remained politically 'obedient' while still offering political advice to the court" and shows that his sermons "reveal that he can more usefully be characterized as one of the major participants in a theological 'middle group'" of church leaders who were "proponents of moderate resistance to absolutism in both Church and State" but who "recognized that their power to offer counsel or to effect change was inextricably (and uncomfortably) tied to their authorized positions within the ecclesiastical hierarchy" (381). Discusses the misuse of Donne's sermons by modern critics, especially the use of them "as means to other ends, rather than as the end of legitimate scholarly inquiry" (384), and the practice of quoting from them in a fragmentary way and/or out of context. Maintains that Donne "developed a casuistical discourse inspired by traditions of both legal interpretation and biblical exegesis in which he was experienced" and that "[t]he conjunction of these interpretive languages made Donne's literal sense a particularly flexible medium through which he adjusted to the dangers of misinterpretation and to his

responsibilities of religious and political counsel" (391). Shows how Donne's sermon defending King James's *Directions to Preachers* is "paradigmatic of the processes by which Donne's casuistry operates" (394). Concludes that "Donne's political casuistry allowed him to develop a language of obedience which resists the 'absolutist' label and which served as a model of the kind of counsel available to one trying to adjust the law of conscience to the laws of political authority" (404).

1561. Shami, Jeanne. "'The Stars in Their Order Fought Against Sisera': John Donne and the Pulpit Crisis of 1622." *JDJ* 14: 1–58.

Appears in a special issue of the *JDJ* on new uses of biographical and historical evidence in Donne studies, edited by Dennis Flynn. Places in an historical context Donne's sermon of 15 September 1622, preached at Paul's Cross defending King James's recently issued *Directions to Preachers,* thereby exploring "Donne's doctrinal and political position immediately preceding and following this extraordinary performance" (2). Through an examination of Donne's pre-1622 sermons argues that "[t]he middle nature of Donne's divinity, the inclusiveness of his spirituality, and his respect for orderly processes and judicial means made Donne particularly well-suited to defend James's *Directions,*" as "did his sustained criticism of Jesuit Scriptural interpretations and other practices, and his fundamental belief that those things necessary for salvation were 'matter without controversie'" (21). In addition to discussing why Donne was selected to deliver the sermon, comments on what he was expected to accomplish—namely, to persuade the people of the King's "good intentions in issuing the directions" and of his "constancy in the reformed religion," to model "the kind of sermon which could be preached from the Paul's Cross pulpit in the wake of the *Directions*," and "to establish the limits within which discreet and religious preachers would be allowed to operate, particularly from the influential Paul's Cross pulpit" (26). Analyzes the sermon, emphasizing that "[t]he modern perception of this sermon as an exercise in bland and unconscientious conformity lacks historical support" (28). Discusses how the last months of 1622 "call into question the modern image of Donne as royal spokesman" (41) and "mark the limits rather than the beginnings of Donne's ambitions" (42).

1562. Shul'piakov, Gleb. "Dzhon Donn: Proshchanie bez prava na pechal." *Literaturnaia Gazeta* 45, no. 5577 (15 November): 7.

Announces to the Russian reading public the publication of Grigorii Kruzkhov's translations of selected *Elegies, Songs and Sonets, Satyres,* and verse epistles. Calls the small volume the first book of Donne's poetry in Russian and describes Kruzkhov's exclusive focus on Donne's early poetry (to 1601). Comments briefly on Donne's life and the critical revival of interest in his work in the twentieth century. Concentrates on Donne's farewell motif and contends that, despite the difficulties in his life (especially economic instability and the death of his wife), Donne never lost his interest in the power of love. Reproduces Kruzkhov's translations of *ElPict, ElWar,* and *ValMourn.*

1563. Smith, Nigel. "What's Inside? Donne, Interiority and Independency," in *John Donne and Modernity,* ed. Armand Himy and Margaret Llasera, 25–35. Confluences XI, Centre de Recherches sur les Origines de la Modernité et les Pays Anglophone. Nanterre: Université Paris X.

Notes that Donne "himself had no part in modernity" and points out that his works, for the most part, "have spoken to those whose views and preferences have been conservative, backward-looking, resistant to the successive waves of innovation in philosophy and social practice that we call the modern." Argues that modernity began during the English Civil War when "interiority became a public issue" (25) and shows how "[t]he uses made of Donne's works during the Civil War and Interregnum illuminate this context" (26). Comments on borrowings and citations from Donne found in the works of Nehemiah Rogers, an ejected Anglican clergyman, and his son John Rogers, his opposite, who was an enthusiastic Puritan, to show how Donne's works were appropriated by both religious groups. Discusses how Donne's "sophisticated rhetoric of selfhood played an important role not only in John Rogers's theorizing of experiential worship, but also in providing a model and a means by which a newly emergent expression of enthusiastic selfhood could grow" (29). Comments also on verses of Robert Overton, a Puritan and republican, who rewrote some of Donne's poems to fit Puritan sensibilities. Maintains that "while Nehemiah Rogers was softening the rigour of Donne's interiority, his son John and Robert Overton were producing a radical Puritan Donne." Concludes that Donne, no doubt, would have been "surprised to see his sermons empowering Independency," but believes that "he had by the end of his life developed an elaborate rhetoric of interiority which was ready to be harvested by a 'new religion'" (35).

1564. Stampino, Maria Galli. "Bodily Boundaries Represented: The Petrarchan, the Burlesque and Arcimboldo's Example." *QI* 16: 61–79.

Briefly discusses *ElAut* as an early example of the "exploitation of Petrarchan topoi in poems other than love ones" (66). Notes that, although the tone of the poem is "far from being mocking and derisive," Donne's use of Petrarchan clichés to describe an old woman would have seemed "eccentric" to his contemporaries, "who could only read these poetic compositions along the lines of the burlesque and the paradoxical" (67).

1565. Stanwood, P. G. "Donne's Earliest Sermons and the Penitential Tradition," in *John Donne's Religious Imagination: Essays in Honor of John T. Shawcross,* ed. Raymond-Jean Frontain and Frances M. Malpezzi, 366–79. Conway, Ark.: UCA Press.

Points out that "[o]f his 160 extant sermons, Donne preached on the Psalms thirty-four times" and that "twenty-one of these sermons are on the penitential psalms," thereby forming "the largest group of related texts in his canon." Suggests that Donne "probably preached a series on the penitential psalms, of which we possess only about one-half of the whole course"; that he "preached these sermons at the beginning of his career, at Lincoln's Inn, as early as 1616 and likely before the beginning of his travel with Doncaster in May 1619"; that his sermons on the penitential psalms "belong to a literary and devotional tradition"; and that "his preaching on these texts represents a particular form of Christian verbal art, of a specific and predictable kind" (366). Holds also that Donne's preaching style "did not markedly change or 'develop' over the period of his ordained ministry" but followed the directives that "he had clearly laid out in his *Essayes in Divinity,* probably composed in the time shortly before his ordination in early 1615, though published posthumously in 1651, and which the sermons

on the penitential psalms also reflect" (366–67). Believes that "Donne's attraction to the penitential psalms may be explained by a cultural and exegetical tradition in which Augustine is central but not [the] single influence," but insists that "the many references Donne makes to him neither provide the structure for a systematic theology nor even the adequate intimation of one" (373).

1566. Stein, Arnold. "Versions of Baroque in Seventeenth-Century English Poetry," in *The Image of the Baroque,* ed. Aldo Scaglione; asst. ed., Gianni Eugenio Viola, 191–202. Studies in Italian Culture: Literature in History, 16. New York: Peter Lang.

Discusses aspects of the baroque and mannerism in the poetry of Donne, Marvell, and Milton in the light of contemporary painting. Maintains that "[i]mages that startle or shock, that present human experience in a harsh light, or express a line of thought that challenges comfortable views . . . seem to be expressing in literature materials that resemble or have some affinity to the Baroque in art" (194). Cites the violent, uncanny, startling, and shocking images in *SecAn* (ll. 7–22, 85–88), passages from *Devotions,* and the sermons as examples of the baroque. Compares and contrasts Donne and Marvell, suggesting that Marvell's poetry seems more manneristic than baroque. Notes that Donne "often reveals little or no preparation for the intensity and scope of the conclusion he is about to bring forth," whereas Marvell "often proceeds as if he had planned every step in advance" (196).

1567. Strier, Richard. "Impossible Radicalism: Donne and the Freedom of Conscience," in *Resistant Structures: Particularity, Radicalism, and Renaissance Texts,* 118–64. The New Historicism: Studies in Cultural Poetics, gen.

ed. Stephen Greenblatt. Berkeley and Los Angeles: University of California Press. Revised and expanded version of "Radical Donne: Satire III," *ELH* 60 (1993): 283–322 (entry 1384).

1568. Sullivan, Ceri. "Donne's Sifted Soul." *N&Q*, n.s. 42: 345–46.

Suggests that Donne's conceit of gluttonous death sifting the soul in *HSScene* (ll. 9–12) may have been suggested by lines from Robert Southwell's "Sinnes heavie loade." Discusses Donne's aquaintaince with Southwell and suggests that manuscript differences in l. 7 perhaps indicate Donne's earlier recusant sympathies.

1569. Sullivan, Ceri. "Seventeenth-Century Wreath Poems." *GHJ* 19, nos. 1–2 (1995–96): 95–101.

Regards *Corona* along with Marvell's "The Coronet," Herbert's "Jordan (II)," and Vaughan's "The Garland" and "The Wreath" as "florilegia of past reading and writing, not only a description of the dilemma of solofidianism." Argues that "the poems' own governing metaphor should be taken literally" (95), noting that "the literary form explicitly used by the poets themselves tends to get ignored" (95–96). Observes that these poets "all describe the creation process as one of gathering flowers" and that "these garlands are the result of past reading." Maintains that they "are remembering their stores of images and expressions for a new purpose" and "are using their anthologies, their gatherings of past flowers of adages, proverbs, similitudes" (96). Notes also that these poets also "dramatize the realization that they have been reading the wrong material," which "leads to a correction of the reading which each garland poet has been engaged in" (98). Sees the "concatenation of each verse" of *Corona* as reflective of this kind of "self-correcting reading" (99).

1570. Suzuki, Kozo. "Donne no Shi ni komerareta Shukyoteki Imi" [John Donne's Religious Messages in Some of his Love Poems], in *17 Seiki to Eikoku Bungaku* [Seventeenth-Century English Literature in Its Cultural Context], 35–55. The Japan Society of Seventeenth-Century English Literature. Tokyo: Kinseido.

Discusses how *Ind, LovDeity, LovExch, LovUsury,* and *WomCon*, though as love poems they seem to have nothing to do with religious problems, do, in fact, clearly reflect Donne's religious position.

1571. Swiss, Margo. "*Lachrymae Christi:* The Theology of Tears in Milton's Lycidas and Donne's Sermon 'Jesus Wept,'" in *Heirs of Fame: Milton and Writers of the English Renaissance,* ed. Margo Swiss and David A. Kent, 135–57. Lewisburg, Pa.: Bucknell University Press; London: Associated University Presses.

Presents an intertextual reading of Donne's sermon "Jesus Wept," preached at Whitehall in Lent (1622/23), and Milton's "Lycidas" "within the context of the theology of tears as described by the Catholic literature of tears and the Protestant literature of contrition" (136). Discusses how Milton's elegy, like Donne's sermon, "advances to and attains its resolution through the three scriptural occasions of Christ's weeping" and how these instances of Christ's compassion "formally authorize Christian bereavement over the human vicissitudes systematically presented in both texts: personal bereavement, worldly commendation or the lack of it, corruption of the religious institution, and the prospect of corporal death." Shows also how the *Lachrymae Christi* tradition accounts for the three-part structure of both works as well as "their parallel thematic constituents" (152). Concludes that, although there is no proof for the direct influence of Donne's sermon on Milton's elegy, an "antiphonal alignment of these two texts" reveals that "Lycidas" is informed not only by the elegiac tradition, but also by "the theology of tears, an orthodox, well-documented and, for the seventeenth century, prominent mode of Christian grief expression" (152–53).

1572. Yen, Julie W. "'What doth Physicke profit thee?': The Pharmakon of Praise in Donne's *Ignatius His Conclave* and the *Holy Sonnets*," in *John Donne's Religious Imagination: Essays in Honor of John T. Shawcross*, ed. Raymond-Jean Frontain and Frances M. Malpezzi, 214–30. Conway, Ark.: UCA Press.

Examines the connection between *Ignatius* and the *Holy Sonnets* "by reading these two texts through the metaphor of the *pharmakon,* or 'physicke,' that is explored in its multivalency of meanings by Derrida in his reading of Plato's *Phaedrus*" (214). Maintains that if "we scrutinize the movement of the *pharmakon,* simultaneously both a poison and a cure," present in *Ignatius*, "we detect within the dramatization of conflicting discourses a play of endless substitutions of meaning" and insists that "[t]his continuous deferral of meaning produces discursive strategies which allowed Donne simultaneously to critique and practice the art of elaborate praise that was a common part of Renaissance court behavior" (214–15). Argues that "these strategies of verbal equivocation . . . are the same devices that he uses in the *Holy Sonnets* to praise and court God" (215). Discusses how in *Ignatius* Donne "exploits the potentialities of language as he successfully manipulates conflicting discourses in the practice of courtly equivocation made available by the example of the king" and shows how he "places his dangerous comments on the practice of flattery in the mouths of various equivocating characters, cautiously criticizing court behavior while remaining inside the power system and availing himself of its strategies of discourse" (222). Maintains that in the *Holy Sonnets* Donne expresses "his profound frustration and disappointment in a system which chose to ignore a man's obvious intellectual abilities and deny him preferment because of his religious affiliation," and shows how "some of the speakers [in the sonnets] resort to the discursive strategies afforded by the *pharmakon* of praise and attempt to court God with 'flattering speeches' but ultimately come to the realization that each cure already carries poisonous side-effects" (223). Concludes that "[t]he language of both flattery and praise that Donne uses to articulate his hopes and disillusionment about his search for political advancement is not different from the language that he uses to dramatize the difficulty of religious belief in the *Holy Sonnets*" (228).

INDEX OF AUTHORS, EDITORS, TRANSLATORS, REVIEWERS AND ILLUSTRATORS

(All references are to Entry Numbers.)

SUBJECT INDEX

(The following is an index of subjects *mentioned in the annotations* in this bibliography.
All references are to Entry Numbers.)

INDEX OF DONNE'S WORKS

(The following is an index of Donne's works *mentioned in the annotations.* See List of Abbreviations, pp. xxi and following, for abbreviations of individual poems. *All references are to Entry Numbers.*)

POEMS

ANNIVERSARIES: 43, 56, 61, 71, 91, 106, 154, 202, 205, 236, 275, 287, 291, 303, 304, 323, 352, 354, 355, 392, 397, 451, 463, 478, 499, 526, 527, 541, 568, 571, 575, 580, 605, 610, 640, 651, 692, 711, 748, 801, 853, 872, 975, 991, 992, 1013, 1023, 1025, 1047, 1063, 1102, 1119, 1138, 1156, 1180, 1194, 1226, 1237, 1261, 1308, 1313, 1319, 1327, 1337, 1363, 1370, 1389, 1391, 1403, 1442, 1463, 1499, 1509

FirAn 55, 140, 158, 187, 198, 268, 352, 371, 384, 392, 393, 411, 421, 465, 495, 499, 533, 541, 656, 687, 711, 748, 768, 847, 872, 893, 899, 975, 981, 1004, 1023, 1047, 1061, 1064, 1118, 1140, 1162, 1194, 1222, 1252, 1499, 1521, 1555

FunEl 371, 711, 748, 815, 975, 1194, 1331, 1499

SecAn 37, 66, 84, 105, 140, 241, 297, 306, 323, 352, 392, 470, 495, 711, 727, 748, 975, 1023, 1047, 1117, 1179, 1194, 1499, 1566

DIVINE POEMS: 46, 61, 91, 94, 219, 258, 266, 272, 281, 291, 304, 352, 372, 413, 468, 470, 568, 569, 575, 576, 593, 627, 651, 656, 853, 905, 967, 991, 992, 1037, 1035, 1073, 1117, 1138, 1220, 1248, 1308, 1337, 1406, 1408, 1420, 1527, 1539

Annun 808, 818, 1212

Christ 62, 87, 122, 127, 153, 208, 220, 304, 371, 727, 803, 811, 1021, 1029, 1039, 1091, 1117, 1184, 1212, 1414, 1432, 1474

Corona 53, 86, 94, 99, 122, 202, 221, 291, 301, 304, 375, 377, 422, 454, 532, 595, 693, 707, 713, 765, 817, 852, 853, 902, 907, 942, 994, 1227, 1241, 1261, 1296, 1302, 1416, 1447, 1460, 1474, 1531, 1569

Cor3 221

Cor5 187

Cross 250, 371, 385, 532, 571, 595, 670, 671, 808, 809, 822, 942, 1022, 1088, 1423, 1470, 1518

ED 53, 94, 765, 888, 907

Father 57, 104, 122, 347, 371, 492, 515, 595, 605, 667, 706, 736, 803, 811, 815, 820, 878, 882, 1011, 1066, 1212, 1225, 1266, 1414, 1447, 1462, 1470

Goodf 9, 46, 70, 102, 106, 187, 194, 196, 229, 250, 268, 281, 304, 319, 371, 397, 527, 532, 600, 670, 727, 758, 785, 808, 828, 839, 848, 853, 1015, 1030, 1031, 1037, 1088, 1124, 1166, 1212, 1213, 1243, 1251, 1266, 1346, 1383, 1437, 1447, 1460, 1484, 1518, 1519, 1531, 1550

Lam 122, 208, 1142, 1181, 1350, 1461, 1509

Lit 31, 84, 86, 102, 187, 197, 501, 503, 703, 853, 942, 1007, 1019, 1088, 1146, 1212, 1261

MHMary 53, 94, 765, 790, 907, 1276

Res 187, 501, 503, 765, 1041, 1447, 1511

Sickness 12, 57, 78, 83, 122, 194, 220, 250, 258, 371, 384, 412, 460, 472, 482, 483, 493, 576, 588, 605, 634, 727, 736, 761, 785, 818, 829, 853, 882, 1021, 1061, 1163, 1240, 1270, 1408, 1414, 1532

Prose Works